HAWAI'I

Where to Stay and Eat
for All Budgets

Must-See Sights
and Local Secrets

Ratings You Can Trust

Fodor's Travel Publications   New York, Toronto, London, Sydney, Auckland
www.fodors.com

FODOR'S HAWAI'I 2004

Editor: Carissa Bluestone

Editorial Contributors: Pablo Madera, John Penisten, Cathy Sharpe, Leslie West-brook, Kim Westerman, Shannon Wianecki, Maggie Wunsch
Maps: David Lindroth, *cartographer*; Rebecca Baer and Bob Blake, *map editors*
Design: Fabrizio La Rocca, *creative director*; Guido Caroti, *art director*; Melanie Marin, *senior picture editor*
Production/Manufacturing: Robert B. Shields
Cover Photo (Nā Pali, Kaua'i): Catherine Karnow

SPECIAL SALES

Fodor's Travel Publications are available at special discounts for bulk purchases for sales promotions or premiums. Special editions, including personalized covers, excerpts of existing guides, and corporate imprints, can be created in large quantities for special needs. For more information, contact your local bookseller or write to Special Markets, Fodor's Travel Publications, 1745 Broadway, New York, NY 10019. Inquiries from Canada should be directed to your local Canadian bookseller or sent to Random House of Canada, Ltd., Marketing Department, 2775 Matheson Boulevard East, Mississauga, Ontario L4W 4P7. Inquiries from the United Kingdom should be sent to Fodor's Travel Publications, 20 Vauxhall Bridge Road, London SW1V 2SA, England.

AN IMPORTANT TIP & AN INVITATION

Although all prices, opening times, and other details in this book are based on information supplied to us at press time, changes occur all the time in the travel world, and Fodor's cannot accept responsibility for facts that become outdated or for inadvertent errors or omissions. So **always confirm information when it matters,** especially if you're making a detour to visit a specific place. Your experiences—positive and negative—matter to us. If we have missed or misstated something, **please write to us.** We follow up on all suggestions. Contact the Hawai'i editor at editors@fodors.com or c/o Fodor's at 1745 Broadway, New York, NY 10019.

PRINTED IN THE UNITED STATES OF AMERICA

10 9 8 7 6 5 4 3 2 1

DESTINATION HAWAI'I

Just try to describe Hawai'i without saying "paradise." In this place of ineffable beauty, the word is not a cliché, but actually an understatement. O'ahu is the most visited island, yet even here the landscape is so rugged that many developers have just shrugged their shoulders and walked away. Maui is dominated by luxury resorts, but also has a dormant volcano and the ultimate scenic drive—Hāna Highway. On the Big Island, ancient ruins and sleepy towns with melodic names punctuate a landscape of tropical forests, pasturelands, and barren lava fields. From Waimea Canyon to the perfect dunes of Polihale Beach, Kaua'i is paradise's prettiest subdivision. Moloka'i is where Hawaiian's themselves unwind, drawn to the island's peace and quiet. Tiny Lana'i is big on natural wonder, including Hulopo'e Beach, where spinner dolphins put on quite a show. Expect to make some tough choices during your trip. Every day you'll have to choose between embarking on high adventure—hiking in a volcano, learning to hang ten at the famous Waikīkī Beach—or simply heading for the nearest crescent of palm-shaded sand to do nothing at all. Only in paradise. Aloha!

Karen Cure, Editorial Director

CONTENTS

ABOUT THIS BOOK

There's no doubt that the best source for travel advice is a like-minded friend who's just been where you're headed. But with or without that friend, you'll have a better trip with a Fodor's guide in hand. Once you've learned to find your way around its pages, you'll be in great shape to find your way around your destination.

SELECTION Our goal is to cover the best properties, sights, and activities in their category, as well as the most interesting communities to visit. We make a point of including local food-lovers' hot spots as well as neighborhood options, and we avoid all that's touristy unless it's really worth your time. You can go on the assumption that everything you read about in this book is recommended wholeheartedly by our writers and editors. Flip to On the Road with Fodor's to learn more about who they are. It goes without saying that no property mentioned in the book has paid to be included.

RATINGS Orange stars ★ denote sights and properties that our editors and writers consider the very best in the area covered by the entire book. These, the best of the best, are listed in the Fodor's Choice section in the front of the book. Black stars ★ highlight the sights and properties we deem Highly Recommended, the don't-miss sights within any region. Fodor's Choice and Highly Recommended options in each region are usually listed on the title page of the chapter covering that region. Use the index to find complete descriptions. In cities, sights pinpointed with numbered map bullets ❶ in the margins tend to be more important than those without bullets.

SPECIAL SPOTS Pleasures & Pastimes focuses on types of experiences that reveal the spirit of the destination. Watch for Off the Beaten Path sights. Some are out of the way, some are quirky, and all are worth your while. If the munchies hit while you're exploring, look for Need a Break? suggestions.

TIME IT RIGHT Wondering when to go? Check On the Calendar up front and chapters' Timing sections for weather and crowd overviews and best days and times to visit.

SEE IT ALL Use Fodor's exclusive Great Itineraries as a model for your trip. (For a good overview of the entire destination, follow those that begin the book, or mix regional itineraries from several chapters.) In cities, Good Walks guide you to important sights in each neighborhood; ▶ indicates the starting points of walks and itineraries in the text and on the map.

BUDGET WELL Hotel and restaurant price categories from ¢ to $$$$ are defined in the opening pages of each chapter-expect to find a balanced selection for every budget. For attractions, we always give standard adult admission fees; reductions are usually available for children, students, and senior citizens. Look in Discounts & Deals in Smart Travel Tips for information on destination-wide ticket schemes.

BASIC INFO Smart Travel Tips lists travel essentials for the entire area covered by the book; city- and region-specific basics end each chapter. To find the best way to get around, see the transportation section; see individual modes of travel ("By Car," "By Train") for details. We assume you'll check Web sites or call for particulars.

ON THE MAPS	Maps throughout the book show you what's where and help you find your way around. Black and orange numbered bullets ❶ ❶ in the text correlate to bullets on maps.
BACKGROUND	In general, we give background information within the chapters in the course of explaining sights as well as in CloseUp boxes and in Understanding Hawai'i at the end of the book. To get in the mood, review the suggestions in Books & Movies. The glossary can be invaluable.
FIND IT FAST	Within the book, chapters are arranged in a roughly clockwise direction starting with O'ahu. Chapters are divided into small regions, within which towns are covered in logical geographical order; attractive routes and interesting places between towns are flagged as En Route. Heads at the top of each page help you find what you need within a chapter.
DON'T FORGET	Restaurants are open for lunch and dinner daily unless we state otherwise; we mention dress only when there's a specific requirement and reservations only when they're essential or not accepted—it's always best to book ahead. Hotels have private baths, phone, TVs, and air-conditioning and operate on the European Plan (a.k.a. EP, meaning without meals). We always list facilities but not whether you'll be charged extra to use them, so when pricing accommodations, find out what's included.

SYMBOLS

Many Listings
- ★ Fodor's Choice
- ★ Highly recommended
- ✉ Physical address
- ✛ Directions
- 🕮 Mailing address
- ☎ Telephone
- 🖷 Fax
- ⊕ On the Web
- ✑ E-mail
- 🎟 Admission fee
- ☉ Open/closed times
- ► Start of walk/itinerary
- 🖃 Credit cards

Outdoors
- ⚠ Camping

Hotels & Restaurants
- 🏨 Hotel
- ⮂ Number of rooms
- ⟁ Facilities
- ⅑ Meal plans
- ✕ Restaurant
- ⟁ Reservations
- 🏛 Dress code
- ⤬ Smoking
- ⑭ BYOB
- ✕🏨 Hotel with restaurant that warrants a visit

Other
- ☺ Family-friendly
- 🛈 Contact information
- ⇨ See also
- ✉ Branch address
- ☞ Take note

ON THE ROAD WITH FODOR'S

A trip takes you out of yourself. Concerns of life at home completely disappear, driven away by more immediate thoughts—about, say, what marvels await the next day, or where you'll have dinner. That's where Fodor's comes in. We make sure that you know all your options, so that you don't miss something that's just around the next bend just because you didn't know it was there. Because the best memories of your trip might well have nothing to do with what you came to Hawai'i to see, we guide you to sights large and small all over the region. You might set out to simply splash around in O'ahu's crystal waters, but back at home you find yourself unable to forget spotting humpback whales off Maui's shores or kayaking along Kaua'i's majestic coast. With Fodor's at your side, serendipitous discoveries are never far away.

Our success in showing you every corner of Hawai'i is a credit to our extraordinary writers. Although there's no substitute for travel advice from a good friend who knows your style, our contributors are the next best thing—the kind of people you would poll for travel advice if you knew them.

Pablo Madera, our Moloka'i updater, is a freelance journalist and editor, a frequent contributor to regional and national publications. A 25-year resident of Maui, he authored Fodor's *Escape to the Hawaiian Islands.* Current projects include alternative airwave programming for a commercial-free radio station.

John Penisten, who updated the Big Island chapter, is a 30-year resident of Hilo. As a freelance travel writer and photographer, he's published in a number of outlets locally, nationally and internationally. His extensive guidebook work includes an adventure guide to Hawaii and guides to Kaua'i and the Big Island for Prima Publishing.

Cathy Sharpe, our Smart Travel Tips updater, was born and reared on O'ahu. For more than 13 years, she worked at a Honolulu public relations agency representing major travel industry clients. Now living in Maryland, she is a public relations and advertising consultant. Cathy returns home at least once a year to visit family and friends, relax at her favorite beaches, and enjoy island cuisine.

Leslie Westbrook, our Big Island dining critic, splits her time between her home in Santa Barbara, where she is the editor of *Santa Barbara Seasons Magazine,* and her apartment on the Big Island. She has contributed to many different publications in her 15 years as a freelance journalist, including *Condé Nast Traveler.*

Even though Maui lodging updater Kim Westerman makes her home in the Sonoran Desert in Arizona, she is an island girl at heart. Her favorite restaurant on Maui is Sansei and she swears by the mai tai recipe at Mama's Fish House. Her favorite beach is a secret.

Shannon Wianecki, who updated the Maui and Lāna'i chapters, was raised on Maui. With a decade of experience working in the Island's tourism industry, she knows its secrets well. She has contributed to various publications including *Maui Time Magazine.*

Maggie Wunsch, our O'ahu and Kaua'i updater, felt the lure of Hawai'i during her first visit to O'ahu as a child. She returned to the island when she started college and has been there ever since. A freelance journalist, Maggie's travelogues, stories, and writings about Hawai'i's people, places, and events can be found on radio, television, in print, and on the Internet.

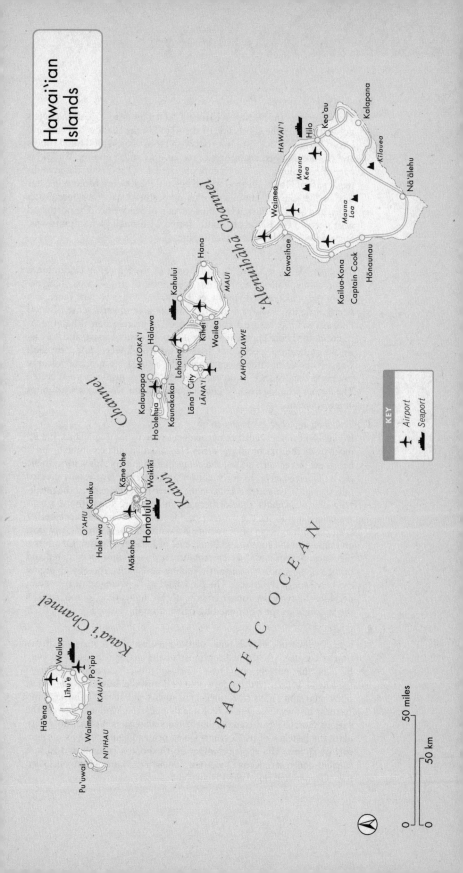

WHAT'S WHERE

1 O'ahu

Third-largest of the Hawaiian Islands, O'ahu is home to 75% of the state's population. On the south side of the island in the shadow of Diamond Head, Waikīkī is a 2½-mi hot spot with more than 31,000 hotel rooms and condominiums, and scores of restaurants and shopping. Waikīkī is part of Honolulu, the state's capital. The East O'ahu ring, the area directly east of Honolulu around and beyond the Ko'olau Mountains, has one of the island's famous snorkeling destinations, some interesting ruins, and Sea Life Park, Hawai'i's version of Sea World. The north and west parts of the island are rural, dotted with small plantation towns. Surfers flock to the famed North Shore.

2 Maui

The lush island of Maui, second-largest of the Hawaiian chain, takes its nickname, Valley Isle, from its topographic profile—an arc slung between the peaks of two volcanoes. Hāna, on Maui's eastern shore, is a sleepy little town where you might still be able to get a sense of what Hawai'i was like before T-shirt tourism. The journey here is half the attraction: the Hāna Highway snakes down the eastern coast, and it's easily one of the most spectacular drives in the world. West Maui, "the Golf Coast," has resort after resort. Haleakalā, a 10,023-ft dormant volcano, towers in the distance—you could fit Manhattan inside its great crater. The former whaling town of Lahaina livens up the west coast with shops and restaurants.

3 The Big Island of Hawai'i

If you like your paradises uncrowded, come to the Big Island. It's almost twice the size of all the other Hawaiian Islands combined, and it hangs off the eastern end of the chain like an anchor. It's a formidable piece of land to cover in one vacation, and therefore is generally divided into six sightseeing areas: Hilo on the eastern side; Hāmākua, the northern seacoast; Kohala, the northern mountainous region with the northwest coastline; Kona, the western seaside village of Kailua-Kona together with the Upcountry coffee region; Ka'u and the vast stretches of lava and desert to the south; and Puna, east of Kīlauea volcano. Of course, the volcano itself is always a major attraction—it's still spewing red and orange lava, which is constantly finding new paths, thereby changing the very face of the island. The Big Island is the youngest of the chain, and like the typical younger sibling, it's biding its time, poised to take the spotlight as the most exciting destination in Hawai'i.

4 Kaua'i

Kaua'i's location may be one of the reasons why it stays off many tourist's radar: it's the westernmost of the major islands, with only Ni'ihau, the sparsely populated "Forbidden Isle," close to it. Dismissing Kaua'i as an afterthought would be a mistake, however. The oldest of the Hawaiian Islands, Kaua'i's 550 square mi are rich in natural and cultural history. The banks of Kaua'i's bubbling Wailua River on the eastern shoreline attracted the first Polynesian settlers. Visitors now populate the beaches of its Coconut Coast or head south to the sunny resort of Po'ipū. The cooler, damper north shore is verdant and lush, a startling contrast to Kaua'i's western side with its Waimea Canyon, called the "Grand Canyon of the Pacific."

5 Moloka'i

Moloka'i is shaped like a slipper, with the toe pointing toward Maui's west shore. Ten miles wide and 38 mi long, Moloka'i is made up of two volcanic mountains connected by a plain. Visitors readily embrace the down-to-earth charm of the "Friendly Isle." In the island's highest reaches you can explore Kamakou Preserve, a 2, 774-acre wildlife refuge. There is also plenty of snorkeling, swimming, and sunbathing.

6 Lāna'i

Lāna'i is the smallest of the populated islands and is below Moloka'i, right off of Maui's west coast. Lāna'i's only population center is Lāna'i City, smack in the middle of the island. The town is surrounded by natural wonders: Garden of the Gods, an eerie hilltop strewn with colorful boulders to the northwest; breathtaking Hulopo'e Beach to the south; and Lāna'ihale, the highest point on the island, to the east. Lāna'i used to be all about pineapples—until the Great Hawaiian Pineapple Crash of the 1980s—but now the fields are mostly gone and the focus is on the two luxury resorts, the Mānele Bay Hotel on the south shore and the Lodge at Kō'ele near Lāna'i City.

GREAT ITINERARIES

Many Hawai'i visitors simply loll in a chaise longue during their stay. If you would prefer to take a peek at several islands, to get a better feeling for the world's most isolated archipelago, let this 14-day itinerary be your guide.

O'ahu in 3 days

O'ahu is a good place to start your tour, with its frequent air service from the mainland and its scores of restaurants and hotels. On the first morning, rise early to make the steep walk to Diamond Head, the summit of an extinct volcano, for a panorama of the city and the beaches. Once you've soaked up the vista, take in a bit of history at the U.S.S. *Bowfin*, a World War II submarine; the U.S.S. *Missouri*, which saw action from World War II to the Persian Gulf War; and the *Arizona* Memorial, commemorating the sinking of this ship on December 7, 1941. Then spend some time exploring the shops, restaurants, and other attractions of Waikīkī—including the Waikīkī Aquarium and the Bishop Museum, known for its collection of Polynesiana.

On day two, drive around Diamond Head to watch the windsurfers, then follow the coast to Hanauma Bay and the windward town of Kailua. Take side trips to the Nu'uanu Pali Lookout, where the view is spectacular, and the Byodo-In Temple, a replica of the Kyoto original, on your way to the Polynesian Cultural Center. Pick up a souvenir or two in its open-air shopping village—it has a good selection of Polynesian handicrafts. It's a long, dark drive back to Waikīkī, so you might want to stay at a local bed-and-breakfast.

On your third day, continue along the North Shore, stopping at Waimea Valley and Waimea Bay, a popular pic-nic spot, en route back to Waikīkī. In Honolulu, explore the lei stands and herb shops in the city's Chinatown. Then take a guided tour of America's only royal residence, 'Iolani Palace, and stroll around Mission Houses Museum, the homes of Hawai'i's first missionaries, and Kawaiaha'o Church, built out of local coral blocks and used for royal ceremonies.

Kaua'i in 2 days

On the Garden Isle, begin by making the 90-minute drive from Līhu'e around the south shore of the island and up to spectacular Waimea Canyon, nicknamed the "Grand Canyon of the Pacific." Lookouts en route give you wonderful views of the entire panorama. Kōke'e State Park is at the northern end of the canyon, a true wilderness full of colorful flowers. Return the way you came, stopping en route as time permits to visit the National Tropical Botanical Gardens and the eclectic shops at Kilohana. Plan your trip to allow time to arrive at Po'ipū Beach and catch the sunset over the Pacific—a sight you won't soon forget.

On your final day, cruise up the Wailua River to the Fern Grotto; take a flightseeing tour; and stop at Kīlauea Lighthouse, built in 1913 and towering over the Kīlauea Point National Wildlife Refuge, and the Hanalei Valley Overlook, where fields of taro stretch before you almost as far as you can see. Spend your last evening watching the sunset at Hanalei Bay, a spectacular way to bring your island sojourn to a close.

Moloka'i in 2 days

This long, small island doesn't take long to explore. The best strategy is to see just a little each day to allow time to kick back and relax. West Moloka'i is mostly given over to the 53,000-acre Moloka'i Ranch, the largest local landholder. In tiny Maunaloa, which anchors the area, start by shopping at the old market and kite shop, on the brief main street. Later head for wide Pāpōhaku Beach, the island's nicest and most private strand and one of the state's most sensational, with its stunning white sand.

At dinnertime head for the nearby Lodge at Moloka'i Ranch. Its restaurant, although the most formal on the island, is casual and comfortable, and if you eat before the sun goes down you can marvel at the spectacular ocean vista through the big picture windows.

The next day—and it will be a full one—reserve ahead to tour Kalaupapa, to which people afflicted with Hansen's disease (leprosy) were once relegated; Father Damien, a Catholic priest, cared for the community's residents until he succumbed to the disease in 1889. Make the tortuous 3-mi trip via the Moloka'i Mule Ride or fly in. Before you catch an evening flight to Maui, take in the stupendous view of the peninsula from Pālā'au State Park.

Maui & Lāna'i in 4 days

Maui, which inspires people to call it the Valley Isle, is the second-largest landfall in the state. Start your Maui sojourn in 'Iao Valley State Park, where a 2,000-ft-high spire known as 'Iao Needle rises from the valley floor and easy hikes lead through forests. The peripatetic Mark Twain, stopping in the area during his peregrinations through the Islands, dubbed it the

"Yosemite of the Pacific." Afterward take 'Iao Valley Road into Wailuku, where it becomes Main Street. Many of the old buildings in this drowsy little town are on the National Register of Historic Places. Bailey House, former home of prominent 19th-century missionaries Edward and Caroline Bailey, displays period furniture and artifacts. Then follow Route 30 south a couple of miles to the 120-acre Maui Tropical Plantation, a sort of agricultural theme park, to tour former sugar-

cane fields, get an overview of the growing processes, and catch lively demonstrations of such activities as lei-making and coconut-husking. Then head over to the Alexander & Baldwin Sugar Museum near Kahului.

The next day, if it's sunny, make the fabulous four-hour drive to Hāna. It's a spectacular 55 mi of bridges and turns and vistas showcasing classic Hawaiian scenery. Keep an eye out en route for waterfalls, pools, swimming holes, hiking trails, lookout points, and other stopping places.

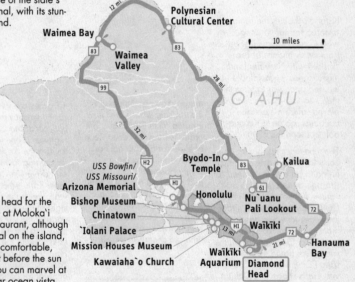

Overnight in Hāna, a onetime company town devoted to the sugar industry that's now almost entirely focused on tourism.

In the morning visit aviator Charles Lindbergh's grave and 'Ohe'o Gulch, where there are many waterfalls more than 100 ft high with idyllic pools at the bottom. The place is perfect for picnicking and sunbathing and can get very crowded. Backtracking along the Hāna Highway, end the day exploring

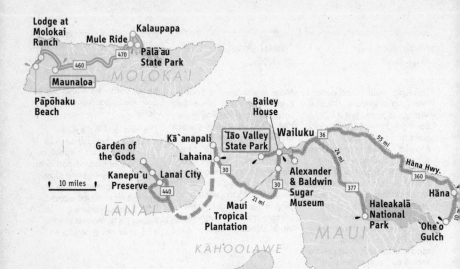

historic Lahaina, the famous restored former whaling town where crusty sailors just back from many months at sea clashed with New England missionaries whose single-minded goal was to save the men's souls. After you've explored Lahaina's antique buildings, go on to Kā'anapali to spend the night.

The next morning, get up early for a ferry ride out of Lahaina to Lāna'i. You'll need to arrange a jeep rental in advance; Adventure Lāna'i Eco Centre is your best bet, since they can, schedule permitting, meet you at the dock with your jeep. Once you're on the road, take Route 440 to Lāna'i City, where you can visit crafts shops and pick up a great picnic basket at Pele's Other Garden. Then take Keōmuku Highway north to Polihua Road through the dryland forest of the Kānepu'u Preserve until you reach Garden of the Gods, a lunar plateau scattered with red boulders of all shapes and sizes. Retrace your steps and end your day with a late afternoon swim at Hulopo'e Beach. Turn in your rental and head back to Lahaina for dinner and a good night's sleep.

If you can handle another early morning, on your last day rise before dawn to see the sun come up over the im-

mense crater of Haleakalā, the volcano whose lava flow created all of East Maui. The crater is now the centerpiece of Haleakalā National Park, which is full of hiking trails. At lovely Hosmer Grove, you can pick up a trail map; the Sliding Sands trail off the top of the crater shows off some amazingly colorful scenery: lush forests keep company with red desertlike terrain.

Big Island in 3 days

After arriving in Hilo, the county seat of the island and the fourth-largest city in the state, drive up Waiānuenue Avenue about a mile (stay to the right) as far as exquisite Rainbow Falls. It's beautiful when the sun is shining, and rainbows form above the mist if the sun is right in the morning. Then travel north of Hilo for 7 mi along Route 19 and turn right onto the 4-mi scenic bypass that skirts Hawai'i Tropical Botanical Garden,

17 acres crowded with such exotic species as ginger and heliconia, before rejoining the highway. Next turn left inland toward the small and unprepossessing town of Honomū and drive 4 mi to 'Akaka Falls State Park, where a 20-minute walk yields the rewarding sight of the park's two cascades—the 400-ft Kahuna Falls and the 442-ft 'Akaka Falls. Spend the afternoon in Hawai'i Volcanoes National Park, exploring its lava tubes, mineral formations, steam vents, and tropical plants—and, if you're lucky, catching the sight of lava flowing from Kīlauea Volcano. Get a feel for the volcanic terrain in just a short time with a visit to Halema'uma'u Crater, a steam-clouded pit inside the Kīlauea Caldera, or with a hike along the blackened Devastation Trail.

Begin day two with a drive up the Hāmākua Coast to Waimea to see the Hawaiiana in the Kamuela Museum and tour the Parker Ranch Visitor Center and Museum. Take the mountain road to the plantation villages of Hāwī and

Kapaʻau to visit the statues of King Kamehameha and his Puʻukoholā Heiau before heading to the sunny Kohala Coast resorts; don't miss the nearby petroglyph carvings, and look for the snowcapped summit of Mauna Keʻa.

The next morning head south through Hōlualoa, Kealakekua, and Captain Cook, stopping for a bit at Puʻuhonua o Hōnaunau National Historic Park, about 20 mi south of Kailua-Kona. Games and crafts demonstra-

tions, among other activities there, teach you about Hawaiian history. If you have time, continue on to Ka Lae, the southernmost point in the United States. This windswept and grassy area gives a realistic glimpse of Hawaiʻi's past. When you've seen it all, head back to Kailua-Kona and the Astronaut Ellison S. Onizuka Space Center, a tribute to Hawaiʻi's first astronaut. Spend the rest of the day shopping and relaxing in Kailua-Kona.

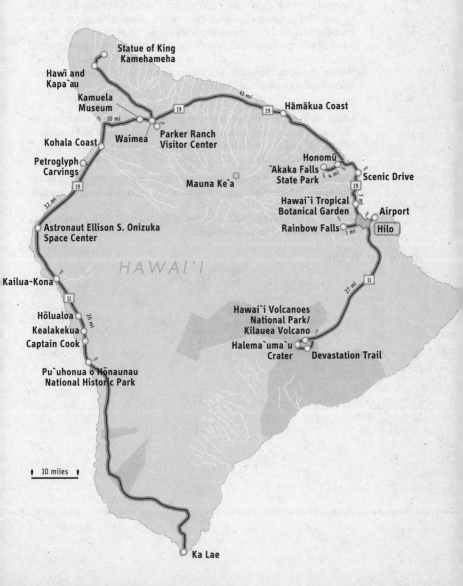

Long days of sunshine and fairly mild year-round temperatures make Hawai'i an all-season destination. Most resort areas are at sea level, with average afternoon temperatures of 75°F–80°F during the coldest months of December and January; during the hottest months of August and September the temperature often reaches 90°F. Only at high elevations does the temperature drop into the colder realms, and only at mountain summits does it reach freezing.

Most travelers head to the Islands during winter. From mid-December through mid-April, visitors from the mainland and other areas covered with snow find Hawai'i's sun-splashed beaches and balmy trade winds appealing. This high season means that fewer travel bargains are available; room rates average 10%–15% higher during this season than the rest of the year.

Rainfall can be high in winter, particularly on the north and east shores of each island. Generally speaking, you are guaranteed sun and warm temperatures on the west and south shores no matter what time of year. Kaua'i's and the Big Island's northern sections get more annual rainfall than the rest of Hawai'i, and so much rain falls on Kaua'i's Mount Wai'ale'ale (approximately 472 inches of rain, or 39 ft), that it's considered the wettest place on earth.

Climate

Moist trade winds drop their precipitation on the north and east sides of the islands, creating tropical climates, while the south and west sides remain hot and dry with desertlike conditions. Higher "Upcountry" elevations typically have cooler, and often misty conditions.

The following are average maximum and minimum temperatures for Honolulu; the temperatures throughout the Hawaiian Islands are similar.

Forecasts **Weather Channel Connection** ☎ 900/932–8437, 95¢ per minute from a Touch-Tone phone ⊕ www.weather.com.

HONOLULU, O'AHU

Jan.	80F	27C	May	85F	29C	Sept.	88F	31C
	65	18		70	21		73	23
Feb.	80F	27C	June	86F	30C	Oct.	87F	31C
	65	18		72	22		72	22
Mar.	81F	27C	July	87F	31C	Nov.	84F	29C
	69	21		73	23		69	21
Apr.	83F	28C	Aug.	88F	31C	Dec.	81F	27C
	69	21		74	23		67	19

ON THE CALENDAR

Hawai'i has so many festivals and special events, that no matter when you go you'll be arriving just in time for the party. You can watch pro surfers and golfers do their thing, sample Island cuisine, learn to hula, or go to a rodeo—just be sure to book way ahead if you're coinciding your trip with any of the major festivals, particularly the Merrie Monarch Festival in April.

WINTER

Dec.

Triple Crown of Surfing O'ahu; ☏ 808/638–7700: The world's top pro surfers gather on the North Shore for big winter waves and tough competition. Nā Mele O Maui Maui; ☏ 808/661–3271: Held the first week in December, this festival in the Kā'anapali Resort features a student art exhibition and schoolchildren competing in Hawaiian song. Honolulu Marathon O'ahu; ☏ 808/734–7200: Watch or run in one of the country's most popular marathons. Bodhi Day all Islands; ☏ 808/536–7044: The traditional Buddhist Day of Enlightenment is celebrated at temples statewide. Kaua'i Products Fair Kaua'i; ☏ 808/ 246–0988: Crafts, fruit, plants, clothes, and entertainment are available at this monthlong outdoor market (weekends only). Festival of Lights all Islands; ☏ 808/523–4674 in O'ahu, 808/828–0014 in Kaua'i, 808/667–9175 in Maui: Islands celebrate the holiday season with electric light parades, decorated city buildings, and events. Christmas (all Islands): Hotels outdo each other in such extravagant exhibits and events as Santa arriving by outrigger canoe. Christmas Lighting of the Banyan Tree Maui; ☏ 808/310–1117: Five thousand lights cover the historic banyan tree on Front Street. Pacific Handcrafters Guild's Annual Christmas Fair O'ahu; ☏ 808/254–6788: Craftspeople display their art and fine crafts at this two-day event at Thomas Square Park. Rainbow Classic O'ahu; ☏ 808/956–6501: The UH Warriors and seven top-ranked mainland college basketball teams compete at the University of Hawai'i between Christmas and New Year's Day. Hawai'i International Film Festival O'ahu and Neighbor Islands; ☏ 808/ 528–3456: The visual feast showcases films from the United States, Asia, and the Pacific and includes seminars with filmmakers and critics. Passport to International Cultures Big Island; ☏ 808/886–8811: A cultural journey of food and fun at the Kings' Shop in Waikoloa, showcases Waikoloa Beach Resort chefs and their cuisine, plus live cultural entertainment and a visit by Santa Claus.

Jan.–Feb.

Chinese New Year Celebrations all Islands; ☏ 808/533–3181 O'ahu, 808/310–1117 Maui, 808/553–3876 Molokai: The Chinese New Year is welcomed with a Narcissus Festival pageant, coronation ball, cooking demonstrations, street fairs, fireworks, and lion dances. HulaFest Week On February 1, the best college football players square off in the Hula Bowl, concluding this five-day festival on Maui which includes a luau, surf classic and Heisman golf tournament. ☏ 808/871–4141. Sony Open Golf in Hawa'i Tournament O'ahu; ☏ 808/523–7888: Top golf pros tee off at the Wai'alae Country Club.

Jan.

Aloha State Square and Round Dance Festival O'ahu; ☏ 808/672–3646: A full week of dancing, workshops, and fun with callers and dancers from around the world. Cherry Blossom Festival O'ahu; ☏ 808/949–2255: This popular celebration of all things Japanese includes a run,

	cultural displays, cooking demonstrations, music, and crafts. It runs through March. **Morey Boogie World Body Board Championships** Oʻahu; ☎ 808/396–2326: The world's best body boarders compete at Banzai Pipeline.
Feb.	**NFL Pro Bowl** Oʻahu; ☎ 808/526–4400: A week after the Super Bowl this annual pro-football all-star game is played at Aloha Stadium. **Punahou Carnival** Oʻahu; ☎ 808/944–5711: Hawaiʻi's most prestigious private school stages an annual two-day fund-raiser with rides, arts and crafts, local food, and a great white-elephant tent. **Pacific Masters & Senior Amateur Golf Tournament** Kauaʻi; ☎ 800/576–1081: This six-day tournament held at Princeville Resort draws golfers from across North America. **Sand-Castle Building Contest** Oʻahu; ☎ 808/956–7225: Students of the University of Hawaiʻi School of Architecture showcase their skills with some amazing and unusual sand sculpture at Kailua Beach Park. **Whale Week** Maui, ☎ 800/942–5311: A parade, run, ocean swim, regatta, children's carnival, silent auction, and celebration honoring the humpback whales that visit Maui each winter.
Feb.–Mar.	**Buffalo's Annual Big Board Surfing Classic** Oʻahu; ☎ 808/951–7877: The event features surfing as it used to be, on old-fashioned 12- to 16-ft boards.

SPRING

Mar.	**Opening Day of Polo Season** Oʻahu; ☎ 808/947–6511: Games are held at Mokuleʻia and Waimānalo every Sunday at 2 PM through August. **Oʻahu Kite Festival** Oʻahu; ☎ 808/661–4766: Kite-flying demonstrations, workshops, and competitions are held at Kapiʻolani Park. **Annual Kona Brewers Festival** Big Island; ☎ 808/334–2739: This gathering of 25 beer brewers and 25 restaurants at the Kona Beach lūʻau grounds is the biggest of its kind in the islands. **East Maui Taro Festival** Maui; ☎ 808/248–8972: Held in Hāna, this three-day festival focuses on all things taro, including poi. **Honolulu Festival** Oʻahu; ☎ 808/926–2424: Dozens of events held at various Oʻahu locations to promote cultural understanding, economic cooperation, and ethnic harmony between the people of Hawaiʻi and Asia-Pacific. The festival culminates with a grand parade down Kalakaua Avenue. **Kauaʻi Marathon** Kauaʻi; ☎ 808/826–6244: The 26.2-mi course begins in Poipu and treks through Kauaʻi Coffee land not normally open to the public. **Prince Kuhio Celebration of the Arts** Kauaʻi; ☎ 808/742–3770: A tribute to a beloved Hawaiʻi monarch. The day includes commemorative ceremonies at the prince's birthplace in Poipu and re-creation of a Hawaiian village at the Hyatt Regency Kauaʻi.
Apr.	**Merrie Monarch Festival** Big Island; ☎ 808/935–9168: A full week of ancient and modern hula competitions begin with a parade the Saturday morning following Easter Sunday. Tickets must be purchased (and hotel rooms reserved) months in advance; the competition is held at the Edith Kanakaʻole Auditorium in Hilo. **Celebration of the Arts** Maui; ☎ 808/669–6200: For three days, the Ritz-Carlton, Kapalua pays tribute to Hawaiʻi's culture with hula, art workshops, a lūʻau, and Hawaiian music concerts. Most activities are free. **The ʻUlupalakua Thing!** Maui; ☎ 808/875–0457: Maui County holds its an-

nual agriculture trade show and sampling with rides, games, and other entertainment at Tedeschi Vineyards, 'Ulupalakua. Buddha Day all Islands; ☎ 808/536–7044: Flower pageants are staged at Buddhist temples to celebrate Buddha's birth. Crazy Shirts Surf Series O'ahu; ☎ 800/550–7873: The Hawai'i Amateur Surfing Association presents this surf competition, including longboarding and bodyboarding. Earth Day Ho'olaule'a and Luau Kaua'i; ☎ 808/826–6404: Five days of celebrations honoring the earth and local culture culminate in a huge, all-you-can-eat lū'au. Hawai'ian Scottish Festival and Games O'ahu; ☎ 808/988–7872: Scottish songs, tartans, crafts, food, and traditional Highland athletic competitions make up this festival at Kapi'olani Park.

May Lei Day all Islands; ☎ 808/547–7393: This annual flower-filled celebration on May 1 includes music, hula, food, and lei-making competitions. Prince Albert Music Festival Kaua'i; ☎ 808/826–7546: Princeville's signature event attracts local musicians and distinguished American composers, plus there are hula performances and art and cultural exhibits. Ka Hula Piko Moloka'i; ☎ 808/672–3220: A community celebration of the birth of hula is marked by performances, storytelling, Hawaiian food, crafts, and lectures at Pāpōhaku Beach Park. World Ocean Games O'ahu; ☎ 808/521–4322: Ten days of events celebrate the sea with lifeguard competitions, boating, and more. Ka Ulu Lauhala O Kona Festival Big Island; ☎ 800/329–5226: A celebration of Hawaiian arts, crafts, and music with Kupuna Elizabeth Lee at the King Kamehameha Kona Beach Hotel. World Fire Knife Dance Competition O'ahu; ☎ 800/367–7060: This international competition of Samoan Fire Knife dancing concludes the Polynesian Cultural Center's weeklong "We Are Samoa" Festival. In Celebration of Canoes Maui ☎ 888/310–1117: Master canoe carvers from around the Pacific carve canoes from logs throughout the week. A parade of canoes, concerts, and cultural demonstrations also are featured.

May–June 50th State Fair O'ahu; ☎ 808/682–5767: Produce, exhibits, food stands, amusement rides, and live entertainment are at Aloha Stadium over several weekends. Hawai'ian Airlines World Ocean Games O'ahu; ☎ 808/521–4322: This 10-day festival includes international lifeguard and water sports competitions. Lantern Floating at Keahi Lagoon O'ahu; ☎ 808/947–2814: A Buddhist ceremony with 700 floating lanterns pays tribute to peace and departed ancestors at Keahi Lagoon Beach Park. Last Monday in May.

SUMMER

June King Kamehameha Day all Islands; ☎ 808/536–0333: Parades and fairs abound, and twin statues of Hawai'i's first king—in Honolulu on O'ahu and in Kapa'au on the Big Island—are draped in giant leis. Taste of Honolulu O'ahu; ☎ 808/536–1015: One of O'ahu's best food events, it includes two days of sampling from the finest restaurants in town and entertainment on the grounds of the Honolulu Civic Center. Pu'uhonua O Hōnunau Festival Big Island; ☎ 808/328–2288: Ancient Hawaiian games, hula, food tasting, lau hala, and coconut-frond weaving demonstrations take place at the historic City of Refuge. The Maui Film Festival at Wailea Maui ☎ 888/999–6330:

Special movie screenings, premieres under-the-stars, contemporary Hawaiian music, and The Taste of Wailea are the highlights of this festival. Kaua'i Annual Hula Exhibition Kaua'i; ☎ 808/335–6466: An evening of Hawaiian and Polynesian chants, music, and hula at the War Memorial Convention Hall.

July	Kapalua Wine and Food Symposium Maui; ☎ 800/669–0244: Wine and food experts and enthusiasts gather for tastings, discussions, and dinners at this four-day event at Kapalua Resort. Makawao Statewide Rodeo Maui; ☎ 808/572–9565: This old-time Upcountry rodeo, held at the Oskie Rice Arena in Makawao on July 4 weekend, includes a parade and three days of festivities. Parker Ranch Rodeo Big Island; ☎ 808/885–7311: In beautiful Waimea, see how the Hawaiian cowboy, the *paniolo,* works the circuit. Independence Day (all Islands): The national holiday on July 4 is celebrated with fairs, parades, and fireworks. Special activities include an outrigger canoe regatta with 30 events held on and off Waikīkī Beach. Prince Lot Hula Festival O'ahu; ☎ 808/839–5334: A whole day of hula unfolds beneath the towering trees of O'ahu's Moanalua Gardens. It is believed to be Hawai'i's oldest and largest non-competitive hula event. Kīlauea Volcano Wilderness Marathon and Rim Runs Big Island; ☎ 808/329–1758: More than 1,000 athletes from Hawai'i, the mainland, and Japan run 26.2 mi across Ka'ū desert, 5 mi around the Kīlauea Caldera rim, and 5.5 mi into Kīlauea Iki Crater. The event takes place in Hawai'i Volcanoes National Park. Queen Lili'uokalani Keiki Hula Competition O'ahu; ☎ 808/521–6905: Tickets for this popular children's hula competition are usually available at the end of June and sell out soon after. Koloa Plantation Days Kaua'i; ☎ 808/822–0734: A weeklong tribute to Kaua'i's plantation heritage on the island's south shore, featuring a sunset *ho'olaule'a, paniolo* rodeo, plantation tennis tournament, Hawaiian Olympics, golf putting tournament, craft fair, and ethnic cooking demonstrations. The festivities end with a parade and festival in Koloa Town with entertainment, local food, and crafts.
July–Aug.	Bon Odori Season all Islands; ☎ 808/661–4304: Buddhist temples invite everyone to festivals that honor ancestors and feature Japanese *o-bon* dancing. Hawai'i State Farm Fair O'ahu; ☎ 808/848–2074: This 10-day fair with farm products, agricultural exhibits, crafts, a petting zoo, contests, and a country market is held at Aloha Stadium.
Aug.	BayFest O'ahu; ☎ 808/254–7653: This event is the largest military festival of its kind in Hawai'i—with rides, water sports, contests, food, and entertainment—at Kane'ohe Marine Corps Base. International Festival of the Pacific Big Island; ☎ 808/934–0177: Music; dance; a lantern parade; floats; sporting events; and food from Japan, China, Korea, Portugal, Tahiti, New Zealand, and the Philippines round out this event. Hawaiian International Billfish Tournament Big Island; ☎ 808/329–6155: This international marlin fishing tournament, held in Kailua-Kona, includes a parade and a full week of cultural events. The Maui Onion Festival Maui; ☎ 808/661–4567: This lighthearted and food-filled celebration of Maui's most famous crop takes place at Whalers Village, Kā'anapali. Poke Contest Maui; ☎ 808/874–1111: Chefs from throughout the Islands convene at the Maui Prince Hotel to compare renditions of this prized local specialty.

FALL	
Sept.	**Maui Writers Conference** Maui; ☎ 808/879–0061: Best-selling authors and powerhouse agents and publishers offer advice—and a few contracts—to aspiring authors and screenwriters at this Labor Day weekend gathering. **Annual Hupuna Beach Prince Hotel Sam Choy Poke Festival** Big Island; ☎ 808/880–3021: Chefs show off their renditions of this local delicacy. **Taste of Lahaina** Maui; ☎ 888/310–1117: Maui's best chefs compete for top cooking honors, and samples of their entries are sold at a lively open-air party. **Hawaiian Canoe Festival** O'ahu; ☎ 808/524–1377: Two weeks of events celebrate the role of the canoe in Polynesian life. **Kaua'i Mokihana Festival** Kaua'i; ☎ 808/822–2166: This two-day islandwide event combines music, crafts, dancing, and hula competitions. **Hawai'i Garlic Festival and "Home Grown" Products** O'ahu, ☎ 808/528–7388: A two-day festival of garlic cuisine created by Hawai'i and mainland chefs, children's games and activities, displays, and entertainment.
Sept.–Oct.	**Aloha Festivals** all Islands; ☎ 808/923–1811 ⊕ www.gohawaii.com: This traditional celebration, started in 1946, preserves Hawaiian native culture. Crafts, music, dance, pageantry, street parties, and canoe races are all part of the festival.
Oct.	**Ironman Triathlon World Championships** Big Island; ☎ 808/329–0063 ⊕ www.ironmanlive.com: This popular annual sporting event has competitors swimming, running, and bicycling. **Moloka'i Hoe Canoe Race** Moloka'i and O'ahu; ☎ 808/259–7112: More than 100 teams from around the world cross the Moloka'i Channel to O'ahu and finish in Waikīkī. **Princess Kaiulani Keiki Hula Festival** O'ahu; ☎ 808/922–5811: Children ages 5–12 perform hulas in honor of Princess Kaiulani. A Hawaiian arts and crafts fair is also held. **Hawaiiana Festival** Kaua'i; ☎ 808/742–3770: A three-day series of educational programs designed to teach the customs, crafts, and spirits of Hawai'i's native people, plus entertainment and lūa'u take place at the Hyatt Regency Kaua'i Resort &Spa.
Nov.	**King Kalakaua Kupuna and Keiki Hula Festival** Big Island; ☎ 808/329–1532: Both children and *kupuna* (adults 55 years and older) compete at this popular hula contest. **Kona Coffee Cultural Festival** Big Island; ☎ 808/326–7820: A weeklong celebration, including two parades and a family day with ethnic foods and entertainment at Hale Halawai Recreation Pavilion, follows the coffee harvest. **Hawai'i's Big Island Festival** Big Island; ☎ 808/326–7820: This celebration of diversity explores the cultures, cuisines, and healing traditions of islanders. **Waikīkī ArtFest** O'ahu; ☎ 808/696–6717: More than 75 of O'ahu's finest artists and handcrafters demonstrate and sell their products at Kapiolani Park. **A Birthday Celebration for a King** O'ahu; ☎ 808/538–1471: 'Iolani Palace commemorates King Kalakaua's birthday with entertainment and decorations of red, white, and blue bunting and Hawaiian flags adorning the palace and grounds. **Hula O Na Keiki** Maui; ☎ 800/262–8450: Children from Hawai'i, California, Las Vegas and Japan compete in this annual contest held at the Kā'anapali Beach Hotel.

PLEASURES & PASTIMES

Acres of Parkland

Like many other states, Hawai'i has sought to protect some of its natural beauty by designating portions of its property national and state parkland. The Islands have a total of seven national parks, national historic parks, and national memorials, along with more than 75 state parks and historic sites.

Hawai'i's two national parks are centered around one of the Islands most exciting attractions: volcanoes. Kīlauea volcano in the Big Island's Hawai'i Volcanoes National Park has been in a state of constant eruption since 1982, and at times, you can catch a glimpse of molten lava hissing into the ocean. Maui's Haleakalā draws a large number of tours who make the two-hour drive to the summit to see the sun rise. Any time of day, however, will find plenty of sights on, in, and around the dormant volcano.

Other national areas run the gamut from royal fishponds to ancient places of worship to Pearl Harbor memorials. State parks range from the 2½-acre wayside stop at O'ahu's Nu'uanu Pali Lookout to the 6,175-acre Nā Pali Coast State Park on Kaua'i.

Golfing

It seems like every square foot of available land has a golf course on it, and many of the Islands' challenging and beautiful links have been designed by such legends as Arnold Palmer, Ben Crenshaw, and Robert Trent Jones Jr.

Maui's greens get the most press due to several nationally televised pro tournaments, especially the EMC Kā'anapali Classic in October, where top Senior PGA players compete. Maui also has a stunning trio of 18-holers clinging to the slopes of Haleakalā volcano.

Not to be outdone, the Big Island has many courses that serve as emerald oases in the midst of black, barren lava fields. On Kaua'i and O'ahu, golf enthusiasts have the enviable task of choosing between fairways that tumble down the sides of mountains, leapfrog across rocky crevices beside the ocean, or serve as nesting areas and playgrounds for black swans. Even Lāna'i has two championship courses.

Lū'au Feasting

Just about everyone who comes to Hawai'i goes to at least one lū'au. Traditionally, lū'au last for days, with feasts, sporting events, hula, and song. But at today's scaled-down version you're as likely to find macaroni salad on the buffet as poi, and heaps of fried chicken beside kālua pig.

If you want authenticity, look in the newspaper to see if a church or civic club is holding a lū'au fund-raiser. You'll not only be welcome, you'll experience some downhome Hawaiiana.

Miles of Beaches

To many O'ahu's Waikīkī Beach epitomizes Hawai'i's beach culture. This hotel-studded strip is tough to beat for convenience to restaurants and shopping, but the big waves are on the North Shore's Sunset Beach and along Waimea Bay. Kailua Beach Park is the site of international windsurfing competitions; its neighbor, Lanikai Beach is often referred to as the most beautiful beach in the world; and, Makapu'u Beach, near Sea Life Park, has some of the best bodysurfing in the state.

The sun arcs slowly over Maui's beaches, because, according to legend, the demigod Maui caught the culprit in his lasso and demanded longer daylight hours. You can catch the rays in seclusion on the sands of Mākena, admire windsurfing skills at Ho'okipa, or people-watch at the resort-lined Kā'anapali Beach.

Kaua'i's beaches have found fame as movie sets. And white, black, and green-sand beaches are attractions in their own right on the Big Island, where Kīlauea Volcano is actively adding to the island's future sandy shores by sending rivers of hot lava steaming into the ocean. Even diminutive Moloka'i and Lāna'i can claim their share of sandy retreats, such as Moloka'i's 3-mi-long Pāpōhaku Beach, the largest white-sand beach in the state; and Lāna'i's Hulopo'e Beach, which has great snorkeling.

Safety deserves a mention here. Ocean waves and currents are often unpredictable, so be careful, even if you are an experienced swimmer. Watch for signs warning of dangerous undertows or occasional invasions of stinging jellyfish, and check to see if your chosen beach has a lifeguard—many do not.

In true aloha spirit, there's no such thing as a private beach in Hawai'i—even those fronting luxury hotels are open to the public.

Scuba Diving

As the Islands emerged millions of years ago, molten lava spilled into the sea and cooled to form cavernous rooms, archways, pinnacles needling skyward, and networks of tunnels called lava tubes. Hawai'i's colorful coral reefs are home to nearly 600 species of tropical fish, including parrot fish, yellow butterfly fish, and the official state fish, the aggressive humuhumunukunukuāpua'a. Other residents include green sea turtles; acrobatic spinner dolphins; graceful manta rays and spotted eagle rays; and cruising white-tip, black-tip, hammerhead, sandbar, and tiger sharks. With all this going on underwater, it's no wonder Hawai'i is among the most popular scuba diving destinations in the world.

A number of areas, such as Molokini Crater off the coast of Maui, are marine preserves where no fishing or shell collecting is allowed. Other great diving spots—where you may become unwitting guests at a scuba wedding ceremony—include the wrecks of sunken ships, aircraft, and World War II vessels. The most popular dive sites are on the south and west shores of each island, which are protected from trade winds; on the north and east shores, beach entry can be dangerous during the winter months. Wherever you dive, you can usually count on visibility of more than 100 ft, and a year-round water temperature of 75°F–80°F.

Surfing

Surfers from around the world come to ride Hawai'i's formidable waves, including the bone-rattling Banzai Pipeline. Indeed, O'ahu's North Shore is an excellent place to view the veterans, especially during high-surf in December and January. For first-time surfers, Waikīkī Beach on O'ahu and Lahaina on Maui are probably the two best spots to pick up the basics; there are plenty of schools staffed by experienced local surfers who will be happy to show you the ropes.

FODOR'S CHOICE

The sights, restaurants, hotels, and other travel experiences on these pages are our editors' top picks—our Fodor's Choices. They're the best of their type in the area covered by the book—not to be missed and always worth your time. In the destination chapters that follow, you will find all the details.

LODGING

$$$$	**The Camps at Moloka'i Ranch, Moloka'i.** City slickers never had it so good in these upscale canvas bungalows.
$$$$	**Four Seasons Resort Huālalai, Big Island.** A resort that movie moguls dream of, with two-story bungalows by the ocean's edge.
$$$$	**Halekūlani, O'ahu.** This resort is one of the world's most sumptuous retreats.
$$$$	**Kaua'i Marriott Resort and Beach Club, Kaua'i.** Oceanfront lagoons, a spa, beachfront dining, golf, and tennis make this resort a destination unto itself.
$$$$	**Lodge at Kō'ele, Lāna'i.** Fireplaces warm this sprawling mountain retreat in the cool highlands.
$$$$	**Princeville Resort, Kaua'i.** This cliffside resort is Kaua'i's most romantic getaway.
$$$$	**Ritz-Carlton, Kapalua, Maui.** A magnificent setting, terraced swimming pools, and exemplary service make for an island ideal.
$$$-$$$$	**Turtle Bay Resort, O'ahu.** At the ocean's edge, cottages offer a private, elegant getaway within steps of fine dining, golf, tennis, and hiking.
$$-$$$	**Old Wailuku Inn, Maui.** This beautiful historic property in a quiet Wailuku neighborhood has been lovingly restored.
$$	**Kilauea Lodge, Big Island.** This rustic country inn is nestled in the cool fern forest near Hawai'i Volcanoes National Park.

BUDGET LODGING

$	**Hotel Moloka'i, Moloka'i.** Nothing can beat this simple seaside hotel for unfeigned, down-home aloha spirit.

RESTAURANTS

$$$-$$$$	**Capische, Maui.** This restaurant is doubly charmed—an exquisite menu paired with the island's best sunset view.
$$$-$$$$	**Orchids at the Halekulani, O'ahu.** Enjoy splendid seafood surrounded by a riot of orchids in this oceanside restaurant.
$$$-$$$$	**Pahui'a at Four Seasons Resort Huālalai, Big Island.** At night, spotlights illuminate the surf—just feet from your table.
$$$	**Formal Dining Room, Lodge at Kō'ele, Lāna'i.** Fresh local ingredients reign in this elegant Upcountry restaurant.

$$–$$$	**Hoku's at the Kāhala Mandarin Oriental, Oʻahu** Endless ocean views, attentive staff, and a menu that travels the world—from Indian nan to Asian stir-frys.
$$–$$$	**Mama's Fish House, Maui.** Mama's mixes the best mai tais on the island, and the fish arrives fresh-off-the-boats every morning.

BUDGET RESTAURANTS

$	**Hamura Saimin, Līhuʻe, Kauaʻi.** Do as approximately 999 others do each day: come here for a delicious bowl of *saimin*.
$	**Kanemitsu Bakery and Restaurant, Molokaʻi.** Don't miss the sweet, round Molokaʻi bread baked on the premises.
¢	**Ba Le, Kahului, Maui.** You'll find the island's best fast food at this popular Vietnamese eatery.

BEACHES

Anaehoʻomalu Beach, Big Island. A beautiful golden-sand crescent complete with ancient fishponds.

Hāpuna Beach, Big Island. In summer this clean, wide white-sand beach is perfect for snorkeling and scuba diving.

Hulopoʻe Beach, Lānaʻi. The island's only swimming beach is great for snorkeling.

Kahaloa and Ulukou Beaches, Oʻahu. The swimming stands out at these strands fronting Waikīkī's big hotels.

Lanikai Beach, Oʻahu. Buttery sand, turquoise waters, and sumptuous sunrises make this a classic postcard beach.

Lydgate State Park, Kauaʻi. This is a family-friendly beach at its best: snorkeling ponds, a playground, and a beach that begs for a good stroll.

Nāpili Beach, Maui. This sparkling white beach forms a secluded cove that's tailor-made for romantics.

Pāpōhaku Beach, Molokaʻi. You can always find a private section of glorious white sand on the island's longest beach.

Polihale Beach Park, Kauaʻi. Come for the breathtaking views of rugged cliffs; surf and currents make swimming dangerous.

Waiʻānapanapa State Park, Maui. Travelers on the Road to Hāna are rewarded with black sand contrasting with green Naupaka leaves.

OUTDOOR ACTIVITIES

Diving at Cathedrals, Lānaʻi. Brilliant fish, rays, and eels dart between the submerged towers of Cathedrals.

Hiking Haleakalā Crater, Maui. You can visit six different climate zones here on the cliffs of this dormant volcano.

Ironman Triathlon, Big Island. The mother of all triathlons takes place each October with 1,500 of the world's top athletes.

Kayaking, Kaua'i. For beginners there's the Wailua River; experienced kayakers can take to the open sea by the majestic Na'pali Coast.

Mule rides, Moloka'i. Meander down some of the highest sea cliffs in the world.

Surfing O'ahu's North Shore. Winter brings giant waves to Sunset Beach and Waimea Bay.

QUINTESSENTIAL HAWAI'I

Garden of the Gods, Lāna'i. This surreal landscape is scattered with red and black lava formations, with the blue Pacific in the background.

Hanauma Bay, O'ahu A magnificent tropical fishbowl, perfect for sunbathing, swimming, or snorkeling.

Kalaupapa National Historical Park, Moloka'i. This park combines natural grandeur with one of the most poignant and inspiring stories in state history.

Mauna Kea, Big Island. Hawai'i's tallest mountain is a sublime experience at both sunrise and sunset.

Road to Hāna, Maui. Fifty-five miles of curvy road forge a path through Maui's rain forest.

U.S.S. *Arizona* Memorial, O'ahu. The gleaming white memorial is a powerful testament.

Waimea Canyon and Kōke'e State Park, Kaua'i. The "Grand Canyon of the Pacific," is a mix of deep red canyons and verdant valleys.

SMART TRAVEL TIPS

Finding out about your destination before you leave home means you won't squander time organizing everyday minutiae once you've arrived. You'll be more streetwise when you hit the ground as well, better prepared to explore the aspects of Hawai'i that drew you here in the first place. The organizations in this section can provide information to supplement this guide; contact them for up-to-the-minute details, and consult the A to Z sections that end each chapter for facts on the various topics as they relate to Hawai'i's many regions. Happy landings!

AIR TRAVEL

Hawai'i is a major destination link for flights traveling to and from the U.S. mainland, Asia, Australia, New Zealand, and the South Pacific. Some of the major airline carriers serving Honolulu fly direct to the islands of Maui, Kaua'i, and the Big Island, allowing you to bypass connecting flights out of Honolulu. For the more spontaneous traveler, island-hopping is easy, with flights departing every 20 to 30 minutes daily until mid-evening. International travelers also have options: O'ahu and the Big Island are gateways into the United States. International visitors can save a considerable amount of time clearing U.S. Customs by entering via the Big Island's Kona International Airport at Keāhole.

BOOKING

When you book, **look for nonstop flights** and **remember that "direct" flights stop at least once.** Try to avoid connecting flights, which require a change of plane. Two airlines may operate a connecting flight jointly, so ask whether your airline operates every segment of the trip; you may find that the carrier you prefer flies you only part of the way. To find more booking tips and to check prices and make on-line flight reservations, log on to www.fodors.com.

CARRIERS

From the U.S. mainland, Delta serves Honolulu and Maui. Continental and Northwest fly into Honolulu. From the West Coast of the United States, American and United fly to Honolulu, Maui, the Big Island, and Kaua'i.

Aloha Airlines flies from California—from Burbank, Oakland, and Orange County—to Honolulu and from Las Vegas to Honolulu and Maui. Aloha flights also connect Vancouver, British Columbia, with Honolulu, and Oakland with the Big Island. Hawaiian Airlines serves Honolulu from Las Vegas, Los Angeles, Toronto, Phoenix, Portland, Sacramento, San Diego, San Francisco, and Seattle. Hawaiian also flies to Maui from Los Angeles, San Francisco, and Seattle. In addition to Aloha and Hawaiian, Island Air and Pacific Wings also provide interisland service. Paragon Airlines offers private charter service to all the Islands.

Major Airlines: American ☎ 800/433-7300. **Continental** ☎ 800/525-0280. **Delta** ☎ 800/221-1212. **Northwest** ☎ 800/225-2525. **United** ☎ 800/241-6522.

Direct Flights from the U.K.: Air New Zealand ☎ 0800/028-4149. **American** ☎ 0208/572-5555. **Continental** ☎ 0800/776-464. **Delta** ☎ 0800/414-767. **United** ☎ 0845/844-4777. **Trailfinders** ✉ 1 Threadneedle St., London EC2R 8JX ☎ 0207/628-7628 can arrange bargain flights.

Interisland Flights: Aloha Airlines ☎ 800/367-5250. **Hawaiian Airlines** ☎ 800/367-5320. **Island Air** ☎ 800/323-3345. **Pacific Wings** ☎ 888/575-4546. **Paragon Airlines** ☎ 800/428-1231.

CHECK-IN & BOARDING

Always **ask your carrier about its check-in policy.** Plan to arrive at the airport about 2 hours before your scheduled departure time for domestic flights and 2½ to 3 hours before international flights. You may need to arrive earlier if you're flying from one of the busier airports or during peak air-traffic times. Plan to **arrive at the airport 45 minutes to 60 minutes before departure for interisland flights.**

Although the Neighbor Island airports are smaller and more casual than Honolulu International, during peak times they can also be quite busy. Allot extra travel time to all airports during morning and afternoon rush-hour traffic periods. Prior to check-in, all luggage being taken out of Hawai'i must pass agricultural inspection. Fruit, plants, and processed foods that have been labeled and packed for export (including pineapples, papaya, coconuts, flowers, and macadamia nuts) are permitted. Fresh fruit and other agricultural items, including seed leis are not, and will be confiscated.

To avoid delays at airport-security checkpoints, try not to wear any metal. Jewelry, belt and other buckles, steel-toe shoes, barrettes, and underwire bras are among the items that can set off detectors.

Assuming that not everyone with a ticket will show up, airlines routinely overbook planes. When everyone does, airlines ask for volunteers to give up their seats. In return, these volunteers usually get a several-hundred-dollar flight voucher, which can be used toward the purchase of another ticket, and are rebooked on the next flight out. If there are not enough volunteers, the airline must choose who will be denied boarding. The first to get bumped are passengers who checked in late and those flying on discounted tickets, so **get to the gate and check in as early as possible,** especially during peak periods.

Always **bring a government-issued photo ID to the airport;** even when it's not required, a passport is best.

CUTTING COSTS

The least-expensive airfares to Hawai'i are priced for round-trip travel and must usually be purchased in advance. Airlines generally allow you to change your return date for a fee; most low-fare tickets, however, are nonrefundable. It's smart to **call a number of airlines and check the Internet;** when you are quoted a good price, **book it on the spot**—the same fare may not be available the next day, or even the next hour. Always **check different routings** and look into using alternate airports. Also, price off-peak flights, which may be significantly less expensive than others. Travel agents, especially low-fare specialists (⇨ Discounts and Deals), are helpful.

Consolidators are another good source. They buy tickets for scheduled flights at reduced rates from the airlines, then sell them at prices that beat the best fare available directly from the airlines. Sometimes you can even get your money back if you need to return the ticket. Carefully read the fine print detailing penalties for changes and cancellations, purchase the ticket with a credit card, and **confirm your consolidator reservation with the airline.**

Check local and community newspapers when you're in the Islands for deals and coupons on interisland flights.

In Hawai'i, Aloha Airlines and Hawaiian Airlines offer travelers multi-island air passes that allow unlimited interisland travel during a specific time period at a reduced rate. Aloha Airlines' passes will save you more money than Hawaiian Airlines', but they must be used between the first and last days of the month—Hawaiian Airlines' passes are valid for any 30 consecutive days.

When you **fly as a courier,** you trade your checked-luggage space for a ticket deeply subsidized by a courier service. There are restrictions on when you can book and how long you can stay. Some courier companies list with membership organizations, such as the Air Courier Association and the International Association of Air Travel Couriers; these require you to become a member before you can book a flight.

Many airlines, singly or in collaboration, offer discount air passes that allow foreigners to travel economically in a particular country or region. These visitor passes usually must be reserved and purchased before you leave home. Information about passes often can be found on most airlines' international Web pages, which tend to be aimed at travelers from outside the carrier's home country. Also, try typing the name of the pass into a search engine, or search for "pass" within the carrier's Web site.

Consolidators: **AirlineConsolidator.com** 📞 888/468-5385 🌐 www.airlineconsolidator.com for international tickets. **Best Fares** 📞 800/576-8255 or 800/576-1600 🌐 www.bestfares.com; $59.90 annual membership. **Cheap Tickets** 📞 800/377-1000 or 888/922-8849 🌐 www.cheaptickets.com. **Expedia** 📞 800/397-3342 or 404/728-8787 🌐 www.expedia.com. **Hotwire** 📞 866/468-9473 or 920/330-9418 🌐 www.hotwire.com. **Now Voyager Travel** ✉ 45 W. 21st St., 5th floor, New York, NY 10010 📞 212/459-1616 🖨 212/243-2711 🌐 www.nowvoyagertravel.com. **Onetravel.com** 🌐 www.onetravel.com. **Orbitz** 📞 888/656-4546 🌐 www.orbitz.com. **Priceline.com** 🌐 www.priceline.com. **Travelocity** 📞 888/709-5983, 877/282-2925 in Canada, 0870/876-3876 in U.K. 🌐 www.travelocity.com.

Courier Resources: **Air Courier Association/Cheaptrips.com** 📞 800/282-1202 🌐 www.aircourier.org or www.cheaptrips.com. **International Association of Air Travel Couriers** 📞 308/632-3273 🌐 www.courier.org.

Discount Passes: **Aloha Airlines** 📞 800/367-5250. **Hawaiian Airlines** 📞 800/367-5320.

ENJOYING THE FLIGHT

State your seat preference when purchasing your ticket, and then repeat it when you confirm and when you check in. For more legroom, you can request one of the few emergency-aisle seats at check-in, if you are capable of lifting at least 50 pounds—a Federal Aviation Administration requirement of passengers in these seats. Seats behind a bulkhead also offer more legroom, but they don't have underseat storage. Don't sit in the row in front of the emergency aisle or in front of a bulkhead, where seats may not recline.

Ask the airline whether a snack or meal is served on the flight. If you have dietary concerns, **request special meals when booking.** These can be vegetarian, low-cholesterol, or kosher, for example. It's a good idea to pack some healthful snacks and a small (plastic) bottle of water in your carry-on bag. On long flights, try to maintain a normal routine, to help fight jet lag. At night, **get some sleep.** By day, **eat light meals, drink water** (not alcohol), and **move around the cabin** to stretch your legs. For additional jet-lag tips consult *Fodor's FYI: Travel Fit & Healthy* (available at bookstores everywhere).

Smoking policies vary from carrier to carrier. Many airlines prohibit smoking on all of their flights; others allow smoking only on certain routes or certain departures. Ask your carrier about its policy.

FLYING TIMES

Flying time is about 10 hours from New York, 8 hours from Chicago, 5 hours from Los Angeles, and 15 hours from London, not including layovers.

HOW TO COMPLAIN

If your baggage goes astray or your flight goes awry, complain right away. Most carriers require that you **file a claim immediately.** The Aviation Consumer Protection Division of the Department of Transportation publishes *Fly-Rights*, which discusses airlines and consumer issues and is available on-line.

Aviation Consumer Protection Division ✉ U.S. Department of Transportation, C-75, Room 4107, 400 7th St. NW, Washington, DC 20590 📞 202/366-2220 🌐 www.dot.gov/airconsumer. **Federal Aviation Administration Consumer Hotline**

✉ for inquiries: FAA, 800 Independence Ave. SW, Room 810, Washington, DC 20591 ☎ 800/322-7873 🌐 www.faa.gov.

RECONFIRMING

Check the status of your flight before you leave for the airport. You can do this on your carrier's Web site, by linking to a flight-status checker (many Web booking services offer these), or by calling your carrier or travel agent.

AIRPORTS

Hawai'i's major airport is Honolulu International, on O'ahu, 20 minutes (9 mi) west of Waikīkī. To travel interisland from Honolulu, you can depart from either the interisland terminal or the commuter-airline terminal, located in two separate structures adjacent to the main overseas terminal building. A free bus service, the Wiki Wiki Shuttle, operates between terminals.

Maui has two major airports: Kahului Airport, which handles major airlines and interisland flights, and Kapalua–West Maui Airport, served by Aloha Airlines and Pacific Wings. If you're staying in West Maui and you're flying in from another island, you can avoid an hour's drive from the Kahului Airport by flying into Kapalua–West Maui Airport. The tiny town of Hāna in East Maui also has an airstrip, served by commuter planes from Honolulu and charter flights from Kahului and Kapalua. Flying here is a great option if you want to avoid the long drive to Hāna from one of the other airports.

Those flying to the Big Island of Hawai'i regularly land at one of two fields. Kona International Airport at Keāhole, on the west side, best serves Kailua-Kona, Keauhou, and the Kohala Coast. Hilo International Airport is more appropriate for those going to the east side. Waimea-Kohala Airport, called Kamuela Airport by residents, is used primarily for commuting among the Islands.

On Kaua'i, visitors fly into Līhu'e Airport, on the east side of the island.

Moloka'i's Ho'olehua Airport is small and centrally located, as is Lāna'i Airport. Both rural airports handle a limited number of flights per day. Visitors coming from the mainland to these islands must first stop in O'ahu and change to an interisland flight.

✈ O'ahu: **Honolulu International Airport** ☎ 808/836-6413. Maui: **Kahului Airport** ☎ 808/872-3893; **Kapalua-West Maui Airport** ☎ 808/669-0623; **Hāna Airport** ☎ 808/248-8208. The Big Island: **Kona International Airport at Keāhole** ☎ 808/329-3423; **Hilo International Airport** ☎ 808/934-5838; **Waimea-Kohala Airport** ☎ 808/887-8126. Kaua'i: **Līhu'e Airport** ☎ 808/246-1448. Moloka'i: **Ho'olehua Airport** ☎ 808/567-6361. Lāna'i: **Lāna'i Airport** ☎ 808/565-6757.

BIKE TRAVEL

Hawai'i's natural beauty, breathtaking coastal routes, and year-round fair weather make it attractive to explore by bike. However, on many roads, bicycle lanes are limited or nonexistent, and cyclists must contend with heavy traffic on the more populated islands; biking on O'ahu and Maui may require some skillful maneuvering. Bike routes on the Neighbor Islands include the challenge of riding the Big Island's 225-mi circle-island route, cycling downhill at Maui's Haleakalā crater, exploring the lush routes of tropical Kaua'i, and mastering off-road mountain biking on Lāna'i and Moloka'i. You can rent bikes for some solo cruising, join local cycling clubs for their weekly rides, or hit the road with outfitters for tours that go beyond the well-traveled paths.

✈ Bike Maps: **Division of Forestry and Wildlife, Kaua'i** ☎ 808/274-3433. **Division of Forestry and Wildlife, Maui** ☎ 808/984-8100. **Honolulu City and County Bike Coordinator** ☎ 808/527-5044.

✈ Rentals: **B&L Bike & Sports** Big Island ☎ 808/329-3309. **Blue Sky Rentals** O'ahu ☎ 808/947-0101. **Kaua'i Cycle and Tour** Kaua'i ☎ 808/821-2115. **Lāna'i Eco Adventure Centre** Lāna'i ☎ 808/565-7737 🌐 www.adventurelanai.com. **Moloka'i Bicycle** Moloka'i ☎ 808/553-3931 🌐 www.molokaibicycle.com. **Outfitters Kaua'i** Kaua'i ☎ 808/742-9667. **West Maui Cycles** Maui ☎ 808/661-9005.

BIKES IN FLIGHT

Most airlines accommodate bikes as luggage, provided they are dismantled and boxed; check with individual airlines about packing requirements. Some airlines sell bike boxes, which are often free at bike shops, for about $15 (bike bags can be considerably more expensive). International travelers often can substitute a bike for a piece of checked luggage at no charge; otherwise, the cost is about $100. U.S. and Canadian airlines charge $40–$80 each way.

BOAT & FERRY TRAVEL

Ferry travel in the Islands is limited to daily service between Lahaina, Maui, and Mānele Bay, Lāna'i. The 9-mi crossing costs about $50 round-trip and takes about 45 minutes or so, depending on ocean conditions (which can make this trip a rough one). Reservations are essential. ⁊ Excursions/Lāna'i Passenger Ferry ☎ 800/695-2624 ⊕ www.go-lanai.com.

BUSINESS HOURS

Even people in paradise have to work. Generally local business hours are weekdays 8–5. Banks are usually open Monday–Thursday 8:30–3 and until 6 on Friday. Some banks have Saturday-morning hours.

Many self-serve gas stations stay open around-the-clock, with full-service stations usually open from around 7 AM until 9 PM. U.S. post offices are open weekdays 8:30 AM–4:30 PM and Saturday 8:30–noon. On O'ahu, the Ala Moana post office branch is the only branch, other than the main Honolulu International Airport facility, that stays open until 4 PM on Saturday.

MUSEUMS & SIGHTS

Most museums generally open their doors between 9 AM and 10 AM and stay open until 5 PM Tuesday–Saturday. Many museums operate with afternoon hours only on Sunday and close on Monday. Visitor-attraction hours vary throughout the state, but most sights are open daily with the exception of major holidays such as Christmas. **Check local newspapers upon arrival for attraction hours and schedules if visiting over holiday periods.** The local dailies carry a listing of "What's Open/What's Not" for those time periods.

SHOPS

Stores in resort areas sometimes open as early as 8, with shopping-center opening hours varying from 9:30 to 10 on weekdays and Saturday, a bit later on Sunday. Bigger malls stay open until 9 weekdays and Saturday and close at 5 on Sunday. Boutiques in resort areas may stay open as late as 11.

BUS TRAVEL

Getting around by bus is an option on O'ahu, but on Neighbor Islands services are limited and car rental is recommended. O'ahu's transportation system, known just as TheBus, is one of the island's best bargains. Fares per ride are $1.50, and with more than 68 bus routes you can even do an O'ahu circle-island tour.

The Big Island's county bus, called Hele-On Bus, travels a Kailua-Kona–to–Hilo route once daily except Sunday. There are limited routes to other areas. On the island of Kaua'i, the Kaua'i Bus travels two main routes, one going north to Hanalei from Līhu'e and one going south from Līhu'e to Kekaha. Routes don't come close to many of the island's resorts or best-known attractions but do wind through residential towns. The Holo Ka'a Public Transit System has routes in South, West, and Central Maui. ⁊ Hele-On Bus on the Big Island ☎ 808/961-8744. Holo Ka'a Public Transit System on Maui ☎ 808/879-2828. Kaua'i Bus on Kaua'i ☎ 808/241-6410. TheBus on O'ahu ☎ 808/848-5555.

CAMERAS & PHOTOGRAPHY

Today's underwater "disposable" cameras can provide terrific photos for those once-in-a-lifetime underwater experiences. Film developing is available on all of the Islands. Many hotel/resort sundries stores offer the service, and larger department stores, such as Long's Drugs, have one-hour service for regular film developing and overnight service for panoramic film.

The *Kodak Guide to Shooting Great Travel Pictures* (available at bookstores everywhere) is loaded with tips. ⁊ Photo Help: Kodak Information Center ☎ 800/242-2424 ⊕ www.kodak.com.

EQUIPMENT PRECAUTIONS

Don't pack film and equipment in checked luggage, where it is much more susceptible to damage. X-ray machines used to view checked luggage are extremely powerful and therefore are likely to ruin your film. Try to **ask for hand inspection of film,** which becomes clouded after repeated exposure to airport X-ray machines, and **keep videotapes and computer disks away from metal detectors.** Always **keep film, tape, and computer disks out of**

the sun. Carry an extra supply of batteries, and **be prepared to turn on your camera, camcorder, or laptop** to prove to airport security personnel that the device is real.

CAR RENTAL

You can rent anything from a $26-a-day econobox to a $1,100-a-day Ferrari. It's wise to make reservations in advance, especially if visiting during peak seasons or for a major convention or sporting event.

Rates in Honolulu begin at $38 a day ($164 a week) for an economy car with air-conditioning, automatic transmission, and unlimited mileage. Rates on Maui begin at $32 a day ($144 a week) for the same. This does not include tax, insurance, and a $2-per-day road tax.

Alamo ☎ 800/327-9633 ⊕ www.alamo.com. **Avis** ☎ 800/331-1212; 800/879-2847 or 800/272-5871 in Canada; 0870/606-0100 in U.K.; 02/9353-9000 in Australia; 09/526-2847 in New Zealand ⊕ www.avis.com. **Budget** ☎ 800/527-0700; 0870/156-5656 in U.K. ⊕ www.budget.com. **Dollar** ☎ 800/800-4000; 0124/622-0111 in U.K., where it's affiliated with Sixt; 02/9223-1444 in Australia ⊕ www.dollar.com. **Hertz** ☎ 800/654-3131; 800/263-0600 in Canada; 0870/844-8844 in U.K.; 02/9669-2444 in Australia; 09/256-8690 in New Zealand ⊕ www.hertz.com. **National Car Rental** ☎ 800/227-7368; 0870/600-6666 in U.K. ⊕ www.nationalcar.com.

CUTTING COSTS

For a good deal, **book through a travel agent, who will shop around.** Also, **price local car-rental companies,** which usually carry pre-owned cars—a popular rental option for the Islands, although the service and maintenance may not be as good as those of a major player. Remember to ask about required deposits, cancellation penalties, and drop-off charges if you're planning to pick up the car in one city and leave it in another. If you're traveling during a holiday period, make sure that a confirmed reservation guarantees you a car.

For a better rental deal, check out local and national promotions as well as discounts offered through frequent-flyer programs, automobile clubs, or business or military affiliations. Many rental companies in Hawai'i also offer coupons for discounts at various attractions that could save you money later on in your trip.

Local Agencies: AA Aloha Cars-R-Us ☎ 800/655-7989 ⊕ www.hawaiicarrental.com. **JN Car and**

Truck Rentals ☎ 800/475-7522, 808/831-2724 on O'ahu, 808/877-7368 on Maui ⊕ www.jnautomotive.com. **NoKa Oi** ☎ 808/877-3300 or 800/567-4659 ⊕ www.mauicarrentals.net on Maui. **VIP Car Rentals** ☎ 808/922-4605 on O'ahu.

INSURANCE

When driving a rented car you are generally responsible for any damage to or loss of the vehicle. You also may be liable for any property damage or personal injury that you may cause while driving. Before you rent, see what coverage you already have under the terms of your personal auto-insurance policy and credit cards.

For about $10 to $25 a day, rental companies sell protection, known as a collision- or loss-damage waiver (CDW or LDW), that eliminates your liability for damage to the car; it's always optional and should never be automatically added to your bill. In most states you don't need a CDW if you have personal auto insurance or other liability insurance. However, **make sure you have enough coverage to pay for the car.** If you do not have auto insurance or an umbrella policy that covers damage to third parties, purchasing liability insurance and a CDW or LDW is highly recommended.

REQUIREMENTS & RESTRICTIONS

In Hawai'i you must be 21 years of age to rent a car and you must have a valid driver's license and a major credit card. Those under 25 will pay a daily surcharge of $15.

In Hawai'i your unexpired mainland driver's license is valid for rental for up to 90 days.

SURCHARGES

Before you pick up a car in one city and leave it in another, **ask about drop-off charges or one-way service fees,** which can be substantial. Note, too, that some rental agencies charge extra if you return the car before the time specified in your contract. To avoid a hefty refueling fee, **fill the tank just before you turn in the car,** but be aware that gas stations near the rental outlet may overcharge. It's almost never a deal to buy the tank of gas that's in the car when you rent it; the understanding is that you'll return it empty, but some fuel usually remains. Surcharges may apply if you're under 25 or if you take the car outside the area approved by the rental agency. You'll pay extra for child seats (about $6 a day), which are compulsory for children under four, and usually for additional drivers (about $10 per day).

CAR TRAVEL

Technically, the Big Island of Hawai'i is the only island you can completely circle by car, but each island offers plenty of sightseeing from its miles of roadways. O'ahu can be circled except for the roadless west-shore area around Ka'ena Point. Elsewhere, major highways follow the shoreline and traverse the island at two points. Rush-hour traffic (6:30 to 8:30 AM and 3:30 to 6 PM) can be frustrating around Honolulu and the outlying areas, as many thoroughfares allow no left turns due to contra-flow lanes. Traffic on Maui can be very bad branching out from Kahului to and from Paia, Kihei, and Lahaina. Drive here during peak hours and you'll know why local residents are calling for restrictions on development. Parking along many streets is curtailed during these times, and towing is strictly practiced. Read curbside parking signs before leaving your vehicle, even at a meter.

GASOLINE

Regardless of today's fluctuating gas prices, you can pretty much count on having to pay more at the pump for gasoline in the Islands than on the U.S. mainland.

ROAD CONDITIONS

It's difficult to get lost in most of Hawai'i. Roads and streets, although they may challenge the visitor's tongue, are well marked. **Keep an eye open for the Hawai'i Visitors and Convention Bureau's red-caped King Kamehameha signs,** which mark major attractions and scenic spots. Ask for a map at the car-rental counter. Free publications containing good-quality road maps can be found on all Islands, too.

The Big Island and O'ahu have well-maintained roads, which can be easily negotiated and do not require a four-wheel-drive vehicle. Kaua'i has a well-maintained highway running south from Līhu'e to Barking Sands Beach; a spur at Waimea takes you along Waimea Canyon to Kōke'e State Park. A northern route also winds its way from Līhu'e to end at Hā'ena, the beginning of the rugged and roadless Nā Pali Coast. Maui also has its share of impenetrable areas, although four-wheel-drive vehicles rarely run into problems on the island. Although Moloka'i and Lāna'i have fewer roadways, car rental is still worthwhile and will allow plenty of interesting sightseeing. **Opt for a four-wheel-drive vehicle** if dirt-road exploration holds any appeal.

RULES OF THE ROAD

Be sure to **buckle up.** Hawai'i has a strictly enforced seat-belt law for front-seat passengers. Children under four must be in a car seat (available from car-rental agencies). Children 18 and under, riding in the backseat, are also required by state law to use seat belts. The highway speed limit is usually 55 mph. In-town traffic moves from 25 to 40 mph. Jaywalking is very common, so be particularly watchful for pedestrians, especially in congested areas such as Waikīkī. Unauthorized use of a parking space reserved for persons with disabilities can net you a $150 fine.

Asking for directions will almost always produce a helpful explanation from the locals, but you should be prepared for an island term or two. Instead of using compass directions, remember that Hawai'i residents refer to places as being either *mauka* (toward the mountains) or *makai* (toward the ocean) from one another. Other directions depend on your location: in Honolulu, for example, people say to "go Diamond Head," which means toward that famous landmark, or to "go 'ewa," meaning in the opposite direction. A shop on the mauka–Diamond Head corner of a street is on the mountain side of the street on the corner closest to Diamond Head. It all makes perfect sense once you get the lay of the land.

CHILDREN IN HAWAI'I

Sunny beaches and many family-oriented cultural sites, activities, and attractions make Hawai'i a very *keiki*- (child-) friendly place. Here kids can swim with a dolphin, surf with a boogie board, check out an active volcano, or ride a sugarcane train. Parents should **use caution on beaches and during water sports.** Even waters that appear calm can harbor powerful rip currents. Be sure to **read any beach-warning guides your hotel may provide. Ask around for kid-friendly beaches** that might have shallow tide pools or are protected by reefs. And remember that the sun's rays are in operation full-force year-round here. Sunblock for children is essential. If you are renting a car, don't forget to **arrange for a car seat** when you reserve. For general advice about traveling with children, consult *Fodor's FYI: Travel with Your Baby* (available in bookstores everywhere).

Most major resort chains in Hawai'i offer children's activity programs for kids ages 5 to 12. These kid clubs provide opportunities to learn about local culture, make friends with children from around the world, and experience age-appropriate activities while giving moms and dads a "time-out." Upon arrival, check out the daily local newspapers for children's events. The *Honolulu Advertiser's* "TGIF" section each Friday includes a section on keiki activities with a local flavor.

FLYING

If your children are two or older, **ask about children's airfares.** As a general rule, infants under two not occupying a seat fly at greatly reduced fares or even for free. But if you want to guarantee a seat for an infant, you have to pay full fare. Consider flying during off-peak days and times; most airlines will grant an infant a seat without a ticket if there are available seats.

Experts agree that it's a good idea to use safety seats aloft for children weighing less than 40 pounds. Airlines set their own policies: if you use a safety seat, U.S. carriers usually require that the child be ticketed, even if he or she is young enough to ride free, because the seats must be strapped into regular seats. And even if you pay the full adult fare for the seat, it may be worth it, especially on longer trips. Do **check your airline's policy about using safety seats during takeoff and landing.** Safety seats are not allowed everywhere in the plane, so get your seat assignments as early as possible.

When reserving, **request children's meals or a freestanding bassinet** (not available at all airlines) if you need them. But note that bulkhead seats, where you must sit to use the bassinet, may lack an overhead bin or storage space on the floor.

LODGING

Families can't go wrong choosing resort locations that are part of larger hotel chains such as Hilton, Sheraton, Outrigger, and Westin. Many of these resorts are on the best beaches on each island, have activities created for children, and are centrally located. Outrigger's "Ohana" brand hotels are off the beachfront but provide great value at good prices. Many condominium resorts now also offer children's activities and amenities during holiday periods. Most hotels allow children under a certain age to stay in their parents' room at no extra charge, but others charge for them as extra adults. Be sure to **find out the cutoff age for children's discounts.** Also **check for special seasonal programs,** such as "kids eat free" promotions.

🇫 Best Choices: Aston Hotels ☎ 800/922-7866 ⊕ www.aston-hotels.com. **Four Seasons Hotels and Resorts** ☎ 800/819-5053 ⊕ www.fourseasons.com. **Hilton** ☎ 800/774-1500 ⊕ www.hilton.com. **Hyatt Hotels & Resorts** ☎ 888/591-1234 ⊕ www.hyatt.com. **Marriott** ☎ 888/236-2427 ⊕ www.marriott.com. **Moloka'i Ranch** ☎ 877/726-4656 ⊕ www.molokai-ranch.com. **Outrigger Hotels** ☎ 800/688-7444 ⊕ www.outrigger.com. **Starwood Hotels and Resorts** ☎ 888/625-5144 for Westin and Sheraton, 800/325-3589 for Luxury Collection, 877/946-8357 for W Hotels ⊕ www.starwood.com.

SIGHTS & ATTRACTIONS

Top picks for children run the gamut from natural attractions kids can enjoy for free to some fairly expensive amusements. On O'ahu, favorites include hiking Diamond Head, snorkeling Hanauma Bay, learning about marine life at Sea Life Park, playing ancient Hawaiian games at Waimea Valley Adventures Park, and touring through South Pacific cultures at the Polynesian Cultural Center. On Maui, kid favorites include the Sugarcane Train that runs between Lahaina and Kā'anapali, snorkeling at Molokini Island, and whale-watching after a visit to the Maui Ocean Center. Visiting Hawai'i Volcanoes National Park, touring the Mauna Loa Macadamia Factory near Hilo, swimming with dolphins at the Hilton Waikoloa, and horseback riding at Parker Ranch are fun things to do on the Big Island.

Kaua'i is where kids go to explore film locations such as Peter Pan's Never-Never Land and Jurassic Park. They can learn to water-ski on the Wailua River, visit Kōke'e National Park, or just spend the day swimming Po'ipū's sunny south shores. Lāna'i and Moloka'i are great islands for adventurous youngsters. At Moloka'i Ranch & Lodge, families can sleep in "tentalows" and tackle the rope-challenge course for excitement. On Lāna'i, four-wheel-drive off-road adventure tours take families to destinations such as Shipwreck Beach and Mānele Bay, where the dolphins sometimes come to play.

Places that are especially appealing to children are indicated by a rubber-duckie icon (☺) in the margin.

CONSUMER PROTECTION

Whether you're shopping for gifts or purchasing travel services, **pay with a major credit card** whenever possible, so you can cancel payment or get reimbursed if there's a problem (and you can provide documentation). If you're doing business with a particular company for the first time, **contact your local Better Business Bureau and the attorney general's offices** in your state and (for U.S. businesses) the company's home state as well. Have any complaints been filed? Finally, if you're buying a package or tour, always **consider travel insurance** that includes default coverage (⇨ Insurance).

🛈 **Council of Better Business Bureaus** ⊠ 4200 Wilson Blvd., Suite 800, Arlington, VA 22203 ☎ 703/ 276-0100 🖷 703/525-8277 ⊕ www.bbb.org.

CRUISE TRAVEL

When Pan Am's amphibious *Hawai'i Clipper* touched down on Pearl Harbor's waters in 1936, it marked the beginning of the end of regular passenger-ship travel to the Islands. From that point on, the predominant means of transporting visitors would be by air, not by sea. Today, however, cruising to Hawai'i is making a comeback.

Norwegian Cruise Lines has a multi-island "freestyle" cruise (no set meal times, less formal clothing, more nightlife choices) on the *Norwegian Star* and *Norwegian Wind*. To get the best deal on a cruise, **consult a cruise-only travel agency.**

Even if you choose, as most travelers do, to travel by air to the Islands, you can get the flavor of what the luxury-cruise era in Hawai'i was like by checking out Aloha Tower Marketplace's Boat Day Celebrations in Honolulu. Vessels stopping here are met upon arrival by hula dancers and the kind of entertainment and floral festivities that once greeted travelers almost a century ago. Contact the Aloha Tower Marketplace for a boat-day schedule upon arrival.

To learn how to plan, choose, and book a cruise-ship voyage, consult *Fodor's FYI: Plan & Enjoy Your Cruise* (available in bookstores everywhere).

🛈 **Aloha Tower Marketplace** ⊠ 1 Aloha Tower Dr., at Piers 8, 9, and 10, Honolulu ☎ 808/528-5700 ⊕ www.alohatower.com. **Carnival** ☎ 888/227-6482 ⊕ www.carnival.com. **Celebrity** ☎ 800/722-5941 ⊕ www.celebritycruises.com. **Crystal Cruises** ☎ 800/820-6663 ⊕ www.crystalcruises.com. **Cunard** ☎ 800/728-6273 ⊕ www.cunard.com. **Holland America** ☎ 877/724-5425 ⊕ www.hollandamerica.com. **Norwegian Cruise Lines** ☎ 800/327-7030 ⊕ www.norwegiancruiselines.com. **Princess** ☎ 800/774-6237 ⊕ www.princess.com. **Royal Caribbean Cruise Line** ☎ 800/398-9819 ⊕ www.royalcaribbean.com. **Seabourn** ☎ 800/929-9391 ⊕ www.seabourn.com.

CUSTOMS & DUTIES

When shopping abroad, **keep receipts** for all purchases. Upon reentering the country, **be ready to show customs officials what you've bought.** Pack purchases together in an easily accessible place. If you think a duty is incorrect, appeal the assessment. If you object to the way your clearance was handled, note the inspector's badge number. In either case, first ask to see a supervisor. If the problem isn't resolved, write to the appropriate authorities, beginning with the port director at your point of entry.

IN AUSTRALIA

Australian residents who are 18 or older may bring home A$400 worth of souvenirs and gifts (including jewelry), 250 cigarettes or 250 grams of cigars or other tobacco products, and 1,125 ml of alcohol (including wine, beer, and spirits). Residents under 18 may bring back A$200 worth of goods. Members of the same family traveling together may pool their allowances. Prohibited items include meat products. Seeds, plants, and fruits need to be declared upon arrival.

🛈 **Australian Customs Service** 🕾 Regional Director, Box 8, Sydney, NSW 2001 ☎ 02/9213-2000 or

1300/363263, 02/9364-7222 or 1800/803-006 quarantine-inquiry line ☎ 02/9213-4043 ⊕ www. customs.gov.au.

IN CANADA

Canadian residents who have been out of Canada for at least seven days may bring in C$750 worth of goods duty-free. If you've been away fewer than seven days but more than 48 hours, the duty-free allowance drops to C$200. If your trip lasts 24 to 48 hours, the allowance is C$50. You may not pool allowances with family members. Goods claimed under the C$750 exemption may follow you by mail; those claimed under the lesser exemptions must accompany you. Alcohol and tobacco products may be included in the seven-day and 48-hour exemptions but not in the 24-hour exemption. If you meet the age requirements of the province or territory through which you reenter Canada, you may bring in, duty-free, 1.5 liters of wine *or* 1.14 liters (40 imperial ounces) of liquor *or* 24 12-ounce cans or bottles of beer or ale. Also, if you meet the local age requirement for tobacco products, you may bring in, duty-free, 200 cigarettes and 50 cigars. Check ahead of time with the Canada Customs and Revenue Agency or the Department of Agriculture for policies regarding meat products, seeds, plants, and fruits.

You may send an unlimited number of gifts (only one gift per recipient, however) worth up to C$60 each duty-free to Canada. Label the package UNSOLICITED GIFT—VALUE UNDER $60. Alcohol and tobacco are excluded.

🛈 **Canada Customs and Revenue Agency** ✉ 2265 St. Laurent Blvd., Ottawa, Ontario K1G 4K3 ☎ 800/ 461-9999, 204/983-3500, 506/636-5064 ⊕ www. ccra.gc.ca.

IN HAWAI'I

Plants and plant products are subject to regulation by the Department of Agriculture, both on entering and leaving Hawai'i. Upon leaving the Islands, you'll have to have your bags X-rayed and tagged at one of the airport's agricultural inspection stations before you proceed to check-in. Pineapples and coconuts with the packer's agricultural inspection stamp pass freely; papayas must be treated, inspected, and stamped. All other fruits are banned for export to the U.S. mainland. Flowers pass except for gardenia, rose leaves, jade vine, and mauna loa. Also banned are insects, snails, soil, cotton, cacti, sugarcane, and all berry plants.

You'll have to **leave dogs and other pets at home.** A strict six-month quarantine is imposed to keep out rabies, which is nonexistent in Hawai'i.

🛈 **U.S. Bureau of Customs and Border Protection** for inquiries ✉ 1300 Pennsylvania Ave. NW, Washington, DC 20229 ☎ 202/354-1000 ⊕ www. customs.gov for complaints ✉ Customer Satisfaction Unit, 1300 Pennsylvania Ave. NW, Room 5.5A, Washington, DC 20229.

IN NEW ZEALAND

All homeward-bound residents may bring back NZ$700 worth of souvenirs and gifts; passengers may not pool their allowances, and children can claim only the concession on goods intended for their own use. For those 17 or older, the duty-free allowance also includes 4.5 liters of wine or beer; one 1,125-ml bottle of spirits; and either 200 cigarettes, 250 grams of tobacco, 50 cigars, *or* a combination of the three up to 250 grams. Meat products, seeds, plants, and fruits must be declared upon arrival to the Agricultural Services Department.

🛈 **New Zealand Customs** ✉ Head office: The Customhouse, 17–21 Whitmore St., Box 2218, Wellington ☎ 09/300-5399 or 0800/428-786 ⊕ www.customs. govt.nz.

IN THE U.K.

From countries outside the European Union, including the United States, you may bring home, duty-free, 200 cigarettes or 50 cigars; 1 liter of spirits or 2 liters of fortified or sparkling wine or liqueurs; 2 liters of still table wine; 60 ml of perfume; 250 ml of toilet water; plus £145 worth of other goods, including gifts and souvenirs. Prohibited items include meat products, seeds, plants, and fruits.

🛈 **HM Customs and Excise** ✉ Portcullis House, 21 Cowbridge Rd. E, Cardiff CF11 9SS ☎ 0845/ 010-9000 or 0208/929-0152, 0208/929-6731 or 0208/910-3602 complaints ⊕ www.hmce.gov.uk.

DISABILITIES & ACCESSIBILITY

The Society for the Advancement of Travel for the Handicapped has named Hawai'i the most accessible vacation spot for people with disabilities. Ramped visitor areas and specially equipped lodgings are relatively common. The Hawai'i Center for Independent Living distributes the "Aloha Guide to Accessibility," which lists addresses and telephone numbers for support-service organizations and rates the Islands' hotels, beaches, shopping and entertainment centers, and major attractions. The guide costs $15 but is available in sections for $3 to $5 per section. Part I (general information) is free. Travelers with vision impairments who use a guide dog don't have to worry about quarantine restrictions. All you need to do is present documentation that the animal is a trained guide dog and has a current inoculation record for rabies.

🖪 Disability and Communication Access Board ✉ 919 Ala Moana Blvd., Room 101, Honolulu, O'ahu 96814 ☎ 808/586-8121. **Hawai'i Center for Independent Living** ✉ 414 Kauwili St., Suite 102, Honolulu, O'ahu 96817 ☎ 808/522-5400.

LODGING

Travelers with disabilities and people using wheelchairs find it easy to get around Hawai'i's resorts and hotels, with indoor-outdoor layouts that are easily navigated. If choosing a smaller hotel or a condo or apartment rental, inquire about ground-floor accommodations and **check to see if rooms will accommodate wheelchairs and if bathrooms are accessible.** Many hotels now offer special-needs rooms featuring larger living spaces and bathrooms equipped for guests who require additional assistance.

Despite the Americans with Disabilities Act, the definition of accessibility seems to differ from hotel to hotel. Some properties may be accessible by ADA standards for people with mobility problems but not for people with hearing or vision impairments, for example.

If you have mobility problems, ask for the lowest floor on which accessible services are offered. If you have a hearing impairment, check whether the hotel has devices to alert you visually to the ring of the telephone, a knock at the door, and a fire/emergency alarm. Some hotels provide these devices without charge. Discuss your needs with hotel personnel if this equipment isn't available, so that a staff member can personally alert you in the event of an emergency.

If you're bringing a guide dog, get authorization ahead of time and write down the name of the person with whom you spoke.

RESERVATIONS

When discussing accessibility with an operator or reservations agent, **ask hard questions.** Are there any stairs, inside *or* out? Are there grab bars next to the toilet *and* in the shower/tub? How wide is the doorway to the room? To the bathroom? For the most extensive facilities meeting the latest legal specifications, **opt for newer accommodations.** If you reserve through a toll-free number, consider also calling the hotel's local number to confirm the information from the central reservations office. Get confirmation in writing when you can.

SIGHTS & ATTRACTIONS

Many of Hawai'i's sights and attractions are accessible to travelers with disabilities. The state's number one attraction, Hawai'i Volcanoes National Park, includes a drive-through volcano. In Waikīkī, the Honolulu Department of Parks and Recreation can assist in obtaining an "all-terrain" wheelchair for strolls down the beach. Accessible Vans of Hawaii rents wheelchairs and scooter vans on O'ahu, Maui, and the Big Island. In addition, the company can arrange accessible accommodations, sightseeing, dining, activities, medical-equipment rentals, and personal care attendants.

🖪 Accessible Vans of Hawaii ☎ 800/303-3750 ⊕ www.accessiblevanshawaii.com. **Honolulu Department of Parks and Recreation** Therapeutic Recreation Unit ☎ 808/522-7034.

TRANSPORTATION

Paratransit Services (HandiVan) will take you to a specific destination on O'ahu—not on sightseeing outings—in vans with lifts and lock-downs. With a HandiVan Pass, one-way trips cost $1.50. Passes are free and can be obtained from the Department of Transportation Services, which is open weekdays 7:45–4:30; you'll need a doctor's written confirmation of your disability or a paratransit ID card. Handi-Cabs of the Pacific also operates ramp-equipped vans with lock-downs in Honolulu. Fares are $10 plus $2.40 per mi for curbside service. Reservations at least 48 hours in advance are required by both companies, so plan ahead.

Those who prefer to do their own driving may rent hand-controlled cars from Avis (reserve 24 hours ahead) and Hertz (24- to 72-hour notice required). You can use the windshield card from your own state to park in spaces reserved for people with disabilities.

Avis ☎ 800/230-4898. **Department of Transportation Services** ✉ 711 Kapi'olani Blvd., Honolulu 96819 ☎ 808/523-4083. **Handi-Cabs of the Pacific** ☎ 808/524-3866. **Hertz** ☎ 800/654-3131. **Paratransit Services (HandiVan)** ☎ 808/456-5555.

TRAVEL AGENCIES

In the United States, the Americans with Disabilities Act requires that travel firms serve the needs of all travelers. Some agencies specialize in working with people with disabilities.

Travelers with Mobility Problems: Access Adventures ✉ 206 Chestnut Ridge Rd., Scottsville, NY 14624 ☎ 585/889-9096 ✍ dltravel@prodigy.net, run by a former physical-rehabilitation counselor. **Accessible Vans of America** ✉ 9 Spielman Rd., Fairfield, NJ 07004 ☎ 877/282-8267, 973/808-9709 reservations ☐ 973/808-9713 ⊕ www. accessiblevans.com. **Accessible Vans of Hawaii** ✉ 296 Alamaha St., Suite C, Kahului, HI 96732 ☎ 808/871-7785 or 800/303-3750 ☐ 808/871-7536 ⊕ www.accessiblevanshawaii.com. **CareVacations** ✉ No. 5, 5110-50 Ave., Leduc, Alberta, Canada, T9E 6V4 ☎ 780/986-6404 or 877/478-7827 ☐ 780/986-8332 ⊕ www.carevacations.com, for group tours and cruise vacations. **Flying Wheels Travel** ✉ 143 W. Bridge St., Box 382, Owatonna, MN 55060 ☎ 507/451-5005 ☐ 507/451-1685 ⊕ www. flyingwheelstravel.com.

Travelers with Developmental Disabilities: New Directions ✉ 5276 Hollister Ave., Suite 207, Santa Barbara, CA 93111 ☎ 805/967-2841 or 888/967-2841 ☐ 805/964-7344 ⊕ www. newdirectionstravel.com.

DISCOUNTS & DEALS

Be a smart shopper and compare all your options before making decisions. A plane ticket bought with a promotional coupon from travel clubs, coupon books, and direct-mail offers or purchased on the Internet may not be cheaper than the least expensive fare from a discount ticket agency. And always keep in mind that what you get is just as important as what you save.

DISCOUNT RESERVATIONS

To save money, look into discount reservations services with Web sites and toll-free numbers, which use their buying power to get a better price on hotels, airline tickets (⇨ Air Travel), even car rentals. When booking a room, always **call the hotel's local toll-free number** (if one is available) rather than the central reservations number—you'll often get a better price. Always ask about special packages or corporate rates.

Airline Tickets: Air 4 Less ☎ 800/AIR4LESS; low-fare specialist.

Hotel Rooms: Accommodations Express ☎ 800/444-7666 or 800/277-1064 ⊕ www. accommodationsexpress.com. **Hotels.com** ☎ 800/246-8357 or 214/369-1246 ⊕ www.hotels.com. **Quikbook** ☎ 800/789-9887 ⊕ www.quikbook.com. **RMC Travel** ☎ 800/245-5738 ⊕ www. rmcwebtravel.com. **Steigenberger Reservation Service** ☎ 800/223-5652 ⊕ www.srs-worldhotels. com. **Turbotrip.com** ☎ 800/473-7829 ⊕ www. turbotrip.com.

PACKAGE DEALS

Don't confuse packages and guided tours. When you buy a package, you travel on your own, just as though you had planned the trip yourself. Fly/drive packages, which combine airfare and car rental, are often a good deal. In cities, ask the local visitor's bureau about hotel packages that include tickets to major museum exhibits or other special events.

EATING & DRINKING

Food in Hawai'i is a reflection of the state's diverse cultural makeup and tropical location. Fresh seafood is the hallmark of Hawai'i regional cuisine, and its preparations are drawn from across the Pacific Rim, including Japan, the Philippines, Korea, and Thailand. But Hawaiian food is a cuisine in its own right. Meals in resort areas are costly but often excellent.

The restaurants we list are the cream of the crop in each price category.

CATEGORY	COST
$$$$	over $30
$$$	$20–$30
$$	$12–$20
$	$7–$12
¢	under $7

Prices are for one main course at dinner.

MEALTIMES

Unless otherwise noted, the restaurants listed in this guide are open daily for lunch and dinner.

RESERVATIONS & DRESS

Hawai'i is decidedly casual. Aloha shirts and shorts or long pants for men and island-style dresses or casual resort wear for women are standard attire for evenings in most hotel restaurants and local eateries. T-shirts and shorts will do the trick for breakfast and lunch.

Reservations are always a good idea; we mention them only when they're essential or not accepted. Book as far ahead as you can, and reconfirm as soon as you arrive. (Large parties should always call ahead to check the reservations policy.) We mention dress only when men are required to wear a jacket or a jacket and tie.

SPECIALTIES

Fish, fruit, and fresh island-grown produce are the base of Hawai'i regional cuisine. The "plate lunch" is the heart of most Hawaiians' days and usually consists of grilled teriyaki chicken, beef, or fish, served with two scoops of white rice and two side salads. *Poke*, marinated raw tuna, is a local hallmark.

WINE, BEER & SPIRITS

Hawai'i has a new generation of microbreweries. Many restaurants also have on-site microbreweries. On Maui, check out the Tedeschi Vineyards, where you can tour a beautiful island estate and get a taste of sweet pineapple wine. The drinking age in Hawai'i is 21 years of age, and a photo ID must be presented to purchase alcoholic beverages. Bars are open until 2 AM; venues with a cabaret license can stay open until 4 AM. No matter what you might see in the local parks, drinking alcohol in public parks or on the beaches is illegal. It is also illegal to have open containers of alcohol in motor vehicles.
🚩 **Tedeschi Vineyards** ✉ Kula Hwy., 'Ulupalakua Ranch, Maui ☎ 808/878-6058 ⊕ www.mauiwine. com.

ECOTOURISM

Hawai'i's connection to its environment is spiritual, cultural, and essential to its survival. You'll find a rainbow of natural attractions to explore, from the ribbons of beaches to volcanic peaks, where lava shows after dark are spectacular. There are 13 climatic regions in the world, and Maui and the Big Island offer ecotravelers a glimpse of 11 of them. Much of Kaua'i's natural beauty can be seen only on foot. Its Nā Pali Coast/Waimea Canyon/Kōke'e trail network includes 28 trails totaling some 45 mi rich in endemic species of flora and fauna. Maui offers the exhilaration of a rain-forest hike in Hāna, the cool Upcountry climes of Kula, and the awe-inspiring Haleakalā Crater. Moloka'i and Lāna'i, two of the least-developed islands, hold adventures best experienced on foot and by four-wheel-drive vehicle, or even by mule. Eco-touring in Hawai'i gives you the opportunity to learn from local guides who are familiar with the *aina* (land) and Hawai'i's unique cultural heritage. Many of these tours take clients to locations less traveled, so it helps to be in good physical shape. The views at the ends of these roads are an exceedingly rich reward.

Nature and all its ornaments are sacred to Hawaiians, so before taking pieces of lava rock home for souvenirs, listen to what residents (and some vacationers) will tell you: don't touch! Hapless travelers who take "souvenir" rocks speak of "bad-luck" consequences in the form of stalled cars, travel delays, and bouts of illness. Park rangers spin tales about lava rocks mailed from around the world with attached tales of woe and pleas for the rocks to be put back. If nothing else, with millions of visitors a year, there aren't enough cool rocks to go around.

During the winter months, be sure to watch the beachfronts for endangered sea turtles, or recently laid nests. If you spot one, notify local authorities—they'll be thankful for your help in tracking these elusive creatures.
🚩 **Alternative-Hawai'i** ☎ 808/695-5113 ⊕ www. alternative-hawaii.com. **Hawai'i Ecotourism Association** ☎ 877/300-7058.

ETIQUETTE & BEHAVIOR

Hawai'i was admitted to the Union in 1959, so residents can be pretty sensitive when visitors refer to their own hometowns as "back in the States." Remember, **when in Hawai'i, refer to the contiguous 48 states as "the mainland" and not as the United States.** When you do, you won't appear to be such a *malahini* (newcomer).

GAY & LESBIAN TRAVEL

A few small hotels and some bed-and-breakfasts in Hawai'i are favored by gay and lesbian visitors; Purple Roofs is a listing agent for gay-friendly accommodations in Hawai'i. In addition, a computerized Gay Community listing compiled by GLEA (Gay & Lesbian Education Advocacy Foundation) is available. Pacific Ocean Holidays specializes in prearranging package tours for independent gay travelers; the organization also publishes the *Pocket Guide to Hawai'i*, distributed free in the state at gay-operated venues and available for $5 by mail for one issue.

For details about the gay and lesbian scene, consult *Fodor's Gay Guide to the USA* (available in bookstores everywhere).

Local Resources: GLEA Box 37083, Honolulu 96837 808/532-9000. **Pacific Ocean Holidays** Box 88245, Honolulu 96830 808/923-2400 or 800/735-6600 www.gayHawaii.com. **Purple Roofs** www.purpleroofs.com.

Gay- & Lesbian-Friendly Travel Agencies: Different Roads Travel 8383 Wilshire Blvd., Suite 520, Beverly Hills, CA 90211 323/651-5557 or 800/429-8747 (Ext. 14 for both) 323/651-3678 lgernert@tzell.com. **Kennedy Travel** 130 W. 42nd St., Suite 401, New York, NY 10036 212/840-8659 or 800/237-7433 212/730-2269 www.kennedytravel.com. **Now, Voyager** 4406 18th St., San Francisco, CA 94114 415/626-1169 or 800/255-6951 415/626-8626 www.nowvoyager.com. **Skylink Travel and Tour** 1455 N. Dutton Ave., Suite A, Santa Rosa, CA 95401 707/546-9888 or 800/225-5759 707/636-0951; serving lesbian travelers.

GUIDEBOOKS

Plan well and you won't be sorry. Guidebooks are excellent tools—and you can take them with you. You may want to check out *Fodor's Exploring Hawaii* and *Compass American Guide: Hawaii*, thorough on culture and history, and *Escape to the Hawaiian Islands* for intriguing ideas. All three have color photos and are available at on-line retailers and bookstores everywhere.

HEALTH

Hawai'i is known as the Health State. The life expectancy here is 79 years, the longest in the nation. Balmy weather makes it easy to remain active year-round, and the low-stress aloha attitude certainly contributes to general well-being. When visiting the Islands, however, there are a few health issues to keep in mind.

The Hawai'i State Department of Health recommends that you drink 16 ounces of water per hour to avoid dehydration when hiking or spending time in the sun. **Use sunblock, wear UV-reflective sunglasses, and protect your head with a visor or hat for shade.** If you're not acclimated to warm, humid weather you should allow plenty of time for rest stops and refreshments. When visiting freshwater streams, be aware of the tropical disease leptospirosis, which is spread by animal urine and carried into streams and mud. Symptoms include fever, headache, nausea, and red eyes. If left untreated it can cause liver and kidney damage, respiratory failure, internal bleeding, and even death. To avoid this, don't swim or wade in freshwater streams or ponds if you have open sores and **don't drink from any freshwater streams or ponds.**

In the Islands, fog is a rare occurrence, but there can often be "vog," an airborne haze of gases released from volcanic vents on the Big Island. During certain weather conditions such as "Kona Winds," the vog can settle over the Islands and wreak havoc with respiratory and other health conditions, especially asthma or emphysema. If susceptible, stay indoors and get emergency assistance if needed.

DIVERS' ALERT

Do not fly within 24 hours of scuba diving.

PESTS & OTHER HAZARDS

The Islands have their share of bugs and insects that enjoy the tropical climate as much as visitors do. Most are harmless but annoying. When planning to spend time outdoors in hiking areas, **wear long-sleeved clothing and long pants** and **use mosquito repellent containing deet.** In very damp places you may encounter the dreaded local centipede. In the Islands they usually come in two colors, brown and blue, and they range from the size of a worm to an 8-inch cigar. Their sting is very painful, and the reaction is similar to bee- and wasp-sting reactions. When camping, **shake out your sleeping bag before climbing in, and check your shoes in the morning,** as the centipedes like cozy places. If planning on hiking or traveling in remote areas, always carry a first-aid kit and appropriate medications for sting reactions.

HOLIDAYS

Major national holidays are New Year's Day (Jan. 1); Martin Luther King Day (3rd Mon. in Jan.); Presidents' Day (3rd Mon. in Feb.); Memorial Day (last Mon. in May); Independence Day (July 4); Labor Day (1st Mon. in Sept.); Columbus Day (2nd Mon. in Oct.); Thanksgiving Day (4th Thurs. in Nov.); Christmas Eve and Christmas Day (Dec. 24 and 25); and New Year's Eve (Dec. 31).

In addition, Hawai'i celebrates Prince Kuhio Day (Mar. 26), King Kamehameha Day (June 11), and Admission Day (3rd Fri. in Aug.). State, city, and county offices as well as many local companies are closed for business.

INSURANCE

The most useful travel-insurance plan is a comprehensive policy that includes coverage for trip cancellation and interruption, default, trip delay, and medical expenses (with a waiver for preexisting conditions).

Without insurance you'll lose all or most of your money if you cancel your trip, regardless of the reason. Default insurance covers you if your tour operator, airline, or cruise line goes out of business. Trip-delay covers expenses that arise because of bad weather or mechanical delays. Study the fine print when comparing policies.

U.K. residents can buy a travel-insurance policy valid for most vacations taken during the year in which it's purchased (but check preexisting-condition coverage).

Always **buy travel policies directly from the insurance company;** if you buy them from a cruise line, airline, or tour operator that goes out of business you probably won't be covered for the agency or operator's default, a major risk. Before making any purchase, **review your existing health and home-owner's policies** to find what they cover away from home.

In the U.S.: **Access America** ✉ 6600 W. Broad St., Richmond, VA 23230 ☎ 800/284-8300 🖶 804/673-1491 or 800/346-9265 ⊕ www.accessamerica.com. **Travel Guard International** ✉ 1145 Clark St.,

Stevens Point, WI 54481 ☎ 715/345-0505 or 800/826-1300 🖶 800/955-8785 ⊕ www.travelguard.com.

FOR INTERNATIONAL TRAVELERS

For information on customs restrictions, *see* Customs and Duties.

CAR RENTAL

When picking up a rental car, non–U.S. residents need a reservation voucher for any prepaid reservations that were made in the traveler's home country, a passport, a driver's license, and a travel policy that covers each driver.

CAR TRAVEL

Gas costs range from $2 to $2.50 a gallon. Stations are plentiful. Most stay open late (24 hours along large highways and in big cities), except in rural areas, where Sunday hours are limited and where you may drive long stretches without a refueling opportunity. Highways are well paved. Interstate highways—limited-access, multilane highways whose numbers are prefixed by "I–"—are the fastest routes. Interstates with three-digit numbers encircle urban areas, which may have other limited-access expressways, freeways, and parkways as well. Tolls may be levied on limited-access highways. So-called U.S. highways and state highways are not necessarily limited-access but may have several lanes.

Along larger highways, roadside stops with rest rooms, fast-food restaurants, and sundries stores are well spaced. State police and tow trucks patrol major highways and lend assistance. If your car breaks down on an interstate, pull onto the shoulder and wait for help, or have your passengers wait while you walk to an emergency phone. If you carry a cell phone, dial *55, noting your location on the small green roadside mileage markers.

Driving in the United States is on the right. Do obey speed limits posted along roads and highways. Watch for lower limits in small towns and on back roads. On weekdays between 6 and 10 AM and again between 4 and 7 PM expect heavy traffic. To encourage carpooling, some freeways have special lanes for so-called high-occupancy vehicles (HOV)—cars carrying more than one passenger.

Bookstores, gas stations, convenience stores, and rest stops sell maps (about $3) and multiregion road atlases (about $10).

CONSULATES & EMBASSIES

🏠 **Australian Consulate** ✉ 1000 Bishop St., Honolulu 96813 ☎ 808/524-5050.

🏠 **British Consulate** ✉ 1000 Bishop St., Honolulu 96813 ☎ 808/524-5050.

🏠 **Canadian Consulate** ✉ 1000 Bishop St., Honolulu 96813 ☎ 808/524-5050.

🏠 **New Zealand Consulate** ✉ 900 Richards St., Room 414, Honolulu 96813 ☎ 808/543-7900.

CURRENCY

The dollar is the basic unit of U.S. currency. It has 100 cents. Coins are the copper penny (1¢); the silvery nickel (5¢), dime (10¢), quarter (25¢), and half-dollar (50¢) and the golden $1 coin, replacing a now-rare silver dollar. Bills are denominated $1, $5, $10, $20, $50, and $100, all green and identical in size; designs vary. In addition, you may come across a $2 bill, but the chances are slim. The exchange rate at this writing was US$1.60 per British pound, US$0.68 per Canadian dollar, US$0.61 per Australian dollar, and US$0.57 per New Zealand dollar.

ELECTRICITY

The U.S. standard is AC, 110 volts/60 cycles. Plugs have two flat pins set parallel to each other.

EMERGENCIES

For police, fire, or ambulance, **dial 911** (0 in rural areas).

INSURANCE

Britons and Australians need extra medical coverage when traveling overseas.

🏠 In the U.K.: **Association of British Insurers** ✉ 51 Gresham St., London EC2V 7HQ ☎ 020/7600-3333 🖷 020/7696-8999 ⊕ www.abi.org.uk. In Australia: **Insurance Council of Australia** ✉ Insurance Enquiries and Complaints, Level 3, 56 Pitt St., Sydney, NSW 2000 ☎ 1300/363683 or 02/9251-4456 🖷 02/9251-4453 ⊕ www.iecltd.com.au. In Canada: **RBC Insurance** ✉ 6880 Financial Dr., Mississauga, Ontario L5N 7Y5 ☎ 800/565-3129 🖷 905/813-4704 ⊕ www.rbcinsurance.com. In New Zealand: **Insurance Council of New Zealand** ✉ Level 7, 111-115 Customhouse Quay, Box 474, Wellington ☎ 04/472-5230 🖷 04/473-3011 ⊕ www.icnz.org.nz.

MAIL & SHIPPING

You can buy stamps and aerograms and send letters and parcels in post offices. Stamp-dispensing machines can occasionally be found in airports, bus and train stations, office buildings, drugstores, and the like. You can also deposit mail in the stout, dark-blue steel bins at strategic locations everywhere and in the mail chutes of large buildings; pickup schedules are posted.

For mail sent within the United States, you need a 37¢ stamp for first-class letters weighing up to 1 ounce (23¢ for each additional ounce) and 23¢ for postcards. You pay 80¢ for 1-ounce airmail letters and 70¢ for airmail postcards to most other countries; to Canada and Mexico, you need a 60¢ stamp for a 1-ounce letter and 50¢ for a postcard. An aerogram—a single sheet of lightweight blue paper that folds into its own envelope, stamped for overseas airmail—costs 70¢.

To receive mail on the road, have it sent c/o General Delivery at your destination's main post office (use the correct five-digit ZIP code). You must pick up mail in person within 30 days and show a driver's license or passport.

PASSPORTS & VISAS

When traveling internationally, **carry your passport** even if you don't need one (it's always the best form of ID) and **make two photocopies of the data page** (one for someone at home and another for you, carried separately from your passport). If you lose your passport, promptly call the nearest embassy or consulate and the local police.

Visitor visas aren't necessary for Canadian or European Union citizens, or for citizens of Australia who are staying fewer than 90 days.

🏠 Australian Citizens: **Passports Australia** ☎ 131-232 ⊕ www.passports.gov.au. **United States Consulate General** ✉ MLC Centre, Level 59, 19-29 Martin Pl., Sydney, NSW 2000 ☎ 02/9373-9200, 1902/941-641 fee-based visa-inquiry line ⊕ usembassy-australia.state.gov/sydney.

🏠 Canadian Citizens: **Passport Office** ✉ to mail in applications: 200 Promenade du Portage, Hull, Québec J8X 4B7 ☎ 819/994-3500 or 800/567-6868 ⊕ www.ppt.gc.ca.

🏠 New Zealand Citizens: **New Zealand Passports Office** ✉ for applications and information: Level 3, Boulcott House, 47 Boulcott St., Wellington

☎ 0800/22-5050 or 04/474-8100 ⊕ www.
passports.govt.nz. **Embassy of the United States**
✉ 29 Fitzherbert Terr., Thorndon, Wellington
☎ 04/462-6000 ⊕ usembassy.org.nz. **U.S. Consulate General** ✉ Citibank Bldg., 3rd floor, 23 Customs St. E, Auckland ☎ 09/303-2724 ⊕ usembassy.
org.nz.

🆔 **U.K. Citizens: U.K. Passport Service** ☎ 0870/
521-0410 ⊕ www.passport.gov.uk. **American Consulate General** ✉ Queen's House, 14 Queen St.,
Belfast, Northern Ireland BT1 6EQ ☎ 028/
9032-8239 🖷 028/9024-8482 ⊕ www.usembassy.
org.uk. **American Embassy** ✉ for visa and immigration information (enclose an SASE): Consular Information Unit, 24 Grosvenor Sq., London W1 1AE
✉ to submit an application via mail: Visa Branch,
5 Upper Grosvenor St., London W1A 2JB ☎ 09068/
200-290 recorded visa information or 09055/444-
546 operator service, both with per-minute charges,
0207/499-9000 main switchboard ⊕ www.
usembassy.org.uk.

TELEPHONES

All U.S. telephone numbers consist of a three-digit area code and a seven-digit local number. Within many local calling areas, you dial only the seven-digit number. Within some area codes, you must dial "1" first for calls outside the local area. To call between area-code regions, dial "1" then all 10 digits; the same goes for calls to numbers prefixed by "800," "888," "866," and "877"—all toll free. For calls to numbers preceded by "900" you must pay—usually dearly.

For international calls, dial "011" followed by the country code and the local number. For help, dial "0" and ask for an overseas operator. The country code is 61 for Australia, 64 for New Zealand, 44 for the United Kingdom. Calling Canada is the same as calling within the United States. Most local phone books list country codes and U.S. area codes. The country code for the United States is 1.

For operator assistance, dial "0." To obtain someone's phone number, call directory assistance at 555-1212 or occasionally 411 (free at public phones). To have the person you're calling foot the bill, phone collect; dial "0" instead of "1" before the 10-digit number.

At pay phones, instructions often are posted. Usually you insert coins in a slot (usually 25¢–50¢ for local calls) and wait for a steady tone before dialing. When you call long-distance, the operator tells you

how much to insert; prepaid phone cards, widely available in various denominations, are easier. Call the number on the back, punch in the card's personal identification number when prompted, then dial your number.

LANGUAGE

English is the primary language in the Islands, so you can get away without knowing much Hawaiian. Making the effort to learn some words of this lyrical language can be rewarding, however. Despite the length of many Hawaiian words, the Hawaiian alphabet is actually one of the world's shortest, with only 12 letters: the five vowels, *a, e, i, o, u,* and seven consonants, *h, k, l, m, n, p, w.* Hawaiian words you are most likely to encounter during your visit to the Islands are *aloha, mahalo* (thank you), *keiki* (child), *haole* (Caucasian or foreigner), *mauka* (toward the mountains), *makai* (toward the ocean), and *pau* (finished, all done). Hawaiian history includes waves of immigrants, each bringing their own language. To communicate with each other, they developed a sort of slang known as "pidgin." If you listen closely, you will know what is being said by the inflections and by the extensive use of body language. For example, when you know what you want to say but don't know how to say it, just say "you know, da kine." For an informative and somewhat-hilarious view of things Hawaiian, check out Jerry Hopkins's series of books titled *Pidgin to the Max* and *Fax to the Max,* available at most local bookstores in the Hawaiiana sections.

LEI GREETINGS

When you walk off a long flight, perhaps a bit groggy and stiff, nothing quite compares with a Hawaiian lei greeting. The casual ceremony ranks as one of the fastest ways to make the transition from the worries of home to the joys of your vacation. Though the tradition has created an expectation that everyone receives this floral garland when they step off the plane, the state of Hawai'i cannot greet each of its nearly 7 million annual visitors.

Still, it's easy to **arrange for a lei ceremony for yourself or your companions before you arrive.** Contact one of the following companies if you have not signed up with a tour company that provides it. If you really want to be wowed by the experience, request a lei of tuberoses, some of the most divine-smelling blossoms on the planet. Greeters of Hawai'i requires 48 hours' notice and charges $20.95 to $30.95 per person; add $10 for late notification. Kama'aina Leis, Flowers & Greeters requires three days' notice and charges $12.65 for a standard greeting on O'ahu and $15 on the Neighbor Islands.

🔲 **Greeters of Hawai'i** ☎ 800/366-8559 🖨 800/ 926-2644 ⊕ www.greetersofhawaii.com. **Kama'aina Leis, Flowers & Greeters** ☎ 808/836- 3246 or 800/367-5183 🖨 808/836-1814.

LODGING

No matter what your budget, there is a place for you in Hawai'i. Large city-size resorts fill the Islands' most scenic shores. Family-style condominiums have many of the amenities of fine hotels, and it's possible to find some at reasonable prices. Vacation rentals and B&Bs are becoming increasingly popular as visitors look for a real slice of Hawai'i away from the crowds. Often tucked into nooks of the Islands you would normally never see, they are competitively priced, highly personalized, and great for relaxing.

The lodgings we list are the cream of the crop in each price category. We always list the facilities that are available, but we don't specify whether they cost extra. When pricing accommodations, always ask what's included and what costs extra.

Assume that hotels operate on the **European Plan** (EP, with no meals) unless we specify that they use the **Continental Plan** (CP, with a Continental breakfast), **Breakfast Plan** (BP, with a full breakfast), **Modified American Plan** (MAP, with breakfast and dinner), or the **Full American Plan** (FAP, with all meals).

CATEGORY	COST
$$$$	over $200
$$$	$150–$200
$$	$100–$150
$	$60–$100
¢	under $60

Prices are for two people in a standard double room in high season, including tax and service.

APARTMENT & HOUSE RENTALS

If you want a home base that's roomy enough for a family and comes with cooking facilities, **consider a furnished rental.** These can save you money, especially if you're traveling with a group. Home-exchange directories sometimes list rentals as well as exchanges.

🔲 **Hideaways International** ⊠ 767 Islington St., Portsmouth, NH 03802 ☎ 603/430-4433 or 800/ 843-4433 🖨 603/430-4444 ⊕ www.hideaways. com; membership $129. **Hometours International** ⊠ 1108 Scottie La., Knoxville, TN 37919 ☎ 865/690- 8484 or 866/367-4668 ⊕ thor.he.net/~hometour. **Vacation Home Rentals Worldwide** ⊠ 235 Kensington Ave., Norwood, NJ 07648 ☎ 201/767-9393 or 800/633-3284 🖨 201/767-5510 ⊕ www.vhrww.com. **Villas and Apartments Abroad** ⊠ 370 Lexington Ave., Suite 1401, New York, NY 10017 ☎ 212/897- 5045 or 800/433-3020 🖨 212/897-5039 ⊕ www. ideal-villas.com.

HOME EXCHANGES

If you would like to exchange your home for someone else's, **join a home-exchange organization,** which will send you its updated listings of available exchanges for a year and will include your own listing in at least one of them. It's up to you to make specific arrangements.

🔲 **HomeLink International** ⊕ Box 47747, Tampa, FL 33647 ☎ 813/975-9825 or 800/638-3841 🖨 813/910-8144 ⊕ www.homelink.org; $110 yearly for a listing, on-line access, and catalog; $40 without catalog. **Intervac U.S.** ⊠ 30 Corte San Fernando, Tiburon, CA 94920 ☎ 800/756-4663 🖨 415/435-7440 ⊕ www.intervacus.com; $105 yearly for a listing, on-line access, and a catalog; $50 without catalog.

HOSTELS

No matter what your age, you can **save on lodging costs by staying at hostels.** Most hostels in Hawai'i cater to a lively international crowd of backpackers, surfers, and windsurfers; those seeking intimacy or privacy should seek out a B&B.

In some 4,500 locations in more than 70 countries around the world, Hostelling International (HI), the umbrella group for a number of national youth-hostel associations, offers single-sex, dorm-style beds and, at many hostels, rooms for couples and family accommodations. Membership in any HI national hostel association, open to travelers of all ages, allows you to stay in HI-affiliated hostels at member rates; one-year membership is about $28 for adults (C$35 for a two-year minimum membership in Canada, £13.50 in the U. K., A$52 in Australia, and NZ$40 in New

Zealand); hostels charge about $10 to $30 per night. Members have priority if the hostel is full; they're also eligible for discounts around the world, even on rail and bus travel in some countries.

🚺 Hostelling International–USA ✉ 8401 Colesville Rd., Suite 600, Silver Spring, MD 20910 ☎ 301/495-1240 🖶 301/495-6697 ⊕ www.hiayh. org. **Hostelling International–Canada** ✉ 400–205 Catherine St., Ottawa, Ontario K2P 1C3 ☎ 613/237-7884 or 800/663-5777 🖶 613/237-7868 ⊕ www. hihostels.ca. **YHA England and Wales** ✉ Trevelyan House, Dimple Rd., Matlock, Derbyshire DE4 3YH, U. K. ☎ 0870/870-8808 🖶 0870/770-6127 ⊕ www. yha.org.uk. **YHA Australia** ✉ 422 Kent St., Sydney, NSW 2001 ☎ 02/9261-1111 🖶 02/9261-1969 ⊕ www. yha.com.au. **YHA New Zealand** ✉ Level 3, 193 Cashel St., Box 436, Christchurch ☎ 03/379-9970 or 0800/278-299 🖶 03/365-4476 ⊕ www.yha.org.nz.

HOTELS

All hotels listed have private bath unless otherwise noted.

🚺 Toll-Free Numbers: Best Western ☎ 800/528-1234 ⊕ www.bestwestern.com. **Choice** ☎ 800/424-6423 ⊕ www.choicehotels.com. **Comfort Inn** ☎ 800/424-6423 ⊕ www.choicehotels.com. **Days Inn** ☎ 800/325-2525 ⊕ www.daysinn.com. **Doubletree Hotels** ☎ 800/222-8733 ⊕ www. doubletree.com. **Embassy Suites** ☎ 800/362-2779 ⊕ www.embassysuites.com. **Fairfield Inn** ☎ 800/228-2800 ⊕ www.marriott.com. **Four Seasons** ☎ 800/332-3442 ⊕ www.fourseasons.com. **Hilton** ☎ 800/445-8667 ⊕ www.hilton.com. **Holiday Inn** ☎ 800/465-4329 ⊕ www.sixcontinentshotels. com. **Howard Johnson** ☎ 800/446-4656 ⊕ www. hojo.com. **Hyatt Hotels & Resorts** ☎ 800/233-1234 ⊕ www.hyatt.com. **La Quinta** ☎ 800/531-5900 ⊕ www.laquinta.com. **Marriott** ☎ 800/228-9290 ⊕ www.marriott.com. **Quality Inn** ☎ 800/424-6423 ⊕ www.choicehotels.com. **Radisson** ☎ 800/333-3333 ⊕ www.radisson.com. **Ramada** ☎ 800/228-2828, 800/854-7854 international reservations ⊕ www.ramada.com or www. ramadahotels.com. **Red Lion and WestCoast Hotels and Inns** ☎ 800/733-5466 ⊕ www.redlion.com. **Renaissance Hotels & Resorts** ☎ 800/468-3571 ⊕ www.renaissancehotels.com. **Ritz-Carlton** ☎ 800/241-3333 ⊕ www.ritzcarlton.com. **Sheraton** ☎ 800/325-3535 ⊕ www.starwood. com/sheraton. **Sleep Inn** ☎ 800/424-6423 ⊕ www.choicehotels.com. **Westin Hotels & Resorts** ☎ 800/228-3000 ⊕ www.starwood.com/westin.

MEDIA

Hawai'i is wired to a variety of media, including network television, cable television, Web-based media, newspapers, magazines, and radio. Many of the resorts and hotels throughout the Islands include an additional visitor-information channel on your in-room television. Consult your in-room directory to get channel and scheduling information and to find out the special activities or events that might be happening during your visit.

NEWSPAPERS & MAGAZINES

Each of the Islands has its own daily newspapers, available through many hotel bell desks; in sundry stores, restaurants, and cafés; and at newsstands. Many hotels will deliver one to your room upon request. The *Honolulu Advertiser* is O'ahu's morning and Sunday paper; the *Honolulu Star-Bulletin* is O'ahu's evening paper. *West Hawai'i Today* is the Big Island's Kona Coast newspaper, and the *Hawai'i Tribune-Herald* serves the Hilo side of the island. On Maui, it's the *Maui News*. On Kaua'i, it's the *Garden Island* and *Kaua'i Times*. The *Honolulu Weekly* is a great guide for arts and alternative events, and the *Pacific Business News* provides the latest in business news. The monthly *Honolulu Magazine* focuses on O'ahu issues and happenings. Check out local bookstores for Neighbor Island magazines, some of which publish on a quarterly schedule.

RADIO & TELEVISION

Radio airwaves on the Islands are affected by natural terrain, so don't expect to hear one radio station islandwide. For Hawaiian music, tune your FM radio dial to 98.5 KDNN (O'ahu), 100.3 KCCN (O'ahu), 99.5 KHUI (O'ahu), 105.1 KINE (O'ahu), 100.3 KAPA (East Hawai'i), 99.1 KAGB (West Hawai'i), 93.5 KPOA (Maui), and 95.9 KSRF (Kaua'i). News junkies can get their fill of news and talk by tuning to the AM radio dial and the following island stations: 590 KSSK (O'ahu), 650 KHNR (O'ahu), 830 KHVH (O'ahu), 670 KPUA (East Hawai'i), 620 KIPA (West Hawai'i), 1110 KAOI (Maui), 570 KQNG (Kaua'i). National Public Radio enthusiasts can tune to the FM dial for NPR programming on 88.1 KHPR (O'ahu) and 90.7 KKUA (Maui). On Kaua'i check out the only commercial-free public radio station in the Islands, KKCR, at 90.9 and 91.9 FM. It broadcasts Hawaiian music, jazz, blues, rock, and reggae, as well as talk shows on local issues.

On Oʻahu, many residents wake up with Perry & Price on KSSK AM 59 or FM 92. The lively duo provides news, traffic updates, and weather reports between "easy-listening" music and phone calls from listeners from 5 to 10 AM.

Television channels in the Islands are plentiful between network and cable channels. Channel allocation varies by island and location. On Oʻahu, you can find the following network programming with its channel and local affiliate call sign: FOX (2) KHON, ABC (4) KITV, UPN/WB (5) KHVE, CBS (9) KGMB, PBS (10) KHET, and NBC (13) KHNL.

MONEY MATTERS

Many of the Islands' best attractions and activities, such as beaches and hiking, can be found in the form of natural beauty and cost nothing to view. You'll pay 50¢ for a daily newspaper, $1.50 to ride the bus anywhere on Oʻahu, and from $45 on up to attend a lūʻau. Large museums cost between $8 and $15 per entry; smaller ones can cost from $3 to $6. Prices throughout this guide are given for adults. Substantially reduced fees are almost always available for children, students, and senior citizens. For information on taxes, see Taxes.

ATMS

Automatic teller machines for easy access to cash are everywhere on the Islands. ATMs can be found in shopping centers, small convenience and grocery stores, inside hotels and resorts, as well as outside most bank branches. For a directory of locations, call 800/424–7787 for the MasterCard Cirrus Maestro network or 800/843–7587 for the Visa Plus network.

CREDIT CARDS

Most major credit cards are accepted throughout the Islands and are required to rent a car. When making reservations, double-check to ensure that the lodging, restaurant, or attraction you are planning to visit accepts them. In smaller concessions, B&Bs, and fast-food outlets, expect to pay cash.

Throughout this guide, the following abbreviations are used: **AE,** American Express; **D,** Discover; **DC,** Diners Club; **MC,** MasterCard; and **V,** Visa.

 Reporting Lost Cards: **American Express** ☎ 800/441–0519. **Diners Club** ☎ 800/234–6377.

Discover ☎ 800/347–2683. **MasterCard** ☎ 800/622–7747. **Visa** ☎ 800/847–2911.

NATIONAL & STATE PARKS

Hawaiʻi has seven national parks. On Maui is the summit and crater of the Haleakalā volcano, at Haleakalā National Park. Molokaʻi's Kalaupapa National Historical Park was once a leper colony where victims of Hansen's disease were sent into exile in the late 1800s and cared for by Father Damien, a Belgian missionary. On the island of Oʻahu, the U.S.S. *Arizona* Memorial at Pearl Harbor is overseen by the National Park Service.

The Big Island, Hawaiʻi's largest island, has four national parks. Hawaiʻi Volcanoes National Park is the state's number one attraction, where vents have been spewing lava for nearly 20 years. The other three are Puʻuhonua O Hōnaunau National Historical Park, Puʻukoholā Heiau National Historical Site, and Kaloko-Honokōhau National Historical Park, all of which give a glimpse into Hawaiʻi's rich cultural history.

Hawaiʻi's 52 state parks encompass more than 25,000 acres on five islands and include many of its most beautiful beaches and coastal areas. The State Parks Division of the Hawaiʻi State Department of Land and Natural Resources can provide information on state parks and historic areas.

 National Parks: **National Park Foundation** ✉ 11 Dupont Circle NW, 6th floor, Washington, DC 20036 ☎ 202/238–4200 ⊕ www.nationalparks.org. **National Park Service** ✉ National Park Service/Department of Interior, 1849 C St. NW, Washington, DC 20240 ☎ 202/208–6843 ⊕ www.nps.gov. **National Parks Conservation Association** ✉ 1300 19th St. NW, Suite 300, Washington, DC 20036 ☎ 202/223–6722 ⊕ www.npca.org.

 Passes by Mail & On-Line: **National Park Foundation** ⊕ www.nationalparks.org. **National Parks Pass** ⊟ Box 34108, Washington, DC 20043 ☎ 888/467–2757 ⊕ www.nationalparks.org; include a check or money order payable to the National Park Service, plus $3.95 for shipping and handling, or call for passes by phone.

 State Parks: **State Parks Division, Hawaiʻi State Department of Land and Natural Resources** ✉ 1151 Punchbowl St., Room 310, Honolulu 96813 ☎ 808/587–0300 ⊕ www.hawaii.gov.

PACKING

Hawai'i is casual: sandals, bathing suits, and comfortable, informal clothing are the norm. In summer synthetic slacks and shirts, although easy to care for, can be uncomfortably warm. You'll easily find a bathing suit in Hawai'i, but **bring a bathing cap with you if you wear one.** You can waste hours searching for one.

Probably the most important thing to tuck into your suitcase is sunscreen. This is the tropics, and the ultraviolet rays are powerful. Doctors advise putting on sunscreen when you get up in the morning. Don't forget to **reapply sunscreen periodically during the day,** since perspiration can wash it away. Consider using sunscreens with a sun protection factor (SPF) of 15 or higher. There are many tanning oils on the market in Hawai'i, including coconut and *kukui* (the nut from a local tree) oils, but they can cause severe burns. Too many Hawaiian vacations have been spoiled by sunburn and even sun poisoning. Hats and sunglasses offer important sun protection, too. Both are easy to find in island shops, but if you already have a favorite packable hat or sun visor, bring it with you, and don't forget to wear it. All major hotels in Hawai'i provide beach towels.

As for clothing in the Hawaiian Islands, there's a saying that when a man wears a suit during the day, he's either going for a loan or he's a lawyer trying a case. Only a few upscale restaurants require a jacket for dinner. The aloha shirt is accepted dress in Hawai'i for business and most social occasions. Shorts are acceptable daytime attire, along with a T-shirt or polo shirt. There's no need to buy expensive sandals on the mainland—here you can get flip-flops for a couple of dollars and off-brand sandals for $20. Golfers should remember that many courses have dress codes requiring a collared shirt; call courses you're interested in for details. If you're not prepared, you can pick up appropriate clothing at resort pro shops. If you're visiting in winter or planning to visit a high-altitude area, **bring a sweater or light- to medium-weight jacket.** A polar fleece pullover is ideal, and makes a great impromptu pillow.

In your carry-on luggage, **pack an extra pair of eyeglasses or contact lenses and enough of any medication** you take to last a few days longer than the entire trip. You may also ask your doctor to write a spare prescription using the drug's generic name, as brand names may vary from country to country. In luggage to be checked, **never pack prescription drugs, valuables, or undeveloped film.** And don't forget to carry with you the addresses of offices that handle refunds of lost traveler's checks. Check *Fodor's How to Pack* (available at on-line retailers and bookstores everywhere) for more tips.

To avoid customs and security delays, carry medications in their original packaging. Don't pack any sharp objects in your carry-on luggage, including knives of any size or material, scissors, and corkscrews, or anything else that might arouse suspicion.

To avoid having your checked luggage chosen for hand inspection, don't cram bags full. The U.S. Transportation Security Administration suggests packing shoes on top and placing personal items you don't want touched in clear plastic bags.

CHECKING LUGGAGE

You're allowed to carry aboard one bag and one personal article, such as a purse or a laptop computer. Make sure what you carry on fits under your seat or in the overhead bin. Get to the gate early, so you can board as soon as possible, before the overhead bins fill up.

Baggage allowances vary by carrier, destination, and ticket class. On international flights, you're usually allowed to check two bags weighing up to 70 pounds (32 kilograms) each, although a few airlines allow checked bags of up to 88 pounds (40 kilograms) in first class. Some international carriers don't allow more than 66 pounds (30 kilograms) per bag in business class and 44 pounds (20 kilograms) in economy. On domestic flights, the limit may be 50 pounds (23 kilograms) per bag. Most airlines won't accept bags that weigh more than 100 pounds (45 kilograms) on domestic or international flights. Check baggage restrictions with your carrier before you pack.

Airline liability for baggage is limited to $2,500 per person on flights within the United States. On international flights it amounts to $9.07 per pound or $20 per kilogram for checked baggage (roughly $640 per 70-pound bag) and $400 per passenger for unchecked baggage. You can buy additional coverage at check-in for about $10 per $1,000 of coverage, but it often excludes a rather extensive list of items, shown on your airline ticket.

Before departure, **itemize your bags' contents** and their worth, and label the bags with your name, address, and phone number. (If you use your home address, cover it so potential thieves can't see it readily.) Include a label inside each bag and **pack a copy of your itinerary.** At check-in, **make sure each bag is correctly tagged** with the destination airport's three-letter code. Because some checked bags will be opened for hand inspection, the U.S. Transportation Security Administration recommends that you leave luggage unlocked or use the plastic locks offered at check-in. TSA screeners place an inspection notice inside searched bags, which are re-sealed with a special lock.

If your bag has been searched and contents are missing or damaged, file a claim with the TSA Consumer Response Center as soon as possible. If your bags arrive damaged or fail to arrive at all, file a written report with the airline before leaving the airport.

ᗕ U.S. Transportation Security Administration Consumer Response Center ☎ 866/289-9673 ⊕ www.tsa.gov.

SAFETY

Hawai'i is generally a safe tourist destination, but it's still wise to follow the same common sense safety precautions you would normally follow in your own hometown. Hotel and visitor-center staff can provide information should you decide to head out on your own to more remote areas. Rental cars are magnets for break-ins, so **don't leave any valuables in the car,** not even in a locked trunk. Avoid poorly lighted areas, beach parks, and isolated areas after dark as a precaution. When hiking, **stay on marked trails,** no matter how alluring the temptation might be to stray. Weather conditions can cause landscapes to become muddy, slippery, and tenuous, so staying on marked trails will lessen the possibility of a fall or getting lost. Ocean safety is of the utmost importance when visiting an island destination. **Don't swim alone, and follow the international signage posted at beaches** that alerts swimmers to strong currents, man-of-war

jellyfish, sharp coral, high surf, sharks, and dangerous shore breaks. At coastal lookouts along cliff tops, heed the signs indicating that waves can climb over the ledges. Check with lifeguards at each beach for current conditions, and **if the red flags are up, indicating swimming and surfing are not allowed, don't go in.** Waters that look calm on the surface can harbor strong currents and undertows, and not a few people who were just wading have been dragged out to sea.

LOCAL SCAMS

Be wary of those hawking "too good to be true" prices on everything from car rentals to attractions. Many of these offers are just a lure to get you in the door for time-share presentations. When handed a flyer, read the fine print before you make your decision to participate.

WOMEN IN HAWAI'I

Women traveling alone are generally safe in the Islands, but always follow the safety precautions you would use in any major destination. When booking hotels, **request rooms closest to the elevator,** and always keep your hotel-room door and balcony doors locked. Stay away from isolated areas after dark; camping and hiking solo are not advised. If you stay out late visiting nightclubs and bars, **use caution when exiting night spots** and returning to your lodging.

SENIOR-CITIZEN TRAVEL

Hawai'i is steeped in a tradition that gives great respect to elders, or *kupuna,* and considers them "keepers of the wisdom." Visitors may not be so esteemed, but senior citizens traveling in Hawai'i will find discounts, special senior citizen–oriented activities, and buildings with easy access. Many lodging facilities have discounts for members of the American Association of Retired Persons (AARP).

To qualify for age-related discounts, **mention your senior-citizen status up front** when booking hotel reservations (not when checking out) and before you're seated in restaurants (not when paying the bill). Be sure to have identification on hand. When renting a car, ask about promotional car-rental discounts, which can be cheaper than senior-citizen rates.

ᗕ Educational Programs: Elderhostel ⊠ 11 Ave. de Lafayette, Boston, MA 02111-1746 ☎ 877/426-8056,

978/323-4141 international callers, 877/426-2167 TTY ☎ 877/426-2166 ⊕ www.elderhostel.org. **Interhostel** ✉ University of New Hampshire, 6 Garrison Ave., Durham, NH 03824 ☎ 603/862-1147 or 800/733-9753 ☎ 603/862-1113 ⊕ www.learn.unh.edu.

SHOPPING

KEY DESTINATIONS

On Oʻahu, Ala Moana Center is one of the largest shopping spots; it's within easy walking distance of the west end of Waikīkī. The Royal Hawaiian Shopping Center is centrally located in Waikīkī itself. Farther away, you'll find Ward Centers, Aloha Tower Marketplace, and the Kāhala Mall.

The Neighbor Islands offer more in the way of smaller strips of shops. Still, it's possible to find larger stores grouped in areas such as Kauaʻi's Kukui Grove Center in Līhuʻe; Maui's Kaʻahumanu Shopping Center in Kahului, the Shops at Wailea, and Whaler's Village in Kāʻanapali; and the Big Island's Prince Kūhiō Shopping Plaza in Hilo, King's Shops in Waikoloa, the Shops at Mauna Lani, and Keauhou Shopping Village and Lanihau Center in Kailua-Kona. Exclusive shops can often be found in the lobbies of luxury hotels.

SMART SOUVENIRS

Aloha shirts and resort wear, Hawaiian-music recordings, shell leis, coral jewelry, traditional quilts, island foods, Kona coffee, and koa-wood products are just a few of the gifts that visitors to Hawaiʻi treasure. For the more elegant gift items, check out the Hawaiian boutiques in major island shopping centers as well as those tucked away in smaller shopping areas in residential districts. Island crafts fairs and swap meets offer a bargain bazaar of standard items such as T-shirts and tiki statues as well as the original works of local artisans.

WATCH OUT

Souvenirs made from coral or tortoise shell may not have been harvested legally, so in the interest of preserving Hawaiʻi's environment, it's best to avoid these.

SPORTS & THE OUTDOORS

If you like to swim, hike, fish, bike, scuba dive, kayak, or play golf, Hawaiʻi is your kind of place. Alternative Hawaiʻi's Web site provides detailed information on hiking, diving, camping, kayaking, and outfitters on each island. The environment is particularly fragile here, so whatever you do outdoors, don't forget to tread lightly. 🎏 **Alternative Hawaiʻi** ☎ 808/695-5113 ⊕ www.alternative-hawaii.com.

BEACHES

Hawaiʻi's beaches are the stuff of legend, with white sand wedged between palm trees and turquoise water, or even colorful black and green stretches of sand. All beaches are free and open to the public unless otherwise noted—even the most luxurious hotels have to share their beachfronts. Note that riptides and strong undertows can challenge even the strongest swimmers, so if you see a beach where no one is swimming, ask a local about its safety before diving in. **Use care when diving into lagoons** as well, as they often are not as deep as they appear. Alcohol is not permitted on most beaches.

GOLF

Hawaiʻi is known for its golf, with many high-profile tournaments on TV each year. To experience the glory for yourself, check with your hotel concierge or golf shop to arrange tee times, or call the courses listed in the chapters directly.

HIKING & CAMPING

Hiking is a wonderful way to explore the Islands, but **don't stray off trails,** and be sure to **wear sturdy hiking shoes,** especially if you're doing lava hikes. When camping, **be prepared for radical weather shifts,** especially at high altitudes. Haleakalā National Park, for example, can reach 85°F by day and drop to 35°F by night. Fog, wind, and rain can and do blow in with little or no warning. Ask local outdoor shops which areas are best for you based on your fitness level and camping experience. Note that Hawaiʻi doesn't have drive-to camping sites; most locations require a hike in or a night on the beach.

KAYAKING

Kayaking is an excellent low-impact way to enjoy the scenery. Kayak rentals are available on each island, and you can arrange guided trips. **Remain close to shore** if you don't want to be whooshed out to sea. Check with the kayak rental shop for weather advisories.

SCUBA DIVING & SNORKELING

Underwater Hawai'i is breathtaking, but diving tends to be pricey. You can arrange trips with countless outfitters, or rent equipment on your own. Whether snorkeling or diving, remember **never to go alone**, and be sure to **ask at the dive shop about rip currents and places to avoid.** Undersea life is extremely fragile, so **don't touch (or take) the coral,** and **watch that your fins don't hit the reefs** behind you.

STUDENTS IN HAWAI'I

Hawai'i is a popular destination for exchange students from around the world, who mainly attend the University of Hawai'i in Honolulu. Contact your hometown university about study and internship possibilities. To check out the student scene in the Islands, stop by any of the University of Hawai'i campuses or community college campuses, and read the *Honolulu Weekly* upon arrival for club and event information. Be sure to ask about discounts for students at all museums and major attractions and be prepared to show ID to qualify.

IDs & Services: STA Travel ✉ 10 Downing St., New York, NY 10014 ☎ 212/627-3111 or 800/777-0112 📠 212/627-3387 ⊕ www.sta.com. **Travel Cuts** ✉ 187 College St., Toronto, Ontario M5T 1P7, Canada ☎ 416/979-2406, 800/592-2887, 866/246-9762 in Canada 📠 416/979-8167 ⊕ www.travelcuts.com.

TAXES

SALES TAX

There is a 4.16% state sales tax on all purchases, including food. A hotel room tax of 7.25%, combined with the sales tax of 4%, equals an 11.25% rate added onto your hotel bill. A $2-per-day road tax is also assessed on each rental vehicle.

TIME

Hawai'i is on Hawaiian Standard Time, 5 hours behind New York, 2 hours behind Los Angeles, and 10 hours behind London.

When the U.S. mainland is on daylight saving time, Hawai'i is not, so add an extra hour of time difference between the Islands and U.S. mainland destinations. You may also find that things generally move more slowly here. That has nothing to do with your watch—it's just the laid-back way called Hawaiian time.

TIPPING

Tip cab drivers 15% of the fare. Standard tips for restaurants and bar tabs run from 15% to 20% of the bill, depending on the standard of service. Bellhops at hotels usually receive $1 per bag, more if you have bulky items such as bicycles and surfboards. Tip the hotel room maid $1 per night, paid daily. Tip doormen $1 for assistance with taxis; tips for concierge vary depending on the service. For example, tip more for "hard-to-get" event tickets or dining reservations.

TOURS & PACKAGES

Because everything is prearranged on a prepackaged tour or independent vacation, you spend less time planning—and often get it all at a good price.

BOOKING WITH AN AGENT

Travel agents are excellent resources. But it's a good idea to collect brochures from several agencies, as some agents' suggestions may be influenced by relationships with tour and package firms that reward them for volume sales. If you have a special interest, find an agent with expertise in that area; the American Society of Travel Agents (ASTA; ⇨ Travel Agencies) has a database of specialists worldwide.

Make sure your travel agent knows the accommodations and other services of the place being recommended. Ask about the hotel's location, room size, beds, and whether it has a pool, room service, or programs for children, if you care about these. Has your agent been there in person or sent others whom you can contact?

Do some homework on your own, too: local tourism boards can provide information about lesser-known and small-niche operators, some of which may sell only direct.

BUYER BEWARE

Each year consumers are stranded or lose their money when tour operators—even large ones with excellent reputations—go out of business. So check out the operator. Ask several travel agents about its reputation, and try to **book with a company that has a consumer-protection program.** (Look for information in the company's brochure.) In the United States, members of the National Tour Association and the

United States Tour Operators Association are required to set aside funds to cover payments and travel arrangements in the event that the company defaults. It's also a good idea to choose a company that participates in the American Society of Travel Agents' Tour Operator Program; ASTA will act as mediator in any disputes between you and your tour operator.

Remember that the more your package or tour includes, the better you can predict the ultimate cost of your vacation. Make sure you know exactly what is covered, and **beware of hidden costs.** Are taxes, tips, and transfers included? Entertainment and excursions? These can add up. ▪ **American Society of Travel Agents** (⇨ Travel Agencies). **National Tour Association** (NTA) ✉ 546 E. Main St., Lexington, KY 40508 ☎ 859/226-4444 or 800/682-8886 🖷 859/226-4404 ⊕ www. ntaonline.com. **United States Tour Operators Association** (USTOA) ✉ 275 Madison Ave., Suite 2014, New York, NY 10016 ☎ 212/599-6599 or 800/468-7862 🖷 212/599-6744 ⊕ www.ustoa.com.

TRANSPORTATION AROUND HAWAI'I

Renting a car is definitely recommended for those who plan to move beyond their hotel lounge chair. With the exception of on O'ahu, public transportation is extremely limited, and even if you are staying in Honolulu or Waikīkī you may want a car if you plan to do any exploring or if you're short on time. **Reserve your vehicle in advance,** particularly during peak travel times and on the smaller islands, where the car-rental fleets are limited. Most major companies have airport counters and complimentary transportation for pickup/drop-off back at the airport upon departure.

Taxis can also be found at island airports, through your hotel doorman, in the more popular resort areas, or by contacting local taxi companies by telephone. Flag-down fees are $2, and each additional mile is $1.70. Most companies will also provide a car and driver for half-day or daylong island tours if you absolutely don't want to rent a car, and a number of companies also offer personal guides. Remember, however, that rates are quite steep for these services, ranging from $100 to $200 per day and up.

TRAVEL AGENCIES

A good travel agent puts your needs first. Look for an agency that has been in business at least five years, emphasizes customer service, and has someone on staff who specializes in your destination. In addition, **make sure the agency belongs to a professional trade organization.** The American Society of Travel Agents (ASTA)—the largest and most influential in the field with more than 20,000 members in some 140 countries—maintains and enforces a strict code of ethics and will step in to help mediate any agent-client disputes involving ASTA members if necessary. ASTA (whose motto is "Without a travel agent, you're on your own") also maintains a Web site that includes a directory of agents. (If a travel agency is also acting as your tour operator, *see* Buyer Beware *in* Tours and Packages.) ▪ Local Agent Referrals: **American Society of Travel Agents** (ASTA) ✉ 1101 King St., Suite 200, Alexandria, VA 22314 ☎ 703/739-2782 or 800/965-2782 24-hr hot line 🖷 703/739-3268 ⊕ www. astanet.com. **Association of British Travel Agents** ✉ 68-71 Newman St., London W1T 3AH ☎ 020/7637-2444 🖷 020/7637-0713 ⊕ www.abtanet.com. **Association of Canadian Travel Agents** ✉ 130 Albert St., Suite 1705, Ottawa, Ontario K1P 5G4 ☎ 613/237-3657 🖷 613/237-7052 ⊕ www.acta.ca. **Australian Federation of Travel Agents** ✉ Level 3, 309 Pitt St., Sydney, NSW 2000 ☎ 02/9264-3299 🖷 02/9264-1085 ⊕ www.afta.com.au. **Travel Agents' Association of New Zealand** ✉ Level 5, Tourism and Travel House, 79 Boulcott St., Box 1888, Wellington 6001 ☎ 04/499-0104 🖷 04/499-0786 ⊕ www. taanz.org.nz.

VISITOR INFORMATION

Before you go, contact the Hawai'i Visitors & Convention Bureau (HVCB) for general information on each island, free brochures that include an accommodations and car-rental guide, and an entertainment and dining listing containing one-line descriptions of bureau members. Take a virtual visit to Hawai'i on the Web, which can be most helpful in planning many aspects of your vacation. The HVCB site has a calendar section that allows you to see what local events are in place during the time of your stay.

Learn more about foreign destinations by checking government-issued travel advisories and country information. For a broader picture, consider information from more than one country.

F **Hawai'i Visitors & Convention Bureau** ✉ 2270 Kalakaua Ave., Suite 801, Honolulu 96817 ☎ 808/923–1811, 800/464–2924 for brochures ⊕ www.gohawaii.com. In the U.K. contact the **Hawai'i Visitors & Convention Bureau** ⌖ Box 208, Sunbury, Middlesex TW16 5RJ ☎ 020/8941–4009 ⊕ www.gohawaii.com. Send a £2 check or postal order for an information pack.

F Government Advisories: **Australian Department of Foreign Affairs and Trade** ☎ 02/6261–1299 Consular Travel Advice Faxback Service ⊕ www.dfat.gov.au. **New Zealand Ministry of Foreign Affairs and Trade** ☎ 04/439–8000 ⊕ www.mft.govt.nz.

WEB SITES

Do check out the World Wide Web when planning your trip. You'll find everything from weather forecasts to virtual tours of famous cities. Be sure to **visit Fodors.com** (⊕ www.fodors.com), a complete travel-planning site. You can research prices and book plane tickets, hotel rooms, rental cars, vacation packages, and more. In addition, you can post your pressing questions in the Travel Talk section. Other planning tools include a currency converter and weather reports, and there are loads of links to travel resources.

For more information on Hawai'i, visit ⊕ www.gohawaii.com, the official Web site of the Hawai'i Visitors & Convention Bureau.

Other sites to check out include ⊕ www.bigisland.org (Big Island Visitors Bureau); ⊕ www.visitmaui.com (Maui County Visitors Bureau); ⊕ www.visit-oahu.com (O'ahu Visitors Bureau); ⊕ www.kauaivisitorsbureau.org (Kaua'i Visitors Bureau); ⊕ www.molokai-hawaii.com (Moloka'i Visitor Information); ⊕ www.thebus.org (O'ahu's public transportation system); and ⊕ www.alohaboatdays.com (for a schedule and information about cruise-arrival celebrations at Aloha Tower, Honolulu Harbor).

The Web site ⊕ www.search-hawaii.com has an engine that can search all linked Hawaiian Web pages by topic or word.

Visit ⊕ www.hshawaii.com for the Hawai'i State vacation planner; ⊕ www.kauai-hawaii.com for Kaua'i visitor information; ⊕ www.honoluluweekly.com for a weekly guide to the arts, entertainment, and dining in Honolulu; ⊕ www.hawaii.gov, the state's official Web site, for all information on the destination, including camping; and ⊕ www.nps.gov for national parks information.

O'AHU
THE GATHERING PLACE

FODOR'S CHOICE

Halekūlani, resort in Waikīkī

Hanauma Bay Nature Preserve, the East O'ahu Ring

Hoku's, restaurant in Honolulu

Kahaloa and Ulukou Beaches, Waikīkī

Lanikai Beach Park, the East O'ahu Ring

Orchids at the Halekūlani, restaurant in Waikīkī

Surfing the North Shore

Turtle Bay Resort, Kahuku

U.S.S. *Arizona* Memorial, Pearl Harbor

HIGHLY RECOMMENDED

BEACHES   Ala Moana Beach Park, Honolulu

Ft. DeRussy Beach, Waikīkī

Kailua Beach Park, the East O'ahu Ring

Kūhiō Beach Park, Waikīkī

Waimānalo Beach Park, the East O'ahu Ring

Waimea Bay, North Shore

SIGHTS   Diamond Head State Monument and Park

Sheraton Moana Surfrider, Waikīkī

Waikīkī Aquarium, Honolulu

Many other great hotels and restaurants enliven this area. For other favorites, look for the black stars as you read this chapter.

Updated by
Maggie
Wunsch

O'AHU IS WHERE THE SPIRIT OF ALOHA WAS BORN, and it's still Hawai'i's most exciting, cosmopolitan gathering place, with an eclectic blend of people, customs, and cuisines. Outside of the urbanity of Honolulu, you'll find all the tropical splendor for which the Islands are famous. Part of O'ahu's dramatic appearance lies in its majestic highlands: the western Wai'anae Mountains rise 4,000 ft above sea level, and the verdant Ko'olau Mountains cross the island's midsection at elevations of more than 3,000 ft. Eons of wind and weather erosion have carved these ranges' sculptured, jagged peaks; deep valleys; sheer green cliffs; and dynamic vistas. At the base of these mountains more than 50 beach parks lie draped like a beautiful lei, each known for a different activity, be it snorkeling, surfing, swimming, or sunbathing.

Third-largest of the Hawaiian Islands and covering 608 square mi, O'ahu was formed by two volcanoes that erupted 4 to 6 million years ago. Honolulu, the nation's 11th-largest city, is here, and 75% of Hawai'i's 1.1 million residents call the island home. Somehow, amid all this urban development, you are never more than a glimpse away from a breathtaking ocean or mountain view.

Hawai'i's last kings and queens ruled from 'Iolani Palace in Downtown Honolulu. Today, 'Iolani stands as an elegant tribute to Hawai'i's rich history as a kingdom, republic, territory, and state. Even in the days of royalty, the virtues of Waikīkī as a vacation destination were recognized. Long processions of *ali'i* (nobility) made their way across streams and swamps, past the duck ponds, to the coconut groves and the beach.

By the 1880s guest houses were scattered along the south shore like so many seashells. The first hotel, the Moana (now the Sheraton Moana Surfrider), was built at the turn of the 20th century and christened the First Lady of Waikīkī. The Moana's inaugural room rates of $1.50 per night were the talk of the town. In 1927 the "Pink Palace of the Pacific," the Royal Hawaiian Hotel, was built by the Matson Navigation Company to accommodate travelers arriving on luxury liners. It was opened with a grand ball, and Waikīkī was officially launched as a first-class tourist destination—duck ponds, taro patches, and all.

December 7, 1941, brought that era to a close with the bombing of Pearl Harbor and America's entry into the war in the Pacific. The Royal Hawaiian was turned over to American military forces and became a respite for war-weary soldiers and sailors. But with victory came the postwar boom, and by 1952 Waikīkī had 2,000 hotel rooms. Today, hundreds of thousands of visitors sleep in the more than 33,000 rooms of Waikīkī's nearly 160 hotels and condominiums. Waikīkī continues to serve as home base for endless possibilities for day trips full of cultural and scenic eco-adventures. Visitors can stroll along Kūhiō Beach and check out the city-sponsored Brunch on the Beach and Sunset on the Beach events each month, as well as meander along the historic Waikīkī walking trail. There are free nightly Hawaiian music and dance performances on the Kūhiō Beach stage. A massive redesign of the Kālia Road and Beachwalk area was scheduled to start in late 2003, with completion set for late 2006. Here, Outrigger Enterprises plans to turn its older hotels from the 1960s into one modern hotel, retail, and entertainment complex that will feature more outdoor gathering places and a Hawaiian-music preservation hall. With Waikīkī leading the way, O'ahu maintains its status as an exciting destination, with more things to see, more places to eat, and more things to do than on all the other Hawaiian Islands combined.

Numbers in the text correspond to numbers in the margin and on the Waikīkī, Downtown Honolulu, and O'ahu maps.

If you have
1 day

If you have a short layover on your way to another island or if you can tear yourself away from a convention (or a honeymoon resort) for just one day of sightseeing, the first thing you should do is treat yourself to a dawn hike up **Diamond Head State Monument and Park** ⑲, then have breakfast at one of Waikīkī's beachfront restaurants. Next, take the bus or drive to nearby Ala Moana Shopping Center, which has stores to satisfy all souvenir needs. Buy a carryout lunch from its eclectic, international food court; cross Ala Moana Boulevard; and picnic, sun, and swim at Ala Moana Beach Park. Go on a late-afternoon outrigger canoe ride with one of Waikīkī's beach attendants, followed by mai tais and Hawaiian music at sunset at the **Halekūlani** ⑦ or **Royal Hawaiian Hotel** ⑧.

If you have
3 days

On your first day, dig in by following the Waikīkī and/or Kapi'olani Park tours described below. Start the second day at the **Hawai'i Maritime Center** ⑳ in Downtown Honolulu, followed by shopping and lunch at the adjacent **Aloha Tower Marketplace** ㉑. For a view from atop the building that was once the tallest structure in Honolulu, go next door for a short elevator ride to the Aloha Tower's observation deck. Explore historic Downtown Honolulu before heading back to Waikīkī for sunset and dinner. On day three, get an early start so you arrive at **Hanauma Bay Nature Preserve** ㊵ by 7:30, before the crowds. Take a break from the sun with a stop a little farther north along the coast at **Sea Life Park** ㊲, which features some splashy marine shows. From here, follow the East O'ahu Ring tour in reverse, back to Waikīkī.

If you have
5 days

Devote the first day to Waikīkī, the second to Downtown Honolulu, and the third to East O'ahu. On the fourth day, get an early start in order to see the **U.S.S. *Arizona* Memorial** and **Battleship *Missouri* Memorial** ㊹, since the lines lengthen throughout the morning. Or take the early morning boat tour to Pearl Harbor. From there, drive to the **Bishop Museum** ㊷ and spend some time immersed in Hawaiiana. Keep the rest of the day low-key until evening, when you can take in a cocktail or dinner show followed by dancing. Devote the fifth day to the North Shore. Drive to **Hale'iwa** ㊼ for breakfast and shopping, then tour **Waimea Falls Park** ㊽, and finish with a late-afternoon or early evening visit to the **Polynesian Cultural Center** ㊿.

Exploring O'ahu

O'ahu is a mixed bag, with enough attractions and adventures to fill an entire vacation. Waikīkī is the center of the island's visitor industry and home to its largest concentration of accommodations, stores, restaurants, and nightclubs. Dominated by Diamond Head crater, Waikīkī's less populated eastern end includes a zoo, an aquarium, and a beautiful park designed for sports from jogging to kite-flying. Take some time to explore the neighborhoods that are just outside of Waikīkī, such as Kaimukī, whose main street, Waialae Avenue, boasts a century of different architectural styles alongside boutique shopping and a world of cuisines to explore in the guise of tiny neighborhood eateries. Kāhala has some of the most luxurious real estate on the island. Ala Moana, west of Waikīkī, is brimming with shops galore that begin with the Ala Moana Center and continue with the five retail complexes of Victoria Ward Centers. Farther west is Downtown Honolulu, the center of Hawaiʻi's capital city, a bustling blend of history and modern-day commerce. Along its edges, historic Chinatown awaits.

The East Oʻahu coast is fringed with white-sand beaches and turquoise seas, and you can drive right over the top of the Koʻolau Mountains. Breeze past modern residential neighborhoods such as Hawaiʻi Kai to the sleepy slopes of Waimānalo. Finally, a circle-island tour takes you to central, northern, and windward Oʻahu, where shoes and cell phones give way to sandy toes and Hawaiian time. Take a time-out to discover the local windward communities of Kailua and Kaneohe, whose beaches are a haven for family fun. On the North Shore, Haleʻiwa is a visit back in time, and in winter, it is the place to catch a glimpse of ocean waves that reach heights of 20 ft and more.

To stay oriented on the island, keep in mind that directions on Oʻahu are often given as *mauka* (toward the mountains) or *makai* (toward the ocean). In Honolulu and Waikīkī, you may also hear people referring to "Diamond Head" (toward that landmark) and *ʻewa*—away from Diamond Head.

About the Restaurants

Oʻahu's cuisines are as diverse as its population, with Asian, European, and Pacific flavors most prevalent. Here, the Asian influence can even be found at the corner fast-food restaurant, where the McDonald's menu is posted in both English and kanji. While you're exploring Oʻahu's banquet of choices, be sure to sample Hawaiʻi regional cuisine, also known variously as Euro-Asian or Pacific Rim.

About the Hotels

Oʻahu's lodgings range from sprawling resorts to intimate, low-rise hideaways. First-time visitors who wish to be in the heart of the island's activity can find it all in Waikīkī. Guests do well by this south-shore tourist mecca, since shops, restaurants, nightlife, and the beach are nearby. Business travelers prefer to stay on the eastern edge of Waikīkī, near the Hawaiʻi Convention Center, or in Downtown Honolulu's sole hotel. Windward and North Shore digs are casual and shorter on amenities but have charms all their own.

WHAT IT COSTS				
	$$$$	$$$	$$	$	¢
RESTAURANTS	over $30	$20–$30	$12–$20	$7–$12	under $7
HOTELS	over $200	$150–$200	$100–$150	$60–$100	under $60

Restaurant prices are for one main course at dinner. Hotel prices are for two people in a standard double room in high season, including tax and service.

Timing

The ideal seasons to visit Oʻahu are spring and fall, when fewer tourists are around and the weather is warm, but not too warm. Fall is additionally fun thanks to the Aloha Festivals, a monthlong program of free Hawaiian-style celebrations and special events. Festival highlights on Oʻahu include a floral parade and evening block parties downtown and in Waikīkī. Come December, Downtown Honolulu is a veritable wonderland during its holiday Festival of Lights.

Scenic Drives A drive around O'ahu brings you face-to-face with its sheer natural beauty. Roll past the wave-dashed eastern shore, with its photogenic beaches and cliffs. Drive through the central plains past acres of red soil, once rich in pineapple and now supporting diversified crops, such as coffee. Head to the North Shore, a reflection of old O'ahu with its rickety storefronts and trees hanging heavy with bananas and papaya. Forget the air-conditioning, roll down the windows, and smell the salt air along the windward coast, where the view is dominated by mountains chiseled by centuries of winds, rains, and waterfalls.

1

Water Sports Whether you soar above them, sail on them, or dive into them, the waters surrounding O'ahu are an ocean lover's dream. The seas off Waikīkī call to novices looking for a surfing lesson or outrigger canoe ride, while the North Shore beckons accomplished wave riders. Snorkeling and scuba diving at Hanauma Bay, on the island's eastern tip, bring you face-to-face with a rainbow of sea creatures. Honolulu's Kewalo Basin is the starting point for most fishing charters, and the Honolulu harborfront piers serve as home port for many luxury cruise excursions. Windsurfers and ocean kayakers head to the beaches of the windward side, Lanikai in particular.

WAIKĪKĪ

If Hawai'i is America's most exotic, most unique state, then Waikīkī is its generator, keeping everything humming. On the dry, sunny side of O'ahu, it incorporates all the natural splendors of the Islands and synthesizes them with elegance and daring into an international playground in the middle of the Pacific.

A tropical retreat since the days of Hawai'i's kings and queens, Waikīkī sparkles along 2½ mi of spangled sea from the famous Diamond Head crater on the east to the Ala Wai Yacht Harbor on the west. Separated on its northern boundary from the sprawling city of Honolulu by the broad Ala Wai Canal, Waikīkī is 3½ mi from Downtown Honolulu and worlds apart from any other city in the world. You may find yourself saying such things as *aloha* and *mahalo* (thank you), and don't be surprised if you find yourself planning your next trip back as you laze on Waikīkī's sunny, hypnotic shores.

a good walk

A good place to start a Waikīkī walking tour is the **Ala Wai Yacht Harbor** ❶ ▶, home to an armada of pleasure boats and two members-only yacht clubs. It's just makai of the Renaissance 'Ilikai Waikīkī at 1777 Ala Moana Boulevard. From here head toward the main intersection of Ala Moana Boulevard and Kālia Road, turn right at the large sculpture of hula dancers signaling the entry to **Hilton Hawaiian Village Beach Resort and Spa** ❷, and wander through this 20-acre resort complex past gardens and waterfalls.

Continue makai on Kālia Road to Ft. DeRussy, home of the **U.S. Army Museum** ❸. Across the street, on Saratoga Road, nestled snugly amid

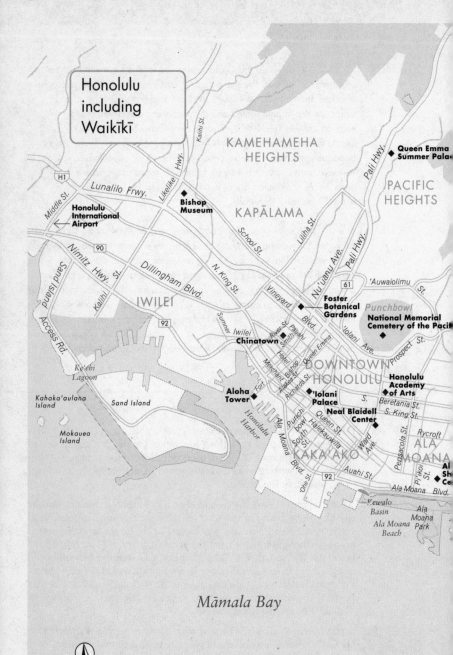

Honolulu
including
Waikīkī

KAMEHAMEHA
HEIGHTS

Queen Emma
Summer Pala

PACIFIC
HEIGHTS

H1

Lunalilo Frwy.

Kalihi St.

Likelike Hwy.

Pali Hwy.

Middle St.

Honolulu
International
Airport

Bishop
Museum

KAPĀLAMA

Nimitz Hwy.

90

Dillingham Blvd.

N. King St.

School St.

Liliha St.

Nu'uanu Ave.

Pali Hwy.

'Auwaiolimu St.

Sand Island

Kalihi

IWILEI

Summer St.

Vineyard

61

Foster
Botanical
Gardens

Punchbowl
National Memorial
Cemetery of the Pacif

Access Rd.

Iwilei

River St.

Pauahi

Smith

'Iolani Ave.

Prospect St.

Ke'ehi
Lagoon

Chinatown

Hotel

Bishop

Queen Emma

DOWNTOWN
HONOLULU

Kahaka'aulana
Island

Sand Island

Merchant

Alakea St.

Richards St.

Honolulu
Academy
of Arts

Mokauea
Island

Aloha
Tower

Fort

'Iolani
Palace

S.

Beretania St.

S. King St.

Honolulu
Harbor

Ala Moana Blvd.

Punch
bowl
St.

Neal Blaidell
Center

Queen St.

Halekauwila

Pensacola St.

Rycroft

ALA
MOANA

South
St.

KAKA'AKO

Auahi St.

Ward
Ave.

Pi'ikoi
St.

Al
Sh
Ce

One St.

92

Ala Moana Blvd.

Kewalo
Basin

Ala
Moana
Park

Ala Moana
Beach

Māmala Bay

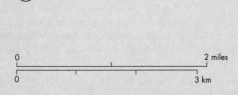

0   2 miles

0   3 km

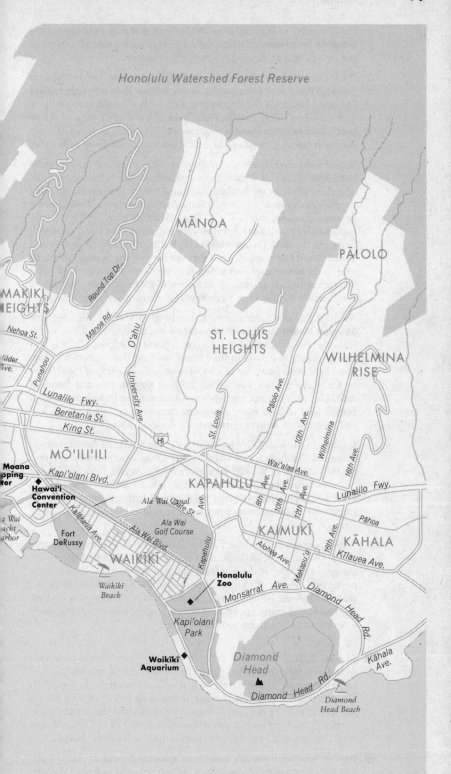

the commerce of Waikīkī, is an oasis of tranquility: the teahouse at the **Urasenke Foundation** ④, where the art of Hawaiian hospitality bows to the art of the centuries-old Japanese tea ceremony.

With a little taste of Asia and some Zen for the road, head mauka on Saratoga Road until you reach Kalākaua Avenue. Then turn right toward Diamond Head. At the intersection with Lewers Street, stop and peer into the lobby of the **First Hawaiian Bank** ⑤ for a quick view of the island's history in six massive wall murals. Diagonally across Kalākaua Avenue is one of Waikīkī's architectural landmarks, the **Gump Building** ⑥.

Walk down Lewers Street toward the ocean. It dead-ends at the impressive **Halekūlani** ⑦, one of Waikīkī's most prestigious hotels, famed for its elegant hospitality. From the Halekūlani stroll toward Diamond Head along the paved oceanside walkway. It leads past the Sheraton Waikīkī to the gracious, historic, and very pink **Royal Hawaiian Hotel** ⑧. Back on the mauka side of Kalākaua Avenue, walk two blocks ʻewa and one block mauka to the **IMAX Theatre Waikīkī** ⑨. Return to Kalākaua Avenue and walk toward Diamond Head. Your next stop on the mauka side of the street is the **International Market Place** ⑩, where artisans display their wares in an open-air bazaar setting. Catch some shade beneath the banyan tree that features its very own Swiss Family Robinson–style tree house.

Across Kalākaua Avenue is the oldest hotel in Waikīkī, the venerable **Sheraton Moana Surfrider** ⑪. Wander through the breezy lobby to the wide back porch, called the Banyan Veranda, or take a quick tour through tourism history in the Moana's second-floor historical room. From here, walk down the beach and head toward Diamond Head. Next to Kalākaua Avenue you'll find the four **Kahuna (Wizard) Stones of Waikīkī** ⑫, just to your right when you are facing the Duke Kahanamoku Statue. Said to hold magical powers, the stones are often overlooked and, more often than not, irreverently draped with wet towels.

Continue your walk four blocks farther down Kalākaua Avenue toward Diamond Head; then turn mauka onto ʻŌhua Avenue and you'll find the only church in Waikīkī with its own building, the Roman Catholic St. Augustine's. In the back of the church is the **Damien Museum** ⑬, a small but fascinating exhibition on the life of Father Damien, a Belgian priest who died while ministering to the victims of Hansen's disease (leprosy) on the island of Molokaʻi.

TIMING Allow yourself at least one full day for this walk, and time it so that you'll wind up on Waikīkī Beach at sunset. Many shops and attractions are open every day of the year from sunup to way past sundown to cater to the body clocks of tourists from around the world. Note, however, that the Urasenke Foundation tea ceremonies take place only on Wednesday and Friday mornings. Waikīkī is most inviting in the cool of the early morning or in late afternoon before sunset.

What to See

▶ ❶ **Ala Wai Yacht Harbor.** Every other summer the Trans-Pacific yacht race from Los Angeles makes its colorful finish here, complete with flags and onboard parties. The next Trans-Pac is estimated to arrive in July 2005. No matter when you visit Hawaiʻi, if you want a taste of what life on the water could be like, stroll around the docks and check out the variety of craft, from houseboats to luxury cruisers. ✉ *1777 Ala Moana Blvd., oceanside across from Renaissance ʻIlikai Waikīkī, Waikīkī.*

⓭ **Damien Museum.** This tiny two-room museum behind St. Augustine's Church contains the personal effects and memorabilia of Father Damien, the Belgian priest who worked with people afflicted with Hansen's disease (leprosy), who were exiled to Moloka'i during the late 1800s. Ask to see the museum's 20-minute videotape—it's not sophisticated by today's standards, but it's well done and emotionally gripping. ⌧ *130 'Ōhua Ave., Waikīkī* ☎ *808/923-2690* ☞ *Free* ☉ *Weekdays 9–3.*

❺ First Hawaiian Bank. Get a glimpse of Hawaiian history kept safe in this Waikīkī bank, where half a dozen murals depict the evolution of Hawaiian culture. The impressive panels were painted between 1951 and 1952 by Jean Charlot (1898–1979), whose work is represented in Florence at the Uffizi Gallery and in New York at both the Metropolitan Museum and the Museum of Modern Art. The murals are beautifully lighted at night, with some panels visible from the street. ⌧ *2181 Kalākaua Ave., Waikīkī* ☎ *808/943-4670* ☞ *Free* ☉ *Mon.–Thurs. 8:30–4, Fri. 8:30–6.*

❻ Gump Building. Built in 1929 in Hawaiian-colonial style, with Asian architectural motifs and a blue-tile roof, this structure once housed Hawai'i's premier store, Gump's, which was known for high-quality Asian and Hawaiian objects. It's now home to a Louis Vuitton boutique. ⌧ *2200 Kalākaua Ave., Waikīkī.*

❼ Halekūlani. Maintaining an air of mystery within its tranquil setting, the modern Halekūlani hotel is centered on a portion of its original (1917) beachfront estate, immortalized as the setting for the 1925 Charlie Chan detective novel, *The House Without a Key*. For a view of an orchid blossom unlike any other, take a peek at the swimming pool with its huge orchid mosaic on the bottom. ⌧ *2199 Kālia Rd., Waikīkī* ☎ *808/923-2311.*

> **need a break?**
>
> If it's lunchtime or close to sunset, linger at the Halekūlani and get a table at **House Without a Key** (⌧ 2199 Kālia Rd., Waikīkī ☎ 808/ 923-2311). The restaurant has a light lunch menu and serves wonderful tropical drinks and *pūpū* (appetizers) before dinner. Enjoy the view and the sounds of the Hawaiian steel guitar, and watch graceful hula performed nightly beneath the centuries-old *kiawe* tree (kiawe is a mesquite-type wood).

❷ Hilton Hawaiian Village Beach Resort and Spa. With a little island in Kahanamoku Lagoon and palm trees all around, this 20-acre Waikīkī resort is the quintessential tropical getaway. The village is a blend of Hawaiian sculpture and Asian architecture, with a Chinese moon gate, a pagoda, and a Japanese farmhouse with a waterwheel, all dominated by a tall mosaic mural of the hotel's Rainbow Tower. You can browse for souvenirs in all price ranges at the 90 different specialty stores throughout the resort. The Kalia Tower is home to a miniature version of Bishop Museum, designed to give visitors an interactive glimpse of the history of Polynesia. ⌧ *2005 Kālia Rd., Waikīkī* ☎ *808/949-4321.*

❾ IMAX Theatre Waikīkī. Immerse yourself in a view of "Hidden Hawai'i" among other films on a screen five stories high and 70 ft wide; 12,000 watts of digital surround sound complete the experience. Call or consult local newspapers for shows and times. ⌧ *325 Seaside Ave., Waikīkī* ☎ *808/923-4629* ⊕ *www.imaxwaikiki.com* ☞ *$9, double feature $13* ☉ *Daily; call for show times.*

❿ International Market Place. It's fun to wander through the open-air setting of this market, where wood-carvers, basket-weavers, and other artisans from various Pacific islands hawk their handicrafts. Intrepid shoppers find fun souvenirs here and at the adjacent Duke's Lane. Free hula performances are given on Monday and Wednesday through Sat-

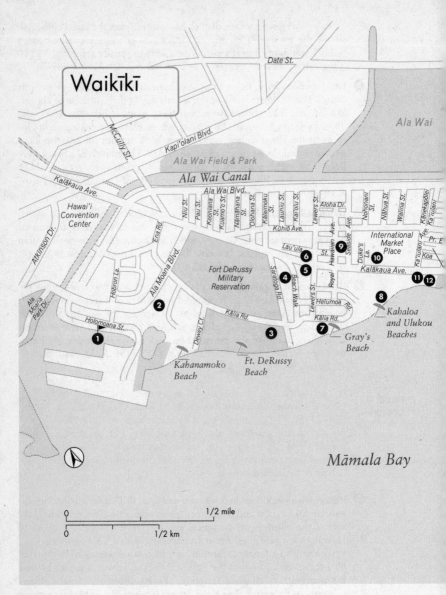

Waikīkī

Date St.

McCully St.

Kapiʻolani Blvd.

Ala Wai

Kalākaua Ave.

Ala Wai Field & Park

Ala Wai Canal

Ala Wai Blvd.

Hawaiʻi Convention Center

Niu St.
Pau St.
Keoniana St.
Kuamoʻo St.
Namahana St.
Olohana St.
Kalaimoku St.
Launiu St.
Kaʻiulani St.
Lewers St.
Aloha Dr.
Nohonani St.
Nāhua St.
Walina St.
Kānekapōlei St.
Kaʻiulani

Atkinson Dr.

Ena Rd.

Hōbron La.

Ala Moana Blvd.

Kūhiō Ave.

Lauʻula

International Market Place

Hawaiian Ave.
Seaside Ave.
Duke's La.
Royal Hawaiian Ave.
Kaʻiulani Ave.
Koa
Pr. E

9
6
5
10
Kalākaua Ave.
11
12

Fort DeRussy Military Reservation

Saratoga Rd.

Beach Walk

2

Dewey Ct.

Kālia Rd.

Helumoa Rd.

8
Kahaloa and Ulukou Beaches

Ala Moana Park Dr.

Holomoana St.

1

3

7

Kālia Rd.

Gray's Beach

Kahanamoko Beach

Ft. DeRussy Beach

Māmala Bay

| 0 | | 1/2 mile |
| 0 | | 1/2 km |

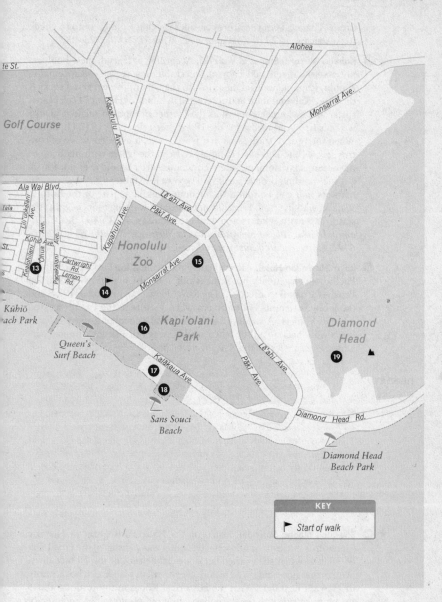

KEY

▶ Start of walk

urday. The food court features cuisines ranging from Filipino to Greek to American. ⌧ *2330 Kalākaua Ave., Waikīkī* ☎ *808/923–9871.*

⑫ Kahuna (Wizard) Stones of Waikīkī. According to legend, these boulders preserve the magnetic legacy of four Tahitian sorcerers—Kapaemahu, Kinohi, Kapuni, and Kahaloa. Just to the west of these revered rocks is the **Duke Kahanamoku Statue**, erected in honor of Hawai'i's celebrated surfer and swimmer. Known as the "father of modern surfing," Duke won his first gold medal for the 100-m freestyle at the 1912 Olympics. When the bronze statue was first placed here, it caused a wave of controversy, as the Duke is facing away from the water with his back to the ocean, something no safety-conscious surfer would ever do. Check out the standing bronze surfboard next to the statue; it's one of several markers that can be found throughout Waikīkī as part of the historic Waikīkī walking trail. Free 90-minute guided walking tours begin at the statue at 9 AM weekdays and 4:30 PM Saturday. ⌧ *Waikīkī Beach, Diamond Head side of Sheraton Moana Surfrider, Waikīkī* ☎ *808/841–6442* ⊕ *www.waikikihistorictrail.com.*

❽ Royal Hawaiian Hotel. Affectionately nicknamed the Pink Palace of the Pacific, this legendary hotel sticks out amid the high-rises on Waikīkī Beach like a pink confection. The Royal Hawaiian opened in 1927, and the lobby is reminiscent of an era when visitors to the Islands arrived on luxury liners. A stroll through the Royal's coconut grove garden is like a walk back to a time when Waikīkī was still a sleepy, tropical paradise. ⌧ *2259 Kalākaua Ave., Waikīkī* ☎ *808/923–7311.*

need a break? When the Royal Hawaiian opened its doors 76 years ago, **Afternoon Tea on the Coconut Grove Lanai** (⌧ Royal Hawaiian Hotel, 2259 Kalakaua Ave., Waikīkī ☎ 808/923–7311) was presented by kimono-clad servers. Restoring this tradition, the Royal has created an "East Meets West" afternoon tea of the highest standards, where 18 blends of tea are offered, including the Royal's signature Hawaiian *lilikoi* (passion fruit) peach tea and its Summer Palace blend of black tea scented with rhubarb cream, lulo-berry, and a hint of Hawaiian vanilla. Finger sandwiches and indulgences like guava-curd scones, pineapple tea cakes, and passion-fruit chocolate tarts sweeten the experience. Reservations are recommended.

★ ⑪ Sheraton Moana Surfrider. Listed on the National Register of Historic Places, this intricate beaux arts–style hotel was christened the First Lady of Waikīkī when she opened her doors at the turn of the 20th century. With period furnishings and historical exhibits, this landmark holds plenty of Hawai'i nostalgia. Visit the **Historical Room** in the rotunda above the main entrance to see the collection of old photographs and memorabilia dating from the opening of the hotel. Then take afternoon high tea on the **Banyan Veranda**. ⌧ *2365 Kalākaua Ave., Waikīkī* ☎ *808/922–3111.*

❹ The Urasenke Foundation. The teahouse here, built in 1951, was the first of its kind to be built outside Japan. If you are looking for a slice of serenity in Waikīkī, this is a good place to find it. The meditative ceremony reflects the influences of centuries of Zen Buddhism. Each ceremony lasts approximately 30 minutes; you can participate or just watch. Wear something comfortable enough for sitting on the floor (but no shorts, please). ⌧ *245 Saratoga Rd., Waikīkī* ☎ *808/923–3059* ⬚ *Minimum donation $3* ⊙ *Wed. and Fri. 10–noon.*

☝ ❸ U.S. Army Museum. This museum at Ft. DeRussy has an intimidating collection of war memorabilia. The major focus is on World War II, but exhibits range from ancient Hawaiian weaponry to displays relating to the Vietnam War. It's within Battery Randolf (Building 32), a bunker built in 1911 as a key to the defense of Pearl Harbor and Honolulu. Some of its walls are 22 ft thick. Guided group tours can be arranged; self-guided audio tours are also available. ⊠ *Ft. DeRussy, Bldg. 32, Kālia Rd., Waikīkī* ☎ *808/438–2822, 808/422–0561 for recorded information* ⊡ *Free* ⊙ *Tues.–Sun. 10–4:15.*

Kapiʻolani Park & Diamond Head

Kapiʻolani Park, established during the late 1800s by King Kalākaua and named after his queen, is a 500-acre expanse where you can play all sorts of sports, enjoy a picnic, see wild animals, or hear live music. It lies in the shadow of Diamond Head crater, perhaps Hawaiʻi's most famous natural landmark. Diamond Head got its name from sailors who thought they had found precious gems on its slopes. The diamonds proved to be volcanic refuse.

a good walk

The ʻewa end of Kapiʻolani Park is occupied by the **Honolulu Zoo** ⑭ ▶, on the corner of Kalākaua and Kapahulu avenues. On weekends look for the Zoo Fence Art Mart, on Monsarrat Avenue outside the zoo, on the Diamond Head side, for affordable artwork by contemporary artists.

Across Monsarrat Avenue, between Kalākaua Avenue and Pākī Avenue in Kapiʻolani Park, is the **Waikīkī Shell** ⑮, Honolulu's outdoor concert venue. Cut across the park toward the ocean to the **Kapiʻolani Bandstand** ⑯, where you'll hear more free island tunes on days when community events are taking place.

Cross Kalākaua Avenue toward the ocean to the **Waikīkī Aquarium** ⑰ and its neighbor, the **Waikīkī War Memorial Natatorium** ⑱, an open-air swimming stadium built in 1927 to commemorate lives lost in World War I.

As it leaves Kapiʻolani Park, Kalākaua Avenue forks into Diamond Head Road, a scenic 2-mi stretch popular with walkers and joggers, and winds around the base of Diamond Head alongside the ocean, passing handsome Diamond Head Lighthouse (not open to the public). Lookout areas offer views of the surfers and windsurfers below. The hike to the summit of **Diamond Head State Monument and Park** ⑲ requires strenuous walking. To save time and energy, drive, don't walk, along Diamond Head Road, turn left at Monsarrat Avenue, head a mile up the hill, and look for a sign on the right to the entrance to the crater. Drive through the tunnel to the inside of the crater. The trail begins at the parking lot.

TIMING Budget a full day to see Kapiʻolani Park and Diamond Head. If you want to hike up to the crater's summit, do it before breakfast. That way you beat not only the heat but the crowds. Hiking Diamond Head takes an hour round-trip, but factor in some extra time to enjoy the views from the top. Keep an eye on your watch if you're there at day's end, because the gates close promptly at 6. If you want to see the Honolulu Zoo, it's best to get there right when it opens, since the animals are livelier in the cool of the morning. Give the aquarium an hour, including 10 minutes in its Sea Visions Theater. For the best seats at the 10 AM Pleasant Hawaiian Hula Show, get to Kapiʻolani Park by 8 or so.

What to See

★ ⑲ **Diamond Head State Monument and Park.** Panoramas from this 760-ft extinct volcanic peak, once used as a military fortification, extend from Waikīkī and Honolulu in one direction and out to Koko Head in the other, with surfers and windsurfers scattered like confetti on the cresting waves below. This 360-degree perspective is a great orientation for first-time visitors. On a clear day you can even see the islands of Maui and Moloka'i if you look to your left. The ¾-mi trail starts at the crater floor, and although most guidebooks say there are 99 steps to the top, that's only true of the first flight—there are four flights altogether! Bring a flashlight to help guide your way through a narrow tunnel and up a very dark flight of winding stairs. And take bottled water with you to ensure that you stay hydrated under the tropical sun. ⊠ *Diamond Head Rd. at 18th Ave., Waikīkī* ☎ *808/587-0285* ☜ *$1* ◷ *Daily 6–6.*

🖐 ▶ ⑭ **Honolulu Zoo.** There are bigger and better zoos, but this one is lovely, and on Wednesday evenings in summer, the zoo puts on "The Wildest Show in Town," a free concert series. The best part of the zoo is its 7½-acre African savanna, where animals roam freely on the other side of hidden rails and moats. If you're visiting during a full moon, check out the "Zoo by Moonlight" tours to get a glimpse of animals who are active only by starlight. At the petting zoo, kids can pet a llama and meet Abbey, the zoo's resident monitor lizard. If your visit is timed right, you might also consider a family sleepover inside the zoo during its "Snooze in the Zoo" events, which take place on a Friday or Saturday night at the end of each month. ⊠ *151 Kapahulu Ave., Waikīkī* ☎ *808/971-7171* ⊕ *www.honoluluzoo.org* ☜ *$6* ◷ *Daily 9–4:30.*

⑯ **Kapi'olani Bandstand.** A replica of the Victorian Kapi'olani Bandstand, which was originally built in the late 1890s, is Kapi'olani Park's centerpiece for community entertainment and concerts. Check out the "Bandstand Jams," held at 5:30 every Friday, with concert performances ranging from contemporary Hawaiian to jazz to reggae. Local newspapers list entertainment information. ⊠ *'Ewa end of Kapi'olani Park, mauka side of Kalākaua Ave., Waikīkī.*

★ 🖐 ⑰ **Waikīkī Aquarium.** This amazing little attraction harbors more than 2,500 organisms and 420 species of Hawaiian and South Pacific marine life, endangered Hawaiian monk seals, sharks, and the only chambered nautilus living in captivity. The Edge of the Reef exhibit showcases five different types of reef environments found along Hawai'i's shorelines. Check out the Sea Visions Theater, the biodiversity exhibit, and the self-guided audio tour, which is included with admission. ⊠ *2777 Kalākaua Ave., Waikīkī* ☎ *808/923–9741* ⊕ *www.waquarium.org* ☜ *$7* ◷ *Daily 9–5.*

⑮ **Waikīkī Shell.** Local people bring a picnic and grab one of the 6,000 "grass seats" (lawn seating) for music under the stars. Here's a chance to enjoy some of Hawai'i's best musicians as well as visiting guest artists. Concerts are held May 1 to Labor Day. Check the newspapers to see who is performing. The Pleasant Hawaiian Hula Show takes place Tuesday–Thursday at 10 AM. ⊠ *2805 Monsarrat Ave., Waikīkī* ☎ *808/924–8934* ⊕ *www.blaisdellcenter.com.*

⑱ **Waikīkī War Memorial Natatorium.** This 1927 World War I monument, dedicated to the 102 Hawaiian servicemen who lost their lives in battle, stands proudly—its 20-ft-tall archway, which was completely restored in 2002, is floodlighted at night. The 100-m saltwater swimming pool is closed to the public; it was the training spot for Olympians Johnny Weissmuller and Buster Crabbe. ⊠ *2777 Kalākaua Ave., Waikīkī.*

need a break? You can enjoy breakfast, lunch, or dinner outdoors beneath the shade of a hau tree at the New Otani Kaimana Beach Hotel, next to the Waikīkī War Memorial Natatorium. Dubbed the **Hau Tree Lānai**

(✉ 2863 Kalākaua Ave. ☎ 808/921–7066), it's a little jewel if you want open-air oceanfront refreshment.

Downtown Honolulu

Honolulu's past and present play a delightful counterpoint throughout the downtown sector. Modern skyscrapers stand directly across from the Aloha Tower, which was built in 1926 and was, until the early 1960s, the tallest structure in Honolulu. Buildings here tell the story of Hawai'i's history in architecture, from the Chinatown buildings of the late 1800s to the 21st-century design of the First Hawaiian Building. Washington Place, built in 1846, was the home of Queen Lili'uokalani until her death in 1917, and until 2003 it served as the residence for Hawai'i's governors. A new governor's residence has been built alongside Washington Place, and plans are under way to open Washington Place to the public as a historical museum.

To reach Downtown Honolulu from Waikīkī by car, take Ala Moana Boulevard to Alakea Street. There are public parking lots (50¢ per half hour for the first two hours) in buildings along Alakea Street and Bethel Street, two blocks 'ewa. Keep in mind that parking in most downtown lots is expensive ($3.50 per half hour).

a good walk

Begin at the **Hawai'i Maritime Center** ⑳ ☞ at the harborfront, across Ala Moana Boulevard from Alakea Street in Downtown Honolulu. This museum traces the history of Hawai'i's love affair with the sea. Just 'ewa of the Hawai'i Maritime Center is **Aloha Tower Marketplace** ㉑, a complex of harborside shops and restaurants where you can also view the luxury cruise liners in port and the traditional Hawaiian Boat Days celebrations that greet each arrival.

Cross Ala Moana Boulevard, walk a block 'ewa, and turn mauka on Ft. Street Mall, a pedestrian walkway, until you reach King Street. Turn left, and in a few blocks you'll reach **Chinatown** ㉒, the old section of Downtown Honolulu. Here you can find a Buddhist temple, a Japanese shrine, shops, art galleries, restaurants, and a big open market.

Walk back toward Diamond Head along King Street until it intersects with Bishop Street. On the mauka side is lovely **Tamarind Park** ㉓, a popular lunchtime picnic spot for Honolulu's workforce, which gathers under its shady plumeria, kukui, and monkeypod trees—and one tamarind. Continue down King Street and hang a left onto Richards Street. At the corner of Richards and Hotel streets, is the No. 1 Capitol District Building, which houses Hawai'i's newest museum, opened in late 2002: the **Hawai'i State Art Museum** ㉔. Walk back along Richards Street toward King Street until you reach **'Iolani Palace** ㉕, on the lefthand side. This graceful Victorian structure was built by King David Kalākaua in 1882. Also on the palace grounds is the Kalākaua Coronation Bandstand, where the Royal Hawaiian Band performs at noon most Fridays.

Across King Street from 'Iolani Palace is Ali'iōlani Hale, the judiciary building that once served as the parliament hall during the kingship era. In front of it is the gilded **Kamehameha I Statue** ㉖, which honors Hawai'i's greatest monarch. Walk one block mauka up Richards Street to tour the **Hawai'i State Capitol** ㉗. Almost across the street from the state capitol is Washington Place, the home of Hawai'i's governor.

Return to King Street via Punchbowl Street, stay on the mauka side, and proceed in a Diamond Head direction. Walk past the palace again until you come to the massive stone **Hawai'i State Library** ㉘, a showcase of architectural restoration. At Punchbowl Street is **Honolulu Hale** ㉙, or City

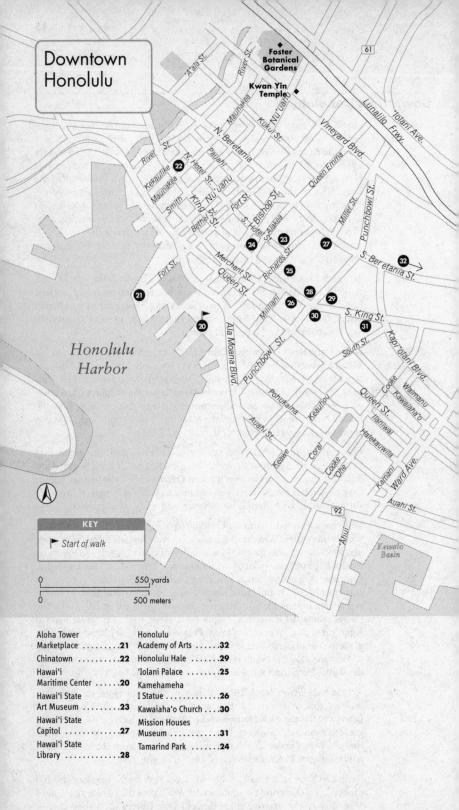

Downtown Honolulu

Foster Botanical Gardens

Kwan Yin Temple

61

ʻIolani Ave.

Lunalilo Frwy.

Vineyard Blvd.

Aʻala St.

River St.

Maunakea

Nuʻuanu

Kukui St.

Queen Emma

N. Beretania

River St.

Kekaulike

Maunakea

Pauahi

N. Hotel St.

Smith

King St.

Nuʻuanu

Bethel St.

Fort St.

Fort St.

Bishop St.

S. Hotel St.

Alakea

Miller St.

Punchbowl St.

S. Beretania St.

22

24

23

27

32

Merchant St.

Queen St.

Richards St.

25

21

20

28

26

29

30

31

Millani

S. King St.

Kapiʻolani Blvd.

Honolulu Harbor

Ala Moana Blvd.

Punchbowl St.

South St.

Queen St.

Cooke

Waimanu

Kawaiahaʻo

Pohukaina

Keaunou

Iliniwai

Halekauwila

Auahi St.

Keawe

Coral

Cooke

Ohe

Kamani

Ward Ave.

Auahi St.

92

Anui

Kewalo Basin

KEY

🚩 *Start of walk*

0   550 yards

0   500 meters

HONOLULU'S 15-BLOCK MELTING POT

HONOLULU'S CHINATOWN was established in the late 1800s by laborers looking for a new life after their contracts with the sugar plantations ended. The neighborhood—bordered by North Beretania Street and North King Street to the north and south and Bethel Street and River Street to the east and west—has a tumultuous and fascinating history. It was twice destroyed by fire, first in 1886 and again in 1900 (the later fire was deliberately set to clear the area of the bubonic plague), but was lovingly rebuilt both times, and by the 1930s it was a real center of influence, namely because of its prime location just minutes from Honolulu Harbor. In the 1940s, however, the neighborhood became notorious as the seedy stomping ground of military personnel, who found their way here to sample the exotic food, as well as the bars, pool halls, tattoo parlors, and prostitution houses. For years after, Chinatown was crime-ridden and many of its historic buildings fell into disrepair. It wasn't until 1973, when the federal government declared the neighborhood a historic area, that Chinatown's slow upswing began. Since then new residential buildings and commercial space have been added and many cultural gems have been restored.

Today, visiting a revitalized Chinatown is like taking a two-hour tour throughout Asia. At its heart is the **O`ahu Marketplace**

(✉ at N. King and Kekaulike Sts.), where everything a Chinese chef could desire is on display. The neighborhood still retains much of its original architecture—notable are the Chinatown Police Station and the Hawai`i Theatre Center. Even amid the flurry of modern retail outlets, including the Maunakea Marketplace, Mahalo Antique Mall, and the more contemporary Chinese Cultural Plaza are places of calm in the Taoist Lum Sai Ho Tong Society Temple, the Shinto Izumo Taisha Mission Cultural Hall, and the Kuan Yin Buddhist Temple. The wild orchid gardens at the **Foster Botanical Garden** (✉ N. Vineyard Blvd. at Nu`uanu Ave. ☎ 808/522–7060), open daily 9–4, are perfect for quiet contemplation.

The contemporary side of Chinatown is just as exciting. Though there's plenty of yesteryear to be found in the herb and antique shops, Chinatown is also a great place to shop for chic modern-day accouterments. Additionally, Nu`uanu Avenue, north of Hotel Street, is packed with art galleries and trendy clubs.

Of course, one of the main reasons to visit this lively neighborhood is the food. Don't miss the udon noodles at the **Yat Hung Chow Noodle Factory** (✉ 150 N. King St. ☎ 808/531–7982). Equally delicious are the pastries at **Shung Chong Yuein** (✉ 1027 Maunakea St. ☎ 808/531–1983).

Hall. Across the street is the **Kawaiaha`o Church** ③⓪, perhaps Hawai`i's most famous religious structure. On the Diamond Head side of the Kawaiaha`o Church is the **Mission Houses Museum** ③①, where the first American missionaries in Hawai`i lived. From here it's three long blocks toward Diamond Head to Ward Avenue and one block mauka to Beretania Street, but the **Honolulu Academy of Arts** ③② is worth the extra mileage (you might choose to drive there instead). It houses a world-class collection of Western and Asian art.

TIMING Downtown Honolulu merits a full day of your time. Be sure to stop by the palace Tuesday–Saturday, the only days tours are offered. Remember that the Mission Houses Museum is closed Sunday and Monday and the Honolulu Academy of Arts is closed Monday. Saturday morning is the best time to walk through Chinatown; that's when the open-air markets do their biggest business with local families. A walk through Chinatown can take at least an hour, as can tours of the Mission Houses and ʻIolani Palace. Wrap up your day at sunset with refreshments or dinner back at the Aloha Tower Marketplace, which stays open late into the evening, with live entertainment on the harborfront.

What to See

㉑ Aloha Tower Marketplace. Two stories of shops and kiosks feature island-inspired clothing, jewelry, art, and home furnishings. The Marketplace, located on the Honolulu Harborfront, also has indoor and outdoor restaurants, as well as live entertainment. For a bird's-eye view of this working harbor, take a free ride up to the observation deck of Aloha Tower, which anchors the market. The Marketplace's location makes it an ideal spot for watching the arrival of cruise ships. On Hawaiian Boat Days, the waterfront comes alive with entertainment and hula dancers who greet and send off the arriving and departing ships. ⊠ *1 Aloha Tower Dr., at Piers 8, 9, and 10,` Downtown Honolulu* ☎ *808/528–5700* ⊕ *www.alohatower.com* ⊘ *Daily 9–9, restaurants 9* AM*–2* AM.

㉒ Chinatown. Noodle factories and herb shops, lei stands and acupuncture studios, art galleries and Chinese and Thai restaurants make up this historic neighborhood. A major highlight is the colorful Oʻahu Market, an open-air emporium with hanging pigs' heads, display cases of fresh fish, row after row of exotic fruits and vegetables, and vendors of all ethnic backgrounds. Check out the Chinese Cultural Plaza's Moongate stage for cultural events, especially around the Chinese New Year. ⊠ *King St. between Smith and River Sts., Chinatown* ⊕ *www. chinatownhi.com.*

> **need a break?** There are Chinese, Thai, Japanese, Korean, and Italian food stalls at **Maunakea Marketplace** (⊠ 1120 Maunakea St., Chinatown ☎ 808/524–3409), one block mauka of King Street. The food is flavorful and reasonably priced. A courtyard has some seating.

㉑ Hawaiʻi Maritime Center. The story of the Islands begins on the seas. The **Kalākaua Boat House** has interactive exhibits where you can learn about Hawaiʻi's whaling days, the history of Honolulu Harbor, the Clipper seaplane, and surfing and windsurfing in Hawaiʻi. Moored next to the Boat House is the *Falls of Clyde.* Built in 1778, this four-masted, square-rigged ship once brought tea from China to the U.S. west coast and is now used as a museum. Also on view is the *Hōkūleʻa,* a reproduction of an ancient Polynesian double-hull voyaging canoe. The *Hōkūleʻa* has completed several journeys throughout the Pacific, during which the crew used only the stars and the sea as navigational guides. Self-guided audio tours are available in English, Japanese, and Korean. ⊠ *Ala Moana Blvd. at Pier 7, Downtown Honolulu* ☎ *808/ 536–6373* 🎫 *$7.50* ⊘ *Daily 8:30–5.*

㉓ Hawaiʻi State Art Museum. Twelve thousand feet of gallery space are dedicated to the art of Hawaiʻi in all its ethnic diversity. The Diamond Head Gallery features new acquisitions and thematic shows from the State Art Collection and the State Foundation on Culture and the Arts programs. The Ewa Gallery houses more than 150 works documenting Hawaiʻi's visual-arts history since becoming a state in 1959. Also included are a sculpture gallery as well as a café, a gift shop, and educational meeting rooms. ⊠ *250 South Hotel St., 2nd Floor, Downtown Honolulu* ☎ *808/ 586–0307* 🎫 *Free* ⊘ *Tues.–Sat. 10–4.*

㉗ Hawaiʻi State Capitol. The capitol's architecture is richly symbolic: the columns look like palm trees, the legislative chambers are shaped like volcanic cinder cones, and the central court is open to the sky, representing Hawai'i's open society. Replicas of the Hawai'i state seal, each weighing 7,500 pounds, hang above both its entrances. The building, which in 1969 replaced 'Iolani Palace as the seat of government, is surrounded by reflecting pools, just as the Islands are embraced by water. ⊠ *215 S. Beretania St., Downtown Honolulu* ☎ *808/586–0146* ⊡ *Free* ⊙ *Guided tours upon request weekday afternoons.*

28 Hawai'i State Library. This beautifully renovated main library, originally built in 1913, is wonderful to explore. Its Samuel M. Kamakani Room, on the first floor in the mauka courtyard, houses an extensive Hawai'i and Pacific book collection and pays tribute to Kamakani, one of Hawai'i's noted historians. ⊠ *478 King St., Downtown Honolulu* ☎ *808/586–3500* ⊡ *Free* ⊙ *Mon. and Fri.–Sat. 9–5, Tues. and Thurs. 9–8, Wed. 10–5.*

32 Honolulu Academy of Arts. The academy dates to 1927 and has an impressive permanent collection that includes Hiroshige's ukiyo-e Japanese prints, donated by James Michener; Italian Renaissance paintings; and American and European art. Six open-air courtyards provide a casual counterpart to the more formal galleries. The Luce Pavilion complex has a traveling-exhibit gallery, a Hawaiian gallery, a café, and a gift shop. The Academy Theatre screens art films. There are select Islamic-art tours from the academy's art center to the Doris Duke Foundation for Islamic Art, located within Duke's former Diamond Head estate, Shangri-La. Guided tours of the academy are available Tuesday–Saturday 11 AM and Sunday 1:15 PM. Call about special exhibits, concerts, and films. ⊠ *900 S. Beretania St., Downtown Honolulu* ☎ *808/532–8700* ⊕ *www.honoluluacademy.org* ⊡ *$7* ⊙ *Tues.–Sat. 10–4:30, Sun. 1–5.*

29 Honolulu Hale. This Mediterranean Renaissance–style building was constructed in 1929 and serves as the center of city government. Stroll through the cool, open-ceiling lobby with exhibits of local artists, and time your visit to coincide with one of the free concerts sometimes offered in the evening, when the building stays open late. During the winter holiday season, the Hale becomes the focal point for the annual Honolulu City Lights Festival program. ⊠ *530 S. King St., Downtown Honolulu* ☎ *808/523–4654* ⊡ *Free* ⊙ *Weekdays 8–4:30.*

25 'Iolani Palace. Built in 1882 on the site of an earlier palace and beautifully restored since, this is America's only royal residence. (Bucking the stereotype of the primitive islander, the palace had electricity and telephone lines installed even before the White House did.) It contains the thrones of King Kalākaua and his successor (and sister) Queen Lili'uokalani. Downstairs galleries showcase the royal jewelry, and kitchen and offices of the monarchy. The palace is open for guided tours only, and reservations are essential. Take a look at the gift shop, formerly the 'Iolani Barracks, built to house the Royal Guard. ⊠ *King and Richards Sts., Downtown Honolulu* ☎ *808/522–0832* ⊕ *www.iolanipalace.org* ⊡ *Grand Tour $20, downstairs galleries only $10* ⊙ *Tues.–Sat. 8:30–2, with tours beginning on the half hour.*

need a break? For an exotic lunch stop by **Duk's Bistro** (⊠ 1188 Maunakea St., Chinatown ☎ 808/531–6325), a tiny three-room eatery facing Chinatown's busiest street and featuring a French-Vietnamese menu. Spring for the shrimp, mushroom, and taro spring rolls or have a "Meal in a Bowl," brimming with rice noodles and fresh island vegetables.

26 Kamehameha I Statue. This downtown landmark pays tribute to the Big Island chieftain who united all the warring Hawaiian Islands into one kingdom at the turn of the 18th century. The statue, which stands with one arm outstretched in welcome, is one of three originally cast in Paris, France, by American sculptor T. R. Gould; the original version is in Kapa'au, on the Big Island, near the king's birthplace. Each year on the king's birthday, June 11, the statue is draped in fresh lei that reach lengths of 18 ft and longer. ⊠ *417 S. King St., outside Ali'iōlani Hale, Downtown Honolulu.*

③⓪ Kawaiaha'o Church. Fancifully called Hawai'i's Westminster Abbey, this 14,000-coral-block house of worship witnessed the coronations, weddings, and funerals of generations of Hawaiian royalty. Each of the building's coral blocks was quarried from reefs offshore at depths of more than 20 ft and transported to this site. Interior woodwork was created from the forests of the Ko'olau Mountains. The upper gallery has an exhibit of paintings of the royal families. The graves of missionaries and of King Lunalilo are in the yard. Services in English and Hawaiian are held each Sunday. Although there are no guided tours, you can look around the church at no cost. ⊠ *957 Punchbowl St., at King St., Downtown Honolulu* ☎ *808/522–1333* ⊠ *Free* ◷ *English service Sun. at 8 AM and Wed. at 6 PM, Hawaiian service Sun. at 10:30 AM.*

③① Mission Houses Museum. The determined Hawai'i missionaries arrived in 1820, gaining royal favor and influencing every aspect of island life. Their descendants became leaders in government and business. You can walk through their original dwellings, including a white-frame house that was prefabricated in New England and shipped around the Horn—it is Hawai'i's oldest wooden structure. The museum hosts living history programs, candlelight museum tours, and crafts fairs. Certain areas of the museum may be seen only on a one-hour guided tour. The museum also offers historic-downtown walking tours on Thursdays at 10 AM; reservations are required 24 hours in advance. ⊠ *553 S. King St., Downtown Honolulu* ☎ *808/531–0481* ⊕ *www.lava.net/~mhm* ⊠ *$10, walking tour $15* ◷ *Tues.–Sat. 9–4; guided tours at 9:45, 11:15, 1, and 2:30.*

②④ Tamarind Park. From jazz and Hawaiian tunes to the strains of the U.S. Marine Band, music fills this pretty park most Fridays at noon. Do as the locals do: pick up lunch at one of the many carryout restaurants and find a bench or patch of grass. ⊠ *Corner of Bishop and S. King Sts., Downtown Honolulu* ⊠ *Free.*

The East O'ahu Ring

At once historic and contemporary, serene and active, the east end of O'ahu holds within its relatively small area remarkable variety and picture-perfect scenery of windswept cliffs and wave-dashed shores.

a good drive

From Waikīkī there are two routes to Lunalilo Freeway (H-1). On the Diamond Head end, go mauka on Kapahulu Avenue and follow the signs to the freeway. On the 'ewa end, take Ala Wai Boulevard and turn mauka at Kalākaua Avenue, staying on it until it ends at Beretania Street, which is one-way going left. Turn right off Beretania Street at Pi'ikoi Street, and the signs will direct you onto the freeway heading west.

Take the freeway exit marked Pali Highway (Route 61), one of three roads that cut through the Ko'olau Mountains. On the right is the **Queen Emma Summer Palace** ③③ ▶. The colonial-style white mansion, which once served as the summer retreat of King Kamehameha IV and his wife, Queen Emma, is now a museum.

As you drive toward the summit of the highway, the road is lined with sweet ginger in summer and red poinsettias in winter. If it has been raining, waterfalls will be tumbling down the chiseled cliffs of the Ko'olau. If it is very windy, those waterfalls can look as if they are traveling up the cliffs, not down, making them a sight to behold.

Watch for the turn to the **Nu'uanu Pali Lookout** ㉞. There is a small parking lot and a lookout wall from which you can see all the way up and down the windward coast—a view that Mark Twain called the most beautiful in the world.

As you follow the highway down the other side of the mountain, continue straight along what becomes Kailua Road. If you're interested in Hawaiian history, look for the YMCA at the Castle Hospital junction of Kalaniana'ole Highway and Kailua Road. Behind it is **Ulupō Heiau** ㉟, an ancient outdoor shrine. Ready for a detour? Head straight on Kailua Road to Kailua Beach Park, which many people consider the best on the island. The road twists and turns, so watch the signs.

Retracing your route back to Castle Junction, turn left at the intersection onto Kalaniana'ole Highway. Soon you will come to the small town of **Waimānalo** ㊱. Waimānalo's two beaches are Bellows Beach, great for swimming and bodysurfing, and Waimānalo Beach Park, also safe for swimming.

Another mile along the highway, on the right, is **Sea Life Park** ㊲, home to the world's only "wholphin," the offspring of a whale and a dolphin. Across the highway from Sea Life Park is Makapu'u Beach, a beautiful cove that is great for seasoned bodysurfers but treacherous for weak swimmers. The road winds up a hill, at the top of which is a turnoff on the makai side to **Makapu'u Point** ㊳.

Next you'll see the inviting Sandy Beach. Tempting as this beach looks, it is not advisable to swim here because the waves are powerful and the rip currents more than tricky. From here the road twists and turns next to steep cliffs along the Koko Head shoreline. Offshore, the islands of Moloka'i and Lāna'i call like distant sirens, and every once in a while Maui is visible in blue silhouette. For the best photos, pull into the parking lot at **Hālona Blowhole** ㊴. At the top of the hill on the makai side of the road is the entrance to **Hanauma Bay Nature Preserve** ㊵, one of O'ahu's most famous snorkeling destinations.

From here back to Waikīkī the highway passes several residential communities called Hawai'i Kai, Niu Valley, and 'Āina Haina, each of which has a small shopping center where you can pick up a soda or a snack. Right before you turn off from Kalaniana'ole Highway there's a long stretch of green on the makai side. This is the private Wai'alae Country Club, scene of the televised annual Sony Open Golf Tournament.

Take the Kīlauea Avenue exit. Turn left at the stoplight onto Kīlauea Avenue. Here you'll see Kāhala Mall, an upscale shopping complex with yuppie eateries, high-fashion stores, and eight movie theaters. A few blocks past the mall, take a left on Hunakai Street and follow it until it dead-ends at Kāhala Avenue. Turn right and drive through **Kāhala** ㊶, O'ahu's wealthiest neighborhood. Kāhala Avenue becomes Diamond Head Road. Follow it straight to Kapi'olani Park. Stay on the right side of the park until you hit Kapahulu Avenue. Take a left, and you're back in Waikīkī.

TIMING   If Hanauma Bay is your main focus, don't try to do the tour on Tuesday, when the park is closed. Also note that the bay is best in the early hours before the waters are churned up. You could reverse the above directions and get there first thing in the morning, before the crowds. Allow two hours for Hanauma Bay, two hours for Sea Life Park, and one for Queen Emma Summer Palace. Another tip: look up to the top

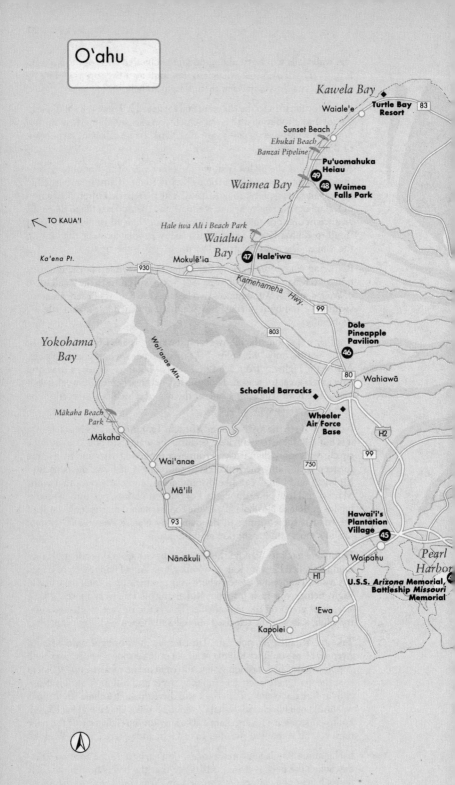

O'ahu

Kawela Bay

Waiale'e

Turtle Bay Resort 83

Sunset Beach

Ehukai Beach
Banzai Pipeline

Pu'uomahuka Heiau

49

48 **Waimea Falls Park**

Waimea Bay

Hale iwa Ali i Beach Park

Waialua Bay

← TO KAUA'I

47 **Hale'iwa**

Ka'ena Pt.

Mokulē'ia

930

Kamehameha Hwy.

99

803

Dole Pineapple Pavilion

Yokohama Bay

46

Wai'anae Mts.

80 Wahiawā

Schofield Barracks

Wheeler Air Force Base

Mākaha Beach Park

H2

Mākaha

99

Wai'anae

750

Mā'ili

93

Hawai'i's Plantation Village

45

Nānākuli

Waipahu

Pearl Harbor

H1

U.S.S. *Arizona* Memorial, Battleship *Missouri* Memorial

'Ewa

Kapolei

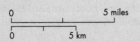

0   5 miles

0   5 km

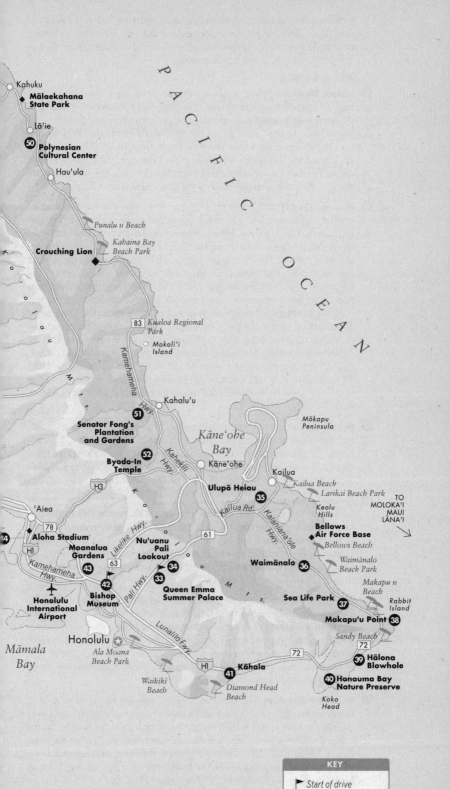

Kahuku

Mālaekahana State Park ◆

Lāʻie

50 **Polynesian Cultural Center**

Hauʻula

Punaluʻu Beach

Kahaina Bay Beach Park

Crouching Lion ◆

83 *Kualoa Regional Park*

Mokoliʻi Island

P A C I F I C   O C E A N

Kahaluʻu

Mōkapu Peninsula

Kāneʻohe Bay

51

Senator Fong's Plantation and Gardens

52

Byodo-In Temple

Kāneʻohe

Kailua

Kailua Beach

Larikai Beach Park

TO MOLOKAʻI MAUI LĀNAʻI

H3

Ulupō Heiau

Keolu Hills

35

Kailua Rd.

ʻAiea

78

Aloha Stadium

Moanalua Gardens

H1

4

Nuʻuanu Pali Lookout

Bellows Air Force Base ◆

Bellows Beach

Waimānalo

36

Waimānalo Beach Park

43

42

63

Bishop Museum

33 **34**

61

Queen Emma Summer Palace

Sea Life Park

37

Makapuʻu Beach

Rabbit Island

Makapuʻu Point **38**

Honolulu International Airport

Honolulu

Ala Moana Beach Park

Sandy Beach

72

39 **Hālona Blowhole**

41

Kāhala

H1

72

40 **Hanauma Bay Nature Preserve**

Māmala Bay

Waikīkī Beach

Diamond Head Beach

Koko Head

KEY

► *Start of drive*

of the mountains and, if it's clear, head directly to the Nu'uanu Pali Lookout. It's a shame to get there only to find the view obscured by clouds or fog. Temperatures at the summit are several degrees cooler than in warm Waikīkī, so bring a jacket along.

What to See

㊴ Hālona Blowhole. Below a scenic turnout along the Koko Head shoreline, this oft-photographed lava tube that sucks the ocean in and spits it out in lofty plumes may or may not perform, depending on the currents. Look to your right to see the tiny beach below that was used to film the wave-washed love scene in *From Here to Eternity*. In winter, it's a good spot to watch whales at play. Take your valuables with you and lock your car, because this scenic location is a hot spot for petty thieves. ⊠ *Kalaniana'ole Hwy., 1 mi east of Hanauma Bay.*

㊵ Hanauma Bay Nature Preserve. This bay was created when the exterior
Fodor'sChoice wall of a volcanic crater collapsed, opening it to the sea and thereby giv-
★ ing birth to O'ahu's most famous snorkeling destination. Even from the overlook, the horseshoe-shape bay is a beauty, and you can easily see the reefs through the clear aqua waters. The wide beach is a great place for sunbathing and picnics. This is a marine conservation district, and regulations prohibit the feeding of the fish. The Hanauma Bay education center and a concession center provide not only modern conveniences but also a cultural history of the bay, and exhibits about the importance of protecting its marine life. Come early to get parking, as the number of visitors allowed per day is limited. Call for current conditions. Weather permitting, Hanauma Bay by Starlight events are held on Saturday, extending the opening hours to 10 PM. ⊠ *7455 Kalaniana'ole Hwy.* ☎ *808/396–4229* ✉ *Donation $3; parking $1; mask, snorkel, and fins rental $6; tram from parking lot down to beach $1.50* ☉ *Wed.–Mon. 6 AM–7 PM.*

㊶ Kāhala. O'ahu's wealthiest neighborhood has streets lined with multimillion-dollar homes and the classy Kāhala Mandarin Oriental Hawai'i hotel, which attracts a prestigious clientele. At intervals along tree-lined Kāhala Avenue are narrow lanes that provide public access to Kāhala's magnificent coastal beaches. ✛ *East of Diamond Head.*

㊳ Makapu'u Point. This spot has breathtaking views of the ocean, mountains, and the windward islands. The peninsula jutting out in the distance is **Mōkapu**, site of a U.S. Marine base. The spired mountain peak is **Mt. Olomana**. In front of you on the long pier is part of the **Makai Undersea Test Range**, a research facility that is closed to the public. Offshore is **Rabbit Island**, a picturesque cay so named because some think it looks like a swimming bunny.

Nestled in the cliff face is the **Makapu'u Lighthouse**, which became operational in 1909 and has the largest lighthouse lense in America. The lighthouse is closed to the public, but near the Makapu'u Point turnout you'll find the start of a mile-long paved road (closed to traffic). Hike up to the top of the 647-ft bluff for a closer view of the lighthouse and, in winter, a great whale-watching vantage point. ⊠ *Kalaniana'ole Hwy., turnout above Makapu'u Beach.*

㉞ Nu'uanu Pali Lookout. This panoramic perch looks out to windward O'ahu. It was in this region that King Kamehameha I drove defending forces over the edges of the 1,000-ft-high cliffs, thus winning the decisive battle for control of O'ahu. From here, you can see views that stretch from Kaneohe Bay to Chinaman's Hat, a small island off the coast, and beyond. It's a windy spot, so hang on to your hat. Lock your car if you get out, because break-ins have occurred here. ⊠ *Top of Pali Hwy.* ☉ *Daily 9–4.*

㉝ Queen Emma Summer Palace. Queen Emma and her family used this stately white home, built in 1848, as a retreat from the rigors of court life in hot and dusty Honolulu during the mid-1800s. It has an eclectic mix of European, Victorian, and Hawaiian furnishings and has excellent examples of Hawaiian quilts and koa-wood furniture as well as the queen's wedding dress and other memorabilia. ✉ *2913 Pali Hwy.* ☎ *808/595–3167* ⊕ *www.daughtersofhawaii.org* ✉ *$5* ☉ *Guided tours daily 9–4.*

㊲ Sea Life Park. Dolphins leap and spin, penguins frolic, and a killer whale performs impressive tricks at this marine-life attraction 15 mi from Waikīkī at scenic Makapuʻu Point. In addition to a 300,000-gallon Hawaiian reef aquarium, you'll find the Pacific Whaling Museum, the Hawaiian Monk Seal Care Center, and a breeding sanctuary for Hawaiʻi's endangered *Honu* sea turtle. There are several interactive activities such as a stingray encounter, an underwater photo safari, and a "Splash University" dolphin-training session. Inquire about the park's behind-the-scenes tour for a glimpse of dolphin-training areas and the seabird rehabilitation center. ✉ *41-202 Kalanianaʻole Hwy., Waimānalo* ☎ *808/259–7933 or 886/365–7446* ⊕ *www.sealifepark.com* ✉ *$24* ☉ *Daily 9:30–5.*

㉟ Ulupō Heiau. Though they may look like piles of rocks to the uninitiated, *heiau* are sacred stone platforms for the worship of the gods and date from ancient times. *Ulupō* means "night inspiration," referring to the legendary *menehune,* a mythical race of diminutive people who supposedly built the heiau under the cloak of darkness. ⊹ *Behind YMCA at Kalanianaʻole Hwy. and Kailua Rd.*

need a break? Generations of children have purchased their beach snacks and sodas at **Kalapawai Market** (✉ 306 S. Kalāheo Ave.), near Kailua Beach. A windward landmark since 1932, the green-and-white market has distinctive charm. It's a good source for your carryout lunch, since there's no concession stand at the beach.

㊱ Waimānalo. This modest little seaside town flanked by chiseled cliffs is worth a visit. Its biggest draw is its beautiful beach, offering glorious views to the windward side. Down the side roads, as you head mauka, are little farms that grow a variety of fruits and flowers. Toward the back of the valley are small ranches with grazing horses. If you see any trucks selling corn and you're staying at a place where you can cook it, be sure to get some in Waimānalo. It may be the sweetest you'll ever eat, and the price is the lowest on Oʻahu. ✉ *Kalanianaʻole Hwy.*

Around the Island

After visiting three historic attractions in populated West Honolulu, you'll find that the Oʻahu landscape turns increasingly rural as you head north. Once carpeted in pineapple and sugarcane plantations, the central plains and the North Shore are now home to ranches, banana farms, and fields of exotic flowers and coffee grown for export. Some plantation towns have become cute with boutiques and little art galleries. Others are just themselves—old, wooden, and picturesque—with small homes surrounded by flowers and tropical-fruit trees.

a good drive Follow H-1 Freeway heading west. Take the exit for Likelike Highway. Stay in the right lane and look for signs to the **Bishop Museum** ㊷ ⚑. Once you're back on the freeway heading west, the road merges into the Moanalua Freeway (Route 78). Stay on this past the Puʻuloa Road–Tripler Hospital exit for **Moanalua Gardens** ㊸, a lovely park with huge monkeypod trees.

Continuing on the freeway, up over what is known as Red Hill, you'll pass Aloha Stadium, a 50,000-seat arena that hosts the annual NFL Pro Bowl, local football and baseball games, and big-name rock concerts. The Aloha Flea Market is also held here. As you approach the stadium on the freeway, bear right at the sign to 'Aiea, and then merge left onto Kamehameha Highway (Route 99), going south to Pearl Harbor. Turn right at the Hālawa Gate for a tour of the **U.S.S. Arizona Memorial, Battleship Missouri Memorial** ㊹, and the U.S.S. *Bowfin*.

Follow H-1 west to Waipahu (Exit 8B) and onto Farrington Highway. Turn right at Waipahu Depot Road and left onto Waipahu Street to reach **Hawai'i's Plantation Village** ㊺, a collection of restored original and replicated homes from a 19th-century plantation town.

Take H-1 to H-2 to Route 80 (Kamehameha Highway), heading to Wahiawā, home of the U.S. Army base at Schofield Barracks. Head north until Route 80 meets Route 99, where you'll see a scrubby patch called the Del Monte Pineapple Variety Garden. Unpromising as it looks, it's actually quite interesting, with varieties of the ubiquitous fruit ranging from thumb-size pink ones to big golden ones.

Merge left on Kamehameha Highway and you'll see the **Dole Pineapple Pavilion** ㊻. From here, Kamehameha Highway cuts through pineapple and sugarcane fields. Close to the bottom of the hill, a traffic-light intersection invites you to take the Hale'iwa bypass road to save time. Don't. Turn left instead and drive to the traffic circle. Go around the circle and continue 7 mi to Mokulē'ia on Route 930. Soon you'll come to Dillingham Airfield, where you can fly in a glider.

Back at the traffic circle, follow the signs to **Hale'iwa** ㊼, a sleepy plantation town with fashion boutiques, surf shops, restaurants, and the best grilled mahimahi sandwich on the North Shore at Kua 'Aina Sandwich. Leaving Hale'iwa and continuing along Kamehameha Highway (Route 83), you'll pass the famous North Shore beaches, where the winter surf comes in size extra large. The first of these is the famous big surf spot Waimea Bay. Across the street, on the mauka side of the road, is **Waimea Falls Park** ㊽. If you're interested in seeing a fine example of an ancient Hawaiian heiau, turn mauka at the Foodland store and take Pūpūkea Road up the steep climb, not quite a mile, to the dirt road on the right, leading to the **Pu'uomahuka Heiau** ㊾.

Continue along the coastal road past more famous surfing beaches, including 'Ehukai and Sunset. If it's wintertime, keep clear of those waves, which sometimes rise as high as 30 ft. Leave the sea to the daring (some say crazy) surfers who ride the towering waves with astounding grace. The only hotel of any consequence in these parts is your next landmark: the Turtle Bay Resort.

As you approach the town of Lā'ie, there is a long stretch of pine trees on the makai side. Look for the entrance to Mālaekahana State Park; on the mauka side is the sprawling **Polynesian Cultural Center** ㊿.

As you continue driving along the shoreline, notice the picturesque little island of Mokoli'i ("little lizard"), a 206-ft-high sea stack. According to Hawaiian legend, the goddess Hi'iaka, sister of Pele, slew the dragon Mokoli'i and flung its tail into the sea, forming the distinct islet. Other dragon body parts—in the form of rocks, of course—were scattered along the base of nearby Kualoa Ridge.

Continue straight on Kahekili Highway (Route 83) and look on your right for **Senator Fong's Plantation and Gardens** 51. Two miles farther on the right is the Valley of the Temples and its lovely **Byodo-In Temple** 52, a replica of a 900-year-old temple outside Uji, Japan.

Follow Kahekili Highway to Likelike Highway (Route 63), where you turn mauka and head back toward Honolulu through the Wilson Tunnel. The highway leads to Lunalilo Freeway going east. Exit at Pali Highway and go south through Downtown Honolulu on Bishop Street. Then turn left on Ala Moana Boulevard, which leads to Kalākaua Avenue in Waikīkī.

TIMING Unless you don't plan on stopping at any of the sights, allot nothing less than a day to circle the island. Try to factor in two or three different excursions and time-outs along this scenic North Shore. Don't rush through the Polynesian Cultural Center; instead, devote an afternoon and evening to the center, perhaps stopping first for a morning at Waimea Valley. Note that the center is closed Sunday.

On another day, allow a full afternoon for the Bishop Museum. Inquire also about the "Behind the Scenes" museum tour. Afternoons, you may have to wait as long as two hours to see the U.S.S. *Arizona* Memorial. The best bet is to head out there early in the day. Security measures at all military sites are now very strict. If you are planning to visit the U. S.S. *Arizona*, U.S.S. *Battleship* Missouri, or U.S.S *Bowfin* Memorial, be prepared to bring only your "self." No purses, backpacks, diaper bags, waist packs, camera bags, or other "items of concealment" are allowed, and locking those items in your vehicle leaves you vulnerable to local petty thieves on the lookout for rental-car targets. Haleʻiwa deserves two hours: factor in some extra North Shore time for hiking, relaxing on a beach, kayaking, taking a glider ride, and having a snack. Wear flip-flops but bring a pair of walking shoes as well.

The weather is mercurial on the North Shore. It can be sunny and clear in Waikīkī and cloudy in the country. Bring along a light jacket, a hat, and sunscreen. Then you'll be ready for anything.

What to See

44 **Battleship** *Missouri* **Memorial.** The U.S.S. *Missouri* saw action from World War II to the Persian Gulf War, and on these decks the agreement for Japanese surrender to end World War II was signed. The famed battleship, now moored about 1,000 ft from the *Arizona*, serves as a museum and interactive educational center. Tours start at the visitor center located between the U.S.S. *Arizona* and U.S.S. *Bowfin* Memorial. A trolley transports you to the navy's Ford Island, where you can board the "Mighty Mo," take a tour, and see how 2,400 sailors lived and worked together in the shadow of its 16-inch guns. Come dressed in attire suitable for climbing up and down the ship's ladders. ⊠ *Pearl Harbor* ☎ *808/423–2263 or 888/877–6477* ⊕ *www.ussmissouri.com* ⊠ *$16, guided tours $22* ⊗ *Daily 9–5.*

▶ 42 **Bishop Museum.** Founded in 1889 by Charles R. Bishop as a memorial to his wife, Princess Bernice Pauahi, the museum began as a repository for the royal possessions of this last direct descendant of King Kamehameha the Great. Today it is the Hawaiʻi State Museum of Natural and Cultural History and houses more than 24.7 million itemsthat tell the history of the Hawaiian Islands and their Pacific neighbors. There are world-famous displays of Polynesian artifacts: lustrous feather capes, the skeleton of a giant sperm whale, photography and crafts displays, and an authentic, well-preserved grass house. Also check out the planetarium, daily hula and Hawaiian crafts demonstrations, special exhibits, and the Shop Pacifica. The building alone, with its huge Victorian turrets and immense stone walls, is worth seeing. ✉ *1525 Bernice St.* ☎ *808/847–3511* ⊕ *www.bishopmuseum.org* 💰 *$14.95* ⊗ *Daily 9–5.*

52 Byodo-In Temple. Tucked away in the back of the Valley of the Temples cemetery is a replica of the 11th-century Temple at Uji in Japan. A 2-ton carved wooden statue of the Buddha presides inside the main temple building. Next to the temple building are a meditation house and gardens set dramatically against the sheer, green cliffs of the Ko'olau Mountains. You can ring the 5-ft, 3-ton brass bell for good luck and feed some 10,000 carp that inhabit the garden's 2-acre pond. ✉ *47-200 Kahekili Hwy., Kāne'ohe* ☎ *808/239–8811* 💰 *$2* ⊗ *Daily 8:30–4:30.*

46 Dole Pineapple Pavilion. Celebrate Hawai'i's famous golden fruit at this promotional, tourist-oriented center with exhibits, a huge gift shop, a snack concession, educational displays, and the world's largest maze. Although much more sophisticated than its original 1950 fruit stand, the Pavilion is filled with souvenir options galore, and kids love the 1.7-mi Pineapple Garden Maze, which is made up of 11,400 tropical plants and trees. ✉ *64-1550 Kamehameha Hwy.* ☎ *808/621–8408* ⊕ *www. dole-plantation.com* 💰 *Pavilion free, maze $5* ⊗ *Daily 9–6.*

47 Hale'iwa. During the 1920s this seaside hamlet was a trendy retreat at the end of a railroad line. During the 1960s hippies gathered here, followed by surfers. Today Hale'iwa is a fun mix, with old general stores and contemporary boutiques, galleries, and eateries. Be sure to stop in at **Lili'uokalani Protestant Church,** founded by missionaries in the 1830s. It's fronted by a large, stone archway built in 1910 and covered with night-blooming cereus. ✥ *Follow H-1 west from Honolulu to H-2 north, exit at Wahiawā, follow Kamehameha Hwy. 6 mi, turn left at signaled intersection, then right into Hale'iwa* ⊕ *www.haleiwamainstreet.com.*

> **need a break?** For a real slice of Hale'iwa life, stop at **Matsumoto's** (✉ 66-087 Kamehameha Hwy. ⊕ www.matsumotoshaveice.com), a family-run business in a building dating from 1910, for shave ice in every flavor imaginable. For something different, order a shave ice with adzuki beans—the red beans are boiled until soft, mixed with sugar, and then placed in the cone with the ice on top.

45 Hawai'i's Plantation Village. Starting in the 1800s, immigrants came to these islands like so many waves against the shore. Tour authentically furnished buildings, both original and replicated, that re-create and pay tribute to Hawai'i's sugar plantation era. See a Chinese social hall; a Japanese shrine, sumo ring, and saimin stand; a dental office; and historic homes at this "living museum" 30 minutes from Downtown Honolulu. ✉ *Waipahu Cultural Gardens Park, 94-695 Waipahu St., Waipahu* ☎ *808/677–0110* 💰 *$7* ⊗ *Weekdays 9–3, Sat. 10–3, with guided hourly tours.*

43 Moanalua Gardens. This lovely park is the site of the internationally acclaimed Prince Lot hula festival on the third weekend in July. Throughout the year, the Moanalua Gardens Foundation sponsors 3-mi guided walks into Kamananui Valley, usually on Sundays; call for specific times. Self-guided tour booklets are also available from the Moanalua Gardens Foundation office. ✉ *1352 Pineapple Pl., Honolulu* ☎ *808/839–5334* ⊕ *www.mgf-hawaii.com* 💰 *Free* ⊗ *Weekdays 8–4:30.*

50 Polynesian Cultural Center. Re-created, individual villages showcase the lifestyles and traditions of Hawai'i, Tahiti, Samoa, Fiji, the Marquesas Islands, New Zealand, and Tonga. This 45-acre center, founded in 1963 by the Church of Jesus Christ of Latter-day Saints, also houses restaurants and lūʻaus and shares cultural traditions such as tribal tattooing, fire dancing, and ancient customs and ceremonies. The expansive open-air shopping village carries Polynesian handicrafts. If you're staying in Honolulu, see the center as part of a van tour so you won't have to drive home late at night after the two-hour evening show. Various packages are available, from basic admission to an all-inclusive deal. ⊠ *55-370 Kamehameha Hwy., Lāʻie* ☎ *808/293–3333* ⊕ *www.polynesia.com* ⊠ *$55–$175* ⊘ *Mon.–Sat. 12:30–9:30.*

49 **Puʻuomahuka Heiau.** Worth a stop for its spectacular views from a bluff high above the ocean overlooking Waimea Bay, this sacred spot was once the site of human sacrifices. It's now on the National Register of Historic Places. ↔ *½ mi north of Waimea Bay on Rte. 83, turn right on Pūpūkea Rd. and drive 1 mi uphill.*

51 **Senator Fong's Plantation and Gardens.** Hiram Fong, the first Asian-American to be elected to Congress, shares his love of Hawaiian flora and fauna by allowing tours of his 700-acre plantation estate. A 45-minute guided tram tour takes you through the estate's five lush valleys, each named for a U.S. president that Fong served under during his 17-year tenure in the Senate. The visitor center has a snack bar and gift shop. ⊠ *47-285 Pūlama Rd., off Kahekili Hwy., 2 mi north of Byodo-In Temple, Kahaluʻu* ☎ *808/239–6775* ⊕ *www.fonggarden.net* ⊠ *$10* ⊘ *Tram tours daily 10–4.*

44 **U.S.S. *Arizona* Memorial.** A simple, gleaming white structure shields the hulk of the U.S.S. *Arizona,* which sank with 1,102 men aboard when the Japanese attacked Pearl Harbor on December 7, 1941. The tour includes a 20-minute documentary with actual news footage from the day of the attack and a shuttle-boat ride to the memorial. Appropriate dress is required (no bathing suits, slippers, or bare feet). ⊠ *National Park Service, Pearl Harbor* ☎ *808/422–0561 or 808/423–2263* ⊕ *www. nps.gov/usar* ⊠ *Free* ☞ *Tour tickets distributed on a first-come, first-served basis, with 1- to 3-hr waits common* ⊘ *Daily 8–3.*

FodorśChoice ★

48 **Waimea Falls Park.** At this 1,800-acre attraction, remnants of an early Hawaiian civilization are surrounded by more than 2,500 tropical plants and trees. The garden trails are well marked, and the plants are labeled. There's a spectacular show of cliff-diving from 45-ft-high falls, and you can take part in Hawaiian games and hula. Tour the backcountry on horseback or by kayak, mountain bike, or all-terrain vehicle. Free "moonwalks" are held two nights at the time of each full moon. ⊠ *59-864 Kamehameha Hwy., Haleʻiwa* ☎ *808/638–8511* ⊕ *www. atlantisadventures.com* ⊠ *$24* ⊘ *Daily 10–5:30.*

off the beaten path

U.S.S. *Bowfin.* Moored near the U.S.S. *Arizona* Memorial visitor center, the *Bowfin,* is one of only 15 World War II subs still in existence. Dubbed the "Pearl Harbor Avenger," the sub saw nine successful war patrols and is credited with sinking 44 enemy ships while in service. Go aboard and see what life was like for its 80-member crew. Children under four are not admitted. ⊠ *11 Arizona Memorial Dr., at Pearl Harbor* ☎ *808/423–1342* ⊕ *www.aloha. net/~bowfin* ⊠ *$8* ⊘ *Daily 9–5.*

BEACHES

For South Seas sun, fun, and surf, Oʻahu is a dream destination, but first some words of caution: when approaching any Hawaiian beach, heed signs indicating current surf conditions. If they warn of dangerous surf

CloseUp

TIE THE KNOT WITH AN ISLAND TWIST

SO MANY COUPLES have gotten married in Hawai'i that an island wedding is starting to become a cliché. However, there's no shortage of reasons to get married in paradise—just think of all the money you'll save if you get hitched in swimsuits—and no matter what your budget or style, you can say your "I dos" on any one of Hawai'i's islands.

First off, you'll need to take care of the legal stuff. Hawai'i state law is fairly forgiving: there are no state-residence or U.S.-citizenship requirements, nor is blood work required. However, both parties must be at least 18 years of age to apply for a marriage license, and proof of age is required—18-year-olds must present a certified copy of a birth certificate; those 19 and older may present a valid ID or driver's license. The State does not issue licenses for same-sex couples.

The prospective bride and groom must appear together before a marriage license agent to apply. The license is issued at the time of application, granted you've been approved and have forked over the $60 fee (bring cash). The license is good within the state of Hawai'i for up to 30 days. You can apply for a marriage license through the **State Department of Health** (✉ Room 101, 1250 Punchbowl St., Honolulu, O'ahu ☎ 808/586-4544 ✉ State Office Building, 75 Aupuni St., Hilo, Big Island ☎ 808/974-6008 ✉ 3040 Umi St., Lihue, Kaua'i ☎ 808/

241-3498 ✉ State Building, 54 High St., Wailuku, Maui ☎ 808/984-8210 for Maui, 808/565-6411 for Lana'i, 808/553-3663 for Moloka'i). The Honolulu office is open weekdays 8-4.

The actual planning of your big day can be just as involved and unromantic as it is on the mainland, and Hawai'i has no shortage of professional wedding planners. The Hawai'i Visitors & Convention Bureau has a wedding and honeymoon registry that will assist with information on everything from finding a location to hiring the caterer and photographer. To register, go to the HVCB Web site at www.gohawaii.com and click on Weddings and Honeymoons. At your request, they can put you in touch with reliable freelance planners. Keep in mind that though there are high-priced planners at all the ritzy resorts, a simple yet memorable outdoor ceremony can be arranged for a few hundred dollars. Don't forget leis for the bride and groom, and be sure to ask the person presiding over the ceremony to give a special blessing in Hawaiian.

Believe it or not, the Hawaiian language has no word for "romance." Instead, islanders live in the spirit of it. Hawai'i is a destination where you can recite your vows at sunset or sunrise, on beaches, on lava rock, on a golf course, or even underwater. Can you imagine a better beginning for the rest of your life?

---

or currents, pay attention. Most beaches have lifeguards, although two exceptions are Kahana and Mālaekahana. Waikīkī is only 21 degrees north of the equator, so the sun here is very strong. No alcoholic beverages are allowed, and no matter which beach you choose, lock your car and never, ever leave your valuables unattended.

Waikīkī Beaches

The 2½-mi strand called Waikīkī Beach actually extends from Hilton Hawaiian Village on one end to Kapi'olani Park and Diamond Head on the other. Areas along this sandy strip have separate names but subtle differences. Beach areas are listed here from west to east.

Kahanamoku Beach. Named for Hawai'i's famous Olympic swimming champion, Duke Kahanamoku, this beach has decent snorkeling and swimming and a gentle surf. Its sandy bottom slopes gradually. The area has a snack concession, showers, a beach-gear and surfboard rental shop, catamaran cruises, and a sand volleyball court. ⊹ *In front of Hilton Hawaiian Village Beach Resort and Spa.*

★ **Ft. DeRussy Beach.** Sunbathers, swimmers, and windsurfers enjoy this beach, one of the widest in Waikīkī, fronting the military hotel, the Hale Koa, and the U.S. Army Museum. It trails off to a coral ocean bottom with fairly good snorkeling. There are volleyball courts, food stands, picnic tables, dressing rooms, and showers. ⊹ *In front of Ft. DeRussy and Hale Koa Hotel.*

Gray's Beach. Named for a little lodging house called Gray's-by-the-Sea, which stood here in the 1920s, this beach is known for two good surfing spots called Paradise and Number Threes just beyond its reef. High tides often cover the narrow beach. ⊹ *In front of Halekūlani.*

Fodor'sChoice **Kahaloa and Ulukou Beaches.** Possibly the best swimming and lots of activities are available along this little stretch of Waikīkī Beach. Take a catamaran or outrigger canoe ride out into the bay, unless you're ready to try your skill at surfing. ⊹ *In front of Royal Hawaiian Hotel and Sheraton Moana Surfrider.*
★

★ **Kūhiō Beach Park.** This beach is a hot spot for shoreline and beach activities. Check out the Kūhiō Beach stage nightly at 6:30 for free hula and Hawaiian-music performances; weekends there's a torch-lighting ceremony at sunset as well. Surf lessons for beginners are available from the beach center here every half hour. ⊹ *Past the Sheraton Moana Surfrider Hotel to Kapahulu Ave. pier.*

Queen's Surf. A great place for a sunset picnic, this beach is beyond the seawall, toward Diamond Head, at what's known as the "other end of Waikīkī." It was once the site of Queen Liliʻuokalani's beach house. A mix of families and gay couples gathers here, and it seems as if someone is always playing a steel drum. There are good shade trees, picnic tables, and a changing house with showers. ⊹ *Across from entrance to Honolulu Zoo.*

Sans Souci. Nicknamed Dig-Me Beach because of its outlandish display of skimpy bathing suits, this small rectangle of sand is nonetheless a good sunning spot for all ages. Children enjoy its shallow, safe waters, and the shore draws many ocean kayakers and outrigger canoeists. Serious swimmers and triathletes also swim in the channel here, beyond the reef. There's no food concession, but near one end is the Hau Tree Lānai restaurant. ⊹ *Makai side of Kapiʻolani Park, between New Otani Kaimana Beach Hotel and Waikīkī War Memorial Natatorium.*

Diamond Head Beach. This narrow strip of beach is not good for swimmers due to the reef just offshore, but it's still a great spot for watching windsurfers and wave boarders strut their skills across the water. Parking is located on Diamond Head Road, just past the Diamond Head Lighthouse. From the parking area, look for an opening in the makai wall where an unpaved trail leads down to the beach.

Beaches Around Oʻahu

Fodor'sChoice **Hanauma Bay Nature Preserve.** The main attraction here is snorkeling. The coral reefs are clearly visible through the turquoise waters of this sunken volcanic crater half open to the ocean. It is a designated marine preserve and features a marine-life education center for visitors. Although the fish are the tamest you'll view while snorkeling, feeding them is not allowed. The bay is best early in the morning (around 7), before the crowds arrive. It can be difficult to park later in the day. There are a busy food and snorkel-equipment concession and changing rooms and showers. No smoking is allowed, and the beach is closed on Tuesday. **Hanauma**
★

Bay Snorkeling Excursions (☎ 808/373–5060) run to and from Waikīkī. ✉ *7455 Kalaniana'ole Hwy.* ☎ *808/396-4229* 🖃 *Donation $3; parking $1; mask, snorkel, and fins rental $6; tram from parking lot down to beach $1.50* ☉ *Wed.–Mon. 6–7.*

Sandy Beach. Strong, steady winds make "Sandy's" a kite-flyer's paradise. There's a changing house with indoor and outdoor showers but no food concessions. Unless you are an expert at navigating rip currents and very shallow shore breaks, this beach is dangerous for the casual swimmer—more neck and spine injuries occur here than anywhere else on the island. ⊹ *Makai of Kalaniana'ole Hwy., 2 mi east of Hanauma Bay.*

Makapu'u Beach. Swimming at Makapu'u should be attempted only by strong swimmers and bodysurfers because the swells can be overwhelmingly big and powerful. Instead, consider this tiny crescent cove—popular with locals—as a prime sunbathing spot. Finding parking in the small lot can be tricky. In a pinch, try parking on the narrow shoulder and walking down to the beach. There is a changing house with indoor and outdoor showers. ⊹ *Makai of Kalaniana'ole Hwy., across from Sea Life Park, 2 mi south of Waimānalo.*

★ **Waimānalo Beach Park.** This is a "local" beach busy with picnicking families and active sports fields. Sometimes folks are not very friendly to tourists here, and there have been some incidents of car theft, but the beach itself is one of the island's most beautiful. Expect a wide stretch of sand; turquoise, emerald, and deep-blue seas; and waves full of boogie boarders. ⊹ *Windward side; look for signs makai of Kalaniana'ole Hwy., south of Waimānalo town.*

Bellows Beach. The waves here are great for bodysurfing. Locals come for the fine swimming on weekends and holidays, when the Air Force opens the beach to civilians. There are showers, abundant parking, and plenty of spots for picnicking underneath shady ironwood trees. There is no food concession, but McDonald's and other take-out fare is available right outside the entrance gate. ⊹ *Entrance on Kalaniana'ole Hwy. near Waimānalo town center; signs on makai side of road.*

★ **Kailua Beach Park.** Steady breezes attract windsurfers by the dozens to this long, palm-fringed beach with gently sloping sands. You can rent equipment in Kailua and try it yourself. This is a local favorite, so if you want the beach to yourself, head here on a weekday. There are showers, changing rooms, picnic areas, and a concession stand. Buy your picnic provisions at the Kalapawai Market nearby. ⊹ *Windward side, makai of Kailua town; turn right on Kailua Rd. at market, cross bridge, then turn left into beach parking lot.*

Fodor'sChoice **Lanikai Beach Park.** A mile of buttery sand ideal for a stroll, this beach ★ fronts some of the most expensive real estate on the windward side. When the trade winds are active, look for windsurfers. Early birds can watch some spectacular sunrises. ⊹ *Windward side, past Kailua Beach Park; street parking on Mokulua Dr. for various public access points to beach.*

Kahana Bay Beach Park. Local parents often bring their children to wade in safety at this pretty beach cove with very shallow, protected waters. A grove of tall ironwood and pandanus trees keeps the area cool, shady, and ideal for a picnic. An ancient Hawaiian fishpond, which was in use until the '20s, is visible nearby. There are changing houses, showers, and picnic tables. ⊹ *Windward side of island, makai of Kamehameha Hwy., north of Kualoa Park.*

Kualoa Regional Park. This is one of the island's most beautiful picnic, camping, and beach areas. Grassy expanses border a long, narrow stretch of beach with spectacular views of Kāne'ohe Bay and the Ko'olau Mountains. Dominating the view is an islet called Mokoli'i, which rises 206 ft above the water. You can swim in the shallow areas year-round.

The one drawback is that it's usually windy. Refreshments are not sold here so bring a cooler. There are places to shower, change, and picnic in the shade of palm trees. ⊹ *Windward side, makai of Kamehameha Hwy., north of Waiāhole.*

Mālaekahana Beach Park. The big attraction here is tiny Goat Island, a bird sanctuary just offshore. At low tide the water is shallow enough—never more than waist high—so that you can wade out to it. Wear sneakers so you don't cut yourself on the coral. Families love to camp in the groves of ironwood trees at Mālaekahana State Park. The beach itself is fairly narrow but long enough for a 20-minute stroll, one-way. The waves are never too big, and sometimes they're just right for the beginning bodysurfer. There are changing houses, showers, and picnic tables. Note that the entrance gates are easy to miss because you can't see the beach from the road. ⊹ *Windward side; entrance gates are makai of Kamehameha Hwy., ½ mi north of Lā'ie.*

Sunset Beach. This is one link in the chain of North Shore beaches that extends for miles. It's popular for its gentle summer waves and crashing winter surf. The beach is broad, and the sand is soft. Lining the adjacent highway there are usually carryout truck stands selling shaved ice, plate lunches, and sodas. ⊹ *North Shore, 1 mi north of 'Ehukai Beach Park on makai side of Kamehameha Hwy.*

'Ehukai Beach Park. 'Ehukai is part of a series of beaches running for many miles along the North Shore. What sets it apart is the view of the famous Banzai Pipeline, where the waves curl into magnificent tubes, making it an experienced wave-rider's dream. In spring and summer, the waves are more accommodating to the average swimmer. The long, wide, and generally uncrowded beach has a changing house with toilets and an outdoor shower. Bring along drinks; the nearest store is a mile away. ⊹ *North Shore, 1 mi north of Foodland store at Pūpūkea, turn makai off Kamehameha Hwy. directly into the small parking lot bordering highway.*

★ **Waimea Bay.** Made popular in that old Beach Boys song "Surfin' U.S.A.," Waimea Bay is a slice of hang-ten heaven and home to the king-size 25- to 30-ft winter waves. Summer is the time to swim and snorkel in the calm waters. The beach is a broad crescent of soft sand backed by a shady area with tables, a changing house, and showers. Parking is almost impossible in the lot on weekends, so folks just park along the road and walk down. ⊹ *North Shore across from Waimea Valley, 3 mi north of Hale'iwa on makai side of Kamehameha Hwy.*

Hale'iwa Ali'i Beach Park. The winter waves are impressive here, but in summer the ocean is like a lake, ideal for family swimming. The beach itself is big and often full of locals. Its broad lawns off the highway invite volleyball and Frisbee games and groups of barbecuers. There is a changing house with showers but no food concessions. Hale'iwa has everything you need for provisions. ⊹ *North Shore, makai side of Kamehameha Hwy., north of Hale'iwa town center and past harbor.*

Yokohama Bay. You'll be one of the few outsiders at this Wai'anae Coast beach at the very end of the road. It feels and looks remote and untouched, which may explain the lack of crowds. Locals come here to fish and swim in waters that are calm enough for children in summer. The beach is narrow and rocky in places. Bring provisions, because the nearest town is a 15-minute drive away. There are showers and a changing house, plus a small parking lot, but most folks just pull over and park on the side of the bumpy road. ⊹ *Wai'anae Coast, northern end of Farrington Hwy. about 7 mi north of Mākaha.*

Mākaha Beach Park. This beach provides a slice of local life most visitors don't see. Families string up tarps for the day, fire up hibachis, set up lawn chairs, get out the fishing gear, and strum 'ukuleles while they "talk story" (chat). The swimming is generally decent in the summer, but avoid the big winter waves. This was home to the island's first professional surf meet, in 1952. The ¼-mi beach has a changing house and showers and is the site of a yearly big-board surf meet. ✥ *Wai'anae Coast, 1½ hrs west of Honolulu on H-1 Fwy. and Farrington Hwy., makai side of hwy.*

★ **Ala Moana Beach Park.** Ala Moana has a protective reef, which keeps the waters calm and perfect for swimming. After Waikīkī, this is the most popular beach among visitors. To the Waikīkī side is a peninsula called Magic Island, with picnic tables, shady trees, and paved sidewalks ideal for jogging. Ala Moana also has playing fields, changing houses, indoor and outdoor showers, lifeguards, concession stands, and tennis courts. This beach is for everyone, but only in the daytime. It's a high-crime area after dark. ✥ *Honolulu, makai side of Ala Moana Shopping Center and Ala Moana Blvd.; from Waikīkī take Bus 8 to shopping center and cross Ala Moana Blvd.*

WHERE TO EAT

If you're looking for a meal with a view, explore the restaurants at the upscale hotels and resorts that line O'ahu's shores. Settings can be as casual as a "barefoot bar" or as elegant as a romantic dinner for two under the stars. Beyond Waikīkī are culinary jewels tucked away in shopping centers and residential neighborhoods that specialize in ethnic cuisines. You'll almost never go wrong if you sample the offerings at any establishment whose name ends in the words "Drive Inn." Here you will find the local grinds, which are the staples of the Hawaiian diet: seafood plate lunches and noodle saimin soups. For snacks and fast food around the island, look for the lunch wagons, usually parked roadside near the beaches.

Waikīkī

Chinese

★ **$–$$$** ✕ **Golden Dragon.** You can't beat the view at this restaurant set by a lagoon. On the menu are nearly 65 à la carte dishes and a six-course dinner menu of fine Cantonese, Szechuan, and nouvelle-Chinese dishes prepared by chef Steve Chiang. Two of the house specialties—the Imperial Peking duck and Imperial beggar's chicken (whole chicken wrapped in lotus leaves and baked in a clay pot)—must be ordered 24 hours in advance. To begin your meal, try the fresh scallop soup end; with a dessert of banana fritter with coconut ice cream and vanilla sauce. ⊠ *Hilton Hawaiian Village, 2005 Kālia Rd., Waikīkī* ☎ *808/946–5336* ⌕ *Reservations essential* ▤ *AE, D, DC, MC, V* ◷ *No lunch.*

Contemporary

★ **$$$–$$$$** ✕ **Bali by the Sea.** In the Hilton Hawaiian Village, this restaurant is breeze-swept, with an oceanside setting offering glorious views of Waikīkī Beach. The menu is a blend of French and Asian influences, with starters like Kula-onion-and-ginger soup; signature dishes are Hawaiian lobster casserole and 'ōpakapaka (blue snapper) with kaffir lime sauce. Another favorite is the roasted-beet salad with caramelized macadamia nuts and goat cheese. ⊠ *Hilton Hawaiian Village, 2005 Kālia Rd., Waikīkī* ☎ *808/941–2254* ⌕ *Reservations essential* ▤ *AE, D, DC, MC, V* ◷ *No dinner Sun.*

$$–$$$ ✕ **Duke's Canoe Club.** This casual beachfront eatery, named after Hawai'i's famous surfer Duke Kahanamoku, is usually crowded (reserve ahead or you'll probably have to wait for a table). Lunchtime is lively, and on the weekend the restaurant hosts sunset concerts on the beach on its out-

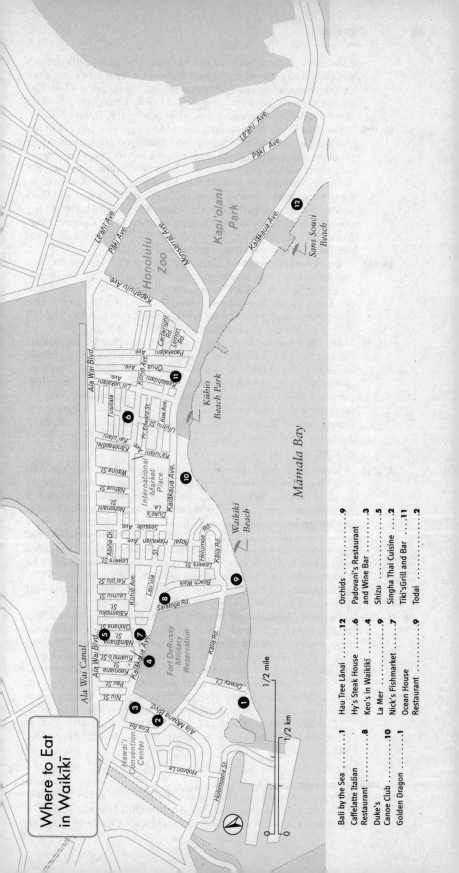

Where to Eat in Waikīkī

½ mile

½ km

Ala Wai Canal

Hawai'i Convention Center

Fort DeRussy Military Reservation

Mamala Bay

Waikiki Beach

Kūhiō Beach Park

Sans Souci Beach

Kapi'olani Park

Honolulu Zoo

International Market Place

door terrace. Fish can be served up Duke's style: baked in a garlic, lemon, and sweet basil glaze to keep it tender and moist. Other Duke's specialties include macadamia-and-crab wontons and the decadent Hula Pie. ⊠ *Outrigger Waikīkī on the Beach, 2335 Kalākaua Ave., Waikīkī* ☎ *808/922–2268* ⊕ *www.dukeswaikiki.com* ⊟ *AE, D, DC, MC, V.*

$$–$$$ ✕ **Hau Tree Lānai.** At breakfast, lunch, or dinner you can eat under graceful hau trees, so close to Kaimana Beach you can hear the whisper of the waves. Breakfast offerings include a huge helping of eggs Benedict, poi pancakes, and a delicious salmon omelet. For dinner, try the moonfish, snapper, the seafood mixed grill with a Thai chili sauce or the popular sesame-crusted hoisin rack of lamb. Every first and third Sunday, the restaurant offers an "East Meets West" brunch buffet in partnership with the hotel's Miyako restaurant. ⊠ *New Otani Kaimana Beach Hotel, 2863 Kalākaua Ave., Waikīkī* ☎ *808/921–7066* ⊕ *www.kaimana. com* ⌕ *Reservations essential* ⊟ *AE, D, DC, MC, V.*

$$–$$$ ✕ **Ocean House Restaurant.** Guests are greeted on the front porch at this re-creation of a 1900s plantation home. The menu puts forth the bounty of the Pacific with such dishes as coconut lobster skewers, seared peppered scallops, and macadamia-nut-crusted sea bass. For beef lovers, there is the slow-roasted prime rib. ⊠ *Outrigger Reef on the Beach hotel, 2169 Kālia Rd., Waikīkī* ☎ *808/923–2277* ⊟ *AE, D, DC, MC, V.*

$–$$ ✕ **Tiki's Grill and Bar.** If you are looking for Hawaiian kitsch, look no further than Tiki's Grill and Bar—you won't find a more fitting tribute to the tiki bars of the '50s and '60s in the rest of Waikīkī. Dishes include a panko-crusted (Japanese bread crumbs) calamari steak, fresh oysters in a fresh crab crust, and seafood fettuccine. Leave a little room for some tropical libations at the Volcano Bar. Outdoor seating gives requisite views of Waikīkī Beach. ⊠ *Aston Waikīkī Beach Hotel, 2570 Kalākaua Ave., Waikīkī* ☎ *808/923–8454* ⊟ *AE, D, DC, MC, V.*

French

★ $$$$ ✕ **La Mer.** In the exotic, oceanfront atmosphere of a Mandalay mansion, you'll be served neoclassic French cuisine that many consider to be the finest in Hawai'i. Here, on the grounds of the Halekūlani hotel, is a room—open to the ocean, and with sweeping views of Diamond Head—as luscious as its menu. French-born chef Yves Garner presides over a menu that includes Hamachi medallions covered with pistachio nuts, roasted Scottish salmon and salmon tartare, and rack of lamb marinated with thyme and garlic cloves. The perfect ending is a symphony of La Mer desserts. Two prix-fixe menus are available for $85 and $115. ⊠ *Halekūlani, 2199 Kālia Rd., Waikīkī* ☎ *808/923–2311* ⌕ *Reservations essential* 🎩 *Jacket required* ⊟ *AE, MC, V* ⊗ *No lunch.*

★ $$–$$$$ ✕ **Padovani's Restaurant and Wine Bar.** Philippe Padovani first gained fame at three top Hawai'i hotels (the Halekūlani, Ritz-Carlton, and Mānele Bay) before opening this hideaway inside the Doubletree Alana Waikīkī. One of the chef's specialties is the salmon confit in extra-virgin olive oil and lemongrass broth. Dessert lovers will savor the ginger crème brûlée. The dining room has rich gold accents against polished wood. An upstairs wine bar offers 50 varietals by the glass, single-malt Scotch, a lighter menu, entertainment on weekend evenings, and an enclosed cigar room. ⊠ *Doubletree Alana Waikīkī, 1956 Ala Moana Blvd., Waikīkī* ☎ *808/ 946–3456 or 808/947–1236* ⌕ *Reservations essential* ⊟ *AE, D, DC, MC, V.*

Italian

$$$$ ✕ **Caffelatte Italian Restaurant.** Every dish at this tiny trattoria run by a Milanese family is worth ordering, from the gnocchi in a thick, rich sauce of Gorgonzola to spinach ravioli served with butter and basil. The tiramisu is the best in town. There's limited seating inside and a few tables outside on the narrow lānai. Be aware that each person must order three courses (appetizer, main course, and dessert). The chef will prepare a special mystery dinner for two for $60. There's no parking, so walk here if you can. ⊠ *339 Saratoga Rd., 2nd level, Waikīkī* ☎ *808/ 924–1414* ▤ *AE, DC, MC, V* ☉ *Closed Tues.*

Japanese

$$$–$$$$ ✕ **Shizu.** Sample the Japanese cooking styles of *teishoku* (traditional preparation of fish, rice, soup, and more, served in lacquer bowls) and tableside *teppanyaki* in a contemporary setting overlooking a Zen-style rock garden. The two teppanyaki rooms have spectacular stained-glass windows with vibrant irises. Here, diners sit around a massive iron grill on which a dexterous chef slices and cooks sizzling meats and vegetables. There are also a sushi bar and traditional dishes such as tempura. Try green-tea cheesecake for dessert. ⊠ *Royal Garden at Waikīkī, 440 'Olohana St., 4th floor, Waikīkī* ☎ *808/943–0202* ▤ *AE, D, DC, MC, V.*

Seafood

★ $$$–$$$$ ✕ **Nick's Fishmarket.** The decor is a little dark and retro, with black booths, candlelight, and formal table settings. But here you can indulge in Beluga caviar, Norwegian salmon marinated in sake and honey, and a sumptuous sourdough lobster bisque. In addition, this is one of the few places with abalone on the menu; it's sautéed and served with lobster risotto. Leave room for Vanbana Pie, a decadent combination of bananas, vanilla Swiss-almond ice cream, and hot caramel sauce. ⊠ *Waikīkī Gateway Hotel, 2070 Kalākaua Ave., Waikīkī* ☎ *808/955–6333* ⌸ *Reservations essential* ▤ *AE, D, DC, MC, V.*

$$$–$$$$ FodorsChoice ★ ✕ **Orchids.** It seems only fitting that you can hear the waves from this orchid-filled dining room that lays out the best seafood bar in town, including sashimi, *poke* (marinated raw fish), and Pacific-crab salad with fresh mango. Try the seared lemongrass Australian prawns or the seafood mixed grill with a lime-ginger sauce. Meat and poultry dishes include a mustard-herb roasted Colorado lamb rack and tandoori-roasted island chicken. Outdoor and indoor seating is available, with the best views from the lānai. ⊠ *Halekūlani, 2199 Kālia Rd., Waikīkī* ☎ *808/923–2311* ⌸ *Reservations essential* ▤ *AE, MC, V.*

★ $$$ ✕ **Todai.** Long on seafood and short on decor, this restaurant is a hit with both local residents and tourists alike. Todai has an 180-ft seafood buffet with 40 different kinds of sushi that include salmon skin, sea urchin, eel, and spicy tuna. You'll also find lobster, shrimp tempura, Alaskan snow crab, salad, barbecued ribs, and much more on the buffet. Save room for a Tokyo crepe stuffed with fresh fruit and chocolate filling and topped with whipped cream. ⊠ *1910 Ala Moana Blvd., Waikīkī* ☎ *808/ 947–1000* ⌸ *Reservations essential* ▤ *AE, D, DC, MC, V.*

Steak

$$$–$$$$ ✕ **Hy's Steak House.** Like most other upscale steak houses, this place has a classic private-club ambience—it's snug and library-like, and the service is outstanding. You can watch the chef perform behind glass. Hy's is famous for its kiawe-broiled New York strip steak, beef Wellington, cold-water lobster tail, and rack of lamb. The Caesar salad is excellent, as are the panfried potatoes. For a final flair, try the flambéed bananas Foster. ⊠ *Waikīkī Park Heights Hotel, 2440 Kūhiō Ave., Waikīkī* ☎ *808/ 922–5555* ⌸ *Reservations essential* ▤ *AE, DC, MC, V* ☉ *No lunch.*

Thai

★ $$–$$$ ✕ **Singha Thai Cuisine.** Dishes here are prepared in traditional Thai fashion, with just a sprinkling of Hawai'i regional flavorings and traditional French cooking techniques. The blackened tuna summer rolls, vegetarian curry dishes, and Thai chili are wonderful. Singha's beautiful Royal

Thai dancers dressed in traditional costume add to the occasion, performing nightly. ✉ *1910 Ala Moana Blvd., Waikīkī* ☎ *808/941–2898* ⌂ *Reservations essential* ▤ *AE, D, DC, MC, V* ☽ *No lunch.*

★ **$–$$** ✕ **Keo's in Waikīkī.** This twinkling little nook, with tables set amid lighted trees, big paper umbrellas, and sprays of orchids, is a favorite of visiting Hollywood celebrities. Most of the herbs, vegetables, fruits, and flowers found here are grown on owner Keo Sananikone's North Shore farm. Favorites include the Evil Jungle Prince (shrimp, vegetables, or chicken in a sauce flavored with Thai basil, coconut milk, and red chili) and the crispy Thai shrimp. The Golden Triangle (tiger prawns wrapped in pastry) and the vegetarian crispy fried noodles are two popular appetizers. For dessert, the apple bananas in coconut milk are wonderful. ✉ *2028 Kūhiō Ave., Waikīkī* ☎ *808/951–9355* ⌂ *Reservations essential* ▤ *AE, D, DC, MC, V* ☽ *No lunch.*

Honolulu

American/Casual

$–$$ ✕ **California Pizza Kitchen.** This duet of dining and watering holes for young fast-trackers is worth the wait for a table. The pizzas have unusual toppings, such as Thai chicken, Peking duck, and Caribbean shrimp. The pastas, like Kung Pao spaghetti, are made fresh daily. At the Kāhala site, a glass atrium with tiled and mirrored walls and one side open to the shopping mall creates a sidewalk-café effect. The location on the top level of the Ala Moana Center offers a great respite for the weary shopper. ✉*Kāhala Mall, 4211 Wai'alae Ave., Kāhala* ☎*808/ 737–9446* ✉ *Ala Moana Shopping Center, 1450 Ala Moana Blvd., Ala Moana* ☎ *808/941–7715* ⌂ *Reservations not accepted* ▤ *AE, D, DC, MC, V.*

$–$$ ✕ **Hard Rock Cafe.** The Honolulu branch of this international chain has its trademark rock-and-roll memorabilia on display along with Hawaiian surfboards and aloha shirts for local flavor. Here, charbroiled burgers hold their own alongside island favorites like 'ahi-steak (yellowfin-tuna-steak) sandwiches and watermelon baby-back ribs. Count on loud music, high energy, and a long wait for a table. ✉ *1837 Kapi'olani Blvd., Ala Moana* ☎ *808/955–7383* ⌂ *Reservations not accepted* ▤ *AE, MC, V.*

¢–$ ✕ **L&L Drive Inn.** On Monsarrat Avenue in Waikīkī and at more than 50 neighborhood locations throughout the island, the Drive Inn serves up an impressive mix of Asian-American and Hawaiian-style plate lunches. Chicken *katsu* (cutlet), shrimp curry, and seafood mix plates include two scoops of rice and macaroni salad. There are also "mini" versions of the large-portion plates that include just one scoop of starch. It's a quick take-out place to pick up lunch before heading to the nearest beach park. ✉ *3045 Monsarrat Ave., Diamond Head* ☎ *808/735–1388* ⌂ *Reservations not accepted* ▤ *No credit cards.*

Barbecue

¢–$$ ✕ **Dixie Grill.** This Southern-inspired eatery emphasizes just how much fun food can be. Why, there's even an outdoor sandbox for the kids! Dixie Grill specializes in all things fried, including okra, catfish, and chicken. Also on the menu are baby-back ribs, whole Dungeness crab, and campfire steak prepared with either wet or dry-rub herb sauces. And if you just can't make up your mind, try the buffet. ✉ *404 Ward Ave., Kaka'ako* ☎ *808/596–8359* ▤ *AE, D, DC, MC, V.*

Chinese

¢–$ ✕ **Legends Seafood Restaurant.** When touring Chinatown, take time out to try some dim sum at Legends, where you'll hear Chinese spoken as

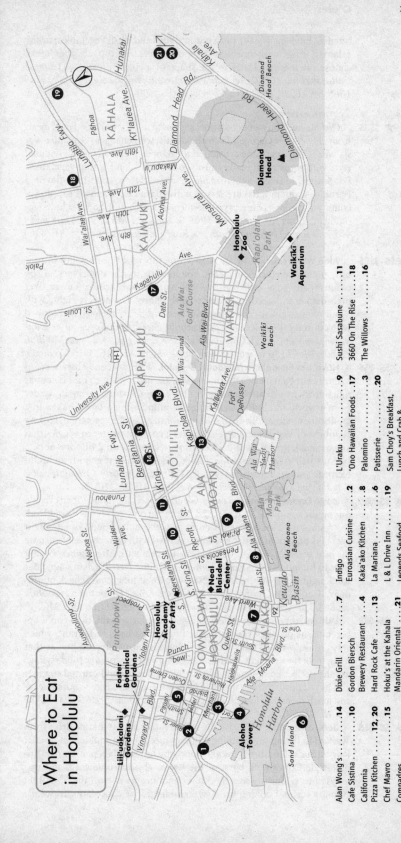

Where to Eat in Honolulu

often as English. Try the prawn dumplings and fresh vegetables, or the calamari rings with northern-Chinese spices. To top off your meal, choose the mango gelatin in the shape of a colorful carp. ⊠ *Chinese Cultural Plaza, 100 N. Beretania St., Downtown Honolulu* ☎ *808/532–1868* ⊟ *AE, D, DC, MC, V.*

Contemporary

★ **$$$$** ✕ **Chef Mavro.** You can expect nothing less than the most creative of meals from chef-owner George Mavrothalassitis, who changes the menu every six weeks. Savor sesame-crusted *uku* (snapper), served Hawai'i regional style with lotus root, enoki mushrooms, and Island spring vegetables. For dessert, Mavro's signature *lilikoi malasadas* (passion-fruit-flavored Portuguese doughnuts) are served with guava coulis and pineapple-coconut ice cream. Three prix-fixe menus, starting at $55, include recommendations for wines. ⊠ *1969 S. King St., Mō'ili'ili* ☎ *808/944–4714* ⊕ *www.chefmavro.com* ⌕ *Reservations essential* ⊟ *AE, DC, MC, V* ⊘ *No lunch.*

★ **$$$–$$$$** ✕ **Alan Wong's.** Chef-owner Alan Wong turns local grinds into beautifully presented epicurean treats. For starters, try the Poki-Pines, crispy wonton 'ahi poke balls on avocado with wasabi sauce. Linger over macadamia-and-coconut-crusted lamb chops. Do dessert right, with Wong Way tiramisu: chocolate espresso *pot de crème* (custard) topped with chiffon cake layers and mascarpone cheese with Kona-coffee *granité* (sugared ice). ⊠ *McCully Court, 1857 S. King St., 3rd floor, Mō'ili'ili* ☎ *808/949–2526* ⊕ *www.alanwongs.com* ⊟ *AE, MC, V* ⊘ *No lunch.*

$$–$$$
Fodor'sChoice
★ ✕ **Hoku's at the Kāhala Mandarin Oriental.** With a second-story view of magnificent Kāhala Beach, this restaurant has a warmth that comes as much from its attentive staff as it does from the sun filtering in. Order from a world of choices that range from Indian nan bread baked in a tandoori oven to a wok-seared Maine lobster. For the vegetarian, Hoku's Rainbow of Vegetables entrée features a colorful platter of veggies that are steamed, grilled, and cooked to perfection. With 24 hours' notice, Hoku's will create a Seafood Tower of shellfish that is both an architectural and epicurean marvel. ⊠ *Kāhala Mandarin Oriental, 5000 Kāhala Ave., Kāhala* ☎ *808/739–8780* ⊟ *AE, D, MC, V.*

★ **$$–$$$** ✕ **Indigo Euroasian Cuisine.** Owner Glenn Chu sets the mood for an evening out on the town: the walls are red brick, the ceilings are high, and from the restaurant's lounge next door comes the sultry sound of late-night jazz. Take a bite of a crispy wonton stuffed with goat cheese or turn up the heat with the Balinese-inspired curried calamari. After dinner, saunter over to Indigo's Green Room lounge or Opium Den & Champagne Bar for a nightcap. If you're touring downtown at lunchtime, check out Indigo's Cool Island Buffet. ⊠ *1121 Nu'uanu Ave., Downtown Honolulu* ☎ *808/521–2900* ⊕ *www.indigo-hawaii.com* ⊟ *AE, D, DC, MC, V.*

$$–$$$ ✕ **L'Uraku.** If you like a little whimsy with your wasabi, then you'll appreciate the decor of this Japanese-European fusion restaurant, which stays sunny with its collection of Kiyoshi hand-painted umbrellas that hang from the ceiling. Chef Hiroshi Fukui's contemporary food stylings are the perfect complement. On the menu are almond-crusted snapper and baked miso-glazed salmon. Check out L'Uraku's three-course weekend lunch menu. ⊠ *1341 Kapi'olani Blvd., Ala Moana* ☎ *808/955–0552* ⊟ *AE, D, MC, V.*

★ **$$–$$$** ✕ **3660 on the Rise.** This casually stylish eatery is a 10-minute drive from Waikīkī in the up-and-coming culinary mecca of Kaimukī. Sample chef Russell Siu's signature Furikake popcorn-shrimp salad, pan-seared Chinese-style Chilean sea bass, or the Kaua'i shrimp, blue crab, and watercress tortellini to see why 3360 continues its rise on the Honolulu culinary scene. Looking for a sweet ending? The chocolate cheesecake

should do the trick. ⊠ *3660 Wai'alae Ave., Kaimukī* ☎ *808/737–1177*
▤ *AE, DC, MC, V.*

★ **$-$$** ✕ **Gordon Biersch Brewery Restaurant.** Snuggling up to Honolulu Harbor, this indoor-outdoor eatery, part of a West Coast–based chain of microbreweries, is Aloha Tower Marketplace's busiest. The menu is American with an island twist, with everything from Tahitian seafood *fafa* (pounded soft taro topped with coconut milk) to a seafood napoleon with crisp wontons and papaya salsa. Ask for tastes of the dark, medium, and light brews before choosing your favorite. ⊠ *Aloha Tower Marketplace, 1 Aloha Tower Dr., Downtown Honolulu* ☎ *808/599–4877* ▤ *AE, D, DC, MC, V.*

$-$$ ✕ **Kaka'ako Kitchen.** If you want the culinary excellence of 3660 on the Rise without the price tag, come to this casual restaurant. Here, the owners of 3660 unleash their skills on the island-style plate lunch. You can order your "two scoops of rice" either white or brown. For vegetarians, the grilled Portobello-mushroom burger served with blue cheese, roasted peppers, lettuce, and tomato on a taro bun is a superb choice. Friday nights, live music adds an additional "local flavor" to the mix. ⊠ *Ward Centre, 1200 Ala Moana Blvd., Kaka'ako* ☎ *808/596–7488* ⌂ *Reservations not accepted* ▤ *No credit cards.*

★ **$-$$** ✕ **La Mariana.** Just past Downtown Honolulu, tucked away in the industrial area of Sand Island, is this friendly South Seas–style restaurant. La Mariana has been around for nearly five decades, and the decor is a hodgepodge of everything from glass floats in fish nets to koa-wood tables. The food here is very surf and turf, but the weekend sing-alongs at the piano bar give the place a nostalgic island charm. ⊠ *50 Sand Island Rd., Iwilei* ☎ *808/848–2800* ▤ *AE, D, DC, MC, V.*

★ **$-$$** ✕ **Palomino.** A Downtown Honolulu favorite, this art deco Euro-bistro, with handblown glass chandeliers, a grand staircase, and a 50-ft marble-and-mahogany bar, features a menu that fuses French, Spanish, and Italian cuisines. Entrées include grilled king salmon with lemon-vermouth butter and roasted prawns. Try the grilled ravioli for a change of pace. ⊠ *Harbor Court, 66 Queen St., 3rd floor, Downtown Honolulu* ☎ *808/ 528–2400* ▤ *AE, D, DC, MC, V.*

German

$-$$ ✕ **Patisserie.** By day, this bakery in the Kāhala Mall serves deli food, but five nights a week it turns into a 24-seat restaurant with great German food, a rarity in Hawai'i. The menu is small—only 10 entrées—but any choice is a good one. The Wiener schnitzel is juicy within its crispy crust, and veal ribs are garnished with a sprig of rosemary. Try the potato pancakes, crisp outside and soft inside, joined by a healthy spoonful of applesauce. ⊠ *Kāhala Mall, 4211 Wai'alae Ave., Kāhala* ☎ *808/735– 4402* ⌂ *Reservations not accepted* ▤ *MC, V* ☉ *Closed Sun.–Mon.*

Hawaiian

$$-$$$ ✕ **The Willows.** The exterior of this garden restaurant gives little clue as to the wonderful ambience that awaits within. Man-made ponds are sprinkled among the thatched dining pavilions, and you'll also find a tiny wedding chapel and a gallery gift shop. The food, served buffet-style, includes the trademark Willows curry along with roasted Portobello mushrooms, *laulau* (a steamed bundle of ti leaves containing pork, butterfish, and taro tops), and pineapple-mango barbecued ribs. ⊠ *901 Hausten St., Mō'ili'ili* ☎ *808/952–9200* ⌂ *Reservations essential* ▤ *AE, D, MC, V.*

¢-$ ✕ **'Ono Hawaiian Foods.** The adventurous in search of a real "local food" experience should head to this no-frills hangout. You know it has to be good if residents are waiting in line to get in. Here you can sample poi, *lomi lomi* salmon (salmon massaged until tender and served with minced onions and tomatoes), laulau, kālua pork (roasted in an undergound oven), and *haupia* (a light, gelatin-like dessert made from co-conut). Appropriately enough, the Hawaiian word *'ono* means delicious. ⊠ *726 Kapahulu Ave., Kapahulu* ☎ *808/737–2275* ⌘ *Reservations not accepted* 💳 *No credit cards* ⊘ *Closed Sun.*

Italian

$–$$ ✕ **Cafe Sistina.** Sergio Mitrotti has gained quite a following with his in-ventive Italian-Mediterranean cuisine, which is as artistic as his draw-ings on the café's walls. The menu combines three generations of family recipes—his grandmother's, his mother's, and his own, which includes a mango fettuccine with shrimp. If you love ravioli, try the asparagus ravioli with a sweet-vermouth cream sauce. On Saturday there's a late-evening menu to feed the lively salsa dance crowd. ⊠ *1314 S. King St., Makīkī* ☎ *808/596–0061* 💳 *AE, MC, V.*

Japanese

$–$$$ ✕ **Sushi Sasabune.** This tiny sushi bar is the home of the island's most famous "trust me" sushi chef, Seiji Kumagawa. Sit back and let him con-coct a great meal for you—and don't expect a California roll. The sushi is authentically Japanese but created from such regional delicacies as Nova Scotia salmon and Louisianna blue crab. You might be presented with something as exotic as teriyaki octopus. Sasabune's sushi specials also include crab, salmon, and tuna and come with miso soup, seaweed salad, and adzuki-bean ice cream. ⊠ *1419 S. King St., Mō'ili'ili* ☎ *808/947–3800* ⌘ *Reservations essential* 💳 *AE, D, DC, MC, V.*

Mexican

$–$$ ✕ **Compadres Mexican Bar and Grill.** The after-work crowd gathers here for potent margaritas and yummy *pūpū.* An outdoor terrace is best for cocktails only. Inside, the wooden floors, colorful photographs, and lively paintings create a festive setting for imaginative Mexican specialties. Fa-jitas, baby-back ribs, pork carnitas, and grilled shrimp are just a few of the many offerings. There's a late-night appetizer menu until midnight. ⊠ *Ward Centre, 1200 Ala Moana Blvd., Ala Moana* ☎ *808/591–8307* 💳 *D, MC, V.*

Seafood

★ $$–$$$ ✕ **Sam Choy's Breakfast, Lunch and Crab & Big Aloha Brewery.** In this ca-sual setting, great for families, diners can get crackin' with crab, chow down on chowders, and fill up with an abundance of both seafood and landlubber fare. This eatery's warehouse size sets the tone for its large portions. An on-site microbrewery brews five varieties of Big Aloha beer. Sam Choy's is in Iwilei past Downtown Honolulu on the highway head-ing toward Honolulu International Airport. ⊠ *580 Nimitz Hwy., Iwilei* ☎ *808/545–7979* ⊕ *www.samchoy.com* 💳 *AE, D, DC, MC, V.*

Around the Island

Hale'iwa

AMERICAN/ CASUAL

$$ ✕ **Haleiwa Joe's.** A day of surfing or just watching the big-wave riders can work up an appetite. Haleiwa Joe's, located just past the Anahulu Stream Bridge, serves up steaks, prime rib, and seafood such as crunchy coconut shrimp and grilled salmon with Asian pesto sauce. Come in time to watch the sun set over Hale'iwa Harbor. The bar serves various "small plate" menu items including black and blue 'ahi, seared tuna with a wasabi-ranch dressing. ⊠ *66-0011 Kamehameha Hwy., Haleiwa* ☎ *808/637–8005* ⌘ *Reservations not accepted* 💳 *AE, DC, MC, V.*

¢ ✕ **Kua 'Aina Sandwich.** A must-stop spot during a drive around the is-land, this tiny North Shore eatery has a few tables inside and a few more on the lānai next to the road. Burgers are heaped with bacon, cheese,

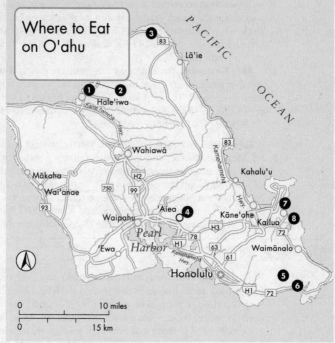

Where to Eat
on O'ahu

salsa, or pineapple, and the grilled mahimahi sandwich comes with a homemade tartar sauce. The crispy shoestring fries alone are worth the trip. You can also check out Kua 'Aina's south-shore location across from the Ward Centre in Honolulu. ⊠ *66-214 Kamehameha Hwy., Haleiwa* ☎ *808/637–6067* ⊠ *1116 Auahi St., Ala Moana, Honolulu* ☎ *808/591–9133* ⌖ *Reservations not accepted* ▭ *No credit cards.*

Hawai'i Kai

AUSTRIAN
$$–$$$
✕ **Chef's Table.** This tiny eatery is good for a lunch break while touring East O'ahu or as a getaway dinner spot. Chef Andreas Knapp, formerly of the Kahala Hilton and the Westin Century Plaza, creates dishes that are true to his Austrian heritage. Daily specials, including luscious homemade soups, salads, sauerbratens, and schnitzels, combined with an atmosphere that is friendly, fun, and casual, make the Chef's Table a neighborhood favorite. A European-style brunch is offered Sunday. ⊠ *Hawai'i Kai Towne Center, 333 Keahole St., Hawai'i Kai* ☎ *808/394–2433* ▭ *AE, D, DC, MC, V.*

CONTEMPORARY
$$–$$$
✕ **Roy's.** Two walls of windows offer views of Maunalua Bay and Diamond Head in the distance, and a glassed-in kitchen affords views of what's cooking at this noisy two-story restaurant with a devoted following. The menu matches Hawaiian flavors with Euro-Asian accents. Dishes with a modern flair—Kahana-style *shutome* (Hawaiian swordfish) with Roy's signature chutney and roasted-peanut Thai-red-curry sauce—share the menu with comfort-food favorites, such as meat loaf with mushroom gravy. ⊠ *Hawai'i Kai Corporate Plaza, 6600 Kalanianaʻole Hwy., Hawai'i Kai* ☎ *808/396–7697* ▭ *AE, D, DC, MC, V.*

Windward O'ahu

AMERICAN
$$–$$$
✕ **Buzz's Original Steakhouse.** This family-owned restaurant is just across the road from Kailua Beach Park and epitomizes the kind of laid-back

style you'd expect to find in Hawai'i. Burgers, salads, and fresh-fish sandwiches are the lunch staples; sirloin steak, rack of lamb, and teriyaki chicken top the dinner choices. Lānai seating allows you to catch an ocean breeze while you dine. ⊠ *413 Kawailoa Rd., Kailua* ☎ *808/261–4661* ▤ *No credit cards.*

$ ✕ **Ahi's Restaurant.** You can't go wrong with the shrimp dishes—steamed, spicy, or tempura-style—at this family-owned restaurant along the rural windward coast. The split-level dining area has views of the lush greenery of this part of the island. ⊠ *53-146 Kamehameha Hwy., Punalu'u* ☎ *808/293–5650* ▤ *No credit cards.*

MEXICAN ✕ **Bueno Nalo.** The owners of this family-run eatery are dedicated to health-
¢–$ ful Mexican cuisine, and the food is reliably good. *Topopo* salad is a heap of greens, tomatoes, onions, tuna, olives, cheese, and beans on top of a tortilla. Combination plates with tacos, enchiladas, and tamales are bargains. Families appreciate the *keiki* (child's) menu for diners 10 and under. Velvet paintings and piñatas add a fun, funky flavor to the setting. ⊠ *20 Kainehe St., Kailua* ☎ *808/263–1999* ▤ *AE, MC, V.*

WHERE TO STAY

If your dream vacation entails getting away from the usual hustle and bustle, look at the listings in the Around the Island category. If you prefer to be close to the action, go for a hotel or condominium in or near Waikīkī, where most of the island's lodgings are. Except for during the peak months of January and February, you'll have little trouble getting a room if you call in advance. Don't be intimidated by published rates. Most hotels offer a variety of package options and special deals, such as sports, honeymoon, room and car, and kids stay/eat free promotions. These extras can make vacations even more affordable, so ask about them when you book.

Below is a selective list of lodging choices in each price category. For a complete list of every hotel and condominium on the island, write or call the Hawai'i Visitors & Convention Bureau for a free *Accommodation Guide.*

Waikīkī

$$$$ ▥ **Aston Waikīkī Beach Tower.** On Kalākaua Avenue, but set back from the street on the mauka side, this 39-story luxury condominium resort has the atmosphere of an intimate vest-pocket hotel. The property has the usual amenities plus views of Waikīkī that you'd expect from a larger beachfront resort. Spacious (1,100–1,400 square ft) one- and two-bedroom suites are appointed with style and feature kitchens that would please a gourmet, twice-daily maid service, washers-dryers, and a private lānai. There's a heated swimming pool. ⊠ *2470 Kalākaua Ave., Waikīkī, Honolulu 96815* ☎ *808/926–6400 or 800/922–7866* 🖷 *808/ 926–7380* ⊕ *www.aston-hotels.com* ➳ *140 suites* ♿ *Room service, kitchens, minibars, cable TV, tennis court, pool, sauna, laundry facilities, concierge* ▤ *AE, D, DC, MC, V.*

$$$$ ▥ **Halekūlani.** The sleek oceanside Halekūlani exemplifies the transla-
FodorsChoice tion of its name—the "house befitting heaven." The service is impec-
★ cable, and the mood is tranquil amid the frenetic activity of Waikīkī. Guest rooms, which are spacious and artfully appointed in marble and wood, have ocean views and dozens of little touches such as fruit baskets, 27-inch flat-screen televisions, DVD and CD players, cordless phones, and complimentary wireless Internet service. The hotel has three of the finest restaurants—House Without a Key, La Mer, and Or-

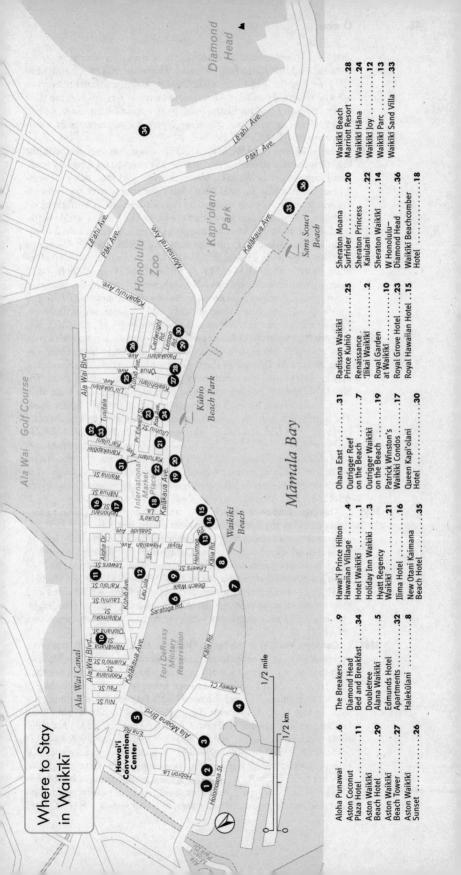

Where to Stay in Waikīkī

Aloha Punawai 6
Aston Coconut
Plaza Hotel 11
Aston Waikīkī
Beach Hotel 29
Aston Waikīkī
Beach Tower 27
Aston Waikīkī
Sunset 26

The Breakers 9
Diamond Head
Bed and Breakfast 34
Doubletree
Alana Waikīkī 5
Edmunds Hotel
Apartments 32
Halekūlani 8

Hawai'i Prince Hilton 4
Hawaiian Village 1
Hotel Waikīkī 3
Holiday Inn Waikīkī 3
Hyatt Regency
Waikīkī 21
Ilima Hotel 16
New Otani Kaimana
Beach Hotel 35

Ohana East 31
Outrigger Reef
on the Beach 7
Outrigger Waikīkī
on the Beach 19
Patrick Winston's
Waikīkī Condos 17
Queen Kapi'olani
Hotel 30

Radisson Waikīkī
Prince Kuhiō 25
Renaissance
'Ilikai Waikīkī 2
Royal Garden
at Waikīkī 10
Royal Grove Hotel 23
Royal Hawaiian Hotel .15

Sheraton Moana
Surfrider 20
Sheraton Princess
Kaiulani 22
Sheraton Waikīkī 14
W Honolulu–
Diamond Head 36
Waikīkī Beachcomber
Hotel 18

Waikīkī Beach
Marriott Resort 28
Waikīkī Hāna 24
Waikīkī Joy 12
Waikīkī Parc 13
Waikīkī Sand Villa 33

chids—in Honolulu and an oceanside pool with a mesmerizing orchid mosaic. ⊠ *2199 Kālia Rd., Waikīkī, Honolulu 96815* ☎ *808/923–2311 or 800/367–2343* 🖷 *808/926–8004* ⊕ *www.halekulani.com* ⊅ *412 rooms, 44 suites* ♨ *3 restaurants, room service, in-room data ports, in-room safes, minibars, pool, gym, hair salon, massage, beach, 3 bars, shops, dry cleaning, concierge, Internet, business services, meeting room* ☰ *AE, DC, MC, V.*

$$$$ 🏨 **Hawai'i Prince Hotel Waikīkī.** The Prince is a slim high-rise with the kind of sophisticated interior design generally reserved for a big-city hotel. You know you're in Waikīkī, however, when you look out your window at the Ala Wai Yacht Harbor—all guest rooms have floor-to-ceiling windows with ocean views. The Prince Court offers a subtle blend of Asian, European, and Hawaiian cooking. The hotel is within walking distance of the Ala Moana Shopping Center and has its own 27-hole Arnold Palmer–designed golf course in Ewa Beach, about a 45-minute hotel-shuttle ride from Waikīkī. ⊠ *100 Holomoana St., Waikīkī, Honolulu 96815* ☎ *808/956–1111 or 800/321–6248* 🖷 *808/946–0811* ⊕ *www.hawaiiprincehotel.com* ⊅ *467 rooms, 57 suites* ♨ *3 restaurants, room service, in-room data ports, in-room safes, minibars, 27-hole golf course, pool, gym, hair salon, hot tub, lobby lounge, shops, baby-sitting, concierge, business services, meeting room* ☰ *AE, DC, MC, V.*

$$$$ 🏨 **Hyatt Regency Waikīkī Resort and Spa.** An open-air atrium with a two-story waterfall, shops, live music, and Atrium Center Stage entertainment daily make this one of the liveliest lobbies anywhere, though you may get lost in it. Guest rooms have private lānai and sitting areas. The Na Ho'ola Spa will pamper you with a poolside massage. The Ciao Mein restaurant mixes it up with a menu of both Italian and Chinese food. The hotel is across from Kūhiō Beach and a short walk from Kapi'olani Park. ⊠ *2424 Kalākaua Ave., Waikīkī, Honolulu 96815* ☎ *808/923–1234 or 800/633–7313* 🖷 *808/923–7839* ⊕ *www.hyattwaikiki.com* ⊅ *1,212 rooms, 18 suites* ♨ *5 restaurants, room service, in-room data ports, in-room safes, minibars, pool, spa, bar, lobby lounge, shops, children's programs (ages 5–12), concierge, business services, meeting rooms* ☰ *AE, D, DC, MC, V.*

$$$$ 🏨 **Outrigger Reef on the Beach.** You can learn to surf or paddle an outrigger canoe at the Reef, which is right on the beach near Ft. DeRussy Park. Ask for an ocean view; the other rooms have decidedly less delightful overlooks. For fun, cook your own meal at the lively Shorebird Beach Broiler or pamper yourself at the oceanside Serenity Spa. ⊠ *2169 Kālia Rd., Waikīkī, Honolulu 96815* ☎ *808/923–3111 or 800/688–7444* 🖷 *808/924–4957* ⊕ *www.outrigger.com* ⊅ *846 rooms, 39 suites* ♨ *2 restaurants, room service, refrigerators, pool, gym, beach, 4 bars, nightclub, children's programs (ages 5–12), meeting room, no-smoking rooms* ☰ *AE, D, DC, MC, V.*

$$$$ 🏨 **Outrigger Waikīkī on the Beach.** Outrigger Hotels & Resorts' star property on Kalākaua Avenue stands on some of the nicest sands in Waikīkī. Rooms have a Polynesian motif, and each has a lānai. For more than 25 years, the main ballroom has been home to the sizzling Society of Seven entertainers. The beachfront Duke's Canoe Club is a dining hot spot. In late May, this hotel is the headquarters for the World Ocean Games competitions that take place on Waikīkī Beach. ⊠ *2335 Kalākaua Ave., Waikīkī, Honolulu 96815* ☎ *808/923–0711 or 800/688–7444* 🖷 *808/921–9749 or 800/688–7444* ⊕ *www.outrigger.com* ⊅ *500 rooms, 30 suites* ♨ *3 restaurants, room service, in-room data ports, in-room safes, kitchenettes, minibars, pool, gym, hot tub, 5 bars, lobby lounge, shops, children's programs (ages 5–13), dry cleaning, laundry facilities, concierge, business services, meeting rooms* ☰ *AE, D, DC, MC, V.*

$$$$ 🏨 **Renaissance 'Ilikai Waikīkī.** Spacious 600-square-ft guest rooms in two towers overlook Ala Wai Harbor and the ocean. The open-air lobby has cascading waterfalls; torches light the walkways for romantic evening strolls. Some guest rooms have kitchenettes and offer Internet access via television screens and cordless keyboards. For sky-high dining, there's Sarento's Top of the "I" Italian restaurant. ⊠ *1777 Ala Moana Blvd., Waikīkī, Honolulu 96815* ☎ *808/949–3811 or 800/245–4524* 🖷 *808/ 947–0892* ⊕ *www.ilikaihotel.com* ➲ *728 rooms, 51 suites* ♨ *3 restaurants, room service, some kitchens, minibars, tennis court, 2 pools, health club, outdoor hot tub, massage, 2 lobby lounges, video game room, shops, laundry facilities, Internet, business services, meeting room, car rental* ☐ *AE, D, DC, MC, V.*

★ **$$$$** 🏨 **Royal Hawaiian Hotel.** Nicknamed the Pink Palace of the Pacific due to its candy-pink exterior, the Royal was built in 1927 by Matson Navigation Company to accommodate its luxury-cruise passengers. It still exudes old-world charm, especially in its rooms in the Historic Wing, which have canopy beds, Queen Anne–style desks, and pink telephones. You can dine by the water's edge at the Surf Room or sip a mai tai at the bar that made that drink famous. ⊠ *2259 Kalākaua Ave., Waikīkī, Honolulu 96815* ☎ *808/923–7311 or 800/782–9488* 🖷 *808/924–7098* ⊕ *www.royal-hawaiian.com* ➲ *472 rooms, 53 suites* ♨ *2 restaurants, room service, minibars, pool, hair salon, spa, beach, bar, children's programs (ages 5–12), concierge, business services, meeting room* ☐ *AE, DC, MC, V.*

$$$$ 🏨 **Sheraton Moana Surfrider.** "The First Lady of Waikīkī" opened its doors in 1901 and became the first resort to make famous a little beach called Waikīkī. It has since merged with the newer Surfrider next door, but you can appreciate its history by requesting a room in the Moana Banyan Wing, where each floor has been restored to its original style (each floor is done in a single kind of wood: mahogany, maple, oak, cherry, or koa). These rooms are small by today's standards, but they're well appointed and charming. The Diamond Head Tower rooms offer full views of Waikīkī Beach. Enjoy high tea and Hawaiian music on the Moana's breeze-swept veranda. ⊠ *2365 Kalākaua Ave., Waikīkī, Honolulu 96815* ☎ *808/922–3111 or 800/782–9488* 🖷 *808/923–0308* ⊕ *www.moanasurfrider.com* ➲ *793 rooms, 46 suites* ♨ *3 restaurants, snack bar, room service, in-room data ports, in room safes, pool, beach, bar, 3 lounges, shops, children's programs (ages 5–12), concierge, meeting room* ☐ *AE, DC, MC, V.*

$$$$ 🏨 **Sheraton Waikīkī.** Towering over its neighbors, the Sheraton takes center stage on Waikīkī Beach. Guest rooms are spacious, and many have grand views of Diamond Head. Be sure to take the glass-walled elevator up to the Hanohano Room, an elegant dining room with breathtaking panoramas of the ocean and Waikīkī. The hotel conducts historical and nature tours, one of which spotlights the Honu sea turtles that can be viewed in the waters at the hotel's edge. ⊠ *2255 Kalākaua Ave., Waikīkī, Honolulu 96815* ☎ *808/922–4422 or 800/325–3535* 🖷 *808/ 923–8785* ⊕ *www.sheraton-hawaii.com* ➲ *1,709 rooms, 130 suites* ♨ *3 restaurants, room service, minibars, 2 pools, health club, beach, lobby lounge, dance club, shops, children's programs (ages 5–12), concierge, business services, meeting rooms* ☐ *AE, DC, MC, V.*

$$$$ 🏨 **W Honolulu—Diamond Head.** The W is on the quiet edge of Waikīkī across from Kapi'olani Park. Guest rooms feature spectacular ocean views, private lānai, 27-inch TVs with Internet access, CD players, and VCRs with a video library. The luxurious trademark W beds wrap you in 250-thread-count sheets, and rooms are elegantly appointed with teak furnishings in a Balinese motif. The hotel's signature restaurant is the Diamond Head Grill. ⊠ *2885 Kalākaua Ave., Waikīkī, Honolulu 96815*

☎ 808/922–1700 or 877/946–8357 🖷 808/923–2249 ⊕ *www.starwood. com* ⇨ *44 rooms, 4 suites ⚬ Restaurant, room service, in-room data ports, in-room VCRs, minibars, beach, bar, lounge, dry cleaning, laundry service, concierge, business services* ☰ *AE, D, DC, MC, V.*

★ $$$$ 🏨 **Waikīkī Beachcomber Hotel.** With an excellent location right across the street from Waikīkī Beach, the Beachcomber is also a short walk from the Royal Hawaiian Shopping Center and the International Market Place. Rooms have tropical motifs and private lānai. Three evening shows are presented here: the venerable "Don Ho," "Blue Hawai'i," and "The Magic of Polynesia." ☒ *2300 Kalākaua Ave., Waikīkī, Honolulu 96815* ☎ *808/922–4646 or 800/622–4646* 🖷 *808/923–4889* ⊕ *www.waikikibeachcomber.com* ⇨ *500 rooms, 7 suites ⚬ Restaurant, snack bar, room service, minibars, refrigerators, pool, outdoor hot tub, lobby lounge, children's program (ages 5–12), laundry facilities, meeting rooms, no-smoking rooms* ☰ *AE, DC, MC, V.*

$$$–$$$$ 🏨 **Aston Waikīkī Beach Hotel.** This Aston hotel is hip to Hawaiiana, paying tribute to the best of paradise: rooms are done in colors ranging from pineapple yellow to hot-lava red and feature teak furnishings and retro hand-painted bamboo curtains. Included with your room is a "breakfast to go" option that allows you to grab prepackaged à la carte breakfast items from the poolside food court that can be easily stashed in your complimentary cooler for a day at the beach. ☒ *2570 Kalākaua Ave., Waikīkī, Honolulu 96815* ☎ *808/922–2511 or 800/922–7866* 🖷 *808/ 922–8785* ⊕ *www.aston-hotels.com* ⇨ *645 rooms, 12 suites ⚬ Restaurant, in-room data ports, in-room safes, pool, shops, laundry facilities, meeting rooms* ☰ *AE, D, DC, MC, V.*

$$$–$$$$ 🏨 **Aston Waikīkī Sunset.** Families enjoy this high-rise condominium resort near Diamond Head, one block from Waikīkī Beach and two blocks from the Honolulu Zoo. One- and two-bedroom suites have complete kitchens, daily maid service, and private lānai. There's also an outdoor barbecue area, a tennis court, a sauna, and a children's playground. ☒229 *Paoakalani Ave., Waikīkī, Honolulu 96815* ☎ *808/922–0511 or 800/ 922–7866* 🖷 *808/922–8580* ⊕ *www.aston-hotels.com* ⇨ *307 suites ⚬ Snack bar, in-room data ports, kitchens, tennis court, pool, sauna, shop, playground* ☰ *AE, D, DC, MC, V.*

$$$–$$$$ 🏨 **Doubletree Alana Waikīkī.** The lobby of this 19-story high-rise is modern and attractive, with rotating exhibits of local artists' work. Guest rooms have private lānai with panoramic views of Waikīkī, the ocean, or the mountains. The staff of this boutique property has a reputation for absolute attention to detail. Those doing business globally like the 24-hour business-center. Also open round-the-clock is the fitness center. ☒ *1956 Ala Moana Blvd., Waikīkī, Honolulu 96815* ☎ *808/941–7275 or 800/ 367–6070* 🖷 *808/949–0996* ⊕ *www.alana-doubletree.com* ⇨ *268 rooms, 45 suites ⚬ Restaurant, room service, in-room data ports, in-room safes, minibars, refrigerators, pool, gym, lobby lounge, concierge, business services, no-smoking rooms* ☰ *AE, D, MC, V.*

★ $$$–$$$$ 🏨 **Hilton Hawaiian Village Beach Resort and Spa.** Sprawling over 22 acres on Waikīkī's widest stretch of beach, this resort is made up of five hotel towers surrounded by lavish gardens, a lagoon, cascading waterfalls, and 60 species of exotic birds, fish, and fauna. Choose from standard hotel guest rooms to one- or two-bedroom condo-style accommodations. Check out the sublime Mandara Spa and Holistic Wellness Center or immerse yourself in Hawaiian culture at the Bishop Museum at the Kalia Hawaiian Cultural Activities Center. The resort has 90 stores where you can get everything from Hawaiian musical instruments to designer clothing. ☒ *2005 Kālia Rd., Waikīkī, Honolulu 96815* ☎ *808/949–4321 or 800/221–2424* 🖷 *808/947–7898* ⊕ *www.hiltonhawaiianvillage.com* ⇨ *3,432 rooms, 365 suites, 264 condominiums ⚬ 18 restaurants,* room service, in-room data ports, in-room safes, minibars, 5 pools, gym, spa, beach, snorkeling, 8 bars, shops, baby-sitting, children's programs (ages 5–12), dry cleaning, laundry service, concierge, Internet, business services, meeting room, car rental, no-smoking rooms ▤ AE, D, DC, MC, V.

★ **$$$–$$$$** ▦ **New Otani Kaimana Beach Hotel.** Polished to a shine, this hotel is open to the trade winds and furnished with big, comfortable chairs. The ambience is cheerful and charming, and the lobby has a happy, unpretentious feel. Best of all, it's right on the beach at the quiet end of Waikīkī, practically at the foot of Diamond Head. Rooms are smallish but very nicely appointed with soothing pastels, off-white furnishings, and private lānai. ⊠ 2863 Kalākaua Ave., Waikīkī, Honolulu 96815 ☎ 808/923–1555 or 800/356–8264 ➮ 808/922–9404 ⊕ www.kaimana.com ➯ 119 rooms, 6 suites ⚐ 2 restaurants, room service, in-room data ports, in-room safes, refrigerators, minibars, gym, hair salon, lobby lounge, baby-sitting, concierge, meeting rooms ▤ AE, D, DC, MC, V.

$$$–$$$$ ▦ **Radisson Waikīkī Prince Kūhiō.** Two blocks from Kūhiō Beach, this 37-story high-rise is on the Diamond Head end of Waikīkī. Hawaiian-print bedspreads and artwork in sepia, cream, and earth tones decorate the rooms. Cupid's, the lobby lounge, plays Hawaiian music, and Trellises, the hotel restaurant, hosts a sumptuous seafood buffet on Friday and Saturday evening. ⊠ 2500 Kūhiō Ave., Waikīkī, Honolulu 96815 ☎ 808/922–8811 or 800/557–4422 ➮ 808/923–0330 ⊕ www.radisson. com/waikikihi ➯ 620 rooms ⚐ Restaurant, room service, in-room data ports, pool, gym, hot tub, lobby lounge, business services ▤ AE, D, DC, MC, V.

$$$–$$$$ ▦ **Royal Garden at Waikīkī.** From the outside, this 25-story boutique hotel looks like a residential Waikīkī high-rise. But step inside and it whispers elegance, from the marble and etched glass in the lobby to the genuine graciousness of the staff. Guest rooms have sitting areas, private lānai, and marble and brass baths. The hotel's Cascada restaurant serves French-inspired island cuisine. There's a free shuttle service to and from Kapiʻolani Park, Ala Moana Shopping Center, Royal Hawaiian Shopping Center, and duty-free shops. ⊠ 440 ʻOlohana St., Waikīkī, Honolulu 96815 ☎ 808/943–0202 or 800/367–5666 ➮ 808/946–8777 ⊕ www.royalgardens.com ➯ 202 rooms, 18 suites ⚐ 2 restaurants, room service, in-room safes, refrigerators, 2 pools, gym, lobby lounge, business services, meeting room ▤ AE, D, DC, MC, V.

$$$–$$$$ ▦ **Sheraton Princess Kaiulani.** Just across from Waikīkī Beach on the land that was once the Ainahau Estate home of Princess Victoria Kaiulani, this hotel keeps alive the traditions of old Hawaiʻi, with furnishings that include Hawaiian quilts and artwork. Arts-and-crafts demonstrations and a historical-hotel tour take place during the day, and at night there's poolside hula on the Lava Stage. The hotel has two restaurants: the Pikake Terrace, for casual outdoor dining, and Momoyama Japanese Restaurant. ⊠ 120 Kaiulani Ave., Waikīkī, Honolulu 96815 ☎ 808/922–5811 or 800/782–9488 ➮ 808/931–4526 ⊕ www.sheraton-hawaii. com ➯ 1150 rooms, 10 suites ⚐ 2 restaurants, room service, in-room data ports, pool, gym, lobby lounge, children's programs (ages 5–12), business services ▤ AE, D, DC, MC, V.

$$$–$$$$ ▦ **Waikīkī Beach Marriott Resort.** On the eastern edge of Waikīkī, this hotel is across from Kūhiō Beach and close to Kapiʻolani Park, the zoo, and the aquarium. Deep Hawaiian woods and bold tropical colors fill the hotel's two towers, which have ample courtyards and public areas open to ocean breezes and sunlight. The Kealohilani Tower's spacious guest rooms are some of the largest in Waikīkī, and the Paokalani Tower's Diamond Head side rooms offer breathtaking views of Diamond Head crater and Kapiʻolani Park. ⊠ 2552 Kalākaua Ave., Waikīkī,

Honolulu 96815 ☎ *808/922–6611 or 800/367–5370* 🖷 *808/921–5222* ⊕ *www.marriottwaikiki.com* ⇙ *1,337 rooms, 9 suites* ♻ *3 restaurants, room service, in-room safes, refrigerators, minibars, tennis court, 2 pools, gym, 2 lounges, concierge, business services, meeting rooms* 🖃 *AE, D, MC, V.*

★ **$$$–$$$$** 🏨 **Waikīkī Parc.** This jewel of a boutique hotel, owned by the same group that manages the Halekūlani across the street, where guests have signing privileges, offers the same attention to detail in service and architectural design as the larger hotel but lacks a beachfront location. The lobby is light and airy, and guest rooms are done in cool blues and whites with sitting areas and large writing desks. The hotel's Japanese restaurant, Kacho, serves Kyoto cuisine, and the lovely Parc Café is known for its bountiful island-style buffets. ⊠ *2233 Helumoa Rd., Waikīkī, Honolulu 96815* ☎ *808/921–7272 or 800/422–0450* 🖷 *808/931–6638* ⊕ *www.waikikiparc.com* ⇙ *298 rooms* ♻ *2 restaurants, room service, in-room data ports, in-room safes, minibars, pool, gym, concierge, business services* 🖃 *AE, D, DC, MC, V.*

$$$ 🏨 **Ohana East.** Formerly the Outrigger East, this hotel is the flagship property for Ohana Hotels in Waikīkī. It's just two blocks from the beach and a quarter mile from Kapi'olani Park, with easy access to Waikīkī activities and trolley and bus routes. You can stay in standard hotel rooms or suites with kitchenettes. All rooms have Nintendo systems for restless kids. ⊠ *150 Kaiulani Ave., Waikīkī, Honolulu 96815* ☎ *808/922–5353 or 800/462–6262* 🖷 *808/926–4334* ⊕ *www.ohanahotels.com* ⇙ *423 rooms, 22 suites* ♻ *4 restaurants, room service, in-room data ports, in-room safes, some kitchenettes, refrigerators, room TVs with video games, pool, gym, hair salon, bar, laundry facilities* 🖃 *AE, D, DC, MC, V.*

$$–$$$ 🏨 **Ilima Hotel.** This 17-story condominium-style hotel has large studios with two double beds and full kitchens; you can also opt for a suite with a spacious lānai. On a side street near the Ala Wai Canal, the Ilima is a short walk away from the International Market Place and the Royal Hawaiian Shopping Center. ⊠ *445 Nohonani St., Waikīkī, Honolulu 96815* ☎ *808/923–1877 or 888/864–5462* 🖷 *808/924–2617* ⊕ *www.ilima.com* ⇙ *99 units* ♻ *In-room safes, kitchens, pool, sauna, laundry facilities* 🖃 *AE, DC, MC, V.*

$$–$$$ 🏨 **Queen Kapi'olani Hotel.** A half block from the shore, this 19-story hotel appeals to those in search of clean, basic accommodations within walking distance of the beach and Waikīkī's main attractions. Some rooms have kitchenettes, and the third floor has a large pool and sundeck. ⊠ *150 Kapahulu Ave., Waikīkī, Honolulu 96815* ☎ *808/922–1941 or 800/367–2317* 🖷 *808/922–2694* ⊕ *www.queenkapiolani.com* ⇙ *307 rooms, 7 suites* ♻ *2 restaurants, room service, in-room data ports, kitchenettes, refrigerators, pool, bar, meeting rooms* 🖃 *AE, D, DC, MC, V.*

$$–$$$ 🏨 **Waikīkī Joy.** This boutique hotel is a lesser-known gem. The location is great, tucked away on a quiet side street next to the DFS Galleria. One tower has all suites, and another has standard hotel rooms. Units have either ocean or partial ocean views. Each has a lānai, an in-room Jacuzzi, a deluxe stereo system, and a control panel by the bed. The hotel's private karaoke rooms are a great place to entertain friends. ⊠ *320 Lewers St., Waikīkī, Honolulu 96815* ☎ *808/923–2300 or 800/922–7866* 🖷 *808/924–4010* ⊕ *www.aston-hotels.com* ⇙ *50 rooms, 44 suites* ♻ *Restaurant, in-room data ports, in-room safes, kitchenettes, minibars, pool, sauna, lobby lounge* 🖃 *AE, D, DC, MC, V.*

$–$$$ 🏨 **Aston Coconut Plaza Hotel.** With its small size and intimate service, Coconut Plaza, on the Ala Wai Canal and three blocks from the beach, is a true boutique hotel. Tropical plantation decor features rattan furnishings and floral bedspreads. Guest rooms have private lānai, and all except standard-view rooms come with kitchenettes. Free Continental breakfast is served daily on the lobby veranda. ⊠ *450 Lewers St., Waikīkī, Honolulu 96815* ☎ *808/923–8828 or 800/922–7866* 🗍 *808/ 923–3473* ⊕ *www.aston-hotels.com* ⬋ *70 rooms, 11 suites* ♿ *In-room data ports, in-room safes, some kitchenettes, pool, hair salon, laundry facilities, meeting rooms* ▤ *AE, D, DC, MC, V.*

$$ 🏠 **Diamond Head Bed and Breakfast.** The two guest rooms at this bed-and-breakfast on the southeastern edge of Kapi'olani Park are big, have private baths, and open to a lānai and large backyard that makes the hustle and bustle of Waikīkī seem miles away. Hostess Joanne Trotter has filled the large living spaces with modern artwork. A minimum two-night stay is required. ⊠ *3240 Noela Dr., Waikīkī, Honolulu 96815* ☎ *808/885–4550* 🗍 *808/885–0559* ⊠ *Reservations:* 🏠 *Hawai'i's Best Bed and Breakfasts, Box 563, Kamuela, 96743* ☎ *808/885–4550 or 800/262–9912* 🗍 *808/885–0559* ⊕ *www.bestbnb.com* ⬋ *2 rooms* ♿ *No a/c, no room phones* ▤ *No credit cards.*

$–$$ 🏠 **Aloha Punawai.** This family-operated apartment hotel is across the street from Ft. DeRussy Beach and within walking distance of shops and restaurants. The studios have bathrooms with showers only, but each unit comes with a full kitchen, cable television, and a lānai. Furnishings are simple and spartan. You can opt for telephone service or forgo the distraction. ⊠ *305 Saratoga Rd., Waikīkī, Honolulu 96815* ☎ *808/923– 5211* 🗍 *808/622–4688* ⊕ *www.alternative-hawaii.com/alohapunawai* ⬋ *19 units* ♿ *Kitchens, cable TV, laundry facilities; no phones in some rooms* ▤ *AE, DC, MC, V.*

$–$$ 🏠 **The Breakers.** The Breakers' six two-story buildings surround the pool and overlook gardens filled with tropical flowers. A throwback to the early 1960s, guest rooms have Japanese-style shoji doors. Rooms come with kitchenettes, bathrooms with shower only, and lānai. Guests return here year after year to soak up the laid-back old Hawai'i atmosphere. It's a half block from the beach and from Waikīkī restaurants. ⊠ *250 Beach Walk, Waikīkī, Honolulu 96815* ☎ *808/923–3181 or 800/ 426–0494* 🗍 *808/923–7174* ⊕ *www.breakers-hawaii.com* ⬋ *64 units* ♿ *Kitchenettes, pool* ▤ *AE, DC, MC, V.*

$–$$ 🏠 **Holiday Inn–Waikīkī.** This Holiday Inn is conveniently located just two blocks from the beach and a 10-minute walk from both the Hawai'i Convention Center and Ala Moana Shopping Center. It offers the standard, reliable chain amenities, with tropical-motif rooms. ⊠ *1830 Ala Moana Blvd., Waikīkī, Honolulu 96815* ☎ *808/955–1111 or 888/992– 4545* 🗍 *808/947–1799* ⊕ *www.holiday-inn-waikiki.com* ⬋ *199 rooms, 6 suites* ♿ *Restaurant, in-room data ports, in-room safes, kitchenettes, hair salon, laundry facilities* ▤ *AE, DC, MC, V.*

$–$$ 🏠 **Patrick Winston's Waikīkī Condos.** This 24-unit condominium complex has budget, standard, and deluxe two-bedroom units. Each has its own individual decor, but all have full kitchens, ceiling fans, sofa beds, and lānai. Owner Patrick Winston can provide everything from exercise equipment to rice cookers to tips on the best places to dine on the island. ⊠ *417 Nohonani St., Waikīkī, Honolulu 96815* ☎ *808/922–3894 or 800/545–1948* 🗍 *808/924–3332* ⊕ *www.winstonwaikikicondos. com* ⬋ *24 units* ♿ *Fans, in-room data ports, kitchens, pool, laundry facilities* ▤ *AE, DC, MC, V.*

$–$$ 🏠 **Waikīkī Hāna.** Smack-dab in the middle of Waikīkī and a block away from the beach, this eight-story hotel is convenient for exploring just about every shop, restaurant, and activity in O'ahu's tourist hub. Accommodations are clean and plain. Many rooms have their own lānai. Pay a little extra per day and you can rent a refrigerator. The Super Chef restaurant on the ground floor offers casual, convenient dining for breakfast, lunch, and dinner. ⊠ *2424 Koa Ave., Waikīkī, Honolulu 96815* ☎ *808/926–*

8841 or 800/367–5004 🖷 808/924–3770 ⊕ *www.castleresorts.com* 🖙70 rooms, 2 suites ⚭ *Restaurant, in-room safes, kitchenettes, hair salon, lobby lounge, laundry facilities* ⊟ *AE, DC, MC, V.*

$–$$ 🏨 **Waikīkī Sand Villa.** The Villa's rooms are definitely on the small side, but they're clean and fairly comfortable. All rooms are equipped with T1 Internet access, and there's even a Webcam set up at the hotel's sand bar so you can chat with friends and family back home. Complimentary breakfast is served daily in the hotel's breakfast room or at tables outside by the swimming pool. Studio accommodations are also available. The hotel is three blocks from the beach across from the Ala Wai Canal. ✉ *2375 Ala Wai Blvd., Waikīkī, Honolulu 96815* 🖀 *808/ 922–4744 or 800/247–1903* 🖷 *808/923–2541* ⊕ *www.sandvillahotel. com* 🖙 *212 rooms* ⚭ *Restaurant, in-room data ports, refrigerators, pool, hot tub, bar, shop* ⊟ *AE, D, DC, MC, V.*

$ 🏨 **Edmunds Hotel Apartments.** Long lānai wrap around the building, so each room has its own view of the pretty Ala Wai Canal and glorious Mānoa Valley beyond—views that look especially lovely at night, when lights are twinkling up in the mountain ridges. This has been a budget alternative for decades, and if you can put up with the constant sounds of traffic on the boulevard, it's a real bargain. The ocean is four blocks away. ✉ *2411 Ala Wai Blvd., Waikīkī, Honolulu 96815* 🖀 *808/923–8381 or 808/732– 5169* 🖙 *8 rooms* ⚭ *Kitchenettes; no a/c* ⊟ *No credit cards.*

¢–$ 🏨 **Royal Grove Hotel.** This flamingo-pink family-oriented hotel is reminiscent of Miami. With just six floors, it is one of Waikīkī's smaller hotels. The lobby is comfortable; the rooms, though agreeably furnished, have neither themes nor views. Go for the higher-end rooms if possible—economy rooms have no air-conditioning and more street noise. The hotel is about two blocks from the beach, and the pool area is bright with tropical flowers. Don't be surprised if members of the Fong family, who own and run the place, cook up a potluck dinner with some 'ukulele entertainment, just so guests can meet each other. Weekly and monthly rates are available. ✉ *151 Uluniu Ave., Waikīkī, Honolulu 96815* 🖀 *808/923–7691* ⊕ *www.royalgrovehotel.com* 🖷 *808/922–7508* 🖙 *78 rooms, 7 suites* ⚭ *Kitchenettes, pool; no a/c in some rooms* ⊟ *AE, D, DC, MC, V.*

Honolulu

★ $$$$ 🏨 **Kāhala Mandarin Oriental Hawai'i.** Minutes away from Waikīkī, on the quiet side of Diamond Head, this elegant oceanfront hotel is hidden in the wealthy neighborhood of Kāhala. Rooms combine touches of Asia and old Hawai'i, with mahogany furniture, teak parquet floors, hand-loomed area rugs, local art, and grass-cloth wall coverings. If you're adventurous, you may want to reserve ahead to interact with dolphins in the hotel's impressive 26,000-square-ft lagoon. For pure indulgence, book a spa suite at the Kahala Spa for the ultimate in pampering. ✉ *5000 Kāhala Ave., Kāhala, Honolulu 96816* 🖀 *808/739– 8888 or 800/367–2525* 🖷 *808/739–8800* ⊕ *www.mandarinoriental.com/ kahala* 🖙 *341 rooms, 29 suites* ⚭ *3 restaurants, room service, minibars, pool, gym, outdoor hot tub, sauna, steam room, beach, dive shop, snorkeling, lobby lounge, concierge, business services, meeting room* ⊟ *AE, D, DC, MC, V.*

$$$–$$$$ 🏨 **Aston at the Executive Centre Hotel.** Here's a great option for the corporate traveler who wants to avoid Waikīkī. Downtown Honolulu's only hotel is an all-suite high-rise in the center of the business district, within walking distance of the Aloha Tower Marketplace and 10 minutes from Honolulu International Airport. Suites are on the top 10 floors of a 40-story glass-walled tower, providing views of downtown and Honolulu

Harbor. Each unit has a separate living area and kitchenette stocked with cold beverages. Some units have washer-dryers. The hotel offers a round-the-clock business center and health spa. ⊠ *1088 Bishop St., Downtown Honolulu 96813* ☎ *808/539–3000 or 800/922–7866* 🖷 *808/523–1088* ⊕ *www.aston-hotels.com* ⟳ *116 suites* ⚹ *Restaurant, in-room data ports, in-room safes, kitchenettes, pool, gym, spa, business services, meeting rooms* ⊟ *AE, DC, MC, V.*

$$–$$$ ▦ **Ala Moana Hotel.** This hotel is at the entrance to Waikīkī near the popular Ala Moana Shopping Center (they're connected by a pedestrian ramp), Victoria Ward Entertainment Complex, the Hawai'i Convention Center, and Ala Moana Beach Park. Each room in this 36-story high-rise has a lānai with a view of Ala Moana Beach, the ocean, or the mountains. Rooms on the 29th to 35th floors provide concierge service, in-room whirlpool baths, and free use of the conference room. The hotel's nightclub, Rumours, is popular with the after-work crowd, and the Plantation Cafe offers a fresh twist on Pacific Rim cuisine in a casual resort setting. ⊠ *410 Atkinson Dr., Ala Moana, Honolulu 96814* ☎ *808/955–4811 or 888/367–4811* 🖷 *808/944–6839* ⊕ *www.alamoanahotel.com* ⟳ *1,150 rooms, 67 suites* ⚹ *4 restaurants, room service, in-room safes, minibars, pool, gym, bar, 2 lobby lounges, dance club, nightclub, meeting room* ⊟ *AE, DC, MC, V.*

$$–$$$ ▦ **Pagoda Hotel.** The location, minutes away from Ala Moana Shopping Center and Ala Moana Beach Park, and moderate rates make this a good choice if you're simply looking for a place to sleep and catch a couple of meals. Studios feature kitchenettes with full-size refrigerators, stoves, microwaves, and cooking and dining ware. There are no memorable views because the hotel is surrounded by high-rises. The restaurant is surrounded by a small lake and is notable for its Japanese gardens and carp-filled waterways. ⊠ *1525 Rycroft St., Ala Moana, Honolulu 96814* ☎ *808/941–6611 or 800/367–6060* 🖷 *808/955–5067* ⊕ *www.hthcorp.com* ⟳ *364 rooms* ⚹ *2 restaurants, room service, in-room data ports, some kitchenettes, refrigerators, 2 pools, hair salon, shop, no-smoking rooms* ⊟ *AE, D, DC, MC, V.*

$$ ▦ **Mānoa Valley Inn.** An intimate surprise is tucked away in Mānoa Valley, just 2 mi from Waikīkī. Built in 1919, this stately home is on the National Register of Historic Places. Linger over the complimentary Continental breakfast buffet on the shady backyard lānai each morning and enjoy tropical fruit and cheese in the afternoon. Rooms are furnished in country-inn style, with antique four-poster beds, marble-top dressers, patterned wallpaper, and fresh flowers. There's a reading room with a TV and VCR. The separate carriage house sleeps four. ⊠ *2001 Vancouver Dr., Mānoa, Honolulu 96822* ☎ *808/947–6019 or 800/634–5115* ⊕ *www.aloha.net/~wery/mvbroch.htm* 🖷 *808/946–6168* ⟳ *7 suites, 4 with bath; 1 house* ⊟ *AE, DC, MC, V.*

Around the Island

★ $$$$ ▦ **J. W. Marriott 'Ihilani Resort & Spa.** The 'Ihilani is in a sleek 17-story building illuminated by a glass-dome atrium. Rooms are 650 square ft and have marble bathrooms with deep soaking tubs, private lānai, teak furnishings, in-room CD players with a selection of CDs, and a high-tech control system (lights, temperature controls, and more). Most rooms have ocean views. Azul is the resort's signature dining room and features contemporary Mediterranean cuisine. The 35,000-square-ft 'Ihilani Spa has everything from green-tea wraps to personalized fitness routines. There's a Ted Robinson–designed 18-hole championship golf facility. ⊠ *92-1001 'Ōlani St., Kapolei 96707* ☎ *808/679–0079 or 800/626–4446* 🖷 *808/679–0080* ⊕ *www.ihilani.com* ⟳ *387 rooms,*

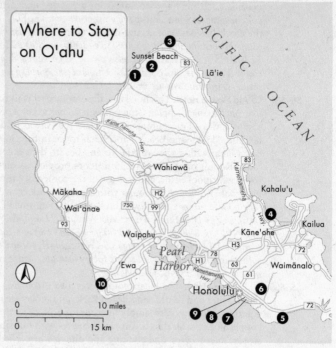

Where to Stay on O'ahu

63 suites ♤ 4 restaurants, room service, minibars, 18-hole golf course, 6 tennis courts, 2 pools, health club, spa, shops, baby-sitting, children's programs (ages 5–12), concierge, business services, meeting rooms ⊟ AE, DC, MC, V.

$$$–$$$$
Fodor'sChoice
★

🏨 **Turtle Bay Resort.** A $35 million renovation has finally restored this resort to a grandeur worthy of its location on O'ahu's scenic North Shore. All rooms now feature lānai to showcase stunning peninsula views. The rooms are stylish and calming, in colors that represent all the shades of the sea and sand. The beach cottages are sumptuous oceanfront retreats complete with Brazilian walnut floors, teak rockers on the lānai, and large marble bathrooms with deep soak tubs. Turtle Bay also has a spa, 12 mi of nature trails, a Hans Heidemann Surf School, and the only 36-hole golf facility on O'ahu. ⊠ 57-091 Kamehameha Hwy. (Box 187), Kahuku 96731 ☎ 808/293–8811 or 800/203–3650 🖷 808/293–9147 ⊕ www.turtlebayresort.com ⥱ 373 rooms, 40 suites, 42 beach cottages ♤ 2 restaurants, room service, refrigerators, 2 18-hole golf courses, 10 tennis courts, 2 pools, gym, beach, horseback riding, lobby lounge, children's programs (ages 5–12), meeting room ⊟ AE, D, DC, MC, V.

$$–$$$$
🏨 **Schrader's Windward Country Inn.** Though billed as "cottages by the sea," the setting is actually more roadside motel than resort. But Schrader's provides a moderately priced lodging alternative with amenities you won't find in Waikīkī, including complimentary biweekly ocean-reef tours that include snorkeling and kayaking the scenic windward coastline. One- to four-bedroom accommodations are available. Units feature microwaves and refrigerators, and some have full kitchens. Ask for the rooms that open onto Kāne'ohe Bay if you relish the possibility of fishing right off your lānai. ⊠ 47-039 Lihikai Dr., Kāne'ohe 96744 ☎ 808/239–5711 or 800/735–5711 🖷 808/239–6658 ⊕ www.hawaiiscene.com/schrader ⥱ 57 rooms ♤ Kitchenettes, pool ⊟ AE, D, DC, MC, V.

¢–$ ⬜ **Backpackers Vacation Inn and Plantation Village.** Spartan in furnishings and definitely very casual in spirit, Backpackers is a surfer's kind of place to catch some sleep between wave sets. It's near Waimea Bay on the North Shore at Three Tables Beach and offers double rooms (some with a double bed, others with two single beds), hostel accommodations, and cottages. Some accommodations have kitchenettes. It's a three-minute walk to the supermarket. ✉ *59-788 Kamehameha Hwy., Haleʻiwa 96712* ☎ *808/638-7838* ⊕ *www.backpackers-hawaii.com* 📠 *808/638-7515* ⇗ *25 rooms* ◊ *Some kitchenettes; no a/c, no phones in some rooms, no TV in some rooms* ▤ *MC, V.*

¢–$ ⬜ **Breck's on the Beach Hostel.** Just north of Sunset Beach Park, Breck's offers convenient digs along the North Shore, with rooms ranging from basic dormitory to ocean-view balcony apartments that sleep eight people. Guests, usually surfer types from many continents, have access to free body boards and snorkeling equipment. Bicycles and surfboards are also available. Studio apartments have refrigerators and private bath, and the larger balcony apartments include kitchens. Airport pickup is available. A three-night minimum stay is required. ✉ *59-043 Huelo St., Sunset Beach 96712* ☎ *808/638-7873* ⇗ *21 units* ◊ *Some kitchens, airport shuttle; no a/c in some rooms* ▤ *No credit cards.*

NIGHTLIFE & THE ARTS

Nightlife on Oʻahu can be as simple as a barefoot stroll in the sand or as elaborate as a dinner show with all the glitter of a Las Vegas production. You can view the vibrant hues of a Honolulu sunset during a cocktail cruise or hear the melodies of ancient chants at a lūʻau on a remote west-shore beach.

Waikīkī's Kalākaua and Kūhiō avenues come to life when the sun goes down. Outside Honolulu, offerings are slimmer but equally diverse. Wafting through the night air of Oʻahu is the sound of music of every kind—from classical to contemporary. Music has been the language of Hawaiʻi from the beginning, and Oʻahu has the best selection. Everywhere there is hula, whether dancers wear sequin skirts in Waikīkī or authentic ti-leaf skirts at Paradise Cove.

The arts thrive alongside the tourist industry. Oʻahu has an established symphony, a thriving opera company, chamber music groups, and community theaters. Major Broadway shows, dance companies, and rock stars also make their way to Honolulu. Check the local newspapers—the *Honolulu Advertiser,* the *Honolulu Star-Bulletin,* or the *Honolulu Weekly*—for the latest events.

Bars, Cabarets & Clubs

The drinking age is 21 on Oʻahu and throughout Hawaiʻi. Many bars will admit younger people but will not serve them alcohol. By law, all establishments that serve alcoholic beverages must close by 2 AM. The only exceptions are those with a cabaret license, which have a 4 AM curfew. Most places have a cover charge of $5 to $10.

Honolulu

Aaron's Atop the Ala Moana. A splendid view, good contemporary dance music, and a sophisticated, well-dressed crowd come together at this Honolulu nightclub, which offers candlelight, a late-night dining menu, and an incomparable 36th-floor view of Honolulu's city lights. ✉ *Ala Moana Hotel, 410 Atkinson Dr., Ala Moana* ☎ *808/955-4466.*

Anna Bannana's. Generations of Hawaiʻi college students have spent more than an evening or two at this legendary two-story, smoky dive. A living-room atmosphere makes it a comfortable place to hang out. Here, the music is fresh, loud, and sometimes experimental. Local favorites deliver ultracreative dance music, and the likes of blues singer Taj Mahal have been known to perform. Live music happens Thursday–Saturday, starting at 9 PM. ⊠ *2440 S. Beretania St., Mō'ili'ili* ☎ *808/946–5190.*

Banana Patch Lounge. This hotel lounge is definitely active—here, the entertainment includes guests strutting their stuff at karaoke. ⊠ *Miramar at Waikīkī Hotel, 2345 Kūhiō Ave., Waikīkī* ☎ *808/922–2077.*

Banyan Court. The Banyan Court is steeped in history. From this location the radio program *Hawaii Calls* first broadcast the sounds of Hawaiian music and the rolling surf to a U.S. mainland audience in 1935. Today, a variety of Hawaiian entertainment, with an emphasis on the sounds of the steel guitar, continues to provide the perfect accompaniment to the sounds of the surf. ⊠ *Sheraton Moana Surfrider, 2365 Kalākaua Ave., Waikīkī* ☎ *808/922–3111.*

Blue Tropix. This nightclub features DJs mixing hip-hop and house for the 18-plus crowd. Check out the Big Teeze Tuesdays and XXX Saturday promotions with DJ Kool-E and the Nocturnal Sound Krew. ⊠ *1700 Kapi'olani Blvd., Ala Moana* ☎ *808/944–0001.*

Café Sistina After Hours. This little Italian restaurant goes "Noche Tropical" after hours on Saturday, when some of the island's most enthusiastic salsa dancers kick up their heels to dance to a DJ spinning Tito Puente, Celia Cruz, and Grupo Niche. ⊠ *Café Sistina, 1314 S. King St., Ala Moana* ☎ *808/596–0061.*

The Cellar Nightclub. Head downstairs to the Cellar to get your groove on with an 18-and-over crowd and music mixed by DJs Big John and Sho. ⊠ *205 Lewers St., Waikīkī* ☎ *808/923–9952.*

Chai's Island Bistro. Chai's welcomes some of Hawai'i's top entertainers, such as the Brothers Cazimero (on Wednesday evening), Hapa, and the Makaha Sons. There's also a Pacific Rim–cuisine menu with a twist of Thai. ⊠ *Aloha Tower Marketplace, 1 Aloha Tower Dr., Downtown Honolulu* ☎ *808/585–0011.*

Dave and Buster's. Located in the Victoria Ward Centers, this restaurant features a stocked bar and lots of amusements ranging from classic billiards to shuffleboard and the latest in video arcade games. ⊠ *Victoria Ward Centers, 1030 Auahi St., Ala Moana* ☎ *808/589–2215.*

Don Ho's Grill. This popular waterfront restaurant in the Aloha Tower Marketplace houses the Tiny Bubbles Bar, famous for its "suck 'em up" mai tai, a Don Ho classic. There's Hawaiian music Wednesday–Sunday at dinnertime with performers like Jerry Santos, Jake Shimabukuro, and Robert Cazimero. On the weekend, dance music plays from 10 PM to 2 AM. ⊠ *Aloha Tower Marketplace, 1 Aloha Tower Dr., Downtown Honolulu* ☎ *808/528–0807.*

Duke's Canoe Club. Oceanfront on Waikīkī Beach, this restaurant presents "Concerts on the Beach" every Friday and Saturday with contemporary Hawaiian musicians like Henry Kapono. National musicians like Jimmy Buffet have also performed here. At Duke's Barefoot Bar, solo Hawaiian musicians take the stage nightly. ⊠ *Outrigger Waikīkī, 2335 Kalākaua Ave., Waikīkī* ☎ *808/922–2268.*

Esprit. Waikīkī's only oceanfront nightclub affords a 180-degree view of the beach. Contemporary dance tunes are spun here nightly. For those who yearn for days gone by, Randy Smith sings the music of Frank Sinatra and friends, Friday and Saturday at 7:45 PM. ⊠ *Sheraton Waikīkī, 2255 Kalākaua Ave., Waikīkī* ☎ *808/922–4422.*

Fusion Waikīkī. This club features a Paper Doll Revue Drag Show and a Men of Fusion Male Revue, with a fun crowd that spans all genders and persuasions. ⊠ *2260 Kūhiō Ave., 3rd floor, Waikīkī* ☎ *808/924–2422.*

Gordon Biersch Brewery Restaurant. Live duos and trios serenade patrons of the outside bar that flanks Honolulu Harbor. Although there's no dancing, this is the place in Honolulu to see and be seen. ⊠ *Aloha Tower Marketplace, 1 Aloha Tower Dr., Downtown Honolulu* ☎ *808/599–4877.*

Hanohano Room. World-class views 30 stories above Waikīkī and music made just for slow dancing make this a romantic spot for honeymooners or those who just like to dance cheek-to-cheek. ⊠ *Sheraton Waikīkī, 2255 Kalākaua Ave., 30th floor, Waikīkī* ☎ *808/922–4422.*

Honu Bar and Terrace. Sophisticated and swank, this lobby lounge presents light jazz and island ensembles during the cocktail and sunset hours. ⊠ *Kāhala Mandarin Oriental Hawai'i, 5000 Kāhala Ave., Kāhala* ☎ *808/739–8888.*

Hula's Bar and Lei Stand. Hawai'i's oldest and best-known gay-friendly nightspot offers calming panoramic outdoor views of Diamond Head and the Pacific Ocean from the bar by day and a high-energy club scene by night. ⊠ *Waikīkī Grand Hotel, 134 Kapahulu Ave., 2nd floor, Waikīkī* ☎ *808/923–0669.*

International Market Place. Tucked away in this outdoor bazaar is a stage where each evening Hawaiian entertainers perform Hawaiian, Maori, and Tahitian songs. The atmosphere is friendly, the dress is casual, and the mood is set by the sounds of the steel guitar, 'ukulele, and Hawaiian falsetto. ⊠ *International Market Place Food Court,2330 Kalākaua Ave., Waikīkī* ☎ *808/923–0669.*

Mai Tai Bar at the Royal Hawaiian. Everything is pink, including the beer, at this outdoor bar, which offers front-row seating for Waikīkī sunsets and an unobstructed view of Diamond Head. Top Hawaiian entertainers like Brother Noland and Keith and Carmen Haugen perform here. ⊠ *Royal Hawaiian Hotel, 2259 Kalākaua Ave., Waikīkī* ☎ *808/923–0669.*

Maze. Three rooms with 10,000 square ft of dance space keep this second-floor nightclub a favorite of the international set. The Arena Room plays hip-hop, progressive, and trance; the Red Room is hot with rare groove; and the Paradox Lounge gets funky with deep house and disco. ⊠ *Waikīkī Trade Center, 2255 Kūhiō Ave., Waikīkī* ☎ *808/921–5800.*

Moana Terrace. Three floors up from Waikīkī Beach, this open-air terrace is the home of Aunty Genoa Keawe, the "First Lady of Hawaiian Music." Her falsetto sessions include jams with the finest of Hawai'i's musicians. The Terrace also features contemporary Hawaiian music and slack-key-guitar-virtuoso George Kuo. ⊠ *Waikīkī Beach Marriott Resort, 2552 Kalākaua Ave., Waikīkī* ☎ *808/922–6611.*

Moose McGillycuddy's Pub and Cafe. Loud bands play for the beach-and-beer gang in a blue-jeans-and-T-shirt setting. ⊠ *310 Lewers St., Waikīkī* ☎ *808/923–0751.*

Nashville Waikīkī. Country music in the tropics? You bet! Put on your *paniolo* (Hawaiian cowboy) duds and mosey on out to the giant dance floor. There are pool tables, dartboards, line dancing, and free dance lessons (nightly at 7 PM) to boot. ⊠ *Ohana Waikīkī West Hotel, 2330 Kūhiō Ave., Waikīkī* ☎ *808/926–7911.*

Opium Den & Champagne Bar at Indigo's. This bar at the edge of Chinatown resembles a joint right out of a film noir. Jazz plays early on in the evening; late nights DJs spin trance, Top 40, funk, disco, and rock. In addition to champagne, happy hour features sake martinis and a sampler menu. ⊠ *Indigo Euroasian Cuisine, 1121 Nu'uanu Ave., Downtown Honolulu* ☎ *808/521–2900.*

Paradise Lounge. Several contemporary Hawaiian acts, including the longtime band Olomana, perform in this pretty outdoor club. ⊠*Hilton Hawaiian Village, 2005 Kālia Rd., Waikīkī* ☎ *808/949–4321.*

Pier Bar. Here's one of the few places in Honolulu where you can hear live music outdoors and dance underneath the stars. It attracts a grab bag of groups; call ahead to find out who's playing. ✉ *Aloha Tower Marketplace, 1 Aloha Tower Dr., Downtown Honolulu* ☎ *808/536–2166.*

Pipeline Cafe and Sports Bar. This is two stories of fun with pool, darts, and more. The upstairs sports bar has TVs galore and a sky-box view of the dancing below. Music includes both live acts and seasoned DJs. ✉ *805 Pohukaina St., Kaka'ako* ☎ *808/589–1999.*

Royal Garden at Waikīkī. Some of O'ahu's top jazz stylists perform in the elegant, intimate lobby lounge of this sophisticated hotel. ✉ *Royal Garden at Waikīkī, 444 'Olohana St., Waikīkī* ☎ *808/943–0202.*

Rumours. The after-work crowd loves this spot, which has dance videos, disco, and throbbing lights. On Saturday "Little Chill" nights, the club plays oldies from the '70s and '80s and serves free pūpū. There is "salsa after dark" dancing Thursday evening. ✉ *Ala Moana Hotel, 410 Atkinson St., Ala Moana* ☎ *808/955–4811.*

Shore Bird Beach Broiler. This Waikīkī beachfront disco spills right out onto the sand. It has a large dance floor and a 10-ft video screen. Karaoke sing-alongs are held nightly. ✉ *Outrigger Reef on the Beach hotel, 2169 Kālia Rd., Waikīkī* ☎ *808/922–2887.*

Venus Nightclub. This high-energy social bar, with leather couches ideal for a night of people-watching, features hip-hop, trance, and reggae with guest DJs five nights a week. Attention, ladies: there's a male dance revue Saturday evenings. ✉ *1349 Kapi'olani Blvd., Ala Moana* ☎ *808/951–8671.*

Virus Entertainment. Here DJs make the music come alive with their mix of house, trance, drum, and bass. On the last Saturday of the month, prepare to get wet at the after-hours foam party. ✉ *1687 Kapi'olani Blvd., Ala Moana* ☎ *808/951–9881.*

Wave Waikīkī. Dance to live rock and roll until 1:30 AM and recorded music after that. It can be a rough scene (the place has seen more than its fair share of drunken fisticuffs), but the bands are tops. Late nights, the music here goes definitely "underground." ✉ *1877 Kalākaua Ave., Waikīkī* ☎ *808/941–0424.*

Wonderlounge at the W Diamond Head. A variety of theme dance nights make Friday and Saturday evenings a wonder to behold here in the lobby of the W Diamond Head. The crowd is full of hip, young professionals who enjoy mai tai martinis and the chance to do some not-so-serious networking. ✉ *W Honolulu—Diamond Head, 2885 Kalākaua Ave., Waikīkī* ☎ *808/922–1700.*

World Cafe. Honolulu's only upscale billiards nightclub also has a sports bar and dancing to Top 40 tunes. ✉ *500 Ala Moana Blvd., Ala Moana* ☎ *808/599–4450.*

Zanzabar. DJs spin top hits, from hip-hop to soul, at this elegant and high-energy nightspot in the Waikīkī Trade Center. ✉ *2255 Kūhiō Ave., Waikīkī* ☎ *808/924–3939.*

Around the Island

The Bay Club. A beautiful place to watch the sun set over the North Shore water, this lounge inside the Turtle Bay Resort hosts a variety of local bands that play contemporary Hawaiian tunes. On weekend nights, dance music keeps things rocking on the North Shore. ✉ *Turtle Bay Resort, 57-091 Kamehameha Hwy., Kahuku* ☎ *808/293–8811.*

Cocktail & Dinner Cruises

Dinner cruises depart either from the piers adjacent to the Aloha Tower Marketplace in Downtown Honolulu or from Kewalo Basin, just 'ewa of Ala Moana Beach Park, and head along the coast toward Diamond Head. There's usually dinner, dancing, drinks, and a sensational sunset. Except as noted, dinner cruises cost approximately $50–$95, cocktail cruises $25–$40. Most major credit cards are accepted.

Ali`i Kai Catamaran. Patterned after an ancient Polynesian vessel, this huge catamaran casts off from Aloha Tower with 1,000 passengers. The deluxe dinner cruise has two open bars, a huge dinner, and an authentic Polynesian show with colorful hula music. The food is good, the after-dinner show loud and fun, and everyone dances on the way back to shore. ⊠ *Pier 5, street level, Honolulu* ☎ *808/539–9400.*

Dream Cruises. The 100-ft motor yacht *American Dream* handles up to 225 guests for evening cruises off the shores of Waikīkī. Decks have plenty of outdoor space for views of the twinkling city lights. The Island Grill dinner cruise includes one mai tai, a grilled-steak and -chicken buffet, and soft drinks. You pay for extra drinks. Vegetarian meals may be ordered in advance. After a hula demonstration, a DJ spins tunes from the '50s through the '70s. ⊠ *306 Kamani St., Honolulu* ☎ *808/592–5200 or 800/400–7300* ⊕ *www.dream-cruises.com.*

Navatek Cruises. The sleek *Navatek* is a revolutionary craft designed to sail smoothly in rough waters, which allows it to power farther along Waikīkī's coastline than its competitors. Choose from sunset dinner or moonlight cruises, or breakfast and lunch whale-watch cruises December–mid-April. Tours leave from Pier 6, next to Aloha Tower Marketplace. ⊠ *Honolulu Harbor* ☎ *808/973–1311* ⊕ *www.goatlantis.com.*

Paradise Cruises. Prices vary depending on which deck you choose on the 1,600-passenger, four-deck *Star of Honolulu.* For instance, a seven-course French-style dinner and live jazz on the top deck cost $164. A steak and crab feast on level two costs $105. This ship also features daily Hawaiiana Lunch cruises that offer lei-making and 'ukulele and hula lessons for $38. Evening excursions also take place on the 340-passenger *Starlet I* and 230-passenger *Starlet II,* which offer three-course dinners beginning at $66. ⊠ *1540 S. King St., Honolulu* ☎ *808/983–7827* ⊕ *www.paradisecruises.com.*

Cocktail & Dinner Shows

Some O'ahu entertainers have been around for years, and others have just arrived on the scene. Either way, the dinner-show food is usually buffet-style with a definite local accent. Dinner shows are all in the $55 to $99 range. Cocktail shows run $30 to $43. The prices usually include one cocktail, tax, and gratuity. In all cases, reservations are essential, and most major credit cards are accepted. Be sure to call in advance. You never know when an artist may have switched venues.

Blue Hawai'i: The Show. Jonathan Von Brana sings Elvis Presley tunes that showcase the King's love of the Islands. ⊠ *Waikīkī Beachcomber Hotel, 2300 Kalākaua Ave., Waikīkī* ☎ *808/923–1245* ☽ *Shows nightly except Tues. at 6:15.*

Creation: A Polynesian Odyssey. This show traces Hawai'i's culture and history, from its origins to statehood. The highlight is a daring Samoan fire knife dancer. ⊠ *'Āinahau Showroom, Sheraton Princess Ka'iulani Hotel, 120 Ka'iulani Ave., Waikīkī* ☎ *808/931–4660* ☽ *Dinner shows nightly except Mon. and Wed. at 6.*

Don Ho. Don Ho is the singer who put Waikīkī entertainment on the map. His song "Tiny Bubbles" would become his trademark. His show, a Polynesian revue (with a cast of young and attractive Hawaiian performers), has found the perfect home in this intimate club inside the Waikīkī Beachcomber Hotel. ⊠ *Waikīkī Beachcomber Hotel, 2300 Kalākaua Ave., Waikīkī* ☎ *808/923–3981* ☽ *Shows Sun.–Thurs. at 7, with cocktail and dinner seatings.*

Magic of Polynesia. Hawai'i's top illusionist, John Hirokawa, displays mystifying sleight of hand in this highly entertaining show, which incorporates contemporary hula and island music into its acts. ⊠ *Waikīkī Beachcomber Hotel, 2300 Kalākaua Ave., Waikīkī* ☎ *808/971–4321* ☉ *Nightly at 6:25 and 8:30.*

Polynesian Cultural Center. Easily one of the best on the Islands, this show has soaring moments and an "erupting volcano." The performers are students from Brigham Young University's Hawai'i campus. ⊠ *55-370 Kamehameha Hwy., Lā'ie* ☎ *808/293–3333 or 800/367–7060* ⊕ *www. polynesia.com* ☉ *Mon.–Sat. 12:30–9:30.*

Society of Seven. This lively, popular septet has great staying power and, after more than 25 years, continues to put on one of the best shows in Waikīkī. They sing, dance, do impersonations, play instruments, and, above all, entertain with their contemporary sound. ⊠ *Outrigger Waikīkī on the Beach, 2335 Kalākaua Ave., Waikīkī* ☎ *808/923–7469* ☉ *Mon.–Sat. at 8:30.*

Dance

Every year at least one of mainland America's finer ballet troupes makes the trip to Honolulu for a series of dance performances at the **Neal Blaisdell Center Concert Hall** (⊠ Ward Ave. at King St., Downtown Honolulu, Honolulu ☎ 808/591–2211). A local company, **Ballet Hawai'i** (☎ 808/ 988–7578), is active during the holiday season with its annual production of *The Nutcracker,* which is usually held at the **Mamiya Theater** (⊠ St. Louis School, 3142 Wai'alae Ave., Kaimukī, Honolulu).

Film

Art, international, classic, and silent films are screened at the little theater at the **Honolulu Academy of Arts** (⊠ 900 S. Beretania St., Downtown Honolulu, Honolulu ☎ 808/532–8768). **Kāhala Mall** (⊠ 4211 Wai'alae Ave., Kāhala, Honolulu ☎ 808/733–6233) has eight movie theaters showing a diverse range of films. It's a 10-minute drive from Waikīkī. **Varsity Twins Theater** (⊠ 1106 University Ave., Mō'ili'ili, Honolulu ☎ 808/973–5834) is the site for showings of internationally acclaimed independent art films. **Ward 16 Entertainment Complex** (⊠ 1044 Auahi St., Ala Moana, Honolulu ☎ 808/593–3000) is a 16-screen entertainment complex that also has restaurants like Dave and Busters and retail outlets like Roxy Sportswear.

The **Hawai'i International Film Festival** (☎ 808/528–3456) may not be Cannes, but it is unique and exciting. During the weeklong festival, held from the end of November to early December, top films from the United States, Asia, and the Pacific are screened day and night at several theaters on O'ahu.

The city-sponsored **Sunset on the Beach** (☎ 808/523–2489) events are held twice a month at various beaches. This is truly a local night out on the town. Find your spot on the beach and enjoy entertainment, food from top local restaurants, and a first-run movie feature on a big screen, all underneath the stars.

Lū'au

Most lū'au emphasize fun over strict adherence to tradition. They generally cost $45–$79. Reservations are essential, and most major credit cards are accepted.

Germaine's Lū'au. This lū'au is billed as being "100 years away from Waikīkī." Expect a lively crowd as you are bused to a private beach 35

BEYOND "TINY BUBBLES"

ASK MOST VISITORS *about Hawaiian music and they'll likely break into a lighthearted rendition of "Little Grass Shack."* When they're finished, lead them directly to a stereo.

First, play them a recording of singer Kekuhi Kanahele, whose compositions combine ancient Hawaiian chants with modern melodies. Then ask them to listen to a CD by guitarist Keola Beamer, who loosens his strings and plays slack-key tunes dating to the 1830s. Share a recording by falsetto virtuoso Amy Hanaiali`i Gilliom, one of the very few singers perpetuating the upper-register vocal style. Or play the late Israel Kamakawiwo`ole's version of "What a Wonderful World," which has appeared on scores of both feature films and national television-series episodes. "Brother Iz," who died in 1997, was a native Hawaiian with a voice so pure, most of his songs were recorded simply with voice and `ukulele. His latest album, Alone In Iz World, released posthumously, has created quite a stir.

These artists, like many others, are proving just how multifaceted Hawaiian music has become. They're unearthing their island roots in the form of revered songs and chants, and they're reinterpreting them for today's audiences. It's "chicken-skin" (goose-bumps) stuff, to be sure, and it's made only in Hawai`i.

Granted, "Little Grass Shack" does have its place in the history books. After Hawai`i became a U.S. territory in 1900, the world discovered its music thanks to touring ensembles who turned heads with swaying hips, steel guitars, and pseudo-Hawaiian lyrics. Once radio and movies got into the act, dreams of Hawai`i came with a saccharine Hollywood sound track.

But Hawaiian music is far more complex. It harks back to the sounds of the ancient islanders who beat rough-hewn drums, blew haunting calls on conch shells, and intoned repetitive chants for their gods. It recalls the voices of 19th-century Christian missionaries who taught islanders how to sing in four-part harmony, a style that's still popular today.

The music takes on international overtones thanks to gifts from foreign immigrants: the `ukulele from Portuguese laborers, for instance, and the guitar from Mexican traders. And it's enlivened by a million renderings of "Tiny Bubbles," as mainstream entertainers such as Don Ho croon Hawaiian-pop hits for Waikīkī tourists.

Island music came full circle in the late 1960s and '70s, a time termed the Hawaiian Renaissance. While the rest of the world was rockin' and rollin', a few dedicated artists began giving voice to a resurgence of interest in Hawaiian culture, history, and traditions.

Today's artistic trailblazers are digging deep to explore their heritage, and their music reflects that thoughtful search. They go one step further by incorporating such time-honored instruments as nose flutes and gourds, helping them keep pace with the past.

Why is Hawaiian music such a well-kept secret? Simply put, it's rarely played outside of the Islands. A handful of local performers are making their mark on the mainland and in Japan. But if you want to experience the true essence of Hawaiian music, you must come to Hawai`i. Check ads and listings in local papers for information on concerts, which take place in indoor and outdoor theaters, hotel ballrooms, and cozy nightclubs. When you hear the sound, you'll know it's Hawaiian because it'll make you feel right at home.

minutes from Waikīkī. The bus ride is actually a lot of fun, and the beach and the sunset are pleasant. The service is brisk in order to feed everyone on time, and the food is the usual multicourse, all-you-can-eat buffet, but the show is warm and friendly. ☎ 808/949–6626 or 800/367–5665 ⊙ Tues.–Sat. at 6.

Paradise Cove Lū'au. There are palms and a glorious sunset, and the pageantry is fun, even informative. The food—well, you didn't come for the food, did you? This is another mass-produced event for 1,000 or so. A bus takes you from one of six Waikīkī hotel pickup points to a remote beachfront estate beside a picturesque cove on the western side of the island, 27 mi from Waikīkī. ☎ 808/842–5911 ⊕ www.paradisecovehawaii.com ⊙ Daily at 5:30, doors open at 5.

Polynesian Cultural Center Ali'i Lū'au. An hour's drive from Honolulu, this North Shore O'ahu lū'au is set amid seven re-created Polynesian villages. Dinner is all-you-can-eat traditional lū'au food such as kālua pig and lomi lomi salmon, followed by a world-class revue. ☎ 808/293–3333 or 800/367–7060 ⊕ www.polynesia.com ⊙ Mon.–Sat. at 5:30.

Royal Hawaiian Lū'au. Waikīkī's only oceanfront lū'au offers an exotic, upscale menu and entertainment. With the setting sun, Diamond Head, the Pacific Ocean, and the legendary Pink Palace as backdrop, this contemporary lū'u might even make you learn to love poi. ☎ 808/923–7311 ⊙ Mon. at 6.

Music

Chamber Music Hawai'i (☎ 808/947–1975) gives 25 concerts a year at the **Honolulu Lutheran Church** (✉ 1730 Punahou St., Makiki Heights, Honolulu), **Honolulu Academy of Arts** (✉ 900 S. Beretania St., Downtown Honolulu, Honolulu), and other locations around the island.

Hawai'i Opera Theater's (✉ Neal Blaisdell Center Concert Hall, Ward Ave. and King St., Downtown Honolulu, Honolulu ☎ 808/596–7372 ⊕ www.hawaiiopera.org) season spans January–March and includes such works as *The Barber of Seville, Tristan and Isolde,* and *Madame Butterfly,* performed by renowned international opera stars and guest conductors. All operas are sung in their original language with projected English translation. Tickets range from $27–$95.

The **Honolulu Symphony Orchestra** (✉ Dole Cannery, 650 Iwilei Rd., Suite 202, Iwilei, Honolulu ☎ 808/792–2000 ⊕ www.honolulusymphony.com ☎ $17–$59) performs at the Neil Blaisdell Concert Hall and is led by the young, dynamic Samuel Wong. The Honolulu Pops series, with some performances underneath the stars summer nights at the Waikīkī Shell, features top local and national artists under the direction of talented conductor-composer Matt Catingub.

Rock concerts are usually performed at the domed **Neal Blaisdell Center Arena** (☎ 808/591–2211). Internationally famous performers pack them in at **Aloha Stadium** (☎ 808/486–9300).

Theater

Because many of today's touring shows and music artists depend on major theatrical sets, lighting, and sound, Hawai'i, already pricey, can be an expensive gig. As a result, not many touring companies manage to stop here—those who do sell out fast. There is strong community support for local performing arts companies. O'ahu has developed several excellent local theater troupes, which present first-rate entertainment on an amateur and semiprofessional level all year long.

Army Community Theatre. This is a favorite for its revivals of musical theater classics, presented in an 800-seat house. The casts are talented, and the fare is great for families. ☒ *Richardson Theater, Fort Shafter, Downtown Honolulu, Honolulu* ☎ *808/438–4480* ☎ *$14–$20.*

Diamond Head Theater. The repertoire includes a little of everything: musicals, dramas, experimental productions, and classics. This company is in residence five minutes from Waikīkī, right next to Diamond Head. ☒ *520 Makapuʻu Ave., Kapahulu, Honolulu* ☎ *808/733–0274* ⊕ *www.diamondheadtheater.com* ☎ *$10–$40.*

Hawaiʻi Theatre Center. Beautifully restored, this Downtown Honolulu theater, built in the 1920s in a neoclassic beaux arts style, hosts a wide variety of performing arts events, including international theatrical productions, international touring acts, festivals, films, and meetings. Historic tours of the theater are offered Tuesday at 11 for $5. ☒ *1130 Bethel St., Downtown Honolulu, Honolulu* ☎ *808/528–0506* ⊕ *www.hawaiitheatre.com* ☎ *Varies.*

ⓒ **Honolulu Theater for Youth.** This group stages delightful productions for children around the Islands from September through May. Call for a schedule. ☒ *2846 Ualena St., Downtown Honolulu, Honolulu* ☎ *808/839–9885* ☎ *$10.*

John F. Kennedy Theater. Eclectic dramatic offerings—everything from musical theater to Kabuki, Nō, and Chinese opera—are performed at this space at the University of Hawaiʻi's Mānoa campus. ☒ *1770 East–West Rd., Mānoa, Honolulu* ☎ *808/956–7655* ☎ *$9–$12.*

Kumu Kahua. This is the only troupe presenting shows and plays written by local playwrights about the Islands. It stages five or six productions a year. ☒ *46 Merchant St., Downtown Honolulu, Honolulu* ☎ *808/536–4441* ☎ *$12–$15.*

Mānoa Valley Theater. Wonderful nonprofessional performances are put on in this intimate theater in Mānoa Valley from September through July. ☒ *2833 E. Mānoa Rd., Mānoa, Honolulu* ☎ *808/988–6131* ☎ *$17–$20.*

SPORTS & THE OUTDOORS

Biking

Coastal roads are flat and well paved. On the downside, they're also awash in vehicular traffic. Frankly, biking is no fun in either Waikīkī or Honolulu, but things are a bit better outside the city. Be sure to take along a nylon jacket for the frequent showers on the windward side and remember that Hawaiʻi is Paradise after the Fall: lock up your bike.

Mountain bikes are available for rent at **Blue Sky Rentals & Sports Center** (☒ 1920 Ala Moana Blvd., across from the Hilton Hawaiian Village, Waikīkī, Honolulu ☎ 808/947–0101). Rates are $18 per day (from 8 to 6), $26 for 24 hours, and $75 per week—a $25 deposit is required for weekly rentals. Prices include bike, helmet, lock, and a water bottle.

If you want to find some biking buddies, write ahead to the **Hawaiʻi Bicycling League** (☒ Box 4403, Honolulu 96813 ☎ 808/735–5756 ⊕ www.bikehawaii.com), which can tell you about upcoming races and club rides (frequent on all the Islands).

For biking information and maps, contact the **Honolulu City and County Bike Coordinator** (☎ 808/527–5044).

Tour Oʻahu's North Shore by bike with guided tours from **Waimea Falls Park** (☒ 59-864 Kamehameha Hwy., Haleʻiwa ☎ 808/638–8511). Admission to the park is $24, with additional charges based on the activity package chosen.

Professional mountain bikers come to Oʻahu each year for the **Outrigger Hotels Hawaiian Mountain Tour** (☎ 808/921–6941), a four-day, five-stage race across the most rugged terrain of the windward coast.

Camping & Hiking

For a free Oʻahu recreation map that outlines the island's 33 major trails, including the visitor-friendly Mānoa Falls Trail, Makapuʻu Lighthouse Trail, Waʻahila Ridge Trail, and Leeward's Oʻahu's Kaena Point, contact the **Hawaiʻi State Department of Land and Natural Resources** (✉ 1151 Punchbowl St., Room 130, Downtown Honolulu, Honolulu 96813 ☎ 808/587–0300 ⊕ www.hawaii.gov).

For a complimentary hiking-safety guide, contact the City and County of Honolulu's **Trails and Access Manager** (☎ 808/973–9782). Ask for a copy of "Hiking on Oʻahu: The Official Guide."

For families, the **Hawaiʻi Nature Center** (✉ 2131 Makiki Heights Dr., Makiki Heights, Honolulu 96822 ☎ 808/955–0100) in upper Makiki Valley conducts a number of programs for both adults and children. The center arranges guided hikes into tropical settings that reveal hidden waterfalls and protected forest reserves. **Oʻahu Nature Tours** (☎ 808/924–2473 or 800/861–6018 ⊕ www.oahunaturetours.com) offers glorious sunrise, rain-forest, and volcanic walking tours with an escort who will explain the wealth of native flora and fauna that is your companion along the way.

When on the North Shore, check out the **Trails at Turtle Bay Resort** (✉ Turtle Bay Resort, 57-091 Kamehameha Hwy. ☎ 808/293–8811 ⊕ www.turtlebayresort.com)—more than 12 mi of trails and oceanside pathways on this 880-acre resort. You can pick up a trail and ocean guide for a self-guided tour of the 5 mi of coastline and its exotic plants and trees.

Camping on Oʻahu is available at four state parks, 12 county beach parks, and within the grounds of one county botanic garden. Stays are restricted to five nights per month in all beach and state recreation areas, and parks are closed to campers on Wednesday and Thursday evenings. To obtain a free camping permit for state parks, write to the **Department of Land and Natural Resources, State Parks Division** (✉ Box 621, Honolulu 96809 ☎ 808/587–0300). For county and beach parks, contact the **Honolulu Department of Parks and Recreation** (✉ 650 S. King St., Honolulu 96813 ☎ 808/523–4525). A word of caution: although some Oʻahu recreation areas have caretakers and gates that close in the evening for your safety, many others can be quite isolated at night.

Mālaekahana State Park on the North Shore is a local favorite and offers a beachfront setting with two areas that include rest rooms, showers, picnic tables, and drinking water. It's on Kamehameha Highway between Lāʻie and Kahuku. On the windward coast, **Hoʻomaluhia Botanic Gardens** (✉ 45-680 Luluku Rd., Kaneohe ☎ 808/523–4525) provides a safe, scenic camping setting at the base of the majestic Koʻolau Mountains. Five grassy camping areas with rest rooms, showers, and drinking water are available on Friday, Saturday, and Sunday evenings only. Permits are free and are issued at the garden daily between 9 and 4.

You can rent everything from tents to backpacks at the **Bike Shop** (✉ 1149 S. King St., Mōʻiliʻili, Honolulu ☎ 808/595–0588 ⊕ www.bikeshophawaii.com).

Fitness Centers & Spas

HONOLULU

Abhasa Spa. Cold laser antiaging treatments, vegetarian lifestyle–spa therapies, color-light therapy, and body cocooning are all available here in this spa tucked away in the Royal Hawaiian Hotel's coconut grove. ⊠ *Royal Hawaiian Hotel, 2259 Kalākaua Ave., Waikīkī* ☎ *808/922–8200.*

Ampy's European Facials and Body Spa. Indulge in this spa's famous custom aromatherapy facials; massages; and day-spa packages, including a Gentlemen's Retreat. It's in the Ala Moana Building, adjacent to Ala Moana Shopping Center. ⊠ *1441 Kapi'olani Blvd., Ala Moana* ☎ *808/946–3838.*

Clark Hatch Physical Fitness Center. Weight-training facilities, an indoor pool, a racquetball court, aerobics classes, and treadmills are all available at this club. ⊠ *745 Fort St., Downtown Honolulu* ☎ *808/536–7205* 🖃 *About $10 per day.*

Hawaiian Rainforest Salon and Spa. Vichy showers; a sauna; facial and massage treatments; and complete hair, nail, and makeup services are available here. ⊠ *Pacific Beach Hotel, 5th floor, 2490 Kalākaua Ave., Waikīkī* ☎ *808/441–4890.*

Na Ho'ola at the Hyatt Waikīkī. Come here for an authentic Hawaiian spa experience with poolside *lomi lomi* (Hawaiian massage), Reiki treatments, ti-leaf and Polynesian aloe body wraps, and La Stone (Swedish massage is combined with the use of hot and cold stones) therapies. The spa also features a fitness center with cardiovascular equipment and an ocean view. ⊠ *2424 Kalākaua Ave., Waikīkī* ☎ *808/921–6097.*

Paul Brown Salon and Day Spa. This is one of the few salons where the principal owner still works the floor. The spa's location makes it an ideal spot to take a break from shopping at the Victoria Ward Centre—get a tropical-fruit facial or mineral body wrap and follow it up with an aromatherapy massage. The spa also has a full-service hair salon. ⊠ *Ward Centre, 1200 Ala Moana Blvd., Ala Moana* ☎ *808/591–1881* ⊕ *www.paulbrownhawaii.com.*

Serenity Spa Hawai'i. Aromatherapy treatments, massages, and facials are provided in an atmosphere of serene calm, only steps off the beach. ⊠ *Outrigger Reef on the Beach, 2169 Kālia Rd., Waikīkī* ☎ *808/926–2882* ⊕ *www.serenityspahawaii.com.*

Spa Suites at the Kāhala Mandarin Oriental. The Kāhala Mandarin Oriental has created spa suites so luxurious you might never want to leave. Each suite features a Jacuzzi, a private vanity area, and a private garden in which to relax between treatments. Treatments are custom designed and merge Hawaiian, Asian, and traditional therapies. ⊠ *Kāhala Mandarin Oriental, 5000 Kāhala Ave., Kāhala* ☎ *808/739–8938.*

24-Hour Fitness. Waikīkī's most accessible fitness center has weight-training machines, cardiovascular equipment, free weights, and a pro shop. Admission is $10 per day for guests of many Waikīkī hotels (call for a list) and $20 for all others. ⊠ *Pacific Beach Hotel, 2nd floor, 2490 Kalākaua Ave., Waikīkī* ☎ *808/971–4653.*

AROUND THE ISLAND

J. W. Marriott 'Ihilani Resort & Spa. About 25 minutes from the airport is O'ahu's largest health and fitness center. There are 35,000 square ft of space for classes, weight rooms, relaxation programs, hydrotherapies, detoxifying wraps, and exotic revitalizing beauty treatments. Call to get prices and to arrange nonguest privileges. ⊠ *J. W. Marriott 'Ihilani Resort & Spa, 92-1001 'Ōlani St., Kapolei* ☎ *808/679–0079* ⊕ *www.ihilani.com.*

The Spa at Turtle Bay Resort. Luxuriate at the ocean's edge at this serene spa, which offers custom massage treatments and beauty rituals, including a full-service hair and nail salon. The Pipeline sports massage provides deep-tissue relaxation, while the seaweed wrap is a soothing way to detox-ify. In addition to in-spa treatments, there are private spa suites, a fit-ness center and an outdoor exercise studio, and a lounge area and juice bar. ⊠ *Turtle Bay Resort, 57-091 Kamehameha Hwy., North Shore* ☎ *808/293–8811* ⊕ *www.turtlebayresort.com.*

Football

Seen nationwide on ESPN on Christmas Day is the collegiate **Hula Bowl** (☎ 808/486–9300) from Aloha Stadium in Honolulu. The nationally tele-vised **NFL Pro Bowl** (☎ 808/486–9300) is held in early February at Aloha Stadium in Honolulu. The **University of Hawai'i Warriors** (☎ 808/956–6508) take to the field at Aloha Stadium in season, with a big local fol-lowing. There are often express buses to games from Kapi'olani Park.

Golf

O'ahu has more than three dozen public and private golf courses. Hotel concierges can assist with tee times and transportation. To get a pre-view before you arrive, check out ⊕ www.808golf.com, which offers a comprehensive on-line guide to Hawai'i golf, including course descrip-tions and tee-time reservations. For last-minute tee times, consult Standby Golf at 888/645–2665. Standby Golf has access to 39 courses on O'ahu, and it is possible to book some courses a day ahead of time at reason-able rates.

Ala Wai Golf Course. One of the most popular municipal 18-hole courses is on Waikīkī's mauka end, across the Ala Wai Canal. It's par 70 on 6,424 yards and has a pro shop and a restaurant. There's always a waiting list for tee times, so if you plan to play, call the minute you land. ⊠ *404 Kapahulu Ave., Waikīkī, Honolulu* ☎ *808/733–7387* ⊠ *Greens fee $42; cart $16.*

Coral Creek Golf Course. Located on the 'Ewa Beach plains, about 40 min-utes from Waikīkī, this 18-hole, 6,808-yard, par-72 course offers wind challenges, ravines, coral rock formations, and lakes. Club rental is avail-able. ⊠ *91-1111 Geiger Rd., 'Ewa Beach* ☎ *808/441–4653* ⊠ *Greens fee $125, cart included.*

Hawai'i Kai Championship Course. Advance reservations are recom-mended at this 18-hole, 6,222-yard course and the neighboring 18-hole, 2,386-yard Hawai'i Kai Executive Course. ⊠ *8902 Kalaniana'ole Hwy., Hawai'i Kai, Honolulu* ☎ *808/395–2358* ⊕ *www.hawaiikaigolf.com* ⊠ *Greens fee weekdays $105 for Championship Course and $37 for Executive Course, weekends $110, cart included.*

Hawai'i Prince Golf Club. This 27-hole Arnold Palmer–designed course welcomes visiting players. ⊠ *91-1200 Ft. Weaver Rd., 'Ewa Beach* ☎ *808/944–4567* ⊠ *Greens fee $90 guests, $135 nonguests, cart in-cluded.*

Kahuku Golf Course. The 9-hole walking-only course is played more by locals than by visitors, but serves up some stunning North Shore natu-ral beauty. ⊠ *56-501 Kamehameha Hwy., Kahuku* ☎ *808/293–5842* ⊠ *Greens fee $20 nonresidents; hand-cart rental $4.*

Ko Olina Golf Club. This club on O'ahu's west side is affiliated with the 'Ihilani Resort. Its 18 holes are beautifully landscaped with waterfalls and ponds where black and white swans serve as your gallery. ⊠ *Ko*

Olina Resort, 92-1220 Ali'inui Dr., Kapolei ☎ 808/676–5300 ⊕ www. koolina.com ✉ Greens fee $145, cart included.

Ko'olau Golf Club. This 18-hole, par-72 course on O'ahu's windward side in Kaneohe is officially rated by the United States Golf Association as the most difficult golf course in the country. Up for the challenge? ✉ 45-550 Kionaole Rd., Kaneohe ☎ 808/236–4653 ✉ Greens fee $100, cart included.

Luana Hills Country Club. The front 9 of this Peter and Perry Dye–designed 18-hole, par-72 course is carved into the slopes of Mount Olomana. ✉ 770 Auloa Rd., Kailua ☎ 808/262–2139 ✉ Greens fee $95, cart included.

Mākaha Valley Country Golf Club. Two exceptional 18-hole courses here offer a beautiful valley setting. ✉ 84-627 Mākaha Valley Rd., Wai'anae ☎ 808/695–9578 ✉ Greens fee $125 until noon, $95 noon–2:30, $80 2:30–closing, cart included.

Mililani Golf Club. The tree-lined greens at this par-72, 6,455-yard course afford magnificent views of the surrounding Ko'olau and Wai'anae mountain ranges. ✉ 95-176 Kuahelani Ave., Mililani ☎ 808/623–2222 ⊕ www.mililanigolf.com ✉ Greens fee $89, cart included.

Olomana Golf Links. This par-72, 6,326-yard course features hills and some interesting water hazards, not to mention a backdrop of the sheer cliffs of the Ko'olau Mountains. ✉ 41-1801 Kalanianaole Hwy., Waimānalo ☎ 808/259–7626 ✉ Greens fee $67, cart included.

Turtle Bay Resort Golf Club. Turtle Bay's renovation has included its two golf courses: both courses have been regrassed and landscaped using the salt-tolerant seashore paspalum grass. The championship par-72 Palmer Course measures 6,225 yards and offers a combination of Scottish links–type play along with a tropical back 9. The Fazio course is the only course in the Islands designed by George Fazio; it has a newly re-vamped back 9 with new 13th and 14th holes and a slightly shorter but more difficult 18th hole that features a 160-yard carry over wetlands. ✉ Turtle Bay Resort, 57-091 Kamehameha Hwy., Kahuku ☎ 808/ 293–8574 ✉ Greens fee $90 guests, $135 nonguests, cart included.

ON THE SIDELINES The giants of the greens return to Hawai'i every January or February (depending on TV scheduling) to compete in the **Sony Open Golf Tour-nament** (☎ 808/734–2151), a PGA tour regular with a $1 million purse. It's held at the exclusive Wai'alae Country Club in Kāhala, and it's al-ways a crowd pleaser.

Horseback Riding

Kualoa Ranch. This ranch across from Kualoa Beach Park leads trail rides in Ka'a'awa, one of the most beautiful valleys in all Hawai'i. Trail rides cost between $35 and $99. Kualoa has other activities as well, such as windsurfing, jet skiing, all-terrain-vehicle trail rides, and children's ac-tivities. ✉ 49-560 Kamehameha Hwy., Ka'a'awa ☎ 808/237–8515 ⊕ www.kualoa.com.

Waimea Falls Park. Take a guided horseback trail ride through the ver-dant Waimea Valley. Admission is $24 to the park, with various addi-tional charges depending on the activity package chosen. ✉ 59-864 Kamehameha Hwy., Haliewa ☎ 808/638–5300.

Jogging

In Honolulu, the most popular places to jog are the two parks, **Kapi'olani** and **Ala Moana**, at either end of Waikīkī. In both cases, the loop around the park is just under 2 mi. You can run a 4½-mi ring around **Diamond Head crater,** past scenic views, luxurious homes, and herds of other joggers. If you're looking for jogging companions, show up for the free **Honolulu Marathon Clinic,** which starts at the Kapi'olani Bandstand March–November, Sunday at 7:30 AM.

Once you leave Honolulu, it gets trickier to find places to jog that are scenic as well as safe. It's best to stick to the well-traveled routes, or ask the experienced folks at the **Running Room** (⊠ 819 Kapahulu Ave., Kapahulu, Honolulu ☎ 808/737–2422) for advice.

The "Honolulu Walking Map" and "The Fitness Fun Map" are free from the **Hawai'i State Department of Health Community Resources Section** (⊠ 1250 Punchbowl St., Room 217, Downtown Honolulu, Honolulu ☎ 808/586–4661). These list more than two dozen routes and suggested itineraries for seeing O'ahu on foot.

ON THE
SIDELINES

The **Honolulu Marathon** is a thrilling event to watch as well as to participate in. Join the throngs who cheer at the finish line at Kapi'olani Park as internationally famous and local runners tackle the 26.2-mi challenge. It's held on the second Sunday in December and is sponsored by the **Honolulu Marathon Association** (☎ 808/734–7200 ⊕ www.honolulumarathon.org).

Tennis

O'ahu has 181 public tennis courts that are free and open for play on a first-come, first-served basis; you're limited to 45 minutes of court time if others are waiting to play. A complete listing is available free of charge from the **Department of Parks and Recreation** (⊠ Tennis Unit, 650 S. King St., Honolulu 96813 ☎ 808/971–7150 ⊕ www.co.honolulu.hi.us).

Kapi'olani Park, on the Diamond Head end of Waikīkī, has two tennis locations. The **Diamond Head Tennis Center** (⊠ 3908 Pākī Ave. ☎ 808/971–7150), on the mauka side of Kapi'olani Park, has nine courts open to the public. There are more than a dozen courts for play at **Kapi'olani Tennis Courts** (⊠ 2748 Kalākaua Ave. ☎ 808/971–2510). The closest public courts to the 'ewa end of Waikīkī are in **Ala Moana Park** (⊠ Makai side of Ala Moana Blvd. ☎ 808/592–7031).

A few Waikīkī hotels have tennis courts that are open to nonguests for a fee. There's one championship tennis court located on the third-floor recreation deck of the **Waikīkī Beach Marriott Resort** (⊠ 2552 Kalākaua Ave. ☎ 808/922–6611). Two tennis courts and tennis lessons are available at the **Pacific Beach Hotel** (⊠ 2490 Kalākaua Ave., Waikīkī ☎ 808/922–1233).

Forty-five minutes from Waikīkī, on O'ahu's Ewa Plain, are two championship tennis courts at the **Hawai'i Prince Golf Club** (⊠ 91-1200 Ft. Weaver Rd., 'Ewa Beach ☎ 808/944–4567); shuttle service is available from the Hawai'i Prince Hotel Waikīkī for hotel guests.

Triathlon

Swim-bike-run events are gaining in popularity and number in Hawai'i. Most fun to watch (or compete in) is the **Tinman Triathlon** (☎ 808/732–7311), held in mid-July in Waikīkī.

Volleyball

Volleyball is extremely popular on the Islands, and no wonder. Both the men's and women's teams of the **University of Hawai'i** have blasted to a number one ranking in years past. Crowded, noisy, and very exciting home games are played from September through December (women's) and from January through April (men's) in the university's 10,000-seat Stan Sheriff Arena. ⊠ *Lower Campus Rd., Honolulu* ☎ *808/956–4481* ⊠ *$8.*

Water Park

Hawaiian Waters Adventure Park. Get wet and wild at this 29-acre water-theme park with a football field–size wave pool, inner-tube cruising, and multistory waterslides. A children's water world of delight has a kids' pool, waterfalls, minislides, and animal floaties. It's in Kapolei, mauka of the H-1 Freeway on Farrington Highway, 15 minutes from the Honolulu International Airport. ⊠ *91-400 Farrington Hwy., Kapolei* ☎ *808/674–9283* ⊕ *www.hawaiianwaters.com* ⊠ *$30.*

Water Sports

The seemingly endless ocean options can be arranged through any hotel travel desk or beach concession. Try the **Waikīkī Beach Center,** next to the Sheraton Moana Surfrider, or the **C & K Beach Service,** by the Hilton Hawaiian Village (no telephones).

DEEP-SEA FISHING **Inter-Island Sportfishing** (☎ 808/591–8888 ⊕ www.fish-hawaii.com) operates four vessels available for exclusive or shared deep-sea fishing charters. Rates range from $165 to $1,000 per day, depending on whether you choose an exclusive charter or share one with five other anglers. If the "big one" doesn't get away, Inter-Island will arrange to have your trophy fish mounted and sent to you. Departures for charters are from Kewalo Basin. **Magic Sportfishing** (☎ 808/596–2998 ⊕ www.magicsportfishing.com) offers shared and private charters; rates range from $120 to $650 per day.

OCEAN KAYAKING This dynamic sport is catching on fast in the Islands. On the North Shore, kayak lessons are available from **Kayak O'ahu Adventures** (⊠ Waimea Valley Adventures Park, 59-894 Kamehameha Hwy. ☎ 808/638–8189). You can kayak the "surfing waters of the kings" off Waikīkī with assistance from **Prime Time Sports** (⊠ Ft. DeRussy Beach ☎ 808/949–8952). Bob Twogood, a name that is synonymous with O'ahu kayaking, runs a shop called **Twogood Kayaks Hawai'i** (⊠ 345 Hahani St., Kailua ☎ 808/262–5656 ⊕ www.aloha.com/~twogood), which makes, rents, and sells the fiberglass craft. Twogood rents solo kayaks for $25 a half day and $32 for a full day. Tandems are $32 a half day and $42 for a full day, including kayak delivery and pickup across from Kailua Beach.

SAILING **Honolulu Sailing Company** (☎ 808/239–3900 ⊕ www.honsail.com) offers a variety of sailing options as well as sailing instruction. Departures are from Pier 2, Honolulu Harbor.

SCUBA DIVING & SNORKELING **South Seas Aquatics** (☎ 808/922–0852) offers two-tank boat dives at various sites for $75. Several certification courses are available; call for rates. On the North Shore, **Surf-N-Sea** (☎ 808/637–3337 ⊕ www.surfnsea.com) conducts a variety of dive excursions, including night dives. A two-tank excursion starts at $65. Night dives begin at $80.

The most famous snorkeling spot in Hawai'i is Hanauma Bay. You can get masks, fins, and snorkels at the **rental stand** (☎ 808/395–4725) right at the park. **Hanauma Bay Snorkeling Excursions** (☎ 808/373–5060) provides transport from Waikīkī and costs $20 round-trip, including park admission, snorkeling gear, and lessons. You can pick up snorkeling equipment and site advice from **Snorkel Bob's** (✉ 700 Kapahulu Ave. ☎ 808/735–7944), conveniently located on the way to Hanauma Bay.

Area dive sites include the following:

Hanauma Bay. East of Koko Head, this bay is an underwater state park and a popular dive site. The shallow inner reef gradually drops from 10 ft to 70 ft at the outer reef. Expect to see butterfly fish, goatfish, parrot fish, surgeon fish, and sea turtles.

Mahi Wai'anae. This 165-ft minesweeper was sunk in 1982 in the waters just south of Wai'anae on Oʻahu's leeward coast to create an artificial reef. It's intact and penetrable. Goatfish, tame lemon butterfly fish, blue-striped snapper, and 6-ft moray eels can be seen hanging out here. Depths are from 50 ft to 90 ft.

Maunalua Bay. East of Diamond Head, Maunalua Bay has several sites, including Turtle Canyon, with lava flow ridges and sandy canyons teeming with green sea turtles of all sizes; *Kāhala Barge,* a penetrable, 200-ft sunken vessel; Big Eel Reef, with many varieties of moray eels; and Fantasy Reef, a series of lava ledges and archways populated with barracuda and eels.

Shark's Cove. You can dive from this North Shore site during summer months only and should be explored only by experienced divers. Sunlight from above creates a stained-glass effect in the large, roomy caverns. Easily accessible from shore, the cove has depths ranging from 15 ft to 45 ft. This is the most popular cavern dive on the island.

Three Tables. Named for the trio of flat rocks that break the surface near the beach, this North Shore site has easy access from the shore. Beneath the waves are large rock formations, caverns, and ledges. It's divable only in the summer months.

SURFING
★
To rent a board in Waikīkī, visit **C&K Beach Service** (☎ no phone), on the beach fronting the Hilton Hawaiian Village. Rentals cost $8 to $10 per hour, depending on the size of the board, and $12 for two hours. Small group lessons are $30 per hour with board, and they promise to have you riding the waves by lesson's end.

Surfing and bodysurfing instruction from the staff of Hans Hedemann—who spent 17 years on the professional surfer World Tour circuit—is available for $50 per hour for group lessons and $90 for private lessons at the Waikīkī **Hans Hedemann Surf Hawaii** (☎ 808/923–7779).

Novice surfers can meet with guaranteed success with lessons from some of Hawai'i's most knowledgeable water-safety experts—off-duty Honolulu firefighters—who man the boards at one of Hawai'i's hottest new surfing schools, **Hawaiian Fire, Inc.** (☎ 808/384–8855). Lessons ($100 per session) include equipment, safety and surfing instruction, and two hours of surfing time (with lunch break) at a secluded beach near Barbers Point. Transportation is available from Waikīkī.

North Shore Eco-Surf Tours (☎ 808/638–9503) will set you up with a surf tour that is not only exhilarating but educational, too. On the North Shore, rent a short board for $5 an hour or a long board for $7 from a shop called **Surf-N-Sea** (☎ 808/637–9887). Lessons cost $65 for three hours and start daily at 1 PM.

In winter head out to the North Shore to watch the best surfers in the world hang ten during the **Van's Triple Crown Hawaiian Pro Surfing Cham-**

pionships (☎ 808/596–7877). This two-day event, scheduled according to wave conditions, is generally held at the Banzai Pipeline and Sunset Beach during November and December.

WATERSKIING **Hawaii Sports Wakeboard and Water Ski Center** (✉ Koko Marina Shopping Center, 7192 Kalaniana'ole Hwy., Hawai'i Kai ☎ 808/395–3773) has a package with round-trip transportation from Waikīkī and a half day of waterskiing in Hawai'i Kai Marina for $110 per hour per person (two-person minimum), with lessons. There are also rides in inflatable banana boats and bumper tubes for children of all ages.

WINDSURFING This sport was born in Hawai'i, and O'ahu's Kailua Beach is its cradle. **Kailua Sailboard and Kayaks Company** (✉ 130 Kailua Rd., Kailua ☎ 808/262–2555) offers small group lessons, rents equipment, and transports everything to the waterfront. World champion Robby Naish and his family build and sell boards, rent equipment, provide accommodations referrals, and offer windsurfing and kiteboarding instruction out of **Naish Hawai'i** (✉ 155A Hamakua Dr., Kailua ☎ 808/261–6067 ⊕ www.naish.com). A four-hour package, including 90 minutes of instruction, costs $55. **North Shore Windsurfing School** (✉ 59-452 Makana Rd., Hale'iwa ☎ 808/638–8198) offers expert instruction, but you have to bring your own board. **Surf-N-Sea** (✉ 7192 Kalaniana'ole Hwy., Hale'iwa ☎ 808/637–9887) rents windsurfing gear for $12 per hour; a two-hour windsurfing lesson costs $58.

Watch the pros jump and spin on the waves during July's **Pan Am Hawaiian Windsurfing World Cup** (☎ 808/734–6999) off Kailua Beach. For windsurfing competitions off Diamond Head point, check out August's **Wahine Classic** (☎ 808/521–4322), featuring the world's best female boardsailors.

SHOPPING

Honolulu is the number one shopping spot in the Islands and an international crossroads of the shopping scene. It has sprawling shopping malls, unique boutiques, hotel arcades, neighborhood businesses, and a variety of other enterprises. Major shopping malls are generally open daily 10–9; smaller neighborhood boutiques are usually 9-to-5 operations.

Shopping Centers

In Honolulu

Ala Moana Shopping Center (✉ 1450 Ala Moana Blvd., Ala Moana ☎ 808/955–9517 special-events and shuttle service) is one of the nation's largest open-air malls and just five minutes from Waikīkī by bus. More than 240 stores and 60 restaurants make up this 50-acre complex. All of Hawai'i's major department stores are here, including Neiman Marcus, Sears, and Macy's. Palm Boulevard features upscale designer fashions, such as Gucci, Louis Vuitton, Gianni Versace, and Emporio Armani.

Aloha Tower Marketplace (✉ 1 Aloha Tower Dr., at Piers 8, 9, and 10, Downtown Honolulu ☎ 808/566–2337 ⊕ www.alohatower.com/atm) cozies up to Honolulu Harbor and bills itself as a festival marketplace. Along with restaurants and entertainment venues, it has 80 shops and kiosks selling mostly visitor-oriented merchandise, from expensive sunglasses to souvenir refrigerator magnets.

DFS Galleria Waikīkī (✉ corner of Kalākaua and Royal Hawaiian Aves., Waikīkī ☎ 808/931–2655) has boutiques of world-class designers—such as Hermès, Cartier, and Calvin Klein—as well as Hawai'i's largest beauty and cosmetic store. An old Hawai'i atmosphere is created by a three-story replica of a 1920s luxury cruise liner; daily Hawaiian music and dance performances; and the Waikīkī Walk, with authentic fashions, arts and crafts, and gifts of the Hawaiian Islands. There is also an exclusive boutique floor available to duty-free shoppers only. The Kalia Grill and Starbucks offer a respite for weary shoppers.

Kāhala Mall (✉ 4211 Wai'alae Ave., Kāhala ☎ 808/732–7736) has 90 retail outlets including Macy's, Gap, Reyn's Aloha Wear, and Barnes & Noble. Restaurants range from quick-bite venues to leisurely meal places. Kāhala Mall's Main Stage spotlights entertaining arts performances ranging from local ballet to contemporary Hawaiian music concerts weekends and evenings. Along with an assortment of gift shops, Kāhala Mall also has **eight movie theaters** (☎ 808/733–6233) for post-shopping entertainment. The mall is 10 minutes by car from Waikīkī in the chic residential neighborhood of Kāhala, near the slopes of Diamond Head.

The fashionable **King Kalākaua Plaza** (✉ 2080 Kalākaua Ave., Waikīkī ☎ 808/955–2878), one of Waikīkī's newer shopping destinations, offers flagship stores Banana Republic and Nike Town as well as the All Sports Hawaii Cafe.

The **Royal Hawaiian Shopping Center** (✉ 2201 Kalākaua Ave., Waikīkī ☎ 808/922–0588 ⊕ www.shopwaikiki.com), fronting the Royal Hawaiian and Sheraton Waikīkī hotels, is three blocks long and contains 150 stores on four levels. Browse through the Hawaiian Heirloom Jewelry Collection by Philip Rickard, which also has a museum with Victorian jewelry pieces. Bike buffs can check out the Harley-Davidson MotorClothes and Collectibles Boutique. The center has 15 restaurants, including the Paradiso Seafood Grill and Villa Paradiso, and even has a post office.

2100 Kalākaua (✉ 2100 Kalākaua Ave., Waikīkī ☎ 808/550–4449 ⊕ www.2100kalakaua.com) is the newest addition to the island retail scene. Many of the world's top designers have boutiques in this unique three-story town-house-style center. Its tenants include Chanel, Tiffany & Co., Yves Saint Laurent, Gucci, and Tod and Bocheron. The bronze statue fronting the center was created by Japanese artist Shige Yamada.

Heading west from Waikīkī toward Downtown Honolulu, you'll run into a section of town with five distinct shopping-complex areas known as the **Victoria Ward Centers**; there are more than 100 specialty shops and 17 restaurants here. The Ward 16 Entertainment Complex features 16 movie theaters. A "Shopping Concierge" can assist you in navigating your way through the center's five complexes, which span four city blocks. Two of the largest and most popular complexes are **Ward Warehouse** (✉ 1050 Ala Moana Blvd., Ala Moana) and **Ward Centre** (✉ Ward Centre, 1200 Ala Moana Blvd., Ala Moana).

Waikīkī Shopping Plaza (✉ 2270 Kalākaua Ave., Waikīkī ☎ 808/923–1111) is across the street from the Royal Hawaiian Shopping Center. Its landmark is a 75-ft-high water-sculpture gizmo, which looks great when it's working. Walden Books, Guess, Clio Blue jewelers, and Tanaka of Tokyo Restaurant are some of the 50 shops and restaurants on six floors.

Waikīkī has three theme park–style shopping centers. Right in the heart of the area is the **International Market Place** (✉ 2330 Kalākaua Ave., Waikīkī ☎ 808/971–2080), a tangle of 150 souvenir shops and stalls under a giant banyan tree. **King's Village** (✉ 131 Ka'iulani Ave., Waikīkī ☎ 808/

944–6855) looks like a Hollywood stage set of monarchy-era Honolulu, complete with a changing-of-the-guard ceremony every evening at 6:15; shops include Hawaiian Island Creations Jewelry, Swim City USA Swimwear, and Island Motor Sports. **Waikīkī Town Center** (✉ 2301 Kūhiō Ave., Waikīkī ☏ 808/922–2724) is an open-air complex with a variety of shops ranging from fashions to jewelry. There are free hula shows here Monday, Wednesday, Friday, and Saturday at 7 PM.

Around the Island

Aloha Flea Market (✉ 99-500 Salt Lake Blvd., 'Aiea ☏ 808/732–9611 or 808/486–1529) is a thrice-weekly outdoor bazaar that attracts hundreds of vendors and even more bargain hunters. Every Hawaiian souvenir imaginable can be found here, from coral shell necklaces to bikinis, as well as a variety of ethnic wares, from Chinese brocade dresses to Japanese pottery. There are also ethnic foods, silk flowers, and luggage in aloha floral prints. Wear comfortable shoes, use sunscreen, and bring bottled water to make this outing even more enjoyable. The flea market takes place in the Aloha Stadium parking lot Wednesday and weekends from 6 to 3; the $6 admission fee includes round-trip shuttle service from Waikīkī.

While playing on the North Shore, check out the **North Shore Marketplace** (✉ 66-250 Kamehameha Hwy., Haleiwa ☏ 808/637–7000) for boutiques like the Silver Moon Emporium for vintage clothing, Patagonia for adventure wear, and North Shore Custom and Design Swimwear for mix-and-match bikinis off the rack.

The **Waikele Premium Outlets** (✉ H-1 Fwy., Waikele, 30 minutes west of Downtown Honolulu, Waikele ☏ 808/676–5656) reflects Hawai'i's latest craze: manufacturer-direct shopping at discount prices. Among its tenants are the Anne Klein Factory, Donna Karan Company Store, Kenneth Cole, and Saks Fifth Avenue Outlet.

Specialty Stores

Clothing

HIGH FASHION Tucked away on the windward side in Kailua, **Adasa** (✉ 25 Maluniu Ave., Kailua ☏ 808/263–8500) offers up some of the world's hippest clothing and accessories from designers like Flavio Olivera and Marc Jacobs. **Anne Namba Designs** (✉ 324 Kamani St., Downtown Honolulu ☏ 808/589–1135) takes the beauty of classic kimonos and creates the most contemporary of fashions. In addition to women's apparel, she also features a men's line and a stunningly beautiful wedding couture line.

Top-of-the-line international fashions for men and women are available at **Mandalay Imports** (✉ Halekūlani, 2199 Kālia Rd., Waikīkī ☏ 808/922–7766), home of Star of Siam silks and cottons, Anne Namba couture, and designs by Choisy, who works out of Bangkok. **Neiman Marcus** (✉ Ala Moana Shopping Center, 1450 Ala Moana Blvd., Ala Moana ☏ 808/951–8887) is the trendy end of the high-fashion scene. For the latest in footwear, **Nordstrom Shoes** (✉ Victoria Ward Centers, Ala Moana Blvd., Ala Moana ☏ 808/973–4620) displays an elegant array of pricey styles. **Pzazz** (✉ 1419 Kalākaua Ave., Waikīkī ☏ 808/955–5800), nicknamed the Ann Taylor of consignment shops, sells high fashion at low prices.

Shanghai Tang (✉ Ala Moana Shopping Center, Ala Moana ☏ 808/942–9800) first opened as a tailoring shop in Hong Kong, and this store is its 11th branch. The emphasis is on workmanship and the luxury of fine fabrics in the tradition of old-Shanghai tailoring. Shanghai Tang offers custom tailoring for men, women, and children.

For vintage aloha shirts, try **Bailey's Antique Clothing and Thrift Shop** (✉ 517 Kapahulu Ave., Waikīkī, Honolulu ☎ 808/734–7628). If you're looking for aloha wear that ranges from the bright-and-bold to the cool-and-classy, try **Hilo Hattie** (✉ 700 N. Nimitz Hwy., Iwilei ☎ 808/535–6500), the world's largest manufacturer of Hawaiian and tropical fashions; it's also a good source for island souvenirs. Free shuttle service is available from Waikīkī. If you plan on surfing or just want to look like a surfer, check out **Local Motion** (✉ 1958 Kalākaua Ave., Waikīkī, Honolulu ☎ 808/979–7873). This outfitter's flagship store has everything from surfboards to surf wear. For contemporary rayon aloha shirts made in the vintage-style patterns, **Locals Only** (✉ Ala Moana Shopping Center, Ala Moana, Honolulu ☎ 808/942–1555) offers an exclusive line by Pineapple Juice and Locals Only sportswear. For stylish Hawaiian wear, the kind worn by local men and women, look in one of the branches of **Macy's** (✉ Ala Moana Shopping Center ✉ Kāhala Mall ✉ 1450 Ala Moana Blvd., Ala Moana ☎ 808/941–2345 for all stores) **Native Books and Beautiful Things** (✉ Ward Warehouse, 1050 Ala Moana Blvd., Ala Moana, Honolulu ☎ 808/596–8885) sells hand-painted, one-of-a-kind clothing created by local artisans.

Ohelo Road (✉ Kāhala Mall, 4211 Wai'alae Ave., Kāhala, Honolulu ☎ 808/735–5525) carries island-print dresses in materials that make living in the tropics cool year-round. For menswear and select women's and children's aloha wear, try **Reyn's** (✉ Ala Moana Shopping Center, 1450 Ala Moana Blvd., Ala Moana, Honolulu ☎ 808/949–5929 ✉ Kāhala Mall, 4211 Wai'alae Ave., Kāhala, Honolulu ☎ 808/737–8313 ✉ Sheraton Waikīkī, 2255 Kalākaua Ave., Waikīkī, Honolulu ☎ 808/923–0331) For contemporary island wear in fabrics made for a tropical climate, try **Tapestries by Hauoli** (✉ Ala Moana Shopping Center, Ala Moana, Honolulu ☎ 808/973–0566), which sells machine-washable dresses, pants, tops, and accessories.

Food

Bring home fresh pineapple, papaya, or coconut to savor or share with friends and family. Jam comes in flavors such as pohā, passion fruit, and guava. Kona- and O'ahu-grown Waialua coffee beans have an international following. There are dried-food products such as saimin, haupia, and teriyaki barbecue sauce. All kinds of cookies are available, as well as exotic teas, drink mixes, and pancake syrups. And don't forget the macadamia nuts, from plain to chocolate-covered and brittled. By law, all fresh-fruit products must be inspected by the Department of Agriculture before export. To really impress those back home, pick up a box of gourmet chocolates from the **Honolulu Chocolate Company** (✉ Ward Centre, 1200 Ala Moana Blvd., Ala Moana ☎ 808/591–2997). Bring home the flavors of Hawai'i, from Kona coffee to macadamia nuts, dipped in the finest of chocolates. For cheap prices on local delicacies, try one of the many **Longs Drugs** (✉ Ala Moana Shopping Center, 1450 Ala Moana Blvd., 2nd level, Ala Moana ☎ 808/941–4433 ✉ Kāhala Mall, 4211 Wai'alae Ave., Kāhala ☎ 808/732–0784). **Tropical Fruits Distributors of Hawai'i** (✉ 651 Ilalo St., Honolulu ☎ 808/847–3224 or 800/697–9100 ⊕ www.dolefruithawaii.com) specializes in packing inspected pineapple and papaya; it will deliver to your hotel and to the airport check-in counter or ship to the mainland United States and Canada.

Gifts

To send home tropical flowers, contact **Hawaiian Greenhouse** (☎ 888/965–8351 ⊕ www.hawaiiangreenhouse.com). To ship exotic orchids, contact the **Kawamoto Nursery** (☎ 808/732–5805 ⊕ www.kawamotoorchids.com).

Pacific-American Gallery (✉ 100 Holomana St., Waikīkī ☎ 808/942–3767), in the Hawai'i Prince Hotel, presents works in all mediums by emerging native Hawaiian and Pacific Island artists, including pottery, sculpture, paintings and drawings, and photography.

Robyn Buntin Galleries (✉ 820 S. Beretania St., Downtown Honolulu, Honolulu ☎ 808/545–5572) presents Chinese nephrite-jade carvings, Japanese lacquer and screens, Buddhist sculptures, and other international pieces.

Takenoya Arts (✉ Halekūlani, 2199 Kālia Rd., Waikīkī ☎ 808/926–1939) specializes in intricately carved netsuke (toggles used to fasten containers to kimonos), both antique and contemporary, and one-of-a-kind necklaces.

Hawaiian Arts & Crafts

Items handcrafted of native Hawaiian wood make lovely gifts. Koa and milo each have a beautiful color and grain. The great koa forests are disappearing because of environmental factors, so the wood is becoming valuable; most koa products you'll encounter are produced from wood grown on commercial farms.

You can purchase traditional island comforters, wall hangings, pillows, and other Hawaiian-print quilt items at **Hawaiian Quilt Collection** (✉ Ala Moana Center, 1450 Ala Moana Blvd., Ala Moana ☎ 808/946–2233). For hula costumes and instruments, try **Hula Supply Center** (✉ 2346 S. King St., Mō'ili'ili ☎ 808/941–5379).

Bring home some aloha you can sink your bare feet into with the exclusive Hawaiian rug collection from **Indich Collection** (✉ Gentry Pacific Design Center, 560 N. Nimitz Hwy., Downtown Honolulu ☎ 808/524–7769), which features designs that include Hawaiian petroglyphs, banana leafs, and heliconia.

Local residents come to **Island Treasures** (✉ Koko Marina Center, 7192 Kalaniana'ole Hwy. ☎ 808/396–8827) to shop for gifts that are both unique and within reach of almost every budget. From koa accessories to original artwork, jewelry, beauty products, and home accessories, the quality is outstanding and the creativity of the work makes this a trove for island gifts.

A wonderful selection of Hawaiian arts, crafts, and children's toys can be found at **My Little Secret** (✉ Ward Warehouse, 1050 Ala Moana Blvd., Ala Moana ☎ 808/596–2990).

Jewelry

Bernard Hurtig's (✉ Hilton Hawaiian Village Ali'i Tower, 2005 Kālia Rd., Waikīkī ☎ 808/947–9399) sells fine jewelry with an emphasis on 18-karat gold and antique jade. **Haimoff & Haimoff Creations in Gold** (✉ Halekūlani, 2199 Kālia Rd., Waikīkī ☎ 808/923–8777) sells the work of jewelry designer Harry Haimoff.

Coral and pearl jewelry is popular, stunning, and fairly affordable. To see where it comes from and how jewelry is designed using these treasures from the sea, take a tour of the **Maui Divers Jewelry Design Center** (✉ 1520 Liona St., Mō'ili'ili, Honolulu ☎ 808/946–7979).

Philip Rickard (✉ Royal Hawaiian Shopping Center, 2201 Kalākaua Ave., Waikīkī ☎ 808/924–7972) features custom Hawaiian wedding jewelry among this famed jeweler's heirloom design collection.

O'AHU A TO Z

To research prices, get advice from other travelers, and book travel arrangements, visit www.fodors.com.

AIR TRAVEL

Most flights to Honolulu International originate in Los Angeles or San Francisco, which means they are nonstop. Flying time from the West Coast is 4½ to 5 hours. Honolulu also has a number of carriers routing to the islands from the United Kingdom.

CARRIERS Carriers flying into Honolulu from the mainland United States include Aloha, American, Continental, Delta, Hawaiian, Northwest, and United. Carriers flying from the United Kingdom to Honolulu include Air New Zealand, American, Continental, Delta, and United.

Charter flights are the least expensive and the least reliable—with chronically late departures and occasional cancellations. They also tend to depart less frequently (usually once a week) than do regularly scheduled flights. The savings may be worth the potential annoyance, however. Charter flights serving Honolulu International Airport are available from American Trans Air and Hawaiian Airlines.

🛈 **Air New Zealand** ☎ 800/262-1234 ⊕ www.airnewzealand.com. **Aloha Airlines** ☎ 808/484-1111 ⊕ www.alohaairlines.com. **American** ☎ 808/833-7600 or 800/433-7300 ⊕ www.aa.com. **American Trans Air** ☎ 800/225-2995 ⊕ www.ata.com. **Continental** ☎ 800/523-3273 ⊕ www.continental.com. **Delta** ☎ 800/221-1212 ⊕ www.delta.com. **Hawaiian Airlines** ☎ 808/838-1555 or 800/367-5320 ⊕ www.hawaiianair.com. **Northwest/KLM** ☎ 808/955-2255 or 800/225-2525 ⊕ www.nwa.com. **United** ☎ 800/241-6522 ⊕ www.ual.com.

AIRPORT

More direct flights, by more domestic and international air carriers, arrive at and depart from Honolulu International than at any other airport in Hawai'i. If you find yourself waiting at the airport with extra time on your hands, be sure to visit the Pacific Aerospace Museum, open daily 8:30–6, in the main terminal. It includes a 1,700-square-ft, three-dimensional, multimedia theater presenting the history of flight in Hawai'i, and a full-scale space-shuttle flight deck. Hands-on exhibits include a mission-control computer program tracing flights in the Pacific.

🛈 **Honolulu International Airport** ☎ 808/836-6411 ⊕ www.ehawaiigov.org. **Pacific Aerospace Museum** ☎ 808/839-0777.

AIRPORT TRANSFERS There are taxis right at the airport baggage-claim exit. At $1.50 start-up plus $2.50 for each mile, the fare to Waikīkī will run approximately $23, plus tip. Drivers are also allowed to charge 30¢ per suitcase. Trans Hawaiian Services runs an airport shuttle service to Waikīkī. The fare is $8 one-way, $15 round-trip. The municipal bus (TheBus) will take you into Waikīkī for only $1.50, but you are allowed only one bag, which must fit on your lap. Some hotels have their own pickup service. Check when you book.

🛈 **TheBus** ☎ 808/848-5555 ⊕ www.thebus.org. **Trans-Hawaiian Services** ☎ 808/566-7300.

BOAT & FERRY TRAVEL

Boat Day used to be the biggest day of the week. Jet travel once obscured that custom, but arriving in Hawai'i by ship is making a comeback. If you have the time, it is one sure way to unwind. Many cruises are planned a year or more in advance and fill up fast. Most cruise-ship companies offer a fare that includes round-trip air travel to the point of embarkation.

Norwegian Cruise Lines' 2,200-passenger *Norwegian Star* vessel offers seven-day cruises to the Hawaiian islands. Ports of call include O'ahu, Maui, Kaua'i, the Big Island, and Fanning Island in Kiribati.

☶ Norwegian Cruise Line (NCL) ⊠ 7665 Corporate Dr., Miami, FL 33126 ☎ 800/327–7030 ⊕ www.ncl.com.

BIKE & MOPED TRAVEL

Blue Sky Rentals & Sports Center rents mopeds for $20 a day (8–6) and $25 for 24 hours. Mountain bikes from Blue Sky Rentals cost $15 a day, $20 for 24 hours, and $75 for the week, plus a $25 deposit. Big Kahuna rents a variety of motorcycles for $125–$250 a day.

☶ Big Kahuna Motorcycle Tours and Rentals ⊠ 404 Seaside Ave., Waikīkī ☎ 808/924-2736. **Blue Sky Rentals & Sports Center** ⊠ 1920 Ala Moana Blvd., across from Hilton Hawaiian Village, Waikīkī ☎ 808/947-0101.

BUS TRAVEL

You can go all around the island or just down Kalākaua Avenue for $1.50 on Honolulu's municipal transportation system, affectionately known as TheBus. You're entitled to one free transfer per fare if you ask for it when boarding. Exact change is required, and dollar bills are accepted. A four-day pass for visitors costs $10 and is sold at the more than 30 ABC stores (Hawaiian chain stores that sell sundries and are geared to tourists) in Waikīkī. Monthly passes cost $25.

There are no official bus-route maps, but you can find privately published booklets at most drugstores and other convenience outlets. The important route numbers for Waikīkī are 2, 4, 8, 19, 20, and 58. If you venture afield, you can always get back on one of these.

There are also a number of brightly painted private buses, many free, that will take you to such commercial attractions as dinner cruises, garment factories, and the like.

☶ TheBus ☎ 808/848-5555 ⊕ www.thebus.org.

CAR RENTAL

If you plan to go beyond Waikīkī to tour O'ahu, renting a car is essential. During peak seasons—summer, Christmas vacations, and February—reservations are necessary. Rental agencies abound in and around the Honolulu International Airport and in Waikīkī. Local agencies rent everything from used cars to classics and pickup trucks.

Cloud Nine Limousine Service provides red-carpet treatment in its chauffeur-driven superstretch limousines. Rates begin at $60 an hour, plus tax and tip, with a two-hour minimum. Another reliable company is Duke's Limousine Service, which offers a choice of luxury superstretches, sedans, or SUV limousines, with rates that begin at $45 per hour, with a two-hour minimum.

☶ Major Agencies: Avis ☎ 808/834-5536 or 800/321-3712 ⊕ www.avis.com. **Budget** ☎ 800/527-0700, 800/527-7000 in Hawai'i ⊕ www.budget.com. **Dollar** ☎ 808/831-2330 or 800/800-4000 ⊕ www.dollarcar.com. **Enterprise** ☎ 808/836-2213 or 800/736-8222 ⊕ www.enterprise.com. **Hertz** ☎ 800/764-4423 ⊕ www.hertz.com. **National** ☎ 808/831-3800 or 800/227-7368 ⊕ www.nationalcar.com. **Thrifty** ☎ 808/831-2277 or 800/367-2277.

☶ Local Agencies: JN Car and Truck Rentals ☎ 808/831-2724 ⊕ www.jnag.com. **Paradise Rent A Car** ☎ 808/946-7777 or 888/882-2277 ⊕ www.paradiserentacar.com. **VIP** ☎ 808/922-4605.

☶ Limousine Rentals: Cloud Nine Limousine Service ☎ 808/524-7999 or 800/524-7999 ⊕ www.cloudninelimos. **Duke's Limousine, Inc.** ☎ 808/738-1878 ⊕ www.dukeslimo.com.

CAR TRAVEL

O'ahu's drivers are generally courteous, and you rarely hear a horn. People will slow down and let you into traffic with a wave of the hand. A friendly wave back is customary. If a driver sticks a hand out the window in a fist with the thumb and pinky sticking straight out, this is a good thing: the Hawaiian symbol for "hang loose," it's called the *shaka* and is often used to say "thanks," as well.

Hawai'i has a seat-belt law for front-seat passengers and those under the age of 18 in the back seats. Children under 40 pounds must be in a car seat, available from your car-rental agency.

It's hard to get lost on O'ahu. Roads and streets, although perhaps unpronounceable to visitors, are at least well marked. Major attractions and scenic spots are marked by the distinctive HVCB sign with its red-caped warrior. Although it's hard to get lost, driving in Honolulu can be frustrating, as many streets are one-way.

Driving in rush-hour traffic (6:30–8:30 and 3:30–5:30) can be exasperating, because left turns are prohibited at many intersections. Parking along many streets is curtailed during these hours, and towing is strictly enforced. Read the curbside parking signs before leaving your vehicle, even at a meter. Remember not to leave valuables in your car. Rental cars are often targets for thieves.

EMERGENCIES

To reach the police, fire department, or an ambulance in an emergency, dial **911**.

A doctor, laboratory-radiology technician, and nurses are always on duty at Doctors on Call. Appointments are recommended but not necessary. Dozens of kinds of medical insurance are accepted, including Medicare, Medicaid, and most kinds of travel insurance.

Kūhiō Pharmacy is Waikīkī's only pharmacy and handles prescription requests only until 4:30 PM. Longs Drugs is open evenings at its Ala Moana location and 24 hours at its South King Street location (15 minutes from Waikīkī by car). Pillbox Pharmacy, located in Kaimukī, will deliver prescription medications for a small fee.

🗎 Doctors & Dentists: **Doctors on Call** ✉ Sheraton Princess Kaiulani Hotel, 120 Kaiulani Ave., Waikīkī ☎ 808/971-6000.

🗎 Emergency Services: **Coast Guard Rescue Center** ☎ 800/552-6458.

🗎 Hospitals: **Castle Medical Center** ✉ 640 Ulukahiki, Kailua ☎ 808/263-5500. **Kapiolani Medical Center for Women and Children** ✉ 1319 Punahou St., Makiki Heights, Honolulu ☎ 808/983-6000. **Queen's Medical Center** ✉ 1301 Punchbowl St., Downtown Honolulu, Honolulu ☎ 808/538-9011. **Saint Francis Medical Center-West** ✉ 91-2141 Ft. Weaver Rd., 'Ewa Beach ☎ 808/678-7000. **Straub Clinic** ✉ 888 S. King St., Downtown Honolulu, Honolulu ☎ 808/522-4000.

🗎 Pharmacies: **Kūhiō Pharmacy** ✉ Outrigger West Hotel, 2330 Kūhiō Ave., Waikīkī ☎ 808/923-4466. **Longs Drugs** ✉ Ala Moana Shopping Center, 1450 Ala Moana Blvd., 2nd level, Ala Moana ☎ 808/949-4010 ✉ 2220 S. King St., Mō'ili'ili ☎ 808/947-2651. **Pillbox Pharmacy** ✉ 1133 11th Ave., Kaimukī ☎ 808/737-1777.

SIGHTSEEING TOURS

AERIAL TOURS Through the bubble top of Honolulu Soaring Club's sleek sail plane you get aerial views of O'ahu's North Shore with its coral pools; sugarcane fields; windsurfers; and, in winter, humpback whales. On-board live videotaping is available. Reservations are not accepted; 20- and 30-minute flights leave every 20 minutes daily 10–5. The charge for one passenger is $90; two people fly for $120. Ask for "Mr. Bill" to make reservations.

Island Seaplane Service takes off from Keahi Lagoon and sets you soaring on an aerial tour that is either a half-hour South and Eastern O'ahu shoreline tour or an hour Circle Island tour. Get the feel of what Hawai'i air transportation was like during the Pan Am Clipper days for $89 to $139.

Makani Kai Helicopters depart from Honolulu International Airport for helicopter tours of O'ahu by daylight or at sunset. A Waikīkī by Night excursion sends you soaring by the breathtaking Honolulu city lights. Tours range from $75 to $190, with customized tours available for $450.
Honolulu Soaring Club ⊠ Dillingham Airfield, Mokulē'ia ☎ 808/677-3404. **Island Seaplane Service** ⊠ Keahi Lagoon, Honolulu ☎ 808/836-6273. **Makani Kai Helicopters** ⊠ 110 Kapalulu Pl., Honolulu ☎ 808/834-5813 ⊕ www.makanikai.com.

BOAT TOURS Dream Cruises offers tours of Pearl Harbor aboard the 100-ft motor yacht *American Dream*. The trip takes place in the early morning—from 7:30 to 10:30—to coincide with the time that Pearl Harbor was attacked on December 7, 1941. It includes a stop near the U.S.S. *Arizona* Memorial, where the captain conducts a brief memorial service and lei placement ceremony. Narration and videos help describe the sights. In winter, this cruise is paired with a whale-watch. The cost is $21.95.

Tradewind Charters is a good bet for half-day private charter tours for sailing, snorkeling, and whale-watching. Traveling on these luxury yachts not only gets you away from the crowds but also gives you the opportunity to "take the helm" if you wish. The cruise also includes snorkeling at an exclusive anchorage as well as hands-on snorkeling and sailing instruction. Charter prices are approximately $495 for up to six passengers.
Dream Cruises ⊠ 306 Kamani St., Honolulu ☎ 808/592-5200. **Tradewind Charters** ⊠ 796 Kalanipuu St., Honolulu ☎ 800/829-4899.

BUS & VAN TOURS There are many ground-tour companies in O'ahu that handle daylong sightseeing excursions. Depending on the size of the tour, travel may be by air-conditioned bus or smaller vans. Vans are recommended because less time is spent picking up passengers, and you get to know your fellow passengers and your tour guide. Ask exactly what the tour includes in the way of actual "get-off-the-bus" stops and "window sights." Most of the tour guides have taken special Hawaiiana classes to learn their history and lore, and many are certified by the state of Hawai'i. Tipping ($2 per person at least) is customary.

E Noa Tours uses minibuses and trolleys and likes to get you into the great outdoors. Polynesian Adventure Tours has motorcoaches, vans, and minicoaches. Polynesian Hospitality provides narrated tours. Roberts Hawai'i has equipment ranging from vans to presidential limousines. Trans Hawaiian Services offers multilingual tours.

Most tour companies offer some version of the following standard O'ahu tours listed below:

There are several variations on the Circle Island Tour theme. Some of these all-day tours, ranging from $45 to $65, include lunch. Little Circle tours cover East O'ahu. This is a half-day tour and costs between $25 and $40.

The comprehensive Pearl Harbor and City tour includes the boat tour to Pearl Harbor run by the National Park Service. These tours cost between $35 and $40.

One of the advantages of the Polynesian Cultural Center tour is that you don't have to drive yourself back to Waikīkī after dark if you take in the evening show. The tour is $70–$80 per person.
⚑ E Noa Tours ☎808/591-9923 ⊕www.enoa.com. **Polynesian Adventure Tours** ☎808/833-3000 ⊕ www.polyad.com. **Polynesian Cultural Center** ☎ 808/293-3333 or 808/923-1861 ⊕ www.polynesia.com. **Polynesian Hospitality** ☎ 808/526-3565. **Roberts Hawaiʻi** ☎ 808/539-9400 ⊕ www.robertshawaii.com. **Trans Hawaiian Services** ☎ 808/566-7300.

THEME TOURS E Noa Tours has certified tour guides who conduct not only Circle Island and Pearl Harbor tours but also shopping tours to the Waikele Premium Outlets.

Hawaiian Island Eco-Tours, Ltd.'s experienced guides take nature lovers and hikers on limited-access trails for tours ranging from hidden waterfalls to bird-watching.

Home of the Brave and Top Gun Tours offers military-history buffs a narrated tour of military bases plus a drive through the National Memorial Cemetery of the Pacific.

Mauka Makai Excursions takes visitors to some of the ancient Hawaiian archaeological, legendary, and nature sites that islanders hold sacred.
⚑ E Noa Tours ☎ 808/591-9923 ⊕www.enoa.com. **Hawaiian Island Eco-tours, Ltd.** ☎808/236-7766 ⊕www.hikeoahu.com. **Home of the Brave and Top Gun Tours** ☎808/396-8112. **Mauka Makai Excursions** ☎ 808/593-3525 ⊕ www.hau-ecotours.com.

UNDERWATER TOURS *Atlantis* Submarines operates two air-conditioned vessels off Waikīkī, which dive up to 100 ft for viewing of a sunken navy-yard oiler, coral gardens, and an artificial reef teeming with tropical fish. Dive cruises are two hours in length and are a popular family activity. Children must be at least 3-ft tall to board. Note: flash photography will not work; use film speed ASA 200 or above without flash. Tours cost $6 and begin from the Hilton Hawaiian Village Resort Pier.
⚑ *Atlantis* **Submarines** ⊠ Hilton Hawaiian Village Beach Resort and Spa, 2005 Kālia Rd., Waikīkī, Honolulu 96815 ☎ 808/973-1296.

WALKING TOURS Meet at the Chinese Chamber of Commerce for a fascinating peek into herbal shops, an acupuncturist's office, open-air markets, and specialty stores. The 2½-hour tour sponsored by the Chamber costs $5 and is available every Tuesday at 9:30. Reservations are required.

The Mission Houses Museum offers a two-hour walk through historic Honolulu that begins with an hour-long tour of the Mission Houses before the downtown stroll. Reservations are required. Tours are $8 and operate Thursday and Friday mornings.

The American Institute of Architects (AIA) offers a tour of Downtown Honolulu from an architectural perspective. Tours cost $15 per person and run Tuesday and Saturday mornings at 9:30 AM.

The Hawaii Geographic Society arranges a unique Downtown Honolulu historic-temple and archaeology walking tour (Sunday only upon request) for $10 per person.

History springs to life for young and old alike during Honolulu Time Walks, which come with appropriately costumed narrators and cost $7 to $45. Tours and seminar programs explore the "mysteries" of Honolulu—its haunts, historic neighborhoods, and the different but not always talked about eras in its colorful history.
⚑ **AIA Downtown Walking Tour** ⊠ American Institute of Architects, 1128 Nuʻuanu Ave., Downtown Honolulu, Honolulu ☎ 808/545-4242. **Chinatown Walking Tour** ⊠ Chinese Chamber of Commerce, 42 N. King St., Downtown Honolulu, Honolulu ☎ 808/

533-3181. **Hawaii Geographic Society** ☎ 808/538-3952. **Historic Downtown Walking Tour** ✉ 553 S. King St., Downtown Honolulu, Honolulu ☎ 808/531-0481. **Honolulu Time Walks** ✉ 2634 S. King St., Suite 3, Downtown Honolulu, Honolulu ☎ 808/943-0371.

TAXIS

You can usually get a taxi right outside your hotel. Most restaurants will call a taxi for you. Rates are $1.50 at the drop of the flag, plus $2.50 per mile. Flat fees can also be negotiated for many destinations—just ask your driver. Drivers are generally courteous, and the cars are in good condition, many of them air-conditioned. For transportation throughout the island, try Charley's Taxi & Tours. SIDA of Hawai'i Taxis, Inc., offers 24-hour island-wide transportation service and multilingual drivers.

☑ **Charley's Taxi & Tours** ☎ 808/531-1333. **SIDA of Hawai'i Taxis, Inc.** ☎ 808/836-0011.

TRANSPORTATION AROUND O'AHU

Waikīkī is only 2½ mi long and ½ mi wide, which means you can usually walk to where you are going. However, if you plan to venture outside of Waikīkī, it's best to rent a car.

TROLLEY TRAVEL

The Waikīkī Trolley has three lines and 40 stops that allow you to design your own itinerary. The Red Line cruises around Waikīkī, Ala Moana, and Downtown Honolulu. The Yellow Line hits major shopping centers and restaurant locations. The Blue Line provides a tour of O'ahu's southeastern coastline, including Hanauma Bay and Sea Life Park. The trolleys depart from the Royal Hawaiian Shopping Center in Waikīkī every 15 minutes daily from 8 to 4:30. Buy an all-day pass from the conductor for $18.

The Rainbow Trolley System picks up riders at the Waikīkī Beachcomber Hotel every 30 minutes and tours "outer Waikīkī" with trolley routes through Kaimukī, Ala Moana shopping district, and Downtown Honolulu.

☑ **Rainbow Trolley** ☎ 808/539-9400. **Waikīkī Trolley** ☎ 808/593-8211 ⊕ www.waikikitrolley.com.

VISITOR INFORMATION

☑ **Hawai'i Attractions Association** ☎ 808/596-7733 ⊕ www.hawaiiattractions.com. **Hawai'i Visitors & Convention Bureau** ✉ Waikīkī Business Plaza, 2270 Kalākaua Ave., Suite 801, Honolulu 96815 ☎ 808/923-1811 or 800/464-2924 ⊕ www.gohawaii.com. **O'ahu Visitor Bureau** ☎ 877/525-6248 ⊕ www.visit-oahu.com. **Surf Report** ☎ 808/973-4383. **Weather** ☎ 808/973-4381.

MAUI
THE VALLEY ISLE

2

FODOR'S CHOICE

Ba Le, restaurant in Kahului

Capische, restaurant in Wailea

Driving the Road to Hāna, East Maui

Hiking Haleakalā Crater, Central Maui

Kā'anapali Beach Hotel, Lahaina

Mama's Fish House, Kū'au

Nāpili Beach, West Maui

Old Wailuku Inn, Wailuku

Ritz-Carlton, Kapalua

Wai'ānapanapa State Park, East Maui

HIGHLY RECOMMENDED

BEACHES   Baldwin Beach, West Maui

Ho'okipa Beach, East Maui

Kā'anapali Beach, West Maui

Mākena, South Shore

Wailea Beach, South Shore

SIGHTS   Alexander & Baldwin Sugar Museum, Pu'unēnē

Bailey House, Wailuku

Baldwin Home, Lahaina

'Īao Valley State Park, Central Maui

Mākena Beach State Park, South Shore

Maui Arts & Cultural Center, Kahului

Maui Ocean Center, Mā'alaea

Tedeschi Vineyards and Winery, Upcountry

Many other great hotels, restaurants, and experiences enliven this area.
For other favorites, look for the black stars as you read this chapter.

Updated by
Shannon
Wianecki

MAUI NŌ KA 'OI" IS WHAT LOCALS SAY—it's the best, the most, the top of the heap. To those who know Maui well, there's good reason for the superlatives. The second-largest island in the Hawaiian chain, Maui has made an international name for itself with its tropical allure, its arts and cultural activities, and miles of perfect-tan beaches. Maui weaves a spell over the more than 2 million people who visit its shores each year, and many decide to return for good.

Maui residents have quite a bit to do with their island's successful tourism story. In the mid-1970s, savvy marketers on Maui saw a way to increase their sleepy island's economy by positioning it as an island apart. Community leaders started promoting their Valley Isle separately from the rest of the state. They nicknamed West Maui the Golf Coast, luring in heavyweight tournaments that, in turn, would bring more visitors. They attracted some of the finest resorts and hotels in the world, and they became the state's condominium experts, emphasizing the luxurious privacy these accommodations can provide. Maui's visitor count swelled, putting it far ahead of that of the other Neighbor Islands.

Quick growth has led to its share of problems. During the busy seasons—from Christmas to Easter and then again during the summer—West Maui can be overly crowded. Although Maui has widened the road that connects Lahaina and Kāʻanapali, the occasional traffic congestion here might not be what you bargained for. And South Maui's Kīhei still has trouble keeping traffic in motion along its one seaside main drive.

But then consider Maui's natural resources. The island is made up of two volcanoes, one now extinct and the other dormant, that both erupted long ago and joined into one island. The resulting depression between the two is what gives Maui its nickname, the Valley Isle. West Maui's 5,788-ft Puʻu Kukui was the first volcano to form, a distinction that gives that area's mountainous topography a more weathered look. Rainbows seem to grow wild over this terrain as gentle mists fill the deeply eroded canyons.

The Valley Isle's second volcano is the 10,023-ft Haleakalā, a mammoth mountain. If you hike its slopes or peer into its enormous crater, you'll witness an impressive variety of nature, with desertlike terrain butted up against tropical forests.

The island's volcanic history gives Maui much of its beauty. The roads around the island are lined with rich red soil, the fertile foothold for sugarcane. Sugar has disappeared from West Maui, as it has nearly everywhere in the state. But Central Maui is still carpeted with grassy green, thanks to HC&S with its last working mill at Puʻunēnē.

Farmers also appreciate the Valley Isle. On the slopes of Haleakalā, the volcanic richness of the soil has yielded lush results. Sweetly scented flowers bloom large and healthy. Grapes cultivated on Haleakalā's slopes are squeezed for wine and champagne. Horses graze languidly on rolling meadows of the best Upcountry grasses, while jacaranda trees dot the hillsides with spurts of luscious lavender. As the big brute of a volcano slides east and becomes the town of Hāna, the rains that lavishly fall there turn the soil into a jungle, and waterfalls cascade down the crags.

Exploring Maui

The island can be split up into five exploring areas—West Maui, Central Maui, the South Shore, Upcountry (including Haleakalā), and the Road to Hāna (East Maui). You can spend a half day to a full day or more in each area, depending on how long you have to visit. The best way to see the whole island is by car, but there are a few good walking tours.

To get yourself oriented, first look at a map of the island. You will notice two distinct circular landmasses. The smaller landmass, on the western part of the island, consists of 5,788-ft Pu'u Kukui and the West Maui Mountains. The interior of these mountains is one of the earth's wettest spots. Annual rainfall of 400 inches has sliced the land into impassable gorges and razor-sharp ridges. Oddly enough, the area's leeward shore—what most people mean when they say "West Maui"—is sunny and warm year-round.

The large landmass on the eastern portion of Maui was created by Haleakalā, the cloud-wreathed volcanic peak at its center. One of the best-known mountains in the world, Haleakalā is popular with hikers and sightseers. This larger region of the island is East Maui. Its dry, leeward South Shore is flanked with resorts, condominiums, beaches, and the busy town of Kīhei. Its windward shore, largely one great rain forest, is traversed by the Road to Hāna.

Between the two mountain areas is Central Maui, the location of the county seat of Wailuku, from which the islands of Maui, Lāna'i, Moloka'i, and Kaho'olawe are governed. It's also the base for much of the island's commerce and industry.

In the Islands, the directions *mauka* (toward the mountains) and *makai* (toward the ocean) are often used.

About the Restaurants

You can eat a great meal every night for a month on Maui without ever dining twice in the same place. The resorts set very high standards, and restaurants elsewhere have risen to the challenge. Maui continues to attract fine chefs, several of whom are known for their trendsetting Hawai'i regional cuisine. This growing movement uses fruits and vegetables unique to Hawai'i in classic European or Asian ways—spawning such dishes as *'ahi* (yellowfin tuna) carpaccio, breadfruit soufflé, and papaya cheesecake. Of course, you can find plain old local-style cooking here—particularly if you wander into the less-touristy areas of Wailuku or Kahului, for example. A good "plate lunch" will fulfill your daily requirement of carbohydrates: macaroni salad, two scoops of rice, and an entrée of, say, curry stew, teriyaki beef, or *kālua* (roasted in an underground oven) pig and cabbage.

About the Hotels

The resorts here re-create whatever is beautiful about Maui on the premises, doing their best to improve on nature. And their best is pretty amazing—opulent gardens and fantasy swimming pools with slide-down waterfalls and hidden grottoes (sometimes with swim-up bars in them). In addition, spas, cultural events, championship golf courses, priceless art collections, and tennis clubs make it hard to work up the willpower to leave the resort and go see the real thing. Kā'anapali, the grande dame, sits next to Lahaina's action. Kapalua, farther north, is more private and serene—and catches a bit more wind and rain. Sprawling Wailea on the South Shore has excellent beaches and designer golf courses, each with a distinct personality. Resort prices are not for everyone. Many people compromise on the luxury and find condominium apartments in Nāpili and Kahana (for West Maui) or in Kīhei (South Shore). With a few exceptions, you'll find that accommodations are all clustered along these leeward shores. If you want to stay elsewhere on the island—say, Upcountry or in Hāna (without using the Hotel Hāna-Maui)—seek out a bed-and-breakfast or a rental property.

2

Numbers in the text correspond to numbers in the margins and on the Maui, Lahaina, Kahului-Wailuku, and Road to Hāna maps.

If you have 1 day

This is a tough choice. But how can you miss the opportunity to see **Haleakalā National Park** ③ and the volcano's enormous, otherworldly crater? Sunrise at the summit has become the thing to do. You'll need an hour and a half from the bottom of **Haleakalā Highway** (Route 37) ③ to the summit. Add to that the time of travel to the highway—at least 45 minutes from Lahaina or Kīhei. *The Maui News* posts the hour of sunrise every day. The best experience of the crater takes all day. Start at the summit, hike down Sliding Sands trail, cross the crater floor, and come back up the Halemau'u switchbacks. (This works out best if you leave your car at the Halemau'u trailhead parking lot and get a lift for the last 20-minute drive to the mountaintop.) If you don't hike, leave the mountain early enough to go explore **'Īao Valley State Park** ②, above Wailuku.

If you have 3 days

Give yourself the Haleakalā volcano experience one day, and then rest up a little with a beach-snorkel-exploring jaunt on either West Maui or the South Shore. The South Shore trip will have to include the **Maui Ocean Center** ③ at Mā'alaea. Then drive east, sampling the little beaches in **Wailea** ③ and getting a good dose of big, golden **Mākena Beach State Park** ③. Be sure to drive on past Mākena into the rough lava fields, the site of Maui's last lava flows, which formed rugged **La Pérouse Bay** ③. The 'Āhihi-Kīna'u Marine Preserve has no beach, but it's a rich spot for snorkeling.

Or take the West Maui trip through Olowalu, **Lahaina** ④–⑯, and **Kā'anapali** ③, and dodge off the highway to find small beaches in Nāpili, Kahana, **Kapalua** ①, and beyond. The road gets narrow and sensational around **Kahakuloa** ②.

On your third day, explore **Hāna** ⑤. Drive up to **Pā'ia** ③ for a meal, pause at **Ho'okipa Beach** ④ for the surf action, and on your way back to Hāna savor the sight of the taro fields of **Ke'anae Arboretum** ⑤ and **Wailua Overlook** ⑤. Nearly everyone keeps going past Hāna town to **'Ohe'o Gulch** ⑥.

If you have 5 days

After you've completed the three-day itinerary above, explore Upcountry. Get to the town of **Makawao** ④ and use it as your pivot point. Head north at the town's crossroads and drive around **Ha'ikū** ④ by turning left at the first street (Kokomo Road), right at Ha'ikū Road, then coming back uphill on any of those leafy, twisting gulch-country roads. After you've explored Makawao town, drive out to Kula on the Kula Highway. Stop in little Kēōkea for coffee, and keep driving on Kula Highway to the 'Ulupalakua Ranch History Room at the **Tedeschi Vineyards and Winery** ④. Add some time in Central Maui to really get to the heart of things, especially **Wailuku** ②–②, with its old buildings and curious shops. From here you can loop out to **Pā'ia** ④ and spend some time enjoying beaches in the Spreckelsville area.

WHAT IT COSTS					
	$$$$	**$$$**	**$$**	**$**	**¢**
RESTAURANTS	over $30	$20–$30	$12–$20	$7–$12	under $7
HOTELS	over $200	$150–$200	$100–$150	$60–$100	under $60

Restaurant prices are for one main course at dinner. Hotel prices are for two people in a standard double room in high season, including tax and service.

Timing

Although Maui has the usual temperate-zone shift of seasons—a bit rainier in the winter, hotter and drier in the summer—these seasonal changes are negligible on the leeward coasts, where most visitors stay. The only season worth mentioning is tourist season, when the roads around Lahaina and Kīhei get crowded. Peak activity occurs from December through March and picks up again in summer. If traffic is bothering you, get out of town and explore the countryside. During high season, the Road to Hāna tends to clog—well, not clog exactly, but develop little choo-choo trains of cars, with everyone in a line of six or a dozen driving as slowly as the first car. The solution: leave early (dawn) and return late (dusk). And if you find yourself playing the role of locomotive, pull over and let the other drivers pass.

WEST MAUI

West Maui, anchored by the amusing old whaling town of Lahaina, was the focus of development when Maui set out to become a premier tourist destination. The condo-filled beach towns of Nāpili, Kahana, and Honokōwai are arrayed between the stunning resorts of Kapalua and Kā'anapali, north of Lahaina.

Lahaina itself has a notorious past. There are stories of lusty whalers who met head-on with missionaries bent on saving souls. Both groups journeyed to Lahaina from New England in the early 1800s. At first, Lahaina might look touristy, but there's a lot that's genuine here as well. The town has renovated most of its old buildings, which date from the time when it was Hawai'i's capital. Much of the town has been designated a National Historic Landmark, and any new buildings must conform in style to those built before 1920.

a good tour

Begin this tour in **Kapalua** ❶ ▶. Even if you're not staying there, you'll want to have a look around the renowned Kapalua Bay Hotel and enjoy a meal or snack before you begin exploring. From Kapalua drive north on the Honoapi'ilani Highway (Route 30). This road is paved, but storms now and then make it partly impassable, especially on the winding 8-mi stretch that is only one lane wide, with no shoulder and a sheer drop-off into the ocean. However, you'll discover some gorgeous photo opportunities along the road, and if you go far enough, you'll come to **Kahakuloa** ❷, a sleepy fishing village tucked into a cleft in the mountain. The road pushes on to Wailuku, but you may be tired of the narrow and precipitously winding course you have to take.

From Kahakuloa turn around and go back in the direction from which you came—south toward Kā'anapali and Lahaina, past the beach towns of Nāpili, Kahana, and Honokōwai. If you wish to explore these towns, get off the Upper Honoapi'ilani Highway and drive closer to the water. If you're not staying there, you may want to visit the planned resort community of **Kā'anapali** ❸, especially the Hyatt Regency Maui and the Westin Maui. To reach them, turn right onto Kā'anapali Parkway. Next, head for Lahaina. Before you start your Lahaina trek, take a short detour by

2

Beaches

Maui's beaches win awards for being the best in the world. (Yes, there are awards for beaches.) Those of Wailea and Kapalua lead the pack. Residents particularly revere Mākena Beach, beyond Wailea—so much so that they launched a successful grassroots campaign to have it preserved as a state park. But don't expect to find the island ringed with sand. In fact, most of the coastline is dramatically craggy; beaches tend to be pockets. Each one has a personality of its own and can be completely explored in a half day. The thin, clean strand of Kā'anapali, though, goes on for 3 mi, past resort after resort. Offshore here, yachts, catamarans, and parasail riders drift across brilliant porcelain-blue water. Many of Maui's beaches are a little difficult to spot from the road, especially where homes and hotels have taken up shoreline property. Just remember that you can go to any beach you want. Access to the sea is a sacred trust in Hawai'i, preserved from ancient times.

Scenic Drives

Maui has bad roads in beautiful places. Lots of visitors take a break from the beach and just go driving, usually taking day trips from their lodgings around Lahaina or Kīhei. Maui's landscape is extraordinarily diverse for such a small island. Your sense of place (and the weather) will seem to change every few miles. If you drive to the top of Haleakalā, you rise from palm-lined beaches to the rare world inhabited by airplanes in only an hour and a half. The Road to Hāna takes you into the tropical rain forest, testing your reflexes behind the wheel on the rain-gouged windward side. Upcountry—around Makawao and Ha'ikū—you can drive into and out of the rain, with rainbows that seem to land on the hood of your car.

Water Sports

The West Maui vacation coast (from Lahaina to Kapalua) centers on Lahaina Harbor, where you can find boats for snorkeling, scuba diving, deep-sea fishing, whale-watching, parasailing, and sunset cocktail–partying. At the harbor, you can learn to surf or you can ride a submarine; catch a ferry ride to Lāna'i or grab a seat on a fast inflatable and explore all the way around it. The South Maui vacation coast has Mā'alaea Harbor and the great snorkeling beaches of Kīhei and Wailea. If you want to walk through the ocean without getting wet, visit the top-notch aquarium in Mā'alaea. If you'd rather watch, drive to Ho'okipa, near Pā'ia, for surfers and windsurfers.

Whale-Watching

One of the best signs of the high intelligence of humpback whales is that they return to Maui every year. Having fattened themselves in subarctic waters all summer, they migrate south in the winter to breed, and thousands of them cruise the Lahaina Roadstead (that is, the leeward Maui sea channel) in particular. From December 15 to May 1 the Pacific Whale Foundation has naturalists stationed in two places—on the rooftop of their headquarters and at the scenic viewpoint on the *pali*, or cliffside stretch, of the highway into Lahaina. The foundation also runs whale-watch boats that depart every hour of the day. In fact, every boat on the island will go out of its way to watch humpbacks when the opportunity arises—which it does often, as the whales themselves seem to have a penchant for people-watching.

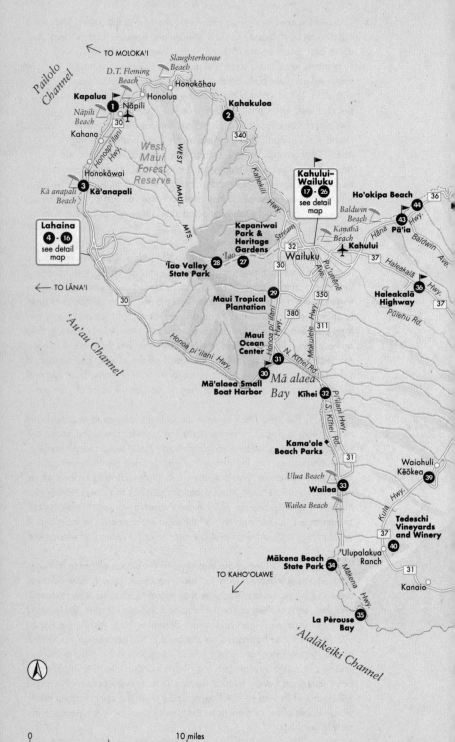

Maui

TO MOLOKA'I

Pailolo Channel

Slaughterhouse Beach

D.T. Fleming Beach

Honokōhau

Kapalua 1

Honolua

Nāpili

Nāpili Beach

Kahakuloa 2

Kahana

30

Honoapi'ilani Hwy.

West Maui Forest Reserve

Honokōwai

340

Kā anapali Beach **Kā'anapali** 3

WEST MAUI MTS.

Kahekili Hwy.

Kahului–Wailuku 17 · 26 *see detail map*

Ho'okipa Beach 44

Baldwin Beach

43

Pā'ia

Hāna Hwy.

Lahaina 4 · 16 *see detail map*

Kepaniwai Park & Heritage Gardens

'Iao Stream

Kanahā Beach

Kahului

36

Baldwin Ave.

TO LĀNA'I

'Iao Valley State Park 28 27

'Iao

Wailuku

30

Pu'unēnē Ave.

37

Haleakalā Hwy.

Haleakalā Highway 36

37

30

Maui Tropical Plantation 29

350

380

Mokulele Hwy.

311

Pūlehu Rd.

Honoapi'ilani Hwy.

Maui Ocean Center

N. Kīhei Rd.

31

Mā'alaea Small Boat Harbor

Mā alaea Bay

Kīhei 32

Pi'ilani Hwy.

S. Kīhei Rd.

Au'au Channel

Honoa pi'ilani Hwy.

Kama'ole Beach Parks

31

Waiohuli Kēōkea 39

Ulua Beach

Wailea 33

Wailea Beach

Kula Hwy.

Tedeschi Vineyards and Winery 40

37

Mākena Beach State Park 34

Ulupalakua Ranch

31

TO KAHO'OLAWE

Mākena Hwy.

Kanaio

La Pérouse Bay 35

'Alalākeiki Channel

0 ————— 10 miles

0 ————— 15 km

PACIFIC OCEAN

365
Rd.
umalu
Kaupakalua
Kokomo
Huelo
Kailua
46
360
Kaumahina State
Wayside Park
Puahokamoa
Stream
48
47
Hui No'eau
Visual Arts
Center
Honomanū
Bay
49
50
Ke'anae Arboretum
wao
lani
Ke'anae Overlook
57
Wailua
52
Wailua Overlook
377
Haleakalā
Crater Rd.
Kōolau
Forest
Reserve
Waikāne
Falls
53
54
Nāhiku
360
Hāna Hwy.
Hāna
Airport
Wai'ānapanapa
State Park
Haleakalā
National Park
Headquarters/
Visitor Center
Ka'eleku Caverns
55
56
57
Leleiwi
Overlook
37
Pi'ilanihale
Heiau
378
Kula Botanical
Gardens
48
Hāna Forest Reserve
Hotel Hāna-Maui
59
Hāna
58
Kalahaku
Overlook
Halemau'u
Trail
Haleakalā
National Park
Kōki Beach
Haleakalā
Pi'ilani Hwy.
Haleakalā Visitor
Center
Hāmoa
Beach
u'u 'Ula'ula
Overlook
Kaupō
Trail
Mū'olea
Kahikinui
Forest
Reserve
'Ohe'o Gulch
60
Kīpahulu
31
Grave of
Charles Lindbergh
61
Pi'ilani Hwy.
Kaupō
31

'Alenuihāhā Channel

TO THE BIG ISLAND OF HAWAI'I

KEY

▶ Start of itinerary

turning left from Honoapiʻilani Highway onto Lahainaluna Road, and stop at the **Hale Paʻi** ④, the printing shop built by Protestant missionaries in 1837. Return down Lahainaluna Road until you reach Front Street and turn left.

Since Lahaina is best explored on foot, use the drive along Front Street to get oriented and then park at or near **505 Front Street** ⑤, at the south end of the town's historic and colorful commercial area. Heading back into town, turn right onto Prison Street and you'll come to **Hale Paʻahao** ⑥, which was built from coral blocks. Return to Front Street, where it's a short stroll north to the **Banyan Tree** ⑦, one of the town's best-known landmarks and, behind it, the old **Court House** ⑧. Next door, also in Banyan Park, stand the reconstructed remains of the waterfront **Fort** ⑨. About a half block northwest, you'll find the site of Kamehameha's **Brick Palace** ⑩. If you walk to the corner of Front and Dickenson streets, you'll find the **Baldwin Home** ⑪, restored to reflect an early-19th-century house. Next door is the **Master's Reading Room** ⑫, Maui's oldest building.

Wander north or south on Front Street to explore Lahaina's commercial side. At the Wharf Cinema Center, you can see the **Spring House** ⑬, built over a freshwater spring. If you head north on Front Street, you'll come to the **Wo Hing Museum** ⑭ on the right. Walk another two blocks north and you'll find the **Seamen's Hospital** ⑮. If it's before dusk and you still have a hankering for just one more stop, try the **Waiola Church and Cemetery** ⑯. Walk south down Front Street, make a left onto Dickenson Street, and then make a right onto Waineʻe Street and walk another few blocks to reach the church.

TIMING You can walk the length of Lahaina's Front Street in less than 30 minutes if you don't stop along the way. Just *try* not to be intrigued by the town's colorful shops and historic sites. Realistically, you'll need at least a half day—and can easily spend a full day—to check out the area's coastal beaches, towns, and resorts. The Banyan Tree in Lahaina is a terrific spot to be when the sun sets—mynah birds settle in here for a screeching symphony, which can be an event in itself. If you arrange to spend a Friday afternoon exploring Front Street, you can dine in town and hang around for Art Night, when the galleries stay open into the evening and entertainment fills the streets.

What to See

★ ⑪ **Baldwin Home.** In 1835 an early missionary to Lahaina, Ephraim Spaulding, built this attractive thick-walled house of coral and stone. In 1836 Dr. Dwight Baldwin—also a missionary—moved in with his family. The home has been restored and furnished to reflect the period. You can view the living room, with the family's grand piano; the dining room; and Dr. Baldwin's dispensary. The Lahaina Restoration Foundation occupies the building, and its knowledgeable staff is here to answer almost any question about historic sites in town. Ask for its walking-tour brochure. ⊠ *696 Front St., Lahaina* ☎ *808/661–3262* ⊕ *www.hawaiimuseums.org* ✉ *$3* ◷ *Daily 10–4.*

⑦ **Banyan Tree.** This massive tree, a popular and hard-to-miss meeting place if your party splits up for independent exploring, was planted in 1873. It's the largest of its kind in the state and provides a welcome retreat for the weary who come to sit under its awesome branches. ⊠ *Front St., between Hotel and Canal Sts., Lahaina.*

⑩ **Brick Palace.** All that's left of the palace built by King Kamehameha I to welcome the captains of visiting ships are the excavated cornerstones and foundation in front of the Pioneer Inn. Hawaiʻi's first king lived only

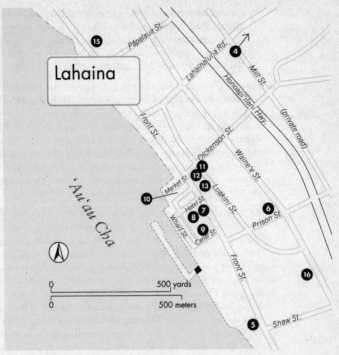

one year in the palace because his favorite wife, Ka'ahumanu, refused to stay here. It was then used as a warehouse, storeroom, and meeting house for 70 years, until it collapsed. ⊠ *Makai end of Market St., Lahaina.*

8 **Court House.** This old civic building was erected in 1859, rebuilt in 1925, and restored to its 1925 condition in 1999. At one time or another it served as a customhouse, post office, vault and collector's office, governor's office, police court, and courtroom. Now it houses museum displays, the Lahaina Arts Society, a visitor center, and, perhaps best of all, a water cooler. ⊠ *649 Wharf St., Lahaina* ☎ *808/661–0111* ⊠ *Free* ☉ *Daily 9–5.*

5 **505 Front Street.** The quaint, New England–style mall on this quiet stretch of Front Street has many treasures—notably a resident endangered sea turtle. In 2002 Turtle No. 5690 awed researchers and tourists alike by laying a record eight nests in the sand just steps from the mall. Catching sight of a nestling is rare, but 505's superb restaurants, galleries, bookstore, day spa, and local designer's shop are much more accessible. ⊠ *South end of Front St. near Shaw St., Lahaina.*

9 **Fort.** Used mostly as a prison, this fortress was positioned so that it could police the whaling ships that crowded the harbor. It was built from 1831 to 1832 after sailors, angered by a law forbidding local women from swimming out to ships, lobbed cannonballs at the town. Cannons raised from the wreck of a warship in Honolulu Harbor were brought to Lahaina and placed in front of the fort, where they still sit today. The building itself is an eloquent ruin. ⊠ *Canal and Wharf Sts., Lahaina.*

6 **Hale Pa'ahao (Old Prison).** This jailhouse dates to rowdy whaling days. Its name literally means "stuck-in-irons house," referring to the wall shackles and ball-and-chain restraints. The compound was built in the 1850s by convict laborers out of blocks of coral that had been salvaged from the demolished waterfront Fort. Most prisoners were sent here for desertion, drunkenness, or reckless horse riding. Today, a wax figure representing an imprisoned old sailor tells his recorded tale of woe. ⊠ *Waine'e and Prison Sts., Lahaina* ⌑ *Free* ⊙ *Daily 8–5.*

❹ Hale Pa'i. Six years after Protestant missionaries established Lahainaluna Seminary as a center of learning and enlightenment in 1831, they built this printing shop. Here at the press, they and their young Hawaiian scholars created a written Hawaiian language and used it to produce a Bible, history texts, and a newspaper. An exhibit displays a replica of the original Rampage press and facsimiles of early printing. The oldest U.S. educational institution west of the Rockies, the seminary now serves as Lahaina's public high school. ⊠ *980 Lahainaluna Rd., Lahaina* ☎ *808/661–3262* ⌑ *Donation requested* ⊙ *Weekdays 10–3.*

❸ Kā'anapali. The theatrical look of Hawai'i tourism—planned resort communities where luxury homes mix with high-rise hotels, fantasy swimming pools, and a theme-park landscape—all began right here in the 1960s. Three miles of uninterrupted white beach and placid water form the front yard for this artificial utopia, with its 40 tennis courts and two championship golf courses. The six major hotels here are all worth visiting just for a look around, especially the Hyatt Regency Maui, which has a multimillion-dollar art collection. At the Whalers Village shopping complex, a small **Whaling Museum** (⊠ Kā'anapali Pkwy., Suite H16 ☎ 808/661–5992 ⌑ donation requested) tells the story of the 19th-century *Moby-Dick* era; it's open daily from 9 AM to 10 PM. ⊠ *2435 Kā'anapali Pkwy.*

❷ Kahakuloa. Untouched by progress, this tiny village is a relic of pre–jet travel Maui. Many remote villages similar to Kahakuloa used to be tucked away in the valleys of this area. This is the wild side of West Maui. True adventurers will find terrific snorkeling and swimming along this coast, as well as some good hiking trails. ✛ *North end of Honoapi'ilani Hwy.*

▶ **❶ Kapalua.** Set in a beautiful secluded spot surrounded by pineapple fields, this resort got its first big boost in 1978, when the Maui Land & Pineapple Company built the luxurious Kapalua Bay Hotel. The hotels host dedicated golfers, celebrities who want to be left alone, and some of the world's richest folks. Kapalua's shops and restaurants are among Maui's finest, but expect to pay high prices. By contrast, the old **Honolua Store** serves informal plate lunches, popular with locals. ⊠ *Bay Dr., Kapalua.*

☼ Lahaina–Kā'anapali & Pacific Railroad. Affectionately called the Sugarcane Train, this is Maui's only passenger train. It's an 1890s-vintage railway that once shuttled sugar but now moves sightseers between Kā'anapali and Lahaina. This quaint little attraction with its singing conductor is a big deal for Hawai'i but probably not much of a thrill for those more accustomed to trains (though children like it no matter where they grew up). A barbecue dinner with entertainment is offered on Thursday at 5 PM. ✛ *1½ blocks north of the Lahainaluna Rd. stoplight (at Hinau St.) on Honoapi'ilani Hwy.* ⊠ *Lahaina* ☎ *808/661–0080* ⌑ *Round-trip $15.75, one-way $11.50, dinner train $59* ⊙ *Daily 10:15– 4.*

⓬ Master's Reading Room. This could be Maui's oldest residential building, constructed in 1834. In those days the ground floor was a mission's storeroom, and the reading room upstairs was for sailors. ⊠ *Front and Dickenson Sts., Lahaina* ☎ *808/661–3262.*

⓯ Seamen's Hospital. Built in the 1830s to house King Kamehameha III's royal court, this property was later turned over to the U.S. government, which used it as a hospital for whalers. Next door is a typical **sugar plantation camp residence**, circa 1900. ⊠ *1024 Front St., Lahaina* ☎ *808/ 661–3262.*

⑮ Spring House. Built by missionaries to shelter a freshwater spring, this historic structure now holds a huge Fresnel lens, once used in a local lighthouse that guided ships to Lahaina. ⊠ *Wharf Cinema Center, 658 Front St., Lahaina.*

need a break? The sandwiches have real Gruyère and Emmentaler cheese at **Maui Swiss Cafe** (⊠ 640 Front St., Lahaina ☎ 808/661–6776)—expensive ingredients with affordable results. The friendly owner scoops the best and cheapest locally made ice cream in Lahaina. Daily lunch specials are less than $6.

⑯ Waiola Church and Cemetery. The Waiola Cemetery is actually older than the neighboring church; it dates from the time when Kamehameha's sacred wife, Queen Keōpūolani, died and was buried here in 1823. The first church here was erected in 1832 by Hawaiian chiefs and was originally named Ebenezer by the queen's second husband and widower, Governor Hoapili. Aptly immortalized in James Michener's *Hawai'i* as the church that wouldn't stand, it was burned down twice and demolished in two windstorms. The present structure was put up in 1953 and named Waiola (water of life). ⊠ *535 Waine'e St., Lahaina* ☎ *808/ 661–4349.*

⑭ Wo Hing Museum. Built by the Wo Hing Society in 1912 as a fraternal society for Chinese residents, this eye-catching building now contains Chinese artifacts and a historic theater that shows Thomas Edison's films of Hawai'i, circa 1898. Upstairs is the only public Taoist altar on Maui. ⊠ *858 Front St., Lahaina* ☎ *808/661–5553* ⚐ *Donation requested* ⊙ *Daily 10–4.*

CENTRAL MAUI

Kahului, an industrial and commercial town in the center of the island, is home to many of Maui's permanent residents, who find their jobs close by. The area was developed in the early '50s to meet the housing needs of workers for the large sugarcane interests here, specifically those of Alexander & Baldwin. The company was tired of playing landlord to its many plantation workers and sold land to a developer who promised to create affordable housing. The scheme worked, and Kahului became the first planned city in Hawai'i. Ka'ahumanu Avenue (Route 32), Kahului's main street, runs from the harbor to the hills. It's the logical place to begin your exploration of Central Maui.

West of Kahului, Wailuku, the county seat since 1950, is certainly the most charming town in Central Maui. Its name means "Water of Destruction," after a battle that pitted King Kamehameha I against Maui warriors in the 'Īao Valley. Wailuku was a politically important town until the sugar industry began to decline in the 1960s and tourism took hold. Nowadays residents are buying and restoring plantation-era bungalows in the foothills of the West Maui Mountains.

a good tour Begin at the **Alexander & Baldwin Sugar Museum** ⑰ ▶ in Pu'unēnē, directly across from the HC&S sugar mill. From here, explore Kahului, which looks nothing like the lush, tropical paradise most people envision as Hawai'i. Head northwest on Pu'unēnē Avenue all the way to its end at Ka'ahumanu Avenue and turn left. Three blocks ahead you'll see the sputniklike canvas domes of Kaʻahumanu Center, Maui's largest shopping center. If you turn right at the signal just before that, you'll follow the curve of Kahului Beach Road and see many ships in port at **Kahului Harbor** ⑱. On your left are the cream-and-brown buildings of the **Maui Arts & Cultural Center** ⑲. Continue past the harbor, turn right at Waiehu Beach Road, and about a mile later as you cross the ʻĪao Stream you'll see **Halekiʻi-Pihana Heiau State Monument** ⑳ on the hilltop to your left. Return along the harbor road and make a right turn at Kanaloa Avenue. Return to Kaʻahumanu Avenue on this road, passing **Keōpūolani Park** ㉑ and the War Memorial Stadium, site of the annual Hula Bowl game. Turn right to reach Wailuku (Kaʻahumanu Avenue eventually becomes Wailuku's Main Street). To get a closer look at **Wailuku's Historic District** ㉒, turn right from Main Street onto Market Street, where you can park for free within view of the landmark ʻĪao **Theater** ㉓. The theater is a good place to begin your walking tour. Many amusing shops line **Market Street** ㉔ between Vineyard and Main streets. From here, it's a short walk along Main Street to **Kaʻahumanu Church** ㉕ on High Street, just around the corner from Main and across the way from the County Court House. Retrieve your car and turn right onto Main Street. After a few blocks, on your left, you'll see **Bailey House** ㉖.

Continue driving uphill, into the mountains. Main Street turns into ʻĪao Valley Road, the air cools, and the hilly terrain gets more lush. Soon you'll come to **Kepaniwai Park & Heritage Gardens** ㉗. ʻĪao Valley Road ends at ʻĪao **Valley State Park** ㉘, home of the erosion-formed gray and moss-green rock called ʻĪao Needle. This is a great place to picnic, wade in the stream, and explore the paths. Then return to Wailuku and, at the traffic light, turn right onto Route 30. Drive south a couple of miles to the **Maui Tropical Plantation & Country Store** ㉙.

TIMING   The complete itinerary will take a full day. But you can explore Central Maui comfortably in little more than a half day if you whiz through the Maui Tropical Plantation, or save it for another day. If you want to combine sightseeing with shopping, you'll need more time. Hikers may want to expand their outing to a full day to explore ʻĪao Valley State Park.

What to See

★ ▶ ⑰ **Alexander & Baldwin Sugar Museum.** "A&B," Maui's largest landowner, was one of the "Big Five" companies that spearheaded the planting, harvesting, and processing of sugarcane. Although Hawaiian cane sugar is now being supplanted by cheaper foreign versions—as well as by sugar derived from inexpensive sugar beets—the crop was for many years the mainstay of the Hawaiian economy. You'll find the museum in a small, restored plantation manager's house next to the post office and the still-operating sugar refinery (black smoke billows up when cane is burning). Historic photos, artifacts, and documents explain the introduction of sugarcane to Hawaiʻi and how plantation managers brought in laborers from other countries, thereby changing the Islands' ethnic mix. Exhibits also describe the sugar-making process. ✉ *3957 Hansen Rd., Puʻunēnē* ☎ *808/871–8058* 🎫 *$5* ⊘ *Mon.–Sat. 9:30–4:30 (last admission at 4).*

★ ㉖ **Bailey House.** This was the home of Edward and Caroline Bailey, two prominent missionaries who came to Wailuku to run the first Hawaiian girls' school on the island, the Wailuku Female Seminary. The school's main function was to train the girls in the "feminine arts." It

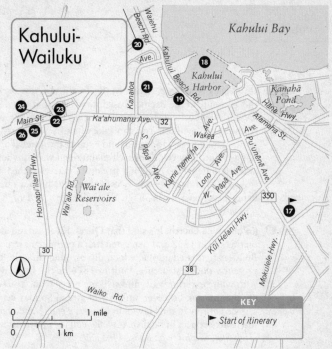

once stood next door to the Baileys' home, which they called
Halehōʻikeʻike (House of Display), but locals always called it the Bailey House, and the sign painters eventually gave in. Construction of
the house, between 1833 and 1850, was supervised by Edward Bailey
himself. The Maui Historical Society runs a museum in the plastered
stone house, with a small collection of artifacts from before and after
the missionaries' arrival and with Mr. Bailey's paintings of Wailuku.
Some rooms have missionary-period furniture. The Hawaiian Room
has exhibits on the making of tapa cloth, as well as samples of pre–Captain Cook weaponry. ⊠ *2375A Main St., Wailuku* ☎ *808/244–3326*
⊕ *www.mauimuseum.org* ⌦ *$5* ⊙ *Mon.–Sat. 10–4.*

㉚ Halekiʻi-Pihana Heiau State Monument. Stand here at either of the two heiau
and imagine the king of Maui surveying his domain. That's what Kahekili, Maui's last fierce king, did, and so did Kamehameha the Great
after he defeated Kahekili's soldiers. Today the view is most instructive.
Below, the once-powerful 'Iao Stream has been sucked dry and boxed
in by concrete. Before you is the urban heart of the island. The subur-
ban community behind you is all Hawaiian Homelands—property
owned solely by native Hawaiians. ✦ *End of Hea Pl., off Kuhio Pl. from
Waiehu Beach Rd. (Rte. 340), Kahului* ⌦ *Free* ⊙ *Daily 7–7.*

㉓ 'Iao Theater. One of Wailuku's most-photographed landmarks, this
charming movie house went up in 1927 and served as a community gathering spot. When restoration work was completed, the Maui Community Theatre resumed its longtime residence here in its historic Wailuku
headquarters. The art deco building is now the showpiece of Wailuku's
Main Street. ⊠ *68 N. Market St., Wailuku* ☎ *808/242–6969.*

Maui Bake Shop (⊠ 2092 Vineyard St., Wailuku ☎ 808/242–0064) serves salads, sandwiches, and a variety of light entrées, but what you're really going to crave are the pastries—a feast for the eyes as well as the palate. The pastel-frosted frogs, chicks, rabbits, and mice, made of orange butter-cream cookie dough, are irresistible.

★ 28 **'Iao Valley State Park.** When Mark Twain saw this park, he dubbed it the Yosemite of the Pacific. Yosemite it's not, but it is a lovely deep valley with the curious 'Iao Needle, a spire that rises more than 2,000 ft from the valley floor. You can take one of several easy hikes from the parking lot across 'Iao Stream and explore the junglelike area. This park has a beautiful network of well-maintained walks, where you can stop and meditate by the edge of a stream or marvel at the native plants and flowers. Mist occasionally rises if there has been a rain, which makes being here even more magical. ⊕ *Western end of Rte. 32* ⊠ *Free* ☉ *Daily 7–7.*

25 **Ka'ahumanu Church.** It's said that Queen Ka'ahumanu attended services on this site in 1832 and requested that a permanent structure be erected. Builders first tried adobe, which dissolved in the rain, then stone. The present wooden structure, built in 1876, is classic New England style, with white exterior walls and striking green trim. You won't be able to see the interior, however, unless you attend Sunday services. There's a service entirely in the Hawaiian language each Sunday morning at 9:30 (there are services in English as well—call for information). ⊠ *Main and High Sts., Wailuku* ☎ *808/244–5189.*

18 **Kahului Harbor.** The island's only deep-draft harbor, Kahului Harbor is Maui's chief port. American Hawaii's 800-passenger S.S. *Independence* and S.S. *Constitution* each stop here once a week, as do cargo ships and smaller vessels, including the occasional yacht. Surfers sometimes use this spot to catch some waves, but it's not a good swimming beach. ⊠ *Kahului Beach Rd., Kahului.*

21 **Keōpūolani Park.** Maui's "Central Park" covers 101 acres, and—reflecting Maui residents' traditional love of sports—it has seven playing fields. Named for the great Maui queen who was born near here and is buried in Lahaina's Waiola Church cemetery, the park is planted with native species that are still growing to reach their potential. The park also includes a native-plant botanical garden and a 3-mi walking path. ⊠ *Kanaloa Ave. next to the YMCA.*

🤚 27 **Kepaniwai Park & Heritage Gardens.** This county park is a memorial to Maui's cultural roots, with picnic facilities and ethnic displays dotting the landscape. Among the displays are an early Hawaiian shack, a New England–style saltbox, a Portuguese-style villa with gardens, and dwellings from such other cultures as China and the Philippines. Next door the Hawai'i Nature Center has an interactive exhibit and hikes good for children.

The peacefulness here belies the history of the area. During his quest for domination, King Kamehameha I brought his troops from the Big Island of Hawai'i to the Valley Isle in 1790 and engaged in a successful and particularly bloody battle against the son of Maui's chief, Kahekili, near Kepaniwai Park. An earlier battle at the site had pitted Kahekili himself against an older Big Island chief, Kalani'ōpu'u. Kahekili prevailed, but the carnage was so great that the nearby stream became known as Wailuku (water of destruction) and the place where fallen warriors choked the stream's flow was called Kepaniwai (the water dam). ⊠ *'Iao Valley Rd., Wailuku* ⊠ *Free* ☉ *Daily 7–7.*

need a break? For lunch try local favorite **Ba Le** (⊠ 270 Dairy Rd., Kahului ☎ 808/ 877–2400), in the Kau Kau Corner food court at the Maui Marketplace. The Vietnamese sandwiches—crisp French rolls piled with fresh herbs, vegetables, and your choice of meat—are cheap and delicious. The food court also offers diner fare and plate lunches.

㉔ Market Street. An idiosyncratic assortment of shops makes Wailuku's Market Street a delightful place for a stroll. Shops such as the Good Fortune Trading Company and Brown-Kobayashi carry affordable antiques and furnishings, while Gallerie Ha and the White Orchid gift shop are more sophisticated. Two good coffee shops provide Internet access. ⊠ *Wailuku.*

★ **⑲ Maui Arts & Cultural Center.** An epic fund drive by the citizens of Maui led to the creation of this $32 million facility. The top-of-the-line Castle Theater seats 1,200 people on orchestra, mezzanine, and balcony levels; rock stars play the A&B Amphitheater. The MACC (as it's called) also includes a small black box theater, an art gallery with interesting exhibits, and classrooms. The building itself is worth the visit: it incorporates work by Maui artists, and its signature lava-rock wall pays tribute to the skills of the Hawaiians. ✛ *Above the harbor on Kahului Beach Rd.* ☎ *808/242–2787, 808/242–7469 box office* ☉ *Weekdays 9–5.*

㉙ Maui Tropical Plantation & Country Store. When Maui's once-paramount crop declined in importance, a group of visionaries decided to open an agricultural theme park on the site of this former sugarcane field. The 60-acre preserve, on Route 30 just outside Wailuku, offers a 30-minute tram ride through its fields with an informative narration covering growing processes and plant types. Children will probably enjoy the historical-characters exhibit as well as fruit-testing, coconut-husking, and lei-making demonstrations, not to mention some entertaining spider monkeys. There's a restaurant on the property and a "country store" specializing in Made in Maui products. ⊠ *Honoapiʻilani Hwy. (Rte. 30), Waikapu* ☎ *808/244–7643* ⊠ *Free; tram ride with narrated tour $9.50* ☉ *Daily 9–5.*

㉒ Wailuku's Historic District. The National Register of Historic Places lists many of the old buildings here. Old Wailuku town, Maui's county seat, is sleepy but undergoing a small renaissance. Some interesting stores, coffee shops, and galleries dot its nostalgic side streets. You can pick up a free brochure that describes a self-guided walking tour at **Wailuku Main Street Association** (⊠ 2062 Main St. ☎ 808/244–3888). ⊠ *High, Vineyard, and Market Sts., Wailuku.*

THE SOUTH SHORE

Twenty-five years ago a scant few adventurers lived in Kīhei. Now about one-third of the Maui population lives here in what was one of the fastest-growing towns in America. Traffic lights and mini-malls may not fit your notion of paradise, but Kīhei does offer sun, heat, and excellent beaches. Besides that, the town's relatively inexpensive condos and small hotels make this a home base for many Maui visitors. Great restaurants are easy to find in any price range. At one end of this populous strip, you have Māʻalaea Small Boat Harbor and the Maui Ocean Center, a world-class seawater aquarium. At the other end, lovely Wailea—a resort community to rival those on West Maui—gives way to truly unspoiled coastline.

CloseUp

THE BOY WHO RAISED AN ISLAND

ACCORDING TO HAWAIIAN LEGEND, the island of Maui was named after a demigod whose father, Akalana, kept the heavens aloft and whose mother, Hina, guarded the path to the netherworld. Of their children, Maui was the only one who possessed magic powers, though he was rather humble in other respects: he wasn't a good fisherman and was teased mercilessly by his brothers for it. Eventually, the cunning young Maui devised a way to catch his own fish: he distracted his brothers and pulled his line across theirs, switching the hooks and stealing the fish they had caught.

When Maui's brothers caught on to his deception, they refused to take him fishing. Maui was dejected about being excluded from this activity, and to console him, his father gave him a magic hook, the Manaiakalani. Akalana said that the hook was fastened to the heavens and when it caught land a new continent would be born. Maui was able to convince his brothers to take him out one more time, and as they paddled deep into the ocean, he chanted a powerful spell, commanding the hook to catch "the Great Fish." The hook caught more than a fish—as they paddled along, mountain peaks were lifted out of the water's depths.

As the mountains began to rise, Maui told his brothers to paddle quickly without looking back. They did so for two days, at which point their curiosity proved too much. One of the brothers looked back, and as he stopped paddling, Maui's magic line snapped, and the hook was lost forever beneath the sea. Maui had intended to raise an entire continent, but because of his brother's weakness, he had only an island to show for his efforts.

a good drive

Start with a look at **Māʻalaea Small Boat Harbor** ㉚ ▶, the setting-out place for many whale-watching trips, snorkel excursions (often out to the tiny crescent island Molokini), and sunset dinner cruises. Then tour the **Maui Ocean Center** ㉛, an aquarium dedicated to the sea life of the North Pacific. When you leave the aquarium, turn right onto Route 30 and then turn right again at the first traffic signal onto North Kīhei Road (Route 31). You're headed toward the town of **Kīhei** ㉜ on a straight road following the long, sandy coastline of Māʻalaea Bay. On your left is marshy Keālia Pond, a state-managed wildlife sanctuary. On your right, ecologically fragile dunes run between the road and the sea. A turnout provides some parking stalls, information about the dunes, and a boardwalk so you can cross the dunes and use the beach. When you get to the long, thin town of Kīhei, you have a choice. You can turn right at the fork in the road and experience the colorful stop-and-go beach route of South Kīhei Road. Or you can turn left and bypass the town on the Piʻilani Highway, hastening to the resort community of **Wailea** ㉝. If you're looking for the best beach, you might as well flip a coin. There are great beaches all along this coast. At Wailea, you'll drive past grand resorts interspersed with stretches of golf courses and access roads leading down to small but excellent beaches. As you head south on Wailea Alanui Drive, the manicured look of Wailea gives way to wildness and, after a couple of miles, to **Mākena Beach State Park** ㉞. Mākena is such a big beach that it has two paved parking areas. Beyond this point the landscape gets wilder and the road gradually fades away in black fields of cracked lava. This is **La Pérouse Bay** ㉟.

TIMING Because it includes so many fine beach choices, this is definitely an all-day excursion—especially if you include a visit to the aquarium. A good way to do this trip is to get active in the morning with exploring and snorkeling, then shower in a beach park, dress up a little, and enjoy the cool luxury of the Wailea resorts. At sunset, settle in for dinner at one of the area's many fine restaurants.

What to See

32 **Kīhei.** This is a community that's still discovering itself. A greenway for bikers and pedestrians is under construction, as is an unchecked surplus of new homes and properties. Moderately priced hotels, condos, and restaurants make the town convenient for visitors. The beaches and the reliably sunny weather are added attractions. The county beach parks such as Kamaʻole I, II, and III have lawns, showers, and picnic tables. Remember: beach park or no beach park, the public has a right to the entire coastal strand, and this one in Kīhei has many off-road delights.

35 **La Pérouse Bay.** Beyond Mākena Beach, the road fades away into a vast territory of black lava flows, the result of Haleakalā's last eruption some 200 years ago. This is where Maui received its first official visit by a European explorer—the French admiral Jean-François de Galaup, Comte de La Pérouse, in 1786. Before it ends, the road passes through ʻĀhihi-Kīnaʻu Marine Preserve, an excellent place for morning snorkel adventures.

▶ **30** **Māʻalaea Small Boat Harbor.** With only 89 slips and so many good reasons to take people out on the water, this active little harbor needs to be expanded. The Army Corps of Engineers has a plan to do so, but harbor users are fighting it—particularly the surfers, who say the plan would destroy their surf breaks. In fact, the surf here is world renowned, especially the break to the left of the harbor called "freight train," said to be the fastest anywhere. ⊠ *Off Honoapiʻilani Hwy. (Rte. 30).*

★ **34** **Mākena Beach State Park.** "Big Beach" they call it—a huge stretch of coarse golden sand without a house or hotel for miles. A decade ago, Maui citizens campaigned successfully to preserve this beloved beach from development. At the right-hand end of the beach rises the beautiful hill called Puʻu Ōlaʻi, a perfect cinder cone. A climb over the rocks at this end leads to "Little Beach," where the (technically illegal) clothing-optional attitude prevails.

★ **31** **Maui Ocean Center.** You'll feel as though you're walking from the seashore down to the bottom of the reef, and then through an acrylic tunnel in the middle of the sea at this aquarium, which focuses on Hawaiʻi and the Pacific. Special tanks get you close up with turtles, rays, and the unusual creatures of the tide pools. The center is part of a growing complex of retail shops and restaurants overlooking the harbor. ✦ *Enter from Honoapiʻilani Hwy. (Rte. 30) as it curves past Māʻalaea Harbor* ⊠ *Māʻalaea* ☎ *808/270–7000* ⊕ *www.mauioceancenter.com* ✉ *$19* ☉ *July–Aug., daily 9–6; Sept.–June, daily 9–5.*

★ **33** **Wailea.** Wailea, the South Shore's resort community, is slightly quieter and drier than its West Side sister, Kāʻanapali. Most visitors cannot pick a favorite and stay at both. The luxury of the resorts (edging on overindulgence) and the simple grandeur of the Shops at Wailea make the otherwise stark coast a worthy destination. A handful of perfect little beaches all have public access, and a paved beach walk allows you to stroll among all the properties, restaurants, and sandy coves. A great place to watch whales in the winter, the makai, or ocean, side of the beach walk is landscaped with exceptionally rare native plants.

HALEAKALĀ & UPCOUNTRY

The west-facing upper slopes of Haleakalā are locally called "Upcountry." This region is responsible for much of Hawai'i's produce—lettuce, tomatoes, and sweet Maui onions—but the area is also a big flower producer. As you drive along you'll notice cactus thickets mingled with purple jacaranda, wild hibiscus, and towering eucalyptus trees. Upcountry is also fertile ranch land, with such spreads as the historic 20,000-acre 'Ulupalakua Ranch and 32,000-acre Haleakalā Ranch. In Makawao each July 4, the Maui Roping Club throws its annual rodeo and parade.

a good drive

Take the **Haleakalā Highway** ㊱ ▶ (Route 37) to **Haleakalā National Park** ㊲ and the mountain's breathtaking summit. Make sure you have a full tank of gas. There are no service stations beyond Kula. Watch the signs: Haleakalā Highway divides. If you go straight it becomes Kula Highway, which is still Route 37. If you veer to the left it becomes Route 377, the road you want. After about 6 mi, make a left onto Route 378. The switchbacks begin here. Near the top of the mountain is the Park Headquarters/Visitor Center, a good spot to stretch your legs and learn a little bit about the park.

Continuing up the mountain, you'll come to several overlooks, including Leleiwi Overlook and Kalahaku Overlook, both with views into the crater. Not far from Kalahaku Overlook you'll find the Haleakalā Visitor Center. Eventually you'll reach the highest point on Maui, the Pu'u 'Ula'ula Overlook.

On the return trip, turn left when you reach Route 377. Drive about 2 mi, and you'll come to **Kula Botanical Gardens** ㊳ on your left. It's worth a stop here to admire the abundant tropical flora. Continue south on Route 377 and you'll soon join Route 37 again. Turn left and soak in the slow pace of life when you stumble upon little **Kēōkea** ㊴. Follow the road as it turns coastward and you'll reach 'Ulupalakua Ranch headquarters and **Tedeschi Vineyards and Winery** ㊵, where you can sample Maui's only homemade wines.

Return toward Kahului on Route 37, the Kula Highway. If you're pressed for time you can take Route 37 from here back to Kahului. Otherwise, head north on Route 365 toward **Makawao** ㊶, a classic old Hawaiian town. The **Hui No'eau Visual Arts Center** ㊷ is about a mile from the Makawao crossroads as you head down Baldwin Avenue. From here it's a 7-mi drive down toward the ocean to the Hāna Highway at the town of Pā'ia. Make a left on the Hāna Highway to return to Kahului.

TIMING   This can be an all-day outing even without the detours to Tedeschi Vineyards and Makawao. If you start early enough to catch the sunrise from Haleakalā's summit, you'll have plenty of time to explore the mountain, have lunch in Kula or at 'Ulupalakua Ranch, and end your day with dinner in Makawao or Ha'ikū.

What to See

▶ ㊱   **Haleakalā Highway.** On this road you'll travel from sea level to an elevation of 10,023 ft in only 38 mi—a feat you won't be able to repeat on any other car route in the world. It's not a quick drive, however. It'll take you about two hours—longer if you can't resist the temptation to stop and enjoy the spectacular views. ⊠ *Rte. 37.*

㊲   **Haleakalā National Park.** Haleakalā Crater is the centerpiece of this 27,284-acre national park, established in 1916. The crater is actually an erosional valley, flushed out by water pouring from the summit

Fodor'sChoice
★

through two enormous gaps. The small hills within the crater are volcanic cinder cones (called *puʻu* in Hawaiian), each with a small crater at its top, and each the site of a former eruption. The mountain has terrific camping and hiking, including a trail that loops through the crater.

Before you head up Haleakalā, call for the latest **park weather conditions** (☎ 808/877–5111). Extreme gusty winds, heavy rain, and even snow in winter are not uncommon. Because of the high altitude, the mountaintop temperature is often as much as 30 degrees cooler than that at sea level. Be sure to bring a jacket.

You can learn something of the volcano's origins and eruption history at the **Park Headquarters/Visitor Center,** at a 7,000-ft elevation on Haleakalā Highway. Maps, posters, and other memorabilia are available at the gift shop here.

Leleiwi Overlook, at about an 8,800-ft elevation on Haleakalā, is one of several lookout areas in the park. If you're here in the late afternoon, it's possible you'll experience a phenomenon called the Brocken Specter. Named after a similar occurrence in East Germany's Harz Mountains, the "specter" allows you to see yourself reflected on the clouds and encircled by a rainbow. Don't wait all day for this, because it's not a daily occurrence.

The famous silversword plant grows amid the desertlike surroundings at **Kalahaku Overlook,** at the 9,000-ft level on Haleakalā. This endangered flowering plant grows only here in the crater at the summit of this mountain. The silversword looks like a member of the yucca family and produces a 3- to 8-ft-tall stalk with several hundred purple sunflowers. At this lookout the silversword is kept in an enclosure to protect it from souvenir hunters and nibbling wildlife.

The **Haleakalā Visitor Center,** at an elevation of 9,740 ft, has exhibits inside, and a trail from here leads to White Hill—a short, easy walk that will give you an even better view of the valley. Hosmer Grove, just off the highway before you get to the visitor center, has campsites and interpretive trails. Park rangers maintain a changing schedule of talks and hikes both here and at the top of the mountain. Call the park for current schedules.

Just before the summit, the **Crater Observatory** offers warmth and shelter, informative displays, and an eye-popping view of the cinder-cone-studded, 7-mi by 3-mi crater. The highest point on Maui is the **Puʻu ʻUlaʻula Overlook,** at the 10,023-ft summit. Here you'll find a glass-enclosed lookout with a 360-degree view. The building is open 24 hours a day, and this is where visitors gather for the best sunrise view. Dawn begins between 5:45 and 7, depending on the time of year. On a clear day you can see the islands of Molokaʻi, Lānaʻi, Kahoʻolawe, and Hawaiʻi (the Big Island). On a *really* clear day you can even spot Oʻahu glimmering in the distance.

On a small hill nearby, you'll see **Science City,** a research and communications center straight out of an espionage thriller. The University of Hawaiʻi and the Department of Defense don't allow visitors to enter the facility. The university maintains an observatory here, and the Department of Defense tracks satellites. ⊠ *Haleakalā Crater Rd. (Rte. 378), Makawao* ☎ *808/572–4400* ⊕ *www.nps.gov/hale* ⌑ *$10 per car* ☉ *Park Headquarters/Visitor Center daily 8–4; Haleakalā Visitor Center daily sunrise–3.*

need a break? **Kula Lodge** (⊠ Haleakalā Hwy., Kula ☎ 808/878–2517) serves hearty breakfasts from 6:30 to 11:15, a favorite with hikers coming down from a sunrise visit to Haleakalā's summit, as well as those on their way up for a late-morning tramp in the crater. Spectacular ocean views fill the windows of this mountainside lodge.

㊷ Hui No'eau Visual Arts Center. The main house of this nonprofit cultural center on the old Baldwin estate, just outside the town of Makawao, is an elegant two-story Mediterranean-style villa designed in the 1920s by the defining Hawai'i architect C. W. Dickey. "The Hui" is the grande dame of Maui's well-known arts scene. The exhibits are always satisfying, and the grounds might as well be a botanical garden. The Hui also offers classes and maintains working artists' studios. ⊠ 2841 Baldwin Ave., Makawao ☎ 808/572–6560 ⊠ Free ☉ Daily 10–4.

㊴ Kēōkea. More of a friendly gesture than a town, this is the last outpost for Maui's cowboys on their way to work at 'Ulupalakua or Kaupō ranch. A coffee tree pushes through the sunny deck at Grandma's Coffee Shop, and tiny Kēōkea Gallery sells some of the most original artwork on the island. The only rest room for miles is across the street at the public park, and the view makes stretching your legs worth it.

㊳ Kula Botanical Gardens. This well-kept garden has assimilated itself naturally into its craggy 6-acre habitat. There are beautiful trees here, including native koa (prized by woodworkers) and *kukui* (the state tree, a symbol of enlightenment). There's also a good selection of proteas, the flowering shrubs that have become a signature flower crop of Upcountry Maui. A natural stream feeds into a koi pond, which is also home to a pair of African cranes. ⊠ R.R. 2, Upper Kula Rd., Kula ☎ 808/878–1715 ⊠ $5 ☉ Daily 9–4.

㊶ Makawao. This once-tiny town has managed to hang on to its country charm (and eccentricity) as it has grown in popularity. The district was settled originally by Portuguese and Japanese immigrants, who came to Maui to work the sugar plantations and then moved "Upcountry" to establish small farms, ranches, and stores. Descendants now work the neighboring Haleakalā and 'Ulupalakua ranches. Every July 4 the *paniolo* (Hawaiian cowboy) set comes out in force for the Makawao Rodeo. The crossroads of town—lined with places to shop, view the work of local artists, and dine—reflects a growing population of people who came here just because they liked it. ⊠ Rte. 365, East Maui.

need a break? One of Makawao's most famous landmarks is **Komoda Store & Bakery** (⊠ 3674 Baldwin Ave. ☎ 808/572–7261)—a classic mom-and-pop store that has changed little in three-quarters of a century—where you can get a delicious cream puff if you arrive early enough. They make hundreds but sell out each day.

★ ㊵ Tedeschi Vineyards and Winery. You can take a tour of the winery and its historic grounds, the former Rose Ranch, and sample the island's only wines: a pleasant Maui Blush, the Maui Brut-Blanc de Noirs Hawaiian Champagne, and Tedeschi's annual Maui Nouveau. The top-selling products, however, are pineapple wines. The tasting room is a cottage built in the late 1800s for the frequent visits of King Kalākaua. The cottage also contains the **'Ulupalakua Ranch History Room,** which tells colorful stories of the ranch's owners, the paniolo tradition that developed here, and Maui's polo teams. The old General Store may look like a museum, but in fact it's an excellent pit stop. The ranch and winery are not too out of the way when you're returning from a visit to

Haleakalā, and they're definitely worth a stop. ⊠ *Kula Hwy., 'Ulupalakua Ranch* ☎ *808/878–6058* ⊕ *www.mauiwine.com* ☎ *Free* ☉ *Daily 9–5, tours at 10:30 and 1:30.*

THE ROAD TO HĀNA

Fodor'sChoice
★

Don't let anyone tell you **Hāna Highway** is impassable, frightening, or otherwise unadvisable. Because of all the hype, you're bound to be a little nervous approaching it for the first time; but once you try it, you'll wonder if maybe there's somebody out there making it sound tough just to keep out the hordes. The 55-mi road begins in Kahului, where it is a well-paved highway. The eastern half of the road, riddled with turns and bridges, is challenging, and you'll want to stop often so the driver can enjoy the view, too. Yet it's not a grueling all-day drive. The challenging part of the road takes only an hour and a half. Don't expect a booming city when you get to Hāna. It's the road, which meanders past lush scenery and waterfalls, that's the draw.

a good drive

Hāna Highway is the main street in the little town of **Pā'ia** ⓸ ▶. You'll want to begin with a full tank of gas. There are no gas stations along Hāna Highway, and the stations in Hāna close by 6 PM. You can also pick up a picnic lunch here. Lunch and snack choices along the way are limited to rustic fruit stands. Once the road gets twisty, remember that many residents make this trip frequently. You'll recognize them because they're the ones who'll be zipping around every curve. They've seen this so many times before that they don't care to linger. Pull over to let them pass.

Two miles east of Pā'ia you'll see **Ho'okipa Beach** ⓸, arguably the windsurfing capital of the world. Two miles later the bottom of Ha'ikū Road offers a right-turn side trip to **Ha'ikū** ⓸, Maui's verdant gulch country. About 6 mi later, at the bottom of Kaupakalua Road, the roadside mileposts begin measuring the 36 mi to Hāna town. The road's trademark noodling starts about 3 mi after that. All along this stretch of road, waterfalls are abundant. Open the windows to enjoy the sounds and smells. There are plenty of places to pull off and park. You'll want to plan on doing this a few times, since the road's curves make driving without a break difficult. When it's raining (which is often), the drive is particularly beautiful.

As you drive on you'll pass the sleepy country villages of **Huelo** and **Kailua** ⓸. At about mile marker 11 you can stop at the bridge over **Puahokamoa Stream** ⓸, where there are more pools and waterfalls. If you'd rather stretch your legs and use a flush toilet, continue another mile to the **Kaumahina State Wayside Park** ⓸. Near mile marker 14 you'll find yourself driving along a cliffside down into deep, lush **Honomanū Bay** ⓸. Another 4 mi brings you to the **Ke'anae Arboretum** ⓹, where you can add to your botanical education or enjoy a challenging hike into a forest. Nearby you'll find the **Ke'anae Overlook** ⓹. Coming up is the halfway mark to Hāna. If you've had enough scenery, this is as good a time as any to turn around and head back to civilization.

Continue from mile marker 20 for about ¾ mi to **Wailua Overlook** ⓹. After another ½ mi you'll hit the best falls on the entire drive to Hāna, **Waikāne Falls** ⓹. At about mile marker 25 you'll see a road that heads down toward the ocean and the village of **Nāhiku** ⓹, once a populous ancient settlement. Just after mile marker 31, turn left onto 'Ula'ino Road. Follow the signs to **Ka'eleku Caverns** ⓹. You'll need to call ahead to book an underground tour. The road doubles back for a mile, loses its pavement, and even crosses a stream just before Kahanu Garden and **Pi'ilani-**

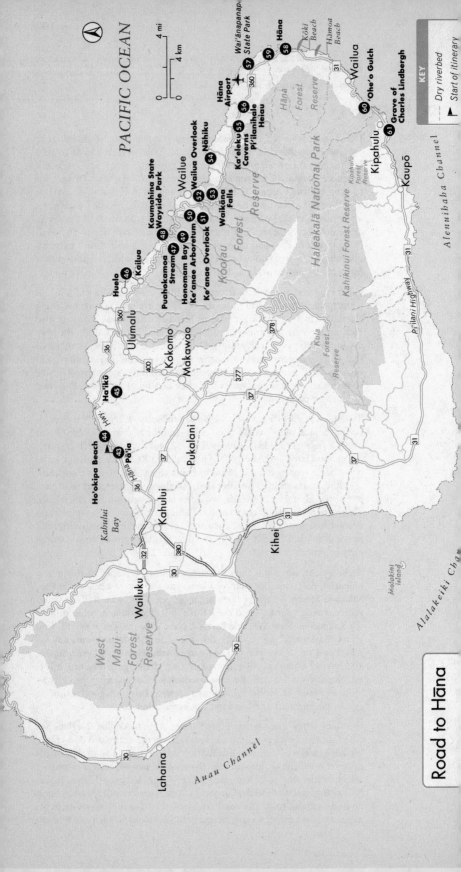

PACIFIC OCEAN

Kaupō

Haleakalā National Park

Kahikinui Forest Reserve

Kula
Forest
Reserve

West
Maui
Forest
Reserve

Wailuku

Kahului

Kahului Bay

Kīhei

Pukalani

Makawao

Kokomo

Ulumalu

Haʻikū 45

Paʻia 43

Huelo

Kailua 46

Puahokamoa
Stream 47

Kaumahina State
Wayside Park 48

Honomanu Bay 49

Keʻanae Arboretum 50

Keʻanae Overlook 51

Wailua 52

Wailua Overlook

Waikāni
Falls 53

Nāhiku 54

Koʻolau
Forest
Reserve

Keʻeleku
Caverns 55

Piʻilanihale
Heiau 56

Hāna
Airport

Waiʻānapanapa
State Park 57

Hāna 58

59

Kōkī
Beach

Hāmoa
Beach

Wailua

ʻOheʻo Gulch 60

Kīpahulu

Grave of
Charles Lindbergh 61

Kipahulu
Forest
Reserve

ʻAlenuihaha Channel

ʻAlalākeiki Channel

Molokini
Island

ʻAuʻau Channel

Lahaina

4 mi
4 km

Road to Hāna

hale Heiau ㊊, the largest in the state. Back on the road and less than ½ mi farther is the turnoff for Hāna Airport. Just beyond mile marker 32 you'll pass **Wai'ānapanapa State Park** ㊐. Stop at the black-sand beach for a swim. **Hāna** ㊝ is just minutes away from here. **Hotel Hāna-Maui** ㊟, with its surrounding ranch, is the mainstay of Hāna's economy.

Once you've seen Hāna, you might want to drive 10 mi past the town to the pools at **'Ohe'o Gulch** ㊿. Many people travel the mile past 'Ohe'o Gulch to see the **Grave of Charles Lindbergh** ㊀. You'll see a ruined sugar mill with a big chimney on the right side of the road and then, on the left, a rutted track leading to Palapala Ho'omau Congregational Church. The simple one-room church sits on a bluff over the sea, with the small graveyard on the ocean side. From here, you'll want to return the way you came. The road ahead is quite rough and not recommended for rental cars.

TIMING With stops, the drive from Pā'ia to Hāna should take you between two and three hours. Lunching in Hāna, hiking, and swimming can easily turn the round-trip into a full-day outing. Since there's so much scenery to take in, try to plan your Road to Hāna drive for a day that promises fair, sunny weather, though the drive can be beautiful when it's raining. For an even more relaxing trip, plan to stay overnight at the Hāna hotel.

What to See

㊀ **Grave of Charles Lindbergh.** The world-renowned aviator chose to be buried here because he and his wife, writer Anne Morrow Lindbergh, spent a lot of time living in the area in a home they'd built. He was buried here in 1974, next to Palapala Ho'omau Congregational Church. Since this is a churchyard, be considerate and leave everything exactly as you found it. Next to the churchyard on the ocean side is a small county park, a good place for a peaceful picnic. ⊠ *Palapala Ho'omau Congregational Church, Pi'ilani Hwy., Kīpahulu.*

㊟ **Ha'ikū.** At one time this town vibrated around a couple of enormous pineapple canneries. Now the place is reawakening and becoming a self-reliant community. At the town center, the old cannery has been turned into a rustic mall. Nearby warehouses are following suit. Continue 2 mi up Kokomo Road to see a large pu'u capped with a grove of columnar pines, and the 4th Marine Division Memorial Park. During World War II American GIs trained here for battles on Iwo Jima and Saipan. Locals have nicknamed the cinder cone Giggle Hill, because it was a popular hangout for Maui women and their favorite servicemen. You might want to return to Hāna Highway by following Ha'ikū Road east. This is one of Maui's prettiest drives, and it passes West Kuiaha Road, where a left turn will bring you to a second renovated cannery. ⊠ *Intersection of Ha'ikū and Kokomo Rds.*

㊝ **Hāna.** The town centers on its lovely circular bay, dominated on the right-hand shore by a pu'u called Ka'uiki. A short trail here leads to a cave, the birthplace of Queen Kā'ahumanu. Two miles beyond town another pu'u presides over a loop road that passes Hāna's two best beaches—Koki and Hāmoa. The hill is called Ka Iwi O Pele (Pele's Bone). This area is rich in Hawaiian history and legend. Offshore here, at tiny 'Ālau Island, the demigod Maui supposedly fished up the Hawaiian islands.

Although sugar was once the mainstay of Hāna's economy, the last plantation shut down in the '40s. In 1946 rancher Paul Fagan built the **Hotel Hāna-Maui** and stocked the surrounding pastureland with cattle. Suddenly, it was the ranch and its hotel that were putting food on most tables. The cross you'll see on the hill above the hotel was put there in memory of Fagan.

For many years, the Hotel Hāna-Maui was the only attraction for diners and shoppers determined to spend some time and money in Hāna after their long drive. Now, the **Hāna Cultural Center Museum** (⊠ Ukea St. ☎ 808/248–8622) also helps to meet that need. Besides operating a well-stocked gift shop, it displays artifacts, quilts, a replica of an authentic *kauhale* (an ancient Hawaiian living complex, with thatch huts and food gardens), and other Hawaiiana. The knowledgeable staff can explain it all to you. ⊠ *Hāna Hwy., mile marker 35.*

Hāna Airport. Think of Amelia Earhart. Think of Waldo Pepper. If these picket-fence runways don't turn your thoughts to the derring-do of barnstorming pilots, you haven't seen enough old movies. Only the smallest planes can land and depart here, and when none of them happen to be around, the lonely wind sock is the only evidence that this is a working airfield. ⊠ *Hāna Hwy. past mile marker 30* ☎ *808/248–8208.*

49 Honomanū Bay. At mile marker 14 the Hāna Highway drops into and out of this enormous valley, with its rocky black-sand beach. The Honomanū Valley was carved by erosion during Haleakalā's first dormant period. At the canyon's head there are 3,000-ft cliffs and a 1,000-ft waterfall, but don't try to reach them. There's not much of a trail, and what does exist is practically impassable. ⊠ *Hāna Hwy. before Ke'anae.*

★ **44 Ho'okipa Beach.** There is no better place on this or any other island to watch the world's best windsurfers in action. The surfers know five different surf breaks here by name. Unless it's a rare day without wind or waves, you're sure to get a show. It's not safe to park on the shoulder. Use the ample parking lot at the county park entrance. ⊹ *2 mi past Pā'ia on Rte. 36.*

59 Hotel Hāna-Maui. It's pleasant to stroll around the lobby of this low-key but beautiful property, perhaps on the way to dinner at the restaurant, drinks at the bar, or shopping in the gift stores. The newer Sea Ranch cottages, built to look like authentic plantation housing from the outside, across the road are also part of the hotel. ⊠ *Hāna Hwy., Hāna* ☎ *808/248–8211.*

46 Huelo. This little farm town has two quaint churches and several lovely B&Bs. It's a good place to stay if you value privacy, but it also provides an opportunity to meet local residents and learn about a rural lifestyle you might not have expected to find in the Islands. The same can be said for nearby **Kailua** (mile marker 6), home to Alexander & Baldwin's irrigation employees. ⊠ *Hāna Hwy. near mile marker 5.*

55 Ka'eleku Caverns. Guided tours with Maui Cave Adventures lead amateur spelunkers into a system of gigantic lava tubes, accentuated by colorful underworld formations. Choose your level of exploration—a one-hour walking tour or a two-hour adventure tour. Gear (gloves, flashlight, and hard hat) is provided, and visitors must be at least eight years of age. ⊹ *1¼ mi down Ulaino Road, off Hāna Hwy.* ☎ *808/248–7308* ⊕ *www.mauicave.com* ⊠ *$29–$59* ⊙ *Tours depart Mon.–Sat. at 11 and 1.*

48 Kaumahina State Wayside Park. The park has a picnic area, rest rooms, and a lovely overlook to the Ke'anae Peninsula. Hardier souls can camp here, with a permit. ⊠ *Hāna Hwy., mile marker 12, Kailua* ☎ *808/984–8109* ⊠ *Free* ⊙ *Weekdays 8–4.*

off the beaten path

Kaupō Road. The road to Hāna continues all the way around Haleakalā's "back side" through 'Ulupalakua Ranch and into Kula. The desertlike area, with its grand vistas, is unlike anything else on the island, but the road itself is bad, sometimes impassable in winter. The car-rental agencies are smart to call it off-limits to their passenger cars. Most of the residents along the road in these wild reaches also prefer that you stick to the windward side of the mountain. The danger and dust from increasing numbers of speeding jeep drivers are making life tough for the residents, especially in Kaupō, with its 4 mi of unpaved road. The small communities around East Maui cling tenuously to the old ways. Please keep them in mind if you do pass this way.

50 Ke'anae Arboretum. Here's a place to learn the names of the many plants and trees now considered native to Hawai'i. The meandering Pi'ina'au Stream adds a graceful touch to the arboretum and provides a swimming pond besides. You can take a fairly rigorous hike from the arboretum if you can find the trail at one side of the large taro patch. Be careful not to lose the trail once you're on it. A lovely forest waits at the end of the hike. ⊠ *Hāna Hwy., mile marker 17, Ke'anae* 🖃 *Free* ☉ *Daily 24 hrs.*

51 Ke'anae Overlook. From this observation point, you can take in the patchwork-quilt effect the taro farms create below. The people of Ke'anae are working hard to revive this Hawaiian agricultural art and the traditional cultural values that the crop represents. The ocean provides a dramatic backdrop for the farms. In the other direction there are awesome views of Haleakalā through the foliage. This is a great spot for photos. ⊠ *Hāna Hwy. near mile marker 17, Ke'anae.*

54 Nāhiku. In ancient times this was a busy settlement with hundreds of residents. Now only about 80 people live in Nāhiku, mostly native Hawaiians and some back-to-the-land types. A rubber grower planted trees here in the early 1900s. The experiment didn't work out, so Nāhiku was essentially abandoned. The road ends at the sea in a pretty landing. This is the rainiest, densest part of the East Maui rain forest. ✛ *Makai side of Hāna Hwy., mile marker 25.*

★ 60 'Ohe'o Gulch. One branch of Haleakalā National Park runs down the mountain from the crater and reaches the sea here, where a basalt-lined stream cascades from one pool to the next. Some tour guides still call this area "Seven Sacred Pools," but in truth there are more than seven, and they've never been considered sacred. You can park here and walk to the lowest pools for a cool swim. The place gets crowded, though, since most people who drive the Hāna Road make this their last stop. If you can hike at all, go up the stream on the 2-mi hike to **Waimoku Falls.** The trail crosses a spectacular gorge, then turns into a boardwalk that takes you through an amazing bamboo forest. You can pitch a tent in the grassy campground down by the sea. ⊠ *Pi'ilani Hwy., 10 mi south of Hāna.*

need a break?

The drive to Hāna wouldn't be as enchanting without a stop or two at one of the countless fruit stands alongside the highway. Every half mile or so a thatched hut tempts passersby with apple bananas, lilikoi, avocados, or starfruit just plucked from the tree. Leave 50¢ or $1 in the can for the folks who live off the land. Definitely take the time to stop just past mile marker 2 on the Hāna Highway, where you can sample fresh sugarcane juice and have a young coconut shucked for you.

About 10 minutes before Hāna town, you can stop for—of all things—espresso. The tiny, colorful **Nahiku Ti Gallery and Coffee Shop** (✛ between mile markers 27 and 28, Hāna Hwy. ☎ 808/248–8800) sells local coffee, dried fruits and candies, and delicious (if pricey) banana bread. Sometimes the barbecue is fired up and you can try fish skewers or baked breadfruit (an island favorite impossible to find elsewhere). The Ti Gallery sells Hawaiian crafts.

★ ▶ **43** **Pā'ia.** This little town on Maui's north shore was once a sugarcane enclave, with a mill and plantation camps. Astute immigrants quickly opened shops to serve the workers, who probably found it easier to buy supplies near home. The town boomed during World War II when the marines set up camp in nearby Ha'ikū. The old HC&S sugar mill finally closed and no sign of the military remains, but the entrepreneurs—in one form or another—are here to stay. In the '70s Pā'ia became a hippie town as dropouts headed for Maui to open boutiques, galleries, and unusual eateries. In the '80s windsurfers discovered nearby Ho'okipa Beach and brought an international flavor to Pā'ia (to the benefit of the unusual eateries). Budget inns have cropped up to accommodate eclectic travelers, and whether you're looking for yoga pants or pumpkin soup, Pā'ia is sure to deliver.

Pā'ia is also home to Lama Tenzin, a Tibetan monk who lives and teaches at a small open temple called **Karma Rimay O Sal Ling,** on Baldwin Avenue a half mile from the traffic light. ⊠ *Rtes. 390 and 36, north shore.*

need a break?
Pā'ia is a great place to find food. A French-Caribbean bistro with a sushi bar in back, a French-Indian creperie, a neo-Mexican gourmet restaurant, and a fish market all compete for your patronage near the intersection of Baldwin Avenue and Hāna Road. This abundance is helpful because Pā'ia is the last place to snack before the pilgrimage to Hāna and the first stop for the famished on the return trip.

Anthony's Coffee Company (☎ 808/579–8340) sells ice cream, smoothies, and picnic lunches. **Charley's Saloon** (☎ 808/579–8085), on Hāna Road, is an easygoing local hangout with pool tables. **Mana Foods** (☎ 808/579–8904) is an admirable natural-foods store. **Pā'ia Fishmarket** (☎ 808/579–8030) has fresh island fish both by the pound and served as tasty lunches and dinners. **Picnics** (☎ 808/579–8021) is a great place to get takeout on Baldwin Avenue. Pā'ia has an excellent wine store, the **Wine Corner** (☎ 808/579–8940).

★ **56** **Pi'ilanihale Heiau.** The largest prehistoric monument in Hawai'i, this temple platform was built for a great 16th-century Maui king named Pi'ilani and his heirs. This king also supervised the construction of a 10-ft-wide road that completely encircled the island. (That's why his name is part of most of Maui's highway titles.) Hawaiian families continue to maintain and protect this sacred site as they have for centuries, and they have not been eager to turn it into a tourist attraction. However, they now offer a brochure so you can tour the property yourself. Parties of four or more can reserve a guided tour by calling 48 hours in advance. Tours include 122-acre **Kahanu Garden,** a federally funded research center focusing on the ethnobotany of the Pacific. ✦ *Left on 'Ula'ino Rd. at mile marker 31 of Hāna Hwy.; the road turns to gravel; continue 1½ mi* ☎ *808/ 248–8912* 🖼 *Self-guided tours $5, guided tours $10* ☉ *Weekdays 10–2.*

47 **Puahokamoa Stream.** The bridge over Puahokamoa Stream is one of many you'll cross en route from Pā'ia to Hāna. It spans pools and waterfalls. Picnic tables are available, so many people favor this as a stopping point, but there are no rest rooms. ⊠ *Hāna Hwy. near mile marker 11.*

57 **Wai'ānapanapa State Park.** The park is right on the ocean, and it's a lovely spot to picnic, hike, or swim. An ancient burial site is nearby, as well as a heiau. Wai'ānapanapa also has one of Maui's only black-sand beaches and some freshwater caves for adventurous swimmers to explore. The water in the tide pools here turns red several times a year.

FodorśChoice
★

FROM MONGOOSE
TO MOUNTAIN APPLE

Hawai'i's Flora & Fauna

Hawai'i has the dubious distinction of claiming more extinct and endangered animal species than all of the North American continent. The Hawaiian crow, or 'alalā, for example, has been reduced to a population of only about 15 birds, and most of these have been raised in captivity on the Big Island. The 'alalā is now facing a serious threat from another endangered bird—the 'io, or Hawaiian hawk. Still "protected" although making a comeback from its former endangered status, the nēnē goose, Hawai'i's state bird, roams freely in parts of Maui, Kaua'i, and the Big Island, where mating pairs are often spotted ambling across roads in Hawai'i Volcanoes National Park.

The mongoose is not endangered, although some residents wish it were. Alert drivers can catch a glimpse of the ferretlike animal darting across country roads. The mongoose was brought to Hawai'i in 1883 in an attempt to control the rat population, but the plan had only limited success, because the hunter and hunted rarely met: mongooses are active during the day, rats at night. Another creature, the rock wallaby, arrived in Honolulu in 1916 after being purchased from the Sydney Zoological Garden. Two escaped, and today about 50 of the small, reclusive marsupials live in remote areas of Kalihi Valley on O'ahu.

At the Kīlauea Point National Wildlife Refuge on Kauai'i, hundreds of Laysan albatross, wedge-tail shearwaters, red-footed boobies, and other marine birds glide and soar within photo-op distance of visitors to Kīlauea Lighthouse. Boobie chicks hatch in the fall and emerge from nests burrowed into cliffside dirt banks and even under stairs—any launching pad from which the fledgling flyer can catch the nearest air current.

Hawai'i has only two native mammals. Threatened with extinction, the rare Hawaiian bat hangs out primarily at Kealakekua Bay on the Big Island. Also on the endangered species list, doe-eyed Hawaiian monk seals breed in the northwestern Islands. With only 1,500 left in the wild, you won't catch many lounging on the beaches of Hawai'i's populated islands, but you can see rescued pups and adults along with "threatened" Hawaiian green sea turtles at Sea Life Park and the Waikīkī Aquarium on O'ahu.

Tropical flowers such as plumeria, orchids, hibiscus, red ginger, heliconia, and anthuriums grow wild on all the Islands. Pīkake blossoms make the most fragrant leis, and fragile orange 'ilima (once reserved only for royalty) the most elegant leis. The lovely wood rose is actually the dried seedpod of a species of morning glory. Mountain apple, Hawaiian raspberry, thimbleberry, and strawberry guava provide refreshing snacks for hikers; and giant banyan trees, hundreds of years old, spread their canopies over families picnicking in parks, inviting youngsters to swing from their hanging vines.

Sprouting ruby pom-pom-like lehua blossoms—thought to be the favorite flower of Pele, the volcano goddess—'ōhi'a trees bury their roots in fields of once-molten lava. Growing on the Big Island as well as the outer slopes of Maui's Haleakalā, exotic protea flourish only at an elevation of 4,000 ft; within Haleakalā's moonscape crater, the rare and otherworldly silversword—a 7-ft stalk with a single white spike and pale yellow flower found nowhere else on earth—blooms once and then dies.

Scientists say it's explained by the arrival of small shrimp, but locals claim the color represents the blood of Popoalaea, who legend says was murdered in one of the caves by her husband, Chief Kaakea. In either case, the dramatic contrast between the rain-forest green of the cliffs and the black volcanic rock is not to be missed. With a permit you can stay in state-run cabins here for less than $30 a night—the price varies depending on the number of people—but reserve early. They often book up a year in advance. ⊠ *Hāna Hwy. near mile marker 32, Hāna* ☎ *808/984–8109* 🖃 *Free.*

⑤③ **Waikāne Falls.** Though not necessarily bigger or taller than the other falls, these are the most dramatic—some say the best—falls you'll find on the road to Hāna. That's partly because the water is not diverted for sugar irrigation. The taro farmers in Wailua need all the runoff. This is a particularly good spot for photos. ⊠ *Hāna Hwy. past mile marker 21, Wailua.*

⑤② **Wailua Overlook.** From the parking lot you can see Wailua Canyon, but you'll have to walk up steps to get a view of Wailua Village. The landmark in Wailua Village is a church made of coral, built in 1860. Once called St. Gabriel's Catholic Church, the current Our Lady of Fatima Shrine has an interesting legend surrounding it. As the story goes, a storm washed just enough coral up onto the shore to build the church but then took any extra coral back to sea. ⊠ *Hāna Hwy. near mile marker 21, Wailua.*

BEACHES

All of Hawai'i's beaches are free and open to the public—even those that grace the front yards of fancy hotels—so you can make yourself at home on any one of them. Blue beach-access signs indicate rights-of-way through condominium and resort properties.

Although they don't appear often, be sure to pay attention to any signs or warning flags on the beaches. Warnings of high surf or rough currents should be taken seriously. Before you seek shade under a coconut palm, be aware that the trade winds are strong enough to knock fruit off the trees and onto your head. Drinking alcoholic beverages on beaches in Hawai'i is prohibited.

West Maui

"Slaughterhouse" (Mokuleia) Beach. The island's northernmost beach is part of the Honolua-Mokuleia Marine Life Conservation District. "Slaughterhouse" is the surfers' nickname for what is officially Mokuleia. When the weather permits, this is a great place for bodysurfing and sunbathing. Concrete steps and a green railing help you get down the sheer cliff to the sand. The next bay over, Honolua, has no beach but offers one of the best surf breaks in Hawai'i. Often you'll see competitions happening there, with cars pulled off the road and parked in the pineapple field. There are no facilities in this wild area. ⊠ *Mile marker 32 on road past Kapalua.*

D. T. Fleming Beach. Because the current can be quite strong, this charming, mile-long sandy cove is better for sunbathing than for swimming. Still it's one of the island's most popular beaches, and there are rest rooms, showers, picnic tables, grills, and paved parking. Part of the beach runs along the front of the Ritz-Carlton, Kapalua. ⊠ *Rte. 30, 1 mi north of Kapalua Resort.*

Kapalua Beach. On the northern side of Nāpili Bay is small, pristine Kapalua Beach. You may have to share sand space with a number of other beach-goers, however, because the area is quite popular for lazing, swimming, and snorkeling. There are showers, rest rooms, and a paved parking lot. ✛ *Past Bay Club restaurant off Lower Honoapi'ilani Hwy., before Kapalua Bay Hotel.*

FodorśChoice **Nāpili Beach.** A sparkling white crescent makes a perfect cove for strolling ★ and sunbathing. It's right outside the Nāpili Kai Beach Club, a popular little resort for honeymooners, but despite this and other condominiums and development around the bay, the facilities here are minimal. There are showers at the far right end of the beach and a tap by the beach-access entrance, where you can wash the sand off your feet, and you're only a few miles south of Kapalua. ✉ *5900 Lower Honoapi'ilani Hwy., from upper highway follow cutoff road closest to Kapalua Resort and look for Nāpili Pl. or Hui Dr.*

★ **Kā'anapali Beach.** If you're looking for peace and quiet, this is not the beach for you. But if you want lots of action, lay out your towel here. The beach fronts the big hotels at Kā'anapali and is one of Maui's best people-watching spots: cruises, windsurfers, and parasailers head out from here while the beautiful people take in the scenery. The area around Black Rock has prime snorkeling, and the bravest of the brave dive off the imposing rock into the calm water below. Although no facilities are available, the nearby hotels have rest rooms and some, like the Marriott, have outdoor showers. You're also close to plenty of shops and concession stands. ✛ *Follow any of 3 Kā'anapali exits from Honoapi'ilani Hwy. and park at any of the hotels.*

The South Shore

Kīhei has excellent beaches right in town, including three beach parks called **Kama'ole I, II,** and **III,** which have showers, rest rooms, picnic tables, and barbecues. Good snorkeling can be done along the rocky borders of the parks. If Kīhei is excellent, though, Wailea is even better. Look for a little road and parking lot between the first two big resorts—the Renaissance and the Marriott. This gets you to **Mōkapu** and **Ulua beaches.** This is a good area for families as the beaches are protected from major swells and several reef formations provide ample tide pools for kids to explore. Note that there have been a lot of break-ins in the parking lot.

★ A road just after the Grand Wailea takes you to **Wailea Beach,** a wide, sandy stretch, with good snorkeling and swimming. There are showers at the north end, though the south end is more accessible and, therefore, more popular with locals. Near the Kea Lani resort, you'll find **Polo Beach,** which is small and uncrowded. You can swim and snorkel here and it's a good place to whale-watch.

★ **Mākena.** Just south of Wailea is the state park at Mākena, with one of the state's most breathtaking beaches. "Big Beach" is a 3,000-ft long and 100-ft wide stretch of deep sand abutting aquamarine sea. It's never crowded, no matter how many cars are crammed into the lots. The water is fine for swimming, but the shore drop-off is steep and swells can get big, so use caution. There are portable toilets at each of the three paved entrances. If you climb the cinder cone near the first entrance, you'll discover "Little Beach"—clothing-optional by popular practice. (Officially, nude sunbathing is illegal in Hawai'i.) On Sunday, free spirits of all kinds crowd Little Beach's tiny shoreline for a drumming circle and bonfire. ✛ *Off Wailea Alanui Dr.*

The North Shore

Kanahā Beach. Local folk and windsurfers like this long, golden strip of sand bordered by a wide grassy area. This is a popular Kahului spot for joggers and picnicking families. Kanahā Beach has toilets, showers, picnic tables, and grills. ✛ *Drive through airport and back out to car-rental road (Koeheke), turn right, and keep going.*

★ **Baldwin Beach.** Another local favorite, just west of Pāʻia town, this beach is a big body of comfortable sand. There's not much wave action for bodysurfing, but this is a good place to stretch out, swim, or jog. The county park at the right side of the beach has picnic areas, rest rooms, showers, and sometimes even a lifeguard. ⊠ *Hāna Rd., 1 mi west of Baldwin Ave.*

★ **Hoʻokipa Beach.** If you want to see some of the world's finest windsurfers, stop at this beach along Hāna Highway. The sport has become an art—and a career, to some—and its popularity was largely developed right at Hoʻokipa. It's also one of Maui's hottest surfing spots, with waves as high as 15 ft. This is not a good swimming beach, nor the place to learn windsurfing, but plenty of picnic tables and barbecue grills are available for hanging out. ✛ *2 mi past Pāʻia on Rte. 36.*

Hāna

Hamoa Beach. This is the beach that James Michener made famous by deeming it the only North Pacific beach he'd ever seen that truly conjures the South Pacific. Indeed, it is idyllic with its perfect half-moon shape shaded by palm trees. And it's rarely crowded, despite the picnic area that the Hotel Hāna-Maui has set up here for its guests. It's also one of the few Hāna beaches with bathroom facilities. It's better for bodysurfing than swimming. ✛ *2 mi past Hāna off Rte. 36.*

Kōkī Beach. This beach in Hāna offers unusually good bodysurfing because the sandy bottom stays shallow for a long way out. On the down side, there are no facilities here. But this is a wild place rich in Hawaiian lore. Watch conditions, because the riptides here can be mean. ⊠ *Haneoʻo Loop Rd. 2 mi east of Hāna town.*

FodorśChoice **Waiʻānapanapa State Park.** The startling contrasts created by white
★ foam, black sand, and green naupaka trees bestow on tired travelers a quick fix of paradise. Swimming here is both relaxing and invigorating. The park has rest rooms, picnic tables, and several cultural sites. A dramatic coastal path continues all the way to Hāna. ⊠ *Hāna Hwy. near mile marker 32.*

WHERE TO EAT

A history of innovative Pacific Rim cuisine has supplied the island with many good restaurants. Fresh fish, island-grown produce, and simple, stylized presentations characterize the very best. Many of the key players have opened restaurants on both resort shores. Roy's, Sansei, Longhi's, and Marco's have all opened second locations in Kīhei and Wailea, making it even easier for visitors to find outstanding meals. Expect to eat well in any price category.

Except as noted, reservations are not required, but it's never a bad idea to phone ahead to book a table. Restaurants are open daily unless otherwise specified. An aloha shirt and pants for men and a simple dress or pants for women are acceptable in all establishments.

West Maui

American

★ **$–$$** ✕ **Lahaina Coolers.** This breezy little café with a surfboard hanging from its ceiling serves such tantalizing fare as Evil Jungle Pasta (pasta with grilled chicken in spicy Thai peanut sauce) and linguine with prawns, basil, garlic, and cream. It also has pizzas, steaks, burgers, and such desserts as a chocolate taco filled with tropical fruit and berry salsa. Pastas are made fresh in-house. Don't be surprised to see a local fisherman walk through or a harbor captain reeling in a hearty breakfast. ⊠ *180 Dickenson St., Lahaina* ☎ *808/661–7082* ⊟ *AE, MC, V.*

¢–$ ✕ **The Gazebo Restaurant.** Even locals will stand in line upward of a half hour for a table overlooking the beach at this restaurant, an actual open-air gazebo. The food is standard diner fare, but it's thoughtfully prepared. Breakfast choices include macadamia-nut pancakes and Portuguese-sausage omelets. There are satisfying burgers and salads at lunch. The friendly hotel staff puts out coffee for those waiting in line. ⊠ *Nāpili Shores Resort, 5315 Lower Honoapi'ilani Hwy., Nāpili* ☎ *808/669–5621* ⊟ *No credit cards* ☉ *No dinner.*

Continental

$$$$ ✕ **Bay Club.** Dinner by candlelight at this spot on a rocky promontory overlooking the ocean is a romantic way to cap off a day in the sun, especially if you've been swimming at Kapalua Beach just a few yards from the door. You won't want to walk through the richly paneled, elegant interior with sandy feet, however. Island seafood is emphasized, starting with 'ahi tartare for appetizers and building to the Hawaiian seafood pan roast of prawns, lobster, and scallops cooked in sweet-basil broth. ⊠ *Kapalua Bay Hotel, 1 Bay Dr., Kapalua* ☎ *808/669–5656* ⊟ *AE, D, DC, MC, V.*

$$$–$$$$ ✕ **Swan Court.** A grand staircase leads down into a cathedral-ceiling ballroom, and black and white swans glide across a waterfall-fed lagoon at this elegant eatery. Try the crispy scallop dim sum in plum sauce; creamy lobster-coconut bisque brimming with chunks of fish, lobster, shrimp, and button mushrooms; or charbroiled lamb chops in macadamia satay sauce. Arrive early and ask for a table on the left side, where the swans linger in the evening. The restaurant also serves a breakfast buffet and hosts the off-Broadway hit *Tony and Tina's Wedding.* ⊠ *Hyatt Regency Maui, Kā'anapali Beach Resort, 200 Nohea Kai Dr., Lahaina* ☎ *808/ 661–1234* ⊟ *AE, D, DC, MC, V.*

French

$$$–$$$$ ✕ **Chez Paul.** Since 1975 this tiny roadside restaurant between Lahaina and Mā'alaea in Olowalu has been serving excellent French cuisine to a packed house of repeat customers. Such dishes as fresh local fish poached in white wine with shallots, cream, and capers typify the classical menu. The restaurant's nondescript exterior belies the fine art, linen-draped tables, and wine cellar. Don't blink or you'll miss this small group of buildings huddled in the middle of nowhere. ⊠ *Honoapi'ilani Hwy., 4 mi south of Lahaina, Olowalu* ☎ *808/661–3843* ⌕ *Reservations essential* ⊟ *AE, D, MC, V* ☉ *No lunch.*

★ $$$–$$$$ ✕ **Gerard's.** Owner and celebrated chef Gerard Reversade started cooking at the age of 10, and at 12 he was baking croissants. He honors the French tradition with such exquisitely prepared dishes as rack of lamb in mint crust with thyme jus, and venison cutlets in a port sauce with confit of chestnuts, walnuts, fennel, and pearl onions. The menu changes once a year, but many favorites—such as the sinfully good crème brûlée—remain. A first-class wine list, a lovely room, and celebrity-spotting round out the experience. ⊠ *Plantation Inn, 174 Lahainaluna Rd., Lahaina* ☎ *808/661–8939* ⊟ *AE, D, DC, MC, V* ☉ *No lunch.*

Hawaiian/Pacific Rim

★ $$$–$$$$ ✕ **The Banyan Tree.** Chef Robert Ciborowski crafts the menu at the Ritz-Carlton's current main restaurant, a beautiful space overlooking the Kapalua coast. The coconut, sweet corn, and lemongrass soup garnished with Dungeness crab is legendary; 'ahi carpaccio with green papaya, and Asian-spiced rock shrimp with chive-mustard dipping sauce highlight the list of appetizers. Main courses include roasted mahimahi with

Where to Eat on Maui

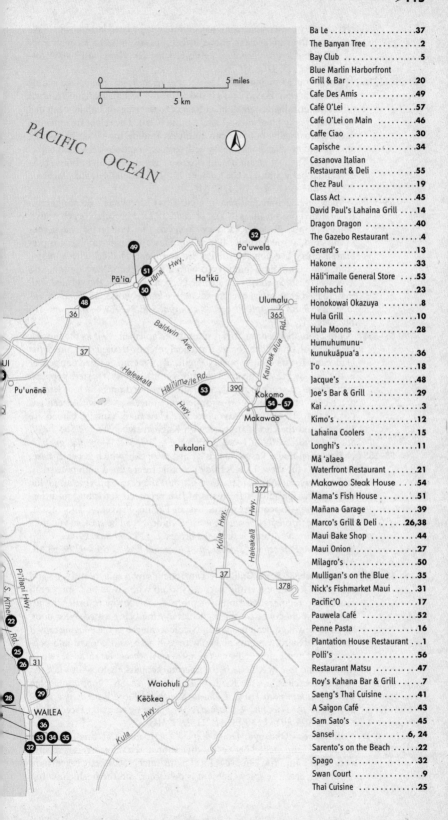

chardonnay butter sauce and macadamia nut–crusted lamb chops. Save room for the vanilla-bean crème brûlée, served in half a baby pineapple. ⊠ *Ritz-Carlton Kapalua, 1 Ritz-Carlton Dr., Kapalua* ☎ *808/669–6200* ⊟ *AE, D, DC, MC, V.*

★ **$$$–$$$$** ✕ **David Paul's Lahaina Grill.** Though the restaurant's namesake is only a consultant now, David Paul's is still a favorite of both locals and tourists alike. Beautifully designed, it's adjacent to the elegant Lahaina Inn in a historic, creaky building on Lahainaluna Road. The celebrated menu is revised seasonally, but you can count on finding the signature tequila shrimp and firecracker rice along with such scrumptious desserts as triple-berry pie. The restaurant has an extensive wine cellar, an in-house bakery, and a baby grand in the lounge. ⊠ *127 Lahainaluna Rd., Lahaina* ☎ *808/667–5117* ⊟ *AE, DC, MC, V.*

$$–$$$ ✕ **Hula Grill.** Genial chef-restaurateur Peter Merriman's bustling, family-oriented restaurant is in a re-created 1930s Hawaiian beach house, and every table has an ocean view. You can also dine on the beach, toes in the sand, at the Barefoot Bar, where Hawaiian entertainment is presented every evening. South Pacific snapper is baked with tomato, chili, and cumin aioli and served with a black bean, Maui onion, and avocado relish. Spareribs are steamed in banana leaves, then grilled with mango barbecue sauce over mesquitelike *kiawe* wood. ⊠ *Whalers Village, 2435 Kā'anapali Pkwy., Kā'anapali* ☎ *808/667–6636* ⊟ *AE, DC, MC, V.*

★ **$$–$$$** ✕ **I'o.** From its opening, this restaurant established itself as the hippest place in Lahaina, both for its theatrical interior designed by the artist Dado and for its contemporary Pacific Rim menu. A prized appetizer is the Silken Purse—steamed wontons stuffed with roasted peppers, mushrooms, macadamia nuts, and tofu. Favorite dinners include lemongrass-coconut fish and nori-wrapped rare tuna, served with green-papaya salad. Desserts to savor are the Hawaiian Vintage Chocolate Mousse and the chocolate pâté with Kula strawberries. ⊠ *505 Front St., Lahaina* ☎ *808/661–8422* ⊟ *AE, D, DC, MC, V* ☽ *No lunch.*

$$–$$$ ✕ **Plantation House Restaurant.** It's hard to decide which is better here, the food or the view. Hills, grassy volcanic ridges lined with pine trees, and fairways that appear to drop off into the ocean provide an idyllic setting. The specialty is fresh island fish prepared according to different "tastes"—Upcountry Maui, Asian-Pacific, Provence, and others. The breeze through the large shuttered windows can be cool, so you may want to bring a sweater or sit by the fireplace. ⊠ *Plantation Course Clubhouse, 2000 Plantation Club Dr., past Kapalua* ☎ *808/669–6299* ⊟ *AE, MC, V.*

★ **$$–$$$** ✕ **Roy's Kahana Bar & Grill.** Roy Yamaguchi's own sake brand "Y" and Hawaiian fusion specialties such as shrimp with sweet-and-spicy chili sauce keep regulars returning for more. Locals know to order the incomparable chocolate soufflé immediately after being seated. Next door, Roy's somewhat quieter restaurant Nicolina caters to a spice-loving crowd with grilled Southwestern chicken with chili hash, and smoked-and-peppered duck with gingered sweet potatoes. All three restaurants, two in Kahana and one in Kīhei, are in supermarket parking lots—it's not the view that excites, it's the food. ⊠ *Kahana Gateway Shopping Center, 4405 Honoapi'ilani Hwy., Kahana* ☎ *808/669–6999 for Roy's, 808/669–5000 for Nicolina* ⊠ *Safeway Shopping Center, 303 Piikea Ave., Kīhei* ☎ *808/891–1120* ⊟ *AE, D, DC, MC, V.*

¢–$ ✕ **Honokowai Okazuya.** Don't expect to sit down at this miniature restaurant sandwiched between a dive shop and a salon—this is strictly a take-out joint. You can order local plate lunches, Chinese, vegetarian, or sandwiches. The spicy eggplant is delicious, and the fresh chow fun noodles are bought up quickly. ✉ *3600-D Lower Honoapi'ilani Hwy. Lahaina* ☎ *808/665–0512* ☰ *No credit cards* ☉ *Closed Sun. and daily 2:30–4:30.*

Italian

$$–$$$ ╳ **Longhi's.** A Lahaina establishment, Longhi's has been around since 1976, serving great Italian pasta as well as sandwiches, seafood, beef, and chicken dishes. The pasta is homemade, and the in-house bakery turns out breakfast pastries, desserts, and fresh bread. Even on a warm day, you won't need air-conditioning with two spacious, breezy, open-air levels to choose from. The black-and-white tile floors are a nice touch. Now there's a branch on the South Shore, at the Shops at Wailea. ✉ *888 Front St., Lahaina* ☎ *808/667–2288* ✉ *The Shops at Wailea, 3750 Wailea Alanui Dr., Wailea* ☎ *808/891–8883* ☰ *AE, D, DC, MC, V.*

★ $–$$ ╳ **Penne Pasta.** Heaping plates of flavorful pasta and low-key, unintrusive service make this restaurant the perfect alternative to an expensive night out in Lahaina. The osso buco (Thursday's special) is sumptuous, and the traditional salad niçoise overflows with generous portions of olives, peppers, garlic 'ahi, and potatoes. It's wise for two people to split a salad and entrée, as portions are large. ✉ *180 Dickenson St., Lahaina* ☎ *808/661–6633* ☰ *AE, D, DC, MC, V* ☉ *No lunch weekends.*

Japanese

★ $$–$$$$ ╳ **Kai.** Master sushi chef Norio Yamamoto sits at the helm of this intimate sushi bar, hidden behind the bar at the Ritz-Carlton, Kapalua. There's a small menu, but your best bet is to let Chef Norio design the meal. He might have yellowtail cheeks, fresh sea urchin, and raw lobster. He also makes lobster-head soup, a Japanese comfort food. ✉ *Ritz-Carlton, Kapalua, 1 Ritz-Carlton Dr., Kapalua* ☎ *808/669–6200* ☰ *AE, D, DC, MC, V.*

★ $$–$$$ ╳ **Sansei.** One of the best-loved restaurants on the island, Sansei is Japanese with a Hawaiian twist. Inspired dishes include *panko*-crusted 'ahi (panko are Japanese bread crumbs), spicy fried calamari, mango-and-crab-salad roll, and a decadent foie gras *nigiri* (served on rice without seaweed) sushi. Desserts often use local fruit; the Kula-persimmon crème brûlée is stunning. The new location in Kīhei is a popular karaoke hangout, serving late-night sushi at half price. ✉ *Kapalua Shops, 115 Bay Dr., Kapalua* ☎ *808/666–6286* ✉ *Kīhei Town Center, 1881 S. Kīhei Rd., Kīhei* ☎ *808/879–0004* ☰ *AE, D, MC, V* ☉ *No lunch.*

Seafood

★ $$$–$$$$ ╳ **Pacific'O.** You can sit outdoors at umbrella-shaded tables near the water's edge, or find a spot in the breezy, marble-floor interior. The exciting menu features fresh 'ahi-and-*ono* tempura (ono is a mackerel-like fish), in which the two kinds of fish are wrapped around *tobiko* (flying-fish roe), then wrapped in nori, and wok-fried. There's a great lamb dish, too—a whole rack of sweet New Zealand lamb, sesame-crusted and served with roasted macadamia sauce and Hawaiian chutney. Live jazz is played Thursday through Saturday from 9 to midnight. ✉ *505 Front St., Lahaina* ☎ *808/667–4341* ☰ *AE, D, DC, MC, V.*

$–$$ ╳ **Kimo's.** On a warm Lahaina day, it's a treat to relax at an umbrella-shaded table on the lānai, sip a mai tai, and watch sailboats glide into and out of the harbor. Outstanding seafood is just one of the options here; also good are Hawaiian-style chicken and pork dishes, and burgers. Try the signature dessert, Hula Pie: vanilla–macadamia nut ice cream topped with chocolate fudge and whipped cream in an Oreo-cookie crust. ✉ *845 Front St., Lahaina* ☎ *808/661–4811* ☰ *AE, DC, MC, V.*

Central Maui

American

★ ¢–$ ✕ **Café O'Lei on Main.** This popular sister restaurant of Café O'Lei in Makawao serves inventive and healthful weekday lunches. The seared 'ahi sandwich with wasabi mayonnaise is always on the menu, and every Friday brings crab cakes with sweet chile aioli. There are daily specials, too, such as curried chicken salad and blackened mahimahi. Also try the Māʻalea and Lahaina locations for lunch or dinner. ⊠ *2051 Main St., Wailuku* ☎ *808/244–6816* ⊠ *839 Front St., Lahaina* ☎ *808/661–9491* ⊠ *300 Māʻalaea Rd., Māʻalaea* ☎ *808/243–2206* ▤ *No credit cards* ☽ *Closed weekends. No dinner at Wailuka location.*

¢ ✕ **Maui Bake Shop.** Wonderful breads baked in brick ovens from 1935, hearty lunch fare, and irresistible desserts make this a popular spot in Central Maui. Baker José Krall was trained in France, and his wife, Claire, is a Maui native whose friendly face you'll often see when you walk in. Standouts include the focaccia and homemade soups. ⊠ *2092 Vineyard St., Wailuku* ☎ *808/242–0064* ▤ *AE, D, MC, V* ☽ *Closed Sun. No dinner.*

Chinese

$ ✕ **Dragon Dragon.** Whether you're a party of 10 or 2, this is the place to share seafood tofu soup or spareribs with garlic sauce. Tasteful, simple decor complements the solid menu. Fresh Dungeness crab is offered with four sauce selections. The restaurant shares parking with the Maui Megaplex and makes a great pre- or postmovie stop. ⊠ *In Maui Mall, 70 E. Kaahumanu Ave., Kahului* ☎ *808/893–1628* ▤ *AE, D, MC, V.*

Eclectic

$$ ✕ **Class Act.** This little-known place offers one of the best values on Maui, as well as a chance to see rising chefs in action. Run by the esteemed Food Service Department at Maui Community College, the restaurant employs student chefs in every position, from the kitchen to the waitstaff. The restaurant is open on Wednesday and Friday for lunch only, and the cuisine changes weekly, so you might find Thai, Moroccan, Austrian, Japanese, or Italian on the menu. No tipping is allowed, but donations to the school are accepted. You must bring your own alcohol. ⊠ *Maui Community College, 310 Kaʻahumanu Ave., Wailuku* ☎ *808/984–3480* ▤ *No credit cards* ☽ *Closed Thurs. and Sat.–Tues. No dinner.*

Hawaiian

¢ ✕ **Sam Sato's.** Locals and tourists sit elbow to elbow at the counter for cheap, delicious saimin and *manju* (pastries with sweetened adzuki beans). The plate lunch of barbecued pork is also popular. Don't miss the fantastic pineapple turnovers. ⊠ *1750 Wili Pa Loop, Wailuku* ☎ *808/244–7124* ▤ *No credit cards* ☽ *Closed Sun. No dinner.*

Italian

$–$$ ✕ **Marco's Grill & Deli.** This convenient eatery outside Kahului Airport (look for the green awning) serves reliable Italian food that's slightly overpriced. Homemade pastas appear on the extensive menu, along with an unforgettably good Reuben sandwich and the best tiramisu on the island. The local business crowd fills the place for breakfast, lunch, and dinner. The Kīhei branch is in a gorgeous new building with a grand piano. ⊠ *444 Hāna Hwy., Kahului* ☎ *808/877–4446* ⊠ *1445 S. Kīhei Rd., Kīhei* ☎ *808/874–4041* ▤ *AE, D, DC, MC, V.*

Japanese

$ ✕ **Restaurant Matsu.** Sit at a common table and eat authentic Japanese fare along with the locals—*katsu* (cutlet) dishes and curries served with white rice, or bowls of saimin or *udon* noodles with tempura. ✉ *161 Ala Maha St., Kahului* ☎ *808/871–0822* ▭ *No credit cards.*

Latin

★ **$$–$$$** ✕ **Mañana Garagé.** Parked in downtown Kahului is this restaurant, which makes the most of its automobile theme—it's probably the only place you'll have your wine served out of buckets with crankshaft stems. Chef Tom Lelli's cuisine ranges from Cuban to Brazilian to Mexican, with a few Hawaiian touches thrown in for good measure. The best dishes include ceviche marinated in coconut milk and lime, 'ahi sashimi, chile adobo pulled pork, and quesadillas made with homemade corn tortillas. For dessert, the pound-cake ice-cream sandwich with sweet potato and praline is a must. There's lively music on the weekends. ✉ *33 Lono Ave., Kahului* ☎ *808/873–0220* ▭ *AE, D, MC, V* ☉ *No lunch weekends.*

Thai

$–$$ ✕ **Saeng's Thai Cuisine.** Choosing a dish from the six-page menu here requires determination, but the food is worth the effort, and most dishes can be tailored to your taste buds: hot, medium, or mild. Begin with spring rolls and a dipping sauce, move on to such entrées as Evil Prince Chicken (cooked in coconut sauce with Thai herbs) or red-curry shrimp, and finish up with tea and tapioca pudding. Asian artifacts, flowers, and a waterfall decorate the dining room, and tables on a veranda satisfy lovers of the outdoors. ✉ *2119 Vineyard St., Wailuku* ☎ *808/244–1567* ▭ *AE, MC, V.*

Vietnamese

★ **$$–$$$** ✕ **A Saigon Café.** The only storefront sign announcing this small, delightful hideaway is one reading OPEN. Once you find it, treat yourself to *banh hoi chao tom,* more commonly known as "shrimp pops burritos" (ground marinated shrimp, steamed and grilled on a stick of sugarcane). Vegetarian fare is also well represented here—try the green-papaya salad. Fresh island fish is always available. The white interior serves as a backdrop for Vietnamese carvings in this otherwise unadorned space. Background music includes one-hit wonders from the early '70s. ✉ *1792 Main St., Wailuku* ☎ *808/243–9560* ▭ *D, MC, V.*

FodorśChoice

★ ¢ ✕ **Ba Le.** Tucked into the mall's food court is the best, cheapest fast food on the island. The famous soups, or *pho,* come laden with seafood or rare beef, fresh basil, bean sprouts, and lime. Tasty sandwiches are served on crisp French rolls—lemongrass chicken is a favorite. The word is out, so the place gets busy at lunchtime, though the wait is never long. ✉ *Kau Kau Corner food court, Maui Marketplace, 270 Dairy Rd., Kahului* ☎ *808/877–2400* ▭ *AE, D, DC, MC, V.*

The South Shore

American

$$–$$$ ✕ **Joe's Bar & Grill.** With friendly service, a great view of Lāna'i, and such dishes as New York strip steak with caramelized onions, wild mushrooms, and Gorgonzola cheese crumble, there are lots of reasons to stop in at this spacious, breezy spot. Owners Joe and Bev Gannon, who run the immensely popular Hāli'imaile General Store, have brought their flair for food home to roost in this comfortable treetop-level restaurant at the Wailea Tennis Club, where you can dine while watching court action from a balcony seat. ✉ *131 Wailea Ike Pl., Wailea* ☎ *808/875–7767* ▭ *AE, MC, V.*

★ **$–$$** ✕ **Maui Onion.** Forget the overrated Cheeseburger in Paradise in Lahaina— Maui Onion has the best burgers on the island, hands down, and phenomenal onion rings as well. They coat the onions in pancake batter, then dip them in panko, then fry them 'til they're golden brown. ✉ *Re-*

naissance Wailea, 3550 Wailea Alanui Dr., Wailea ☎ *808/879–4900* ▤ *AE, D, DC, MC, V.*

Hawaiian/Pacific Rim

$$$–$$$$ ✕ **Humuhumunukunukuāpua'a.** Wrestle with the restaurant's formidable name—the name of the state fish—or simply watch the fish swim by in the 2,100-gallon tank at the bar. The thatch-roofed building actually floats on a lagoon. Sweet-corn and lobster soup with poached rock shrimp and basil puree is a standout, as is the sesame-crusted mahimahi with coconut rice, baby bok choy, and black bean miso sauce. You can fetch your own spiny lobster (which is best simply grilled) from a cage below the water's surface. ⊠ *Grand Wailea Resort, 3850 Wailea Alanui Dr., Wailea* ☎ *808/875–1234* ▤ *AE, D, DC, MC, V.*

★ $$$–$$$$ ✕ **Spago.** Celebrity chef and owner Wolfgang Puck wisely brought his fame to this gorgeous locale. Giant sea-anemone prints, modern-art-inspired lamps, and views of the shoreline give diners something to look at while waiting. The solid menu, under the direction of chef Adam Condon, delivers with dishes like seared scallops with asparagus and pohole fern, and "chinois" lamb chops with Hunan eggplant. The beef dish, with braised celery, Armagnac, and horseradish potatoes, may be the island's priciest—but devotees swear it's worth every cent. ⊠ *Four Seasons Resort, 3900 Wailea Alanui Dr., Wailea* ☎ *808/879–2999* ▤ *AE, D, DC, MC, V* ☾ *No lunch.*

$$–$$$ ✕ **Hula Moons.** This delightful oceanside spot is full of memorabilia chronicling the life of Don Blanding, an artist and poet who became Hawai'i's unofficial ambassador of aloha in the 1930s. The vegetarian appetizer of fresh pohole ferns, Hāna tomatoes, and Kula onions is fabulous. Try the bamboo-steamed whole *moi*, a fish once reserved for Hawaiian royalty, or the tangy braised short ribs. Sunday brunch is one of the most lavish on the island, and the wine list is extensive. You can dine inside, poolside, or on the terrace. ⊠ *Marriott Wailea Resort, 3700 Wailea Alanui Dr., Wailea* ☎ *808/879–1922* ▤ *AE, D, DC, MC, V.*

Irish

$–$$ ✕ **Mulligan's on the Blue.** If you're hankering for bangers and mash or shepherd's pie, stop in here. You'll be greeted by a nearly all-Irish staff, and before you know it, you'll be sipping a heady pint of Guinness. Breakfast is a good value for the area, and the view is one of the best. Live music makes evenings fun. ⊠ *100 Kaukahi St., Wailea* ☎ *808/874–1131* ▤ *AE, D, DC, MC, V.*

Italian

$$$–$$$$ ✕ **Capische.** Hidden up at the quiet Blue Diamond Resort, this restaurant is one local patrons would like to keep secret. A circular stone atrium gives way to a small piano lounge, where you'll find the best sunset view on the island. You can count on the freshness of the ingredients in superb dishes like the quail saltimbocca, and the saffron *vongole*—a colorful affair of squid-ink pasta and spicy saffron broth. Intimate and well conceived, Capische, with its seductive flavors and ambience, makes for a romantic night out. ⊠ *Blue Diamond Resort, 555 Kaukahi St., Wailea* ☎ *808/879–2224* ▤ *AE, D, DC, MC, V* ☾ *No lunch.*

FodorsChoice
★

$$$–$$$$ ✕ **Sarento's on the Beach.** Chef George Gomes, formerly of A Pacific Café, heads the kitchen at South Maui's newest Italian restaurant. The beachfront setting is irresistible, and the menu features both traditional Italian dishes—like penne Calabrese and seafood fra diavolo—as well as inventions such as swordfish saltimbocca, a strangely successful entrée with a prosciutto, Bel Paese, radicchio, and porcini-mushroom sauce. The wine list includes some affordable finds. ⊠ *2980 S. Kīhei Rd., Kīhei* ☎ *808/875–7555* ▤ *AE, D, DC, MC, V* ☾ *No lunch.*

$–$$ ✕ **Caffe Ciao.** Chef Dino Bugica brings Italy to the Fairmont Kea Lani. Authentic, fresh gnocchi and lobster risotto taste especially delicious in the open-air café, which overlooks the swimming pool. For casual European fare, try a poached-tuna salad, grilled panini, or pizza from the wood-burning oven. Additionally, locals have long known Caffe Ciao's sister deli as the sole source for discerning palates: delectable pastries, tapenades, mustards, and even $50 bottles of truffle oil. ⊠ *Fairmont Kea Lani, 4100 Wailea Alanui Dr., Wailea* ☎ *808/875–4100* ▭ *AE, D, DC, MC, V.*

Japanese

$$$–$$$$ ✕ **Hakone.** Well-regarded Japanese food is served at this restaurant in the Maui Prince hotel. A full six-course *kaiseki* meal—with small dishes of raw, cooked, hot, cold, sweet, and savory items—is $58, a good value for the quality of food presented. Impeccably fresh sushi, traditional cooked dishes, and an impressive sake list round out the menu. The Sunday-night sushi buffet is popular. ⊠ *Maui Prince, 5400 Mākena Alanui Rd., Mākena* ☎ *808/874–1111* ▭ *AE, MC, V* ☻ *No lunch.*

★ **¢–$$** ✕ **Hirohachi.** A stone's throw from the flashier Sansei, Hirohachi has been serving authentic Japanese fare for years. Owner Hiro has discerning taste—he buys only the best from local fishermen and imports many ingredients from Japan. Order with confidence—even if you can't read the Japanese specials posted on the wall—everything on the menu is high quality. ⊠ *1881 S. Kīhei Rd., Kīhei* ☎ *808/875–7474* ▭ *AE, MC, V* ☻ *Closed Mon.*

Seafood

★ **$$$–$$$$** ✕ **Nick's Fishmarket Maui.** This romantic spot serves fresh seafood in the simplest preparations: mahimahi with Kula-corn relish, 'ahi pepper fillet, and *opakapaka* with rock shrimp in a lemon-butter-caper sauce. Everyone seems to love the Greek Maui Wowie salad made with local onions, tomatoes, avocado, feta cheese, and bay shrimp. Service is somewhat formal, but it befits the beautiful food presentations and extensive wine list. ⊠ *Fairmont Kea Lani, 4100 Wailea Alanui Dr., Wailea* ☎ *808/879–7224* ▭ *AE, D, DC, MC, V* ☻ *No lunch.*

$$–$$$ ✕ **Mā'alaea Waterfront Restaurant.** At this harborside establishment, fresh fish is prepared in a host of sumptuous ways: baked in buttered parchment paper; imprisoned in ribbons of angel-hair potato; or topped with tomato salsa, smoked chili pepper, and avocado. The varied menu also lists an outstanding rack of lamb and veal scallopini. Tourists come early to dine at sunset on the outdoor patio. Enter Mā'alaea at the Maui Ocean Center and then follow the blue WATERFRONT RESTAURANT signs to the third condominium. ⊠ *50 Hau'oli St., Mā'alaea* ☎ *808/244–9028* ▭ *AE, D, DC, MC, V* ☻ *No lunch.*

$–$$ ✕ **Blue Marlin Harborfront Grill & Bar.** This is a casual, less expensive alternative to the Mā'laea Waterfront Restaurant. It's as much a bar as it is a grill, but the kitchen nonetheless sends out well-prepared, substantial servings of fresh fish, burgers, and salads. The sidewalk tables have a lovely view of the harbor. ⊠ *Mā'alaea Harbor Village, corner of Old Mā'alaea Rd. and Honoapiilani Hwy., next to the Maui Ocean Center* ⊠ *Mā'alaea* ☎ *808/244–8844* ▭ *AE, MC, V.*

Thai

★ **$–$$** ✕ **Thai Cuisine.** Fragrant tea and coconut-ginger chicken soup begin a satisfying meal at this excellent Thai restaurant. The care that goes into the decor here (reflected in the glittering Buddhist shrines, fancy napkin folds, and matching blue china) also applies to the cuisine. The lean and moist meat of the red-curry duck rivals similar dishes at resort restaurants, and the fried bananas with ice cream are wonderful. ⊠ *In Kukui Mall, 1819 S. Kīhei Rd., Kīhei* ☎ *808/875–0839* ▭ *AE, D, DC, MC, V.*

East Maui

American

¢–$ ✕ **Café O'Lei.** Your best bet for a casual lunch in Makawao, this restaurant paved the way for three other popular locations island-wide. Especially recommended are the quinoa salad and the snow-crab-and-avocado sandwich on focaccia. Seating is outdoors only. ⊠ *Paniolo Courtyard, 3673 Baldwin Ave., Makawao* ☎ *808/573–9065* ▭ *No credit cards* ⊘ *Closed Sun. No dinner.*

★ ¢–$ ✕ **Pauwela Café.** Ultracasual and ultrafriendly, this spot just off Hāna Highway is worth the detour. Order a kālua-pork sandwich and a piece of coffee cake and pass the afternoon. The large breakfast burritos and homemade soups are also good. ⊠ *375 W. Kuiaha Rd., off Hāna Hwy. past Ha'ikū Rd., Ha'ikū* ☎ *808/575–9242* ▭ *No credit cards* ⊘ *No dinner.*

Eclectic

$–$$ ✕ **Jacque's.** Jacque, an amiable French chef, won the hearts of the windsurfing crowd when he opened this hip, ramshackle bar and restaurant. French-Caribbean dishes like Jacque's Crispy Little Poulet reveal the owner's expertise. The outdoor seating can be a little chilly at times; coveted spots at the sushi bar inside are snatched up quickly. ⊠ *120 Hāna Hwy., Pā'ia* ☎ *808/579–8844* ▭ *AE, D, MC, V.*

¢–$ ✕ **Cafe Des Amis.** Papier-mâché wrestlers pop out from the walls at this small creperie. French crepes with Gruyère and Indian wraps with lentil curry are among the choices, all served with wild greens and sour cream or chutney on the side. For dessert, of course, are more crepes—filled with chocolate, Nutella, cane sugar, and banana. ⊠ *42 Baldwin Ave., Pā'ia* ☎ *808/579–6373* ▭ *AE, D, MC, V.*

Hawaiian/Pacific Rim

★ $$–$$$ ✕ **Hāli'imaile General Store.** What do you do with a lofty wooden building that was a tiny town's camp store in the 1920s and is surrounded by sugarcane and pineapple fields? If you're Bev and Joe Gannon, you invent a legendary restaurant. The Szechuan barbecued salmon and rack of lamb Hunan-style are classics, as is the sashimi napoleon appetizer: a tower of crispy wontons layered with 'ahi and salmon. Pastry chef Teresa Gannon makes an unbelievable pineapple upside-down cake. The restaurant even has its own cookbook. ⊠ *900 Hāli'imaile Rd., left at exit off Rte. 37, 5 mi from Hāna Hwy., Hāli'imaile* ☎ *808/572–2666* ▭ *MC, V.*

Italian

$$–$$$ ✕ **Casanova Italian Restaurant & Deli.** The pizzas, baked in a brick wood-burning oven imported from Italy, are the best on the island. This is a good Italian dinner house in an out-of-the-way location. Casanova is also known for its daytime deli and, at night, for its extra-large dance floor and entertainment by well-known island and mainland musicians. ⊠ *1188 Makawao Ave., Makawao* ☎ *808/572–0220* ▭ *D, DC, MC, V.*

Mexican

$–$$ ✕ **Milagro's.** Delicious fish tacos are found at this corner hangout, along with a selection of fine tequilas. Latin fusion recipes ignite fresh fish and vegetables. The people-watching can be fun here, under the awning shade at the junction of Baldwin Avenue and Hāna Highway. Lunch and happy hour (3–5) are the best values; the prices jump at dinnertime. ⊠ *3 Baldwin Ave., Pā'ia* ☎ *808/579–8755* ▭ *AE, D, DC, MC, V.*

$–$$ ✕ **Polli's.** This Mexican restaurant in the paniolo town of Makawao not only offers standards such as enchiladas, chimichangas, and fajitas but will also prepare any item on the menu with seasoned tofu or vegetarian taco mix—and the meatless dishes are just as good. A special treat are the *bunuelos*—light pastries topped with cinnamon, maple syrup, and ice cream. The intimate interior is plastered with colorful sombreros and other cantina knickknacks. ⊠ *1202 Makawao Ave., Makawao* ☎ *808/572–7808* ⊟ *AE, D, DC, MC, V.*

Seafood

$$$–$$$$ ✕ **Mama's Fish House.** Check out the stone path engraved with whimsi-
Fodor's Choice   cal Hawaiian geckos as you approach this cliff-top restaurant. The
   ★   Hawaiian nautical theme inside is just as fun, but the real treat here is the fish, prepared seven ways—baked in a creamy herb sauce or grilled with spicy wasabi butter, for example. The chicken, steak, and kālua pig dishes are worth trying as well. And the restaurant serves the best mai tais on the island, bar none. The restaurant, about 1½ mi east of Pa'ia on Hāna Highway, is marked by a tiny fishing boat perched above the entrance. ⊠ *799 Poho Pl., Kū'au* ☎ *808/579–8488* ⌣ *Reservations essential* ⊟ *AE, D, DC, MC, V.*

Steak

$$–$$$ ✕ **Makawao Steak House.** A restored 1927 house on the slopes of Haleakalā is the setting for this paniolo restaurant, which serves consistently good prime rib, rack of lamb, and fresh fish. Three fireplaces, friendly service, and an intimate lounge create a cozy, welcoming atmosphere. ⊠ *3612 Baldwin Ave., Makawao* ☎ *808/572–8711* ⊟ *D, DC, MC, V* ☉ *No lunch.*

WHERE TO STAY

Updated by
Kim
Westerman

Maui has the highest percentage of upscale hotel rooms and the highest average accommodation cost of any Hawaiian island. The quality level—and the opulence quotient—is way up there, making this one of the best places in the world to indulge in a first-class resort vacation. But Maui also has the state's highest concentration of condominium units; many are oceanfront and offer the amenities of a hotel suite without the cost.

The county officially sanctions relatively few B&Bs, not wanting to siphon business from the hotels. However, many alternative accommodations offer seclusion and a countryside experience, especially Upcountry and in Hāna. Most of these are better described as guest cottages—or guest houses—that skip the breakfast part of B&B and offer instead provisions and privacy. Rates for most B&Bs range from $40 to as much as $150 per night.

West Maui

$$$$ ▥ **Hyatt Regency Maui.** This resort underwent a $19 million room renovation in 2002, which has resulted in a softer color scheme and colonial-style furniture, rounded out by Hawaiian-quilt wall hangings. There are also a museum-quality art collection; a seemingly endless swimming pool, with swim-through grottoes and a 130-ft water slide; fantasy landscaping (the builders used 10,000 tons of rock to fabricate the environment) with splashing waterfalls; and the Spa Moana, an oceanfront, full-service facility. ⊠ *Kā'anapali Beach Resort, 200 Nohea Kai Dr., Lahaina 96761* ☎ *808/661–1234 or 800/233–1234* ▤ *808/667–4499* ⊕ *www.mauihyatt.com* ↝ *815 rooms* ⌂ *4 restaurants, in-room safes, 2 18-hole golf courses, 6 tennis courts, pool, health club, spa, beach, 6 bars, library, children's programs (ages 3–12), Internet, no-smoking floors* ⊟ *AE, D, DC, MC, V.*

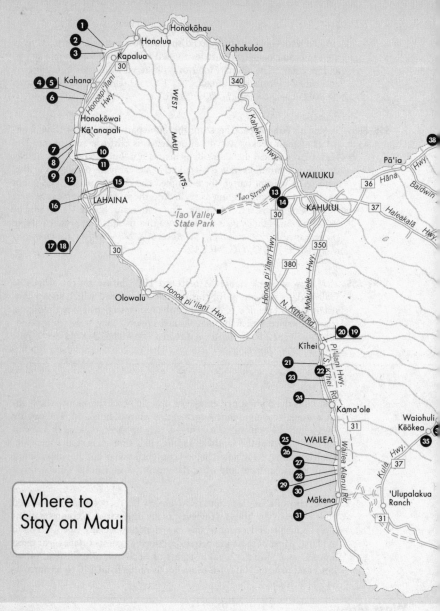

Where to Stay on Maui

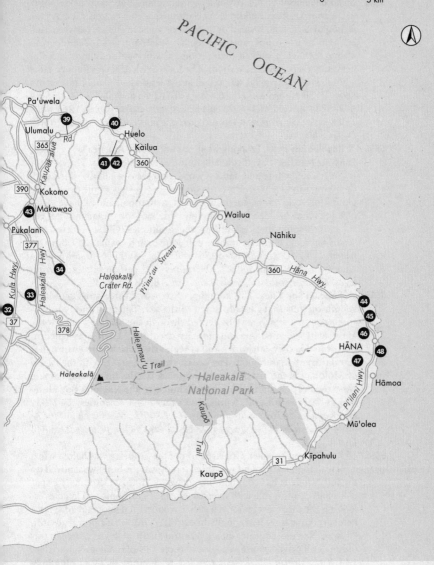

PACIFIC OCEAN

Pa'uwela

Ulumalu
365
39
40
Huelo
Kailua
41 **42**
360

390
Kokomo

43 Makawao

Pukalani
377
34

Kula Hwy.
Haleakalā Hwy.

33
32
37
378

Haleakalā
Crater Rd.

Pi'ina'au Stream

Wailua

Nāhiku

360 Hāna Hwy.

44
45

Haleamau'u Trail

46

HĀNA **48**

47

Haleakalā ▲

Haleakalā
National Park

Kaupō Trail

Piʻilani Hwy.

Hāmoa

Mū'olea

31 Kīpahulu

Kaupō

$$$$ 🏨 **Kāʻanapali Aliʻi.** Yes, this is a condominium, but you'd never know it: the four 11-story buildings are put together so well you still have the feeling of seclusion. Instead of tiny rooms you can choose between one- and two-bedroom apartments. Each has lovely amenities: a chaise in an alcove, a bidet, a sunken living room, a whirlpool, oak kitchen cabinets, and a separate dining room. The Kāʻanapali Aliʻi is maintained like a hotel, with daily maid service, an activities desk, and a 24-hour front desk. ✉ *50 Nohea Kai Dr., Lahaina 96761* ☎ *808/667–1400 or 800/ 642–6284* 🖨 *808/661–1025* ⊕ *www.classicresorts.com* ➪ *264 units* ⛳ *18-hole golf course, 6 tennis courts, 2 pools, sauna, beach* ☰ *AE, D, DC, MC, V.*

$$$$ 🏨 **Kapalua Bay Hotel.** Fronting what was once voted America's best beach, at lovely Kapalua Bay, this hotel has a real Maui feel to it. The exterior is understated white and natural wood, and the open lobby, filled with flowering vanda and dendrobium orchids, has a view of the ocean. The plantation-style rooms are decorated in earth tones, and all have views of Lānaʻi and Molokaʻi. A shopping plaza outside the main hotel entrance has some fine restaurants and boutiques. Guests receive preferred rates and tee times at three golf courses in Kapalua. ✉ *1 Bay Dr., Kapalua 96761* ☎ *808/669–5656 or 800/367–8000* 🖨 *808/669–4694* ⊕ *www.kapaluabay.com* ➪ *209 rooms* ⛳ *3 restaurants, golf privileges, 6 tennis courts, 2 pools, beach* ☰ *AE, DC, MC, V.*

$$$$ 🏨 **Kapalua Bay Villas.** This complex of two- and three-story buildings is built on hills that cascade down to the sea. The one- and two-bedroom condos, which may be rented through the Kapalua Bay Hotel, are privately owned and individually decorated. Each is assigned to one of five luxury categories and is regularly inspected to ensure that standards are maintained. The ocean views are great, with the island of Molokaʻi in the distance and humpback whales (in season) passing close to shore. Renters enjoy a free shuttle to the Kapalua Bay Hotel and guest rates for golf, tennis, and other hotel amenities. ✉ *1 Bay Dr., Kapalua 96761* ☎ *808/669–5656 or 800/367–8000* 🖨 *808/669– 4694* ⊕ *www.kapaluabay.com* ➪ *125 units* ⛳ *Golf privileges* ☰ *AE, D, DC, MC, V.*

$$$$ 🏨 **Ritz-Carlton, Kapalua.** Construction of the property was halted when
Fodor's Choice a Hawaiian burial ground was discovered, and the hotel was moved up
★ the hill, where it has commanding views of Molokaʻi. Rooms are spacious and comfortable with oversize marble bathrooms and lānai overlooking the three-level pool. There's a wonderful democracy of service here: everyone is treated equally like a VIP. A full-time cultural advisor, Clifford Naeʻole, educates employees and guests alike in Hawaiian tradition. Golf privileges are available at three 18-hole courses in Kapalua. ✉ *1 Ritz-Carlton Dr., Kapalua 96761* ☎ *808/669–6200 or 800/262– 8440* 🖨 *808/665–0026* ⊕ *www.ritzcarlton.com* ➪ *548 rooms* ⛳ *3 restaurants, in-room safes, 18-hole golf course, golf privileges, 10 tennis courts, pool, hair salon, health club, massage, beach, lobby lounge, shops, children's programs (ages 5–12), laundry service, Internet, business services* ☰ *AE, D, DC, MC, V.*

$$$$ 🏨 **Royal Lahaina Resort.** What distinguishes the Royal Lahaina are the two-story cottages, each divided into four units; the bedrooms open to the trade winds on two sides. The upstairs units each have a private lānai, and downstairs units share—all lānai have stunning ocean or golf-course views. The walkway to the courtyard wedding gazebo is lined with stepping-stones engraved with the names of past brides and grooms and their wedding dates. ✉ *2780 Kekaʻa Dr., Lahaina 96761* ☎ *808/ 661–3611 or 800/447–6925* 🖨 *808/661–3538* ⊕ *www.hawaiihotels. com* ➪ *592 rooms* ⛳ *3 restaurants, 18-hole golf course, 11 tennis courts, 3 pools, beach* ☰ *AE, D, DC, MC, V.*

$$$$ 🏨 **Sheraton Maui.** The six buildings that make up this understated resort are set among dense gardens on Kā'anapali's best stretch of beach. Rooms come with ocean, mountain, or garden views. One of the two swimming pools looks like a natural lagoon, with rock waterways and wooden bridges. Best of all is that the hotel sits next to 80-ft-high "Black Rock," from which divers leap in a nightly torch-lighting ritual. ⊠ *2605 Kā'anapali Pkwy., Lahaina 97671* ☎ *808/661–0031 or 800/782–9488* 📠 *808/661–0458* ⊕ *www.sheraton-maui.com* 🛏 *510 rooms* ⚬ *3 restaurants, in-room safes, refrigerators, 3 tennis courts, 2 pools, hair salon, health club, hot tub, spa, beach, lobby lounge, children's programs (ages 5–12), laundry facilities, business services* ⊟ *AE, D, DC, MC, V.*

$$$$ 🏨 **Westin Maui.** This is a hotel for active people who won't want to spend much time in their rooms, which are rather small for the price. But compensations are provided—an "aquatic playground" with five heated swimming pools, privileges at two 18-hole golf courses in Kā'anapali, and Tropica, one of Maui's few night spots. The landscaping has a jungle theme, with abundant waterfalls (15 at last count) and lagoons. A valuable Asian and Pacific art collection is displayed throughout the property. ⊠ *2365 Kā'anapali Pkwy., Lahaina 96761* ☎ *808/667–2525 or 800/228–3000* 📠 *808/661–5831* ⊕ *www.westinmaui.com* 🛏 *761 rooms* ⚬ *3 restaurants, golf privileges, 5 pools, hair salon, health club, hot tub, beach, lobby lounge, baby-sitting, children's programs (ages 12 and under)* ⊟ *AE, D, DC, MC, V.*

$$$–$$$$ 🏨 **Aston at Papakea Resort.** Though there's no beach on the premises, there are several nearby, and with classes on swimming, snorkeling, pineapple cutting, and more, you'll have plenty to keep you busy at this resort. Papakea has built-in privacy because its units are spread out among 11 low-rise buildings on some 13 acres of land; bamboo-lined walkways between buildings and fish-stocked ponds add to the serenity. Note that there's a two-night minimum stay. ⊠ *3543 Honoapi'ilani Hwy., Lahaina 96761* ☎ *808/669–4848 or 800/922–7866* 📠 *808/922–8785* ⊕ *www.aston-hotels.com* 🛏 *36 studios, 224 1-bedroom units, 104 2-bedroom units* ⚬ *Kitchens, putting green, 4 tennis courts, 2 pools, hot tub, sauna* ⊟ *AE, MC, V.*

★ $$$–$$$$ 🏨 **Plantation Inn.** Charm and luxury set apart this inn, which is on a quiet street in the heart of Lahaina. Filled with Victorian and Asian furnishings, it's reminiscent of a southern plantation home. Secluded lānai draped with hanging plants face a central courtyard, pool, and a garden pavilion perfect for morning coffee. Each guest room or suite is decorated differently, with hardwood floors, French doors, antiques, four-poster beds, and ceiling fans. Some have kitchenettes and whirlpool baths. A generous breakfast is included in the room rate, and one of Hawai'i's best French restaurants, Gerard's, is on-site. ⊠ *174 Lahainaluna Rd., Lahaina 96761* ☎ *808/667–9225 or 800/433–6815* 📠 *808/667–9293* ⊕ *www.theplantationinn.com* 🛏 *18 rooms* ⚬ *Restaurant, fans, refrigerators, in-room VCRs, pool, hot tub, free parking* ⊟ *AE, MC, V.*

★ $$$ 🏨 **Kā'anapali Beach Hotel.** This attractive, old-fashioned hotel is full of aloha. Locals say that it's the only resort on the island where visitors can get a true Hawaiian experience. The vintage-style Mixed Plate restaurant, known locally for its native cuisine program, has displays honoring the many cultural traditions represented by the staff: the employees themselves contributed the artifacts. The spacious rooms are simply decorated in wicker and rattan and face the beach beyond the courtyard. There are complimentary classes in authentic hula dancing, lei-making, and 'ukulele playing. ⊠ *2525 Kā'anapali Pkwy., Lahaina 96761* ☎ *808/661–0011 or 800/262–8450* 📠 *808/667–5978* ⊕ *www.*

kaanapalibeachhotel.com 🛏 *430 rooms* 🍴 *3 restaurants, golf privileges, pool, beach, lobby lounge* ☰ *AE, D, DC, MC, V.*

$$$ ▥ **Mauian Hotel.** If you're looking for a quiet place to stay, this sedate hotel way out in Nāpili may be for you. The rooms have neither televisions nor telephones—such noisy devices are relegated to the 'Ohana Room, where a Continental breakfast is served daily. The simple two-story buildings date from 1959, but the current owners have renovated the place for comfort and convenience, including fully equipped kitchens. Best of all, the 2-acre property opens out onto lovely Napīli Bay. ⊠ *5441 Lower Honoapi'ilani Hwy., Napīli 96761* ☎ *808/669–6205 or 800/367–5034* 🖷 *808/669–0129* ⊕ *www.mauian.com* 🛏 *44 rooms* 🍴 *Pool, hair salon, shuffleboard, laundry facilities; no room phones, no room TVs* ☰ *AE, D, MC, V.*

$$$ ▥ **Nāpili Kai Beach Club.** On 10 beautiful beachfront acres—the beach here is one of the best on the West Side for swimming and snorkeling—the Nāpili Kai draws a loyal following. Hawaiian-style rooms are done in sea-foam green, mauve, and rattan; shoji doors open onto your lānai, with the beach and ocean right outside. The rooms closest to the beach have no air-conditioning, but ceiling fans usually suffice. This is a family-friendly place, with children's programs and free classes in hula and lei-making. Packages that include a car, breakfast, and other extras are available if you stay five nights or longer. ⊠ *5900 Lower Honoapi'ilani Hwy., Nāpili Bay 96761* ☎ *808/669–6271 or 800/367–5030* 🖷 *808/669–5740* ⊕ *www.napilikai.com* 🛏 *162 rooms* 🍴 *Fans, kitchenettes, 2 putting greens, 4 pools, exercise equipment, hot tub, beach, shuffleboard, children's programs (ages 6–12), dry cleaning, concierge, Internet; no a/c in some rooms* ☰ *AE, MC, V.*

★ $$–$$$ ▥ **Lahaina Inn.** This antique jewel right in the heart of town is classic Lahaina—a two-story wooden building that will transport you back to the turn of the 20th century. The nine small rooms and three suites shine with authentic period restoration and furnishings, including quilted bedcovers, antique lamps, and Oriental carpets. You can while away the hours in a wicker chair on your balcony. An excellent Continental breakfast is served in the parlor. ⊠ *127 Lahainaluna Rd., Lahaina 96761* ☎ *808/661–0577 or 800/669–3444* 🖷 *808/667–9480* ⊕ *www.lahainainn.com* 🛏 *9 rooms, 3 suites* 🍴 *No room TVs, no smoking* ☰ *AE, D, MC, V.*

The South Shore

★ $$$$ ▥ **Fairmont Kea Lani Hotel Suites & Villas.** This dramatic resort with a gleaming white exterior is a replica of Las Hadas in Manzanilla, Mexico, and it's the best value in upscale Wailea. Spacious one-bedroom suites in the main hotel have dining lānai and marble bathrooms. Two- and three-bedroom villas on the beach offer more seclusion; each has a private plunge pool and a full kitchen. Service here is as good as what you'd find at hotels with double the price tag, and such special touches as guava juice and cool towels at check-in set this hotel apart. Another plus: one of Maui's best restaurants, Nick's Fishmarket, is on the premises. ⊠ *4100 Wailea Alanui Dr., Wailea 96753* ☎ *808/875–4100 or 800/882–4100* 🖷 *808/875–1200* ⊕ *www.kealani.com* 🛏 *413 suites, 37 villas* 🍴 *3 restaurants, snack bar, microwaves, refrigerators, in-room VCRs, golf privileges, 3 pools, hair salon, health club, 2 hot tubs, beach, lobby lounge, shops, children's programs (ages 5–12), Internet* ☰ *AE, D, DC, MC, V.*

★ $$$$ ▥ **Four Seasons Resort.** This is a Maui favorite, partly because of its location, on one of the Valley Isle's finest beaches. Access to three 18-hole golf courses and "Wimbledon West," with 11 championship tennis courts, is included. The property itself has great appeal, with terraces, courtyards, gardens, waterfalls, and fountains. Nearly all the rooms have an ocean view and combine traditional style with tropical touches. You'll find terry robes and whole-bean coffee grinders in each room. ⊠ *3900 Wailea Alanui Dr., Wailea 96753* ☎ *808/874–8000 or 800/334– 6284* 🖷 *808/874–6449* ⊕ *www.fshr.com* 🕿 *380 rooms* ⚶ *3 restaurants, in-room safes, refrigerators, golf privileges, 2 tennis courts, pool, health club, massage, spa, beach, bicycles, badminton, croquet, volleyball, 2 bars, recreation room, baby-sitting, Internet* ⊟ *AE, D, DC, MC, V.*

$$$$ 🏨 **Grand Wailea.** Sunny opulence is everywhere at this 40-acre resort. Elaborate water features include a 2,000-ft multilevel "canyon riverpool" with slides and grottoes. The Spa Grande offers guests everything from aerobics classes to hydrotherapy massage. Spacious ocean-view rooms are outfitted with overstuffed chaises, comfortable writing desks, and oversize tubs. Access to three 18-hole golf courses and tennis privileges are available. The resort also has one of Maui's most legendary—and least pronounceable—restaurants, Humuhumunukunukuāpua'a. ⊠ *3850 Wailea Alanui Dr., Wailea 96753* ☎ *808/875–1234 or 800/888–6100* 🖷 *808/874–2442* ⊕ *www.grandwailea.com* 🕿 *779 rooms* ⚶ *5 restaurants, in-room safes, cable TV with movies, golf privileges, 3 pools, health club, spa, beach, windsurfing, 6 bars, recreation room, shops, children's programs (ages 5–12), Internet* ⊟ *AE, D, DC, MC, V.*

$$$$ 🏨 **Kama'ole Sands.** Eleven four-story buildings wrap around 15 acres of grassy slope on which are clustered swimming pools, a small waterfall, whirlpool baths, and barbecues. It's a good choice for the active traveler, with tennis and volleyball courts that always seem full. Condos are well appointed with all the modern conveniences, but there's a relaxed, almost retro feel to the place. All units have kitchens, laundries, and private lānai. The property has a 24-hour front desk and an activities desk, and it is across the road from Kīhei Beach. ⊠ *2695 S. Kīhei Rd., Kīhei 96753* ☎ *808/874–8700 or 800/367–5004* 🖷 *808/879– 3273* ⊕ *www.castle-group.com* 🕿 *11 studios; 211 1-bedroom, 83 2- bedroom, and 4 3-bedroom units* ⚶ *Restaurant, 4 tennis courts, pool, wading pool, volleyball* ⊟ *AE, D, DC, MC, V.*

$$$$ 🏨 **Marriott Wailea Resort.** The Marriott (formerly the Outrigger) was built before current construction laws were put in place, so rooms sit much closer to the crashing surf than at most resorts—Wailea Beach is just a few steps away. The tropical lobby and interior spaces showcase a remarkable collection of Hawaiian and Pacific Rim artifacts. All of the spacious rooms have private lānai and are styled with a tropical theme. The grounds are accented with palm, banana, and torch ginger. There are golf privileges at three nearby courses, as well as tennis privileges at the Wailea Tennis Club. The Mandara Spa provides beauty and relaxation treatments as well as massage. ⊠ *3700 Wailea Alanui Dr., Wailea 96753* ☎ *808/879–1922 or 800/922–7866* 🖷 *808/874–8331* ⊕ *www. outriggerwailea.com* 🕿 *516 rooms* ⚶ *3 restaurants, in-room safes, cable TV with video games, golf privileges, 3 pools, hair salon, 2 hot tubs, massage, spa, beach, children's programs (ages 5–12), dry cleaning, laundry service, Internet, business services* ⊟ *AE, D, DC, MC, V.*

$$$$ 🏨 **Maui Prince.** The attention to service, style, and presentation is apparent from the minute you walk into the delightful open-air lobby of this hotel. Rooms on five levels surround the courtyard, which has a Japanese garden with a bubbling stream. Room decoration is understated, in tones of mauve and beige. ⊠ *5400 Mākena Alanui Rd., Mākena 96753* ☎ *808/874–1111 or 800/321–6284* 🖷 *808/879–8763* ⊕ *www. princeresortshawaii.com* 🕿 *310 rooms* ⚶ *4 restaurants, in-room safes, some in-room VCRs, 2 18-hole golf courses, 6 tennis courts, 2 pools, exercise equipment, hot tub, beach, badminton, croquet, shuffleboard, children's programs (ages 5–12), business services* ⊟ *AE, DC, MC, V.*

$$$–$$$$ 🏨 **Maui Coast Hotel.** You might never notice this elegant hotel because it's set back off the street. The standard rooms are fine—very clean and modern—but the best deal is to pay a little more for one of the suites. In these you'll get an enjoyable amount of space and jet nozzles in the bathtub. You can lounge by the large, heated pool and order food and drinks from neighboring Jameson's Grill & Bar. Or walk across the street to 6-mi-long Kama'ole Beach. There's an activities desk, too, to help you plan your time. ✉ 2259 S. Kīhei Rd., Kīhei 96753 ☎ 808/874–6284, 800/895–6284, or 800/426–0670 🖷 808/875–4731 ⊕ www. westcoasthotels.com ➟ 265 rooms, 114 suites ⚲ Restaurant, in-room safes, refrigerators, cable TV with movies, 2 tennis courts, pool, 2 hot tubs, dry cleaning, laundry service ⊟ AE, D, DC, MC, V.

$$$–$$$$ 🏨 **Renaissance Wailea Beach Resort.** Most of the rooms here are in a seven-story, T-shape building positioned on fantastic Mōkapu Beach. Tapestries and gorgeous carpets enhance the public areas. Outside, you'll find exotic gardens, waterfalls, and reflecting ponds. The VIP Mōkapu Beach Club building has 26 luxury accommodations and its own concierge, pool, and beach cabanas. Guest rooms are decorated in shades of cream and each has a lānai. Guests have access to the nearby golf and tennis facilities. ✉ 3550 Wailea Alanui Dr., Wailea 96753 ☎ 808/879–4900 or 800/992–4532 🖷 808/874–6128 ⊕ www.renaissancehotels.com ➟ 345 rooms ⚲ 4 restaurants, refrigerators, 2 pools, health club, hot tub, beach, basketball, Ping-Pong, shuffleboard, lobby lounge, children's programs (ages 5–12) ⊟ AE, D, DC, MC, V.

$$$–$$$$ 🏨 **Wailea Villas.** The Wailea Resort started out with three fine condominiums, named, appropriately, Wailea 'Ekahi, Wailea 'Elua, and Wailea 'Ekolu (Wailea One, Two, and Three). Since then, Wailea has added the Grand Champions Villas, and the adjoining Mākena Resort has built Mākena Surf and Polo Beach Club. All have large units with exceptional views and access to five of the island's best beaches. The Wailea 'Elua Village, Polo Beach Club, and Mākena Surf are the more luxurious properties, with rates to match. ✉ 3750 Wailea Alanui Dr., Wailea 96753 ☎ 808/879–1595 or 800/367–5246 🖷 808/874–3554 ⊕ www.drhmaui. com ➟ 9 studios, 94 1-bedroom, 157 2-bedroom, and 10 3-bedroom apartments ⚲ 6 pools ⊟ AE, MC, V.

$$ 🏨 **Maui Lu Resort.** This was the first hotel in Kīhei; the main lobby was the summer home of the original owner, a Canadian logger. Over the years the Maui Lu has added numerous wooden buildings and cottages to its 28 acres. It's a little reminiscent of a rustic lodge, but the rooms are modern and comfortable. Of the 120 rooms, 50 are on the beach, and some have their own private coves. The rest are across Kīhei Road on the main property. ✉ 575 S. Kīhei Rd., Kīhei 96753 ☎ 808/879–5881 or 800/922–7866 🖷 808/879–4627 ⊕ www.aston-hotels.com ➟ 120 rooms ⚲ Restaurant, in-room safes, refrigerators, 2 tennis courts, pool, beach, lounge ⊟ AE, D, DC, MC, V.

$–$$ 🏨 **Luana Kai.** Here's a prime example of the condominium-by-the-sea, perfect for setting up house for at least four days (the required minimum). There are three different room plans, suited for couples, families, or friends traveling together. Each one comes with everything you need to make yourself at home—a fully stocked kitchen, dishwasher, laundry, television, VCR, and stereo equipment. The pool's a social place, with five gas grills, a full outdoor kitchen, and saunas. There's no beach on-site—for that, you have to go down the road a ways—but the place adjoins a grassy county park with tennis courts. ✉ 940 S. Kīhei Rd., Kīhei 96753 ☎ 808/879–1268 or 800/669–1127 🖷 808/879–1455 ⊕ www.luanakai.com ➟ 113 units ⚲ Putting green, 4 tennis courts, pool, sauna, shuffleboard ⊟ AE, DC, MC, V.

$ 🏨 **Maui Sunseeker Resort.** This hotel is a great value for the area, with renovations completed in 2002, including new paint and carpeting. You can opt for a studio, a one-bedroom, or the two-bedroom penthouse; all have kitchenettes and full baths, as well as barbecue facilities and easy access to the 4-mi stretch of beach outside. ⊠ *551 S. Kīhei Rd., Kīhei 96753* ☎ *808/879–1261 or 800/532–6284* 🖶 *808/874–3877* ⊕ *www.mauisunseeker.com* ⇨ *3 units* ⚲ *Kitchenettes, refrigerators, cable TV, laundry facilities* ⊟ *MC, V.*

East Maui

★ $$$$ 🏨 **Hotel Hāna-Maui.** A small, secluded hotel surrounded by a 7,000-acre ranch, the Hotel Hāna is a departure from the usual resort-style accommodations. The original hotel buildings have verandas with trellises; inside, the spacious rooms have bleached-wood floors, furniture upholstered in natural fabrics, and such welcome touches as fine art and orchids. The newer Sea Ranch Cottages, surrounding a state-of-the-art fitness center across the road, are the best value. A shuttle takes you to beautiful Hamoa Beach. Hunton Conrad's redesign of the interior spaces utilizes the colors of the landscape. The once-maligned restaurant has had a makeover, too. Chef Larry Quirit, an island native who has worked in California and Italy, is introducing organic produce and locally caught fish to the Pacific Rim menu. ⊠ *Hāna Hwy.* ⊘ *Box 9, Hāna 96713* ☎ *808/248–8211 or 800/321–4262* 🖶 *808/248–7264* ⊕ *www.hotelhanamaui.com* ⇨ *19 rooms, 47 cottages, 1 house* ⚲ *Restaurant, 2 tennis courts, 2 pools, exercise equipment, gym, massage, beach, horseback riding, bar, library* ⊟ *AE, D, DC, MC, V.*

$$$–$$$$ 🏨 **Heavenly Hāna Inn.** An impressive Japanese gate marks the entrance to this small upscale inn. Lush gardens surround the three suites, all under one roof, but each with a separate entrance. Rooms are lovingly spare, with Japanese overtones, and the furniture was built with exotic woods by Hāna residents. There is also a traditional Japanese tearoom. ⊠ *Hāna Hwy. near mile marker 32* ⊘ *Box 790, Hāna 96713* ☎ *808/248–8442* ⊕ *www.heavenlyhanainn.com* ⇨ *3 suites* ⚲ *No a/c, no room phones, no room TVs, no kids under 15, no smoking* ⊟ *AE, D, MC, V.*

$$ 🏨 **Kula Lodge.** This hotel isn't typically Hawaiian: the lodge inexplicably resembles a chalet in the Swiss Alps, and two units even have gas fireplaces. Charming and cozy in spite of the nontropical ambience, it's a good spot for a romantic stay. Units are in two wooden cabins; four have lofts in addition to the ample bed space downstairs. On 3 wooded acres, the lodge has views of the valley and ocean enhanced by the surrounding forest and tropical gardens. The property has a protea store that will pack flowers for you to take home. ⊠ *Haleakala Hwy. (Rte. 377)* ⊘ *R.R. 1, Box 475, Kula 96790* ☎ *808/878–2517 or 800/233–1535* 🖶 *808/878–2518* ⊕ *www.kulalodge.com* ⇨ *5 units* ⚲ *Restaurant, shop; no room phones, no room TVs* ⊟ *AE, MC, V.*

Guest Houses & Bed & Breakfasts

Despite the name, many of these small-scale accommodations (both rooms and cottages) choose not to interrupt your privacy with breakfast. Instead they'll provide you with Upcountry or tropical surroundings that will enchant you and a kitchen that will let you do your own thing.

$$$–$$$$ 🏨 **Cliff's Edge at Huelo Point.** This beautiful 2-acre estate is located at Huelo Point, next door to Huelo Point Flower Farm. It's a lower-priced alternative and a good choice when the Flower Farm is booked. There's a private two-bedroom house with a multilevel sundeck, a barbecue grill, and a hot tub. The main house also has two rooms, each with private

entrance, lānai, and kitchenettes. The views from the property are breathtaking, and you are free to pick fruit and flowers from the lush grounds. ⌖ *Box 1095, Haiku 96708* ☎ *808/572–4530* ⊕ *www. cliffsedge.com* ↩ *2 rooms, 1 house* ♨ *Pool* ▤ *No credit cards.*

$$$–$$$$ 🏠 **Ekena.** "Ekena" means Garden of Eden, and the grounds here are full of tropical fruit trees and exotic flowers; a hillside location makes for commanding views of the ocean. There are two houses, each with a fully equipped kitchen. Jasmine, the smaller of the two, is suited to parties of two or four. The main house, Sea Breeze, is huge (2,600 square ft), with two large suites, but occupancy is restricted to a maximum of four people. In order to ensure privacy, the owners rent to only one party at a time. There's a minimum stay of three days. ⌖ *Off Hāna Hwy.* ⌖ *Box 728, Hāna 96713* ☎☎ *808/248–7047* ⊕ *www.maui.net/~ekena* ↩ *2 houses* ♨ *Cable TV, in-room VCRs, laundry facilities; no kids under 14* ▤ *No credit cards.*

★ **$$$–$$$$** 🏠 **Hamoa Bay House & Bungalow.** This Balinese-inspired property is sensuous and secluded—a private sanctuary in a fragrant jungle. There are two buildings: the main house is 1,300 square ft and contains two bedrooms, one of them a suite set apart by a breezeway; there's a screened veranda with an ocean view and also an outdoor lava-rock shower. The 600-square-ft bungalow is a treetop perch with a giant bamboo bed and a hot tub on the veranda. Hamoa Beach is a short walk away. ✉ *Hāna Hwy.* ⌖ *Box 773, Hāna 96713* ☎ *808/248–7884* 🖷 *808/248–7047* ⊕ *www.hamoabay.com* ↩ *1 house, 1 bungalow* ♨ *Kitchen, in-room VCRs, laundry facilities; no kids under 14, no smoking* ▤ *No credit cards.*

$$$–$$$$ 🏠 **Huelo Point Flower Farm.** Set on a 300-ft cliff overlooking Waipo Bay, this 2-acre estate is one of the most secluded inns on the island. The Gazebo Cottage is a large studio with a half bath inside and an outdoor shower. The Carriage House has 15-ft cathedral ceilings, a loft bedroom with a queen-size bed, a den with a double bed, and two spacious decks. The Guest House is a two-bedroom, one-bath home with 18-ft cathedral ceilings, floor-to-ceiling glass facing the ocean, a spacious ocean-view patio, and a private hot tub. Most luxurious of all is the Main House, with 22-ft cathedral ceilings, a sunken tub in the master bath, a large patio, and a private hot tub; it can accommodate up to eight. ⌖ *Off Hāna Hwy. in Huelo* ⌖ *Box 1195, Paia 96779* ☎ *808/572–1850* ⊕ *www. maui.net/~huelopt* ↩ *4 units* ♨ *In-room VCRs, pool* ▤ *No credit cards.*

$$–$$$$ 🏠 **Olinda Country Cottage & Inn.** The restored Tudor home and adjacent cottage are so far up Olinda Road above Makawao you'll keep thinking you must have passed it. The inn, which sits amid an 8½-acre protea farm surrounded by forest and some wonderful hiking trails, has five accommodations: two upstairs bedrooms with private baths; the downstairs Pineapple Sweet; a romantic cottage, which looks like a dollhouse from the outside; and best of all, Hidden Cottage, which has a private hot tub. Bring warm clothes—the mountain air can be chilly. ✉ *2660 Olinda Rd., Olinda 96768* ☎☎ *808/572–1453* ☎ *800/932–3435* ⊕ *www.mauibnbcottages.com* ↩ *3 rooms, 2 cottages* ♨ *No smoking* ▤ *No credit cards.*

★ **$$$** 🏠 **ʻAinahau.** Hidden away next to Hāna Bay, this cottage looks so-so until you get inside and start looking around. The place is ingeniously and lovingly crafted and furnished with works of art. The kitchen is set up with all the details of home, including a loaded spice rack and a coffee grinder, and the cottage is equipped with cable TV and a CD player. Hāna Settings manages this and several other getaways, provides catered meals at your order, and organizes custom Hāna weddings. ⌖ *Off Hāna Hwy.* ⌖ *Box 970, Hāna 96713* ☎ *808/248–7849* 🖷 *808/248–*

8267 ✉ *hanawed@maui.net* ➥ *1 cottage* ⚒ *Kitchen, in-room VCR* ⊟ *AE, MC, V.*

$$$ ▦ **Kū'au Cove Plantation.** Here's a rare and handy location for a Maui visit—on a secluded cove midway between the town of Pā'ia and Ho'okipa Beach Park. The home is quite handsome, dating from the late 1930s and lovingly renovated by the current owners. In classic B&B style, the owners rent two large bedrooms in the main house, both set apart from the family living area and each with private baths and queen-size beds. There are also two private studio apartments with kitchens. Continental breakfast is served. ✉ *2 Wa'a Pl., Kū'au 96779* ☎ *808/579–8988* 🖷 *808/579–8710* ⊕ *www.maui.cc/KuauCovePlantation.html* ➥ *2 rooms, 2 apartments* ⊟ *MC, V.*

$$–$$$ ▦ **Old Wailuku Inn.** This historic home, built in 1924, may be the ulti-
Fodor'sChoice mate Hawaiian B&B. Each room is decorated with the theme of a
★ Hawaiian flower, and the flower motif is worked into the heirloom Hawaiian quilt on each bed. Other features include 10-ft ceilings, floors of native hardwoods, and (depending on the room) some delightful bathtubs. The first-floor rooms have private gardens. A hearty breakfast is included. ✉ *2199 Kaho'okele St., Wailuku 96793* ☎ *808/244–5897 or 800/305–4899* ⊕ *www.mauiinn.com* ➥ *7 rooms* ⚒ *In-room VCRs, library, Internet* ⊟ *AE, D, DC, MC, V.*

$$ ▦ **Bambula Inn.** This casual sprawling house in a quiet Lahaina residential area has two studio apartments, one attached to the house and one freestanding. No breakfast is served; this is a move-in-and-hang-out beach house. Just across the street is a small beach, and moored just offshore is a sailboat hand-built by the owner. He likes to take his guests out for whale-watching and sunset sails, no charge. He also provides bicycles and snorkel equipment. This is a friendly, easygoing way to visit Lahaina. ✉ *518 Ilikahi St., Lahaina 96761* ☎ *808/667–6753 or 800/544–5524* 🖷 *808/667–0979* ⊕ *www.bambula.com* ➥ *2 studios* ⚒ *Fans, kitchens, kitchenettes, cable TV; no a/c in some rooms* ⊟ *D, MC, V.*

$$ ▦ **Bloom Cottage.** The name comes from the abundance of roses and other flowers that surround this well-run, classic B&B. This is life in the slow lane, with privacy and quiet and a fireplace for when the evenings are nippy. The furnishings are very Ralph Lauren with a cowhide flourish suited to this ranch-country locale. The 1906 house has three rooms and is good for four to six people willing to share a single bathroom. The cottage is ideal for a couple. ✉ *229 Kula Hwy., Kula 96790* ☎ *808/878–1425* 🖷 *661/393–5015* ⊕ *www.hookipa.com/bloom_cottage.html* ➥ *3 rooms, 1 cottage* ⚒ *No smoking* ⊟ *AE, D, MC, V.*

$–$$ ▦ **Silver Cloud Guest Ranch.** Silver Cloud is in cowboy country, on the high mountainside beyond Kula and just 5 mi before 'Ulupalakua Ranch. The noble Plantation House, with six rooms, surveys pasturelands and a spellbinding panorama of islands and sea. Silence is a chief attraction in this offbeat but magnificent part of Maui. In addition to the main house, the ranch has the separate Lānai Cottage and five studios with kitchenettes (good for families) arranged like a bunkhouse in a horseshoe shape. A complete breakfast with fresh fruit and juice is served out of the Plantation House kitchen every morning. ✉ *1373 Thompson Rd.* ⌖ *R.R. 2, Box 201, Kula 96790* ☎ *808/878–6101 or 800/532–1111* 🖷 *808/878–2132* ⊕ *www.maui.net/~slvrcld* ➥ *11 rooms, 1 cottage* ⚒ *Some kitchenettes, horseback riding* ⊟ *AE, D, DC, MC, V.*

$ ▦ **By the Sea B&B.** You'll be amazed at the romance the owner has managed to create in a small lot in Kīhei, hemmed in by apartments and commercial buildings. The private yard is a cool little Eden with a large pond and waterfall—a good place to hang out in the hammock by day or the hot tub by night. There are three self-contained apartments in the house. The honeymoon-style Palm Room on the second floor has a king bed and its own lānai. All accommodations have separate entrances, and the owners provide beach equipment, fishing gear, and Continental breakfast. ✉ *20 Wailana Pl., Kīhei 96753* ☎ *808/879–2700 or 888/879–2700* 🖶 *808/879–5540* 🗗 *3 rooms* ⬧ *Hair salon, laundry facilities* ▭ *AE, DC, MC, V.*

$ 🏠 **Hale Hoʻokipa Inn.** This handsome 1924 Craftsman-style house is right in the heart of Makawao town, a good home base for excursions to the crater or to Hāna. The owner has lovingly furnished it with antiques and fine art. (She's also a certified tour guide who likes to take guests on hikes.) She has divided the house into three single rooms, each prettier than the next, and the South Wing, which sleeps four and includes the kitchen. All rooms have private bath, and Continental breakfast is served. This inn matches most people's notion of Grandma and Grandpa's house. ✉ *32 Pakani Pl., Makawao 96768* ☎ *808/572–6698* 🖶 *808/572–2580* ⬥ *www.maui.net/~mauibnb* 🗗 *3 rooms, 1 2-bedroom suite* ⬧ *Cable TV* ▭ *No credit cards.*

$ 🏠 **Halfway to Hāna House.** A private country studio on Maui's lush rural north coast, this serene retreat comes with surrounding gardens and great ocean views. It's a short walk from here to natural pools and waterfalls, hiking areas, and horseback riding. The room comes with optional Continental breakfast and a well-supplied kitchenette—all the equipment you need to do your own thing. A three-night minimum stay is required. ✉ *Hāna Hwy.* ⬧ *Box 675, Haʻikū 96708* ☎ *808/572–1176* 🖶 *808/572–3609* ⬥ *www.halfwaytohana.com/paradise.html* 🗗 *1 room* ⬧ *Kitchenette* ▭ *No credit cards.*

$ 🏠 **Kula View.** This affordable home-away-from-home sits in comfortable, peaceful rural Kula. The 2,000-ft elevation makes for a pleasantly temperate climate and a panorama that takes in the West Maui Mountains and the ocean on either side. Guests stay in the entire upper floor of a simple but tastefully decorated house with Laura Ashley fabrics, a breakfast nook full of wicker furnishings, a private entrance, and a deck. The hostess provides an "amenity basket," a very popular Continental breakfast, advice on touring, and even beach towels or warm clothes for your crater trip. ✉ *140 Holopuni Rd., Kula 96790* ☎ *808/878–6736* ⬥ *www.angelfire.com/hi3/mauibedandbreakfast* 🗗 *1 room* ▭ *No credit cards.*

$ 🏠 **Makani ʻOluʻolu Cottage.** These folks offer both a cottage and an *ʻohana* (an apartment attached to the house). The location is unusual—the heart of lush rural Haʻikū. Both rentals are suited to one or two people, with queen-size beds, complete kitchens, and delightful frescoes on the walls depicting tropical scenes—original works by the multitalented landlady. The tiled ʻohana is downstairs, with its own entrance and a lānai that looks over green pastures. The cottage has decoupage shelves and an antique upright piano. ✉ *925 Kaupakalua Rd., Haʻikū 96708* ☎ *808/572–8383* 🗗 *2 rooms* ⬧ *Kitchens* ▭ *No credit cards.*

¢–$ 🏠 **Aloha Lani Inn.** This accommodation operates rather like the classic European homestay. You share a bathroom with another guest, or perhaps with the home owners, and you're welcome to the kitchen, the lānai, the laundry facilities, the phone, the snorkel gear, the kayak, and so on. It's a casual, friendly, and inexpensive way to visit the West Side. The inn is in a quiet neighborhood within walking distance of Lahaina town. There's a two-night minimum stay. ✉ *13 Kauaula Rd., Lahaina 96761* ☎ *808/662–0812 or 800/572–5642* 🖶 *808/661–8045* ⬥ *www.maui-vacations.com/aloha* 🗗 *2 rooms* ⬧ *Fans, laundry facilities* ▭ *AE, D, MC, V.*

¢–$ 🏠 **Peace of Maui.** The small Upcountry community of Haliʻimaile, 2 mi closer to the coast than Makawao and near both Baldwin Avenue and Haleakalā Highway, is well situated for accessing the rest of the island.

This small inn is a good choice for budget-minded travelers who want to be out and active all day. Six rooms in a "lodge" have pantries and mini-refrigerators. The kitchen and bathroom are shared. There's also a separate cottage with its own kitchen and facilities. You'll have sweeping views of the north shore and the mountains here. ⊠ *1290 Hali'imaile Rd., Hali'imaile 96768* ☎ *808/572–5045 or 888/475–5045* ⊕ *www. peaceofmaui.com* ⇆ *6 rooms, 1 cottage* ⊛ *Cable TV, car rental* ⊟ *No credit cards.*

¢ ▦ **Banana Bungalow Maui Hostel.** The only owner-operated hostel on the island, Banana Bungalow offers the cheapest private accommodations in Wailuku. Each room has one queen-size or two single beds; clean bathrooms are down the newly carpeted hallway. Dorm-style accommodations are also available for $17.50 per night. The property's amenities include free high-speed Internet access in the common room and free local phone calls, as well as kitchen privileges, a Jacuzzi, and fruit trees that you are welcome to pick from. ⊠ *310 N. Market St., Wailuku 96793* ☎ *808/244–5090 or 800/846–7835* ⊕ *www.mauihostel.com* ⇆ *38 rooms* ⊛ *Kitchen, laundry facilities, Internet* ⊟ *MC, V.*

NIGHTLIFE & THE ARTS

Nightlife on Maui might be better labeled "evening life." The quiet island has little of Waikīkī's after-hours decadence. But before 10 PM there's a lot on offer, from lū'au shows and dinner cruises to concerts. Lahaina still tries to uphold its reputation as a party town and succeeds wildly every Halloween when thousands converge on Front Street.

The **Maui Arts & Cultural Center** (✦ Above the harbor on Kahului Beach Rd. ☎ 808/242–2787) is the backbone of Maui's arts and entertainment. The complex includes the 1,200-seat Castle Theater, which hosts international performances and weekly film showings; a 4,000-seat amphitheater for large outdoor concerts; and the 350-seat McCoy Theater for plays and recitals. For information on current programs, check the **Events Box Office** (☎ 808/242–7469) or the *Maui News.*

For nightlife of a different sort, children and astronomy buffs should try stargazing at **Tour of the Stars,** a one-hour program held nightly on the roof of the Hyatt Regency Maui in Kā'anapali. You can look through giant binoculars and a deep-space telescope. The program is run by an astronomer. A romantic program for couples, with roses and chocolate, is held on Friday and Saturday nights at 11. Check in at the hotel lobby 15 minutes prior to starting time. ⊠ *Lahaina Tower, Hyatt Regency Maui, 200 Nohea Kai Dr., Lahaina* ☎ *808/661–1234 Ext. 4727* ▨ *$25* ☉ *Nightly at 8, 9, and 10; Fri. and Sat. romantic program at 11.*

Bars & Clubs

With a little homework, good music and high times can be had on Maui. *Maui Times Magazine,* a free publication found at most stores and restaurants, will help you find out who's playing where. The *Maui News* also publishes an entertainment schedule in its Thursday edition of "Maui Scene."

Contemporary Music

Kahale's Beach Club. A friendly, informal hangout, Kahale's offers live music (usually Hawaiian), drinks, and burgers every day from 10 AM 'til 2 in the morning. ⊠ *36 Keala Pl., Kīhei* ☎ *808/875–7711.*

Lobby Lounge. In the comfort of the Four Seasons lobby, you can listen to contemporary and Hawaiian music played by some of the island's best musicians. At sunset, a hula dancer joins the performance. In addition, the menu is far superior to regular lounge fare—it offers selections from all of the resort's restaurants. ⊠ *Four Seasons Resort, 3900 Wailea Alanui Dr., Wailea* ☎ *808/874–8000.*

Tropica. This restaurant at the Westin Maui is the latest and hottest, more for its Thursday-night dance mix than its food. ⊠ *Westin Maui, 2365 Kā'anapali Pkwy., Lāhaina* ☎ *808/667–2525.*

Jazz

Le Jazzerie. The newest (and tiniest) hot spot on the South Shore is entered through the back door, reminiscent of jazz-era speakeasies. Comfy couches encourage patrons to relax—or spontaneously perform on the available microphone. Meals from the adjacent creperie are available until 10 PM. ⊠ *Behind Le Creperie, 1913 S. Kīhei Rd., off Keala Pl., Kīhei* ☎ *808/891–0822.*

Pacific'O. This highly recommended restaurant is also the most reliable place to hear live jazz on the beach. It's a mellow, pacific sort of jazz—naturally—and it plays from 9 until midnight Thursday through Saturday. Guest musicians—George Benson, for example—often sit in. ⊠ *505 Front St., Lahaina* ☎ *808/667–4341.*

Rock

Casanova Italian Restaurant & Deli. Popular Casanova claims to be the best place on the island for singles. When a DJ isn't spinning, contemporary musicians play blues, country and western, rock and roll, and reggae. Past favorites have included Kool and the Gang, Los Lobos, and Taj Mahal. Expect a cover charge on nights featuring live entertainment. ⊠ *1188 Makawao Ave., Makawao* ☎ *808/572–0220.*

Cheeseburger in Paradise. This Front Street hangout is known for—what else?—big beefy cheeseburgers (not to mention a great spinachnut burger). Locals also know it as a great place to tune in to live bands playing rock and roll, Top 40, and oldies from 4:30 PM to closing. There's no dance floor, but the second-floor balcony is a good place to watch Lahaina's Front Street action. ⊠ *811 Front St., Lahaina* ☎ *808/661–4855.*

Hapa's Brewhaus & Restaurant. Well-loved local performer Willi K. owns Monday nights at this club, which has a large stage, a roomy dance floor, state-of-the-art light and sound systems, and tier seating. Crowds pile in on this and other nights for live music, televised sports, and fine brews. ⊠ *Lipoa Center, 41 E. Lipoa St., Kīhei* ☎ *808/879–9001.*

Hard Rock Cafe. Maui's version of the Hard Rock is popular with young locals as well as visitors who like their music *loud.* ⊠ *Lahaina Center, 900 Front St., Lahaina* ☎ *808/667–7400.*

Maui Brews. Live bands serve up Top 40, reggae, salsa, or rock weeknights; a DJ spins hits on weekends. This is a big place, with a complete bar menu of appetizers, pastas, burgers, and entrées. There are 16 kinds of draft beer and 10 specialty martinis. ⊠ *Lahaina Center, 900 Front St., Lahaina* ☎ *808/667–7794.*

Moose McGillycuddy's. The Moose offers no-cover live music on Tuesday and Thursday and draws a young crowd that comes to enjoy the burgers and beer, dancing and mingling. ⊠ *844 Front St., Lahaina* ☎ *808/667–7758.*

Mulligan's on the Blue. Perfect pints of Guinness and late-night fish-and-chips—who could ask for more? Add to that live entertainment (including Sunday-evening Irish jams), gorgeous sunset views, an optimal resort location, and a dance floor, and you've got one of Maui's busiest nighttime hangouts. ⊠ *100 Kaukahi St. (on Blue Golf Course), Wailea* ☎ *808/874–1131.*

The Sly Mongoose. Off the beaten tourist path, the Sly Mongoose is the seediest dive bar in town, and one of the friendliest. The bartender will know your name and half your life history inside of 10 minutes, and she makes the strongest mai tai on the island. ⊠ *1036 Limahana Pl., Lahaina* ☎ *808/661–8097.*

Tsunami's. You can dance to hip-hop, house, techno, reggae, and Top 40 hits in this sophisticated, high-tech disco, where laser beams zigzag high above a futuristic dance floor. The music plays from 9 to 1 on Friday and Saturday nights. Expect a dress code—no jeans or T-shirts—and a $10 cover charge. ⊠ *Grand Wailea, 3850 Wailea Alanui Dr., Wailea* ☎ *808/875–1234.*

Dinner & Sunset Cruises

America II Sunset Sail. The star of this two-hour cruise is the craft itself—a 1987 America's Cup 12-m class contender that is exceptionally smooth and steady. ⊠ *Lahaina Harbor, Lahaina* ☎ *808/667–2195* ☜ *$30–$33.*

Kaulana Cocktail Cruise. This two-hour sunset cruise (with a bit of whale-watching in season) has a *pūpū* (appetizers) menu, open bar, and live music. ⊠ *Lahaina Harbor, Lahaina* ☎ *808/871–1144* ☜ *$39.*

Pride Charters. A 65-ft catamaran built specifically for Maui's waters, the *Pride of Maui* has a large cabin, a large upper sundeck for unobstructed viewing, and a stable, comfortable ride. Breakfast, lunch, and beverages are provided. For later departures, there is an optional barbecue. ⊠ *Māʻalaea Harbor, Māʻalaea* ☎ *808/242–0955* ☜ *$40.*

Scotch Mist Charters. A two-hour champagne sunset sail is offered on the 25-passenger Santa Cruz 50 sloop *Scotch Mist II.* ⊠ *Lahaina Harbor, Lahaina* ☎ *808/661–0386* ☜ *$55.*

Windjammer Cruises. This cruise includes a prime-rib and Alaskan-salmon dinner and live entertainment on the 70-ft, 93-passenger *Spirit of Windjammer,* a three-masted schooner. ⊠ *283 Wili Ko Pl., Suite 1, Lahaina* ☎ *808/661–8600* ☜ *$69.*

Film

There are megaplexes showing first-run movies in Kukui Mall, Lahaina Center, Maui Mall, and Kaʻahumanu Shopping Center. Check local papers for showtimes.

Maui Film Festival. In this ongoing celebration, quality films that may not show up at the local megaplex are screened weekly. Most screenings are in Maui's most luxurious movie house—Castle Theater at Maui Arts & Cultural Center. On Wednesday night the usual movies are followed by live music and poetry readings in the Candlelight Cafe. The schedule varies, and the program is expanding. In summer the festival comes to Wailea for cinema under the stars in a program that includes music, hula, and Hawaiian storytelling. ☎ *808/572–3456 for recorded program information* ⊕ *www.mauifilmfestival.com.*

Lūʻau & Revues

★ **The Feast at Lele.** "Lele" is an older, more traditional name for Lahaina. This "feast" is redefining the lūʻau by crossing it with fine dining island-style in an intimate beach setting. Both the show and the four-course meal express the spirit of a specific island culture—Hawaiian, Samoan, Tongan, or Tahitian. The wine list and liquor selections are excellent. ⊠ *505 Front St., Lahaina* ☎ *808/667–5353* ↺ *Reservations essential* ☜ *$89* ⊙ *Mon.–Sat. at 5:30 in winter and 6:30 in summer.*

Maui Myth & Magic Theatre. One of Maui's hottest tickets, "ʻUlalena" is a 75-minute musical extravaganza that is well received by audiences and Hawaiian-culture experts alike. The ensemble cast (20 singer-dancers and a five-musician orchestra) mixes native rhythms and stories with acrobatic performance and high-tech stage wizardry to give an inspiring introduction to island culture. It has auditorium seating, and beer and wine are for sale at the concession stand. There are dinner-theater packages in conjunction with top Lahaina restaurants. ⊠ *878 Front St., Lahaina* ☎ *808/661–9913 or 877/688–4800* ⌂ *Reservations essential* ▦ *$45* ⊙ *Tues.–Sat. at 6 and 8:30.*

Nāpili Kai Beach Club Keiki Hula Show. Expect to be charmed as well as entertained when 30 children ages 6 to 17 take you on a dance tour of Hawai'i, New Zealand, Tahiti, Samoa, and other Polynesian islands. The talented youngsters make their own ti-leaf skirts and fresh-flower leis. They give the leis to the audience at the end of the show. This is a non-professional but delightfully engaging review, and the 80-seat oceanfront room is usually sold out. ⊠ *Nāpili Kai Beach Club, 5900 Lower Honoapi'ilani Hwy., Nāpili* ☎ *808/669–6271* ▦ *$50* ⊙ *Dinner Fri. at 6, show at 7:30.*

Old Lahaina Lū'au. This is the best lū'au you'll find on Maui. It's small, personal, and authentic and is performed in an outdoor theater designed specifically for traditional Hawaiian entertainment. The setting feels like an old seaside village. In addition to fresh fish and grilled steak and chicken, you'll get all-you-can-eat traditional lū'au fare: kālua pig, chicken long rice, *lomi lomi* salmon (massaged until tender and served with minced onions and tomatoes), *haupia* (coconut pudding), and other treats. You'll also get all you can drink. Guests sit either on tatami mats or at tables. Then there's the entertainment: a musical journey from old Hawai'i to the present with hula dancing, chanting, and singing. ⊠ *1251 Front St., Lahaina (makai of the Lahaina Cannery Mall)* ☎ *808/667–1998* ▦ *$79* ⊙ *Nightly 5:30–8:30.*

Warren & Annabelle's. Magician Warren Gibson entices his guests into a swank nightclub with red carpets and a gleaming mahogany bar and plies them with appetizers (coconut shrimp, crab cakes), desserts (rum cake, crème brûlée), and "smoking cocktails." Then he performs tableside magic while his ghostly assistant, Annabelle, tickles the ivories. The show is fun, and all the better for being not too slick. Note that this is a nightclub, so no one under 21 is allowed. ⊠ *Lahaina Center, 900 Front St.* ☎ *808/667–6244* ⌂ *Reservations essential* ▦ *$39.95* ⊙ *Mon.–Sat. at 6.*

Music

Maui Symphony Orchestra. The symphony orchestra usually performs at the Maui Arts & Cultural Center, offering six seasonal concerts and a few special programs as well. The regular season includes a Christmas concert, an opera gala, a classical concert, and two pop concerts outdoors. At the season's end, in June, the International Music Festival takes over, bringing renowned musicians to the island—each of whom plays for a pittance and the pleasure of performing on Maui. ☎ *808/244–5439* ⊕ *www.mauisymphony.com.*

Theater

Baldwin Theatre Guild. Dramas, comedies, and musicals are presented by this group about eight times a year. The guild has staged such favorites as *The Glass Menagerie, Brigadoon,* and *The Miser.* Musicals are held in the 1,200-seat Community Auditorium. All other plays are presented in the Baldwin High School Mini Theatre. ⊠ *1650 Ka'ahumanu Ave., Kahului* ☎ *808/984–5673* ▦ *$8.*

Maui Academy of Performing Arts. For a quarter-century this group has offered fine performances as well as dance and drama classes for children and adults. It has presented such plays as *Peter Pan, Jesus Christ*

Superstar, and *The Nutcracker.* Call ahead for performance venue. ✉ *81 N. Church St., Wailuku* ☎ *808/244–8760* 🖅 *$10–$12.*

Maui Community Theatre. Now staging about six plays a year, this is the oldest dramatic group on the island, started in the early 1900s. Each July the group also holds a fund-raising variety show, which can be a hoot. ✉ *'Iao Theatre, 68 N. Market St., Wailuku* ☎ *808/242–6969* 🖅 *Musicals $10–$15, nonmusicals $8–$13.*

Seabury Hall Performance Studio. This college-preparatory school above Makawao town offers a season of often supercharged shows in its satisfying small theater and two dance studios. The school's formula is to mix talented kids with seasoned adults and innovative, even offbeat, concepts. Dance concerts are always a hit. ✉ *480 Olinda Rd., 1 mi north of Makawao crossroads* ☎ *808/573–1257* 🖅 *$7–$12.*

Tony and Tina's Wedding. The longest-running off-Broadway hit ever, this show couldn't have found a more apt backdrop than the Hyatt's Swan Court. If you didn't come to Maui with a wedding party, or you need relief from the party you did come with, immerse yourself in the hilarity of a faux Italian wedding. Typical reception fare is served—lasagna, fish, Caesar salad, and wedding cake. Heckling is allowed; the more you participate, the more fun you have. ✉ *Hyatt Regency Maui, Kā'anapali Resort, 200 Nohea Kai Dr., Lahaina* ☎ *808/661–1234* 🖅 *$76.50* 🕑 *Mon.–Sat. at 6:30.*

SPORTS & THE OUTDOORS

Biking

Maui County has designated hundreds of miles of bike paths on Maui's roads, making biking safer and more convenient than in the past. Painted bike lanes make it possible for a rider to travel all the way from Mākena to Kapalua, and you'll see dozens of hardy souls pedaling under the hot Maui sun. Some people rent a bike just to ride around the resort where they're staying. Bikes rent for $10 to $20 a day. Several companies offer downhill bike tours from the top of Haleakalā all the way to the coast.

Extreme Sports Maui (✉ 397 Dairy Rd., Kahului ☎ 808/871–7954) rents front-suspension bikes for $29 per day or $162 per week. Full-suspension bikes run $39 per day or $218 per week. All rates include helmets. **Island Biker** (✉ 415 Dairy Rd., Kahului ☎ 808/877–7744) rents standard front-shock bikes and road bikes for $29 a day or $95 per week; helmets are included. **West Maui Cycles** (✉ 840 Waine'e St., Lahaina ☎ 808/ 661–9005) rents front-suspension bikes for $25 per day, full-suspension bikes for $45 per day, and standard hybrid bikes for $20 per day. It also organizes bike tours of the island.

Camping & Hiking

FodorśChoice ★ Let's start with the best—hiking **Haleakalā Crater** (✉ Haleakalā Crater Rd., Makawao, ☎ 808/572–4400) at Haleakalā National Park. The recommended way to explore the crater is to go in two cars and ferry yourselves back and forth between the head of Halemau'u Trail and the summit. This way, you can hike from the summit down Sliding Sands Trail, cross the crater floor, investigate the Bottomless Pit and Pele's Paint Pot, then climb out on the switchback trail (Halemau'u). When you emerge, the shelter of your waiting car will be very welcome. Give yourself eight hours for the hike; take a backpack with lunch, water, and a reliable jacket for the beginning and end of the hike. This is a demanding trip, but you will never regret or forget it.

If you want to stay longer than a day, plan on overnighting in one of the national park's three cabins or two campgrounds. The cabins are equipped with bunk beds, wood-burning stoves, fake logs, and kitchen gear. To reserve a cabin you have to plan at least three months in advance and hope the lottery system is kind to you. Contact the **National Park Service** (🖃 Box 369, Makawao 96768 ☎ 808/572–9306). The tent campsites are easy to reserve on a first-come, first-served basis. Just make sure to stop at park headquarters to register on your way in.

Just as you enter Haleakalā National Park, **Hosmer Grove** offers an hour-long loop trail into the cloud forest that will give you insight into Hawai'i's fragile ecology. You can pick up a map at the trailhead. Park rangers conduct guided hikes on a changing schedule. There are six campsites (no permit needed), pit toilets, drinking water, and cooking shelters.

Another good hiking spot—and something totally unexpected on a tropical island—is **Polipoli Forest.** During the Great Depression the government began a program to reforest the mountain, and soon cedar, pine, cypress, and even redwood took hold. It's cold here and foggy, and often wet or at least misty. To reach the forest, take Route 37 all the way out to the far end of Kula. Then turn left at Route 377. After about a half mile, turn right at Waipoli Road. First you'll encounter switchbacks; after that it's just plain bad—but passable. There are wonderful trails, a small campground, and a cabin that you can rent from the Division of State Parks. Write far in advance for the **cabin** (🖃 Box 1049, Wailuku 96793 ☎ 808/244–4354); for the campground, you can wait until you arrive in Wailuku and visit the **Division of State Parks** (🖃 54 High St. ☎ 808/984–8109).

'**Ohe'o Gulch** is a branch of Haleakalā National Park past Hāna on the Pi'ilani Highway. This is the starting point of one of the best hikes on Maui—the 2-mi trek upstream to 400-ft **Waimoku Falls.** Along the way you can take side trips and swim in the stream's basalt-lined pools. Then the trail bridges a sensational gorge and passes onto a boardwalk through a mystifying forest of giant bamboo. Down at the grassy sea cliffs, you can camp, no permit required, although you can stay only three nights. Toilets, grills, and tables are available here, but there's no water and open fires aren't allowed.

For excursions into remote areas, contact **Maui Eco Adventures** (🖃 180 Dickenson St., Suite 101, Lahaina ☎ 808/661–7720 or 877/661–7720). The ecologically minded company leads hikes into private or otherwise inaccessible areas. Hikes, which can be combined with kayaking, mountain biking, or sailing trips, explore botanically rich valleys in Kahakuloa and East Maui.

Fitness & Spa Centers

Most spas and fitness centers on Maui are in hotels. Generally, spa services are available to both guests and nonguests, whereas fitness centers are for guests only. If your hotel does not have a facility, ask whether privileges are available at another hotel. Those listed provide the most comprehensive services.

The Spa at Four Seasons Resort. This fully renovated, comprehensive spa offers massage, facials, wraps, and signature services such as the Mango Salt Glow (an exfoliating body scrub using mango sorbet) in a relaxing new treatment facility. Oceanside and couples massage are available. 🖃 *3900 Wailea Alanui Dr., Wailea* ☎ *808/874–8000 or 800/334–6284.*

THE HUMPBACK'S WINTER HOME

THE HUMPBACK WHALES' *attraction to Maui is legendary. More than half the North Pacific's humpback population winters in Hawai`i. At* one time there were thousands of the huge mammals, but a history of overhunting and marine pollution dwindled the world population to about 1,500. In 1966, humpbacks were put on the endangered species list, which restricts boats and airplanes from getting too close.

Experts believe the humpbacks keep returning to Hawaiian waters because of the warmth. Winter is calving time, and the young whales, born with little blubber, probably couldn't survive in the frigid Alaskan waters. No one has ever seen a whale give birth here, but experts know that calving is their main winter activity, since the 1- and 2-ton youngsters suddenly appear while the whales are in residence.

Between November and April boats leave the wharves at Lahaina and Mā`alaea in search of the massive creatures, merely to observe and enjoy their awe-inspiring size in closer proximity. As it's almost impossible not to see whales during winter on Maui, you'll want to prioritize: is adventure or comfort your aim? If close encounters with the giants of the deep are your desire, pick a smaller boat that guarantees sightings. Afternoon trips are generally rougher as the wind picks up, but some say this is when the most surface action occurs. If an impromptu marine-biology lesson sounds fun, go with Pacific Whale Foundation. For those wanting to

sip mai tais as whales cruise calmly by, stick with a sunset cruise on a boat with a full bar and buffet.

Every captain aims to please during whale season, getting as close as legally possible. Crew members know when a whale is about to dive (after several waves of its heart-shape tail) but rarely can predict breaches (when the whale hurls itself up and almost entirely out of the water). On snorkel trips, crew members will sometimes volunteer to dive with your underwater camera, catching especially exciting photos of sea life. Don't forget to bring sunscreen, light long sleeves, and a hat you can secure. Weather can be extreme at sea, especially as the wind picks up. Arrive early to find parking—this can be a particular challenge at Mā`alaea Harbor.

Pacific Whale Foundation (✉ Kealia Beach Plaza, 101 N. Kīhei Rd., Kīhei ☎ 808/ 879–8811) pioneered whale-watching back in 1979 and now runs four boats. During humpback season PWF has a marine naturalist stationed at McGregor Point Lookout (on the cliffs heading into Lahaina).

Whale-watching trips can be booked by the **Ocean Activities Center** (✉ 1847 S. Kīhei Rd., Suite 203A, Kīhei ☎ 808/ 879–4485). **Island Marine** (✉ 658 Front St., Lahaina ☎ 808/661–8397) takes passengers out on the West Side. **Pride Charters** (✉ 208 Kenolio Rd., Kīhei ☎ 808/874–8835) offers two-hour cruises narrated by a naturalist.

★ **Spa Grande, Grand Wailea.** At 50,000 square ft, this is the largest spa on the island. The "Termé Circuit," with five different therapeutic baths, is a bargain at $50, and prices for spa services—massages, facials, wraps, and the like—go up from there. The gym, which has state-of-the art cardio equipment, is a separate facility, and use is free to hotel guests. ✉ *3850 Wailea Alanui Dr., Wailea* ☎ *808/875–1234 or 800/ 888–6100.*

★ **Spa Kea Lani, Fairmont Kea Lani Hotel Suites & Villas.** One of the island's smallest spas may well be its nicest. There are only nine treatment rooms, but each is state-of-the-art. Massage tables are hydraulic, so your therapist can move you into the perfect position for your specific needs. The signature Ilíili Stone Massage is practiced by experts who harvest their own stones nearby. Use of the gym, open 24 hours a day, is free to hotel guests. ✉ *4100 Wailea Alanui Dr., Wailea* ☎ *808/875–4100 or 800/659–4100.*

Spa Luna. If hotel spa prices are a little intimidating, try this day spa, which is also an aesthetician's school. Located in the former Hāʻiku Cannery, it offers services ranging from facials to massage to microdermabrasion. You can opt for professional services or take advantage of the student clinics. The students are subject to rigorous training, and their services are offered at a fraction of the regular cost. ✉ *Hāʻiku Cannery, 810 Hāʻiku Rd., Hāʻiku* ☎ *808/575–2440.*

Spa Moana, Hyatt Regency Maui. Spa Moana has oceanfront views from the gym, which is free to hotel guests. Treatment areas are serene. The spa offers traditional treatments such as Thai massage and shiatsu, as well as its own signature services, such as the Káanapali Coffee Scrub (treatment times come in Tall, Grande, and Vente). ✉ *200 Nohea Kai Dr., Lahaina* ☎ *808/661–1234 or 800/233–1234.*

Waihua, Ritz-Carlton, Kapalua. The gym here is the island's most elegant, right down to the chilled washcloths waiting for you after your workout. Unique services include butler-drawn baths in your room, complete with theme music and champagne, mai tais, or fresh juice. All the traditional spa services are offered, too, including massages from Swedish to lomi lomi. ✉ *1 Ritz-Carlton Dr., Kapalua* ☎ *808/669–6200 or 800/ 262–8440.*

Outside the resorts, the most convenient and best-equipped fitness center is **24-Hour Fitness** (✉ 150 Hāna Hwy., Kahului ☎ 808/877–7474); day passes are $20. The **Maui Family YMCA** (✉ 250 Kanaloa Ave., Kahului ☎ 808/242–9007) offers $10 day passes.

Golf

How do you keep your mind on the game in a place like Maui? The views make it very hard. Nonetheless Maui has become one of the world's premier golf-vacation destinations. The island's major resorts all have golf courses, each of them stunning. They're all open to the public, and most lower their greens fees after 2 PM on weekday afternoons.

Elleair Golf Course. Bill Newis designed this privately owned course, which is independent of the resorts, to take advantage of its lofty location above Kīhei town. You'll get panoramic views not only out to sea but also across Haleakalā. ✉ *1345 Piʻilani Hwy., Kīhei* ☎ *808/874–0777* ⛳ *Greens fee $85, cart included.*

Kāʻanapali Golf Courses. Two of Maui's most famous courses are here: the North Course, designed by Robert Trent Jones, Sr., and the South Course, laid out by Arthur Jack Snyder. ✉ *Kāʻanapali Beach Resort, Kāʻanapali* ☎ *808/661–3691* ⛳ *Greens fee $130 guests, $150 nonguests; cart included.*

Kapalua Golf Club. The club has three 18-holers—the Village Course and the Bay Course, both designed by Arnold Palmer, and the Plantation Course, designed by Ben Crenshaw. Kapalua is well known to television-sports watchers. ✉ *300 Kapalua Dr., Kapalua* ☎ *808/669–8044* ⛳ *Greens fee $115 guests, $160 nonguests, $99 special 11 AM–2 PM; cart included; club rental $40–$50.*

Mākena Golf Course. There are two lovely 18-hole courses here, North and South, designed by Robert Trent Jones, Jr. Of all the resort courses, this one is the most remote. At one point, golfers must cross a main road, but there are so few cars that this poses no problem. ✉ *5415 Mākena Alanui Rd., Kīhei* ☎ *808/879–3344* ⛳ *Greens fee $95–$105 guests, $155–$175 nonguests; cart included.*

Sandalwood Golf Course. Sandalwood has a unique location on the slopes of the West Maui Mountains just south of Wailuku, with elevated views of Haleakalā. ✉ *2500 Honoapi'ilani Hwy., Wailuku* ☎ *808/ 242–4653* ✆ *Greens fee $80, $50 after 12 PM; cart included.*

Wailea Golf Club. The club has three courses: the Gold and the Blue, which were designed by Arthur Jack Snyder, and the newer Emerald, designed by Robert Trent Jones, Jr. In his design, Snyder incorporated ancient lava-rock walls to create an unusual golfing experience. ✉ *100 Wailea Golf Club Dr., Wailea* ☎ *808/875–5111* ✆ *Greens fee $115 guests, $140 nonguests; cart included.*

Maui has municipal courses, where the fees are lower. Be forewarned, however, that the weather can be cool and wet, and the locations may not be convenient. The **Waiehu Municipal Golf Course** is on the northeast coast of Maui a few miles past Wailuku. ✚ *Off Rte. 340, West Maui* ☎ *808/244–5934* ✆ *Greens fee $25 weekdays, $30 weekends; cart $15.*

ON THE
SIDELINES   Maui has a number of golf tournaments, most of which are of professional caliber and worth watching. Many are also televised nationally. One attention-getter is the **Mercedes Championships** (☎ 808/669–2440), formerly called the Lincoln-Mercury Kapalua International, held in January. This is the first official PGA tour event, held on Kapalua's Plantation Course. The Aloha Section of the Professional Golfers Association of America hosts the **GTE Hawaiian Tel Hall of Fame** (☎ 808/669–8877) championship at the Plantation Course in May. A clambake feast on the beach tops off the **Kapalua Clambake Pro-Am** (☎ 808/669–8812) in July.

At Kā'anapali the **EMC Maui Kā'anapali Classic SENIOR PGA Golf Tournament** (☎ 808/661–3691) pits veteran professionals in a battle for a $1 million purse each October.

Over in Wailea, in June, on the longest day of the year, self-proclaimed "lunatic" golfers start out at first light to play 100 holes of golf in the annual **Ka Lima O Maui** (☎ 808/875–5111), a fund-raiser for local charities. The nationally televised **Senior Skins** (☎ 808/875–5111) in January pits four of the most respected Senior PGA players against one another.

Hang Gliding

Armin Engert of **Hang Gliding Maui** (☎ 808/572–6557 ⊕ www. hangglidingmaui.com) will take you on an instructional powered hang-gliding trip out of Hāna Airport. A 25- to 30-minute flight lesson costs $95, and a 50- to 60-minute lesson is $165. Snapshots of your flight from a wing-mounted camera cost an additional $25.

Outrigger-Canoe Races

Polynesians first traveled to Hawai'i by outrigger canoe, and racing the traditional craft has always been a favorite pastime in the Islands. Canoes were revered in old Hawai'i, and no voyage could begin without a blessing, ceremonial chanting, and a hula performance to ensure a safe journey. At Whalers Village in May, the two-day launch festivities for the **Ho'omana'o Challenge Outrigger Sailing Canoe World Championship** (☎ 808/661–3271) also include a torch-lighting ceremony, arts-and-crafts demonstrations, and a chance to observe how the vessels are rigged—as well as the start of the race.

Parasailing

Parasailing is an easy and fun way to earn your wings: just strap on a harness attached to a parachute, and a powerboat pulls you up and over the ocean from a launching dock or from a boat's platform. Note that to reduce interference with whales, no "thrill craft"—including parasails—are allowed in Maui waters from December 15 to April 15.

West Maui Para-Sail (☎ 808/661–4060) offers both 400- and 800-ft flights, ranging from $38 to $51—early-bird flights are cheapest. For safety reasons, passengers must weigh more than 100 pounds, or two must be strapped together in tandem. The group will be glad to let you experience a "toe dip" or "freefall" if you request it.

Polo

Polo is popular on Maui. From April through June Haleakalā Ranch hosts "indoor" contests on a field flanked by side boards. The field is on Route 377, 1 mi from Route 37. During the "outdoor" polo season, mid-August to the end of October, matches are held at Olinda Field, 1 mi above Makawao on Olinda Road. There is a $3 admission charge for most games, which start at 1 PM on Sunday. The sport has two special events. The **Oskie Rice Memorial Tournament** occurs on Memorial Day. The **High Goal Benefit,** held on the last Sunday in October, draws challengers from Argentina, England, South Africa, New Zealand, and Australia. For information, contact **Emiliano** (☎ 808/572–4915).

Rodeos

With dozens of working cattle ranches throughout the Islands, many youngsters learn to ride a horse before they can drive a car. Mauians love their rodeos and put on several for students at local high schools throughout the year. Paniolos get in on the action, too, at three major annual events: the Oskie Rice Memorial Rodeo, usually staged the weekend after Labor Day; the Cancer Benefit Rodeo in April, held at an arena 3 mi east of Pāʻia; and Maui's biggest event, drawing competitors from all the Islands as well as the U.S. mainland, the 4th of July Rodeo, which comes with a full-on parade and other festivities that last for days. Spectator admission fees to the competitions vary from free to $7. Cowboys are a tough bunch to tie down to a phone, but you can try calling the **Maui Roping Club** (☎ 808/572–2076) for information.

Sporting Clays

Skillfully designed to fit inside the crater of a large cinder cone, **Papaka Sporting Clays** (✉ 1325 S. Kīhei Rd., Kīhei ☎ 808/879–5649) is an outdoor arcade dedicated to the art of shooting. The 40 stations include "Springing Teal," "High Pheasant," and "Busting Bunnies" (no real bunnies involved; the targets are clay disks). Certified instructors outfit you with a vest, earplugs, eye protection, a shotgun, and instruction. They can pick you up in the Kīhei-Wailea area or at ʻUlupalakua Ranch by appointment any morning or afternoon. The cost is $95 for 75 targets. Spectators can come along for free.

Tennis

Most courts charge by the hour but will let players continue after their initial hour for free, provided no one is waiting. In addition to the facilities listed below, smaller hotels and condos usually have one or two courts open only to their guests. The best free courts are the five at the **Lahaina Civic Center** (✉ 1840 Honoapiʻilani Hwy., Lahaina ☎ 808/661–4685), near Wahikuli State Park. They're available on a first-come, first-served basis.

Hyatt Regency Maui. The Hyatt has six premium Plexipave courts and provides clinics, private lessons, and rentals. All-day passes cost $20 for guests, $25 for nonguests. ✉ *200 Nohea Kai Dr., Lahaina* ☎ *808/661–1234 Ext. 3174.*

Kapalua Tennis Garden. This complex serves the Kapalua Resort with 10 courts and a pro shop. You'll pay $10 an hour if you're a guest, $12 if you're not. ✉ *100 Kapalua Dr., Kapalua* ☎ *808/669–5677.*

Mākena Tennis Club. This club at the Mākena Resort, just south of Wailea, has six courts, with two lighted for night play. Rates are $20 per court hour for guests, $24 for nonguests. ✉ *5400 Mākena Alanui Rd., Kīhei* ☎ *808/879–8777.*

Maui Beach & Tennis Club. The Maui Marriott's club has five Plexipave courts, with three lighted for night play, and a pro shop. Daily rates are $10 per hour for guests and nonguests. ✉ *100 Nohea Kai Dr., Kā'anapali* ☎ *808/667–1200 Ext. 8689.*

Royal Lahaina Tennis Ranch. In the Kā'anapali Beach Resort on West Maui, the Royal Lahaina has 11 courts and a pro shop. Rates are a flat $10 per person per day whether you are a guest or not. ✉ *2780 Keka'a Dr., Lahaina* ☎ *808/661–3611 Ext. 2296.*

Wailea Tennis Club. The club has 11 Plexipave courts (its famed grass courts are, sadly, a thing of the past), lessons, rentals, and ball machines. On weekday mornings clinics are given to help you improve your ground strokes, serve, volley, or doubles strategy. Rates are $27 per hour per court. ✉ *131 Wailea Ike Pl., Kīhei* ☎ *808/879–1958 or 800/332–1614.*

ON THE SIDELINES At the Kapalua Jr. Vet/Sr. Tennis Championships in May, where the minimum age is 30, players have been competing in singles and doubles events since 1979. On Labor Day, the Wilson Kapalua Open Tennis Tournament, Maui's grand prix of tennis, calls Hawai'i's hottest hitters to volley for a $12,000 purse at Kapalua's Tennis Garden and Village Tennis Center. Also at the Tennis Center, Women's International Tennis Association professionals rally with avid amateurs in a week of pro-am and pro-doubles competition during the Kapalua Betsy Nagelsen Tennis Invitational in December. All events are put on by the **Kapalua Tennis Club** (☎ 808/669–5677).

The Wailea Open Tennis Championship is held in spring or summer on the Plexipave courts at the **Wailea Tennis Club** (☎ 808/879–1958).

Water Sports

DEEP-SEA FISHING If fishing is your sport, Maui is the place for it. You'll be able to throw in hook and bait for fish such as 'ahi, *aku* (skipjack tuna), barracuda, bonefish, *kawakawa* (bonito), mahimahi, Pacific blue marlin, *ono* (wahoo), and *ulua* (jack crevalle). On Maui you can fish throughout the year, and you don't need a license.

Plenty of fishing boats run out of Lahaina and Mā'alaea harbors. If you charter a boat by yourself, expect to spend in the neighborhood of $600 a day. But you can share the boat for about $100 per person.

Finest Kind Inc. (✉ Lahaina Harbor, Slip 7 ☐ Box 10481, Lahaina 96767 ☎ 808/661–0338) has three boats: *Finest Kind,* a 37-ft Merritt; *Reel Hooker,* a 35-ft Bertram; and *Exact,* a 31-ft Bertram. The company specializes in live bait. **Hinatea Sportfishing** (✉ Lahaina Harbor, Slip 27, Lahaina 96761 ☎ 808/667–7548) has a 41-ft Hatteras, and offers full-day, shared-boat tours beginning at $160 per person. **Luckey Strike Charters** (✉ Lahaina Harbor, Slip 50, Lahaina 96767 ☎ 808/661–4606 ⊕ www.luckeystrike.com) has two boats, the *Luckey Strike II,* a 50-ft Delta sportfishing vessel, and the *Kanoa,* a 31-ft Uniflite Sport

Fisher. It offers four-, six-, and eight-hour trips. **Ocean Activities Center** (✉ 1847 S. Kīhei Rd., Suite 203A, Kīhei 96753 ☎ 808/879–4485 or 800/798–0652) offers full-day tours for as low as $115 per person on a 37-ft Tolleycraft.

KAYAKING   The sport has been gaining popularity on the island, and kayaking off the coast of Maui can be a leisurely paddle or a challenge, depending on your location, your inclination, and the weather of the day. The company to contact is **Maui Sea Kayaking** (☎ 808/572–6299 ⊕ www.maui. net/~kayaking). It takes small parties to secret spots and takes great care in customizing its outings. For example, the guides accommodate kayakers with disabilities as well as senior kayakers, and they also offer kid-size gear. Among their more unusual programs are kayak surfing and wedding-vow renewal.

RAFTING   These high-speed inflatable craft are nothing like the raft that Huck Finn used to drift down the Mississippi. While passengers grip straps, these rafts fly, skimming and bouncing, across the sea. Because they're so maneuverable, they go where the big boats can't—secret coves, sea caves, and unvisited beaches. **Ocean Riders** (✉ Lahaina 96767 ☎ 808/661–3586 ⊕ www.mauioceanriders.com), in Lahaina, takes people all the way around the island of Lāna'i. For snorkeling or gawking, the "back side" of Lāna'i is one of Hawai'i's unsung marvels.

SAILING   Because of its proximity to the smaller islands of Moloka'i, Lāna'i, Kaho'olawe, and Molokini, Maui can provide some of Hawai'i's best sailing experiences. Most sailing operations like to combine their tours with a meal, some throw in snorkeling or whale-watching, and others offer a sunset cruise.

The best and longest-running operation is the Coon family's **Trilogy Excursions** (✉ Lahaina ☎ 808/661–4743 or 800/874–2666). They have six beautiful multihulled sailing craft, and the crews treat passengers with genuine warmth and affection. A full-day catamaran cruise to Lāna'i includes a guided van tour of the island, a barbecue lunch, beach volleyball, and a "Snorkeling 101" class, in which you can test your skills in the waters of Hulopo'e Marine Preserve. (Trilogy has exclusive commercial access.) Snorkeling gear is supplied. The company also offers a Molokini snorkel cruise.

The Hyatt Regency Maui's **Kiele V** (☎ 808/661–1234), a 55-ft luxury catamaran, does daily (except Wednesday) snorkel sails; afternoon cocktail sails; and, in season, whale-watching sails. **Mahana Na'ia** (✉ Mā'alaea Harbor ☎ 808/871–8636) provides good service and food on its comfortable catamaran cruise. This boat specializes in snorkel trips to Molokini.

Maui–Moloka'i Sea Cruises (☎ 808/242–8777) features the 92-ft *Prince Kuhio*, one of the largest air-conditioned cruise vessels in Maui waters. Programs include snorkeling and whale-watching cruises. **Scotch Mist Charters** (☎ 877/464–6284 or 808/661–0386) takes a maximum of 25 on snorkeling, sunset, or whale-watching trips aboard a 50-ft Santa Cruz sailing yacht.

SCUBA DIVING   Maui is just as scenic underwater as it is on dry land. In fact, some of the finest diving spots in Hawai'i lie along the Valley Isle's western and southwestern shores. If you're a certified diver, you can rent gear at any Maui dive shop simply by showing your PADI or NAUI card. Unless you're familiar with the area, however, it's probably best to hook up with a dive shop for an underwater tour.

Dive shops island-wide sell and rent equipment and give lessons and certification. Before signing on with any of these outfitters, however, it's a good idea to ask a few pointed questions. All provide equipment with proof of certification, as well as introductory dives ($100–$160) for those who aren't certified.

Ed Robinson's Diving Adventures (⊠ Kīhei ☎ 808/879–3584 or 800/635–1273) offers diving instruction, charters, and underwater photo trips. **Happy Divers** (⊠ 888 Puiki St., Lahaina ☎ 808/669–0123) specializes in small group trips; beginners can get their feet wet with single dives or take a three-day PADI certification course. **Lahaina Divers** (⊠ 143 Dickenson St., Lahaina ☎ 808/667–7496 ⊕ www.lahainadivers.com) offers tours of Maui, Molokini, and Lāna'i; boats are accessible for passengers with disabilities. **Maui Dive Shop** (⊠ 1455 S. Kīhei Rd., Kīhei ☎ 808/873–3388) offers scuba charters, diving instruction, and equipment rental from six locations island-wide, with its main office in Kīhei.

Area dive sites include the following:

Honolua Bay. In West Maui, this marine preserve is alive with many varieties of coral and tame tropical fish, including large ulua, *kāhala,* barracuda, and manta rays. With depths of 20 ft to 50 ft, this is a popular spot for introductory dives. Dives are generally made only during the summer months.

Molokini Crater. At 'Alalākeiki Channel, this is a crescent-shape islet formed by the top of a volcano. This marine preserve's depth range (10 ft to 80 ft), combined with the attraction of the numerous tame fish dwelling here that can be fed by hand, make it a popular introductory dive site.

SNORKELING The same dive companies that take scuba aficionados on tours will take snorkelers as well. One of Maui's most popular snorkeling spots can be reached only by boat: Molokini Crater, that little bowl of land off the coast of Wailea. For about $55, you can spend a half day at Molokini, with meals provided.

For a personal introduction to Maui's undersea universe, the undisputable authority is **Ann Fielding's Snorkel Maui** (⊠ Box 1107, Makawao 96768 ☎ 808/572–8437). A marine biologist, Fielding—formerly with the University of Hawai'i, Waikīkī Aquarium, and the Bishop Museum and the author of several guides to island sea life—is the Carl Sagan of Hawai'i's reef cosmos. She'll not only show you fish, but she'll also introduce you to *individual* fish. This is a good first experience for dry-behind-the-ears types. Snorkel trips, which cost $75, include lunch.

You can find some good snorkeling spots on your own. Secluded **Windmill Beach** (✛ take Rte. 30 3½ mi north of Kapalua; then turn onto the dirt road to the left) has a superb reef for snorkeling. A little more than 2 mi south of Windmill Beach, a dirt road leads to **Honolua Bay.** The coral formations on the right side of the bay are particularly dramatic. You'll find **Nāpili Bay,** one beach south of the Kapalua Resort, quite good for snorkeling.

Almost the entire coastline from Kā'anapali south to Olowalu offers fine snorkeling. Favorite sites include the area just out from the cemetery north of Wahikuli State Park, near the lava cone called **Black Rock,** on which Kā'anapali's Sheraton Maui Hotel is built; and the shallow coral reef south of Olowalu General Store.

The coastline from Wailea to Mākena is also good. The best snorkeling is found near the rocky fringes of Wailea's **Mōkapu, Ulua, Wailea,** and **Polo** beaches.

Between Polo Beach and Mākena Beach (turn right on Mākena Road just past Mākena Surf Condo) lies **Five Caves,** where you'll find a maze of underwater grottoes below offshore rocks. This spot is recommended for experienced snorkelers only, since the tides can get rough. At Mākena, the waters around the **Puʻu Ōlaʻi** cinder cone provide great snorkeling.

If you need gear, **Snorkel Bob's** (⊠ Nāpili Village Hotel, 5425 Lower Honoapiʻilani Hwy., Nāpili ☎ 808/669–9603 ⊠ 2411 S. Kīhei Rd., Kīhei ☎ 808/879–7449 ⊠ 1217 Front St., Lahaina ☎ 808/661–4421) will rent you a mask, fins, and a snorkel and throw in a carrying bag, map, and snorkel tips for as little as $5 per day.

SURFING   Although on land it may not look as if there are seasons on Maui, the tides tell another story. In winter the surf is up on the northern shores of the Hawaiian Islands, and summer brings big swells to the southern side. Near-perfect winter waves on Maui can be found at **Honolua Bay,** on the northern tip of West Maui. To get there, continue 2 mi north of D. T. Fleming Park on Route 30 and take a left onto the dirt road next to a pineapple field; a path takes you down the cliff to the beach.

Hoʻokipa Beach Park (✛ 2 mi past Pāʻia on Rte. 36) is where the modern-day sport of surfing began on Maui. This is the easiest place to watch surfing, because there are paved parking areas and picnic pavilions in the park. A word of warning: the surfers who come here are pros, and if you're not, they may not take kindly to your getting in their way.

Viewers with a good pair of binoculars might be able to see out past the windsurfers to view an example of tow-in surfing: Jet Ski pilots pull state-of-the-art big-wave surfers out to the 1-mi marker, where the waves can average 30 ft to 40 ft during winter swells.

Hāna Highway Surf (⊠ 69 Hāna Hwy., Paia ☎ 808/579–8999) rents boards for a little as $20 per day. **Second Wind** (⊠ 111 Hāna Hwy., Kahului ☎ 808/877–7467) rents surfboards for $18 per day or $90 per week.

Check out www.mauisurf.com for information on surf schools and surf rules on Maui. **Hawaiʻi Ultimate Adventures** (✆ Box 12467, Lahaina 96761 ☎ 808/669–3720 ⊕ www.hawaiiultimate.net) offers specialized instruction for kids and watchful instruction for all ages. The **Nancy Emerson School of Surfing** (⊠ 358 Papa Pl., Suite F, Kahului ☎ 808/244–7873 ⊕ www.surfclinics.com) will get even the most shaky novice riding the waves with its pioneering "Learn to Surf in One Lesson" program. A private lesson with Nancy herself—a pro surfer and occasional stunt double—will cost you $200 for one hour or $305 for two hours; a private lesson with one of her equally qualified instructors costs $95 for one hour and $150 for two hours. Group lessons are $75 for two hours. The endless patience of the **Surf Dog Maui** (✆ Box 501, Lahaina 96767 ☎ 808/250–7873) instructors will help you learn to surf like the locals do. And at $58 for a two-hour beginner course, they offer one of the best deals on the island.

WINDSURFING   It's been about two decades since Hoʻokipa Bay was discovered by windsurfers, who gave this windy beach 10 mi east of Kahului an international reputation. The spot is blessed with optimal wave-sailing wind and sea conditions and, for experienced windsurfers, can offer the ultimate experience. Other locations around Maui are good for windsurfing as well—Kanahā, for example—but Hoʻokipa is absolutely unrivaled.

Even if you're a windsurfing aficionado, chances are good you didn't bring your equipment. You can rent it—or get lessons—from these shops. Lessons range from $30 to $60 and can last anywhere from one to three hours. Equipment rental also varies—from no charge with lessons to $20 an hour. For the latest prices and special deals, it's best to call around once you've arrived. **Maui Ocean Activities** (✉ Whalers Village, Kāʻanapali ☎ 808/667–1964) rents windsurfing equipment for $45 a day. **Maui Windsurf Company** (✉ 22 Hāna Hwy., Kahului ☎ 808/877–4816) has a drive-through service and a no-hassle pickup and drop-off system. **Maui Windsurfari** (✉ 425 Koloa St., Kahului ☎ 808/871–7766 or 800/736–6284 ⊕ www.windsurfari.com) specializes in windsurfing vacation packages, offering a full range of services including accommodation bookings and high-tech-gear rental. **Second Wind** (✉ 11 Hāna Hwy., Kahului ☎ 808/877–7467) rents boards with two sails for $43 per day. Boards with three sails go for $48 per day.

ON THE SIDELINES Not many places can lay claim to as many windsurfing tournaments as Maui. The Valley Isle is generally thought to be the world's preeminent windsurfing location and draws boardsailing experts from around the globe who want to compete on its waves. In March the **Hawaiian Pro Am Windsurfing** competition gets under way. In April the **Da Kine Hawaiian Pro Am** lures top windsurfers, and the **Aloha Classic World Wave Sailing Championships** takes place in October. All are held at Hoʻokipa Bay, right outside the town of Pāʻia, near Kahului. For competitions featuring amateurs as well as professionals, check out the **Maui Race Series** (☎ 808/877–2111), six events held at Kanahā Beach in Kahului in summer, when winds are the strongest and a lack of big waves makes conditions excellent for the slalom (speed-racing) course. Competitors maneuver their boards close to shore, and the huge beach provides plenty of seating and viewing space. Hoʻokipa Bay's large waves are also prime territory for surfers. The **Local Motion Surfing** competition heats up the action in May, and in January the **Maui Rusty Pro**, held jointly at Honolua Bay, invites professionals to compete for a $40,000 purse.

SHOPPING

Shopping is, of course, abundant in the resort areas. Whether you're searching for a dashboard hula dancer or something a little more upmarket, you can probably buy it on Front Street in Lahaina or South Kīhei Road in Kīhei. But don't miss the great boutiques lining the streets of small towns like Pāʻia and Makawao. You can purchase upscale fashions and art while strolling through these charming, quieter communities.

Local artisans turn out gorgeous work in a range of prices. Special souvenirs include rare hardwood bowls and boxes, prints of sea life, Hawaiian quilts, and specialty food products like Kona coffee. A group that calls itself Made on Maui exists solely to promote the products of its members—items ranging from pottery and paintings to Hawaiian teas and macadamia caramel corn. You can identify the group by its distinctive Haleakalā logo.

Business hours for individual shops on the island are usually 9 to 5, seven days a week. Shopping centers tend to stay open later (until 9 or 10 at least one night of the week).

Shopping Centers

Azeka Place Shopping Center. Kīhei offers this large and bustling place. Azeka I is the older half, on the makai side of the street. Azeka II, on the mauka side, has a Longs Drugs and several good lunch stops. ✉ *1280 S. Kīhei Rd., Kīhei.*

Kaʻahumanu Center. This is Maui's largest mall and a showplace with more than 75 stores and a gorgeous glass-enclosed atrium entrance topped by an umbrella-shaded food court. Stop at Camellia Seed Shop for what the locals call "crack seed," a delicacy made from dried fruits, nuts, and sugar. Other interesting stops here include Maui Hands—purveyor of prints, paintings, woodwork, and jewelry by some of the island's finest artists—and such mall standards as Macy's, Gap, and Waldenbooks. ✉ *275 Ka'ahumanu Ave., Kahului* ☎ *808/877–3369.*

Kama'ole Shopping Center. Residents of Kīhei favor the locally owned shops at this small shopping center. ✉ *2463 S. Kīhei Rd., Kīhei.*

Lahaina Cannery Mall. Set in a building reminiscent of an old pineapple cannery are 50 shops and an active stage. The mall hosts fabulous free events year-round (like the International Jazz Festival). Recommended stops include Na Hoku, purveyor of striking Hawaiian heirloom jewelry and pearls; Totally Hawaiian Gift Gallery; and Kite Fantasy, one of the best kite shops on Maui. An events schedule is available on the Web site. ✉ *1221 Honoapi'ilani Hwy., Lahaina* ☎ *808/661–5304* ⊕ *www.lahainacannery.com.*

Lahaina Center. Island department store Hilo Hattie Fashion Center anchors the complex and puts on a free hula show at 2 PM every Wednesday and Friday. In addition to Hard Rock Cafe, Banana Republic, and a four-screen cinema, you will find a replica of an ancient Hawaiian village complete with three full-size thatch huts built with 10,000 ft of Big Island 'ōhi'a wood, 20 tons of *pili* grass, and more than 4 mi of hand-woven coconut *senit* (twine). There's all that *and* validated parking. ✉ *900 Front St., Lahaina* ☎ *808/667–9216.*

Maui Mall. The anchor stores here are Longs Drugs and Star Market, and there's a good Chinese restaurant, Dragon Dragon. The Tasaka Guri Guri Shop is an oddity. It's been around a hundred years, selling an ice cream–like confection called "guri guri." The mall also has a whimsically designed 12-screen megaplex. ✉ *70 Ka'ahumanu Ave., Kahului* ☎ *808/877–7559.*

Maui Marketplace. On the busy stretch of Dairy Road, just outside the Kahului Airport, this behemoth marketplace couldn't be more conveniently located. The 20-acre complex houses several outlet stores and big retailers, such as Pier One Imports, Sports Authority, and Borders Books & Music. Sample local food at the Kau Kau Corner food court. ✉ *270 Dairy Rd., Kahului* ☎ *808/873–0400.*

Rainbow Mall. This mall is one-stop shopping for condo guests—it offers video rentals, Hawaiian gifts, pizza, and a liquor store. ✉ *2439 S. Kīhei Rd., Kīhei.*

The Shops at Wailea. Stylish, upscale, and close to most of the resorts, this mall brings high fashion to Wailea. Luxury boutiques such as Gucci, Fendi, Cos Bar, and Tiffany & Co. have shops, as do less expensive chains like Gap, Guess, and Tommy Bahama's. Several good restaurants face the ocean, and regular Wednesday-night events have live entertainment, art exhibits, and fashion shows. ✉ *3750 Wailea Alanui Dr., Wailea* ☎ *808/ 891–6770.*

Whalers Village. Chic Whalers Village has a whaling museum and more than 50 restaurants and shops. Upscale haunts include Louis Vuitton, Prada, Ferragamo, Versace, and Chanel Boutique. The complex also offers some interesting diversions: Hawaiian artisans display their crafts daily, hula dancers perform on an outdoor stage weeknights from 7 to 8, and three films spotlighting whales and marine history are shown daily for free at the Whale Center of the Pacific. ✉ *2435 Kā'anapali Pkwy., Kā'anapali* ☎ *808/661–4567.*

Grocery Stores

Foodland. In Kīhei town center, this is the most convenient supermarket for those staying in Wailea. It's open round-the-clock. ✉ *1881 S. Kīhei Rd., Kīhei* ☎ *808/879–9350.*

Hawaiian Moons Natural Foods. You'll find the best selection of organic produce on the island, as well as Maui-made products to take home, at this health food store. ⊠ *2411 S. Kīhei Rd., Kīhei* ☎ *808/875–4356.*

Lahaina Square Shopping Center Foodland. This Foodland serves West Maui and is open daily from 6 AM to midnight. ⊠ *840 Waine'e St., Lahaina* ☎ *808/661–0975.*

Safeway. Safeway has three stores on the island open 24 hours daily. ⊠ *Lahaina Cannery Mall, 1221 Honoapi'ilani Hwy., Lahaina* ☎ *808/667–4392* ⊠ *170 E. Kamehameha Ave., Kahului* ☎ *808/877–3377* ⊠ *277 Piikea Ave., Kīhei* ☎ *808/891–9120.*

Specialty Stores

Art

Maui has more art per square mile than any other Hawaiian island—maybe more than any other U.S. county. There are artists' guilds and co-ops and galleries galore all over the island. Art shows are held throughout the year at the Maui Arts & Cultural Center. The Lahaina Arts Society presents **Art in the Park** under the town's historic banyan tree every Friday and Saturday from 9 to 5. Moreover, the town of Lahaina hosts **Art Night** every Friday from 7 to 10. Galleries open their doors (some serve refreshments) and musicians stroll the streets. Similar festivities occur at **WOW!** on Wednesday, from 6:30 to 9:30 at the Shops at Wailea.

Avalene Gallery. Avalene Gallery shows the work of Jan Kasprzycki, Steve Smeltzer, and Lisa Kasprzycki. Jan Kasprzycki, one of Hawai'i's best-known colorists, is currently working on "NightScapes," a series of large portraits of cities and towns worldwide. Smeltzer's sculpture is whimsical and colorful. Kasprzycki's daughter, Lisa, is a wonderful painter in her own right, working mostly in oil on canvas and wood. ⊠ *1156 Makawao Ave., Makawao* ☎ *808/572–8500.*

Hot Island Glassblowing Studio & Gallery. With the glass-melting furnaces glowing bright orange and the shop loaded with mesmerizing sculptures and functional pieces, this is an exciting place to visit. The working studio, set back from Makawao's main street in "The Courtyard," is owned by a family of glassblowers. ⊠ *3620 Baldwin Ave., Makawao* ☎ *808/572–4527.*

★ **Hui No'eau Visual Arts Center.** Not only are the grounds a pleasure to visit, but the Hui's gift shop sells unique pieces from local artists, as does the pottery studio in back. ⊠ *2841 Baldwin Ave., Makawao* ☎ *808/572–6560.*

Lahaina Galleries. Works of both national and international artists are displayed at the gallery's two locations in West Maui. ⊠ *728 Front St., Lahaina* ☎ *808/667–2152* ⊠ *Kapalua Resort, Bay Dr., Kapalua* ☎ *808/669–0202.*

Martin Lawrence Galleries. Martin Lawrence displays the works of noted mainland artists, including Andy Warhol and Keith Haring, in a bright and friendly gallery. ⊠ *Lahaina Market Place, Front St. and Lahainaluna Rd., Lahaina* ☎ *808/661–1788.*

★ **Maui Crafts Guild.** This is one of the most interesting galleries on Maui. Set in a two-story wooden building alongside the highway, the Guild is crammed with treasures. Resident artists craft everything in the store—from Norfolk-pine bowls to *raku* (Japanese lead-glazed) pottery to original sculpture. The prices are surprisingly low. Upstairs, gorgeous pieces of handcrafted hardwood furniture are on display. ⊠ *43 Hāna Hwy., Pā'ia* ☎ *808/579–9697.*

★ **Maui Hands.** This gallery shows work by dozens of local artists, including paniolo-theme lithographs by Sharon Shigekawa, who knows whereof she paints: she rides each year in the Kaupō Roundup. ⊠ *3620 Baldwin Ave., Makawao* ☎ *808/572–5194* ⊠ *Ka'ahumanu Center, 275 Ka'ahumanu Ave., Kahului* ☎ *808/877–0368.*

Viewpoints Gallery. Viewpoints calls itself Maui's only fine-arts collective; it is a cooperative venture of about two dozen Maui painters and sculptors. ⊠ *3620 Baldwin Ave., Makawao* ☎ *808/572–5979.*

Village Gallery. This gallery, with two locations on the island, showcases the works of such popular local artists as Betty Hay Freeland, Wailehua Gray, Margaret Bedell, George Allen, Joyce Clark, Pamela Andelin, Stephen Burr, and Macario Pascual. ⊠ *120 Dickenson St., Lahaina* ☎ *808/661–4402* ⊠ *Ritz-Carlton, 1 Ritz-Carlton Dr., Kapalua* ☎ *808/669–1800.*

Clothing

ISLAND WEAR   **Hilo Hattie Fashion Center.** Hawai'i's largest manufacturer of aloha shirts and mu'umu'u also carries brightly colored blouses, skirts, and children's clothing. ⊠ *Lahaina Center, 900 Front St., Lahaina* ☎ *808/661–8457.*

Tommy Bahama's. It's hard to find a man on Maui who *isn't* wearing a TB-logo aloha shirt. For better or worse, here's where you can get yours. Make sure to grab a Barbados Brownie on the way out at the restaurant, which is attached to the shop. ⊠ *The Shops at Wailea, 3750 Wailea Alanui Dr., Wailea* ☎ *808/875–9983.*

RESORT WEAR   If you're not in the mood for a matching aloha shirt and mu'umu'u ensemble, check out the malls and franchise stores like **Honolua Surf Company** (⊠ 845 Front St., Lahaina ☎ 808/661–8848). This chain is popular with young men and women for surf trunks, casual clothing, and accessories.

Some of the smaller boutiques around the island offer a great selection of upscale resort wear and casual sportswear. Head to Baldwin Avenue in Makawao, and Hāna Highway in Pā'ia for a string of several good shops.

Maggie Coulombe. Maggie Coulombe's cutting-edge fashions have the style of SoHo and the heat of the Islands. The designs here are unique and definitely worth a look, even if you don't buy. ⊠ *505 Front St., Lahaina* ☎ *808/662–0696.*

Maui Girl. This is the place for swimwear, cover-ups, beach hats, and sandals. Maui Girl designs its own suits and imports teenier versions from Brazil as well. Whatever your size, tops and bottoms can be purchased separately. ⊠ *13 Baldwin Ave., Pā'ia* ☎ *808/579–9266.*

Nell. The Fairmont Kea Lani's boutique carries stylish resort wear for women. ⊠ *Fairmont Kea Lani, 4100 Wailea Alanui Dr., Wailea* ☎ *808/875–4100.*

Sisters & Company. Opened by four sisters, this little shop has a lot to offer—current brand-name clothing such as Tamara Katz and ener-chi, locally made jewelry, beach sandals, and gifts. Sister No. 3, Rhonda, runs a tiny, ultrahip hair salon in back. ⊠ *1913 S. Kīhei Rd., Kīhei* ☎ *808/875–9888.*

Flea Market

Maui Swap Meet. This Saturday flea market is the biggest bargain on Maui, with crafts, gifts, souvenirs, fruit, flowers, jewelry, antiques, art, shells, and lots more. ⊠ *Rte. 350, off S. Pu'unēnē Ave., Kahului* ☜ *50¢* ☉ *Sat. 5:30 AM–noon.*

Food

Local produce—pineapples, papayas, coconuts, or Maui onions—and Made in Maui jams and jellies make great souvenirs. Cook Kwee's Maui Cookies have gained quite a following, as have Maui Potato

Chips. Both are available in most Valley Isle grocery stores. Coffee sellers now have Maui-grown and -roasted beans alongside the better-known Kona varieties.

Remember that fresh fruit must be inspected by the U.S. Department of Agriculture before it can leave the state, so it's safest to buy a box that has already passed muster.

Airport Flower & Fruit Co. Ready-to-ship pineapples, Maui onions, papayas, and fresh coconuts are available by phone. ☎ *808/243–9367 or 800/922–9352.*

Maui Coffee Roasters. This café and roasting house near Kahului Airport is the best stop for Kona and Island coffees. The salespeople give good advice and will ship items. You even get a free cup of joe in a signature to-go cup when you buy a pound of coffee. ✉ *444 Hāna Hwy., Unit #B, Kahului* ☎ *808/877–2877* ⊕ *www.hawaiiancoffee.com.*

Take Home Maui. These folks will supply, pack, and deliver produce free to the airport or your hotel. ✉ *121 Dickenson St., Lahaina* ☎ *808/661–8067 or 800/545–6284.*

Gifts

Lahaina Printsellers Ltd. Hawai'i's largest selection of original antique maps and prints pertaining to Hawai'i and the Pacific is available here. It also sells museum-quality reproductions and original oil paintings from the Pacific Artists Guild. A second, smaller shop is open at 505 Front Street. ✉ *Whaler's Village, 2435 Kā'napali Pkwy., Kā'anapali* ☎ *808/667–7617.*

Lei Spa. In addition to being a day spa, this is a wonderful place to buy soaps, lotions, and shampoos, almost all of which are made on Maui. ✉ *505 Front St., Lahaina* ☎ *808/661–1178.*

White Orchid. Maui's wedding-business boom prompted White Orchid Wedding to expand its business by opening a gift shop. It offers tasteful gifts including colorful home furnishings, photo albums, Maui-made products, and art objects. ✉ *1961 Vineyard St., Wailuku* ☎ *808/242–8697.*

Hawaiian Crafts

The arts and crafts native to Hawai'i are first on the list for many visiting shoppers. Such woods as koa and milo grow only in certain parts of the world, and because of their increasing scarcity, prices are rising. Artisans turn the woods into bowls, trays, and jewelry boxes that will last for years. Look for them in galleries and museum shops.

★ **Hāna Coast Gallery.** One of the best places to shop on the island, this 3,000-square-ft gallery has fine art and jewelry on consignment from local artists. ✉ *Hotel Hāna-Maui, Hāna Hwy., Hāna* ☎ *808/248–8636 or 800/637–0188.*

Hāna Cultural Center. The center sells distinctive island quilts and other Hawaiian crafts. ✉ *Ukea St., Hāna* ☎ *808/248–8622.*

Kīhei Kalama Village Marketplace. This is a fun place to investigate. Shaded outdoor stalls sell everything from printed and hand-painted T-shirts and sundresses to jewelry, pottery, wood carvings, fruit, and gaudily painted coconut husks—all made by local craftspeople. ✉ *1941 S. Kīhei Rd., Kīhei* ☎ *808/879–6610.*

Jewelry

Haimoff & Haimoff Creations in Gold. This shop carries the original work of several jewelry designers, including the renowned Harry Haimoff. ✉ *Kapalua Resort* ☎ *808/669–5213.*

Jessica's Gems. Jessica's has a good selection of Hawaiian heirloom jewelry, and its Lahaina store specializes in black pearls. ✉ *Whalers Village, 2435 Kā'anapali Pkwy., Kā'anapali* ☎ *808/661–4223* ✉ *858 Front St., Lahaina* ☎ *808/661–9200.*

Lahaina Scrimshaw. Here you can buy brooches, rings, pendants, cuff links, tie tacks, and collector's items adorned with this intricately carved sailors' art. ⊠ *845A Front St., Lahaina* ☎ *808/661-8820* ⊠ *Whalers Village, 2435 Kāʻanapali Pkwy., Kāʻanapali* ☎ *808/661-4034.*

Master Touch Gallery. The exterior of this shop is as rustic as all the old buildings of Makawao, so there's no way to prepare yourself for the elegance of the handcrafted jewelry displayed within. Owner David Sacco truly has the "master touch." The extravagant new shop in Wailea is perhaps more befitting to the designs. ⊠ *3655 Baldwin Ave., Makawao* ☎ *808/572-6000* ⊠ *The Shops at Wailea, 3750 Wailea Alanui Dr., Wailea* ☎ *808/875-5555.*

Maui Divers. This company has been crafting gold and coral into jewelry for more than 20 years. ⊠ *640 Front St., Lahaina* ☎ *808/661-0988.*

MAUI A TO Z

To research prices, get advice from other travelers, and book travel arrangements, visit www.fodors.com.

AIR TRAVEL

You can fly to Maui from the mainland United States or from Honolulu. Flight time from the West Coast to Maui is about 5 hours; from the Midwest, expect about an 8-hour flight; and coming from the East Coast will take about 10 hours, not including layovers. Maui is the most visited of the Neighbor Islands and therefore the easiest to connect to on an interisland flight. Honolulu–Kahului is one of the most heavily traveled air routes in the nation.

CARRIERS United flies nonstop to Kahului from Los Angeles and San Francisco. American also flies into Kahului, with one stop in Honolulu, from Dallas and Chicago and nonstop from Los Angeles. Delta has through service to Maui daily from Salt Lake City, Atlanta, and Los Angeles and one nonstop flight daily from Los Angeles. Hawaiian Airlines has direct flights to Kahului from the U.S. West Coast.

Continental, Hawaiian, and Northwest fly from the mainland to Honolulu, where Maui-bound passengers can connect with a 40-minute interisland flight. Flights generally run about $75 one-way between Honolulu and Maui and are available from Hawaiian Airlines, Aloha Airlines, and Island Air.

🛪 **Aloha Airlines** ☎ 808/244-9071, 800/367-5250 from U.S. mainland ⊕ www.alohaairlines.com. **American** ☎ 800/433-7300 ⊕ www.aa.com. **Continental** ☎ 800/523-3273 ⊕ www.continental.com. **Delta** ☎ 800/221-1212 ⊕ www.delta.com. **Hawaiian Airlines** ☎ 800/882-8811 ⊕ www.hawaiianair.com. **Island Air** ☎ 800/652-6541 ⊕ www.islandair.com. **Northwest** ☎ 800/225-2525 ⊕ www.nwa.com. **United** ☎ 800/241-6522 ⊕ www.ual.com.

AIRPORTS

Kahului Airport is efficient and remarkably easy to navigate. Its main disadvantage is its distance from the major resort destinations in West Maui. Kahului is the only airport on Maui that has direct service from the mainland.

If you're staying in West Maui, you might be better off flying into the Kapalua–West Maui Airport. The only way to get to the Kapalua–West Maui Airport is on an interisland flight from Honolulu because the short runway accommodates only small planes. Set in the midst of a pineapple field with a terrific view of the ocean far below, the little airport provides one of the most pleasant ways to arrive on the Valley Isle.

Hāna Airport isn't much more than a landing strip. Only commuter Aloha Island Air flies here, landing twice a day from Honolulu (via Moloka'i and Kahului) and departing 10 minutes later. The morning flight originates in Princeville, Kaua'i. When there is no flight, the tiny terminal usually stands eerily empty, with no gate agents, ticket takers, or other people in sight.

🔹 **Kahului Airport** ☎ 808/872-3800 or 808/872-3830. **Kapalua–West Maui Airport** ☎ 808/669-0623. **Hāna Airport** ☎ 808/248-8208.

AIRPORT TRANSFERS

The best way to get from the airport to your destination—and to see the island itself—is in your own rental car. Most major car-rental companies have desks or courtesy phones at each airport. They also can provide a map and directions to your hotel from the airport.

It will take you about an hour, with traffic in your favor, to get from Kahului Airport to a hotel in Kapalua or Kā'anapali and 30 to 40 minutes to go to Kīhei or Wailea.

Shuttles also run between the airport and the Kā'anapali and Kapalua resorts during daylight hours at regular intervals.

If you are flying into Hāna Airport and staying at the Hotel Hāna-Maui, your flight will be met. If you have reserved a rental car, the agent will usually know your arrival time and meet you. Otherwise you can call Dollar Rent A Car to pick you up.

Maui has more than two dozen taxi companies, and they make frequent passes through the Kahului and Kapalua–West Maui airports. If you don't see a cab, you can call La Bella Taxi for island-wide service from the airport. Call Kīhei Taxi if you're staying in the Kīhei, Wailea, or Mākena area. Charges from Kahului Airport to Kā'anapali run about $49; to Wailea, about $31; and to Lahaina, about $42.

🔹 **Kīhei Taxi** ☎ 808/879-3000. **La Bella Taxi** ☎ 808/242-8011.

BOAT & FERRY TRAVEL

Approaching the Valley Isle on the deck of a ship is an unforgettable experience. Watching the land loom ever larger conjures up the same kinds of feelings the early Polynesians probably had on their first voyage—except they didn't get the kind of lavish treatment those on board a luxury cruise ship routinely receive. You can book passage through American Hawai'i Cruises, which offers seven-day interisland cruises departing from Honolulu on the S.S. *Constitution* and the S.S. *Independence*. Or ask about the company's seven-day cruise-resort combination packages.

🔹 **American Hawai'i Cruises** ✉ 2 North Riverside Plaza, Chicago, IL 60606 ☎ 312/466-6000 or 800/765-7000.

BUS TRAVEL

Maui has a limited bus system, run by a private company, Akina Tours. Air-conditioned buses transport visitors around the West Maui and South Maui areas only. Inexpensive one-way, round-trip, and all-day passes are available. The Holo Ka'a Public Transit System has routes in South, West, and Central Maui.

🔹 **Akina Bus Service/Holo Ka'a Public Transit System** ☎ 808/879-2828 ⊕ www.akinatours.com

CAR RENTAL

During peak seasons—summer, and Christmas through Easter—be sure to reserve your car well ahead of time if you haven't booked a room-car package with your hotel. Expect to pay about $35 a day—before taxes, insurance, and extras—for a compact car from one of the major companies. You can get a less-expensive deal from one of the locally owned budget companies. There is a $2 daily road tax on all rental cars in Hawai'i.

Budget, Dollar, and National have courtesy phones at the Kapalua–West Maui Airport; Hertz and Alamo are nearby. All of the above, plus Avis, have desks at or near Maui's major airport in Kahului. Roberts Tours offers car rentals through package tours. Quite a few locally owned companies rent cars on Maui, including Aloha Rent-A-Car, which will pick you up at Kahului Airport or leave a vehicle for you if your flight comes in after-hours.

Arthur's Limousine Service offers a chauffeured superstretch Lincoln complete with bar and two TVs for $88 per hour. Arthur's fleet also includes less grandiose Lincoln Town Cars for $65 per hour with a two-hour minimum. If you want to stretch out with a company on the South Shore, call Wailea Limousine Service. Despite the name, this company also provides limousines to the Lahaina area.

Major Agencies: Alamo ☎ 800/327-9633 ⊕ www.alamo.com. **Avis** ☎ 800/331-1212, 800/879-2847 in Canada ⊕ www.avis.com. **Budget** ☎ 800/527-7000, 800/268-8900 in Canada ⊕ www.budget.com. **Dollar** ☎ 808/248-8237 or 800/800-4000 ⊕ www.dollar.com. **Hertz** ☎ 800/654-3011, 800/263-0600 in Canada ⊕ www.hertz. com. **National** ☎ 800/227-7368 ⊕ www.nationalcar.com.

Local Agencies: Aloha Rent-A-Car ☎ 808/877-4477 or 877/452-5642. **Arthur's Limousine Service** ☎ 808/871-5555 or 800/345-4667. **Rent-A-Jeep** ☎ 808/877-6626. **Roberts Tours** ☎ 808/523-9323. **Wailea Limousine Service** ☎ 808/875-4114, 808/661-4114 in Lahaina.

CAR TRAVEL

Maui has some 120 mi of coastline, not all of which is accessible. Less than one-quarter of its land mass is inhabited. To see the island, your best bet is a car. Most of the roads on the island have two lanes. If you're going to attempt the partially paved, patched, and bumpy road between Hāna and 'Ulupalakua, you'll be better off with a four-wheel-drive vehicle, but be forewarned: rental-car companies prohibit travel on roads they've determined might damage the car, so if you break down, you're on your own for repairs. There are two other difficult roads on Maui: one is Route 36, or Hāna Highway, which runs 56 mi between Kahului and Hāna and includes more twists and turns than you can count. The other is an 8-mi scenic stretch of one-lane highway between Kapalua and Wailuku on the north side of the West Maui Mountains.

EMERGENCIES

In an emergency, dial **911** to reach an ambulance, the police, or the fire department.

For emergency road service, there is a Honolulu-based AAA. A dispatcher will send a tow truck, but you will need to tell the driver where to take your car. Don't forget to carry your membership card with you.

For medical assistance in West Maui, call Doctors on Call. Or try a walk-in clinic at Whalers Village, West Maui Health Care Center, which was created by two doctors in 1980 to treat visitors to West Maui. It is open daily from 8 AM to 10 PM. Kīhei Clinic Medical Services is in the central part of the Valley Isle and is geared toward working with visitors in Kīhei and Wailea.

Doctors: Doctors on Call ✉ Hyatt Regency Maui, Nāpili Tower, Suite 100, 200 Nohea Kai Dr., Lahaina ☎ 808/667-7676. **Kīhei Clinic Medical Services** ✉ 2349 S. Kīhei Rd., Suite D, Kīhei ☎ 808/879-1440. **West Maui Health Care Center** ✉ 2435 Kā'anapali Pkwy., Suite H-7, Kā'anapali ☎ 808/667-9721.

🔢 Emergency Services: **AAA** ☎ 800/222-4357. **Coast Guard Rescue Center** ☎ 800/552-6458.

🔢 Hospitals: **Hāna Medical Center** ✉ Hāna Hwy., Hāna ☎ 808/248-8294. **Kula Hospital** ✉ 204 Kula Hwy., Kula ☎ 808/878-1221. **Maui Memorial Hospital** ✉ 221 Mahalani St., Waiḷuku ☎ 808/244-9056.

LODGING

APARTMENT
RENTALS

Besides the condos listed in the Where to Stay section, which operate like hotels and offer hotel-like amenities, Maui has condos you can rent through central booking agents. Most agents represent more than one condo complex (some handle single-family homes as well), so be specific about what kind of price, space, facilities, and amenities you want. The following are multiproperty agents.

🔢 **Aston Hotels & Resorts** ✉ 2255 Kūhiō Ave., 18th floor, Honolulu 96815 ☎ 800/342-1551 ⊕ www.aston-hotels.com. **Captain Cook Resorts** ✉ 1024 Kapahulu Ave., Honolulu 96816 ☎ 808/738-5507 or 800/854-8843. **Destination Resorts** ✉ 3750 Wailea Alanui Dr., Wailea 96753 ☎ 800/367-5246 ⊕ www.drhmaui.com. **Hawai'i Condo Exchange** ✉ 1817 El Cerrito Pl., Los Angeles, CA 90068 ☎ 800/442-0404. **Kīhei Maui Vacations** 📭 Box 1055, Kīhei 96753 ☎ 800/542-6284 ⊕ www.kmvmaui.com. **Marc Resorts Hawai'i** ✉ 2155 Kalakaua Ave., Suite 706, Honolulu 96815 ☎ 800/535-0085 ⊕ www.marcresorts.com. **Maui Windsurfari** ✉ 425 Koloa St., Kahului 96732 ☎ 808/871-7766 or 800/736-6284 ⊕ www.windsurfari.com.

BED-AND-
BREAKFASTS

The Maui Visitors Bureau refers callers to Bed & Breakfast Hawai'i. Bed and Breakfast Honolulu has statewide listings, with about 50 B&Bs on Maui. Bed & Breakfast Maui-Style has listings for about 50 B&Bs on Maui. Island Bed & Breakfast, headquartered on Kaua'i, has listings throughout the state and handles about 35 B&Bs on Maui. A directory is available for $12.95.

🔢 **Bed & Breakfast Hawai'i** ☎ 808/733-1632 ⊕ www.bandb-hawaii.com. **Bed and Breakfast Honolulu** ☎ 808/595-7533 or 800/288-4666 ⊕ www.hawaiibnb.com. **Bed & Breakfast Maui-Style** ☎ 808/879-7865. **Island Bed & Breakfast** ☎ 808/822-7771 or 800/733-1632.

MOPED TRAVEL

You can rent mopeds on the West Side at Wheels R Us for $26 a day. On the South Shore, try Wheels USA at Rainbow Mall. Rates are $16.95 a day. Expect to pay a hefty deposit, up to $300, if you don't use a credit card. Be especially careful navigating roads where there are no designated bicycle lanes. Note that helmets are optional on Maui, but eye protection is not.

🔢 **Wheels R Us** ✉ 741 Waine'e St., Lahaina ☎ 808/667-7751. **Wheels USA** ✉ 2439 S. Kīhei Rd., Kīhei ☎ 808/875-1221.

SHUTTLE TRAVEL

If you're staying in the right hotel or condo, there are a few shuttles that can get you around the area. Akina Tours double-decker West Maui Shopping Express ferries passengers to and from Kā'anapali, Kapalua, Honokōwai, and Lahaina from 8 AM to 10 PM. The fare is $1 per person each way, and schedules are available at most hotels.

The free Kā'anapali Trolley Shuttle runs within the resort between 9 AM and 11 PM and stops automatically at all hotels and at condos when requested. All Kā'anapali hotels have copies of schedules, or you can call the Kā'anapali Operation Association.

The Wailea Shuttle and the Kapalua Shuttle run within their respective resorts and are free. Schedules are available throughout each resort.

🔢 **Akina Bus Service** ☎ 808/870-2828 ⊕ www.akinatours.com. **Kā'anapali Operation Association** ☎ 808/661-7370.

SIGHTSEEING TOURS

BUS & VAN TOURS This is a big island to see in one day, so tour companies combine various sections—either Haleakalā, 'Iao Needle, and West Maui, or Hāna and its environs. Contact companies for their current offerings. Often hotels have tour desks to facilitate arrangements.

A tour of Haleakalā and Upcountry is usually a half-day excursion and is offered in several versions by different companies for about $50 and up. The trip often includes stops at a protea farm and at Tedeschi Vineyards and Winery, the only place in Maui where wine is made. A Haleakalā sunrise tour starts before dawn so that you can get to the top of the dormant volcano before the sun peeks over the horizon. Some companies throw in champagne to greet the sunrise.

A tour of Hāna is almost always done in a van, since the winding road to Hāna just doesn't provide a comfortable ride in bigger buses. Of late, Hāna has so many of these one-day tours that it seems as if there are more vans than cars on the road. Still, to many it's a more relaxing way to do the drive than behind the wheel of a car. Guides decide where you stop for photos. Tours run from $70 to $120.

Ground tour companies are usually statewide and have a whole fleet of vehicles. Some use air-conditioned buses, whereas others prefer smaller vans. Then you've got your minivans, your microbuses, and your minicoaches. The key is how many passengers each will hold. Be sure to ask how many stops you'll get on your tour, or you may be disappointed to find that all your sightseeing is done through a window.

Most of the tour guides have been in the business for years. Some were born in the Islands and have taken special classes to learn more about their culture and lore. They expect a tip ($1 per person at least), but they're just as cordial without one.

Polynesian Adventure Tours uses large buses with floor-to-ceiling windows. The drivers are fun and really know the island. Roberts Hawai'i Tours is one of the state's largest tour companies, and its staff can arrange tours with bilingual guides if asked ahead of time.

Temptation Tours' president, Dave Campbell, has targeted members of the affluent older crowd (though almost anyone would enjoy these tours) who don't want to be herded onto a crowded bus. He provides exclusive tours in his plush six-passenger limovan and specializes in full-day tours to Haleakalā and Hāna, ranging from $110 to $249. Dave's "Ultimate" Hāna tour includes lunch at Hotel Hāna-Maui.
Polynesian Adventure Tours ⊠ 400 Hāna Hwy., Kahului 96732 ☎ 808/877-4242 or 800/622-3011 ⊕ www.polyad.com. **Roberts Hawai'i Tours** ⊘ Box 247, Kahului 96732 ☎ 808/871-6226 or 800/767-7551 ⊕ www.roberts-hawaii.com. **Temptation Tours** ⊠ 211 'Āhinahina Pl., Kula 96790 ☎ 808/877-8888.

HELICOPTER TOURS Helicopter flight-seeing excursions can take you over the West Maui Mountains, Hāna, and Haleakalā. This is a beautiful, exciting way to see the island, and the *only* way to see some of its most dramatic areas. Tour prices usually include a videotape of your trip so you can relive the experience at home. Prices run from about $125 for a half-hour rainforest tour to $340 for a two-hour mega-experience that includes a champagne toast on landing.

It takes about 90 minutes to travel inside the volcano, then down to the village of Hāna. Some companies stop in secluded areas for refreshments. Helicopter-tour operators throughout the state come under sharp scrutiny for passenger safety and equipment maintenance. Don't be afraid to ask about a company's safety record, flight paths, age of equipment, and level of operator experience. Noise levels are a concern as well; residents have become pretty vocal about regulating this kind of pollution.

The highly recommended Blue Hawaiian Helicopters has provided aerial adventures in Hawai'i since 1985, and it has the best service and safety record. Its ASTAR helicopters are air-conditioned and have noise-blocking headsets for all passengers. Sunshine Helicopters offers a Moloka'i flight in its *Black Beauty* aircraft.

🚁 **Blue Hawaiian Helicopters** ✉ Kahului Heliport, Hangar 105, Kahului 96732 ☎ 808/871-8844 ⊕ www.bluehawaiian.com. **Sunshine Helicopters** ✉ Kahului Heliport, Hangar 107, Kahului 96732 ☎ 808/871-0722 or 800/544-2520 ⊕ www.sunshinehelicopters.com.

HIKING & WALKING TOURS Hike Maui is the oldest hiking company in the Islands, and its rain-forest, mountain-ridge, crater, coastline, and archaeological-snorkel hikes are led by such knowledgeable folk as ethnobotanists and marine biologists. Prices range from $59 to $135 for hikes of 5 to 10 hours, including lunch. Hike Maui supplies waterproof day packs, rain ponchos, first-aid gear, water bottles, and transportation to the site.

Paths in Paradise is a small company offering specialized hikes into wetlands, rain-forest areas, and the crater. The owner, Renate Gassman-Duvall, is an expert birder and biologist. She helps hikers spot native honeycreepers feeding on lehua blossoms and supplies them with bird and plant check cards. Half-day hikes run $110, and full-day hikes are $135, with lunch and gear provided.

In 'Iao Valley, the Hawai'i Nature Center leads interpretive hikes for children and their families.

🚶 **Hawai'i Nature Center** ✉ 875 'Iao Valley Rd., Wailuku 96793 ☎ 808/244-6500. **Hike Maui** 🖃 Box 330969, Kahului 96733 ☎ 808/879-5270 ⊕ www.hikemaui.com. **Paths in Paradise** 🖃 Box 667, Makawao ☎ 808/579-9294 ⊕ www.mauibirdhikes.com.

HORSEBACK TOURS Several companies on Maui offer horseback riding that's far more appealing than the typical hour-long trudge over a dull trail with 50 other horses.

Adventures on Horseback conducts five-hour outings into secluded parts of Maui. The $185 tours traverse ocean cliffs on Maui's north shore, follow the slopes of Haleakalā, and pass along streams, through rain forests, and near waterfalls, where riders can stop for a dip in a freshwater pool. Tours include breakfast, lunch, and refreshments.

Charley's Trail Rides & Pack Trips require a stout physical nature—but not a stout physique: riders must weigh less than 200 pounds. Overnight trips go from Kaupō—a *tiny* village nearly 20 mi past Hāna—up the slopes of Haleakalā, where you spend the night in the crater. Charley is a bona fide paniolo, and tours with him include meals, park fees, and camping supplies for $250 per person. Book several weeks in advance if you'd prefer a cabin instead of a tent.

Pony Express Tours will take you on horseback into Haleakalā Crater. The half-day ride goes down to the crater floor for a picnic lunch. The full-day excursion covers 12 mi of terrain and visits some of the crater's unusual formations. You don't need to be an experienced rider, but the longer ride can be tough if you're unathletic. The company also offers one- and two-hour rides on Haleakalā Ranch for $55 to $155.

🐎 **Adventures on Horseback** 🖃 Box 1419, Makawao 96768 ☎ 808/242-7445 ⊕ www.mauihorses.com/aoh. **Charley's Trail Rides & Pack Trips** 🖃 c/o Kaupō Kaupō Ranch, Kaupō 96713 ☎ 808/248-8209. **Pony Express Tours** 🖃 Box 535, Kulā 96790 ☎ 808/667-2200 or 808/878-6698 ⊕ ponyexpresstours.com.

Once you have your bearings, you may want a tour that's a bit more specialized. For example, you might want to bike down a volcano, ride an ATV, or immerse yourself in art.

Art lovers will admire the spectacular resort collections. A free tour of the Hyatt Regency Maui's art collection and gardens starts at 11 on Monday, Wednesday, and Friday and winds through the multimillion-dollar collection of Asian and Pacific art. Among the treasures are Chinese cloisonné, Japanese dragon pots, Thai elephant bells, Hawaiian quilts, and contemporary work. If you're not fond of group tours, just pick up a copy of the hotel's "Art Guide" for a fascinating do-it-yourself experience.

The diverse art collection at the Grand Wailea rivals that of an international art museum. Sculptures, artifacts, stained-glass windows, a 200,000-piece ceramic-tile mosaic, paintings, and assorted works by Léger, Warhol, Picasso, Botero, and noted Hawaiian artists decorate the grounds. Tours leave from the resort's Napua Gallery at 10 on Tuesday and Friday. Nonguests pay $6.

If biking down the side of Haleakalā Crater sounds like fun, several companies are ready to assist you. Maui Downhill vans will shuttle you to the mountaintop, help you onto a bike, and follow you as you coast down through clouds and gorgeous scenery. Lunch or breakfast is included, depending on your trip's start time; treks cost $150. Maui Mountain Cruisers bike trips are $125 including lunch; nonbikers can ride down Haleakalā in a van for $55.

Haleakalā ATV Tours explore the mountainside in their own unique way: propelled through the forest on 350 cc, four-wheel-drive Honda Rancher all-terrain vehicles. The adventures begin at Haleakalā Ranch and rev right up to the pristine Waikamoi rain-forest preserve. Kids under 15 ride alongside in the exciting Argo Conquest, an eight-wheeled amphibious vehicle. Two-hour trips go for $90, and 3½-hour trips are $139.

The Maui Pineapple Plantation Tour takes you right into the fields in a company van. The 2½-hour, $26 trip gives you first-hand experience of the operation and its history, some incredible views of the island, and the chance to pick a fresh pineapple for yourself. Tours depart weekday mornings and afternoons from the Kapalua Logo Shop.

Grand Wailea ✉ 3850 Wailea Alanui Dr., Wailea 96753 ☎ 808/875-1234. **Haleakalā ATV Tours** ✆ Box 703, Kula 96790 ☎ 808/661-0288 ⊕ www.atvmaui.com. **Hyatt Regency Maui** ✉ Kā'anapali Beach Resort, 200 Nokea Kai Dr., Lahaina 96761 ☎ 808/661-1234. **Maui Downhill** ✉ 199 Dairy Rd., Kahului 96732 ☎ 808/871-2155 or 800/535-2453 ⊕ www.mauidownhill.net. **Maui Mountain Cruisers** ✆ Box 1356, Makawao 96768 ☎ 808/871-6014 ⊕ www.mauicruisers.com. **Maui Pineapple Plantation Tour** ✉ Kapalua Resort Activity Desk, 500 Office Rd., Kapalua 96761 ☎ 808/669-8088.

TAXIS

For short hops between hotels and restaurants, taxis can be a convenient way to go, but you'll have to call ahead. Even busy West Maui doesn't have curbside taxi service. Long distances between towns spike the prices; you'd be smart to use taxis just for the areas in which they're located. Ali'i Cab covers West Maui, and Kīhei Taxi serves Central Maui.

To really arrive in style, you might consider Classy Taxi. The company offers limos, convertibles, and a 1929 Model A Ford Phaeton for a regular cab's fare.

Ali'i Cab ☎ 808/661-3688. **Classy Taxi** ☎ 808/665-0003. **Kīhei Taxi** ☎ 808/879-3000.

VISITOR INFORMATION

The Maui Visitors Bureau can provide you with brochures and information. Visitor Channel 7 televises visitor information 24 hours a day, including video tours, restaurant previews, and activities information.

National Weather Service/Maui Forecast covers the islands of Maui, Moloka'i, and Lāna'i.

🚩 **Maui Visitors Bureau** ✉ 1727 Wili Pā Loop, Wailuku 96793 ☎ 800/525-6284 🖷 808/244-1337 ⊕ www.visitmaui.com. **National Weather Service/Maui Forecast** ☎ 808/877-5111.

THE BIG ISLAND OF HAWAI'I

THE VOLCANO ISLE

3

FODOR'S CHOICE

'Anaeho'omalu Beach, Kohala

Four Seasons Resort Hualālai, Kona

Hāpuna Beach State Recreation Area, Kohala

Ironman Triathlon, Kailua-Kona

Kīlauea Lodge, Volcano Village

Mauna Kea, Hāmākua Coast

Pahu i'a, restaurant in Kona

HIGHLY RECOMMENDED

BEACHES Green Sand (Mahana) Beach, Kona Coast

Kahalu'u Beach Park, Kona Coast

Kaloko–Honokōhau National Historical Park, Kailua-Kona

Kauna'oa Beach, Kohala

Kiholo Bay, Kohala

Leleiwi Beach Park, Hāmākua Coast

Punalu'u Beach Park, Kona Coast

Spencer Beach Park, Kohala

White Sands Beach Park, Kailua-Kona

RESTAURANTS The Batik at Mauna Kea Beach Hotel, Kohala

CanoeHouse at the Mauna Lani Bay Hotel, Kohala

Coast Grille at Hāpuna Beach Prince Hotel, Kohala

The Grill at The Fairmont Orchid, Kohala

Hakone Steakhouse and Sushi Bar, Waimea

Hale Samoa at Kona Village Resort, Kohala

Imari at the Hilton Waikoloa Village, Waimea

Kīlauea Lodge, Volcano Village

Merriman's, Waimea

Roy's Waikoloa Bar and Grill, Waikoloa

Many other great hotels and experiences enliven this area.
For other favorites, look for the black stars as you read this chapter.

Updated by
John Penisten

NEARLY TWICE AS LARGE AS ALL THE OTHER Hawaiian Islands combined, Hawai'i (known as the Big Island to avoid confusion with the state name) is used to setting records. Perhaps most dramatically, it has the world's most active volcano: the east rift zone below Halema'uma'u on Kīlauea has been spewing lava intermittently since January 3, 1983. The island's southern tip is the southernmost point in the United States, although to the southeast, far beneath the ocean's surface, Lōihi, a sea mount bubbling lava, is slowly building another Hawaiian island, due to emerge in about 100,000 years. If you measure Mauna Kea from its origins 32,000 ft beneath the ocean's surface to its 13,796-ft peak, it is the tallest mountain in the world. The Keck Observatory on its summit, with one of the world's most powerful telescopes, searches the universe from the clearest place on earth for peering into the heavens.

With its diverse climate and terrain, the Big Island offers skiing (but only for experts) in winter and year-round sunshine on its southern and western shores, where the temperature averages 69°F to 84°F in July and 53°F to 75°F in January. So much rain falls near Hilo, the island's major city, that a botanical garden at Onomea Bay provides umbrellas to enter its tropical jungle. By contrast, land along the Kona-Kohala Coast feels desertlike, with uninhabited stretches of lava.

In earlier times, Hawai'i's kings and queens lived and played along the Kona-Kohala Coast. King Kamehameha I was born close to its northern shores, near Mo'okini Heiau, built around the end of the 5th century (a *heiau* is a stone platform that was used as a site of worship). All along the water's edge are reminders of earlier inhabitants. At Kawaihae, two heiaus—Pu'ukoholā and Mailekini—mark the site of Kamehameha's final victory in 1810 in his battle to unite the Hawaiian Islands.

Developers are becoming increasingly aware of the cultural significance and rich history of the '*āina* (land). They attempt to preserve and restore the bits and pieces of Hawai'i's past that come to light when a bulldozer rakes the land. You'll find historic markers scattered along trails and roadways, at hotel grounds, and in parks. Resorts, such as the Waikoloa Beach Marriott, the Fairmont Orchid Hawai'i, Kona Village, and Ohana Keauhou Beach Resort, conduct tours of petroglyph fields and historic sites. The Waikoloa Beach Marriott, the Four Seasons Resort Hualālai, and the Mauna Lani Bay Hotel and Bungalows have restored the fishponds that once supplied the tables of Hawaiian royalty.

The drive along the Hāmākua Coast from Hilo, the island's county seat and the fourth-largest city in the state, to Waimea, a fast-growing wealthy cowboy town, shows recent developments on the island. Sugarcane stalks no longer wave in the breeze. They have been replaced by orchards of macadamia-nut trees, eucalyptus, and specialty crops (from lettuce to strawberries) raised for chefs who prepare Hawai'i regional cuisine. Macadamia nuts are big business on the Big Island, supplying 90% of the state's yield. Diversification—coffee; anthuriums and orchids; ginger; tomatoes; sweet corn; papayas; bananas; kava (used in the pharmaceutical industry); and even goat cheese, vanilla, and cacao—is adding a new chapter to the agricultural history of the state.

Although Kīlauea Volcano remains the greatest attraction to visitors, one other thing is certain: business owners in all sections of the economy have combined efforts to make the island exciting, welcoming, and fun. Ongoing airport expansions in the Kona area reflect their success. In Hilo, despite the rain, the farmers' market remains the most inspiring in the state, displaying colorful produce reflecting the island's full range of climates and ethnic traditions. In North Kohala, the statue of King Kamehameha I has been spruced up in the red and yellow colors of royalty, and the area draws an increasing number of visitors to its plantation past. Gated communities are sprouting up along the entire coast, and even remote South Point has become well worth the long drive.

Exploring the Big Island

The first secret to enjoying the Big Island: rent a car. The second: stay more than three days, or return again and again until you have seen all the facets of this fascinating place. With 266 mi of coastline made up of white-coral, black-lava, and a dusting of green-olivine beaches, and with its cliffs of lava and emerald gorges slashing into jutting mountains, the Big Island is so large and so varied that it is easiest to split your stay and your sightseeing into excursions from Hilo and excursions from Kona when planning a visit.

If your schedule allows a week or 10 days on the island, you might want to spend a couple of nights in the historic town of Hilo, followed by two nights at a bed-and-breakfast near Hawai'i Volcanoes National Park and another night in Waimea before finishing up your vacation at a resort on the sunny west side of the island. It's best to follow this in east coast–to–west coast order for accommodations, although the itinerary could be easily reversed. If you're short of time, head straight for Hawai'i Volcanoes National Park on your first day, and briefly visit Hilo before traveling the Hāmākua Coast route and making your new base in Kailua-Kona that night.

Directions on the island are often referred to as *mauka* (toward the mountains) and *makai* (toward the ocean).

A word of caution: the Big Island is truly big; some areas are largely undeveloped and without amenities for miles on end. Each year, unmarked trails and dangerous currents claim the lives of unprepared adventurers. Swim and hike only in areas that are established and designated as safe. Take plenty of drinking water when hiking, along with proper footwear and clothing for the area. And always let someone know where you are going.

About the Restaurants

In resort restaurants along the Kohala Coast, upscale eateries in Waimea, and elsewhere, cutting-edge chefs cook with the freshest local produce, fish, and herbs, creating intriguing blends of flavors that reflect the island's varied ethnic background. Events such as the Great Waikoloa Food, Wine and Music Fest at the Hilton Waikoloa Village, and Cuisines of the Sun at Mauna Lani Bay Hotel draw hundreds of guests to starlit open-air dinners celebrating the bounty of the isle's land and waters.

About the Hotels

Accommodations vary tremendously: from sunny "destination" resorts to condominiums on cool mountaintops to family-style B&Bs in green little towns geared more toward fishing and farming than vacationing. This is the beauty of a trip to this island: you can sample that elusive thing called "the real Hawai'i" and also have time to experience the ultimate luxury vacation. But be aware that you'll need a car or a taxi if you choose to stay outside the resort areas. Also, quality and prices vary enormously away from the resorts.

Numbers in the text correspond to numbers on the Hilo Vicinity, Hawai'i Volcanoes National Park and Puna, Hāmākua Coast, Kailua-Kona, South Kona and Ka'u, and Kohala District maps.

If you have 1 day

Fly directly to Hilo and rent a car or take a prearranged tour to see **Hawai'i Volcanoes National Park** 29 – 34. Ask about area hikes to explore Halema'uma'u Crater, Thurston Lava Tube, fern forests, and Devastation Trail.

If you have 3 days

Start in **Kailua-Kona** 48 – 55, learning about Big Island history. Then spend the afternoon at a beach. On the second day, head for **Hawai'i Volcanoes National Park** 29 – 34 early so you'll have time to sightsee along the way. Take Queen Ka'ahumanu Highway, turning inland to **Waimea** 76 – 79. If you have time take a side trip to the **Waipi'o Valley Overlook** 47.

On your third day, consider a morning snorkel cruise to Kealakekua Bay. As an alternative, drive down to **Ka Lae** 64, through **South Kona and Ka'u** 56 – 66, to get an impression of what Hawai'i was like before developers changed the land. Stretch your legs hiking to Green Sand Beach. If you prefer to sightsee, head north and explore the **Kohala District** 67 – 79. As you wind your way up the coast, stop at the **Pu'ukoholā Heiau National Historic Site** 67. There are several restaurants in Kawaihae, and the sugar-plantation towns of **Hāwī and Kapa'au** 72 have several little galleries and eateries that are worth investigating. Pause in Kapa'au to snap a photo of the **King Kamehameha Statue** 73 and then continue to the **Pololū Valley** 74 overlook.

If you have 8 days

Split your stay between three hotels. Stay the first night in **Hilo** 1 – 18, where you can do a little sightseeing and visit the farmers' market. Rise early the second day to move to new accommodations closer to the volcano. Explore the town of **Pāhoa** 19 and its surroundings on your way to **Hawai'i Volcanoes National Park** 29 – 34, where you'll want to spend most of the third day.

On the fourth day, move on to the southwestern shore. Drive back through Hilo to enjoy sightseeing along the **Hāmākua Coast** 38 – 47. If time permits, take a guided tour into Waipi'o Valley. Make day five primarily a beach day, adding a snorkel cruise or a run into **Kailua-Kona** 48 – 55 for lunch and some souvenir shopping. Save the morning of the sixth day to discover North Kohala. After hiking, biking, or horseback riding in the area, check out the little towns of **Hāwī and Kapa'au** 72. On the return drive, history comes alive at **Mo'okini Heiau** 71, **Lapakahi State Historical Park** 70, and the **Pu'ukoholā Heiau National Historic Site** 67.

On the seventh day, take the high road through Kona coffee country and head south from Kailua-Kona via the artists' colony of Hōlualoa to **Kainaliu** 56. Visit the **Greenwell Site** 57; then drive down to **Kealakekua Bay** 58 and check out **Hikiau Heiau** 59 and the **Captain Cook Monument** 60. Even if you skip everything else, be sure to explore **Pu'uhonua O Hōnaunau** 61. Finally take a spin through Ka'u past lava fields and coffee orchards to **Ka Lae** 64, the United States's most southern point.

The last day of your trip should be one of rest and relaxation—a leisurely breakfast and a brief trip to the beach, golf, or last-minute shopping before departing.

WHAT IT COSTS					
	$$$$	**$$$**	**$$**	**$**	**¢**
RESTAURANTS	over $30	$20–$30	$12–$20	$7–$12	under $7
HOTELS	over $200	$150–$200	$100–$150	$60–$100	under $60

Restaurant prices are for a main course. Hotel prices are for two people in a standard double room, including tax and service.

Timing

Touring the Big Island is appealing at any time of year. Although traffic can be heavy in town areas at times, the country roads are far less busy. The weather remains basically stable year-round. It's a rare day when Kailua-Kona and the Kohala Coast are not sunny and warm; however, deluges can occur in January and February. It's difficult to predict weather in Hilo. If you are traveling in winter, you are apt to get wet on the Hāmākua side. The volcano area is always cooler because of the higher elevation, so bring a sweater or light jacket.

HILO

Hilo is a town of both modern and rustic buildings stretching from the banks of the Wailuku River to Hilo Bay, where a few hotels rim stately Banyan Drive. Nearby, the 30-acre Lili'uokalani Gardens, a formal Asian garden with arched bridges and waterways, was created in the early 1900s to honor the area's Japanese sugar plantation laborers. It also became a safety zone after a devastating tidal wave swept away businesses and homes on May 22, 1960, killing 60 people.

Though the center of government and commerce for the island, Hilo is primarily a residential town. Mansions with perfectly kept yards of lush tropical foliage surround older wooden houses with rusty corrugated roofs. It's a friendly community, populated primarily by descendants of the contract laborers—Japanese, Chinese, Filipino, Puerto Rican, and Portuguese—brought in to work the sugarcane fields during the 1800s. Bring your umbrella: the rainfall averages 130 inches per year!

When the sun shines and the snow glistens on Mauna Kea, 25 mi in the distance, Hilo sparkles. In the rain the town takes on the look of an impressionist painting—greenery muted alongside weather-worn brown, red, and blue buildings. Several of these buildings have been spruced up to revitalize the downtown area. Often the rain blows away by noon and a colorful arch appears in the sky. One of Hilo's nicknames is the City of Rainbows.

The whole town has fewer than 1,000 hotel rooms, most of them strung along Banyan Drive. By contrast, the eight Kohala Coast resorts alone have more than 3,704 rooms combined. Nonetheless, Hilo, with a population of almost 50,000 in the entire district, is the fourth-largest city in the state and home to the University of Hawai'i at Hilo.

a good tour

Historic downtown Hilo is best explored on foot. Start your excursion at the Public Library, on Waiānuenue Avenue, four blocks from Kamehameha Avenue, on your right. Here are the ponderous **Naha and Pinao stones** ① ▶, which legend says King Kamehameha I was able to lift as a teenager, thus foretelling that someday he would be a powerful king. Cross the road to walk southeast along Kapi'olani Street, and turn right on Haili Street to visit the historic **Lyman Mission House and Museum** ②. Back on Haili Street, follow this busy road toward the ocean; on your right you'll pass **Haili Church** ③.

3

Flora & Fauna

On the Big Island, 11 distinct climatic zones across 4,038 square mi are home to hundreds of indigenous plants and birds that are today among the most endangered species on Earth. Even the warm waters are unlike oceans elsewhere. More than 30% of marine mammals, such as the Hawaiian monk seal and Hawaiian spinner dolphins, are endemic. Humpback whales, which can be seen from late December to early April, and green sea turtles, visible year-round, are Big Island attractions.

Hitting the Links

Many of the Big Island's courses are emerald oases in the midst of black, barren lava fields. They were designed by world-renowned architects, and on several of the courses—which range from mountainsides to green seaside havens—the challenges are as extraordinary as the views. Towering over them is snowcapped, 13,796-ft Mauna Kea, home of Poli'ahu, the Hawaiian snow goddess. The course at Hualālai hosts the Senior PGA MasterCard Championship.

Hiking

The ancient Hawaiians blazed many trails across their archipelago, and many of these paths can still be hiked today. Part of the King's Trail at 'Anaeho'omalu winds through a field of lava rocks covered with prehistoric carvings meant to communicate stories of births, deaths, marriages, and other family events. In Hawai'i Volcanoes National Park, trails crisscross the volcanic landscape. You can explore a lava tube or cave, or circle a *kīpuka* (verdant island surrounded by lava). In addition, the serenity of remote beaches, such as the black-sand beach at Pololū, is accessible only to hikers.

Horseback Riding

With its *paniolo* (cowboy) heritage, the Big Island is a great place for equestrians. Riders can gallop through green Upcountry pastures, ride to Kealakekua Bay to see the Captain Cook Monument, saunter into Waipi'o Valley for a taste of old Hawai'i, or venture around the rim of Pololū Valley on mules.

Scuba Diving

Kealakekua Bay State Historical and Underwater Park Marine Preserve has depths from 15 ft to more than 110 ft and is popular with experienced divers. Pine Trees, in North Kona, is an area that includes such sites as Carpenter's House, Golden Arches, and Pyramid Pinnacles—two underwater lava towers with tubes, arches, false Moorish idols, and large schools of butterfly fish. Plane Wreck Point, off Keāhole Point, is for expert divers only. Damselfish, fantail, and filefish hover around in the shadows. Red Hill, south of Kona, encompasses large caverns and lava tubes.

Shopping

Galleries abound in Kailua-Kona, North Kohala, Waimea, Holualoa, Volcano, Hilo, and even in such out-of-the-way burgs as Kukuihaele and Honomū. Coffee drinkers will also want to bring back some Kona coffee, grown on the western slopes of the Big Island. Look for the "100% Pure Kona Coffee" label to make sure you're getting the best. Another local product that makes a great gift are macadamia nuts. You'll find them everywhere and processed in every way—from chocolate-covered to garlic-dusted.

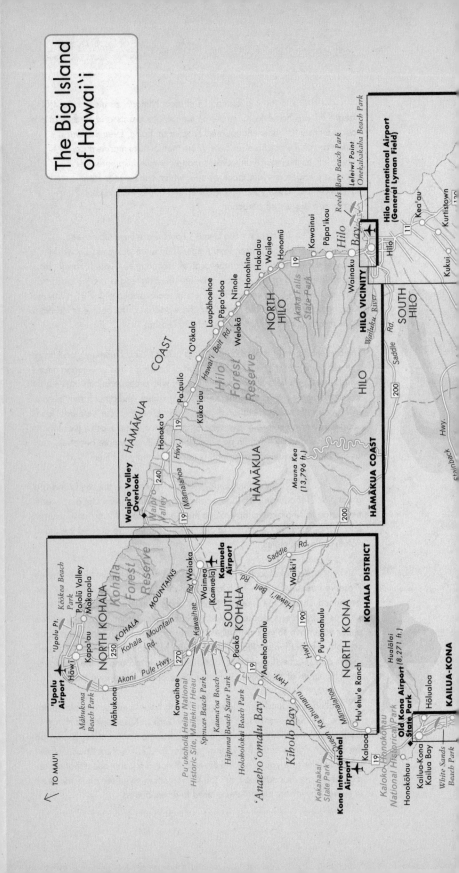

The Big Island
of Hawai'i

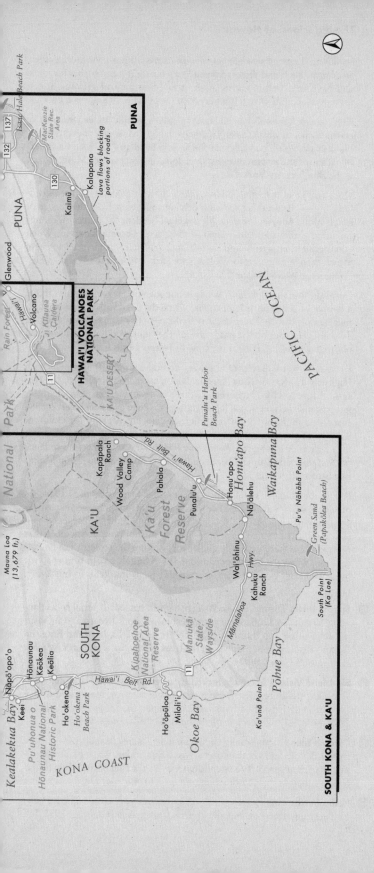

Soon you'll reach **Keawe Street** ❹ with its plantation-style architecture. Stop at the **Big Island Visitors Bureau** ❺ on the right-hand corner for maps and brochures before taking a left. You'll bump into Kalākaua Street; for a quick respite turn left and rest on the benches in **Kalākaua Park** ❻.

Continue makai on Kalākaua Street to visit the **Pacific Tsunami Museum** ❼ on the corner of Kalākaua and Kamehameha Avenue. After heading three blocks east, you'll come across the **S. Hata Building** ❽, which has interesting shops and restaurants; just next door, on either side of Mamo Street, is the **Hilo Farmers Market** ❾.

Once you've fully explored Hilo, take a drive to some of the area's outlying sights. Begin this excursion driving southwest from the cluster of hotels along **Banyan Drive** ❿. **Lili'uokalani Gardens** ⑪, on the right, has Japanese gardens and an arched footbridge to **Coconut Island** ⑫. When you reach Hilo Bayfront and Kamehameha Avenue, turn left onto Pauahi Street, then left again into Wailoa State Park. Close to the Waiakea Fish Pond is the **Wailoa Center** ⑬.

Continue and turn left onto Waiānuenue Avenue for two popular sights a couple of miles outside of town. When the road forks, after about a mile in a southwest direction, stay to the right to reach **Rainbow Falls** ⑭. Two miles farther up the road, also on the right, you'll come across the photogenic Boiling Pots at the base of **Pe'epe'e Falls** ⑮.

Drive back to the Bayfront Highway and take a right. It intersects with Highway 11, Kanoelehua Avenue, which takes you directly to the volcano. Close to Hilo, however, are three more attractions. On the right, just past mile marker 4, you'll pass the sign for **Pana'ewa Rain Forest Zoo** ⑯. Just five minutes up Stainback Highway, it's a great stop for children. Back on Highway 11, 5 to 6 mi south of Hilo, turn left when you reach the marker for **Mauna Loa Macadamia Factory** ⑰. On your return to Hilo, find serenity and tropical beauty at the **Nani Mau Gardens** ⑱ on Makalika Street off Route 11.

TIMING   Rain is inevitable in Hilo. Expect to get rained on here, as the 130 inches of annual precipitation are equally distributed throughout the year. Allow a full day to explore Hilo if you try to take in all the sights, less if you skip the museums and have little interest in shopping. Remember that morning hours are generally cooler for walking the streets than late afternoon, when the humidity can soar. It's definitely worth timing a visit for a Wednesday or Saturday, when the farmers' market is in full swing.

What to See

★ ❿ **Banyan Drive.** The more than 50 leafy banyan trees with aerial roots dangling from their limbs were planted some 60 to 70 years ago by visiting celebrities; you'll find such names as Amelia Earhart and Franklin Delano Roosevelt on plaques on the trees. ⊹ *Begin at Hawai'i Naniloa Resort* ⊠ *93 Banyan Dr.*

❺ **Big Island Visitors Bureau.** Marked by a red-and-white Hawaiian-warrior sign, the bureau is worth a visit for brochures, maps, and up-to-date, friendly insider advice. ⊠ *250 Keawe St. (corner of Haili St.)* ☎ *808/961-5797* ⊕ *www.bigisland.org* ⊙ *Weekdays 8–4:30.*

★ ⑫ **Coconut Island.** This small (approximately 1 acre) island, just offshore from Lili'uokalani Gardens and across a footbridge, was a place of healing in ancient times. Today children play in the tide pools while fisherfolk try their luck. ⊠ *Lili'uokalani Gardens, Banyan Dr.*

❸ **Haili Church.** This church was originally constructed in 1859 by New England missionaries, but the church steeple was rebuilt in 1979 fol-

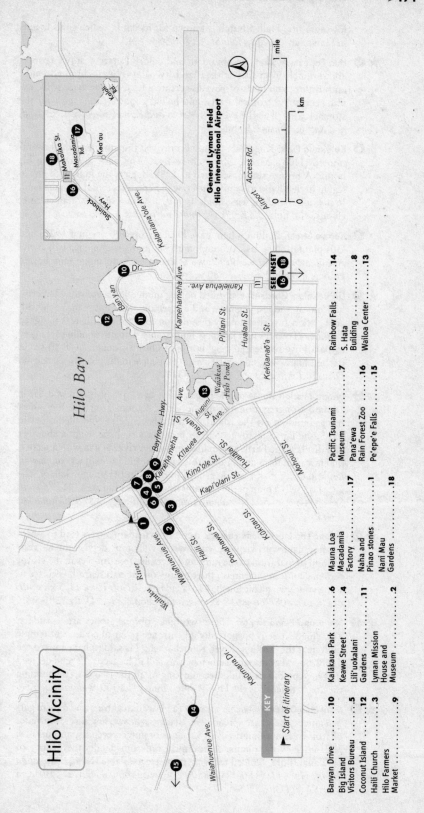

Hilo Vicinity

Hilo Bay

Wailuku River

Waiānuenue Ave.

Kaūmana Dr.

Hāʻili St.

Ponahawai St.

Kīlauea Ave.

Kamehameha Ave.

Pauahi St.

Kinoʻole St.

Kapiʻolani St.

Kīlauea Ave.

Kūkau St.

Mohouli St.

Huālālai St.

Kamehameha Ave.

Bayfront. Hwy.

ʻAupuni St.

Kekūanaōʻa St.

Huālālai St.

Piʻilani St.

Kamehameha Ave.

Kanielehua Ave.

Kalanianaʻole Ave.

Banyan Dr.

Waiākea Fish Pond

**General Lyman Field
Hilo International Airport**

Airport Access Rd.

SEE INSET 16 — 18

Steinback Hwy.

Keaʻau

Macadamia Rd.

Makalika St.

Kolob Rd.

KEY

▶ *Start of itinerary*

Banyan Drive **10**
Big Island
Visitors Bureau **5**
Coconut Island **12**
Haili Church **3**
Hilo Farmers
Market **9**

Kalākaua Park **6**
Keawe Street **4**
Liliʻuokalani
Gardens **11**
Lyman Mission
House and
Museum **2**

Mauna Loa
Macadamia
Factory **17**
Naha and
Pinao stones **1**
Nani Mau
Gardens **18**

Pacific Tsunami
Museum **7**
Panaʻewa
Rain Forest Zoo **16**
Peʻepeʻe Falls **15**

Rainbow Falls **14**
S. Hata
Building **8**
Wailoa Center **13**

lowing a fire. Haili Church is known for its choir, which sings hymns in Hawaiian. ⊠ *211 Haili St.* ☏ *808/935–4847.*

★ ❾ **Hilo Farmers Market.** An abundant and colorful market draws farmers and shoppers from all over the island. Two days a week, bright orchids, anthuriums, and birds-of-paradise create a feast for the eyes, while exotic vegetables, tropical fruits, and baked goods create a feast for the stomach as well as the eyes. ⊠ *Mamo and Kamehameha Sts.* ☉ *Wed. and Sat. 6:30 AM–2:30 PM.*

❻ **Kalākaua Park.** King Kalākaua, who revived the hula, was the inspiration for Hilo's Merrie Monarch Festival. The park is named in his honor. A bronze statue, sculpted in 1988, depicts the king with a taro leaf in his left hand to signify the Hawaiian peoples' bond with the land. In his right hand the king holds an *ipu*, a symbol of Hawaiian culture, chants, and hula. ⊠ *Kalākaua and Kino'ole Sts.*

❹ **Keawe Street.** Buildings here have been restored to original 1920s and '30s plantation styles. Although most shopping is along Kamehameha Avenue, the ambience on Keawe Street offers a nostalgic sampling of Hilo as it might have been 80 years ago.

★ ⓫ **Lili'uokalani Gardens.** Fish-filled ponds, unique Japanese stone lanterns, half-moon bridges, pagodas, and a ceremonial tea house make this 30-acre park a favorite Sunday destination for residents. It was designed to honor Hawai'i's first Japanese immigrants. The surrounding area used to be a busy residential neighborhood until a tsunami in 1960 swept the buildings away, taking the lives of 60 people in the process. ⊠ *Banyan Drive at Lihiwai St.* ☏ *808/961–8311.*

❷ **Lyman Mission House and Museum.** Built in 1839 by David and Sarah Lyman, Congregationalist missionaries, Lyman House is the oldest frame building on the island. In the adjacent museum, dedicated in 1973, the Earth Heritage Gallery includes a realistic magma chamber and displays the Earth's formation and the arrival of life, with a section on Hawaiian flora and fauna. You can view unique artifacts of Hawaiian and other major ethnic groups in the Island Heritage Gallery. The gift shop sells a map of the tsunami flows in the Hilo area. ⊠ *276 Haili St.* ☏ *808/935–5021* ⊕ *www.lymanmuseum.org* ⊠ *$7* ☉ *Mon.–Sat. 9–4:30.*

★ ⓱ **Mauna Loa Macadamia Factory.** Acres of macadamia trees lead to a processing plant with viewing windows. A videotape depicts the harvesting and preparation of the nuts, and there are free samples in the visitor center. Children can run off their energy on the nature trail. Feel free to bring your own picnic lunch. ⊠ *Macadamia Rd. off Hwy. 11, 5 mi south of Hilo* ☏ *808/966–8618* ⊕ *www.maunaloa.com* ☉ *Daily 8:30–5:30.*

🚩 ❶ **Naha and Pinao stones.** These two huge, oblong stones are legendary. The Pinao stone is purportedly an entrance pillar of an ancient temple built near the Wailuku River. Kamehameha I is said to have moved the 5,000-pound Naha stone when he was still in his teens. Legend decreed that he who did so would become king of all the islands. The building they're in front of is the Hilo Public Library. ⊠ *300 Waiānuenue Ave.*

★ ⓲ **Nani Mau Gardens.** Theme gardens (a Hawaiian garden and a palm garden among them) are spread over 20 acres, showcasing several varieties of fruit trees and hundreds of varieties of ginger, orchids, anthuriums, and other exotic plants. A botanical museum details the history of Hawaiian flora. Guided tours by tram are available. ⊠ *421 Makalika St., off Hwy. 11* ☏ *808/959–3500* ⊕ *www.nanimau.com* ⊠ *$10, tram tour $7* ☉ *Daily 8:30–5.*

IF TREES COULD TALK

THE HISTORY OF THE TREES lining Hilo's Banyan Drive is one of the Big Island's most interesting and least-known stories. Banyan Drive was named for these trees, which were planted by VIP visitors to Hilo. Altogether, some 50 or so banyans were planted between 1933 and 1972.

The majority are Chinese banyans (Fiscus retusa), and each one is marked with a sign naming the VIP who planted it and the date on which it was planted. The tradition was conceived of by the parks commission, and the first banyan trees were planted on October 20, 1933, by a Hollywood group led by director Cecil B. DeMille, who were in Hilo making the film Four Frightened People. Soon after, on October 29, 1933, another banyan was planted by the "Sultan of Swat," the one and only George Herman "Babe" Ruth, who was in town playing exhibition games.

President Franklin D. Roosevelt planted a tree on his visit to Hilo on July 25, 1934. And in 1935, famed aviatrix Amelia Earhart put a banyan in the ground just days before she became the first person to fly solo across the Pacific Ocean.

Trees continued to be planted along Banyan Drive until World War II. The tradition was then revived in 1952 when a young and aspiring U.S. senator, Richard Nixon of California, planted a banyan tree. Nixon's tree was later toppled by a storm and was replanted by his wife, Pat, during a Hilo visit in 1972.

On a bright, sunny day, strolling down Banyan Drive is like going through a green, shady tunnel. The banyans form a regal protective canopy over Hilo's own "Walk of Fame."

★ ❼ **Pacific Tsunami Museum.** A memorial to all who lost their lives in the tragedies that have struck this side of the island, this small museum offers a poignant history of tsunamis. In a 1931 C. W. Dickey–designed building—the former First Hawaiian Bank—you'll find an interactive computer center, a science room, a theater, a replica of Old Hilo Town, a *keiki* (children's) corner, and a knowledgeable, friendly staff. In the background, a striking quilt tells a silent story. ⊠ *130 Kamehameha Ave.* ☎ *808/935–0926* ⊕ *www.tsunami.org* ☞ *$5* ☉ *Mon.–Sat. 9–4.*

☝ ⓰ **Pana'ewa Rain Forest Zoo.** Children enjoy the monkeys and the white tiger in this quiet, often wet zoo, which also hosts native Hawaiian species such as the state bird—the nēnē. It's the only rain-forest zoo in the United States. Trails have been paved, but take an umbrella for protection from the frequent showers. ⊠ *Stainback Hwy. off Hwy. 11* ☎ *808/959–7224* ☞ *Free* ☉ *Daily 9–4.*

⓯ **Pe'epe'e Falls.** Four separate streams drop into a series of circular pools. The resultant turbulent action—best seen after a good rain when the water is high—has earned these the name Boiling Pots. ⊹ *3 mi northwest of Hilo on Waiānuenue Ave.; keep to the right when road splits and look for a green sign.*

★ ⓮ **Rainbow Falls.** After a Hilo rain, these falls thunder into Wailuku River gorge. If the sun peeks out in the morning hours, rainbows form above the mist. ⊹ *Take Waiānuenue Ave. west of town 1 mi; when road forks, stay on right of Waiānuenue Ave.; look for Hawaiian-warrior sign.*

❽ **S. Hata Building.** Erected as a general store in 1912 by Sadanosuke Hata and his family, this historic structure now houses shops, restaurants, and offices. During World War II the Hatas were interned and the building confiscated by the U.S. government. When the war was over, a daughter repurchased it for $100,000. A beautiful example of Renaissance-revival architecture, it won an award from the state for the authenticity of its restoration. ⊠ *308 Kamehameha Ave., at Mamo St.*

need a break? Wander inside the S. Hata Building and get a table at **Café Pesto** (⊠ 308 Kamehameha Ave. ☎ 808/969–6640). Enjoy lunch or dinner from a menu of creative Italian fare including pastas, sandwiches, and the house special: wood-fired pizzas scented with native 'ōhi'a and guava hardwoods.

⑬ Wailoa Center. This circular exhibition center, adjacent to Wailoa State Park, has shows by local artists that change monthly. There's also a photographic exhibit of the 1946 and 1960 tidal waves. Just in front of the center is a 12-ft-high bronze statue of King Kamehameha I, made in Italy in the late 1980s. Check out his gold Roman sandals. ⊠ *Pi'opi'o St. off Kamehameha Ave.* ☎ *808/933–0416* ◷ *Mon.–Tues. and Thurs.–Fri. 8:30–4:30, Wed. noon–4:30.*

PUNA

The Puna District includes the southeast section of the Big Island. It's an area of open lava lands, rugged coastline, quiet villages, and rainforest slopes leading up to Hawai'i Volcanoes National Park, which straddles the Puna border. Before you head off to Hawai'i Volcanoes National Park, take some time to explore Puna, where farmers grow everything from orchids and anthuriums to papayas, bananas, and macadamia nuts; numerous farms and orchards are located throughout the Puna District. Several of the island's larger, rural residential subdivisions are located between Kea'au and Pāhoa, including Hawaiian Paradise Park, Orchidland Estates, Hawaiian Acres, Hawaiian Beaches, and others. Tide pools and natural springs dot the coastal area here.

a good drive Heading out from Hilo, turn right at Kea'au—or take the new bypass road (Highway 130) just south of this little town—and drive about 11 mi; then take the turnoff to **Pāhoa** ⑲ ▶.

At the bypass intersection of Pāhoa, continue on Highway 132 in the direction of Kapoho. Take a break at **Lava Tree State Park** ⑳. Just south of the park entrance is the intersection of the highway and Pāhoa-Pohoiki Road. Continue southeast on Highway 132, passing papaya and orchid farms. As you near the coast, you'll pass through recent lava flows that cover the former town of Kapoho. The highway intersects with the coastal road, Highway 137, which turns south along the Kapoho–Opihikao coast, linking up with Highway 130 in the Kalapana area to complete the loop back to Pāhoa.

At the intersection of Highways 132 and 137 at Kapoho, the gravel road straight to the coast leads to **Cape Kumukahi Lighthouse** ㉑. Turn right and follow Highway 137 along the coast, stopping for a dip in the pond at **Ahalanui Park** ㉒.

Highway 137 is a magnificent drive along a very narrow and winding coastal road. There are some great views of rugged coastline plus relaxing stops at **Isaac Hale Beach Park** ㉓, **MacKenzie State Recreation Area** ㉔, and **Kehena Beach** ㉕. After passing through the settlements of Pohoiki and Opihikao on the coast, the road links up with Highway 130 at the Kaimu-Kalapana area. This area marks the eastern expanse of lava flows of the early 1990s, which covered the Kalapana residential area and several fine black-sand beaches and parks. Take Highway 130 north back to Pāhoa. About a mile north of the intersection of Highways 130 and 137, stop at **Star of the Sea Painted Church** ㉖.

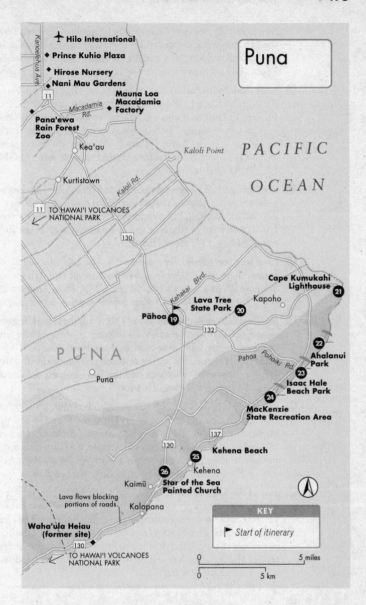

✈ **Hilo International**

◆ **Prince Kuhio Plaza**

◆ **Hirose Nursery**
◆ **Nani Mau Gardens**

[11]

Macadamia Rd.

◆ **Mauna Loa
Macadamia
Factory**

◆ **Pana'ewa
Rain Forest
Zoo**

○ Kea'au

Puna

Kaloli Point

PACIFIC

OCEAN

○ Kurtistown

Kaloli Rd.

[11] **TO HAWAI'I VOLCANOES
NATIONAL PARK**

[130]

Kahakai Blvd.

**Cape Kumukahi
Lighthouse** [21]

Kapoho

**Lava Tree
State Park** [20]

Pāhoa [19]

[132]

P U N A

○ Puna

Pahoa Pohoiki Rd.

[22] **Ahalanui
Park**

[23] **Isaac Hale
Beach Park**

[24] **MacKenzie
State Recreation Area**

[137]

[130] [25] **Kehena Beach**

Kehena

[26] **Star of the Sea
Painted Church**

Kaimū

**Lava flows blocking
portions of roads.**

Kalapana

**Waha'ula Heiau
(former site)**

[130]

**TO HAWAI'I VOLCANOES
NATIONAL PARK**

KEY

▶ *Start of itinerary*

0 —————— 5 miles
0 —————— 5 km

TIMING The Pāhoa to Kapoho and Kalapana coast drive is a loop that's about 25 mi long; driving times are from two to three hours, depending on the number of stops you make and the length of time at each stop.

What to See

㉒ Ahalanui Park. This park was established with a federal grant in the mid-1990s to replace parks lost at Kalapana to the lava flows. It's 2½ mi south of the intersection of Highways 132 and 137 on the Kapoho coast, southeast of Pāhoa town. There is a half-acre pond fed by thermal freshwater springs mixed with seawater. Facilities include portable rest rooms, outdoor showers, and picnic tables; no drinking water is available. ⊠ *Hwy. 137, Puna District.*

㉑ Cape Kumukahi Lighthouse. The lighthouse, 1½ mi east of the intersection of Highways 132 and 137, was unharmed during the 1960 volcano eruption here that destroyed the town of Kapoho. The lava flowed around the lighthouse but did not touch it. According to Hawaiian legend, Pele, the volcano goddess, protected the Hawaiian fisherfolk by sparing the lighthouse. ⊠ *Past the intersection of Hwys. 132 and 137, Kapoho.*

㉓ Isaac Hale Beach Park. This beach park on Highway 137, south of Cape Kumukahi, has a busy boat-launching ramp used by local commercial fisherfolk. The bay is also used for water sports like body boarding, surfing, and swimming. The beach has small pebbles and rocks—no fine sand. The Pohoiki Warm Springs is a natural warm-water bathing pool behind the beach area. Rest rooms and showers are available. ⊠ *Hwy. 137, Puna District.*

㉕ Kehena Beach. This is a nice black-sand crescent beach just off the highway; it's reached via a steep, rough trail down the cliff face. The beach is good for sunning, but swimming is dangerous due to strong currents. No facilities are available; there is a parking area at the Kehena Lookout. ⊠ *Hwy. 137, Puna District.*

㉒ Lava Tree State Park. Tree molds that rise like blackened smokestacks formed here in 1790 when a lava flow swept through the 'ōhi'a forest. Some reach as high as 12 ft. ⊠ *Hwy. 132, Puna District* ☎ *808/974–6200* 🖅 *Free* ⊙ *Daily 30 mins before sunrise–30 mins after sunset.*

㉔ MacKenzie State Recreation Area. This is a coastal park located on rocky shoreline cliffs in a breezy, cool ironwood grove. There are picnic tables, rest rooms, and a tent-camping area; bring your own drinking water. The park is significant for the restored section of the old "King's Highway" trail system, which circled the island along the coast in the old days. ⊠ *Hwy. 137, Puna District.*

⑲ Pāhoa. This little town still has wooden boardwalks and rickety buildings reminiscent of the Wild West. The secondhand stores, tie-dye clothing boutiques, and art galleries in quaint old buildings are fun to wander through. Little eateries, such as **Sawasdee**, a Thai restaurant that's open for lunch, may pleasantly surprise you. ✛ *Turn southeast onto Hwy. 130 at Kea'au, drive 11 mi to right turn marked Pāhoa.*

★ ㉖ Star of the Sea Painted Church. This historic church, now a community center, was moved to its present location in 1990 just ahead of the advancing lava flow that destroyed the Kalapana area. The church, which dates from the early 1900s, was built by a Belgian Catholic missionary priest who also did the detailed paintings of religious scenes on the interior. The building has several lovely stained-glass windows. ⊠ *Hwy. 130, 1 mi north of Kalapana.*

HAWAI'I VOLCANOES NATIONAL PARK

The most popular attraction on the Big Island, Hawai'i Volcanoes National Park holds the active Kīlauea Volcano. The 359-square-mi park, established in 1916, provides an unmatched volcanic experience. The current eruption has been ongoing since January 3, 1983, primarily from a vent called Pu'u O'o. It's steady and slow, appearing and disappearing from view. Even when there is no fiery display or lava flowing, you'll have plenty to see in the park, which includes the summit caldera and gently sloping northeast flank of 13,677-ft Mauna Loa volcano. With more than 150 mi of trails passing tree ferns and other tropical plants, lava tubes, cinder cones, odd mineral formations, steam vents, and the vast barren craters along Chain of Craters Road, this is the ultimate ecotour. Don't forget to take a sweater (or a jacket in winter), as temperatures can get nippy at the park's 4,000-ft elevation. Also take a flashlight if you plan to visit the shoreline lava flow around sunset.

Before setting out on any hike in the eruption area, check with the park staff for the latest lava flow and eruption information. Be sure to follow all rules and posted signs and markers, stay on the marked trails, and don't wander off by yourself. The risk of injury from falling into a lava crack is real, as is the threat of becoming disoriented and lost due to volcanic fumes, smoke, and haze clouds.

Yellow, acrid-smelling sulfur banks and gaping vents emitting warm steam are found throughout the cool environs of the park. Pregnant women and anyone with heart or respiratory problems should avoid both the sulfur banks and the noxious fumes. The park and Chain of Craters Road are open 24 hours a day, but you must obtain a backcountry hiker's permit to remain in the park area overnight. Admission is $10 per car for seven days.

a good tour

From Hilo take Highway 11, Kanoelehua Avenue, which takes you directly to the park, 30 mi to the southwest. The drive is uphill all the way, through the towns of Kurtistown, Mountain View, and Volcano. **Dan Deluz Woods** ㉗ ⌐, just past mile marker 12, is a perfect place for handmade hardwood crafts. Just ½ mi past mile marker 22 you'll find **Akatsuka Orchid Gardens** ㉘.

About 1½ mi west past the turnoff to Volcano Village is the entrance sign to the park. Stop first at the **Kīlauea Visitor Center** ㉙ to find the latest information on volcanic activity and hiking trails. Across the street is **Volcano House** ㉚.

You can drive the crater's circumference via the 11 mi of **Crater Rim Drive** ㉛. Scenic stops include the yellow, acrid-smelling sulfur banks; steam vents; and the park's **Thomas A. Jaggar Museum** ㉜, on the edge of Kīlauea Caldera. You'll find several easy walks along the way: Halemaʻumaʻu Overlook (a 10-minute walk), Devastation Trail (30 minutes), and Thurston Lava Tube (20 minutes).

If you have time, drive from the center of the park down **Chain of Craters Road** ㉝. A sign midway down on the left marks a trail across the lava to **Puʻu Loa Petroglyphs** ㉞, a field of lava etchings left by early Hawaiians. It's about a 25-minute walk to the petroglyph field.

Chain of Craters Road stops abruptly after about 22 mi. Turn around and head back, making one last stop in the park at **Volcano Art Center** ㉟. Exiting the park, turn left onto Highway 11 then take a right at the first crossroads toward the Volcano Golf & Country Club. Less than a mile beyond the club you'll find **Volcano Winery** ㊱.

Back on Highway 11 drive southwest to the next right and turn onto Mauna Loa Road. A sign marks Tree Molds. Each chimneylike formation was created when molten lava hardened around a tree, burning it away in the process. About 2 mi in, you can take a self-guided mile-long walk around **Kīpuka Puaulu** ㊲.

Head back toward Hilo via the Old Volcano Highway, which runs parallel to Highway 11.

TIMING Open daily, this is a national park, ideal for families and therefore busier during the summer months, holidays, and weekends. Count on spending at least three-quarters of a day at the park, and keep in mind that a round-trip from Kona or the resorts takes four to six hours. You may want to plan an overnight stay at one of the charming B&Bs tucked into the fern forest.

It'll take you about 45 minutes to drive the distance from Hilo to the park. Allow two hours for the trip up and back down the 22 mi of the Chain of Craters Road. Check with park staff on the latest lava-flow

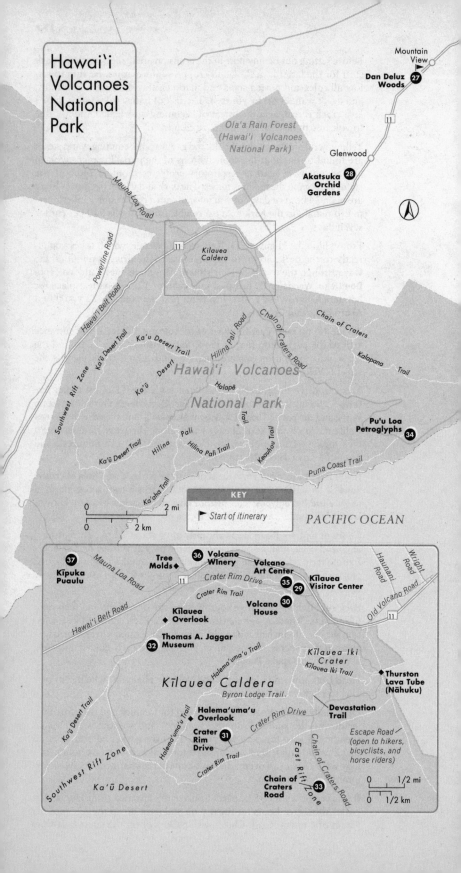

Hawai'i Volcanoes National Park

Ola'a Rain Forest
(Hawai'i Volcanoes
National Park)

Mountain View ▶

Dan Deluz Woods 27

11

Glenwood

Akatsuka Orchid Gardens 28

11

Mauna Loa Road

Powerline Road

11

Kīlauea Caldera

Hawai'i Belt Road

Southwest Rift Zone

Ka'ū Desert Trail

Ka'ū Desert Trail

Ka'ū Desert Trail

Hilina Pali Road

Chain of Craters Road

Chain of Craters

Kalapana Trail

Hawai'i Volcanoes

Ka'ū Desert

Ka'ū

Holapē

Trail

National Park

Keauhou Trail

Hilina Pali

Hilina Pali Trail

Ka'aha Trail

Pu'u Loa Petroglyphs 34

Puna Coast Trail

KEY
▶ *Start of itinerary*

0 ——— 2 mi
0 ——— 2 km

PACIFIC OCEAN

---

37 **Kīpuka Puaulu**

Mauna Loa Road

Tree Molds ◆

36 **Volcano Winery**

Volcano Art Center 35 29

Kīlauea Visitor Center

Crater Rim Drive

11

Crater Rim Trail

30 **Volcano House**

Hawai'i Belt Road

Kīlauea Overlook ◆

Haunani Road

Wright Road

Old Volcano Road

11

32 **Thomas A. Jaggar Museum**

Kīlauea Iki Crater

Kīlauea Iki Trail

◆ **Thurston Lava Tube (Nāhuku)**

Ka'ū Desert Trail

Kīlauea Caldera

Byron Lodge Trail

Halema'uma'u Trail

Halema'uma'u Overlook ◆

Crater Rim Drive

31

Crater Rim Trail

Halema'uma'u Trail

Devastation Trail

Crater Rim Drive

Escape Road (open to hikers, bicyclists, and horse riders)

Southwest Rift Zone

Ka'ū Desert

East Rift Zone

Chain of Craters Road

Chain of Craters Road 33

0 ——— 1/2 mi
0 ——— 1/2 km

viewing conditions and accessibility. You may need to allow two or three extra hours to walk to any active lava-flow sites.

What to See

28 Akatsuka Orchid Gardens. This is one of the largest collections of orchids in Hawai'i. The greenhouse includes a covered garden where you can take a self-guided tour and enjoy the beauty of hundreds of orchids and exotic tropical flowers. The cool Volcano climate provides the ideal conditions for orchid cultivation. The floral shop sells orchid plants and cut flowers and can pack and ship to anywhere in the world. ⊠ *Hwy. 11, just past mile marker 22, Volcano* ☎ *808/967–8234* ⊠ *Free* ⊙ *Daily 8:30–5.*

★ **33 Chain of Craters Road.** No food, water, or gasoline is available along this road, which descends 3,700 ft in 22 mi to the Kalapana Coast. You'll pass barren fields and thick 'ōhi'a forests, which are quite stirring when in full blossom. At road's end, you may be able to walk to where the lava flows into the ocean; ask at the Kīlauea Visitor Center before starting out, but be forewarned that it's a long, hot trek, often over very difficult and dangerous terrain, and there are no facilities. ✛ *Begins in Hawai'i Volcanoes National Park.*

★ **Crater Rim Drive.** This scenic 11-mi drive provides panoramic vistas of the national park's vast lava deserts, steaming craters, and forests. Start from the visitor center and drive southwest past the sulfur banks and Kīlauea Caldera overlooks to the Thomas A. Jaggar Museum. View observatory displays and the vastness of the caldera and then continue the drive across a huge, open lava desert and old lava flows to a turnout to view Halema'uma'u Crater. It's a ¼-mi hike from the road to the crater overlook. The drive continues past other craters into the forest, past Devastation Trail, Thurston Lava Tube, and Kīlauea Iki Crater, before coming full circle back at the visitor center.

▶ **27 Dan Deluz Woods.** This country craftshop is the place to stop for handmade native-Hawaiian-hardwood crafts. The shop features fine woodwork crafts including bowls, carvings, picture frames, furniture, jewelry and jewelry boxes and a variety of accessory items made from koa, monkeypod, mango, kiawe, and other fine local hardwoods. Dan's wife, Mary Lou, operates the Koa Shop Kaffee restaurant next to the woodshop. ⊠ *64-1013 Māmalahoa Hwy. (Hwy. 11), at mile marker 12, Mountain View* ☎ *808/968–6607* ⊙ *Daily 9–5.*

Devastation Trail. This trail was created after a 1959 eruption, when fiery lava from the adjacent Kīlauea Iki Crater burned the surrounding 'ōhi'a forest. The 30-minute walk on a paved path across the cinder outfall off Crater Rim Drive is self-guided.

Kīlauea Caldera. Halema'uma'u Crater is the steaming pit within this gaping caldera in the national park. You can hike around or into the crater. You can also drive around the crater's 11-mi circumference to **Halema'uma'u Overlook** for another view of the crater.

need a break? For a decent meal, a drink, or Internet access, head to **Lava Rock Café** (⊠ Old Volcano Hwy., behind Kīlauea General Store ☎ 808/ 967–8526), which serves breakfast and lunch daily and dinner Tuesday through Saturday in a breezy, pinewood-lattice setting. You'll find a variety of dishes, from chicken salad to New York steak, cappuccino to wine.

Kīlauea Iki Crater. If you're in the park for a full day or more, you could venture on an exhilarating hike into Kīlauea Iki (*iki* means little). It takes less than a half day, but get information and maps first at the Kīlauea Visitor Center. On the 4-mi loop you'll descend 400 ft through rain forest and cross the crater floor. A 20-minute walk will take you 450 ft into **Thurston Lava Tube,** a natural tunnel about 10 ft high that formed when the cooling top and sides of a lava flow hardened and the lava inside drained away.

㉙ Kīlauea Visitor Center. The visitor center lies just beyond the park's entry booth. You can learn about park wildlife and vegetation and get updates on the flow. If you can't see a real eruption, don't miss the movie shown on the hour from 9 to 4. Hikers can obtain information about trails, ranger-escorted scenic walks, and camping permits at the center. ⊠ *Hawai'i Volcanoes National Park, Volcano 96785* ☎ *808/985–6000* ⊕ *www.nps.gov/havo* ☉ *Daily 7:45–5.*

★ ☙ ㊲ Kīpuka Puaulu. A *kīpuka* is a forested island surrounded by a sea of lava. This unique and diverse 100-acre mesic forest is also known as Bird Park, although its real beauty lies in its rare flora. Native birds, such as the 'apapane and the 'elepaio, call from their hiding places in the thick canopy. A written guide is available at the Kīlauea Visitor Center in Hawai'i Volcanoes National Park. ⊠ *Hawai'i Volcanoes National Park, Mauna Loa Rd.*

㉞ Pu'u Loa Petroglyphs. It's a 25-minute walk across the lava to where etchings of people, boats, and animals made by early Hawaiians are spread over a vast area of black lava. The round depressions are thought to be *piko* holes, where umbilical cords of newborns were buried. ✛ *Hawai'i Volcanoes National Park, Chain of Craters Rd., on left past mile marker 16.*

☙ ㉜ Thomas A. Jaggar Museum. Children can enjoy hands-on fun at this free museum at the edge of Kīlauea Caldera. Seismographs that measure the Earth's movement will also record a child's footfall. And fascinating filmstrips document current and previous eruptions. ⊠ *Crater Rim Dr., Volcano* ☎ *808/985–6049* ✎ *Free* ☉ *Daily 8:30–5.*

★ ㉟ Volcano Art Center. This celebrated gallery displays the work of Big Island photographers, artists, and craftspeople. The building was originally constructed to be the Volcano House in 1877, replacing a thatch-roof hut built in 1846. ⊠ *Hawai'i Volcanoes National Park, Crater Rim Dr., Volcano 96785* ☎ *808/967–7565* ☉ *Daily 9–5.*

㉚ Volcano House. This old lodge, with its huge stone fireplace, 42 rooms, the Ka 'Ōhelo Dining Room, and a snack bar, dates from 1941. The windows in the dining room overlook Kīlauea, and, in the center of the caldera, you'll see Halema'uma'u Crater. The dining room is busy with tour groups for the buffet lunch, but dinner can be a quieter experience. ⊠ *Hawai'i Volcanoes National Park, Crater Rim Dr.* ☎ *808/967–7321.*

★ ㊱ Volcano Winery. Have a tasting and shop at this unusual winery, which creates white table wines made from symphony grapes grown nearby. Also on offer are honey wines, a red Pele Delight, Guava or Passion Chablis, and Volcano Blush. Experiments with traditional varietals such as pinot noir are under way. ⊠ *35 Pi'imauna Dr., Volcano 96785* ☎ *808/967–7772* ⊕ *www.volcanowinery.com* ☉ *Daily 10–5:30.*

> **need a break?** Coffee and a steaming bowl of saimin at **Volcano Golf & Country Club Restaurant** (⊠ Volcano Golf & Country Club, 35 Pi'imauna Dr., Volcano ☎ 808/967–8228) can be a soul-saving meal on a cool, wet day.

HĀMĀKUA COAST

The Hilo–Hāmākua Heritage Coast leads past green cliffs and gorges, jungle vegetation, open emerald fields, and stunning ocean scenery along Highway 19, which runs north-northwest from Hilo. Brown signs featuring a sugarcane tassel point out this area's history: thousands of acres of sugar land are now idle, as the area's sugar mills all went out of business by the late 1990s. "King Sugar," which once dominated daily life here, is no longer the economic backbone of the Hāmākua Coast community. The 45-mi drive winds through little plantation towns—Pāpaʻikou, Laupāhoehoe, and Paʻauilo among them. It veers to the right at Honokaʻa, taking you to the end of the road bordering Waipiʻo Valley. The isolated valley floor has maintained the ways of old Hawaiʻi, with taro patches, wild horses, and a handful of houses. This is a great drive if you're on your way from Hilo to one of the resorts along the Kohala Coast. To Kailua-Kona, count on a total of 95 mi via this shorter of the two coastal routes from Hilo.

a good drive

Seven miles north of Hilo, turn right off Highway 19 onto a 4-mi scenic drive to reach **Hawaiʻi Tropical Botanical Garden** ㊳ ▶. After the scenic drive rejoins Highway 19, turn left toward **Honomū** ㊴ to travel 4 mi inland to **ʻAkaka Falls State Park** ㊵. As you continue north on Highway 19, stop at **Kolekole Beach Park** ㊶: it's a nice place for a picnic, and it has facilities. Head north on Highway 19 and turn left to visit the 300 acres of the still-growing **World Botanical Gardens** ㊷. From here you'll see stunning views of triple-tiered Umauma Falls, one of the prettiest waterfalls on the isle.

As you continue north on Highway 19, enjoy the ride through sleepy little villages with music in their names: Honohina, Niʻnole, Pāpaʻaloa. The **Laupāhoehoe Train Museum** ㊸ takes you back to the time when sugar reigned along the Hāmākua Coast.

Just beyond the museum is **Laupāhoehoe Point Park** ㊹, which is good for fishing but not swimming. Farther inland, hikers will enjoy the nature walk through the cool upland forest of **Kalōpā State Park** ㊺.

Next, you'll reach the turnoff to **Honokaʻa** ㊻. Secondhand and antiques stores, with dusty dishes, fabrics, and crafts, line Honokaʻa's main street along with a few cafés and island-style eateries.

Just before the road (Route 240) ends, 8 mi beyond Honokaʻa, a sign directs you to the right to Kukuihaele, on a coastal loop with no name. On your way to **Waipiʻo Valley Overlook** ㊼, passing the old Plantation Managers House, you can make arrangements for tours to explore the 6-mi-deep valley at the Last Chance building, and Waipiʻo Valley Artworks gallery. At the end of Route 240, the once heavily populated Waipiʻo Valley is a tropical Eden bounded by 2,000-ft cliffs. There are spectacular views of the valley and coast from the overlook.

TIMING   If you've stopped to explore the quiet little villages with wooden boardwalks and dogs dozing in backyards, or if you've spent several hours in Waipiʻo Valley, night will undoubtedly be falling by the time you complete this journey. Don't worry: the return to Hilo via Highway 19 takes only about an hour, or you can continue on the same road to stop for dinner in Waimea (30 minutes) and head to the Kohala Coast resorts (another 25 to 45 minutes).

What to See

★ ㊵ **ʻAkaka Falls State Park.** A meandering 20-minute trail takes you to the best spots to see the two falls, **ʻAkaka** and **Kahuna.** The downhill part

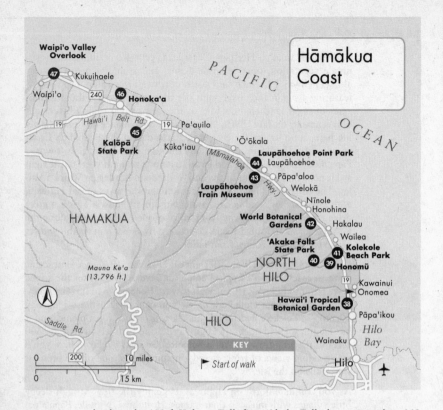

leads to the 400-ft Kahuna Falls first. 'Akaka Falls drops more than 442 ft, tumbling far below into a pool drained by Kolekole Stream amid a profusion of fragrant white, yellow, and red torch ginger. ✛ *4 mi inland off Hwy. 19, near Honomū* ☎ *808/974–6200* ✉ *Free* ☾ *Daily 7–7.*

★ ⚐ ③⑧ **Hawai'i Tropical Botanical Garden.** Eight miles north of Hilo, stunning coastline views appear around each curve of the 4-mi scenic jungle drive that accesses the privately owned, nonprofit, 17-acre nature preserve beside Onomea Bay. Paved pathways lead past waterfalls, ponds, and more than 2,000 species of plants and flowers, including palms, bromeliads, ginger, heleconia, orchids, and ornamentals. ✉ *27-717 Old Māmalahoa Hwy., Pāpa'ikou* ☎ *808/964–5233* ⊕ *www.hawaiigarden. com* ✉ *$15* ☾ *Daily 9–4.*

④⑥ **Honoka'a.** In 1881, Australian William Purvis planted the first macadamia-nut trees in Hawai'i in what is now this funky little town. But the macadamia-nut-processing factory has long since closed. Honoka'a's true heyday came when sugar thrived, in the early and mid-1900s. During World War II, this was also the place for soldiers stationed around Waimea to cut loose. Its historic buildings are home today to little eateries and stores crammed with knickknacks and antiques. ✉ *Mamane St. (Hwy. 240).*

need a break? A quick stop at **Tex Drive In** (✉ Pakalana St. and Hwy. 19 ☎ 808/ 775–0598) will give you a chance to taste the snack it is famous for: *malasada*, a puffy, doughy Portuguese doughnut (sans hole), deep-fried and rolled in sugar and best eaten hot. For mouthwatering pastries and a strong espresso in Honoka'a, stop in at **Mamane Street Bakery** (✉ Mamane St. ☎ 808/775–9478), where residents from as far as Waimea and Hilo gladly shop. **Café il Mondo**

(⊠ Mamane St. ☎ 808/775–7711) serves stone oven–baked pizzas and calzones until 9 PM.

㊴ Honomū. A plantation past is reflected in the wooden boardwalks and tin-roof buildings of this small, struggling town. It's fun to poke through old, dusty shops such as Glass from the Past, where you'll find an assortment of old bottles. The Woodshop Gallery/Café showcases fine local art. ✛ *2 mi inland from Hwy. 19 en route to 'Akaka Falls State Park.*

★ ㊺ Kalōpā State Park. At a cool 2,000-ft elevation, past the old plantation town of Pa'auilo, a lush, forested area with picnic tables and rest rooms hides an easy ¾-mi loop trail with additional paths in the adjacent 100-acre forest reserve. Small signs identify some of the plants. Cabins are available. ✛ *12 mi north of Laupāhoehoe and 3 mi inland off Hwy. 19* ☎ *808/974–6200* ✉ *Free* ☉ *Daily 7–7 or by permit.*

㊶ Kolekole Beach Park. This rocky beach at the mouth of the Kolekole River is not safe for inexperienced swimmers, but when the river runs low, it might just make for a chilly, refreshing dip. Facilities at the park include rest rooms, barbecue pits, and covered picnic areas. A scenic drive takes you from the top of the park through the old town of Wailea back to Highway 19. ✛ *Off Hwy. 19* ☎ *808/961–8311* ✉ *Free* ☉ *Daily 7 AM–sunset.*

㊸ Laupāhoehoe Point Park. Come here to watch the surf pound the jagged black rocks at the base of the stunning point, but remember that this is not a safe place for swimming. Still vivid in the minds of longtime area residents is the 1946 tragedy in which 21 schoolchildren and three teachers were swept to sea by a tidal wave. The park has bathrooms, picnic tables, and stone barbecue pits. ✛ *On northeast coastline, Hwy. 19, makai side, north of Laupāhoehoe* ☎ *808/961–8311* ✉ *Free* ☉ *Daily 7 AM–sunset.*

㊷ Laupāhoehoe Train Museum. Behind the stone loading platform of the once-famous Hilo Railroad, constructed around the turn of the 20th century, the former manager's house is a poignant display of the era when sugar was king. The railroad, one of the most expensive built in its time, was washed away by the tidal wave of 1946. Today, one of the old engines is running again on a short Y-track at the museum. ⊠ *Hwy. 19, Laupāhoehoe, mauka side* ☎ *808/962–6300* ✉ *$3* ☉ *Weekdays 9–4:30, weekends 10–2.*

Fodor'sChoice **Mauna Kea.** Mauna Kea is the antithesis of the typical island experience.
★ Freezing temperatures and arctic conditions are common at the summit, and snow storms can occur year-round. It's also home to Lake Waiau, one of the highest lakes in the world. The summit—at 13,796 ft—is reputedly the clearest place in the world for viewing the night sky; it's also an outstanding place to see the sun rise and set. If you're driving to the summit on your own, stop in first at the **Onizuka Center for International Astronomy Visitor Information Station** (☎ 808/961–2180 ⊕ www.ifa.hawaii.edu/info/vis), at a 9,300-ft elevation, open from 9 AM to 10 PM daily. (Technically it can be reached in a standard automobile, though you'll need four-wheel drive to get to the summit.) To reach this station from Hilo, which is about 34 mi away, take Highway 200, Saddle Road, and turn right at mile marker 28 onto Summit Access Road. The observatory patio here is the best amateur observation site on Earth, with three telescopes and a knowledgeable staff, so you might not need to go farther. However, free summit tours are also available at the center. Whether you're hiking or driving to the summit, take the change in altitude seriously—don't overexert yourself, especially at the top. Note

that scuba divers must wait at least 24 hours before attempting a trip to the summit to avoid getting the bends.

★ ㊼ **Waipi'o Valley Overlook.** Bounded by 2,000-ft cliffs, the Valley of the Kings—Waipi'o—was once a favorite retreat of Hawaiian royalty. Waterfalls drop 1,200 ft from the Kohala Mountains to the valley floor. Sheer cliffs make access difficult. Only four-wheel-drive vehicles should attempt the steep road from the overlook. A handful of families still cultivate taro in the pastoral valley, a few residents find refuge here, and horses roam narrow trails and rocky streams. A crescent of black sand makes it a popular spot for surfers, but the beach is not safe for swimming due to strong currents and undertows. ⊹ *Follow Hwy. 240 8 mi northwest of Honoka'a.*

off the
beaten
path

Waipi'o Valley. Today completely off the grid, Waipi'o was once the center of Hawaiian life, when somewhere between 4,000 and 20,000 people made it their home between the 13th and 17th centuries. In 1823, the first white visitors found 1,500 people living in this Eden-like environment amid fruit trees, banana patches, taro fields, and fishponds. Here, in 1780, Kamehameha I was singled out as a future ruler by reigning chiefs. In 1791 he fought Kahekili in his first naval battle at the mouth of the valley. The 1946 tidal wave drove most residents to higher ground. Now, as then, waterfalls frame the landscape, but the valley has become one of the most isolated places in the state. To preserve this pristine part of the island, commercial transportation permits are limited—only four outfits offer organized valley trips—and Sunday the valley rests. The walk down into the valley is less than a mile—start at the four-wheel-drive road leading down from the lookout point—but the climb back up is strenuous in the hot sun.

㊷ **World Botanical Gardens.** About 300 acres of former sugarcane land are slowly giving way to a botanical center, which includes native Hawaiian plants. In the 10-acre arboretum children love to wind their way through a maze of 5-ft shrubs. From within the gardens you have access to splendid views of one of the prettiest waterfalls on the isle, triple-tiered **Umauma Falls.** ✉ *Hwy. 19, from Hilo just past mile marker 16* ☎ *808/963–5427* ⊕ *www.wbgi.com* ✉ *$7* ☉ *Mon.–Sat. 9–5:30.*

KAILUA-KONA

The touristy seaside village of Kailua-Kona, at the base of the 8,271-ft Mt. Hualālai, has many historic sites tucked among the open-air shops and restaurants that line Ali'i Drive, its main oceanfront street. This is where King Kamehameha I died in 1819 and where his successor, Liholiho, broke the *kapu* (taboo) system, a rigid set of laws that had provided the framework for Hawaiian government. The following year, on April 4, 1820, the first Christian missionaries from New England came ashore at Kailua-Kona.

The easiest place to park your car (a fee is charged) is at King Kamehameha's Kona Beach Hotel. Some free parking is available: when you enter Kailua via Palani Road, or Highway 190, turn left onto Kuakini Highway; drive for a half block, and turn right (it's marked) and then immediately left into the parking lot. Walk makai on Likana Lane a half block to Ali'i Drive.

a good walk

This ½-mi walk follows Aliʻi Drive south. Begin at **King Kamehameha's Kona Beach Hotel** ㊽ ▶ at the northern end of town. The hotel, which borders the last residency of King Kamehameha I, **Kamakahonu** ㊾, offers free tours of a replica of the king's temple, Ahuʻena Heiau. You can also wander around the two stone platforms at the ocean's edge to view the site on your own. Next, investigate **Kailua Pier** ㊿. Walk a short distance and take in **Huliheʻe Palace** ⑤, on your right, and **Mokuʻaikaua Church** ㊾, on your left. Tackle a plethora of shops in the block-long **Kona Inn Shopping Village** ㊿. End your walk at **St. Michael's Church** ㊾, on your left, across the street from the wooden restaurant complex known as Waterfront Row, or continue a few blocks down to Coconut Plaza.

If you have a car, return to it to complete your historical tour; drive to the end of Aliʻi Drive past Disappearing Sands Beach Park, the tiny blue-and-white St. Peter's Catholic Church, the ruins of a heiau, and Kahaluʻu Beach Park. There, a jagged lava lake on the edge of a bay outlines the **Kuamoʻo Battlefield and Lekeleke Burial Grounds** ㊿.

TIMING You can walk the whole ½-mi length of "downtown" Kailua-Kona and back again in an hour, or else spend an entire day here, taking time to browse in the shops, do the historical tours, and have lunch. The drive to the Kuamoʻo Battlefield and Lekeleke Burial Grounds takes less than 10 minutes. If you want to know more about Kailua's fascinating past, arrange for a guided tour by the Kona Historical Society.

Kailua-Kona enjoys year-round sunshine—except for the rare deluge. Mornings offer cooler weather, smaller crowds, and more birds singing in the banyan trees, but afternoon outings are great for cool drinks while gazing out over the ocean.

What to See

off the beaten path

Astronaut Ellison S. Onizuka Space Center. This informative museum 7 mi north of Kailua-Kona, at the airport, was opened as a tribute to Hawaiʻi's first astronaut, who was killed in the 1986 *Challenger* disaster. The space center has computer-interactive exhibits. You can launch a miniature rocket and rendezvous with an object in space, feel the effects of gyroscopic stabilization, participate in hands-on science activities, and view educational films. ⊠ *Keāhole–Kona International Airport, Kailua-Kona* ☎ *808/329–3441* ⊕ *www.planet-hawaii.com/astronautonizuka* ⊠ *$3* ⊙ *Daily 8:30–4:30.*

★ ⑤ **Huliheʻe Palace.** Fronted by a wrought-iron gate decorated with the royal crest, Huliheʻe Palace is one of only three royal palaces in America. The two-story residence was built of lava, coral, koa wood, and ʻohiʻa timber in 1838 by the island's governor, John Adams Kuakini, a year after he completed Mokuʻaikaua Church. During the 1880s it served as King David Kalākaua's summer palace. The oversize doors and koa-wood furniture bear witness to the size of some of the Hawaiian people. During weekday afternoons hula schools rehearse on the grounds. ⊠ *75-5718 Aliʻi Dr.* ☎ *808/329–1877* ⊠ *$5* ⊙ *Weekdays 9–4, weekends 10–4.*

㊿ **Kailua Pier.** Though most fisherfolk use Honokōhau Harbor, north of Kailua-Kona, Kailua Pier, built in 1918, is still a hub of ocean activity. Outrigger canoe teams practice, and tour boats depart. Each October close to 1,500 international athletes swim 2.4 mi from the pier to begin the grueling Ironman Triathlon competition.

Along the seawall fisherfolk and children daily cast their lines. For youngsters, a bamboo pole and hook are easy to come by, and plenty

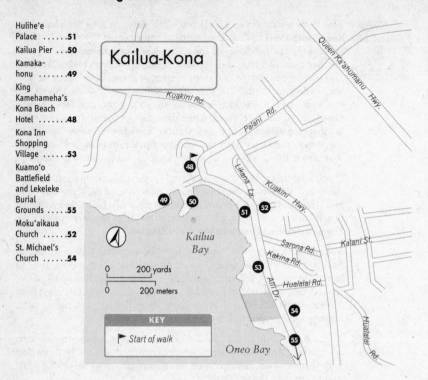

of locals are willing to give pointers. ✛ *Next to King Kamehameha's Kona Beach Hotel; the seawall is between Kailua Pier and Hulihe'e Palace on Ali'i Dr.*

㊾ Kamakahonu. King Kamehameha I chose to spend his last years, from 1812 until his death in 1819, in this area, just outside of what is now King Kamehameha's Kona Beach Hotel, adjacent to the little beach and lagoon. Part of what was once a 4-acre homestead complete with several houses and religious sites has been swallowed by Kailua Pier, but

★ a replica of the temple, **Ahu'ena Heiau**, keeps history alive. Free tours start from King Kamehameha's Kona Beach Hotel. ✉ *75-5660 Palani Rd.* ☎ *808/329–2911* 🎫 *Free* ☉ *Tours weekdays at 1:30.*

⚑ **㊽ King Kamehameha's Kona Beach Hotel.** Stroll through the high-ceiling lobby of this Kailua-Kona fixture, built in the mid-'70s, to view displays of Hawaiian artifacts and mounted marlin from Hawaiian International Billfish tournaments (from when Kailua Pier was still the weigh-in point). One tournament winner, a marlin that weighed in at 1,062 pounds, hangs on a wall. An even larger, 1,166-pound record-setter is a floor display. These "granders," marlin weighing 1,000 pounds or more, are the big attraction for Kona fisherfolk. Classes in Hawaiian arts and crafts take place regularly. ✉ *75-5660 Palani Rd.* ☎ *808/329–2911.*

off the beaten path

Kona Brewing Company & Brewpub. A few blocks mauka of King Kamehameha's Kona Beach Hotel, Kona Brewing Company offers thirst-quenching tours and tastings. Its wheat ale, flavored with liliko'i, is a staple of the pub here, which is eclectic in its architecture, with a koa-wood bar, driftwood benches, and a historic tin roof. The pub uses local and organic produce for its pizzas. For nondrinkers, an exquisite sparkling ginger ale hits the spot. ✉ *North Kona Shopping*

Center, 75-5629 Kuakini Hwy. ☎ *808/334–2739* ⊙ *Mon.–Thurs. 11–10, Fri.–Sat. 11–11, Sun. 4–10.*

🔵 **Kona Inn Shopping Village.** This shopping arcade was once the Kona Inn, a hotel built in 1928 to attract a new wave of wealthy travelers. As new vacation condos and resorts opened along the Kona and Kohala coasts, the old Kona Inn lost much of its appeal and finally closed in 1976. The former hotel was renovated into a shopping complex with dozens of clothing boutiques, art stores, gifts shops, and island-style eateries. Prior to the construction of the inn, the personal heiau of King Liholiho was on this shore. Today, shops and restaurants line the boardwalk. Broad lawns with coconut trees on the ocean side are lovely for afternoon picnics. ⊠ *75-5744 Ali'i Dr.*

🔵 **Kuamo'o Battlefield and Lekeleke Burial Grounds.** In 1819, an estimated 300 Hawaiians were killed on this vast, desolate black-lava field now filled with terraced graves. After the death of his father, King Kamehameha I, Liholiho became king; shortly thereafter King Liholiho ate at the table of women, thereby breaking an ancient kapu. Chief Kekuaokalani, vying for the throne and with radically different views about traditions and religion, unsuccessfully challenged King Liholiho in battle. In breaking the ancient kapu, Liholiho forced a final battle between not just him and his opponent but, more importantly, between traditional and new religious beliefs in Hawai'i. ⊹ *South end of Ali'i Dr.*

★ 🔵 **Moku'aikaua Church.** The earliest Christian church on the Islands was founded here as a thatch hut by Hawai'i's first missionaries in 1820. The present incarnation of the church was built in 1836 with black stone from an abandoned heiau. The stone was mortared with white coral and topped by an impressive steeple. Inside, at the back, behind a panel of gleaming koa wood, is a model of the brig *Thaddeus.* ⊠ *75-5713 Ali'i Dr.* ☎ *808/329–0655.*

> **need a break?** Sample some 100% pure Konà coffee at the **Kona Coffee Café** (⊠ 75-5744 Ali'i Dr. ☎ 808/329–7131). For cocktails at sunset head to the **Kona Inn Restaurant** (⊠ 75-5744 Ali'i Dr. ☎ 808/329–4455), a traditional favorite.

🔵 **St. Michael's Church.** The site of the first Catholic church built in Kona, in 1840, is marked by a small thatch structure to the left of the present church, which dates from 1850. In front of the church a coral grotto shrine holds 2,500 coral heads, harvested in 1940, when preservation was not yet an issue. ⊠ *75-5769 Ali'i Dr.* ☎ *808/326–7771.*

SOUTH KONA & KA'U

South of Kailua-Kona, Highway 11 leaves busy streets behind, hugging splendid coastlines. Cradled against the slopes of Mauna Loa, coffee plantations alternate with arid landscapes in the surreal emptiness of the most southern part of the United States. The 50-mi drive to windswept South Point, where the first Polynesians came ashore as early as AD 750, passes a national historic park, Pu'uhonua O Hōnaunau, the only remaining Hawaiian place of refuge, as well as a whimsically painted church. Below the highway shimmers Kealakekua Bay, where Captain James Cook arrived in 1778, bringing radical change to Hawai'i. Narrow, steep roads off the main highway lead to isolated fishing towns where life unfolds far removed from the modern world. To the east of Highway 11, an 11,000-acre development overgrown with ohelo berries, Ocean View Estates, testifies to the struggle it takes to survive in this land crisscrossed

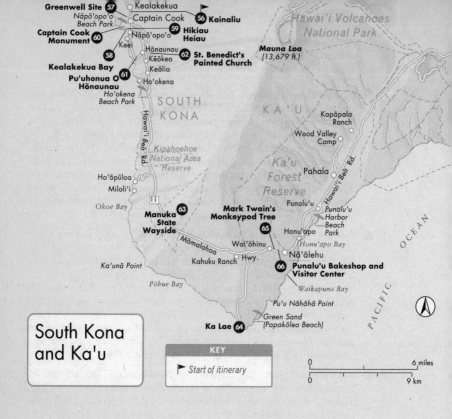

South Kona
and Ka'u

KEY

► Start of itinerary

0   6 miles

0   9 km

by lava flows. Mark Twain, however, wrote some of his finest prose here, and macadamia-nut farms, fine beaches, and tiny villages offer as yet largely undiscovered beauty.

a good
drive

From Kailua-Kona, drive south on Highway 11, also known as Hawai'i Belt Road or Māmalahoa Highway, to historic **Kainaliu** ⑤⑥ ►. Just outside the town, on your right, you'll find the **Greenwell Site** ⑤⑦, now headquarters of the Kona Historical Society. Pick up brochures and guides here and arrange for a tour of the D. Uchida Farm.

At the junction in the town of Captain Cook, turn right and follow the steep descent along Nāpō'opo'o Road to **Kealakekua Bay** ⑤⑧. Park your car and walk to **Hikiau Heiau** ⑤⑨. A moderately difficult three-hour hike from the top of Nāpō'opo'o Road on a rough trail takes you to **Captain Cook Monument** ⑥⓪. Dip into the calm, dolphin-friendly waves that lap onto rocky Nāpō'opo'o Beach before taking Route 160, which hugs the coast, to **Pu'uhonua O Hōnaunau** ⑥①. Plan to spend some time walking around this ancient Hawaiian sanctuary. Visit the restored royal Hale-o-Keawe Heiau, built circa 1650, and wander to the tide pools south of the park. Back in your car, head mauka on Route 160 toward Kēōkea, and turn left at Painted Church Road to visit the whimsical **St. Benedict's Painted Church** ⑥②.

Continue south on Highway 11; after about 2 mi, you'll pass the turnoff to Ho'okena Beach Park, a busy steamer port in the 19th century. About 12 mi farther south, at mile marker 88, the infamous Mauna Loa lava flow of 1926 destroyed an entire Hawaiian fishing village. Turn left here for a 2-mi scenic drive along the old Māmalahoa Highway; then take a break at **Manuka State Wayside** ⑥③.

Drive another 12 mi on Māmalahoa Highway to reach the windswept South Point Road, which leads to the southernmost part of the United

States, **Ka Lae** ⑥. You must have a four-wheel-drive vehicle and a per-mit to get beyond the gate to reach Green Sand Beach, or you can take an exhilarating 5-mi round-trip hike.

For the last leg of this drive, head east on Highway 11 to the wetter, windward towns of Waiʻōhinu and Nāʻālehu, small communities strug-gling in the aftermath of sugar-plantation closures. Be sure to stop first at **Mark Twain's Monkeypod Tree** ⑥ for inspiration, then at **Punaluʻu Bakeshop and Visitor Center** ⑥.

TIMING Start your day early, as it takes 2½ hours from Kona just to get to the southern end of the island. You may want to make this a two-day ex-cursion and stay in one of the many cozy B&Bs at Hawaiʻi Volcanoes National Park—a short 45-minute drive away from Nāʻālehu. Fill up on gasoline and pack some snacks, as there are few amenities along the way. Chances are it'll be close to dinnertime by the time you've com-pleted this tour, but eateries in Kona remain open late.

What to See

★ ⑥ **Captain Cook Monument.** No one knows for sure what happened on February 14, 1779, when English explorer Captain James Cook was killed here. He chose Kealakekua Bay as a landing place in November 1778 and initiated Hawaiʻi's dramatic change. Cook was welcomed at first, arriving during the celebration of Makahiki, the harvest season. Some Hawaiians saw him as an incarnation of the god Lono, and he was re-ceived with great reverence. Cook's party reprovisioned and sailed away in February 1779. But a freak storm off the Kona Coast forced him back to Kealakekua Bay for repairs. The Hawaiians were not so welcoming this time, and various confrontations arose between them and Cook's sailors. The theft of a longboat brought Cook and an armed party ashore to reclaim the boat. One thing led to another: shots were fired, daggers and spears were thrown, and Captain Cook fell, mortally wounded. Suffice it to say, Captain James Cook and his party introduced the Hawaiian Islands to the world. Soon after, Western influences ar-rived on Hawaiʻi's shores: whalers, sailors, traders, missionaries, and more, and they brought with them crime, debauchery, alcohol, disease, and a world unknown to the Hawaiians. A 27-ft-high obelisk marks the spot where Captain Cook died on the shore of Kealakekua Bay. The three-hour 2½-mi hike to get to the monument begins at the trailhead 100 yards off Highway 11 on Nāpōʻopoʻo Road. Look for the downslope trail opposite three large royal palm trees.

⑤ **Greenwell Site.** Established in 1850, the homestead of Henry N. Green-well served as cattle ranch, sheep station, post office, store complex, and family home all in one. Now, all that remains is the 1875 stone store, which is listed on the National Register of Historic Places. It is head-quarters for the **Kona Historical Society** and its fascinating museum, with ranching and coffee-farming photographs and exhibits. ✉ *81-6551 Māmalahoa Hwy.* ☎ *808/323–3222* ⊕ *www.konahistorical.org* ✉ *By donation* ⊙ *Weekdays 9–3.*

⑤ **Hikiau Heiau.** The remains you see of the stone platform and walls were once an impressive state temple, a large and sacred site enclosed by stone walls, dedicated to the god Lono. When Captain Cook arrived in 1778, ceremonies in his honor were held here. ✉ *Bottom of Nāpōʻopoʻo Rd.*

★ ⑥ **Ka Lae.** Windswept Ka Lae, the southernmost point of land in the United States, has a few abandoned structures once used in the 19th and early 20th centuries to lower cattle and produce to ships anchored below the cliffs. It is thought that the first Polynesians came ashore here. Check out the old canoe-mooring holes that are carved through the rocks, possibly by settlers from Tahiti as early as AD 750. Some artifacts, thought to have been left by early voyagers who never settled here, date to AD 300. Driving down the 12-mi road, you pass Kamoa Wind Farm; turn off your engine and listen to the eerie sound of the wind hitting the white wings of the windmills high above you. ✛ *Turn right just past mile marker 70 on Māmalahoa Hwy. and drive for 12 mi down South Point Rd.*

▶ **56 Kainaliu.** It doesn't seem like much, this ribbon of funky old stores, but Kainaliu hosts a wealth of traditional-Japanese family-operated shops. Browse around Heritage Stores such as Oshima's, established in 1926, and Kimura's, established in 1927, to find authentic Japanese goods beyond tourist trinkets. When times were tough, these stores survived by accepting coffee as tender. Peek into Aloha Theatre, built in 1932, where community-theater actors might be practicing a Broadway review. ⊠ *Hwy. 11, mile markers 112–114.*

★ **58 Kealakekua Bay.** Before the arrival of Captain Cook in the late 18th century, this now tranquil state marine park and sanctuary with its old steamer landing lay at the center of Hawaiian life. Historians consider Kealakekua Bay as the birthing ground for the postcontact era. ⊠ *Bottom of Nāpō'opo'o Rd.*

need a break? Treat yourself to awesome views of Kealakekua Bay at the **Coffee Shack** (⊠ 83-5799 Māmalahoa ☎ 808/328–9555), a deli and pizza place with just nine tables on an open, breezy la'nai. The bread is home-baked, the sandwiches are generous, and the staff is friendly.

☾ **63 Manuka State Wayside.** This is a dry, upland native forest spread across several lava flows. It has a well-maintained arboretum. A rugged trail follows a 2-mi loop past a pit crater and winds around ancient trees such as *hau* and *kukui.* Kids love the trees, so large you can't get your arms around them, but pathways aren't well maintained. Rest rooms, picnic areas, and telephones are available. ⊠ *Hwy. 11, north of mile marker 81* ☎ *808/974–6200* ⊠ *Free* ◷ *Daily 7–7.*

65 Mark Twain's Monkeypod Tree. Legend has it that Mark Twain, who gained inspiration for some of his writings during his travels in this area, planted this robust, gnarled tree in 1866. In the 1950s a storm blew the tree down. New shoots have since developed into an impressive tree again. Next door is a little take-out restaurant, Mark Twain Square. ⊠ *Hwy. 11, just before mile marker 64.*

off the beaten path Pahala. About 16 mi east of Na'lehu, beyond Punalu'u Beach Park, Highway 11 flashes past this little town. You'll miss it if you blink. Pahala is a perfect example of a sugar-plantation town. Behind it, along a wide cane road, you enter Wood Valley, once a prosperous community, now a mere road heavily scented by night-blooming jasmine, coffee blossoms, and eucalyptus trees. Here you'll find Wood Valley Temple (☎ 808/928–8539), a quiet Tibetan Buddhist retreat that welcomes guests who seek serenity and solitude.

66 Punalu'u Bakeshop and Visitor Center. They say it's the best sweetbread—of course, it's the only sweetbread—in this area. While here, browse for rare *pohā*-berry (gooseberry) jam, look up at the old tamarind tree outside, and be sure to take some of that sweetbread home. ⊠ *Mamalahoa Hwy. at Kaalaiki Rd., Na'alehu* ☎ *808/929–7343* ◷ *Daily 9–5.*

★ **61 Pu'uhonua O Hōnaunau.** This 180-acre National Historic Park, about 20 mi south of Kailua-Kona, was, in early times, a place of refuge and healing. It was a safe haven for women in times of war as well as for kapu breakers, criminals, and prisoners of war—anyone who could get inside the 1,000-ft-long wall, which was 10 ft high and 17 ft thick, was safe and could avoid punishment. **Hale-o-Keawe Heiau,** built in 1650 as the burial place of King Kamehameha I's ancestor Keawe, has been restored. South of the park, tide pools offer another delight. Demonstrations of Hawaiian skills, games, poi pounding, canoe making, and more are scheduled occasionally. ⊠ *Rte. 160* ☎ *808/328–2326* ⊕ *www.nps.gov* ✑ *$3–$5* ◷ *Park grounds Mon.–Thurs.* 6 AM–8 PM, *Fri.–Sun.* 6 AM–11 PM; *visitor center daily* 8 AM–4:30 PM.

★ ⓰ **St. Benedict's Painted Church.** Whimsical, bright, and creative, the ceiling, columns, and walls of this Roman Catholic church depict Bible scenes through the paintbrush of Belgium-born priest Father Velghe. Mass is still held every weekend. The view of Kealakekua Bay from the entrance is amazing. ⊠ *Painted Church Rd., off Hwy. 160* ☎ *808/328–2227.*

THE KOHALA DISTRICT

Along the roadside of Highway 19, brightly colored bougainvillea stands out in relief against the chunky black-lava landscape that stretches as far as the eye can see. Most of the lava flows, spreading from the mountain to the sea, are from the last eruptions of Mt. Hualālai, in 1800–01. They are interrupted only by the green oases of irrigated golf courses surrounding the glamorous luxury resorts rising along the Kona-Kohala Coast. The landscape along this long stretch of coastline changes considerably, from the cool 2,500-ft altitude of the cowboy town of Waimea to the green rolling fields that compose much of North Kohala. During the winter months, glistening humpback whales cleave the waters just offshore. On the coast you'll see ancient stone heiau and the remains of a fishing village, moving legacies of the Hawaiian people who still inhabit the area.

a good drive

If you're staying in Kona or at a Kohala Coast resort, begin this tour early in the morning by driving north on Queen Ka'ahumanu Highway 19 along the base of Mt. Hualālai. When you get to the split in the road 33 mi from Kailua-Kona, turn left on Highway 270 toward Kawaihae and stop at **Pu'ukoholā Heiau National Historic Site** ⓰ ▶. Continue on to **Kawaihae Harbor** ⓰: go straight when Highway 270 veers sharply to the right. Here, in 1793, British captain George Vancouver brought on land the cattle that would proliferate beyond control and draw the first paniolo (cowboys).

Rejoin Highway 270 to drive north through an arid landscape. The sweeping coastline offers great places to spot whales. Just after mile marker 6, you'll see the red warrior sign for **Pua Mau Botanical Garden** ⓰. At **Lapakahi State Historical Park** ⓰, a 1-mi trail meanders through the site of once-prosperous Koai'e, an ancient fishing village. Back on the highway, past Māhukona Beach Park and Kapa'a Beach Park, turn left at the sign for the remote, old 'Upolu Airport. At the bottom of the paved road you'll need a four-wheel-drive vehicle or good hiking shoes to traverse a 1½-mi dirt lane to **Mo'okini Heiau** ⓰. About 1,000 yards away from the heiau is King Kamehameha I's birthplace.

Continue north on the highway. Your next stops are in the old sugar-plantation villages of **Hāwī and Kapa'au** ⓰. Browse through the many galleries and gift shops, have some lunch, and make sure to visit the original **King Kamehameha Statue** ⓰. Highway 270 ends farther east at an overlook with a stunning view of **Pololū Valley** ⓰. A rugged, steep hiking trail leads down into the valley. Drive back toward Hāwī to complete the loop via Highway 250, better known as Kohala Mountain Road.

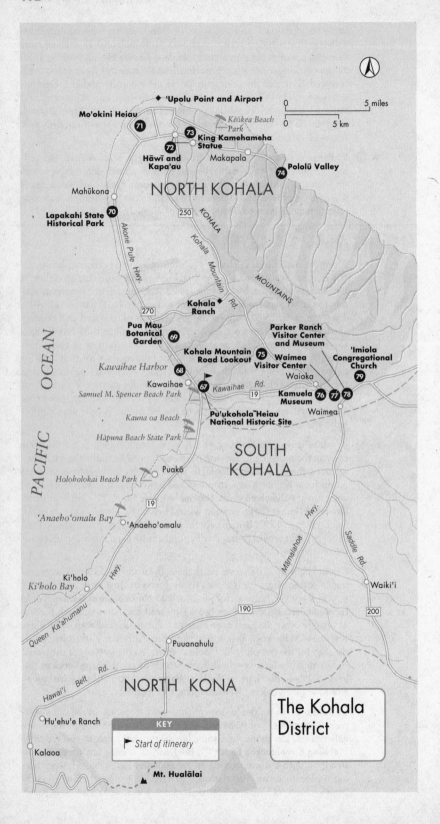

'Upolu Point and Airport

0 ____ 5 miles
0 ____ 5 km

Mo'okini Heiau

71

Kēōkea Beach Park

73 King Kamehameha Statue

72

Hāwī and Kapa'au

Makapala

74 Pololū Valley

NORTH KOHALA

Mahūkona

250

70 Lapakahi State Historical Park

Akone Pule Hwy.

KOHALA

Kohala Mountain Rd.

MOUNTAINS

270

Kohala Ranch

Pua Mau Botanical Garden

69

Parker Ranch Visitor Center and Museum

Kohala Mountain Road Lookout

75 Waimea Visitor Center

'Imiola Congregational Church

79

Kawaihae Harbor

68

Waiaka

Kawaihae

67 Kawaihae Rd.

19

76 77 78

Samuel M. Spencer Beach Park

Kamuela Museum

Waimea

Kauna oa Beach

Pu'ukoholā Heiau National Historic Site

Hāpuna Beach State Park

SOUTH KOHALA

Holoholokai Beach Park

Puakō

19

'Anaeho'omalu Bay

'Anaeho'omalu

Māmalahoa Hwy.

Saddle Rd.

Ki'holo

Ki'holo Bay

Waiki'i

Queen Ka'ahumanu Hwy.

190

200

Puuanahulu

NORTH KONA

Hawai'i Belt Rd.

KEY

Hu'ehu'e Ranch

Start of itinerary

Kalaoa

The Kohala District

PACIFIC OCEAN

Mt. Hualālai

This scenic ride across high elevations and through ironwood trees that act as windbreaks along a narrow, twisting road passes an exclusive country-home subdivision called Kohala Ranch as well as active working ranches such as Kahuā. Take a break at **Kohala Mountain Road Lookout** 75 for a view of the entire coastline, including the protective breakwater, directly below. The road slopes down toward Waimea. Where the road bumps into Highway 19, take a sharp right and turn into the first open gate on your left to visit **Kamuela Museum** 76.

Next, head for Upcountry Waimea, a bustling, affluent town with a cowboy heritage. Behind the shops of High Country Traders on your right on Highway 19, **Waimea Visitor Center** 77 offers detailed information on the cultural and historic sites of Kohala. On the other side of the traffic lights are the **Parker Ranch Visitor Center and Museum** 78 and the Parker Ranch Shopping Center.

Drive northeast on Highway 19. On the left lies Church Lane—stop to peek into the cream-color **ʻImiola Congregational Church** 79 to see its unique koa-wood interior. Make sure to browse through Cook's Discoveries at the third traffic light for exquisite local-theme gifts.

Reverse directions and head west on Highway 19; follow the road down to get back to the resorts along the coast.

TIMING   This is an all-day excursion covering many miles over ground that ranges from lava-covered flatlands with glorious seaside views to lush mountain pastures. If you're short on time, head either straight for Waimea to shop and dine and to visit the Parker Ranch Museum or drive to Hāwī and Kapaʻau via Highway 270 to see the dramatic history of these sugar towns. Allow a half day or more for the abbreviated trip.

What to See

72 **Hāwī and Kapaʻau.** These two neighboring villages thrived during plantation days. There were hotels, saloons, and theaters—even a railroad. Today, both towns are blossoming once again, honoring their past. Old historic buildings have been restored and now hold shops, galleries, and eateries. In Kapaʻau, browse through the Hawaiian collection of **Kohala Book Shop** (✉ 54-3885 Akoni Pule Hwy. ☎ 808/889–6400), the second-largest book store in the state. ✉ *Kohala Mount Rd., off Hwy. 270.*

need a break?   It can get hot and humid in North Kohala. A great place to feel the breeze is on the lawn of the **Nanbu Courtyard** (✉ Kapaʻau ☎ 808/889–5546), behind the historic Old Nanbu Hotel. Open as early as 6:30 on weekdays, this friendly espresso shop serves toasted bagels, salads, and grilled sandwiches along with soft ice cream. If you're looking for something sweet, head to **Kohala Coffee Mill** (✉ Akone Pule Hwy. ☎ 808/889–5577), an espresso café in bustling Hāwī that whips up Kona coffee, espresso drinks, and luscious iced *chai* (Indian tea).

79 **ʻImiola Congregational Church.** Stop here to admire the dark koa interior and the unusual wooden calabashes hanging from the ceiling. Be careful not to walk in while a service is in progress, as the front entry of this church, which was established in 1832 and rebuilt in 1857, is behind the pulpit. ✉ *Off Hwy. 19, Waimea* ☎ 808/885–4987.

off the beaten path   **Fire House Gallery.** Walk across the Parker Ranch Shopping Center parking lot to a historic 77-year-old fire station, now a gallery, to glimpse what the artists in Hāmākua and Kohala are up to. The Waimea Arts Council sponsors free *kaha kiʻis* (one-person shows).

✛ *Near main stoplight in Waimea, toward Kailua-Kona on Hwy. 190* ☎ *808/887–1052.*

76 Kamuela Museum. This small private museum has a fascinating collection of artifacts from Hawai'i and around the world. The eclectic collection includes Hawaiian weapons and a satiny-smooth koa table that once graced 'Iolani Palace in Honolulu. There are also period furniture pieces, artwork, and military and war memorabilia. ⊠ *Hwys. 19 and 250, Waimea* ☎ *808/885–4724* ✑ *$5* ☉ *Daily 8–4.*

68 Kawaihae Harbor. This commercial harbor, where in 1793 the first cattle came on land, setting the course of the Big Island's ranching history, is a hub of activity, especially on weekends, when paddlers and local fishing boats seek the waves. Second in size only to Hilo Harbor on the east coast, the harbor is often home to the *Makali'i,* one of three Hawaiian sailing canoes. King Kamehameha I and his men launched their canoes from here when they set out to conquer the island chain. ⊠ *Kawaihae Harbor Rd. off Hwy. 270.*

75 Kohala Mountain Road Lookout. The lookout here provides a splendid view of the Kohala Coast and Kawaihae Harbor far below. On clear days, you can see well beyond the resorts. It's one of the most scenic spots on the island and great for a picnic. Often, thick mists drift in, casting an eerie feeling. ⊠ *Kohala Mountain Rd. (Hwy. 250).*

73 King Kamehameha Statue. This is the original of the statue in front of the Judiciary Building on King Street in Honolulu. It was cast in Florence in 1880 but lost at sea when the German ship transporting it sank near the Falkland Islands. A replica was shipped to Honolulu. Two years later an American sea captain found the original in a Port Stanley (Falkland Islands) junkyard and brought it to the Big Island. The legislature voted to erect it near Kamehameha's birthplace. Every year, on King Kamehameha Day (June 11), a magnificent abundance of floral lei adorns the image of Hawai'i's great king. ⊠ *Hwy. 270, Kapa'au.*

> **need a break?**
>
> **Jen's Kohala Café** (☎ 808/889–0099), across from the King Kamehameha statue in Kapa'au, serves wraps and sandwiches all day long. Try the Greek spinach wrap—stuffed with organic baby greens, black olives, feta cheese, and pickled *pepperoncini* (small, hot chili peppers).

★ **70 Lapakahi State Historical Park.** A self-guided, 1-mi walking tour leads through the ruins of the once-prosperous fishing village Koai'e, which dates as far back as the 15th century. Displays illustrate early Hawaiian fishing, salt gathering, legends, games, shelters, and crops, and a park guide is often on-site to answer questions. Since the shores off Lapakahi are now mostly a Marine Life Conservation District, and part of the site itself is considered sacred, swimming is discouraged. ✛ *Makai side of Hwy. 270, between Kawaihae and Māhukona, North Kohala* ☎ *808/974–6200 or 808/882–6207* ✑ *Free* ☉ *Daily 8–4.*

★ **71 Mo'okini Heiau.** This National Historic Landmark, an isolated *luakini* (sacrificial) heiau, is so impressive in size it may give you goose bumps. Its foundations date to about AD 480, but the high priest Pa'ao from Tahiti built the heiau in earnest several centuries later to sacrifice people to please his gods. You can still see the lava slab. A nearby sign marks the place where Kamehameha I was born in 1758. The area is now part of the Kohala Historical Sites State Monument. ✛ *Turn off Hwy. 270 at sign for 'Upolu Airport, near Hāwī, and hike or drive in a four-wheel-drive vehicle 1½ mi southwest* ☎ *808/974–6200.*

78 **Parker Ranch Visitor Center and Museum.** The center chronicles the life of John Palmer Parker (and his descendants), who founded Parker Ranch in 1847. Parker married the granddaughter of King Kamehameha and bought 2 acres of land from the king for the sum of $10. Purchase your tickets here for the **Parker Ranch Historic Homes,** a couple of miles south of town: Mānā is the original koa-wood family residence, and Puʻōpelu, added to the Parker estate in 1879, was the residence of Richard Smart, a sixth-generation Parker who expanded the house to make room for his European art collection. Fridays, Hawaiian crafts demonstrations take place at the homes. A wagon ride allows you a comfortable, albeit old-fashioned, visit to the pastures. Also available are horseback rides and walking tours. ☒ *Parker Ranch Shopping Center, Hwy. 19, Waimea* ☎ *808/ 885–7655 or 808/885–5433* ⊕ *www.parkerranch.com* ☒ *Museum $6, homes $8.50, both $12* ☉ *Museum daily 9–5, homes daily 10–5.*

74 **Pololū Valley.** A steep trail leads into this once heavily populated valley, which edges a rugged coastline ribboned by silver waterfalls. The valleys beyond provide water for the Kohala Ditch, the ingenious project that used to bring water to the sugar plantation. The former ditch trails have become inaccessible and dangerous. A kayak cruise through the old irrigation ditch, a mule ride, and a ditch-trail hike reveal more of this dramatic part of Kohala history. ✛ *End of Hwy. 270.*

69 **Pua Mau Botanical Garden.** Virgil and Irina Place are slowly transforming 45 acres of arid land into a desert garden of everblooming plants, plumeria trees, and bronze sculptures modeled after Kohala's desert bugs. A maze of 200-plus hibiscus varieties leads to a magic circle—in accordance with Celtic traditions, a configuration of stones placed to follow the path of the sun through the seasons. Self-guided tours pass inviting picnic spots with sweeping coastal views. ☒ *Kohala Estates, 10 Ala Kahua Dr., off Hwy. 270 at mile marker 6, Kawaihae* ☎ *808/882–0888* ⊕ *www. puamau.com* ☒ *$5* ☉ *Wed.–Sun. 10–5.*

★ ▶ **67** **Puʻukoholā Heiau National Historic Site.** In 1790 a prophet told King Kamehameha I to build a heiau on top of Puʻukoholā (Hill of the Whale) and dedicate it to the war god Kūkāʻilimoku by sacrificing his principal Big Island rival, Keōua Kūahuʻula. By doing so the king would achieve his goal of conquering the Hawaiian Islands. The prophecy came true in 1810. A short walk over arid landscape leads from the visitor center to **Puʻukoholā Heiau** and to **Mailekini Heiau,** constructed about 1550. An even older temple, dedicated to the shark gods, lies submerged just offshore. The center organizes Hawaiian arts-and-crafts programs on a regular basis. ☒ *Hwy. 270, Kawaihae* ☎ *808/882–7218* ⊕ *www. nps.gov* ☒ *Free* ☉ *Daily 7:30–4.*

77 **Waimea Visitor Center.** The old Lindsey House—a restored ranch cabin built in 1909 and now listed on the Hawaiʻi Register of Historic Places— serves as a visitor center. Part of the Waimea Preservation Association, it offers detailed information on Kohala's many historic and cultural sites. (Note: technically, the name of the Waimea post office is Kamuela, and the name of the town is Waimea. Therefore, you'll see Kamuela in many addresses. Some say the post office is named for the son of the founder of Parker Ranch.) ☒ *65-1291 Kawaihae Rd., behind High Country Traders, Waimea* ☎ *808/885–6707* ⊕ *www.northhawaii.net* ☉ *Mon.–Sat. 9:30–4:30.*

need a break? At **Aioli's** (☒ ʻOpelo Plaza, Hwy. 19 and ʻOpelo Rd., Waimea ☎ 808/885–6325) you can pick up ready-to-go box lunches or opt for a custom-made sandwich. **Tako Taco Taqueria** (☒ Kawaihae Rd. next to Parker Sq., Waimea ☎ 808/887–1717) serves superb fresh,

CloseUp

HAWAIIAN MYTHS & LEGENDS

THE BEST-KNOWN DEITY in Hawaiian lore is Pele, the beautiful volcano goddess. Although visitors are warned not to remove lava rocks from Pele's domain without her permission, some do and find themselves dogged by bad luck until they return the stolen items. The Hawai`i Volcanoes National Park Service often receives packages containing chunks of lava along with letters describing years of misfortune.

Tales of Pele's fiery temper are legendary. She battled Poli`ahu, ruler of snowcapped Mauna Kea on the Big Island, in a fit of jealousy over the snow goddess's extraordinary beauty. She picked fights with her peace-loving sister, Hi`iaka, turning the younger goddess's friends into pillars of stone. And her recurring lava-flinging spats with suitor Kamapua`a, a demigod who could change his appearance at will, finally drove him into the sea, where he turned into a fish to escape from her wrath.

But Pele can be kind if the mood suits her. It is said that before every major eruption, she appears in human form as a wrinkled old woman walking along isolated back roads. Those who offer her a ride home return home to find a river of boiling magma abruptly halted inches from their property or diverted around their houses. Those who pass her by find their homes devastated by molten lava. Many hula hālau still make pilgrimages to the rim of Kīlauea—Pele's home on the Big Island—where they honor the fickle goddess with prayers, chants, and offerings of gin and flower leis.

In addition to battling the elements and each other, gods were thought to have intervened in the daily lives of early Hawaiians. Storms that destroyed homes and crops, a fisherman's poor catch, or a loss in battle were blamed on the wrath of angry gods. And according to legend, an industrious race of diminutive people called menehune built aqueducts, fishponds, and other constructs requiring advanced engineering knowledge unavailable to early Hawaiians. Living in remote hills and valleys, these secretive workers toiled only in darkness and completed complex projects in a single night. Their handiwork can still be seen on all the Islands.

Also at night, during certain lunar periods, a traveler might inadvertently come across the Night Marchers—armies of dead warriors, chiefs, and ancestral spirits whose feet never touch the ground. They float the ancient highways, chanting and beating their drums, pausing only to claim the spirits of their brethren who died that night. It was believed that such an encounter would bring certain death unless a relative among the marchers pleaded for the victim's life.

organic Mexican fare. If you're in the mood for a mug of steaming caffe latte with a hot croissant, stop by **Waimea Coffee & Company** (⊠ Parker Sq., off Kawaihae Rd., Waimea ☎ 808/885–4472).

BEACHES

Don't believe anyone who tells you the Big Island lacks beaches. It actually has 80 or more, and new ones appear—and disappear—regularly. In 1989 a black-sand beach, Kamoamoa, formed when molten lava shattered as it hit cold ocean waters. Kamoamoa was the largest of the black-sand beaches, more than ½ mi long and 25 yards wide, until it was closed by new lava flows in 1992. Some beaches are just a little hard to get to—several are hidden behind elaborate hotels or down unmarked roads.

Note that many beaches have dangerous undertows—rip currents and pounding shore breaks may cause serious risk anywhere at any time. The surf tends to get rough in winter. To be safe, swim only when you see other visitors swimming in the area. Local surfers are not an indication that the area is safe. Few public beaches have lifeguards.

That said, the most beautiful, swimmable white-sand beaches stretch along the Kohala coastline. Beaches below are listed in a counterclockwise direction around the island, starting from the northern tip. For overnight permits, necessary at all parks, contact the Department of Land and Natural Resources for state parks and the Department of Parks and Recreation for county parks.

Keōkea Beach Park. Driving back from the end of Highway 270 at the Pololū overlook to the north, you'll see a curvy road angle off to the right. Follow it for a mile, past the cemetery with the weathered old stones, and you'll come upon the green lawns and large picnic pavilion of Keōkea Beach Park. You can fish from the black boulders, but heavy surf makes this a hazardous swimming beach. This is a popular weekend destination for local folks. ✛ *Off Hwy. 270, near Pololū overlook* ☎ *808/961–8311.*

Māhukona Beach Park. Next to the abandoned Port of Māhukona, in the Kohala District, where sugar was once shipped by rail to be loaded on boats, Māhukona Beach's old docks and buildings are a treat for photographers. You can still view remnants of shipping machinery in the clear water, but heavy surf makes swimming dangerous at times. It's a pleasant picnicking spot, with rest rooms and showers but no sandy beach. ⊠ *Off Hwy. 270, Māhukona* ☎ *808/961–8311.*

★ **Spencer Beach Park.** This spot is popular with local families because of its reef-protected, gently sloping white-sand beach, and it's safe for swimming year-round. Close to large shade trees are cooking facilities, showers, and a large pavilion with electrical outlets. You can walk from here to the Puʻukoholā and Mailekini heiaus. ✛ *Entry road off Hwy. 270, uphill from Kawaihae Harbor* ☎ *808/961–8311.*

★ **Kaunaʻoa Beach at Mauna Kea Beach Hotel.** It's a toss-up whether this or neighboring Hāpuna is the most beautiful beach on the island. Kaunaʻoa unfolds like a white crescent, and it slopes very gradually. It's a great place for snorkeling. In winter, however, the powerful waves can be dangerous. Amenities are hotel-owned. Public parking places are limited. ✛ *Entry through gate to Mauna Kea Beach Resort, off Hwy. 19.*

Fodor'sChoice **Hāpuna Beach State Recreation Area.** This beach, part of a 61-acre park,
★ forms a ½-mi crescent of glistening sand guarded by rocky points at either end. The surf can be hazardous in winter, but in summer the gradual slope of the beach can stretch as wide as 200 ft into a perfectly blue

ocean—ideal for swimming, snorkeling, and bodysurfing. State cabins are available. There's even a little restaurant. Lifeguards are not always on duty, so take care. ✛ *Between Mauna Kea Beach and Mauna Lani resorts, off Hwy. 19* ☎ *808/974–6200.*

Holoholokai Beach Park. This rocky beach of black-lava formations and white-coral clinkers, with bathrooms, picnic tables, barbecue grills, and a small grassy area nearby, makes for a pleasant snorkeling and sunbathing afternoon. Just before the beach park, you can explore historic Puakō Petroglyph Park: Malama Trail meanders ⁷⁄₁₀ mi through brush and *kiawe* trees to an area of lava covered with the ancient etchings of Hawaiian figures and animals. ✛ *Off Hwy. 19 at the Fairmont Orchid Hawai'i.*

Fodor'sChoice **'Anaeho'omalu Beach, at Waikoloa Beach Marriott.** This expansive beach
★ on the west coast, also known as A-Bay, is perfect for swimming, windsurfing, snorkeling, and diving. Some equipment is for rent at the north end. Be sure to wander around the ancient fishponds and petroglyph fields. ✛ *Follow Waikoloa Beach Dr. to Royal Waikoloan Resort, then signs to park and beach right-of-way to south.*

★ **Kiholo Bay.** A 20-minute hike across lava leads to an oceanfront with private homes but no public facilities. The huge, spring-fed Luahinewai Pond anchors the south end of the bay, and the three black-pebble beaches are fine for swimming in calm weather. At the northern end, Wainānāli'i Pond (a 5-acre lagoon) is a feeding site for green sea turtles. The two ponds are off-limits to swimmers. Kamehameha I had a well-stocked fishpond here that was destroyed by lava in 1859. ⊠ *Hwy. 19, mile marker 81, unmarked road.*

Kekaha Kai State Park. Beyond the park's entrance, at the end of separate, unpaved roads, about 1½ mi each, await two sandy beaches, Mahai'ula, to the south, and Kua Bay, to the north. In calm weather, they are great for swimming. You can hike along a historic 4½-mi trail from one to the other, but be prepared for the heat and bring lots of drinking water. Mahai'ula has a picnic area and portable toilets. ✛ *Sign about 2 mi north of Keāhole–Kona International Airport, off Hwy. 19, marks rough 1½-mi road to beach* ☎ *808/327–4958 or 808/974–6200.*

★ **Kaloko–Honokōhau National Historical Park.** Part of a 1,160-acre park, two beaches, rich in archaeology and good for swimming, are down the road from Honokōhau Harbor. 'Alula is a slip of white sand, a short walk over lava to the left of the harbor entrance. Honokōhau Beach, a ¾-mi stretch with ruins of ancient fishponds, is north of the harbor. At the north end of the beach, a historic trail leads mauka across the lava to a freshwater pool. A Hawaiian settlement up until the 19th century, the park is being developed as a cultural and historical site. For information about the park, visit its headquarters, a 5- to 10-minute drive away. ✛ *Off Hwy. 19, at Honokōhau Harbor, or via park access between mile markers 96 and 97* ⊠ *Park Headquarters, Kaloko New Industrial Park, 73-4786 Kanalani St., No. 14* ☎ *808/329–6881* ⊕ *www. nps.gov* ☉ *Park road gate 8 AM–3:30 PM.*

Old Kona Airport State Recreation Area. The unused runway—great for jogging—is still visible above this beach at Kailua Park, which has picnic tables, showers, bathroom facilities, tennis courts, and palm trees strung along the shore. The beach has a sheltered, sandy inlet with tide pools for children, but for adults it's better for snorkeling than it is for swimming. An offshore surfing break known as Old Airport is popular with Kona surfers. ⊠ *North end of Kuakini Hwy., Kona* ☎ *808/ 327–4958 or 808/974–6200.*

★ **White Sands, Magic Sands, or Disappearing Sands Beach Park.** Now you see it, now you don't. Overnight, winter waves wash away this small white-sand beach on Ali'i Drive just south of Kailua-Kona. In summer you'll know you've found it when you see the body- and board surfers. Rest rooms, showers, a lifeguard tower, and a coconut grove create a convenient summer hangout, but this isn't a great beach for swimming. ✛ *4½ mi south of Kailua-Kona on Ali'i Dr.* ☎ *808/961–8311.*

★ **Kahalu'u Beach Park.** This spot was a favorite of King Kalākaua, whose summer cottage is on the grounds of the Ohana Keauhou Beach Resort next door. Kahalu'u is popular with commoners, too, and on weekends there are just too many people. On the other hand, this is one of the best snorkeling spots—it's a good place to see reef fish up close, as the fish are used to snorkelers. But beware: a strong riptide during high surf pulls swimmers away from shore. Facilities include a pavilion, rest rooms, showers, a lifeguard tower, and limited parking. A narrow path takes you directly to the resort's beach bar, which serves sandwiches and plate lunches. ✛ *5½ mi south of Kailua-Kona on Ali'i Dr.* ☎ *808/961–8311.*

Ho'okena Beach Park. You'll feel like an adventurer when you come upon Ho'okena, at the northern end of Kauhakō Bay. When Mark Twain visited, 2,500 people populated the busy seaport village. You can still find gas lampposts dating from the early 1900s. This dark-gray coral-and-lava-sand beach offers good swimming, snorkeling, and bodysurfing. Rest rooms, showers, and picnic tables are available at the park. The access road is narrow and bumpy. ✛ *2-mi drive down road bordered by ruins of stone wall off Hwy. 11, 23 mi south of Kailua-Kona* ☎ *808/961–8311.*

Nāpō'opo'o Beach Park. The best way to enjoy this marine preserve is to take a snorkel, scuba, or glass-bottom boat tour from Keauhou Bay. A 27-ft white obelisk indicates where Captain James Cook was killed in 1779. Although this 6-acre beach park has a picnic pavilion, the beach consists of rocks, making access to the water difficult. ✉ *Kealakekua Bay* ☎ *808/961–8311.*

★ **Green Sand (Mahana) Beach.** You need a permit, good hiking shoes, and a four-wheel-drive vehicle to get to this green crescent, one of the most unusual and prettiest beaches on the island. The beach lies at the base of Pu'u o Mahana, a cinder cone formed during an early eruption of Mauna Loa. The greenish tint is caused by an accumulation of olivine that forms in volcanic eruptions. Swimming is dangerous in this windy, remote area, and there are no facilities. Still, in calm water close to the shore, the aquamarine surf feels great and you find yourself in a surreal grass-plain landscape. Follow the trail 2 to 3 mi along the shoreline. Permits can be obtained from **Hawaiian Homelands** (✉ 160 Baker Ave., Hilo 96720 ☎ 808/974–4250). There you can get a key to the gate for a $25 deposit. ✛ *2½ mi northeast of South Point, off Hwy. 11.*

★ **Punalu'u Beach Park.** The endangered Hawaiian green sea turtle nests in the black sand of this beautiful and easily accessible beach. You can see the turtles feeding on the seaweed along the surfbreak. Fishponds are just inland. At the northern end of the beach near the boat ramp lie the ruins of a heiau and a flat sacrificial stone. This used to be a sugar and army port until the tidal wave of 1946 destroyed the buildings. Offshore rip currents are extremely dangerous, though you'll see a few local surfers riding the waves. There are rest rooms across the road. Inland is a memorial to Henry Opukaha'ia. In 1809, when he was 17, Opukaha'ia swam out to a fur-trading ship in the harbor and asked to sail as a cabin boy. When he reached New England, he entered the Foreign Mission School in Connecticut, but he died of typhoid fever in 1818. His dream of bringing Christianity to the Islands inspired the American Board of Missionaries in 1820 to send the first Protestant missionaries to Hawai'i. ✉ *Hwy. 11, 27 mi south of Hawai'i Volcanoes National Park* ☎ *808/ 961–8311.*

MacKenzie State Recreation Area. This 13-acre park shaded by iron-woods is good for picnicking. You can't swim here, but there are rest rooms. ⊕ *Off Hwy. 137, 9 mi northeast of Kaimū* ☒ *Puna District* ☎ *808/974–6200.*

Isaac Hale Beach Park. Oceanfront park facilities include rest rooms and picnic areas. It's a good place for an afternoon nap but is dangerous for swimming. ⊕ *Off Hwy. 137, about 10 mi northeast of Kaimū* ☒ *Puna District* ☎ *808/961–8311.*

Ahalanui Park. This 3-acre beach park, also known as Pū'āla'a, has a ½-acre pond heated by volcanic steam. There's nothing like swimming in this warm pool, but the nearby ocean is rough. Note: the thermal pool has had bacterial-contamination problems recently; check with the life-guard/attendant on safety and heed all posted signs. Drinking water and a few tables are available for picnicking, and there are portable rest rooms. ⊕ *Southeast of Pāhoa, 2½ mi south of junction of Hwys. 132 and 137* ☒ *Puna District* ☎ *808/961–8311.*

★ **Leleiwi Beach Park and Richardson Ocean Park.** Along Hilo's Keaukaha shoreline laced with bays, inlets, lagoons, and pretty parks, these two beaches are adjacent to each other. The grassy area is ideal for picnics. The beaches are rocky and dangerous for swimming, though you can dip your feet in the shallow areas. ☒ *2349 Kalaniana'ole Ave., follow Kalaniana'ole Ave. along the water about 4 mi east of Hilo* ☎ *808/961–8311.*

Onekahakaha Beach Park. A protected, white-sand beach makes this a favorite for Hilo families with small children. Lifeguards are on duty. The park has picnic pavilions, rest rooms, and showers. ⊕ *Follow Kalaniana'ole Ave. 3 mi east of Hilo* ☎ *808/961–8311.*

Reeds Bay Beach Park. Rest rooms, showers, drinking water, calm and safe swimming, and proximity to downtown Hilo are the enticements of this cove. Cold freshwater springs seep from the bottom of a nearby pond and rise in the saltwater. ☒ *Banyan Dr. and Kalaniana'ole Ave., Hilo* ☎ *808/961–8311.*

WHERE TO EAT

Updated by
Leslie
Westbrook

Choosing a place to eat in the western part of the Big Island is difficult, as there are many good, established restaurants and ethnic eateries. All along Ali'i Drive in Kailua-Kona, sunny little cafés with indoor-outdoor seating serve numerous cuisines as well as regular American and Hawai'i regional food. Hotels along the Kohala Coast invest in top chefs, and between that and the opulent settings, diners are rarely disappointed. Kawaihae Harbor offers some fun choices, and upcountry Waimea—just a 40-minute drive inland from the resorts—also has a variety of pop-ular restaurants. Although Hilo's dining scene may seem less exciting, restaurants are often inexpensive family places where good, substantial food makes up for lack of atmosphere.

Hilo

American/Casual

$$–$$$ ✕ **Harrington's.** A great view and a daily happy hour make this steak and seafood restaurant on Reed's Bay a popular place. You can't go wrong with the catch of the day served in a tangy citrus-wasabi beurre blanc or the New York peppercorn steak. For lunch try the Harrington's Burger, served with a cream cheese aioli. ☒ *135 Kalaniana'ole Ave.* ☎ *808/961–4966* ☐ *MC, V.*

$$–$$$ ✕ **Seaside Restaurant.** The Nakagawa family has been running this home-based eatery and aquafarm since the early 1920s. The decor is bare-bones, with plastic chairs and wooden tables, but Seaside serves

some of the best and freshest fish on the island. Locals travel far for the fried *āholehole* (young Hawaiian flagtail). Not a fish eater? Try the grilled lamb chops, pasta, or chicken. Arrive before sunset and request a table on the patio for a view of fishponds and egret roosting. ⊠ *1790 Kala-niana'ole Ave.* ☎ *808/935–8825* ▤ *AE, DC, MC, V* ☉ *Closed Mon. No lunch.*

$–$$ ✕ **Uncle Billy's Restaurant.** Uncle Billy's is pure Hawaiian kitsch—right out of 1930s Hollywood—but the thatch roofs, tinkling capiz-shell wind chimes, and Tahitian-print curtains add to the fun, as does a free nightly hula show. Choose from mahimahi meunière, teriyaki chicken, pastas, soup and salad, and local specialties. ⊠ *Hilo Bay Hotel, 87 Banyan Dr.* ☎ *808/935–0861* ▤ *AE, D, DC, MC, V* ☉ *No lunch.*

$ ✕ **Ken's House of Pancakes.** For years this 24-hour coffee shop between the airport and the Banyan Drive hotels has been a gathering place for Hilo residents. As its name implies, Ken's serves good pancakes and omelets, but there are close to 180 items to choose from on the menu. Wednesday is paniolo prime-rib night. ⊠ *1730 Kamehameha Ave.* ☎ *808/935–8711* ▤ *AE, D, DC, MC, V.*

Chinese

$–$$ ✕ **Ting Hao.** This Mandarin restaurant on the edge of Hilo Bay empha-sizes fresh island fish with offerings that change daily. Entrées include spicy Szechuan and Hunan dishes and scrumptious specialties from Tai-wan and Beijing. The special slow-roasted Peking duck, wrapped in a Mandarin pastry layer and served with plum sauce, must be ordered a day in advance. ⊠ *Hawai'i Naniloa Resort, 93 Banyan Dr.* ☎ *808/935–8888* ▤ *AE, D, DC, MC, V* ☉ *Closed Tues.*

Eclectic

$$–$$$ ✕ **Restaurant Kaikodo.** This ground-floor restaurant will serve as the an-chor for an art museum scheduled to open on the second floor in the spring of 2004. A 20-ft-long Victorian bar graces the lounge area, Italian chan-deliers hang from the 17-ft ceilings, and 19th-century Chinese doors add to the dining room. The menu is just as diverse as the decor, with Chi-nese, French, and Indian cuisines featured. The historic building has gone through a couple of different incarnations—the last was as a bank, and the restaurants 2,000 bottles of wine are stored in the former vaults. ⊠ *60 Keawe St.* ☎ *808/961–2558* ▤ *AE, D, DC, MC, V.*

Hawaiian

¢–$ ✕ **Kuhio Grille.** There is no ambience to speak of, and your water is served in unbreakable plastic, but if you're searching for local fare—that eclec-tic and undefinable fusion of ethnic cuisines—Kuhio Grille is a must. Sam Araki serves a 1-pound *laulau,* made with Waipi'o Valley–grown taro leaves and pork, alongside "loco" plate lunches and grilled meats. This diner at the edge of Hilo's largest shopping mall opens as early as 6 AM. ⊠ *Prince Kūhiō Shopping Plaza, 111 E. Puainako St., at Hwy. 11* ☎ *808/959–2336* ▤ *AE, MC, V.*

Italian

$$–$$$ ✕ **Pescatore.** Intimately Italian, with dim lights, stately high-backed chairs, and dark wood, Pescatore serves traditional dishes such as a clas-sic cioppino. Families love the pastas made to please choosy children. In addition to lunch and dinner daily, the restaurant serves breakfast on weekends. ⊠ *235 Keawe St., at Haili St.* ☎ *808/969–9090* ▤ *AE, D, DC, MC, V.*

Japanese

$–$$$ ✕ **Ocean Sushi Deli/Tsunami Grill and Tempura.** Fresh seafood dishes and superb sushi rolls will make you quickly forget the Formica tables and

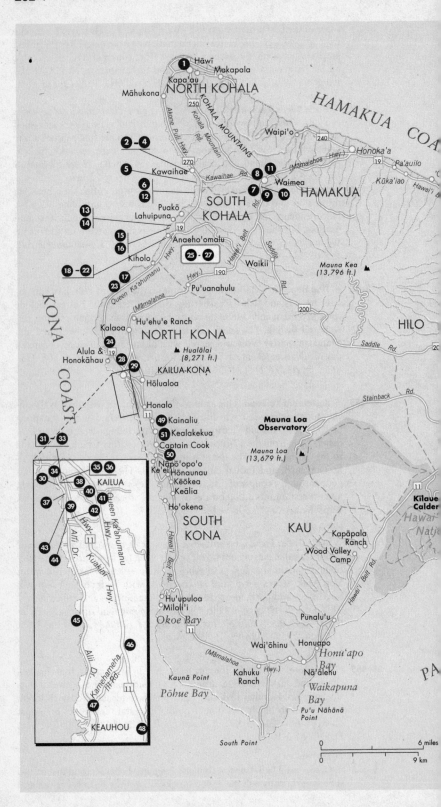

Where to Eat
on the Big Island

neon lights. 'Ahi *poke* (seasoned raw tuna), fried limpets, and chewy *taco* (octopus) salad are favorites with the local crowd, but there are also more familiar, equally delectable dishes, such as sake-steamed scallops. The place is popular and almost always crowded. You can also choose from the menu at Tsunami Grill and Tempura—tempura, saimin, and the like— and your waitress will pop across the street to get your order. Both menus are offered at both restaurants. ⊠ *239 Keawe St.* ☎ *808/961–6625* ⊟ *AE, MC, V* ☉ *Closed Sun.*

Thai

$ ✕ **Naung Mai.** This restaurant in downtown Hilo is nothing more than five tables, three booths, and owner-chef Alisa Rung Khongnok hard at work in the visible kitchen. It's hard to find, but a colorful exterior, a cozy interior with mellow music and original art on the walls, and fresh, reasonably priced meals greet intrepid customers. It just may be the best Thai food on the island. ⊠ *86 Kīlauea Ave.* ☎ *808/934–7540* ⊟ *MC, V* ☉ *Closed Sun. No lunch Wed. or Sat.*

$ ✕ **Royal Siam.** A downtown Hilo fixture, this authentic Thai eatery offers little ambience in its straightforward dining room. But you don't need a dramatic view when you can choose from a menu that includes five curries and plenty of stir-fry—the tangy stir-fried garlic shrimp with coconut milk and wild mushrooms is particularly good. ⊠ *70 Mamo St.* ☎ *808/961–6100* ⊟ *AE, D, DC, MC, V* ☉ *Closed Sun.*

Volcano

Contemporary

★ $$–$$$ ✕ **Kīlauea Lodge.** Chef Albert Jeyte combines contemporary trends with traditional cooking styles from the mainland, France, and his native Hamburg, Germany. Built in 1937 as a YMCA camp, the restaurant still has the original "Friendship Fireplace" made from stones from around the world. The roaring fire, koa tables, and warm lighting create a lodge feel inside the sunny main building. Entrées include venison, duck à l'orange with an apricot-mustard glaze, and authentic hasenpfeffer (braised rabbit served with Jeyte's signature sauerbraten) to name a few. ⊠ *Old Volcano Hwy., Volcano Village* ☎ *808/967–7366* ⊟ *AE, MC, V* ☉ *No lunch.*

Continental

$$–$$$ ✕ **Ka 'Ōhelo Dining Room.** Eat here just for the incomparable views of Kīlauea Caldera. During the day this old, well-worn locale serves up breakfast and luncheon buffets primarily for tour groups. Roast prime rib, king crab legs, lamb chops, seafood, and pasta are on the dinner menu. Art aficionados appreciate several magnificent early-19th-century oil paintings of the volcano. ⊠ *Volcano House, Hawai'i Volcanoes National Park* ☎ *808/967–7321* ⊟ *AE, D, DC, MC, V.*

Thai

$–$$ ✕ **Thai Thai.** Tucked behind the hardware store, this modest little eatery offers simple but savory Thai dishes. Try mahimahi in one of the five curries or opt for a refreshing shrimp and green-papaya salad with lime juice, chili, and garlic. The staff is friendly, and there is a full bar. ⊠ *19-4084 Old Volcano Rd.* ☎ *808/967–7969* ⊟ *AE, D, MC, V.*

Kailua-Kona & South Kona

American/Casual

$$$ ✕ **Beachcomber's & Paradise Lounge.** Many come to this casual, oceanfront restaurant (formerly the Charthouse) at the far end of Waterfront Row for the happy hour (5 to 7) drinks, *pūpū* (appetizers), and sunset

views. The menu features a crunchy coconut-shrimp appetizer. Steak, seafood, and prime-rib entrées include the popular salad bar. ☒ *75-5770 Ali'i Dr., Kailua-Kona* ☏ *808/329–2451* ⊟ *AE, MC, V* ☯ *No lunch.*

$$$ ✕ **Jameson's by the Sea.** Sit outside next to the ocean or just inside the picture windows for glorious sunset views over Magic Sands Beach. You can choose between three or four daily fish specials, some prepared Cajun-style. Sautéed scallops with lemon butter and capers and Jameson's special creamy clam chowder are popular as well. Hawaiian music accompanies dinner five nights a week. ☒ *77-6452 Ali'i Dr., Kailua-Kona* ☏ *808/329–3195* ⊟ *AE, D, DC, MC, V* ☯ *No lunch weekends.*

$$–$$$ ✕ **Kona Beach Restaurant at King Kamehameha's Kona Beach Hotel.** The buffet-style meals at this Kailua-Kona hotel are themed and great for families: Monday it's Hawaiian, Tuesday and Thursday feature crab dishes and tempura, and Friday and Saturday are for prime rib and seafood. Tables overlook a torchlighted lawn. Beyond is the beach, with outrigger canoes and a thatch house built on a restored heiau. A Sunday champagne brunch is served from 9 to 1. ☒ *75-5660 Palani Rd., Kailua-Kona* ☏ *808/329–2911* ⊟ *AE, D, DC, MC, V.*

$$–$$$ ✕ **Kona Inn Restaurant.** In the historic Kona Inn, this open-air restaurant, which faces a wide lawn with the ocean beyond, has been a longtime favorite for cocktails at sunset in the café. A more formal menu is served in the main dining area; fresh fish—'ahi and mahimahi—and beef entrées are consistently delectable. ☒ *75-5744 Ali'i Dr., Kailua-Kona* ☏ *808/329–4455* ⊟ *AE, MC, V.*

$ ✕ **Manago Hotel.** Manago offers a full time-warp experience: a vintage neon sign identifies the hotel, and Formica tables, ceiling fans, and venetian blinds add to the flavor of this film noir spot. Pork chops are popular, but the *ono* (an albacore-like fish) is the best deal. The restaurant is about 20 minutes south of Kailua-Kona. ☒ *82-6155 Māmalahoa Hwy., Captain Cook* ☏ *808/323–2642* ⊟ *D, DC, MC, V* ☯ *Closed Mon.*

¢–$ ✕ **Ocean View Inn.** To those on a tight budget, this local hangout facing the pier at Kailua Bay has been a lifesaver for breakfast, lunch, and dinner since the 1920s. Chinese and American food are on the plate-lunch menu, and you can get Hawaiian specialties à la carte. The atmosphere is pure old-time diner, with a funky full bar. Note that the "ocean view" is across the road. ☒ *75-5683 Ali'i Dr., Kailua-Kona* ☏ *808/329–9998* ⊟ *No credit cards* ☯ *Closed Mon.*

Contemporary/Hawaiian

$$$ ✕ **Huggo's.** Open windows extend out over the rocks at the ocean's edge, and at night you can almost touch the manta rays drawn to the spotlights. Relax with a Kīlauea cocktail for two, or feast on fresh local seafood. **Huggo on the Rocks,** next door, has become Kailua-Kona's hot spot for drinks, wraps, sandwiches, pizza, and burgers. ☒ *75-5828 Kahakai Rd., off Ali'i Dr., Kailua-Kona* ☏ *808/329–1493* ⊟ *AE, D, DC, MC, V.*

$$–$$$ ✕ **Aloha Angel Café.** The lānai is the spot for breakfast or a healthful lunch; dinner is best had in the airy dining room, with its green wicker furniture, Hawaiian-print tablecloths, and vintage signage on the walls. The Hawaiian sweet-potato coconut salad is certainly unique, and entrées range from succulent lamb chops in a mushroom-merlot sauce to simple seafood curries. Don't miss the desserts from the on-site bakery. This is the perfect place to do dinner and a movie: the café is in the historic Aloha Theater & Performing Arts Center, which shows current releases and independent films. ☒ *79-7384 Māmalahoa Hwy., Kainaliu* ☏ *808/322–3383* ⊟ *AE, MC, V.*

$–$$ ✕ **Ke'ei Café.** This casual restaurant is in a plantation-style building 15 minutes south of Kona. Delicious dinners with Brazilian, Asian, and

European flavors utilize fresh ingredients provided by local farmers. Try the Thai red curry or wok-seared 'ahi accompanied by a selection from the extensive wine list. ☒ *Hwy. 11, ½ mi south of Kainaliu, Hōnaunau* ☎ *808/328–8451* ⌂ *Reservations essential* ▤ *No credit cards* ◷ *Closed Sun.*

¢–$ ✕ **Sam Choy's Kaloko Restaurant.** Locals come here to fuel up on the huge breakfast, *loco moco* (rice, gravy, and grilled onions topped with 13 choices ranging from Spam to teriyaki chicken), and home-style plate lunches. The restaurant is cavernous and cafeteria-like and is adorned with photos of celebrity visitors. It's in the Kaloka Light Industrial Park, off Highway 19, between Kona and the airport. ☒ *73-5576 Kauhola St., Kailua-Kona* ☎ *808/326–1545* ▤ *MC, V* ◷ *No dinner.*

¢ ✕ **Kona Mix Plate.** Don't be surprised if you find yourself rubbing elbows with lots of hungry locals at this inconspicuous Kona lunch spot. The antithesis of a tourist trap, this casual island favorite with fluorescent lighting and stark wooden tables is all about the food. Try the teriyaki chicken, shrimp tempura, or the *katsu*—a chicken breast fried with Japanese bread crumbs and served with a sweet, rich sauce. ☒ *341 Palani St., Kailua-Kona* ☎ *808/329–8104* ▤ *No credit cards.* ◷ *Closed Sun.*

Continental

$–$$$ ✕ **Tropics Café at Royal Kona Resort.** You'll have a lovely view from the open-air dining room of boats bobbing in Kailua Bay, outlined by the sun. The restaurant serves daily breakfast buffets and is open nightly for à la carte dinners, but the place is best known for its ample seafood and prime-rib buffets on Tuesday, Friday, and Saturday nights, a good-value feast for big eaters. The resort is within walking distance of central Kailua-Kona. ☒ *75-5852 Ali'i Dr., Kailua-Kona* ☎ *808/329–3111* ▤ *AE, D, DC, MC, V.*

Eclectic

$$$–$$$$ ✕ **Edward's at Kanaloa.** What is essentially a covered patio next to the pool of a condo complex also happens to be (weather permitting) a fabulous restaurant overlooking the ocean. Real tablecloths, fresh flowers, and candles on the tables make this a romantic spot as well. The Mediterranean menu includes wild game, fresh fish, rack of lamb, pork tenderloin, and a 16-ounce T-bone steak. Edward's is discretely tucked away inside a residential community just south of the Keahou Shopping Center; it's a good idea to call for directions. Reservations are recommended. ☒ *Kanaloa at Kona, 78-261 Manukai St., Kailua-Kona* ☎ *808/322–1003* ▤ *MC, V.*

$$–$$$ ✕ **Oodles of Noodles.** Chef Amy Ferguson-Ota combines Southwestern flavors with Hawai'i regional cuisine and a touch of French cooking. There are noodles of all types, in all shapes, from all ethnic backgrounds—be it as delicate spring rolls, a crisp garnish to an exquisite salad, or as orecchiette in Ota's tuna casserole with wok-seared spiced 'ahi and shiitake cream. ☒ *Crossroads Shopping Center, 75-1129 Henry St., Kailua-Kona* ☎ *808/329–9222* ▤ *AE, D, DC, MC, V.*

French

$$$–$$$$ ✕ **La Bourgogne.** A genial husband-and-wife team owns this relaxing, country-style restaurant with dark-wood walls and private, romantic booths. The traditional French menu has classics such as beef fillet with a cabernet sauvignon sauce, escargots, rack of lamb with roasted garlic and rosemary, and a less-traditional venison with a pomegranate glaze. ☒ *Kuakini Plaza S on Hwy. 11, 77-6400 Nālani St., Kailua-Kona* ☎ *808/329–6711* ⌂ *Reservations essential* ▤ *AE, D, DC, MC, V* ◷ *Closed Sun. and Mon. No lunch.*

Greek

\$\$ ✕ **Cassandra's Greek Taverna.** The blue and white colors of the Greek flag decorate Cassandra's. Greek salads, a gyro plate of sliced beef with roast potatoes, *dolmades* (grape leaves stuffed with meat and rice), moussaka, and a variety of souvlaki (lamb, beef, chicken) keep dinners interesting, but the restaurant's main attraction is the occasional belly-dancing performance on Saturday night. ⊠ *75-5719 W. Ali'i Dr., Kailua-Kona* ☎ *808/334–1066* ▭ *AE, D, DC, MC, V* ☉ *No lunch weekends.*

Indonesian

\$\$ ✕ **Sibu.** This restaurant is inside a tiny shopping mall (and nearly hidden by a large stone fountain) close to the pier in central Kailua-Kona. Try shrimp satay flavored with coconut milk, and red chili and served with peanut sauce. Be forewarned: the tasty Ayum Panggang Pedis (spicy grilled chicken fillets with black and red pepper) really packs a punch! ⊠ *75-5695 Ali'i Dr., Kailua-Kona* ☎ *808/329–1112* ▭ *No credit cards.*

Italian

\$\$–\$\$\$ ✕ **Ambrosia.** Save your appetite for this cozy restaurant—portions are generous, to say the least. The dining area is a mix of old-world Italian and tropical; the patio, which has candlelit tables, a fountain, and small twinkling lights strung around the foliage, is especially lovely in the evening. Chicken, seafood, and steak entrées and the obligatory pastas give you a lot to choose from, but the superb osso buco—falling-off-the-bone veal served with roasted asparagus and a Portobello-mushroom risotto—won't disappoint. Sunday evenings, when the Big Island Jazz Quartet jams in the bar, are lively. ⊠ *75-5719 Ali'i Dr., Kailua-Kona* ☎ *808/329–2002* ▭ *AE, D, DC, MC, V* ☉ *No lunch Sun.*

Japanese

\$–\$\$ ✕ **Teshima's.** Locals show up at Teshima's whenever they're in the mood for sashimi, beef *hekka* (beef and vegetables cooked together in an iron pot), and puffy shrimp tempura at a reasonable price. You might also want to try a *teishoku* (tray) of assorted Japanese delicacies. Service is laid-back and friendly. The restaurant is 15 minutes south of Kailua-Kona. ⊠ *Māmalahoa Hwy., Honalo* ☎ *808/322–9140* ▭ *No credit cards.*

¢–\$ ✕ **Hayashi's You Make the Roll.** This is your basic sushi take-out hole-in-the-wall, with a handful of plastic tables outside. The food is tasty, the service is fast, and the price is right. ⊠ *Kona Marketplace, 75-5725 Ali'i Dr., Kailua-Kona* ☎ *808/326–1322* ▭ *MC, V* ☉ *Closed Sun.*

Mexican

¢ ✕ **Tacos El Unico.** At last, Mexican food at the right price on the Big Island. You'll find an array of soft taco choices (carnitas, chicken, tongue, and more), burritos, tortas, great homemade tamales, quesadillas, and taquitos. Order at the counter, take a seat outside at one of a dozen yellow tables with blue umbrellas, and enjoy all the good flavors served up in those red plastic baskets. ⊠ *Kona Marketplace, 75-5725 Ali'i Dr., Kailua-Kona* ☎ *808/326–4033* ▭ *No credit cards.*

Thai

\$–\$\$ ✕ **Orchid Thai Cuisine.** This reasonably priced, family-run restaurant is off the beaten track in a small strip mall in Kona's old industrial area. It's cheerfully decorated with purple and gold Thai fabrics, and orchids (real and fake) abound. Entrées range from barbecue hen with lemongrass and garlic to basic curries (red, green, yellow, and "evil"); don't miss the summer rolls. Top off your meal with mango and sticky rice. ⊠ *77-5563 Kaiwi St., Suite B 27-28, Kailua-Kona* ☎ *808/327–9437* ▭ *MC, V* ☉ *Closed Sun.*

$-$$ ✕ **Thai Rin Restaurant.** The Thai chef-owner at this old-timer in Ali'i Sunset Plaza is likely to take your order, cook it, and bring it to your table himself. The menu includes five curries, a green-papaya salad, and a popular Thai Rin platter, which combines spring rolls, satay, *tom yum* (lemongrass soup), and beef salad. ✉ *75-5799 Ali'i Dr., Kailua-Kona* ☎ *808/329–2929* 🖃 *AE, D, DC, MC, V.*

Kohala Coast

American/Casual

$$-$$$$ ✕ **Big Island Steak House.** The walls here are adorned with Hawaiian kitsch dating from the '30s, '40s, and '50s—'ukuleles, steamer trunks, and a zany grass-skirted gorilla. As the name implies, the place serves steak—large portions in different styles, straight from the grill and without much fanfare. Also on the menu are local fish (charbroiled, sautéed, or blackened) and live lobster. There's an outdoor dining area overlooking the golf-course lake. The Merry Wahine Bar serves tropical libations. ✉ *King's Shops, Waikoloa Resort, Waikoloa Beach Dr., Waikoloa* ☎ *808/886–8805* 🖃 *AE, D, MC, V* ☺ *No lunch.*

$-$$$ ✕ **Kawaihae Harbor Grill and Seafood Bar.** This popular little restaurant is always packed—the enticing aromas alone would draw anyone in. Both the Harbor Grill and the new hot spot, the Seafood Bar (upstairs in a separate building), are housed in historic buildings from the 1850s. Errol Flynn was here—a life preserver off his yacht hangs in the thatched bar along with old records, hula skirts, a surfboard, and other vintage Hawaiiana. The bar is a good place to wait before your table is ready, or you can just feast from the all-pūpū menu. Fresh island fish (charbroiled, sautéed, and Cajun-style), ribs, chicken, and more are served at the equally atmospheric restaurant. ✉ *Kawaihae Harbor, Hwy. 270, Kawaihae* ☎ *808/882–1368* 🖃 *MC, V.*

Chinese

$$-$$$$ ✕ **Kirin at Hilton Waikaloa Village.** Rare Chinese artifacts fill the intimate dining room. Dozens of exotic dishes appear on the menu, many with unusual ingredient combinations. How about prawns with honey-glazed walnuts and a citrus dressing, or a whole open-flame-roasted Peking duck? ✉ *425 Waikoloa Beach Dr., Waikoloa* ☎ *808/886–1288* 🖃 *AE, D, DC, MC, V.*

$-$$$ ✕ **Grand Palace Chinese Restaurant.** A reasonable alternative in a land of high-price hotel dining, this restaurant offers dishes from most regions, including such standards as egg foo yung, wonton soup, chicken with snow peas, and beef with broccoli. More adventurous are sautéed local seafood, lobster, and sizzling shrimp with garlic sauce. Etched-glass panels are a nice embellishment. ✉ *King's Shops, Waikoloa Resort, Waikoloa Beach Dr., Waikoloa* ☎ *808/886–6668* 🖃 *AE, DC, MC, V.*

Contemporary/Hawaiian

★ $$$$ ✕ **Hale Samoa at Kona Village Resort.** Formal and romantic, this Kona Village restaurant has a magical atmosphere, especially at sunset. In a Samoan setting with tapa screens and candles, you can feast on five-course prix-fixe dinners that change daily. Specialties may include papaya-and-coconut bisque, duck stuffed with andouille sausage, or wok-charred prime strip loin. Reservations can be made only on the day you want to dine. ✉ *Kona Village, 12 mi north of Kailua-Kona on Hwy. 19, Kohala Coast* ☎ *808/325–5555* ⌚ *Reservations essential* 🖃 *AE, DC, MC, V* ☺ *Closed Wed., Fri., and 1 wk in Dec.*

★ $$$-$$$$ ✕ **The Batik at Mauna Kea Beach Hotel.** For the hotel's elegant signature restaurant—with its glass-enclosed, split-level waterfront dining room—executive chef Thomas Woods combines French-Mediterranean elements with Indonesian influences to create dazzling dishes such as a macadamia-nut-crusted ono with lemongrass-coconut emulsion. Most of the staff has been here for 15 years, so the service is seamless. ☒ 62-100 Mauna Kea Beach Dr., Kohala Coast ☎ 808/882–5810 ▤ AE, D, DC, MC, V ☉ Closed nights vary. No lunch.

★ $$$–$$$$ ✕ **CanoeHouse at the Mauna Lani Bay Hotel and Bungalows.** This award-winning, open-air beachfront restaurant belongs to Hawai'i's best. Its cuisine is Pacific Rim the way it used to be: a matching of pure Asian and Western flavors with imaginative entrées such as Shanghai lobster, spiced lacquered tofu with Chinese greens and jasmine rice, and the popular seafood salad. ☒ 68-1400 Mauna Lani Dr., Kohala Coast ☎ 808/885–6622 ▤ AE, D, DC, MC, V.

★ $$$–$$$$ ✕ **Coast Grille at Hāpuna Beach Prince Hotel.** This spacious, high-ceiling restaurant has a lānai overlooking the ocean. Oyster lovers should head straight to the oyster bar. The creative Pacific Rim menu has such seafood dishes as pan-seared *opah* (moonfish) in cardamom sauce and, when available, delicate farm-raised *moi*, in ancient times enjoyed only by chiefs. Don't overlook the appetizer sampler with seared 'ahi and tempura sushi, and save room for warm Valrhona chocolate cake. ☒ Hāpuna Beach Prince Hotel, 62-100 Kauna'oa Dr., Kohala Coast ☎ 808/880–3192 ▤ AE, D, DC, MC, V ☉ No lunch.

$$$–$$$$ ✕ **Hawai'i Calls at Waikoloa Beach Marriott.** With its retro art, Hawai'i Calls offers a nostalgic taste of the past, from the '20s to the '50s. The menu, however, is contemporary and fresh, changing seasonally, with specialties such as moi, seared crispy and served with coconut rice, pickled ginger, and spicy cucumber salad. Don't miss the macadamia chocolate tart with vanilla ice cream. The spacious outdoor setting is lovely—ask for a table near the koi pond and waterfall—and a great place to watch the sun set as tiki torches light up the gardens. The adjacent Clipper Lounge serves tropical drinks and features a bistro menu. ☒ 69-275 Waikoloa Beach Dr., Waikoloa ☎ 808/886–6789 ▤ AE, D, DC, MC, V.

$$$–$$$$ ✕ **Kamuela Provision Company at the Hilton Waikoloa Village.** Quiet guitar music, tables along a breezy lānai, and a sweeping view of the Kohala-Kona coastline are the perfect accompaniments to KPC's elegant yet down-to-earth Hawai'i regional cuisine. Popular are the bouillabaisse with nori *crostini* (toasted bread) and the Parker Ranch rib-eye steak with green peppercorn sauce. KPC is a great place to sip cocktails—the adjacent Wine Bar makes for a romantic evening in itself, with an appetizer menu and more than 40 labels available by the glass. ☒ 425 Waikoloa Beach Dr., Waikoloa ☎ 808/886–1234 ▤ AE, D, DC, MC, V ☉ No lunch.

$$$–$$$$ ✕ **Pahu i'a at Four Seasons Resort Hualālai.** The English translation for
Fodor'sChoice *pahu i'a* is "aquarium," and the 9- by 4-ft aquarium in the entrance casts
★ a dreamy light through this exquisite restaurant. Presentation is paramount—tables are beautifully set, with handblown glassware—and the food tastes as good as it looks. Asian-influenced dishes on the menu stand out for their layers of flavor. Don't miss the three sashimi and three caviar appetizers or the crispy whole moi served with Asian slaw, black beans, and sweet chili-lime vinaigrette. Reserve a table on the patio and you may be able to spot whales while dining. ☒ Four Seasons Resort Hualālai, 100 Ka'ūpūlehu Dr., Ka'ūpūlehu/Kona ☎ 808/325–8000 ▤ AE, D, DC, MC, V ☉ No lunch.

$$–$$$ ✕ **Bamboo Restaurant.** It's out of the way, but the food is good and the service has a country flair. Creative entrées feature fresh island fish prepared several ways. Thai-style fish, for example, combines lemongrass, kaffir lime leaves, and coconut milk—best washed down with a passion-fruit margarita or passion-fruit iced tea. Bamboo finishes, bold art-

work, and an old unfinished wooden floor make the restaurant cozy. Local musicians entertain on Friday and Saturday night. ⊠ *Old Takata Store, Hwy. 270, Hāwī* ☎ *808/889–5555* ☰ *MC, V* ⏱ *Closed Mon. No dinner Sun.*

$$–$$$ ✕ **Gallery Restaurant at Mauna Lani Bay Hotel and Bungalows.** You wouldn't expect such first-class food in what's essentially a clubhouse bordering the rolling greens of a golf course. You'll find open-air tables, an impressive koa bar, and professional staff. This upscale chop house has a simple menu that features prime rib, porterhouse steak, and fresh seafood. ⊠ *68-1400 Mauna Lani Dr., Kohala Coast* ☎ *808/885–7777* ☰ *AE, D, DC, MC, V* ⏱ *No dinner Sun.–Mon.*

★ **$$–$$$** ✕ **Roy's Waikoloa Bar and Grill.** You can easily fill up just on the enormous selection of appetizers at Roy Yamaguchi's cool and classy place overlooking a golf course lake. If you want a full meal, try the blackened island 'ahi with spicy soy-mustard-butter sauce or jade-pesto steamed Hawaiian whitefish with cilantro, ginger, garlic, and peanut oil. An extensive wines-by-the-glass list offers good pairing options. Be forewarned that the place tends to get noisy. ⊠ *King's Shops, Waikoloa Resort, Waikoloa Beach Dr., Waikoloa* ☎ *808/886–4321* ☰ *AE, D, DC, MC, V.*

Eclectic

★ **$$$–$$$$** ✕ **Brown's Beach House at the Fairmont Orchid.** The gorgeous torchlighted setting at this waterfront restaurant makes this the quintessential splurge. The restaurant combines a casual beach vibe with elegant resort dining at night. Wok-seared Kona lobster, farm-raised on the island and served with lobster ravioli in a wasabi-butter sauce, is rich and delicious. Leave room for the chocolate hazelnut soufflé. ⊠ *1 N. Kanikū Dr., Kohala Coast* ☎ *808/885–2000* ☰ *AE, D, DC, MC, V* ⏱ *No lunch.*

★ **$$$–$$$$** ✕ **The Grill at the Fairmont Orchid.** With a superb wine list and menu, this steak restaurant has earned its stellar reputation. Rich koa-wood paneling and a piano next to a small dance floor give it an old-world vibe. Entrées include robust dishes such as filet mignon of certified black Angus beef, wild game, and whole Keāhole-Maine lobster. Open-air seating is available, and the service is impeccable. ⊠ *The Fairmont Orchid, 1 N. Kanikū Dr., Kohala Coast* ☎ *808/885–2000* ⌔ *Reservations essential* ☰ *AE, D, DC, MC, V.*

$–$$$ ✕ **Café Pesto.** Both branches of Café Pesto—in the quaint harbor town of Kawaihae and in Hilo—are equally popular. Fresh local seafood, exotic pizzas (with chili grilled shrimp, shiitake mushrooms, and cilantro crème fraîche, for example), and Asian-inspired pastas and risottos reflect the ethnic diversity of the island. Local microbrews and a full-service bar make this a good place to end the evening. ⊠ *Kawaihae Shopping Center, Kawaihae* ☎ *808/882–1071* ⊠ *S. Hata Bldg., 308 Kamehameha Ave., Hilo* ☎ *808/969–6640* ☰ *AE, D, DC, MC, V.*

Italian

$$$–$$$$ ✕ **Donatoni's at the Hilton Waikoloa Village.** This romantic restaurant overlooking the boat canal resembles an Italian villa and serves scrumptious dishes with the subtle sauces of northern Italy. From mahimahi with marinated artichokes to fettuccine with Hawaiian lobster, this intimate place sets out to please. Be sure to look over the Italian-wine and champagne list. ⊠ *425 Waikoloa Beach Dr., Waimea* ☎ *808/886–1234* ☰ *AE, D, DC, MC, V* ⏱ *No lunch.*

Japanese

★ **$$$–$$$$** ✕ **Hakone Steakhouse and Sushi Bar at Hāpuna Beach Prince Hotel.** It's hard not to start whispering in this tranquil and graceful restaurant. Choose from exquisite Japanese sukiyaki, *shabu shabu* (thin slices of beef cooked in broth), and an elaborate sushi bar. The broad selection of sake (try a sakitini, a martini made with sake) is guaranteed to enliven your meal. ⊠ *Hāpuna Beach Prince Hotel, 62-100 Kaunaʻoa Dr., Waimea* ☎ *808/880–3192* ⊟ *AE, D, DC, MC, V* ◌ *No lunch.*

★ $$$–$$$$ ✕ **Imari at the Hilton Waikoloa Village.** This elegant restaurant, complete with waterfalls and a teahouse, serves sukiyaki and tempura aimed to please mainland tastes. Beyond the impressive display of Imari porcelain at the entrance, you'll find *teppanyaki* (beef or shrimp cooked table-side), shabu shabu, and an outstanding sushi bar. Impeccable service by kimono-clad waitresses adds to the quiet refinement. ⊠ *425 Waikoloa Beach Dr., Waimea* ☎ *808/886–1234* ⊟ *AE, D, DC, MC, V* ◌ *No lunch.*

Mexican

$–$$ ✕ **Tres Hombres Beach Grill.** This casual restaurant serves the usual Mexican combination plates (enchiladas, tacos, chiles rellenos) as well as burgers and sandwiches at lunch. Dinner items include bean-and-rice combinations, fresh fish, salads, and steaks. The separate bar is known for its Mexican beer and tequila selection. ⊠ *Kawaihae Shopping Center, Kawaihae* ☎ *808/882–1031* ⊠ *Aliʻi Dr. and Wālua Rd., Kailua-Kona* ☎ *808/329–2173* ⊟ *MC, V.*

Waimea

American/Casual

$$–$$$ ✕ **Koa House Grill.** In the heart of cowboy country, this bar and grill has developed into a busy stop for Waimea's residents. Local Parker Ranch Angus beef is a favorite, and a full salad bar has fresh Waimea greens. Large windows open out onto the Keck Observatory headquarters. ⊠ *Waimea Shopping Center, 65-1144 Māmalahoa Hwy.* ☎ *808/885–2088* ⊟ *AE, D, MC, V.*

$$–$$$ ✕ **Parker Ranch Grill.** With cowhides serving as wallpaper and riding boots as doorknobs, this popular restaurant makes no mistake about its paniolo identity and Parker Ranch heritage. In front of a blazing fire, the koa tables are a perfect setting for, of course, Parker Ranch beef entrées. A separate bar area offers a variety of pūpū. ⊠ *Parker Ranch Shopping Center, 67-1185 Māmalahoa Hwy.* ☎ *808/887–2624* ⊟ *AE, D, MC, V.*

Contemporary

$$$–$$$$ ✕ **Daniel Thiebaut.** Underneath 11-ft-high ceilings, the space once known as the historic Chock In Store (built in 1900) has been transformed into seven dining areas. Collectibles abound, such as antique porcelain, original bar stools, and a long redwood community dining table, once the store's countertop. Chef Daniel Thiebaut's French-Asian creations include an amazing appetizer of sweet-corn crab cake with a lemongrass, coconut, and lobster sauce. Other signature dishes include Hunan-style rack of lamb served with eggplant compote, and Big Island goat cheese. ⊠ *65-1259 Kawaihae Rd.* ☎ *808/887–2200* ⊟ *AE, D, DC, MC, V.*

★ $$$ ✕ **Merriman's.** This is the signature restaurant of Peter Merriman, one of the pioneers of Hawaiʻi regional cuisine. Merriman's is the home of the original wok-charred ʻahi, usually served with buttery Wainaku corn. If you prefer meat, try the Kahuā Ranch lamb, raised to the restaurant's specifications, or opt for the prime Kansas City Cut steak, grilled to order. The wine list includes 22 selections poured by the glass, and the staff is refreshingly knowledgeable. ⊠ *ʻOpelo Plaza, Hwy. 19 and ʻOpelo Rd.* ☎ *808/885–6822* ⌕ *Reservations essential* ⊟ *AE, MC, V.*

Continental

$$$–$$$$ ✕ **Edelweiss.** Faithful local diners and visitors alike flock to this relaxed, family-oriented restaurant with rustic redwood furnishings. The

rack of lamb is always excellent. Soup, salad, and coffee or tea are included in dinner prices. A varied menu includes 15 to 20 daily specials (such as a sausage platter and fresh seafood), many rich and with a German flavor. ⊠ *Hwy. 19, entering Waimea* ☎ *808/885–6800* ♠ *Reservations essential* ▤ *MC, V* ⊘ *Closed Sun. and Mon. and Sept.*

WHERE TO STAY

You'll almost always be able to find a room on the Big Island, but you might not get your first choice if you wait until the last minute. Make reservations six months to a year in advance if you're visiting during the winter season, December 15 through April 15. The week after Easter Sunday, when the Merrie Monarch Festival is in full swing, all of Hilo's rooms are taken. Kailua-Kona bursts at the seams in mid-October during the Ironman World Triathlon Championship. (Even tougher than trying to find a room at these times is trying to find a rental car.)

Hotel package deals are often available in all price categories and may include a rental car, meals, spa treatments, golf, and other activities. Children under 17 can sometimes stay for free. Check with a travel agent or visit the listed Web sites. All rooms have air-conditioning, a TV, and a phone unless otherwise indicated.

If you choose a B&B, inn, or an out-of-the-way hotel, explain your expectations fully and ask plenty of questions before booking. Be clear about your travel and location needs. Some places require stays of two or three days. Many B&Bs close to Hawai'i Volcanoes National Park are not the best locations for beach and sun worshipers; rain forests come with the price of humid conditions. When booking, ask about car-rental arrangements, as many B&B networks can offer discounted rates.

Hilo

★ $$–$$$$ ▦ **Hilo Hawaiian Hotel.** With large bay-front rooms offering spectacular views of Mauna Kea and Coconut Island, this is one of the most pleasant lodgings on Hilo Bay. Streetside rooms overlook the golf course. Most accommodations have private lānai, and kitchenettes are available in some one-bedroom suites. Views of the bay are showcased in the Queen's Court dining room, and the Wai'oli Lounge has entertainment Thursday through Saturday. ⊠ *71 Banyan Dr., 96720* ☎ *808/935–9361, 800/367–5004 from the mainland, 800/272–5275 interisland* ⎙ *808/961–9642* ⊕ *www.hilohawaiian.com* ⇌ *286 rooms, 6 suites* ♠ *Restaurant, some kitchenettes, refrigerators, pool, bar, meeting room* ▤ *AE, D, DC, MC, V.*

★ $$$ ▦ **Shipman House Bed & Breakfast Inn.** You'll have a choice between one of three rooms in the main house—a 100-year-old turreted "castle"— or one of two rooms in a separate cottage unit. The B&B is on 5½ verdant acres on Reed's Island; the house is furnished with antique koa and period pieces, some dating from the days when Queen Lili'uokalani came to tea. On Tuesday night, an authentic hula school practices Hawai'i's ancient dances in the house. ⊠ *131 Kaiulani St., 96720* ☎ *808/934–8002 or 800/627–8447* ⎙ *808/934–8002* ⊕ *www.hilo-hawaii.com* ⇌ *3 rooms, 2 cottage rooms* ♠ *Fans, refrigerators, library; no a/c, no room phones, no room TVs, no smoking* ▤ *AE, MC, V* ⊚ *CP.*

$$–$$$ ▦ **Hawai'i Naniloa Resort.** This is probably the most contemporary hotel on Hilo's waterfront. What you get is a great view of Hilo Bay— ask for a room with an ocean view—and a feeling of open space. With its glass walls, white-painted lānai, and rooms in pastel shades of green and coral, the hotel is more than adequate for business travelers and

for those who seek a touch of the luxury resort. Paradise Spa specializes in Hawaiian treatments. ⊠ *93 Banyan Dr., 96720* ☎ *808/969–3333 or 808/969–1175 on the Big Island, 800/367–5360 from the mainland, 800/442–5845 interisland* 🖨 *808/969–6622* ⊕ *www.naniloa.com* ➪ *325 rooms, 15 suites* ⚒ *2 restaurants, in-room safes, refrigerators, 9-hole golf course, tennis court, 2 pools, health club, spa, bar, dance club, laundry facilities* ▤ *AE, DC, MC, V.*

$$ 🏨 **Hilo Seaside Hotel.** It's as close to the airport as you can get, which means it can get noisy during the day. It's also a friendly, laid-back, and otherwise peaceful place, with neutral rooms that have private lānai. The nicest ones overlook the koi-filled lagoon or are around the pool. The staff is friendly, the restaurant is local-style, and the tropical foliage around you gives you a sense of old Hawai'i. ⊠ *126 Banyan Way, 96720* ☎ *808/935–0821 or 800/560–5557* 🖨 *808/969–9195* ⊕ *www. hiloseasidehotel.com* ➪ *135 rooms* ⚒ *Restaurant, fans, some kitchenettes, refrigerators, pool, laundry facilities* ▤ *AE, D, DC, MC, V.*

$–$$ 🏨 **Hale Kai.** On a bluff above Hilo Bay, just 2 mi from downtown Hilo, this 5,400-square-ft modern home has four impeccable rooms with patios and a private loft that is ideal for families—all with grand ocean views and within earshot of lapping waves. Fresh flowers add a warm, European touch. The Norwegian-Hawaiian hosts, Evonne and Paul Bjornen, serve a delightful breakfast—fruits, breads, and special egg dishes—on an outdoor deck or in the kitchen's bay-window dining area. ⊠ *111 Honoli'i Pali St., 96720* ☎ *808/935–6330* 🖨 *808/935–8439* ⊕ *www.interpac.net/~halekai* ➪ *4 rooms, 1 suite* ⚒ *Fans, pool, hot tub, laundry service; no smoking* ▤ *No credit cards.*

$–$$ 🏨 **Hilo Bay Hotel, Uncle Billy's.** Don't expect more than a casual, inexpensive place to stay at this friendly, easygoing hotel—a popular stopover for Neighbor Islanders who enjoy proprietor Uncle Billy Kimo's Hawaiian hospitality. A nightly hula show and entertainment during dinner are part of the fun. ⊠ *87 Banyan Dr., 96720* ☎ *808/935–0861, 800/ 367–5102 from the mainland, 800/442–5841 interisland* 🖨 *808/935–7903* ⊕ *www.unclebilly.com* ➪ *145 rooms* ⚒ *Restaurant, some kitchenettes, refrigerators, pool, bar, laundry facilities, Internet, meeting room, free parking* ▤ *AE, D, DC, MC, V.*

$ 🏨 **Dolphin Bay Hotel.** True, the units are modest, but they are clean and inexpensive, and the staff has plenty of aloha. Coffee and fresh fruit are offered daily. Just four blocks from Hilo Bay, in a residential area called Pu'ue'o, the private hotel borders a verdant 2-acre Hawaiian garden with jungle trails and shady places to rest. The owner loves the Volcano and the camera: stunning lava pictures adorn the common area. Guests of the hotel return repeatedly, and it's ideal for families who seek a home base. ⊠ *333 'Iliahi St., 96720* ☎ *808/935–1466* 🖨 *808/935–1523* ⊕ *www.dolphinbayhotel.com* ➪ *13 rooms, 4 1-bedroom units, 1 2-bedroom unit* ⚒ *Fans, kitchens, kitchenettes, microwaves; no a/c, no room phones, no room TVs* ▤ *MC, V.*

$ 🏨 **The Inn at Kulaniapia.** With an awesome view of Hilo Bay 4 mi below, as well as access to a magnificent 120-ft waterfall that tumbles into a 300-ft-wide swimming pond, this inn is an oasis of beauty and tranquility. Trails meander to the river, and Hilo is just a 15-minute drive away over sugarcane roads. Hosts Jane and Len Sutton added Asian accents, koa, and eucalyptus wood floors to the inn. Complete breakfasts are served, and you can cook an informal dinner on the barbecue. ⊙ *Box 11338, 96721* ☎ *808/966–6373 or 888/838–6373* ⊕ *www.waterfall.net* ➪ *4 rooms* ⚒ *No smoking* ▤ *AE, MC, V.*

¢–$ 🏨 **Maureen's Bed & Breakfast.** This historic, old family mansion is opposite Kealoha Beach Park and just 4 mi from Hilo. The house is surrounded by gardens and has lovely redwood and cedar woodwork

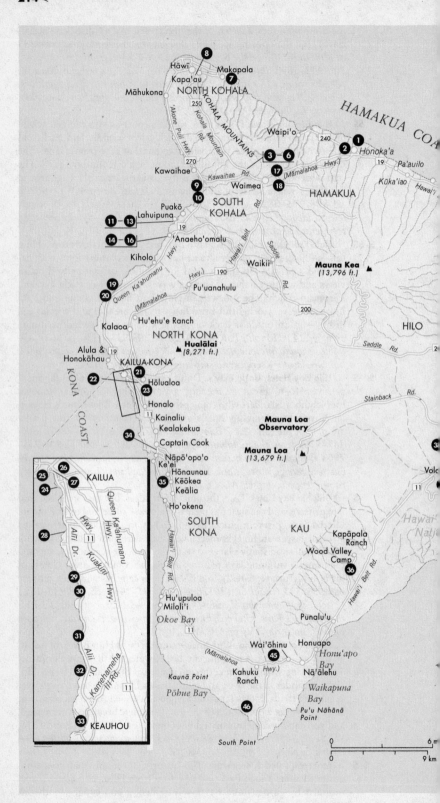

Where to Stay on the Big Island

throughout as well as an open-beam cathedral ceiling in the main room. Dual staircases wind up to open balconies, and guest rooms have antique furniture, artwork, and bookcases for a rustic, gallery-like feel. ⊠ *1896 Kalaniana'ole St., Hilo 96720* ☎ *808/935–9018 or 800/953–9018* 🖷 *808/961–5596* ⊕ *www.maureenbnb.com* ⇨ *5 rooms with shared baths* ⚓ *Beach, lounge; no kids under 7* 🚫 *No credit cards.*

¢–$ 🖷 **Wild Ginger Inn Bed & Breakfast.** Funky and wildly pink with turquoise trim, this inn is reminiscent of '40s Hawai'i. The old, wooden building has simple plantation-style rooms that appeal to a younger crowd. Most rooms have double and twin beds. A big lawn and a jungle garden run along a stream bank. A complimentary buffet breakfast is served on the lānai lobby. ⊠ *100 Pu'u'eo St., 96720* ☎ *808/935–5556 or 887/212–8276* 🖷 *808/593–8183* ⊕ *www.wildgingerinn.com* ⇨ *28 rooms* ⚓ *Fans, some microwaves, refrigerators, hair salon, laundry facilities, Internet, free parking, some pets allowed; no a/c, no room phones, no smoking, no TV in some rooms* 🚫 *D, MC, V* 🍽️ *CP.*

¢ 🖷 **Arnott's Lodge.** Owner Doug Arnott runs a budget lodge for backpackers that manages to combine the joy of oceanside wilderness with the convenience of being just minutes away from the airport. You can choose to tent on the lawn or stay in dormitory-style bunk beds, semiprivate rooms, or private accommodations. Four rooms in an adjacent house have private tile bathrooms. There's a shared kitchen and a separate video gazebo for all. Young travelers take advantage of guided activities provided by the lodge. Arnott's latest addition is an Internet café. ⊠ *98 'Apapane Rd., 96720* ☎ *808/969–7097* 🖷 *808/961–9638* ⊕ *www.arnottslodge.com* ⇨ *12 semiprivate units, 6 private units, 36 bunks* ⚓ *Some microwaves, hair salon, bicycles, hiking, laundry facilities, Internet, airport shuttle, travel services; no room phones, no room TVs* 🚫 *AE, D, DC, MC, V.*

Puna

$–$$$$ 🖷 **Kalani Oceanside Retreat.** An unusual tropical getaway, Kalani is an out-of-the-way retreat with healthful cuisine, nearby thermal springs, and programs on Hawaiian culture, healing, gay relationships, and Watsu-therapy (water shiatsu) training. Accommodations include campsites; shared rooms; cottage units with shared kitchen; lodge rooms; and private, luxurious tree-house units. Bathing suits are optional both on the nearby beach and at the Olympic-size pool. ⊠ *Pāhoa-Beach Rd. (Hwy. 137), Pāhoa 96778* ☎ *808/965–7828 or 800/800–6886* 🖷 *808/965–0527* ⊕ *www.kalani.com* ⇨ *24 rooms with shared bath, 9 cottages, 4 tree-house units, 3 guest-house rooms* ⚓ *Fans, some refrigerators, tennis court, pool, hair salon, hot tub, sauna, laundry facilities, laundry service, no-smoking room; no room TVs* 🚫 *AE, D, MC, V.*

$–$$ 🖷 **Yoga Oasis.** This center, on 26 tropical acres, isn't your average vacation rental: with an expensive design of Mexican tiles, finished redwood, Balinese doorways, and imported art, it draws those who seek rejuvenation, and perhaps a free yoga lesson or two. You're close to hot springs and black-sand beaches; the Volcano is a 45-minute drive away. Bathrooms are shared. A 1,600-square-ft state-of-the-art yoga and gymnastics space, with 18-ft ceilings, crowns this friendly retreat. ⊠ *Pohoiki Rd., Pāhoa 96778* ☎ *808/965–8460 or 800/274–4446* ⊕ *www.yogaoasis.org* ⇨ *5 rooms with shared bath, 4 bungalows, 1 cottage* ⚓ *Some fans, massage, laundry service; no a/c, no room phones, no room TVs, no smoking* 🚫 *MC, V.*

★ ¢–$ 🖷 **Bed & Breakfast Mountain View.** This modern home is surrounded by rolling forest and farmland. The secluded 4-acre estate has extensive floral gardens and a fishpond. Owners Linus and Jane Chao are longtime

Big Island art educators and have an art studio on the lower level, where they conduct ongoing classes. Inquire about special packages that include art lessons. The house itself is a virtual art gallery with varied displays in oil, acrylic, watercolor, and Oriental brush paintings. ⊠ *South Kulani Rd., Kurtistown 96760* ☎ *808/968–6868 or 888/698–9896* ⊠ *808/968–7017* ⊕ *www.bbmtview.com* ⮑ *4 rooms, 2 with shared bath* ♢ *Pond, fishing, billiards, laundry facilities* ⊟ *MC, V.*

¢–$ ▥ **Hale Nui Bed & Breakfast.** This large alpine-style country home is in a rural subdivision 14 mi south of Hilo and 1 mi off Highway 11, near the village of Mountain View. It's just a few miles to Hawai'i Volcanoes National Park and close to other east Hawai'i attractions like Hilo shopping and dining and tropical-flower gardens. A generous Continental breakfast is provided each morning. ⊠ *18-7879 Leonaka Rd., Mountain View 96771* ☎ *808/968–6577 or 888/968–4253* ⊠ *808/968–8900* ⊕ *www.bbonline.com/hi/halenui* ⮑ *4 rooms, 2 with shared bath* ♢ *Fans, cable TV, massage, library* ⊟ *No credit cards.*

Volcano/South Point

$–$$$$ ▥ **Chalet Kīlauea Collection.** The Collection comprises five inns and lodges and five vacation houses in and around Volcano Village; the theme rooms, suites, and vacation homes range from no-frills dorm-style bedrooms in a funky old house to a plantation mansion with its own six-person Jacuzzi. Best known is the Inn at Volcano, a "boutique resort." The two-story Treehouse Suite, with wraparound windows, a marble wet bar, and a fireplace, gives one the impression of floating on the tops of the trees. Afternoon tea is served before a fireplace. A candlelit breakfast under a glittering chandelier adds a touch of elegance. ⊠ *Wright Rd., Volcano Village 96785* ☎ *808/967–7786 or 800/937–7786* ⊠ *808/ 967–8660* ⊕ *www.volcano-hawaii.com* ⮑ *11 rooms, 9 suites, 5 houses* ⊟ *AE, D, DC, MC, V.*

$$–$$$ ▥ **Carson's Volcano Cottages.** You can choose the privacy of a romantic hideaway with a full kitchen and a hot tub in the midst of hapu ferns; a deluxe oceanfront cottage down at Kapoho, an hour away; or the intimate rooms and cottages around the property itself. Each unit has its own theme decor, from country-style to Hawaiian. Elaborate breakfasts in the main house's cozy dining room include home-baked breads and such dishes as spinach quiche and poi doughnuts. ⊡ *Box 1120, Volcano 96785* ☎ *808/967–7683 or 800/845–5282* ⊠ *808/967–8094* ⊕ *www.carsonscottage.com* ⮑ *5 rooms, 6 cottages* ♢ *Dining room, no-smoking room; no phones in some rooms* ⊟ *AE, D, MC, V.*

$$–$$$ ▥ **Colony One at Sea Mountain.** Avid golfers and seekers of seclusion will appreciate these modest condominiums bordered by the ocean and fairways. A 30-minute drive from Hawai'i Volcanoes National Park, the property is adjacent to the black-sand Punalu'u Beach Park, home of the green sea turtle preserve. Condominium units are not plush but have a country feel, with rattan furnishings, complete kitchens in the larger units, and lānai. Higher rates apply for one-night stays. ⊠ *95-789 Ninole Loop Rd. (turn off Hwy. 11 at Punalu'u), Pahala 96777* ☎ *808/ 928–6200 or 800/344–7675* ⊠ *808/928–8075* ⊕ *www.sunterra.com* ⮑ *17 1-bedroom units, 6 2-bedroom units, 5 studios* ♢ *Snack bar, fans, some kitchens, 18-hole golf course, 4 tennis courts, pool* ⊟ *MC, V.*

$$–$$$ ▥ **Volcano House.** The rooms look a bit tired with their old-fashioned white wallpaper and faded, flowered carpets, but they're clean, and bright teal-and-peach quilts and gorgeous koa rocking chairs add some class. Besides, nothing beats the view of the crater from the higher-end rooms: the Volcano House, built in 1941, perches on the edge of Kīlauea Caldera. The Ka 'Ōhelo Dining Room is convenient after a day of hik-

ing, and a drink in front of the 'ōhi'a-wood fire in the lobby's stone fireplace is great on a cold, misty day. ⊠ *Crater Rim Dr. (Box 53), Hawai'i Volcanoes National Park 96718* ☎ *808/967–7321* 🖷 *808/967–8429* 🛏 *42 rooms* ⚭ *Restaurant, snack bar, shops* ▤ *AE, D, DC, MC, V.*

$$ ⊡ **Hydrangea Cottage & Mountain House.** On a landscaped jungle estate about a mile away from Hawai'i Volcanoes National Park, the private cottage has a wraparound covered deck and floor-to-ceiling windows looking out over giant tree ferns. The Mountain House has three bedrooms with antique furnishings, each with its own bath. Both units have a kitchen as well as breakfast fixings provided. *Reservations:* ⚲ *Pacific Islands Reservations, 571 Pauku St., Kailua-Kona 96734* ☎ *808/262–8133* 🖷 *808/262–5030* ⊕ *www.aloha.com/~pir/hydcott.html* 🛏 *1 3-bedroom house, 1 cottage* ⚭ *Kitchen, cable TV, in-room VCRs, laundry facilities* ▤ *No credit cards.*

$$ ⊡ **Kīlauea Lodge.** A mile from the Hawai'i Volcanoes National Park en-
FodorsChoice   trance, this country inn is possibly the most elegant place to stay in the
★   area. The original building dates from the 1930s, and rooms have rich quilts, Hawaiian photographs, and European antiques, as well as their own wood-burning fireplaces. Two cottages off the main property include the two-bedroom Tutu's Place, and Pīi Mauna House on the 6th fairway of the Volcano Golf Course. On property, a charming one-bedroom cottage with a gas fireplace and a deluxe honeymoon room with a private balcony are perfect for romance. ✛ *Old Volcano Hwy. about 1 mi northeast of Volcano Store* ⚲ *Box 116, Volcano Village 96785* ☎ *808/967–7366* 🖷 *808/967–7367* ⊕ *www.kilauealodge.com* 🛏 *11 rooms, 3 cottages* ⚭ *Restaurant, dining room, hot tub, shop; no smoking* ▤ *AE, MC, V.*

★ $–$$ ⊡ **Hale Ohia Cottages.** This peaceful estate was built in 1931 as a vacation home for the Dillingham family. It has a Japanese hot tub surrounded by ancient trees and glorious gardens. Antique furnishings, stained glass, unique collectibles, and fireplaces abound. The luxurious Ihilani Cottage is an octagonal hideaway with a private garden. Another luxury unit, prosaically named Number 44 but poetic as can be with skylights and a see-through fireplace, has a bedroom that incorporates an old water tank. ⊠ *Hale Ohia Rd. off Hwy. 11, Volcano Village 96785* ☎ *808/967–7986 or 800/455–3803* 🖷 *808/967–8610* ⊕ *www.haleohia. com* 🛏 *4 suites, 4 cottages* ⚭ *Some microwaves, refrigerators, hot tub; no room phones, no room TVs, no smoking* ▤ *D, DC, MC, V.*

$–$$ ⊡ **My Island Bed & Breakfast Inn.** Gordon, Joann, and daughter Ki'i Morse opened their historic century-old home and 7-acre botanical estate to visitors in 1985. The house is the oldest in Volcano, built in 1886 by the Lyman missionary family. Three rooms, sharing two baths, are available in the main house. Scattered around the area are five fully equipped guest houses and another three rooms in private garden apartments. You won't start the day hungry after a deluxe all-you-can-eat breakfast. ⊠ *19-3896 Old Volcano Hwy., Volcano Village* ⚲ *Box 100, Volcano 96785* ☎ *808/967–7216 or 808/967–7110* 🖷 *808/967–7719* ⊕ *www.myislandinnhawaii.com* 🛏 *6 rooms, 3 with bath; 5 guest houses* ⚭ *No phones in some rooms* ▤ *No credit cards.*

$–$$ ⊡ **Volcano Inn.** Nestled among tree ferns within a rain forest, Volcano Inn offers a choice of private cedar cottages with enormous picture windows, or rooms in the main building, which is a 15-minute walk from the center of Volcano Village. Either way, the owners provide a breakfast every morning that includes fresh eggs and whole-grain breads. Guests of the main-building rooms must share a pay phone. ⊠ *19-3820 Old Volcano Hwy., Volcano Village* ⚲ *Box 490, Volcano 96785* ☎ *808/ 967–7293 or 800/997–2292* 🖷 *808/985–7349* ⊕ *www.volcanoinn.*

com ⇔ *5 rooms, 4 cottages* ⚐ *Refrigerators; no phones in some rooms* ▤ *AE, D, DC, MC, V.*

$ ⊞ **Bougainvillea Bed & Breakfast.** This large country home is off Highway 11 at Ocean View Estates (between mile markers 77 and 78). The remote, quiet area is close to South Point and the rural charm of Ka'u District but within easy distance of Hawai'i Volcanoes National Park, hiking, and black- and green-sand beaches. Breakfast is served on the lānai. There are restaurants, a Laundromat, a grocery store, and a gas station nearby. ⌂ *Box 6045, Ocean View 96737* ☎ *808/929–7089 or 800/688–1763* ⊕ *hi-inns.com/bouga* ⇔ *3 rooms* ⚐ *Pool, hot tub, massage, lounge* ▤ *MC, V.*

¢ ⊞ **Shirakawa Motel.** In the remote Ka'ū District, midway between Kona and Hilo near Nā'ālehu, the southernmost town in the United States, this bare and basic motel has been run by the same family since 1921. Families can get connecting units with cooking facilities, though there are places to eat nearby in town. A large one-bedroom unit has a full kitchen. ⊠ *95-6040 Māmalahoa Hwy. 11, Wai'ōhinu* ⌂ *Box 467, Nā'ālehu 96772* ☎ *808/929–7462* ⊕ *www.shirakawamotel.com* ⇔ *12 rooms* ⚐ *No a/c, no room phones, no room TVs* ▤ *No credit cards.*

Upcountry Kona District

$$$ ⊞ **Hōlualoa Inn.** Six spacious rooms are available in this cedar home on a 40-acre Upcountry orchard estate with glorious coastal views, 4 mi above Kailua Bay. The artists' town of Hōlualoa is steps away. Each room has an island theme. The premium Balinese suite has wraparound windows with stunning views. A lavish breakfast includes estate-grown coffee as well as homemade breads and macadamia-nut butter. Rooftop gazebos inspire quiet, relaxing moments, and for stargazers there's a telescope. ⊠ *76-5932 Māmalahoa Hwy. (Box 222), Hōlualoa 96725* ☎ *808/324–1121 or 800/392–1812* ▤ *808/322–2472* ⊕ *www.konaweb. com/hinn* ⇔ *6 rooms* ⚐ *Fans, pool, hot tub, billiards; no kids under 13, no smoking* ▤ *AE, D, DC, MC, V.*

$$ ⊞ **Hale Maluhia.** This expansive country home occupies a quiet tree-shaded plot above Kailua-Kona. Choose from several guest rooms or opt for the private cottage. There's a Japanese gazebo with a hot tub for relaxing. Kailua-Kona's restaurants and shops are minutes away. ⊠ *76-770 Hualalai Rd., Kailua-Kona 96740* ☎ *808/329–1123, 808/329–5773, or 800/559–6627* ▤ *808/326–5487* ⊕ *www.hawaii-bnb.com/halemal. html* ⇔ *5 rooms, 1 cottage* ⚐ *Billiards, library, recreation room* ▤ *MC, V.*

Kailua-Kona & South Kona

$$$$ ⊞ **Aston Kona by the Sea.** Complete modern kitchens, tile lānai, and a washer-dryer can be found in every suite of this comfortable oceanfront condo complex. Despite being near the bustling town of Kailua-Kona, this four-story place is quiet and relaxing. The nearest sandy beach is 2 mi away, but the pool is next to the ocean. ⊠ *75-6106 Ali'i Dr., Kailua-Kona 96740* ☎ *808/327–2300 or 800/922–7866* ▤ *808/922–8785* ⊕ *www.aston-hotels.com* ⇔ *37 1-bedroom units, 41 2-bedroom units* ⚐ *Kitchens, pool, hot tub* ▤ *AE, D, DC, MC, V.*

★ $$$$ ⊞ **Horizon Guest House.** About 30 mi south of Kona, at an elevation of 1,100 ft on 40 acres overlooking the Kona Coast, this private luxury retreat offers tranquility, comfort, sweeping views, and a state-of-the-art solar-heated pool. Hawaiian quilts, collectibles, and antiques give personality and warmth to the four spacious suites, all with private lānai. Host Clem Classen's generous breakfast starts your day. The estate borders the native forests of the 15,000-acre McCandless Ranch. ⌂ *Box 268, Hōnaunau 96726* ☎ *808/328–2540 or 888/*

328–8301 ⌕ 808/328–8707 ⊕ www.horizonguesthouse.com ⊃ 4 suites ⌂ Refrigerators, pool, hot tub, library, Internet; no kids under 14, no smoking ⊟ MC, V.

★ $$$$ ⊞ **Kanaloa at Kona.** The 16-acre grounds provide a verdant background for this low-rise condominium complex bordering the Keauhou-Kona Country Club. Large one-, two-, and three-bedroom apartments have koa-wood cabinetwork and washer-dryers; oceanfront villas have private hot tubs. Edward's at Kanaloa Restaurant serves excellent Mediterranean cuisine. ✉ 78-261 Manukai St., Kailua-Kona 96740 ☎ 808/322–9625, 808/322–2272, or 800/688–7444 ⌕ 808/322–3818 ⊕ www.outrigger.com ⊃ 166 units ⌂ Restaurant, kitchenettes, 2 tennis courts, 3 pools ⊟ AE, D, DC, MC, V.

$$$–$$$$ ⊞ **Kona Bali Kai.** Though slightly older, with rattan furnishings and a basic layout, these condominium units do have a pretty good location, just a couple of minutes from Kailua-Kona and popular White Sands beach. And they are great for families. Kitchens are fully equipped, and there's a little convenience store. If you can afford it, choose an oceanfront unit for the luxury of quiet sunsets. ✉ 76-6246 Ali'i Dr., Kailua-Kona 96740 ☎ 808/329–9381 or 800/535–0085 ⌕ 808/326–6056 ⊕ www.marcresorts.com ⊃ 62 condominiums (13 studios, 25 1-bedroom, 24 2-bedroom) ⌂ Fans, kitchens, in-room VCRs, pool, hair salon, hot tub, laundry facilities ⊟ AE, D, DC, MC, V.

★ $$$–$$$$ ⊞ **Ohana Keauhou Beach Resort.** This oceanfront hotel with sage-green rooms is just 5 mi south of Kailua-Kona. It has won awards for the preservation of its unique history: its grounds include a heiau, a sacred fishpond, and a replica of the summer home of King David Kalākaua. Consider a nightcap at the Verandah bar, just a few feet away from lapping waves and turtles. The hotel is adjacent to Kahalu'u, one of the Big Island's best snorkeling beaches; the rooms on that side may get noisy. ✉ 78-6740 Ali'i Dr., Kailua-Kona 96740 ☎ 808/322–3441 or 800/462–6262 ⌕ 808/322–3117 ⊕ www.ohanahotels.com ⊃ 311 rooms, 6 suites ⌂ Restaurant, 6 tennis courts, pool, health club, beach, bar, meeting room ⊟ AE, D, DC, MC, V.

$$$–$$$$ ⊞ **Royal Kona Resort.** The spacious Royal Kona Resort, a steady downtown landmark, remains ever popular with travelers. Rooms, all with lānai, have natural stone, sand, and green tones. The resort is within walking distance of Kailua and right across from shops and restaurants. Little artificial streams and a private lagoon with a sandy beach create an ambience of carefree tropical living. The resort hosts a weekly lū'au with Polynesian entertainment. ✉ 75-5852 Ali'i Dr., Kailua-Kona 96740 ☎ 808/329–3111 or 800/222–5642 ⌕ 808/329–9532 ⊕ www.royalkona.com ⊃ 452 rooms, 8 suites ⌂ Restaurant, in-room data ports, in-room safes, refrigerators, 4 tennis courts, pool, health club, spa, beach, bar, meeting room ⊟ AE, D, DC, MC, V.

$$–$$$ ⊞ **King Kamehameha's Kona Beach Hotel.** Rooms are not particularly special here (the fifth- and sixth-floor oceanfront rooms are best), but what you get instead of the luxury of upscale Kohala resorts is a great central Kailua-Kona location with a small white-sand family beach and a calm swimming bay, right next to Kailua Pier. There are several resort shops in the lobby. Visitors can explore the grounds and Ahu'ena Heiau, which King Kamehameha I had reconstructed in the early 1800s. The hotel serves an ample champagne brunch every Sunday and hosts a fabulous beachfront Polynesian lū'au several nights a week. ✉ 75-5660 Palani Rd., Kailua-Kona 96740 ☎ 808/329–2911 or 800/367–6060 ⌕ 808/329–4602 ⊕ www.konabeachhotel.com ⊃ 455 rooms ⌂ 2 restaurants, tennis courts, pool, hot tub, sauna, beach, 2 bars ⊟ AE, D, DC, MC, V.

$$ ⊞ **Hale Kona Kai.** Its name means "House by the Kona Sea," and it's indeed just a small, friendly, clean three-story building, right on the ocean.

Each unit has different furnishings and fixtures. The corner units with wraparound lānai have the best views. You must book a three-day minimum stay. Adjacent to the Royal Kona Resort, Hale Kona Kai is close to restaurants and shops. ⊠ *75-5870 Kahakai Rd., Kailua-Kona 96740* ☎ *808/329–2155 or 800/421–3696* 🖷 *808/329–2155* 📧 *hkk@kona. net* 🖵 *22 units* ⚲ *Pool* ⊟ *AE, MC, V.*

$$ 🖼 **Kona Seaside Hotel.** If you're on a budget, want a central location, and don't need resort extras, spacious rooms, or lavish bathrooms, you'll feel at home in this casual hotel. It's on a busy intersection, right across the street from Kailua Bay. Rooms nearest the main street are built around a private pool. The staff is very friendly. ⊠ *75-5646 Palani Rd., Kailua-Kona 96740* ☎ *808/329–2455 or 800/560–5558* 🖷 *808/329– 6157* ⊕ *www.konaseasidehotel.com* 🖵 *223 rooms, 1 suite* ⚲ *Restaurant, refrigerators, 2 pools, bar, laundry facilities, meeting room* ⊟ *AE, D, DC, MC, V.*

$–$$ 🖼 **Kona Bay Hotel, Uncle Billy's.** These two- and four-story motel-type units are right in the center of town, across the street from the ocean. The mood is friendly and casual, with relaxed open-air dining around the pool. Some rooms have kitchenettes. The place is owned and managed by the same local family that owns the Hilo Bay Hotel, Uncle Billy's. ⊠ *75-5739 Ali'i Dr., Kailua-Kona 96740* ☎ *808/329–1393 or 800/367– 5102* 🖷 *808/329–9210* ⊕ *www.unclebilly.com* 🖵 *146 rooms* ⚲ *Restaurant, refrigerators, pool, bar* ⊟ *AE, D, DC, MC, V.*

$–$$ 🖼 **Kona Magic Sands.** Cradled between two small beach parks, one of which is Magic Sands, this condo complex is great for swimmers and sunbathers in summer (the sand washes away in winter). Units vary because they are individually owned, but all are oceanfront, spacious, and light. Some units have enclosed lānai, and all have an ocean view. ⊠ *77-6452 Ali'i Dr., Kailua-Kona 96740* ☎ *808/329–9393 or 800/622–5348* 🖷 *808/326–4137* ⊕ *www.konahawaii.com* 🖵 *37 rooms* ⚲ *Restaurant, kitchens, kitchenettes, pool, bar; no a/c in some rooms* ⊟ *MC, V.*

$ 🖼 **Kona Tiki Hotel.** The best thing about this three-story walk-up budget hotel, about a mile south of Kailua-Kona, is that all the units have lānai right next to the ocean. The rooms are modest but pleasantly decorated nonetheless. You can sunbathe by the seaside pool, where a buffet breakfast is also served. Some would call this place old-fashioned; others would say it's local and the best deal in town, with glorious sunsets no different from those at the resorts. ⊠ *75-5968 Ali'i Dr., Kailua-Kona 96745* ☎ *808/329–1425* 🖷 *808/327–9402* ⊕ *www.wheretostay. com* 🖵 *15 rooms* ⚲ *Grill, fans, refrigerators, pool; no room phones, no room TVs* ⊟ *No credit cards* ⏀ *CP.*

¢–$ 🖼 **Manago Hotel.** You'll get a great ocean view high above the Kona Coast in the newer wing of this family-run three-story hotel, the oldest operating hotel in the area. To honor his grandparents, Kinzo and Osame Manago, who built the main hotel in 1917, Dwight Manago has maintained one Japanese-style room with tatami mats and a *furo,* a traditional Japanese bath. The other rooms are nothing special, but the friendly Manago Hotel has an authentic old Hawai'i vibe, especially in the bar and local-style restaurant. ⊠ *81-6155 Māmalahoa Hwy. (Box 145), Captain Cook 96704* ☎ *808/323–2642* 🖷 *808/323–3451* ⊕ *www. managohotel.com* 🖵 *64 rooms, 42 with bath* ⚲ *Restaurant, bar* ⊟ *D, MC, V.*

Kohala Coast & Waikoloa

$$$$ 🖼 **Aston the Shores at Waikoloa.** These red-tile-roof villas are set amid landscaped lagoons and waterfalls at the edge of the championship Waikoloa Village Golf Course. The spacious villas and condo units—

the ground floor and upper floor are available separately—are privately owned, so all furnishings are different. Sliding glass doors open onto large lānai. Large picture windows look out on rolling green fairways. Units have complete kitchens with washer-dryer and come with maid service. ☒ 69-1035 Keana Pl., Waikoloa 96738 ☎ 808/886–5001 or 800/922–7866 🖶 808/922–8785 ⊕ www.aston-hotels.com ✍75 1- and 2-bedroom units ♻ Fans, kitchens, kitchenettes, putting green, 2 tennis courts, pool, hot tub, shop ☰ AE, D, DC, MC, V.

★ $$$$ 🏨 **The Fairmont Orchid Hawai'i.** This elegant, romantic hotel stretches along 32 beachfront acres, incorporating botanical gardens and waterfall ponds. Rooms are refined, with European luxury; marble bathrooms and fluffy robes are just part of the pampering. The Spa Without Walls incorporates traditional and contemporary treatments, including Tibetan yoga, body and facial rejuvenations, and massage practices ranging from Swedish to Hawaiian. The resort offers 2½-hour voyages aboard an authentic Polynesian double-hulled sailing canoe, the *Hahalua Lele*, or "Flying Manta Ray." ☒ 1 N. Kanikū Dr., Kohala Coast 96743 ☎ 808/885–2000 or 800/845–9905 🖶 808/885–5778 ⊕ www.fairmont. com ✍ 539 rooms, 54 suites ♻ 3 restaurants, 2 18-hole golf courses, 10 tennis courts, pool, health club, sauna, spa, beach, snorkeling, boating, 4 bars, children's programs (ages 5–12) ☰ AE, D, DC, MC, V.

$$$$ 🏨 **Four Seasons Resort Hualālai.** Slate floors, Hawaiian artwork, warm
Fodor'sChoice earth and cool white tones, and spacious bathrooms create peaceful re-
★ treats, tucked into four clusters of oceanfront bungalows. Ground-level rooms have outdoor garden showers. Natural ponds dot the property. The Hawaiian Cultural Center honors the grounds' spiritual heritage, and the Sports Club and Spa offers guests top-rate health and fitness options. Hualālai's golf course hosts the Senior PGA Tournament of Champions. ☒ 100 Ka'ūpūlehu Dr., Ka'ūpūlehu/Kona ☜ Box 1269, Kailua-Kona 96745 ☎ 808/325–8000, 800/332–3442, or 888/340–5662 🖶 808/325–8200 ⊕ www.fourseasons.com ✍243 rooms, 31 suites ♻3 restaurants, 18-hole golf course, 8 tennis courts, 5 pools, health club, spa, beach, recreation room, baby-sitting, children's programs (ages 5–11), laundry service, concierge, Internet, business services, meeting rooms, airport shuttle ☰ AE, DC, MC, V.

★ $$$$ 🏨 **Hāpuna Beach Prince Hotel.** This luxury hotel—a glitzy beauty with floors of slate tile—fronts white-sand Hāpuna, one of the best beaches in the United States. Spacious, with marble bathrooms and private lānai, all rooms have at least a partial ocean view. Meandering pathways lead to restaurants, beach facilities, and a spectacular golf course. The showpiece of the hotel is the 8,000-square-ft, four-bedroom Hāpuna Suite, with its own swimming pool and 24-hour butler service. A hiking trail and an easier, frequent shuttle connect Hāpuna with its partner, the Mauna Kea Beach Hotel. ☒ 62-100 Kauna'oa Dr., Kohala Coast 96743 ☎ 808/880–1111 or 800/882–6060 🖶 808/880–3142 ⊕ www.hapunabeachprincehotel.com ✍ 314 rooms, 36 suites ♻ 5 restaurants, refrigerators, 18-hole golf course, 13 tennis courts, pool, hair salon, health club, hot tub, spa, 2 bars, children's programs (age 5–12), Internet, business services, convention center, meeting rooms ☰AE, D, DC, MC, V.

★ $$$$ 🏨 **Hilton Waikoloa Village.** Shaded pathways pass by artifacts from a multimillion-dollar Pacific Island art collection to connect the three tall buildings that make up this 62-acre resort. Trams and boats shuttle you around if you don't want to walk. The pool has a 175-ft water slide and a meandering river that connects smaller pools. A man-made sand beach borders a 4-acre lagoon, a playground for dolphins. The Kohala Spa has some of the finest fitness facilities on the island. ☒ 425 Waikoloa Beach Dr., Waikoloa 96738 ☎ 808/886–1234 or 800/445–8667 🖶 808/886–

2900 ⊕ *www.hiltonwaikoloavillage.com* ⤢ *1,240 rooms, 57 suites*
♨ *9 restaurants, 2 18-hole golf courses, putting green, 8 tennis courts,
3 pools, health club, spa, beach, 7 bars, shops, children's programs (ages
5–12), Internet* ⊟ *AE, D, DC, MC, V.*

★ **$$$$** 🏨 **Kona Village Resort.** Without phones, TVs, or radios, it's easy to feel
like you are part of an extended Polynesian *ohana* (family), with your
own thatch-roof *hale* (house) near the resort's sandy beach. Built on the
grounds of an ancient Hawaiian village, the modern bungalows reflect
styles of South Seas cultures—Tahitian, Samoan, Tongan, Maori, Fijian,
or Hawaiian. The extralarge Royal rooms have private hot tubs. Rates
include meals, an authentic Polynesian Friday-night lūau, ground tours,
tennis, sports activities, and rides in the resort's glass-bottom boat.
⊠ *Queen Ka'ahumanu Hwy., Kailua-Kona 96745* ☎ *808/325–5555 or
800/367–5290* 🖷 *808/325–5124* ⊕ *www.konavillage.com* ⤢ *125 bungalows* ♨ *2 restaurants, fans, 3 tennis courts, 2 pools, health club, hot
tub, beach, boating, 3 bars, children's programs (ages 6–17; not available in May or Sept.), meeting room, airport shuttle; no room phones,
no room TVs* ⊟ *AE, DC, MC, V* ⦿ *FAP.*

★ **$$$$** 🏨 **Mauna Kea Beach Hotel.** The Mauna Kea Beach is the grande dame
of Kohala Coast hotels. Opened in 1965, it has long been regarded as
one of the world's premier vacation resort hotels. It borders one of the
islands' finest white-sand beaches. Rare works of art, such as a 7th-cen-
tury Buddha, enhance walkways and open spaces. The rooms have a
natural look with pastel tones and natural woods. Shuttles operate between the Mauna Kea and the adjacent Hāpuna Beach Prince Hotel, allowing guests to use the facilities at both hotels. ⊠ *62-100 Mauna Kea
Beach Dr., Kohala Coast 96743* ☎ *808/882–7222 or 800/882–6060*
🖷 *808/882–5700* ⊕ *www.maunakeabeachhotel.com* ⤢ *300 rooms,
10 suites* ♨ *5 restaurants, in-room safes, refrigerators, 2 18-hole golf
courses, 13 tennis courts, pool, hair salon, health club, beach, children's programs (age 5–12), Internet* ⊟ *AE, D, DC, MC, V.*

★ **$$$$** 🏨 **Mauna Lani Bay Hotel and Bungalows.** Ninety percent of the spacious
rooms in this elegant hotel have ocean views, and all have a large lānai.
Comfortable furnishings grace rooms with natural fabrics and teak. The
resort is known for its two spectacular golf courses. The new Mauna
Lani Spa offers mud wraps with volcanic ash, hot-stone therapies, massage, and more. Some of the best Pacific Rim cuisine is served at the oceanfront CanoeHouse. ⊠ *68-1400 Mauna Lani Dr., Kohala Coast 96743*
☎ *808/885–6622 or 800/367–2323* 🖷 *808/885–1484* ⊕ *www.
maunalani.com* ⤢ *335 rooms, 10 suites, 5 bungalows* ♨ *6 restaurants, in-room safes, refrigerators, in-room VCRs, 2 18-hole golf courses,
16 tennis courts, pool, spa, 5 bars, children's programs (ages 5–12), Internet* ⊟ *AE, D, DC, MC, V.*

$$$$ 🏨 **Mauna Lani Point Condominiums.** Surrounded by the emerald greens
of a world-class oceanside golf course, spacious two-story suites offer a
private, independent home away from home. The privately owned units,
individually decorated according to the owners' tastes, have European
cabinets and oversize soaking tubs in the master bedrooms. The pool sports
a little waterfall. You're just a few steps away from the Mauna Lani Bay
Hotel and Bungalows, where you have access to golf, tennis, spa facilities, and restaurants. ⊠ *68-1050 Mauna Lani Point Dr., Kohala Coast
96743* ☎ *808/885–5022 or 800/642–6284* 🖷 *808/885–5015* ⊕ *www.
classicresorts.com* ⤢ *24 1-bedroom units, 37 2-bedroom units* ♨ *Kitchens,
kitchenettes, pool, hot tub, sauna* ⊟ *AE, DC, MC, V.*

★ **$$$$** 🏨 **Waikoloa Beach Marriott.** The most affordable of the Kohala Coast resorts, this hotel covers 15 acres, and encompasses ancient fishponds, historic trails, and petroglyph fields. All rooms have Hawaiian art and
bamboo-type furnishings. The oversize cabana rooms overlook the lagoon.

Reliable dining is available at the Hawai'i Calls restaurant. The Hawaiian Rainforest Salon & Spa offers a full range of treatments. Bordering the white-sand beach of 'Anaeho'omalu Bay, the hotel has a range of ocean activities, including wedding-vow renewals on a catamaran. ✉ 69-275 *Waikoloa Beach Dr., Waikoloa 96738* ☎ 808/886–6789 *or* 800/688–7444 📠 808/886–7852 ⊕ *www.outrigger.com* ⟿ *524 rooms, 21 suites* ♿ *Restaurant, refrigerators, 2 18-hole golf courses, 6 tennis courts, pool, hair salon, health club, 2 hot tubs, sauna, spa, beach, 2 bars, children's programs (ages 5–12), laundry facilities, Internet, business services, meeting rooms* ⊟ *AE, D, DC, MC, V.*

$$ ▦ **Hale Ho'onanea.** The Hawaiian translation of this comfortable home's name is "House of Relaxation." It sits on 3 acres in the Kohala Estates hills, above the ocean. From here you can watch the sun rise over Mauna Kea and the sun set over the Pacific, and view the sparkling beauty of Hawai'i's night sky. It's minutes away from dining and shopping at Waimea and the attractions of the Kohala Coast resorts. ✉ *Kohala Estates, Ala Kahua Dr., Waimea 96743* ☎ 808/882–1653 *or* 877/882–1653 📠 808/882–1653 ⊕ *www.houseofrelaxation.com* ⟿ *3 suites* ♿ *Kitchenette, library* ⊟ *No credit cards.*

¢–$$ ▦ **Kohala Guest House.** In rural North Kohala, the birthplace of King Kamehameha, contemporary comforts and the aloha style of old meet in the tropical orchard property of Don and Nani Svendsen. The cozy studio and rental houses, adorned with Svendsen's flowers, are minutes away from Pololū Valley. It's just 30 minutes to the white-sand beaches of the resorts. Close to the shops, eateries, and activities in Hāwī and Kapa'au, but sheltered from heavy tourism, you can live like the locals here. ✉ *Box 172, Hāwī 96719* ☎ 808/889–5606 📠 808/889–5572 ⊕ *home1.gte.net/svendsen* ⟿ *1 cottage, 3 houses (for families or rented as separate room units)* ⊟ *No credit cards.*

¢–$ ▦ **Kohala Village Inn.** Located in the heart of Hāwī town in the rural far-north peninsula of the Big Island, this budget no-frills country lodge offers clean and simple rooms. It's perfect for backpackers or those seeking the opposite of the resort experience. Some rooms accommodate up to six. It's steps away from Hāwī dining and shops. There's easy access to Pololū Valley, Kapa'au, Mo'okini Heiau, King Kamehameha's birthplace, and whale-watching spots. ✉ *55-514 Hāwī Rd., Hāwī 96719* ☎ 808/889–0404 ⊕ *www.kohalavillageinn.com* ⟿ *17 rooms* ♿ *Cable TV* ⊟ *No credit cards.*

Waimea/Hāmākua Coast

$$–$$$$ ▦ **Jacaranda Inn.** Built in 1897, this sprawling, historic estate was once the home of the Parker Ranch manager; it has been completely restored in raspberry and lavender colors, with lots of koa wood and Upcountry Victorian elements. The units are booked under two separate plans. Plan A includes daily maid service, full breakfasts, and a bottle of wine; Plan B is simpler, with Continental breakfast and less service. The Jacaranda is close to Waimea shops as well as to beaches. ✉ *65-1444 Kawaihae Rd., Waimea 96743* ☎ 808/885–8813 📠 808/885–6096 ⊕ *www.jacarandainn.com* ⟿ *8 suites, 1 cottage* ♿ *Some in-room hot tubs, recreation room; no smoking* ⊟ *MC, V.*

★ $$ ▦ **Cook's Discoveries Waimea Suite.** Patti Cook, owner of the well-known Cook's Discoveries arts-and-crafts shop in Waimea, has opened her elegant Waimea country home to guests. The private lower apartment unit opens onto an expansive lawn with beautiful trees framing views of Mauna Kea. The common living room has beautiful antique furniture and decorative artwork. The double and twin bedrooms are tastefully furnished. Make a direct booking and receive a $20 gift certificate to Cook's

Discoveries; stay six nights and you get the seventh night free. ✉ *Hwy. 19 at Kamamalu St., Waimea 96743* ☎ *808/937–2833* ⊕ *www.hawaii-island.com/cooks.htm* ⇨ *2 rooms* ♨ *Kitchen* 🗏 *AE, D, MC, V.*

★ $$ 🏨 **Waimea Country Lodge.** In the heart of cowboy country, next door to the Paniolo Country Inn, this quiet, modest lodge offers views of the green, rolling slopes of Mauna Kea yet is close to the activity of busy Waimea town. The rooms are adequate and clean, with Hawaiian quilts lending them a personal touch. You can arrange to sign meals at Merriman's Restaurant and the Inn to your room. ✉ *65-1210 Lindsey Rd., Waimea* ⌂ *Box 2559, Kamuela 96743* ☎ *808/885–4100 or 800/367–5004* 🖷 *808/885–6711* ⊕ *www.castleresorts.com/wcl* ⇨ *21 rooms* ♨ *Some kitchenettes* 🗏 *AE, D, DC, MC, V* ❑ *CP.*

$$ 🏨 **Waimea Gardens Cottage.** These two charming streamside country cottages have French doors, antique furnishings, window boxes spilling over with flowers, fireplaces, and kitchens stocked with your choice of breakfast items. Though 8 mi from the island's beaches, the property is on the sunny side of Waimea. You can awake on cool Upcountry mornings to collect your own eggs from the quiet flock of miniature hens outside. *Reservations:* ⌂ *Hawai'i's Best Bed and Breakfasts, Box 520, Kamuela 96743* ☎ *808/885–4550 or 800/262–9912* 🖷 *808/885–0559* ⊕ *www.bestbnb.com* ⇨ *2 cottages* 🗏 *No credit cards* ❑ *CP.*

$$ 🏨 **Waipi'o Wayside.** Nestled amid avocado and kukui trees, on a plantation estate, this serene inn provides a retreat close to Waipi'o Valley. Hostess Jacqueline Horne has given each room its own character with, for example, rare Chinese antiques or patchwork quilts. A sprawling garden with an orchid-covered deck and a little gazebo have hammocks to help you indulge your lazy side. ✉ *Waipi'o Valley Rd. (Hwy. 240), Honoka'a 96727* ☎ *808/775–0275 or 800/833–8849* 🖷 *808/775–0275* ⊕ *www.waipiowayside.com* ⇨ *5 rooms* ♨ *Snack bar; no room phones, no room TVs, no smoking* 🗏 *MC, V.*

★ $ 🏨 **Kamuela Inn.** The rooms in this unpretentious, peaceful inn, just 20 minutes from the island beaches, are basic but clean. Small lānai look out over the inn's gardens. Depending on your needs, you can choose anything from a no-nonsense single bedroom to two connecting penthouse suites with a lānai and full kitchen. ✉ *65-1300 Kawaihae Rd. (Box 1994), Kamuela 96743* ☎ *808/885–4243 or 800/555–8968* 🖷 *808/885–8857* ⊕ *www.kamuelainn.com* ⇨ *20 rooms, 11 suites* ♨ *Some kitchenettes; no phones in some rooms* 🗏 *AE, D, DC, MC, V.*

¢–$ 🏨 **Hotel Honoka'a Club.** This basic bargain hotel is 45 minutes from Hilo and close to Waipi'o Valley. Rustic rooms range from lower-level dormitory-style hostel units—bring your own sleeping bag—with shared bathrooms to upper-story rooms with private bath, queen-size beds, an ocean view, and a complimentary Continental breakfast. ✉ *45-3480 Māmane St. (Box 247), Honoka'a 96727* ☎ *808/775–0678 or 800/808–0678* ⊕ *www.hotelhono.com* ⇨ *13 rooms, 5 hostel rooms* ♨ *Restaurant; no room phones, no smoking, no TV in some rooms* 🗏 *MC, V.*

NIGHTLIFE & THE ARTS

If you're the sort of person who doesn't come alive until after dark, you're going to be pretty lonely on the Big Island. Blame it on the plantation heritage. People did their cane-raising in the morning.

Clubs & Cabarets

Honu Bar. This elegant spot at the Mauna Lani Bay Hotel and Bungalows on the Kohala Coast has a nice dance floor for weekend revelers; the music varies, so call ahead. Regardless, appetizers, imported cigars, and fine cognacs make this a popular, upscale gathering spot. ⊠ *68-1400 Mauna Lani Dr., Kohala Coast* ☎ *808/885–6622.*

Ho'omalimali Lounge. This lounge and dance club at the Hawai'i Naniloa Resort in Hilo competes with the crashing surf on Friday and Saturday night with live music from 9 to midnight. ⊠ *93 Banyan Dr., Hilo* ☎ *808/969–3333.*

Huggo's. Jazz, country, and even rock bands perform at this popular restaurant, so call ahead of time to find out what's on. Outside, people often dance in the sand to Hawaiian songs. ⊠ *75-5828 Kahakai Rd., at Ali'i Dr., Kailua-Kona* ☎ *808/329–1493.*

Koa House Grill. A popular hangout for Waimea's residents, this old-fashioned bar has live music Friday and Saturday night—until 2 in the morning at times. ⊠ *Waimea Shopping Center, 65-1144 Māmalahoa Hwy., Waimea* ☎ *808/885–2088.*

Lulu's. A young crowd gyrates until 1:30 AM Friday and Saturday to hot dance music—hip-hop, R&B, and rock—spun by a professional DJ. ⊠ *75-5819 Ali'i Dr., Kailua-Kona* ☎ *808/331–2633.*

Michaelangelo's. On the second level of the Waterfront Row complex, this Italian restaurant starts rocking after 10 every night with a live DJ. ⊠ *75-5770 Ali'i Dr., Waterfront Row, Kailua-Kona* ☎ *808/329–4436.*

Film

Recorded **showtime information** (☎ 808/961–3456) is available for all movie houses.

Hilo

Kress Cinemas (⊠ 174 Kamehameha Ave. ☎ 808/961–3456) screens selected art films. After decades of being closed, the historic **Palace Theatre** (⊠ 38 Haili St. ☎ 808/934–7010), built in 1925, now shows movies. First-run films are shown regularly at the state-of-the-art **Prince Kuhio Stadium Cinemas** (⊠ Prince Kūhiō Plaza, 111 E. Puainako St. ☎ 808/959–4595).

Kailua-Kona

Keauhou 7 Cinemas (⊠ Keauhou Shopping Center, 78-6831 Ali'i Dr. ☎ 808/324–7200) is a splendid seven-theater complex. The 10-screen **Makalapua Stadium Cinemas** (⊠ Makalapua Ave., next to Big Kmart ☎ 808/327–0444) has stadium seating and digital surround sound.

Around the Island

Aloha Theatre (⊠ Hwy. 11, Kainaliu ☎ 808/322–2323 or 808/322–2323) shows plays and movies in a 320-seat historic arts center built in 1923. **Honoka'a Peoples Theaters** (⊠ Māmame St., Honoka'a ☎ 808/775–0000) screens movies on weekends only. **Kahilu Theatre** (⊠ Parker Ranch Shopping Center, Hwy. 19, Waimea ☎ 808/885–6868) occasionally shows best-selling or foreign movies on weekends. **Na'alehu Theater** (⊠ Hawai'i Belt Rd., Hwy. 11, Na'alehu ☎ 808/929–9133) sometimes shows movies Friday, Saturday, and Sunday nights.

Hula

★ For hula lovers, the biggest show of the year and the largest event of its kind in the world is the annual **Merrie Monarch Hula Festival** (⊠ Hawai'i Naniloa Resort, 93 Banyan Dr., Hilo 96720 ☎ 808/935–9168). Honoring the legacy of King David Kalākaua, Hawai'i's last king, the festival is staged in Hilo at the spacious Edith Kanaka'ole Stadium during the first week following Easter Sunday. Hula hālau compete in various classes of ancient and modern dance styles. You need to reserve accommodations and tickets up to a year in advance.

HAWAI'I'S HIPPY HIPPY SHAKE

EGENDS IMMORTALIZE LAKA as the goddess of hula, portraying her as a gentle deity who journeyed from island to island, sharing the dance with all who were willing to learn. Laka's graceful movements, spiritual and layered with meaning, brought to life the history, the traditions, and the genealogy of the islanders. Ultimately taught by parents to children and by kumu (teachers) to students, the hula preserved without a written language the culture of these ancient peoples.

Some legends trace the origins of hula to Moloka'i, where a family named La'ila'i was said to have established the dance at Ka'ana. Eventually the youngest sister of the fifth generation of La'ila'i was given the name Laka, and she carried the dance to all the Islands in the Hawaiian chain.

Another legend credits Hi'iaka, the volcano goddess Pele's youngest sister, as having danced the first hula in the hala groves of Puna on the Big Island. Hi'iaka and possibly even Pele were thought to have learned the dance from Hōpoe, a mortal and a poet also credited as the originator of the dance.

In any case, hula thrived until the arrival of puritanical New England missionaries, who with the support of Queen Ka'ahumanu, an early Christian convert, attempted to ban the dance as an immoral activity throughout the 19th century.

Though hula may not have been publicly performed, it remained a spiritual and poetic art form, as well as a lively celebration of life presented during special celebrations in many Hawaiian homes. David Kalākaua, the popular "Merrie Monarch" who was king from 1874 to 1891, revived the hula. Dancers were called to perform at official functions. In 1906, Nathaniel Emerson wrote about hula, "Its view of life was idyllic, and it gave itself to the celebration of those mythical times when gods and goddesses moved on earth as men and women, and when men and women were as gods."

Gradually, ancient hula, called kahiko, was replaced with a lively, updated form of dance called 'auana (modern). Modern costumes of fresh ti-leaf or raffia skirts replaced the voluminous pa'u skirts made of kapa (cloth made of beaten bark), and the music became more melodic, as opposed to earlier chanted routines accompanied by pahu (drums), 'ili 'ili (rocks used as castanets), and other percussion instruments. Such tunes as "Lovely Hula Hands," "Little Grass Shack," and the "Hawaiian Wedding Song" are considered hula 'auana. Dancers might wear graceful holomu'u with short trains or ti-leaf skirts with coconut bra tops.

In 1963 the Merrie Monarch Festival was established in Hilo on the Big Island and has since become the most prestigious hula competition in the state. It's staged annually the weekend after Easter, and contestants of various halau (hula schools) from Hawai'i and the mainland compete in the categories of Miss Aloha Hula, hula kahiko (ancient), and hula 'auana (modern). For more information, contact the **Merrie Monarch Hula Festival** (✉ Hawai'i Naniloa Resort, 93 Banyan Dr., Hilo 96720 ☎ 808/935–9168).

Moloka'i stages its own Ka Hula Piko festival every May to celebrate the birth of hula. Singers, musicians, and dancers perform in a shaded glen at Pāpōhaku Beach State Park; nearby, islanders sell food and Hawaiian crafts. During the week preceding the festival, John Kaimikaua, the founder, and his halau present hula demonstrations, lectures, and storytelling at various Moloka'i sites.

For more information, contact the **Moloka'i Visitors Association** (✉ Box 960, Kaunakakai 96748 ☎ 808/553–3876 or 800/800–6367).

Lū'au & Polynesian Revues

Kailua-Kona

★ **King Kamehameha's Kona Beach Hotel's Island Breeze Lū'au.** Witness the arrival of the Royal Court by canoe and have pictures taken at this beach-front event, which includes a 22-item buffet, an open bar, and a show. ⊠ 75-5660 *Palani Rd.* ☎ 808/326–4969 *or* 808/329–2911 ⊠ *$55* ☉ *Tues.–Thurs. and Sun. 5–8:30.*

★ **Kona Village Resort.** In its utter isolation, the lū'au here is one of the most authentic and traditional in the Islands. As in other lū'au, activities include the steaming of a whole pig in the *imu* (ground oven). A Polynesian show on a stage over a lagoon is magical. ✛ *6 mi north of Kona International Airport, off Queen Ka'ahumanu Hwy.* ⊠ *Kailua-Kona* ☎ 808/325–5555 ⊠ *$76, including open bar* ☉ *Fri. from 5; walking tour at 5:30, imu ceremony at 6:30, dinner at 7, show at 8.*

Royal Kona Resort. This resort lights lū'au torches for a full Polynesian show and a Hawaiian-style oceanfront buffet four times a week. ⊠ *75-5852 Ali'i Dr.* ☎ 808/329–3111 *Ext. 4* ⊠ *$52, including beer and wine* ☉ *Mon., Wed., and Fri.–Sat. at 5.*

Kohala Coast & Waikoloa

Hilton Waikoloa Village. The Hilton seats 400 people outdoors at the Kamehameha Court, where the acclaimed Polynesian group Tihati performs a lively show. A buffet dinner provides samplings of Hawaiian food as well as fish, beef, and chicken to appeal to all tastes. ⊠ *425 Waikoloa Beach Dr., Waikoloa* ☎ 808/886–1234 ⊠ *$65* ☉ *Fri. at 6.*

Mauna Kea Beach Hotel. Every Tuesday chefs come together here to create a traditional Hawaiian *pa'ina* (dinner feast), which includes the classic *kālua* (roasted in an underground oven) pig. On the gracious North Pointe Lū'au Grounds of the Mauna Kea Beach Hotel, you can sample the best of Hawaiian cuisine while listening to the enchanting songs of Nani Lim. ⊠ *62-100 Mauna Kea Beach Dr., Kohala Coast* ☎ 808/882–7222 ⊠ *$74* ☉ *Tues. at 6.*

Waikoloa Beach Marriott. The Marriott offers a great-value lū'au at the Lū'au Grounds, where entertainment includes a Samoan fire dance as well as songs and dances of various Pacific cultures. Traditional Hawaiian dishes are served alongside more familiar fare. ⊠ *69-275 Waikoloa Beach Dr., Waikoloa* ☎ 808/886–6789 ⊠ *$65, including open bar* ☉ *Wed. and Sun. 5:30–8:30.*

Sunset Cruises

★ **Captain Beans' Polynesian Dinner Cruise.** This is the ever-popular standby in sunset dinner cruises. You can't miss it—as the sun sets in Kailua, look out over the water and you'll see a big gaudy boat with distinctive orange sails. This cruise is corny, and dinner is nothing great, but it's an experience, with unlimited drinks and a Hawaiian show. This is for adults only. ⊠ *Kailua Pier, Kailua-Kona* ☎ 808/329–2955 ⊕ *www.robertshawaii.com* ⊠ *$52–$63, including dinner, entertainment, and open bar* ☉ *Tues.–Sun. at 5:15.*

🐚 **Hawai'i Ocean Adventures.** The *Pacific Passion*, a 40-ft-long single-hull boat, takes you from Honokōhau Harbor to dolphin-rich waters while the sun sets in the distance. Appetizers and beverages are part of the three-hour cruise. No alcohol is served, but you may bring your own if you wish. The captain and crew are eager to share local legends and knowledge about the area. ⊠ *Honokōhau Harbor, Slip J-38, Kailua-Kona* ☎ 808/325–0766 *or* 877/566–2786 ⊕ *www.hawaiioceanadventures.com* ⊠ *$53* ☉ *Tues. and Thurs. 5–8.*

Theater

Aloha Performing Arts Center. Local talent stages musicals and Broadway plays at this center near Kailua-Kona. ✉ *Aloha Theatre Café, Hwy. 11, Kainaliu* ☎ *808/322–9924.*

Hilo Community Players. This group stages plays on an occasional basis. ✉ *141 Kalākaua Ave., Hilo* ☎ *808/935–9155.*

Kahilu Theater. For legitimate theater, the little town of Waimea is your best bet. The Kahilu Theater hosts regular internationally acclaimed performances. ✉ *Parker Ranch Center, Hwys. 19 and 190, Waimea* ☎ *808/885–6868.*

SPORTS & THE OUTDOORS

Biking

Backroads Bicycle Touring. This company has been pushing pedaling in Hawai'i since 1985. One six-day biking trip on the southern part of the island includes a day of hiking in Hawai'i Volcanoes National Park. The other choice, also six days, allows for kayaking and snorkeling. Lodgings alternate between luxury resorts and old Hawaiian inns. Fees starting at $2,400 include meals and accommodations, but bicycles and airfare are extra. ✉ *801 Cedar St., Berkeley, CA 94710-1800* ☎ *510/527–1555 or 800/462–2848* ⊕ *www.backroads.com.*

Bicycle Adventures, Inc. Eight-day tours of the Big Island accommodate both easygoing bikers and hard-core enthusiasts. You'll enjoy beach time, snorkeling, hiking excursions, comfortable accommodations, and fine dining in addition to visits to Kīlauea Volcano and Pu'uhonua O Hōnaunau. The cost of $2,400 doesn't include bicycle rental or airfare. ✆ *Box 11219, Olympia, WA 98508* ☎ *360/786–0989 or 800/443–6060* ⊕ *www.bicycleadventures.com.*

C&S Outfitters. These folks in Waimea have a wealth of knowledge about the island's biking trails. They have a shop for accessories and repair needs, plus they rent kayaks and can equip you for paintball and archery sports held at a nearby range. ✉ *64-1066 Māmalahoa Hwy. (Box 2338), Kamuela 96743* ☎ *808/885–5005.*

Kona Coast Cycling Tours. Kona Coast leads a number of bike tours all over the Big Island. See the wonders of the Big Island up close on a tour including the Kohala Coast, Hāmākua Coast, historical Māmalahoa Highway, Kona coffee country, and backcountry Mauna Kea via the Mana Road. Custom tours are also available. Rates for standard tours range from $50 to $150. ✉ *74-5588 Pawai Pl., Suite 1, Kailua-Kona 96740* ☎ *808/327–1133 or 877/592–2453* ⊕ *www.cyclekona.com.*

Mauna Kea Mountain Bikes, Inc. Daily tours down the upper slopes of Mauna Kea—chances are you'll start out in the snow—and downhill along the Kohala Mountains, as well as bike rentals are offered by this company. Tour prices range from $50 to $120. ✆ *Box 44672, Kamuela 96743* ☎ *808/883–0130 or 888/682–8687.*

Vermont Bicycle Tours. Bruce Starbuck, your experienced guide, has biked every road and trail on the Big Island. His eight-day winter tours cruise mostly downhill and visit Hawai'i's cultural sites, including Hawai'i Volcanoes National Park, Pu'uhonua O Hōnaunau, and Parker Ranch. Tour fees start at $1,800. ✉ *614 Monkton Rd. (Box 711), Bristol, VT 05443* ☎ *802/453–4811 or 800/245–3868* ⊕ *www.vbt.com.*

BIKE RENTAL If you want to strike out on your own, there are several rental shops in Kailua-Kona and a couple in Waimea and Hilo. Resorts rent bicycles that can be used around the properties. Most outfitters listed can provide a bicycle rack for your car.

B&L Bike and Sports (⊠ 75-5699 Kopiko Pl., Kailua-Kona ☎ 808/329–3309), in downtown Kailua-Kona, rents various bikes, with prices for mountain bikes starting around $30 for 24 hours.

Upcountry, close to trails that flank the slopes of Mauna Kea, **C&S Outfitters** (⊠ 64-1066 Māmalahoa Hwy., Waimea ☎ 808/885–5005) has both road and mountain bikes.

Dave's Bike & Triathlon Shop (⊠ 75-5669 Ali'i Dr., Kailua-Kona ☎ 808/329–4522) specializes in road and race bikes.

Hawaiian Pedals (⊠ Kona Inn Shopping Village, 75-5744 Ali'i Dr. ☎ 808/329–2294) rents road and mountain bikes, starting at $15 for five hours or $20 for the whole day.

Hilo Bike Hub (⊠ 318 E. Kawili St., Hilo ☎ 808/961–4452) caters to bike enthusiasts ready to explore Volcano and its surroundings.

Experienced riders will find rugged mountain bikes at **HP BikeWorks** (⊠ 74-5599 Luhia St., Suite F-3, Kailua-Kona ☎ 808/326–2453) for $25 a day for front-suspension bikes and $30 a day for full-suspension bikes.

At the Hilton Waikoloa Village, **Red Sail Sports** (⊠ 425 Waikoloa Beach Dr., Waikoloa ☎ 808/886–2876) rents out bikes to guests of the resort for $7 per hour or $20 for the whole day.

Fitness & Spa Centers

Several health clubs around the island offer inexpensive day passes for your routine workout; they have showers and lockers. With 10 spas encircling the island, you can find rejuvenation easily. Six of the major hotels have spa facilities that may be used by nonguests.

The Club. High-tech fitness facilities, with a pool and sauna, are available here for a daily rate of $15. ⊠ 75-5699 Kopiko Rd., Kailua-Kona ☎ 808/326–2582.

The Fairmont Orchid Hawai'i. The Spa Without Walls program offers an ever-expanding choice of treatments, indoors and outdoors. Ancient Hawaiian techniques, fragrant herbal wraps, and Hawaiian-coffee and vanilla scrubs are just a sampling of what's available. A pass for the gym and hot tub is $20. ⊠ 1 N. Kanikū Dr., Kohala Coast ☎ 808/885–2000.

Four Seasons Resort Hualālai. This may well be the most beautiful spa on the island, but you have to be a guest of the hotel to indulge in the top-rate health and fitness options. ⊠ 100 Ka'ūpūlehu Dr., Ka'ūpūlehu/Kona ☎ 808/325–8000.

Hāpuna Beach Prince Hotel. The hotel provides daily $15 passes for its Fitness Center at the Clubhouse and offers herbal treatments and massages, including a soothing poi body wrap. ⊠ 62-100 Kauna'oa Dr., Waimea ☎ 808/880–1111.

Hawai'i Naniloa Resort. Nonguests can use the spa and fitness center for $15. ⊠ 93 Banyan Dr., Hilo ☎ 808/969–3333.

Hilton Waikoloa Village. The hotel lays claim to the well-known and spacious Kohala Spa ($33 daily), where you can even find a healthful smoothie at the Spa Café. ⊠ 425 Waikoloa Beach Dr., Kohala Coast ☎ 808/886–1234.

Kona Village Resort. Kona Village remains true to its secluded, romantic, and luxurious isolation with a health club open to resort guests only. ⊠ Queen Ka'ahumanu Hwy., Kailua-Kona ☎ 808/325–5555.

Mauna Kea Beach Hotel. A state-of-the-art fitness center for guests only is in the hotel's private beachfront building. ⊠ 62-100 Mauna Kea Beach Dr., Kohala Coast ☎ 808/882–7222.

Mauna Lani Spa. This indoor-outdoor spa is a combination of Hawaiian gardens, thatch hales, and slate-floor state-of-the-art treatment rooms. The "Fire & Ice" theme influences the treatments, which include, among others, mud wraps using volcanic ash and hot-stone therapies. Facilities are available to nonguests; a minimum 60-minute treatment is required. ⊠ *68-1400 Mauna Lani Dr., Francis H. I'i Brown Golf Courses, Kohala Coast* ☎ *808/881–7922.*

Ohana Keauhou Beach Resort. At the Kalona Salon & Spa you can opt for spa or beauty treatments and gardenside massages. The resort's fitness room is for hotel guests only. ⊠ *78-6740 Ali'i Dr., Kailua-Kona* ☎ *808/322–9373.*

Pacific Coast Fitness. This fitness center in Upcountry Waimea offers daily classes and has state-of-the-art equipment; the fee is $8 daily. ⊠ *65-1298A Kawaihae Rd., Waimea* ☎ *808/885–6270.*

Spencer Health and Fitness Center. Exercise addicts can try this $10-a-day health club in Hilo. ⊠ *197 Keawe St., Hilo* ☎ *808/969–1511.*

Waikoloa Beach Marriott. The Hawaiian Rainforest Salon & Spa features traditional Hawaiian healing arts as well as the latest spa therapies and aromatherapy facials. The spa facilities are for hotel guests only. ⊠ *69-275 Waikoloa Beach Dr., Waikoloa* ☎ *808/886–6789.*

Golf

If there is one thing the Big Island is known for, it's beautiful golf courses. Five of the courses—two at the Mauna Kea Beach Hotel, two at the Mauna Lani Hotel, and the course at the Four Seasons Resort Hualālai—are repeatedly chosen by golfing magazines as the best.

Big Island Country Club. At a 2,500-ft elevation, this 18-hole course has a dramatic layout and stunning views. Formerly a private-membership course, it's now open to the public. ⊠ *71-1420 Māmalahoa Hwy., Kailua-Kona* ☎ *808/325–5044* ⚑ *Greens fee $85, twilight (after 11 AM) $55.*

Discovery Harbor Golf Course. At this course, designed by Robert Trent Jones, Sr., on the southern end of the island, you can play 18 holes, par 72. It can get windy here, but the cost is hard to beat. ⊠ *Kamaoa Rd., take South Point Rd., off Hwy. 11* ☎ *808/929–7353* ⚑ *Greens fee $28, cart included.*

★ **Francis H. I'i Brown Golf Course at the Mauna Lani Hotel.** This demanding and beautiful course was redesigned by Nelson Wright Haworth and now has two 18-hole courses (North and South). The men's tee at the 15th hole of the South Course is famous among golfers because they must carry their tee shot over a stretch of open ocean to reach the green. ⊠ *68-1400 Mauna Lani Dr., Kohala Coast* ☎ *808/885–6655* ⚑ *Greens fee for either course for nonguests $200, cart included.*

Hāmākua Country Club. At this friendly 9-hole course, designed in 1925, greens fees are deposited into a drop box on an honor system. You pay for the day—feel free to go into town for lunch and then come back. ⊠ *41 mi north of Hilo makai of Hwy. 19, Honoka'a* ☎ *808/775–7244* ⚑ *Greens fee $15; no carts available.*

★ **Hāpuna Golf Course.** Landscaped with indigenous plants, trees, and grasses, this course at the Hāpuna Beach Prince Hotel aims to be environmentally sensitive. It's also one of the best, a challenging par-72 course designed by Arnold Palmer and Ed Seay. Both the 1st and 18th holes are within easy walking distance of Mauna Kea Beach Hotel. ⊠ *62-100 Kauna'oa Dr., Waimea* ☎ *808/880–3000* ⚑ *Greens fee $195, twilight $105, cart included.*

Hilo Municipal Golf Course. On the east side of the island is this 18-hole, inexpensive course with four sets of tees. It's near the airport. Bring both water and an umbrella. ⊠ *340 Haihai St., Hilo* ☎ *808/959–7711* ☐ *Greens fee $25 weekdays, $30 weekends.*

★ **Hualālai Golf Course.** Designed by Jack Nicklaus, this 18-hole course is a masterpiece. Players can see the ocean from every hole. Play here is a treat reserved for Four Seasons Resort Hualālai guests and resort residents, so the course is seldom crowded. ⊠ *100 Ka'ūpūlehu Dr., Ka'ūpūlehu/Kona* ☎ *808/325–8480* ☐ *Greens fees $160.*

Kona Country Club. Choose from two Kailua-Kona 18-hole courses, both with awesome views of the Kona Coast: the **Ali'i Course** (Mountain Course) or the **Ocean Course.** The pros try to avoid the lava. ⊠ *78-7000 Ali'i Dr., Kailua-Kona* ☎ *808/322–2595* ☐ *Greens fee $130 for Ocean Course (twilight $85), $115 for Mountain Course (twilight $75).*

Mākālei Hawai'i Country Club. On the cool slopes of Hualālai Mountain, the 18-hole course climbs from 1,800 ft to 2,800 ft and is interrupted by peacocks, wild turkeys, and pheasants that wander across the bent-grass greens. ⊠ *72-3890 Hawai'i Belt Rd., Kailua-Kona* ☎ *808/325–6625* ☐ *Greens fee $110, twilight $50, cart included.*

★ **Mauna Kea Beach Resort Golf Course.** This extremely challenging championship par-72, 18-hole course receives award after award from golf magazines. It was designed by Robert Trent Jones Sr. ⊠ *62-100 Mauna Kea Beach Dr., Kohala Coast* ☎ *808/882–5400* ☐ *Greens fee $185, twilight $105.*

Naniloa Country Club Golf Course. The Naniloa is a 9-hole course convenient to Hilo's major hotels. For one fee you may take the course twice. ⊠ *120 Banyan Dr., Hilo* ☎ *808/935–3000* ☐ *Greens fee weekday $25, weekend $30; cart $7.*

Sea Mountain Golf Course. This course overlooks the shores of a black-sand beach about 30 mi south of Volcano Village. The 18-hole, par-72 course stretches from the Pacific coast up the slopes of Mauna Loa. ⊠ *Hwy. 11, Ninole Loop Rd., Punalu'u* ☎ *808/928–6222* ☐ *Greens fee weekdays $42, weekend $45, cart included.*

★ **Volcano Golf & Country Club.** This 18-hole, par-72 course perches on the rim of Kīlauea Volcano, at an elevation of 4,000 ft. It is comfortably cool, and on clear days you'll have glamorous views. It was originally built in 1922. Three grass bunkers and a pond have been added since. ⊠ *Hawai'i Volcanoes National Park* ☎ *808/967–7331* ☐ *Greens fee $63, twilight $50; cart included.*

★ **Waikoloa Beach Golf Course.** Designed by Robert Trent Jones, Jr., in 1981, this course sprawls over historical grounds at the two Waikoloa resorts. An 18-hole, par-70 course with three sets of tees, it wends through lava formations and has beautiful ocean views. ⊠ *Waikoloa Beach Dr., Waikoloa* ☎ *808/886–6060* ☐ *Greens fee for nonguests $195 for 18 holes, $105 for 9 holes; cart included.*

★ **Waikoloa King's Golf Course.** This par-72, 18-hole course, designed by Tom Weiskopf and Jay Morrish, has four large lakes and four sets of tees and is adjacent to the Hilton Waikoloa Village. ⊠ *600 Waikoloa Beach Dr., Waikoloa* ☎ *808/886–7888* ☐ *Greens fee for nonguests $195 for 18 holes, $105 for 9 holes, cart included.*

Waikoloa Village Golf Club. You'll have beautiful views at this 1,000-ft elevation. The club is 6 mi up from the resorts and is the second of the two Waikoloa courses designed by Robert Trent Jones Jr. ⊠ *68-1792 Melia St., Waikoloa Village* ☎ *808/883–9621* ☐ *Greens fee $80, twilight $55, cart included.*

Waimea Country Club. Wedged inside a eucalyptus forest is this 18-hole, bent-grass-greens, par-72 course. It lies in the cool, misty highlands on the Hilo side of Waimea and often gets rainy in the afternoon. ⊠ *47-5220 Māmalahoa Hwy., Waimea* ☎ *808/885–8053* ☐ *Greens fee $65,* *twilight $50, cart included (call for reduced rates for senior citizens or for golfers who want to walk).*

ON THE
SIDELINES
Ample celebrity-spotting is possible at golf tournaments held at resort golf courses in the Kohala area. The biggest and best is the **MasterCard Championship** (☎ 800/417–2770 ⊕ www.pga.com), a Senior PGA Tour event hosted by **Four Seasons Resort Hualālai** (☎ 808/325–8000) in January.

Hiking & Camping

For the fit adventurer, hiking is a great way to explore the Big Island's natural beauty. If you're eager to learn as you hike through pristine wilderness, you may want to book a guided nature trek with experienced naturalists and bird-watchers.

Trails crisscross the slopes of **Mauna Kea.** Hiking up here is particularly rigorous because of the change in altitude. Hikers should make sure they have plenty of water and warm clothes—sunscreen, sunglasses, and a compass are also good items to bring. The most popular hike is up to the summit, a difficult, four-hour journey that rewards the stalwart with glimpses of endangered species and amazing views. The trail begins at the Onizuka Center and makes a stop at Lake Waiau before bringing you to the summit.

The best—but also the most dangerous—overnight backcountry hikes follow the steep, isolated trails in **Hawai'i Volcanoes National Park.** Conditions are often extremely hazardous, and you must register to obtain a free permit at Kīlauea Visitor Center first. One trek leads to the top of 13,677-ft **Mauna Loa;** it's 20 mi one-way, with overnight stops at two cabins, one at 10,000 ft and the other at the summit. You should count on spending three to four days on this hike, which is possibly the hardest in the Hawaiian Islands, with arctic conditions. The **Nāpau Trail** takes you through the Kīlauea rain forest to a campsite close to the percolating stream around Pu'u O'o cone, itself active and, therefore, extremely dangerous. The **Coastal and East Rift Backcountry** descends to isolated beach sites that hide sea turtles but are not safe for swimming. ✉ *Hawai'i Volcanoes National Park, Kīlauea Visitor Center, Volcano 96785* ☎ *808/985–6000* ⊕ *www.nps.gov* ☽ *Daily 7:45–5.*

Dozens of trails at the center of Hawai'i Volcanoes National Park make for great day hikes. A ranger will be happy to help you choose according to your fitness level and time frame. Consider staying at the inexpensive **Nāmakani Paio Cabins,** at a 4,000-ft elevation, managed by Volcano House, a concession of the National Park Service. Each cabin has a double bed, two bunk beds, and electric lights. Bring extra blankets, as it gets cold in these basic units. Each cabin also has a grill outside, but you must bring your own firewood. ☽ *Volcano House, Box 53, Hawai'i Volcanoes National Park, 96718* ☎ *808/967–7321* ☐ *808/967–8429* ✍*Single or double $40; a $32 refundable deposit allows guests to pick up bedding and keys (for cabins and separate bath facilities) at Volcano House.*

For information about the Big Island's state parks, including Hāpuna Beach and Kalopa Park, contact the **Department of Land and Natural Resources, State Parks Division** (☐ 75 Aupuni St., Hilo 96720 ☎ 808/974–6200 ⊕ www.hawaii.gov).

For general hiking information, topographic and other maps, as well as up-to-date hiking guides, contact **Hawai'i Geographic Society** (☐ Box 1698, Honolulu 96806 ☎ 800/538–3950).

For information on camping at county parks, including Spencer Beach Park, contact the **Department of Parks and Recreation** (⚏ 25 Aupuni St., Hilo 96720 ☎ 808/961–8311 ⊕ www.hawaii-county.com).

Horseback Riding

In addition to the companies listed below, the Mauna Kea Beach Hotel maintains stables in Upcountry Waimea.

King's Trail Rides O'Kona, Inc. Riders take a 4½-hour excursion to Captain Cook Monument in Kealakekua Bay. The trip includes snorkeling and lunch for $95. Custom rides can also be arranged. ⊠ *Hwy. 11, mile marker 111, Kealakekua* ☎ *808/323–2388* ⊕ *www.konacowboy.com.*
Kohala Na'alapa. Here, adjacent to the white fence of Kohala Ranch, riders of all levels are invited to take open-pasture rides on historic Kahuā Ranch. Forested areas alternate with splendid panoramic views. Excursions range from $55 to $75. ⊠ *Kohala Mountain Rd. (Hwy. 250)* ☎ *808/ 889–0022.*
Paniolo Riding Adventures. Trail rides for beginners to buckaroos pass through lush Kohala ranch land. You'll never be nose-to-tail on these rides. A 1½-hour ride costs $63, a 2½-hour ride costs $89, and a 4-hour adventure costs $130. Custom rides are available. ⊠ *Kohala Mountain Rd. (Hwy. 250)* ☎ *808/889–5354* ⊕ *www.panioloadventures.com.*
Waipi'o Na'alapa Trail Rides. Deep in Waipi'o Valley, riders meander past waterfalls and rivers over lush, secluded trails on these twice-daily rides. Expeditions cost $75 and depart from Waipi'o Valley Artworks in Kukuihaele. ⊠ *Waipi'o Valley Artworks, off Hwy. 240, Kukuihaele* ☎ *808/775–0419 for information about trail rides, 808/775–0958 for Artworks.*
Waipi'o on Horseback and Taro Farm. Only two riding outfits venture into the green jungle of the valley floor. Waipi'o on Horseback takes you to an authentic taro farm. Rides depart twice daily from the Last Chance Store and cost $78. ⊠ *Last Chance Store, off Hwy. 240, Kukuihaele* ☎ *877/775–7291 or 808/775–7291.*
Waipi'o Ridge Stables. Two different rides around the rim of Waipi'o are offered—a 2½-hour trek for $75 and a 5-hour hidden-waterfall adventure for $145. Riders meet at Waipi'o Valley Artworks. ⊠ *Waipi'o Valley Artworks, off Hwy. 240, Kukuihaele* ☎ *808/775–1007 or 877/757– 1414 for information about trail rides, 808/775–0958 for Artworks* ⊕ *www.topofwaipio.com.*

Skiing

Skiing on Mauna Kea is for experienced skiers only. Currently the ski area has no lodge or lifts.

Ski Guides Hawai'i. Christopher Langan of Mauna Kea Ski Corporation is the only outfitter licensed to furnish transportation, guide services, and ski equipment on Mauna Kea. Snow can fall from Thanksgiving through June, but the most likely months are February and March. Langan charges $450 per person for a full-on daylong experience that includes refreshments, lunch, equipment, guide service, transportation from Waimea, and four-wheel-drive shuttle back up the mountain after each ski run. He also offers a $250 mountain ski service without the frills and ski or snowboard rentals. ⚏ *Box 1954, Kamuela 96743* ☎ *808/885–4188, 808/884–5131 off-season* ⊕ *www. skihawaii.com.*

Tennis

School and park courts are free and open to anyone who wishes to play, though students have first priority during school hours at high school courts. Listed below are the most popular courts. Resort courts often rent rackets, shoes, and balls. Nonguests can play for a fee at the **Royal Kona Resort**, at the **Ohana Keauhou Beach Resort**, and at the **King Kamehameha's Kona Beach Hotel**. **Waikoloa Beach Marriott**, **Hilton Waikoloa Village**, and the **Fairmont Orchid Hawai'i** also have superb courts you can book as a nonguest. Contact the **Department of Parks and Recreation** (⌂ 25 Aupuni St., Hilo 96720 ☎ 808/961–8311 ⊕ www.hawaii-county.com) for a full list of all public Big Island tennis courts.

On the Hilo side, the eight courts (three lighted for night play) at **Hilo Tennis Stadium** (⊠ Ho'olulu County Park, Pi'ilani and Kalanikoa Sts., Hilo ☎ 808/961–8720) require a small fee. There are four free (two lighted) courts at **Lincoln Park** (⊠ Kino'ole and Ponahawai Sts., Hilo). You will find well-maintained courts at the **University of Hawai'i–Hilo** (⊠ 200 Kawili St., Hilo ☎ 808/974–7520). **Waiākea Racquet Club** (⊠ 400 Hualani St., Hilo ☎ 808/961–5499) is open to the public for a reasonable fee.

In Kailua-Kona, you can play for free at the **Kailua Playground** (⊠ 75-5794 Kuakini Hwy., Kailua-Kona). Tennis courts are available at the **Old Kona Airport** (⊠ north end of Kuakini Hwy., Kailua-Kona).

There are two free, lighted courts at **Waimea Park** (⊠ Kawaihae and Lindsey Rds., Waimea). Courts at **Colony One at Sea Mountain** (⊠ 95-789 Ninole Loop Rd., turn off Hwy. 11 at Punalu'u, Punalu'u ☎ 808/928–6200 or 800/344–7675) are available at an hourly charge.

Mauna Kea Beach Hotel (⊠ 62-100 Mauna Kea Beach Dr., Kohala Coast) maintains 13 courts open to nonguests in a beautiful 12-acre oceanside tennis park.

ON THE SIDELINES The world's best players compete in January in the **USTA Challenger** (⊠ Kohala Coast ☎ 518/274–1674 ⊕ www.tesports.com) on the courts of **Hilton Waikoloa Village** (☎ 808/886–1234).

Triathlon

Fodor'sChoice ★ The highly popular **Ironman Triathlon** (☎808/329–0063 ⊕www.ironmanlive. com), with a $430,000 purse, is limited to 1,500 competitors, who swim 2.4 mi, bicycle 112 mi, and run a 26.2-mi marathon. Entrants must qualify through other international competitions. The grueling event begins with the ocean swim from Kailua Pier at 7 AM, usually on the third Saturday in October. Close to 7,000 volunteers along Ali'i Drive, Queen Ka'ahumanu Highway, and the turnaround in Hāwī provide encouragement and much-needed water to the world's top athletes.

Water Sports

DEEP-SEA FISHING Along the Kona Coast you'll find some of the world's most exciting "blue-water" fishing. Although July, August, and September are peak months, with a number of tournaments, charter fishing goes on year-round. You don't have to compete to experience the thrill of landing a big Pacific blue marlin or other game fish. More than 60 charter boats, averaging 26 ft to 58 ft, are available for hire, most of them out of **Honokōhau Harbor,** just north of Kailua. Prices for a full day of fishing range from $200 for shared charters to $900 for private trips. Half-day charters are also available in the $175 to $550 range. Tackle, bait, and ice are furnished, but you'll have to bring your own lunch. Most boats do not allow you to keep your entire catch, although if you ask, many captains will send you home with a few fish fillets. In addition, be sure to describe your expectations when you book your charter so the booking agent can match you with a captain and a boat you will like.

Make arrangements for deep-sea fishing at your hotel activities desk or stop by at the **Charter Desk** (✉ Kailua-Kona ☎ 808/329–5735) at Honokōhau Harbor; you can pick up a lunch-to-go for the trip at the **Fish Dock Deli & Store** (☎ 808/329–8389) next door.

With its varied fleet, the **Charter Locker** (☎ 808/326–2553 ⊕ www.aerialsportfishingkona.com) has been in business since 1964. **Charter Services Hawai'i** (☎ 808/334–1881 or 800/567–2650 ⊕ www.konazone.com) represents nine boats ranging from 33 ft to 46 ft. **Kona Activities Center** (☎ 808/329–3171 or 800/367–5288) provides bookings and information for several charter companies. Book charters directly or get information about tournaments at **Kona Charter Skippers Association** (☎ 808/329–3600 or 800/762–7546 ⊕ www.konabiggamefishing.com). **Notorious Sport Fishing** (☎ 808/322–6407 ⊕ www.interpac.net/-jackc) favors small groups of up to six people. For the true fishing enthusiast, **Reel Action Light-Tackle Sportfishing** (☎ 808/325–6811) runs an open-center console boat and offers light-tackle fishing, including fly-fishing.

The biggest of the fishing competitions is the five-day **Hawaiian International Billfish Tournament** (✎ Box 4800, Kailua-Kona 96745 ☎ 808/329–6155 ⊕ www.konabillfish.com), held annually in August since 1959. Tournament results can serve as a helpful guide in choosing which boat to charter.

Big fish are weighed in daily at **Honokōhau Harbor's Fuel Dock.** Try to be there in the afternoon between 4 and 5 to watch the weigh-in of the day's catch. It might just be another "grander" (more than 1,000 pounds).

KAYAKING Kayaks are great for observing Hawai'i's diverse marine life and serene shores. When you venture out, however, be sure to respect Hawai'i's waters: 30% of marine mammals are unique to the Big Island, and coral reefs are endangered; as a result, many bays are protected marine preserves. A reputable kayak shop can point out friendly locations, as currents can be dangerous.

Hawai'i Ocean Adventures (✉ Honokōhau Harbor, Slip J-38, Kailua-Kona ☎ 808/325–0766 or 877/566–2786 ⊕ www.hawaiioceanadventures.com) offers a variety of snorkeling and kayaking expeditions, often in dolphin-rich waters, from its vessel *Pacific Passion.* Fees start at $53.

Kona Boy's Kayaks/Ocean Eco Tours (✉ Honokohau Harbor, 74-425 Kealekehe Pkwy., Kailua-Kona ☎ 808/328–1234 or 808/324–7873 ⊕ www.oceanecotours.com) provides kayak sales and rentals, complete with gear and coolers, as well as guided tours. A tandem kayak costs $45 for the day. Daily tours are $95 per person. A $250 overnight trip takes you to a secluded black-sand beach.

JET SKIING Kailua Bay in Kona has generally calm waters that are perfect for jet skiiing. **Aloha Jet Ski Rentals** (✉ Kailua Pier, Ali'i Dr. at Palani Rd., Kailua-Kona ☎ 808/329–2754) charges $75 per hour for up to three riders.

SAILING & PARASAILING Ralph Blancato and Kalia Potter of **Maile Charters** (✉ Kawaihae Harbor, Kawaihae ☎ 808/326–5174 or 800/726–7245 ⊕ www.adventuresailing.com) offer unique around-the-Islands sailing adventures that range from half-day to five-day journeys. Island-cuisine meals, itineraries, and activities are custom-designed. Private cabins and hot showers keep you comfortable. Fees start at $575 for six passengers for a half day.

Parasailers sit in a harness attached to a parachute that lifts off from the boat deck and sails aloft. Passengers can choose to glide 7 or 10 minutes at 400-, 800-, or 1,200-ft heights. Call **UFO Parasail** (⊠ across the street from Kailua Pier, Kailua-Kona ☎ 808/325–5836 or 800/359–4836 ⊕ www.ufoparasailing.com) to make arrangements. Costs range from $48 to $58.

SCUBA DIVING & SNORKELING Two-tank dives average $80 to $135, depending on whether or not you're certified and whether you're diving from a boat or from the shore. Many dive outfits have underwater cameras for rent. Instruction with PADI, SDI, or TDI certification in three to five days is $400 to $650. The Kona Coast has calm waters for diving, and dive operators are helpful about suggesting dive sites as far south as Pu'uhonua O Hōnaunau. Some companies also teach surfing, and most rent out dive equipment, snorkel gear, and other water toys. A few organize otherworldly mantaray dives at night or whale-watching cruises in season.

A reputable scuba charter in Kailua-Kona is **Big Island Divers** (⊠ 75-5467 Kaiwi St., Kailua-Kona ☎ 808/329–6068 or 800/488–6068 ⊕ www.bigislanddivers.com). **Body Glove Cruises** (⊠ Kailua Pier, Kailua-Kona ☎ 808/326–7122 or 800/551–8911 ⊕ www.bodyglovehawaii.com) has a 55-ft catamaran that sets off from the Kailua Pier daily for a 4½-hour dive and snorkel cruise, which includes breakfast and a buffet lunch. Children are welcome. **Eco-Adventures Dive & Adventure Programs** (⊠ King Kamehameha's Kona Beach Hotel, 75-5660 Palani Rd., Kailua-Kona ☎ 808/329–7116 or 800/949–3483 ⊕ www.eco-adventures.net) creates daylong experiences with three dives as well as discovery trips, packages that include snorkeling and kayaking, and charter vacations. **Kohala Divers Ltd.** (⊠ Kawaihae Shopping Center, downstairs, Kawaihae ☎ 808/882–7774 ⊕ www.kohaladivers.com) offers complete diving services. **Kona Coast Divers** (⊠ Honokohau Harbor, 74-425 Kealekehe Pkwy., Kailua-Kona ☎ 808/329–8802 or 800/562–3483 ⊕ www.konacoastdivers.com) is a reputable, friendly outfit that has been around a long time. **Ocean Eco Tours** (⊠ Honokohau Harbor, 74-425 Kealekehe Pkwy., Kailua-Kona ☎ 808/324–7873 ⊕ www.oceanecotours.com) is an ecofriendly, full-service outfit eager to share a wealth of knowledge. At 'Anaeho'omalu Bay, at the Hilton Waikoloa Village on the Kohala ★ Coast, **Red Sail Sports** (⊠ 425 Waikoloa Beach Dr. ☎ 808/886–2876 ⊕ www.redsail.com) certifies divers and organizes dives from the 38-ft *Lani Kai*. **Sandwich Isle Divers** (⊠ 75-5729 Ali'i Dr., Kailua-Kona ☎ 808/329–9188 or 800/743–3483 ⊕ www.sandwichisledivers.com) is central and well established.

Colorful tropical fish frequent the lava outcroppings along many Big Island shorelines, so it's easy to arrange a do-it-yourself snorkeling tour by renting masks and snorkels from any of the many diving outfits in Kona or at the resorts. If you are island-hopping and want to drop off your equipment on O'ahu, Maui, or Kaua'i, consider **Snorkel Bob's** (⊠ 75-5831 Kahakai Rd., next to the Royal Kona Resort, Kailua-Kona ☎ 808/329–0770 or 800/262–7725 ⊕ www.snorkelbob.com), where prices start at $9 a week for a simple set.

Many snorkel cruises are available. Shop for prices at kayak, scuba, and sailing outfitters; ask about the size of the boat, and make sure you know what is included and how much the extras, such as underwater cameras, cost.

Among the Big Island's wet-and-wild offerings is the **Captain Zodiac Raft Expedition** (✉ Honokōhau Harbor, Kailua-Kona ☎ 808/329–3199 🌐 www.captainzodiac.com). The exciting four-hour 14-mi trip on this inflatable raft takes you along the Kona Coast to explore gaping lava-tube caves, search for dolphins and turtles, and drift through Kealakekua Bay for snorkeling. The cost is $78.

★ At Keauhou Bay **Fair Wind Snorkel and Orca Raft Adventures** (✉ Keauhou Bay, Kailua-Kona ☎ 808/322–2788 or 800/677–9461 🌐 www.fair-wind.com) offers 4½-hour morning and 3½-hour afternoon excursions as well as special tours and packages. *Fair Wind* is a 60-ft double-decker catamaran with a 15-ft water slide and a dive tower. Gear includes prescription masks. Morning sails feature a barbecue lunch. The *Orca,* a 28-ft inflatable raft, cleaves the waves in a high-thrill, fast-pace ride not for the weak at heart. It also makes time for snorkeling and gentler floating opportunities. Morning sails cost around $87 on the *Fair Wind* and $73 on the *Orca*; afternoon trips are around $55 for both vessels.

WINDSURFING　One of the best windsurfing locations on the Big Island is at 'Anaeho'omalu Bay, at the beach in front of the Waikoloa Beach Marriott. Call **Ocean Sports** (☎ 808/886–6666) to obtain information.

SHOPPING

Residents like to complain that there isn't much to shop for on the Big Island, but unless you're searching for winter coats or high-tech toys, you'll find plenty to deplete your pocketbook. Kailua-Kona has a range of souvenirs from far-flung corners of the globe. Resorts along the Kohala Coast have high-quality exclusive clothing, art, and accessories. Galleries and boutiques, many with the work of local artists, fill historic buildings in Waimea and North Kohala.

In general, stores and shopping centers on the Big Island open at 9 or 10 AM and close by 6 PM. Hilo's Prince Kūhiō Shopping Plaza stays open until 9 weekdays. In Kona, most shops in shopping plazas that are geared toward tourists remain open until 9. Big outlets such as KTA (a supermarket in Kona Coast Shopping Center) or Wal-Mart on Henry Street are open until midnight.

Shopping Centers

HĀMĀKUA COAST　Developed for local consumers, **Kaloko Industrial Park** (✛ off Hwy. 19 and Hina Lani St., near Keāhole-Kona International Airport) has outlets such as Costco Warehouse. It's useful for industrial shopping, off-the-beaten-path finds, and wholesale prices.

HILO　In Hilo the most comprehensive mall, similar to mainland malls, is **Prince Kūhiō Shopping Plaza** (✉ 111 E. Puainako St., at Hwy. 11). Here you'll find Macy's for fashion, Safeway for food, and Longs Drugs for just about everything else, along with several other shops and boutiques. The older **Hilo Shopping Center** (✉ Kekuanaoa St. at Kīlauea Ave.) has several air-conditioned shops and restaurants; great cookies, cakes, and baked goodies at Lanky's Pastries; and plenty of free parking. Hilo's **Waiakea Center** (✉ Makaala St., across from Prince Kūhiō Shopping Plaza, at Hwy. 11) has a Borders Books & Music, Island Naturals, a food court, and a Wal-Mart.

KAILUA-KONA　**Coconut Plaza** (✉ 75-5795–75-5825 Ali'i Dr.), just south of Kona Inn Shopping Village, hides coffee shops, boutiques, ethnic restaurants, and an exquisite gallery in its meandering labyrinth of airy buildings.

Shopping in Kailua-Kona has begun to go the way of mainland cities with Wal-Mart, a huge Safeway, Borders Books & Music, and an eclectic collection of restaurants at **Crossroads Shopping Center** (⊠ 75-1000 Henry St.). **Keauhou Shopping Center** (⊠ 78-6831 Ali'i Dr.) has a variety of stores and boutiques and a few island-style eateries.

On the makai side of Ali'i Drive, extending for an entire block, is **Kona Inn Shopping Village** (⊠ 75-5744 Ali'i Dr. ☎ 808/329–6573), crammed with boutiques selling bright pareos (beach wraps) and knickknacks. Here **Island Salsa** (☎ 808/329–9279) has great tropical toppers and T-shirts, and **Honolua Surf Company** (☎ 808/329–1001) is filled with cool beachwear. In Kailua-Kona, head north on **Palani Road** from Kailua Pier toward the intersection with Highway 19; **Kopiko Plaza** and **Lanihau Center,** on your right, house Longs Drug, gift stores, sandwich shops, and a budget-friendly Sack 'n Save Foods. On your left, you'll find **North Kona Center** and **Kona Coast Shopping Center.**

Just north of Kona, off Highway 19, islanders find bargains at Big Kmart in the **Makalapua Center** (⊠ Makalapua Ave.). Of more interest might be the large Macy's; although a mainland chain, it keeps nice selections in apparel and gifts from local vendors.

KOHALA The harborside **Kawaihae Center** (⊠ Hwy. 270, Kawaihae) houses restaurants, a dive shop, a bathing-suit store, and art galleries, including the Harbor Gallery.

King's Shops (⊠ 250 Waikoloa Beach Dr., Waikoloa ☎ 808/886–8811) houses fine stores such as Under the Koa Tree, with its upscale gift items by artisans. You'll also find high-end outlets such as DFS Galleria and Louis Vuitton.

The 60,000-square-ft **Shops at Mauna Lani** (⊠ between the Mauna Lani and the Fairmont Orchid resorts) has top-of-the-line retail outlets and restaurants.

WAIMEA **Parker Ranch Shopping Center** (⊠ Hwy. 19) sports a ranch-style motif. Anchors include a Foodland supermarket, Starbucks Coffee, and Natural Foods Store. Other shops in the mix are clothing boutiques and food outlets. The Parker Ranch Store and Parker Ranch Visitor Center and Museum are also here.

In Waimea, browse around boutiques in **Parker Square** (⊠ Kawaihae Rd. ☎ 808/331–1000) and in the adjacent **High Country Traders,** where you may find hand-stitched Hawaiian quilts. **Waimea Center** (⊠ Hwy. 19) has an eclectic mix of stores, including a large KTA supermarket, an unusual San Francisco–style gift shop, and a travel service, Without Boundaries.

Specialty Stores

Books & Maps

Basically Books (⊠ 160 Kamehameha Ave., Hilo ☎ 808/961–0144 or 800/903–6277 ⊕ www.basicallybooks.com) stocks one of Hawai'i's largest selections of maps and charts, including USGS, topographical, and raised relief maps. It also has Hawaiiana books, with great choices for children. **Kohala Book Shop** (⊠ 54-3885 Akoni Pule Hwy., Kapa'au ☎ 808/889–6400 ⊕ www.abebooks.com/home/kohalawind) in the historic Old Nanbu Hotel is the largest used-book store in the state, with one of the most complete Hawaiian and Pacific collections in the nation and rare first editions. **Middle Earth Bookshoppe** (⊠ 75-5719 Ali'i Dr., Kailua-Kona ☎ 808/329–2123) is an independent bookstore with superb maps and an esoteric collection of literary works.

Candies & Chocolates

★ The chocolate factory **Big Island Candies** (⊠ 585 Hinano St., Hilo ☎ 808/935–8890 ⊕ www.bigislandcandies.com) lets you tour and taste before you buy. **Kailua Candy Company** (⊠ 74-5563 Kaiwi St., Kailua-Kona ☎ 808/329–2522) sells chocolate made with locally grown cacao beans from the Original Hawaiian Chocolate Factory. Of course, tasting is part of the fun. Through a glass wall you can watch the chocolate artists at work.

Hawaiian Art & Crafts

HAWAI'I VOLCANOES NATIONAL PARK On your way to Hawai'i Volcanoes National Park, be sure to visit the workshop of **Dan DeLuz's Woods, Inc.** (⊠ Hwy. 11, mile marker 12, Mountain View ☎ 808/968–6607 ⊠ 64-1013 Māmalahoa Hwy., Waimea ☎ 808/885–5856), where master bowl-turner Dan DeLuz creates works of art from 50 types of exotic wood grown on the Big Island.

★ In Hawai'i Volcanoes National Park, **Volcano Art Center** (☎ 808/967–7565) remains a favorite with everyone. The Art Center represents more island artists than any other gallery and carries a selection of fine art prints and oils as well.

HILO Step into **Dragon Mama** (⊠ 266 Kamehameha Ave. ☎ 808/934–9081) to find authentic Japanese fabrics, futons, and antiques. You'll find exquisite ceramics, Japanese tea sets, and affordable bamboo ware at **Ets'ko** (⊠ 35 Waiānuenue Ave. ☎ 808/961–3778). Hilo's **Most Irresistible Shop** (⊠ 256 Kamehameha Ave. ☎ 808/935–9644 ⊠ Prince Kuhio Plaza, 111 E. Puainako St., at Hwy. 11, ☎ 808/959–6515) lives up to its name with unique gifts from the Pacific, be it coconut-flavored butter or a whimsical wind chime.

If you're driving north from Hilo, take time to browse through **Hoaloha** (⊠ Last Chance Store, off Hwy. 240, Kukuihaele ☎ 808/775–0502) and pick up a colorful pareo or accessory. In the remote **Waipi'o Valley Artworks** (⊠ off Hwy. 240, Kukuihaele ☎ 808/775–0958) you'll find finely crafted wooden bowls, koa furniture, paintings, and jewelry—all made by local artists.

KAILUA-KONA For hula instruments, intricate feather headbands, and other original art, head to **Alapaki's Hawaiian Gifts** (⊠ Keauhou Shopping Village, 78-6831 Ali'i Dr. ☎ 808/322–2007). Geared toward cruise-ship passengers

★ with little time, **Made on the Big Island** (⊠ King Kamehameha's Kona Beach Hotel, 75-5660 Palani Rd., at Kailua Pier ☎ 808/326–4949) is one-stop shopping for traditional Big Island gifts. You'll find quite a few treasures here, such as koa boxes and bonsai trees that may be exported. At **Rift Zone** (⊠ Coconut Plaza, 75-5801 Ali'i Dr. ☎ 808/331–1100), owned by ceramist Robert Joiner and his wife, Kathy, you'll find ceramics but also exquisite jewelry, bowls, ornaments, and handblown glass.

KOHALA **Cook's Discoveries** (⊠ 64-1066 Māmalahoa Hwy., Waimea ☎ 808/885–

★ 3633) is one of the best places in the state to shop for high-end Hawaiian gifts. In the **Gallery of Great Things** (⊠ Kawaihae Rd. ☎ 808/885–7706) at Parker Square, you might fall in love with the Ni'ihau shell leis ($150–$7,000) it occasionally carries. More affordable perhaps are koa mirrors and other high-quality artifacts from all around the Pacific basin. For fine art, furniture, and decorative pieces made with koa and other native woods, make sure to stop in Kawaihae and visit the **Harbor Gallery** (⊠ Kawaihae Shopping Center, Kawaihae ☎ 808/882–1510). **Mauna Kea Galleries** (⊠ 65-1298 Kawaihae Rd., Waimea ☎ 808/887–2244) specializes in rare vintage collectibles, including hula dolls, prints, and koa furniture.

Upcountry of Kailua-Kona, in the little coffee town of Hōlualoa, several galleries crowd the narrow street. **Hōlualoa Gallery** (✉ Māmalahoa Hwy., Hōlualoa ☎ 808/322–8484) has stunning *raku* (Japanese lead-glazed pottery). Men can pick up an authentic *lauhala* hat for some top-level sun protection at **Kimura's Lauhala Shop** (✉ Māmalahoa Hwy., Hōlualoa ☎ 808/324–0053). The **Kona Arts Center** (✉ Māmalahoa Hwy., Hōlualoa) has drawn an entire community of artists; feel free to drop in if the doors are open.

Remote North Kohala has dozens of artists and hosts a remarkable number of galleries in its old restored plantation buildings. At **Ackerman Gallery** (✉ Akoni Pule Hwy., Kapaʻau ☎ 808/889–5971), painter Gary Ackerman; his wife, Yesan; and their daughter, Camille, have a fine and varied collection of gifts for sale in two locations near the King Kamehameha statue. Be sure to stop at the Old Nanbu Hotel, a historic building constructed in 1898. Here, working in the front window of his store, **Elements** (✉ 54-3885 Akoni Pule Hwy., Kapaʻau ☎ 808/889–0760), John Flynn creates exquisite jewelry such as delicate, silver-maile lei and gold waterfalls. The shop also showcases carefully chosen gift items, including unusual ceramics and glass. Inside the Bamboo Restaurant in Hāwī, the **Gallery at Bamboo** (✉ Hāwī Rd., Hāwī ☎ 808/889–1441) seduces visitors with koa-wood pieces such as rocking chairs and writing desks. It also has a wealth of gift items such as boxes, jewelry, and Hawaiian wrapping paper. **Nanbu Gallery** (✉ 54-3885 Akoni Pule Hwy., Kapaʻau ☎ 808/889–0997) shows the paintings of owner Patrick Sweeney and other island artists. Watercolorist and oil painter Patrick Louis Rankin runs **Rankin Gallery** (✉ 53-4380 Akoni Pule Hwy., Kapaʻau ☎ 808/889–6849) in the old Wo On Store, next to the Chinese temple.

Vintage & Resort Wear

Hotel shops generally offer the most attractive and original resort wear, but prices run higher than elsewhere.

HILO **Hilo Hattie** (✉ Prince Kūhiō Plaza, 111 E. Puainako St., Hilo ☎ 808/961–3077 ✉ Kopiko Plaza, Kailua-Kona ☎ 808/329–7200) matches his-and-her aloha wear and carries a huge selection of casual clothes, slippers, jewelry, and souvenirs. Call for free transportation from selected hotels. The well-known **Sig Zane Designs** (✉ 122 Kamehameha Ave., Hilo ☎ 808/935–7077) sells distinctive island wearables with bold colors and motifs.

KAILUA-KONA For rare vintage clothing and authentic antique jewelry, browse through the selection at **Flamingo's** (✉ Kona Inn Shopping Village, 75-5744 Aliʻi Dr. ☎ 808/329–4122). In **Keauhou Shopping Center** (✉ 76-6831 Aliʻi Dr.) in Kailua-Kona, stop in at **Borderlines** (☎ 808/322–5003) for colorful women's apparel. **Laneke Boutique** (☎ 808/322–9100) carries a great variety of aloha attire and resort wear.

KOHALA At **Adasa** (✉ 3 Opelo Plaza, Waimea ☎ 808/887–0997), designer Donna Lore carries high-end couture, her own designs, and matching accessories. Custom design is also possible. In North Kohala, in the historic 1932 Toyama Building, **As Hāwī Turns** (✉ Akoni Pule Hwy., Hāwī ☎ 808/889–5023) adds a sophisticated touch to breezy resort wear, pareos, and hand-painted silk clothing. There are vintage and secondhand treasures, crafts, and gifts as well. If you'd like to take home some of Hawaiʻi's splashy material, stop in at **Kimura's Fabrics** (✉ Māmalahoa Hwy. 11, Kainaliu ☎ 808/322–3771). Upcountry on the one-street town of Kainaliu—and in Kailua-Kona's shopping centers—**Paradise Found** (✉ Māmalahoa Hwy. 11 ☎ 808/322–2111 ✉ Lanihau Center, Kailua-

Kona ☎ 808/329–2221 ✉ Keauhou Shopping Center, Kailua-Kona ☎ 808/324–1177) has contemporary silk and rayon clothing.

Tropical Flowers & Produce

★ You can buy tropical blooms at **Akatsuka Orchid Gardens** (✉ Hwy. 11, Volcano ☎ 808/967–8234) and have them shipped home. The nursery is in Volcano, a 10-minute drive from Hawai'i Volcanoes National Park.

At **Ali'i Gardens Market Place** (✉ 75-6129 Ali'i Dr., 1½ mi south of Kona Inn Shopping Village, Kailua-Kona ☎ 808/334–1381), open from Wednesday through Sunday, individual entrepreneurs sell everything from tropical flowers to Kona coffee, baskets, souvenirs, and crafts. It's more of a flea market than a farmers' market.

In addition to selling and shipping miniature brassaia lava plantings and other bonsai plants, **Fuku-Bonsai Cultural Center** (✉ Ola'a Rd., Kurtistown ☎ 808/982–9880 ⊕ www.fukubonsai.com), which is on the way to Volcano, has free educational exhibits of different ethnic styles of pruning.

★ At **Hilo Farmers Market** (✉ Kamehameha Ave. and Mamo St., Hilo) farmers sell a profusion of tropical flowers, high-quality produce, and macadamia nuts. This colorful, open-air market—the most popular in the state—takes place on Wednesday and Saturday from 6:30 AM to 2:30 PM.

The low-key **Kona Inn Farmers' Market** (✉ 75-7544 Ali'i Dr., Kona Inn Shopping Village parking lot, Kailua-Kona) is filled with colorful tropical flowers and locally grown produce, including macadamia nuts and coffee. It takes place Wednesday and Saturday from 7 AM until 3 PM.

In North Kohala, **Na Pua O Kohala** (✉ 55-3413 Akoni Pule Hwy. ☎ 808/889–5541 or 877/889–5571 ⊕ www.kohalaflowers.com) you can order leis or let owner Johanna Bard help you create a memorable bouquet. She'll ship your selections for you.

The old stone **Volcano Store** (✉ Old Volcano Hwy., Volcano Village ☎ 808/967–7210), near Hawai'i Volcanoes National Park, has excellent bargains in cut flowers such as anthuriums and will ship them for you.

THE BIG ISLAND A TO Z

To research prices, get advice from other travelers, and book travel arrangements, visit www.fodors.com.

AIR TRAVEL

Several domestic and international airlines serve the Big Island's two airports from the mainland as well as from the other islands. Charters around the Islands are available from any airport location through Big Island Air, in nine-passenger aircraft at hourly rates starting at $770.

CARRIERS Both national and local airlines offer daily flights to several cities on the mainland. Connections of airlines listed are direct, but keep in mind that you can fly from anywhere as long as you're willing to transfer on O'ahu or Maui. Hawaiian Airlines, for example, now serves San Diego, San Francisco, Portland, Phoenix, Las Vegas, Los Angeles, and Seattle from Honolulu. Aloha Airlines has daily trips connecting Oakland, Orange County, Burbank, Phoenix, Vancouver, and Las Vegas with the Islands.

United offers daily direct flights from San Francisco and Los Angeles to Kona International Airport.

Between the Neighbor Islands, Aloha and Hawaiian airlines offer frequent jet flights that take about 40 minutes from Honolulu to either Hilo or Kona. Fares are approximately $120 to $180.

Aloha Airline's sister commuter carrier Island Air provides frequent, direct flights from Kona to Hawai'i's resort and smaller community destinations, including Lāna'i, Moloka'i, and Kapalua.

🛫 **Aloha Airlines** ☎ 800/367-5250 or 808/935-5771 ⊕ www.alohaairlines.com. **Big Island Air** ☎ 808/329-4868 or 800/303-8868. **Hawaiian Airlines** ☎ 800/882-8811 in Hawai'i, 800/367-5320 from the mainland ⊕ www.hawaiianair.com. **Island Air** ☎ 800/652-6541 in Hawai'i, 800/323-3345 from the mainland ⊕ www.islandair.com. **United** ☎ 800/241-6522 ⊕ www.ual.com.

AIRPORTS

The Big Island has two main airports: Kona International Airport, near Kailua-Kona, and Hilo International Airport. Visitors whose accommodations are on the west side of the island normally fly into Kona. If you're staying on the eastern side, in Hilo or near Volcano, fly into Hilo. Midway between Hilo and Kailua-Kona, a small airstrip is used primarily by residents of Waimea. In North Kohala a deserted airstrip, Upolo Point, services small, private planes only.

🛫 **Hilo International Airport** ✉ General Lyman Field ☎ 808/934-5838, 808/934-5840 for visitor information. **Kona International Airport** ☎ 808/329-1190, 808/329-3423 for visitor information. **Waimea-Kohala Airport** ☎ 808/887-8126.

AIRPORT TRANSFERS Kona International Airport is about 7 mi (a 10-minute drive) from Kailua-Kona. The Keauhou resort area stretches another 6 mi to the south beyond Kailua. It takes about 30 to 45 minutes by car to reach the upscale resorts along the Kona-Kohala Coast.

Hilo International Airport is just 2 mi from Hilo's Banyan Drive hotels. If you have chosen a B&B closer to Hawai'i Volcanoes National Park, plan on a 40-minute drive from Hilo International Airport.

If you have booked accommodations in the Waimea area, expect an hour's drive north from either the Kona or Hilo airport.

Limousine service with a chauffeur who will act as your personal guide averages $100 an hour, with a two-hour minimum. A few have all the extras—TV, bar, and narrated tours, plus Japanese-speaking guides.

There is no regularly scheduled shuttle service from either main airport, although private service is offered by the Kohala Coast resorts to the north of Kona International Airport. The rates for this service vary depending on the distance but are less than a taxi. Check-in is at the Kohala Coast Resort Association counters at the Aloha and Hawaiian airlines arrival areas. SpeediShuttle arranges shared rides from Kona International Airport and may be less expensive than a taxi, but you must call ahead of time.

If you're staying in Kailua or at the Keauhou resort area to the south of the airport, check with your hotel upon booking to see if shuttle service is available.

Taxis are on hand for plane arrivals at both major airports. Taxis from Hilo International Airport to Hilo charge about $10 for the 2-mi ride to the Banyan Drive hotels. At Kona International Airport, fares start at about $20 for transport to King Kamehameha's Kona Beach Hotel and are slightly more expensive for other Kailua-Kona hotels and condos. Taxi fares to Kohala Coast resorts range from $45 to $60. Several taxis offer guided tours.

🚖 In Hilo: **A-1 Bob's Taxi** ☎ 808/959-4800. **Hilo Harry's Taxi** ☎ 808/935-7091.
🚖 In Kona: **Aloha Taxi** ☎ 808/325-5448. **Elsa Taxi** ☎ 808/887-6446. **Luana Limousine** ☎ 808/326-5466. **Marina Taxi** ☎ 808/329-2481. **Paradise Taxi** ☎ 808/329-1234. **SpeediShuttle** ☎ 808/329-5433.

BOAT & FERRY TRAVEL

Many luxury cruise ships visit the Islands throughout the year. Currently only Norwegian Cruise Lines sails its luxury vessel among the Islands exclusively, pausing in Kailua-Kona and Hilo on the Big Island. Point of departure and of final return is Honolulu. Costs for seven- or eight-day cruises range from $1,160 to more than $5,000, depending on your choice of cabin and the time of year.

🚢 **Norwegian Cruise Lines:** *Norwegian Star* ☎ 800/327-7030 ⊕ www.ncl.com.

BUS TRAVEL

Hele-On Bus operates Monday through Saturday between Hilo and Kailua-Kona, for $5.25 each way or $7 round-trip. The once-daily connection takes about three hours each way and stops in numerous locations. An additional $1 is charged for luggage and backpacks that do not fit under the seat. The Hele-On operates in the Hilo and Kailua-Kona town areas themselves for 75¢ and up; exact fare is required. The bus also services the regions of North Kohala, Waimea, and Ka'u. The county Web site shows complete schedules, additional services, and fees.

The Ali'i Shuttle operates a bus service in the Kona resort area between Keauhou Bay and Kailua-Kona town Monday through Saturday, 8:30 AM to 7 PM. The shuttle connects all major hotels, condos, attractions, and shopping centers along Ali'i Drive. The cost is $3.

🚌 **Ali'i Shuttle** ☎ 808/938-1112. **Hele-On Bus** ☎ 808/961-8744 ⊕ www.hawaii-county.com/mass_transit/transit_main.htm.

CAR RENTAL

To get the best rate on a rental car, book it in conjunction with an interisland Hawaiian or Aloha Airlines flight, or ask your travel agent to check out room-and-car packages. Drivers must be 25 years or older. Note that dropping off a rental at a different airport from where you originally rented may cost you as much as $85 extra.

Most agencies make you sign an agreement that you won't drive on Saddle Road between Hilo and Waimea: it's a bumpy route that can be dangerous, and there are no gas stations or emergency phones. On the other hand, if you're thinking about stargazing, you'll have to take the road up to Mauna Kea off Saddle Road for the clearest views. Alamo, Budget, Dollar, and Harper Rentals let you do this in their four-wheel-drive vehicles. You might consider a four-wheel-drive vehicle anyway to reach rugged shoreline sights.

Two companies on the island rent RVs. Island RV gives you a ready-to-go vacation that includes a complete itinerary, equipment rentals, and customized care; Harper Rentals just gets you the RV as is. Linens are available at both outfits.

🚗 Major Agencies: **Alamo** ☎ 800/327-9633. **Avis** ☎ 800/321-3712. **Budget** ☎ 800/527-0700. **Dollar** ☎ 800/800-4000. **Enterprise** ☎ 800/736-8222. **Hertz** ☎ 800/654-3011. **National** ☎ 800/227-7368. **Thrifty** ☎ 800/367-2277.
🚗 Local Agencies: **Harper Car and Truck Rental** ☎ 808/969-1478 or 800/852-9993 ⊕ www.harperhawaii.com. **Island RV** ☎ 808/334-0464 or 800/406-4555 ⊕ www.islandrv.com.

CAR TRAVEL

You need a car to see the sights of the Big Island in any reasonable amount of time. Even if you're solely interested in relaxing at your self-contained megaresort, you may still want to rent a car, simply to travel to Kailua-Kona or to the restaurants in Waimea.

Though there are nine car-rental companies from which to choose, cars can be scarce during holiday weekends, special events, and peak seasons—from mid-December through mid-March. It is best to book well in advance.

EMERGENCIES

Dial **911** in an emergency to reach the police, fire department, or an ambulance. Call one of the hospitals listed for a doctor or dentist close to you. The Volcano Update Hotline provides 24-hour recorded information.

🆘 Emergency Services: **Police** ☎ 808/935-3311. **Poison Control Center** ☎ 800/362-3585. **Volcano Update Hotline** ☎ 808/985-6000.

🆘 Hospitals: **Hilo Medical Center** ✉ 1190 Waiānuenue Ave., Hilo ☎ 808/974-4700. **Kona Community Hospital** ✉ Hwy. 11 at Hau Kapila St., Kealakekua ☎ 808/322-9311. **Kona-Kohala Medical Associates** ✉ 75-137 Hualalai Rd., Kailua-Kona ☎ 808/329-1346. **North Hawai'i Community Hospital** ✉ 67-1125 Māmalahoa Hwy., Waimea ☎ 808/885-4444.

LODGING

B & BS Members of the Big Island–based Hawai'i Island Bed and Breakfast Association are listed with phone numbers and rates in a comprehensive on-line brochure from the Hawai'i Island Bed and Breakfast umbrella organization. Or you can go with several network booking agencies that try to meet your needs on an individual basis.

🏠 **Bed & Breakfast Honolulu (Statewide)** ☎ 800/288-4666 🖨 808/595-2030 ⊕ www.hawaiibnb.com. **Go Native Hawai'i** ☎ 800/662-8483 ⊕ www.gonativehi.com. **Hawai'i Island Bed and Breakfast Association** ⊕ www.stayhawaii.com. **Hawai'i's Best Bed and Breakfasts** ☎ 808/885-4550 or 800/262-9912 🖨 808/885-0559 ⊕ www.bestbnb.com.

MOTORCYCLE TRAVEL

Scooters and motorcycles can be rented in Hilo and Kailua-Kona. Some words of warning: Big Island roads often have narrow shoulders, and the drafts from oversize tour buses swooping by can unexpectedly double the excitement of a simple Sunday ride. Helmets are advised but not mandatory in Hawai'i.

🏍 **DJ's Rentals** ✉ 75-5563A Palani Rd., Kailua-Kona ☎ 808/329-1700 or 800/993-4647. **Hilo Harley Davidson** ✉ 100 Kanoelehua Ave., Hilo ☎ 808/934-9090. **Kona Harley Davidson** ✉ 74-5615 Luhia St., Kailua-Kona ☎ 808/326-9887.

SIGHTSEEING TOURS

AIRPLANE & HELICOPTER TOURS There's nothing quite like gazing at a waterfall that drops a couple of thousand feet into multiple pools. You can also fly above the lava lake on Kīlauea, then follow the flow to the ocean, where clouds of steam billow into the air. (The lava flow has been changing locations and sometimes goes underground, so ask exactly what you'll see when you book your flight.) For a fee, some tour companies will record your flight as a souvenir if you wish. You can go in small planes that carry three to nine passengers or helicopters that carry up to six passengers. Expect to pay anywhere from $150 for 50-minute flights to $325-plus for two hours, and make reservations in advance.

Big Island Air and Island Hoppers Hawai'i offer plane tours. Island Hoppers Hawai'i leaves from Hilo airport for 50-minute flights and from Kailua-Kona for 2- and 2½-hour flights. Blue Hawaiian Helicopters, Sunshine Helicopters, Tropical Helicopters, and Volcano Helicopters all offer helicopter tours leaving from one of the two major airports or a private landing pad.

Big Island Air ⊠ Kona International Airport ☎ 808/329-4868 or 800/303-8868. **Blue Hawaiian Helicopters** ⊠ Hilo International Airport or Waikoloa Helipad ☎ 808/961-5600 or 800/786-2583 ⊕ www.bluehawaiian.com. **Island Hoppers Hawai'i** ⊠ Hilo and Kona International Airports ☎ 808/969-2000 or 800/538-7590 ⊕ www.fly-hawaii.com/above. **Sunshine Helicopters** ⊠ Helipad at the Hāpuna Beach Prince Hotel and Hilo International Airport ☎ 808/882-1223 or 800/622-3144 ⊕ www.sunshinehelicopters.com. **Tropical Helicopters** ⊠ Hilo International Airport ☎ 808/961-6810 ⊕ www.tropicalhelicopters.com. **Volcano Helicopters** ⊠ Hilo International Airport ☎ 808/961-3355.

<table>
<tr><td>ALL-TERRAIN-VEHICLE TOURS</td><td>A different way to experience the Big Island's rugged coastline and wild ranch lands is through an off-road adventure. At higher elevations, weather can be nippy and rainy, but views can be awesome. You can ride in your own all-terrain vehicle or share a Hummer. Protective gear is provided. Prices range from $85 to $125 per person, depending on tour length and specifics.</td></tr>
</table>

ATV Outfitters Hawai'i ⊠ Old Sakamoto Store, Hwy. 270, Kapa'au ☎ 808/889-6000 or 888/288-7288 ⊕ www.outfittershawaii.com. **Bedrock Ranch ATV Adventure** ⊠ Hwy. 11, Ka'u District, Waiohinu ☎ 808/929-8157 ⊕ www.bedrockranchatv.com. **HMV Tours** ⊠ Hwy. 250, Hāwī ☎ 808/889-6922 or 877/449-6922 ⊕ www.hmvtours.com. **Kahuā Ranch ATV Rides** ⊠ Hwy. 250, 10 mi north of Waimea ☎ 808/882-7954 or 808/882-4646 ⊕ www.kahuaranch.com. **Kukui ATV & Adventures** ⊠ Pickup from Waipi'o Valley Artworks, Kukuihaele ☎ 808/775-1701 or 877/757-1414 ⊕ www.topofwaipio.com.

BOAT TOURS A voyage on a traditional double-hulled sailing canoe is available on the *Hahalua Lele* along the Kohala shores near the Fairmont Orchid Hawai'i. The crew spices up the tour with Hawaiian history and legends. Expect to pay $100.

Unique among the abundance of water adventures is the *Atlantis IV* one-hour submarine tour from Kailua Pier, across from King Kamehameha's Kona Beach Hotel in Kona. A large glass dome in the bow and 13 viewing ports on the sides allow clear views of the watery world. Children must be at least 3 ft tall. Fees for adults range from $75 to $90.

Atlantis IV Submarine ☎ 808/329-6626 or 800/548-6262 ⊕ www.atlantisadventures.com. **Hahalua Lele** ☎ 808/885-2000 ⊕ www.fairmont.com.

BUS TOURS Local tour-bus operators conduct volcano tours and circle-island tours, with pickup at the major resorts. Costs range from $38 to $68, depending on pickup location.

Jack's Tours ☎ 808/886-2202 in Kona, 808/961-6666 in Hilo, 800/442-5557. **Polynesian Adventure Tours** ☎ 808/329-8008 in Kona, 800/622-3011 ⊕ www.polyad.com. **Roberts Hawai'i** ☎ 808/329-1688 in Kona, 808/966-5483 in Hilo, 800/831-5541 ⊕ www.robertshawaii.com.

COFFEE-FARM TOURS Several coffee farms around the South Kona and Upcountry Kona coffee-belt area from Hōlualoa to Hōnaunau welcome visitors. You'll learn about the whole process, from green beans to packaging. Often, macadamia nuts are for sale, and the brew, of course, is always ready. Some tours are self-guided, and most are free. The exception is the Kona Coffee Living History Farm (known as the D. Uchida Farm), unique in its heritage of coffee pioneers. The site, which has been preserved and restored by the Kona Historical Society, includes a 1913 farmhouse surrounded by coffee trees, a Japanese bathhouse, Kuriba (coffee processing mill), and Hoshidana (traditional drying platform). Tours of the farm are available by reservation only and cost $20.

🏠 **Bay View Farms** ⊹ ½ mi past St. Benedict's Painted Church, 83-5249 Painted Church Rd. ⊠ Hōnaunau ☎ 808/328-9658. **Greenwell Farms** ⊠ 81-6581 Māmalahoa Hwy., Kealakekua ☎ 808/323-2862. **Holualoa-Kona Coffee Company** ⊠ 77-6261 Old Māmalahoa Hwy. (Hwy. 180), Hōlualoa ☎ 808/322-9937 or 800/334-0348. **Kona Coffee Living History Farm** (known as the D. Uchida Farm) ⊠ Kona Historical Society, 81-6551 Māmalahoa Hwy., Kealakekua ☎ 808/323-3222 ⊕ www.konahistorical.org. **Royal Kona Coffee Museum and Coffee Mill** ⊠ 83-5427 Māmalahoa Hwy., next to tree house in Hōnaunau ☎ 808/328-2511.

GARDEN TOURS Several botanical gardens across the island welcome you to meander along the trails and study the diversity of the local flora. Often overlooked is the Amy B. H. Greenwell Ethnobotanical Garden, with its wealth of Hawaiian cultural traditions. It has on 12 acres 250 types of plants, including food and fiber crops, that were typical in an early Hawaiian *ahupuaʻa*, a pie-shape land division that ran from the mountains to the sea. Call to find out about guided tours or drop in between 8:30 AM and 5 PM.

🏠 **Amy B. H. Greenwell Ethnobotanical Garden** ⊠ 82-6188 Māalahoa Hwy., Captain Cook ☎ 808/323-3318 ⊕ www.bishopmuseum.org/greenwell.

MAUNA KEA ASTRONOMY TOURS On the weekend, the Onizuka Center offers an escorted summit tour using four-wheel-drive vehicles. Departure is at 1 PM, and reservations are not required. You must be 16 or older, in good health, and not pregnant.

As an easier alternative, book a tour with a reliable company. Tour operators usually provide parkas, as well as telescopes, snacks, and meals when appropriate. They pick you up at convenient locations, including the resorts. Excursion fees range from about $75 to $155.

🏠 **Arnott's Lodge & Hiking Adventures** ☎ 808/969-7097 ⊕ www.arnottslodge.com. **Hawaiʻi Forest & Trail** ☎ 808/331-8505 or 800/464-1993 ⊕ www.hawaii-forest.com. **Onizuka Center for International Astronomy Visitor Information Station** ⊠ Summit Access Rd. ☎ 808/961-2180 ⊕ www.ifa.hawaii.edu/info/vis. **Paradise Safaris** ☎ 808/322-2366 or 888/322-2366 ⊕ www.maunakea.com.

RANCH TOURS Three historic, working ranches have opened their lands to guided activities. The verdant Kohala Mountains land stretches down to the sea from the rim of Pololū Valley high in the rain forest and holds legendary stories about King Kamehameha and his troops. Here, the owners of the 8,000-plus acres of Kahuā Ranch—known for its lamb, beef, and hydroponic vegetables—provide horseback riding, operations tours, ATV adventures, mountain biking, hiking, and clay shooting. There is even a guest house.

Paniolo Riding Adventures offers horseback rides, mountain-bike tours, and guided hikes in Ponoholo Ranch, an 11,000-acre cattle ranch that shelters prehistoric sites and ancient ruins.

A covered wagon pulled by a pair of draft horses leads you through a portion of the 225,000-acre Parker Ranch. If you are a reasonably experienced horseback rider, you can also participate in a two-hour trek that includes a cattle drive. Hiking tours and other adventures are available as well.

🏠 **Kahuā Ranch Tours** ⊠ Kahuā Ranch, Hwy. 250 ☎ 808/882-7954 or 808/882-4646 ⊕ www.kahuaranch.com. **Paniolo Riding Adventures** ⊠ Hwy. 250, close to mile marker 13, Kohala Mountain Rd. ☎ 808/889-5354 ⊕ www.panioloadventures.com. **Parker Ranch** ⊠ Parker Ranch Visitor Center, Hwy. 19, Waimea ☎ 808/885-7655 ⊕ www.parkerranch.com.

VALLEY TOURS Although you certainly can hike down into the Waipi'o and Pololū valleys that frame the Kohala Mountains, a horseback-riding tour might be more fun. Or consider a guided tour around Waipi'o rim by a four-wheel-drive vehicle and around Pololū by mule. You'll be treated to breathtaking views along historic trails, and experienced guides are happy to recount the ancient history of this land. Costs range from about $40 to $85.

🖪 Four-Wheel, Wagon, Shuttle Tours: **Waipi'o Rim Backroad Adventures** ☎ 808/775-1122 or 877/757-1414 ⊕ www.topofwaipio.com. **Waipi'o Valley Shuttle** ☎ 808/775-7121. **Waipi'o Valley Wagon Tours** ☎ 808/775-9518.

🖪 Horseback Riding Tours: **Waipi'o on Horseback** ☎ 808/775-7291. **Waipi'o (Na'alapa) Stables** ☎ 808/775-0419.

🖪 Mule Tours: **Hawaii Forest and Trail** ☎ 808/331-8505 or 800/464-1993 ⊕ www.hawaii-forest.com.

WALKING & HIKING TOURS Maps and brochures for self-guided walking tours in historic areas or parks are often available on-site or at locations listed below. In Kailua-Kona, interpretive guides from the Kona Historical Society conduct various guided tours for a small fee.

As for nature hikes, to get to some of the best trails and places, it's worth going with a skilled guide. Costs range from $75 to $180, and hikes include picnic meals and gear such as binoculars, ponchos, and walking sticks. The outfitters mentioned here also offer customized adventure tours. Expert naturalist guides from Hawai'i Forest and Trail take you to 500-ft Kalopa Falls in North Kohala and on bird-watching expeditions. They, as well as Hawai'i Volcanoes National Park rangers, also offer tours into lava tubes and through normally inaccessible areas of Hawai'i Volcanoes National Park and rain forests. Hawaiian Walkways conducts several tours—waterfall hikes, coastal adventures, flora and fauna explorations, and jaunts through Hawai'i Volcanoes National Park—as well as custom-designed trips.

🖪 Historic Tours: **Big Island Visitors Bureau** ✉ 250 Keawe St., Hilo ☎ 808/961-5797 ✉ King's Shops, 250 Waikoloa Beach Dr., Suite B 15, Waikoloa ☎ 808/886-1655. **Kona Historical Society** ✉ 81-6551 Māmalahoa Hwy., Kealakekua ☎ 808/323-3222 ⊕ www.konahistorical.org.

🖪 Nature Hikes: **Hawai'i Forest and Trail** ☎ 808/331-8505 or 800/464-1993 ⊕ www.hawaii-forest.com. **Hawai'i Volcanoes National Park** ☎ 808/985-6010. **Hawaiian Walkways** ☎ 808/775-0372 or 800/457-7759 ⊕ www.hawaiianwalkways.com.

WHALE-WATCHING TOURS Most Hawaiian whale-watching cruises focus on the migratory humpbacks that are seen here only from December through April. You can contact any one of the many snorkeling, scuba diving, sailing, and kayaking companies as well: in season they adapt their adventures. Captain Dan McSweeney's offers three-hour trips year-round to find six other species of whales that rarely stray far from the Kona Coast. The cost is about $55.

🖪 **Captain Dan McSweeney's Year-Round Whale Watching Adventures** ✉ Honokōhau Harbor, Kailua-Kona ☎ 808/322-0028 or 888/942-5376 ⊕ www.ilovewhales.com.

WATER-SPORTS TOURS You can sail, cruise the ocean, fish, and snorkel to your heart's content on the Big Island, but two unique water tours stand apart from the others. One is an $89 kayak adventure down the pitch-black, eerie tunnels of the 22½-mi Kohala Ditch—irrigation ditches, built in 1905 by Japanese workers. You'll emerge now and then to pristine rain forests. "Flumin the ditch" in an inner tube used to be a dangerous and exciting pastime for sugar-plantation children. The other tour, provided by Hawaiian Adventure Tours, is a land-and-water package that combines hiking, swimming, snorkeling, and kayaking in 7-day ($1,750) or 10-day ($2,100) adventures on two or three Islands. **Flumin' Da Ditch** ✉ 55-519 Hāwī Rd. (Hwy. 250), Hāwī ☎ 808/889-6922 or 877/449-6922 🌐 www.flumindaditch.com. **Hawaiian Adventure Tours** ✉ Kapaʻau ☎ 808/889-0227 or 800/659-3544 🌐 www.hawaiianadventuretours.com.

TAXIS

Several companies advertise guided tours by taxi, but it is an expensive way to travel, with a trip around the island totaling about $350.

VISITOR INFORMATION

You can find lots of information and brochures at the Big Island Visitors Bureau (BIVB) booths at Big Island airports and at the offices in Hilo and King's Shops. If you rent a car, be sure to get a "Drive Guide." These handy booklets have all the maps you'll probably need to navigate the island. Several state, county, and resort organizations and Web sites are invaluable.

Visit the bookstores below for detailed street maps, and call the weather hot line for daily reports. **Basically Books** ✉ 160 Kamehameha Ave., Hilo ☎ 808/961-0144. **Borders Books & Music** ✉ 75-1000 Henry St., Kailua-Kona ☎ 808/331-1668 ✉ 301 Makaʻala, Hilo ☎ 808/933-1410. **Middle Earth Bookshoppe** ✉ 75-5719 Aliʻi Dr., Kailua-Kona ☎ 808/329-2123.

Big Island Visitors Bureau ✉ 250 Keawe St., Hilo 96720 ☎ 808/961-5797 📠 808/961-2126 ✉ 250 Waikoloa Beach Dr., B12, King's Shops, Waikoloa 96738 ☎ 808/886-1655 🌐 www.bigisland.org. **Destination Hilo** ✉ 2109F Kaiwiki Rd., Hilo 96720 ☎ 808/935-5294. **Destination Kona Coast** 📦 Box 2850, Kailua-Kona 96745 ☎ 808/329-6748 🌐 www.destinationkonacoast.com. **Hawaiʻi Visitors and Convention Bureau** 🌐 www.gohawaii.com. **Kohala Coast Resort Association** ✉ 69-275 Waikoloa Beach Dr., Waikoloa 96743 ☎ 808/886-4915 or 800/318-3637 🌐 www.kkra.org. **Weather** ☎ 808/961-5582.

KAUA'I
THE GARDEN ISLE

4

FODOR'S CHOICE

Hamura Saimin, Līhu'e

Kaua'i Marriott Resort & Beach Club, Līhu'e

Lydgate Beach Park, South Shore

Polihale Beach Park, the West Side

Princeville Resort, North Shore

Waimea Canyon and Kōke'e State Park, the West Side

HIGHLY RECOMMENDED

BEACHES 'Anini Beach County Park, North Shore

Ke'e Beach, North Shore

Tunnels Beach, North Shore

SIGHTS Ft. Elisabeth, Waimea

Kalalau Lookout, the West Side

Kīlauea Point National Wildlife Refuge, North Shore

Kilohana Plantation, Līhu'e

Limahuli Gardens, Hā'ena

The town of Līhu'e, South Shore

'Ōpaeka'a Falls, Wailua

Spouting Horn, Po'ipū

Many other great hotels and restaurants enliven this area. For other favorites look for the black stars as you read the chapter.

Updated by
Maggie
Wunsch

NICKNAMED THE GARDEN ISLE, Kaua'i is Eden epitomized. In the mountains of Kōke'e, lush swamps ring with songs of rare birds, and the aroma of ginger blossoms sweetens the rain forests of Hā'ena. Time carved the elegant spires along the remote northwestern shore known as Nā Pali (The Cliffs) Coast as seven coursing rivers gave life to the valleys where ancient Hawaiians once dwelled. Today you can explore this Pacific paradise by land, sea, and air—hiking along the Kalalau Trail, kayaking up the Hanalei River, or hovering in a helicopter high above 5,148-ft Wai'ale'ale, the wettest spot on earth.

The Garden Isle is a laid-back, restful retreat—an island of unmatched physical beauty that rewards those who love the outdoors. You can take a boat trip up Nā Pali Coast to snorkel in azure waters; ride a horse-drawn coach around a plantation-era sugar estate; or play golf on the world-class greens of Princeville Resort, where a majestic mountain peak, nicknamed Bali Hai, rises just beyond the fairways. Then again, you might want to saddle up and go horseback riding into the steep ridges and ravines of Waimea Canyon.

One road runs almost all the way around the island but dead-ends on either side of a 15-mi stretch of the rugged Nā Pali Coast. Driving from one end to the other takes you past lustrous green stands of sugarcane, which are gradually being replaced with coffee and macadamia-nut orchards. Dating from 1836, when Hawai'i's first sugar mill was built in Kōloa, sugar was a key economic force on the island until the early 1990s. Patches of taro are found around Hanalei Valley. This longtime staple of the Hawaiian diet is grown for its root (to make poi, a puddinglike accompaniment for fish and meat) as well as its leaves (used to wrap and cook food).

Kaua'i, the fourth-largest island in the Hawaiian chain, has its capital in Līhu'e, the island's commercial center. Its collection of businesses—a pair of banks, a library, a school, a museum, some family-run restaurants, and hotels—is small enough to keep the pace unhurried.

On the south coast the sunny beaches and clear skies around Po'ipū have spawned a crop of condos and hotels. The area has also come into its own as a golf destination, and several fine restaurants have found a home here as well. Head west, beneath the slopes of the Hoary Head Mountains, to encounter such storybook plantation villages as Hanapēpē, Kalāheo, and Waimea—where Captain James Cook first landed back in 1778. Beyond Waimea lies Polihale Beach, an idyllic stretch of golden sand sprawled beneath the cool highlands of Kōke'e State Park.

From the southwestern part of Kaua'i you can see the island of Ni'ihau 17 mi off the coast. Until 1987 no uninvited guests were allowed to visit this family-owned island. Most people who live in Hawai'i still consider Ni'ihau off-limits, but its mysteries can now be breached by helicopter.

North of Līhu'e the climate turns cooler and wetter, and everything sparkles green. In Wailua and Kapa'a, resort complexes huddle along a picturesque shoreline called the Royal Coconut Coast for its abundance of palms. As you head farther north to Anahola, Kīlauea, Princeville, and Hanalei, vines and flowers flourish. At the end of the road, in Hā'ena, you encounter a misty otherworldliness conjuring up the legends of the ancients.

More myths are attached to the natural landscape of Kaua'i than to any other Hawaiian island. A favorite among locals is the legend of the Mene-hune, a community of diminutive yet industrious workers said to have lived on Kaua'i before the Polynesians. Few people actually saw the Menehune because they worked in privacy at night—practicing, it seems, their impressive stoneworking skills. There are bridges, walls, fishponds, and other solid constructions attributed to the engineering skill of these mysterious mythical stonemasons.

Kaua'i is the oldest of the Hawaiian Islands, and its 550 square mi are rich in natural history and the resonance of the past. A sense of relaxation and natural beauty calmly welcomes all who step off the plane at the Līhu'e Airport and wraps them in a lei of traditional Hawaiian hospitality. In fact, many feel that Kaua'i's people are the friendliest in all the Islands.

Exploring Kaua'i

The main road tracing the island's perimeter takes you past easily explored landscapes and attractions. There are magical mountains, cascading waterfalls, mist-shrouded caves, a fern grotto, and a lighthouse designated a National Historic Landmark. All around the island are highway overlooks where you can take in the view.

Directions on the island are often referred to as *mauka* (toward the mountains) and *makai* (toward the ocean).

About the Restaurants

Sugar plantations of 19th-century Kaua'i brought together a universe of cultures as workers from other countries sought new jobs in Hawai'i. Today tourism, technology, and agriculture set the scene for 21st-century Kaua'i. With these influences comes an array of foods and preparations that constitute a purely Hawaiian style of cuisine, known to some as Pacific Rim. This style is typified by fresh local seafood prepared with hints of Asian cooking. Into this melting pot, add a bit of Mexican, Italian, French, and American influence to both food choice and cooking technique. The hallmark of Hawaiian regional cuisine is *poke,* fresh raw tuna, marinated with combinations of sesame oil, soy sauce, onions, and pickled seaweed. No trip to Kaua'i is complete without it.

When it's time for a snack, look for the carryout wagons that are often parked at major beaches. They serve local foods, such as the ubiquitous plate lunch.

About the Hotels

Part of the appeal of the Garden Isle is its range of accommodations— from swanky resorts to rustic cabins. In the older, low-budget locations, what you lose in modernity you gain in authenticity. They can be kitschy and outdated, filled with bamboo and tikis, but they really give you the feeling of old Hawai'i. Bed-and-breakfasts and vacation rentals reflect current island life, with peaceful settings and plenty of aloha welcome. The major hotels have numerous activities and amenities, often catering to families.

Sunseekers head south to the condo-studded shores of Po'ipū, where three- and four-story complexes line the coast and the surf is ideal for swimming. Po'ipū has more condos than hotels, with prices in the moderate to expensive range, though several oceanfront cottages are in demand with budget travelers.

Interested in the history of the Islands? Stay on the east coast near the Wailua River, where Kaua'i's first inhabitants resided. Many of the lodgings here place an emphasis on the legends and lore of the area. The beaches are so-so for swimming but nice for sunbathing. Farther north are the swanky hotels and condominiums of Princeville Resort; golfers should head here. There are lots of B&Bs and rentals hiding out in the

4

Numbers in the text correspond to numbers in the margin and on the Kaua'i map.

If you have
2 days

Beginning your trek in **Līhu'e** ⑮, drive around the harbor at **Nāwiliwili** ⑰, then head up the hill to the lookout for a view of **Menehune Fishpond** ⑱, connecting with Route 50 until a left turn on Route 520 takes you through the Tunnel of Trees to **Kōloa** ㉑ for shopping and **Po'ipū** ㉒ for sightseeing. Follow the signs to **Spouting Horn** ㉕ for a quick look and then continue on to Po'ipū for a beach or food break. Proceed to **Waimea Canyon** ㉟, giving yourself enough time to take in the view and maybe a short walk. It's a 36-mi return to Līhu'e. You can catch dinner and the sunset on the way back.

On your second day, make your goal the end of the road at Hā'ena State Park, 40 mi northwest of Līhu'e. On the way, stretch your legs at the **Kīlauea Lighthouse and Kīlauea Point National Wildlife Refuge** ⑧. Stop briefly at the **Maniniholo Dry Cave** ⑪ and at **Waikapala'e and Waikanaloa Wet Caves** ⑬ before turning around and heading to Hanalei for lunch. Spend the afternoon at the beach before heading back.

If you have
4 days

Spend the first day exploring **Līhu'e** ⑮ more thoroughly. Get a feeling for Kaua'i's history at the **Kaua'i Museum** ⑯ and then drive south to **Kōloa** ㉑ for some leisurely shopping. Have lunch and soak up some rays on the beach in **Po'ipū** ㉒.

A drive to **Waimea** ㉝ and Kōke'e on the second day will allow time for longer hikes and lunch and gallery hopping in **Hanapēpē** ㉙. The third day should be devoted to Kaua'i's north shore. Head to **Kīlauea Lighthouse and Kīlauea Point National Wildlife Refuge** ⑧. Then stop in Hanalei for lunch before stretching out at **Ke'e Beach State Park** ⑭. Along the way, you can check out **Maniniholo Dry Cave** ⑪, **Limahuli Gardens** ⑫, and **Waikapala'e and Waikanaloa Wet Caves** ⑬.

On your fourth day stick close to Kapa'a. In the morning, make the Fern Grotto your destination, either going aboard one of the Wailua river boats or renting a kayak. Then drive up Mā'alo Road to see the **Pōhaku-ho'ohānau and Pōhaku Piko** ④ and **'Ōpaeka'a Falls** ⑤. If you follow the road nearly to its end, you come upon the Keāhua Forestry Arboretum, where you can picnic before you head back.

If you have
6 days

Consider splitting your vacation between two hotels, spending the first two nights on the south shore and the last three on the north shore. On the first day, explore the **Waimea Canyon** ㉟, stopping at **Ft. Elisabeth** ㉛, or the main street (one block off the highway) of **Hanapēpē** ㉙. Leave the afternoon for a boat trip out of Port Allen.

Spend the morning of the second day in **Līhu'e** ⑮, touring **Grove Farm Homestead** ⑲ and the **Kaua'i Museum** ⑯. In the afternoon take time to explore **Kōloa** ㉑ and see **Spouting Horn** ㉕.

Pack and get away early on the third day so you can take in the Fern Grotto, the **Pōhaku-ho'ohānau and Pōhaku Piko** , and **'Ōpaeka'a Falls** ⑤. Alternatively, you could take a helicopter tour.

On day four, you might simply want to revel in your north-shore surroundings: play golf, paddle a kayak up Hanalei River, or soak in the pool. For hikers, the fifth day could involve a several-hour-long trek along the Kalalau Trail to Hanakāpī'ai Beach. If you prefer a less strenuous stroll, investigate the grounds at **Limahuli Gardens** ⑫. In any case, this fifth afternoon is the time to drive to the end of the road at Hā'ena, visiting **Maniniholo Dry Cave** ⑪ and **Waikapala'e and Waikanaloa Wet Caves** ⑬ along the way.

Reserve your sixth and final day to see sights you missed along the northeast shore or just relax.

jungles of the north shore. They can be an attractive option if you're looking for a more settled-in and residential experience. A good booking service can be a big help.

WHAT IT COSTS				
$$$$	**$$$**	**$$**	**$**	**¢**
RESTAURANTS over $30	$20–$30	$12–$20	$7–$12	under $7
HOTELS over $200	$150–$200	$100–$150	$60–$100	under $60

Restaurant prices are for a main course. Hotel prices are for two people in a standard double room, including tax and service.

TIMING   Kaua'i is beautiful in every season; however, if you prefer hot beach weather, you might schedule your visit from June through October, when rainfall is at its lightest. The northern coast of Kaua'i receives more precipitation than the rest of the island, particularly from December through February. Sometimes it can be downright soaking. To avoid family crowds, time a visit for months when school is in full session, May or October, for example, when the weather is generally fine and plenty of rooms are available.

THE NORTH SHORE

Traveling north from Līhu'e, you encounter green pastureland and valleys of Kīlauea, an area rich in history and legend. It was one of the first communities of the Polynesians who settled here more than 1,000 years ago. As the road turns west, tracing the island's shore, you time-travel through historic plantation towns, then past Princeville, winding up in the mist-shrouded primeval wilds around Ke'e Beach and Nā Pali Coast State Park.

a good drive   Head north out of Līhu'e on Route 56, the main artery that traces the eastern and northern coasts of Kaua'i. For an early scenic side trip turn left on Mā'alo Road (Route 583) before you reach Kapa'a. Then drive 4 mi to **Wailua Falls** ① ▶. Backtrack to Route 56 and continue north. A short drive will take you to **Lydgate County Park** ②.

On the mauka side of Route 56, follow the sign directing you to Wailua Marina, where cruise boats depart for the Fern Grotto. Continue north on Route 56. You can head up to **Wailua** ③ for a bite to eat or for some shopping or you can turn left past the mouth of the Wailua River onto

Kuamoʻo Road (Route 580). Just beyond Wailua River State Park on your left is one of seven revered *heiau* (stone platforms that were the site of worship) and the royal birthing stones, **Pōhaku-hoʻohānau and Pōhaku Piko** ④. Farther up Kuamoʻo Road, you reach the most intact of the stone temples, Poliʻahu, complete with storyboards. On clear days you can see Waiʻaleʻale, the misty peak that is the source of the Wailua River. Across the road is the spectacular **ʻŌpaekaʻa Falls** ⑤. Drive farther on to get to the viewing area.

You can follow Kuamoʻo Road another 7 or 8 mi to its end in Keāhua Forestry Arboretum for a picnic.

Head back to Route 56 and drive north toward Waipouli. On your left you pass a mountain ridge resembling the mythical **Sleeping Giant** ⑥. Follow the highway along the eastern coast to Kapaʻa, Kauaʻi's largest town.

To the north you pass Keālia and the turnoff to Anahola Beach Park. Seven miles farther is **Kīlauea** ⑦, another former plantation town. Turn right on Kolo Road when you see the Menehune Foodmart next to Christ Memorial Episcopal Church. Take the first left onto Kīlauea Road, and follow it to the end for **Kīlauea Lighthouse and Kīlauea Point National Wildlife Refuge** ⑧.

After Kīlauea, continue west until you reach mile marker 25 on Route 56. Kalihi Wai Valley Overlook is a splendid place to photograph the valley and the waterfall across the road. As you drive farther along you pass Princeville Airport (on the mauka side of the road) before you reach **Hanalei Valley Overlook** ⑨, across the street from the Princeville Shopping Center. From here you can look out across acres of taro fields in the valley below. The road descends and comes to a rustic, one-lane bridge dating from 1912, then heads into the town of Hanalei and the 19th-century **Waiʻoli Mission House** ⑩.

West of Hanalei the highway (now labeled 560 on street signs) winds its way between the mountains and the sea and crosses a series of old one-lane bridges. When the road rises and curves left, and you see hosts of rental cars on the side of the road, you've reached Lumahaʻi Beach.

As you continue west, past mile marker 8, there's a right turn through a grove of trees. This takes you to Tunnels Beach. A little farther, on the mauka side, is **Maniniholo Dry Cave** ⑪. A few miles farther, on the mauka side, is **Limahuli Gardens** ⑫. Less than ½ mi up the highway, a five-minute walk uphill takes you to **Waikapalaʻe and Waikanaloa Wet Caves** ⑬. At the end of Route 560 in Hāʻena, the Kalalau trailhead is near **Keʻe Beach State Park** ⑭.

TIMING Without stopping, you can drive the 40 mi from Līhuʻe to Hāʻena in less than 90 minutes if you avoid traveling during rush hour. Including meal breaks, allow a full day to stop and explore the sights along the way and take a short hike or swim.

What to See

Fern Grotto. A 3-mi boat ride up the Wailua River culminates at a yawning lava tube covered with enormous fishtail ferns. You can rent a kayak, hire a boat and captain, or take one of the popular boat tours to this site, which is approachable only via the river. ✛ *Depart from Wailua Marina on mauka side of Rte. 56.*

off the beaten path

Guava Kai Plantation. Come have a look around the orchard, and sample all kinds of guava goodies—jellies, juices, and marinades—at the visitor center. This 480-acre farm is one of the most productive guava plantations in the world. Here you can see how guava is grown and processed and ends up on your table. ✣ *Rte. 56, north of mile marker 23 on Kūhiō Hwy.; turn mauka onto Kuawa Rd., near Kīlauea, and follow signs* ☎ 808/828–6121 ☑ *Free* ◷ *Daily 9–5.*

❾ Hanalei Valley Overlook. Mountains form the backdrop to a 900-acre National Wildlife Refuge for endangered waterfowl. In the 1850s Robert Wyllie attempted to establish a coffee plantation below. After that failed the Chinese farmed rice in the valley until the early 1900s. Now, the valley floor is a patchwork of more than ½ mi of taro ponds. ☒ *Rte. 56, Princeville.*

★ ⑭ Ke'e Beach State Park. The stunning beach here is also the trailhead for Nā Pali's **Kalalau Trail;** another path leads from the sand to an open, grassy meadow with a stone altar called **Lohi'au's Hula Platform,** which is still revered for its historical and spiritual *mana* (power). It's said that Laka, goddess of the hula, originated her dancing on this very spot. Hula practitioners sometimes leave offerings for her. ✣ *Drive to western end of Rte. 560.*

❼ Kīlauea. A former plantation town, Kīlauea is known today for its aquacultural successes, especially with prawns. It has also distinguished itself in guava cultivation. One of Kīlauea's most notable buildings, **Christ Memorial Episcopal Church** on Kolo Street, dates from 1941. The church is constructed of native lava rock, and its stained-glass windows came from England. Also in town is the Kong Lung Center, which houses the unique Kong Lung Co. boutique and Kīlauea Bakery and Pau Hana Pizza, known for its pizza and tropical pastries. ✣ *Take Rte. 56, 25 mi north of Līhu'e.*

★ ❽ Kīlauea Lighthouse and Kīlauea Point National Wildlife Refuge. A beacon for passing air and sea traffic since it was built in 1913, and a National Historic Landmark, this lighthouse has the largest clamshell lens of any lighthouse in the world. The Kīlauea Wildlife Refuge surrounds the lighthouse, and several species of seabirds, some endangered, roost here. Two-hour guided hikes are conducted through the refuge from Monday through Thursday; reserve ahead. ☒ *Kīlauea Lighthouse Rd., Kīlauea* ☎ *808/828–0168* ⊕ *www.kilauea-point.com* ☑ *$3* ◷ *Daily 10–4.*

> **need a break?** Banana Joe's Tropical Fruit Stand (☒ 5-2719 Kūhiō Hwy., Kīlauea ☎ 808/828–1092) occupies a rustic yellow shelter on the mauka side of Route 56, past the turnoff to Kīlauea. Sample the Kaua'i-grown fruit here (fresh, dried, or in smoothies and salads). It's the perfect tropical energy booster. Banana Joe's also sells fresh corn and other vegetables in season.

★ ⑫ Limahuli Gardens. Early Hawaiians lived in this area known for its mana. Today the botanical garden here focuses on preserving the integrity, appearance, and environment of the native flora and fauna. Several endangered plants call Limahuli home. The gardens are an archaeological site, and restoration projects are under way. The agricultural areas and taro patches are, in fact, actual working farms in the ancient Hawaiian tradition. Picnicking is not allowed. You must call for reservations to join the guided tour, which starts at 10 AM. ☒ *Rte. 560, Hā'ena* ☎ *808/826–1053* ⊕ *www.ntbg.org* ☑ *Self-guided tour $10, guided tour $15* ◷ *Tues.–Fri. and Sun. 9:30–4.*

☺ ❷ Lydgate County Park. The park, named for the Reverend J. M. Lydgate, founder of the Līhu'e English Union Church, houses a children's playground and the remains of a heiau. In pre–Captain Cook days, the area was a city of refuge for Hawaiians who had violated one of the religious

Beaches

The island is surrounded by stretches of magnificent ivory sand, many with breathtaking mountain backdrops. Pay attention to the surf conditions, and heed any warnings. Some beaches are just perfect for swimming, and some are just perfect for looking. Check which one you are at before diving in.

Hitting the Links

4

Princeville Resort's stunning Robert Trent Jones Jr.–designed Prince Course is rated the second-most difficult course in Hawai'i. The resort's (and Jones's) neighboring Makai Course is also beautiful, with the so-called Zen bunker (a boulder in the middle of a huge sand trap) and an 8th hole played across an ocean chasm. As you play the four closing holes of Jones's Po'ipū Bay course you will hear the crashing surf on your left. Kiahuna Plantation, Jones's fourth design on Kaua'i, is a challenging inland course that winds over streams, through woods, and past lava formations.

Jack Nicklaus's Kiele course, adjoining the Kaua'i Marriott Resort & Beach Club, has many greens positioned diagonally to the fairway. His Mokihana course is less dramatic and wider. Endangered wildlife, such as the nēnē goose, monk seal, and sea turtle, can often be spotted (the geese in ponds on the back 9, and the seals and turtles on the beach or in the water below).

Hiking

Kaua'i is best known to hikers for the challenging north-shore Kalalau Trail. Trails at Kōke'e State Park cover all skill levels and overlook the green ramparts of the Nā Pali coastline or Waimea Canyon. For easy excursions, traipse through Keāhua Forestry Arboretum, Limahuli Gardens, and other tropical gardens.

Horseback Riding

Kaua'i offers possibly the broadest selection of equestrian outings of all the Islands. You can saddle up to ride along the rim of Waimea Canyon, to a secluded waterfall, along the edge of a moonlit beach, or through green mountain pastures.

Water Sports

Safe yet exciting water adventures are possible through companies that rent equipment or have guided excursions. Kayaking is big here—this is the only island where you have the choice of kayaking on rivers, in ancient fishponds, or on the ocean. Fishing and snorkel guides are quick to locate the spots where the biggest or most colorful fish hang out. Surfing and windsurfing instructors can help you get on the waves in no time.

There are three great dive sites on the north shore's Cannon's Reef, which drops quickly from the shoreline, forming a long ledge permeated with lava tubes. Plate coral is found here, turtles are a common sight, and you may come across white-tip sharks sleeping in caverns or patrolling the ledge. General Store, at Kukui'ula, is the site of a 19th-century shipwreck. The horseshoe-shape ledge and two caverns teem with schools of lemon butterfly fish that follow divers around. There are also green moray eels and black coral at this site, which runs to depths of 65 ft to 80 ft. Sheraton Caverns, off Po'ipū, are formed by three immense, parallel lava tubes. There is a lobster nursery in one cavern, sea turtles swim in all three, and the occasional white-tip shark cruises by. Depths range from 35 ft to 60 ft.

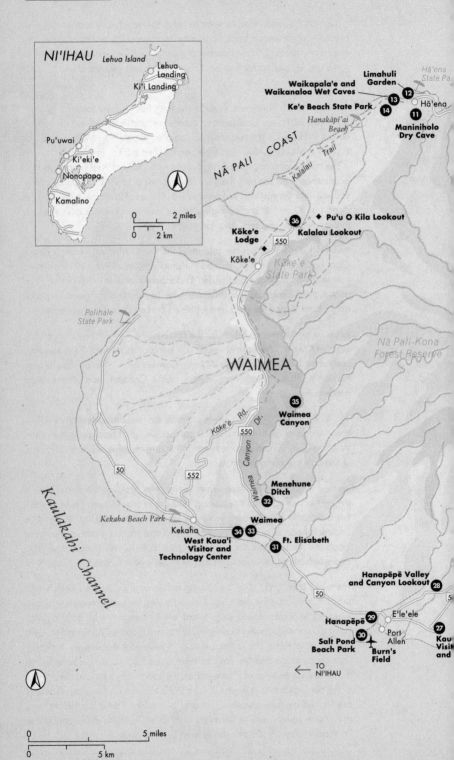

PACIFIC OCEAN

HANALEI

Tunnels Beach

Lumahaʻi Beach

Hanalei Beach Park

Anini Beach

560

Hanalei

Kalihi Wai Valley Overlook

Secret Beach

Kīlauea Lighthouse and Kīlauea Point National Wildlife Refuge ❽

Waiʻoli Mission House ❿

Hanalei Valley Overlook ❾

Princeville

Princeville Airport

❼ **Kīlauea**

■ **Guava Kai Plantation**

Waipā Valley

Mamalahoa Heleleʻa Forest Reserve

Hanalei River

Anahola

Anahola Beach Park

KAWAIHAU

Keālia

581

Kapaʻa

Waipouli

Waiʻaleʻale (5148 ft.)

Sleeping Giant

❻

Smithʼs Tropical Paradise

❺ 580

ʻŌpaekaʻa Falls

Wailua Falls

❶

❸ **Wailua**

● **Wailua Marina**

❹

Fern Grotto

❷ **Lydgate County Park**

Pōhaku-hoʻohānau and Pōhaku Piko

Wailua R.

56

583

Lihue-Koloa Forest Reserve

LĪHUʻE

Hanamāʻulu

■ **Kapaiʻa**

Kauaʻi Museum

❶❻ **Līhuʻe**

❶❺

Līhuʻe Airport

Kilohana Plantation

❷⓿

Puhi

58

❶❾

Grove Farm Homestead

❶❼ **Nāwiliwili**

Kalapaki Beach

KŌLOA

50

Tunnel of Trees

Huleʻia River

❶❽ **Menehune Fishpond**

Kalāheo

National Tropical Botanical Gardens

Lāwaʻi

HOARY HEAD RANGE

■ **Queen Victoriaʼs Profile**

Māhāʻulepū Beach

Shipwreck Beach

❷❺ **Kukui o Lono Park**

530

520

❷❶

Prince Kūhiō Park

Kōloa

Kauaʻi Channel

ʻi Coffee r Center Museum

❷❹

❷❺ **Spouting Horn**

❷❸

❷❷ **Poʻipū**

Brenneckeʼs Beach

Poʻipū Beach Park

TO OʻAHU →

kapu (taboos). If they made their way to this beachfront haven, they could escape banishment or death by remaining until their families arranged for their forgiveness. ✛ *Before mouth of Wailua River turn makai off Rte. 56 onto Lehu Dr. and left onto Nalu Rd.* ✉ *Free* ☾ *Daily.*

⓫ **Maniniholo Dry Cave.** An ancient place of worship, this cave was said to have been dug by a Menehune chief searching for an evil spirit. Don't be spooked; one or another Hawaiian goddess removed the traces of evil that lurked here long ago, most likely Laka and her hula followers. Across the highway from Maniniholo Dry Cave is **Hā'ena State Park,** a fine beach for swimming when there's no current. The well-protected **Tunnels Beach** adjoins Hā'ena State Park. ✉ *Rte. 560, Hā'ena.*

off the beaten path

Nā Pali Coast and State Park. This park contains Kaua'i's ultimate adventure hike: the Kalalau Trail. Even if you plan to complete only the first 2 mi of the 11-mi trek—from Ke'e Beach to Hanakāpī'ai Beach—start early, wear rugged shoes, carry a picnic lunch, and don't forget plenty of drinking water. Note that swimming is too dangerous off the white-sand beach at the head of Hanakāpī'ai Valley. If you're in good shape you may want to follow an unmaintained trail the additional 2 mi to the waterfall and freshwater river pool at the back of the valley. The permit waiting list for the Hanakāpī'ai campsite is long.

Serious backpackers can continue on the entire 11-mi coastal trail. The hike crosses streams that bisect a series of valleys and then passes waterfalls and wild fruit trees until 4 mi later you reach another campsite at Hanakoa Valley. Hanakoa Falls, ⅓ mi inland, provides a refreshing, cool shower.

The last 5 mi of the trail culminate at Kalalau Valley and Beach. Nearby, after the final stream crossing, a red-dirt trail leads uphill to an old heiau. A nearby campsite can be crowded in fine weather, when many adventurers seek out Kalalau's legendary beauty.

Backpackers headed to Kalalau must obtain permits from the Department of Land and Natural Resources and are limited to five nights in Nā Pali State Park. Hiking the trail during the rainy winter season should not be attempted, as flash floods are a danger. Tour boats no longer take passengers along Nā Pali shore from Hanalei on the north side of the island, but in the summer months, when the ocean is calm, boats run from Port Allen on the west coast, and kayakers can take a guided tour or explore the coastline in their own rental kayaks. ✉ *Department of Land and Natural Resources, 3060 Eiwa St., Līhu'e 96766* ☎ *808/274–3444* ⊕ *www.kauai-hawaii.com.*

★ ❺ **'Ōpaeka'a Falls.** A dramatic waterfall plunges hundreds of feet to the pools below. 'Ōpaeka'a means "rolling shrimp," which refers to the little creatures that are said to have been so abundant at one time that they could be seen tumbling in the falls to the pool below. ✉ *Rte. 580 (Kuamo'o Rd.), Wailua.*

❹ **Pōhaku-ho'ohānau and Pōhaku Piko.** These two rocks make Wailua one of the most sacred sites in all Hawai'i, as it was here that all the royal births of Kaua'i took place. An expectant royal mother supported her back against the birthing stone Pōhaku-ho'ohānau. After the newborn's umbilical cord fell off, it was wrapped in *kapa* (cloth made from bark) and deposited in the crevices of the Pōhaku Piko for safekeeping. Just up the road is Poli'ahu Heiau, where storyboards tell about the heiau, the Wailua River area, and its former inhabitants. ✉ *Rte. 580 (Kuamo'o Rd.), Wailua.*

6 **Sleeping Giant.** Puni, a mythical giant, is said to be represented in this formation on Mount Nounou. His back outlining the mountain ridge, he has dozed here undisturbed since hungry villagers fed him stones after he ate all their taro and fish. ⊹ *Rte. 56, about 1 mi north of Wailua River.*

☙ **Smith's Tropical Paradise.** Right next to Wailua Marina in the lush Wailua Valley, this 30-acre botanical and cultural garden offers a glimpse at exotic foliage, rare birds like the "singing tree ducks," fruit orchards, and tropical lagoons. Take the tram and enjoy a narrated tour or stroll along the mile-long pathways. A lū'au and show are held Monday, Wednesday, and Friday from 5 to 9, and there is free shuttle service from Wailua. Reservations are essential for the evening events and shuttle. ✉ *174 Wailua Rd., Kapa'a* ☎ *808/821–6895* ✆ *$5.25, lū'au and show $56* ⊙ *Daily 8:30–4.*

▶ **1** **Wailua Falls.** You may recognize this impressive cascade from the opening sequences of the *Fantasy Island* television series. Kaua'i has plenty of picturesque waterfalls, but this one surpasses most. ⊹ *End of Rte. 583 (Ma'alo Rd.), 4 mi west of Rte. 56.*

10 **Wai'oli Mission House.** This 1837 mission was once the home of teachers Lucy and Abner Wilcox. Its tidy architecture feels as if it belongs back in New England, and the prim and proper koa-wood furnishings epitomize missionary Hawai'i. Half-hour guided tours are available. ✉ *Kūhiō Hwy., Hanalei* ☎ *808/245–3202* ✆ *Donations accepted* ⊙ *Tues., Thurs., and Sat. 9–3.*

LĪHU'E & THE SOUTH SHORE

As you follow the main road south from Līhu'e the air heats up and dries out. This is one way to tell you're nearing the region called Po'ipū, named after the south-shore resort town that is its unofficial center. The sun shines steadily on the condo- and hotel-lined beaches, and there's plenty of water sports to engage in.

a good drive

Begin in **Līhu'e** ⑮ ▶ and visit the **Kaua'i Museum** ⑯. Head southeast on Rice Street, the town's main road, until it drops you off at **Nāwiliwili** ⑰, Kaua'i's major port. From what's now Wa'apā Road, turn right onto Hulemalu Road and follow the Hulē'ia River to view **Menehune Fishpond** ⑱.

Return to Nāwiliwili, take a left on Nāwiliwili Road (Route 58), and look on your right for **Grove Farm Homestead** ⑲. At the intersection of Nāwiliwili Road and Route 50, turn left and head west on Route 50. Two miles farther on the right is the entrance to **Kilohana Plantation** ⑳.

Continuing west on Route 50, you pass the majestic slopes of the Hoary Head Mountains. On the top of the range to your right is a formation called Queen Victoria's Profile, indicated by a Hawaiian-warrior marker. When you get to the intersection of Routes 50 and 520, you have reached Kōloa Gap, a natural pass between Mt. Wai'ale'ale on your right and the Hoary Heads on your left. Turn left onto Route 520 (Maluhia Road), also known as the Tunnel of Trees because of the eucalyptuses that border the road to form a canopy overhead.

Route 520 takes you to **Kōloa** ㉑, site of Kaua'i's first sugar mill, dating from 1835. Head south on Route 520, which here is also called Po'ipū Road. At the fork stay to the left.

From here turn right onto Honowili Road, which takes you through the heart of sunny **Po'ipū** ㉒. On the makai side of the road are Po'ipū

Beach Park and Brennecke's Beach, prime spots for sunbathers and bodysurfers. Return to Po'ipū Road and follow it past the stunning Hyatt Regency Kaua'i, which fronts Shipwreck Beach. The road abruptly turns to dirt, but 3 mi farther awaits beautiful Māhā'ulepū Beach. To reach it, follow the road to the T intersection, turn right, stop at the gates to sign in (this is private property), and park at the end of the dirt road to walk to the beach. Explorers willing to search can find an interesting cave site at the far end of this beach if they hike inland beside a little stream.

When you head back on Po'ipū Road, instead of turning to Kōloa go left onto Lāwa'i Road just after you cross the bridge over Waikomo Stream. You soon come to **Prince Kūhiō Park** ㉓. Beyond the park is the visitor center for the **National Tropical Botanical Gardens** ㉔. At the end of this beachfront road is **Spouting Horn** ㉕. Its rising plume signals your drive's end.

TIMING   From Līhu'e to Po'ipū is only 14 mi, but since there is plenty to see, you can easily devote a day or two to this itinerary. If you have only a half day, be sure you watch the sunset from Brennecke's Beach. The bodysurfers on this legendary beach are something to see.

What to See

⑲ **Grove Farm Homestead.** One of Kaua'i's oldest plantation estates, founded in 1864, now offers a look at 19th-century life on Kaua'i. On the 80 acres composing this living museum are the original family home filled with turn-of-the-20th-century memorabilia, workers' quarters, and elaborate tropical flower gardens. The homestead is accessible only by tour, three days per week, twice per day. The two hours they take may be too long for young children. Reservations are essential, as there's a six-person limit per tour. ⊠ *Rte. 58 (Nāwiliwili Rd.), Līhu'e* 🕾 *808/ 245–3202* 🖙 *$5* ☉ *Tours Mon. and Wed.–Thurs. at 10 and 1.*

⑯ **Kaua'i Museum.** A permanent display, "The Story of Kaua'i," provides an overview of the Garden Isle and traces its mythology and its geological and cultural history. A highlight is the 30-minute aerial-view movie. Works by local artists are on display in the Mezzanine Gallery, and the gift shop carries impressive Ni'ihau shell leis and wooden bowls. ⊠ *4428 Rice St., Līhu'e* 🕾 *808/245–6931* 🖙 *$5* ☉ *Weekdays 9–4, Sat. 10–4.*

★ ⑳ **Kilohana Plantation.** This 35-acre estate, the site of the old Wilcox sugar plantation, dates from 1935. It's a beautiful showpiece from earlier days. At one time, it was the most expensive manor built on the island and was originally filled with furnishings brought in from Gump's of San Francisco. Today the 16,000-square-ft Tudor mansion is host to specialty shops and art galleries, as well as Gaylord's, a courtyard restaurant with an island-wide reputation. Tours of the sugarcane fields and carriage rides are available. ⊠ *3-2087 Kaumuali'i Hwy. (Rte. 50), Līhu'e* 🕾 *808/ 245–5608* 🖙 *Free* ☉ *Mon.–Sat. 9:30–9:30, Sun. 9:30–5.*

㉑ **Kōloa.** Kaua'i's first sugar mill began operating in this town in 1835. You can see the remains of the old stone smokestack on the right side of the road. A sculpture depicting the various ethnic groups that made their mark on the sugar industry on Kaua'i sits on a small green nearby. The main street of Kōloa is lined with old plantation-style buildings that have been preserved to house boutiques, a general store, and a selection of restaurants. Placards outside each building describe the original tenants and tell about life in the old mill town. Here you'll find Kōloa Ice House and Deli, which sells shaved ice laced with tropical syrups, and Kōloa Fish Market, which offers poke and sashimi takeout. ⊠ *Rte. 520.*

need a
break?

Pizzetta (✉ 5408 Kōloa Rd., Kōloa ☎ 808/742–8881) concocts the best mai tai cocktail on the island. A rustic wood-panel room at the back, with an open deck, makes up the bar area. When you're ready for dinner, order a pizza, try a Hawaiian calzone, or choose freshly made fettuccine.

★ ▶ ⑮ **Līhuʻe.** The commercial and political center of Kauaʻi County, which includes the islands of Kauaʻi and Niʻihau, Līhuʻe is the home of the island's major airport and harbor. The main thoroughfare, Rice Street, offers a short, pleasant stroll from the War Memorial and Convention Hall (Rice and Hardy streets), past government offices, to the Līhuʻe Shopping Center (Rice Street and Route 50). ✉ *Rtes. 56 and 50.*

⑱ **Menehune Fishpond.** A diminutive race of ancient Hawaiians is said to have built this intricate aquaculture structure for a princess and prince. Today the 4-ft-thick and 5-ft-high walls, also known as ʻAlekoko, still contain placid waters where mullet thrive and kayakers glide. ✉ *Hulemalu Rd., Niumalu.*

㉔ **National Tropical Botanical Gardens.** Tucked away beneath the cliffs of the Lāwaʻi Valley, these gardens were once a favorite of Hawaiʻi's Queen Emma. Today they contain a 252-acre scientific research center (McBryde Gardens) and a 100-acre estate property (Allerton Gardens) dedicated to preserving Hawaiʻi's natural flora as found in its exotic botany and horticulture. McBryde Gardens tours are self-guided and require no reservations. Visitation to the Allerton Gardens is restricted—reservation-only guided tours are given three times a day, except Sundays. At Allerton, kids enjoy getting a close-up view of the *Jurassic Park* trees, otherwise known as Moreton Bay Figs. ✉ *Lāwaʻi Rd., Poʻipū, across from Spouting Horn parking lot* ☎ 808/742–2623 ✉ *Self-guided tour (McBryde) $15, guided tour (Allerton) $30* ⏰ *McBryde Gardens Mon.–Sat. 9:30–4, Allerton Gardens tours Mon.–Sat. at 9, 10, and 1.*

⑰ **Nāwiliwili.** At Kauaʻi's major port, numerous fishing and private boats come and go. Tour boats also set out for snorkeling and sightseeing adventures along the coast. This is a port of call for container ships, U.S. Navy vessels, and passenger cruise lines. Nearby there's protected swimming at **Kalapakī Beach.** ✉ *Makai end of Waʻapā Rd., Līhuʻe.*

㉒ **Poʻipū.** The major resort destination of the south shore remains irrepressibly sunny. Anchored by the Sheraton Kauaʻi Resort and a half dozen condominiums, including Kiahuna Plantation, Poʻipū is famous for its golden sandy beaches. ✉ *Rte. 520.*

㉓ **Prince Kūhiō Park.** The park behind the Prince Kūhiō Condominium honors the birthplace of one of Hawaiʻi's most beloved congressional representatives, Prince Jonah Kūhiō Kalanianaʻole, a man who might have become Hawaiʻi's king if Queen Liliʻuokalani had not been overthrown in 1893. ✉ *Lāwaʻi Rd., Poʻipū.*

★ ㉕ **Spouting Horn.** This ocean waterspout shoots up like Old Faithful from an ancient lava tube. Follow the paved walkways around; the rocks can be slippery and people have been known to fall in. Vendors sell inexpensive souvenirs and costume jewelry, in addition to one of the best selections of rare and treasured Niʻihau shell necklaces. When purchasing a Niʻihau shell lei, ask for a certificate of authenticity and an address in case you need to reorder or repair your purchase at a later date. ✉ *Lāwaʻi Bay, Lāwaʻi Rd., Poʻipū.*

CloseUp

KAUA'I: UNDERCOVER MOVIE STAR

Though Kaua'i has played itself in the movies (you may remember Nicolas Cage frantically shouting "Is it Kapa'a or Kapa' a-a?" into a pay phone in Honeymoon in Vegas [1992]), most of its screen time has been as a stunt double for a number of tropical paradises. The island's remote valleys and waterfalls portrayed a Costa Rican dinosaur preserve in Steven Spielberg's Jurassic Park (1993). Spielberg was no stranger to Kaua'i, having filmed Harrison Ford's escape via seaplane from

Menehune Fishpond in Raiders of the Lost Ark (1981). The fluted cliffs and gorges of Kaua'i's rugged Nā Pali Coast play the misunderstood beast's island home in King Kong (1976), and a jungle dweller of another sort, in George of the Jungle (1997), frolicked on Kaua'i. Harrison Ford returned to the island for 10 weeks during the filming of Six Days, Seven Nights (1998), a romantic adventure set in French Polynesia.

THE WEST SIDE

Heading west along Kaua'i's south shore, you'll pass through old plantation towns and historical sites, each with a story to tell: Hanapēpē, whose salt ponds have been harvested since ancient times; Ft. Elisabeth, from which an enterprising Russian tried to take over the island in the early 1800s; and Waimea, home of the Menehune Ditch, supposedly built by the legendary race of little people.

From Waimea town you can drive along the rim of magnificent Waimea Canyon to reach the crisp, cool climate of Kōke'e, which ranges from 3,200 ft to 4,200 ft above sea level. The staff at a mountain lodge here welcomes guests with old-style warmth and hospitality.

a good drive

The west side of the island offers a look at the sleepiest—as well as the most dramatic—sections of Kaua'i. Begin this tour by heading west on Route 50 out of Līhu'e. The first town you come to is tiny Lāwa'i, which once housed the Kaua'i Pineapple Cannery. In its wake, Lāwa'i has emerged as a significant producer of tropical fruits and plants. The next town along Route 50 is Kalāheo. Turn left on Pāpālina Road to make the climb to **Kukui o Lono Park** 26 .

Beyond Kalāheo, a left turn onto Route 540 takes you to the **Kaua'i Coffee Visitor Center and Museum** 27 . Route 540 loops back to Route 50. You'll pass acres of shiny-leaf coffee trees, but if you travel the loop, you miss the **Hanapēpē Valley and Canyon Lookout** 28 . Backtrack to Route 50 to see this dramatic divide, which holds a place in Hawaiian history as the site of Kaua'i's last battle, in 1824.

Hanapēpē 29 lies west of the lookout. At the fork turn right to drive down Hanapēpē's dusty main street and visit a surprising number of galleries or pick up a plate lunch. If you want to bypass Hanapēpē, angle left and follow Route 50 past the town. Then turn makai on Lele Road to reach **Salt Pond Beach Park** 30 . Nearby is Burns Field, Kaua'i's first airfield. Just around the bend and across the bay from the airstrip is Port Allen, the shipping center for the west side of the island and home base for snorkeling excursions.

Head west again on Route 50 and look on the makai side of the road for the Hawaiian-warrior marker to **Ft. Elisabeth** 31 . Cross the Waimea River Bridge and take your first right on Menehune Road, which leads you 2½ mi up Waimea Valley to **Menehune Ditch** ㉜. As you enter **Waimea** ㉝ you might spot the statue commemorating Captain Cook's arrival here in 1778. The remains of a missionary church built in 1846 should hold your interest as well. On the right, **West Kaua'i Visitor and Technology Center** ㉞ has information on Kaua'i.

Route 50 meanders through the sugar town of Kekaha. Eventually it passes the Pacific Missile Range Facility. Take the right fork after you pass the missile range and you can follow Route 50 to where it ends near Polihale State Park. The park is accessible only by a long, bumpy dirt road through sugarcane fields. During or after heavy rain—or if you're more inclined to smooth, pleasant rides—you might want to skip it. At the end of the road is a long, arching beach with few people. It's quiet, striking, and private, and a good place to watch the sunset, but not well suited for swimming. Be careful not to get your car stuck in the sand or you could be seeing the sunrise from here, too.

You have two choices for visiting **Waimea Canyon** ㉟. Kōke'e Road (Route 55) makes a steep climb from Kekaha. The other, more scenic option is Waimea Canyon Drive (Route 550), which you pick up near the western edge of Waimea, by the church. It's narrow but well paved and climbs quickly for immediate views of the town and ocean below. A few miles up, the roads converge and continue the steep ascent with spectacular bird's-eye views out over the canyon. Be sure to stop at the Pu'u-ka-Pele and Pu'u-hinahina lookouts for the most appealing views. As the road rises to 4,000 ft, it passes through Kōke'e State Park, with its cozy Kōke'e Lodge. The road out of the park leads past the NASA Tracking Station.

Waimea Canyon Drive ends 4 mi above the park at the **Kalalau Lookout** ㊱. This is the beginning of a beautiful hiking trail that passes Pu'u-o-Kila Lookout. Be sure to bring a jacket for the cooler weather here.

TIMING The 36-mi drive from Līhu'e to Waimea Canyon takes about 90 minutes with no stops for botanical gardens, beaches, or quaint little towns. If you want to spend a half day or more hiking in the canyon, you might save south-shore sightseeing for another day. In winter be prepared for chilly temperatures in the heights above the canyon, especially in the early morning.

What to See

★ ㉛ **Ft. Elisabeth.** The ruins of this stone fort, built in 1816 by an agent of the imperial Russian government named Anton Scheffer, are reminders of the days when Scheffer tried to conquer the island for his homeland. King Kaumuali'i eventually chased him off the island. The crumbling walls of the fort are not particularly interesting, but the informative placards are. ✉ *Rte. 50, Waimea.*

㉙ **Hanapēpē.** This quiet farming town on the south coast supplies Kaua'i with much of its produce and all of the Islands with Lappert's famous ice cream. **Hanapēpē Road** had a featured role (as an Australian town) in the television miniseries *The Thorn Birds.* Today shops sell koa-wood crafts and other artwork. Just to the east is the main boat-excursion departure point, **Port Allen.** The harbor is still the shipping center for the west side of Kaua'i and headquarters of the McBryde Company, which has replaced sugarcane fields with coffee trees. If you want further proof that Hanapēpē was once a power center, check out 'Ele'ele Shopping Center on Lele Road. It was the first "modern" shopping center built on Kaua'i. ✉ *Rte. 50.*

You can sit at the spiffy black-and-white bar for a quick espresso or relax at one of a dozen tables while you dine on vegetarian food with French-Italian flair at **Hanapēpē Café and Espresso** (⊠ 3830 Hanapēpē Rd., Hanapēpē ☎ 808/335–5011).

㉘ Hanapēpē Valley and Canyon Lookout. This dramatic divide once housed a thriving Hawaiian community, and some remains of its taro patches still exist. Hanapēpē is a historic canyon: it's the site of Kaua'i's last battle, led in 1824 by Humehume, son of the island's King Kaumuali'i. ⊠ *Rte. 50.*

★ **㊱ Kalalau Lookout.** Near the end of the road high above Waimea Canyon, Kalalau Lookout marks the start of a challenging one-hour, 2-mi hike to **Pu'u-o-Kila Lookout.** On a clear day at either spot you can gaze right down into the gaping valley at sawtooth ridges and waterfalls. But stick around for a few minutes if clouds are obscuring the view. Winds are strong up here and just might blow away the clouds so you can snap a photo. If you turn your back to the valley and look to the northwest, you might pick out the shining sands of Kalalau Beach, gleaming like a tiny golden thread against the Pacific. ⊠ *Waimea Canyon Dr., 4 mi north of Kōke'e State Park.*

㉗ Kaua'i Coffee Visitor Center and Museum. Two restored camp houses, dating from the days when sugar was the main agricultural crop in the Islands, have a museum, visitor center, and gift shop. About 3,400 acres of McBryde sugar land have become Hawai'i's largest coffee plantation. You can walk among the trees, view old grinders and roasters, watch a video to learn how coffee is processed, sample various estate roasts, and check out the gift store. On the way to Waimea Canyon in Ele'ele, take Highway 50 and veer right onto Highway 540, west of Kalāheo. The center is 1½ mi from the Highway 50 turnoff. ⊠ *870 Halawili Rd.,* ☎ *808/ 335-3237* 🎟 *Free* ⊙ *Daily 9–5.*

Kōke'e State Park. At the north end of Waimea Canyon, this park rises 4,000 ft above sea level. Here, the air is cool and crisp, and the vegetation turns to evergreens and ferns. This 4,345-acre wilderness park is full of wild fruit, flowers, and colorful rare birds that make these forests their home. A 45-mi network of hiking trails takes you to some of Kaua'i's most remote places. Before you set off, ask about trail conditions. **Kōke'e Natural History Museum** has displays of plants, native birds, and other wildlife, as well as a weather exhibit that describes the formation of hurricanes. ⊠ *Rte. 550* ☎ *808/335-9975* 🎟 *Donation suggested* ⊙ *Daily 10–4.*

Treat yourself to a cup of coffee or a sandwich at the rustic mountaintop inn, **Kōke'e Lodge** (⊠ Kōke'e State Park, 3600 Kōke'e Rd., mile marker 15 ☎ 808/335–6061). Peruse the gift shop for T-shirts, postcards, or other Kōke'e memorabilia.

▶ **㉖ Kukui o Lono Park.** Translated as "light of the god Lono," Kukui o Lono has serene Japanese gardens and a display of significant Hawaiian stones—an anchor stone and salt pan—collected by Walter McBryde, the sugar-plantation heir who founded the estate in the 1900s. Spectacular panoramic views make this one of Kaua'i's most scenic park areas and an ideal picnic spot. There's also a golf course. ⊠ *Pāpālina Rd., Kalāheo* ☎ *808/332-9151* 🎟 *Free* ⊙ *Daily 6–6.*

㉜ Menehune Ditch. Archaeologists claim that this aqueduct was built before the first Hawaiians lived on Kaua'i, and it is therefore attributed to the industrious hands of the legendary, tiny Menehune. The way the flanged and fitted cut-stone bricks are stacked and assembled indicates a knowledge of construction that is foreign to Hawai'i, and the ditch is inscribed with mysterious markings. Until someone comes up with a better suggestion, the Menehune retain the credit for this engineering feat. ⊠ *Menehune Rd., Waimea Valley.*

30 Salt Pond Beach Park. Hawaiians harvested salt for almost 200 years here. They let the sun evaporate the seawater in mud-lined drying beds, then gathered the salt left behind. This is a safe area for swimming. ⊠ *Lele Rd., Hanapēpē.*

33 Waimea. This is the town that first welcomed Captain James Cook to the Sandwich Islands in 1778. An easy-to-miss monument on the mauka side of the road commemorates his landfall, as does a statue near the entry to town. Waimea was also the place where Kaua'i's King Kaumuali'i ceded his island to the unifying efforts of King Kamehameha. Waimea played host to the first missionaries on the island, and you can still see what's left of the old **Waimea Christian Hawaiian and Foreign Church** on Mākeke Road. Constructed in 1846, the church was made of huge timbers brought down from the mountains 8 mi away, as well as limestone blocks from a nearby quarry. The church suffered severe damage from Hurricane 'Iniki in 1992, but the beautiful stonework of its front and side walls is worth a photo. ⊠ *Rte. 50.*

35 Waimea Canyon. Created by an ancient fault in the Earth's crust, the canyon has been eroding over the centuries due to weather, wind, and the water of its rivers and streams. The "Grand Canyon of the Pacific" is 3,600 ft deep, 2 mi wide, and 10 mi long. The earth's deep reds, greens, and browns are ever changing in the light. Be sure to allow time to soak up the views from **Pu'u-ka-Pele** and **Pu'u-hinahina** lookouts.

34 West Kaua'i Visitor and Technology Center. Local photos and informational computers with touch screens bring to life the island's history and attractions. ⊠ *9565 Kaumualii Hwy. (Rte. 50), Waimea* ☎ *808/338–1332* ⊕ *www.kauaivisitorscenter.com* ☒ *Free* ☉ *Mon.–Sat. 9–5, Sun. 9–2.*

BEACHES

The waters that hug the island are clean, clear, and inviting, but be careful to go in only where it's safe. All beaches on Kaua'i are free and open to the public, and none have a phone number.

The north shore has some of the most spectacular beaches on the island, but they can be treacherous in winter. Many of these beaches require a hike in or walk down, but are worth the effort. There's great snorkeling here in summer.

The south shore has the softest, sandiest, most consistently sunny beaches with excellent snorkeling and swimming. You may come across endangered monk seals or turtles basking on the beach—don't touch or disturb these creatures in any way.

The beaches fronting the hotels and condos along the eastern shore are conducive to seaside strolling but not swimming. The strong surf and rip currents of the winter months are unpredictable, and it's often windy.

If you want wide-open spaces, drive to the west coast beyond Waimea where many locals go to fish and swim. Plus, you can catch the best sunsets from this side. Waimea has a black-sand beach, and a dazzling white-sand beach starts beneath the cliffs at Polihale. The current here can be tricky.

Beaches along the northwest shore are inaccessible except to those who hike the rugged Nā Pali trail from the opposite end of the road at Hā'ena or who book a boat tour. Some operators offer a hiker-camper drop-off service from May through September, transporting passengers one way so they can enjoy a secluded beach, then hike back on their own. After a 2-mi hike, it's tempting to dive into the water at Hanakāpī'ai Beach, but the memorial to those lost at sea while swimming here might convince you that a dip in the river is perfectly fine.

For general information about beaches around the island, call the **County Department of Parks and Recreation** (☎ 808/241–6670). The **Department of Land and Natural Resources** (☎ 808/274–3446) is the source for beach-camping permits.

The list of beaches below starts from the western end of Route 50 and goes counterclockwise around the island to the end of the road on the north shore.

FodorśChoice
★

Polihale Beach Park. This large-grain sand beach stretches almost 15 mi from the town of Kekaha to within the 140-acre Polihale State Park. The wide beach, with mountains ⅓ mi away in the distance, is beautiful for sunbathing, beachcombing, and surf-casting, but the rip currents and crashing waves are too rough for swimming, and there are no lifeguards. Locals dune-buggy here on weekends. The road here is rough and rugged; many first-timers turn around before finishing the 35-minute drive from the end of Route 50. Be careful not to get stuck. Bring your own drinking water. ✛ *Drive to end of Rte. 50 and turn left at Hawaiian-warrior marker onto dirt road, which leads several mi through sugarcane fields; turn left at small national park sign.*

Kekaha Beach Park. On the south shore, this miles-long strip of sand brings to mind the endless beaches of southern California. Dune-buggying is popular. If you don't like the noise, stay away. There are no lifeguards, rest rooms, or showers. ✛ *Take Rte. 50 west of Kekaha.*

Salt Pond Beach Park. The protected bay at Salt Pond is particularly safe for swimmers, so its crescent-shape beach is popular with families. There are picnic tables under covered pavilions, showers, rest rooms, lifeguards, and a large grassy lawn. Camping is allowed. The beach derives its name from the ancient salt ponds that can still be seen to the left as you enter the park. ✛ *Follow Lele Rd., on makai side off Rte. 50 in Hanapēpē.*

Po'ipū Beach Park. A popular bodysurfing and swimming spot, Po'ipū Beach has clean white sand. It's a fun place for a picnic or a barbecue under the palm trees. There are lifeguards, showers, rest rooms, and a take-out deli across the street. A stroll on the beach takes you past a half dozen condominiums to the Sheraton Kaua'i Resort, which has an inviting cocktail lounge overlooking the beach. ✛ *Po'ipū Rd. on south shore, opposite Ho'ōne and Pane Rds.*

Brennecke's Beach. A steady stream of small- to medium-size waves makes this a bodysurfer and boogie-boarder heaven. Waves are bigger here in summer than in winter. Showers, rest rooms, and lifeguards are on hand, and there are food stands nearby. It's also a great place to catch a glimpse of sea turtles. ✛ *Po'ipū Rd. on south shore.*

Shipwreck Beach. Nicknamed for an old wooden boat that wrecked on the 2-mi stretch of sand fronting the Hyatt Regency, this beach, also known as Keoneloa, is popular with surf casters who fish from Makawehi Point on the east side. Sea turtles and monk seals like the coves, but strong rip currents and shore breaks can make swimming dangerous. The winds here are a magnet for windsurfers, who head to the beach's east end. ✣ *Turn into Hyatt Regency Kaua'i Resort, drive along the east side of the hotel, and turn right.*

Kalapakī Beach. This sheltered bay is ideal for swimming, surfing, and windsurfing in the small waves, and offers a magnificent view of cruise ships plying Nāwiliwili Harbor. It fronts the Kaua'i Marriott Resort & Beach Club. Rest rooms, lifeguards, showers, and concessions are steps away. ✣ *Off Wapa'a Rd., which runs from Līhu'e to Nāwiliwili.*

Fodor'sChoice
★ **Lydgate Beach Park.** One of the island's busiest beach parks, Lydgate sits at the mouth of the Wailua River and offers two fishponds and an iron-wood-tree grove in addition to its oceanfront setting. A rock wall protects the swimming area here, and there are lifeguards at this family-friendly beach. Picnic under the covered pavilion or send the kids to romp on the large playground. Rest rooms and showers are available. ✣ *Before mouth of Wailua River turn makai off Rte. 56 onto Lehu Dr. and left onto Nalu Rd.*

Anahola Beach Park. A grassy park on the east end of the beach offers sometimes-calm waters for swimming and snorkeling. The Makalena Mountains are your backdrop here. There are rest rooms and showers but no lifeguards. ✣ *After mile marker 13 on Rte. 56, turn makai on Anahola Rd.*

★ **'Anini Beach County Park.** Safest of the north-shore beaches, this 3-mi stretch of golden sand lies beside a reef-protected blue lagoon, making it ideal for beginning windsurfers, snorkelers, and swimmers. A beachside park, polo field, campground, public rest rooms, showers, grills, and picnic tables keep families happy year-round. There are no lifeguards. Sunsets here can be spectacular. ✣ *Turn makai off Rte. 56 onto Kalihi Wai Rd. on Hanalei side of Kalihi Wai Bridge; road angles left along beach onto 'Anini Rd.*

Hanalei Bay Beach Park. This perfectly curved beach is a marvel of natural beauty. Views of the Nā Pali Coast and tree-shaded picnic tables attract plenty of beach bums, but swimming here can be treacherous, even in summer months, due to strong currents. Stay near the old pier, where the water is a bit calmer. There are rest rooms, showers, and lifeguards. ✣ *In Hanalei turn makai at Aku Rd. and right at dead end.*

Lumaha'i Beach. Lumaha'i is flanked by high mountains and lava rocks. In the movie *South Pacific,* this is where Mitzi Gaynor sang "I'm Gonna Wash That Man Right Outta My Hair." There are no lifeguards, showers, or rest rooms. The currents here have a habit of sweeping people out to sea. ✣ *On winding section of Rte. 56 west of Hanalei between mile markers 4 and 5. Park on makai side of road and walk down a steep path to the beach.*

★ **Tunnels Beach.** Kaua'i's best-protected, big, deep lagoon for swimming and snorkeling is surrounded by a gently sloping beach shaded with iron-wood trees. There are no lifeguards, showers, or rest rooms. ✣ *½ mi past mile marker 8 on Rte. 56. Turn makai onto dirt road that runs through grove of trees. If parking lot is full, continue ½ mi to Hā'ena Beach Park and walk back.*

Hā'ena Beach Park. This beach on Maniniholo Bay was once a popular site for net fishing. Today it is good for swimming but only in summer when the surf is down. There are rest rooms, showers, camping facilities, picnic tables, and food wagons, but no lifeguards. ✣ *On north shore near end of Rte. 56 across from lava-tube sea caves.*

CloseUp

SEAL-SPOTTING ON THE SOUTH SHORE

WHEN SIGHTSEEING or strolling on one of Kaua'i's magnificent beaches, don't be surprised if you find yourself in some unusual company. Although it is thought that there are fewer than 1,500 Hawaiian monk seals in existence today, which lands this animal on the endangered species list, the seals have been known to come ashore, and impromptu sightings are not uncommon. Heavy rains tend to bring them out; they also come ashore to give birth on sandy coral beaches that have sheltering vegetation.

If you see a monk seal, keep your distance and do not attempt to assist the seal back into the water. They are usually not sick or injured but just resting or happily digesting a big meal (the monk seal can eat up to 10% of its own body weight per day). It is illegal to capture or harass these wonderful creatures, and you can incur heavy fines if you do so. If you do have concerns about the health or safety of a seal—or just want more information about these creatures—contact the **Kaua'i Monk Seal Watch Program** (Box 1898, Koloa 96756 808/938–5715 to report seal harassment www.kauaimonkseal.com)

Hawaiian monk seals are usually sighted on the leeward (southwest) shores of Hawai'i's northwestern islands. They have been known to dive to depths of 500 ft and stay at sea for long periods of time before they come ashore. If you are lucky enough to see one of these exotic sea creatures, enjoy the view and let them be. After all, monk seals got their name not only because they have round, shiny heads but also because they are solitary creatures who like to lead a "monk-like" existence at sea.

★ **Ke'e Beach.** In summer this is a fine swimming beach, with a reef lagoon made for snorkeling. In winter, big waves wash away the sand, so stay out of the water and enjoy the views of Nā Pali Coast. This is where the Kalalau Trail begins. Changing facilities are available, as are showers and rest rooms, but there are no lifeguards. ✦ *Northern end of Rte. 56, 7 mi west of Hanalei.*

Hanakāpī'ai Beach. It's a 2-mi hike to this crescent of beach, which changes length and width throughout the year as fierce winter waves rob the shoreline of sand and summer's calm returns it. Be very careful swimming here in summer, and don't even think of going in during the winter swells. Hike an additional 2 mi inland beside the adjacent stream and you find Hanakāpī'ai Falls, which splashes into a freshwater pool perfect for shutterbugs or a cool dip. ✦ *Mi 2 of Kalalau Trail, which begins near Ke'e Beach, at northern end of Rte. 56.*

WHERE TO EAT

In addition to preparing all kinds of ethnic dishes, restaurateurs use the produce grown on native soil and local seafood to create regional dishes. Dining out can be costly, and the menus begin to blur after a while, but you can find inspired cuisine. Romance is a big part of Kaua'i dining, with oceanfront dining rooms, orchids, tiki torches as decorations, and elaborate food presentation. Reservations are always a good idea if you'd like a table with a view.

The East Side

American/Casual

$–$$ ✕ **The Eggbert's.** If you're big on breakfasts, try Eggbert's, in the Coconut Marketplace. This sunny restaurant with a soft-yellow interior, lots of windows, and lānai seating is a great spot for omelettes, banana pancakes, and eggs Benedict in five styles, all of which are served until 3 PM. Lunch and dinner feature club sandwiches, stir-fry, and fresh fish. ✉ *Coconut Marketplace, 4-484 Kūhiō Hwy., Kapa'a* ☎ *808/822–3787* ⊟ *MC, V.*

Contemporary

★ **$$$** ✕ **A Pacific Cafe.** Chef Jean-Marie Josselin serves up cutting-edge cuisine in a setting of cool white calm amid a busy shopping center. Here, East meets West as Asian cooking styles fuse with Josselin's European roots and his commitment to fresh, Kaua'i-grown ingredients. The menu changes daily. Josselin might present lemongrass macadamia-crusted 'ahi (yellowfin tuna) with a vanilla, basil, coconut vinaigrette, or crispy Salmon Firecracker—a signature dish. ✉ *Kaua'i Village Shopping Center, 4-831 Kūhiō Hwy., Kapa'a* ☎ *808/822–0013* ⊟ *AE, D, DC, MC, V* ☻ *No lunch.*

$–$$ ✕ **Caffé Coco.** This little restored plantation cottage is set back off the highway and is surrounded by a riot of tropical foliage. You'll know it by its bright lime-green storefront. An attached black-light art gallery and an artful shop called Bambulei make this a fun stop for any meal. Occasional live music attracts a down-to-earth local crowd. Pot stickers filled with tofu and chutney, 'ahi wraps, Greek salads, fresh fish, and vegetarian items take center stage here. ✉ *4-369 Kūhiō Hwy., Wailua* ☎ *808/822–7990* ⊟ *MC, V* ☻ *Closed Mon.*

Eclectic

$–$$ ✕ **Wailua Family Restaurant.** The 25,000 Christmas lights along the roof might catch your attention, as will the "bars"—as in the all-you-can-eat hot-and-cold salad bar; tostada, taco, and pasta bar; sushi bar; and dessert bar. Steaks, chops, and seafood fill out the menu. Emphasis is on low price rather than high quality, so it's a good place to come with children or if your wallet needs a break. ✉ *4-361 Kūhiō Hwy., Kapa'a* ☎ *808/822–3325* ⊟ *AE, D, MC, V.*

¢–$ ✕ **Ono Family Restaurant.** This local joint is a cross between a country diner and a Hawaiian plantation home. It has faded yellow walls, wooden booths and tables, and local antiques. Breakfast packs 'em in with specialties such as eggs Canterbury (poached eggs, ham, turkey, jack cheese, tomato, hollandaise sauce, and mushrooms on an English muffin), banana macadamia-nut pancakes, and a breakfast burrito. The lunch menu has burgers, meat-loaf sandwiches, salads, fish, and stir-fries. Try the Portuguese bean soup. ✉ *4-1292 Kūhiō Hwy., Kapa'a* ☎ *808/ 822–1710* ⊟ *AE, D, DC, MC, V* ☻ *No dinner.*

Japanese

$–$$ ✕ **Restaurant Kintaro.** Come find out what the locals know: Kintaro's has a great sushi menu. Try the Bali Hai, a roll of eel and smoked salmon, baked and topped with wasabi mayonnaise. *Teppan* (grilled) dinners include tender hibachi shrimp sautéed in lemon butter and served with bean sprouts and steamed rice. Tatami-mat seating is available behind shoji screens, as is lots of black-lacquered table seating by a giant fish tank. ✉ *4-370 Kūhiō Hwy., Kapa'a* ☎ *808/822–3341* ⊟ *AE, D, DC, MC, V* ☻ *Closed Sun. No lunch.*

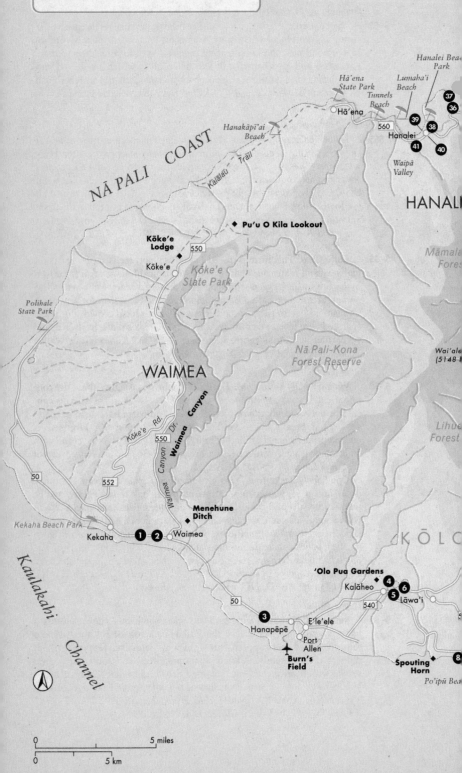

Where to Eat on Kaua'i

Pan-Asian

$$–$$$ ✕ **Lemongrass Grill, Seafood and Sushi Bar.** The owner of this two-story restaurant is of Chinese heritage and raised in Laos. His food is inventive and exciting, combining elements of Burmese, Chinese, Lao, and Japanese cuisine with those of Thai cooking. The focus is on seafood, from Togorashi scallops with sweet potato to salmon grilled with lemongrass and ginger. Orders from the sushi bar are presented on tiny surfboards that make their way to you via a waterway that surrounds the bar. The dining room is rich with Asian art, sculptures, and fresh orchids. ⊠ 4-885 Kūhiō Hwy., Kapa'a ☎ 808/821–2888 ⊟ AE, D, DC, MC, V ☽ No lunch.

Steak & Seafood

$$–$$$ ✕ **Bull Shed.** The A-frame design of this popular restaurant imparts a distinctly rustic feel, but the interior is brightened by light-color walls and unobstructed ocean views. Although it's known especially for its prime rib, Australian rack of lamb, and fresh fish, the Alaskan king crab and homemade desserts are also very good. The view of the surf as it hits the rocks is magnificent. Arrive early before dinner service begins at 5:30 for your best chance at getting a window seat. ⊠ 796 Kūhiō Hwy., Kapa'a ☎ 808/822–3791 or 808/822–1655 ⊟ AE, D, DC, MC, V ☽ No lunch.

$–$$$ ✕ **Wailua Marina Restaurant.** Boats chug along the Wailua past the riverview lānai of this marina restaurant, a great stop on the way to or from Fern Grotto. For the large number of people it serves, the restaurant has a surprisingly inspired menu and generous portions. Stuffed chicken is baked in plum sauce, and the 'ahi is stuffed with crab. There's a good choice of steak and fresh seafood dishes as well. ⊠ Wailua River State Park, Wailua Rd., Wailua ☎ 808/822–4311 ⊟ AE, DC, MC, V ☽ Closed Mon.

Thai

$–$$ ✕ **Mema Thai Chinese Cuisine.** Sophisticated and intimate, Mema Thai serves its dishes on crisp white linens accented by tabletop orchid sprays. Menu items such as broccoli with oyster sauce and cashew chicken reveal Chinese origins, but the emphasis is on Thai dishes. A host of curries—red, green, yellow, and house—made with coconut milk and kaffir lime leaves runs from mild to mouth-searing. ⊠ Wailua Shopping Plaza, 4-369 Kūhiō Hwy., Kapa'a ☎ 808/823–0899 ⊟ AE, D, DC, MC, V ☽ No lunch weekends.

Vegetarian

¢–$ ✕ **Papaya's.** This well-stocked natural foods market also offers vegetarian dining and ethnic specialties that range from baked tofu to spicy Kung Pao stir-fry. Expect a crowd inside the store if you crave some solitude with your chai latte, and check out the seating in the courtyard. ⊠ Kaua'i Village Shopping Center, 4-831 Kūhiō Hwy., Kapa'a ☎ 808/823–0190 ⊟ AE, D, MC, V ☽ Closed Sun.

The North Shore

American/Casual

$–$$ ✕ **Hanalei Gourmet.** The decor in this restaurant in the old school building at Hanelei Center may be basic, but it suits the somewhat rowdy, sports-watching weekend crowd that comes here. Lunch and dinner feature pūpū (appetizer) platters and everything from soups and sandwiches to crab cakes. They also will prepare a picnic and give it to you in an insulated cooler. Happy hour starts at 3:30, and there is live music after dark. ⊠ 5-5161 Kūhiō Hwy., Hanalei ☎ 808/826–2524 ⊟ D, DC, MC, V.

$-$$ ✕ **Kīlauea Bakery and Pau Hana Pizza.** The bakery has garnered tons of press for its Hawaiian sourdough loaf made with guava starter, and such pizzas as the Pomodoro (fresh tomatoes with Kīlauea goat cheese, marinated artichokes, black olives, and mozzarella). To begin your day on a sweet note, check out the tropical danish assortment with fillings that include mango, guava, and macadamia nut. Open at 6:30 AM, the bakery serves as "coffee central" in Kīlauea. ⊠ *Kong Lung Center, 2490 Keneke St., Kīlauea* ☎ *808/828–2020* ▭ *MC, V.*

Contemporary

$$$–$$$$ ✕ **Cafe Hanalei and Terrace.** You're in for a very romantic evening here: the view from the Princeville Resort overlooking Hanalei Bay is mesmerizing, and the attention to detail and service are outstanding. The Sunday brunch and the daily breakfast buffet are enormous feasts. Lunch includes Japanese specialties, lobster bisque, Cobb salad, and sandwiches. For dinner, be adventurous and try the Japanese *unaju,* a broiled freshwater eel served over steamed rice, or opt for Friday night's seafood buffet. ⊠ *Princeville Resort, 5520 Ka Haku Rd., Princeville* ☎ *808/826–2760* ⌂ *Reservations essential* ▭ *AE, D, DC, MC, V.*

$$–$$$ ✕ **Lighthouse Bistro.** Tucked into the heart of Kīlauea, but with no real view of the Kīlauea Lighthouse, this plantation-style restaurant has terra-cotta floors, bamboo chairs, and Hawaiian artwork on the walls for sale. Some entrées have an Italian flair, such as seafood linguine or tortellini. Others, such as stuffed shrimp in phyllo and chicken *satay* (chicken grilled on skewers) with Thai peanut sauce, are more Pacific Rim. ⊠ *2484 Keneke St., at Lighthouse Rd., Kīlauea* ☎ *808/828–0480* ▭ *MC, V.*

★ $$–$$$ ✕ **Postcards Cafe.** Pretty as a picture postcard, this plantation-cottage restaurant, with its beamed ceilings, light interiors, and postcard artwork, has a menu featuring mostly organic, additive-free foods. But don't get the wrong idea—this isn't simple cooking: specials might include carrot ginger soup, Thai coconut curry, or fresh fish served with peppered pineapple sage sauce. Their signature breakfast is a seven-grain English muffin topped with sautéed greens, tempeh strips, and hollandaise—all dairy free. ⊠ *5-5075A Kūhiō Hwy., Hanalei* ☎ *808/826–1191* ▭ *AE, MC, V* ⊗ *No lunch.*

$–$$ ✕ **Bamboo Bamboo.** Locally grown produce, island fish, and homemade desserts are served in this restaurant that features outdoor courtyard seating overlooking Hanalei's lush green taro fields. 'Ahi spring rolls, potato-crusted mahimahi (dolphin fish), and Kīlauea-goat-cheese salad are choices to fit any appetite. Save room for the blackberry cheesecake. ⊠ *Hanalei Center, 5-5161 Kūhiō Hwy., Hanalei* ☎ *808/826–1177* ▭ *AE, MC, V.*

Eclectic

$–$$ ✕ **Zelo's Beach House.** Call the menu eclectic—what else could you say about its American-Italian-Thai-Creole leanings? The decor, however, is strictly South Seas tropical. A bamboo bar, *lau hala* (pandanus leaf) mats on the walls, a kayak overhead, and Tahitian-print bar stools add to the relaxed family atmosphere. Burgers and burritos are served on an open-air deck. For dinner, large salads, fresh fish, pasta, steak, and seafood artichoke fettuccine fit the bill. ⊠ *5-5156 Kūhiō Hwy., Hanalei* ☎ *808/826–9700* ▭ *MC, V.*

Italian

$$$–$$$$ ✕ **La Cascata.** Terra-cotta floors, hand-painted murals, and trompe l'oeil paintings give La Cascata an Italian-villa flair, and picture windows offer dazzling views of Hanalei Bay. The menu emphasizes light sauces, plenty of pastas, plus fresh seafood, beef, and lamb. Savor fettuccine with

Kona lobster or sample sautéed shrimp, clams, and scallops on pasta with a spicy tomato-fennel sauce. Come early for sunset views of Bali Hai. ⊠ *Princeville Resort, 5520 Ka Haku Rd., Princeville* ☎ *808/826–2761* ⌕ *Reservations essential* ⊟ *AE, D, DC, MC, V* ⊘ *No lunch.*

Mexican

$–$$ ✕ **Roadrunner Bakery and Café.** Casual with a capital "C," the Roadrunner has a counter where you can order fresh-baked taro rolls or bread in addition to breakfast pastries and espresso. Sit down to check out the *huevos rancheros* (eggs with a piquant red sauce) or a burrito, such as the Black Dog (stuffed with pork, grilled taro, and black beans). Sizzling fajitas and enchiladas are popular dinner items. The dining room is a concrete-block room covered with Mexican murals and plastic patio furniture. ⊠ *2430 Oka St., Kīlauea* ☎ *808/828–8226* ⊟ *MC, V.*

Steak & Seafood

$$$–$$$$ ✕ **Bali Hai.** Views of the bay are as memorable as the cuisine at this open-air restaurant, richly appointed with natural wood. Specialties include the Kaua'i-onion soup topped with melted provolone cheese, grilled-Portobello-mushroom salad, and fresh fish pan-seared and served over a crispy crab cake. Breakfast includes poi pancakes, fried taro, and eggs. ⊠ *Hanalei Bay Resort, 5380 Honoiki Rd., Princeville* ☎ *808/826–6522* ⊟ *AE, D, DC, MC, V.*

$$–$$$ ✕ **Chuck's Steak House.** A *paniolo* (Hawaiian cowboy) feeling permeates this split-level eatery, with saddles and blankets hanging from the open-beam ceiling. Barbecued baby-back ribs, lobster, chicken, and Alaskan king crab are all good, but fresh island seafood and Angus beef are what Chuck's is known for. You can put steak alongside almost any other entrée on the menu, and a salad bar comes with them all. Save room for dessert—the special mud pie is a winner. ⊠ *Princeville Shopping Center, 5-4280 Kūhiō Hwy., Princeville* ☎ *808/826–6211* ⊟ *AE, D, DC, MC, V* ⊘ *No lunch weekends.*

Līhu'e

American/Casual

$$–$$$ ✕ **JJ's Broiler.** Overlooking Kalapakī Bay, this spacious, low-key local favorite has two levels: downstairs is a bar and lānai with hearty American fare; upstairs you can feast on fancier Pacific Rim dishes, including sugarcane shrimp and Peking chicken tacos in a garlic oyster sauce. The house specialty is Slavonic steak, a broiled sliced tenderloin dipped in a buttery wine sauce. ⊠ *Anchor Cove, 3146 Rice St., Nāwiliwili* ☎ *808/246–4422* ⊟ *D, MC, V.*

$–$$ ✕ **Līhu'e Barbecue Inn.** This local-style hangout features booths and tables and a menu that ranges from classic American fare to Asian. Try the baby-back ribs, the shrimp tempura, or the Cajun seafood medley with king crab. If you can't make up your mind, the Inn's tri-sampler is a good compromise. This venue has been a mainstay on Kaua'i since 1940. ⊠ *2982 Kress St., Līhu'e* ☎ *808/245–2921* ⊟ *No credit cards.*

Eclectic

$$$–$$$$ ✕ **Gaylord's.** Located in what was at one time Kaua'i's most expensive plantation estate, Gaylord's pays tribute to the elegant dining rooms of 1930s society. Candlelit tables on a cobblestone patio overlook a wide lawn with a fountain. The menu pairs classic American cooking with an island twist. A popular Sunday brunch has innovative dishes like sweet-potato hash and Cajun 'ahi in addition to the standard omelettes and pancakes. You can also arrange for a pre- or postmeal horse-drawn carriage ride of the plantation. ⊠ *Kilohana Plantation, 3-2087 Kaumuali'i Rd., Līhu'e* ☎ *808/245–9593* ⊟ *AE, D, DC, MC, V.*

$$$–$$$$ ✕ **Kukui's Restaurant and Bar.** With an imaginative menu that focuses on healthful choices and cross-cultural flavors, Kukui's offers a casual, open-air oceanfront dining experience. For lunch, try the blackened Pacific salmon with grilled-pineapple scallion salsa, the *kālua* (roasted) pork quesadillas, or Thai-chicken pizza. Dinner is more formal, with an island-influenced menu that includes a shrimp boat buffet, served from a real island canoe. At breakfast the temptations are twofold: a buffet or a full à la carte menu. ⊠ *Kaua'i Marriott Resort & Beach Club, 3610 Rice St., Līhu'e* ☎ *808/245–5050* ▭ *AE, D, DC, MC, V.*

Hawaiian

¢–$ ✕ **Dani's Restaurant.** Kaua'i residents often frequent this big and bare come-as-you-are eatery near the Līhu'e Fire Station. Dani's is a good place to try lū'au food without commercial lū'au prices. You can order Hawaiian-style *laulau* (pork wrapped in ti leaves and steamed) or kālua pig and rice. Other island-style dishes include Japanese-prepared *tonkatsu* (pork cutlet) and teriyaki beef, and there's always the all-American New York steak. ⊠ *4201 Rice St., Līhu'e* ☎ *808/245–4991* ▭ *No credit cards* ☉ *Closed Sun. No dinner.*

¢ ✕ **Hamura Saimin.** It doesn't look like much from the outside, but inside this old plantation diner each day, the Hiraoka family serves 1,000 orders of saimin, a steaming bowl of broth and noodles with varying garnishes. This little landmark also turns out tasty chicken and beef grilled on barbecue sticks, as well as liliko'i (Passion fruit) chiffon pie. ⊠ *2956 Kress St., Līhu'e* ☎ *808/245–3271* ▭ *No credit cards.*

FodorsChoice
★

Italian

$$–$$$ ✕ **Café Portofino.** Owner Giuseppe Avocadi's menu has garnered this little Italian restaurant in the Harbor Mall a host of culinary awards. The cuisine is northern Italian and features fresh 'ahi carpaccio, along with pasta, scampi, and veal dishes, each enhanced by sauces "with an Italian soul." If you get a table out on the lānai, you can enjoy beautiful views of Kalapakī Bay and live harp music while you eat. ⊠ *Harbor Mall, 3501 Rice St., Nāwiliwili* ☎ *808/245–2121* ▭ *AE, D, DC, MC, V* ☉ *No lunch.*

Japanese

$–$$ ✕ **Hanamā'ulu Restaurant, Tea House, Sushi Bar, and Robatayaki.** This truly Japanese restaurant is spartan; it's not the furnishings but the food that is popular. Traditional Japanese fare such as sashimi; sushi; *teishoku* (set meal) platters with miso soup, tempura shrimp, fish, and vegetables; chicken katsu; and *robatayaki* (grilled seafood and meat) is the main attraction. Call ahead to reserve one of the private teahouse dining rooms for soothing views of the Japanese garden and ponds. ⊠ *1-4291 Kūhiō Hwy. (Rte. 56), Hanamā'ulu* ☎ *808/245–2511* ▭ *MC, V* ☉ *Closed Mon.*

Seafood

$–$$$ ✕ **Duke's Canoe Club.** Surf legend Duke Kahanamoku would be proud: a bi-level beachfront restaurant replete with indoor garden and waterfall, the happening Barefoot Bar (a bar menu is available), and the biggest salad bar on the island. The best order here is the fresh catch of the day—prepared as you like it, from broiled plain to Thai-chili-glazed. Strolling musicians are a fun accompaniment, as is the view of Kalapakī Bay and Nāwiliwili Harbor at sunset. ⊠ *Kalapakī Beach, Līhu'e* ☎ *808/246–9599* ▭ *AE, D, DC, MC, V.*

The South Shore & The West Side

American

$$ ✕ **Camp House Grill.** A simple plantation-style camp house with squeaky wooden floors has become a simple, down-home restaurant. The food is basic: hamburgers, chicken, pork ribs, and fresh fish aimed to please families. Barbecued specialties include chicken marinated in a blend of Chinese, Cajun, and Hawaiian spices. Huge sandwiches are served at lunchtime. Large breakfasts are available, and pies are baked fresh daily. As you enter Kalāheo heading west, look for the blue building on the right. ⊠ *Kaumuali`i Hwy. (Rte. 50), Kalāheo* ☎ *808/332–9755* ⊠ *Kaua`i Village, Kūhiō Hwy., Kapa`a* ☎ *808/822–2442* ⊟ *AE, D, MC, V.*

Contemporary

★ $$$–$$$$ ✕ **The Beach House.** Though this restaurant may have the best ocean view of any on the south shore, it's equally possible to get swept away by the cuisine. The menu changes more often than the work of local artists on the walls, but you might find Kaua`i-asparagus salad and Local Boy paella, fire-roasted `ahi, or lemongrass-and-kaffir-lime-leaf-crusted scallops on the menu. A coconut-butter *mochi* (doughy Japanese rice cake) sundae is the sweetest finale. ⊠ *5022 Lawai Rd., Kōloa* ☎ *808/742–1424* ⊟ *AE, D, DC, MC, V* ⊗ *No lunch.*

$$–$$$ ✕ **Shells Restaurant.** Chandeliers made from big shells light the way for a tropically influenced meal. Crab cakes, rack of lamb with herb and hoisin crust, and fresh fish prepared three ways are among your choices. Friday evenings there is a bountiful seafood buffet. Shells is one of three signature restaurants in the Sheraton's Oceanfront Galleria. Each of these restaurants has been designed to embrace the view of the Pacific Ocean from sunrise to sunset. ⊠ *Sheraton Kaua`i Resort, 2440 Ho`onani Rd., Po`ipū Beach, Kōloa* ☎ *808/742–1661* ⊟ *AE, D, DC, MC, V* ⊗ *No lunch.*

$–$$$ ✕ **Tomkats Grille.** Tropical ponds, a waterfall, a large bar area, and a porch overlooking an inner courtyard give this grill its casual island ambience. You can have a blackened "katch of the day" with tropical salsa, or a homemade chili, and wash it down with a glass of wine or a choice of 35 ales, stouts, ports, and lagers. Plenty of Tomkats' Nibblers—buffalo wings, stuffed mushrooms, sautéed shrimp—enliven happy hour from 3 to 6. ⊠ *Old Kōloa Town, 5402 Kōloa Rd., Kōloa* ☎ *808/742–8887* ⊟ *DC, MC, V.*

$$ ✕ **Waimea Brewing Company.** Housed within the Waimea Plantation Cottages, this brewpub-restaurant is spacious, with hardwood floors and open-air decks. Dine indoors amid rattan furnishings or at a bar decorated with petroglyphs and colored with Kaua`i red dirt. Smoked-chicken quesadillas, grilled Portobellos, hamburgers, kalbi beef short ribs, and fresh fish are highlights. Entrées come in two sizes (small and big!) and are reasonably priced. It's a good place to pick up a picnic basket. ⊠ *9400 Kaumuali`i Hwy., Waimea* ☎ *808/338–9733* ⊟ *MC, V.*

Eclectic

★ $$$–$$$$ ✕ **Roy's Po`ipū Bar & Grill.** Hawai`i's culinary superstar Roy Yamaguchi created a sleek restaurant that quickly became a mecca for fans of his Euro-Asian Pacific cuisine. Who but Roy would turn smoked duck into *gyoza* (Japanese dumplings), or team fresh seared `ōpakapaka with orange shrimp butter and Chinese black bean sauce? There are 15 to 20 or more specials nightly. ⊠ *Po`ipū Shopping Village, 2360 Kiahuna Plantation Dr., Po`ipū Beach* ☎ *808/742–5000* ⊟ *AE, D, DC, MC, V* ⊗ *No lunch.*

$–$$ ✕ **Green Garden.** A favorite since 1948, this plantation-house restaurant is surrounded by tropical greenery that seems to hug its very foundation. Green Garden is very low-key: servers treat you like longtime friends, and the food is solid, no-frills fare. Dinner includes some 30 items of native Hawaiian, Asian, and American influence. Mahimahi, scallops, oysters, and shrimp are key ingredients. The homemade desserts are the best part of a meal here, particularly the liliko'i chiffon pie. ✉ *Rte. 50, Hanapēpē* ☎ *808/335–5422* ▭ *AE, MC, V* ☺ *Closed Tues.*

Italian

$$–$$$$ ✕**Dondero's.** Inlaid marble floors, ornate tile work, and Italianate murals make it difficult to choose between indoor and outdoor dining. The choice of food is no less enticing: porcini-mushroom crepes with Parmesan sauce, a perfectly seasoned Caesar salad, and *spiedini* (skewered lobster, scallops, and shrimp suspended over tender gnocchi pillows), for example. ✉ *Hyatt Regency Kaua'i Resort and Spa, 1571 Po'ipū Rd., Po'ipū Beach* ☎ *808/742–1234* ▭ *AE, D, DC, MC, V* ☺ *No lunch.*

$$–$$$ ✕**Casa di Amici.** Ceiling fans whirl above rattan furnishings at the "House of Friends." Outside deck seating has a sweeping ocean view. Order your favorite pasta with your choice of sauce, or savor the scents of the Orient with a Thai lobster bisque. The menu hints of French, Thai, Japanese, and Vietnamese influences. Live classical music plays on the weekends. ✉ *2301 Nalo Rd., Po'ipū* ☎ *808/742–1555* ▭ *AE, D, DC, MC, V* ☺ *No lunch.*

$$–$$$ ✕**Plantation Gardens.** A former plantation manager's residence, this historic structure now serves Italian food in a Polynesian atmosphere—an interesting mix. There are torch-lit gardens, wood interiors, and veranda dining. Fish right off the boat is prepared with fresh herbs straight from the garden. Outstanding dishes include marinated grilled eggplant with goat cheese and sun-dried tomatoes, shrimp and wasabi ravioli, and the tender osso buco served with saffron risotto. ✉ *Kiahuna Plantation, 2253 Po'ipū Rd., Kōloa* ☎ *808/742–2216* ▭ *AE, DC, MC, V* ☺ *No lunch.*

$–$$ ✕**Pomodoro.** Begin with prosciutto and melon, and then proceed directly to the lasagna, a favorite of the chefs, who are two Italian-born brothers. Highlights include eggplant or veal parmigiana, chicken saltimbocca, and scampi in a garlic, caper, and white wine sauce. Two walls of windows brighten this intimate second-story restaurant. ✉ *Upstairs at Rainbow Plaza, Kaumuali'i Hwy. (Rte. 50), Kalāheo* ☎ *808/332–5945* ▭ *MC, V* ☺ *No lunch.*

Steak & Seafood

$$$–$$$$ ✕**Tidepools.** The Hyatt Regency Kaua'i has three superb restaurants, but this one delivers the most. Dine in one of the grass-thatch huts that float on a koi-filled pond, and enjoy views of the romantic torch-lit grounds and starry Po'ipū skies. A major advocate of Hawai'i regional cuisine, which utilizes Kaua'i-grown products, the chef prepares fish with local flavors. Specialties include macadamia-crusted fish, prime rib, and filet mignon. ✉ *Hyatt Regency Kaua'i Resort and Spa, 1571 Po'ipū Rd., Po'ipū Beach* ☎ *808/742–1234 Ext. 4260* ▭ *AE, D, DC, MC, V* ☺ *No lunch.*

$$–$$$ ✕**Kalāheo Steak House.** Prime rib, tender top sirloin, Cornish game hen in citrus marinade, Alaskan king crab legs, and Portuguese bean soup bring in the locals. The interior is Upcountry casual—a room designed for hearty eating. Fresh-baked rum cake comes with Lappert's ice cream (made at a factory up the road). Wines range from $8 to $25 a bottle. ✉ *4444 Papalina Rd., Kalāheo* ☎ *808/332–9780* ▭ *AE, D, MC, V* ☺ *Reservations not accepted* ☺ *No lunch.*

$$–$$$ ✕**Keoki's Paradise.** Built to resemble a dockside boathouse, this is an active, boisterous place that fills up quickly on weekend nights because of live music. Ocean-originating appetizers range from sashimi to fisherman's chowder. The day's fresh catch is available in half a dozen styles

and sauces. And there's a sampling of beef, chicken, and pork-rib entrées especially for the committed carnivore. ⊠ *Po'ipū Shopping Village, 2360 Kiahuna Plantation Dr., Po'ipū Beach* ☎ 808/742–7534 ⊟ *AE, D, DC, MC, V.*

$$–$$$ ✕ **Wrangler's Steakhouse.** Denim-cover seating, decorative saddles, and a stage coach in a loft helped to transform this former historic Ako General Store in Waimea into a west-side steak house. You can eat under the stars on the deck out back. The 16-ounce steak comes sizzling with either garlic, capers, peppers, or teriyaki. Local folks love the tin lunch: soup, rice, beef teriyaki, and shrimp tempura served in a three-tier lunch pail (the kind that sugar-plantation workers once carried). A gift shop has local crafts (and sometimes a craftsperson). ⊠ *9852 Kaumuali'i Hwy., Waimea* ☎ 808/338–1218 ⊟ *AE, MC, V* ☉ *Closed Sun.*

$$ ✕ **Brennecke's Beach Broiler.** Brennecke's is decidedly casual and fun, with a busy bar, windows overlooking the beach, and a cheery blue-and-white interior. It specializes in big portions of *kiawe*-wood-broiled (kiawe is a mesquitelike wood) foods such as New York steak, spiny lobster, and the fresh catch of the day. Fresh mussels, pasta, and deluxe fish sandwiches are other options. There's a take-out deli downstairs. ⊠ *2100 Ho'one Rd., Po'ipū* ☎ 808/742–7588 ⊟ *AE, D, DC, MC, V.*

WHERE TO STAY

Make reservations in advance, whether you choose to stay at a plush Po'ipū resort or a condo on the south shore, where you can bask all day in the sun; at the posh Princeville Resort on the north shore, where you can enjoy world-class golfing; at a Coconut Coast guest house on the east side, where you can take advantage of an abundance of nearby shops and restaurants; or at a rustic cabin on Kaua'i's west side. Peak months are February and August. When booking your accommodations, ask about such extras as tennis, golf, honeymoon, and room-and-car packages.

BED-AND-
BREAKFASTS

Two B&B reservation services are based in Kaua'i. **Bed and Breakfast Kaua'i** (⊠ 105 Melia St., Kapa'a 96746 ☎ 808/822–1177 or 800/822–1176 🖷 808/826–9292 ⊕ www.bnb-kauai.com) has been in operation on the Garden Isle for many years and offers a network of more than 200 homes.

Island-wide reservations services, such as **Hawaii's Best Rentals** (🏠 Box 790450, Paia 96779 ☎ 808/929–9557 or 866/772–5642 ⊕ www. hawaiisbestrentals.com), can book B&B rooms and exclusive vacation rentals for a Kaua'i or multi-island trip. **Bed and Breakfast Honolulu** (⊠ 3242 Kā'ohinani Dr., Honolulu 96817 ☎ 808/595–7533 or 800/288–4666 🖷 808/595–2030 ⊕ www.hawaiibnb.com) advertises more than 400 host homes on all major islands and can assist with interisland airfares and car rental.

The North Shore

$$$$ 🏨 **Kīlauea Lakeside Estate.** Imagine having your own private island retreat where the amenities and activities are custom-designed to meet your every vacation dream. At Kīlauea Lakeside Estate, a private 20-acre freshwater lake teeming with bass and catfish awaits your fishing pole. You'll also have your own three-par golf hole and putting green and 3 acres of botanical gardens to stroll through. The modern three-bedroom house has a romantic master suite and bath. The proprietors can arrange for personal chefs, windsurfing lessons, lakeside spa treatments, and on-site weddings. ⊠ *4613 Waiakalua Rd., Kīlauea 96754* ☎ 310/379–7842 🖷 *310/379–0034* ⊕ *www.kauaihoneymoon.com* ⌁ *1 house* ♨ *Grill,*

fans, kitchen, cable TV, in-room VCRs, putting green, lake, beach, fishing, laundry facilities; no a/c ⊟ *AE, D, MC, V.*

$$$$ 🏨 **Princeville Resort.** Ornate guest rooms have views of Hanalei Bay, marble bathrooms with gold-plated fixtures, and a privacy window—flip a switch and it goes from clear to opaque. A sunset drink in the Living Room is an event complete with a traditional Hawaiian ceremony. There are two top-ranked golf courses on the resort grounds; a spa and tennis center can be reached by shuttle. ⊠ *5520 Ka Haku Rd. (Box 3069), Princeville 96722* 🕾 *808/826–9644 or 800/826–4400* 🖷 *808/826–1166* ⊕ *www.princeville.com* ⟿ *201 rooms, 51 suites* ♨ *3 restaurants, room service, minibars, 2 18-hole golf courses, 8 tennis courts, pool, gym, health club, massage, spa, beach, 2 bars, children's programs (ages 5–12), dry cleaning, laundry service, concierge, business services, meeting rooms, travel services* ⊟ *AE, D, DC, MC, V.*

FodorsChoice
★

$$$$ 🏨 **Secret Beach Hideaway.** Start a romance or write the great American novel—anything seems possible at these three sumptuous one-bedroom, one-bath retreats. The cottages feature custom furniture and flooring in island-hewn hardwoods, gourmet kitchens with European appliances, indoor-outdoor garden showers, and picture windows designed to offer the most stunning ocean and mountain views. Four private paths lead down to Secret Beach. ⊠ *2884 Kauapea Rd. (Box 781), Kīlauea 96754* 🕾 *808/828–2862 or 800/820–2862* 🖷 *808/828–0899* ⟿ *3 cottages* ♨ *Fans, in-room fax, kitchens, microwaves, cable TV, in-room VCRs, tennis court, pool, hot tub, beach; no a/c.*

$$$–$$$$ 🏨 **Hanalei Bay Resort.** Three-story buildings angle down the cliffs overlooking Hanalei Bay and the famed Bali Hai. Units are extremely spacious, with high, sloping ceilings and large private lānai. Rattan furniture and island art add a casual feeling to rooms. Studios have small kitchenettes not meant for serious cooking. The resort's upper-level pool has lava-rock waterfalls, an open-air hot tub, and a kid-friendly sand "beach." Guests have golf privileges at Princeville Resort. ⊠ *5380 Honoiki Rd., Princeville 96722* 🕾 *808/826–6522 or 800/827–4427* 🖷 *808/826–6680* ⊕ *www.hanaleibayresort.com* ⟿ *137 units* ♨ *Restaurant, in-room safes, kitchenettes, refrigerators, cable TV, 8 tennis courts, 2 pools, hot tub, beach, lobby lounge, baby-sitting, children's programs (ages 5–12), laundry facilities* ⊟ *AE, D, DC, MC, V.*

$$$–$$$$ 🏨 **Hanalei Colony Resort.** This 5-acre property is a laid-back, go-barefoot kind of place sandwiched between towering mountains and the sea. There are no neighbors to speak of, no phones in the rooms, and no stereos or TVs. Each of the two-bedroom condominium units can sleep a family of four. The units are modern and well maintained, with Hawaiian-style furnishings, full kitchens, and lānai. ⊠ *5-7130 Kūhiō Hwy. (Box 206), Hā'ena 96714* 🕾 *808/826–6235 or 800/628–3004* 🖷 *808/826–9893* ⊕ *www.hcr.com* ⟿ *48 units* ♨ *Grill, fans, kitchens, pool, hot tub, beach, laundry facilities; no a/c, no room phones, no room TVs* ⊟ *AE, MC, V.*

The East Side

$$$$ 🏨 **Outrigger Laenani.** Ruling Hawaiian chiefs once returned from ocean voyages to this spot, now host to condominiums comfortable enough for minor royalty. An oceanside heiau and hotel-sponsored Hawaiiana programs, with a booklet for self-guided historical tours, are nice extras. Units are all decorated differently, with bright, full kitchens and expansive lānai. Your view of landscaped grounds is interrupted only by a large pool before ending at a sandy, swimmable beach. ⊠ *410 Papaloa Rd., Kapa'a 96746* 🕾 *808/822–4938 or 800/688–7444* 🖷 *808/*

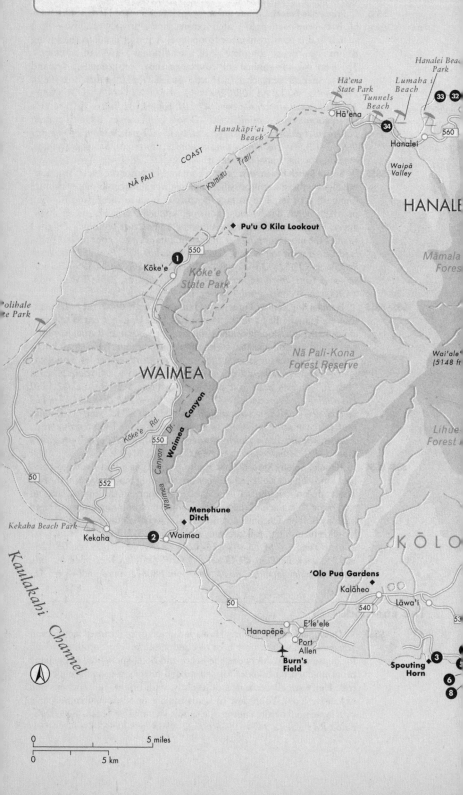

Where to Stay on Kaua'i

Hanalei Beach Park

Hā'ena State Park

Lumaha'i Beach

Tunnels Beach

Hanakāpi'ai Beach

Hā'ena

33 32

560

Hanalei

Waipā Valley

NĀ PALI

COAST

Kalalau Trail

34

HANALE

Pu'u O Kila Lookout

Māmala Fores

550

Kōke'e 1

Kōke'e State Park

Nā Pali-Kona Forest Reserve

Wai'ale (5148 ft

Polihale e Park

WAIMEA

Lihue Forest

Kōke'e Rd.

550

Waimea Canyon Dr.

Waimea Canyon

50

552

Menehune Ditch

Kekaha Beach Park

Kekaha 2 Waimea

KŌLO

'Olo Pua Gardens

Kalāheo

Lāwa'i

540

53

50

Hanapēpē

E'le'ele

Port Allen

Burn's Field

Spouting Horn

3

5

6

8

Kaulakahi Channel

0   5 miles

0   5 km

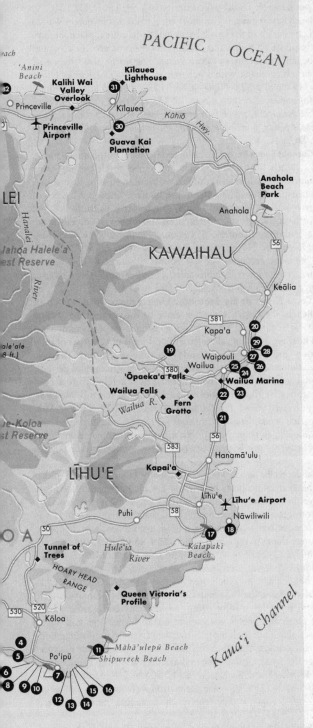

822–1022 ⊕ *www.outrigger.com* ↩ *84 condominiums (52 rentals)* ☆ *Picnic area, fans, in-room safes, kitchens, microwaves, cable TV, tennis court, pool, beach, laundry facilities; no a/c* ▭ *AE, D, DC, MC, V.*

$$$–$$$$ ▣ **Aloha Beach Resort Kaua'i.** The short walk from this resort on Wailua Bay to Lydgate Park and the beach helps make this a great place for families. It's also close to shops and restaurants. Rooms are in two wings and have beach, mountain, or ocean views. The resort also offers one-bedroom beach cottages with kitchenettes. ⊠ *3-5920 Kūhiō Hwy., Kapa'a 96746* ☎ *808/823–6000 or 888/823–5111* 🖷 *808/823–6666* ⊕ *www.alohabeachresortkauai.com* ↩ *188 rooms, 2 suites, 24 beach cottages* ☆ *Restaurant, snack bar, in-room data ports, in-room safes, 2 tennis courts, 2 pools, gym, hot tub, shuffleboard, volleyball, lobby lounge* ▭ *AE, D, DC, MC, V.*

$$$–$$$$ ▣ **Kaua'i Coconut Beach Resort.** Considered the most authentic by many, this resort's nightly lū'au and free hula and sunset torch-lighting show perpetual native spirit. Modern rooms have plantation-style furnishings and floral bedspreads. Set back from the highway amidst 11 acres of coconut grove and on Waipouli Beach, this resort is centrally located between north- and south-shore attractions and within walking distance of three major shopping centers. ⊠ *Coconut Plantation on Kūhiō Hwy. (Box 830), Kapa'a 96746* ☎ *808/822–3455 or 800/222–5642* 🖷 *808/ 822–0035* ⊕ *www.kcb.com* ↩ *307 rooms, 2 suites* ☆ *Restaurant, room service, refrigerators, 3 tennis courts, pool, hot tub, shuffleboard, lobby lounge, meeting room* ▭ *AE, D, DC, MC, V.*

$$–$$$$ ▣ **Kaua'i Coast Resort at the Beachboy.** On an uncrowded stretch of Waipouli Beach, the resort is a quick drive to Kapa'a and the Wailua Municipal Golf Course, and within walking distance of the Coconut Marketplace. The three-building, three-story condominium consists of fully furnished one- and two-bedroom, and some time-share units. They are decorated in rich woods with tropical prints and Hawaiian-quilt designs. Each unit has a kitchen and private lānai. The 8 acres feature a pool with waterscapes, a children's pool, and an oceanside hot tub. ⊠ *4-484 Kūhiō Hwy., Kapa'a 96746* ☎ *808/822–3441 or 877/977–4355* 🖷 *808/ 822–0843* ⊕ *www.kauaicoasthawaii.com* ↩ *108 1- and 2-bedroom condos* ☆ *Restaurant, in-room data ports, kitchens, microwaves, refrigerators, tennis court, 2 pools, gym, hot tub, lobby lounge* ▭ *AE, D, DC, MC, V.*

$$–$$$ ▣ **Aston Islander on the Beach.** The eight three-story buildings of this pleasant 6-acre beachfront property have a low-key Hawai'i-plantation look. Rooms have showers but not tubs. The dark carpeting is brightened by the light from glass doors leading to the lānai and lovely green lawns outside. A free-form pool sits next to a golden-sand beach, and you can take the lounge chairs to the ocean's edge. ⊠ *4-484 Kūhiō Hwy., Kapa'a 96746* ☎ *808/822–7417 or 800/922–7866* 🖷 *808/822–1947* ↩ *194 rooms, 2 suites* ☆ *Restaurant, tennis court, pool, hair salon, hot tub, volleyball, bar, laundry facilities, meeting room* ▭ *AE, D, DC, MC, V.*

$$–$$$ ▣ **Best Western Plantation Hale Suites.** These attractive plantation-style one-bedroom units have fully equipped kitchens and garden lānai. Rooms are clean and pretty, with white rattan furnishings and pastel colors. You couldn't ask for a more convenient location for dining, shopping, and sightseeing: it's across from Waipouli Beach and near Coconut Marketplace. Request a unit on the makai side, away from Kūhiō Highway. ⊠ *484 Kūhiō Hwy., Kapa'a 96746* ☎ *808/822–4941 or 800/775– 4253* 🖷 *808/822–5599* ⊕ *www.plantation-hale.com* ↩ *145 units* ☆ *In-room safes, kitchens, kitchenettes, microwaves, putting green, 3 pools, hot tub* ▭ *AE, D, DC, MC, V.*

$$ ▣ **Kapa'a Sands.** An old rock etched with kanji, Japanese characters, reminds you that the site of this condominium gem formerly contained

a Shinto temple. Two-bedroom rentals—equipped with full kitchens and private lānai—are a fair deal. Studios feature pull-down Murphy beds to create more daytime space. Ask for an oceanfront room to get the breeze. ⊠ *380 Papaloa Rd., Kapa'a 96746* ☎ *808/822–4901 or 800/ 222–4901* ☐ *808/822–1556* ⊕ *www.kapaasands.com* ⤶ *24 condominiums* ♿ *Fans, kitchens, microwaves, cable TV, in-room VCRs, pool; no a/c* ☐ *MC, V.*

$–$$ 🏨 **Kaua'i Sands.** Hawaiian owned and operated, this oceanfont inn is a real example of the Hawai'i before megadevelopers. The carpets are sea-foam green, the bedspreads floral prints, the furniture spare and simple. It's so retro it's unintentionally hip. A big grassy courtyard opens to the beach. For dining and shopping, the Coconut Marketplace is adjacent. ⊠ *420 Papaloa Rd., Kapa'a 96746* ☎ *808/822–4951 or 800/ 560–5553* ☐ *808/822–0978* ⊕ *www.sand-seaside.com* ⤶ *198 rooms, 2 suites* ♿ *Some kitchenettes, cable TV, 2 pools, gym, lobby lounge, laundry facilities* ☐ *AE, D, DC, MC, V.*

¢–$ 🏨 **Hotel Coral Reef.** Coral Reef has been in business since the 1960s and is something of a beachfront landmark. The well-maintained, no-frills hotel sits right on the sand's edge. Upper units have carpeting, while ground-level rooms are done in terrazzo tile with patios that lead out to the beach and barbecue grills. Rooms have showers only, not tubs. There are two two-room units, good for families. ⊠ *1516 Kūhiō Hwy., Kapa'a 96746* ☎ *808/822–4481 or 800/843–4659* ☐ *808/822–7705* ⊕ *www.hotelcoralreef.com* ⤶ *24 rooms, 2 suites* ♿ *Picnic area, some refrigerators, cable TV, beach, laundry facilities; no a/c, no room phones* ☐ *MC, V* ⋈ *CP.*

¢–$ 🏨 **Rosewood Bed and Breakfast.** This charming B&B on a macadamia-nut plantation estate offers four separate styles of accommodations, including a two-bedroom Victorian cottage, a little one-bedroom grass-thatch cottage, a bunkhouse with three rooms and a shared bath, and the traditional main plantation home. ⊠ *872 Kamalu Rd., Kapa'a 96746* ☎ *808/822–5216* ☐ *808/822–5478* ⊕ *www.rosewoodkauai. com* ⤶ *3 cottages, main home with 1 room* ♿ *Kitchens, cable TV in some rooms; no room phones, no smoking* ☐ *No credit cards.*

Līhu'e

$$$$ 🏨 **Kaua'i Marriott Resort & Beach Club.** An elaborate tropical garden, waterfalls right off the lobby, and an enormous 26,000-square-ft swimming pool characterize the grand scale of this resort, which is oceanfront on stunning Kalapakī Bay. This resort has it all, with fine dining, shopping, spa, golf, tennis, water activities of all kinds, and Hawaiian-cultural activities that embrace the island's revered heritage. Rooms are appointed with tropical touches, and most have expansive ocean views. ⊠ *3610 Rice St., Kalapakī Beach, Līhu'e 96766* ☎ *808/245–5050 or 800/220– 2925* ☐ *808/245–5148* ⊕ *www.marriotthotels.com* ⤶ *356 rooms, 11 suites, 232 time-share units* ♿ *2 restaurants, room service, minibars, 2 18-hole golf courses, 7 tennis courts, pool, health club, outdoor hot tub, spa, beach, boating, lobby lounge, children's programs (ages 5–12), airport shuttle* ☐ *AE, D, DC, MC, V.*

Fodor'sChoice
★

$$$$ 🏨 **Radisson Kaua'i Beach Hotel.** A low-rise, horseshoe-shape hotel, the Radisson surrounds a pool complex with rock-sculpted slopes, waterfalls, tropical flowers, and a cave resembling the Fern Grotto. The sand-bottom swimming pool makes up for the rough coastline. There are lots of little extras here, such as the 5 PM complimentary mai tai happy hour, followed by a torch-lighting ceremony and live Hawaiian music. Guest rooms are attractive in rich tones with maroon accents and dark wood. The lānai have views of mountains, gardens, or the sea. ⊠ *4331 Kaua'i*

Beach Dr., Līhu'e 96766 ☎ *808/245–1955 or 888/805–3843* 🖷 *808/ 246–9085* ⊕ *www.radissonkauai.com* ☞ *347 rooms, 8 suites* 🕭 *2 restaurants, room service, in-room safes, some refrigerators, cable TV, in-room VCRs, 18-hole golf course, 4 tennis courts, 2 pools, wading pool, health club, hot tub, beach, lobby lounge, pub, airport shuttle* ⊟ *AE, D, DC, MC, V.*

$–$$ 🏨 **Garden Island Inn.** This handy three-story inn, near Kalapakī Beach and Anchor Cove shopping center, is a bargain. From here you can sneak over and enjoy the majesty and facilities of the Marriott across the street. The orchid suites on the top floor, and tropical rooms on the second, have lānai and glimpses of the bay. Budget accommodations are on the ground floor. The innkeepers lend out boogie boards and snorkeling and golf equipment and give away fruit from their trees. ⊠ *3445 Wilcox Rd., Kalapakī Bay 96766* ☎ *808/245–7227 or 800/648–0154* 🖷 *808/ 245–7603* ⊕ *www.gardenislandinn.com* ☞ *21 rooms, 2 suites, 1 condominium* 🕭 *Fans, kitchens, kitchenettes, microwaves, refrigerators, cable TV; no a/c in some rooms* ⊟ *AE, DC, MC, V.*

The South Shore

★ **$$$$** 🏨 **Gloria's Spouting Horn Bed & Breakfast.** The most elegant oceanfront B&B on Kaua'i, this cedar home was built specifically for guests. The comfortable common room has a soaring A-frame ceiling and deck. Waves dash the black rocks below, while just above the ocean's edge, the beach invites sunbathers. All three bedrooms have four-poster beds with romantic canopies and Hawaiian quilts, oceanside lānai, and bathrooms with deep soaking tubs and separate showers. ⊠ *4464 Lawai Rd., Po'ipū* ☎ *808/742–2850* 🖷 *808/742–6995* ⊕ *www.gloriasbedandbreakfast. com* ☞ *3 rooms* 🕭 *Fans, refrigerators, cable TV, in-room VCRs, pool* ⊟ *No credit cards.*

★ **$$$$** 🏨 **Hyatt Regency Kaua'i Resort and Spa.** Step into this superbly designed and dramatically handsome, classic Hawaiian low-rise, built right into the cliffs overlooking Shipwreck Beach. Spacious rooms, two-thirds with ocean views, have a plantation theme with bamboo and wicker furnishings and island art. Five acres of meandering fresh- and saltwater swimming lagoons are beautifully set amid landscaped grounds. ⊠ *1571 Po'ipū Rd., Kōloa 96756* ☎ *808/742–1234 or 800/633–7313* 🖷 *808/ 742–1557* ⊕ *www.kauai.hyatt.com* ☞ *565 rooms, 37 suites* 🕭 *5 restaurants, room service, in-room data ports, minibars, refrigerators, 18-hole golf course, 4 tennis courts, pool, health club, hot tub, massage, spa, beach, 4 bars, 3 lobby lounges, nightclub, concierge* ⊟ *AE, D, DC, MC, V.*

$$$$ 🏨 **Outrigger Kiahuna Plantation.** Forty-two plantation-style low-rise buildings arc around a large, grassy field leading to the beach at this 35-acre oceanfront condominium resort. The individually decorated one- and two-bedroom units vary in style, but all are nice and clean, have lānai, and get lots of ocean breezes. This is a popular destination for families who take advantage of the swimmable beach and of the lawn, for picnics and games. Great sunset and ocean views are available from some units. The Sheraton is next door, and there are facility-use agreements between the two locations. ⊠ *2253 Po'ipū Rd., Kōloa 96756* ☎ *808/742–6411 or 800/688–7444* 🖷 *808/742–1698* ⊕ *www.outrigger. com* ☞ *333 condominiums* 🕭 *Restaurant, fans, in-room data ports, kitchens, kitchenettes, microwaves, cable TV, in-room VCRs, 18-hole golf course, 6 tennis courts, pool; no a/c* ⊟ *AE, DC, MC, V.*

$$$$ 🏨 **Po'ipū Kapili.** Spacious one- and two-bedroom condo units are minutes from Po'ipū restaurants. White-frame exteriors and double-pitched roofs complement the tropical landscaping. Interiors include full kitchens and entertainment centers. There are garden and across-the-street ocean views to choose from. Three deluxe 2,600-square-ft penthouse suites have enormous lānai, private elevators, and cathedral ceilings. You can mingle at a weekly coffee hour held beside the ocean-view pool, or grab a good read from the resort library. ⊠ *2221 Kapili Rd., Kōloa 96756* ☎ *808/742–6449 or 800/443–7714* 🖷 *808/742–9162* ⊕ *www.poipukapili.com* 🖙 *57 condominiums, 3 penthouse suites* ⚘ *Kitchens, microwaves, cable TV, in-room VCRs, 2 tennis courts, pool, library* ⊟ *MC, V.*

$$$$ 🏨 **Po'ipū Shores.** Sitting on a rocky point above pounding surf, this is a perfect spot for whale- or turtle-watching. Weddings are staged on a little lawn beside the ocean, and a sandy swimming beach is a 10-minute walk away. There are three low-rise buildings, with a pool in front of the middle one. Condo units are individually owned and decorated, but all have large windows and many of them have bedrooms on the ocean side; they either share a sundeck or have a lānai. ⊠ *1775 Pe'e Rd., Kōloa 96756* ☎ *808/742–7700 or 800/367–5004* 🖷 *808/742–9720* ⊕ *www.castle-group.com* 🖙 *39 condominiums* ⚘ *Fans, kitchens, kitchenettes, microwaves, cable TV, pool, laundry facilities; no a/c* ⊟ *AE, MC, V.*

$$$$ 🏨 **Sheraton Kaua'i Resort.** One of the jewels of the south shore, this resort has ocean wings so close to the water you can practically feel the spray of the surf as it hits the rocks below. Beachfront rooms have muted sand and eggshell colors and are as soothing as the room's comfortable lounge seating. Brighter palettes enliven the garden rooms. Dining rooms, king beds, and balconies differentiate the suites. Hawaiian artisans stage crafts demonstrations under a banyan tree in the central courtyard. ⊠ *2440 Ho'onani Rd., Po'ipū Beach, Kōloa 96756* ☎ *808/742–1661 or 800/782–9488* 🖷 *808/742–9777* ⊕ *www.sheratonkauai.com* 🖙 *399 rooms, 14 suites* ⚘ *4 restaurants, room service, in-room safes, some minibars, refrigerators, cable TV, 3 tennis courts, 2 pools, gym, massage, beach, bar, children's programs (ages 5–12), meeting rooms* ⊟ *AE, D, DC, MC, V.*

$$$$ 🏨 **Sunset Kahili.** On a bluff, this five-story ocean-edge building catches great sunsets—and a glimpse of the spray from Spouting Horn. Privately owned apartments are individually furnished in an island motif. Narrow kitchens include microwaves and washers and dryers. There's a barbecue area on the grounds, and complimentary coffee is served each morning in the central recreation room. Rates decrease the longer you stay. ⊠ *1763 Pe'e Rd., Po'ipū 96756* ☎ *808/742–7434 or 800/827–6478* 🖷 *808/742–1559* ⊕ *www.sunsetkahili.com* 🖙 *24 condominiums* ⚘ *Fans, kitchenettes, in-room VCRs, pool* ⊟ *AE, D, DC, MC, V.*

$$$$ 🏨 **Whalers Cove.** All of the two-bedroom condos face the water and share a swimming pool, which is almost near enough to the surf to cast out a fishing line. The rocky beach is good for snorkeling, and a short drive or brisk walk will get you to a sandy stretch. A handsome koa-bedecked reception area offers services for the plush units. Two barbecue areas, big picture windows, spacious living rooms, lānai, and modern kitchens with washer-dryers make this a home away from home. ⊠ *2640 Pu'uholo Rd., Kōloa 96756* ☎ *808/742–7571 or 800/225–2683* 🖷 *808/742–1185* ⊕ *www.whalers-cove.com* 🖙 *39 condominiums* ⚘ *Fans, kitchens, kitchenettes, microwave, pool, hot tub, laundry facilities; no a/c* ⊟ *AE, MC, V.*

$$$–$$$$ 🏨 **Makahuena at Po'ipū.** Large, tastefully decorated two- and three-bedroom suites with white tile and sand-color carpets are housed in white wood buildings on well-kept lawns. Each unit has a kitchen and washer and dryer; there are also a small pool and shared barbecue area on the property. Situated close to the center of Po'ipū, on a rocky point over the ocean, the Makahuena is near Shipwreck and Po'ipū beaches.

✉ *1661 Pe'e Rd., Po'ipū 96756* ☎ *808/742–2482 or 800/367–5004* 🖨 *808/742–2379* ⊕ *www.castle-group.com* ➷ *79 suites* ♨ *Fans, kitchenettes, tennis court, pool, hot tub* 🖃 *AE, MC, V.*

$$$–$$$$ ▦ **Suite Paradise Po'ipū Kaī.** Condominiums, many with cathedral ceilings and all with big windows overlooking the lawns, give this property the feeling of a spacious, quiet retreat inside and out. Large furnished lānai have views to the ocean and across the 110-acre grounds. All of the condos are furnished with modern kitchens. Some units are two-level; some have sleeping lofts. Three-, four-, and five-bedroom units are also available. A two-night minimum stay is required. ✉ *1941 Po'ipū Rd., Kōloa 96756* ☎ *808/742–6464 or 800/367–8020* 🖨 *808/742–9121* ⊕ *www.suite-paradise.com* ➷ *130 1- and 2-bedroom condominiums* ♨ *Restaurant, fans, kitchens, in-room data ports, in-room safes, in-room VCRs, 9 tennis courts, 6 pools, hot tub; no a/c in some rooms* 🖃 *AE, D, DC, MC, V.*

$$–$$$$ ▦ **Po'ipū Plantation Resort.** Plumeria, ti, and other tropical foliage fill the 1-acre grounds of this resort, which has one B&B–style plantation home and nine one- and two-bedroom cottage apartments. All cottage units have vaulted ceilings and full kitchens and are decorated in light, airy shades. The 1930s plantation home has three rooms with private baths and one suite. A full complimentary breakfast is served daily for those staying in the main house. Rates decrease with the length of stay. ✉ *1792 Pe'e Rd., Kōloa 96756* ☎ *808/742–6757 or 800/634–0263* 🖨 *808/742–8681* ⊕ *www.poipubeach.com* ➷ *3 rooms, 9 cottages* ♨ *Fans, kitchens, in-room VCRs, hair salon, hot tub, laundry facilities* 🖃 *D, MC, V* ⦿*BP.*

$$–$$$ ▦ **Garden Isle Cottages.** Tropical fruit trees and flower gardens surround these spacious oceanside accommodations. Contemporary Hawaiian furnishings include some rattan, but the best part of the cottages is the ocean view. Five of seven units have kitchens with microwaves, ceiling fans, and washers and dryers. It's a five-minute walk to the restaurants of nearby Po'ipū. ✉ *2666 Pu'uholo Rd., Kōloa 96756* ☎ *808/742–6717 or 800/742–6711* ⊕ *www.oceancottages.com* ➷ *7 cottages* ♨ *Fans, some kitchens, microwaves, laundry facilities; no a/c, no room phones* 🖃 *No credit cards.*

$–$$ ▦ **Kaua'i Cove Cottages.** Three modern studio cottages sit side by side at the mouth of Waikomo Stream, beside an ocean cove that offers super snorkeling. The studios, with complete kitchens, have airy tropical decor under cathedral ceilings. Private patios on the ocean side have their own gas grills. There is a $25 cleaning fee for stays of fewer than three nights. VCRs are available upon request. ✉ *2672 Pu'uholo Rd., Po'ipū 96756* ☎ *808/742–2562 or 800/624–9945* ⊕ *www.kauaicove.com* ➷ *3 cottages* ♨ *Fans, kitchens, cable TV, snorkeling, laundry facilities; no a/c* 🖃 *D, MC, V.*

$–$$ ▦ **Kōloa Landing Cottages.** You'll be treated like family here. Kōloa Landing has five cottages, including a studio that's about a five-minute walk to a swimming beach. The cottages are also across the street from Kōloa Landing, a popular location for diving, snorkeling, and fishing. Accommodations sleep two to eight; all cottages have showers only. Open-beam ceilings and fans keep the interiors cool. Book well in advance. ✉ *2704-B Ho'onani Rd., Kōloa 96756* ☎ *808/742–1470 or 800/779–8773* ⊕ *www.koloa-landing.com* ➷ *5 cottages, 2 rooms* ♨ *Fans, kitchens, kitchenettes, hair salon, laundry facilities; no a/c* 🖃 *No credit cards.*

The West Side

$$–$$$$ ▦ **Waimea Plantation Cottages.** Tucked into a coconut grove, these reconstructed sugar-plantation cottages, near the stunning Waimea Canyon and many beautiful beaches, make for a laid-back vacation experience. The one- to five-bedroom cottages are rustic but spacious and all have porches. Plantation-era furnishings are updated with modern kitchens and cable TV. Barbecue grills, hammocks, porch swings, a gift shop, a spa, and a museum are on the property. Cottages are steps away from a black-sand beach with equally murky water. ⊠ *9400 Kaumuali'i Hwy. (Box 367), Waimea 96796* ☎ *808/338–1625 or 800/992–4632* 🖷 *808/338–2338* ⊕ *www.waimea-plantation.com* ⤴ *48 cottages* ☄ *Restaurant, fans, some kitchens, pool, beach, horseshoes, bar; no a/c* ⊟ *AE, D, DC, MC, V.*

¢ ▥ **Kōke'e Lodge.** If you're an outdoor enthusiast, you may appreciate Kaua'i's mountain wilderness from this lodge. Wood-burning stoves in the 12 rustic cabins ward off any chill from the mountain air (wood is a few dollars extra). The Lodge restaurant serves a light breakfast and lunch between the hours of 9 and 3:30 daily. Many locals fill up Kōke'e on the weekend, so make your reservations early. ⊠ *3600 Kōke'e Rd., mile marker 15, Kekaha* ⌖ *Box 819, Waimea 96796* ☎ *808/335–6061* ⤴ *12 cabins* ☄ *Restaurant, hiking; no a/c* ⊟ *D, DC, MC, V.*

NIGHTLIFE & THE ARTS

People on Kaua'i take great pride in their culture and enjoy sharing their traditions with those who come to call. As a result, on the Garden Isle you will find more traditional Hawaiiana and less glitz than on neighboring O'ahu.

Most of the island's dinner and lū'au shows take place within a hotel or resort. Hotel lounges and restaurant bars offer live music with no cover charge. True to Kaua'i's agricultural roots of "early to bed, early to rise," most evening events around the island, outside of major hotels, wrap up by 9 PM.

Check the local newspaper, the *Garden Island Times*, for listings of weekly happenings. Free publications such as *Kaua'i Gold, This Week on Kaua'i*, and *Kaua'i Magazine* also list entertainment events. You can pick them up at the Kaua'i Visitors Bureau and at Līhu'e Airport.

Bars & Clubs

Night clubs that stay open to the wee hours are rare on Kaua'i, and the bar scene is pretty limited. The major resorts generally host their own live entertainment and happy hours. All bars and clubs that serve alcohol must close at 2 AM, except for those with a cabaret license, which allows them to close at 4 AM.

Duke's Barefoot Bar. Contemporary Hawaiian music is performed in the beachside bar on Thursday and Friday, and upstairs a traditional Hawaiian trio plays nightly for diners, making this bar one of the liveliest on Kalapakī Beach. The bar closes at 11 PM most nights. ⊠ *Kalapakī Beach, Līhu'e* ☎ *808/246–9599.*

Hanalei Gourmet. The sleepy north shore stays awake—until 10:30 PM, that is—each evening in this small, convivial setting. The emphasis here is on local live jazz, rock, and folk music. ⊠ *5-5161 Kūhiō Hwy., Hanalei Center, Hanalei* ☎ *808/826–2524.*

Tropics. A sports bar on the weekends, this funky hangout presents live island-style music several nights a week. It closes at 11 PM. ⊠ *4-1330 Kūhiō Hwy., at Kauwila St., Kapa'a* ☎ *808/822–7330.*

Lū'au

Drums of Paradise Lū'au. More than music and dance, the Hyatt lū'au displays Hawaiian artwork and includes the dances of Polynesia and a traditional and contemporary menu to suit all tastes. ☒ *Hyatt Regency Kaua'i Resort and Spa, 1571 Po'ipū Rd., Po'ipū Beach* ☎ *808/742–1234* ☒ *$65* ☉ *Thurs. and Sun. 5:45–9.*

Kaua'i Coconut Beach Resort Lū'au. The evening begins with a traditional *imu* (underground oven) ceremony. After dark, Polynesian culture comes to life on a musical tour through the culture and legends of the island told in song and dance. ☒ *Coconut Plantation, Kūhiō Hwy., Kapa'a* ☎ *808/822–3455 Ext. 651* ☒ *$55* ☉ *Nightly 6–9.*

Lū'au Kilohana. This lū'au—on an old sugar plantation, with 35-acre grounds, gardens, workers' homes, and a 16,000-square-ft Tudor mansion—has a kick: all guests arrive at the feast by horse-drawn carriage (reservations are staggered to prevent lines). Families especially seem to enjoy the food and fun here. The evening's theme is the history of sugar in the Islands. ☒ *3-2087 Kaumuali'i St., Līhu'e* ☎ *808/245–9593* ☒ *$58* ☉ *Tues. and Thurs. wagon rides begin at 5:15, dinner at 6, show at 6:30.*

Pa'ina o Hanalei. The blowing of the conch calls revelers to the beach at Hanalei Bay for a gourmet lū'au feast. Entertainment includes a celebration of the songs and dances of the islands of the South Pacific. ☒ *Princeville Resort, 5520 Ka Haku Rd.* ☎ *808/826–2788* ☒ *$68* ☉ *Mon. and Thurs. at 6.*

Smith's Tropical Paradise Lū'au. Amid 30 acres of tropical flora and fauna, this lū'au begins with the traditional blowing of the conch shell and imu ceremony, followed by cocktails, an island feast, and an international show in the amphitheater overlooking a torch-lighted lagoon. ☒ *174 Wailua Rd., Kapa'a* ☎ *808/821–6895* ☒ *$56* ☉ *Mon., Wed., and Fri. 5–9:15.*

Tahiti Nui Lū'au. This venerable institution in sleepy Hanalei is a welcome change from the standard commercial lū'au. It's intimate (about 40 guests), casual, and put on by an island family that really knows how to throw a party. The all-you-can-eat buffet includes kālua pig that has been slow-roasted in an imu, and the show has plenty of dancing, music, and laughs. ☒ *Kūhiō Hwy., Hanalei* ☎ *808/826–6277* ☒ *$62* ☉ *Wed. at 5.*

Music

Check the local papers for outdoor reggae and Hawaiian-music shows, or one of the numbers listed below for more formal performances.

Kaua'i Community College Performing Arts Center (☒ 3-1901 Kaumuali'i Hwy., Līhu'e ☎ 808/245–8270) provides a venue for Hawaiian music and dance as well as visiting performers. **Kaua'i Concert Association** (☒ 3-1901 Kaumuali'i Hwy., Līhu'e ☎ 808/245–7464) offers a seasonal program at the arts center. The **Līhu'e Public Library** (☒ 4344 Hardy St., Līhu'e ☎ 808/241–3222) sometimes plays host to storytelling, music, and arts-and-crafts events.

Film & Theater

The **Kaua'i Community Players** (☒ Līhu'e Parish Hall, 4340 Nāwiliwili Rd., Līhu'e ☎ 808/245–7700) is a talented local group that presents plays throughout the year.

Kaua'i Village Theatre (☒ Kaua'i Village Shopping Center, 4831 Kūhiō Hwy., Kapa'a ☎ 808/823–6789) presents six shows per season plus concerts and feature films in a 62-seat, air-conditioned theater.

THE FORBIDDEN ISLE

SEVENTEEN MILES *and a world away from Kaua'i across the Kaulakahi Channel sits one of the most Hawaiian islands of all, the* privately owned Ni'ihau. *It's commonly called the "Forbidden Isle," because access is limited to the 200 residents who live and work here and their invited guests.*

Ni'ihau was first bought from King Kamehameha in 1864 by a Scottish widow, Eliza Sinclair, who was looking for a quiet, safe place to raise her young family of five children. Sinclair was first introduced to the island after an unusually wet winter; she saw nothing but green pastures and thought it would be an ideal place to raise cattle. The cost for this 23-mi-long, 3-ft-wide island was $10,000. It was a real deal, or so Sinclair thought.

Unfortunately, Ni'ihau's usual rainfall is about 12 inches a year, and with its lack of fresh water, the land soon returned to its normal desertlike state. Regardless, Sinclair did not abandon her venture and today the island is owned by the Robinson family, and a marginally successful ranching operation is overseen by Bruce Robinson, Eliza Sinclair's great-great-grandson. What makes this island so unique is that here, the traditions of ancient Hawai'i are still observed. The 200 residents speak Hawaiian, and there is no indoor plumbing or electricity, save a few personal generators. Bikes and horses are the preferred modes of transportation.

Everyone who lives on the island works on the ranch and lives in the single town of Pu'uwai. One of Ni'ihau's best-known exports is its tiny seashells that have been fashioned into shell lei. These rare, delicate lei can sell for up to thousands of dollars each.

Although visits to the island are still very much restricted, the Robinson family does operate one Ni'ihau Helicopter flightseeing tour, which includes a bird's-eye view of the island as well as a stopover at one of Ni'ihau's more secluded beaches.

The tiny **Kīlauea Theater and Community Event Center** (✉ 2490 Keneke St., Kīlauea ☎ 808/828–0438) is the site of north-shore live concert events, first-run movies, and art films.

SPORTS & THE OUTDOORS

Biking

Kaua'i Adventure Trek. This 4½-hour bike, hike, and beach adventure follows an old cane road through Grove Farm Plantation, stops for a tour of the island's first sugar mill, then heads for Māhā'ulepū Beach, where a picnic lunch is served. Trips are geared to novice and intermediate-level bikers. This is one of the few bike companies to furnish electric bikes for riders who prefer to take the easy way. Vans carry bikers back to Kilohana Plantation, which has upscale shops and Gaylord's restaurant. ✉ *3-2087 Kaumuali'i Hwy., Līhu'e 96766* ☎ *808/245-3440 or 808/635-8735* ⊕ *www.kauaiadventuretrek.com.*

Outfitters Kaua'i. Ride right out the door to tour Po'ipū on a rented bike or get information on how to do a self-guided tour of Kōke'e State Park and Waimea Canyon. The company also leads coasting tours (under the name Canyon to Coast) from Waimea Canyon to the island's west-side beaches. Rentals cost between $20 and $40. ✉ *2827-A Po'ipū Rd., Po'ipū 96756* ☎ *808/742-9667.*

Pedal 'n' Paddle. This company rents bicycles for $20 a day. Hourly and weekly rates are also available. ✉ *Ching Young Village, Kūhiō Hwy., Hanalei* ☎ *808/826-9069* ⊕ *www.pedalnpaddle.com.*

MOUNTAIN BIKING The 12-mi Power Line Trail, which begins in the mountains above Wailua in Keāhua Forestry Arboretum and ends mauka of Princeville Resort, is a challenge even for the seasoned biker. It's a muddy, difficult ride, but you have views of Wai'ale'ale that are usually seen only from the air. Be sure your mountain bike is in top condition, take plenty of water and energy bars, and let someone know when and where you are going. If you rent a mountain bike, explain what you've got in mind and heed any advice offered by the experts.

Fitness & Spa Centers

Alexander Day Spa at the Kaua'i Marriott. This spa offers body treatments utilizing the Epicuren Discovery skin-care line, including a microderm body scrub and a green-tea-and-ginger sea-enzyme body wrap. The spa also provides facials, massage, and custom spa packages. Day passes for the Kaua'i Marriott pool, spa, and fitness center are available for $25 with spa treatments. ✉ *Kaua'i Marriott Resort & Beach Club, 3610 Rice St., Līhu'e* ☎ *808/246-4918.*

Anara Spa. Nonguests are welcome to use the spa facilities at this Po'ipū resort. For $30 per day you have use of the weight room, lap pool, steam room, sauna, and hot tub in the deluxe 25,000-square-ft facility. The spa offers massage, yoga, and classic Hawaiian spa treatments. Spa cuisine is available from 11 to 2 at Kupono Café next door. ✉ *Hyatt Regency Kaua'i Resort and Spa, 1571 Po'ipū Rd., Po'ipū* ☎ *808/742-1234.*

Hanalei Yoga Center. Get into the healthy north-shore groove with one of several daily yoga classes offered here. ✉ *Hanalei Center, Hwy. 56, Hanalei* ☎ *808/826-9642.*

Kaua'i Athletic Club. This centrally located facility offers a $12 day pass that grants you access to saunas, racquetball, aerobics classes, swimming, cardio-fitness instruction, and a hot tub. ✉ *4370 Kukui Grove, Līhu'e* ☎ *808/245-5381.*

Princeville Health Club & Spa. State-of-the-art workout equipment, saunas, and hot tubs are surrounded by inspiring views of mountains, sea, and sky; a day pass is $15. Facials, body treatments including body bronzing, and massage treatments are available for total relaxation. A round of golf at a Princeville course entitles you to a free day at the spa. ✉ *Princeville Resort, 53-900 Kūhiō Hwy., Princeville* ☎ *808/826-5030.*

Golf

Greens fees vary according to season, time of day, whether you're a Hawai'i resident, and whether you are a guest of a particular hotel. Playing in the afternoon and staying at a partner hotel can save you a bundle of money—up to 60%.

Kaua'i Lagoons Golf Club. Two Jack Nicklaus–designed par-72 courses adjoin the Kaua'i Marriott Resort & Beach Club. The championship Kiele course challenges golfers of all levels. The links-style Mokihana course promises a satisfying round for everyone. Forty acres of tropical lagoons provide breathtaking views. A shared cart and the same-day use of a practice facility are included. ⊠ *3351 Ho'olaulea Way, Līhu'e* ☎ *808/241–6000* ⚑ *Greens fee $170 for Kiele, $120 for Mokihana.*

Kiahuna Plantation Golf Club. On the southern side of the island is this Robert Trent Jones Jr.–designed 18-hole course. This course could be the longest short course you've ever had the pleasure to play on. It includes unique archaeological features like a Hawaiian heiau, a lava-tube entrance, a crypt, and an ancient pigpen—as well as the usual water hazards, 68 bunkers, and the challenge of playing to prevailing tradewinds. There are equipment rentals, a pro shop, a restaurant, and a bar. A shared cart is included in the greens fee. ⊠ *2545 Kiahuna Plantation Dr., Po'ipū* ☎ *808/742–9595* ⚑ *Greens fee $75.*

Kukui o lono Golf Course. You can play 9 holes or a full round here on a peaceful wooded hilltop setting with spectacular views of Kaua'i's eastern shore. A cart is $6 for 9 holes; club rental is $6. ⊠ *854 Pu'u Rd., Kalāheo* ☎ *808/332–9151* ⚑ *Greens fee $7.*

Po'ipū Bay Resort Golf Course. This 18-hole links-style course has been the site of the PGA Grand Slam for almost a decade. It's next to the Hyatt Regency Kaua'i, and many of the distractions on this course come not only from its Robert Trent Jones Jr. design, but also from its naturally inspiring location on Po'ipū Bay. A shared cart is included in the price. ⊠ *2250 'Ainakō St., Po'ipū Beach* ☎ *808/742–8711 or 800/ 858–6300* ⚑ *Greens fee $130 Hyatt Regency guests, $185 nonguests.*

Princeville Resort Makai Course. This is Kaua'i's best-known golf facility. The Makai Course, designed by Robert Trent Jones Jr., features an ocean 9, lakes 9, and woods 9 that combine the best of human ingenuity with Princeville's natural beauty. The facility includes a pro shop, driving range, practice area, lessons, club rental and storage, tennis facilities, and a snack bar. ⊠ *Off Rte. 56, at Princeville Resort, 5520 Ka Haku Rd., Princeville* ☎ *808/826–1105* ⚑ *Greens fee $110 Princeville guests, $125 nonguests.*

Princeville Resort Prince Course. Spectacular ocean and mountain views are some of the delights at this 18-hole, Robert Trent Jones Jr.–designed course. It is also rated Kaua'i's toughest course, with a USGA course rating of 75.3 and a 145 slope. A restaurant and bar are open for breakfast and lunch. A shared cart, a pass to the Princeville Spa, and use of the driving range are included in the fee. ⊠ *Off Rte. 56, at Princeville Resort, 5520 Ka Haku Rd., Princeville* ☎ *808/826–5000* ⚑ *Greens fee $125 Princeville guests, $175 nonguests.*

Puakea Farm Golf Course. Developed on the lush lands of the former Grove Farm Homestead sugar plantation, Kaua'i's youngest course was, at this writing, in the final phase of its expansion from a 10-hole beauty into what promises to be a challenging 18-hole layout by golf architect Robin Nelson. Puakea also offers food and beverage services, a pro shop, a natural-grass practice facility, and lessons. A cart is included in the greens fee. ⊠ *4315 Kalepa St., Līhu'e* ☎ *808/245–8756* ⚑ *Greens fee $65.*

Wailua Municipal Golf Course. This municipal course sits next to the Wailua River and beach and has a pro shop, driving range, and restaurant. Its 18 holes have hosted national tournaments, and golfers here play to undulating fairways and the sounds of the ocean, which borders four of the greens. Carts cost $14. ⊠ *3-5351 Kūhiō Hwy., Wailua* ☎ *808/241–6666* ⚑ *Greens fee $32 weekdays, $44 weekends.*

Hiking & Camping

For your safety, wear sturdy shoes, bring plenty of water, never hike alone, stay on the trail, and avoid hiking when it's wet and slippery. All hiking trails on Kaua'i are free.

Before planning any hike or camping trip on Kaua'i, contact the **Department of Land and Natural Resources** for information on trail conditions and camping permits. ⊠ *State Parks Division, 3060 'Eiwa St., Room 306, Līhu'e 96766* ☎ *808/274–3446.*

Kalalau Trail. Kaua'i's prize hike begins at the western end of Route 56 and proceeds 11 mi to Kalalau Beach. With hairpin turns, sometimes very muddy conditions, and constant ups and downs, this hike is a true test of endurance and can't be tackled round-trip in one day. For a good taste of it, hike the first 2 mi to Hanakāpī'ai Beach. For the best trail and weather conditions, hike Kalalau between May and September.

If you plan to hike beyond Hanakāpī'ai Beach to Kalalau, a camping permit must be obtained from the Department of Land and Natural Resources. Permits must also be obtained to camp at Miloli'i, Kōke'e, and Polihale. Permits, which are issued for five nights maximum, are free and can be requested up to a year in advance. These state campsites assess a charge of $10 for those along the Kalalau Trail, $5 for other locations. ⊹ *Western end of Rte. 56* ☎ *no phone.*

Kōke'e State Park. The park contains a 45-mi network of hiking trails of varying difficulty that take you through acres of native forests, home to many rare species of birds. The Kukui Trail leads down the side of Waimea Canyon. Awa'awapuhi Trail descends 4 mi to a spectacular overlook into the canyons of the north shore. Pleasant, shaded campsites can be reserved through the Parks Department. All hikers should register at Kōke'e Park headquarters, which offers trail maps and information. Camping permits from the land department are $5 per night. ⊠ *Kōke'e Rd., 20 mi north of Hwy. 50, Kekaha* ☎ *808/335–6061.*

Polihale Beach Park. Tent camping is permitted here, at the westernmost beach in the United States. Three sets of numbered campsites have rest rooms, outdoor showers, picnic tables, and grills. Swimming can be dangerous when the waves are rough. Permits are $5 per night. ⊹ *Drive to end of Rte. 50 and turn left at Hawaiian-warrior marker onto dirt road, which leads several mi through sugarcane fields; turn left at small national park sign* ☎ *808/274–3446.*

Waimea Canyon State Park. Four tent campsites are hidden along the floor of Waimea Canyon near the Waimea River. The Kukui trailhead is along Waimea Canyon Road. You may want to hike beyond the first campsite to Lonomea Camp, about 6 mi in, where there are pit toilets, roofed shelters, and a picnic table. Near Hipalau Camp are two waterfall-fed pools worth hiking to even if you don't camp at the site. There's no fee to camp in Waimea. ⊹ *Drive 7½ mi north on Waimea Canyon Rd., then hike approximately 6 mi on Kukui Trail* ☎ *808/274–3433.*

Horseback Riding

Exploring by horseback is a great way to get an up-close look at rolling green pastures, sandy shorelines, and the hidden spots of Kaua'i. Escorted rides often provide meals or a snack and guides who are full of local lore.

CJM Country Stables. This company in Po'ipū charges $75 to $95 for each of three guided rides: a 2-hour ranch ride with ocean scenery, a 3-hour hidden-valley beach breakfast ride, and a 3½-hour swim and picnic ride.

Children age seven and older are permitted to ride, and two weekends a month, CJM sponsors rodeo events that are free and open to the public. ⊠ *1731 Kekaukia St., Kōloa, 1½ mi from Hyatt Regency Kauaʻi Resort and Spa at east end of Poʻipū Rd.* ☎ *808/742–6096.*

Esprit de Corps. In Kapaʻa, Esprit de Corps offers private lessons, pony parties for children, and half-day horse camps, as well as trail rides that range from three-hour jaunts for $112 to eight-hour excursions for $350 that include lunch. Group trail rides require some experience, as they allow trotting and cantering. Weddings on horseback can be arranged, and custom rides for less-experienced riders are available. ⊠ *Wailua Homesteads, end of Kualapa Pl., Kapaʻa* ☎ *808/822–4688.*

Princeville Ranch Stables. Guided horseback tours from this very professional operation take riders into the less-explored northern reaches of the island. A 90-minute country ride is $65 per person. A three- or four-hour waterfall picnic ride is $125 to $170, including lunch. Individual tours and riding time are available. ⊠ *5-4430 Kūhiō Hwy., Princeville* ☎ *808/826–6777.*

Silver Falls Ranch. You can take a private lesson at this Kīlauea ranch, join a two-hour Hawaiian Discovery ride with refreshments ($78), or try a three-hour Silver Falls ride ($105) that includes picnicking by a waterfall and a swim in a secluded freshwater pool. ⊠ *2818 Kamookoa Rd., Kīlauea* ☎ *808/828–6718.*

Tennis

Kauaʻi has 20 lighted public tennis courts and more than 70 private courts at hotels.

Hanalei Bay Resort. Nonguests pay $6 per hour to play at Hanalei Bay; there are eight courts. ⊠ *5380 Honoiki Rd., Princeville* ☎ *808/826–6522.*

Hyatt Regency Kauaʻi Resort and Spa. The Hyatt has four courts, a pro shop, and a tennis pro. The cost is $20 per hour. ⊠ *1571 Poʻipū Rd., Poʻipū Beach* ☎ *808/742–1234.*

Kauaʻi Coconut Beach Resort. Guests play for free and nonguests pay $7 to use the four courts at this resort. ⊠ *Coconut Plantation, Kūhiō Hwy., Kapaʻa* ☎ *808/822–3455.*

Princeville Tennis Center. The six courts here cost $12 for resort guests and $15 for nonguests for 90 minutes (you can extend your play as long as the courts are not in demand). Weekly rates are available. ⊠ *4080 Lei-o-papa Rd., Princeville* ☎ *808/826–1230.*

The Tennis Club at the Kauaʻi Lagoons. The island's only tennis stadium is here, as well as seven courts for mere mortals. An hour of court time costs $20. Private lessons, lessons for two, and a daily clinic are available. ⊠ *3351 Hoʻolaulea Way, Līhuʻe* ☎ *808/241–6000.*

Water Sports

FISHING Kauaʻi waters are home to marlin, tuna, and mahimahi (dolphin fish), with many charter boats berthed at Nāwiliwili Harbor. No matter which company you choose for ocean fishing, plan to spend $135 to $165 for almost a full day of charter fishing on a shared basis, $95 to $110 for a half day on a shared basis, and $475 to $1,100 for exclusive charters ranging from half-day excursions to 10-hour trips fishing off Niʻihau.

For freshwater fishing, head for the bass- and trout-filled streams near Kōkeʻe and Waimea Canyon. A seven-day visitor license for $10 or a 30-day license for $20 must be obtained from the **Department of Land and Natural Resources.** ⊠ *3060 ʻEiwa St., Līhuʻe 96766* ☎ *808/274–3344.*

'Anini Fishing Charters. Skipper Bob Kutkowski completed his 33-ft sport cruiser, *Sea Breeze V,* himself for sport- or bottom-fishing charters, as well as Nā Pali Coast tours. The boat launches from Princeville. ☐ *Box 594, Kīlauea 96754* ☎ *808/828–1285 or 808/639–8415.*

Sportfishing Kaua'i. This outfitter runs 33-ft and 38-ft six-passenger custom sportfishers for shared or private charters for half,- three-quarter-, or full-day trips. ☐ *Box 1195, Kōloa 96756* ☎ *808/639–0013.*

True Blue. True Blue offers charters on a roomy 55-ft Delta, the *Konane Star,* which features some of the luxuries of home, like television and hot and cold running showers. This vessel is certified to carry 32, but fishing trips are limited to 10 anglers. ✉ *Nāwiliwili Harbor entrance, Slip 112* ☐ *Box 1722, Kalapakī Beach, Līhu'e 96766* ☎ *808/245–9662.*

KAYAKING
Fodor'sChoice
★
Guided trips are ideal for novices; renting a kayak for ocean journeys is more popular with experienced paddlers. Rentals include roof padding and straps for your car. Be sure to inquire with an outfitter about weather conditions and trips suitable for your ability. Nā Pali trips are for experienced, seaworthy paddlers only, unless accompanied by a knowledgeable guide.

Aloha Canoes and Kayaks. This Hawaiian-owned and -operated company offers guided Hawaiian double-hull canoe and kayak trips, with guides whose families have lived here for generations. Adventures lasting 3½ hours take you up the Wailua River to a mountain pool, including lunch. One tour combines helicopter sightseeing, a kayak trip up the Hulē'ia River, and a hike through tropical forestland on Kipu Ranch. Tours range from $60 to $199, depending on the activity. ✉ *3366 Wa'apa Rd., Suite 106, Līhu'e 96766* ☎ *808/246–6804 or 877/473–5446* ⊕ *www.hawaiikayaks.com.*

Island Adventures. These one-way, guided kayak trips up the Hulē'ia River lead to the heart of a national wildlife refuge, whose only access is by this river trip. The 2½-hour excursion ($59) includes a snack and ends with a hike and van transportation back to civilization. ✛ *Take Hwy. 58 to Wilcox St. Continue past main pier to opening of Nāwiliwili Small Boat Harbor* ☐ *Box 3370, Līhu'e 96766* ☎ *808/245–9662 or 808/639–9333.*

Kayak Kaua'i. In addition to renting kayaks, this outfit also offers professionally guided half- and full-day tours along the Nā Pali Coast and up the Hanalei and Wailua rivers. Snorkeling is included in the Hanalei excursion. These guys are the favored choice for *National Geographic* excursions. One-day tours range from $60 to $175; six-night, seven-day packages are $1,550, including accommodations, transportation, boats, and meals. They also rent camping equipment, surfboards, bicycles, canoes, and kayaks. It's the third building to your right as you enter Hanalei, 1 mi west of the Hanalei Bridge. ☐ *Box 508, Hanalei 96714* ☎ *808/826–9844 or 800/437–3507.*

Outfitters Kaua'i. This company runs guided kayak excursions for novices as well as longer Nā Pali Coast and jungle-stream paddles. If you're an experienced paddler, you can rent a kayak, grab a plastic-coated map, and discover a romantic waterfall on your own. For a family adventure, consider the Kipu Falls Safari ($119), which includes a short kayak trip up a jungle steam, a ¾-mi hike, a covered-wagon ride, a picnic at a swimming hole with a waterfall, and a double-hull canoe ride back to civilization. Other guided tours range from $94 to $165, and kayak rentals cost $40 to $65. ✉ *2827-A Po'ipū Rd., Po'ipū 96756* ☎ *808/742–9667 or 888/742–9887.*

Paradise Outdoor Adventures. Paradise provides topographical maps, motorboat and kayak rentals, and guided excursions. A half-day guided

Wailua Jungle-River Safari includes a hike to a waterfall and lunch for $85. Tour vessels range from one-person kayaks to six-person Boston Whaler powerboats. A two-person kayak costs $50 per day. ✉ *1-561 Kūhiō Hwy., Kapa'a 96746* ☎ *808/822–1112 or 877/422–6287.*

Wailua River Kayak Adventures. Rent a kayak that holds two adults and two small children, bring your own picnic lunch, and follow the map to your own adventure. It's the most convenient place to get a kayak for use on the river. These folks also specialize in guided tours to Wailua's Secret Falls. A guided tour is $60; kayak rentals are $15 to $30. ✉ *411 Kaholalele St., Kūhiō Hwy., Kapa'a 96746* ☎ *808/822–5795.*

SCUBA DIVING   **Dive Kaua'i Scuba Center.** Introductory, half-day scuba excursions are $98 at Dive Kaua'i. Two-tank shore dives for certified divers cost $98, a refresher course is $89, and a three- to five-day PADI (scuba-diving certification) course is $395. A boat dive with two tanks costs $115, including equipment. Excursions to dive locations on each of Kaua'i's coastlines are available. ✉ *1038 Kūhiō Hwy., Kapa'a 96746* ☎ *808/ 822–0452 or 800/828–3483* ⊕ *www.divekauai.com.*

Ocean Odyssey. Ocean Odyssey will arrange lessons, shore dives, night dives, and even underwater videotaping for you. Packages range from a simple one-tank shore dive starting at $105 for noncertified divers to three- to five-day PADI certification courses. ⌂ *Box 869, 'Ele'ele 96705* ☎ *808/245–8681* ⊕ *www.bluedolphincharters.com.*

Seasport Divers. This full-service PADI, NAUI, and SSI training facility's dive options range from daily shore dives to dives off Ni'ihau, from beginner lessons and introductory dives to private charters. It also offers equipment rental and repair service, as well as SASY (Supplied Air Snorkeling for Youths) programs for children ages five and older. ✉ *2827 Po'ipū Rd., Kōloa 96756* ☎ *808/742–9303 or 800/685–5889* ⊕ *www. kauaiscubadiving.com.*

SNORKELING &   Snorkeling cruises run along the south shore and Nā Pali Coast. Most
WHALE-   trips depart from Port Allen. Whale-watching is possible during the win-
WATCHING   ter months, and curious dolphins are a regular sight. Inquire about sun-
set and dinner cruises as well.

Captain Andy's Sailing Adventures. Captain Andy's can accommodate up to 49 passengers on its 55-ft catamaran *Spirit of Kaua'i*; cruises depart from Port Allen and Kukui'ula Harbor in Po'ipū. The rate for the four-hour morning snorkel-picnic tour is $109, including gear and lunch. Whale-watching excursions are run during the winter months. Seasonal Nā Pali Coast tours are offered that include Continental breakfast, lunch, snorkeling gear, and instruction for $109, or try the afternoon Nā Pali sunset snorkel excursion that includes snack and buffet. ✉ *'Ele'ele Shopping Center, 4469 Waialo Rd., 'Ele'ele* ☎ *808/335–6833.*

Catamaran Kahanu. This Hawaiian-owned and -operated company has been in business since 1985. It offers a 4½-hour Nā Pali Coast cruise on a 36-ft power catamaran. The trip includes snorkeling, whale- or dolphin-watching, buffet lunch, and a bit of Hawaiian history and culture. The price is $105 for adults, and cruises departs from Port Allen. ✉ *43 Waialo Rd., 'Ele'ele* ☎ *808/335–3577 or 888/335–3577.*

Hanalei Watersports. You can take scuba and surfing lessons in addition to guided kayak and snorkel tours. Accommodating guides can craft a full day's land-and-sea adventure to suit your whims. There's also an idyllic $85 sunset cruise from the Princeville Resort aboard a Hawaiian outrigger canoe equipped with a traditional sail and a paddling canoe. Prices run the gamut. ✉ *Princeville Resort, 53-900 Kūhiō Hwy., Princeville* ☎ *808/826–7509.*

HoloHolo Charters. A deluxe snorkel cruise with this charter takes in the majesty of the Nā Pali Coast and anchors off the private island of Ni'ihau. Continental breakfast and a deluxe lunch buffet are served on the 61-ft power catamaran during the seven-hour excursion. Wine, beer, soda, and juice are included in the $156 fee. Three other shorter (and less expensive) excursions are offered on the 48-ft sailing catamaran *Leila* and the 61-ft high-speed Power Cat *HoloHolo*. ⊠ *'Ele'ele Shopping Center, Rte. 541 at Waialo Rd., 'Ele'ele* ☎ *808/335–0815 or 800/ 848–6130.*

Kaua'i Sea Tours. During the winter Kaua'i Sea Tours runs marine-ecology whale-watching tours; it also has year-round snorkeling tours on Power Cats and rigid-hull inflatable rafts. Narrated sightseeing trips range from $80 to $150 and take from two hours to a full day. Longer cruises include snorkeling gear, Continental breakfast, lunch, and cold drinks. ⊠ *4610 Waialo Rd., 'Ele'ele* ☎ *808/826–7254 or 800/733–7997.*

SURFING & WINDSURFING
Just about any of the outfitters who handle kayaking and snorkeling also arrange surfing and windsurfing lessons and excursions. Below is one of the real specialists.

Margo Oberg Surfing School. Seven-time world surfing champion Margo Oberg furnishes surfboards, and she and her staff give dry-land and wave instruction to beginning surfers. Lessons are $48 for 1½ hours. The surf shop is next to Brennecke's Beach Broiler, between Kiahuna Plantation and the Sheraton Kaua'i. ⊠ *Nukumoi Surf Shop, Po'ipū Beach* ☎ *808/ 742–8019.*

SHOPPING

Along with a few major shopping malls, Kaua'i has some really delightful mom-and-pop shops and family-run boutiques with loads of character.

Kaua'i also offers one-of-a-kind options for souvenirs. For instance, the famous shell jewelry from nearby Ni'ihau is sometimes sold on Kaua'i for less than it is on other islands. For such a small island, there is an abundance of art galleries that showcase the creative works of the many artisans who live here. The Garden Isle is also known for its regular outdoor markets where you can find bargain prices on various souvenirs and produce and get a chance to mingle with island residents.

Mainland-style discount and department stores reached Kaua'i years ago, carrying an all-inclusive selection of moderately priced merchandise. Kaua'i's major shopping centers are open daily from 9 or 10 to 5, although some stay open until 9. Stores are basically clustered around the major resort areas and Līhu'e.

Department Stores

Big Kmart (⊠ Kukui Grove Center, 3-2600 Kaumuali'i Hwy., Līhu'e ☎ 808/245–7742) has groceries, film, flip-flops, a souvenirs section, beach items, sunscreen products, and more. **Sears** (⊠ Kukui Grove Center, 3-2600 Kaumuali'i Hwy., Līhu'e ☎ 808/246–8301) sells electronics and homeware, plus a line of casual clothes. **Wal-Mart** (⊠ 3-3300 Kūhiō Hwy., Līhu'e ☎ 808/246–1599) has Hawaiian-print tropical-style clothing and a variety of Hawaiian souvenir items ranging from books to stationery to food products.

Shopping Centers

Ching Young Village. In the heart of Hanalei, Ching Young draws people to its Village Variety Store with cheap prices on beach towels, macadamia nuts, film and processing, wet suits—you name it. There's also the well-stocked Hanalei Natural Foods store, and a few steps away is Evolve Love Artists Gallery, where you can find work by local artisans. ✉ *5-1590 Kūhiō Hwy Hanalei* ☎ *808/826–7222.*

Coconut Marketplace. This tourist-oriented complex is near resort hotels. Here 70 shops sell everything from snacks and slippers to scrimshaw. There are also two movie theaters with first-run features and a free nightly Polynesian show at 5. ✉ *4-484 Kūhiō Hwy., Kapaʻa* ☎ *808/822–3641.*

ʻEleʻele Shopping Center. Kauaʻi's west side has a scattering of stores, including those at this no-frills strip-mall shopping center where several tour-boat companies have offices. It's a good place to rub elbows with local folk or to grab a quick bite to eat at the casual Grinds Cafe or McDonald's. ✉ *Rte. 50 near Hanapēpē, ʻEleʻele* ☎ *808/246–0634.*

Hanalei Center. Listed on the Historic Register, the old Hanalei School has been refurbished and rented out to boutiques and restaurants. After you dig through '40s and '50s vintage clothing and memorabilia in the Yellow Fish Trading Company or search for that unusual gift at Sand People, you can grab a shaved ice (the Hawaiian version of a snow cone) or catch a class at the Hanalei Yoga Center. ✉ *5-5161 Kūhiō Hwy., Hanalei* ☎ *808/826–7677.*

Kauaʻi Village Shopping Center. The buildings of this Kapaʻa shopping village are in the style of 19th-century plantation towns. ABC Discount Store sells sundries; Safeway carries groceries and alcoholic beverages and has a pharmacy. Wyland Gallery sells island art, and Kauaʻi One-Hour Photo provides speedy film processing. Worth a look is the Kauaʻi Heritage Center, which sponsors cultural workshops and dance and displays authentic crafts for sale. ✉ *4-831 Kūhiō Hwy., Poʻipū Beach* ☎ *808/822–4904.*

Kilohana Plantation. This 35-acre parcel of a former sugar plantation is buttressed by a 16,000-square-ft Tudor mansion, which now contains five art galleries and a restaurant. There are a craft shop and a Hawaiian-clothing shop in restored plantation quarters as well. The house itself is worth a look, filled with antiques from its original owner. Gaylord's restaurant is located in the house. Horse-drawn carriage rides are available, with knowledgeable guides reciting the history of sugar on Kauaʻi. ✉ *3-2087 Kaumualiʻi Hwy., 1 mi west of Līhuʻe* ☎ *808/245–7818.*

Kinipopo Shopping Village. Kinipopo is on Kūhiō Highway in Kapaʻa, across from Wailua Family Restaurant. The Goldsmith's Gallery sells handcrafted Hawaiian-style gold jewelry, and Tin Can Mailman bookstore is filled with an eclectic collection of books, Hawaiiana, and paper ephemera. You can also rent water skis and beach paraphernalia here at Kauaʻi Water Ski, or dig in at Korean Barbeque. ✉ *4-356 Kūhiō Hwy., Kapaʻa* ☎ *no phone.*

Kong Lung Co. The heart of Kīlauea town houses Kong Lung Co., a shop and gallery featuring amazing gifts from around the world. Homegrown shops include Island Soap and Candle Works and the Kīlauea Farmers Market grocery, where you can pick up a picnic lunch. Kīlauea Bakery is legendary for pizza and its tropical-fruit-filled pastries. ✉ *2490 Keneke St., Kīlauea* ☎ *no phone.*

Kukui Grove Center. This is Kauaʻi's largest mall. Besides Sears and Kmart, it offers a Longs Drugs and Star Market for groceries. Island-inspired garb is for sale at Hawaiian Islands Creations, Kauaʻi-made gifts at Kauaʻi Products Store, and girls' and women's surfwear at Chicks Who Rip Clothing. Restaurants range from fast food and deli takeout to La Bamba Mexican and Ho's Chinese. ✉ *3-2600 Kaumualiʻi Hwy., west of Līhuʻe* ☎ *808/245–7784.*

Poʻipū Shopping Village. Convenient to nearby hotels and condos on the south shore, the two dozen shops here sell resort wear, gifts, souvenirs, and art. The upscale Black Pearl Kaua'i shop and the Hale Manu store, with "gifts for the spirited," are particularly appealing. Restaurants within include Roy's, Po'ipū Tropical Burgers, and Pattaya Asian Cafe. ⊠ *2360 Kiahuna Plantation Dr., Po'ipū Beach* ☎ *808/742–2831.*

Princeville Shopping Center. A busy little gathering of shops includes Kaua'i Kite and Hobby Shop, Princeville Music, and JM's Jewels. Stock up on groceries and a bottle of wine at Foodland. Eateries include Bourbon Street Cafe, Chuck's Steakhouse, and Lappert's Ice Cream and Coffee. Also located within are a post office and two banks. ⊠ *5-4280 Kūhiō Hwy., Princeville* ☎ *808/826–7513.*

Waimea Canyon Plaza. The little town of Kekaha is proud of its tidy complex of shops selling local foods, souvenirs, and island-made gifts for all ages. It is also the last stop for supplies before heading up to Waimea Canyon. ⊠ *Kōke'e Rd. at Rte. 50, Kekaha* ☎ *no phone.*

Waipouli Town Center. On the east coast of the island in Kapa'a is a modest collection of 10 shops. Buy a T-shirt at Waipouli Variety, pick up a video at Blockbuster, and then grab a good-value plate lunch or other local food at Waipouli Restaurant. Libations and a grill menu can be found at the Lizard Lounge Bar and Grill. ⊠ *4-901 Kūhiō Hwy., Kapa'a* ☎ *808/524–2023.*

Specialty Stores

Books

Borders Books & Music. There's a large section of books focused on Hawai'i, plus plenty of magazines for beach reading, a music section, and a café. ⊠ *Kukui Grove Shopping Center, 4303 Nāwiliwili Rd., Līhu'e* ☎ *808/246–0862.*

Kaua'i Museum. The gift shop at the museum sells some fascinating books, maps, and prints. ⊠ *4428 Rice St., Līhu'e* ☎ *808/245–6931.*

Tin Can Mailman Books and Curiosities. Both new and used books can be found here, along with an extensive collection of Hawaiian and South Pacific literature. Tin Man also houses stamps and coins, rare prints, and vintage maps. ⊠ *Kinipopo Shopping Village, 4-356 Kūhiō Hwy., Kapa'a* ☎ *808/822–3009.*

Clothing

Bambulei. Two 1930s-style plantation homes have been transformed into this unique boutique featuring vintage and contemporary clothing, antiques, jewelry, and accessories. ⊠ *4-369 Kūhiō Hwy., Wailua* ☎ *808/ 823–8641.*

Crazy Shirts. This chain has a wide variety of shirts, from classy to genuinely crazy designs. It's a good place for active wear. ⊠ *Po'ipū Shopping Village, 2360 Kiahuna Plantation Dr., Po'ipū Beach* ☎ *808/742–9000* ⊠ *Anchor Cove, 3416 Rice St., Līhu'e* ☎ *808/245–7073* ⊠ *Kaua'i Village Shopping Center, 4-831 Kūhiō Hwy., Kapa'a* ☎ *808/823–6761* ⊠ *5356 Kōloa Rd., Kōloa* ☎ *808/742–7161.*

Kilohana Clothing Company. This store, located in the guest cottage by Gaylord's restaurant, offers vintage Hawaiian clothing as well as contemporary styles using traditional Hawaiian designs. The store also features a wide selection of home products in vintage fabrics. ⊠ *Kilohana Plantation, 3-2087 Kaumuali'i Hwy., Līhu'e* ☎ *808/246–6911.*

Macy's. You can purchase high-quality designer labels usually found in this store's mainland counterparts along with those from top Hawaiian designers. ⊠ *Kukui Grove Center, 3-2600 Kaumuali'i Hwy., Līhu'e* ☎ *808/245–7751.*

M. Miura Store. A great assortment of clothes for outdoor fanatics is available at M. Miura, including tank tops, visors, swimwear, and Kaua'i-style T-shirts. ⊠ *4-1419 Kūhiō Hwy., Kapa'a* ☎ *808/822–4401.*

Paradise Sportswear. This is the retail outlet of the folks who invented Kaua'i's popular "red dirt" shirts, which are dyed and printed with the characteristic local soil. Do let the salesperson tell you the charming story behind these shirts. Sizes from infants up to 5X are available. ⊠ *4350 Waialo Rd., Port Allen* ☎ *808/335–5670.*

ISLAND WEAR **Hilo Hattie Fashion Factory.** This is the big name in aloha wear for tourists throughout the Islands. You can visit the factory, a mile from Līhu'e Airport, to pick up cool, comfortable aloha shirts and mu'umu'us in bright floral prints, as well as other souvenirs. ⊠ *3252 Kūhiō Hwy., Līhu'e* ☎ *808/245–3404.*

Tropical Shirts. Come here for the beautiful clothing embroidered by local artists. There's also a selection of the island's unique "red dirt" T-shirts. ⊠ *Po'ipū Shopping Village, 2360 Kiahuna Plantation Dr., Po'ipū Beach* ☎ *808/742–6691.*

Flowers

Kaua'i Tropicals. You can have this company ship heliconia, anthuriums, ginger, and other tropicals directly from its flower farm in 5-ft-long boxes. ⊠ *3870 Waha Rd., Kalāheo* ☎ *808/332–9071 or 800/303–4385.*

Food

Kaua'i produces more coffee than any other island in the state, and the local product, somewhat milder than the Big Island's better-known Kona coffee, makes a worthy souvenir.

Kaua'i Coffee Visitor Center and Museum. Coffee can be purchased from the source at the grower's visitor center. ⊠ *870 Halawili Rd., off Rte. 50, west of Kalāheo* ☎ *808/335–0813 or 800/545–8605.*

Kaua'i Fruit and Flower Company. Near Līhu'e you can buy fresh pineapple, sugarcane, ginger, coconuts, local jams, jellies, and honey, plus Kaua'i-grown papayas, bananas, and mangos in season. Special gift packs are available, inspected, and certified for shipment out of the state. ⊠ *3-4684 Kūhiō Hwy., Kapa'a* ☎ *808/245–1814.*

Kaua'i Products Council. They'll tell you the best places to find Kaua'i Kookies, taro chips, Kaua'i boiled peanuts, salad dressings, and jams and jellies made from locally grown fruit, as well as nonfood items handcrafted on the island. ✑ *Box 3660, Līhu'e 96788* ☎ *808/823–8714.*

Kaua'i Products Fair. Open weekends, this outdoor market features craftspeople, artisans, fresh produce, tropical plants and flower, aloha wear, collectibles, and food along with wellness practitioners who will give you a massage right on the spot. ✢ *Outside next to 4-1621 Kūhiō Hwy., in Kapa'a* ☎ *808/246–0988.*

Lappert's Ice Cream. Don't forget to try a scoop of Hawai'i's own ice cream. Created by Walter Lappert of Hanapēpē in 1983, it's now a favorite on all the Islands. Lappert shops also sell locally produced coffees, which are easier to ship home than the ice cream. ⊠ *1-3555 Kaumuali'i Hwy., Hanapēpē* ☎ *808/335–6121* ⊠ *Coconut Marketplace, 4-484 Kūhiō Hwy., Kapa'a* ☎ *808/822–0744* ⊠ *5242 Kōloa Rd., Kōloa* ☎ *808/742–1272* ⊠ *Princeville Shopping Center, 5-4280 Kūhiō Hwy., Princeville* ☎ *808/826–7393.*

Star Market. Some of the best prices on Hawai'i's famous macadamia nuts are available at Star Market. ⊠ *Kukui Grove Center, 3-2600 Kaumuali'i Hwy., Līhu'e* ☎ *808/245–7777.*

Gifts

Hilo Hattie Fashion Factory. This is the place where you can buy all the hats, baskets, inexpensive shell jewelry, rubber slippers, golf towels, and other trinkets you need to carry home to friends and family. The location is perfect for a last-minute stop en route to Līhu'e Airport. ⊠ *3252 Kūhiō Hwy., Līhu'e* ☎ *808/245–3404.*

Kong Lung Co. Sometimes called the Gump's of Kaua'i, this gift store combines elegant clothing, exotic glassware, ethnic books, gifts, and artwork mainly of Asian heritage. There's a working artists' studio upstairs where you can purchase works fresh off the easel. The shop is housed in a beautiful 1892 stone structure on the way to the lighthouse in Kīlauea. ⊠ *2490 Keneke St., Kīlauea* ☎ *808/828–1822.*

Lee Sands' Eelskin. You can buy the popular eel skin wholesale here at this rural spot at the Hawaiian Trading Post. It's an unusual store, with other skin lines such as sea snake, chicken feet, and frog. A lizard card case is available for about $12. ⊠ *Rte. 50 at Kōloa Rd., Lāwa'i* ☎ *808/ 332–7404.*

Village Variety Store. How about a fun beach towel for the folks back home? That's just one of the gifts you can find here, along with shell leis, Kaua'i T-shirts, macadamia nuts, and other great souvenirs at low prices. ⊠ *Ching Young Village, Kūhiō Hwy., Hanalei* ☎ *808/826- 6077.*

Hawaiian Arts & Crafts

Art Shop. This intimate gallery in Līhu'e sells original oils, photos, and sculptures. ⊠ *3196 'Akahi St., Līhu'e* ☎ *808/245–3810.*

Kahn Galleries. You can purchase the works of many local artists—including seascapes by George Sumner and Roy Tabora—at this gallery's locations. ⊠ *Coconut Marketplace, 4-484 Kūhiō Hwy., Kapa'a* ☎ *808/ 822-3636* ⊠ *Kilohana Plantation, 3-2087 Kaumuali'i Hwy., Līhu'e* ☎ *808/246–4454* ⊠ *Kaua'i Village Shopping Center, 4-831 Kūhiō Hwy., Kapa'a* ☎ *808/822–4277* ⊠ *Koloa Rd., Old Kōloa Town* ☎ *808/ 742-2277* ⊠ *Hanalei Center, 5-5161 Kūhiō Hwy., Hanalei* ☎ *808/826- 6677.*

Kapaia Stitchery. Quilts and other fabric arts are featured in this cute little red plantation-style structure. The starter kits are great gifts for crafters. ⊠ *Kūhiō Hwy., in red building ½ mi north of Līhu'e* ☎ *808/ 245–2281.*

Kaua'i Heritage Center. Authentic reproductions of old (and new) Hawaiian crafts by Kaua'i artisans are displayed here: feather hatbands, nose flutes, *konane* (a Hawaiian game similar to checkers) boards and playing pieces, calabashes, and woven lau hala hats and pocketbooks. Sales help to support the center's cultural workshops and programs, which sometimes take place in the courtyard by the clock tower. ⊠ *Kaua'i Village, 4-831 Kūhiō Hwy., No. 838, Kapa'a* ☎ *808/821–2070.*

Kaua'i Products Store. Every seed lei, every finely crafted koa-wood box, every pair of tropical-flower earrings in this boutique is handcrafted on Kaua'i. Other gift items include koa oil lamps, pottery, hand-painted silk clothing, sculpture, and homemade fudge. ⊠ *Kukui Grove Center, 3- 2600 Kaumuali'i Hwy., Līhu'e* ☎ *808/246–6753.*

★ **Kebanu Gallery.** Original works by Island artists at this stunning space definitely lean toward the contemporary. Words can't do the rare wood sculptures, whimsical ceramics, beaded jewelry, and colorful glassware justice. The Kebanu may just be the artistic pinnacle of your trip. ⊠ *Hee Fat Marketplace, 4-1354 Kūhiō Hwy., Kapa'a* ☎ *808/823–6820* ⊕ *www. aloha.net/~kebanu.*

★ **Piece of Paradise Gallery.** Fine art, koa-wood clocks and sushi platters, carved island tikis, handblown glass, and unique jewelry are available here, all designed by talented Kaua'i-based artisans. ⊠ *Radisson Kaua'i Beach Hotel, 4331 Kaua'i Beach Dr., Līhu'e* ☎ *808/246–2834* ⊕ *www. apieceofparadise.org.*

Ye Olde Ship Store & Port of Kaua'i. Scrimshaw-decorated pocket and army knives, boxes, and other gift items are available at this store in the Coconut Marketplace. The shop carries the work of nearly 40 scrimshaw artists and sponsors an annual contest celebrating the art form. ⊠ *Coconut Marketplace, 4-484 Kūhiō Hwy., Kapa'a* ☎ *808/822–1401.*

Jewelry

Jim Saylor Jewelers. Jim Saylor has been designing beautiful keepsakes for more than 20 years on Kaua'i. Gems from around the world appear in his unique settings, including black pearls and diamonds. ⊠ *1318 Kūhiō Hwy., Kapa'a* ☎ *808/822–3591.*

Kaua'i Gold. A wonderful selection of the rare Ni'ihau shell leis ranges in price from $20 to $200. Ask about how these remarkable necklaces are made to appreciate the craftsmanship, understand the sometimes high prices, and learn to care for and preserve them. The store also sells a selection of 14-karat gold jewelry. ⊠ *Coconut Marketplace, 4-484 Kūhiō Hwy., Kapa'a* ☎ *808/822–9361.*

Remember Kaua'i. Pick up a memento of your trip in the form of jewelry, Ni'ihau shell necklaces, or other gift items here. It also runs a booth at Po'ipū Spouting Horn. ⊠ *Radisson Kaua'i Beach Hotel, 4331 Kaua'i Beach Dr., Līhu'e* ☎ *808/639–9622.*

KAUA'I A TO Z

To research prices, get advice from other travelers, and book travel arrangements, visit www.fodors.com.

AIR TRAVEL

Several short daily flights can take you from Honolulu to Kaua'i, and there is limited service from Los Angeles and San Francisco.

CARRIERS Two main carriers, Aloha Airlines and Hawaiian Airlines, offer daily round-trip flights from Honolulu and Neighbor Islands to Līhu'e Airport. Rates fluctuate from $70 to $100 one-way. It's generally a 20- to 40-minute flight, depending on where you start. United Airlines has a daily direct flight from Los Angeles and San Francisco to Līhu'e Airport. ▱ **Aloha Airlines** ☎ 808/245-3691 or 800/367-5250 ⊕ www.alohaairlines.com. **Hawaiian Airlines** ☎ 808/838-1555 or 800/882-8811 ⊕ www.hawaiianair.com. **United Airlines** ☎ 800/241-6522 ⊕ www.ual.com.

AIRPORTS

The Līhu'e Airport is 3 mi east of the town of Līhu'e. There's a Visitor Information Center outside each baggage-claim area.

Used primarily by private planes, the Princeville Airport is a tiny strip on the north shore, set within rolling ranches and sugarcane fields. It's a five-minute drive from the Princeville Resort and condo development, and a 10-minute drive from the shops and accommodations of Hanalei. ▱ **Līhu'e Airport** ☎ 808/246-1488 or 888/697-7813 for Visitor Information Center. **Princeville Airport** ☎ 808/826-3040.

AIRPORT TRANSFERS Līhu'e Airport is a five-minute drive from Līhu'e. If you're staying in Wailua or Kapa'a, your driving time from Līhu'e is 15 minutes; to Princeville and Hanalei it's about 45 minutes. A charter flight into Princeville might save you a few minutes, but it's not worth the additional cost.

To the south, it's a 30-minute drive from Līhu'e to Po'ipū, the major resort area. To Waimea it takes one hour, and if you choose the rustic accommodations in the hills of Kōke'e, allow a good hour and a half of driving time from Līhu'e.

Check with your hotel or condo to see if it offers free shuttle service from the airport.

For luxurious transportation between the airport and your accommodations, contact Custom Limousine Service. Rates are $75 per hour, with a two-hour minimum. It also has packages that include lei greetings, wedding arrangements, and tours. North Shore Limousine specializes in service in the Hanalei and Princeville areas; it can pick you up at Princeville Airport.

Taxi fares around the island are $2 at the meter drop plus $2 per mile. That means a taxicab from Līhu'e Airport to Līhu'e town runs about $6 and to Po'ipū about $32, excluding tip. Akiko's Taxi offers its services from the east side of the island. Po'ipū Taxi will take you to Līhu'e and Po'ipū. Scotty Taxi provides quick service around the airport and Līhu'e. From the Princeville Airport to Hanalei, you pay about $14 when you ride with the North Shore Cab Company, which serves only the northeast portion of the island.

🚖 **Akiko's Taxi** ☎ 808/822-7588. **Custom Limousine Service** ☎ 808/246-6318. **North Shore Cab Company** ☎ 808/826-6189. **North Shore Limousine** ☎ 808/826-6189. **Po'ipū Taxi** ☎ 808/639-2042 or 808/639-2044. **Scotty Taxi** ☎ 808/245-7888 or 808/639-9807.

BIKE TRAVEL

A two-wheeler is an exciting way to cruise around the Garden Isle. Kaua'i's country roads are generally uncrowded, so you can ride along at your own pace and enjoy the views. There are few designated bike lanes, but as long as you exercise caution on the busier thoroughfares, you should be fine. You can rent bikes from the activities desks of certain hotels and at sports outfitters.

CAR RENTAL

Unless you plan to do all of your sightseeing as part of guided tours, you will want a rental car on Kaua'i, since the attractions are sprinkled from one end of the island to the other. Reserve your vehicle in advance, especially during the peak seasons of summer, the Christmas holidays, and February.

Right across from baggage claim at Līhu'e Airport are several rental-car counters, as well as vans that will shuttle you to rental offices nearby. Rental companies also have desks at Princeville Airport. Prices for a car from the major-name companies begin at $40, unless you rate a discount through AAA, AARP, or by other means. A fly/drive deal can sometimes reduce that cost, and many hotels—and even some condos—offer packages that include rental cars. There is a $3 daily surcharge on all rentals.

Several companies operate small reservation desks at major hotels, but spur-of-the-moment rentals will cost you more than pre-arranged ones. Alamo, Avis, Budget, Dollar, Hertz, National, and Thrifty have offices at the Līhu'e Airport. Avis has offices at the Hyatt Regency.

You may get some good deals on a car if you book with one of Kaua'i's local budget or used-car rental companies. Westside U-Drive, which rents cars and jeeps, is reliable. It keeps its vehicles in good shape and offers free delivery and pickup of your car at your hotel or condo in Po'ipū.

🚗 **Major Agencies: Alamo** ✉ Līhu'e Airport ☎ 808/246-0646 or 800/327-9633 🌐 www.alamo.com. **Avis** ✉ Līhu'e Airport ☎ 800/831-8000 🌐 www.avis.com ✉ Hyatt Regency Kaua'i Resort and Spa, 1571 Po'ipū Rd., Kōloa ☎ 808/742-1627. **Budget** ✉ Līhu'e Airport ☎ 800/527-0700 🌐 www.budget.com. **Dollar** ✉ Līhu'e Airport ☎ 800/342-7398, 800/800-4000 from outside HI 🌐 www.dollar.com. **Hertz** ✉ Līhu'e Airport ☎ 800/654-3011 🌐 www.hertz.com. **National** ✉ Līhu'e Airport ☎ 800/227-

7368 ⊕ www.nationalcar.com. **Thrifty** ⊠ Līhuʻe Airport ☎ 808/246-6252 or 800/847-4389 ⊕ www.thrifty.com.

🔳 Local Agency: **Westside U-Drive** ⊠ 4552 Ehako St., Kalaheo ☎ 808/332-8644.

CAR TRAVEL

Although Kauaʻi is relatively small, its sights stretch across the island. You can walk to the stores and restaurants in your resort area, but major attractions are not within walking distance.

It's easy to get around on Kauaʻi—it has one major road almost encircling the island. Your rental-car company will supply you with a map with enlargements of each area of the island. The traffic on Kauaʻi is pretty light most of the time, except in the Līhuʻe and Kapaʻa areas during rush hour (6:30 AM to 8:30 AM and 3:30 PM to 5:30 PM), and heading south to Poʻipū. Major attractions are indicated by road signs depicting King Kamehameha wearing a red cape.

Although Kauaʻi looks like paradise, it has its fair share of crime. Lock your car wherever you park it. Don't leave valuables in the car, even in the trunk. Pay attention to parking signs, particularly in Līhuʻe.

CRUISE TRAVEL

A romantic way to visit Kauaʻi for a short time is to book passage on an interisland cruise ship. Norwegian Cruise Lines has introduced a 7- and 10-day Hawaiian Island cruise on its luxurious *Norwegian Sky,* which departs each week and stops at the other four main Hawaiian islands. Sightseeing and shore excursions are available at each port. On Kauaʻi, the ships dock at Nāwiliwili on the southeast coast. Optional extension packages allow you to add a hotel stay before or after the cruise in the port of your choice.

🔳 **Norwegian Cruise Lines** ⊠ 7665 Corporate Center Dr., Miami, FL 33126 ☎ 800/343-0098 ⊕ www.ncl.com.

EMERGENCIES

To reach the police, ambulance, or fire department in case of any emergency, dial **911.**

Kauaʻi's Wilcox Memorial Hospital is one of the top 100 in the country. Its Kauaʻi Medical Clinic (KMC) has a staff with 32 different specialties. It has lab and X-ray facilities, physical therapy, optometry, and emergency rooms. The main clinic is in Līhuʻe. Other KMC clinics are in Kīlauea, Kukui Grove, ʻEleʻele, Kōloa, and Kapaʻa. Major emergency cases are often air-lifted to Oʻahu. West Kauaʻi Medical Center serves the area from Poʻipū to Kekaha.

Except for Longs Drugs, which often stays open until 9, most pharmacies close about 5 PM on Kauaʻi. The Kauaʻi Medical Clinic has a well-stocked pharmacy at its main clinic.

🔳 Doctors: **Kauaʻi Medical Clinic** ⊠ 3420-B Kūhiō Hwy., Līhuʻe ☎ 808/245-1500, 808/245-2471 for pharmacy, 808/245-1831 for 24-hr on-call physicians, 808/338-9431 for after-hours emergencies ⊠ North Shore Clinic, Kīlauea and Oka Rds., Kīlauea ☎ 808/828-1418 ⊠ 4392 Waialo Rd., ʻEleʻele ☎ 808/335-0499 ⊠ 5371 Koloa Rd., Kōloa ☎ 808/742-1621 ⊠ 4-1105 Kūhiō Hwy., Kapaʻa ☎ 808/822-3431.

🔳 Hospitals: **West Kauaʻi Medical Center** ⊠ 4643 Waimea Canyon Dr., Waimea ☎ 808/338-9431. **Wilcox Memorial Hospital** ⊠ 3420 Kūhiō Hwy., Līhuʻe ☎ 808/245-1100.

🔳 Pharmacies: **Longs Drugs** ⊠ Kukui Grove Center, Rte. 50, Līhuʻe ☎ 808/245-8871. **Safeway Food and Drug** ⊠ Kauaʻi Village Shopping Center, 4-831 Kūhiō Hwy., Kapaʻa ☎ 808/822-2191. **Shoreview Pharmacy** ⊠ 4-1177 Kūhiō Hwy., Suite 113, Kapaʻa ☎ 808/822-1447. **Westside Pharmacy** ⊠ 1-3845 Kaumualiʻi Hwy., Hanapēpē ☎ 808/335-5342.

SIGHTSEEING TOURS

There are three major methods for getting a good guided look at the Garden Isle: by land, by sea, and by air. You can book these tours through the travel desk of your hotel or call directly.

Tour companies use big air-conditioned buses as well as smaller, more personalized vans. When making reservations, ask what vehicle it is and which tours let you get off and look around. Guides are friendly and generally know their island inside out—tip them $10 or more per person for their efforts.

If you're interested in a north-shore sea excursion, be forewarned that big winter waves often cause trips to be canceled, so call first to find out if the company you're interested in is operating.

BOAT TOURS   A great way to take a look at Kaua'i is by boat, including kayak rentals and half-day tours. Intrepid explorers can traverse mountains, rivers, and ocean on a Kayak Kaua'i Discovery Tour. For $1,550 (including accommodations, ground transportation, and meals), you get a seven-day paddling and hiking adventure with six nights spent in out-of-the-way inns and cottages.

Cruise boats depart Wailua Marina at the mouth of the Wailua River for the Fern Grotto. Round-trip excursions, on 150-passenger flat-bottom riverboats, take an hour and a half, including time to walk around the grotto and environs. During the boat ride, guitar and 'ukulele players regale you with Hawaiian melodies and tell the history of the river. The 3-mi upriver trip culminates at a yawning lava tube that is covered with enormous fishtail ferns. Two companies offer several trips daily to Fern Grotto. Wai'ale'ale Boat Tours is well known for its Fern Grotto expedition ($16). Smith's Motor Boat Services ($16) tours get passengers involved in singing and learning hula while on board.

Captain Andy's Sailing Adventures' 55-ft catamaran *Spirit of Kaua'i* takes passengers on a two-hour sunset sail along the south shore. Hors d'oeuvres and beverages are included in the $59 cost. Captain Andy also offers a five-hour Nā Pali Coast cruise from Port Allen with breakfast and lunch for $109. This is Kaua'i's best-known boat operator, famous for big buffet meals.

Liko Kaua'i Cruises tour the northern coastline in a 49-ft powered catamaran while captains share Hawaiian history and legends. Boats depart for four-hour tours—with time for snorkeling, a deli lunch, and whale-watching in season—from Kīkīaola Harbor in Waimea for $110.

Nā Pali Explorer departs at 7:30 AM from Kīkīaola Harbor in Waimea to tour the Nā Pali Coast (weather permitting) in a 48-ft adventure craft with an onboard toilet, freshwater shower, and shade canopy. Scenic 3½-hour cruises include a snack; longer snorkel trips include Continental breakfast and a picnic lunch, snorkel gear, and a Hawaiian cultural specialist to answer questions. Zodiac boat trips make a Nā Pali beach landing. Rates range from $79 to $118, and charters are available.

Captain Andy's Sailing Adventures ⌂ Box 876, 'Ele'ele 96705 ☎ 808/335-6833 or 800/535-0830 ⊕ www.captainandys.com. **Kayak Kaua'i** ⌂ Box 508, Hanalei 96714 ☎ 808/826-9844 or 800/437-3507 ⊕ www.kayakkauai.com. **Liko Kaua'i Cruises** ⌂ 9875 Waimea Rd., Waimea 96796 ☎ 808/338-0333 or 888/732-5456 ⊕ www. liko-kauai.com. **Nā Pali Explorer** ✉ 9935 Kaumuali'i Hwy., Waimea 96796 ☎ 808/338-9999 or 877/335-9909 ⊕ www.napali-explorer.com. **Smith's Motor Boat Services** ✉ 174 Wailua Rd., Kapa'a 96746 ☎ 808/821-6892. **Wai'ale'ale Boat Tours** ✉ 6455 Makana Rd., Kapa'a 96746 ☎ 808/822-4908.

ALL-TERRAIN-
VEHICLE TOURS

You get *way* off the beaten track on Aloha Kaua'i Tours' four-wheel-drive van excursions into Kōke'e, along the rugged side of Waimea Canyon, to the top of Kilohana Crater, or into the rain forests and the crater of Wai'ale'ale. Also offered are a half-day back-roads tour, bike and hike tours, and a "SeaFun" snorkeling tour. Prices range from $60 to $125.

You must be 16 or older to operate your own ATV, but Kaua'i ATV Tours also offers its "Mud Hog" six-passenger dune-buggy vehicle that can accommodate families with kids age five and older. The $90 three-hour jaunt takes you through a private sugar plantation and historic cane-haul tunnel. The $145 four-hour tour visits secluded waterfalls and includes lunch. The longer excursion includes a hike through a bamboo forest and a swim in a freshwater pool at the base of the falls.
Aloha Kaua'i Tours ⊠ 1702 Haleukana St., Līhu'e 96766 ☎ 808/245-6400 or 800/452-1113 ⊕ www.alohakauaitours.com. **Kaua'i ATV Tours** ⊠ 3412 Weliweli Rd., Kōloa 96756 ☎ 808/742-2734 or 877/707-7088 ⊕ www.kauaiatv.com.

HELICOPTER
TOURS

From the air, the Garden Isle blossoms wth views you cannot see by land, foot, or sea. In an hour you can see waterfalls, craters, and places that are inaccessible even by hiking trails. Expect to pay $125 or more per person for the longest, most comprehensive tours, but call around for itineraries. A shorter, less-expensive flight might suit your needs. Don't be afraid to ask about the pilot's experience and safety record. Most, but not all, companies use top-of-the-line equipment, and the operators listed below have reliable flight experience. There are 20 companies flying on Kaua'i, so if you don't like what you see, keep looking. Ask about special discounts sometimes available with coupons from free visitors' pamphlets. For both safety and comfort, single passengers weighing 250 pounds or more, or couples with a combined weight of 450 pounds or more, are required to purchase an additional seat.

Jack Harter Helicopters is the originator of heli-tours on Kaua'i. In the air since the early 1960s, it has a perfect safety record and a modern fleet and offers both 60- and 90-minute air tours. Air Kaua'i has A-Star choppers with all-glass doors for amazing views. Island Helicopters gives you a free video of your tour. South Sea Tour Co. has a choice of tours available from Līhu'e. Will Squyres Helicopter Tours offers group rates and charters from Līhu'e Airport.
Air Kaua'i ⊠ 3651 Ahukini Rd., Līhu'e 96766 ☎ 808/246-4666 or 800/972-4666 ⊕ www.airkauai.com. **Island Helicopters** ⊠ Līhu'e Airport, Līhu'e 96766 ☎ 808/245-8588 or 800/829-5999 ⊕ www.islandhelicopters.com. **Jack Harter Helicopters** ⊠ 4231 Ahukini Rd., Līhu'e 96766 ☎ 808/245-3774 or 888/245-2001 ⊕ www.helicopters-kauai.com. **South Sea Tour Co.** ⊠ 4480 Ahukini Rd., Suite 204, Līhu'e 96766 ☎ 808/245-2222 or 800/367-2914 ⊕ www.southseashelicopters.com. **Will Squyres Helicopter Tours** ⊠ 3222 Kūhiō Hwy., Līhu'e 96766 ☎ 808/245-8881 or 888/245-4354 ⊕ www.helicopters-hawaii.com.

NI'IHAU TOUR

It takes only 12 minutes to fly from Kaua'i to an island that few outsiders have set foot on since 1864. This 72-square-mi island 17 mi from Kaua'i is now run by the Robinson family, who raise cattle and sheep on the barren land. Bruce Robinson initiated Ni'ihau Helicopters in 1984 in order to supplement the cost of medical evacuation via helicopter for residents. Tours avoid the western coastline, especially the village of Pu'uwai, where the island's 200 residents live. Flights depart from and return to Kaumakani. There's a four-passenger minimum for each flight, and reservations are essential. Ground transportation is not available. A picnic lunch on a secluded Ni'ihau beach is included along with time for swimming and snorkeling. The half-day tour is $280 per person.
Ni'ihau Tours ✈ Ni'ihau Helicopters, Box 690370, Makaweli 96769 ☎ 808/335-3500 or 877/441-3500.

ORIENTATION
TOURS The Round-the-Island Tour, sometimes called the Wailua River/Waimea Canyon Tour, gives a good overview of the island including Ft. Elisabeth, 'Ōpaeka'a Falls, and Menehune Fishpond. Guests are transported in air-conditioned 17-passenger minivans. The trip includes a boat ride up the Wailua River to Fern Grotto, and then a drive around the island to lookouts above Waimea Canyon. Companies offering Round-the-Island ground tours include Roberts Hawai'i Tours.

The Best of Kaua'i is a whirlwind daylong tour, sponsored by Kaua'i North Shore Limousine and Tours, for $175 per person. It includes a visit to Kilohana, a refurbished plantation mansion in Līhu'e; a boat ride to the Fern Grotto; a tour of Kīlauea Lighthouse; and a helicopter tour. Ground transportation is in 15-passenger, air-conditioned vans. They will pick you up at Līhu'e Airport or at your hotel if it's on the north or east side of the island.

Kaua'i Island Tours will arrange charter tours around Kaua'i in anything from a passenger car to a 57-person motorcoach.
🏠 **Kaua'i Island Tours** 🏠 2960 Aukele St., Līhu'e 96766 ☎ 808/245-4777 or 800/733-4777. **Kaua'i North Shore Limousine and Tours** 🏠 Box 109, Kīlauea 96754 ☎ 808/826-6189 or 808/634-7260. **Roberts Hawai'i Tours** 🏠 Box 3389, Līhu'e 96766 ☎ 808/245-9101 or 800/831-5541 🌐 www.robertshawaii.com.

THEME TOURS Gay and Robinson can take you on a sugar plantation, field, and factory tour. Venturing into where the cane is grown, you learn about the history of sugar in Hawai'i; then you head to Kaua'i's last working sugar mill to see the refining process. Tours are offered weekdays at 8:45 and 12:45 for $30. Another option is the sugar and ranch-land tour, which revisits old ranch roads and Waimea Canyon destinations that were popular prior to World War II. The views include the rugged Olokele Canyon. The cost is $60, including lunch.

Hawai'i Movie Tours' minibuses with in-van television monitors let you see the actual scenes of films while visiting the real locations used for the filming of *Jurassic Park, Raiders of the Lost Ark, South Pacific, Blue Hawaii, Gilligan's Island,* and more. One stop is for a picnic lunch at 'Anini Beach. The standard land tour is $95, and the four-wheel-drive Off Road Tour is $113.
🏠 **Gay and Robinson Tours** ✉ 423 Kaumakani Ave., Kaumakani 96747 ☎ 808/335-2824 🌐 www.gandrtours-kauai.com. **Hawai'i Movie Tours** ✉ 356 Kūhio Hwy., Kapa'a 96746 ☎ 808/822-1192 or 800/628-8432 🌐 www.hawaiimovietour.com.

WALKING TOURS History buffs curious about Kapa'a's sugarcane-, pineapple-, and rice-growing past and the World War II years will enjoy Kapa'a History Tour's 90-minute laid-back stroll from the Pono Kai Resort at the gateway of Kapa'a town. This insider's look led by locals tells the story of Kapa'a's Japanese stone lantern. Tours take place on Tuesday, Thursday, and Saturday at 10 AM and 4 PM and cost $15.

To see a rapidly vanishing lifestyle, take the unique, volunteer-led Plantation Lifestyles Walking Tour through the residential housing of a real mill camp. In the shadow of the old sugar mill, the dirt lanes of the 70-year-old camp are shaded by fruit trees and tropical gardens, and sometimes elderly residents come out to say aloha. Reservations are needed for the $10 1½-hour to 2-hour tours that begin at 9 AM every Tuesday, Thursday, and Saturday at Waimea Plantation Cottages.
🏠 **Kapa'a History Tour–Kaua'i's Historical Society** ✉ 4-1250 Kūhiō Hwy., Kapa'a 96746 ☎ 808/245-3373. **Plantation Lifestyles Walking Tour** 🏠 Box 1178, Waimea 96796 ☎ 808/335-2824 🌐 www.gandrtours-kauai.com.

TAXIS

Cabs can be costly on Kaua'i. Each mile is $2, after a $2 meter drop; from Līhu'e to Po'ipū the price is $32, so from Līhu'e to Princeville is $60, excluding tip. Use a cab for short distances only (to a restaurant, for instance).

Akiko's Taxi operates from Kapa'a and offers minivans in its fleet. City Cab is a reliable taxi company with island-wide services it uses Līhu'e as a home base. Based in Princeville, the North Shore Cab Company provides complete ground handling services for the north and east sections of the island.

🚕 **Akiko's Taxi** ✉ 5258 Laipo Rd. ☎ 808/822-7588 or 808/634-6018. **City Cab** ✉ 2979 Ohiohi St. ☎ 808/245-3227 or 808/639-7932. **North Shore Cab Company** ✉ 4480 Ka Haku Rd. ☎ 808/826-4118 or 808/639-7829.

VISITOR INFORMATION

The Kaua'i Visitors Bureau, the local island chapter of the Hawai'i Visitors and Convention Bureau, is on Rice Street, Līhu'e's main thoroughfare, near the Kaua'i Museum.

Activity centers such as Pahiō Activities will help you book tours, arrange sporting excursions, rent cars, reserve rooms in hotels and condos, and even plan weddings. There are four locations in Princeville and one at the Radisson.

Po'ipū Beach Resort Association is the central source of information about the south shore. You can make on-line reservations through the organization's Web site, and maps and brochures are sent on request.

🚕 **Kaua'i Visitors Bureau** ✉ 4334 Rice St., Suite 101, Līhu'e 96766 ☎ 808/245-3971 or 800/262-1400 🖷 808/246-9235 ⊕ www.kauaivisitorsbureau.com. **Pahiō Activities** ✉ 3970 Wyllie Rd., Princeville 96722 ☎ 808/826-6549 ⊕ www.pahio.com. **Po'ipū Beach Resort Association** 🖃 Box 730, Kōloa 96756 ☎ 808/742-7444 or 888/744-0888 🖷 808/742-7887 ⊕ www.poipu-beach.org.

MOLOKA'I
THE FRIENDLY ISLE

5

FODOR'S CHOICE

The Camps at Moloka'i Ranch, Maunaloa

Hotel Moloka'i, Kaunakakai

Kalaupapa National Historical Park

Kanemitsu Bakery and Restaurant, Kaunakakai

Moloka'i Mule Ride

Pāpōhaku Beach, West Moloka'i

HIGHLY RECOMMENDED

Kaloko'eli Fishpond, East Moloka'i

Kamakou Preserve, Kualapu'u

The Lodge at Moloka'i Ranch, Maunaloa

Maunaloa Room, restaurant in Maunaloa

Pālā'au State Park, Central Moloka'i

Paniolo Hale, hotel in Maunaloa

The town of Kaunakakai

The town of Maunaloa

Updated by
Pablo Madera

MOLOKA'I'S ROUGH-AND-TUMBLE LANDSCAPE—much of it inaccessible by conventional means—spans climatic zones from rain forest to desert, encompassing misty mountain peaks and parched windblown ranch land. Beaches are untrammeled and often empty enough to call your own. The Kalaupapa Peninsula, home to a former colony of leprosy patients, is guarded by the tallest sea cliffs in the world. Mountain bikers ply the dry open pastures of the west end. Divers revel in black coral reefs.

Pulling out of Moloka'i's Ho'olehua Airport you see a hand-painted sign that reads ALOHA! SLOW DOWN, THIS IS MOLOKA'I. It doesn't refer just to road speed but also to your internal pace and expectations. Heeding this advice is the best way to enjoy the island on its own terms.

Moloka'i residents resist strongly the unchecked growth of neighboring islands, even at the expense of the economy, and struggles with the influence of development are common. The 6,680 inhabitants focus more on family, community, and the retention of Hawaiian culture than on the eradication of the past for a high-rise future. Because of this, some areas can seem outdated and stuck. But as you sit quietly on a deserted west end beach looking at the lights of Honolulu twinkling across the channel 25 mi away, you realize that being lost in time can be a beautiful thing.

Exploring Moloka'i

Moloka'i is long and shaped like a slipper, with the "heel" facing west and the "toe" pointing to the east. Two dormant volcanoes are connected by a long plain. The imaginary dividing line is the town of Kaunakakai, in the center of the island's southern shore. West, Central, and East Moloka'i are used as natural divisions in this chapter.

Nature is the main attraction—waterfalls, valleys, cliffs, and the like. A rental car is the best way to explore at your own pace.

Directions on the island are often referred to as *mauka* (toward the mountains) and *makai* (toward the ocean).

About the Restaurants

During a week's stay, you might easily hit all the dining spots worth a visit, then return to your favorites for a second round. The dining scene is fun, nevertheless, because it's a microcosm of Hawai'i's diverse cultures. You can find locally grown vegetarian foods, spicy Filipino cuisine, and Hawaiian fish with a Japanese influence—such as *'ahi* or *aku* (types of tuna), mullet, and moonfish, grilled, sautéed, or sliced and mixed with seaweed and eaten raw as *poke* (marinated raw fish). It's all on Ala Malama Street in Kaunakakai, with pizza, pasta, and ribs only a block away. What's more, the price is right. For something a bit fancier (but casual just the same), try dinner at the Lodge at Moloka'i Ranch.

About the Hotels

Moloka'i appeals more to travelers who appreciate genuine Hawaiian hospitality than to those who like swanky digs. Hotel and condominium properties range from adequate to funky. Kaunakakai's accommodations are ideal if you're on a tight budget and want a central location. There's also a handful of bed-and-breakfasts around the island.

If you want activity and a bit of adventure, you can stay in a bungalow-size luxury tent at the Camps at Moloka'i Ranch. The resort has horseback riding, mountain biking, snorkeling, kayaking, and other activities. The Lodge at Moloka'i Ranch in Maunaloa has spa treatments and added creature comforts. Ke Nani Kai and Wavecrest have guest-only tennis courts.

	$$$$	$$$	$$	$	¢
WHAT IT COSTS					
RESTAURANTS	over $30	$20–$30	$12–$20	$7–$12	under $7
HOTELS	over $200	$150–$200	$100–$150	$60–$100	under $60

Restaurant prices are for one main course at dinner. Hotel prices are for two people in a standard double room in high season, including tax and service.

Timing

Moloka'i's weather is good year-round. There are seldom crowds, but the island gets an influx of visitors during festivals. For a real taste of Hawaiian culture, you might want to visit during event weekends anyway. Be sure you make reservations for accommodations and a rental car well in advance if you schedule a trip during any major holiday.

WEST MOLOKA'I

The region is largely made up of the 53,000-acre Moloka'i Ranch. The rolling pastures and farmlands are presided over by Maunaloa, a sleepy little plantation town with a dormant volcano of the same name. West Moloka'i has another claim to fame: Pāpōhaku, the island's best beach.

a good drive

This driving tour focuses on two of Moloka'i's tourist areas. If you're approaching the west end from Kaunakakai on Route 460 (also called Kamehameha V Highway), turn right at mile marker 15 down Kaluako'i Road and right again at the sign for **Kaluako'i Hotel and Golf Club** ❶ ▶. Take time to enjoy the grounds and the beach.

Back behind the wheel, turn right out of Kaluako'i Hotel and Golf Club and follow Kaluako'i Road 2 mi west until it dead-ends. This shoreline drive takes you past a number of lovely parks, including **Pāpōhaku Beach** ❷, the largest white-sand beach on the island. Look for a big sign on the side of the road.

Turn around and follow Kaluako'i Road back past the resort entrance, and continue uphill to the intersection with Route 460. Turn right and drive 2 mi on Route 460 (Maunaloa Highway) to **Maunaloa** ❸, a former plantation town that was torn down and replaced with—guess what—buildings resembling a plantation town. Much controversy surrounds development in this area. Landowners in favor of large-scale development come up against residents who resist the loss of their lifestyle. Raise this subject with locals, and you may hear a lively debate.

TIMING   If you follow this excursion at a leisurely Moloka'i pace, it will take you the better part of a day, particularly if your accommodations are not on the west end of the island. A walk around Kaluako'i Hotel and Golf Club can take an hour or more.

Another hour can fly by at Pāpōhaku Beach as you dig your toes in its sands and picnic on its shady grassy area. Allow one hour for exploring Maunaloa's main street to shop for souvenirs and chat with local shop owners. Don't try to do your shopping on Sunday, or you may find many CLOSED signs on the doors.

What to See

▶ ❶ **Kaluako'i Hotel and Golf Club.** This late-1960s resort passed through several owners, and the hotel itself is now closed, awaiting its next incarnation. Some very nice shops and condos are still operating here. Stroll the grounds—an impressive 6,700 acres of beachfront property, in-

Numbers in the text correspond to numbers in the margin and on the Moloka'i map.

If you have 1 day

Book a **Moloka'i Mule Ride** ❹ and a tour of **Kalaupapa** ❻ prior to leaving home. Fly into Ho'olehua Airport and drive to Kala'e, where the steep, 26-switchback mule trail begins. The tour of the former leper colony, where some 43 people live with the now manageable illness currently known as Hansen's disease, is the most emotionally moving experience on Moloka'i. If you ask nicely, you might be able to persuade your driver to stop at **Pālā'au State Park** ❺ for a photo of the Phallic Rock before you head back to the airport in the afternoon. For less-adventurous souls, flights directly to Kalaupapa can be arranged, thereby eliminating the grueling mule ride.

5

If you have 2 days

Maunaloa ❸ on West Moloka'i makes a good starting point, particularly because there are many places to stay in the area. Spend a little time poking through the jumble of treasures at the Big Wind Kite Factory and Plantation Gallery, and you've just about seen the town. Moloka'i Ranch, and its activities base, is also here. It would be a good time to enjoy skeet shooting, a kayak ride, world-class mountain-biking trails, or maybe a horseback trip on the 58,000-acre ranch. By afternoon, head for the nearest beach. This could be the former Kaluako'i Hotel and Golf Club's own Kawākiu Beach (the hotel is closed, but the beach is open). Or, if you prefer privacy, try **Pāpōhaku Beach** ❷, just a few miles southwest of the hotel. Reserve the second day for the **Moloka'i Mule Ride** ❹ and a tour of **Kalaupapa** ❻, taking in **Pālā'au State Park** ❺ and the Phallic Rock afterward. If you're up to it after the ride, you can stop by **Coffees of Hawai'i** ❽, **R. W. Meyer Sugar Mill and Moloka'i Museum** ❼, or **Purdy's Macadamia Nut Farm** ❾. If not, pause for some island-style corned beef hash or a burger with the locals at the Kamuela's Cookhouse before heading back to your hotel.

If you have 4 days

Follow the itinerary above for your first two days, and then visit **Kaunakakai** ⓬ on your third day to pick up souvenirs, sample ethnic foods, and stop at the Kanemitsu Bakery, a local institution, for a loaf of its famous Moloka'i sweet bread, pastries, or snacks for the road. Check out **Kaunakakai Wharf** ⓭; you might set out on a fishing or scuba excursion from here. Otherwise, continue on a leisurely drive to Moloka'i's east end. Along the way, sightseeing points include **Kaloko'eli Fishpond** ⓮, St. Joseph's church near **Kamalō** ⓯, and 'Ili'ili'ōpae Heiau. Turn around for the return drive when you reach **Hālawa Valley** ⓳. Your final day should be reserved for your own pleasures—perhaps a morning game of golf, an easy hike, a return to the beach, or a drive to see anything you might have missed.

---

cluding the newly revived golf course and 5 mi of coastline. ✉ *Kaluako'i Rd., Maunaloa* ☎ *808/552–2555 or 888/552–2550.*

★ ❸ **Maunaloa.** This sleepy town was developed in 1923 to support the island's pineapple plantation. Although the fields of golden fruit have gone fallow, some of the workers' dwellings still stand, anchoring the west end of Moloka'i. Colorful local characters run the half-dozen businesses (including a kite shop and an eclectic old market) along the town's short main street. This is also the headquarters for Moloka'i Ranch, with an outfitters center, rodeo arena, and luxury lodge. ✛ *Western end of Maunaloa Hwy. (Rte. 460).*

② **Pāpōhaku Beach.** The most splendid white-sand beach on Moloka'i, Pāpōhaku is also the island's biggest—it stretches 3 mi along the western shore. On busier days you're likely to see a handful of other people. If the waves are up, swimming is dangerous. ✉ *Kaluako'i Rd., 2 mi beyond Kaluako'i Hotel and Golf Club, look for sign on makai side of road.*

CENTRAL MOLOKA'I

The center of the island is where the action is, relatively speaking. If you opt to do the Moloka'i Mule Ride in the morning and still feel up to exploring afterward, you can make quick stops at the places along the drive that follows. Central Moloka'i has the shops and eateries of Kaunakakai, water sports based at Kaunakakai Wharf, and the attractions and natural beauty of the central highlands.

a good drive

If you have reserved the **Moloka'i Mule Ride** ❹, go directly to Kala'e, north on Route 470. The highway ends at **Pālā'au State Park** ❺ ▶, where you can admire knockout views of **Kalaupapa** ❻ and the Kalaupapa Peninsula. Bring along a light jacket for cooler upland weather in the fall and winter.

On the way back down the hill on Route 470, stop at the **R. W. Meyer Sugar Mill and Moloka'i Museum** ❼ to see photos and machinery from earlier times. Then turn right on Farrington Highway to visit the little town of Kualapu'u, where **Coffees of Hawai'i** ❽ has a plantation store and espresso bar and offers tours of its coffee fields and processing plant. A five-minute drive west takes you to **Purdy's Macadamia Nut Farm** ❾ in Ho'olehua.

Head back on Farrington Highway, and then take a right onto Route 470; go down the rest of the hill and turn left on Route 460. Near the ocean on Route 460 are two stops of note that are practically right across the road from each other: **Kapuāiwa Coconut Grove** ❿ and **Church Row** ⓫. Follow Route 460 east to reach **Kaunakakai** ⓬, Moloka'i's "big city." **Kaunakakai Wharf** ⓭ is the home base for deep-sea fishing excursions and other aqua adventures.

TIMING   Allow at least a day to explore. If you save the Moloka'i Mule Ride for another day, there's no need to rush. Otherwise many shops in Kaunakakai may be closed by the time you get there. During your tour of the highlands, take an hour to visit the sugar museum and another hour or more for the macadamia-nut farm and plantation store. Both are closed on Sunday. Once you hit Kaunakakai, indulge yourself: take an hour or two to stroll around town and *talk story* (chat) with the locals. Be sure to save a half hour for snacks at the Kanemitsu Bakery, a local institution.

What to See

⓫ **Church Row.** Standing cheek by jowl along the highway are several houses of worship with primarily native Hawaiian congregations. Notice the unadorned, boxlike style of architecture so familiar to missionary homes. ✛ *Mauka side of Rte. 460, 5½ mi southwest of airport.*

❽ **Coffees of Hawai'i.** Take a self-guided tour of 500 acres of shiny-leaf coffee trees, after which you can head over to the espresso bar for a fresh-brewed cup of java and *liliko'i* (passion fruit) cheesecake. Or you can buy

5

Festivals & Seasonal Events

The year kicks off with the Ka Moloka'i Makahiki Festival in January, a day when islanders and visitors get together to compete in ancient Hawaiian games. In May, Moloka'i Ka Hula Piko, an annual daylong event, brings performances by some of the state's best hula troupes, musicians, singers, lecturers, and storytellers. It's all in tribute to Kā'ana, on the slopes of Maunaloa Mountain, which is reputed to be the birthplace of the hula. Late September's Aloha Week has live music, hula, and fashion shows in front of the town library. It tops off with a big (by Moloka'i standards) parade down Ala Malama Street. The autumn Moloka'i-to-O'ahu Canoe Race is the world's major long-course outrigger canoeing event. It begins near the harbor of Haleolono. After paddling across the rough Kaiwi Channel, participants finish at Ft. DeRussy Beach in Waikīkī. The event takes place each September (women) and October (men). Thanksgiving Day weekend, the Moloka'i Ranch Rodeo draws cowpokes for contests ranging from bull riding to barrel racing.

Sports & the Outdoors

Moloka'i's beauty, sunny skies, and fragrant winds beckon. A mule ride down a narrow 1,664-ft cliff over a 3-mi, 26-switchback trail leads to Kalaupapa National Historical Park. At Kamakou Preserve, a Hawai'i Nature Conservancy property protecting endangered plants and birds, you can embark on a challenging guided trek. Arrange for a fishing charter, a sailing-snorkeling-scuba outing, or a whale-watching cruise at Kaunakakai Wharf. Mokuho'oniki Island, at the east end of the island, is a great dive spot. It was once a military bombing target, and artifacts from World War II are scattered throughout its many pinnacles and drop-offs. The area is home to barracuda and gray reef sharks. Black coral grows in depths ranging from 30 to 100 ft.

---

roasted beans to go from the gift shop. The Muleskinner is a great, low-acid, dark roast. ✉ *Farrington Hwy., off Rte. 470, Kualapu'u* ☎ *808/567-9241* ⊕ *www.coffeehawaii.com* ✉ *$14* ☉ *Tours Mon.–Sat. 10–1.*

6 Kalaupapa. The Kalaupapa Peninsula was once a community of about 1,000 victims of Hansen's disease (leprosy) who were banished from other parts of Hawai'i. A Belgian man named Joseph de Veuster, ordained in Hawai'i in 1864 and known as Father Damien, committed himself to the care of the afflicted until he died here of the same disease in 1889. There are about 40 patients still living in Kalaupapa—now by choice, as the disease is controlled by drugs and patients are no longer carriers. You will most likely not see any patients other than perhaps the tour guide. The history of the community is fascinating and heart wrenching. Kalaupapa is the name of a peninsula, a town, and a park. Views of the peninsula from Kalaupapa Lookout in Pālā'au State Park are a standout. Note that no one under the age of 16 is allowed to visit Kalaupapa. Whether you hike down, take a mule ride down, or fly in, you must be part of a tour to visit. You can book through Moloka'i Mule Ride, or through **Damien Tours** (☎ 808/567–6171) if you want to hike or fly in. Book before getting to the island. Hikers need to start walking by 8 AM to connect with a tour. ⊹ *North end of Rte. 470.*

FodorśChoice
★

⑩ Kapuāiwa Coconut Grove. At first glance this looks like a sea of coconut trees. Close-up you'll see that the tall, stately palms are planted in long rows leading down to the sea. This is one of the last surviving royal groves planted by Prince Lot, who ruled Hawai'i as King Kamehameha V from 1863 until his death in 1872. Watch for falling coconuts; protect your head and your car. ⊕ *Makai side of Rte. 460, 5½ mi south of airport.*

★ ⑫ **Kaunakakai.** Kaunakakai looks like an Old West movie set. Along the one-block main drag is a cultural grab bag of restaurants and shops. People are friendly and willing to supply directions. The preferred dress is shorts and a tank top, and no one wears anything fancier than a mu'umu'u or aloha shirt. ✉ *Rte. 460, about 3 blocks north of Kaunakakai Wharf.*

⑬ **Kaunakakai Wharf.** Docks, once bustling with watercraft exporting pineapples, now host boats shipping out potatoes, tomatoes, baby corn, herbs, and other produce. The wharf is also the starting point for excursions, including deep-sea fishing, sailing, snorkeling, whale-watching, and scuba diving. ⊕ *Rte. 450 and Ala Malama St.; drive makai on Kaunakakai Pl., which dead-ends at the wharf.*

Fodor'sChoice
★ ④ **Moloka'i Mule Ride.** Mount a friendly mule and wind along a 3-mi, 26-switchback trail to reach the town of Kalaupapa. The path was built in 1886 as a supply route for the settlement below. Once in Kalaupapa, you'll take a guided tour of the town and have a picnic lunch. The trail is very steep, down some of the highest sea cliffs in the world. It's narrow and has no rails, so if it's muddy, the ride is cancelled. Only those in good shape should attempt the ride, as two hours each way on a mule can take its toll. The entire event takes seven hours. It's wise to make reservations ahead of time, as spots are limited. The same outfit can also arrange for you to hike down or fly in, or some combination of a hike in and fly out. ✉ *100 Kala'e Hwy. (Rte. 470), Kualapu'u* ☎ *808/567–6088* ⊕ *www.muleride.com* ✆ *$150* ☾ *Mon.–Sat. 8–3:30.*

★ ▶ ⑤ **Pālā'au State Park.** One of the island's few formal recreation areas, this cool retreat covers 233 acres at a 1,000-ft elevation. A short path through a heady pine forest leads to **Kalaupapa Lookout,** a magnificent overlook with views of the town of Kalaupapa and the 1,664-ft-high sea cliffs protecting it. Informative plaques have facts about leprosy, Father Damien, and the colony itself. The park is also the site of **Phallic Rock,** known as Kauleonānāhoa to the ancient Hawaiians. It's said that if women sit by this large rock formation they will become more fertile. The park is well maintained, with camping facilities, washrooms, and picnic tables. ⊕ *Take Rte. 460 west from Kaunakakai and then head mauka on Rte. 470, which ends at the park* ☎ *No phone* ✆ *Free* ☾ *Daily dawn–dusk.*

⑨ **Purdy's Macadamia Nut Farm.** Moloka'i's only working macadamia-nut farm is open for educational tours hosted by the knowledgeable and entertaining owner. A family business on Hawaiian homestead land in Ho'olehua, the farm takes up 1½ acres with a flourishing grove of some 50 trees more than 70 years old. Taste a delicious nut right out of its shell, or fresh macadamia-blossom honey; then buy some at the shop on the way out. Look for Purdy's sign behind Moloka'i High School. ✉ *Lihipali Ave., Ho'olehua* ☎ *808/567–6601* ✆ *Free* ☾ *Weekdays 9:30–3:30, Sat. 10–2.*

⑦ **R. W. Meyer Sugar Mill and Moloka'i Museum.** Built in 1877, this old mill has been reconstructed to signify Moloka'i's agricultural history. The equipment is still in working order, including a mule-driven cane crusher, redwood evaporating pans, some copper clarifiers, and a steam engine.

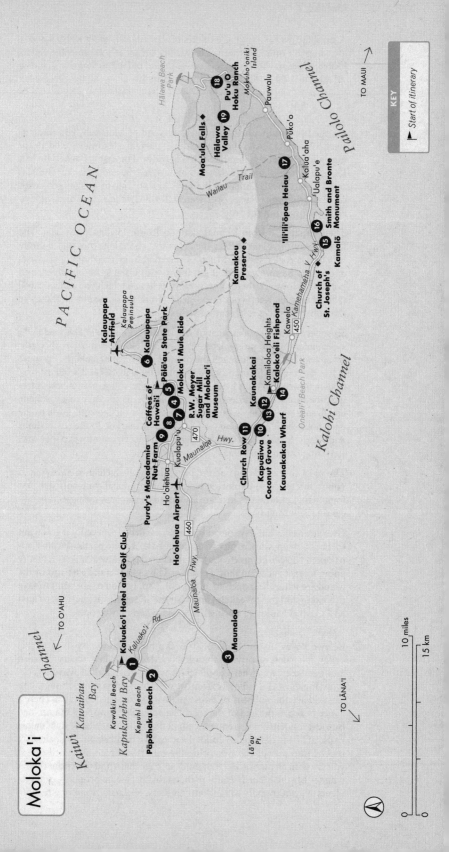

Moloka'i

KEY
▲ *Start of Itinerary*

Kaiwi Channel

TO O'AHU

Kawaihau Bay

Kapukahehu Bay

Kawākiu Beach

Kepuhi Beach

Pāpōhaku Beach

Kaluako'i Hotel and Golf Club ▲

Kaluako'i Rd.

① ▲

②

PACIFIC OCEAN

Iā'au Pt.

TO LĀNA'I

Maunaloa ③

Maunaloa Hwy.

460

Ho'olehua Airport

Ho'olehua

Maunaloa Hwy.

470

Kualapu'u

Purdy's Macadamia Nut Farm

Coffees of Hawai'i

⑨ ⑧ ④ ⑤ ▲

⑦

R.W. Meyer Sugar Mill and Moloka'i Museum

Moloka'i Mule Ride

Pāla'au State Park

⑥ **Kalaupapa**

Kalaupapa Peninsula

Kalaupapa Airfield ✈

Kamakou Preserve ◆

Church Row ⑪

Kapuāiwa Coconut Grove ⑩

Kaunakakai ⑫ ⑬

Kaunakakai Wharf

Kamiloloa Heights

Kaloko'eli Fishpond ⑭

Kawela

Oneali'i Beach Park

450 Kamehameha V Hwy.

Church of St. Joseph's ◆

Kamalō ⑮

Smith and Bronte Monument ⑯

'Ualapu'e

Kalua'aha

'Ili'ili'ōpae Heiau ⑰

Pūko'o

Pauwalu

Mokoho'oniki Island

Pu'u O Hoku Ranch ⑱

Hālawa Valley ⑲

Moa'ula Falls ◆

Wailau Trail

Hālawa Beach Park

Pailolo Channel

TO MAUI

Kalohi Channel

0 10 miles

0 15 km

A museum with changing exhibits on the island's early history and a gift shop are on-site as well. The facility serves as a campus for Elderhostel programs. ⊠ *Rte. 470, 2 mi southwest of Pālā'au State Park, Kala'e* ☎ *808/567–6436* ⊠ *$2.50* ☉ *Mon.–Sat. 10–2.*

EAST MOLOKA'I

On the beautifully undeveloped eastern end of Moloka'i, you find ancient fishponds, a magnificent coastline, splendid ocean views, and a gaping valley that's been inhabited for centuries. The east is flanked by Mt. Kamakou, the island's highest point at 4,961 ft, and home to The Nature Conservancy's Kamakou Preserve. Miles of rain forests burgeon with tropical fruit, mist hangs over waterfall-filled valleys, and ancient lava cliffs jut out from the sea.

a good drive

The journey east from Kaunakakai, on Route 450, is 30 mi long. The farther you drive, the wilder the coastline, changing from white sandy beaches to rocky shores. Much of the road hugs the shore as it twists and turns. Be forewarned: it's fraught with bumps, blind curves, and potholes. However, there are several bays beside which you can stop and take a breather. Keep your eyes open for mile markers: at times, they're the only references for locating sights.

Six miles east of Kaunakakai, look offshore to see **Kaloko'eli Fishpond** ⑭ ⌐, surrounded by the most picturesque of Moloka'i's historic rock walls. After another 5 mi you reach the natural harbor of **Kamalō** ⑮. En route is the stark white Church of St. Joseph's, built in 1876. It's one of four houses of worship built by Father Damien. The statue of him here is frequently adorned with flower leis. A mile later is the easy-to-miss **Smith and Bronte Monument** ⑯. At mile marker 15, a hidden trail leads to the enormous **'Ili'ili'ōpae Heiau** ⑰. Close to mile marker 20 the road climbs and winds through **Pu'u O Hoku Ranch** ⑱, a vast Upcountry expanse with sparkling ocean panoramas.

The road east dead-ends at the beach in the lush **Hālawa Valley** ⑲. If you're interested in exploring trails, contact a local tour outfitter first for a map. Landowners here are known to chase away unsuspecting hikers on the wrong trail.

TIMING Give yourself a full day for this meandering drive, especially if you want to break it up with a picnic at one of the beach parks. From Kaunakakai, you can complete the tour in a half day; allow a full day if you're going to visit the Kamakou Preserve. The sights on the east end of the island are natural, so opening hours don't apply. You might want to save this excursion for a weekend and visit the shops and attractions of East and Central Moloka'i during the week, when they're open.

What to See

⑲ **Hālawa Valley.** As far back as AD 650 a busy community lived in this valley, the oldest recorded habitation on Moloka'i. Hawaiians grew fruit and taro and fished here until 1946, when a fierce tidal wave struck. Now much of the valley is overrun with lush vegetation, though you can still see the remains of house platforms and garden walls. There's a nice beach at the end of the road. An accessible 3-mi trail maintained by local residents, who request a small donation, leads back to Moa'ula Falls, a 250-ft cascade. A hidden art gallery and botanical garden are tucked into the jungle. Exploring the trail is not recommended unless you are with an authorized tour guide or have maps and directions. Don't wander off the hiker-friendly path, as this is private property, and residents are not friendly to random ramblers. ⊹ *Eastern end of Rte. 450.*

17 **'Ili'ili'ōpae Heiau.** Human sacrifices once took place at this hidden heiau. As long as a football field, it's a well-preserved example of Hawai'i's ancient outdoor shrines. This revered site is said to hold great power to this day. Please act with respect by speaking in a soft voice. The sacrifices were introduced by Tahitian immigrants who came between AD 1090 and 1240, but the heiau could have existed before then—as early as AD 650, the time of the first island habitation. The old religion, which included human sacrifice, has not been practiced since 1819. Don't wander off the designated trail. The whole area is private property. The owners don't object to people simply visiting the heiau, but permission should be requested by phone. ✢ *15 mi east of Kaunakakai and ½ mi inland of Rte. 450; park on the side of road, look for Wailau Trail sign, and walk about 10 mins mauka until you see sign on left for heiau* ☎ *808/ 558-8380.*

★ ▶ **14** **Kaloko'eli Fishpond.** With its narrow rock walls connecting two points of the shore, Kaloko'eli is typical of the numerous fishponds that define southern Moloka'i. Many of them were built around the 13th century. This early type of aquaculture, particular to Hawai'i, exemplifies the ingenuity of precontact Hawaiians. Fishpond walls were built of lava rocks or coral or both; usually they were built on fringing reefs. You can see the tops of the dark circular stone walls a foot or two above the surface of the water all along the coast. One or more openings were left in the wall, where gates with grills (wooden slats side by side) called *makaha* were installed. These gates allowed seawater and tiny fish to enter the enclosed pond, kept larger predators out, and allowed water to circulate so the pond didn't get stagnant. The ponds were stocked with fish too big to escape through the slats, but tiny fish that entered and were not eaten by bigger ones often grew too big to get out. When fish were needed, they were harvested by net. At one time there were 62 fishponds around Moloka'i's coast. ✉ *Rte. 450 about 6 mi east of Kaunakakai.*

★ **Kamakou Preserve.** Tucked away on the slopes of Mt. Kamakou, Moloka'i's highest peak, the 2,774-acre preserve is a dazzling wonderland full of wet *'ohi'a* (hardwood trees of the myrtle family, with red blossoms called lehua flowers) forests, rare bogs, and native trees and wildlife. Monthly guided hikes, limited to eight people, are held on Saturday. Hikers meet at Ho'olehua Airport at 8:30 and return by 4. Reservations are required well in advance. You can visit the park without a tour, but you need a good four-wheel-drive vehicle, and the Nature Conservancy requests that you sign in at the office and get directions first. ✉ *The Nature Conservancy, 23 Pueo Pl., Kualapu'u* ☎ *808/553-5236* ✑ *Free; donation suggested for guided hike, $10 members, $25 nonmembers (includes one-year membership).*

15 **Kamalō.** A natural harbor used by small cargo ships during the 19th century, this is also the site of the **Church of St. Joseph's,** a tiny white church built by Father Damien in the 1880s. ✉ *Rte. 450 about 11 mi east of Kaunakakai, on makai side.*

18 **Pu'u O Hoku Ranch.** A 14,000-acre private spread in the highlands of East Moloka'i, Pu'u O Hoku was developed in the '30s by wealthy industrialist Paul Fagan. Route 450 cuts right through this rural gem with its green pastures and grazing horses and cattle. As you drive along, enjoy the splendid views of Maui and Lāna'i. The small island off the coast is Mokuho'oniki, where the military practiced bombing techniques during World War II. ✉ *Rte. 450 about 20 mi east of Kaunakakai* ⊕ *www. puuohoku.com.*

⑯ Smith and Bronte Monument. This humble site tucked away in a grove of trees and bushes is dedicated to Ernest Smith and Emory Bronte, Americans who crash-landed here in 1927. They were the first civilians to complete a transpacific flight from California, a noteworthy feat even if it did have a bumpy ending. They ran out of fuel over Moloka'i and ended up in a grove of *kiawe* (mesquite trees), both wings having been sheared off the airplane and the fuselage broken in two. Amazingly, the aviators walked away with only scratches. ⊠ *Rte. 450, 12 mi east of Kaunakakai, makai side.*

> **need a break?**
>
> The best place to grab a snack or stock up on picnic supplies is the **Neighborhood Store 'N Counter** (⊠ Rte. 450, 16 mi east of Kaunakakai, Puko'o 🕾 808/558–8498). It's the last store on your drive east from Kaunakakai. There's no pay phone here, or in the neighborhood, in case you're looking.

BEACHES

Moloka'i has numerous beaches, many of them quite remote and undisturbed. The largest and most beautiful beaches are along the west coast, but steer clear of their high winter waves. Beaches fronting the Kaunakakai hotels and condominiums are narrow and the shore is not appealing for swimmers, yet the shallow waters are almost always calm for a beginning kayak trip. At the extreme east end of the island is the beach fronting Hālawa Valley, a nice place to relax after the long drive.

Island beaches are free and open to the public. None have telephones or lifeguards. They're all under the jurisdiction of the **Department of Parks, Land and Natural Resources** (🖃 Box 153, Kaunakakai 96746 🕾 808/567–6083).

The beaches below are listed counterclockwise.

West Moloka'i

Kawākiu Beach. Seclusion is the reason to come to this remote beach, accessible only by four-wheel drive or a 45-minute walk. The white-sand beach is beautiful, but rocks and undertow make swimming really dangerous. Head past the Ke Nani Kai condominiums, and look for the dirt road off to the right. Park here and hike in. ⊠ *Kaluako'i Rd.*

Kapukahehu Bay. Locals like to surf just out from this bay in a break called Dixie's or Dixie Maru. The sandy protected cove is usually completely deserted during the weekdays but can fill up when the surf is up. There are no facilities. ⊕ *Drive about 3½ mi beyond Pāpōhaku Beach to end of Kaluako'i Rd. on northwest end of island; beach-access sign on makai side of road points to parking lot.*

Kepuhi Beach. Ideal for strolling, sunbathing, and watching the sunset, this white-sand beach stretches about ½ mi in front of Kaluako'i Hotel and Golf Club. It's fairly windy here, which makes the swimming somewhat dangerous during high tide. There are outdoor showers at the resort and a few shops selling snacks and beachwear. ⊠ *Kaluako'i Hotel and Golf Club, Kaluako'i Rd.*

FodorśChoice ★ **Pāpōhaku Beach.** One of the most sensational beaches in Hawai'i, Pāpōhaku is a 3-mi-long strip of white sand, the longest of its kind on the island. Some places are too rocky for swimming; look carefully before entering the water and go in only when the waves are small (generally in summer). Between the parking lot and the beach are outdoor showers, picnic facilities, and a rest room. ⊠ *Kaluako'i Rd., 2 mi beyond Kaluako'i Hotel and Golf Club, look for sign on makai side of road.*

Central Moloka'i

Oneali'i Beach Park. Smashing views of Maui and Lāna'i across the Pailolo Channel dominate this, the only decent beach park on the island's south-central shore. A narrow and long stretch of sand, Oneali'i has adequate swimming in calm waters year-round, along with rest rooms, outdoor showers, and tree-shaded picnic tables. ⊠ *Rte. 450, east of Hotel Moloka'i.*

East Moloka'i

Hālawa Beach Park. The long drive to Hālawa Valley is worth it, in part because it culminates in this pretty, curving beach flanked by cliffs. Swimming is safe only during the summer. Watch out for hazardous currents and high surf in winter. ✛ *Drive east on Rte. 450 until it dead-ends.*

WHERE TO EAT

West Moloka'i

★ **$$–$$$** ✕ **Maunaloa Room.** Order haute cuisine appetizers such as coconut-crusted shrimp, Moloka'i *'opihi* (a crunchy limpet), or *lumpia* (egg roll) stuffed with *kālua* duck (roasted in an underground oven). Entrées follow a steak-and-seafood theme, and the catch of the day can be prepared with *alae* (a pale-orange salt found in Moloka'i and Kaua'i). Inside, wagon-wheel chandeliers with electric candles typify the hotel restaurant's ranch fixtures. A dinner on the outside deck can't be beat. ⊠ *The Lodge at Moloka'i Ranch, 8 Maunaloa Hwy., Maunaloa* ☎ *808/ 660–2725* ▭ *AE, MC, V.*

Central Moloka'i

$$ ✕ **Oceanfront Dining Room.** This is *the* place to hang out on Moloka'i. Locals relax at the bar listening to live music on weekends, or they come in for theme-night dinners (posters around town tell you what's in store for the week). Prime-rib specials on Friday and Saturday nights draw a crowd. Try the broiled baby-back ribs smothered in barbecue sauce. ⊠ *Hotel Moloka'i, Kamehameha V Hwy., Kaunakakai* ☎ *808/553–5347* ▭ *AE, D, DC, MC, V.*

$–$$ ✕ **Moloka'i Pizza Cafe.** A cheerful, busy restaurant, Moloka'i Pizza is a popular gathering spot for families. Pizza, sandwiches, salads, pasta, fresh fish, and homemade pies are simply prepared and tasty. Kids keep busy on a few little coin-operated rides. ⊠ *Kaunakakai Pl. on Wharf Rd., Kaunakakai* ☎ *808/553–3288* ⌨ *Reservations not accepted* ▭ *No credit cards.*

$–$$ ✕ **Ziggy's.** This comfortable and casual restaurant on a side street near central Kaunakakai starts serving at dawn. Specialties include ribs, fresh fish, and fresh Moloka'i-raised shrimp, not to mention Auntie Rosie's homemade chocolate–macadamia-nut pie. In a separate room, the bar provides a good perch to swap fishing stories—until 2 AM on weekends. Ziggy's also has take-out and even delivers. ⊠ *19 N. Mohala St., Kaunakakai* ☎ *808/553–8166* ▭ *AE, D, MC, V.*

$ ✕ **Oviedo's.** This spare lunch counter specializes in *adobos* (stews) with traditional Filipino spices and sauces. Try the tripe, pork, or beef adobo for a real taste of tradition. You can eat in or take out. ⊠ *145 Ala Malama St., Kaunakakai* ☎ *808/553–5014* ▭ *No credit cards* ☉ *No dinner.*

¢–$ ✕ **Kamuela's.** Local food at a reasonable price is the draw at this Kaunakakai restaurant, which is little more than a crowded room set with rows of simple tables. Family operated, it's a place where you can hang out with the islanders, and selections are also unpretentious: noodles, chicken wings, and the like. Take-out meals are available. ⊠ *93-B Ala*

Malama St., Kaunakakai ☎ *808/553–4826* 🖃 *No credit cards* ☾ *No dinner Sun.*

¢–$ ✕ **Kamuela's Cookhouse.** Kamuela's is the only eatery in rural Kualapu'u. The cozy, casual family-owned restaurant looks like a little plantation house; paintings of hula dancers and island scenes enhance the green-and-white furnishings. The Works, a humongous breakfast with buttermilk pancakes, eggs, and home fries, can keep you fueled all day. At lunch, plates of chicken and pork *katsu* (breaded cutlets) are served with rice. Nightly special favorites are prime rib and pork chops. It's across the street from the Kualapu'u Market. 🖂 *Farrington Hwy., 1 block west of Rte. 470, Kulapūu* ☎ *808/567–9655* 🖃 *No credit cards* ☾ *Closed Mon. No dinner weekends.*

¢–$ ✕ **Kanemitsu Bakery and Restaurant.** Come here for a taste of *lavosh*, a
FodorsChoice pricey flatbread flavored with sesame, taro, Maui onion, Parmesan
★ cheese, or jalapeño. Or try the round Moloka'i bread—a sweet, pan-style white loaf that makes excellent cinnamon toast. 🖂 *79 Ala Malama St., Kaunakakai* ☎ *808/553–5855* 🖃 *No credit cards* ☾ *Closed Tues.*

¢–$ ✕ **Moloka'i Drive Inn.** Fast food Moloka'i-style is served at a walk-up counter. Hot dogs, fries, and sundaes are on the menu, but residents usually choose the foods they grew up on, such as *saimin* (noodle soup), plate lunches, shave ice (snow cone with flavored syrup), and the beloved *loco moco* (rice topped with a hamburger and a fried egg, covered in gravy). 🖂 *857 Ala Malama St., Kaunakakai* ☎ *808/553–5655* 🖃 *No credit cards.*

¢–$ ✕ **Sundown Deli.** This clean little rose-color deli focuses on freshly made take-out food. Sandwiches come on a half-dozen types of bread, and the Portuguese bean soup and chowders are rich and filling. Specials, which might include the likes of vegetarian quiche, change daily. The deli sells vitamins and local-theme T-shirts. 🖂 *145 Ala Malama St., Kaunakakai* ☎ *808/553–3713* 🖃 *AE, MC, V* ☾ *Closed Sun. No dinner.*

¢ ✕ **Outpost Natural Foods.** The heart of Molokai's health-food community, Outpost is a well-stocked store. At the counter you can get fresh juices and delicious sandwiches geared toward the vegetarian palate. It's a great place to pick up local produce and all the ingredients you need for a picnic lunch. 🖂 *70 Makaena St., Kaunakakai* ☎ *808/553–3377* 🖃 *No credit cards* ☾ *Closed Sat. No dinner.*

WHERE TO STAY

Several of the lodging establishments listed in this chapter arrange outdoor excursions and have sports facilities that aren't accessible to nonguests and are hard to find elsewhere.

West Moloka'i

$$$$ 🏨 **The Camps at Moloka'i Ranch.** The "camps" actually consist of one-
FodorsChoice and two-unit canvas tent bungalows, mounted on wooden platforms.
★ Don't let the presence of ecotravelers fool you—the rooms are unexpectedly luxurious, with queen-size beds, self-composting flush toilets, and private outdoor showers. A full buffet breakfast is included; lunch and dinner, served family-style in an open-air pavilion, cost extra. Extensive activities, including snorkeling, kayaking, clay shooting, and mountain biking, are available with discounted rates to guests. Shuttle transport is available for a fee. 🖂 *Maunaloa Hwy. (Box 259), Maunaloa 96770* ☎ *808/552–2791 or 877/726–4656* 🖷 *808/534–1606* ⊕ *www.molokai-ranch.com* ⇆ *100 tents* ⚲ *Restaurant, fans, beach, snorkeling, boating, mountain bikes, hiking, horseback riding, airport shuttle; no a/c, no room phones, no room TVs* 🖃 *AE, D, MC, V* ⦿ *BP.*

$$$$ 🔲 **Hale Aloha.** This spacious four-bedroom, three-bath vacation rental is on 12 secluded acres, has ocean views, and is surrounded by an orchard and woodlands. Wood floors stretch the length of the house, connecting the two kitchens. A wraparound porch leads to a gazebo-covered hot tub. Rooms are open and simple, with wood-beam ceilings. The managers of this property, 1-800-Molokai, also have other rentals in the area. ✉ *Kaluako'i Rd. (Box 20), Maunaloa 96770* ☎ *800/665–6524* ⊕ *www.1-800-molokai.com* 🛏 *1 house* ⟁ *Fans, kitchen, cable TV, in-room VCRs, pool, hot tub; no a/c* ▭ *AE, MC, V.*

★ **$$$$** 🔲 **The Lodge at Moloka'i Ranch.** Moloka'i's plushest accommodation is this Old West–style lodge. Ranching memorabilia and local artwork adorn guest-room walls, with each of the 22 suites individually decorated. All rooms have private lānai and some have skylights. An impressive stone fireplace warms up the central great room, and there's a games room for pleasant socializing during cool Moloka'i evenings. Pathways and a greenhouse delineate the grounds. Spa facilities include massage rooms, a juice bar, and men's and women's saunas. ✉ *Maunaloa Hwy. (Box 259), Maunaloa 96770* ☎ *808/660–2722 or 877/726–4656* 🖷 *808/534–1606* ⊕ *www.molokai-ranch.com* 🛏 *22 suites* ⟁ *Restaurant, in-room data ports, in-room safes, refrigerators, pool, gym, massage, sauna, spa, beach, boating, fishing, mountain bikes, billiards, croquet, hiking, horseback riding, horseshoes, bar, lounge, library, recreation room, children's programs (ages 5–12), concierge* ▭ *AE, D, MC, V.*

★ **$$–$$$$** 🔲 **Paniolo Hale.** Perched high on a ledge overlooking the beach, Paniolo Hale is one of Moloka'i's best condominium properties. Some units have spectacular ocean views. Studios and one- or two-bedroom units all have beautiful screened lānai and kitchens; some have hot tubs for an additional charge. Kitchens are well equipped, and the rooms are tidy and simple. Adjacent to the Kaluako'i Golf Course and a stone's throw from the Kaluako'i Hotel and Golf Club, the property is some nights a playground for wild turkeys and deer. ✉ *Lio Pl. (Box 190), Maunaloa 96770* ☎ *808/552–2731 or 800/367–2984* 🖷 *808/552–2288* ⊕ *www.paniolohaleresort.com* 🛏 *77 condominiums (22 rentals)* ⟁ *Kitchens, microwaves, 18-hole golf course, golf privileges, pool, paddle tennis* ▭ *AE, MC, V.*

$$$ 🔲 **Ke Nani Kai.** These pleasant one- and two-bedroom condo units have ocean views and use of the facilities at the former Kaluako'i Hotel and Golf Club. Furnished lānai have flower-laden trellises, and the spacious interiors are decorated with rattans and pastels. Each unit has a washer-dryer and a fully equipped kitchen. The beach is a five-minute walk away. ✉ *Kaluako'i Rd. (Box 289), Maunaloa 96770* ☎ *808/552–2761 or 800/535–0085* 🖷 *808/552–0045* ⊕ *www.marcresorts.com* 🛏 *120 condominiums (22 rentals)* ⟁ *Fans, kitchens, cable TV, 18-hole golf course, 2 tennis courts, pool, laundry facilities; no a/c* ▭ *AE, D, DC, MC, V.*

$$–$$$ 🔲 **Kaluako'i Villas.** Studios and one-bedroom ocean-view suites are decorated in blue and mauve, with island-style art, rattan furnishings, and private lānai. Units are spread out in 21 two-story buildings covering 29 acres, adjacent to the now defunct Kaluako'i Resort. The view toward the ocean looks across the newly revived golf course. The seclusion and sunsets make this a great find. ✉ *1131 Kaluako'i Rd. (Box 200), Maunaloa 96770* ☎ *808/552–2721 or 800/367–5004* 🖷 *808/552–2201* ⊕ *www.castleresorts.com* 🛏 *36 rooms, 11 suites, 2 1-bedroom cottages* ⟁ *Fans, kitchens, in-room VCRs, 18-hole golf course, pool, beach, shops; no a/c* ▭ *AE, MC, V.*

Central Moloka'i

$$ 🔲 **Moloka'i Shores.** Every room in this oceanfront, three-story condominium complex has a view of the water. One-bedroom, one-bath units or two-bedroom, two-bath units all have full kitchens and furnished lānai, which look out on 4 acres of manicured lawns with picnic tables. There's a great view of Lāna'i in the distance. ⊠ *450 Kamehameha Hwy. (Box 1037), Kaunakakai 96748* ☎ *808/553–5954 or 800/535–0085* ◻ *800/ 633–5085* ⤏ *100 units* ⬧ *Fans, kitchens, cable TV, pool, shuffleboard; no a/c* ▭ *AE, D, MC, V.*

$–$$ 🏨 **Hotel Moloka'i.** Friendly staff members here embody the aloha spirit.
FodorśChoice Low-slung Polynesian-style buildings with wood roof shingles are set
★ waterside. Simple, tropical furnishings with white rattan accents fill the rooms, and a basket swing awaits on the lānai. The Oceanfront Dining Room serves breakfast, lunch, dinner, and libations—with entertainment on weekend nights. Ask about deals in conjunction with airlines and rental-car companies when you make your reservation. ⊠ *Kamehameha V Hwy. (Box 1020), Kaunakakai 96748* ☎ *808/553–5347 or 800/367–5004* ◻ *808/553–5047* ⊕ *www.hotelmolokai.com* ⤏ *45 rooms* ⬧ *Restaurant, fans, some kitchenettes, cable TV, pool, lounge, laundry facilities; no a/c* ▭ *AE, D, DC, MC, V.*

¢–$ 🏨 **A Hawaiian Getaway.** If you want to learn about Moloka'i's history and culture, consider staying here: gracious hosts Lawrence and Catherine Aki have an extensive library and also conduct cultural hikes. Two rooms in the home are available. Small and simply decorated, both have double beds and one has a TV and VCR. Guests use the same entrance, bathroom, and living room as the proprietors. It's within walking distance of Kaunakakai town. ⊠ *270 Kaiwi St., Kaunakakai 96748* ☎ *808/ 553–9803 or 800/274–9303* ✉ *mcai@aloha.net* ⤏ *2 rooms with shared bath* ⬧ *Fans, some cable TV, some in-room VCRs, hair salon, library, laundry facilities; no a/c* ▭ *No credit cards.*

East Moloka'i

$$–$$$ 🏨 **Pu'u O Hoku Ranch.** At the east end of Moloka'i, near mile marker 25, are three ocean-view accommodations on 14,000 isolated acres of pastures and forest. One country cottage has two bedrooms, basic wicker furnishings, and *lau hala* matting on the floors. An airy four-bedroom cottage has a small deck and a somewhat Balinese air. The lodge, which has 11 rooms and seven bathrooms, is similarly decorated. Groups can book the full lodge for $1,000 nightly. Inquire about horseback riding on the property. ⊠ *Rte. 450 (Box 1889), Kaunakakai 96748* ☎ *808/ 558–8109* ◻ *808/558–8100* ⊕ *www.puuohoku.com* ⤏ *1 2-bedroom cottage, 1 4-bedroom cottage, 11 rooms in lodge* ⬧ *Kitchens, pool, hiking, horseback riding; no a/c* ▭ *No credit cards.*

$$ 🏨 **Dunbar Beachfront Cottages.** These two spotlessly clean two-bedroom, one-bath cottages with complete kitchens—each with its own secluded beach—are set near the ocean, about ¼ mi apart. The beach is good for swimming and snorkeling during the summer months and great for whale-watching during the winter. Covered lānai have panoramic vistas of Maui, Lāna'i, and Kaho'olawe across the ocean. ⊠ *King Kamehameha V Hwy., mile marker 18 (HC01, Box 901), Kauanakakai 96748* ☎ *808/ 558–8153 or 800/673–0520* ◻ *808/558–8153* ⊕ *www.molokai-beachfront-cottages.com* ⤏ *2 cottages* ⬧ *Fans, kitchens, in-room VCRs, beach; no a/c* ▭ *No credit cards.*

$–$$ 🏨 **Kamalo Plantation Cottage and Moanui Beach House.** Both of these Polynesian-style cottages have a fully equipped kitchen, living room, dining room, and deck. Kamalo, with one king-size bed, is at the base of a mountain. Moanui has two king-size beds, a TV, and a VCR. It's on a good snorkeling beach and has great views from its huge deck. Homegrown fruit and fresh-baked bread are provided for breakfast. ⊹ *East of Kaunakakai off Rte. 450* 🖉 *HC 01, Box 300, Kaunakakai 96748*

808/558–8236 ⊕ *www.molokai.com/kamalo* ⇌ *2 cottages* ⚘ *Fans, kitchens; no a/c* ⊟ *No credit cards* ⊚ *BP.*

$–$$ ⊞ **Wavecrest.** This oceanfront condominium complex is convenient if you want to explore the east side of the island—it's 3 mi east of Kaunakakai. Individually decorated one- and two-bedroom units have full kitchens. Each has a furnished lānai, some with views of Maui and Lāna'i. Be sure to ask for an updated unit when you make your reservation. The shallow water here is bad for swimming but good for fishing. ⊠ *Rte. 450 near mile marker 13* ⊕ *Friendly Isle Realty, 75 Ala Malama, Kaunakakai 96748* ☎ *808/553–3666 or 800/600–4158* ⊟ *808/553–3867* ⊕ *www.molokairealty.com* ⇌ *126 1- and 2-bedroom condominiums (10 rentals)* ⚘ *Fans, kitchens, 2 tennis courts, pool, beach, shuffleboard; no a/c* ⊟ *V.*

$ ⊞ **Honomuni House.** One acre of tropical garden is complemented by waterfalls and a freshwater stream. Inside the rental are a kitchen, one bedroom, one bath, and a large living-dining room with pull-out couch. An outdoor shower with hot water is an added bonus. It's 17 mi east of Kaunakakai on Route 450. ⊠ *Rte. 450 (HC 1, Box 700), Kaunakakai 96748* ☎ *808/558–8383* ⇌ *1 house* ⚘ *Kitchen; no a/c, no room TVs* ⊟ *No credit cards.*

NIGHTLIFE & THE ARTS

Local nightlife consists mainly of gathering with friends and family, sipping a few cold ones, strumming 'ukulele and guitars, singing old songs, and talking story. Still, there are a few ways to kick up your heels for a festive night out. Go into Kaunakakai, pick up a copy of the weekly *Moloka'i Dispatch*—available along Ala Malama Street at Misaki's Inc., Friendly Market Center, or Moloka'i Wines 'n' Spirits—and see if there's a church supper or square dance. The bar at the Hotel Molokai is always a good place to drink by the tiki torches. For the most part, big events such as fashion shows, New Year's galas, and Hawaiian celebrations are held poolside at the hotel.

Film

Maunaloa Town Cinemas. Folks from all around Moloka'i come here nightly for current blockbusters. ⊠ *Maunaloa Hwy., Maunaloa* ☎ *808/552–2707.*

SPORTS & THE OUTDOORS

Fitness & Spa Centers

The **Spa Venture** is Moloka'i's closest thing to a full-service spa. With natural-wood decor lending a rustic feeling to locker rooms and saunas, the spa fits right in with the low-key ranch hotel. A swimming pool and an exercise room are here, and massages are available. ⊠ *The Lodge at Moloka'i Ranch, Maunaloa Hwy., Maunaloa* ☎ *808/660–2710* ⊚ *Free admittance for lodge guests or nonguests with massage appointment.*

Turning Point Therapeutic Massage has herbal remedies, and the staff offers nutritional advice to keep you at the top of your form. Allana Noury has been studying natural medicine for more than 30 years and is a licensed massage therapist and naturopathic physician. A 30-minute massage is $30; one hour is $50. It's just across the street from the post office in Kaunakakai. ⊠ *125 Puali Pl., Kaunakakai* ☎ *808/553–8034.*

Golf

Compared with the more commercialized Neighbor Islands, Moloka'i has a relatively mellow golf scene.

Although west-end Kaluako'i Hotel remains closed, the **Kaluako'i Golf Club** has reopened with enthusiasm and with the boost of drought-ending rains. In the basking heat, golfers can look out over the Kaiwi Channel, with O'ahu in the background. The 18-hole course includes a driving range and rentals of clubs, shoes, and pull carts. ✛ *Kaluako'i Rd.,* ⊠ *Maunaloa* ☎ *808/552–0255* ⌸ *Greens fee $35, cart $20.*

The **Ironwood Hills Golf Club** in Upcountry Kala'e is a public 9-hole course. This was pastureland until the Del Monte Corporation turned it into a golf course for plantation workers in 1928. It gets windy in the afternoons, so call for a morning tee time. ✛ *Turn off Rte. 460 onto 470 and go north uphill 3½ mi; dirt road to golf course is on left side* ⊠ *Kualapu'u* ☎ *808/567–6000* ⌸ *Greens fee $14, cart $14.*

Hiking

You can make a day of hiking to Kalaupapa and back along the 3-mi, 26-switchback trail that is also used for the Moloka'i Mule Ride. The trail is well maintained by the **National Park Service** (⊡ Box 2222, Kalaupapa 96742 ☎ 808/567–6802). You need a confirmed reservation with **Damien Tours** (☎ 808/567–6171) to see Kalaupapa village.

Historical Hikes of West Moloka'i has six guided hikes, ranging from two to six hours, focusing on Moloka'i's cultural past. One takes you to an ancient quarry; another follows the remains of an ancient paved trail. Other hikes investigate the remains of an early fishing village at Kaupoa Bay and explore high sea cliffs where Hawaiian chiefs played games during the Makahiki season. Backpacks are provided, as is lunch on intermediate and advanced hikes. You meet at Moloka'i Ranch Outfitters Center. Guides Lawrence and Catherine Aki also run A Hawaiian Getaway vacation rental. ⊠ *Moloka'i Ranch Outfitters Center, Maunaloa Hwy., Maunaloa* ☎ *808/552–2797, 808/553–9803, or 800/274–9303* ⊕ *www.molokai-aloha.com/hikes* ⌸ *$45–$125.*

Horseback Riding

Hitting the trail since 1983, **Moloka'i Horse and Wagon Ride** offers a 1½-hour ride ($50) that takes in a heiau, a mountain-top whale-watching lookout, an enormous mango grove, and a beach. Trips take six riders and start at 10 AM. Call at least a day in advance to make arrangements. ✛ *15 mi east of Kaunakakai off Rte. 450* ⊠ *Kaunakakai* ☎ *808/558–8380.*

Set on the prow of the island's Maui-facing east end, **Pu'u O Hoku Ranch** keeps a stable of magnificent, amiable brown horses that are available for trail rides starting at $55 an hour. The peak experience is a four-hour beach ride ($120) that culminates at a secluded cove where the horses are happy to swim, rider and all. Bring your own lunch. ✛ *Rte. 450, 20 mi east of Kaunakakai* ☎ *808/558–8109.*

Water Sports

FISHING   The six-passenger, 31-ft cruiser **Alyce C.** (⊠ Kaunakakai Wharf ☎ 808/558–8377) runs excellent sportfishing excursions. The cost is $400 for a nine-hour trip, $300 for five to six hours. Shared charters are available.

Fun Hogs Hawai'i (⊠ Kaunakakai Wharf ☎ 808/567–6789) takes out the 27-ft *Ahi* for half-day ($350), six-hour ($400), and full-day ($450) sportfishing. Full-day bottom-fishing trips, all equipment furnished, are $500.

SAILING   The 42-ft Cascade sloop *Satan's Doll* is your craft with **Moloka'i Charters** (⊠ Kaunakakai Wharf ☎ 808/553–5852). The company arranges two-hour sails for $40 per person. Half-day sailing trips cost $50 per person, including soft drinks and snacks. A minimum of four people is required, but shared charters can be arranged.

SNORKELING &   **Bill Kapuni's Snorkel & Dive** (☎ 808/553–9867 or 877/553–9867) leaves
SCUBA DIVING   Kaunakakai Wharf daily for two-hour snorkeling excursions. Whale-watching cruises in season, underwater massages, and diving certification can all be arranged. Prices vary with the length of dive and number of people involved.

Spectacular north-shore sightseeing trips with **Fun Hogs Hawai'i** (⊠ Kaunakakai Wharf ☎ 808/567–6789) cost $500 and are only for the sea hardy. Whale-watching trips from December to April take 2½ hours, depart at 8 and 10:30, and cost $65 per person. Bring your own snacks and drinks. You can also book a snorkeling excursion or a custom cruise.

Moloka'i Charters (⊠ Kaunakakai Wharf, Kaunakakai 96748 ☎ 808/553–5852) takes people via sailboat on full-day snorkeling excursions to the island of Lāna'i for $90 per person. Soft drinks and a picnic lunch are included.

Jim Brocker, owner of **Moloka'i Fish and Dive** (⊠ 61 Ala Malama St., Kaunakakai ☎ 808/553–5926), can fill you in on how to find the best snorkel sites, rent you the gear, then send you home with an armful of custom Moloka'i souvenirs. Jim is also the author of two books about Moloka'i, *A Portrait of Molokai* and *The Lands of Father Damien*.

SHOPPING

Moloka'i has one main commercial area: Ala Malama Street in Kaunakakai. There are no department stores or shopping malls, and the clothing available is typical island wear.

Most stores in Kaunakakai are open Monday through Saturday between 9 and 6. In Maunaloa most shops close by 4 in the afternoon and all day Sunday.

West Moloka'i

A handful of family-run businesses line the main drag of Maunaloa, a rural plantation town.

Arts & Crafts

The **Big Wind Kite Factory and Plantation Gallery** (⊠ 120 Maunaloa Hwy., Maunaloa ☎ 808/552–2364) has custom-made appliquéd kites you can fly or display. Designs range from hula girls to tropical fish. Also in stock are kits, paper kites, minikites, and wind socks. Ask to go on the factory tour, or take a free kite-flying lesson. The gallery is intermingled with the kite shop and carries everything from locally made crafts to Hawaiian books and CDs, sunglasses, and incense.

Clothing

A Touch of Moloka'i (⊠ Kaluako'i Hotel and Golf Club, Kaluako'i Rd., Maunaloa ☎ 808/552–0133) sells high-end resort wear with tropical prints. This is some of the nicer clothing on Moloka'i and worth the drive to take a look.

Grocery Store

Victuals and travel essentials are available at the **Maunaloa General Store** (✉ 200 Maunaloa Hwy., Maunaloa ☎ 808/552–2346). Open Monday–Saturday 8–6, it's convenient for guests staying at the nearby condos of Kaluako'i Hotel and Golf Club, who shop here for meat, produce, dry goods, drinks, and all the little things you find in a general store.

Central Moloka'i

You can walk from one end of Kaunakakai's main street, Ala Malama, to the other in about five minutes—unless you like to browse, of course. Ho'olehua has just one must-shop stop, the Plantation Store, next to Coffees of Hawai'i.

Arts & Crafts

Kamakana Fine Arts Gallery (✉ 110 Ala Malama Ave., Kaunakakai ☎ 808/553–8520) represents only artists who live on the island, including world-class talent in photography, wood carving, ceramics, and Hawaiian musical instruments. This business actively supports the local community by showcasing talents that may otherwise go undiscovered. It's above American Savings Bank.

Clothing

Casual, knockabout island wear is sold at **Imports Gift Shop** (✉ 82 Ala Malama St., Kaunakakai ☎ 808/553–5734), across from Kanemitsu Bakery. **Moloka'i Island Creations** (✉ 62 Ala Malama St., Kaunakakai ☎ 808/553–5926) carries exclusive swimwear, beach cover-ups, sun hats, and tank tops. **Moloka'i Surf** (✉ 130 Kamehameha Hwy., Kaunakakai ☎ 808/553–5093) is known for its wide selection of Moloka'i T-shirts, swimwear, and sports clothing.

Grocery Stores

Friendly Market Center (✉ 93 Ala Malama St., Kaunakakai ☎ 808/553–5595) is the best-stocked supermarket on the island. Its slogan—"Your family store on Moloka'i"—is truly credible: hats, T-shirts, and sun-and-surf essentials keep company with fresh produce, meat, groceries, liquor, and sundries. Locals say the food is fresher here than at the other major supermarket in town. It's open weekdays 8:30–8:30 and Saturday 8:30–6:30.

Misaki's Inc. (✉ 78 Ala Malama St., Kaunakakai ☎ 808/553–5505) is a grocery with authentic island allure. It has been in business since 1922. Pick up housewares and beverages here, as well as your food staples, Monday–Saturday 8:30–8:30 and Sunday 9–noon.

Don't let the name **Moloka'i Wines 'n' Spirits** (✉ 77 Ala Malama St., Kaunakakai ☎ 808/553–5009) fool you. Along with a surprisingly good selection of fine wines and liquors, the store also carries gourmet cheeses and snacks. It's open Sunday–Thursday 9 AM–10 PM, Friday and Saturday until 10:30.

Island Goods

The **Plantation Store** (✉ Kualapu'u Base Yard, Farrington Hwy., Ho'olehua ☎ 808/567–9023) has Moloka'i-made products, including Moloka'i-grown coffee. In the market for jewelry made from coconut shells and wiliwili seeds? This is your place. You can also buy local artwork, homemade jellies and jams, island soaps, pen-and-ink drawings of Moloka'i landscapes, and handcrafted pottery.

Jewelry

Imports Gift Shop (✉ 82 Ala Malama St., Kaunakakai ☎ 808/553–5734) sells a decent collection of 14-karat-gold chains, rings, earrings, and bracelets, plus a jumble of Hawaiian quilts, pillows, books, and post-cards. It also carries Hawaiian heirloom jewelry, unique replicas of popular Victorian pieces. These stunning gold pieces are made to order with your Hawaiian name inscribed on them.

Moloka'i Island Creations (✉ 62 Ala Malama St., Kaunakakai ☎ 808/553–5926) carries its own unique line of jewelry, including sea opal, coral, and sterling silver, as well as other gifts and resort wear.

Sporting Goods

Moloka'i Bicycle (✉ 80 Mohala St., Kaunakakai ☎ 808/553–3931 ⊕ www.molokaibicycle.com) rents and sells mountain and road bikes as well as jogging strollers, kids' trailers, helmets, and racks. It supplies maps and information on biking and hiking and will drop off and pick up equipment for a fee nearly anywhere on the island.

Moloka'i Fish and Dive (✉ 61 Ala Malama St., Kaunakakai ☎ 808/553–5926) is *the* main source for your sporting needs, from snorkeling rentals to free and friendly advice. Ask to see the owner's original-design Moloka'i T-shirts and his books about Moloka'i.

MOLOKA'I A TO Z

To research prices, get advice from other travelers, and book travel arrangements, visit www.fodors.com.

AIR TRAVEL

If you're flying in from the mainland United States, you must first make a stop in Honolulu. From there, it's a 25-minute trip to the Friendly Isle.

CARRIERS Hawaiian Airlines flies its DC-9 jet aircraft daily between O'ahu and Moloka'i. A round-trip ticket can cost up to $200 per person. Island Air, the puddle-jumper arm of Aloha Airlines, provides daily flights between Molokai and O'ahu or Maui on its 18-passenger de Haviland Dash-8 Twin Otters. Pacific Wings flies an eight-passenger Cessna daily between O'ahu and Moloka'i.

Pacific Wings also flies from Honolulu to Ho'olehua Airport and from Honolulu to the airstrip in Kalaupapa. Your arrival there should coincide with one of the authorized ground tours of the area. Otherwise you'll be asked to leave. Paragon Air runs commuter and charter flights and trips to Kalaupapa. Moloka'i Air Shuttle flies from Honolulu to Kalaupapa.

🛫 **Hawaiian Airlines** ☎ 800/367-5320 ⊕ www.aa.com. **Island Air** ☎ 800/323-3345 ⊕ www.islandair.com. **Moloka'i Air Shuttle** ☎ 808/567-6847 in Honolulu. **Pacific Wings** ☎ 808/873-0877 or 888/575-4546 ⊕ www.pacificwings.com. **Paragon Air** ☎ 808/244-3356 or 800/428-1231 ⊕ www.paragon-air.com.

AIRPORTS

Moloka'i's transportation hub is Ho'olehua Airport, a tiny airstrip 8 mi west of Kaunakakai and about 18 mi east of Maunaloa. An even smaller airstrip serves the little community of Kalaupapa on the north shore.

🛫 **Ho'olehua Airport** ☎ 808/567-6140. **Kalaupapa Airfield** ☎ 808/567-6331.

AIRPORT TRANSFERS From Ho'olehua Airport, it takes about 10 minutes to reach Kaunakakai and 25 minutes to reach the condominiums of Kaluako'i Hotel by car. Since there's no rush hour, traffic won't be a problem. There's no public bus.

Shuttle service for two passengers costs about $18 from Ho'olehua Airport to Kaunakakai and about $18 to Kaluako'i Hotel and Golf Club. A trip to Molokai Ranch costs $28, divided by the number of passengers. For shuttle service via a car or a van, call Moloka'i Off-Road Tours and Taxi or Molokai Outdoor Activities. Kukui Tours and Limousines has drivers available daily 8–5:

🔷 Kukui Tours and Limousines ☎ 808/553-8022. Moloka'i Off-Road Tours and Taxi ☎ 808/553-3369. Molokai Outdoor Activities ☎ 808/553-4477 or 877/553-4477.

CAR RENTAL

Budget maintains a counter near the baggage claim area at the airport. Dollar also has offices at Ho'olehua Airport, and your rental car can be picked up in the parking lot. Expect to pay from $30 to $50 per day for a standard compact and from $36 to $55 for a midsize car. Rates are seasonal and may run higher during the peak winter months. It's best to make arrangements in advance. If you're flying on Island Air or Hawaiian Airlines, see whether fly-drive package deals are available—you might luck out on a less-expensive rate. Hotels and outfitters might also offer packages.

Locally owned Island Kine Rent-a-Car offers airport or hotel pickup and sticks to one rate year-round for vehicles ($35 to $50 per day) in a broad spectrum from two- and four-wheel drives to 15-passenger vans.

🔷 Major Agencies: **Budget** ☎ 808/451-3600 or 800/527-7000 ⊕ www.budget.com. **Dollar** ☎ 808/567-6156 or 800/367-7006 ⊕ www.dollar.com.

🔷 Local Agency: **Island Kine Rent-a-Car** ☎ 808/553-5242 ⊕ www.molokai-aloha.com/cars.

CAR TRAVEL

If you want to explore Moloka'i from one end to the other, it's best to rent a car. With just a few main roads to choose from, it's a snap to drive around here. From the Ho'olehua Airport, turn right on the main road, Route 460 (also called Maunaloa Highway), to reach Kaluako'i and left if you're staying in Kaunakakai.

The gas stations are in Kaunakakai and Maunaloa. When you park your car, be sure to lock it—thefts do occur. Drivers must wear seat belts or risk a $42 fine. Children under three must ride in a federally approved child passenger restraint device, easily leased at the rental agency. Ask your rental agent for a free *Moloka'i Drive Guide*.

EMERGENCIES

Round-the-clock medical attention is available at Moloka'i General Hospital. Severe cases or emergencies are often air-lifted to Honolulu.

🔷 Emergency Services: **Ambulance and general emergencies** ☎ 911. **Coast Guard** ☎ 808/552-6458 on O'ahu. **Fire** ☎ 808/553-5601 in Kaunakakai, 808/567-6525 at Ho'olehua Airport. **Police** ☎ 808/553-5355.

🔷 Hospital: **Moloka'i General Hospital** ⊠ 280A Puali St., Kaunakakai ☎ 808/553-5331.

TOURS

ADVENTURE TOURS
Walter Naki is a friendly, knowledgeable guide who custom-designs tours through his Moloka'i Action Adventures. One of his most popular excursions is a north-shore cruise aboard a 21-ft Boston Whaler. He is also a competent guide for year-round fishing trips.

The Moloka'i Ecoadventure Centre, headquartered at the Ke Nana Kai Resort, rents jeeps, kayaks, bikes, and scuba equipment and can provide experienced guides for all activities, including four-wheel-drive trips.

Moloka'i Outdoors is a "one-stop shop" provider of customized visits to this unusual island. The company will shuttle you from the airport, set you up with one of its own rental cars, rent you a bike or kayak, and guide you where you want to go—with particular emphasis on the east end of the island.

If you want a smart island resident to set you up with a unique vacation rental, a car to drive, a kayak tour, private cooking, and personalized help with tours of any kind, you should call Moloka'i Rentals and Tours. It's like having a close friend on the island.

🏠 **Moloka'i Action Adventures** ☎ 808/558-8184. **Moloka'i Ecoadventure Centre** ☎ 808/552-2277. **Moloka'i Outdoors** ☎ 808/553-4477 or 877/553-4477 ⊕ www.molokai-outdoors.com. **Moloka'i Rentals and Tours** ☎ 808/553-5663 or 800/553-9071 ⊕ www.molokai-rentals.com.

BIKE TOURS   Moloka'i Bicycle's guides have the exclusive right to take mountain bikers to Pu'u O Hoku Ranch. You might ride along an eastern ridge rimming Hālawa Valley to four waterfalls and a remote pool for swimming or pedal on sea cliffs to a secluded beach. Daily tours for a minimum of two people cost $45 per person for a half day and $65 for a full day, including lunch.

🏠 **Moloka'i Bicycle** ☎ 808/553-3931.

KALAUPAPA TOURS   Tours of this former leper colony are lead through Damien Tours by longtime residents of Kalaupapa, who are well versed in its history. The four-hour van tour begins and ends at Kalaupapa Airfield if you arrive by air, or at the foot of the 3-mi trail if you hike down the mountain. Tours depart at 10:15 Monday–Saturday and cost $30. Reservations are essential. No one under 16 is allowed. Bring your own lunch and water.

You can contact Damien Tours directly, and it can arrange everything including flights. Moloka'i Mule Ride can also make all of your arrangements—transport, flight or mule ride, and tour. Moloka'i Air Shuttle also offers packages, or flights can be arranged separately from the tour through several airlines.

🏠 **Damien Tours** ☎ 808/567-6171. **Moloka'i Air Shuttle** ☎ 808/567-6847 in Honolulu. **Moloka'i Mule Ride** ☎ 808/567-6088.

MO'OMOMI DUNE TOURS   The Nature Conservancy conducts about 12 tours annually of Mo'omomi Dunes, a fine example of a pristine coastal ecosystem on West Moloka'i. These educational walks are for those interested in geology, archaeological sites, rare plants, snails, and bird life, many of which are endangered. Tours are held one Saturday per month and must be booked in advance. Directions are provided on booking. The suggested donation is $10 for members and $25 for nonmembers, which includes an annual membership.

🏠 **The Nature Conservancy** ✉ 23 Pueo Pl., Kualapu'u ☎ 808/553-5236.

VAN TOURS   Visit Hālawa Valley, Kalaupapa Lookout, Maunaloa town, and other points of interest in the comfort of an air-conditioned van on four- or six-hour tours. At Moloka'i Off-Road Tours and Taxi, Pat and Alex Pua'a are your personal guides. They'll even help you mail a coconut back home. Tours cost $36 to $49 and begin at 9 AM. Charters are also available.

Moloka'i Outdoor Activities, based in the lobby of the Hotel Moloka'i, can organize island van tours with experienced guides who focus on local culture, customs, and history. It can also arrange trips to Kamakou Preserve.

Kukui Tours and Limousines offers half-day and full-day tours to various points of interest on the island in seven-passenger vehicles.

🏠 **Kukui Tours and Limousines** ☎ 808/553-8022. **Moloka'i Off-Road Tours and Taxi** ☎ 808/553-3369. **Molokai Outdoor Activities** ☎ 808/553-3369.

WAGON TOURS   Island residents Junior and Nani Rawlins take folks on a scenic and informative amble in a horse-drawn wagon. The first stop is 'Ili'ili'ōpae Heiau, the largest outdoor shrine in Hawai'i. Next, tour the largest mango grove in the world before hitting the beach for coconut husking, barbecuing, and fishing. Call for arrangements and directions. Tours cost $50, include lunch, and are available daily.

🎏 **Moloka'i Wagon Ride** ☎ 808/558-8132 or 808/558-8380.

VISITOR INFORMATION

There's tourist information available in kiosks and stands at the airport in Ho'olehua or at the Moloka'i Visitors Association. The Maui Visitors Bureau has travel information for Maui County, of which Moloka'i is a part.

Molokaievents.com, Inc., has information on island events and can help you plan your own events on the island.

Car-rental agencies distribute the free *Moloka'i Drive Guide* along with maps and other up-to-date information.

🎏 **Maui Visitors Bureau** ✆ Box 580, Wailuku, Maui 96793 ☎ 808/244-3530 ⊕ www. visitmaui.com. **Molokaievents.com, Inc.** ☎ 808/567-6789 ⊕ www.molokaievents. com. **Moloka'i Visitors Association** ✉ 10 Kamehameha V Hwy. (Box 960), Kaunakakai ☎ 808/553-3876 or 800/800-6367 ⊕ molokai-hawaii.com.

LĀNAʻI

FODOR'S CHOICE

Scuba diving at Cathedrals, South Lānaʻi

Formal Dining Room, restaurant in East Lānaʻi

Garden of the Gods, North Lānaʻi

Hulopoʻe Beach, South Lānaʻi

Lodge at Kōʻele, East Lānaʻi

HIGHLY RECOMMENDED

Hiking the Munro Trail, East Lānaʻi

ʻIhilani, restaurant in South Lānaʻi

Mānele Bay Hotel, South Lānaʻi

Shipwreck Beach, North Lānaʻi

Updated by
Shannon
Wianecki

ALTHOUGH TODAY LĀNA'I is an island that welcomes visitors with its rustic charm, it hasn't always been so amiable. The earliest Polynesians believed it to be haunted by evil ghosts who gobbled up unsuspecting souls. In 1836, a pair of missionaries named Dwight Baldwin and William Richards came and went after failing to convert the locals to Christianity. In 1854, a group of Mormons tried to create the City of Joseph here, but they were forced to abandon their mission after a drought in 1857.

With the Mormons came Walter Gibson, who managed to acquire ownership of much of the land and transformed Lāna'i into a ranching colony: by 1892 close to 50,000 sheep grazed the dry hillsides, competing for food with goats and cattle. Eighteen years later a New Zealander, George Munro, was hired by an investment group that later formed the Lāna'i Company to reforest the land, which marked the first effort to protect Lāna'i's eroding watershed. The hundreds of Cook pines that define the profile of Lāna'i today form part of his legacy.

There were also attempts to grow sugar, but they never took hold in Lāna'i: on the east side, the ruins of a boat landing and an abandoned church tell the story of this ill-fated crop.

In 1922, American-born Jim Dole's Hawaiian Pineapple Company bought the island for $1.1 million, thus marking a time of great transition for Lāna'i. Hundreds of people, mostly of Asian descent, moved to the island. To accommodate them, Dole built Lāna'i City on the flatlands, where the crater floor is flanked by volcanic slopes. He also planned the harbor at Kaumalapau, from which his pineapples would be shipped. Four years later, as he watched the first harvest sail away to Honolulu, the enterprising businessman could safely say that Dole Plantation was a success.

For decades, Lāna'i was known as the Pineapple Island, with hundreds of acres filled with the golden fruit. But in the late 1980s pineapples ceased to be profitable. The solution? Dole's Lāna'i Company, currently known as Castle & Cooke Resorts, built two sophisticated resorts and developed a tourism industry that has started to thrive.

Lāna'i City, the island's only population center, with about 2,800 residents, remains an old plantation town with a few family-run shops, diner-style eateries, and an art center. Tall Cook pines shade streets filled with tiny houses with colorful facades, tin roofs, and tidy gardens.

Lāna'i is home to many natural wonders. To the northwest lies the Garden of the Gods, where rocks and boulders are scattered across a crimson landscape. Adjacent is a trail leading through the Kānepu'u Preserve, a dryland forest with some 48 native species, including the endangered Hawaiian gardenia. On the southern tip, the waters at Hulopo'e Beach are so clear that within a minute of snorkeling you can see turquoise and jade fish. After hiking or driving to the summit of Lāna'ihale, a 3,370-ft-high windswept perch in the eastern reaches, you'll find a splendid view of nearly every Hawaiian island.

Though Castle & Cooke still owns 98% of this 141-square-mi island, pineapple fields have given way to open, rolling green lands and championship golf courses. Despite the changes, Lāna'i remains remote and intimate, earning its new nickname, Hawai'i's Most Secluded Island.

If you have 1 day

If you can squeeze in just one day of exploring, rent a four-wheel-drive vehicle and get to know the back roads, where the landscape's power and beauty are immutable. If you're staying at or close to the Lodge at Kō'ele, take a look here at the solitary **Norfolk Pine** ① and the little historic **Ka Lokahi o Ka Mālamalama Church** ② before heading out to the **Garden of the Gods** ⑮ and the **Kānepu'u Preserve** ⑯ . After lunch in **Lāna'i City** ③, drive down to **Lu'ahiwa Petroglyphs** ⑤ and **Kaunolū** ⑦; then head for a late-afternoon swim at Hulopo'e Beach at **Mānele Bay** ⑧. If you're a guest at the Mānele Bay Hotel, reverse the itinerary.

If you have 3 days

On the first day, follow the above itinerary. On the second day, take an adventurous tour of the undeveloped east shore. Pack a picnic lunch and start the day with a drive to **Shipwreck Beach** ⑬ for a morning walk. Then drive along a bumpy coastal road to explore **Keōmuku** ⑫, **Kahe'a Heiau** ⑩, **Naha** ⑨, and Lōpā Beach. Start your third day with a cool morning hike up the **Munro Trail** ⑭ to Lāna'ihale. A drive out to **Kaumalapau Harbor** ④ shows you the departure point of Lāna'i's barge since the early pineapple days.

If you have 5 days

Follow the three-day itinerary and dedicate the fourth day to the sport of your choice. On the fifth day, rent a jeep to drive out to spectacular Polihua Beach or take a half-day fishing trip or snorkeling–scuba diving expedition.

Exploring Lāna'i

Most of Lāna'i's sights are out of the way—rent a four-wheel-drive vehicle, ask your hotel's concierge for a road map, make sure you have a full tank, and bring a snack. Don't stray from marked paths, and ask your hotel's concierge about road conditions before you set out. Admission is free to all sights mentioned.

The main road in Lāna'i, Route 440, is also called Kaumalapau Highway or Mānele Road.

In the Islands, the directions *mauka* (toward the mountains) and *makai* (toward the ocean) are often used.

About the Restaurants

Lāna'i has developed its own version of Hawai'i regional cuisine. The upscale menus at the Lodge at Kō'ele and Mānele Bay Hotel draw on the bounty provided by local hunters and fisherfolk—everything from *'ahi* (yellowfin tuna) to venison. Lāna'i City's eclectic fare ranges from local-style plate lunches to Louisiana ribs and pizza.

About the Hotels

Though Lāna'i has few properties, it does have a range of price options. The Lodge at Kō'ele and Mānele Bay Hotel are luxury resorts, which their rates reflect. If you're on a budget, seek out a bed-and-breakfast or consider the Hotel Lāna'i. House rentals, a great option for families, give you a taste of everyday life on the island.

WHAT IT COSTS					
	$$$$	**$$$**	**$$**	**$**	**¢**
RESTAURANTS	over $30	$20–$30	$12–$20	$7–$12	under $7
HOTELS	over $200	$150–$200	$100–$150	$60–$100	under $60

Restaurant prices are for one main course at dinner. Hotel prices are for two people in a standard double room in high season, including tax and service.

Timing

Lāna'i is generally warm and clear, though winter weather is cooler and less predictable. It's sunniest at sea level, while up-country, in Lāna'i City, the nights and mornings can be chilly and the fog can settle in.

SOUTH & WEST LĀNA'I

Pineapples once blanketed the Pālāwai Basin, the flat area south of Lāna'i City. Today it's used primarily for agriculture and grazing and holds historic treasures. You'll need a four-wheel-drive vehicle to explore this rugged area.

a good drive

Start at the Lodge at Kō'ele to get a glimpse of early ranching history. The lone **Norfolk Pine** ❶ ▶ in front of the Lodge, planted in 1875, was the source of inspiration for the island's current watershed of pines. On the left stands **Ka Lokahi o Ka Mālamalama Church** ❷.

Pause in **Lāna'i City** ❸ for an espresso, and then drive south on Route 440 until you reach a major intersection. Go straight, following the highway west to **Kaumalapau Harbor** ❹, the island's main seaport. Backtrack to the intersection, turn right, and take Route 440 south. After about a mile you'll see a dirt road on your left leading to the **Lu'ahiwa Petroglyphs** ❺, ancient rock carvings.

Return to Highway 440 and drive 2 mi south until the road veers left. Here, go straight on unpaved Kaupili Road; then take the fourth left and navigate your jeep down to the well-preserved archaeological sites of **Halulu Heiau** ❻ and **Kaunolū** ❼.

Back on Highway 440, drive down the long, steep hill. At the bottom awaits **Mānele Bay** ❽. The road ends at the island's only true swimming area, Hulopo'e Beach.

TIMING   You could explore this small area in just half a day, but if you like water sports, you may want to count on a few hours at Hulopo'e Beach. The south is almost always sunny, clear, and warm, so wear sunscreen and head for shade at midday.

What to See

❻ **Halulu Heiau.** The carefully excavated remains of an impressive heiau, which was actively used by Lāna'i's earliest residents, attest to this spot's sacred history. As late as 1810, this hilltop sight was also considered a place of refuge, where those who had broken *kapu* (taboos) were forgiven and where women and children could find safety in times of war. ✛ *From Lāna'i City follow Hwy. 440 (Mānele Rd.) south; when road makes sharp left, continue straight on Kaupili Rd.; turn makai onto fourth dirt road.*

❷ **Ka Lokahi o Ka Mālamalama Church.** This picturesque church was built in 1938 to provide Hawaiian services for Lāna'i's growing population—for many people, the only other Hawaiian church, in coastal Keōmuku, was too far away. Typical of plantation days, the church had

Hitting the Links

Lāna'i has two championship golf courses. The pine-covered fields of the Experience at Kō'ele stretch across hills punctuated by lakes, streams, and waterfalls. At the Challenge at Mānele, the Pacific Ocean makes a daunting water hazard: dolphins and whales have been known to distract even the most serious golfer.

Hiking & Biking

Only 30 mi of Lāna'i's roads are paved. But red-dirt roads and trails, ideal for hiking and mountain biking, will take you to abandoned villages with historic *heiau* (stone altars), isolated beaches, and forest preserves. Follow a self-guided walk through Hawai'i's largest native dryland forest, explore the Munro Trail over Lāna'ihale with views of plunging canyons, or participate in a guided hike along an old, coastal fisherman trail or across Koloiki Ridge.

6

Snorkeling & Scuba Diving

When you have a dive site such as Cathedrals—with pinnacle formations and mysterious caverns—it's no wonder that snorkeling and scuba diving buffs consider exploring the waters off Lāna'i akin to having a religious experience. For the best underwater viewing, try Hulopo'e Beach, a Marine Conservation Area, or go on an excursion with Trilogy or the Adventure Lāna'i Eco Centre.

---

to be moved from its original Lānāi Ranch location when the Lodge at Kō'ele was built. Services are still held, in Hawaiian and English. ✛ *Left of entrance to Lodge at Kō'ele.*

④ Kaumalapau Harbor. Built in 1926 by the Hawaiian Pineapple Company, which later became Dole, this is Lāna'i's principal seaport. The cliffs that flank the western shore are as much as 1,000 ft tall. No water activities are allowed here, but if you're in the area on Thursday, you'll witness the arrival of the barge: the island depends on its weekly deliveries. ✛ *From Lāna'i City follow Hwy. 440 (Kaumalapau Hwy.) west as far as it goes; turn left and drive about 7 mi makai.*

❼ Kaunolū. Atop the island's highest cliffs, Kaunolū was once a prosperous fishing village. This important archaeological site includes terraces, stone floors, and platforms. The impressive 90-ft drop to the ocean is called **Kahekili's Leap.** Warriors would make the death-defying jump into the mere 12 ft of water below to show their courage to Hawai'i's King Kamehameha I, who used the island as his summer hideaway. ✛ *From Lāna'i City follow Hwy. 440 (Mānele Rd.) south; when road makes sharp left, continue straight on Kaupili Rd. through pineapple fields; turn makai onto fourth dirt road.*

❸ Lāna'i City. This tidy plantation town was built in 1924 by Jim Dole. It reflects his wish to create a model plantation village: a simple grid of roads lined with tall Cook pines and all the basic services a person might need. Visit the **Lāna'i Arts Program** (⊠ 339 7th Ave.) to get a glimpse of this island's creative abundance.

❺ Lu'ahiwa Petroglyphs. On a steep slope overlooking the Pālāwai Basin are 34 boulders with carvings. Drawn in a mixture of ancient and historic styles dating to the late 1700s and early 1800s, the simple stick-

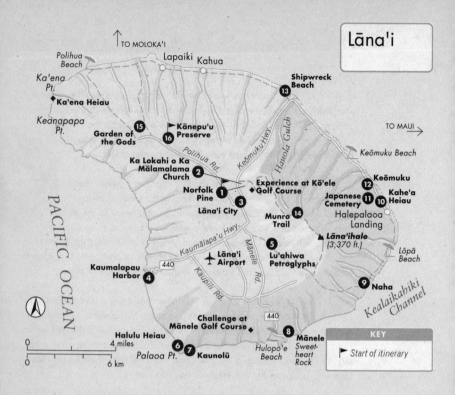

figure illustrations depict life on Lāna'i. Some of the stones are believed to possess the spiritual power of rain gods. ✣ *From Lāna'i City follow Hwy. 440 (Mānele Rd.) south 1 mi to an unmarked dirt road that leads left through pineapple fields; at end of that road, walk up unmarked trail to petroglyphs.*

⑧ Mānele Bay. The site of a Hawaiian village dating from AD 900, Mānele Bay is flanked by lava cliffs that are hundreds of feet high. Though a Marine Life Conservation District, it's the island's only public boat harbor and was the location of most post contact shipping until Kaumalapau Harbor was built in 1926. The ferry to and from Maui also pulls in here.

Just offshore you can catch a glimpse of **Pu'upehe.** Often called Sweetheart Rock, the isolated 80-ft-high islet carries a sad Hawaiian legend. The rock is named after Pehe, a woman so beautiful that her husband, afraid that others would steal her away, kept her hidden in a sea cave. One day, while Pehe was alone, the surf surged into the cave and she drowned. With the help of the gods, her grief-stricken husband buried her offshore on the summit of this rock and then jumped to his own death. ✣ *From Lāna'i City follow Hwy. 440 (Mānele Rd.) south to bottom of hill and look for harbor on your left.*

▶ ① Norfolk Pine. More than 100 ft high, this majestic pine tree was planted here, at the former site of the manager's house, in 1875. Almost 30 years later, George Munro, then the ranch manager, would observe how, in foggy weather, water collected on its foliage, forming a natural rain. This drip led to the planting of Cook pines along the ridge of Lāna'ihale and across town. ✉ *Entrance of Lodge at Kō'ele.*

NORTH & EAST LĀNA'I

The north and east sections of Lāna'i are wild and untouched. A ghost town and deserted heiau are the only traces of civilization. You'll need a four-wheel-drive vehicle to explore this side of the isle. Pack a picnic lunch and bring plenty of drinking water.

a good drive

Set out north of the Lodge at Kō'ele on Keōmuku Highway: turn left on the road between the Stables at Kō'ele and the tennis courts. Follow the dirt road a couple of miles and turn right at the crossroads onto Polihua Road, which heads north through the dryland forest of **Kānepu'u Preserve 16** ▶ and, 1½ mi beyond, the **Garden of the Gods 15**.

Return to Keōmuku Highway and head east. After about 1 mi, make a right onto the only road in sight, and you're on your way to the **Munro Trail 14**, a 9-mi route that runs over the top of Lāna'ihale, the mountain that rises above Lāna'i City.

Back on Keōmuku Highway, head makai—at an unofficial scenic point between mile markers 4 and 5 you'll find awesome views of Moloka'i, Maui, and Kaho'olawe and a first glimpse of the stranded World War II oiler at **Shipwreck Beach 13**.

If you feel adventurous, head southeast at the fork in the road where the beach starts, and follow the dirt road along the coast. The landscape changes from coastal dunes to *kiawe* forest (kiawe is a mesquite-type wood; watch for thorns!). Along the way, you'll come across abandoned Hawaiian homesteads. Five miles later, dozens of tall coconut trees announce the site of the old village **Keōmuku 12**, once a bustling sugar-mill town. Pause at the **Japanese Cemetery 11**. Nearby are the ruins of a temple called **Kahe'a Heiau 10**, but you may need an experienced guide to find it. The road passes the often-deserted Lōpā Beach and ends 3 mi later at the remnants of an old Hawaiian fishpond at **Naha 9**.

TIMING Give yourself a day to tour the island's northern and eastern reaches. Keep your eye on the sky: the highlands tend to attract heavy fog. If you're a hiker, you'll want a day just to enjoy the journey up to Lāna'ihale. Since many of the roads are bumpy, it takes more time to reach sights than it does to actually experience them. But getting there is half the fun.

What to See

15 Garden of the Gods. This preternatural plateau is scattered with boulders of different sizes, shapes, and colors, the products of a million years

Fodor'sChoice ★

of wind erosion. Its lunar appearance changes colors from rich red to purple as the sun sets. Magnificent views of the Pacific Ocean, Moloka'i, and, on clear days, O'ahu provide the perfect backdrop for photographs. ⊹ *From The Stables at Kō'ele, follow dirt road through hay fields 2 mi; turn right at crossroads and head through ironwood forest 1½ mi.*

11 Japanese Cemetery. In 1899, sugar came to this side of Lāna'i. A plantation took up about 2,400 acres and seemed a profitable proposition, but that same year, disease wiped out the labor force. This authentic Buddhist shrine commemorates the Japanese workers who died. ⊹ *6½ mi southeast from where Keōmuku Hwy. dead-ends at Shipwreck Beach, on dirt road running along north shore.*

10 Kahe'a Heiau. What was once a central place of worship for the people of Lāna'i now may be hard to find through the kiawe overgrowth. Equally hidden are the remaining stone platforms of the **Halepaloa Landing**, a wharf used by the Maunalei Sugar Company (1899) to ship cane. Some say that the company failed because attempted construction of a railroad disturbed the sacred stones of the heiau, which angered the gods, who then turned the drinking water salty, forcing closure in 1901. ✢ *6½ mi southeast from where Keōmuku Hwy. dead-ends at Shipwreck Beach, on dirt road running along north shore.*

▶ **⑯ Kānepu'u Preserve.** The 590 acres of this native dryland forest are under the stewardship of the Nature Conservancy of Hawai'i. Kānepu'u contains the largest remnant of this rare forest type. More than 45 native species of plants, including the endangered Hawaiian gardenia, grow in the shade of such rare trees as Hawaiian sandalwood, olive, and ebony. A short self-guided loop trail, with eight signs illustrated by local artist Wendell Kaho'ohalahala, reveals this ecosystem's beauty and the challenges it faces. ⊠ *Polihua Rd., 6 mi north of Lāna'i City* ☎ *808/537–4508* ⊘ *Daily 9–4.*

⑫ Keōmuku. There's an eerie beauty about Keōmuku, with its crumbling, weed-choked stone walls and homes. During the late 19th century, this busy Lāna'i community of some 900 to 2,000 residents served as the headquarters of Maunalei Sugar Company. After the company failed, the land was used for ranching, but by 1954 the area lay abandoned. Its church, **Ka Lanakila O Ka Mālamalama,** the oldest on the island, was built in 1903. It has been partially restored by volunteers. ✢ *5 mi along unpaved road southeast of Shipwreck Beach.*

★ **⑭ Munro Trail.** This 9-mi path along a pine-covered ridge was named after George Munro, manager of the Lāna'i Ranch Co., who began a reforestation program in the 1950s to provide a much-needed watershed. The trail climbs Lāna'ihale (House of Lāna'i), which, at 3,370 ft, is the island's highest point; on clear days you'll be treated to a panorama of canyons and almost all of the Hawaiian Islands. Be careful: the roads get very muddy, and trade winds can be strong. This is a difficult hike in general: it's steep, the ground is uneven, and there is little shade. ✢ *From Lodge at Kō'ele head north on Keōmuku Hwy. for 1¼ mi, then turn right onto dirt road; trailhead is ½ mi past cemetery on right.*

⑨ Naha. An ancient rock-walled fishpond—visible at low tide—lies here, where the sandy shorelines end and the cliffs begin their rise along the island's shores. The beach is a frequent resource for local fisherfolk, but the treacherous tides make this a dangerous place for swimming. ✢ *East side of Lāna'i, at end of dirt road that runs from end of Keōmuku Hwy. along eastern shore.*

★ **⑬ Shipwreck Beach.** The rusting World War II tanker may be a clue that the waters off this 8-mi stretch of sand aren't friendly. Strong trade winds have propelled innocent vessels onto the reef ever since 1824, when the first shipwreck was recorded. Some believe that the unknown oiler you see stranded today, however, was merely abandoned. ⊠ *End of Keōmuku Hwy. heading north.*

BEACHES

Though all of Lāna'i's beaches provide peaceful strolls, sunbathing, and, of course, sunsets, only Hulopo'e Beach is safe for swimming. To reach most of the beaches, listed clockwise from the south, you will need a four-wheel-drive vehicle; note that it is illegal to go four-wheeling on the beaches themselves.

Fodor'sChoice **Hulopo'e Beach.** A five-minute walk from the Mānele Bay Hotel, Hu-
★ lopo'e is one of the best beaches in all of Hawai'i. The sparkling crescent of this Marine Life Conservation District beckons with clear waters

that are safe for swimming, great snorkeling reefs, tide pools, and, often, spinner dolphins. Shady grassy expanses are perfect for picnics, and there are showers, rest rooms, and changing facilities. ⊹ *From Lāna'i City follow Hwy. 440 (Mānele Rd.) south to bottom of hill; road dead-ends at beach's parking lot.*

Lōpā Beach. A popular surfing spot for locals, Lōpā is also an ancient fishpond. With majestic views of West Maui and Kaho'olawe, this remote, white-sand beach is a great place for a picnic. Don't let the sight of surfers fool you: the channel's currents are too strong for swimming. ⊹ *East side of Lāna'i, 7 mi down dirt road that runs from end of Keōmuku Hwy. along eastern shore.*

Polihua Beach. This often-deserted beach should get a star for beauty with its long, wide stretch of white sand and the clear views of Moloka'i. The drive to get here isn't easy, though, and frequent high winds whip up sand and waves. Strong currents and a sudden drop in the ocean floor make swimming extremely dangerous. ⊹ *Northwest shore, 11 mi from Lāna'i City, past Garden of the Gods.*

★ **Shipwreck Beach.** Beachcombers come to this windswept area for shells and washed-up treasures; photographers for great shots of Moloka'i, just across the 9-mi wide Kalohi Channel; and walkers for the broad, 8-mi-long stretch of sand. Kaiolohia, as it's also called, is not, however, for swimmers. ⊹ *North shore, 10 mi north of Lāna'i City at end of Keōmuku Hwy.*

WHERE TO EAT

Although Lāna'i's restaurant choices are limited, the menus are wide-ranging. If you dine at the Lodge at Kō'ele or Mānele Bay Hotel, you'll be treated to top-notch cuisine served in upscale surroundings. Lāna'i City's restaurants are unpretentious, with simple fare. A lesser-known alternative is the clubhouse at the Challenge golf course, which, seasonally, stays open until 9 PM.

South & West Lāna'i

★ **$$$$** ✕ **'Ihilani.** The Mānele Bay Hotel's dining room shimmers with crystal and silver as light filters through the glass ceiling. Executive chef Pierre Bellon prepares fresh island ingredients in the tradition of the Mediterranean, in particular southern France. Sterling choices on the menu include the crispy whole *moi,* a fish once reserved for Hawaiian royalty, and a lavender-honey-glazed Muscovy duck breast. You can opt for a five-course food-and-wine pairing menu. ⊠ *Mānele Bay Hotel* ☎ *808/565–7700* ☖ *Reservations essential* ▭ *AE, DC, MC, V* ☾ *No lunch.*

North & East Lāna'i

$$$$ ✕ **Formal Dining Room.** Reflecting the elegant country atmosphere of the
Fodor'sChoice Lodge at Kō'ele, this romantic octagonal restaurant offers intimate ta-
★ bles close to a roaring fireplace. The walls are hand-stenciled by local artists. The changing menu is an expansion of Hawai'i regional cuisine that includes specialties such as pancetta-wrapped roasted Lāna'i venison loin and seared Hawaiian snapper with gingered crab. ⊠ *Lodge at Kō'ele* ☎ *808/565–7300* ☖ *Reservations essential* ⌂ *Jacket required* ▭ *AE, DC, MC, V* ☾ *No lunch.*

$$$–$$$$ ✕ **Henry Clay's Rotisserie.** With the only bar and fine dining in Lāna'i City, this is a busy spot, right at the Hotel Lāna'i. Louisiana-style ribs, Cajun-style shrimp, and gumbo add up to what chef Henry Clay Richardson calls "American country," but he brings it back home with island venison and locally caught fish. A fireplace and paintings by local artists add to the country feel. ✉ *Hotel Lāna'i, 828 Lāna'i Ave., Lāna'i City* ☎ *808/565–7211* ☰ *MC, V.*

$–$$ ✕ **Pele's Other Garden.** Mark and Barbara Zigmond's dynamic little eatery is a deli and bistro all in one. For lunch, mile-high sandwiches and fresh-baked breads are a great reward after an arduous hike. You can also order picnic lunches served in a convenient cooler bag. At night, the tiny spot turns into an intimate tablecloth-dining bistro, complete with soft jazz music. Bring your own wine, start with bruschetta, then choose from a selection of pasta dishes or pizzas. ✉ *811 Houston St., Lāna'i City* ☎ *808/565–9628 or 888/764–3354* ☰ *AE, DC, MC, V.*

¢–$ ✕ **Blue Ginger Café.** This small, no-frills eatery may look run-down with its bare floor and plastic tablecloths, but the menu is diverse, and the wonderful owner, Georgia Abilay, has turned this place into one of the town's most popular hangouts. At breakfast, try a three-egg omelet with rice or fresh pastries, which are available each morning. Lunchtime selections range from burgers and pizza to Hawaiian staples such as saimin and *spam musubi* (fried spam on rice). Try a stir-fry with mahimahi for dinner. ✉ *409 7th Ave., Lāna'i City* ☎ *808/565–6363* ☰ *No credit cards.*

¢–$ ✕ **Petro's Pizza and Subs.** New to Lāna'i is the convenience of pizza delivery. Petro's serves pizza and hot and cold subs. Fresh cookies and breads are baked on the premises. If you happen to need a helium balloon for a festive occasion, you can find it here, too. ✉ *408 8th St., Lāna'i City* ☎ *808/565–6622* ☰ *D, DC, MC, V.*

WHERE TO STAY

For years the island's only accommodation was the no-fuss Hotel Lāna'i in Lāna'i City. Today, you can choose among classy resorts, pleasant B&Bs, and a few rental houses.

South & West Lāna'i

★ $$$$ ▥ **Mānele Bay Hotel.** This property has spectacular views of Lāna'i's dramatic coastline and beyond. Courtyard gardens, arcades, breezeways, and bridges connect guest-room buildings. The architecture combines Mediterranean and traditional Hawaiian elements. Asian art, as well as work by local artists, fills the common areas. The crescent of Hulopo'e Bay is just minutes away, and a *keiki* (children's) program focuses on the island's cultural and environmental heritage, with petroglyph walks, crab hunting, 'ukulele playing, and more. ✍ *Box 310, Lāna'i City 96763* ☎ *808/565–7700 or 800/321–4666* 🖷 *808/565–3868* 🌐 *www.manelebayhotel.com* ⇆ *222 rooms, 28 suites* ⧖ *4 restaurants, room service, in-room safes, minibars, cable TV with movies and video games, 18-hole golf course, 6 tennis courts, pool, health club, spa, archery, billiards, bar, library, baby-sitting, children's programs (ages 5–13), Internet, convention center* ☰ *AE, DC, MC, V.*

North & East Lāna'i

$$$$ ▥ **Captain's Retreat.** This private two-story cedar home is always popular. Within walking distance of town, it provides a great family or friends' getaway, with 3,000 square ft, four bedrooms (including one master suite with private bath and patio), a redwood deck, an outside shower, and a roomy kitchen. The house accommodates 10 comfortably; single-room bookings aren't available. Okamoto Realty may have other rentals available as well. ✉ *Okamoto Realty, 730 Lāna'i Ave., Lāna'i City 96763*

☎ 808/565–7519 or 888/565–6106 ⊕ www.lanairental.com 📶 1 4-bedroom unit ⊟ MC, V.

$$$$
Fodor'sChoice
★

🏨 **Lodge at Kō'ele.** On 21 acres, in the highlands at the edge of Lāna'i City, this grand country estate is a luxurious and romantic mountain retreat. Secluded by old pines, 1½ mi of paths meander through gardens with a pond and an orchid greenhouse. Inside, beamed ceilings, stone fireplaces, a music room, a tea room, and the magnificent Great Hall create an old-world feel. The porch offers views of spectacular sunsets. 🏠 Box 310, Lāna'i City 96763 ☎ 808/565–7300 or 800/321–4666 🖷 808/565–3868 ⊕ www.lodgeatkoele.com 📶 88 rooms, 14 suites ♻ 2 restaurants, room service, in-room safes, minibars, cable TV with movies and video games, 8-hole golf course, 3 tennis courts, pool, health club, archery, croquet, horseback riding, bar, lobby lounge, baby-sitting, children's programs (ages 5–12), Internet ⊟ AE, DC, MC, V.

$–$$
🏨 **Hotel Lāna'i.** Built in 1923 to house visiting plantation executives, this 11-room inn was once the only accommodation on the island. The rooms, with country quilts, light pine woods, and watercolors by a local artist, make you feel like you're staying in someone's home. Those rooms with patios that look out over the garden and Lāna'i City are especially nice. A Continental breakfast with fresh-baked breads is included in the rate. ✉ 828 Lāna'i Ave., Lāna'i City 96763 ☎ 808/565–7211 or 800/795–7211 🖷 808/565–6450 ⊕ www.hotellanai.com 📶 11 rooms ♻ Restaurant; no a/c, no room TVs, no smoking ⊟ AE, MC, V.

$
🏨 **Dreams Come True.** Michael and Susan Hunter's B&B in the heart of Lāna'i City has canopy beds, antique furnishings, and memorabilia from their many years in Asia and on Lāna'i. Fresh fruit from their own trees and passion fruit lemonade make breakfast a special occasion. Susan is a trained massage therapist and provides in-house massage for $35 an hour. Vehicle rental is also available. The Hunters also rent out the four-bedroom, four-bathroom Lāna'i Avenue Plantation Home. It's available in its entirety as a vacation rental or as individual guest rooms. ✉ 1168 St., Lāna'i City 96763 ☎ 808/565–6961 or 800/566–6961 🖷 808/565–7056 ⊕ www.circumvista.com/dreamscometrue.html 📶 3 rooms ♻ Massage, car rental; no room phones, no room TVs, no smoking ⊟ AE, D, MC, V.

NIGHTLIFE & THE ARTS

Nightlife

Lāna'i is certainly not known for its nightlife. Less than a handful of places stay open past 9 PM. At the resorts, excellent piano music or light live entertainment makes for a quiet, romantic night.

At the **Hotel Lāna'i** (☎ 808/565–7211), a lively bar stays open until the last dinner guest leaves. The cozy cocktail lounge at the **Lodge at Kō'ele** (☎ 808/565–7300) stays open until 11 PM. The lodge also features music in its Great Hall every evening from 7 to 10. Hale Aheahe (House of Gentle Breezes), the classy lounge at the **Mānele Bay Hotel** (☎ 808/565–7700), offers entertainment every evening from 5:30 to 9:30.

The Arts

A surprising number of talented artists have made Lāna'i their home. Their work enhances both resorts and restaurants in town and is for sale in gift stores.

The **Visiting Artist Program** (☎ 800/321–4666), at either the Lodge at Kō'ele or the Mānele Bay Hotel, brings authors, chefs, and musicians to the island for informal presentations. Participants are often famous chefs, such as Rick Tramonto, owner and chef of Chicago's nationally acclaimed restaurant Tru. Other celebrity visits have included the Eroica Trio, Clint Eastwood, and Ellen Goodman. **Lāna‘i Art Program** (⊠ 339 7th Ave., Lāna‘i City ☎ 808/565–7503) is the center for local artists to practice and display their crafts. You can book 2½-hour art sessions via the resorts.

Film

The 153-seat **Lāna‘i Theater and Playhouse** (⊠ 465 7th Ave., Lāna‘i City ☎ 808/565–7500), a '30s landmark, presents first-run movies.

SPORTS & THE OUTDOORS

Camping

Camping isn't encouraged on Lāna‘i outside the one, official campground at Hulopo‘e: the isle's ecosystem is fragile; islanders are keen on privacy; and, unless you know about tides, winds, and undertows, camping on the beach can be hazardous. The companies below will help you play it safe and be respectful of the island.

Adventure Lāna‘i Eco Centre (☎ 808/565–7373 ⊕ www.adventurelanai. com) in town can set you up with complete camping packages and provides a wealth of inside tips. **Castle & Cooke Resorts** (☎ 808/565–3982 for permits) operates one great, little campground at Hulopo‘e Beach with clean rest rooms, fire pits, and showers. You must call first to obtain a permit. **Destination Lāna‘i** (☎ 808/565–7600 or 800/947–4774) can help you locate no-frills camp sites.

Fitness & Spa Centers

The Fitness Center at the Lodge at Kō‘ele. The center is small, but it provides state-of-the-art equipment as well as yoga classes. In conjunction with the Spa at Mānele, specialty treatments and massages are available. A heated pool keeps you agreeably warm. Nonguests are not permitted to use the fitness center but may book treatments at the spa. ⊠ *Lodge at Kō‘ele* ☎ *808/565–7300.*

The Spa at Mānele. With granite stone floors, onyx marble countertops, and lots of natural wood, this spa offers an outstanding menu of state-of-the-art pampering, such as the Ali‘i Banana Coconut Scrub and the Hehi Lani-Royal Foot Treatment. Massages start at $95 for 50 minutes. A fitness center with cardiovascular equipment, free weights, whirlpools, and a steam room is also on-site. ⊠ *Mānele Bay Hotel, Lāna‘i City* ☎ *808/ 565–7700.*

Golf

Cavendish Golf Course. This 9-hole course in the pines is free, but a donation for upkeep is requested. Call the Lodge at Kō‘ele concierge for information and directions. Bring your own clubs. ☎ *808/565–7300.*

Challenge at Mānele. This world-class 18-hole course was designed by Jack Nicklaus. The clubhouse serves lunch and, in the busier season, light dinners as well. ⊠ *Mānele Bay Hotel* ☎ *808/565–2222* 🖼 *Greens fee $165 for guests of the Lodge at Kō‘ele or Mānele Bay Hotel, $205 for nonguests; cart included.*

Experience at Kō‘ele. The Lodge at Kō‘ele has an 18-hole championship course designed by Greg Norman. There's also an 18-hole executive putting course, free to guests but not accessible to nonguests. The clubhouse serves lunch. ⊠ *Lodge at Kō‘ele* ☎ *808/565–4653* 🖼 *Greens fee $165 guests, $205 nonguests; cart included.*

Hiking

Lāna'i is a hiker's paradise with remote trails snaking through dryland forest, over rugged grasslands, and along splendid shores. Make sure to get a good map before setting out.

Koloiki Ridge, a wide, easy trail of about 2 ½ mi behind the Lodge at Kō'ele, overlooks the island's north side. Ask the concierge at the Lodge about guided, interpretative hikes.

Lāna'i Fisherman Trail takes about an hour and follows the oceanside perimeter of Mānele Bay Hotel, along cliffs bordering the golf course. Mānele Spa offers early morning fitness hikes along the trail; if you're lucky, you may see dolphins leaping offshore.

★ The **Munro Trail**, a strenuous 9-mi trek that takes about eight hours, is the island's most popular hike. There is an elevation gain of 1,400 ft, leading you to the lookout at Lāna'i's highest point, Lāna'ihale.

Horseback Riding

The **Stables at Kō'ele** (☎ 808/565–4424) takes you through scenic high-country trails. It has a corral full of well-groomed horses for riders of all ages and skill levels. Your options include sunset rides, private saunters, and four-hour adventures. Prices start at $50 for one hour. You can also arrange lessons or customized daylong rides.

Mountain Biking

John, the friendly owner of **Adventure Lāna'i Eco Centre** (☎ 808/565–7373 ⊕ www.adventurelanai.com), rents 21-speed mountain bikes for less than $30 per day. He and his team also offer downhill bike treks for $89 and multitreks ($129) that get you into a variety of island sports.

Sporting Clays & Archery

At **Lāna'i Pine Sporting Clays and Archery Range** (⊹ off Keōmuku Hwy. ☎ 808/559–4600), a rustic, 14-station sporting-clays course, lies in a pine-wood valley overlooking the sea. A single shooter can complete the course in an hour. The cost is $145 for 100 targets and $85 for 50 targets. Beginners can start with a 25-target lesson for $75. The Archery Range has 14 straw-bale stations at 15- or 35-yard ranges. Private and group lessons are offered. The $45 introduction includes an amusing "pineapple contest"—contestants are given five arrows with which to hit a pineapple. The winner takes home a lovely crystal prize. Additionally, an air-rifle range is under construction. When it's completed, compressed air rifles will be available for shooting stationary targets with moving parts.

Water Sports

DEEP-SEA FISHING Jeff Menzie captains the *Kila Kila* (☎ 808/565–2387 or 808/565–4555), a 53-ft fishing vessel with a spacious cockpit and the comforts of a luxury ship. Its heritage includes world records for sportfishing in Florida and Kona. A four-hour deep-sea-fishing trip with up to six passengers costs $825; a full day runs $1,200. Book your expedition with the concierges at the resorts.

Sherry Menzie (Captain Jeff's wife) pilots **Spinning Dolphin Fishing Charters** (☎ 808/565–6613); charters are a little harder to book, as she's also the island's harbormistress. Make advance reservations for her 28-ft diesel-powered Omega sportfisher, which handles both heavy- and light-tackle fishing. Half-day ($400) and full-day ($600) charters out of Mānele Bay are private, with a six-person maximum. Bring your own lunch. Juice and ice are provided.

**Hulopo`e Beach** is one of Hawai`i's most outstanding snorkeling destinations. Several companies offer snorkeling tours, and the hotels rent equipment as well.

★ Some say scuba diving doesn't get better than off the shores of Lāna`i. The dive site **Cathedrals,** off the south shore, gets its name from the spacious caverns created by numerous pinnacles that rise from depths of 60 ft to just below the water's surface. In these beautiful chambers lurk spotted moray eels, lobster, and ghost shrimp. **Sergeant Major Reef,** on the south shore, is made up of three parallel lava ridges, a cave, and an archway, with rippled sand valleys between the ridges. Depths range from 15 ft to 50 ft.

Adventure Lāna`i Eco Centre (☎ 808/565–7373 ⊕ www.adventurelanai. com) offers unique kayaking, scuba diving, and snorkeling adventures in remote locations, often excellent whale-watching spots. The four-hour excursions cost around $89. You can also opt for surf safaris and learn to navigate wooden long boards with local instructors.

Spinning Dolphin Fishing Charters (☎ 808/565–6613) offers private snorkeling and sightseeing tours. When the whales are here (December through April), three-hour whale-watching tours are available.

Trilogy Oceansports Lāna`i (☎ 808/667–7721 or 888/628–4800 ⊕ www. sailtrilogy.com) offers a daily four-hour morning snorkel sail on a 51-ft catamaran with lessons, equipment, and meals included. It charters two-tank dives on their catamarans for experienced divers for $160— ask about the availability of introductory dives. You can also sign up for ocean kayaking adventures or book a blue-water dolphin watch, a whale-watching sail, or a sunset cruise. It's best to book trips through your hotel concierge.

SHOPPING

Except for the boutiques at the Lodge at Kō`ele and Mānele Bay Hotel, which sell high-end gifts and sundries, Lāna`i City is the island's only place to shop. Its main streets, 7th and 8th streets, have friendly general stores straight out of the '20s. Stores are closed on Sunday, during lunch, and after 5.

General Stores

International Food and Clothing Center. You may not find everything the name implies, but this old-fashioned emporium does stock items for your everyday needs, from fishing gear to beer. ✉ 833 `Ilima Ave., Lāna`i City ☎ 808/565–6433.

**Lāna`i City Service.** In addition to being a gas station and car-rental operation, this outfit sells sundries, T-shirts, and island crafts in the **Plantation Store.** ✉ 1036 Lāna`i Ave., Lāna`i City ☎ 808/565–7227.

Pine Isle Market. You can get everything from cosmetics to canned vegetables here at one of Lāna`i City's two supermarkets. It's a great place to buy fresh fish. ✉ 356 8th St., Lāna`i City ☎ 808/565–6488.

Richard's Shopping Center. Richard Tamashiro founded this store in 1946, and the Tamashiro clan continues to run the place. Along with groceries, the store has a fun selection of Lāna`i T-shirts. ✉ 434 8th St., Lāna`i City ☎ 808/565–6047.

Clothing

Local Gentry. This tiny, classy store has clothing for every need, from casual men's and women's beachwear to evening resort wear, shoes, jewelry, and hats. A small selection of children's apparel can also be found here. ⊠ *363 7th St., Lāna'i City* ☎ *808/565–9130.*

Crafts

Gifts with Aloha. Hand-painted clothing and casual resort wear is sold alongside a great collection of Hawaiiana books and the work of local artists, including ceramic ware, *raku* (Japanese-style lead-glazed pottery), fine handblown glass, and watercolor prints. ⊠ *811-B Houston St., Lāna'i City* ☎ *808/565–6589.*

Lāna'i Art Program. The center offers art classes and has a gift shop that sells unique Lāna'i handicrafts, from painted silk scarves to beaded jewelry. ⊠ *339 7th St., Lāna'i City* ☎ *808/565–7503.*

LĀNA'I A TO Z

To research prices, get advice from other travelers, and book travel arrangements, visit www.fodors.com.

AIR TRAVEL

You can reach Lāna'i from O'ahu's Honolulu International Airport, Maui's Kahului Airport, or the Big Island's Keāhole-Kona International Airport. The flight takes about a half hour. Round-trip tickets start at $170.

CARRIERS Hawaiian Airlines offers two round-trip flights daily on DC-9 jets. Island Air offers several flights daily on 18-passenger Dash-6s and 37-seat Dash-8s.
🛫 **Hawaiian Airlines** ☎ 800/882-8811 ⊕ www.hawaiianair.com. **Island Air** ☎ 808/484-2222 or 800/323-3345 ⊕ www.islandair.com.

AIRPORTS

The small Lāna'i Airport is in the southwest area of the island. There's a federal agricultural inspection station so that guests departing to the mainland can check luggage directly.
🛫 **Lāna'i Airport** ☎ 808/565-6757.

AIRPORT Lāna'i Airport is a 10-minute drive from Lāna'i City. If you're staying
TRANSFERS at the Hotel Lāna'i, the Lodge at Kō'ele, or the Mānele Bay Hotel, you'll be met by a shuttle. If you're staying elsewhere in Lāna'i City, make arrangements with your hosts. There are no public buses on the island, but you can arrange a taxi transfer or, if you want to travel in style, splurge on a private limousine—$42 to the Lodge at Kō'ele or $81 to Mānele Bay Hotel.
🛫 **Rabaca's Limousine Service** ☎ 808/565-6670.

BOAT & FERRY TRAVEL

Ferries cross the channel five times daily, departing from Lahaina on Maui and Mānele Bay Harbor on Lāna'i. The crossing takes 45 minutes and costs $25 each way. Lāna'i City Service offers shuttle service to the harbor.
🛫 **Expeditions** ☎ 808/661-3756 or 800/695-2624 ⊕ www.golanai.com.

CAR RENTAL

Renting a car is essential if you plan to do a lot of exploring. Compact cars are available, but most of Lāna'i's sights require a four-wheel-drive vehicle. Make your reservations way in advance of your trip, because Lāna'i's fleet of vehicles is limited. Lāna'i City Service, a subsidiary of Dollar Rent A Car, is open daily 7–7. Its fees for Jeep Wranglers run around $130 a day, and compact cars are about $60. Four-wheel-drive Cherokees are also available for about $145 per day. Adventure Lāna'i Eco Centre offers Safari Jeep Wranglers for about $100 per day; weekly rentals are also available. You can also rent four-wheel-drive vehicles from Michael and Susan Hunter, proprietors of Dreams Come True.

Local Agencies: Adventure Lāna'i Eco Centre ☎ 808/565-7373 ⊕ www. adventurelanai.com. **Dreams Come True** ☎ 808/565-6961 or 800/566-6961. **Lāna'i City Service** ✉ Lāna'i Ave. at 11th St. ☎ 808/565-7227 or 800/533-7808.

CAR TRAVEL

There are only 30 mi of paved road on the island, and secondary roads usually aren't marked. From Lāna'i City, the streets extend outward as paved roads with two-way traffic. Keōmuku Highway runs north to Shipwreck Beach, and Highway 440, also known as Mānele Road or Kaumalapau Highway, runs south down to Mānele Bay and Hulopo'e Beach and west to Kaumalapau Harbor. The rest of your driving takes place on bumpy, muddy roads.

The island doesn't have traffic lights, and you'll never find yourself in a traffic jam, but it's easy to get lost; before heading out on your explorations, ask for a map at your hotel desk, and verify that you're headed in the right direction. The only gas station on the island is in Lāna'i City, at Lāna'i City Service.

EMERGENCIES

In an emergency, dial **911** to reach an ambulance, the police, or the fire department. The Lāna'i Community Hospital is the island's health-care center. It has 24-hour ambulance service and a pharmacy.

Lāna'i Community Hospital ✉ 628 7th St., Lāna'i City ☎ 808/565-6411.

SIGHTSEEING TOURS

Adventure Lāna'i Eco Centre's popular 4x4 Adventure Trek takes you to the island's most scenic places, stopping where and when you want. Guides "talk story" about local history and flora and fauna. They even provide binoculars, snorkeling gear, snacks, and drinks. Expect to pay around $90. Kayak adventures and bike treks also start at around $90.

Rabaca's Limousine Service offers four-wheel-drive tours that start at $50 per hour, with a three-hour minimum.

Adventure Lāna'i Eco Centre ☎ 808/565-7373 ⊕ www.adventurelanai.com. **Rabaca's Limousine Service** ☎ 808/565-6670.

VISITOR INFORMATION

Destination Lāna'i, the island's visitors bureau, is your best bet for general information and maps. Feel free to stop in, but be aware that opening hours are erratic. The Maui Visitors Bureau also has some information on the island.

Destination Lāna'i ✉ 730 Lāna'i Ave., Suite 102, Lāna'i City 96763 ☎ 808/565-7600 ⊕ www.aloha.net/~dlanai. **Maui Visitors Bureau** ☎ 808/244-3530 ⊕ www. visitmaui.com.

UNDERSTANDING HAWAI'I

THE ALOHA SHIRT:
A COLORFUL SWATCH
OF ISLAND HISTORY

ELVIS PRESLEY had an entire wardrobe of them in the '60s films *Blue Hawaii* and *Paradise, Hawaiian Style.* During the '50s, entertainer Arthur Godfrey and bandleader Harry Owens often sported them on television shows. John Wayne loved to lounge around in them. Mick Jagger felt compelled to buy one on a visit to Hawai'i in the 1970s. Dustin Hoffman, Steven Spielberg, and Bill Cosby avidly collect them.

The roots of the aloha shirt go back to the early 1930s, when Hawai'i's garment industry was just beginning to develop its own unique style. Although locally made clothes did exist, they were almost exclusively for plantation workers and were constructed of durable palaka or plain cotton material.

Out of this came the first stirrings of fashion: Beachboys and schoolchildren started having sport shirts made from colorful Japanese kimono fabric. The favored type of cloth was the kind used for children's kimonos—bright pink and orange floral prints for girls; masculine motifs in browns and blues for boys. In Japan, such flamboyant patterns were considered unsuitable for adult clothing, but in the Islands such rules didn't apply, and it seemed the flashier the shirt, the better—for either sex. Thus, the aloha shirt was born.

It was easy and inexpensive in those days to have garments tailored to order; the next step was moving to mass production and marketing. In June 1935, Honolulu's best-known tailoring establishment, Musa-Shiya, advertised the availability of "Aloha shirts—well tailored, beautiful designs and radiant colors. Ready-made or made to order . . . 95¢ and up." This is the first known printed use of the term that would soon refer to an entire industry. By the following year, several local manufacturers had begun full-scale production of "aloha wear." One of them, Ellery Chun of King-Smith, registered as local trademarks the terms "Aloha Sportswear" and "Aloha Shirt" in 1936 and 1937, respectively.

These early entrepreneurs were the first to create uniquely Hawaiian designs for fabric as well—splashy patterns that would forever symbolize the Islands. A 1939 *Honolulu Advertiser* story described them as a "delightful confusion [of] tropical fish and palm trees, Diamond Head and the Aloha Tower, surfboards and leis, ukuleles and Waikīkī beach scenes."

The aloha wear of the late 1930s was intended for—and mostly worn by—tourists, and interestingly, a great deal of it was exported to the mainland and even Europe and Australia. By the end of the decade, for example, only 5% of the output of one local firm, the Kamehameha Garment Company, was sold in Hawai'i.

World War II brought this trend to a halt, and during the postwar period, aloha wear really came into its own in Hawai'i itself. A strong push to support local industry gradually nudged island garb into the workplace, and kama'āina began to wear the clothing that previously had been seen as attire for visitors.

In 1947, for example, male employees of the City and County of Honolulu were first allowed to wear aloha shirts "in plain shades" during the summer months. Later that year, the first observance of Aloha Week started the tradition of "bankers and bellhops . . . mix[ing] colorfully in multihued and tapa-designed Aloha shirts every day," as a local newspaper's Sunday magazine supplement noted in 1948. By the 1960s, "Aloha Friday," set aside specifically for the wearing of aloha attire, had become a tradition. In the following decade, the suit and tie practically disappeared as work attire in Hawai'i, even for executives.

"The Aloha Shirt: A Colorful Swatch of Island History" first appeared in ALOHA magazine. Reprinted with permission of Davick Publications.

Most of the Hawaiian-theme fabric used in manufacturing aloha wear was designed in the Islands, then printed on the mainland or in Japan. The glowingly vibrant rayons of the late '40s and early '50s (a period now seen as aloha wear's heyday) were at first printed on the East Coast, but manufacturers there usually required such large orders, local firms eventually found it impossible to continue using them. By 1964, 90% of Hawaiian fabric was being manufactured in Japan—a situation that still exists today.

Fashion trends usually move in cycles, and aloha wear is no exception. By the 1960s, the "chop suey print" with its "tired clichés of Diamond Head, Aloha Tower, outrigger canoes [and] stereotyped leis" was seen as corny and garish, according to an article published in the *Honolulu Star-Bulletin*. But it was just that outdated aspect that began to appeal to the younger crowd, who began searching out old-fashioned aloha shirts at the Salvation Army and Goodwill thrift stores. These shirts were dubbed "silkies," a name by which they're still known, even though most of them were actually made of rayon.

Before long, what had been 50¢ shirts began escalating in price, and a customer who had balked at paying $5 for a shirt that someone had already worn soon found the same item selling for $10—and more. By the late 1970s, aloha-wear designers were copying the prints of yesteryear for their new creations.

The days of bargain silkies are now gone. The few choice aloha shirts from decades past that still remain are offered today by specialized dealers for hundreds of dollars apiece, causing many to look back to the time when such treasures were foolishly worn to the beach until they fell apart. The best examples of vintage aloha shirts are now rightly seen as art objects, worthy of preservation for the lovely depictions they offer of Hawai'i's colorful and unique scene.

— DeSoto Brown

THESE VOLCANIC ISLES

DAWN AT THE CRATER on horseback. It's cold at 10,023 ft above the warm Pacific—maybe 45°F. The horses' breath condenses into smoky clouds, and the riders cling to their saddles. It's eerily quiet except for the creak of straining leather and the crunch of volcanic cinders underfoot, sounds that are absurdly magnified in the vast empty space that yawns below.

This is Haleakalā, the "house of the sun." It's the crown of east Maui and the largest dormant volcanic depression in the world. The park encompasses 28,665 acres, and the valley itself is 21 mi in circumference and 19 square mi in area. At its deepest, it measures 3,000 ft from the summit, and could fit all of Manhattan. What you see here isn't actually a crater at all but something called a caldera, formed by the collapsing of the main cone, the result of eons of wind and rain wearing down what was once a small dip at the original summit peak. The small hills within the valley are volcanic cinder cones, each the site of an eruption.

Every year thousands of visitors drive the world's steepest auto route to the summit of Haleakalā National Park. Sunrise is extraordinary here. Mark Twain called it "the sublimest spectacle" he had ever witnessed.

But sunrise is only the beginning.

Hiking Haleakalā is like walking on the moon, with thirty-two miles of trails weaving around volcanic rubble, crater cones, frozen lava flows, vents, and tubes. The colors are muted yet dramatic—black, yellow, russet, orange, lavender, brown, even a pinkish blue—and change throughout the day.

This ecosystem sustains the surefooted mountain goat; the rare nēnē goose (no webbing between its toes, the better to negotiate this rugged terrain); and the strange, delicate silversword. A spiny, metallic-leaf plant, the silversword once grew abundantly on Haleakalā's slopes. Today it survives in small numbers at Haleakalā and at high elevations on the Big Island of Hawai'i. The plants live up to 40 years, bloom only once, scatter their seeds, and die.

It's not difficult to see this place as a bubbling, sulfurous cauldron, a direct connection to the core of the earth. Haleakalā's last—and probably final—eruption occurred in 1790, a few years after a Frenchman named Jean-François de Galaup, Comte de La Pérouse, became the first European to set foot on Maui. The rocky area on the southwest side of east Maui known as La Pérouse Bay is the result of that flow.

Large and small, awake or sleeping, volcanoes are Hawai'i's history and heritage. Behind their beauty is the story of the flames that created this ethereal island chain. The islands in the Hawaiian archipelago are actually the upper bodies of immense mountains rising from the bottom of the sea. Formed by molten rock known as magma, the islands have slowly grown from the earth's volatile mantle, lava forced through a "hot spot" in the thin crust of the ocean floor. The first ancient eruptions cooled and formed pools on the Pacific bottom. Then as magma spilled from the vents over millions of years, the pools became ridges and grew into crests. The latter built upon themselves over the eons, until finally they towered above the surface of the sea. This type of volcano, with its slowly formed, gently sloping sides, is known as a shield volcano. All of the Hawaiian Islands were created this way.

As the Islands cooled in the Pacific waters, the lava slopes slowly bloomed, over centuries, with colorful flora. About once every 35,000 years, a seed, spore, bird, or insect arrived here on the winds or waves. They found a fertile, sun-and-rain-drenched home, free of predators. Over time, these migrants developed into highly specialized organisms. A land with no predatory species breeds a population of plants and animals devoid of biological protections, making them especially fragile and vulnerable to foreign species and human development. Today Hawaii suffers from one of the world's highest species extinction rates; eighty percent of native Hawaiian birds are now gone.

B UT FOR ALL THE TALK OF GEOLOGY, Hawaiian myth casts a different history of the islands. Pele, the beautiful and tempestuous daughter of Haumea, the Earth Mother, and Wakea, the Sky Father, is the Hawaiian goddess of fire, the maker of mountains, melter of rock, eater of forests—a creator and a destroyer. Legend has it that Pele came to the Islands long ago to flee from her cruel older sister, Na Maka o Kahai, goddess of the sea. Pele ran first to the small island of Ni'ihau, making a crater home there with her digging stick. But Na Maka found her and destroyed her hideaway, so Pele again had to flee. On Kaua'i she delved deeper, but Na Maka chased her from that home as well. Pele ran on—from O'ahu to Moloka'i, Lana'i to Kaho'olawe, Molokini to Maui—but always Na Maka pursued her.

Pele came at last to Halema'uma'u, the vast firepit crater of Kīlauea, and there, on the Big Island, she dug deepest of all. There she is said to remain, all-powerful, quick to rage, and often unpredictable; the mountain is her impenetrable fortress and domain—a safe refuge, at least for a time, from Na Maka o Kahai.

The chronology of the old tales of Pele's flight from isle to isle closely matches the reckonings of modern volcanologists regarding the ages of the various craters. Today, the Big Island's Kīlauea and Mauna Loa retain the closest links with the earth's superheated core and are active and volatile. The other volcanoes have been carried beyond their magma supply by the movement of the Pacific Plate. Those on Kaua'i, O'ahu, and Moloka'i are completely extinct. Those at the southeasterly end of the island chain—Haleakalā, Mauna Ke'a, and Hualālai—are dormant and slipping away, so that the implacable process of volcanic death has begun. As erosion continues, the islands will someday melt back into the sea.

T HE LARGEST ISLAND of the archipelago, the Big Island of Hawai'i rises some 13,796 ft above sea level at the summit of Mauna Ke'a. Mauna Loa is nearly as high at 13,667 ft. Geologists believe it required more than 3 million years of steady volcanic activity to raise these peaks up above the waters of the Pacific. From their bases on the ocean floor, these shield volcanoes are the largest mountain masses on the planet.

Mauna Loa's little sister, Kīlauea, at about 4,077 ft, is the most active volcano in the world. Between the two volcanoes, they have covered nearly 200,000 acres of land with their red-hot lava flows over the past 200 years. In the process, they have ravished trees, fields, meadows, villages, and more than a few unlucky humans. For generations, Kīlauea, in a continually eruptive state, has pushed molten lava up from the earth's magma at 1,800°F and more. But as active as she and Mauna Loa are, their eruptions are comparatively safe and gentle, producing continuous small flows rather than large bursts of fire and ash. The exceptions were two explosive displays during recorded history—one in 1790, the other in 1924. During these eruptions, Pele came close to destroying the Big Island's largest city, Hilo.

I T IS AROUND THESE MAJOR VOLCANOES that the island's Hawai'i Volcanoes National Park was created. A sprawling natural preserve, the park attracts visitors from around the world for the unparalleled opportunity to view lava up close and personal. Geology experts and volcanologists have been coming for a century or more to study and to improve methods for predicting the times and sites of eruptions.

Thomas Augustus Jaggar, preeminent volcanologist and student of Kīlauea, built his home on stilts wedged into cracks in the volcanic rock of the crater rim. Harvard-trained and universally respected, he was the driving force behind the establishment of the Hawaiian Volcano Observatory at Kīlauea in 1912. When he couldn't raise research funds from donations, public and private, he raised pigs to keep the scientific work going. After Jaggar's death, his wife scattered his ashes over the great fiery abyss.

The park is on the Big Island's southeastern flank, about 30 minutes out of Hilo on the aptly named Volcano Highway. Wear sturdy walking shoes and carry a warm sweater. It can be a long hike across the lava flats to see Pele in action, and at

4,000 ft above sea level, temperatures can be brisk, however hot the volcanic activity. So much can be seen at close range along the road circling the crater that Kīlauea has been dubbed the "drive-in volcano."

At the park's visitor center sits a large display case. It contains dozens of lava-rock "souvenirs"—removed from Pele's grasp and then returned, accompanied by letters of apology. They are sent back by visitors who say they regret having broken the *kapu* (taboo) against removing even the smallest grain of native volcanic rock from Hawai'i. A typical letter might say: "I never thought Pele would miss just one little rock, but she did, and now I've wrecked two cars . . . I lost my job, my health is poor, and I know it's because I took this stone." The letters can be humorous, or poignant and remorseful, requesting Pele's forgiveness.

It is surprisingly safe at the crater's lip. Unlike Japan's Mount Fuji or Washington State's Mount Saint Helens, Hawai'i's shield volcanoes spew their lava downhill, along the sides of the mountain. Still, the clouds of sulfur gas and fumes produced during volcanic eruptions are noxious and heady and can make breathing unpleasant, if not difficult. It has been pointed out that the chemistry of volcanoes—sulfur, hydrogen, oxygen, carbon dioxide—closely resembles the chemistry of the egg.

It's an 11-mi drive around the Kīlauea crater via the Crater Rim Road, and the trip takes about an hour. But it's better to walk a bit. There are at least eight major trails in the park, ranging from short 15-minute strolls to the three-day, 18-mi (one way) Mauna Loa Trail. An easy, comfortable walk is Sulfur Banks, with its many steaming vents creating halos of clouds around the rim of Kīlauea. The route passes through a forest of sandalwood, flowers, and ferns.

Just ahead is the main attraction: the center of Pele's power, Halema'uma'u. This yawning pit of flame and burning rock measures some 3,000 ft wide and is a breathtaking sight. When Pele is in full fury, visitors come in droves, on foot and by helicopter, to see her crimson expulsions coloring the dark earth and smoky sky. Kīlauea's most recent violent activity has occurred at mountainside vents instead of at the summit crater. Known as rift zones, they are lateral conduits that often open in shield volcanoes.

Kīlauea has two rift zones, one extending from the summit crater toward the southwest, through Kau, the other to the east-northeast through Puna, past Cape Kumakahi, into the sea. In the last two decades, repeated eruptions in the east rift zone have blocked off 12 mi of coastal road—some under more than 300 ft of rock—and have covered a total of 10,000 acres with lava. Where the flows entered the ocean, roughly 200 acres have been added to the Big Island.

Farther along the Crater Rim Road is the Thurston Lava Tube, an example of a strangely beautiful volcanic phenomenon common on the Islands. Lava tubes form when lava flows rapidly downhill. The sides and top of this river of molten rock cool, while the fluid center flows on. Most formations are short and shallow, but some measure 30 ft to 50 ft high and hundreds of yards long. Lava tubes were often used to store remains of the ancient Hawaiian royalty—the *ali'i*. The Thurston Lava Tube sits in a beautiful prehistoric fern forest called Fern Jungle.

Throughout the park, new lava formations are continually being created. These volcanic deposits exhibit the different types of lava produced by Hawai'i's volcanoes: *'a'ā*, the dark, rough lava that solidifies as cinders of rock; and the more common *pāhoehoe*, the smooth, satiny lava that forms the vast plains of black rock in ropy swirls known as lava flats, which in some areas go on for miles. Other terms that help identify what may be seen in the park include *caldera*, which are the open, bowllike lips of a volcano summit; *ejecta*, the cinders and ash that float through the air around an eruption; and *olivine*, the semiprecious chrysolite (greenish in color) found in volcanic ash.

* * *

BUT THIS VOLCANIC LANDSCAPE isn't all fire and flash, cinders, and devastation. Hawai'i Volcanoes National Park is also the home of some of the most beautiful of the state's black-sand beaches; forest glens full of lacy butterflies and colorful birds such as the dainty flycatcher, called the *'elepaio*;

and exquisite grottoes sparked with bright wild orchid sprays and crashing waterfalls. Even as the lava cools, still bearing a golden, glassy skin, lush, green native ferns—*ama'uma'u, kupukupu,* and *'ōkupukupu*—spring up in the midst of Pele's fallout, as if defying her destructiveness or simply confirming the fact that after fire she brings life.

Some 12 centuries ago, in fact, Pele brought humans to her verdant islands: the fiery explosions that lit Kīlauea and Mauna Loa probably guided the first explorers to Pele's side from the Marquesas Islands, some 2,400 mi away across the ocean.

Once settled, they worshiped her from a distance. Great numbers of religious *heiau* (outdoor stone platforms) dot the landscapes near the many older and extinct craters scattered throughout Hawai'i, demonstrating the reverence the native islanders have always held for Pele and her creations. But the ruins of only two heiau are to be found near the very active crater at Halema'uma'u. There, at the center of the capricious Pele's power, native Hawaiians caution one even today to "step lightly, for you are on holy ground."

In future ages, when mighty Kīlauea is no more, this area will still be a volcanic isle. Beneath the blue Pacific waters, fiery magma flows and new mountains form and grow. Off the south coast of the Big Island, a new island is forming. Still ½ mi below the water's surface, it won't be making an appearance any time soon, but already has a name: Lōihi.

— Gary Diedrichs

BOOKS & MOVIES

Books

If you like your history in novel form, you'll enjoy James A. Michener's *Hawaii* for its overall perspective. Captain James Cook's *A Voyage to the Pacific Ocean,* one of the first guidebooks to the Islands, contains many valid insights; *Shoal of Time,* by Gavan Daws, chronicles Hawaiian history from Cook's time to the 1960s. History also comes to life in the pages of *Travels in Hawaii,* by Robert Louis Stevenson. To gain familiarity with the gods and goddesses who have also had a hand in this land's development, read *Hawaiian Mythology* by Martha Beckwith. *Hawai'i's Story by Hawai'i's Queen,* the tale of the overthrow of the Hawaiian monarchy in Queen Lili'uokalani's own words, is poignant and thought-provoking. For a truly Hawaiian perspective, *Voices of Wisdom: Hawaiian Elders Speak* by M. J. Harden shares interviews with some of Hawai'i's most respected elders. Albert J. Schütz's *All About Hawaiian* is a good introduction to the language of the Islands and efforts to preserve it.

Paul Wood's essays, collected in *Four Wheels, Five Corners: Facts of Life in Upcountry Maui,* are quirky tales of life on a rock in the middle of the Pacific. Writers Paul Theroux, Barbara Kingsolver, and Maxine Hong Kingston are among those who share stories about the Islands in *Hawai'i: True Stories of the Island Spirit,* a collection edited by Rick and Marcie Carroll. *Call for Hawaiian Sovereignty,* by Michael Kioni Dudley, traces the growing movement for a sovereign Hawaiian nation. *Kamehameha and the Warrior Kekūhoaupi'o* is a classical Hawaiian epic, translated by Naomi Sodetani. For kids, pick up *Beautiful Hawaiian Day,* by Henry Kapono, a story about a little girl who finds a seashell that takes her back through the history of Hawai'i.

The *Handbook of Hawaiian Fishes,* by W. A. Gosline and Vernon Brock, is great for snorkelers. *Hawai'i's Birds,* put out by the Hawai'i Audubon Society, is perfect for bird-watchers. *Hawaiian Hiking Trails,* by Craig Chisholm, is just the guide for day hikers and backpackers. *Surfing: The Ultimate Pleasure,* by Leonard Lueras,

covers everything about the sport. Geographers greatly appreciate the maps, social and geological history, and biology in *Atlas of Hawai'i,* by Sonia Juvik.

The New Cuisine of Hawaii, by Janice Wald Henderson, features recipes from the 12 chefs credited with defining Hawai'i regional cuisine. One of these pioneers, celebrity chef Roy Yamaguchi, provides an in-depth taste of the Islands with his cookbook *Roy's Feasts from Hawaii. Hawaiian Country Tables* by Kaui Philpotts spotlights vintage Island recipes and dishes.

For swaying musicologists, there's *Hula Is Life, The Story of Maiki Aiu and Hālau Hulo o Maiki,* by Rita Aryioshi; it's the definitive book on hula's origins and development. Hawaiian-music lovers might take note of the ideas presented in *Strains of Change: Impact of Tourism on Hawaiian Music* by Elizabeth Tatar.

Instead of just taking home a lei, learn how to make one: *Hawaiian Lei Making,* by Laurie Shimizu Ide, offers a photographic guide for making floral leis.

Movie buffs enjoy *Made in Paradise: Hollywood's Films of Hawaii and the South Seas,* by Luis Reyes. It points out movie locations and pokes gentle fun at some of the misinformation popularized by Tinseltown's version of Island life. Guided tours of Kaua'i locations used in filming are provided by **Hawai'i Movie Tours** (☎ 800/628–8432).

Movies

For a preview of your vacation, take a look at *Forever Hawaii,* a video portrait of Hawai'i's six major islands.

The video *Hawaii on Foot,* with Robert Smith, gives hikers a peek at some of the best trails on O'ahu, Maui, the Big Island, and Kaua'i. It is available from **H.O.A. Publications** (✉ 102-16 Kaui Pl., Kula 96796 ☎ 808/678–2664 ⊕ www.maui. net/~hionfoot). Hula comes alive in the **1999 Merrie Monarch Festival Highlights.** The video is available from ⊕ *www. BooklinesHawaii.com* ☎ 877/828–4852.

Most people automatically think of Elvis when the words "Hawai'i" and "movie" are mentioned in the same sentence. Elvis Presley's Hawaiian-filmed movies are *Girls! Girls! Girls!* (1962), *Paradise, Hawaiian Style* (1966), and *Blue Hawaii* (1962), which showcases Oʻahu's picturesque Hanauma Bay and Kauaʻi's Coco Palms Resort.

Films such as Shirley Temple's *Curly Top* (1935); *Waikiki Wedding* (1937), with Bing Crosby; and *Gidget Goes Hawaiian* (1962) feature Hawaiʻi's beaches, palm trees, and hula dancers. The Islands' winter waves have taken center stage in a legion of hang-ten films of which only *North Shore* (1987) is on video.

Mitzi Gaynor washed that man right out of her hair on Kauaʻi's Lumahaʻi Beach in *South Pacific* (1958). And the tempestuous love scene between Burt Lancaster and Deborah Kerr in *From Here to Eternity* (1954) took place on Oʻahu's Halona Cove beach.

Military-theme movies filmed in Hawaiʻi include *Mister Roberts* (1955), starring Henry Fonda, Jack Lemmon, and James Cagney; and *Lt. Robin Crusoe, USN* (1966), with Dick Van Dyke. *Tora! Tora! Tora!* (1971) re-created the December 7, 1941, bombing of Pearl Harbor. For *Flight of the Intruder* (1991), director John Milius turned taro farms at the base of Kauaʻi's Mount Waiʻaleʻale into the rice paddies of Southeast Asia.

The film version of James A. Michener's story *Hawaii* (1967) chronicles the lives of the Islands' missionary families. *Picture Bride* (1995) tells the story of a young Japanese girl who arrives on the Islands to face harsh realities as the wife of a sugar-plantation laborer.

Other movies with Hawaiʻi settings include *Black Widow* (1987), in which journalist Debra Winger travels to the Big Island's lava fields to prevent a murder; *Honeymoon in Vegas* (1992); *Under the Hula Moon* (1995); *Blue Crush* (2002); Disney's animated *Lilo & Stitch* (2002); and, of course, *Pearl Harbor* (2001).

CHRONOLOGY

ca. AD 500–750 The first humans to set foot on Hawaiian shores are Polynesians, who travel 2,400 mi in 60- to 80-ft canoes in search of a land revered in ancient mythology. Researchers today believe they were originally from Southeast Asia and that they discovered the South Pacific islands of Tahiti and the Marquesas before ending up in Hawai'i.

ca. 750–1200 The Islands are well populated with well-defined social and political structures brought by the Polynesians. Ali'i (chiefs) own the land, and the citizens tend to it and are taxed. Kahuna (priests) are the link between the gods; their oracular advice is sought for matters of all types.

ca. 1200 Tahitian voyagers arrive, bringing with them rituals of human sacrifice, as well as highly developed ecosystem-management techniques for livestock and agriculture.

ca. 1758 Kamehameha, the Hawaiian chief who unifies the Islands, is born.

1778 In January, Captain James Cook, commander of the H.M.S. *Resolution* and the consort vessel H.M.S. *Discovery*, lands on the island of Kaua'i. He arrives during a festival honoring the god Lono, and he himself is revered as a god prophesied to appear. He names the archipelago the Sandwich Islands after his patron, the Earl of Sandwich. In November, he returns to the Islands for the winter, anchoring at Kealakekua Bay on the Big Island.

1779 In February, Cook is killed in a battle with Hawai'i's indigenous people at Kealakekua.

1785 The isolation of the Islands ends as British, American, French, and Russian fur traders and New England whalers come to Hawai'i. Tales spread of thousands of acres of sugarcane growing wild, and farmers come in droves from the United States and Europe.

1790 Kamehameha begins his rise to power with a series of bloody battles.

1791 Kamehameha builds Pu'ukoholā Heiau (temple) on the Big Island and dedicates it by sacrificing a rival chief, Keoua Kuahu'ula, whom he has killed.

1795 Using Western arms, Kamehameha wins a decisive confrontation on O'ahu. Except for Kaua'i, which he tries to invade in 1796 and 1804, this completes his military conquest of the Islands.

1810 The chief of Kaua'i acknowledges Kamehameha's rule, giving him suzerainty over Kaua'i and Ni'ihau. Kamehameha becomes known as King Kamehameha I, and he rules the unified Kingdom of Hawai'i with an iron hand.

1819 Kamehameha I dies, and his oldest son, Liholiho, rules briefly as Kamehameha II, with Ka'ahumanu, Kamehameha I's favorite wife, as co-executive. Ka'ahumanu persuades the new king to abandon old religious *kapu* (taboos), including those that forbade women to eat with men or to hold positions of power. The first whaling ships land at Lahaina on Maui.

1820 By the time the first missionaries arrive from Boston, Hawai'i's social order is beginning to break down. First, Ka'ahumanu and then Kamehameha II defy kapu without attracting divine retribution. Hawaiians, disillusioned with their own gods, are receptive to the ideas of Christianity. The influx of Western visitors also introduces to Hawai'i Western diseases, liquor, and what some view as moral decay.

1824 King Kamehameha II and his favorite wife die of measles during a visit to England. Honolulu missionaries give both royals a Christian burial outside Kawaiaha'o Church, inspiring many Hawaiians to convert to the Protestant faith. The king's younger brother, Kau'ikea'ōuli, becomes King Kamehameha III, a wise and gentle sovereign who reigns for 30 years with Ka'ahumanu as regent.

1832 Ka'ahumanu is baptized and dies a few months later.

1840 The Wilkes Expedition, sponsored by the U.S. Coast and Geodetic Survey, pinpoints Pearl Harbor as a potential naval base.

1845 Kamehameha III and the legislature move Hawai'i's seat of government from Lahaina, on Maui, to Honolulu, on O'ahu.

1849 Kamehameha III turns Hawai'i into a constitutional monarchy, and the United States, France, and Great Britain recognize Hawai'i as an independent country.

1850 The Great Mahele, a land commission, reapportions the land to the crown, the government, chiefs, and commoners, introducing for the first time the Western principle of private ownership. Commoners are now able to buy and sell land, but this great division becomes the great dispossession. By the end of the 19th century, white men own 4 acres for every 1 owned by a native Hawaiian. Some of the commission's distributions continue to be disputed to this day.

1852 As Western diseases depopulate the Islands, a labor shortage occurs in the sugarcane fields. For the next nine decades, a steady stream of foreign labor pours into Hawai'i, beginning with the Chinese. The Japanese begin arriving in 1868, followed by Filipinos, Koreans, Portuguese, and Puerto Ricans.

1872 Kamehameha V, the last descendent of the king who unified the Islands, dies without heirs. A power struggle ensues between the adherents of David Kalākaua and William Lunalilo.

1873 Lunalilo is elected Hawai'i's sixth king in January. The bachelor rules only 13 months before dying of tuberculosis.

1874 Kalākaua vies for the throne with the Dowager Queen Emma, the half-Caucasian widow of Kamehameha IV. Kalākaua is elected by the Hawai'i Legislature, against protests by supporters of Queen Emma. American and British marines are called in to restore order, and Kalākaua begins his reign as the "Merrie Monarch."

1875 The United States and Hawai'i sign a treaty of reciprocity, assuring Hawai'i a duty-free market for sugar in the United States.

1882 King Kalākaua builds 'Iolani Palace, an Italian renaissance–style structure, on the site of the previous royal palace.

1887 The reciprocity treaty of 1875 is renewed, giving the United States exclusive use of Pearl Harbor as a coaling station. Coincidentally, successful importation of Japanese laborers begins in earnest (after a false start in 1868).

1891 King Kalākaua dies and is succeeded by his sister, Queen Lili'uokalani, the last Hawaiian monarch.

1893 After a brief two-year reign, Lili'uokalani is removed from the throne by American business interests led by Lorrin A. Thurston (grandson

of the missionary and newspaper founder Asa Thurston).
Lili'uokalani is imprisoned in 'Iolani Palace for nearly eight months.

1894   The provisional government converts Hawai'i into a republic and
proclaims Sanford Dole president.

1898   With the outbreak of the Spanish-American War, President William
McKinley recognizes Hawai'i's strategic importance in the Pacific and
moves to secure the Islands for the United States. On August 12,
Hawai'i is officially annexed by a joint resolution of Congress.

1901   Sanford Dole is appointed first governor of the territory of Hawai'i.
The first major tourist hotel, the Moana (now called the Sheraton
Moana Surfrider), is built on Waikīkī Beach.

1903   James Dole, a cousin of Sanford Dole, produces nearly 2,000 cases of
pineapple, marking the beginning of Hawai'i's pineapple industry.
Pineapple eventually surpasses sugarcane as Hawai'i's number one
crop.

1907   Fort Shafter Base on O'ahu, headquarters for the U.S. Army, becomes
the first permanent military post in the Islands.

1908   Dredging of the channel at Pearl Harbor begins.

1919   Pearl Harbor is formally dedicated by the U.S. Navy. Representing
the Territory of Hawai'i in the U.S. House of Representatives, Prince
Jonah Kūhiō Kalaniana'ole—the adopted son of Kapi'olani, the wife
of Kalākaua, and with his brother one of the designated heirs to the
throne of the childless Lili'uokalani—introduces the first bill
proposing statehood for Hawai'i.

1927   Army lieutenants Lester Maitland and Albert Hegenberger make the
first successful nonstop flight from the mainland to the Islands.
Hawai'i begins to increase efforts to promote tourism, the industry
that eventually dominates development of the Islands. The Matson
Navigation Company builds the Royal Hawaiian Hotel as a
destination for its cruise ships.

1929   Hawai'i's commercial interisland air service begins.

1936   Pan American World Airways introduces regular commercial
passenger flights to Hawai'i from the mainland.

1941   At Pearl Harbor the U.S. Pacific Fleet is bombed by the Japanese,
forcing U.S. entry into World War II. Nearly 4,000 men are killed in
the surprise attack.

1942   James Jones, with thousands of others, trains at Schofield Barracks
on O'ahu. He later writes about his experience in *From Here to
Eternity*.

1959   Congress passes legislation granting Hawai'i statehood. In special
elections the new state sends to the U.S. House of Representatives its
first American of Japanese ancestry, Daniel Inouye, and to the U.S.
Senate its first American of Chinese ancestry, Hiram Fong. Later in
the year, the first Boeing 707 jets make the flight from San Francisco
in a record five hours. By year's end 243,216 tourists visit Hawai'i,
and tourism becomes Hawai'i's major industry.

1986   Hawai'i elects its first native Hawaiian governor, John Waihe'e.

1992   Hurricane 'Iniki, the most devastating hurricane to hit Hawai'i, tears
through Kaua'i on September 11. The island's people, infrastructure,
gardens, and tourism industry have happily all since recovered.

1993 After native Hawaiians commemorate the 100th anniversary of the overthrow of Queen Lili'uokalani with a call for sovereignty, Congress issues an apology to the Hawaiian people for the annexation of the Islands.

1997 After 34 years of planning, construction, and endless litigation, O'ahu's H-3 "Trans-Koolau" freeway linking Pearl Harbor to the windward side of O'ahu finally opens. Opposition to the highway centered on the route through the Hālawa and Haiku valleys, areas of historical and religious significance to native Hawaiians. The price tag for this scenic roadway with a million-dollar view? More than 1 billion in state and federal tax dollars.

1998 The U.S.S. *Missouri* comes to her final resting place in Pearl Harbor. The battleship, on whose decks the Japanese signed their surrender agreement in World War II, is now a floating museum, permanently docked at Ford Island.

2001 Kīlauea Volcano on the Big Island of Hawai'i reaches the 19th year of its current eruptive phase and the longest phase of such activity in recorded volcanic history.

2002 Kīlauea is still at it.

VOCABULARY

Although an understanding of Hawaiian is by no means required on a trip to the Aloha State, a *malihini,* or newcomer, will find plenty of opportunities to pick up a few of the local words and phrases. Traditional names and expressions are widely used in the Islands, thanks in part to legislation enacted in the early '90s to encourage the use of the Hawaiian language. You're likely to read or hear at least a few words each day of your stay. Such exposure enriches a trip to Hawai'i.

With a basic understanding and some uninhibited practice, anyone can have enough command of the local tongue to ask for directions and to order from a restaurant menu. One visitor announced she would not leave until she could pronounce the name of the state fish, the *humuhumunukunukuāpua'a.* Luckily, she had scheduled a nine-day stay.

Simplifying the learning process is the fact that the Hawaiian language contains only eight consonants—H, K, L, M, N, P, W, and the silent *'okina,* or glottal stop, written '—plus one or more of the five vowels. All syllables, and therefore all words, end in a vowel. Each vowel, with the exception of a few diphthongized double vowels such as *au* (pronounced "ow") or *ai* (pronounced "eye"), is pronounced separately. Thus *'Iolani* is four syllables (ee-oh-la-nee), not three (yo-la-nee). Although some Hawaiian words have only vowels, most also contain some consonants, but consonants are never doubled.

Pronunciation is simple. Pronounce A "ah" as father; E "ay" as in weigh; I "ee" as in marine; O "oh" as in no; U "oo" as in true.

Consonants mirror their English equivalents, with the exception of W. When the letter begins any syllable other than the first one in a word, it is usually pronounced as a V. *'Awa,* the Polynesian drink, is pronounced "ava"; *'ewa* is pronounced "eva."

Nearly all long Hawaiian words are combinations of shorter words; they are not difficult to pronounce if you segment them into shorter words. *Kalaniana'ole,* the highway running east from Honolulu, is easily understood as *Kalani ana 'ole.* Apply the standard pronunciation rules—the stress falls on the next-to-last syllable of most two- or three-syllable Hawaiian words—and Kalaniana'ole Highway is as easy to say as Main Street.

Now about that fish. Try *humu-humu nuku-nuku āpu a'a.*

The other unusual element in Hawaiian language is the *kahakō,* or macron, written as a short line (ˉ) placed over a vowel. Like the accent (´) in Spanish, the kahakō puts emphasis on a syllable that would normally not be stressed. The most familiar example is probably *Waikīkī.* With no macrons, the stress would fall on the middle syllable; with only one macron, on the last syllable, the stress would fall on the first and last syllables. Some words become plural with the addition of a macron, often on a syllable that would have been stressed anyway. No Hawaiian word becomes plural with the addition of an S, since that letter does not exist in the *'ōlelo Hawai'i* (which is Hawaiian for "Hawaiian language").

What follows is a glossary of some of the most commonly used Hawaiian words. Don't be afraid to give them a try. Hawaiian residents appreciate visitors who at least try to pick up the local language.

ʻaʻā: rough, crumbling lava, contrasting with *pāhoehoe,* which is smooth.

ʻae: yes.

aikane: friend.

āina: land.

akamai: smart, clever, possessing savoir faire.

akua: god.

ala: a road, path, or trail.

aliʻi: a Hawaiian chief, a member of the chiefly class.

aloha: love, affection, kindness; also a salutation meaning both greetings and farewell.

ʻānuenue: rainbow.

ʻaʻole: no.

ʻapōpō: tomorrow.

ʻauwai: a ditch.

auwē: alas, woe is me!

ʻehu: a red-haired Hawaiian.

ʻewa: in the direction of ʻEwa plantation, west of Honolulu.

hala: the pandanus tree, whose leaves (*lau hala*) are used to make baskets and plaited mats.

hālau: school.

hale: a house.

hale pule: church, house of worship.

ha mea iki or **ha mea ʻole:** you're welcome.

hana: to work.

haole: ghost. Since the first foreigners were Caucasian, *haole* now means a Caucasian person.

hapa: a part, sometimes a half; often used as a short form of *hapa haole,* to mean a person who is part-Caucasian; thus, the name of a popular local band, whose members represent a variety of ethnicities.

hauʻoli: to rejoice. *Hauʻoli Makahiki Hou* means Happy New Year. *Hauʻoli lā hānau* means Happy Birthday.

heiau: an outdoor stone platform; an ancient Hawaiian place of worship.

holo: to run.

holoholo: to go for a walk, ride, or sail.

holokū: a long Hawaiian dress, somewhat fitted, with a yoke and a train. Influenced by European fashion, it was worn at court, and at least one local translates the word as "expensive muʻumuʻu."

holomū: a post–World War II cross between a *holokū* and a muʻumuʻu, less fitted than the former but less voluminous than the latter, and having no train.

honi: to kiss; a kiss. A phrase that some tourists may find useful, quoted from a popular hula, is *Honi Kaʻua Wikiwiki:* Kiss me quick!

honu: turtle.

hoʻomalimali: flattery, a deceptive "line," bunk, baloney, hooey.

huhū: angry.

hui: a group, club, or assembly. A church may refer to its congregation as a *hui* and a social club may be called a *hui.*

hukilau: a seine; a communal fishing party in which everyone helps to drive the fish into a huge net, pull it in, and divide the catch.

hula: the dance of Hawaiʻi.

iki: little.

ipo: sweetheart.

ka: the. This is the definite article for most singular words; for plural nouns, the definite article is usually *nā.* Since there is no S in Hawaiian, the article may be your only clue that a noun is plural.

kahuna: a priest, doctor, or other trained person of old Hawai'i, endowed with special professional skills that often included the gift of prophecy or other supernatural powers; the plural form is kāhuna.

kai: the sea, saltwater.

kalo: the taro plant from whose root poi is made.

kama'āina: literally, a child of the soil; it refers to people who were born in the Islands or have lived there for a long time.

kanaka: originally a man or humanity in general, it is now used to denote a male Hawaiian or part-Hawaiian, but is occasionally taken as a slur when used by non-Hawaiians. *Kanaka maoli,* originally a full-blooded Hawaiian person, is used by some native Hawaiian rights activists to embrace part-Hawaiians as well.

kāne: a man, a husband. If you see this word on a door, it's the men's room. If you see *kane* on a door, it's probably a misspelling; that is the Hawaiian name for the skin fungus tinea.

kapa: also called by its Tahitian name, *tapa,* a cloth made of beaten bark and usually dyed and stamped with a repeat design.

kapakahi: crooked, cockeyed, uneven. You've got your hat on *kapakahi.*

kapu: keep out, prohibited. This is the Hawaiian version of the more widely known Tongan word *tabu* (taboo).

kapuna: grandparent; elder.

kēia lā: today.

keiki: a child; *keikikāne* is a boy, *keikiwahine* a girl.

kona: the leeward side of the Islands, the direction (south) from which the *kona* wind and *kona* rain come.

kula: upland.

kuleana: a homestead or small plot of ground on which a family has been installed for some generations without necessarily owning it. By extension, *kuleana* is used to denote any area or department in which one has a special interest or prerogative. You'll hear it used this way: If you want to hire a surfboard, see Moki; that's his *kuleana.* And conversely: I can't help you with that; that's not my *kuleana.*

lā: sun.

lamalama: to fish with a torch.

lānai: a porch, a balcony, an outdoor living room. Almost every house in Hawai'i has one. Don't confuse this two-syllable word with the three-syllable name of the island, Lāna'i.

lani: heaven, the sky.

lau hala: the leaf of the *hala,* or pandanus tree, widely used in Hawaiian handicrafts.

lei: a garland of flowers.

limu: sun.

lolo: stupid.

luna: a plantation overseer or foreman.

mahalo: thank you.

makai: toward the ocean.

malihini: a newcomer to the Islands.

mana: the spiritual power that the Hawaiian believed inhabited all things and creatures.

manō: shark.

manuwahi: free, gratis.

mauka: toward the mountains.

mauna: mountain.

mele: a Hawaiian song or chant, often of epic proportions.

Mele Kalikimaka: Merry Christmas (a transliteration from the English phrase).

Menehune: a Hawaiian pixie. The *Menehune* were a legendary race of little people who accomplished prodigious work, such as building fishponds and temples in the course of a single night.

moana: the ocean.

muʻumuʻu: the voluminous dress in which the missionaries enveloped Hawaiian women. Now made in bright printed cottons and silks, it is an indispensable garment in a Hawaiian woman's wardrobe. Culturally sensitive locals have embraced the Hawaiian spelling but often shorten the spoken word to "muʻu." Most English dictionaries include the spelling "muumuu," and that version is a part of many apparel companies' names.

nani: beautiful.

nui: big.

ohana: family.

ʻono: delicious.

pāhoehoe: smooth, unbroken, satiny lava.

Pākē: Chinese. This *Pākē* carver makes beautiful things.

palapala: document, printed matter.

pali: a cliff, precipice.

pānini: prickly pear cactus.

paniolo: a Hawaiian cowboy, a rough transliteration of *español,* the language of the Islands' earliest cowboys.

pau: finished, done.

pilikia: trouble. The Hawaiian word is much more widely used here than its English equivalent.

puka: a hole.

pupule: crazy, like the celebrated Princess Pupule. This word has replaced its English equivalent in local usage.

puʻu: volcanic cinder cone.

waha: mouth.

wahine: a female, a woman, a wife, and a sign on the ladies' room door; the plural form is *wāhine.*

wai: freshwater, as opposed to saltwater, which is *kai.*

wailele: waterfall.

wikiwiki: to hurry, hurry up (since this is a reduplication of *wiki,* quick, neither *W* is pronounced as a *V*).

Note: Pidgin is the unofficial language of Hawaiʻi. It is a Creole language, with its own grammar, evolved from the mixture of English, Hawaiian, Japanese, Portuguese, and other languages spoken in 19th-century Hawaiʻi, and it is heard everywhere: on ranches, in warehouses, on beaches, and in the hallowed halls (and occasionally in the classrooms) of the University of Hawaiʻi.

MENU GUIDE

Much of the Hawaiian language encountered during a stay in the Islands will appear on restaurant menus and lists of lūʻau fare. Here's a quick primer.

ʻahi: yellowfin tuna.

aku: skipjack, bonito tuna.

ʻamaʻama: mullet; it's hard to get but tasty.

bento: a box lunch.

chicken lūʻau: a stew made from chicken, taro leaves, and coconut milk.

haupia: a light, gelatin-like dessert made from coconut.

imu: the underground ovens in which pigs are roasted for lūʻau.

kālua: to bake underground.

kaukau: food. The word comes from Chinese but is used in the Islands.

kimchee: Korean dish of pickled cabbage made with garlic and hot peppers.

Kona coffee: coffee grown in the Kona district of the Big Island.

laulau: literally, a bundle. *Laulau* are morsels of pork, butterfish, or other ingredients wrapped with young taro shoots in ti leaves for steaming.

lilikoʻi: passion fruit, a tart, seedy yellow fruit that makes delicious desserts, jellies, and sherbet.

lomilomi: to rub or massage; also a massage. *Lomilomi* salmon is fish that has been rubbed with onions and herbs, commonly served with minced onions and tomatoes.

lūʻau: a Hawaiian feast, also the leaf of the taro plant used in preparing such a feast.

lūʻau leaves: cooked taro tops with a taste similar to spinach.

mahimahi: mild-flavored dolphinfish, not the marine mammal.

mai tai: potent rum drink with orange and lime juice, from the Tahitian word for "good."

malasada: a Portuguese deep-fried doughnut without a hole, dipped in sugar.

manapua: dough wrapped around diced pork.

manō: shark.

niu: coconut.

ʻōkolehao: a liqueur distilled from the ti root.

onaga: pink or red snapper.

ono: a long, slender mackerel-like fish; also called wahoo.

ʻono: delicious; also hungry.

ʻopihi: a tiny shellfish, or mollusk, found on rocks; also called limpets.

pāpio: a young *ulua* or jack fish.

pohā: Cape gooseberry. Tasting a bit like honey, the pohā berry is often used in jams and desserts.

poi: a paste made from pounded taro root, a staple of the Hawaiian diet.

poke: chopped, pickled raw tuna, tossed with herbs and seasonings.

pūpū: Hawaiian hors d'oeuvre.

saimin: long thin noodles and vegetables in broth, often garnished with small pieces of fish cake, scrambled egg, luncheon meat, and green onion.

sashimi: raw fish thinly sliced and usually eaten with soy sauce.

ti leaves: a member of the agave family, used to wrap food in cooking and removed before eating.

uku: deep-sea snapper.

ulua: a member of the jack family that also includes pompano and amberjack. Also called crevalle, jack fish, and jack crevalle.

INDEX

NOTES

NOTES

NOTES

NOTES

GLACIER
National Park
and
Waterton Lakes
National Park

★★

Edited by ROBERT SCHARFF
with the cooperation of
NATIONAL PARK SERVICE

★★

DAVID McKAY COMPANY, INC.
NEW YORK

GLACIER NATIONAL PARK
and
Waterton Lakes National Park

COPYRIGHT © 1967 BY ROBERT SCHARFF

LIBRARY OF CONGRESS CATALOG CARD NUMBER: 67-10608

MANUFACTURED IN THE UNITED STATES OF AMERICA

foreword

THE unheralded line that separates Canada and the United States is the longest unfortified border in the world, today, and perhaps in all of history. It says to mankind: Let not the cartographers rule, elevate nature and human friendship.

This is what I think when I visit Glacier National Park, in Montana. For, somewhere, as I wander through its wilderness and wildness, I know I must have left my country. At least I think it possible. Yet nothing stops me. There is no line, no meaningful barrier. The earth does not end at a sudden cliff transformed from its natural condition into an escarpment. I think I may be in Canada, but I cannot be sure. The wind and the sun and the sky—the things in which man had no hand, at all—these remain as they were in my own land.

If, as I think, I am in Canada, then I am in Waterton Lakes National Park. It is across the border. It is maintained and loved by our neighbors to the North. Think of it: two nations, at peace across a common border . . . and two great National Parks, back-to-back, to prove it.

This knowledge, this realization, alone, would be sufficient reason to visit the Glacier and Waterton Parks. Here is the greatest international monument to peace . . . and strangely, it is natural and not man-made in its detail, in its scope.

And here, in these two utterly beautiful Parks, where the snows hang on the peaks through the summer, where there are lush valleys and flower-covered slopes, here is an overpowering experience to be seen and sensed: It is nature unviolated, and man humanized, and both at peace.

There is little else one could ask for.

STEWART L. UDALL
Secretary of the Interior

acknowledgments

WHILE assembling and verifying the information in this book, I received a great deal of help from the National Park Service and the concessioners at both Glacier and Waterton Lake National Parks. Glacier's Chief Naturalist Francis H. Elmore, and S. L. Roberts of Department of Northern Affairs and National Resources helped greatly in the gathering of material and checked both the manuscript and proofs for accuracy. In addition, I would like to thank Superintendent Keith Neilson, and other members of the Glacier staff including John J. Palmer and B. Riley McClelland. I am indebted to the Glacier Natural History Association for use of certain material from their publications. In Waterton Lakes National Park, Superintendents Al Pettis and R. H. Kendall, Naturalist Kurl Seel and Chief Warden Frank Camp deserve special thanks. William L. Perry and O. L. Wallis of the National Park Service made valuable suggestions to assure accuracy.

Among the concessioners, Don Hummel, A. S. Donau, William Trimble, and Robert Hayes, Jr. of Glacier Park Inc., Robert Toelke of Rocky Mountain Outfitters, Inc., and Dee Olsen of the Timberline Horse Stables have been especially helpful in the preparation of the book. Mel Ruder of the *Hungry Horse News,* Roland Meyer of H. S. Crocker Company, Inc., and C. W. Moore and Frank Perrin of Great Northern Railway also have contributed greatly to the book's completion. Of all the people outside of the National Park Service personnel, however, Peter A. Tufts of Glacier Park, Inc., deserves special acknowledgment. He made all the arrangements and acted as coordinator of my research missions to the Parks.

ROBERT SCHARFF

Contents

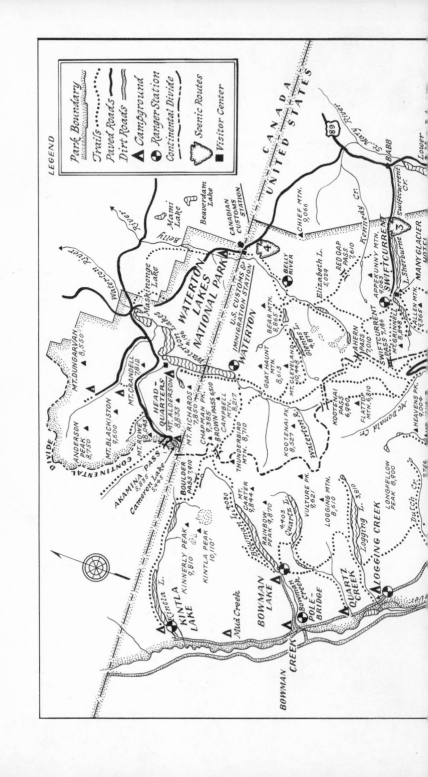

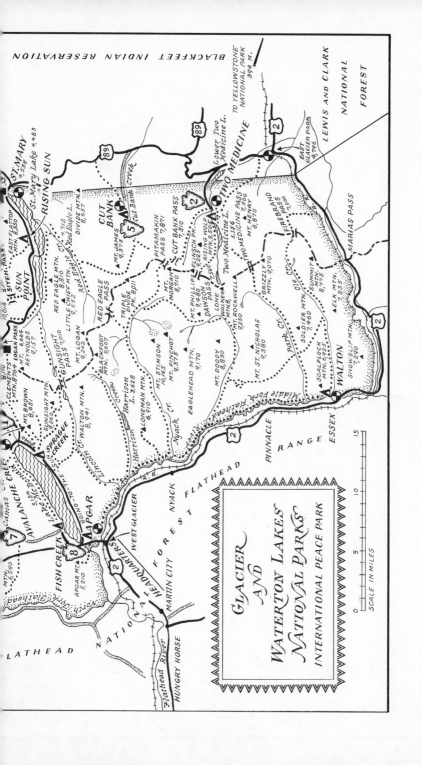

GLACIER
AND
WATERTON LAKES
NATIONAL PARKS
INTERNATIONAL PEACE PARK

SCALE IN MILES
0   5   10   15

BLACKFEET INDIAN RESERVATION

LEWIS AND CLARK
NATIONAL FOREST

TO YELLOWSTONE
NATIONAL PARK
394 M.

EAST GLACIER PARK 4,796

MARIAS PASS

FIREBRAND PASS 7,000

TWO MEDICINE PASS 7,500

Lower Two Medicine L.

TWO MEDICINE

MT. HENRY 8,870

Two Medicine L.

TWO MEDICINE PASS 5,156

GRIZZLY MTN. 9,070

ELK MTN. 7,835

SUMMIT MTN. 8,773

SOLDIER MTN. 7,760

Ole Cr.

Park Cr.

MT. ROCKWELL 9,250

RISING WOLF MTN. 9,513

LONE WALKER 7,560

DAWSON 8,830

MT. HELEN

FLINSCH PK. 9,225

MT. PHILLIPS 9,480

PITAMAKIN PASS

CUT BANK PASS 7,510

LITTLE CHIEF MTN. 9,552

89

89

ST. MARY 4,483

St. Mary Lake 4,483

RISING SUN

SUN POINT

SIYEH PASS 10,014

EAST FLATTOP MTN. 8,350 8,539

LOGAN PASS 6,664 6,712

CLEMENTS MTN. 8,764

MT. REYNOLDS 9,125

Red Eagle L.

Red Eagle Cr.

RED EAGLE PASS

Cut Bank Creek

Red Eagle

Divide Mtn. 8,657

CUT BANK 5

MT. JAMES 9,375

RED EAGLE MTN. 8,880

GUNSIGHT PASS 7,010

MT. LOGAN 9,262

MT. BROWN 8,651

GUNSIGHT MTN. 9,260

BLACKFOOT MTN. 9,607

TRIPLE DIVIDE PK. 8,011

MT. MORGAN 8,710

MT. STIMSON 10,165

MT. PINCHOT 9,315

MT. DOODY 8,830

EAGLEHEAD MTN. 9,170

MT. NICHOLAS

MT. ST. NICHOLAS 9,380

SCALPLOCK MTN. 6,925

SNOW SLIP MTN. 7,290

WALTON

ESSEX

PINNACLE RANGE

Middle Fork Flathead

FLATHEAD NATIONAL FOREST

NYACK

WEST GLACIER

MARTIN CITY

HUNGRY HORSE

Flathead River

HEADQUARTERS

APGAR

APGAR MTN. 5,210

FISH CREEK

AVALANCHE CREEK

Lake McDonald

GOING-TO-THE-SUN

SPRAGUE CREEK

MT. CANNON

Camas Creek

LINCOLN OF WALTON MTN. 8,941

LONEMAN MTN. 6,910

Harrison Cr.

Nyack Cr.

Harrison L. 3,528

North Fork Flathead

FLATHEAD

2

2

2

2

Chapter 1.

The Land of Shining Mountains

A MONG these mountains, those that lie to the west of the
river St. Pierre are called the Shining Mountains, from
an infinite number of crystal stones, of an amazing size, with
which they are covered, and which, when the sun shines full
upon them, sparkle so as to be seen at a very great distance. . . .
Probably in future ages they may be found to contain more riches
in their bowels than those of Indostan and Malabar, or that are
produced on the Golden Coast of Guinea; nor will I except even
the Peruvian mines." Thus spoke Jonathan Carver, soldier-ex-
plorer-writer, two hundred years ago. His river St. Pierre, which
he thought had its source in the mountains, is the present day
Minnesota; and his description of the unknown country to the west
was obtained from the Cree Indians, in whose country he was
traveling at the time.

Carver's sense of the dramatic often overshadowed his veracity,
but the "Shining Mountains" of his fancy have turned out to be
real, and his guess as to the riches contained in them is accurate
enough to make it seem a prophesy. The Shining Mountains are
the Rockies of Northwestern Montana and Southwestern Alberta,
now set aside as the Glacier National Park and Waterton Lakes
National Park. Carver's "crystal stones of an amazing size" are
living glaciers; and the riches of the mountains are far greater than
those of Indostan and Malabar, for they consist of transcendent
and imperishable beauty. Here the mountains tumble and froth

*Trick Falls in Two Medicine Valley is so named because of
an underground cavern into which part of the Two Medicine
River loses itself for brief seconds, only to reappear in a cloud
of spray rejoining main falls.* Glacier Park, Inc., photo.

like a wind-whipped tide as they careen off to the northwest. Here is the backbone of the continent and the little and big beginning of things. Here, huddled close together, are tiny streams, that, leagues to the north, the south, and the west, flow as mighty rivers into Hudson Bay, the Gulf of Mexico, and the Pacific Ocean. Here peak after peak, named and unnamed, rear their sawtooth edges to the clouds. Threescore glaciers are slowly and silently grinding away at their epochal task. Three hundred lakes in valley and in mountain pocket give back to the sky its blue, gray, or green. Half a thousand waterfalls cascade from everlasting snow in misty torrents or milk-white traceries. Rainbows flicker and vanish in the everlasting play of waters, while the clear sun does tricks of light and shade on pine and rock. High up on some gale-swept crag the shy goat pauses for a moment and plunges from view. Lower down the bighorn sheep treads his surefooted way. The powerful silvertip prowls in the upper reaches of the alpine meadows. The clownish black bear shuffles to his huckleberry patch. Far up in the blue, between mountain and sun, the golden eagle sails his rounded periods, peering down for the timid creature beneath the leaves and shadows of the rocks. Here indeed are riches. There are other canyons as deep, other mountains as high, but those who have roamed the world with open eyes say earnestly that there is no other place where nature has so condensed her wonders and run riot with such utter abandon, where she has carved and hewn with such unrestrained fancy and scattered her jewels with so reckless a hand. Here is the realization of Jonathan Carver's fanciful dream—the Land of Shining Mountains.

MAN IN GLACIER NATIONAL PARK

Glacier National Park forms the United States section of this magnificent mountain area. It lies astride the Continental Divide along the Livingstone and Lewis Ranges of the Rocky Mountains in northwestern Montana and contains nearly 1,600 square miles of spectacular scenery and primitive wilderness which President Theodore Roosevelt once called the "Great American Alps." But not even Switzerland can boast a million forest-green acres containing over 250 lakes, some sixty honest-to-goodness glaciers, over 1,100 different native flowers, and some fifty-seven species of wild animals and many varieties of birds.

While the Land of Shining Mountains is geologically over two billion years old, the archeology of the region is not well known.

2

There is evidence, however, that Indians have occupied the area for about ten thousand years. Stone weapon points, ranging in age from those used by hunters of extinct species of bison to the arrowheads of historic tribes, have been found throughout the region. But the occupants of the northern Montana plains during prehistoric times have not been identified. The Blackfeet, known to have been in the Eagle Hills of South Saskatchewan about 1720, penetrated this region before they acquired the horse. With the acquisition of the horse and possession of firearms, they consolidated their hold on the area. The Kootenai Indians, who now dwell only west of the Continental Divide, were displaced by the better armed and more mobile Blackfeet. A Siouan-speaking group, the Crows, who might have been pushing into the area from the southeast at about the same time, were driven beyond the Yellowstone River. The Blackfeet dominated the region until curbed and confined to reservations.

The first white men to see what is now Glacier National Park were probably French traders and trappers working for the Hudson's Bay Fur Company. This northeast part of the Park, which is in the Hudson Bay drainage, was granted the company in the 1700's, and it was undoubtedly the eloquent French who named these mountains "The Land of Shining Mountains." They probably saw them in the spring when there was lots of snow on their slopes and were very thrilled at the sight.

In 1806, the explorer Meriwether Lewis, of the Lewis and Clark Expedition, reached a point on the Marias about 30 miles from the present Park boundary. He named the river in honor of his cousin, Maria Wood. Subsequently someone (probably a printer) dropped the apostrophe, and Maria's River became the Marias; thus Miss Wood's one chance for fame was gone.

The valuable furs to be acquired around the upper tributaries of the Missouri River attracted venturesome fur trappers and traders from St. Louis, beginning in 1807. The trappers explored the region of the Three Forks of the Missouri, but the continuing hostility of the Blackfeet prevented their entry into the Glacier National Park area. It must be remembered, however, that trappers came after the beaver, and also the buffalo hides were plentiful and easy to hunt. It was, of course, only natural that the Blackfeet were displeased with the white man, who often took only the hide and the tongue of the buffalo, leaving the rest to rot in the heat of the prairie sun.

One of the first white men to make friends with the Blackfeet

3

ST. MARY LAKE from THE NARROWS

At left, Wahtotopa; (1) Little Chief; (2) Citadel; (3) Gunsight; (4) Fusillade; (5) Reynolds; (6) Heavy Runner; (7) Going-to-the-Sun; (8)

was Hugh Monroe, a French-Canadian trapper, who befriended the Blackfeet and married into the tribe. For many years he made his home with the Indians on the shore of St. Mary Lake. The tribe called this the "inside lake" because it was surrounded by mountains, and Lower St. Mary was called the "outside lake" as it had no mountains around it. Some historians believe that Hugh Monroe with the Jesuit Priest Father Peter De Smet named St. Mary Lake as such in 1834. Many landmarks in the Two Medicine area are named for Hugh Monroe or his family. Sinopah, the mountain across Two Medicine Lake, was Hugh Monroe's Indian wife. There is a mountain near called Never Laughs; this was Hugh Monroe's father-in-law. Monroe's Indian name was Rising Wolf, and there is a mountain there by that name, too. He got that name because he allegedly got up in the morning on all fours uttering guttural sounds out of his throat.

Between the Lewis and Clark Expedition of 1806 and the United States presidential campaign of 1844, nothing much was done to, in, or about what was to become Glacier National Park. The conflicting claims of England and the United States to the Pacific Northwest produced hotter and hotter arguments, but none of them melted the Glacier snows and ice. In 1844, the two countries were at the brink of war after James K. Polk, a Democrat, campaigned successfully on the slogan, "Fifty-Four Forty or Fight." By that he meant that the boundary between Canada and the United States would have to cross the Rockies at about the latitude of Prince Rupert, British Columbia. Polk settled for less. The powers agreed in 1846 on the 49th parallel as a boundary, all the way from Lake of the Woods between Minnesota and Manitoba to Point Roberts on Puget Sound. That put Glacier Park inside the United States.

The period from 1850 to 1900 could be called the "period of discovery" of Glacier National Park. Although a few white persons did set foot in the Park area prior to 1850, most of the early effort was spent in establishing, consciously or otherwise, a solid line of approach to the mountains. Now, for the first time, organized parties actually began to enter the mountains and explore them. The railroad surveys, boundary survey parties, the U. S. Army, and various others interested in the region pushed farther and farther into the area, finding new routes across the mountains.

In 1853, A. W. Tinkham, a Government engineer, exploring a route for a Pacific railroad, traveled up Flathead Lake and the Middle Fork of the Flathead River to what is now known as

5

Nyack Creek. Here Tinkham's guide, for reasons known only to himself, turned off up Nyack Creek and led the party over Cut Bank (Pitamakan) Pass. From here, the party proceeded down to Fort Benton. While Tinkham reported the country as being impractical for railroad purposes, his was the first accurate journal of a trip through what is now the Park.

Another early penetration of the Park area was by international boundary survey parties. With the settlement of the boundary disputes between the United States and Great Britain, plans were made to survey and mark the boundary dividing the two countries along the 49th parallel. In 1861 a survey party of the newly-formed Northwest Boundary Commission, led by Archibald Campbell, and a corresponding British party, reached the Continental Divide and established a station there on the north edge of the park, completing the first survey of the 49th parallel from the Pacific Ocean to the summit of the Rockies. In March, 1872, President Ulysses S. Grant signed the bill authorizing the remainder of the survey, between the Lake of the Woods, Minnesota, and the summit of the Rockies, to complete the boundary survey between the United States and Canada. In 1874 the survey parties from the east reached the Continental Divide, connecting with the survey of 1861.

Just prior to the survey of the second section of the international boundary, a series of incidents occurred that effectively put an end to the Indian troubles east of the mountains and paved the way for a steadily increasing number of exploration parties in the area. In 1855, following his return from the northwest and numerous conferences with different Indian tribes of the area, Governor Isaac I. Stevens of Washington Territory called a great council of the northwestern Indians on the Judith River, including tribes from both east and west of the mountains, for the purpose of establishing hunting grounds and promoting peace between them. The result of this treaty was the establishment of a common hunting ground for all tribes east and west of the mountains and closure of the passes leading across the mountains into the remainder of the Blackfeet territory. The western Indians did not like being told where they could hunt, and this really touched off the fireworks. The treaty was condemned by the western tribes and was never kept, resulting in warfare between 1855 and 1870.

In 1869, Malcolm Clark, one of the early factors for the fur companies in the Missouri, then operating a stage station near Helena, Montana, was shot down in the door of his home by two Piegan Indians. Clark's wife and one son, Horace, were also

6

wounded in the fray. Major Clark's murder, coupled with the cold-blooded killing of Mountain Chief's brother and a young Blood Indian on the streets of Fort Benton, led to the open combat between whites and Indians sometimes known as the Piegan War.

Following numerous Indian raids and much agitation for action by Clark's two sons, Horace and Nathan, a column of infantry and cavalry under Colonel Eugene M. Baker, accompanied by the two Clark boys, left Fort Shaw January 19, 1870, to find Mountain Chief and his band of some 1,500 Blackfeet Indians and punish them. Four days later they came upon an Indian village on the Marias River in the dark and surrounded it, presumably thinking it was the camp of Mountain Chief, who was camped farther down the river.

The camp was, in reality, a smallpox camp headed by Heavy Runner, an Indian who had been unswervingly friendly to the whites. The troops were ordered to open fire and not let anyone escape. Upon hearing the shooting, Heavy Runner ran out in an attempt to stop the fighting and was shot down. The troops then descended upon the camp and massacred nearly everyone in it, killing 173 and wounding 20, nearly all of whom were women and children or men too ill to defend themselves. It was one of the blackest deeds perpetrated upon the Indians by white men of the region. But the Baker Massacre, horrible though it was, marked the end of organized Indian uprising as well as the Treaty of 1855, which had caused cessation of further attempts to enter this part of the Rockies.

In the 1880's, the railroads showed renewed interest in finding a northwest pass through the mountains. Roads farther south were rapidly pushing rails westward, but so far there had been no indication of iron reaching toward the Park area. Then, James J. Hill, the famous railroad magnate, directed one of his young engineers, John F. Stevens, to locate the elusive Marias Pass described by early traders and trappers such as Finan McDonald. In December of 1889, accompanied by a Flathead Indian named Coonsah, Stevens started out to locate this pass. The bitter cold proved too much for Coonsah, who became exhausted and had to be left behind near the location of the station of Lubec. Thus Stevens proceeded on alone and by evening had reached the pass and crossed it far enough to be certain that it was the true pass and that it was usable for the railway. Since it was too late to return that night to the camp, Stevens remained in the pass until morning, tramping in a runway beaten out of the snow to keep from freezing. The next morning he found that Coonsah had allowed the campfire to go out and was almost frozen. Stevens revived him, and they returned to the Blackfeet agency on Badger Creek. A monument was erected by the Great Northern Railway on Marias Pass, near the headwaters of what Lewis had intended to call Maria's River, which now commemorates Stevens' location of the pass.

In 1890, copper ore was found at the head of Quartz Creek, and there was a rush of prospectors. The east side of the Continental Divide, being part of the Blackfeet Indian Reservation, was closed to prospectors, and Congress was importuned to take steps that would open the area to investigation of the mineral resources. In 1896, this land was purchased from the Indians for $1½ million and was opened to exploration. For a short while there was considerable activity in the valleys of the St. Mary and the Swiftcurrent. The mining villages of Altyn and St. Mary flourished for a time, and then, when it was found that minerals did not exist in sufficient quantity to make mining profitable, they died out. A few weather-beaten log cabins and prospect holes here and there in the mountains are all that remain to mark the points where hopes once high had grown fainter and had been abandoned.

After the excitement over the copper had died down, the region was visited only by big-game hunters and occasional sightseers until it was made a National Park in 1910. Actually, it was through the efforts of George Bird Grinnell that the latter occurred.

Often called "the father of Glacier Park," Grinnell first came to the area in 1885 and became captivated with the region and returned annually for many years. He saw the possibilities of the area, and for twenty-five years he labored courageously to have it set aside as a National Park. He contended against Indian problems, opposition from those who wished to further their private interests, and even arguments of Congressional committees. Finally, in the spring of 1910, after previously rejecting two bills to make the area a National Park, Congress passed and sent to President William Howard Taft a bill establishing Glacier National Park. The President signed the bill on May 11, 1910.

Glacier National Park in the United States and Waterton Lakes National Park in Canada are formally known as the International Peace Park. The idea to link the two Parks originated at the first goodwill meeting of the Rotary Clubs of Alberta and Montana in 1931. By their efforts laws were passed the following year by Canada and the United States to link the two Parks into the first international peace park in the world. The association formed by the original Rotarians meets annually on alternate sides of the border to renew their pledge of friendship and foster goodwill.

8

HISTORY OF WATERTON LAKES
NATIONAL PARK

Waterton Lakes National Park, situated in the extreme south-west corner of the Province of Alberta, was set apart in 1895. It covers an area of 202.8 square miles along the eastern slope of the Rocky Mountains immediately north of the international boundary. It is one of the most colorful of Canada's playgrounds.

The Park derives its name from the lakes that form the main valley. These lakes were named in honor of Charles Waterton, famed eighteenth-century English naturalist, by Lieutenant Thomas Blakiston, who led a section of the Palliser Expedition of 1857-1860. This expedition was looking for a pass to traverse in the Rockies so that eastern Canada could be connected with her west coast settlement.

The Palliser Expedition marked a turning point in the history of the region which hitherto had been practically unknown territory and a stronghold of the hostile Blackfeet Indian Federation. In 1886, traces of oil were discovered in Lineham Creek, and Alberta's first oil well was drilled there in 1902. The location of the well can still be seen from the Akamina Highway some 5 miles from Waterton townsite. The gradual settlement of the region ultimately led to the filing of a petition to make this area a Canadian national park. Most active in the promoting of this objective was John George "Kootenai" Brown, who was later to become the first park warden and subsequently the acting park superintendent.

Kootenai was a dashing, swashbuckling fellow about whom many tales are told similar to those surrounding Davy Crockett of American fame. For example, one tale is that at his cabin in Waterton he had an immense tame bear that he had released from a trap and domesticated. So well did he train bruin that the animal used to come when called and serve as a pack horse whenever Kootenai decided on an expedition back into the mountains. One morning he stepped outside the cabin door and called for his pet. This time he received no response to his call, and when his patience was finally exhausted, he saw the big bear quite unconcerned at the edge of the clearing. Dashing over he grabbed bruin by the scruff of his neck and gave him the thrashing of his life. When he decided that he had administered enough punishment, he turned toward the cabin, and there to his amazement he saw his own pet bear ambling amiably from the back of his cabin. He had thrashed the wrong bear!

There is an old saying that if one would learn a man's back-

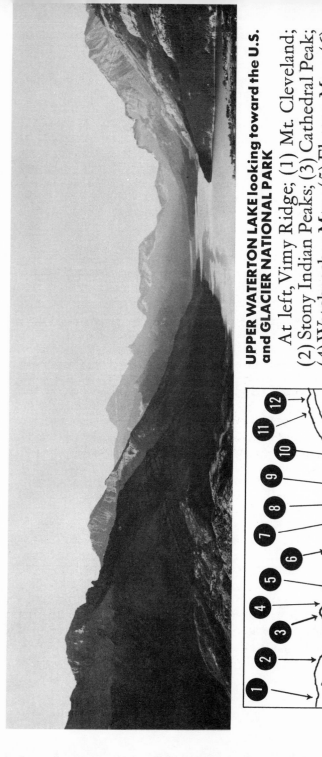

UPPER WATERTON LAKE looking toward the U.S. and GLACIER NATIONAL PARK

At left, Vimy Ridge; (1) Mt. Cleveland; (2) Stony Indian Peaks; (3) Cathedral Peak; (4) Watcheechee Mtn.; (5) Flattop Mtn.; (6) West Flattop Mtn.; (7) Citadel Peaks; (8) Porcupine Ridge; (9) Campbell Mtn.; (10) Bertha Peak; (11) Mt. Crandell; (12)

ground one should see him intoxicated. If such is the test of man-hood, then Kootenai Brown measured up completely. No matter what the in-between years had been, his birthright and culture as a young man were genuine. (He was once an officer in the British Army and a great favorite at the English royal court.) Let no man scoff because he was a squaw-man; his Indian wives received the courtesy and consideration due the wife of a white man, and the man who, drunk or sober, uttered a disparaging remark about either Mary Delano Brown or "Nee-Pa-Tha-Qua-Ka-Soon" had to deal with the indignant wrath of Kootenai. He now lies buried in a little picket-fenced plot near the lower Waterton Lakes, with his Indian wives on either side of him; it is also said that a good bottle of contraband whiskey rests more closely to him.

THE BLACKFEET AND THE LAND OF SHINING MOUNTAINS

Any presentation of Glacier and Waterton Lakes National Parks would be inadequate and incomplete that did not have regard for the primitive and picturesque tribesmen who live in the very shadows of the "Shining Mountains" and whose traditions and history have so enriched these areas with Indian lore.

These people are, of course, the Blackfeet Indians. Actually this tribe is made of three subtribes. The northern tribe, which has its reservation today in northern Alberta, are called the Siksika, or Blackfeet proper, from the black moccasins they wore. The central subtribe, who have their reservation today in southern Alberta close to Waterton Lakes National Park, are called the Kainah, or Blood, because of the way they painted their faces and arms with bright red paint made from clay or possibly berries. The southern subtribe, who have their reservation bordering the eastern edge of Glacier National Park, are called the Piegans. This word literally translated means "Far-off Robe"; its more idiomatic equivalent is "Poorly dressed relations."

Only a century or so ago the Blackfeet, in bands of restless, predatory warriors and hunters, dominated the rich buffalo plains that spread from the Saskatchewan to the southernmost head-streams of the Missouri and eastward along the Missouri from the Rockies to the mouth of the Yellowstone. They protected the Sarsi and Atsina, but they waged constant and relentless warfare against the Flatheads, Nez Percés, Shoshones, Crees, Crows, Sioux, Assiniboin, Kootenai, and Snakes. They maintained no permanent habitations but lived in skin tepees which, with their other belongings, were easily packed on travois and transported from place to place. First, they used dog travois, which were constructed by taking two short poles and fastening them together over the dogs' fore shoulders and then tying them beneath under their front legs. The Blackfeet secured their belongings to the travois, which the dogs pulled when called. With the introduction of the horse by the Spanish in the 1500's, the Indians soon captured many horses, and they spread over the western part of the United States. This animal changed the Indians' way of life somewhat. Now they could carry more of their belongings farther and faster. They oftentimes used the lodgepoles of their tepees for the poles of the travois. The horse also brought them a source of exchange or barter, and horses became very valuable and wars were fought over them.

The Blackfeet used the buffalo for all their needs. They used the hide for their tepees and for clothing. The meat, of course, was used for food both fresh and smoked, or pounded into pemmican with berries and dried—a sort of dehydrating process. The horns were used for cups, the bones for scraping tools and shallow dishes, the intestines for strings on their bows, the hooves for glue, and even the tail was used, and for the same purpose as the buffalo used it—as a fly-swatter.

Killing the buffalo was quite difficult before the horse was acquired. One way to get them was to drive them over cliffs. The younger warriors would drive the buffalo over a cliff, and then the older men would be at the base of the cliff to kill those that were not killed in the fall. The women would then set to work cleaning and preparing the meat and skin. Near the site of the Holy Family Mission on the Two Medicine River, one of these cliffs has been found with thousands of bleached buffalo bones at its base. There is another cliff, or piskun, which has been found in Waterton Park along the Pass Creek Highway.

Communal life centered around just a few lodges, and the head of each household was a chief. A man had to prove himself as a brave warrior, and then when his possession of horses, wives, and other goods was great he was a chief. And so it was that from these villages the Blackfeet ranged to make war and steal horses from their enemies. They painted their bodies and rode their horses off into the mountains to find fame and to prove their bravery. Crossing the mountains was very difficult on horseback. One of the passes that horses could be taken across was Pitamakan Pass near the Two Medicine area. This pass was named for an Indian maiden, Pitamakan, who proved to be as brave in combat as any of the men; and she led the men on many forays over this pass into the Flathead Valley near the "Lake of Sacred Dancing

12

Waters," which is today called Lake McDonald. Here the Flathead were met and engaged in battle. Today we can see the stories of these battles as painted on buffalo hides. These can be seen in the lobby of the Prince of Wales Hotel and the Museum of the Plains Indian in Browning, Montana.

The Blackfeet believed that their principal deity, "Napi," lived in the sun. They ascribed both human and supernatural attributes and magical power to many animals and inanimate things. Individual acts were influenced largely by dreams, and each Indian had his personal "medicine" or manito, an animal or an object, through which he warded off the ill will of the spirit world and sought the aid of magic powers. The tribe had many "sacred bundles," with ceremonies consisting of songs, dances, and incantations surrounding each. They practiced polygamy; and their dead were lashed in trees or laid away in tepees erected for the purpose on prominent hills. Their great tribal festival was the Sun Dance, at which they erected a "Sun Lodge" and made sacrifices of food, clothing, and other valuables, and for participation in which they prepared by fasting and self-inflicted penances.

The principal hero of their mythology is a curious semisupernatural creature known as "Napi" or "Old Man." Many of the living members of the Piegan and Blood tribes have rich funds of stories concerning Napi. Some of them portray him as a beneficent power working for the benefit of the tribes; sometimes he assumes the cleverness of a demon in working mischievous pranks, and in other myths he is the grotesque butt of some Blackfoot mortal's farcical humor.

Writers do not agree as to what use the Blackfeet made of the mountainous areas of their domain which are now included in Glacier and Waterton Lakes Parks. Some say the Indians feared the mountains. The lofty peaks, the gloom of the forests, the roar of waterfalls, and the shriek of winds in storm-swept defiles were believed the expression of a malignant force that could be wisely avoided by remaining on the plains—those plains they loved—whose wide vistas could conceal no lurking enemy, supernatural or otherwise. Others tell us the Blackfeet went on many hunting excursions into that matchless area where elk, pastured in the high flower-starred valleys, and mountain sheep and goats, perched on dizzy ledges, offered worthy targets for their arrows.

One of the Indian legends of the area was "proved" by Henry L. Stimson, who is best known for his service to the United States as Secretary of War during World War I. In 1891, he was a member of the party that discovered the mountain that was later to

13

bear his name. The following year Stimson and Dr. Walter B. James of New York City, accompanied by an Indian guide named "Indian Billy," ascended the precipitous east face of Chief Mountain. Upon reaching the summit they found the remains of an old bison skull, decayed except for the frontal bone and the horn stubs, securely anchored by rocks on the highest point, and protected from the wind. The presence of the skull may be accounted for by a story told by the Flathead Indians. One of their braves went across the mountains to make his "warrior's sleep" and to prepare for his "medicine vision." He climbed to the top of a large mountain overlooking the plains and stayed for days, fasting and praying until he had received the vision that was to govern his life. Then he returned, leaving the skull on the mountaintop. Since no white man had previously set foot on the peak before Stimson climbed it and since no bull bison could have climbed it, the story is the logical explanation for the presence of the skull on 9,066-foot Chief Mountain.

Today the Blackfeet on the reservation adjoining the park on the east remain a picturesque reminder of their former glory. They have laid aside their intense hostility to the white man and have reconciled themselves to the march of civilization. Some of them, dressed in colorful native costume, demonstrate their traditional dances occasionally at Glacier Park Lodge, St. Mary, and Babb during the summer season. At Browning, 12 miles east of East Glacier Park, a museum is maintained to interpret the customs and ways of life of the Indians of the Great Plains through many murals, exhibits, and dioramas. The museum is operated by the Bureau of Indian Affairs of the U. S. Department of the Interior. An arts and crafts center in the building serves as a central market for handicraft articles made by the present-day Indians of the reservations of the northern plains. The Flathead Indian Reservation is west of the park on U. S. Highway 93, between the towns of Polson and Missoula.

PARK ADMINISTRATION

The Waterton-Glacier International Peace Park is a non-administrative arrangement since each Park is under separate administrations. For instance, Glacier National Park is administered by the National Park Service, U. S. Department of the Interior. A superintendent is in immediate charge; his address is Glacier National Park, West Glacier, Montana 59936.

Park rangers and naturalists are here to help you learn and

understand the natural and human history of Glacier (see Chapter 3), to enforce Park regulations, and to help and advise you; therefore, you should consult them if you have any questions about the Park or are in any difficulty. Rangers also protect animals from poachers and guard United States property. They have complete authority. Everybody in the Park is trained in fighting forest fires —Glacier's woods get powder-dry every summer and are explosively susceptible to devastating burns. When fire does come, rangers are aided by Forest Service smoke jumpers from Missoula, Montana, and by other professionals flown in from all over the West.

In winter the rangers' duties require them to do lots of skiing and snowshoeing. They forecast that the Park will have a fabulous winter-sport future. Even now it is used a lot by a few hardy connoisseurs of cross-country and alpine skiing. Maintenance and engineering divisions keep roads plowed free of snow until winter storms make this impossible—the Going-to-the-Sun Road, for example, often has big drifts of up to 80 feet. In order to get this road open for visitor travel by June 15, each year an average of some 100,000 cubic yards of snow must be removed from it.

Waterton Lakes National Park is administered by the Department of Indian Affairs and Northern Development of Canada. A superintendent, with headquarters in Waterton townsite, is in immediate charge. The uniformed Park Warden Service is basically a protection organization with primary responsibility for:

1. Protecting the natural scene or features of the Park, including the forests and wildlife.

2. Advising visitors to the Park of the regulations established for their guidance, protection, and safety.

3. Assisting and directing visitors in their use of the Park.

Within Waterton Lakes National Park the maintenance of law and order is the responsibility of the Royal Canadian Mounted Police. Park wardens (and any other park officers so appointed by the Parks Service) also have all the powers of a police constable and are concerned with the enforcement of the Park regulations.

HOW TO REACH THE PARKS

The Land of Shining Mountains can be reached by automobile, train, bus, or airplane. Bus, train, and airline schedule information is available from your local travel agent or from Glacier Park, Inc. (see page 165 for address). See Mileage Table next page.

Road Mileages—Glacier National Park and Vicinity

	Whitefish	West Glacier	Waterton Lakes National Park	Two Medicine	St. Mary	Rising Sun	Polebridge	Park hdqrts.	Many Glacier	Logan Pass	Lake McDonald Lodge	Kiowa Junction	Kintla Lake	Kalispell	Going-to-the-Sun Point	East Glacier Park	Browning	Babb Junction	Avalanche Campground	Apgar
Apgar	29	3	94	72b 83a	47	41	28	3	68	29	8	67a 72b	44	35	37	60b 79a	73b 80a	56	13	
Avalanche Campground	42	16	81	70a 85b	34	28	41	16	55	16	5	54	57	48	24	66c 73b	67c 86b	43		13
Babb Junction	87a 123c	59	38	45	9	15	84	59	12	27	48	29	100	91a 130c	19	41	42		43	56
Browning	99b	70b 83a	80	25	33	39	101b 108a	71b 83a	54	51	72a 81b	13	117b 124a	102b	43	13		42	67c 86b	73b 80a
East Glacier Park	86b 108a	57b 82a	79	12	32	38	88b 107a	58b 82a	53	50c	68b 71a	12	104b 123a	89b 114a	42		13	41	66c 73b	60b 79a
Going-to-the-Sun Point	66a	40	57	46	10	4	65	40	31	8	29	30	87a	72a		42	43	19	24	37
Kalispell	16	32	129a	101b 118a	82a 121b	76a	63d	33	103a 142c	64	43	102a 101b	79d		72	89b 114a	102b	91a 130c	48	35
Kintla Lake	73d	47	138a	116b 127a	91a	85a	16	47	112a	73	52	111a 116b		79d	81	104b 123a	117b 124a	100	57	44
Kiowa Junction	96a 95b	70a 69b	67	16	20	26	95a 100c	70a 70b	41	38	59a 80b		111a 116b	102a 101b	30	12	13	29	54	67a 72b

Glacier National Park — Distance Chart (in miles)

Lake McDonald Lodge	8	5	48	72a 81b	68b 71a	29	43	52	59a 80b	21	60	11	36	33	39	75a 80b	86	11	37
Logan Pass	29	16	27	51	50c	8	64	73	38		39	32	57	12	18	54	65	32	58
Many Glacier	68	55	12	54c	53	31	103a 142c	112	41	39		71	96	27	21	57	50	71	97a 139c
Park hdqtrs.	3	16	59	71b 83a	58b 82a	40	33	47	70a 70b	32	71		31	44	50	70b 86a	97a	1	27
Polebridge	28	41	84	101a 108a	88b 107a	65	63d	16	95a 100b	57	96	31		69	75	100b 111a	122a	31	57d
Rising Sun	41	28	15	39	38	4	76a	85	26	12	27	44	69		6	42	53	44	70a
St. Mary	47	34	9	33c	32	10	82a	91	20	18	21	50	75	6		36	47	50	76a 115b
Two Medicine	72b 83a	70a 85b	45	25	12	46	101b 118a	116b 127a	16	54	57	70b 86a	100b 111a	42	36		83	69b 86a	95b 112a
Waterton Lakes Park	94	81	38	80c	79	57	129a	138a	67	65	50	97a	122a	53	47	83		97a	123a 165b
West Glacier	3	16	59	70b 83a	57b 82a	40	32	47	70a 69b	32	71	1	31	44	50	69b 86a	97a		26
Whitefish	29	42	87a 123c	99b 108a	86b 108a	66a	16	73d	96a 95b	58	97a 139c	27	57d	70a	76a 115b	95b 112a	123a 165b	26	

(a) Via Going-to-the-Sun Road
(b) Via U.S. Highway 2
(c) Via Kiowa Junction
(d) Via Apgar

GLACIER NATIONAL PARK

By automobile. You can reach Glacier National Park over a number of modern, well-marked roads. It is on U. S. 2 and 89 and near U. S. 91 and 93. From Canada, it is a choice of Alberta Highways 2, 3, 5, and 6. Automobile associations, touring services, travel bureaus, chambers of commerce, and leading gasoline stations can furnish road information and maps. You should make local inquiry concerning road conditions and snow in high mountain passes in May and June and in September and October.

By train. The park is on the main transcontinental line of the Great Northern Railway. For information about railroad fares and services, inquire of local ticket agents or travel bureaus, or write the Passenger Traffic Manager, 175 East Fourth Street, St. Paul, Minnesota. Regular bus service is provided by Glacier Park, Inc., for those who arrive by train.

By bus. The Glacier Transportation Company operates buses both to West Glacier and East Glacier Park from Kalispell, Shelby, and Great Falls. (This line connects with Greyhound Lines.) On the north, Glacier Park, Inc., buses connect at Waterton Lake with the Central Canadian Greyhound Lines from Lethbridge or Fort Macleod.

By airplane. West Coast Airlines serves Flathead County Airport, 26 miles west (by road) of West Glacier. Northwest Orient Airlines, Western Airlines, and West Coast Airlines also serve the Park. All three lines have regular schedules to Great Falls, which is an easy 143 miles to East Glacier Park by bus or rental car. Glacier Park, Inc., will provide on-call service for air passengers, but you should make arrangements for such service with the airlines before you start your trip.

WATERTON LAKES NATIONAL PARK

By automobile. Waterton Lakes National Park is reached by the Provincial Highway System of Alberta, which connects with the park highways. From the east, approach may be made from Medicine Hat via Lethbridge and Fort Macleod to Pincher Creek (town) and from there south to the park (Route 6). An alternative route from Lethbridge is through Cardston (Route 5). From British Columbia on the west, approach may be made via Crowsnest Pass and Pincher. From the north, a hard-surfaced route may be followed from Edmonton to Calgary and Fort Macleod, and from there to the Park, via Pincher. The most direct approach to

18

Waterton Lakes National Park from the United States is over the Chief Mountain International Highway (Route 17) from Glacier National Park. Glacier Park, Inc., operates a frequent service over this route. This highway also forms a link in the new hard-surfaced route between Glacier National Park and Banff National Park and the other Canadian Mountain National Parks.

By train. The Park is accessible via the Canadian Pacific Railway to Pincher Creek or Cardston, and by a convenient bus service from these points. Buses leave Lethbridge for the Park twice daily in summer, one by way of Cardston and one by way of Pincher Creek. The trip takes approximately three hours. A station bus operates between Pincher Station and Pincher Creek for the convenience of those traveling by train. The bus also makes a daily round trip to Waterton Park.

By airplane. Visitors traveling by air are served by Trans-Canada Airlines and Western Airlines, which make scheduled stops at Lethbridge. A small landing field for private craft is also located near Pincher Creek.

Border Crossing Stations

United States citizens do not need a passport to enter Canada. However, it would be helpful to carry some proof of United States citizenship, such as a birth or baptismal certificate, or voter's registration card. Naturalized citizens should carry documentary evidence of citizenship. Alien permanent residents in the United States are advised to carry their alien registration receipt card (U. S. Form 1-151).

Information on the hours that the Ports of Entry are open may be obtained at both Parks' Entrance Stations.

ENTRANCE PERMIT

Glacier National Park has been designated as a federal recreation area pursuant to the Land and Water Conservation Fund Act of 1965, as amended. This means that the $7.00 *Annual Federal Recreation/Conservation Area Entrance* permit admits the individual paying such fee and all those who accompany him in a private noncommercial automobile. This permit is good until March 31 of the year following issuance and admits the purchaser to all national parks, national forests, and other federal areas designated as "recreation areas."

If you do not purchase an annual permit, a temporary 30-day

permit or a day-use permit may be purchased. All permits can be obtained at any entrance station.

Motorists entering Waterton Lakes National Park must register and obtain Park motor licenses. Licenses are issued for motor vehicles not used for commercial purposes on the basis of:

(1) Single trip license: Automobile, 25 cents; auto with trailer, 50 cents.

(2) License good for entire season, which is also honored at Elk Island, Prince Albert, Riding Mountain, and Point Pelee National Parks: Automobile, $1.00; auto with trailer, $2.00.

(3) Special license for entire season, honored in *all* national parks of Canada: Automobile, $2.00; auto with trailer, $3.00.

Special licenses may be obtained for motor vehicles used for commercial purposes.

PARK SEASON

The park season in Glacier is usually from May 15 to October 15, inclusive. As a rule, the Park roads at lower elevations are open by May 15, and every attempt is made to have the Going-to-the-Sun Road over Logan Pass open by June 15. While Waterton Lakes National Park is officially open the year around, its *actual* season is the same as Glacier's.

In spite of extensive snowfields in the high country during early summer, the weather is seldom cold in July or August. Good clear weather, with temperatures in the 70's and 80's, is customary almost every day from July 1 to September 1. Before and after these dates the visitor is likely to be rained upon or snowed in for a few days, but the beauty of the snowy peaks on occasional clear days more than compensates for the inconvenience. But, even during the summer, sudden rain squalls or thundershowers may occur, and so—a word to the wise for hikers—add a raincoat to your equipment. You will need warm clothing while hiking in the higher elevations at all times of the year. Days are warm, but when the sun sets or during storms you will reach for a sweater, and nights are chilly!

Another plus for summer visitors is the Parks' pollen count. Hay fever sufferers hear about the Waterton-Glacier region's pollen count of less than .001 and hasten to make their reservations.

Chapter 2.

A Playground—Millions of Years in the Making

THE spectacular beauty of the Glacier and Waterton Lakes section of the Rocky Mountains is partially explained by the structural history of the country. The geological story of how these rocky peaks thrust up and folded over in what the books call "the archetype of overthrusts" is a scientific thriller.

This story began better than a half-billion years ago. At that time, a long, narrow, shallow arm of the sea extended south from the Arctic Ocean, covering much of western Montana and perhaps joining, farther south, a similar arm of the Pacific Ocean. The region of Glacier and Waterton Parks formed part of the flat bottom of this sea. For millions of years the sea persisted with little change. Throughout this time, clay, lime, silt, sand, and other sediments were carried by streams into this sea and settled on the bottom, just as deposits of sediment are everywhere accumulating on the bottoms of seas and lakes today.

With the passing of time, the sea withdrew from the great trough that extended throughout the Rocky Mountain area. Pressure, heat, and chemical changes eventually solidified the sediment into argillites, quartzites, and limestones, forming the multicolored strata that now make up Glacier's spectacular scenery. Later, molten rock penetrated into cracks and between the rock layers; lava oozed along the ancient sea floor. Also scattered throughout these rocks are remains of deposits made by colonies of algae.

The story of the elevation of these rocks from sea bottom to soaring heights is a dramatic chapter in the formation of the landscape of Waterton Lakes and Glacier National Parks. Long after the seas had disappeared, the region became dry land. But the crust of the earth is nowhere absolutely at rest. Geologists have much evidence that the earthball is gradually shrinking. As its surface gets smaller and smaller, great wrinkles or folds develop. Rocks, however, are relatively plastic, but, in some places, break under the stresses set up by shrinkage or otherwise. So the strata in the Glacier-Waterton region were wrinkled and folded; so too, great fractures occurred that parallel its two mountain regions of today. Meanwhile, increasingly great pressure was being exerted on the rocky block from the southwest, a pressure that grew so irresistible that the strata gradually gave way to the strain; a huge mass was not only uplifted as a gigantic mountain range, but also shoved far over the beds adjoining it on the east, presenting the lofty mountain wall with an absence of foothills that is so striking.

A fracture of the earth's crust with slippage of one portion with respect to an adjacent portion is known as a fault. A horizontal thrusting of a faulted block over another is known as an overthrust. From the mountain range that was formed by it, the local overthrust fault is termed the *Lewis Overthrust*. It is traceable throughout the entire length of the Parks. The horizontal encroachment of mountain over plain, which must have occupied millions of years, is estimated as having been at least thirty-five miles in this region. Greater overthrusts throughout the world are known to geologists. The fault caused by Lewis Overthrust possibly extends as far south as the vicinity of Helena, Montana, and as far north as Canada's Banff National Park. But nowhere is there a fault which is so readily apparent to those who are not physiographers; nowhere one that can be so easily traced for such a great distance. It is well exposed on the eastern side of Glacier Park, and Chief Mountain, standing out by itself near the Canadian border, is a remnant of this overthrust mass.

Coincident with or consequent upon the overthrust came uplift of the region. This uplift stimulated all the streams to increased activity, and the great mass of the mountains was deeply scored by the canyons they cut. Running water is the most powerful agent known in carving mountains and other features of high relief. Where the streams have a sharp descent the cutting is rapid, but the force slowly becomes less effective as the grade is reduced, until the stream becomes sluggish, and then its cutting power ceases, and it builds up instead of wearing down its channel. This process, which is known as erosion, may be witnessed by anyone in small rills or brooks after a hard rain. Each stream is swollen with water which, if the ground or rock over which the stream passes is soft, is heavily charged with mud and sand that act as cutting and scouring agents, effectively rasping the walls and deepening the channel of the stream. Where it reaches a lowland or

22

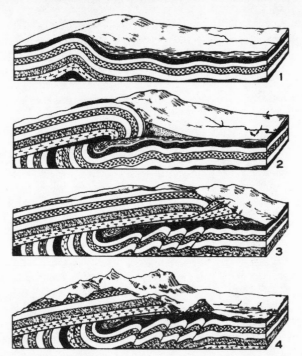

The first of these diagrams shows the sea-bed layers being arched upward. In 2, the surface has bent so far that it has broken and older layers are moving over the younger ones. Figure 3 shows a section after the thrust ended. The mountains as they are today, with rocks carved into peaks and valleys, are shown in Figure 4.

---

pond, the coarser sediment carried by the water is deposited, being spread out over the flat land or built out as a delta in a pond or lake. While the process of stream erosion may seem to be slow, in reality it is rapid for the streams, especially in a mountain country, are constantly charged with abrasive sand or gravel and so are always at work. There is no cessation, no relief from the endless rasping of the grains of sand on the beds of the streams, and as a result the hardest and most massive rocks are rapidly worn away. The streams cut deep gorges, which at first may have nearly vertical walls and be true canyons, but which in a region of considerable precipitation will sooner or later take on, in cross section, the form of a V.

23

As time goes on the streams cut farther and farther back into the mountain mass until they completely dissect it, leaving instead of an upland plateau a region of serrate ridges and sharp peaks. In this manner most of the mountains of the world have been produced—not by volcanic eruption and sudden movement, but by gradual uplift and the dissection of the uplifted mass into rugged mountain forms by the streams.

The final chapter of the Parks begins with the ice age, about a million years ago. A change in climate resulted in the formation of vast ice sheets over much of northern North America and Europe. Heavy snows accumulating in the area of Glacier National Park began to form individual ice masses, or mountain glaciers. In the upper valleys at high elevations, the snow and ice formed small glaciers. These in turn joined to form larger glaciers.

In Glacier National Park, during the Ice Age, it is evident, due to recent studies, that ice did not cover the entire range, but that the higher peaks stood out above the ice, which probably never reached a thickness of over 3,000 feet in this region. The V-shaped valleys which had been produced by stream erosion were filled with valley glaciers. The weight of the ice caused the ice masses to move slowly down the valleys that were first cut by streams.

Glaciers are powerful agents of erosion—the process resulting mainly from plucking and abrasion. Plucking takes place mainly near the head of the glacier, where the ice freezes to the rock walls and pulls off huge slabs as it moves forward. Usually a large crevasse, the bergschrund, develops in the ice at the head of the glacier. The bergschrund of most glaciers in the Park consists of an opening 10 to 15 feet wide at the top and about 50 feet deep. This continuous plucking action of a glacier results in the formation of a deep amphitheater called a cirque.

Abrasion takes place due to the rock fragments frozen into the bottom and sides of the glacier. These fragments act as a huge file or rasp as the ice mass moves down its course. Valleys eroded by streams are V-shaped. Glaciers scour and grind the sides and bottoms to form a characteristic U-shaped cross section, such as is found in practically all the valleys of the Park, including Two Medicine, Cut Bank, St. Mary, Swiftcurrent, McDonald, Waterton Lakes, and Belly River. Since the main glaciers were at least a half-mile thick, the results of glaciation can be seen far up the sides of the large valleys.

Sperry Glacier is the second largest one in the Parks. Great Northern Railway photo.

The tributaries of glacial valleys are also peculiar in that they usually enter high above the floor of the main valley and thus are known as hanging valleys. The thicker a stream of ice, the more erosion it is capable of performing; consequently the main valley becomes greatly deepened, whereas the smaller glacier in the tributary valley does not cut down so rapidly, leaving its valley hanging high above the floor of the major valley. The valleys of Virginia and Florence Creeks, tributary to the St. Mary Valley, are good examples of hanging valleys. The valley above "Bird Woman Falls" as seen from Going-to-the-Sun Road is a spectacular illustration of hanging valley. In addition there are many others, such as Preston Park and the Hanging Gardens near Logan Pass, and Cameron Falls in Waterton Park.

Even more conspicuous than the large U-shaped valleys and their hanging tributaries are the long sharp-crested ridges which form most of the backbone of the Lewis Range. These features, of which the Garden Wall is one of the most notable, are known as arêtes and owe their origin also to glaciers. As the former long valley glaciers enlarged their cirques and cut farther in toward the center of the range, the latter finally was reduced to a very narrow steep-sided ridge, the arête. In certain places glaciers on opposite sides of this ridge, by headward cutting, created a low place which is referred to as a col, locally known as a pass. Gunsight, Logan, Red Eagle, Stony Indian, and Piegan are only a few of many such passes in the Park. At certain places three or more glaciers plucked their way back toward a common point leaving at their heads a conspicuous, sharp-pointed peak known as a horn. Innumerable such horn peaks occur throughout both the Lewis and Livingstone Mountains, Kinnerly Peak, Mount St. Nicholas, and Mount Wilbur.

Had it not been for the ice there would not have been the beautiful lakes found high on the mountains or in the long valleys. In general, the lakes of the region may be divided into four main groups, according to their origin. First are the cirque lakes, which fill the depressions plucked out by glaciers at their source. Iceberg, Cracker, Hidden, Avalanche, and Ellen Wilson Lakes are good examples. Second are the rock-bound lakes, where the glacier's excavating was lessened by harder rock material which

View from Lake McDonald. Lake McDonald's clear waters offer sports lovers boating, swimming, sun bathing, and summer fun in a sylvan setting. Glacier Park, Inc., photo.

formed a dam. Swiftcurrent and Josephine Lakes are of this type. Third are the lakes held in by outwash of gravel or morainal material as a result of glacial dumping. Most of the large lakes on the west side of Glacier Park, such as McDonald and Bowman, are of this type. A fourth type of lake is found where alluvial fans form a dam. A good example is found at St. Mary where deposits of gravel from side streams have separated Upper and Lower St. Mary Lakes. It is also interesting to note that the Waterton townsite is built on an alluvial fan or delta formed by Cameron Creek.

Another feature of the area which must be attributed partly to glaciation is the waterfall. There are two principal types, one which occurs in the bottom of the main valleys and one at the mouth of the hanging tributary valleys. The former, exemplified by Swiftcurrent, Redrock, Dawn Mist, Trick, Morning Eagle, and others, is located where streams drop over the risers of the glacial staircase. In other words, resistant layers of rock which the glaciers were unable to entirely wear away give rise to this type of fall. Examples of the hanging tributary type of fall, which is due directly to the activity of glaciers, are Florence, Cameron, Virginia, Grinnell, Lincoln, Bird Woman Falls, and many others.

Glacier National Park contains over 1,000,000 acres or more than 1,600 square miles. Waterton Lakes National Park has an area of 202.8 square miles. The width of Glacier National Park along the international boundary is 40 miles, that of Waterton Lakes Park is 23 miles. It is 53 miles in a straight line from the international boundary to Nimrod (Java), located at the most southerly tip of the Park. The longest north-south distance in the Canadian Park is 14 miles. The lowest point in the American Park is the confluence of the Middle and North Forks of the Flathead River in the southwestern corner, 3,150 feet; in the Canadian Park, it is on the Waterton River at the Park boundary, 4,050 feet. The highest elevations for the two parks are Mount Cleveland (10,448) and Mount Blakiston (9,600).

You may see many of these geological features from the Park roads (see Chapter 3), but the farther you get from the roads, the greater the reward. Travel into the less accessible but most spectacular parts can be by foot, horse, or boat. By such means, you may easily obtain firsthand views of the rock formations or the glaciers; in fact, free guided trips are available to both Sperry and Grinnell Glaciers. See Chapter 4 for full details on back-country travel.

THE ROCK FORMATIONS

You have already seen how the rocks in the Glacier-Waterton region were almost all laid down as sediments in a succession of seas that covered the area in the very distant geological past. If you could find a place in the area where a drill could penetrate the entire rock section—from the very youngest rocks on the top to the very oldest ones deep below—we could study the whole history in one place. But because these rocks have been folded and broken along great splits or faults, this is not possible. You can, however, piece together the broken parts of the record from different areas and thus figure out almost exactly what the whole sequence of rocks looked like before it was broken. Within the rock sequence, units of various sizes with different names occur.

You can easily distinguish four differently colored rock formations (and the igneous sill) in the two Parks. The fact that these formations occur in alphabetical order, with the oldest formation the lowest, will help you.

The lowest easily recognizable formation is the *Altyn limestone*. About 2,000 feet thick, it is gray-blue and weathers to pale buff. Good places to examine this formation are: on the ridge immediately behind Many Glacier Hotel; above Swiftcurrent Falls; at the narrows of St. Mary Lake; and the area around Hell Roaring Creek in Waterton. In the Two Medicine area, it forms the terrace over which Trick Falls drops. Altyn limestone is quite hard and forms steep cliffs. It also contains fossil algae colonies (see page 31).

On top of Altyn limestone is a 2,000- to 5,000-foot layer of *Appekunny argillite*. This formation is similar to shale but is somewhat harder. Green and greenish gray are the usual colors, though there are some white and dull red beds. It may be seen along the Going-to-the-Sun Road near McDonald Falls on the west side and for several miles east of Sun Point on the east side, especially on the side of Singleshot Mountain. You can hike over it on the lower part of the Grinnell Glacier Trail. Appekunny argillite is also well displayed in the lower and middle slopes of Vimy Peak opposite Waterton townsite, at Mount Galwey, and in Ruby Ridge.

The *Grinnell argillite,* the next formation, is nearly 3,000 feet thick. Red to purplish, it is the most colorful formation in the Parks. Actually, the Grinnell formation seems to be everywhere. In the Many Glacier region it comprises the bulk of Grinnell

Point, Altyn Peak, and Mount Allen, and is no less striking in the bases of Mount Wilbur and the Garden Wall. Ptarmigan Tunnel is drilled through it, and the trails to Grinnell Glacier and Cracker and Iceberg Lakes cross it. Redrock Falls, on the trail to Swift-current Pass, and Ptarmigan Falls, on the Iceberg Lake Trail, drop over several of its highly colored layers. From the Blackfeet Highway on top of Two Medicine Ridge one can see the dark red rocks of this formation capping the summits of Rising Wolf and Red Mountains. Even from the valley floor it is just as noticeable. Sinopah Mountain, standing alone and impressive across the lake from the Two Medicine parking area, carries the red banner of the Grinnell formation. These red rocks also constitute an important scenic feature for many miles along Going-to-the-Sun Road. If you begin your trip on this road at St. Mary, you soon find yourself in the midst of a group of imposing red peaks— Goat and Going-to-the-Sun on the right, Red Eagle and Mahtotopa on the left across St. Mary Lake. The road crosses the formation along a mile and a half stretch just west of Baring Creek Bridge. Innumerable loose slabs of red rock along the side of the road contain excellent mud cracks and ripple marks. Near Avalanche Creek on the west side of Logan Pass the road crosses the Grinnell argillite where it comes to the surface on the western limb of the big syncline. In addition, the formation is well exposed in the vicinity of Sperry Chalets and Glacier. It forms all the mountains surrounding the basin in which the chalets are located, and the trail from chalets to glacier lies wholly on it. At the glacier, intensely folded white quartzite layers and red argillites are very conspicuous.

The fourth of these formations, the *Siyeh,* ranges from 1,800 to 5,000 feet in thickness. It is a dark, bluish-gray formation, weathering to buff. It caps most of the taller peaks of the parks. For example, in the Many Glacier area such peaks are Mount Gould and the Garden Wall, Mounts Siyeh, Grinnell, Allen, Wilbur, and Henkel. A number of others, including Little Chief, Jackson, Gunsight, Fusillade, Going-to-the-Sun, Piegan, Pollock, Cannon, and Heavens Peak, are visible from Going-to-the-Sun Road. The huge peaks—Kinnerly, Kintla, Carter, and Rainbow—which stand guard at the heads of Kintla and Bowman Lakes are composed of the Siyeh. This list also includes Mount Cleveland, Mount Blakiston, and Anderson Peak.

Through most of the Siyeh formation runs an igneous sill (layer of volcanic rock), which few persons fail to notice. This sill, which is called the *metagabbro sill,* is most evident on the face of the

Garden Wall and on Mount Wilbur in the Many Glacier area. Passengers on the Waterton Lake launch can also see it cutting across the stupendous north face of Mount Cleveland. It is most accessible at Logan Pass, where you may examine it on the trail to Granite Park Chalets, about 200 yards from the pass. The sill, about 100 feet thick, has turned the limestone on either side of it to marble by the tremendous heat it gave off while still molten.

Several other formations occur above the Siyeh, but they are very localized. One of these is the *Shepard formation,* which weathers yellow-brown. Although named for outcrops on the cliff above Shepard Glacier (south of Stoney Indian Pass) the formation is exposed on the summit of Swiftcurrent Mountain at the head of Swiftcurrent Valley, in the Hanging Gardens at Logan Pass, and on nearby Reynolds and Clements Mountains and on Citadel and Almost-a-Dog, visible from Going-to-the-Sun Road in the St. Mary Valley. The formation is replete with mud cracks and ripple marks. Some rock surfaces exhibit two or three sets of the latter.

Another is the *Kintla formation,* which outcrops on a few peaks in the northwest portion of Glacier Park. Visitors to Cameron Lake in Waterton Lakes National Park can see it in the red north wall of Mount Custer. The mountains around colorful Boulder Pass and Hole-in-the-Wall Basin are likewise composed of it. Still another formation is that of *Purcell lava,* which was laid down under the sea, and one of the best exposures of it is on the west side of Swiftcurrent Pass and in Granite Park just west and northwest of the chalets. In fact it is this lava flow which gives the name, albeit wrongly, to Granite Park. The material of the flow is basalt and is very fine-grained and dark, in contrast to the light color and coarse grain of granite. Nonetheless, many prospectors are wont to call every igneous rock, regardless of its composition, a granite.

How do we know these mountains that we see in the parks were once under the ocean? You can find many mud cracks in most of the shale rocks. These are formed when tide flats are dry and the mud contracts as it dries. The water returns and new sediments fill up these cracks. You can also find ripple marks in some of the rocks. These are formed by the continued wave action on the beaches of oceans. You can see this going on today on the shores of our oceans. The Siyeh formation also shows us some colonial algae. These fossils can be found in many of the limestones, and there is a roadside exhibit about a mile below the switchback on the road on the west side of Glacier National Park which shows these very well.

THE GLACIERS OF
GLACIER NATIONAL PARK

Within the boundaries of Glacier National Park there are fifty to sixty glaciers, of which only one has a surface area greater than one-half square mile, and not more than seven others exceed one-fourth square mile in area. All these bodies of ice lie on east- or north-facing slopes at elevations between 6,000 and 9,000 feet, in all cases well below the regional snowline. Thus they are alimented almost entirely by wind-drifted snow.

Excessive cold is not essential to the existence of glaciers. The main requirement is a winter snow accumulation so large that some of it will survive the summer, to be covered by more snow during the succeeding winter. That is, on the high areas of the glacier, the winter snow accumulation exceeds the summer snow ablation (the loss due to melting, evaporation, and erosion). Thus a portion of the winter snowpack remains at the end of each summer. The snow flows downhill, compacting into solid ice as it moves, and is buried by subsequent snows, until it reaches an area where ablation exceeds accumulation, and where it will eventually disappear. Thus, the glacier may be viewed as a river of ice flowing downhill, that is constantly replenished at its source and wasted at its terminus. The equilibrium line, which divides the area of predominant accumulation from the area of predominant ablation, varies from year to year according to the complicated interplay of a number of meteorological factors: snowfall, sunshine, wind, cloud cover, etc. In a year of high snowfall or a very cool summer, the equilibrium line will be found at a low elevation. This indicates that the mass of the glacier increased that year, and the glacier is said to be healthy (growing). Conversely, an equilibrium line at a high elevation indicates that the mass has decreased that year, and the glacier is unhealthy (shrinking). If the glacier grows in mass over a period of many years, the terminus will advance. Thus the terminus responds to average conditions over a period of many years or decades, not to individual years of high or low snowfall. It is quite possible in any one year for a glacier to increase in mass (especially in thickness), while the terminus continues to retreat.

Glaciers do not flow uniformly. The ice flow within a glacier and on its surface varies in a complicated manner depending upon such factors as ice thickness, surface slope, bottom roughness, and meltwater lubrication. The speed varies from day to day, winter to summer, and year to year. The average speed near the margins of small glaciers in the Park may be only several inches per year, while the larger ones may move at speeds of 30 feet or more per year. Ice in a valley glacier flows fastest at the center of the glacier, and speeds at the surface are greater than speeds below the surface, exactly as in a river. Unequal speeds at different places in a glacier give rise to stresses, which in turn cause crevasses. These dangerous, gaping cracks in the ice surface rarely extend to depths of greater than 100 feet or so, because the ice pressure at that depth is so great that it tends to close all open holes or cracks. The faster the ice is stretched, due to unequal flow speeds, the deeper the crevasses will extend.

Grinnell is the largest glacier in the Park, and with the possible exception of one or more of the Dinwoody glaciers in Wyoming's Wind River Range, is the largest in the Rocky Mountains south of the Canadian boundary. Its present surface area is somewhat less than 315 acres. The second largest glacier in the Park is Sperry with a surface area of about 287 acres. Both Sperry and Grinnell have probably maximum thickness of 400 or 500 feet.

Other important Park glaciers, although much smaller than the first two mentioned, are Chaney, Sexton, Jackson, Blackfoot, Siyeh, Harrison, Agassiz, and Ahern. Several others approach some of these in size, but because of isolated locations they are seldom seen. As a matter of fact, there are persons who visit Glacier National Park without seeing a single glacier, while others, although they actually see glaciers, leave the park without realizing they have seen them. This is because the roads afford only distant views of the glaciers, which from a distance appear much like mere accumulations of snow. A notable example is Grinnell as seen from the roads along the shore of Sherburne Lake and from the vicinity of the Many Glacier Entrance Station. The glacier, despite its length of almost a mile, appears merely as a conspicuous white patch high up on the Garden Wall at the head of the valley. Several of the glaciers, however, are accessible by trail and are annually visited by many persons, either on foot or by horse. See Chapter 4 for details on these trails to the glaciers.

Although the observer will see the glaciers of the Park as static bodies of gleaming ice, he should realize that they are dynamic units in a state of constant flow and that they exist in a sensitive balance of climatic factors. Although science is rapidly gaining knowledge of glacier behavior and finds glaciers a useful tool in research, a full understanding of glaciers and their relation to their environment will come only after many years of intensive and persevering research.

NORTHWEST from LOGAN PASS

At left, Oberlin; (1) East Flattop; (2) Cathedral Peak; (3) Kipp; (4) Pyramid, with tip of Cleveland to right; (5) Swift-current; (6) Haystack Butte; (7) Garden Wall; (8) Gould.

Chapter 3.

Sight-Seeing from the Roads*

G LACIER National Park is one of the outstanding wilderness areas in the National Park System and one of the few remaining unspoiled primitive regions left in the United States. Here, in the rugged fastness, amid tranquil forests or beside lakes of almost unbelievable solitude and beauty, man can find peace and quiet to soothe jangled nerves and ease the tensions produced by the rush and stress of our high-speed, mechanized civilization. There are only about 70 miles of improved roads *within* the Park itself. But there are excellent roads around its boundaries.

The Blackfeet Highway (U. S. Highway 89), for example, is an all-weather road leading from Browning to the international boundary, along the entire east side of the Park. The picturesque Chief Mountain International Highway branches from U. S. 89 at Kennedy Creek, leading around the base of Chief Mountain and across the international boundary to Waterton Lakes National Park. Hard-surfaced branch roads lead from State 49 into the Two Medicine Valley and from U. S. 89 into the Many Glacier Valley. U. S. Highway 2 follows the southern boundary of the Park between the villages of East Glacier Park and West Glacier, a distance of 57 miles. The only road that is completely within the Park and which links the west and east sides, is the famous Going-to-the-Sun Road (Glacier Route 1). But, in spite of the lack of great road lengths, motoring is the most popular method of seeing the Park.

* *Note:* All distances given in this chapter are in miles and tenths of miles. Since speedometers are not always accurately calibrated, reasonable allowances must be made.

Going-to-the-Sun Road (Glacier Route 1)

The 50-mile Going-to-the-Sun Road which links the west and east sides of the Park is one of the world's great scenic drives, crossing the Continental Divide at its most spectacular point. (The Continental Divide is an imaginary line, which follows the backbone of the Rocky Mountains from Alaska to Mexico. Water drainage from the west side of the Divide flows into the Pacific Ocean. Water from the east side drains into the Arctic or Atlantic Oceans.) An engineering marvel, the road had to be carved from sheer rock walls. The tremendous impact it provides the traveler comes from penetrating to the very heart of the highest peaks and valleys. Although the surrounding beauty is transcendental in any weather, if you see it during the misty period before or after a rainstorm, when the highest peaks disappear mysteriously in the clouds, you can easily see why the Indians believe this to be the dwelling place of the great spirits. But mountains are not all you see as you climb toward the summit at *Logan Pass* (6,664 feet). Broad meadows speckled with alpine flowers and the racing waters of *Avalanche Creek* and other streams are seen at the lower elevations. As you climb, you pass redcedar forests carpeted with ferns, beautiful glacier-fed lakes, and active waterfalls. It matters little whether you choose to follow the Going-to-the-Sun Road from west to east or vice versa—the scenery and the perspective are equally impressive from either direction.

The construction of the Going-to-the-Sun Road could be written as a complete book by itself. As with any engineering marvel, many difficulties had to be surmounted. For instance, when it was constructed along the sides of cliffs, above the main switchbacks on the east and west side of the Divide, men had to be lowered over the faces of the cliffs by ropes in order to set the initial stakes. In this work often a centerline distance of 50 to 100 feet was a big day's work for a staking party. Next, men with boxes of dynamite carried on their shoulders descended vertical ladders 75 to 100 feet, and perching precariously on narrow ledges, set the initial charges of dynamite to make the start on the safe and comfortable road which you travel over today. In constructing this road, sufficient maximum grade without curvature compensation was established. As an indication of what an effort it was to maintain this favorable grade, the fact can be cited that from Logan Pass to *Logan Creek,* a distance of 10.3 miles, the average grade is 5.6 percent. This is a very small working margin and indicates how closely they had to hold to the maximum gradient. When the highway was completed, it cost in the neighborhood of $4,000,000 or an average of $80,000 a mile. Naturally, the miles along the floors of the valleys cost much less, making the cost of 20 miles along the *Garden Wall* and along other mountain walls, correspondingly much higher.

What makes these costs additionally high are the years in which the highway was built. The actual work began on the western portion in 1921 and on the eastern section in 1924. In June of 1929, it was opened to Logan Pass from the west, and the through road was opened to public use on July 13, 1933. Former Chief Park Naturalist George C. Ruhle suggested the name "Going-to-the-Sun Highway" for the new road, and the name was later adopted by the National Park Service. Since that time it has been termed a "road" to avoid the connotation of speed indicated in the word "highway."

In describing the points of interest along the Going-to-the-Sun Road, we will start at *park headquarters* at *West Glacier* and head toward *St. Mary* on the east side of the park. The mileage given at the end of this description is given for both the west-east and east-west trips.

The park headquarters area contains the residences of the permanent park employees, warehouses, shops, and the administration building. In the latter are the offices of the superintendent, assistant superintendent, chief engineer, chief naturalist, chief ranger, and their assistants. The Park headquarters remain open all year. A short distance beyond is the *West Entrance Station,* where rangers record all vehicles entering the Park and collect the prescribed fees for motor vehicles using Park roads.

For about the next 2 miles you pass through flats that were scarred by a forest fire in 1929. A few scattered trees which survived the fire are larch and aspen. The new growth is mostly lodgepole pine. While only a small portion of the Park was affected by this fire, do not be the cause of the next one, which could destroy the entire area. Help the rangers protect the forests and the scenic beauty of the Park by being careful. *Do not throw cigarettes or other burning material from your automobile.*

After passing two road junctions, you will arrive at *Lake McDonald* viewpoint. This lake, the largest in the Park, is 10 miles long, 1½ miles wide, and over 400 feet deep in some locations. In about the year 1878, Duncan McDonald, while camping overnight on the shores of this beautiful lake, carved his name upon the trunk of a hardwood tree. This tree, bearing his name, remained standing for many years near what is now the site of *Apgar*.

37

Visitors saw the name upon the tree by his campsite, spoke of the lake in terms of his name, until gradually it acquired it permanently, Lake McDonald.

At the *McDonald Valley* viewpoint, you can see the U-shape which is common to the glaciated valleys of the Park. Lake McDonald itself is probably a product of both glacial erosion which carved a basin, and of damming by glacial deposition in the lower end of the valley. A number of cirques can be observed in the region, the most prominent being that occupied by *Avalanche Lake*. Above this lake lies *Sperry Glacier,* whose meltwater cascades over the steep cirque walls into the lake below. The peaks visible from the viewpoint (left to right) are *Stanton Mountain, Mount Vaught, McPartland Mountain, Mount Gould on The Garden Wall, Mount Cannon, Mount Brown, Edwards Mountain,* and *Lincoln Peak.*

Passing the road junctions that will take you to *Lake McDonald Lodge* and *McDonald Ranger Station,* you will come to *McDonald Falls,* a series of cascades in the *McDonald Creek.* This creek flows through Lake McDonald, the Flathead River and Lake, and the Clark Fork and Columbia Rivers into the Pacific. A little farther along, you will come to the *Avalanche Creek Campground* junction. Here you can take the interesting *Trail of the Cedars* self-guiding nature walk. This easy 20-minute walk takes you through a cool, shady, deep-forest plant community typical of the upper McDonald Valley. You may start from the footbridge at the mouth of *Avalanche Gorge* (at rear of campground near start of trail to Avalanche Lake) or at the road near the entrance to Avalanche Campground. There are also many other trails that start near the Going-to-the-Sun Road which will take you to many interesting spots in McDonald Valley (see page 89).

There are several good viewpoints along this section of the road, too. At one you can see Sperry Glacier, one of the largest in the Park. At another you receive an excellent view of Mount Gould and the Garden Wall. The latter is the long, knife-edged ridge that forms a section of the Continental Divide between *Logan* and *Swiftcurrent Passes,* so named by one of George Bird Grinnell's parties which was camped at *Grinnell Lake* in the late 1890's. One

Weeping Wall, which truly "weeps" most of the summer, is one of the many scenic rarities in Glacier National Park. Melting snow flows in never-ending rivulets all along this sheer wall portion of the Going-to-the-Sun Highway. Glacier Park, Inc., photo.

evening, around a campfire, they were singing the then popular song, "Over the Garden Wall," when one of the party remarked, "There is one wall we cannot get over," and the name was immediately applied to the ridge. Going-to-the-Sun Road may be seen for a considerable distance ahead along the side of the wall. The opposite side of the Garden Wall is seen from *Many Glacier*.

Eastward along the road, you will note a fine example of the power of a snow avalanche. At about the 18½-mile point, you can see downed trees and treeless swaths down the mountainside. This damage was caused by the 1953-54 snow avalanche which crashed down the mountainside, gaining momentum and mass, and swept everything before it.

After crossing Logan Creek, you will note that the road starts to climb fairly rapidly. At a roadside exhibit—at which you surely will want to stop—there is an algae colony in the rock from the "dawn of life" period. The formation here is a concentration of single-celled plants associated together in colonies. The oldest Precambrian rocks show remains of life developed from the simplest single-celled forms. Much of this development must have taken place during the time that the earlier Precambrian rocks were being formed. Yet the evidences of life in the Precambrian rocks are scanty. In the Precambrian rocks of Glacier National Park are structures believed to be the tracks of primitive worms and globular limey masses (Cryptozoa) probably built up by one-celled plants called algae.

Your next major point of interest is the *West-side Tunnel,* the first of two along Going-to-the-Sun Road. Two openings have been cut in this tunnel, and the upper one frames *Heavens Peak* effectively for photography. Parking is *prohibited* within the tunnel, but space is available on either side.

There are several excellent viewpoints along this stretch of road where you should plan to stop. The first is the *Bird Woman Falls* viewpoint. Between *Mount Cannon* and *Mount Oberlin* there is an excellent example of a hanging valley. The water from a snowfield in this valley (it cannot be seen from the road) drains over Bird Woman Falls. At one time it was called Oberlin Falls, but it was renamed several years ago in honor of the woman Indian guide of the Lewis and Clark Expedition, Bird Woman. At another

Two tunnels were necessary when Swiss engineers built the Going-to-the-Sun Road in Glacier National Park. Here is an unusual view of Mount Clements through one of the tunnel openings. Glacier Park, Inc., photo.

stop, you can see McDonald Valley, some 2,500 feet below. The panorama of peaks in the Livingstone Range to the north are: (left to right) *Heavens Peak, Longfellow Peak, Anaconda Peak, Mount Geduhn, Trapper Peak, Vulture Peak* and Glacier, *Rainbow Peak* and Glacier, and *Mount Carter.*

Farther on is the McDonald Valley viewpoint with its roadside exhibit; then the road takes you past the *Weeping Wall.* For hundreds of feet, the icy-cold water drips off the side of the mountain onto the side of the road. The "weeping" goes on all summer long, but is at its best early in the season. As the road continues to climb, it takes you through an alpine meadow which is carpeted with yellow glacier lilies in early summer. White and red heather, globeflower, and wild heliotrope may also be found growing with the lilies; Rocky Mountain parnassia and blue gentians follow later.

Your next important stop is at *Logan Pass,* which is one of the choicest spots of the Park accessible by car. There is a new visitor's center here, and naturalists are on duty to give you information and to help point out the mountain goats on nearby slopes of Oberlin, Clements, or Reynolds. There is a free telescope available to aid you in the latter task.

Logan Pass was named for Major William R. Logan, the first superintendent of Glacier National Park (1910-1912). Until work began on the Going-to-the-Sun Road, the pass had been practically unknown and unused. Here the winter snowfall averages about 10 feet on the level, but in years of exceptional snowfall, drifts of over 80 feet occur.

From Logan Pass, the Continental Divide can be traced north from *Pollock Mountain,* along the *Garden Wall* to *Swiftcurrent Mountain* and beyond. It can be followed from Logan Pass, across meadows, ascending *Clements Mountain* before continuing south over *Hidden Lake Pass* and *Reynolds Mountain.* The alpine meadows between Logan Pass, and Clements and Reynolds Mountains are called the *Hanging Gardens.*

A fitting climax to your visit at Logan Pass is a 2-mile walk on the *Hidden Lake Overlook Trail.* This self-guided nature trail wanders across icy brooks, through gardens of wildflowers, and on glacial moraine until it reaches the unsurpassed view 800 feet above sapphire-blue *Hidden Lake.* Other trails that may be taken while in the Logan Pass area include the scenic Highline Trail along the Garden Wall to *Granite Park* and *Waterton Lakes.*

Dropping down the east side of the Continental Divide, you get your first view of the *Upper St. Mary Valley.* The peak to the left is *Piegan Mountain*, while *Citadel, Little Chief, Mahtotopa*, and *Red Eagle Mountains* can be seen down valley. *Going-to-the Sun Mountain* is ahead. Then the road swings around a flower-carpeted cirque with the red tabular summit of Pollock Mountain in the back, flanked by Piegan Mountain on the right. Snow remains in shady portions of this basin throughout most of the summer.

Farther along you will come to a tunnel through *Piegan Mountain,* named for the Piegan subtribe of Blackfeet. But, just above the tunnel, the road crosses a dark-colored igneous intrusion of metagabbro, the same black bands that show so strikingly on some of the park's mountains. This intrusion, about 100 feet thick, dropping from the heights of Piegan and Pollock Mountains down to the south across the road and thence southward, may be seen interbedded with limestone in the upper part of the cliff below the Hanging Gardens.

At the *Siyeh Creek* viewpoint, *Blackfoot Mountain, Mount Siyeh,* and *Jackson Glacier* are visible. Upstream may be seen the trail to *Many Glacier* high on *Cataract Mountain*. Downstream and across the valley the mountains are: left, *Citadel;* middle, *Blackfoot* and the upper portion of *Blackfoot Glacier;* far right, over the forested ridge of *Heavy Runner Peak* is *Mount Jackson*. Blackfoot Glacier, once one of the largest glaciers in the Rocky Mountains, has melted so rapidly in recent years that it is now divided into several smaller ice bodies. Jackson Glacier, which lies between Mount Jackson and Blackfoot Mountain, is one of these bodies. It was named for William Jackson, a scout for General Custer on the Little Bighorn who later guided early visitors in the Glacier Park area.

The next viewpoint after Jackson Glacier is that of *St. Mary Lake*. Farther along you come to one for *Baring Creek* and *Sunrift Gorge*. This gorge was the result of lift or upraising of the mountains in this area. Baring Creek makes a 90 degree turn to follow an old fault line for 800 feet, where it makes another 90 degree turn to plunge on down over *Baring Falls* into St. Mary Lake. This gorge is 80 feet deep and only 4 feet wide. The falls is located about a quarter of a mile down the gorge and is reached by a self-guiding nature trail. Because Baring Creek is a favorite haunt of the water ouzel, or dipper, this trail is known as the *Water Ouzel Trail*. The falls itself is about 37 feet high, and is a good example of the almost constant erosional work of a mountain stream. Through such processes the rough topography of Glacier

43

National Park is carved. Layering of the rocks is quite apparent around the falls, providing evidence of sedimentary origin.

St. Mary Lake—often called the Upper Lake—is 10 miles long and from a quarter-mile to a mile wide. In some places this bow-shaped lake is over 300 feet deep. The small rocky island in it was for years the nesting site for wild geese, hence its name *Wild Goose Island*. There is also a *Lower St. Mary Lake*.

St. Mary Valley is one of the largest valleys of the Park. Its steep sides and curved floor speak of glaciation. In the lower end of the valley where the rocks are soft, the glacier cut a broad valley floor, while above *The Narrows*, where the rocks are more resistant, the valley remained relatively narrow. The Lewis Overthrust fault line follows the base of Red Eagle Mountain, crosses the lake at The Narrows and extends north along the base of the steep slopes of *Otokomi, Singleshot,* and *East Flattop Mountains*. Actually, following the road up St. Mary Valley, you have a splendid opportunity to distinguish the four formations making up the Lewis Overthrust rock. The original sequence of rocks is remarkably undisturbed, and as you ascend the valley, you observe in the road cuts progressively younger rocks. From The Narrows, where the Altyn limestone, weathered to a light buff, is seen beside the road, you climb through the layer of Appekunny argillite (dominantly green, but some red beds), the layer of Grinnell argillite (dominantly maroon argillite, but some light-colored quartzite), and finally into the lower limestone member of the Siyeh formation. This limestone, gray weathered to buff, is the rock exposed at Logan Pass. The argillitic (reddish and greenish) upper members of the Siyeh formation, the youngest of our present mountain rocks, may be observed, above the limestone, on the high peaks—Clements, Pollock, Piegan Mountains, etc.

One of the most interesting viewpoints along Going-to-the-Sun Road is that of *Triple Divide Peak*. At this peak the Hudson Bay Divide meets the Continental Divide. Water from here flows into three drainages: through the Mississippi system to the Atlantic; through the Columbia system to the Pacific; and through the Saskatchewan-Nelson system to Hudson Bay and the Arctic. Straight across the lake are: (left to right) *Divide Mountain,* which marks the eastern boundary of the Park at that point, and *Curley Bear Mountain*. The mountain behind you is *Singleshot,* so named because Grinnell is reported to have killed a running bighorn sheep there with a single shot.

On the road again, you pass across the *St. Mary River,* which flows into Lower St. Mary Lake a mile away; then you will go by

44

the *St. Mary Visitor Center* and *Entrance Station;* and finally you cross *Divide Creek,* a stream which forms the east boundary of Glacier Park at this point. A few minutes later, the Going-to-the-Sun Road has a junction with the Blackfeet Highway (U. S. Highway 89 and Montana 287). This highway parallels the Park boundary going north to Many Glacier, Waterton Lakes National Park, and Canada, and south to Cut Bank Valley, Two Medicine, and East Glacier Park, and connects with U. S. Highway 2.

Miles	*Points of Interest*	*Miles*
0.0	*Junction.* Going-to-the-Sun Road and U. S. Highway 2	50.3
0.2	Glacier National Park boundary (west)	50.1
0.5	*Junction.* Road to Park headquarters	49.8
0.8	West Entrance Station	49.5
1.0	*Junction.* Flathead Ranger Station Road	49.3
2.0	*Junction.* North Fork Road (Glacier Route 8) to Apgar village, Apgar Campground, and Village Inn	48.3
2.8	*Junction.* Road to Apgar. Also serves campground, picnic area, and amphitheater	47.5
3.4	Lake McDonald viewpoint	46.9
5.7	McDonald Valley viewpoint	44.6
10.0	*Junction.* Entrance to Sprague Creek Campground	40.3
10.5	*Junction.* Road to Lake McDonald Lodge	39.8
10.9	Snyder Creek crossing	39.4
11.0	*Junction.* Road to Lake McDonald Lodge, parking area, post office, general store, coffee shop, etc. Trails start from this point to Sperry Chalets, Sperry Glacier, Fish Lake, Snyder Lake, and Mount Brown Lookout	39.3
12.2	*Junction.* McDonald Ranger Station Road (3 miles)	38.1
12.5	McDonald Falls viewpoint	37.8
12.9	*Trail Head.* Cascades and Johns Lake Trail	37.4
13.6	Roadside exhibit—Moose	36.7
14.1	*Trail Head.* Big Cedar Trail	36.2
16.2	*Junction.* Entrance to Avalanche Creek Campground and picnic area. Starting point of Avalanche Lake Trail and the Trail of the Cedars self-guiding nature trail	34.1
16.5	Sperry Glacier viewpoint	33.8
18.5	Snow avalanche damage area	31.8
19.1	Garden Wall viewpoint	31.2
20.8	Logan Creek crossing	29.5
22.9	*Junction.* Packers Roost Road	27.4
23.3	Roadside exhibit—Algae Colony	27.0
23.5	Tunnel	26.8
24.1	Roadside exhibit. Start of Granite Park Trail (Loop)	26.2
24.5	Glaciated ledges. The rock strata at this point were rounded and polished by the McDonald Creek Glacier.	25.8

24.9	Crystal Point. Named from the iron pyrite crystals embedded in the red quartzite member of the rock wall on the right	25.4
26.2	*Trail Head.* Granite Park Chalets Trail	24.1
27.0	Bird Woman Falls viewpoint	23.3
27.7	McDonald Valley viewpoint	22.6
28.9	Weeping Wall	21.4
29.1	Marmot Colony viewpoint	21.2
32.0	Logan Pass. Park area and visitor center. Start of Highline Trail along the Garden Wall to Granite Park and Waterton Lakes. Branching trails lead to McDonald Valley, Many Glacier, Belly River, and Kintla and Bowman Lakes.	18.3
32.3	St. Mary Valley viewpoint	18.0
32.8	Piegan Cirque viewpoint	17.5
33.2	Piegan Mountain Tunnel	17.1
34.9	Siyeh Creek viewpoint	15.4
36.7	Jackson Glacier viewpoint	13.6
36.8	Piegan Pass Trail Underpass. The trail system from Sun Point over Piegan Pass to Many Glacier and Granite Park passes through this subway under the road	13.5
38.8	St. Mary Lake viewpoint. Virginia Falls may be seen across St. Mary Valley. Start of trail for St. Mary Falls, Virginia Falls, and Gunsight Pass	11.5
39.5	Sunrift Gorge viewpoint	10.8
40.2	*Junction.* Road to Sun Point	10.1
40.6	Lost Lake viewpoint	9.7
41.6	Wild Goose Island viewpoint	8.7
43.2	St. Mary Lake viewpoint	7.1
43.5	Narrows of St. Mary Lake	6.8
43.9	*Junction.* Road to public boat launching ramp, lake boat rentals, lakes cruises	6.4
44.0	*Junction.* Road to Rising Sun Campground, Rising Sun Motor Inn, coffee shop, store, and gas station. Roes Creek	6.3
44.1	*Junction.* Road to gas station, coffee shop, store, Rising Sun Motor Inn, and Rising Sun Campground. Road to picnic area	6.2
45.9	Triple Divide Peak viewpoint	4.4
49.3	*Junction.* Entrance road to St. Mary Campground	1.0
49.5	St. Mary River crossing	0.8
49.7	St. Mary Entrance Station and Visitor Center	0.6
49.9	*Junction.* Road to St. Mary Ranger Station. Start of trail to Red Eagle Lake	0.4
50.2	Divide Creek crossing. E. boundary of Glacier National Pk.	0.1
50.3	*St. Mary Junction.* Eastern terminus of the Going-to-the-Sun Road. Joins U. S. 89 and Montana State 287	0.0

East Glacier Park to International Border via Blackfeet and Chief Mountain Highways

East Glacier Park, while not in the Park, is one of its most important eastern centers. Here is found *East Glacier Park Railway Station* and only a few hundred feet from it, the *East Glacier Park Lodge.* The latter is called the "Big Trees Lodge" by the Indians. It is a very apt name since the lodge is fashioned out of huge fir trees and immense cedars, many of them 5 feet in diameter and 45 feet high—monarchs of the forest requiring from five to eight hundred years to grow.

The main road north from East Glacier Park, the *Blackfeet Highway,* crosses the Indian reservation and parallels the main range of the Rockies, traversing the sparsely forested but richly flowered valleys of the Two Medicine, the Cut Bank, the headwaters of the Milk, the St. Mary, the Swiftcurrent, and the Belly Rivers.

A mile and a half after leaving the lodge, you cross the *Old North Trail.* This famous old Indian trail followed the eastern slope of the Rockies from Edmonton, Alberta, to Old Mexico. Upon close inspection, you can still find travois' tracks along the route. The Old North Trail crosses the Blackfeet Highway at this point and is here easily traceable today. This trail is the title to the best popular book on the Blackfeet Indians, *The Old North Trail,* by Walter McClintock.

At the *Two Medicine Valley* viewpoint, both *Two Medicine* and *Upper Two Medicine Lakes* can be seen. *Rising Wolf, Sinopah,* and *Painted Tepee* are the principal mountains. *Rising Bull* is the long ridge, whose outline against the sky is like that of a buffalo bull. The head is toward the south. The ridge extends northward from the summit of *Mount Rockwell,* which is in back of Sinopah Mountain.

At the 10½-mile point you will find a series of folds along the road with faults on both ends. This area shows in miniature the type of folding and faulting responsible for Glacier Park's mountains. This is not, however, in any sense an exact replica of the Lewis Overthrust; however, this crumpling of the weak shales was done at the time the mountains were pushed eastward on the Lewis Overthrust fault. The surface of the earth appears stable to us because its motions are usually very slow. The motion of one part relative to another results in folds and faults. Folds are bends in the original rock structures in which the rocks have acted as

47

flexible or plastic material. Faults are fractures or breaks along which slipping has taken place. Folds and faults are found in all types of rock, but are most easily seen in banded rocks such as a sedimentary series.

Of the major streams in the vicinity, the *Two Medicine River* and the *Cut Bank Creek* flow into the Marias River and thence into the Missouri. Cut Bank Creek derives its name from its steep banks of white clay east of Browning. The *Milk River* flows northeastward into Canada, reenters the States near Havre, flows east through northern Montana, and empties into the Missouri River in eastern Montana. It was named Milk River by the Lewis and Clark Expedition because of its turbid white color at its mouth.

At about 25 miles out from Glacier Park Lodge the road climbs to the top of a big lateral moraine, the *Hudson Bay Divide* (St. Mary Ridge). This is the highest elevation reached on the Blackfeet Highway, 6,077 feet. This long ridge, a prominent landmark which includes St. Mary Ridge and Divide Mountain, separates the headwaters of the Missouri from those flowing to Hudson Bay. That is, the north and west drainage is via the St. Mary, Saskatchewan, and Nelson Rivers into Hudson Bay. The country south and east of this divide is drained by tributaries which empty into the Missouri, the Mississippi, and the Gulf of Mexico. From the summit of the ridge the road enters a forest of Engelmann spruce and lodgepole pine, and a few miles farther on it takes a course beside the hurrying but pellucid waters of *Divide Creek*. Emerging from the timber, the traveler gets a real thrill from the first comprehensive picture that reveals the marvelous beauty of Glacier Park—the mountains massed at the head of St. Mary Lake suddenly brought into view, with the blue water of the lake in the foreground.

From the St. Mary junction with the Going-to-the-Sun Road, the Blackfeet Highway follows the shoreline of the lower lake for 9 miles, with the lake and the precipitous crags of Singleshot and East Flattop Mountains in view all the way. (The eastern end of Flattop Mountain forms the profile of a St. Bernard dog.) Crossing the St. Mary River a few miles beyond the outlet of Lower St. Mary Lake, the road turns north to the small village of *Babb*. At Babb junction, a road leads to Many Glacier, while the Blackfeet Highway follows the course of the St. Mary River to

---

Glacier Park Lodge, which is silhouetted against snow-capped peaks, as seen from Glacier Park railway station. Great Northern Railway photo.

Miles	Points of Interest	Miles
0.0	East Glacier Park (Glacier Park Lodge)	59.2
1.5	The Old North Trail crossing	57.7
2.6	Two Medicine River crossing	56.6
4.2	*Junction.* Two Medicine Road (Glacier Route 2)	55.0
7.9	Two Medicine Valley viewpoint	51.3
8.4	Summit of Two Medicine Ridge (5,972 feet)	50.8
8.6	Mountain viewpoint. The mountains on the northwest side of the highway are (left to right): Spot, Basin, Mad Wolf, White Calf, and Divide, which takes its name from its location on the Hudson Bay Divide.	50.6
10.5	Folded rock	48.7
11.9	*Kiowa Junction.* Montana 49 joins U. S. 89 here. U. S. 89 joins U. S. 2 at Browning. U. S. 89 continues north as the Blackfeet Highway.	47.3
15.6	Top of Cut Bank Ridge (5,404 feet)	43.6
17.1	Cut Bank Creek crossing	42.1
17.2	*Junction.* Left—Cut Bank Road (Glacier Route 5) to Cut Bank Valley Campground (5.8 miles). Right—road to airplane landing field (7.9 miles) and to Browning (16 miles)	42.0
18.7	View up Cut Bank Valley. Mountains are (left to right): Mad Wolf, Eagle Plume, Stimson, Razoredge, James, and Kupunkamint. Cut Bank Pass was the best-known one in this region during the early days.	40.5
19.7	Top of Milk River Ridge (5,563 feet)	39.5
20.9	South Fork of the Milk River	38.3
25.3	Hudson Bay Divide viewpoint. Rest stations are available here.	33.9
25.6	Mount Siyeh viewpoint	33.6
27.4	Going-to-the-Sun Mountain viewpoint	31.8
29.2	View of both St. Mary and Lower St. Mary Lakes	30.0

the international boundary. From *Carway,* the Canadian port of entry, it leads to the little city of Cardston, Alberta.

Just north of Babb, you will come to the canal of the *Milk River Irrigation Project.* The water in this canal has been diverted from the St. Mary River and flows to a point about 8 miles below Babb, where it is carried in tubes over the St. Mary River and over the Hudson Bay Divide into the Milk River. This water is used in eastern Montana. This is a reclamation project, of which the *Sherburne Reservoir* is a part, being initiated prior to the establishment of Glacier National Park.

Most visitors to Glacier Park leave the Blackfeet Highway just north of *Kennedy Creek,* and head for *Waterton Lakes National*

Miles	Points of Interest	Miles
31.6	*St. Mary Junction.* Going-to-the-Sun Road (Glacier Route 1)	27.6
31.9	Blackfeet Indian Craft Shop	27.3
32.9	Lower St. Mary Lake viewpoint	26.3
35.3	Thunderbird Island viewpoint. The Indians believed that thunder was made by a large partridge-like bird flapping its wings and that this creature lived on this tiny island in Lower St. Mary Lake.	23.9
37.9	First good view of Chief Mountain (ahead)	21.3
38.6	Mount Merritt and Old Sun Glacier viewpoint. This glacier, named after one of the ancient Blackfoot men, is the largest one visible from Blackfeet Highway.	20.6
39.1	St. Mary River crossing	20.1
40.4	*Babb Junction.* Many Glacier Road (Glacier Route 3)	18.8
41.8	Canal of the Milk River Irrigation Project	17.4
44.6	Kennedy Creek crossing	14.6
44.7	*Junction.* Chief Mountain International Highway. Blackfeet Highway (U. S. 89) goes to Carway, international border, 5.2 miles; and Cardston, a Canadian Mormon settlement, 25 miles. Kennedy Creek road follows the creek. Chief Mountain Highway (Glacier Route 4) continues as follows:	14.5
46.5	Chief Mountain viewpoint	12.7
53.7	East face of Chief Mountain viewpoint	5.5
51.1	*Junction.* Otatso Creek Road	8.1
55.5	Park boundary. Leaving Blackfeet Indian Reservation. Mount Cleveland, the highest in the park and the summit of the Lewis Range can be seen ahead. It was named for President Grover Cleveland.	3.7
57.1	Lee Creek crossing	2.1
59.1	U. S. Customs and Immigration Office	0.1
59.2	International boundary	0.0

Park over the *Chief Mountain International Highway* (Glacier Route 4). *Chief Mountain,* for which the road was named, is prominent because it lies isolated on the plains east of the main mountain front. It is not one of the Park's highest mountains, but its prominent position, its awe-inspiring east face, and its unique geology have made it the most widely known topographic feature of the Montana Rockies. It consists of an isolated mass of old Precambrian rock, resting on a base of relatively young plains rock. Chief Mountain (called "Chief of the Mountains" by the Indians) was once joined with *Gable Mountain* behind it, as part of the Lewis Overthrust; but erosion has removed all the overthrust rock around the "Chief," leaving it an "island" surrounded and underlain by much younger plains rocks. The Lewis Over-thrust fault line lies at the base of the mountain at about 7,000 feet. The sheer mountain walls rise more than 2,000 feet to an elevation of 9,066. The mountain is composed entirely of hard Altyn limestone. For more than two-thirds of the mountain's height—up to the prominent ledge on the east face—the beds of limestone are not horizontal, but are considerably crumpled and faulted, the rock having piled up on itself to its present height. The upper 600 feet of the peak consists of almost horizontal, relatively undistorted beds.

The Chief Mountain Highway takes you past United States Customs and to the Waterton and Glacier National Park bounda-ries. The boundary is marked by a 20-foot swath through the trees. This cut is present in all wooded areas over the entire length of the boundary between Canada and the United States.

Two Medicine Road (Glacier Route 2)

The valley of the Two Medicine was in ancient times, and still is, a favorite summer campground of the Blackfeet Indians. Here they found good water, poles for their lodges, and a plentiful sup-ply of game. In the upper valley, berries were plentiful to cure and mix with buffalo fat for their pemmican. Here, too, their women and children were secure from prowling war parties of Crees and Crows. Each summer they held their "Medicine Lodge" ceremonies and made their sacrifices to the sun. According to Blackfeet tradition, the tribe at one time experienced factional strife, and the two factions built separate "medicine lodges" in the valley. Since that time the river has been called "The-River-Where-the-Two-Medicine-Lodges-Were-Built." White men have shortened the name to Two Medicine.

Trick Falls, which is found in Two Medicine Valley, is one of nature's geological oddities and is a favorite with visitors to the Park. This beautiful waterfall is over a ledge of Altyn limestone at the base of the Lewis Overthrust. It is paneled by the tall spires of fir and spruce with the brilliant red Rising Wolf Mountain form-ing a background. The quarter-mile self-guiding nature walk from the road to the base of the fall is over a level, shady forest path and is easily traversed in ten minutes. At times of high water, as in May or early June, the fall appears very regular and sym-metrical; in mid-season the volume of water coming over the top has diminished to a small fraction of its maximum, but much

52

pours forth from a cavernous opening which was hidden by the full flow. In late season, water no longer comes over the top, but all filters through fissures in the limestone to emerge from the cave. Trick Falls, because of its unusual nature, was held in great awe by the Indians. They believed it to be a favored haunt of the sprites they knew as the "Under Water People."

At *Two Medicine Lake,* there is a panorama of lake, mountain, and forest of unforgettable grandeur. The base of Rising Wolf Mountain forms the north shore of the lake, and the red, snow-patched summit of the mountain towers 4,340 feet above the lake level. Opposite Rising Wolf, on the west side of the lake, is Appistoki Peak. The bold cliffs of Sinopah Mountain are the center of vision at the far end of the lake. Actually, as you look down the lake, the mountains, left to right, are: *Scenic Point, Appistoki Peak, Never Laughs Mountain, Grizzly Mountain, Painted Tepee Peak, Sinopah Mountain, Lone Walker Mountain, Helen Mountain, Pumpelly Pillar,* and *Rising Wolf Mountain.*

There are a number of fine objectives for rides or hikes which can be made in the Two Medicine area (see page 83); there is a boat livery where rowboats can be rented by the hour or by the day; and the launch *Rising Wolf* makes regular trips between the Two Medicine Lake boat dock and the upper end of the lake. The boat is docked at the upper end of Two Medicine Lake to give passengers an opportunity to visit *Twin Falls.*

Miles	*Points of Interest*	*Miles*
0.0	*Junction.* Blackfeet Highway	7.8
0.5	Irrigation dam. This irrigation project was started before Glacier National Park was established in 1910. The water is used on the Blackfeet Indian Reservation.	7.3
3.1	Boundary of Glacier National Park. The trees have been cut out along the boundary line.	4.7
3.8	Two Medicine Entrance Station	4.0
4.2	Two Medicine Ranger Station	3.6
4.4	Scenic Point. This is the point of the mountain, a spur of Mount Henry, on the opposite side of the valley.	3.4
5.6	Start of trail to Trick Falls	2.2
5.7	Two Medicine River crossing	2.1
7.6	*Junction.* Road to Two Medicine Campground	0.2
7.7	Appistoki Creek crossing. Appistoki is Blackfoot for "Peeping over something."	0.1
7.8	Two Medicine Lake parking area. Camp store and boat dock are located near here.	0.0

Many Glacier Road (Glacier Route 3)

The next valley north of St. Mary is the *Swiftcurrent,* drained by the *Swiftcurrent Creek* to Hudson Bay. The area at the head of the valley and contiguous to it is known as the *Many Glacier* region. This is the focal point from which trails radiate in all directions.

Leaving Babb, the Many Glacier Road enters the lower end of *Swiftcurrent Valley.* At several points road cuts reveal the black shale (one of the relatively young plains rocks) which, together with glacial deposit, composes *Swiftcurrent Ridge.* This shale is a weak rock, subject to landsliding and slow downslope creep, and is responsible for occasional obstruction of the highway and for actual slow movement of parts of the highway downslope near *Sherburne Lake.*

The outstanding geologic feature of Swiftcurrent Valley is the excellent exposure of the Lewis Overthrust fault on both sides of the valley below the head of Sherburne Lake. The ridges underlying the overthrust are composed of plains rocks. The lower Altyn limestone bed of the overthrust block is marked by steep cliffs which form the bases of the mountains on both sides of the valley, contrasting with the gentle slopes of the ridges below them. The exact line of fault contact, lying near the foot of the cliffs, is generally partially obscured by rock debris. The fault line follows the base of the cliffs on the north side of *Mount Wynn* and *Mount Allen,* crosses the valley at the head of Sherburne Lake and extends northeast along the base of the cliffs of *Appekunny Mountain.* Appekunny (Spotted Robe) is the Indian name of James Willard Schultz, the well-known author of Blackfeet stories.

Altyn limestone, the lowest formation of the overthrust, is exposed on the valley floor in the area between *Sherburne* and *Swiftcurrent Lakes. Many Glacier Hotel* is built on this rock. The lower slopes around Swiftcurrent Lake consist of greenish Appekunny argillite. Above it are the red beds of the Grinnell argillite which form the top of Altyn Mountain. The higher peaks, such as *Grinnell, Wilbur,* and *Gould* are capped with part of the Siyeh formation, the same rock which is found at Logan Pass. Between two

Many Glacier Hotel along the shores of Swiftcurrent Lake. Mount Gould (left) and Grinnell Peak (right) are the two major peaks, while the clouds lie atop the Garden Wall. Glacier Park, Inc., photo.

Miles	*Points of Interest*	Miles
0.0	*Babb Junction.* Blackfeet Highway	11.9
1.5	Devil's Slide Rodeo Grounds (right) where rodeos are held in summer by Blackfeet Indians. (Left) Swiftcurrent Creek which flows into St. Mary River	10.4
1.8	Boulder Creek crossing	10.1
2.0	Timber burned in 1933. This fire was caused by a shepherd (locally: "sheepherder") who was herding sheep up Boulder Canyon, and who let his campfire get away during high fire hazard.	9.9
4.7	Reclamation dam—part of the Milk River Irrigation Project	7.2
4.8	Sherburne Lake. Before the dam was built there were two natural lakes in the valley, and most of the valley floor was covered by heavy timber. Also, Glacier Park boundary—leaving Blackfeet Indian Reservation	7.1
7.1	Grinnell Glacier viewpoint. Facing west the mountains (left to right) are: Wynn, Allen, Gould, Grinnell, Altyn, and Appekunny.	4.8

beds in this formation a black band representing a metagabbro igneous intrusion, crosses the face of Mount Gould, extends under Grinnell Glacier, and reappears on Mount Grinnell. This same intrusion may be noted in other valleys of the park.

The *Swiftcurrent Valley* was profoundly altered by glaciation. Evidences of glacial erosion include the broad U-shape of the valley floor, the many cirques, and the chain of lakes. The cirque at the head of *Cracker Canyon* accommodates Cracker Lake, the cirque wall on Mount Siyeh rising 4,000 feet above the lake. *Grinnell Glacier,* the largest body of ice in the valley, lies in a small cirque in the wall of the large major cirque, which holds Grinnell Lake. The glacier consists of two parts separated by a cliff several hundred feet high. The lower part, or main glacier, covers about one square mile and is about three-fourths of a mile in length. It may be 200 or more feet thick in places.

At *Swiftcurrent Falls,* the ledge of rock which the stream plunges over is the lowest or oldest formation in the mountains of the Park. The Lewis Overthrust fault is just below this ledge. Swiftcurrent Lake itself occupies a basin scooped by glacial action out of the Altyn limestone whose dip is to the southwest. Formerly the lake was much larger, and the falls were higher, but as the stream cut back into the rim of the basin, it left dry the tilted ledge on which the hotel stands today.

56

7.5	Swiftcurrent Entrance Station	4.4
8.7	Cracker Canyon and Mount Siyeh viewpoint	3.2
10.5	*Trail Head.* Appekunny Falls Trail	1.4
10.6	Appekunny Creek crossing	1.3
10.8	Grave of Altyn Woman (right). Stones surround the grave of a woman who died in the old mining town of Altyn. Altyn, a boom mining town of the late nineties, was located at the base of Mount Wynn. At one time the town had a population of 200 people.	1.1
11.2	*Junction.* Road to horse corral. Buildings here are all that remain of the old mining camp of Altyn.	0.7
11.4	Swiftcurrent Falls viewpoint	0.5
11.6	*Junction.* Road to Many Glacier Campground, Swiftcurrent Motor Inn, gift shop, general store, coffee shop (1¼ miles). Also Swiftcurrent Lake viewpoints. Facing west, the mountains (left to right) are: Swiftcurrent, Wilbur, Ptarmigan Wall, Henkel and Altyn.	0.3
11.7	Water Gage Station	0.2
11.9	Many Glacier Hotel	0.0

Chief Mountain International Highway
(Border to Waterton Lakes Entrance Station)

The Chief Mountain Highway, which enters Canada at the southeasternmost corner of Waterton Lakes National Park, follows along the eastern side of the valley of the *Belly River* for about 4 miles. This river drains a large sector of Glacier National Park, then flows northward through Alberta, picking up the drainage from the eastern flank of the southern Canadian Rockies, and eventually empties into Hudson Bay. The origin of the name is in dispute, although the names of Belly River, the Gros Ventre Indians, and Big Belly Buttes upon the river between Cardston and MacLeod are connected. One belief is as follows: The Blackfeet people had a custom of apportioning the anatomy of Napi all over the landscape. His elbow was the Bow River at Calgary. His knees were the Teton Buttes. Midway lay his stomach, and what more appropriate than the aforementioned buttes, which to the Indian resembled the contorted stomach of a buffalo? Hence they became Mokowanis, or Big Belly Buttes. The river that flowed at their base became Mokowanis River, and later, when Indians from the southeast drifted into the region, and established themselves upon the river, these, too, became Mokowanis or simply

57

Miles	*Points of Interest*	*Miles*
0.0	International boundary	14.9
0.1	Canadian Customs and Immigration Station	14.8
1.1	Belly River Valley viewpoint	13.8
2.7	*Junction.* Road to Belly River Campground	12.2
3.9	Belly River crossing. Near the west end of bridge a wagon road leads to the various Belly River trails.	11.0
4.0	Entering Blood Indian Reservation	10.9
7.2	Leaving Blood Indian Reservation	7.7
8.0	Crooked Creek beaver dams	6.9
8.5	Belly River District Warden's Station; *emergency* telephone	6.4

translated into the French, the Gros Ventres. Another version has it that the Gros Ventres were so called because they "eat much and have big paunches." Certainly their alternative name, Atsena, or Gut People, gives this interpretation support. The river which flowed through their country simply took its name from them. The Arrowsmith map of 1802 called this river Moo-coo-wans, by which name it was sometimes referred to later. On David Thompson's map of 1814, it was marked Stee-muk-ske-picken, signifying bullhead. The Palliser map of 1865 labeled it Oldman River. The reconnaissance maps of the United States Northern Boundary Commission, 1872-76, labeled it Belly River, which name has been officially adopted by both the United States and Canada.

The *Waterton Valley* viewpoint provides an excellent view of the gap made by the *Waterton Lakes.* The brown slopes of *Sofa Mountain* rise to the south and southwest. To the right, *Vimy Peak* with its complicated rock structures forms the southern entrance to the Waterton Lakes Valley. As you look farther to the northwest, directly over the end of the main lake, the valley of *Blakiston Brook* (Pass Creek) stretches off into the distance. The *Pass Creek Highway* follows this valley, with trails leading from its end to the Continental Divide and the boundaries of the park. On its right the low flank in front is *Bellevue Hill,* and the spike with a patch of red rock debris before it is *Mount Galwey,* with the high ridge of *Mount Dungarvan* to its right. Directly up the valley is *Anderson Peak,* which lies fairly close to *Red Rock Canyon.* To the left of the valley, part of the eastern peaks of *Mount Blakiston* show over and behind the mass of *Mount Crandell,* whose front end and top show great folds making a giant S pattern. The light gray slope on the left side of Mount Crandell

58

Miles	Points of Interest	Miles
10.2	Waterton Valley viewpoint	4.7
14.0	*Junction.* Road to Camp INUSPI (YMCA) and Knight's L.	0.9
14.3	*Junction.* Alberta Route 5 from Lethbridge. East boundary of park is 2.2 miles east on Route 5. (Cardston 32 miles eastward)	0.6
14.7	Maskinonge Lake and picnic area	0.2
14.9	Waterton Lakes Entrance Station	0.0

Miles	Points of Interest	Miles
0.0	Waterton Lakes Entrance Station	1.5
0.1	Waterton River crossing	1.4
1.3	*Junction.* Road to buffalo paddock (½ mile)	0.2
1.5	North boundary of park	0.0

as you look at it from Waterton Valley viewpoint makes the light-colored hill that is conspicuous in Waterton Park townsite. A little to the left of this, a dark wooded slope with light-green stripes made by snowslides is part of *Bertha Peak,* and the high peak just to the left of it is *Mount Alderson.*

Just before reaching the Waterton Lakes National *Park Entrance Station,* you pass *Maskinonge Lake,* which is the Indian name for the large species of pike found in this lake.

On the *Northern Entrance Road* (Alberta Route 6), there is a *buffalo paddock* which is a popular point of interest for visitors. The herd of bison, or buffalo, which usually numbers about twenty-six, may often be seen from vantage points along the road in the paddock. A special cattle gate on the west fence allows motorists to drive right into the paddock, but be sure *not* to get out of your auto while in the paddock. These bison are wild animals and can be dangerous even though held in captivity. Of course, pedestrians and cyclists are not permitted in the paddock.

Waterton Townsite Road

Heading up Waterton Valley toward the townsite, you will pass *Knight's Lake* and *Kootenai Brown's* grave (see page 9). At the junction with the Pass Creek Highway (Red Rock Canyon Road), you can see Vimy Peak looming to the southeast. As your eyes swing to the right, you will see the low, light-gray dolomite ridge between the main body of the Waterton Lakes, which runs generally north and south, and the northern arm, which runs more

east–west. This ridge must have made sort of a threshold for the glaciers filling the main Waterton valley. Above the ridge in the distance you can see the jagged spikes of *Citadel Peaks* in Glacier National Park, and next to it the bulk of *Mount Campbell* with strata sloping to the right. Still farther to the right looms *Mount Richards,* with grayish rocks in the lower part interrupted by a layer of limestone that sticks out and shows a general dip of the strata away from you. The great rock wall which extends from *Mount Richards* to *Mount Alderson* can be seen to be layered even from here. The snow avalanche-scarred slopes of *Bertha Peak* rise above and to the right of the *Prince of Wales Hotel.* Light-colored limestones and dolomites of the nearer peak to the right change along fault lines to darker grays and reds to the west of you in the slopes of *Mount Crandell.* Straight out the Pass Creek Highway the sharp peak is *Mount Galwey,* with various ridges and spurs of *Bellevue Hill* to the right. The road junction here lies within a few hundred feet of the Lewis Overthrust line. It thus separates the whole pile of older rocks above and to the west from the younger rocks below and to the east.

Waterton Lakes is noteworthy for its glacial sculpturing, which is well illustrated in the prominent cirques, rock-basin lakes or tarns, U-shaped valleys, hanging valleys, and waterfalls. One of the most conspicuous features of the Park area is the main chain of lakes. The largest lake, *Upper Waterton,* is 7 miles long and one-half mile wide. In places it is over 450 feet deep. This lake, which spans the international boundary, occupies part of a valley that has been considerably deepened and widened by valley glaciers. A hanging valley formed by this deepening caused *Cameron Falls* in the townsite area.

The townsite itself is built on a delta deposited by *Cameron Creek.* It is believed that most of the delta deposit was made while the Cameron and Alderson Glaciers were still present farther up the valleys. The grinding of the Waterton Glacier against Bertha Mountain produced a sharp bank over which Cameron Falls now drops. The old delta can be seen from the viewpoint at the top of the Bear's Hump Trail. For complete information on the facilities and accommodations in Waterton townsite site, see Chapter 8.

Cameron Creek Falls is a short distance out from the Waterton Townsite. Glacier Park, Inc., photo.

Miles	Points of Interest	Miles

Miles	Points of Interest	Miles
0.0	Waterton Lakes Entrance Station	5.8
0.9	Knight's Lake Picnic Area	4.9
1.8	Knight's Lake viewpoint	4.0
2.0	*Junction.* Road to John "Kootenai" Brown's grave (first acting superintendent of the park). His memorial cairn is at south end of Main Street, opposite R.C.M.P. Barracks	3.8
2.8	*Junction.* Road to ball field, trail to the Dardanelles and Camp Tee-La-Dow (Latter Day Saints)	3.0
3.3	*Junction.* Pass Creek Highway (Red Rock Canyon Road)	2.5
3.4	Blakiston Brook (Pass Creek) crossing	2.4
3.5	Pass Creek (Blakiston Brook) Picnic Area	2.3
3.8	*Junction.* Road to golf course	2.0
4.3	*Junction.* Road to Lower Waterton Lake, Marquis Hole, and Camp Columbus (Roman Catholic)	1.5
4.5	*Junction.* Road to Timberline Saddle Horse Stables (left). Also boat trailer storage area (right)	1.3
4.8	*Junction.* Road to Government Compound and Lonesome Lake	1.0
4.9	Linnet Lake Picnic Area	0.9
5.2	*Junction.* Prince of Wales Hotel. Also, information center and start of trail to Bear's Hump are located here.	0.6
5.4	*Junction.* Akamina Highway. Emerald Bay Picnic Area on left	0.4
5.8	Waterton Lake Park Administration Building in townsite	0.0

Pass Creek Highway (Red Rock Canyon Road)

The drive to Red Rock Canyon along Pass Creek Highway is a very beautiful motor trip. This road follows the old Hudson's Bay Company Trail through the mountains. This company's fur traders and trappers used the trail for over a hundred years to supply their trading posts and forts on the Pacific coast, and in their dealings with the Indian tribes. Numerous wild animals, particularly bighorn sheep, moose, and mule deer, are often seen in this area. The low cliff, near *Buffalo Jump Picnic Area,* was employed by the Indians to kill buffalo (see page 12).

Another interesting picnic area is the one at *Copper Mine Creek.* This creek gets its name from traces of copper found along its banks some time ago in a sill of igneous rock in the Grinnell Formation. A view to the south from here shows a low pass that leads through the Crandell Lake Valley into the upper valley of Cameron Creek and the *Akamina Highway* to *Cameron Lake.* The various peaks of *Buchanan Ridge* (7,966 to 8,499 feet) fill the skyline through the gap.

At Red Rock Canyon, the 1½-mile self-guiding nature trail is very popular with visitors. This canyon has been cut into soft red argillites of the Grinnell Formation by the small brook flowing off the high mountains to the northeast. Nearly horizontal layering in the rock is marked by slight variations in the red color and by sharply contrasting pale gray-green and yellow-green layers. The pale gray-green occurs also in spots and irregular patches. These light patches all represent places where the iron compound in the rock has been changed in composition because of the presence of some other chemical substance. Ordinarily it is in the same form as the iron in reddish iron rust, but where it comes in contact with some organic matter or "reducing agent" it changes to a different composition which has this pale yellow-green or gray-green color. Along the canyon walls some of the gray layers appear to be a little harder than the reddish rocks in which they occur, and they stick out as ledges. Along the brook you may also notice that smooth, nearly vertical faces seem to intersect the canyon wall. These are joints made when the rock fractured from large stresses, perhaps set up during the making of the mountains themselves. On the right side of the canyon going upstream, one of the light-colored layers shows fairly well-developed ripple marks on one surface and here and there some shrinkage cracks—the kind formed when wet sediments dry out at low tide or at a time of year when streams are low. Just above the bridge some parts of the canyon bottom are quite well rounded and appear to have been parts of "potholes"—made when hard boulders are whirled round and round by the moving water and gradually bore their way into the softer rock beneath. A few hundred feet above the bridge the canyon shallows rapidly and gradually becomes a normal brook valley.

Riding and walking trails and a fire road, which may be driven only with a permit from the Park authorities, lead to the west and northwest corner of the Park.

Miles	Points of Interest	Miles
0.0	*Junction.* Waterton Townsite Road	9.2
1.3	Pass Creek beaver dams viewpoint	7.9
2.5	Blakiston Brook (Pass Creek) viewpoint	6.7
3.1	Buffalo Jump Picnic Area	6.1
4.4	*Junction.* Road to Mount Crandell Campgrounds	4.8
5.1	Coppermine Creek Picnic Area	4.1

(*Continued*)

(*Continued from page 63*)

5.2 *Junction.* Road to Canyon Church Camp (United Church) 4.0
and trail to Crandell Lake
6.0 Ruby Falls viewpoint 3.2
7.7 Lost Horse Picnic Site 1.5
8.9 Horse stables 0.3
9.2 Red Rock Canyon. Picnic area, self-guided nature trail, 0.0
Red Rock District Warden, *emergency* telephone. Trail to
South Kootenai Pass, Blakiston Falls, Twin Lakes, Lone
Lake, Goat Lake, Lost Lake, and Castle River Divide. Also,
Snowshoe fire road to campsite

Akamina Highway

The Akamina Highway provides a scenic 10-mile drive up *Cameron Valley*. The highway rises more than 1,000 feet from the floor of the Waterton Lakes Valley to Cameron Lake. Along the road, there are several viewpoints which permit you to look down into the gorge of Cameron Creek. This gorge, cut mostly in yellow-brown dolomite of the lower Altyn Formation, shows how very slow solution of the rock, combined with abrasion by the passage of boulders and sand over the bottom, gradually wears away the land and, after thousands of years, produces considerable change in the landscape.

About 5 miles from the start of the Akamina Highway is *Oil City,* the site of Alberta's first oil discovery. The only remains of the "city" are a few pieces of rusted wire rope, bits and pieces of old iron and wood, and two pieces of well casing sticking out of the ground. One of these has a railing around it and a piece of drill stem stuck firmly in the hole.

The Akamina Highway ends at *Cameron Lake,* a glacially carved body of water right up against the Continental Divide. That is, the eastward drainage from the lake goes into the Waterton Lakes via Cameron Creek and thence northeastward into the Saskatchewan River toward Hudson Bay; water from this divide also flows westward through Akamina Brook and Kintla Creek and eventually into the Pacific Ocean via the Columbia River. It is also interesting to note that the high back wall of Mount Custer at the south end of Cameron Lake is in the United States, with the international boundary cutting across the southern tip of the lake. The south-trending ridge to the right or west of Cameron Lake is the boundary between the Province of Alberta and the Province of British Columbia; at a three-way boundary point it intersects the international boundary.

Miles	Points of Interest	Miles
0.0	*Junction.* Waterton Townsite Road	10.2
0.4	Waterton Townsite viewpoint	9.8
1.6	Cameron Canyon and Creek viewpoint	8.6
2.3	Cameron Canyon and Creek viewpoint	7.9
2.5	Cameron Canyon and Creek viewpoint	7.7
2.8	Bridal Veil Falls viewpoint	7.4
4.1	McNeely Picnic Area	6.1
4.4	Trail head to Crandell Lake	5.8
4.8	Cameron Creek viewpoint	5.4
5.1	Oil City. Site of Alberta's first oil discovery (1886)	5.1
5.7	High Falls viewpoint	4.5
5.9	Trail head to Lineham Lake	4.3
6.2	Trail head to Rowe Lakes	4.0
8.4	Little Prairie Picnic Area	1.8
9.3	*Junction.* Road to Akamina Pass, an access route into the southeast corner of British Columbia	0.9
9.6	Park warden cabin	0.3
10.2	Cameron Lake. Picnic area. Trails to Summit Lake and Carthew Lakes. Self-guiding nature trail	0.0

Theodore Roosevelt Highway (U. S. Highway 2)

This highway connects West Glacier with East Glacier Park, and, if you stretch the rules of geometry, it could be said to parallel the Going-to-the-Sun Road. The latter road is a great deal more spectacular and much more interesting. U. S. Highway 2, however, is quicker. Only a short portion of the road—2.7 miles—is really in the park. The western portion of the highway takes you through Flathead National Forest, but once crossing the Continental Divide at Marias Pass, you are in the Lewis and Clark National Forest. Completed in 1930 and rebuilt in 1966, this route is the most northerly *year-round* route over the Continental Divide in the United States. The highway parallels the Great Northern Railway tracks throughout its length.

Other Roads

There are a few narrow, unimproved, dirt roads that will take you into various portions of Glacier National Park. These include the Otatso Creek, Kennedy Creek, Camas Creek (Glacier Route 7), Cut Bank (Glacier Route 5), and North Fork (Glacier Route 8) Roads. The latter three with route designations are the ones most often used by visitors to the Park. Because of the number of campgrounds along the North Fork Road, a mileage log of that road is given here:

0.0	*Junction.* Going-to-the-Sun Road	39.9
0.7	Apgar village. Apgar Campground, Village Inn, general store, etc.	39.2
0.8	McDonald Creek crossing	39.1
1.2	*Junction.* Camas Creek Road (Glacier Route 7)	38.7
2.3	Fish Creek Campground. McGee Creek Trail to Huckleberry Mountain starts here.	37.6
8.0	Trail head to Howe Lake	31.9
9.3	Camas Creek crossing. Trail head to Camas Lake	30.6
12.3	*Junction.* Road to private homes. Dutch Creek crossing	27.6
14.9	Anaconda Creek crossing. Anaconda Creek Trail begins.	25.0
20.1	Logging Ranger Station and Logging Creek Campground. Trail to Logging and Grace Lakes starts here.	19.9
22.9	Quartz Creek crossing. Quartz Creek Campground is here as well as start of Quartz Lake Trail.	17.0
23.4	Mud Lake. Mud Creek Campground	16.5
28.0	*Junction.* Polebridge Park Entrance Road. Polebridge Ranger Station	11.9
28.3	Bowman Creek Campground. *Junction.* Road to Bowman Lake Campground (6.3 miles)	11.6
39.7	Kintla Creek crossing	0.2
39.9	*Junction.* Road (right) leads to Kintla Lake Campground (2 miles). Left fork is not recommended.	0.0

Traffic Regulations. The speed limit in the parks is 45 miles per hour, unless otherwise posted; 1½-ton trucks or over, 35 miles per hour. Keep gears meshed and out of overdrive on grades. Signal when leaving the road to park on overlooks. Do not park so as to interfere with travel on the road. Drive slowly and do not park on curves. Report all accidents to the nearest ranger or warden station or to Park headquarters.

TRANSPORTATION WITHIN THE PARKS

For those without their own motor transportation, bus service is maintained by Glacier Park, Inc., between the hotels and the Parks' major points of interest. Typical bus tours in famous open-top motor coaches are as follows:

One of Glacier's famed 1936 model "vista-view" buses at a McDonald Valley viewpoint along the Going-to-the-Sun Road. Bus tops are rolled back to permit an unrestricted view. These buses have been in use for over 30 years and are still going strong. Glacier Park, Inc., photo.

Glacier Park Lodge	to	Two Medicine Lake area
" " "	"	Logan Pass
" " "	"	Lake McDonald Lodge (both ways via Logan Pass)
" " "	"	Lake McDonald Lodge (going via Logan Pass, return via West Glacier & U. S. Highway No. 2)
" " "	"	Many Glacier Hotel
" " "	"	Prince of Wales Hotel, Waterton Lakes National Park
Many Glacier Hotel	to	Lake McDonald Lodge
" " "	"	Prince of Wales Hotel, Waterton Lakes National Park
" " "	"	Logan Pass
Lake McDonald Lodge	to	Logan Pass

For rates and time schedules between points check the information desks in each of the hotel lobbies.

Glacier Park, Inc., also offers a series of all-expense tours of Glacier and Waterton Lakes National Parks. These tours are of two- to ten-day duration and include motor coach transportation, meals, and lodging at the hotels. Some tours include launch trips and horseback trips. They start daily from June 15 to September 9, commencing at East Glacier Park, West Glacier, and the Prince of Wales Hotel. A brief itinerary description of two- and three-day tours is shown below. Write to Glacier Park, Inc., for details.

One-Day Tour. From West Glacier over Going-to-the-Sun Road to East Glacier Park, with side trip to Two Medicine Lake in afternoon. Four meals and one night's stay in lodge. From East Glacier Park, tour takes side-trip to Two Medicine, then is routed the following day to West Glacier via Going-to-the-Sun Road.

Two-Day Tour. This tour offers all that the one-day tour provides, plus a trip to Many Glacier Hotel on Swiftcurrent Lake.

Three-Day Tour. This tour offers all that the two-day tour provides, plus a trip to Prince of Wales Hotel, Waterton Lakes.

Rates. All-expense tour rates and bus fares will be quoted by Glacier Park, Inc., upon request. Information and rates may also be obtained by writing the Great Northern Railway, St. Paul, Minnesota, 55102, or their passenger representatives. Tour and travel agencies throughout the United States and Canada also have this information available.

If you do not have your own transportation and would like to do some independent exploring of the Parks, you can obtain rental cars from Glacier Park, Inc.

Chapter 4.

Seeing the Parks' Wilderness

ONE of the best ways to experience what Thoreau called "the tonic of wildness" is to follow the trails of Glacier-Waterton Lakes Parks, either on foot or on horse. For family groups it is an ideal vacation from the pressures of modern-day living.

On Foot

Glacier National Park is one of the greatest trail parks in the United States, with more than 1,000 miles of wilderness trails inviting your exploration. To this, you must also add Waterton Lakes Park's more than 100 miles of trails. Almost the entire area of both Parks is accessible to hikers from all campgrounds, chalets, and hotels. The trails are well marked, and you need not worry about venomous snakes or such unpleasant plants as poison oak or poison ivy. We suggest that you pack your lunch, leave your automobile in a parking area, and spend a day or as much time as you can spare in the out-of-doors.

Trail trips range in length from short, 15-minute walks along self-guiding nature trails to hikes that may extend over a period of several days. In Glacier, you are invited to join the Park naturalists on two-hour, half-day, all-day, and overnight trips. These trips are free except for lodging and meals in connection with overnight hikes. Or you may bring or organize your own party. Organized groups desiring special naturalist services for hikes should make arrangements *in advance* with the Chief Park Naturalist, Park Headquarters, West Glacier, Montana 59936.

In addition, Rocky Mountain Outfitters, Inc., operates equipped camping trips for hiking groups which include the services of a packer or guide and cook per party, and one pack horse carrying approximately 150 pounds for each three guests. Food and commissary equipment are supplied. Hikers are to furnish their own

69

sleeping bags and personal camp gear. There are also camping trips for hiking groups where hikers furnish their own food, commissary and camping equipment, while the concessionaire furnishes just the guides and the pack horse required. Rates are reasonable and approved by the National Park Service. See page 72.

Since the trails are so well marked, your party can hike them without guides. (It is *never* wise to hike all alone.) If you would like to take an interesting overnight hike without being burdened with camping equipment, you may hike to either Sperry Chalets or Granite Park Chalets, where meals and overnight accommodations are available. (A new chalet, or mountain hotel, is being planned at Fifty Mountain—so named because fifty mountain peaks can be seen from this great open area.)

In Glacier Park, there are shelter cabins at Gunsight Lake and Pass, Waterton Lake, Arrow Lake, Fifty Mountain, and Mokowanis Junction. The shelter cabins are equipped with cots and cooking stoves, but you will have to bring your own food, and sleeping and cooking gear.

For backcountry travel, you will need a topographic map or trail map that shows trails, streams, lakes, mountains, and glaciers. You may purchase either the topographic map or a trail map at park headquarters, hotels, and by mail (see page 178).

By Horseback

It is to the leisurely traveler, the hiker, and the horseback rider, that the Parks bestow their greatest gifts. After you have seen the easily accessible things, and if you do not care to hike, you may choose to engage a competent guide, take horses and camping outfit, and follow the trails. If you do, you are likely to gain a better understanding of the increasing importance of our areas of unspoiled wilderness.

You can rent saddle horses for trips within Glacier Park at Many Glacier Hotel, Lake McDonald Lodge, Apgar Village, East Glacier Park Lodge, and St. Mary. Information and tickets for the regularly scheduled rides may be obtained at the transportation desks in the hotel lobbies within the Park, or from the saddle-horse

---

The best way to see the International Peace Park is by foot or on horseback and camping out. It is a good idea to take your fish pole so that you can catch your dinner. This photo was taken at Grinnell Lake and its glacier is in the background. Great Northern Railway photo.

guides or wranglers at the corrals. Guides are required for all horseback trips within the Park.

In addition to the scheduled rides, trips for private parties or family groups may be arranged from any of the starting points in the Park. Arrangements or reservations for trips of long duration should be made well in advance to secure the best possible guides, camp cooks, and necessary equipment. These services include the furnishing of saddle horses, pack horses, guides, packers and/or cooks, food, and camp equipment. Guests bring their personal necessities, camera, fishing gear, etc. For further information about either trail rides or equipped camping trips (see page 69) in Glacier, write to Rocky Mountain Outfitters, Inc., Ronan, Montana 59864 (winter), or Babb, Montana 59411 (summer).

The Timberline Horse Stables have about the same services available for the visitors to Waterton Lakes National Park. Corrals are located adjacent to the Waterton Townsite and at Red Rock Canyon. Scheduled rides leave from both locations daily. Special pack trips are also available. For complete data, write Dee Olson, Cardston, Alberta, Canada (winter), or Timberline Horse Stables, Waterton Lakes, Alberta, Canada (summer).

TRAILS IN GLACIER

Trails are almost everywhere in Glacier National Park, and they take you to scenic wonders that cannot be seen from the Park's road system. It is impossible to describe all the trails, but we have selected the popular ones and have given trail mileages of these.

MANY GLACIER AREA

The Many Glacier region is often called "the heart of Glacier's trail system." Here the trails vary from those that are relatively level to those that contain some steep climbs. Of the level type, the Swiftcurrent Lake Self-Guiding Nature Trail is interesting. This trail is a pleasant walk of one mile along the south and east shores of Swiftcurrent Lake between the Many Glacier Hotel and the boat dock at the head of the lake. Features along the trail include a wide variety of shrubs, trees, and flowering plants combined with scenic vistas which present an opportunity for explaining the story of the rocks and glaciers.

Another interesting short trail is the one around Swiftcurrent Falls. It starts by the water-gauging station, and follows the Swift-

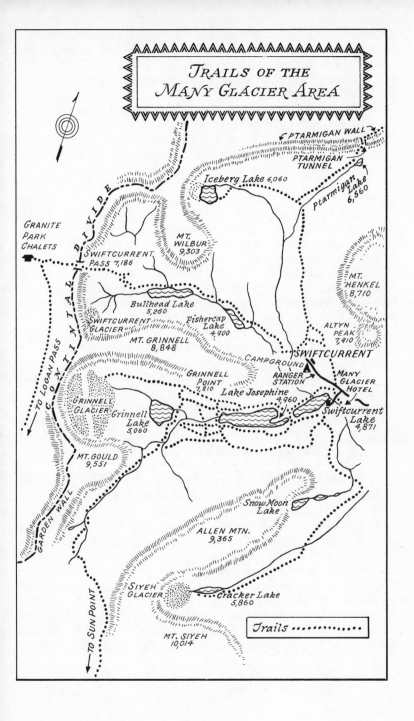

Trails of the Many Glacier Area

PTARMIGAN WALL

PTARMIGAN TUNNEL

Ptarmigan Lake 6,560

Iceberg Lake 6,060

GRANITE PARK CHALETS

CONTINENTAL DIVIDE

MT. WILBUR 9,303

MT. HENKEL 8,710

SWIFTCURRENT PASS 7,186

Bullhead Lake 5,260

ALTYN PEAK 7,910

Fishercap Lake 4,900

SWIFTCURRENT GLACIER

MT. GRINNELL 8,848

CAMPGROUND

SWIFTCURRENT

TO LOGAN PASS

GRINNELL POINT 7,810

RANGER STATION

MANY GLACIER HOTEL

Lake Josephine 4,960

GRINNELL GLACIER

Grinnell Lake 5,060

Swiftcurrent Lake 4,871

MT. GOULD 9,551

GARDEN WALL

Snow Moon Lake

ALLEN MTN. 9,365

SIYEH GLACIER

Cracker Lake 5,860

Trails ··············

TO SUN POINT

MT. SIYEH 10,014

current Creek for about a half-mile. The creek has cut an attractive gorge in the yellow Altyn limestone. The trail terminates just past the powerhouse.

Following are short descriptions of the more popular trails in the Many Glacier region:

Ptarmigan Tunnel (*Ptarmigan Falls and Lake*). This trail leaves from in front of the hotel, passes in back of Swiftcurrent Motor Inn, and goes on to Ptarmigan Falls. After passing the Iceberg Lake Trail junction, it climbs up Ptarmigan Creek valley to Ptarmigan Lake, at the head of the deep, narrow canyon below Ptarmigan Wall. The term "wall" is applied to the ridge north of the lake. The top is 1,000 feet above the lake. It is only about a mile climb to the tunnel, which was carved through the face of Ptarmigan Wall in 1931. The trail is steep but safe, even for the novice. The south portal of the tunnel offers a splendid view of Mounts Wilbur, Grinnell, Gould, and the Garden Wall. Coming out of the north end of the 183-foot opening, you overlook the beautiful valley containing Elizabeth Lake and the Belly River country. A quarter-mile past the tunnel, you will be rewarded with an excellent view of Mount Merritt with its glistening Old Sun Glacier and its many sparkling waterfalls. If you were to continue on this trail it would lead to Elizabeth and Crossley Lakes and then on to Waterton Lakes National Park.

Appekunny Falls. The Appekunny Falls Trail—a short, interesting walk—begins from the Many Glacier Road, about 1½ miles east of the hotel. The trail follows up the east bank of Appekunny Creek to the foot of a beautiful little waterfall. There is a naturalist-conducted walk every morning along this trail, which is *not* suitable for saddle horse travel.

Lake Sherburne. Starting from in front of the Many Glacier Hotel, this trail follows the south shore of beautiful Lake Sherburne. It concludes at the Park boundary line on the Many Glacier Road. A trail starts at this point and leads to Boulder Creek.

Iceberg Lake. A 6-mile ride or walk from Many Glacier Hotel over open level trail will take you to Iceberg Lake, a miniature polar sea. This little turquoise lake, covering perhaps 100 acres, is backed up by a head wall 3,000 feet above the surface of the water. It is never free from ice. During the warm days of July and August, huge chunks of ice break off the face of a permanent snowfield at the head of the lake, and these icebergs float around for days before they melt or become sufficiently small to find their way over the falls at the outlet. A naturalist-conducted nature hike is made each morning, starting from the Swiftcurrent Camp Store.

Grinnell Glacier. Another 6-mile trail leads to Grinnell Glacier, and of all the glaciers in this region, this is the most accessible and the best field for exploration and study of glacial action. The trip to Grinnell Glacier is more strenuous than other short trips in the Many Glacier region, due to the fact that for some distance the trail is steep, but the trip furnishes thrills that cannot be experienced elsewhere. Grinnell Glacier is small enough to be easily comprehended; it has many of the characteristics of the prehistoric ice rivers that carved the beauty of Glacier National Park, but it is not repellent and forbidding as the more expansive ice sheets must have been. Over the serrated surface of the glacier a Park naturalist will lead you to the edge of a great crevasse. As you look down into the depths you are astounded to find that the ice is so thick, for at this point it measures all of 250 feet in depth, and it stretches away for over a mile to the edge of the rocky face of Mount Gould. The view from the glacier over the lovely lakes in the valley below is unforgettable.

Actually, the most popular naturalist-conducted trip in the park is the one to Grinnell Glacier. This all-day trip can be a straight hiking trip, hiking trip combined with a boat ride (see page 175), or a trip on horseback. All of these parties meet on the trail; and after lunch at a picnic area, naturalists accompany the party on to Grinnell Glacier itself.

Josephine and Grinnell Lakes. Below Grinnell Glacier lies Grinnell Lake, and a little lower down in the valley is lovely Josephine Lake. A short river forms a connecting link between Lakes Josephine and Swiftcurrent. These three lakes are fed by the meltings which flow in lacy cascades down the precipice that shelves Grinnell Glacier. The gray-green color of the water is due to the presence of fine, pulverized rock-silt ground by the moving ice mass.

Josephine Lake is, in the opinion of many, the most charming lake in Glacier Park. No other combination of mountain, glacier, waterfall, and lake in Glacier, or perhaps in all America, is more perfectly composed. The lake and its surroundings form a symphony in water, rock, and foliage that has taken nature millions of years to produce.

There are two naturalist-conducted combination boat-and-trail trips daily to Grinnell Lake, which also offers great vistas of nature.

The distance to the head of Josephine Lake is 1.2 miles, while Grinnell is 3.6 miles. The trails are mostly level.

Cracker Lake. Seven miles of trail in another direction will bring you to the head of Cracker Canyon where Cracker Lake lies bowled in a gray limestone cirque at the bottom of Mount Siyeh's highly colored and almost perpendicular wall. Siyeh towers 10,000 feet into the blue, and the wall that rises from the shore of Cracker Lake is a sheer cliff almost 4,000 feet high. The trail to Cracker Lake follows an interesting route up Canyon Creek to its source in the lake. Of special interest on the Cracker Lake trip are the hanging glacier of Siyeh with its huge terminal moraine, the alpine wildflowers, dwarf alpine trees perhaps hundreds of years old and but 3 or 4 feet high, and the goats and sheep which pick their way along the cliffs above the trail.

Morning Eagle Falls and Piegan Pass. Piegan Pass trail winds along the west side of Allen Mountain from Many Glacier Hotel, following the valley floor to Grinnell Lake, and continuing past Hidden Falls. It then goes up Cataract Creek to Morning Eagle Falls. The distance from Many Glacier to this charming cascade and return to Many Glacier is a little over 5.3 miles. The horseback ride or hike to Morning Eagle Falls is one of Glacier's most fascinating trips, and it is recommended as a splendid one-day outing from Many Glacier, especially suitable for those who do not care for the higher altitudes. Farther along you pass Feather Plume Falls.

The trail, by means of switchbacks, makes its way above the falls to the summit of Piegan Pass. From the summit, Blackfoot Glacier, 5 miles south, is seen sparkling in the sunlight, accentuated by the irregular peaks of Jackson, Almost-a-Dog, Citadel, and Blackfoot Mountains. After crossing the pass and stopping an hour for lunch, two routes are available; both of them fascinating. One is directly down the west side of Going-to-the-Sun Mountain and then down to Siyeh Creek to the Going-to-the-Sun Road. The other is by a trail through Siyeh Pass which leads across Preston Park, a beautiful meadow, over the pass, and down the north side of Sun Mountain past Sexton Glacier, and by way of Baring Creek to Sunrift Gorge. The total distance from Many Glacier to Sunrift Gorge via Piegan and Siyeh Passes is 18.0 miles, which is slightly longer than the Siyeh Creek Trail. The former, however, is more spectacular, but a more difficult trail.

Swiftcurrent Pass and Granite Park. A never-to-be-forgotten trip is up the switchbacks of Glory Trail and across Swiftcurrent Pass to Granite Park. The trail from Many Glacier winds along the Swiftcurrent Creek, past Fishercap and Redrock Lakes, Redrock

Falls, and Bullhead Lake, to the foot of Swiftcurrent Mountain. (There is a daily naturalist-conducted walk up this trail as far as Redrock Falls.) At the foot of the mountain, the trail zigzags up 1,000 feet to Nine-Lake Point, a sharp, projecting shoulder of the mountain. From this point, about two-thirds of the distance to the summit of the pass, an impressive view is obtained. Looking down the Swiftcurrent Valley, nine blue lakes can be counted, the last one—Duck Lake—being 20 miles to the east on the Blackfeet Indian Reservation. Another short climb brings one to the summit of the pass, and after crossing several large snow patches that resist old Sol's summer rays, a signboard indicates that an altitude of 7,186 feet above sea level has been attained—the top of the Continental Divide. From here a foot-trail leads up to the top of Swiftcurrent Mountain, which offers a view that is one of the broadest and most inspiring vistas in any mountain land. To the south beyond the goat-haunted ledges of the Garden Wall, the embattled summits of Haystack Butte, Pollock, Brown, Oberlin, and Cannon appear as a jumbled collection of discarded fortresses. To the east there is the same extravagant piling-up of resplendent, lofty ridges, the same unequal line of spires and peaks, of points and crags—their deep sun-protected recesses vast receptacles for the inevitable masses of snow.

On the main trail, it is only seven-tenths of a mile from Swiftcurrent Pass to Granite Park Chalets. Granite Park itself is a wide plateau bulging from the west side of the Continental Divide wall, 6,500 feet above sea level, at the edge of the timberline. From here, the unobstructed outlook west across the deep wooded valley of McDonald Creek to Heavens Peak, south toward Logan Pass, and north up Mineral Creek and over Flattop Mountain is a sight so inspiring that the memory of it lives long years afterward. The glorious view from Granite Park across the horizon for 180 degrees is particularly impressive at evening when the peaks are bathed in the azure, pink, mauve, and lavender glory of the setting sun, when the vast trailless, tenantless, unexplored region to the west and north is blanketed in semidarkness, and the sharp ridges and ice fields are silhouetted against a sky dimly lit by the afterglow of the sun and by myriads of stars. Only occasionally may one see so sublime a panorama as this.

North Circle Trip. From Many Glacier, too, the wonderful "North Country" of Glacier Park is accessible, and a journey through it affords accustomed riders a most exhilarating and satisfactory outing. One such backcountry journey, usually called the

"North Circle Trip," through this vast and little explored section of Glacier Park may be made in about five days.

The first day of the trip has already been described in the ride over Swiftcurrent Pass to Granite Park. From Granite Park the trail generally follows the 7,000-foot contour north to Fifty Mountain. Here a shelter cabin, close under the pinnacles of Mount Kipp, is reached late in the afternoon. On the third day the way is still northward down the valley of the Little Kootenai to Waterton Lake Trail Shelter at the south end of Waterton Lake. Here the mountains pile up in awe-inspiring masses, culminating in the bold magnificent cliffs of Mount Cleveland, the highest mountain in Glacier Park. On the fourth day travel is back over the previous day's trail for about 5 miles, then past the blue of Stoney Indian Lake and up the switchbacks to the summit of Stoney Indian Pass. Here a view unfolds that has made many acclaim this defile between Cathedral Peak and Wahcheechee Mountain on one side and Stoney Indian Peaks on the other as the most beautiful of Glacier's passes. Ahead are the cliffs of Mount Kipp with a wonderful series of cascades dropping from the glacier above. Below and to the east opens up the wonderful valley of the Belly River, with Glenns Lake and Crossley Lake filling up the middle distance and Pyramid Peak in the foreground. As the visitor winds down into the valley he is almost under the spray from the many lovely waterfalls that fling their way down from the ice imprisoned in the upper cirques. The last few miles of the trail are through forest, with glimpses of mountain peaks and water. Crossley Lake Campsite—or at Mokowanis Junction Shelter Cabin—where the day's travel ends, looks northward, and the pass crossed during the day is seen framed by the tremendous cliffs of Mount Cleveland on the right and the almost equally fine mass of Mount Merritt on the left. On the fifth day, there is a choice of two trails. One is through the Ptarmigan Tunnel, which has already been described. The second trail crosses and recrosses the Belly River, gives a glimpse of Dawn Mist Falls, leads past Elizabeth Lake, up the steep windswept sides of Red Gap Pass with its stunning view of Mount Merritt, past the banks of Kennedy Creek and Poia Lake, then over Swiftcurrent Ridge, and into the Swiftcurrent Valley in the glory of the setting sun.

Morning Eagle Falls, a feature of the Piegan Pass Trail. National Park Service photo.

Many Glacier Area Trail Log

Trail	Distance in Miles	Official Trail Numbers***
Many Glacier Hotel to		
Josephine Lake (head)	1.2	**** 168
Ptarmigan Falls	3.7 *	152
Ptarmigan Lake	5.7 *	152
Ptarmigan Tunnel	6.7 *	152
Iceberg Lake	6.2 *	152 (4.1), 155
Grinnell Lake	3.6	**** 168 (2.6), 169
Grinnell Glacier	6.1	**** 168 (2.6), 169 (1.0), 170
East boundary via Sherburne Lake	8.3 **	165 (1.8), 162
Cracker Lake	5.6 **	165
Morning Eagle Falls	5.1 **	113
Sun Point via Reynolds Creek	17.8 **	113
Sun Point via Siyeh Pass	18.5 **	113 (10.1), 117
Redrock Falls	2.8 **	157
Swiftcurrent Pass	6.8 *	157
Swiftcurrent Pass to summit of		
Swiftcurrent Mountain	1.4	158
Many Glacier Road to		
Appekunny Falls	1.6	166
Boundary Creek	1.6	110

North Circle Route

Trail	Distance in Miles	Official Trail Numbers***
Many Glacier Hotel to Granite Park Chalets	7.5	157
Granite Park Chalets to Fifty Mountain Shelter Cabin	11.9	121
Fifty Mountain Shelter Cabin to Waterton Lake Shelter Cabin	11.0	122
Waterton Lake Shelter Cabin to Crossley Lake Campsite	18.8	122 (5.4), 131
Crossley Lake Campsite to Many Glacier Hotel via Ptarmigan Tunnel	14.8	152
Crossley Lake Campsite to Many Glacier Hotel via Redgap Pass	21.9	152 (5.7), 154

*When starting from Swiftcurrent Motor Inn distance is about 1 mile less.

** When starting from Swiftcurrent Motor Inn distance is about 1 mile more.

*** Numbers in parentheses are the mileage distance to trail junction.

**** When starting from Swiftcurrent Motor Inn substitute trail #167 for #168.

80

EAST GLACIER PARK–TWO MEDICINE–
CUT BANK AREA

Several trails start near Glacier Park Lodge, but the most popular is the one to Two Medicine Lake. This 10-mile hike, often called the Mount Henry Trail, takes you up Bald Hill, across Fortymile Creek and down in Two Medicine Valley via Appistoki Creek. Near the end of the trail, this creek makes a tortuous drop, creating the attractive Appistoki Falls.

At Two Medicine Lake, you can easily reach all parts of the valley by trail. You can go up the north side of the lake by a trail with beautiful views of the lake and high peak on the opposite side (Sinopah Mountain) reflected in its placid waters. If you follow the trail, you will climb up through Bighorn Basin, from which you may look back at the valley nestling at your feet and finally reach the Continental Divide at Dawson Pass. If you wish to go in the other direction, you can proceed by a good trail up Paradise Creek and cross the range at Two Medicine Pass, or you can climb the east wall of the valley and enjoy the beauties of Buttercup Park just under Bearhead Mountain. Another interesting glacial cirque, or park, is at Aster.

From Two Medicine Lake, there are two trails to Cut Bank. One is via Dawson and Cut Bank Passes, while the other is easier going, just through the latter pass. You may also wish to take the trail to Nyack Ranger Station on the west side of the park via famous Pitamakan Pass.

At one time there were chalets at both Two Medicine and Cut Bank. Both were razed in the early fifties, and there are only improved campgrounds at these locations now. One campground is located in a very pretty spot near the Cut Bank River in the shadow of Twin Buttes, and facing the sculptured cirque of Amphitheater Mountain. Ten miles up the valley is the Continental Divide, while 8 miles away, hemmed in by Mount James and Norris Mountain, is Triple Divide Peak, a "three ocean" watershed. As stated in Chapter 3, from its 8,000 foot summit the water from the melting snow flows three ways—down the south slope via Atlantic Creek to the Missouri River and the Gulf of Mexico, by way of Pacific Creek to the Flathead River and the Pacific Ocean, and via Hudson Bay Creek and the St. Mary River to Hudson Bay It is about an hour's walk from the trail and somewhat of a climb to the summit. Triple Divide has its own message that can only be appreciated or understood when you stand on its summit and watch the water at your feet "flow three ways."

East Glacier Park–Two Medicine–Cut Bank Area Trail Log

Trail	Distance in Miles	Official Trail Numbers*
Glacier Park Lodge to		
Lubec Lake Ranger Station	9.4	93 (8.4), 90
Summit Marias Pass	16.6	93 (15.6), 94
Autumn Creek	19.8	93
Walton Ranger Station	29.3	93 (7.4), 89
Midvale Creek	2.0	95
Fortymile Creek	4.4	96
Two Medicine Lake Camp Store	10.0	96
Two Medicine Lake Camp Store to		
Appistoki Falls	0.5	96
Aster Park	2.0	98 (1.3), 101
Buttercup Park	4.2	98 (2.0), 88
Rockwell Falls	3.5	98 (2.4), 87
Cobalt Lake	5.8	98 (2.4), 87
Two Medicine Pass	8.0	98 (2.4), 87
Lake Isabel	14.1	98 (2.4), 87 (9.4), 86
Walton Ranger Station	26.5	98 (2.4), 87 (21.8), 67
Twin Falls	4.3	98
Upper Two Medicine Lake	5.5	98
Around Two Medicine Lake	7.9	98 (4.2), 99
Two Medicine Campgrounds to		
No Name Lake	3.9	99
Dawson Pass	5.8	99
Pitamakan Pass	8.7	99
Nyack Ranger Station (Via Upper Nyack)	30.5	99 (8.7), 80 (5.0), 73 (16.1), 67
Buffalo Woman Lake	20.7	99 (8.7), 80 (5.0), 74 (5.6), 76
Beaver Woman Lake	20.9	99 (8.7), 80 (5.0), 74 (5.6), 76
Nyack Ranger Station (Via Coal Creek)	38.6	99 (8.7), 80 (5.0), 74 (5.6), 75 (14.5), 67
Cut Bank Campground (via Dawson Pass)	18.9	99 (9.1), 102
Old Man Lake	6.5	102

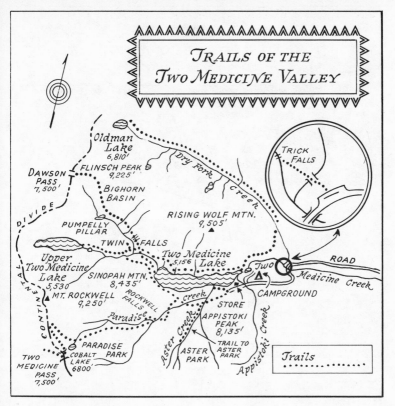

TRAILS OF THE
Two Medicine Valley

Cut Bank Pass	7.7	102
Cut Bank Campground (via Inside Trail)	17.5	102
Cut Bank Campground to		
Medicine Grizzly Lake	5.9	102 (3.9), 104 (0.1), 260
Triple Divide Pass	6.6	102 (3.9), 104
Red Eagle Lake	14.9	102 (3.9), 104
St. Mary Lake Boat Landing	18.2	102 (3.9), 104 (11.0), 107 (1.8), 109
Sun Point	27.4	102 (3.9), 104 (11.0), 107 (1.8), 109 (8.8), 113

* Numbers in parentheses are the mileage distance to trail junction.

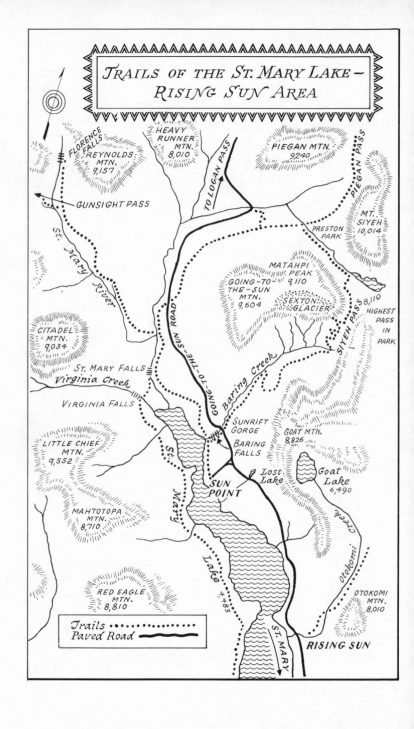

Trails of the St. Mary Lake – Rising Sun Area

FLORENCE FALLS

REYNOLDS MTN. 9,157

HEAVY RUNNER MTN. 8,010

PIEGAN MTN. 9240

PIEGAN PASS

TO LOGAN PASS

GUNSIGHT PASS

MT. SIYEH 10,014

PRESTON PARK

St. Mary River

MATAHPI PEAK 9,110

GOING-TO-THE-SUN MTN. 9,604

SEXTON GLACIER

SIYEH PASS 8,110

HIGHEST PASS IN PARK

CITADEL MTN. 9,034

St. Mary Falls

Virginia Creek

Baring Creek

GOING-TO-THE-SUN ROAD

VIRGINIA FALLS

LITTLE CHIEF MTN. 9,552

Sunrift Gorge

Baring Falls

GOAT MTN. 8,826

St. Mary

Lost Lake

Goat Lake 6,490

SUN POINT

MAHTOTOPA MTN. 8,710

Otokomi Creek

RED EAGLE MTN. 8,810

Lake 4,485

OTOKOMI MTN. 8,010

Trails · · · · · · · · · ·
Paved Road ▬▬▬▬▬

St. Mary

RISING SUN

ST. MARY–RISING SUN–SUN POINT AREA

Sun Point is the junction point of the park's trail system. Here trails can be taken north through Siyeh and Piegan Passes to Many Glacier Hotel (see map). This so-called "Inside Trail" also heads south to Glacier Park Lodge. In addition, there is a trail that leads west to Lake McDonald. If you are staying at Rising Sun—either the campground or Motor Inn—a launch leaves Rising Sun dock and will take you to Sun Point (the starting point for most trails in the area), thus saving you almost 2 miles of walking. This boat service is rather frequent during the day. (See page 157).

On the south of St. Mary Lake, Red Eagle and Little Chief Mountains project their shiplike prows into the water. On the north shore, Singleshot, Goat, and Otokomi Mountains expose their red, green, and purple hues to the mirror-like surface of the lake. Far up the valley the tilted cone of Fusillade Mountain disputes the right of way to Gunsight Pass, and Reynolds Peak, with its green slopes, is strongly contrasted against the frosted summit of the Continental Divide.

Once at Sun Point—either by horse, foot, boat, or auto—one of the interesting hikes is to visit the many falls in the area. Baring, St. Mary, and Virginia Falls are easily reached on a mostly level trail. Actually, a park naturalist conducts a tour to these beauties every morning.

Unfortunately few visitors to the Park make the spectacular trail trip to Sexton Glacier. Sexton is a small glacier, but late in the summer after its snow cover has melted off, it exhibits many of the features seen on much larger bodies of ice. A naturalist-accompanied all-day trip is made from Sunrift Gorge. This hike is through the spectacular alpine gardens at Preston Park and over Siyeh Pass, returning to Sunrift Gorge. The party makes a side trip to Sexton Glacier. On all-day nature walks, be sure to carry a lunch.

One of the Park's most interesting and beautiful trails is that at Gunsight Pass. (Gunsight Pass was named in 1891 by George Grinnell for its resemblance to the rear sight of a rifle, with the peak of a distant mountain showing through it like the front sight.) Leaving from Sun Point, this trail crosses Baring Creek below Baring Falls and moves up Reynolds Creek. At the foot of Fusillade Mountain the trail leaves the conifer forest and ascends the slope covered with smaller trees and shrubs. There are excellent views of Mount Jackson, Blackfoot Glacier, Siksika Falls (a large waterfall below the glacier), and Gunsight Pass. The trail climbs up along Gunsight Lake and then through the pass itself. Upon leaving Gunsight Pass, the trail swings down past Lake Ellen Wilson, named for the wife of former President Woodrow Wilson. There are several lofty waterfalls that can be seen from the trail; the most spectacular is Beaver Chief Falls, where water drops over 1,000 feet. The trail soon leads to Sperry Chalets, and in another 6 miles you will be at Lake McDonald.

St. Mary–Rising Sun–Sun Point Area Trail Log

Trail	Distance in Miles	Official Trail Numbers*
Sun Point		
Sexton Glacier	6.2	117 (5.5), 118
Siyeh Pass	6.4	117
Baring Falls	0.8	113
St. Mary Falls	2.5	113 (1.8), 109
Virginia Falls	3.0	113 (1.8), 109
Florence Falls	6.7	113 (3.2), 52 (2.7), 54
Gunsight Lake	8.1	113 (3.2), 52
Blackfoot Glacier	10.0	113 (3.2), 52 (5.0), 53
Gunsight Pass	11.1	113 (3.2), 52
Lake Ellen Wilson	12.8	113 (3.2), 52
Lincoln Pass	14.7	113 (3.2), 52
Sperry Chalet	15.5	113 (3.2), 52
Lake McDonald Lodge	21.3	113 (3.2), 52
Rising Sun Camp Store to		
Otokomï Lake	5.0	112

* Numbers in parentheses are the mileage distance to trail junction.

LAKE MC DONALD–AVALANCHE AREA

The number-one hike in this area is to Sperry Glacier and Chalets. The chalets overlook the deep valley of Sprague Creek, and a portion of Lake McDonald is visible from the verandas. An easy side trip from the chalets is the climb to Lincoln Pass and Peak. From this lookout there is a fine view south toward the Flathead Range and an equally striking view toward Lake McDonald.

The Sperry Glacier Trail is gouged out of the cirque wall before it begins its climb up between Edwards and Gunsight Mountains. The surface of the glacier itself is smooth in early season, but becomes deeply crevassed and covered with slush and streams of meltwater in midsummer. Seracs, wells, bergschrunds, dust wells, tables, and other features develop as the season progresses. The most interesting, but more distant, are near the front of the glacier. Naturalist-conducted overnight trips leave Lake McDonald Lodge three times a week to Sperry Glacier. Overnight accommodations are at Sperry Chalets. This glacier was named for Dr. Lyman B. Sperry of Oberlin College (Ohio), the "Gentleman Explorer," who led the first party to reach the glacier in 1896, and who later was responsible for the building of the first trail to the glacier over approximately the same route as the present one.

The hike to Avalanche Lake may be accomplished from either Lake McDonald Lodge or Avalanche Campground. Avalanche Basin is one of the finest examples of a glacial cirque in the Park. The walls at the back of the basin are over 3,000 feet high. At the top of this wall is Sperry Glacier, and water from the melting ice of the glacier spills over the precipice in a half-dozen torrential streams. Most of the water reaches the lake, but a great quantity is blown away in mist as it dashes against the rocks in its downward plunge. A naturalist-conducted walk leaves from the rear of Avalanche Campground every morning and afternoon.

There are many other lakes to visit while in this area including Snyder, Fish, Trout, Arrow, Camas, Rogers, Lincoln, and Johns Lakes. To the latter, there is a daily naturalist-conducted walk that leaves from the Johns Lake Trail Parking Area. This delightful walk takes you through a red cedar–hemlock forest to a sphagnum-sedge bog surrounding Johns Lake.

Lake McDonald–Avalanche Area Trail Log

Trail	Distance in Miles	Official Trail Numbers*
Lake McDonald Lodge to		
Mount Brown Lookout	5.0	52 (1.3), 49
Snyder Lake	3.9	52 (1.3), 50
Sperry Chalets	5.8	52
Sperry Glacier	9.3	52 (5.6), 51
Sun Point	21.3	52 (18.1), 113

(Continued)

(*Continued from page 87*)

Trail	Distance in Miles	Official Trail Numbers*
Fish Lake	1.8	45
Snyder Ridge	11.1	45
Lincoln Lake	10.2	45 (3.9), 47 (2.7), 68
Lincoln Creek (mouth)	12.4	45 (3.9), 47 (2.7), 68
Johns Lake	1.6	56
Lake McDonald Ranger Station	2.3	56 (1.5), 9
Avalanche Campgrounds	6.6	56 (1.6), 57 (0.7), 59
Avalanche Lake	7.8	56 (5.8), 60
Avalanche Campgrounds to Avalanche Lake	2.3	256 (0.3), 60
Lake McDonald Ranger Station to		
Trout Lake	4.3	9
Rogers Lake	5.1	9
Arrow Lake	7.3	9 (4.3), 39
Camas Lake	10.5	9 (4.3), 39
Lake Evangeline	11.3	9 (4.3), 39
Johns Lake Parking Area to		
Johns Lake	1.1	57 (0.7), 56

* Numbers in parentheses are the mileage distance to trail junction.

LOGAN PASS–GRANITE PARK AREA

The summit of Logan Pass is another of those surprising contradictions so often found in Glacier's construction. It is not a pass in the way these defiles are commonly pictured, but a broad flat plateau cut with silvery streams, luxuriant grass growing from the surplus moisture of the melting snow, and wildflowers, brighter, bigger, and more plentiful than at any other place in the Park. From the pass, the hanging gardens on the slopes of Mount Reynolds and a sea of nearby and distant peaks are in full view. Hidden Lake Overlook, high up on the slopes of Mount Reynolds and a short distance from Logan Pass, is an objective of unusual

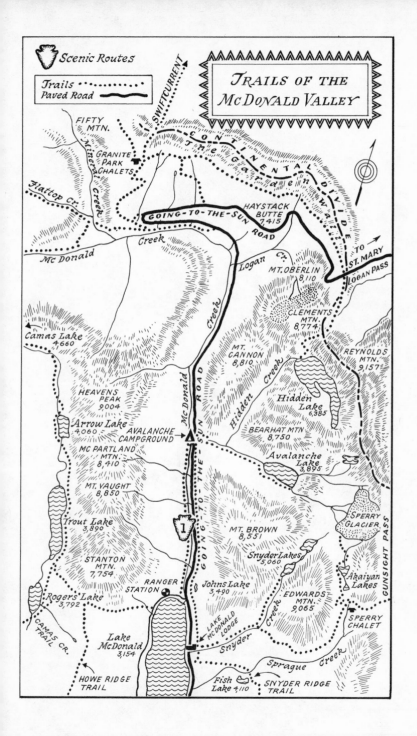

Scenic Routes

Trails · · · · · · · ·
Paved Road 〰〰〰〰

TRAILS OF THE
McDONALD VALLEY

SWIFTCURRENT

FIFTY MTN.

CONTINENTAL DIVIDE

The Garden Wall

GRANITE PARK CHALETS

Mineral Creek

Flattop Cr.

GOING-TO-THE-SUN ROAD

HAYSTACK BUTTE 7,415

TO ST. MARY

McDonald Creek

Logan Cr.

MT. OBERLIN 8,110

LOGAN PASS

Camas Lake 4,660

CLEMENTS MTN. 8,774

REYNOLDS MTN. 9,157

HEAVENS PEAK 9,004

MT. CANNON 8,810

Hidden Creek

Hidden Lake 6,385

Arrow Lake 4,060

AVALANCHE CAMPGROUND

McDonald Road

BEARHAT MTN. 8,750

Avalanche Lake 3,895

McPARTLAND MTN. 8,410

MT. VAUGHT 8,850

Trout Lake 3,890

SPERRY GLACIER

GOING-TO-THE-SUN ROAD

MT. BROWN 8,551

STANTON MTN. 7,754

Snyder Lakes 5,060

Akaiyan Lakes

1

RANGER STATION

Johns Lake 3,490

EDWARDS MTN. 9,065

GUNSIGHT PASS

Rogers Lake 3,792

LAKE McDONALD LODGE

Snyder Creek

SPERRY CHALET

CAMAS CR. TRAIL

Lake McDonald 3,154

Snyder Creek

Sprague Creek

HOWE RIDGE TRAIL

Fish Lake 4,110

SNYDER RIDGE TRAIL

and surprising beauty for hikers. A self-guiding natural trail leads to the cirque overlook.

The unanimous opinion of the thousands who have traveled the Garden Wall Trail is that it is the most dramatic spectacle of any of the well-traveled routes. Contrary to the common conception of mountain trails, it is not steep; in fact, its entire distance is almost a level grade, but it hugs closely the mile-high rim of the Garden Wall. Starting out from Granite Park at about the 6,000-foot level, it holds closely to this contour until the last few hundred feet approaching Logan Pass. For a considerable distance it is a ledge trail, carved out of the sides of the precipitous cliffs which form the Garden Wall and which tower above one from 1,000 to 2,000 feet. It is not the trail itself but the imposing, impressive panorama of deep canyons, and the piling up of massive rock strata in splendid disarray, brilliant in color, streaked with snow, and carved in majestic proportions, that hold one spellbound.

Earlier in this chapter the North Circle Trail, which leads from Granite Park Chalet to Fifty Mountain, was described. There are two other trails that will lead to the same destination. One is the long, but beautiful trail via Kootenai Pass, and the other is via Mineral Creek. Both of these trails start at the end of Packers Roost Road, which is 5 miles from the chalets and 2.4 miles from the Going-to-the-Sun Road. From Fifty Mountain the trail leads to Waterton Lake.

Logan Pass–Granite Park Area Trail Log

Trail	Distance in Miles	Official Trail Numbers*
Logan Pass Visitor Center to		
Hidden Lake Overlook	2.0	120
Hidden Lake	3.0	120
Granite Park Chalets	7.6	121
Going-to-the-Sun Road to		
Granite Park Chalets via Loop	4.0	62
Granite Park Chalets	3.9	126 (2.7), 121
		(Continued)

A naturalist-conducted tour of Sperry Glacier takes hikers up for a close-up view of a crevasse. Great Northern Railway photo.

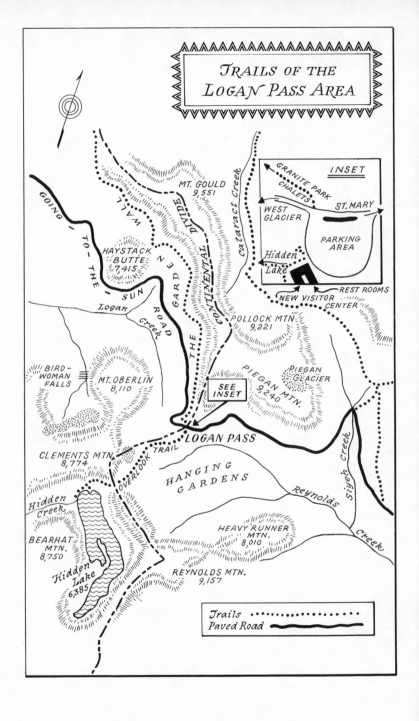

TRAILS OF THE LOGAN PASS AREA

INSET

GRANITE PARK CHALETS

ST. MARY

WEST GLACIER

PARKING AREA

Hidden Lake

REST ROOMS

NEW VISITOR CENTER

GOING - TO - THE - SUN

THE WALL

GARDEN

THE CONTINENTAL DIVIDE

Cataract Creek

MT. GOULD 9,551

HAYSTACK BUTTE 7,415

Logan Creek

ROAD Creek

POLLOCK MTN. 9,221

PIEGAN GLACIER

PIEGAN MTN. 9,240

BIRD-WOMAN FALLS

MT. OBERLIN 8,110

SEE INSET

LOGAN PASS

Siyeh Creek

CLEMENTS MTN. 8,774

OVERLOOK TRAIL

HANGING GARDENS

Reynolds Creek

Hidden Creek

BEARHAT MTN. 8,750

Hidden Lake 6,385

HEAVY RUNNER MTN. 8,010

REYNOLDS MTN. 9,157

Trails ••••••••
Paved Road ━━━━━

(*Continued from page 91*)

Granite Park Chalets to		
Packers Roost Road (end)	5.0	62 (4.2), 63
Packers Roost Road (end) to		
Fifty Mountain via Flattop		
Mountain and Kootenai Pass	17.0	63
Fifty Mountain via Mineral Creek	9.8	63 (0.3), 128
Flattop Creek	5.7	63 (0.3), 128 (0.5), 66

* Numbers in parentheses are the mileage distance to trail junction.

NORTH FORK AREA

Along the North Fork Road there are several trail heads. These are all noted on page 67.

North Fork Area Trail Log

Trail	Distance in Miles	Official Trail Numbers*
From North Fork Road to		
Huckleberry Mountain		
Lookout	6.4	35
Howe Lake	2.0	38
Trout Lake via Howe		
Ridge	10.7	38
Trout Lake via Camas		
Creek	6.9	39
Camas Lake	13.9	39
Dutch Lakes	12.3	34
Anaconda Creek	7.5	33
Logging Lake	4.4	24
Grace Lake	12.3	24 (4.4), 9 (1.9), 20
Lower Quartz Lake	6.7	17
Upper Quartz Lake	10.0	17
Bowman Lake (end of road) to		
Brown Pass	12.8	15
Waterton Ranger Station	21.4	15 (12.8), 6
Numa Lookout	5.6	15 (0.7), 14
Kintla Lake Ranger Station to		
Upper Kintla Lake	8.8	6
Boulder Pass	17.6	6
Hole-in-the-Wall Basin	19.9	6
Brown Pass	22.7	6
Waterton Ranger Station	31.3	6

* Numbers in parentheses are the mileage distance to trail junction.

HEADQUARTERS–APGAR AREA

A trail follows the Flathead River from the headquarters of Glacier National Park to the Walton Ranger Station. From this trail, several others take off to interesting spots along the southern boundary of the Park.

Headquarters–Apgar Area Trail Log

Trail	Distance in Miles	Official Trail Numbers*
Headquarters to		
Lincoln Creek (mouth)	5.3	67
Lincoln Lake	14.7	67 (5.3), 68
Harrison Creek (mouth)	7.1	67
Harrison Lake (foot)	10.0	67 (7.1), 69
Harrison Creek (head)	15.8	67 (7.1), 69
Loneman Lookout	16.3	67 (11.0), 70
Nyack Ranger Station	12.0	67
Coal Creek (mouth)	16.8	67
Walton Ranger Station	30.7	67
Apgar Lookout	4.2	Flathead Ranger Station Road (1.4), 42

* Numbers in parentheses are the mileage distance to trail junction.

WATERTON LAKES TRAILS

This Park contains, someone has said, a maximum of scenery in a minimum of space. More than 100 miles of graded and well-maintained trails form a network throughout the over 200 square miles of the Park's area, offering an introduction to unique alpine scenery impossible to reach by automobile. The following notes are offered to provide information on distances, problems, and other details of interest. The trails are separated into different groups in relation to their locations within the various sections of the Park. The townsite section consists of these radiating from the Waterton Park Townsite; the Akamina Highway–Cameron Lake section, those which extend from the Akamina Highway and Cameron Lake; the Red Rock Canyon section, those radiating from the area of Red Rock Canyon; and the Belly River section, those which extend from the Chief Mountain Highway, which passes through the most easterly section of the Park. Horse stables are located adjacent to the townsite and at Red Rock Canyon.

TRAILS IN WATERTON
LAKES NATIONAL PARK

TOWNSITE SECTION

Trail	Location	Length in Miles
Bear's Hump	From parking lot at information center, trail climbs up slope of Mount Crandell and to Bear's Hump.	0.8
Lake Linnet	Off main entrance road—100 yards east of Akamina Highway junction—a foot path emerges near information center, crosses road leading to Prince of Wales Hotel, and continues on along north shoreline of Lake Linnet.	0.5
Bosporus	Starting at picnic area on north shore of Emerald Bay, the trail follows shoreline in southeasterly direction to the Bosporus.	0.7
Bosporus-Stoney Flats Trail	After crossing the Bosporus (depth of water is enough to make horses swim), trail proceeds to Stoney Flats.	3.3
From townsite to Vimy Peak	Via Bosporus-Stoney Flats Trail which leads to summit.	6.8
From townsite to Vimy Peak	Via Pass Creek Flats. Follow main road from townsite to junction of Pass Creek Flats secondary road. Follow road to Marquis Hole picnic site. Ford Dardanelles here, and follow well-marked trail to Stoney Flats and Vimy Peak.	8.0
From townsite to Vimy Peak	Via Waterton River Bridge and Camp INUSPI. Turn off Chief Mountain Highway to Camp INUSPI. Then follow trail to Stoney Flats and hence on to Vimy Peak.	13.2

Townsite to Crypt Lake	Follow Bosporus-Stoney Flats Trail to sign indicating Crypt Lake Trail. This trail leads past Hell Roaring Canyon Warden's Cabin and ascends to Crypt Lake. Many hikers charter a boat from the townsite to take them to warden's cabin.	7.5
Alderson Lake (Carthew Trail)	Trail begins about 200 yards south of Cameron Fall.	4.6
Lower Carthew Lake (Carthew Trail)	Near Alderson Lake a sign indicates trail to Lower Carthew Lake. Upper Carthew is ¼-mile beyond lower lake.	1.5
Cameron Lake (Carthew Trail)	The Carthew Trail continues past Upper Carthew Lake, over Carthew Summit, and then drops down to Summit Lake where it joins the trail connecting Cameron Lake with Upper Waterton Lake (Waterton Ranger Station) via West Boundary Creek (Glacier Park trail #137).	6.0
From townsite to Bertha Lake	Follow Lakeshore Trail at the end of Cameron Falls Bridge in townsite to junction at Bertha Creek, and then continue on as indicated by trail markers.	3.6
From townsite to International boundary line	The Lakeshore Trail continues southeast from the junction at Bertha Creek until it reaches the warden's patrol cabin near the international boundary line.	5.1

TRAILS IN WATERTON
LAKES NATIONAL PARK

| From townsite to Goathaunt | The Lakeshore Trail terminates at the head of Upper Waterton Lake (called Goathaunt). Trails at Waterton Ranger Station branch off from here south and west into Glacier Park. | 9.3 |

| Crandell Lake | Trail begins about 400 yards south of the Akamina Highway junction and continues along southwest slope of Crandell Mountain to Crandell Lake. | 3.9 |

AKAMINA HIGHWAY-CAMERON LAKE SECTION

| Lineham Brook | From mile 5.9 on Akamina Highway, a *very* steep trail leads to five beautiful lakes. While a steep cliff must be climbed, a cable has been installed to make this easier. *Alternate routes:* via Lower Rowe Lake, climbing Lineham Mountain; via Red Rock Canyon, Lone Lake, and over Hawkins Mountain. | 3.6 |

| Rowe Lakes | From mile 6.2 on Akamina Highway, a trail follows Rowe Brook to Lower Rowe Lake. Upper Rowe Lake is 1¼-mile farther on the trail. | 2.5 |

| Mother Duck Trail | This trail commences across the bridge at the north end of Cameron Lake. It is 14½-miles from Cameron Lake to townsite via the Mother Duck and Lakeshore Trails. | 6.4 |

| Cameron Lake | This footpath trail leads down the west side of the lake to nearly its upper end. | 1.2 |

South Kootenai Pass	This trail begins at the Red Rock Canyon Warden's Station and follows a well-marked route to South Kootenai Pass and British Columbia.	7.0
Twin Lakes	A secondary road (permission from the warden must be obtained before private vehicle can travel on it) leads from Red Rock Canyon Warden's Station to within 2 miles of Twin Lakes. At mile 2.5 on this road, a trail leads to Goat Lake.	2.2
	At termination of fire road, trail leads to Lost Lake and another leads to Twin Lakes.	1.2

THE BELLY RIVER SECTION AND FOOTHILLS

The Belly River area within the extreme eastern section of the Park is approximately 35 square miles in area. The Chief Mountain International Highway passes through the entire length of this district, making its most attractive feature, the Belly River, very accessible.

The North Fork Trail (5.1 miles from the Belly River Bridge to the North Fork Cabin). This trail commences as a wagon road which begins at the west end of the Belly River Bridge and follows the west bank of the river south for nearly a mile onto a large open area known as "Bebee Flats." The wagon road crosses these flats in a westerly direction and, at their extreme west side, terminates near the edge of the creek. This creek is named "North Fork of the Belly River." From this point the trail climbs to a higher level on the north bank of the creek and enters the forest. It more or less parallels the creek extending in a southwesterly direction as far as the international boundary, and the North Fork Cabin.

The Belly River Wagon Road (2.6 miles from Belly River Campground to international boundary). This is an original route

---

Fording the middle fork of the Belly River as it leaves Crossley Lake. Great Northern Railway photo.

into the headwaters of Belly River which are in Glacier National Park. The wagon road continues due south from the Belly River Campground. It connects with Glacier Park Trail #148, which leads to the Belly River Ranger Station (5.3 miles). From here you can go to Crossley Lake (#148—2 miles) or Dawn Mist Falls (#151—1.8 miles). The North Circle route is then picked up at either of these points (see page 77). Other Glacier National Park trails in the Belly River area are the ones to Miche Wabun Lake (#140) and the Gable Pass (#149), which goes to Slide Lake and to the end of the Otatso Creek Road. The Red Gap Pass Trail (#154 and #161) leads to the Kennedy Road.

There are other trails in Waterton Lakes that follow along the eastern boundary of the Park from the Chief Mountain Customs to the extreme north end at Yarrow Creek. A large prairie area lies between the Pincher Creek park entrance and the golf course. This area offers lots of room for riders who enjoy the wide-open spaces in which to gallop. At its north end is the buffalo paddock. Between the paddock and Bellevue Hill a trail climbs the grassy slope of a ridge (an outrun of Bellevue Hill) and enters the Horseshoe Basin to the northwest of the paddocks and the prairie area. The trail eventually crosses a creek bed, then turns north following the north branch of the valley to its head. Here, it is carried by switchbacks over the west portion of Lakeview Ridge, then down into the Oil Basin in the north portion of the Park. It is 12 miles from the Waterton River Bridge to Yarrow Creek.

APPROVED BACKCOUNTRY CAMPSITES

Backcountry visitors in Glacier Park must have a campfire permit in their possession if they wish to build a fire, and they must build fires only in established places at approved campfire sites. Campfire permits may be used for the following backcountry campsites in Glacier:

West Lakes District

North Fork Area

Akokala Lake
Bowman Lake, head
Dutch Lakes
Grace Lake, head

Logging Lake, foot
Logging Lake, head
Lower Quartz Lake, foot
Quartz Lake, foot

North Fork Area Continued

Hole-in-the-Wall Basin

Kintla Lake, head

Upper Kintla Lake, foot

Upper Kintla Lake, head

McDonald Area

Arrow Lake Trail Shelter

Camas Lake

Granite Park, near the trails cabin

Howe Lake, foot

Lake Ellen Wilson

Lake Evangeline, foot

Lincoln Lake, foot

McDonald Boat Picnic Sites
(Nos. 1, 2 or 3; west shore)

Rogers Lake

Snyder Lake, foot

Sperry Chalets (¼ mile northeast
of Chalets)

Trout Lake, foot

Trout Lake, head

Walton Area

Beaver Woman Lake

Buffalo Woman Lake

Coal Creek at Fielding Trail

Harrison Lake, head

Harrison Lake, foot

Lake Isabel

Martha's Basin

Nyack Creek, Lower

Nyack Creek, Upper

Nyack Meadow (3½ miles below
Lower Nyack Patrol Cabin)

Ole Creek at Fielding Trail

Ole Lake, gravel bar (near Skeleton Mountain)

Park Creek, Lower

Park Creek, Upper

Hudson Bay District

Two Medicine Area

Cobalt Lake, outlet

Katoya Lake, outlet

Medicine Grizzly Lake (headwaters of Atlantic Creek)

Morning Star Lake, east shore

No-Name Lake, northeast shore

Old Man Lake, northeast shore

Pitamakan Lake, outlet (north of
Cut Bank Pass)

Triple Divide Trail, at Cut Bank
Trail junction

Two Medicine Lake, Paradise
Point

Upper Two Medicine Lake, east
shore

St. Mary Area

Gunsight Lake Trail Shelter

Gunsight Pass Trail Shelter

Otokomï Lake

Piegan Pass

Preston Park

Red Eagle Lake, foot

Red Eagle Lake, head

Many Glacier Area

Bullhead Lake, above head of
lake

Cracker Lake, foot

Grinnell Glacier, base of moraine

Grinnell Lake, foot

Iceberg Lake, foot

Otatso Creek Trail Shelter

Poia Lake, head

Ptarmigan Lake, foot

Slide Lake, northeast corner

Hudson Bay District (Continued)

Belly River Area

Atsina Lake
Crossley Lake, north shore
Elizabeth Lake, foot
Elizabeth Lake, head
Glenns Lake, foot
Glenns Lake, head
Helen Lake, foot
Miche Wabun Lake, foot

Mokowanis Junction Trail Shelter
  (above head)
Mokowanis Lake, foot
Paiota Falls, top (between Atsina
  Lake and Stoney Indian Pass)
Three Mile Campground (be-
  tween Chief Mtn. Customs and
  Belly River Ranger Station)

Waterton Area

Fifty Mountain Trail Shelter
Kootenai Lakes (north of mouth
  of Valentine Creek)
Lake Francis, above head of lake
Lake Janet, above head of lake

Pass Creek
Stoney Indian Lake
Waterton Lake Trail Shelter
Waterton River (across from
  Waterton Ranger Station)

In Waterton Park, backcountry campsites can be found at the various lakes such as Alderson, Bertha, Crandell, Crypt, and Twin Lakes. These sites contain kitchen shelters and sanitary facilities.

BACKCOUNTRY ETIQUETTE
AND REGULATIONS

If you desire to make either a horseback or hiking trip into the backcountry, on your own without benefit of a guide, you must do the following:

1. Go to a ranger (warden) station and obtain a campfire permit for the area or areas you will be in.

2. Give your itinerary to the ranger (warden). This is necessary for several reasons, including protection of the visitor and protection of the Parks. Never hike alone.

3. Always report the completion of your trip to prevent a needless search, and turn in the campfire permit at the same time.

When going into the backcountry of Glacier Park, you should by all means obtain either a topographic map or a hiking trail map of the Park that you are in and should have a compass. You must know how to use them to avoid becoming lost or getting into difficult situations requiring the help of a rescue party. Obtain a topographic map of the Park from the Geological Survey, U. S. Department of the Interior, Washington, D. C. 20240, or at one of the visitor centers in the Park. A good compass, such as the

Silva with an azimuth face on which the magnetic declination can be set off, is preferable to the small pocket type.

Keep the following backcountry rules of etiquette in mind:

1. In general, there are several things that you may do as a camper or hiker to conserve the wild beauty of the Glacier-Waterton country. First, in choosing a campsite, pick one that already has the scar of an old campfire and build your fire there. If you are traveling with stock, unpack at your campsite, and then hobble your horses well away from campsites, lakes, and trails.

2. When making camp, do not "ditch" your tent or dig a level area. These scars last several years, even if the soil is carefully replaced (and no two parties have the same size tents). Of course, cutting fir boughs for beds has long been a poor practice.

3. Sanitation at high campsites is a tough problem. There is literally no place left to bury cans and foil. Marmots have invariably become civilized enough to dig up such refuse. Burn that which is flammable, and then pack out your flattened cans and foil with you. For personal sanitation, walk well away from campsites, trails, and streams, and bury all human waste.

4. For campfires, you may gather only wood that is dead and fallen to the ground. In some locations, fuel is definitely scarce, so use small fires—or carry a Primus stove. Fires should not be kindled near the roots of trees, dead wood, moss, or forest duff, but in some open space on rock or earth. When breaking camp, let your fire burn all garbage and fuel completely so as to leave the smallest possible fire scar, then be sure it is completely out. Be sure to clean your campsite. Never throw bottles, cans, jars, or refuse in streams or lakes.

5. Do not try to cover too much country in one day. Carry a light pack. Keep warm. Include in your pack a flashlight, waterproof matches, and a pocket first-aid kit. Your trip in the mountains should be a pleasant experience, not an ordeal.

6. Trails penetrate most areas in both Parks and are maintained for your benefit. Avoid shortcutting, especially on switchbacks, since this greatly accelerates the erosion along trails. Rock climbing is hazardous due to the composition of the formations. It is a good idea to stay on established trails.

7. If you are lost or injured, do not panic; keep your head. Sit down, rest, think. If you are lost, try to figure out where you are. If it is close to dark, find a place to camp, gather firewood, keep warm, and rest. Three smoke signals, three fires, three shouts, or three of almost anything that will attract attention will start help on the way.

8. Picking flowers or collecting specimens of plants, animals, or other natural or historical objects is prohibited without written authorization obtained in advance from the superintendent. (No permits are issued for personal collections.)

9. On the trails, saddle and pack stock have the right of way at all times. Hikers shall move off the trail and remain still until the stock passes. Guides will proceed slowly with stock party after the hikers are in a safe location off the trail. Horses should not be permitted to walk on the oil-surfaced roads except where designated trails cross such roads.

10. Motorcycles, other motor vehicles, or bicycles are prohibited from operating on the trails. You must not operate a vehicle outside the roadways or designated parking areas. Dogs or cats are not permitted on any trail in either Park. (Not even on a leash.)

The foregoing regulations and suggestions have evolved through many years of Park management. Obviously, they are meant to protect both you as a backcountry traveler and both Parks themselves so that your visits will be worthwhile. Know and abide by them to get the most enjoyment from your trail trips.

MOUNTAIN CLIMBING

Mountain climbing is a healthful but more strenuous form of sport than either horseback riding or hiking. In this book we will not involve ourselves in the controversy of whether or not the Parks' mountains are unsuitable for climbing because their sedimentary rocks are too crumbly to be safe. But, in order to keep the sport within the customary limits of mountaineering safety, the National Park Service in Glacier must insist upon adherence to certain policies and procedures. No one should attempt climbs without first consulting the rangers, discussing the proposed expedition, and registering at the ranger station both before and after the trip.

The same type of regulations holds true in Waterton Lakes National Park. This it, Park regulations require that all persons before climbing a mountain shall register with the district warden indicating their proposed route and the duration of the climb. Inexperienced climbers should obtain the services of a guide and full information concerning the necessary equipment. They must also report in to the Warden Service on returning.

Chapter 5.

Plant Life in the Parks

As you drive along the Going-to-the-Sun Road, you will note that there are changes in the kinds of plants and animals found at lower elevations as compared to those at higher elevations. Very few plants that are found on the mountain tops grow in the valleys. For example, the dense red cedar–hemlock–larch forests around Lake McDonald stand out in striking contrast to the sparse subalpine fir growth found at Logan Pass.

Animal and plant life not only changes with the different altitudes, but it also changes with difference in latitude. Plants and animals of the tropics differ from those of the temperate or Arctic regions. It has been found that every 1,000 feet rise in elevation is equivalent to traveling 300 miles north from the equator. Biologists have tried to correlate such facts by advancing the life zone concept. Roughly speaking, the vegetation is divided into belts or zones depending upon the temperature and moisture.

A journey along the Pacific coast of North America from the state of Sonora in Mexico to the Arctic Circle is equivalent to climbing from the base to the top of a high snow-capped peak in Sonora. In making either trip several life zones are traversed. The first or lowest zone, with the climate typical of the state of Sonora, is called the Sonoran (*Desert*) zone. In it are found desert and semidesert types of plants. Needless to say, such a zone does not occur in the Glacier-Waterton region.

Each of the other zones occur in the Parks. The lowest of these, with a temperate climate resembling that found in the Great Plains area and that covered by the ponderosa pine forests of the Pacific coast, is called the Transition (*Prairie*) zone, since it is transitional between the hot semiarid regions and the cool, moist, timbered regions of Canada. This latter zone is known as the

Canadian (*Forest*) zone. The Hudsonian (*Scrub Forest*) zone, above the Canadian zone, is typified by stunted alpine forest growth as found at Logan Pass or in the Hudson Bay area in Canada. The Arctic-Alpine (*Alpine*) zone has no trees, and plant growth found there is comparable to that found in the Arctic regions. Everything above timberline is considered in this life zone.

The Transition zone embraces most of the Great Plains and extends up into the mountains in some places, especially farther south. The prairies may be broken up by aspens in damper areas or by stands of pine where moisture is more abundant. Prairies exist along the entire eastern edge of both Parks as well as in a few isolated areas west of the Continental Divide in Glacier. The small western areas are distinctive and sharply defined, and in places they support small groves of ponderosa pine, such as those along the North Fork of the Flathead River.

The Canadian zone is slightly higher and considerably damper than the Transition zone. It covers most of both Waterton Lakes and Glacier National Parks, including all the heavily forested areas. Characteristic trees, in order of their abundance, are Engelmann spruce, lodgepole pine, western red cedar, western hemlock, western white pine, Douglas fir, western larch, and black cottonwood poplar. The line of demarcation between these two life zones is very indistinct along the eastern edge of the Parks, with slender arms of prairie extending several miles into the larger valleys and wooded ridges stretching down into the prairies in a few places.

The dense forests of the Canadian zone gradually thin out at higher elevations, and almost imperceptibly the trees with more or less stunted growth become predominant. The major climatic factors causing trees to be dwarfed at high elevations are decreased atmospheric pressure, lowered temperatures, and increased wind. The approximate elevation at which climatic conditions prevent trees from exceeding 10 to 15 feet in height may be referred to as "timberline," and this narrow altitudinal band contains the true Hudsonian zone. In the Parks, timberline would probably occur at 7,000 to 7,500 feet above sea level, if inhabitable slopes

---

Beargrass (Xerophyllum tenax), *gorgeous creamy-white spikes of four to six feet, bloom profusely in the Parks during June and July. The beargrass shown here is blooming near Two Medicine Lake. Mount Sinopah is the predominant mountain, while Painted Tepee Peak can be seen at its left, and Rising Bull Ridge and Pumpelly Pillar to its right.* Glacier Park, Inc., photo.

extended that high. However, almost everywhere in the Parks the upper limit of trees is regulated, not by the actual altitudinal and climatic factors, but rather by the amount of soil on the high talus slopes and the amount of wind buffeting the passes and high ridges. The trees growing in the Hudsonian zone are mostly sub-alpine fir, but whitebark pine or limber pine trees are usually also present. Logan Pass is a typical region of this sort, with fir thickets scattered throughout broad expanses of snowy meadows.

The Arctic-Alpine zone is marked by wide alpine meadows or rocky open places where all woody plants become increasingly smaller until there are no trees. Plant species such as are found along the trail to Hidden Lake Pass and in the Hanging Gardens are typical of the Arctic-Alpine zone.

THE FORESTS OF THE PARKS

From the dawn of history forests have aroused in man a variety of conflicting emotions. He has feared their dark pathways, yet traveled them in search of game. They have furnished fuel and wood for his home, yet occupied land needed for his crops. He has fought them with axe and fire, yet enjoyed the peacefulness of their cool depths. Perhaps this paradoxical association over centuries of time is responsible for the unmistakable appeal forests hold for us today. The stately, verdant forests of the valleys and lower mountain slopes, and the twisted, weather-beaten trees of the higher and arid regions, are an integral part of the scenic beauty of Glacier and Waterton Lakes National Parks.

Trees, like people, may be sturdy and strong or delicate and weak. Among the many factors affecting the growth or very existence of trees are soil, moisture, temperature, and light. The type, size, and condition of a tree or forest is indicative of the soil and climatic condition of the area in which it is found. Hence, in Glacier National Park the contrast will be noted between the exuberant growth of beautiful trees common to the moist Pacific slopes (west side of the Continental Divide), and the slower growing, smaller trees of the more arid east side.

Cone-bearing trees dominate the lower landscapes of both Glacier and Waterton. Fifteen species are found, two of which have fleshy "cones" and one of which loses its needles in the winter. There are also about ten broad-leaved species in the region. Following is a short description of the trees of the Parks:

WESTERN WHITE PINE (*Pinus monticola*)

The fine, slender needles, five in a bundle, are blue-green in color and from 2 to 4 inches long. The bark on young trees is smooth and light gray. On old trees it darkens to a purplish tinge and checks into regular squares or rectangles. The slender, thin-scaled cones are from 6 to 10 inches long (the cones of western white pine are the longest found in the Park) and are borne on the upper branches. Mature trees in the Park often attain heights of 100 feet and occasionally reach 150 feet. Diameters of mature trees ordinarily vary from 1 to 3 feet; however, a few are larger. The range of western white pine in Glacier National Park is limited to the lower elevations of the west side and occurs only occasionally north of Dutch Creek. It grows most abundantly in the upper McDonald Valley, where it is found in association with fir and spruce although it occurs in mixture with other conifers.

LODGEPOLE PINE (*Pinus contorta*)

One of the most characteristic trees of the Rocky Mountains is lodgepole pine. It grows in various forms from sea level to 11,000 feet and from Lower California almost to Alaska, and is the most abundant tree in the Parks. Lodgepole pine bears its needles two in a bundle; they are yellow-green in color and generally about 2 inches long, though sometimes they may be found as short as 1 inch or as long as 4 inches. The small, hard cones persist on the tree for many years and often remain closed. The tree never reaches a large size. Heights seldom exceed 70 to 80 feet and diameters are generally less than 18 inches in mature stands. But because of their slender straight trunks, the Indians used this pine for their lodges. This practice has given the tree its common name.

In Rocky Mountain forests, lodgepole pine ranks first as a "fire" tree; that is, when an area is swept by fire, this pine reseeds and restocks the ground in greater abundance than any other species. The reasons for this are apparent. When a fire passes through the forest, many of the tightly closed lodgepole cones escape the fire or are merely scorched. The heat, however, is sufficient to open the scales, and almost before the ground has cooled, thousands of seeds are fluttering down. Other cones buried in the litter on the forest floor may have lain, their scales closed and seeds dormant, for many years. Then, opened by the heat, the cones free the seeds,

109

which germinate the next spring. Finally, the blackened earth seems to form an ideal seed bed for this species, and within a few years, under favorable conditions, the scar left by the fire has been at least partially erased by the green and thrifty lodgepole saplings. When a stand of lodgepole reaches maturity, instead of young trees of this species replacing dying veterans, we find an encroachment of spruce, fir, or some other species, and an almost total lack of healthy lodgepole reproduction. It is apparent, then, that lodgepole pine seldom succeeds itself except after fires, and it is safe to assume that most pure stands of lodgepole pine are indirectly the result of fire. Thus the term "fire species"—a tree whose role in nature seems to be one of protection and preparation. It first restocks the barren ground left by fire, protecting it from erosion, and then prepares a site for other species to gain a foothold.

LIMBER PINE (Pinus flexilis) and
WHITEBARK PINE (Pinus albicaulis)

Somewhat similar to the western white pine are the limber and whitebark pines, found most commonly on the east side of the Continental Divide and above 5,000 feet in both Parks. Generally speaking, the limber pine is more abundant at middle elevations; the range of the whitebark extends through the Hudsonian zone, where it occurs as a stunted timberline tree. The two trees otherwise are distinguished from each other with difficulty, unless they are bearing mature cones. Those of the limber pine are yellowish green in color, while those of the whitebark are purple. The branches are very limber and can be tied into a tight knot without breaking. The crowns are loose and bushy; the foliage is dark yellow to gray-green, having considerably more blue than the lodgepole pines, the only pine with which they are associated. The foliage is densely set at the ends of branches. The leaves, 1½ to 3 inches long, are set five needles in a bundle. The bark of old limber pines becomes blackish with deep furrows; on old whitebark pines it is little broken except near the base of the tree.

PONDEROSA PINE (Pinus ponderosa)

The visitor who takes the time to walk the trails in Glacier National Park is often rewarded by sights not usually seen by those who follow the main arteries of travel. In the valley of the North

110

Fork of the Flathead River are found the beautiful stands of mature ponderosa pine, a sight that, unfortunately, is not seen from the main roads in the other parts of the Park. Along the North Fork Road and trails leading from it these large pines present a picture that is not soon forgotten. Its stout needles, in bundles of three (occasionally two), are from 5 to 11 inches long and persist on the branches for three years. The light-brown cones are 3 to 6 inches long, and cone scales are armed with prickles. The bark is nearly black on trees up to 12 or 14 inches. On larger trees the bark is a cinnamon red and deeply divided into large plates 4 to 8 inches wide and 12 to 18 inches long. This tree, in the Park, grows up to 3½ feet in diameter and 140 feet high. It occurs in pure stands or mixed with lodgepole pine, Douglas fir, Engelmann spruce and western larch. As previously stated, it may be best observed along the North Fork Road from Anaconda Creek to Kintla Lake. The most beautiful stand of ponderosa pine (often called the western yellow pine) in the Park is on this road between Anaconda and Logging Creeks.

WESTERN LARCH (*Larix occidentalis*)

You can easily recognize western larch by its pale, feathery foliage, its deeply furrowed, cinnamon-colored bark, the tapering limb-free trunk, and short, open pyramidal crown. The cones are small, 1 to 1½ inches long, and each scale is overlaid by a slender elongated bract. Trees over 100 feet high and 3 feet in diameter are common, a few reaching 180 feet. Found throughout the west side of Glacier Park in the Transition and Canadian zones, this species occurs in mixture with other conifers. When mixed with ponderosa pine, one must sometimes look to the tree crowns as a means of separating the two species because of the similarity of their bark. Occasionally larch is found east of the Continental Divide, most notably on the west side of Upper Waterton Lake and in the Roes Creek drainage.

Though a conifer, the western larch is *not* an evergreen; it loses its foliage in winter. In the autumn, its golden-yellow needles stand out in bright contrast against a background of forest greenery.

SUBALPINE LARCH (*Larix lyallii*)

Near timberline, in small scattered groups, the rare subalpine larch occurs. Its foliage is similar to the western larch, but the

111

branchlets are hairy and the cones are larger. It is a small and often stunted tree, but its brilliant green foliage forms a striking contrast to the bare rock ledges where it is commonly found. It has been chosen as the official tree of Glacier National Park and may be seen nearest a highway at Preston Park, above the switchback on Siyeh Creek.

ENGELMANN SPRUCE (*Picea engelmannii*)

From the Park boundaries to timberline, on either side of the Continental Divide, Engelmann spruce is an important forest constituent. Under optimum conditions it is a large, rapidly tapering tree with a close short crown, but frequently it is found with branches almost to the ground. At timberline it may appear almost shrublike.

The bark of Engelmann spruce varies from a dark purplish-brown to a russet red and is broken into thin, small, loose scales. The branches are in regular whorls, generally drooping, then turning upwards at the ends. In the upper elevations it is found in pure stands and at the lower elevations in varied mixtures and associations. Along the Middle and North Forks of the Flathead River are picturesque spruce-cottonwood associations. Engelmann spruce foliage is often bluish in color and may easily be mistaken for blue spruce. However, the latter species is not native to the Glacier-Waterton region.

SUBALPINE FIR (*Abies lasiocarpa*)

The foliage of the subalpine fir is dark green in color, and the needles are 1 to 1¾ inches long. The erect cones are 2¼ to 4 inches long, dark purple, and covered with sticky resin. The buds are short, blunt, and yellowish. The smooth blue-gray bark is thickly set with blisters formed by resin. On old trees the bark has a purplish tinge. Subalpine fir, as one would guess from its name, grows at high elevations. Though frequently found at lower altitudes, it is characteristically a timberline tree. Its most common associate is Engelmann spruce. Subalpine fir ranges throughout the Rocky Mountains from Mexico to Alaska and is common to all forests in Glacier and Waterton Lakes National Parks.

GRAND FIR (*Abies grandis*)

This species has the characteristic smooth, ashy-gray bark of the true firs, covered with the "balsam" blisters when small, and

112

the typical erect cones. On older trees the bark may become rough and shallowly furrowed, reddish brown, with occasional chalky patches, often flinty hard and rarely over 1 inch thick. The branches droop down and out from the trunk, much like the subalpine fir, giving the younger trees a spirelike crown. Older individuals often lose this spire. The yellow-green foliage is less dense than that of the subalpine fir, and the needles appear to grow straight out from opposite sides of the twig, giving it a two-ranked appearance. The needles are flat and blunt at the tips, from 1 to 2 inches in length, with a whitish cast on their under surfaces. The cones vary from 2½ to 4½ inches in length, yellow-green in color and cylindrical in shape, like those of the subalpine fir. Actually, the Park visitor will rarely see this tree because of its relative scarcity, although some people frequently mistake the more common subalpine fir for the grand fir, particularly on the valley floors where it is sometimes quite hard to distinguish except for the cones.

DOUGLAS-FIR (*Pseudotsuga menziesii*)

In youth this tree has much the same appearance as a true fir, and at maturity it resembles a spruce. Fortunately for the amateur naturalist, the species bears cones very different from any of its associates. Elongated, three-pointed bracts protrude from between and beyond the cone scales. The long-stemmed cones hang pendant from the branches of the upper half of the crown and vary in length from 1½ to 4½ inches. The needles of Douglas-fir are flat, blunt, and between ¾ and 1½ inches long. The bark is very rough and thick on old trunks. On the Pacific coast Douglas-fir often attains a huge size, being exceeded only by the sequoias. In the Rocky Mountains, trees 100 feet high are common, and they occasionally reach heights of 150 feet. This species grows on both sides of the Continental Divide and in both Parks, generally in mixture with other conifers. A typical east-side stand may be seen in and near the Rising Sun Campground and along the Going-to-the-Sun Road on the rock point overlooking St. Mary Lake, just west of the Rising Sun Campground. A typical west-side stand may be seen along the North Fork Road, just before one reaches Logging Ranger Station.

WESTERN REDCEDAR (*Thuja plicata*)

The fernlike twigs of western redcedar are covered with tiny, flat, scalelike, yellowish-green leaves. The cones, borne on all limbs, are very small, usually less than ½ inch and are formed of eight scales, six of which bear seeds. The fast tapering trunk is buttressed at the base and covered with thin, shreddy, reddish-brown bark. Western redcedar, often called *giant arborvitae,* is easily recognized because of its distinctive foliage.

This is another Pacific coast tree whose eastern limit is found in Glacier National Park. On the coast it grows to a height of 250 feet and attains diameters up to 15 feet. The trees in the Park, though sometimes of large size, do not approach such proportions. It is most abundant in the McDonald Valley, where it is found growing in moist, protected sites of the lower elevations. Western redcedar does not occur east of the Divide and is seldom seen north of Howe Ridge.

PACIFIC YEW (*Taxus brevifolia*)

In Glacier, it is usually a shrub 3 to 10 feet high, but occasionally it is a small tree. Its foliage resembles hemlock's, the needles being two-ranked, linear and sharp-pointed, deep yellow-green in color. The branches are spreading or sprawling. Its growth is restricted to the west slope of the Continental Divide at elevations below 5,000 feet.

WESTERN HEMLOCK (*Tsuga heterophylla*)

Along the shore of Lake McDonald, especially above Avalanche Campground, the observant person will note the pleasing effect of the dark-green, shelflike boughs of young hemlock under the lighter-green canopy of red cedar and larch. The soft, flat needles are very short, ¼ inch to ¾ inch long, and crowded. They are dark green and lustrous above and silvery below. Cones are small, generally less than an inch in length. The tree at maturity is from 40 to 60 feet tall (occasionally taller) and less than 2 feet in diameter. The range in Glacier is limited also entirely to the lower elevations of McDonald Valley.

ROCKY MOUNTAIN JUNIPER (*Juniperus scopulorum*)

This tree has scalelike leaves varying in color from brownish green to dark green. The trunk is fluted, tapers abruptly, and is covered with shreddy gray bark. The crown is long, open, and often irregular. Trees seldom exceed 30 feet in height or 1 foot in diameter. Trees of this species are found scattered along the North

114

Fork of the Flathead River, a few growing along the Middle Fork. Some individuals are exceptionally long-lived; one tree in Logan Canyon is estimated to be more than 3,000 years old.

COMMON JUNIPER (*Juniperus communis*)
and CREEPING JUNIPER (*Juniperus horizontalis*)

The two other species of juniper that occur in both Parks are quite common, extending from the river valleys to and often above timberline. They are small creeping shrubs, seldom over 3 feet in height, and often form dense carpets or mats that are very difficult to walk through. Both species resemble each other very closely and differ from the Rocky Mountain juniper mainly in their form and growing habits. Common juniper also differs from the other two by having short, sharp-pointed, awl-like needles instead of being small and closely appressed to the twig. All three species bear the characteristic blue, berry-like cone or fruit.

BLACK COTTONWOOD (*Populus trichocarpa*)

Most common deciduous trees (those that lose their leaves in winter) of the Rocky Mountains belong principally to the poplar group. The black cottonwood is typically a Pacific Coast tree, seldom reaching as far east as the Rocky Mountains. In the Glacier-Waterton region it is found along watercourses and lakes at low elevations. On the west slopes of Glacier Park it grows much larger than on the east, mainly because of the less severe weather and heavier forest cover.

The broadly ovate leaves of black cottonwood are dark green above and pale below. They vary in length from 3 to 4 inches. The bark on young trees is smooth and yellowish white. On old trees it turns ashy gray and is broken into rounded ridges. Black cottonwood is the largest poplar native to North America. Trees 80 to 125 feet high with diameters 3 to 4 feet are common in Glacier National Park. The largest known specimen of this species may be seen at the north end of Quartz Creek Bridge on the North Fork Road, just across the road from the campground. This tree measures better than 14 feet in circumference at 4½ feet above ground.

QUAKING ASPEN (*Populus tremuloides*)

The leaves of the aspen are nearly round, from 1 to 3 inches across, and are borne on long, thin petioles. They are almost con-

115

stantly quivering or trembling, now showing their pale, dull undersides, now their lustrous, darker upper surfaces. The bark of aspen is greenish white, smooth, and broken by black, elliptic branch scars. Aspen at a distance may be confused with paper birch, but the difference at close range is readily apparent—birch bark peels off in thin, papery layers.

WILLOWS (Salix spp.)

Some 25 species of willows are listed for the Parks, but most of these are shrub or dwarf form. The SCOULER WILLOW (Salix scouleriana) and the PEACHLEAF WILLOW (Salix amygdaloides) reach tree size and are found at low and middle elevations. Leaves alternate, usually long and narrow, and occasionally with fine teeth along the margin or near the tip of the leaf. Willow leaves characteristically have a pair of small or large ear-shaped leaflike growths at the base of the leaf stem. This is usually a point of positive identification, especially during the leaf-growing stage.

NORTHWESTERN PAPER BIRCH
(Betula papyrifera subcordata)

This is the tree that furnished the bark which Indians used for making canoes; hence, it is often called canoe birch. The bark on young trees and twigs is bronze or orange-brown. On older trees it is chalky or creamy white, peeling easily in horizontal strips. Seldom a large tree, heights generally vary from 30 to 40 feet, with diameters up to 1 foot. The bole, or trunk, is long, slender, and inclined to be curved. In the Parks its range is generally limited to the west side and to Waterton Valley, though a few trees are reported growing in Belly River and Many Glacier Valley. Paper birch is often found in mixture with spruce or fir and frequently comes in after fire.

There are two other birches found in the Parks—WATER BIRCH (Betula occidentalis) and BOG BIRCH (Betula glandulosa)—but both are classed as shrubs rather than trees because of their size.

COMMON CHOKECHERRY (Prunus virginiana)

In the Parks, the common chokecherry usually grows in large shrub form, up to 15 feet in height, but occasionally reaching tree size in sheltered locations. The bark is reddish brown, smooth,

116

becoming scaly on older trees. The leaves are relatively thick, somewhat leathery, about 3 or 4 inches long, deep green on the upper side and paler below. The leaf margins are rimmed with small, sharp teeth. The five-petaled, white flowers are about ⅓ inch across and are borne in attractive cylindrical clusters 3 to 4 inches long. The fruits, which gradually become bright red and finally almost black, ripen during August or early September. But the fruit is harshly astringent to the taste and is nearly all pit. Chokecherry is fairly common at low and middle altitudes, particularly along stream bottoms and watercourses of the eastern slopes in Glacier and in Waterton Lakes Park.

PIN CHERRY (Prunus pensylvanica)

Pin cherry is usually a small, single-stemmed shrub 5 to 8 feet high, but reaching small tree size in favorable locations. The leaves are somewhat smaller than a chokecherry, ranging up to 3 inches in length, with rounded teeth on the margin. The flowers are white and smaller than, but closely resembling, the domestic cherry blossom. The fruit is a small, red or red and yellow cherry scattered along the branch or occurring in small clumps, and very bitter to the taste. The pin cherry is common on the western side of Glacier National Park on open slopes at lower elevations.

BLACK HAWTHORN (Cratægus douglasii)

In either tree or shrub form, black hawthorn varies from 5 to 25 feet high and is fairly common in both Parks at low elevations, mainly along lakes and streams. Its bark is reddish brown, often becoming scaly on older trees. The leaves are relatively thick and leathery, smooth, deep green above and paler below, margins toothed and often deeply lobed. The flowers are white, similar to the pear or apple, forming a small, purplish black, occasionally red, apple-like fruit. Numerous long, sharp thorns are scattered along the trunk and branches.

THINLEAF ALDER (Alnus tenuifolia)

This is a small tree or shrub, 3 to 16 feet high, with smooth, reddish-brown bark. The leaves are oval or ovate, 1½ to 4 inches long, thick, and dull green. Alder cones (or fruit) are woody and persist on the tree throughout the winter. It is a typical streamside species and may be found in any moist situation, particularly in avalanche paths. It is fairly common at low altitudes in both Parks. The SITKA ALDER (*Alnus sinuata*) can be found in the Parks, generally in shrub form, but at higher elevations.

DOUGLAS MAPLE (*Acer glabum douglasii*)

This shrubby representative of the maple group is easily distinguished from other trees in the Parks. The leaves of this small tree are three to five lobed, the slender twigs are red in color and are arranged in pairs, one opposite the other. The conspicuous winged seeds (samaras), also in pairs, are attached to the twig by a common stem. Trees are many-stemmed or often a small shrub. Mountain maple, as it is often called, grows throughout the Canadian and Hudsonian zones of the Northwest and is common to all timbered portions of the Parks.

The preservation of the Parks' forests has always been a matter of anxious solicitude on the part of the authorities. Extreme precautions are taken to prevent fires, and severe penalties are inflicted upon anyone who is careless in this respect. Forest fires in the Parks arise from two principal causes: lightning and man. Lightning is undoubtedly a frequent cause of fires and one which cannot be eliminated. But the agency of man in causing forest fires is something that can be *greatly* reduced, or eliminated.

The accumulation of leaves, twigs, and decaying logs forms a loose layer of material called *duff,* which covers the average forest floor. It is simply an intermediate stage in the return of this material to soil. This duff serves as a soil mulch and helps absorb water and keep the soil from drying out. When the weather is very dry, the duff constitutes something of a hazard, for fires easily start in this tinder-like material. A cigarette or match dropped in dry duff may smolder for hours before it actually breaks out into a going fire. *Please be careful with your smokes—do not be a flipper!*

WILDFLOWERS IN THE PARKS

The colorful display of wildflowers is one of the greatest attractions in Glacier and Waterton Lakes National Parks. Few areas in western United States and Canada have a richer variety and greater abundance of trees and wildflowers. Here, southern forms mingle with northern ones, and western varieties meet those of the East. In all, over 1,000 species of trees and wildflowers may be found in the Glacier-Waterton region.

Wildflower shows begin in early spring at the lower elevations of Glacier National Park and progress up the mountainsides as the snow recedes, culminating in the alpine floral displays when the season is well advanced. At no time from early spring to early autumn can you fail to find a flower display somewhere within the Park. And with the coming of autumn, the scarlet berries and yellow and orange leaves make the Park a colorful spectacle.

Early in the spring just after the snow leaves the ground, the glacier lilies spread a beautiful yellow carpet over large areas along the Blackfeet Highway, particularly around the Hudson Bay Divide. Other early-blooming flowers along the east-side highways are purple pasqueflower with flowers sometimes 2 inches across, and the blue camas lily. The western pasqueflower may be seen at Logan Pass during early July soon after Going-to-the-Sun Road is opened for travel. At about the time the meadows at higher elevations start to bloom, those below have finished or changed their pattern. During the latter part of June and early July there are pink geraniums, blue and yellow pentstemons, purple-flowered silky phacelias, pale-blue bur forget-me-nots, yellow arnicas, and a host of others including the moss silene (carpet pink) with tiny rose-colored flowers that form low matted cushions on the ground hence another name—cushion pinks.

Gradually as summer presses on, many of these are replaced with other species such as the gaillardia (exactly alike in appearance to the cultivated variety), yellow and bronze false dandelions, yellow sulphur plant, showy-purple fleabane, brilliant red paintbrush, red-purple fireweed, blue harebell, shrubby cinquefoil with bright yellow flowers, white spirea, wild roses, purple horsemint, and the mountain spray, composed of a mass of tiny cream-colored flowers. The pink-flowered wild hollyhock is one of the most admired plants along the Going-to-the-Sun Road and in the Many Glacier region.

Showiest of all the park's myriad flowers is the beargrass, usually "unofficially" considered Glacier Park's flower. It neither belongs to the bears, nor is it a grass. Unfortunately, we do not know who named it or why they decided on "beargrass." It belongs to the lily family. It sometimes covers acres of open, dry forest. In June, it commences to bloom on the valley floors, and it continues into August at the higher elevations. The tough grasslike leaves were used by the Indians in weaving baskets. For this reason, it is sometimes called "squaw grass."

During the latter part of the season, purple asters with their numerous showy flower heads are among the most conspicuous roadside flowers, especially on the east side. Goldenrod also makes its appearance, as well as the tall slender stalks of mullein.

Following the early flowers at Logan Pass, the meadows blossom out with myriads of colors, and the Hanging Gardens present as fine a display of flowers as can be seen in Glacier. Many of the species are the same as those seen in the lower meadows earlier in the season, but others may be seen only at the higher elevations. Here, and in the alpine meadows of the region, snow lingers so long that the growing season is exceedingly short, sometimes being less than three weeks for many plants. Glacier lilies, globeflowers, pasqueflowers, and spring beauties often force their way through the edges of melting snowbanks, and always bloom within a few days after the snow has uncovered them. As the glacier lilies and globeflowers wane, other species replace them. By mid-August the meadows are a riot of color. Everywhere are flowers of blue pentstemon, purple pentstemon, red and yellow monkeyflower, Indian paintbrush (red, orange, or greenish), buttercup, purple onion, moss pink, alpine forget-me-not, yellow-flowered St.-John's-wort with its bright red buds, valerian, blue gentian, red heather, white heather, mountain laurel, bistort, yellow stonecrop, arnica, beargrass, yellow columbine, aster, fleabane, shooting star, Indian warrior, purple elephanthead, yellow alpine lousewort, and dozens of others. While in these alpine gardens, remember that it has taken several hundred years to reach the growth that you see here. Please stay on the trail and do not step on the plants.

In Waterton Lakes National Park, the flowers are very similar to Glacier and present an ever-changing carpet of color for most of the summer season, too. Amongst the better known flowers are the wild rose, large-flowered gaillardia ("brown-eyed Susan"), sulphur plant, harebell, cow parsnip, aster, Indian paintbrush, larkspur, wild geranium, western pasqueflower, windflower, false hellebore, yellow columbine, avalanche (glacier) lily, and Jacob's ladder. Balsamroot, beargrass, and mariposa lily are special features among the wildflowers of the Park. Some of the more common shrubs found in the Park are shrubby cinquefoil, bearberry (kinnikinnick), Canadian buffaloberry, silver-berry, whortleberry, red-osier dogwood, and Sitka mountain-ash.

It would be quite impossible, within the limits of this chapter, to give a full description of the 1,000 or more wildflowers of the Parks. Excellent books on the subject include Sharpe's *101 Wildflowers of Glacier National Park,* Moss's *Flora of Alberta,* and Craigheads' *A Field Guide to Rocky Mountain Wildflowers.*

Chapter 6.

The Animals of the Parks

THE extreme variety of terrain in the Glacier-Waterton region—from open prairies, through brush land and deep forest, to alpine meadows and rocky crags—provides habitats for a great variety of animal life. Herds of bison and pronghorn lived in the prairies where the Blackfeet Indians hunted before the white man entered the area. Now both are gone from this area. (A herd of bison is kept in the buffalo paddock at Waterton Lakes National Park. These are the only animals in captivity in either Park.) Wanton slaughter of the buffalo by both white man and Indians brought about extermination of the last great herd in 1883. Since the buffalo was the main item of Indian sustenance, the Blackfeet declined in numbers with the decline of buffalo population. Today coyotes, wolves, and sometimes (in winter) elk roam the plains adjacent to the Parks, while golden eagles are sometimes seen soaring overhead or swooping to pick up a fat ground squirrel. In the forested areas are deer, bear, elk, a few mountain lions, and several smaller fur bearers such as beaver, mink, marten, otter, badger, and weasel. In broken forest areas ground squirrels and grouse are numerous, with moose found in swampy areas and around lakes. An amazing variety of animals inhabit areas way above timberline where existence is cold and bleak for all but about four months out of the year. In this zone are mountain goats, bighorn sheep, pikas, marmots, etc. Specific types of birds and other animals inhabit watercourses at various elevations, and will never be found far from water.

In all National Parks, the policy is to maintain an area as a wilderness zone just as it would operate naturally, with as little artificial interference as possible. Thus the Park Service limits road building and all types of construction to a minimum, permitting only unavoidable artificial disturbance, so that you may enter the area and see the way nature cares for its own. In all nature there is what is called a biotic balance: a balance between different species of animals, and between animals and plant life within an area. Briefly, as an example, it might be said that although many deer are killed each year by predators such as coyotes or cougars, the Park Service does not try to eliminate the predator, or interfere in any way in its pursuit of food and shelter. They realize that if they were to eliminate all predators of one planteater, such as a deer, the latter would increase in abundance above all capacity of the range to support it, and would weaken and die of disease and starvation.

As a whole the Park Service interferes very little with the normal lives of the animals within the parks. You may help them to keep the biotic balance by not feeding the bears, because when bears expect handouts from humans and depend on them for their food, they gradually become dangerous and pestiferous, as well as less healthy. Rangers sometimes have to trap such bears, removing them from the area, or sometimes disposing of them by shooting. Generally speaking, all wild animals will be much healthier if they are left to forage rather than depending on man for their proper nutritive balance. Fires also upset the biotic balance and destroy homes for wildlife, as well as the animals themselves. Therefore, be careful with smokes, matches, and campfires while in the Parks.

The automobile is the most difficult enemy in the Parks for an animal to cope with. A great many of the squirrels are destroyed by speeding cars, and some of the larger animals are not immune, especially at night when the glare from the headlights of an approaching car seems to blind the animals and cause them to leap in front of the automobile to become another victim.

PARK MAMMALS

Mammals are the warm-blooded backboned members of the animal kingdom that possess hair. Most of them give birth to living young, and all nourish their offspring with milk produced by special glands known as "mammary glands," whence the name "mammals." Fifty-seven species exist in Glacier and Waterton Lakes National Parks. A short description of them follows.

122

The "official" Glacier Park animal—the mountain goat—and bird—white-tailed ptarmigan—are common in the Parks. The latter are shown in winter plumage.

MOUNTAIN GOAT (*Oreamnos americanus*)

The mountain goat is the most distinctly representative animal of Glacier National Park, an imperturbable, daring ungulate; a mountaineer possessing unexcelled qualities for alpine climbing. Its love of the high places, its surefootedness and excellent equanimity while scaling the steepest precipice and the most formidable mountain challenge the spirit of who- or whatever might follow in its footsteps. Only one other national Park in the United States, Mount Rainier, has mountain goats. This eccentric animal is the symbol of Glacier Park, Inc., and other Park operators. The Great Northern Railway, a transportation system closely interwoven with the history of the Park, also uses the mountain goat as a symbol. Though the name "mountain goat" is well entrenched, this species is actually an antelope—the only antelope found in the United States. The "pronghorn antelope" found in some national parks is not a true antelope.

The mountain goat is the only large white mammal found in the Glacier-Waterton area and cannot be confused with any other animal during the summer months. The white shaggy coat and the slender black horns will readily distinguish it. In weight and size, it is about the same as the domestic sheep. Adult males weigh on an average of 150 pounds, exceptional goats exceeding 300 pounds; the female "nanny" goats are lighter in weight. The kids are born in May or early June and weigh about 6 or 7 pounds. In Glacier, one kid per mother appears to be the normal number, but twins are not rare and triplets sometimes occur. In a very short time the young goats follow their mothers and traverse the most precipitous areas in the Parks.

Mountain goats are common in both Parks. Park visitors can spot them on open slopes above mountain passes or as white specks on apparently sheer cliffs where they rest during the heat of the day. Early in the season, people in automobiles and buses see them frequently on the declivities of Mount Cannon above Avalanche Campground. Often they can be identified for the Park visitor by the naturalists stationed at Logan Pass Visitor Center. They have been found on the Going-to-the-Sun Road above 4,500 feet elevation and on Marias Pass of U. S. Route 2. They are common at Iceberg Lake, Sexton Glacier, Porcupine Ridge, and Goat Haunt Mountain. At Sperry Chalets, they ordinarily come down during the night to rummage about the quarters.

In Waterton Lakes National Park, these animals may occasionally be seen near Cameron Lake, Bertha Lake, Crypt Lake, Lineham Lakes, on Sofa Mountain, and at high altitudes in remote areas along the Continental Divide. If *all* these locations fail, it is possible, of course, to see goats on the sides of Great Northern boxcars at either East or West Glacier.

BIGHORN SHEEP (*Ovis canadensis*)

The ram, or male, of the bighorn sheep lives among the rocky crags during the time when most visitors are in the Parks, in a habitat with the mountain goat. The female bighorn sheep, or ewe, with her lamb, or two, grazes in meadows below timberline. Both sexes are dirty yellow, or light grayish-brown, with a characteristic creamy-white rump patch. The rams may be differentiated by their long, curled, dark horns, whereas the ewes have much smaller, only slightly curved brown horns. The ram weighs from 200 to 300 pounds, while the ewe is only between 125 and 175 pounds.

In Glacier Park, the largest number of bighorn sheep are in the Many Glacier area. The ewes and lambs graze in the meadow near the corral and parking area behind the hotel. The slopes of any of the surrounding peaks, including Wilbur, Altyn, Grinnell, Wynn, or Appekunny, if they are carefully scanned with a pair of binoculars, may sometimes reveal a band of sheep. Observations of bighorn sheep have also been made on Mt. Henry in the Two Medicine area, on Cut Bank Pass and on Curley Bear Mountain in the St. Mary area. Occasionally hikers along the Highline Trail to Granite Park Chalets encounter sheep in the saddle between Haystack Butte and the Garden Wall or on the slopes above the chalets.

They may usually be found near the Waterton Park Information Bureau, along the Akamina and Pass Creek Highways, and near Carthew, Goat, and Lineham Lakes.

THE BEAR FAMILY (*Ursidae*)

There are two types of bears in Glacier-Waterton region: the BLACK BEAR (*Evarctos americanus*) and GRIZZLY BEAR (*Ursus horribilis*). The latter bear may be differentiated by its larger size, hump on the shoulders, and silver-tipped hair along the back. The grizzly also has a massive, thick skull. Its claws are longer than the black bear's, but not as curved. Grizzlies rarely climb trees except when young. Although not uncommon, grizzlies in the Glacier-Western area are rarely found around human habita-

125

tion, and are usually seen near timberline far away from the trails.

Black bear, as well as grizzlies, have several color variations, usually ranging from light brown to black. A few individuals are quite light-colored, almost blond.

Do *not* feed or tease the bears. There are several very good reasons for this restriction, one being your own personal safety. Many people, upon observing the activities of the Parks' "hold-up" bears, fail to realize that the bear is a *wild* animal. An angry bear can rip your arm or chest open with its curved claws, inflicting painful and costly injuries, if you try to fool it about food. Sometimes the bear thinks your camera is food, so be careful when you attempt to photograph a bear. Then, too, remember that a mother bear usually never leaves her cubs very far away, even during the second summer, and will attack anyone she thinks is trying to molest them. If you happen to meet a bear on the trail, pay attention to your own business, and the bear will try to get out of your way.

Bears that become too much of a nuisance around areas of human habitation are trapped in special bear traps and transported to remote sections of the Parks. Sometimes the same bear will return to the location where it was trapped 40 or 50 miles away and continue to be a pest, and is trapped again. This may happen four or five times, and finally rangers (wardens) may have to shoot the bear if it causes too much damage. You can help rangers to keep down the number of bears they have to dispose of by respecting park regulations, and thus not attracting bears to areas of artificial feeding. The natural food of bears varies considerably, including berries, tender plant shoots, and lily bulbs, as well as several types of animal life, including ground squirrels, grubs, ants, and other insect life.

Bears are usually born in litters of two, but one to three or even four have been recorded. They are born during the female's "winter sleep," around the first of February, and are very helpless at birth, being nearly hairless and weighing less than a pound. The cubs stay with their mother through the second summer, receiving much instruction and discipline during all that time, so that every other year is a cub year for the mother.

Black bears occur in almost all regions of both Parks below the upper limits of tree growth, but seldom do they wander higher into the alpine meadows where grizzlies may be found.

Photo by the author.

THE DEER FAMILY (Cervidae)

This family is represented in Glacier and Waterton Parks by the mule and white-tailed deer, American elk and moose. The MULE DEER (*Odocoileus hemionus*) is characterized by big mule-like ears, white rump patch, and black tip on its tail. It lives in both Parks, usually in forest or broken forest and brush land, and sometimes in alpine meadows. The mule deer is tame around Waterton Townsite and can be seen walking streets with the mammal called "man."

The WHITE-TAILED DEER (*Odocoileus virginianus*) has a somewhat bigger tail, white-tipped and white underneath; its body is white underneath and brown on top. They run through the dense woods on the west side of Glacier during twilight, with white tail standing up and bobbing from side to side, so that the onlooker sees mainly flashes of white. Antlers of the white-tailed buck are composed of a single beam with upright prongs, whereas the antlers of the mule deer are branched or forked. The white-tailed deer are generally found only on the west side of the Continental Divide, probably because they seem to prefer a denser forest. White-tailed deer, however, are commonly seen at Granite Park Chalets, just one mile west of Swiftcurrent Pass, in timberline habitat. Both black-tailed and white-tailed deer are primarily browsers, feeding on many types of shrubs and young trees.

Usually one fawn is born in the early summer. Its white spots greatly aid in protective coloration, and during the early days of its life it also escapes the search of predators because it has absolutely no scent. Natural enemies of the deer are coyotes and the few mountain lions still in the Parks. During the summer season, does and their fawns are commonly seen around areas of human habitation, but most of the bucks are back in the higher country.

Another, somewhat larger member of the deer family is the AMERICAN ELK (*Cervus canadensis*), known as *wapiti* to the Indians. This animal is characterized by its dark-brown neck and lighter-brown sides and back. A good-sized male will stand about 5 feet high at the shoulders, and has a set of widely spreading antlers.

Baby wapiti, called calves, are born in May or June. Usually one calf is born to each cow. Sometimes there are two calves, but

The bighorn sheep is another common animal in the Parks.

seldom three. The calves are spotted, and they keep their spotted coats until fall, when they grow brown winter coats. Elk are primarily grazers, and thus are often found in herds in open meadows, especially in winter. Elk are generally distributed throughout both Parks in summer, but are rarely seen by visitors because they hide under the forest cover. They herd together at lower elevations in winter, often migrating out of the Parks.

In Waterton Lakes National Park, elk are common in the Stoney Flats, Horseshoe Basin, Belly River, and Oil Basin areas during most of the year. They often move out into the open prairie areas around the buffalo paddock during the winter. Elk are rather scarce in the remainder of the Park.

The fourth member of this family requires water as part of its habitat, at least in summer. The MOOSE (*Alces alces*) is commonly seen with its head underwater, feeding on the sedges and rushes or other underwater plant growth, only coming up when necessary for a breath of air. Often in the summer months the moose will stand mostly submerged in water to ward off the hordes of insects which swarm about it. The moose has a long, thick muzzle which more closely resembles that of a mule than a deer or wapiti; it also has a characteristic hump on the shoulders, an average-sized bull standing about 6 feet high at this point. The bull has a very large set of flattened, or more or less spoon-shaped antlers, with a number of long sharp points.

The female moose is quite a bit smaller, and the females of all members of the deer family do not normally grow antlers, whereas the males grow and shed a set each year.

During mating season the bull moose is quite ferocious, especially toward other males of the same species. Battles employing antlers and sometimes hoofs are not uncommon. Unlike the young of many of the deer family, baby moose are unspotted at birth. Twins are the rule, but sometimes only a single calf is born.

In Glacier, most of the moose population is located on the west side of the Continental Divide, and the greatest concentration is along the North Fork of the Flathead River and its various tributaries such as Camas, Dutch, Anaconda, Logging, Quartz, Bowman, Kintla, and Kishenehn Creeks. Mud Lake and Howe Lake usually have one or two moose along their shores during the visitor season. McDonald Creek normally has one to several of the animals somewhere along its banks, and occasionally one or two are seen along the Going-to-the-Sun Road at the swampy area between McDonald Lodge and Avalanche Campground. (A roadside ex-

130

hibit marks the spot.) On the east side of the Park, moose are sometimes seen in the St. Mary, Many Glacier, and Belly River Valleys. In Waterton Park, they can usually be observed near Cameron Lake, Red Rock Canyon, and the lakehead area of the Waterton Lakes.

THE DOG FAMILY (Canidae)

For each animal that lives on grass and other vegetation there is an enemy that uses it as food. The grass-eater makes use of the forage it finds, while the meat-eater gets its nutrients from the flesh of the grass-eater. Chief among the carnivores in the Parks are two members of the dog family: the coyote and the timber wolf.

The COYOTE (*Canis latrans*) looks somewhat like a small collie dog, with long fur and a bushy tail. It is buff-gray in color with black tips on its guard hairs. While common in both Parks, they are seldom seen along the main roads. The coyote eats any animal that he can catch and overpower. The list is long and varied, starting with the smallest of the mice or even insects and going up as far as the elk, providing the latter is sick or wounded.

The GRAY WOLF (*Canis lupus*) resembles a rather large dog, standing from 2 to 2½ feet at the shoulder and weighing from 50 to 120 pounds. The ears are rounded rather than pointed, and the body color is dark gray to almost black. It is rarely seen, although occasional reports drift in from various parts of both Parks, indicating at least passing visits from the lobo. Park visitors frequently mistake one of the larger coyotes for a wolf, however, and report it as such. But the average wolf is nearly two to three times as heavy as a coyote and is taller.

The RED FOX (*Vulpes fulva*) is a small doglike animal, weighing 10 to 15 pounds. There are many color variations, but the normal is a reddish brown, with the feet and backs of the ears black, and the tip of the tail white. The red fox, at one time a common resident in this region, is rarely seen today.

THE CAT FAMILY (Felidae)

The cat family in the Parks swells the list of carnivorous animals by three: the COUGAR (*Felis concolor*), the BOBCAT (*Lynx rufus*), and the CANADIAN LYNX (*Lynx canadensis*). The latter two are very similar, yet have definite differences. Both animals are catlike in general appearance, but have proportionately longer, stouter legs, and larger feet than a house cat. These animals weigh about 20 pounds—the lynx is somewhat larger than the bobcat. The fur of the lynx is a grayish color, while the fur of the bobcat ranges from pale brown to reddish brown. The bobcat has shorter tufts on its ear tips than does the lynx, and the bobcat's tail tip is striped black on top and pale underneath. The tail of the lynx has black rings on it and is tipped with a single black cap.

The cougar is a large, lithe, unspotted cat with a long cylindrical tail. The coat is soft, short, and a tawny brown or gray in color. The muzzle, backs of the ears, and tip of the tail may be almost black, and the underparts are much paler than the upper parts. The young are spotted until about one year old, at which time the spots disappear. The males resemble the females but are larger and may weigh up to 200 pounds, but the average weight is closer to 150 pounds.

While all three members of the cat family occur in both Parks, they are in quite limited numbers and are only rarely seen, although their tracks have been observed.

THE WEASEL FAMILY (Mustelidae)

The Glacier-Waterton area has many members of the weasel family present, but the actual number of each species is fairly limited. The chances of a visitor seeing a member of this group are also greatly reduced because of their nocturnal habits. All can be classed as beneficial predators.

The STRIPED SKUNK (Mephitis mephitis) is probably the best known member of the weasel family. This large cat-sized animal, with a long bushy tail and a black body with two white stripes along the back that form a V at its shoulders, frequently causes uneasiness around human habitations in the Parks, usually because of some untoward event in the life of the skunk. If not disturbed, their presence often goes unnoticed, for their offensiveness is reserved for those who, through evil intent or ignorance, overstep the bounds. Striped skunks are relatively rare within the Parks, but are occasionally seen in the lower valleys, particularly on the east side of the Continental Divide.

The MARTEN (Martes americana) and the FISHER (Martes pennanti) are alike in many respects. In proportion, they resemble

132

a large squirrel. Marten weigh up to 2½ pounds; fisher up to 10 pounds. The length of the animals varies from 2 feet for the marten to 3½ feet for the fisher; the tail constitutes about one-third that length. The head is broad and narrows rapidly to a sharp muzzle, and the ears are large, erect, and prominent. The feet are large with stout toes and long, sharply-curved claws. The marten is colored a rich, golden brown over most of its body, while the fisher is colored an ashy, brownish gray with an overwash of black. The fisher is very rare in the park area, but the marten is possibly the most common carnivore in the region. It is fairly well distributed throughout the forested areas of Glacier, being most common along the North Fork of the Flathead River. They are often seen along the numerous trails which cross this area, such as those to Logging and Quartz Lakes. In recent years they have been reported by visitors near the Lake McDonald Lodge on the west side and near Sun Point on the east side of the Continental Divide.

RIVER OTTER (*Lutra canadensis*) is one of the largest members of the weasel family, adults weighing up to 25 pounds. The body is long and rather plump; the feet are large and webbed for swimming. The short, thick, soft fur is colored rich, dark chocolate brown, fading to a lighter shade on the underside of the animal. The aquatic habits of the otter allow it to exist in both marine and freshwater environments. Otter build dens in banks of streams and ponds, usually in protected spots such as beneath roots of trees or under overhanging vines. While not too common in the area, they have been seen along streams and lakes, especially the Middle and North Forks of the Flathead River and its tributary creeks.

The LONG-TAILED WEASEL (*Mustela frenata longicauda*), the SHORT-TAILED WEASEL (*Mustela erminea*), and the MINK (*Mustela vison*) are similar in appearance and habits. All have a rather long, slim body with short, thick, soft fur. The feet are large with curved claws, and the legs are short and stout. The head is placed low, narrowing abruptly to the muzzle, and the tail is well furred. These animals are found throughout the Parks in wet, lowland areas. They characteristically establish a home base, but travel a wide area away from their dens, which are used for nesting and storing food. These dens are burrows usually dug under rocks, logs, or stumps; the animals may make use of deserted burrows. Weasels and mink all have a reputation for being agile and able hunters; all climb and swim well.

133

Weighing 7 to 8 ounces and averaging 18 inches in length, the long-tailed weasel is colored golden to dark brown on its back and sides throughout most of the year. The tip of the tail is black, and the underside of the body is yellow-orange. The short-tailed weasel, or ermine (in winter), is smaller—weighing 3 to 4 ounces and averaging 11 inches in length—and is a darker color than the long-tailed species. Its back and sides are a chocolate brown, the underside is white or pale yellow, and the tail has a black tip.

In the winter both these weasels may turn entirely white, except for the black tip on the tail. The mink—averaging 2 pounds in weight and 24 inches in length—is colored a rich, dark reddish or chocolate brown; the underside is slightly paler than the back of the animal. Mink do not show any marked seasonal color change as do weasel and ermine. The tail is bushier than that of the weasel. Both the ermine and mink are common in the Parks, but the long-tailed weasel is rare and has only been reported on the east side of the Continental Divide. Minks prefer the stream banks and lake shores at lower and middle elevations; the ermine may be found in a variety of habitats from the valley floors up to the high mountain meadows.

The BADGER (*Taxidea taxus*) is a short, stocky animal with long, shaggy fur, and it may weigh up to 25 pounds. The general coloration is silver-gray grizzled with black. The face has a distinct black-and-white appearance due to a base of brownish black divided by a median white stripe and white hairs on the jaw areas. The under body parts are much lighter than the top, blending from dull gray to white. The head is comparatively small and flat. The badger is not common within Glacier Park boundaries; some have been observed in the meadows along McDonald Creek from the foot of Lake McDonald to the junction with the Middle Fork of the Flathead River. In Waterton Lakes Park, however, they have been frequently observed along the main entrance roads and the Pass Creek Highway, and anywhere on the prairie-land portion of the Park where populations of Columbian ground squirrels exist.

Of the rarer members of the weasel group the rarest is the WOLVERINE (*Gulo luscus*), a sturdy animal on the order of a small bear, and probably the most powerful animal for its size of any North American mammal. They are about 42 inches long and weigh up to 36 pounds. The color varies from brown to nearly black with a broad yellowish stripe along each side and meeting over the hips. Nearly exterminated from this region, its wide-

134

spread, bearlike tracks are sometimes seen in the Parks during the winter months.

THE RODENTS (*Rodentia*)

This is the largest order of mammals found in the two Parks, both in numbers of species and in numbers of individuals. They also adapt to all types of habitat to be found in the Parks.

The BEAVER (*Castor canadensis*) is the largest rodent in North America. Actually, the beaver, the embodiment of industry, may occasionally be seen at work on one of its numerous projects throughout both the Parks. Along the smaller streams dams are built to conserve the water for its protection, canals are dug to its timber-cutting operations, and large, well-constructed houses are built. Its value as a soil conservationist and flood control agent is beginning to be truly appreciated. This animal has an uncanny sense when it comes to logging operations. It knows just how to undercut a tree to make it fall where it wants it, and it usually fells trees as close as possible to watercourses, so that they may be easily transported to build the dam or its home, or provide food during the long winter months. In its home the beaver has two underwater doors, thus providing escape without detection from would-be predators by swimming out its front door underwater. It knows just how high to build the dam in order to maintain sufficient depth of water; its house is usually upstream from the dam.

The beaver is a robust animal, brown in color, with a flat, paddle-shaped, leatherlike tail, which helps it to maneuver while swimming. It also has webbed hind feet. Its principal food is the soft bark of the young broad-leaved trees, mainly aspen, willow, and cottonwood. However, when these favorite foods are not available, the beaver will sometimes work on other trees.

The MUSKRAT (*Ondatra zibethica*) is a large aquatic rodent, but it is not overly common in the Parks. It may occasionally be observed along some of the slower-moving streams or near some of the ponds or lakes of Glacier's west side. The general body proportions of the muskrat are like those of a mouse; weights run up to 4 pounds. The head, eyes, and ears are small in comparison with the well-furred plump body. This animal is easily identified by its scaly tail, which is vertically compressed, and bears a few

135

hairs. The underfur is dense and soft, while the guard hair is stiff and shiny. The back and sides of the body are colored a rich, dark brown, but the underside tends to be grayish.

The PORCUPINE (*Erethizon dorsatum*) is a large rodent with a most effective means of defense. This heavy-bodied, short-legged, clumsy animal feeds principally on the tender inner bark and foliage of conifers and of many broad-leaved trees and shrubs. It also gnaws on bones, apparently as a means of getting needed minerals; and on wooden tools and furniture that have been handled by humans, apparently because of its taste for salt. The porcupine, principally nocturnal in its habits, is common in timbered areas of both Parks, particularly at higher elevations. If you have occasion to drive over Logan Pass any time at night, you will likely see as many as a dozen porcupines waddling slowly along the side of the road trying to get out of your way. And certainly it is not the porcupine's speed which it relies on to get out of danger. If cornered or pursued at too fast a rate, it will turn around with tail facing you so that you can see the many exposed barbs thereon. The porcupine's quills only become dislodged when they come into contact with some other object. One or two barbs may fall off as it switches its tail, but the porcupine *cannot throw* its quills.

Alpine rockslides and meadows yield several forms of rodent life. Most conspicuous is the HOARY MARMOT (*Marmota caligata*). In appearance it is a large, ungainly ground squirrel. It is silvery-gray in color, with the head, feet, and bushy tail dark, but with a white band around the nose in front of the eyes. The marmot soon becomes quite bold and friendly with people, and visitors to the Parks can often take good pictures of it. Equipment must be kept away from their teeth, for they quickly seize upon leather or other articles which suit their fancy. Most of their time is spent in gathering food to make fat to carry them through the long mountain winter. The marmot is often called a "whistling" marmot because of the rather shrill piercing sound uttered while sitting up.

At nearly all elevations, the COLUMBIAN GROUND SQUIRREL (*Citellus columbianus*) is most abundant in both Parks, except in the Belly River Valley. About the size of a large house rat, its coloration is mottled grizzled-gray, with legs and underparts rusty yellowish-brown. The front part of the head, extending from the nose to the ears, is generally a bright reddish-brown. They are very active for only about three or four months of the year, fattening

136

up by eating tremendous quantities of food, including seeds, berries, roots, nuts, etc., and begin to go into hibernation as early as mid-August. While hibernating they are very inactive, almost in a hypnotic state, and often in September and October are eaten by bears who come around and dig them up. Many ground squirrels fall prey in this manner to bears, who are themselves trying to fatten up before they go into their winter sleep about two months later than the ground squirrels.

Another species is the RICHARDSON GROUND SQUIRREL (*Citellus richardsonii*), which was common along the east boundaries of both Parks but now seems to be replaced by the Columbian ground squirrel. The Richardson ground squirrel is similar to the Columbian but has a shorter tail and is more yellow in color. It is now considered rare in the Parks.

Two other species of ground squirrels are found in the region, but neither is numerous. The GOLDEN-MANTLED GROUND SQUIRREL (*Citellus lateralis*) has a heavy body with wide black and buff stripes on its back; it occurs mainly on the eastern slopes of the Rockies and at higher elevations. The THIRTEEN-LINED GROUND SQUIRREL (*Citellus tridecemlineatus*) is the smallest and slimmest of the ground squirrels, and its color is a pale chestnut-brown with some black intermingled, through which there are about thirteen longitudinal, solid and interrupted stripes running from the shoulder onto the rump. The underparts are much lighter, and the tail is an almost reddish-brown color toward the tip.

The RED SQUIRREL (*Tamiasciurus hudsonicus*) is one of the common forest dwellers in the Parks and is a tree squirrel, in contrast to the ground squirrels, which never climb trees. A reddish coat and light underparts make it one of the most attractive creatures of the woods. Its food is obtained from the cones of the various evergreens, and its feeding places are marked by piles of cone scales discarded in the process of obtaining the seeds.

The NORTHERN FLYING SQUIRREL (*Glaucomys sabrinus*) is most common on the western slope of Glacier Park, but it is not often seen by visitors due to its nocturnal habits. It can be readily identified by its pale-brown coloration, large eyes, and the thin membranes connecting the front and hind legs. This squirrel cannot fly in the true sense of the word, but it is an excellent glider and can sail for distances over 50 feet. It generally jumps from the top of a tall tree and glides downward, checking its speed abruptly as it approaches the trunk of the tree on which it lands. The flattened tail serves as a rudder, and it can make sharp turns in the direction of its "flight."

Three different species of CHIPMUNKS (*Eutamias* spp.) in the Parks are too much alike to be differentiated by the casual observer, and their habits are practically identical. They are nervous creatures, skipping about over logs in the liveliest fashion, chattering with excitement when an intruder approaches. The chipmunk is sometimes confused with the golden-mantled ground squirrel but may be distinguished by its smaller body and several white lines on his back, with lines extending to tip of pointed nose. It does not live in the ground but often inhabits trees, sometimes actually raiding bird nests, although usually feeding on seeds, buds, insects, etc.

The NORTHERN POCKET GOPHER (*Thomomys talpoides*) is a short-legged, stout-bodied brown rodent about 7 inches in total length, with extremely small eyes and ears. The tail is short (about 2 inches) and sparsely haired. The fur is a grayish brown and buff-white below. They dig their burrows just below the surface of the ground in the soft soil, eating on the roots of plants growing above the tunnel system. They push the earth from the tunnels up onto the surface, and these characteristic mounds may be seen in many meadows of the Parks. The mounds are often called "mole hills," which has led to the misconception that these animals are moles. (There are no members of the mole family known to occur in the Parks.) Gophers are abundant. However, because of their subterranean habits they are seldom seen, although their works are a conspicuous feature of the dry meadows of middle and high elevations.

The MOUSE–RAT–VOLE–LEMMING (*Cricetidae*) family is an extremely large and varied group of rodents. They range from a small mouse size to medium muskrat size, but they are difficult for the visitor to identify to species. The species reported in the Parks are as follows: LONGTAIL VOLE (quite abundant in fields and meadows throughout the Parks); MEADOW VOLE (very common in meadows and grasslands); BOREAL RED-BACKED VOLE (very common in meadows and grasslands); NORTHERN BOG LEMMING (rare in both Parks); DEER MOUSE (occurs only on the prairie country along the eastern edge of Glacier Park); WATER VOLE (largest of the voles and common along streams and wet places at high elevations). MOUNTAIN HEATHER VOLE (a vole that is found commonly in alpine meadows and around rock slides at high elevations); and BUSHY-TAILED WOOD RAT (common at lower elevations).

LAGOMORPHA

There are two members of the hare-rabbit family in the Parks. The largest is the WHITE-TAILED JACK RABBIT—actually a hare (*Lepus townsendi*). It is large, heavy-bodied (about 7 pounds) with large ears, long legs, and a good-sized fluffy tail that is all white throughout the year. The color above is fairly uniform buff-gray, underparts white. Its winter coat is much the same as the summer, though paler in tone. These jack rabbits are primarily prairie dwellers in this region. They are common on the Blackfeet Indian Reservation to the east of Glacier National Park, and occasionally individuals are seen in the open areas of the eastern valleys in the Parks. They are most often seen in St. Mary, Cut Bank, Many Glacier, and Belly River Valleys, and prairie areas of Waterton Lakes Park.

SNOWSHOE HARE (*Lepus americanus*) is a medium-sized hare (about 3 pounds), but it is differentiated by its relatively much larger hind feet and its change in color to white in the winter. With hind feet much larger than fore feet, this hare would appear to be unbalanced or awkward, but to watch one run through the brushland or aspen groves will convince anyone that such an assumption is quite false. The summer coloration is brown on the upper parts blending to a white underneath, with the tips of the ears and the upper surface of the tail black. Snowshoe hares are common throughout the Parks at lower elevations.

The smallest member of this order in the Parks is the PIKA (*Ochotona princeps*). A high country dweller, it is a buff- or gray-colored, round-eared, tailless mammal about the size of a guinea pig. Often called a cony or rock rabbit, it really "makes hay while the sun shines," and is quite busy all summer gathering grasses and drying them for winter use in its den. It is quite timid and runs around quite noiselessly except for an occasional cheeping cry.

THE SHREWS

The shrew (*Soricidae*) family is the primitive group of mammals that can be observed in the Parks. While they resemble mice—small, with grayish fur, long tails, and short feet—they are totally different and are completely unrelated. In contrast to mice, all shrews have long pointed snouts, pinpoint eyes, and almost invisible ears. The three found in this area are: the COMMON SHREW (the smallest park mammal, quite common but rarely seen); VAGRANT SHREW (a medium-sized brown shrew that is fairly common); and WATER SHREW (largest shrew in the Parks and common along streams and water courses).

THE BATS

Members of the bat (*Chiroptera*) order are the only mammals capable of true flight. Other mammals that are referred to as flying mammals are actually capable only of gliding motions made possible by various body membranes. The forelegs of bats are modified into rather effective wings by a membrane of skin which extends from the greatly elongated bones of the hand and the forearm to the sides of the body and back to the hind legs. In all species of bats in the Parks there is also a thin skin membrane connecting the hind limbs to the tail. The ears of bats are in general quite large for such small mammals and have in their center a rather long leaflike appendage referred to as the tragus. The species found in the Park region are: BIG BROWN BAT (apparently uncommon); LONG-LEGGED BROWN BAT (rare, but known to exist in the Parks); LITTLE BROWN BAT (fairly common at lower elevations); LONG-EARED BAT (very rare); and SILVER-HAIRED BAT (probably the most common bat in the area).

BIRDS OF THE PARKS

The Glacier and Waterton Lakes region possesses a wealth of bird life, varied and interesting. In Glacier Park, for instance, over 210 species of birds have been recorded. Actually, this Park with its heavy forest cover and its snowbanks and glaciers would seem an unlikely place for birds to spend the summer, as few species care for either deep forests or snow-clad mountains; but while general conditions limit the abundance of birds found within the boundaries of the Parks, certain local conditions increase their

140

numbers, so that by knowing where to look one may find a richly varied bird population. While birds breed within fairly definite boundaries governed by temperature during the breeding season, many of them wander widely afterwards in the Parks.

Around the warm outer margins of Glacier Park—in the Lake McDonald and the North Fork of the Flathead regions on the west, and the St. Mary, Sherburne Lake, and Belly River regions on the east—and the entrance station area of Waterton Lakes Park, islands and tongues of Transition zone prairie together with swampy meadows, sloughs, and large lakes affording more or less marshy cover invite a variety of birds.

Notable among birds on record are the western grebe, horned grebe, red-necked grebe, common merganser, mallard, gadwall, green-winged teal, blue-winged teal, bufflehead, canvasback, scaup, sora, American coot, snipe, great blue heron, upland plover, killdeer, sharp-tailed grouse, mourning dove, marsh hawk, Swainson's hawk, ferruginous hawk, prairie falcon, ring-necked pheasant, gray partridge, California gull, short-eared owl, saw-whet owl, downy woodpecker, red-headed woodpecker, cliff swallow, barn swallow, nighthawk, magpie, crow, raven, brown-headed cowbird, western meadowlark, red-winged blackbird, bobolink, Brewer's blackbird, vesper sparrow, Savannah sparrow, song sparrow, black-headed grosbeak, lazuli bunting, cedar waxwing, yellowthroat, yellow warbler, white-crowned sparrow, robin, American redstart, catbird, common grackle, house wren, red-breasted nuthatch, chestnut-backed chickadee, veery (willow thrush), and chestnut-collared longspur. While by no means all of these birds will be seen by visitors, since most of Park areas are too high for them, and generally frequented trails follow through the deep forest or over the rocky passes, it is interesting to know of the presence of these lowlanders. And the fact that the birds of the Parks range from such familiar friends as the catbird, kingbird, and red-headed woodpecker of the low country in the Transition zone to the unfamiliar ptarmigan, water pipit, and gray-crowned rosy finch of the alpine slopes above timberline affords an interesting and striking illustration of the vertical variation of the Parks' fauna.

Many of the birds of the prairie can be found in the Canadian (Forest) zone. In this zone, a great deal of the bird life centers around the lakes and streams with their bordering willow and alder thickets, together with the burned-over brushy slopes. Flying over the rivers and lakes, ospreys and swallows—either the

141

tree, the cliff, the bank, or the northern violet-green—may occasionally be seen. Even on the most frequented lakes numerous broods of (both common and Barrow's) golden-eye, mallards and other ducks may be found, and on the less frequented lakes the harlequin may sometimes be seen, although it prefers rapid rivers and streams to the quieter waters. On lakes where safe, secluded nesting sites are to be had, a few Canada geese may perhaps be discovered. Along the lake shores the spotted sandpiper, northern (Grinnell) water-thrush, and now and then the belted kingfisher and dipper (water ouzel) may be noted, although both kingfisher and ouzel are more generally seen along rivers and streams, the ouzel especially near waterfalls or cascades.

On the brushy slopes above the lakes where the forest cover has been replaced by scrub trees, among other birds may be found slate-colored fox sparrows, white-crowned and chipping sparrows, juncos, Swainson's thrush, Audubon's and MacGillivray's warblers, and some of the smaller flycatchers, such as the thrush and Traill's.

In the open a variety of hawks—the sparrow hawk, olive-sided sharp-shinned, Cooper's, and goshawk—may be noted, and now and then among the cliffs and canyons a golden eagle. On occasions a nighthawk, a swift (the black, Vaux's, or possibly the white-throated), or a hummingbird (generally the rufous but possibly the calliope or broad-tailed) may be caught sight of in passing.

Inside the forest three species of grouse—the blue (dusky), spruce (Franklin's), and ruffed—may be flushed. Campers may be fortunate enough to discover some of the resident owls, including the great horned owl, pygmy owl, great gray owl, and saw-whet owl. A number of woodpeckers are also to be closely watched for, among them the hairy, northern three-toed, black-backed three-toed, red-breasted sapsucker, Williamson's sapsucker, pileated woodpecker, Lewis' woodpecker, and the red-shafted flicker. Among other birds that may be seen are the Steller's jay, evening grosbeak, Oregon junco, western tanager, winter wren, brown creeper, red-breasted nuthatch, mountain chickadee, chestnut-backed chickadee, golden-crowned kinglet, Townsend's solitaire, Swainson's (olive-backed) thrush, hermit thrush, varied thrush, mountain bluebird, robin, and ruby-crowned kinglet.

In the narrow Scrub Forest or Hudsonian zone where the white-barked pine is the dominant tree, there are relatively few characteristic birds. Among them are the gray jay, Clark's nutcracker, pine grosbeak, Cassin's purple finch, red crossbill, white-winged

142

crossbill, pine siskin, and Bohemian waxwing. Above timberline the number of characteristic summer birds is reduced to three: the white-tailed ptarmigan, gray-crowned rosy finch, and water pipit.

While most of the birds found in the Parks in summer are merely summer visitants, coming north in the spring to nest and returning south in the fall or winter, there are some permanent residents, such as the grouse, some of the hawks, owls, and woodpeckers, together with the jays, ravens, eagles, crossbills, juncos, kingfishers, nutcrackers, nuthatches, and chickadees, which presumably never leave the Parks. Similarly, the birds found in the Parks in winter may be either permanent residents or winter visitants from farther north, such as the snowy owl, boreal owl, redpoll, and snow bunting, which come south during the fall or winter and return north on the approach of spring. In still another category come the spring and fall visitants, which merely pass through the Parks on their northward and southward migrations, as some of the ducks, snow geese, swans, phalaropes, snipes, and doubtless many of the smaller birds, overlooked or unrecognized by casual observers. Some of these migrants—namely the Canada goose and blue-winged teal—are known even to have nested at times in the Parks.

No attempt is made in this book to give descriptions of the over 210 bird species found in the Parks. There are several complete books on the subject, including Parratt's *Birds of Glacier National Park,* Munro's *Birds of Canada's Mountain Parks,* and Peterson's *A Field Guide to Western Birds.* The checklists are available at the Visitor Centers in both Parks.

REPTILES AND AMPHIBIANS

The Parks' long cold winters, high elevations, and short, cool summers offer little encouragement to animals that assume the temperature of their environment. Thus, less than a dozen species of reptiles and amphibians can be found, and most of these are extremely rare.

REPTILES

Snakes are not at all common in the Glacier-Waterton Lakes Parks, and *none* is poisonous. Two species of snakes—GREAT BASIN GARTER SNAKE and GREAT PLAINS RED-SIDED GARTER SNAKE —are the only ones that have been positively identified in the

143

Parks. On the hypothetical list are the GOPHER SNAKE, the YELLOW-BELLIED BLUE RACER (both of which *may* occur along the border of the Great Plains along the eastern boundaries of the Parks), and the RUBBER BOA (which *may* occur either side of the Continental Divide in rock slides or possibly even in forested areas.)

AMPHIBIANS

The WESTERN SPOTTED FROG (also known as the western or Pacific frog) is the most abundant amphibian in the Parks. This drab mottled or spotted frog with an obscure eye mark and white lip line is found along streams, ponds, and sloughs up to the subalpine regions. The GREEN FROG and TAILED FROG are found in some areas of the Parks.

There are two species of toads found in the Parks: the WESTERN TOAD (also known as the Columbian, northern, or northwestern toad) and PACIFIC TREE TOAD. The latter can be easily identified by its small size and the disks on its fingers and toes. The western toad is quite common in a variety of habitats up to the lower edge of the Alpine zone.

Two species of salamanders have been observed in the Parks. The TIGER SALAMANDER, with a ground color of either black or bluish black and large spots or blotches of yellow, is the most often reported. The other species—the LONG-TOED SALAMANDER—has a ground color of black or dark brown with a wide band of yellow extending from the back of the head to the tip of the tail.

Chapter 7.

Fishing and Boating in the Parks

ANGLING amidst such scenic grandeur can be an exhilarating experience. Awaiting your skill are sport fishes such as the cutthroat, rainbow, Dolly Varden, lake, and brook trouts, kokanee salmon, whitefish, grayling, and pike. The lakes of both Parks offer good fishing. The streams of the two Parks, however, are likely to be disappointing to the angler for a number of reasons. Except for the branches of the Flathead and Belly Rivers the streams are mainly small and extremely rapid. The many beautiful waterfalls and cascades seen everywhere in the Parks do not provide a very good home for trout. The falls prevent free movement of the fish up- and downstream, and the swift water furnishes very few resting places for fish. In addition, some glacier-fed streams carry quantities of rock flour which make them perpetually roily, preventing the proper development of fish food. Furthermore, and this is extremely important, most of the streams in the Parks have been found to be too cold to produce good crops of trout. Although this may sound odd, it has been determined that trout do not grow well unless the water temperature ranges from 55 to 65 degrees F. during the summer months. Many streams never reach 55 degrees even during the warmest days in summer. A good example is Cut Bank Creek. Only in the beaver ponds and immediately below them does the stream yield any trout worth catching.

Another factor which probably makes for poor trout production in streams is the character of the soil through which they flow. Fed by the pure water from snowfields and glacial lakes, they contain very little mineral and organic matter essential to the growth of fish food organisms. Only in the lower reaches do these streams have the proper richness to support the algae which supply the food upon which aquatic insects depend and which in turn make up the staple diet of trout.

Fishing along McDonald Creek with the Garden Wall in the distance. Glacier Park, Inc., photo.

The numerous and beautiful lakes in the Parks offer conditions suitable for trout and other game fish. Nowhere can you find a greater variety of lakes than in Glacier National Park. The range extends from small, permanently ice-filled lakes in the glacial cirques high in the mountains (most not suitable for fish) to the richer, warmer lakes in the lowland. In between these extremes is a great range of conditions. In Iceberg Lake, for example, although open water is present on part of the lake during August, the temperature at the surface is only 42 degrees and no sign of plant or animal life can be found. Ptarmigan Lake is at an even greater elevation (6,560 feet), but the glacial cirque in which it lies has a southern exposure, and consequently the water warms more rapidly. Brook trout can be found living in this lake, many reaching a fair size.

In general, however, the lower lakes are the best fishing lakes. They are warmer and have larger drainage basins than the higher lakes. The soil at lower elevations is richer, and the waters consequently produce more fish food. Also, the shallower lakes in the Parks are found to be the most productive. The deep, clear types of lake having a very limited amount of shallow water, such as Lake McDonald, are beautiful to the eye but do not provide the excellent fishing that is found in Red Eagle or Swiftcurrent.

FISH OF THE PARKS

The fish of Waterton Lakes and Glacier National Parks are plentiful in certain lakes but extremely limited in *number* of species. In Glacier, for instance, only twenty-two species of fish have been found or have been reported, and of these at least five—the rainbow trout, brook trout, lake whitefish, grayling, and kokanee salmon—were introduced. The sport fish are the cutthroat trout, the rainbow trout, the brook trout, the Dolly Varden, the lake trout, the Arctic grayling, the mountain whitefish, the kokanee, and the northern pike. Three species of suckers (largescale, longnose, and white), five species of minnows (longnose dace, northern dace, streamline chub, redside shiner, and northern squawfish—the latter often reaching a weight of 1 to 2 pounds), two species of sculpins (mottled sculpin and spoonhead sculpin), two species of whitefish (lake and pygmy), and burbot or ling (the only representative of the cod family found in fresh waters) complete the list of fishes in the Parks. Incidentally, the pygmy whitefish, which seldom exceeds 6 inches in length, has been discovered in only a few widely separated localities in North America.

147

This number of species seems small when it is remembered that three major drainage systems head in Glacier Park, but the cold water and presence of many high falls have undoubtedly restricted the natural distribution of fish in this area. In fact, the majority of the lakes on the east side of the Park and a number on the west were originally barren of all fish life because falls in the course of the principal streams prevented access to the waters above. Many of the lakes have been planted with trout and salmon, and now furnish good fishing. A description of the sport fish found in the two-Park area is as follows:

CUTTHROAT TROUT (Salmo clarki)

This is the native trout of the Rocky Mountains and the most widespread in the Parks. It is also known as native, black-spotted, Columbia River, redthroated, red-belly, mountain, and speckled trout.

The name "cutthroat" is derived from the two red or orange slash marks or streaks on the underside of the lower jaw. This color is weaker in young fish and fades rapidly after death. Coloration is generally dark green above, olive on sides, and silvery below. Numerous distinct black spots appear on the head, back and sides, and on the dorsal, adipose, and caudal fins. The lip bone on the upper jaw of the cutthroat extends well beyond the hind margin of the eye. Weights will run up to 3 pounds, with larger fish occasionally taken. For example, they grow to about 6 pounds in Red Eagle and Hidden Lakes, but the average size is about 1 pound in the Parks. They can be caught on flies, spoons, spinners, or bait.

RAINBOW TROUT (Salmo gairdneri)

The rainbow trout, like other *true* trout, char, salmon, grayling, and whitefish, has an adipose fin (small fatty fin just forward of the tail). True trout, like the rainbow, have dark spots on lighter-colored bodies. In general, the rainbow is bluish-green on the back, silvery on the sides and belly. A generous sprinkling of small black spots appears along the back, and on the dorsal, adipose, and caudal fins. A purplish-red band or stripe usually extends along the sides. Rainbows have short heads, the lip bone on the upper jaw seldom extending beyond the hind margin of the eye. Unlike the cutthroat trout, the rainbow lacks teeth on the back of the

148

Gamefish of the Parks

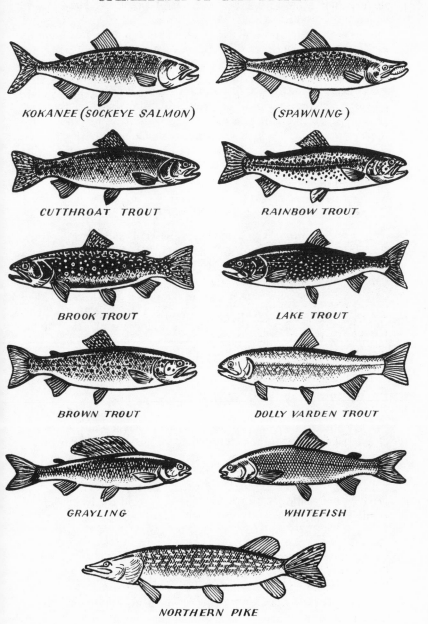

KOKANEE (SOCKEYE SALMON)

(SPAWNING)

CUTTHROAT TROUT

RAINBOW TROUT

BROOK TROUT

LAKE TROUT

BROWN TROUT

DOLLY VARDEN TROUT

GRAYLING

WHITEFISH

NORTHERN PIKE

tongue. They are found mainly in waters of the Park east of the Divide, and grow to a fair size (1 to 4 pounds). They can be taken on the same lures as cutthroat trout.

DOLLY VARDEN (Salvelinus malma)

It is locally known as bull trout. In reality, "Dolly" is a char, not a trout. Named after the colorful "Dolly Varden" ladies' hats of early fashion, bull trout are greenish to brownish on the back and sides, cream colored on the belly. Small cream to yellow spots appear on the back and sides. Some spots along the sides may be deep orange to reddish. The leading edges of the lower fins are white. They take worms, plugs, and spinners; occasionally, they will go for flies.

BROOK TROUT (Salvelinus fontinalis)

It is also known as speckled char, squaretail, and speckled trout. Probably the most colorful of the chars, the brook trout is dark green above, with wormlike markings on the back and dorsal fin. Cream and red spots appear on the sides, with the red spots bordered with blue. The lower fins are reddish, the leading edges bordered with a white and a black stripe. Generally, the weights run up to 3 pounds. Brook trout are found mainly east of the Divide, except for Lake Ellen Wilson and Harrison Lake. Wet and dry flies, spinning lures, spinner and bait combinations, and worms can be employed to take "brookies."

LAKE TROUT (Salvelinus namaycush)

They are known locally as "Mackinaw." They are also known as Great Lakes trout, forktail trout, longe, togue, Great Lakes char, and namaycush. They are gray to dark grayish-green in color with light spots over much of their body. The body is slender with a long head. The tail is deeply forked. Except for short periods when in the shallows, lake trout must be angled for by trolling at great depths. They are found in the larger east-side lakes such as St. Mary, Crossley, Glenns, and Waterton, and specimens of 15 pounds and up have been taken.

MOUNTAIN WHITEFISH (Coregonus williamsoni)

It is also called Rocky Mountain whitefish, mountain herring, Williamson's whitefish, Rocky Mountain herring, and—erroneously—"grayling." It is closely related to the trout and chars and is often included in this family. Troutlike in appearance, the body is silvery in color with a bronze or darkish back—no spots or specklings. The mouth is small. They run up to 18 inches in length and 3 pounds in weight.

Many sportsmen look with disfavor on the mountain whitefish and often throw it back as undesirable. However, it has much to recommend it. In addition to bait, it will often rise to artificial flies, and in swift, cold streams will show the spirit and dash characteristic of sport fish. The flesh of the whitefish is of the best quality, being firm, palatable, and tasty.

KOKANEE (Oncorhynchus nerka)

The kokanee is a landlocked form of the well-known Pacific red salmon. It also goes by the names of silver trout, little redfish, walla, yank, blueback, and Kennerley's landlocked, silver, or sockeye salmon. Its color is greenish blue on black with fine black specklings, but no *distinct* black spots. The mature males develop humps on their backs, hooked snouts, deep red on backs and sides. The kokanee salmon seldom grows bigger than 1 pound in Glacier.

ARCTIC GRAYLING (Thymallus arcticus)

Grayling are close relatives of the salmon and trout. While it is like the trout in its general shape, the grayling's large dorsal fin distinguishes it from all other game fish in the Parks. The general color is gray to silver with black spots, many of which are X-shaped. The eyes are large and the mouth is small. The length is up to 18 inches and weight up to 2 pounds. While grayling have been introduced into numerous lakes in the Parks, they are now pretty well confined to Elizabeth Lake and the Belly River drainage.

NORTHERN PIKE (Esox lucius)

This fish, often called a pickerel, has an overall coloration varying from a greenish cast to olive-gray shading to a lighter color on lower sides, becoming yellow-white on the belly. Body is profusely covered with lighter oval or bean-shaped spots; the fins are usually spotted with darker markings. It has a long, flattened snout, and numerous, needle-like teeth. This voracious feeder usually can be caught on bright spoons, spinners, plugs, and most baits.

They seldom take a fly. Pike are found only in Sherburne, Waterton, and Maskinonge Lakes in the two Parks, and they average from 2 to 4 pounds in weight—a few go as high as 15 pounds.

WHERE TO FISH

The western drainages from the Continental Divide were stocked principally with cutthroat trout. The larger lakes and streams support Dolly Varden. This species is quite frequently taken in the North and Middle Forks of the Flathead River and in Kintla, Upper Kintla, Bowman, and Logging Lakes.

Several lakes and streams on the eastern slope of the Divide also support cutthroat trout. In addition, good rainbow trout fishing may be had in Two Medicine, Elizabeth, Medicine Grizzly, Francis, and Gunsight Lakes. Brook trout are plentiful in many of the lakes and streams on the east side of the mountains. Two Medicine Lake, Two Medicine River, Josephine, Swiftcurrent, and Kootenai Lakes are well populated. Lake trout, the largest of the chars, are frequently taken in St. Mary, Waterton, Glenns, and Crossley Lakes, and occasionally in Lake McDonald west of the Divide.

The native trout are caught during the entire open season extending from late May through October 15. The best catches are, however, made during June, the first part of July, and during the cooler part of September. Trout fishing remains good during the entire season in some of the interior lakes and streams. Early- and late-season fishing yields superior catches of the other species. The comparatively warm weather occurring during the latter part of July and August appears to drive the fish to the bottom of the deeper pools, where additional skill is necessary to make successful catches. Many fishermen bring in their limits regardless of weather conditions.

The fly fishing in Waterton Lakes and Glacier National Parks is a pleasure which, once experienced, forever reappears in the smoke of the fisherman's pipe. In hook sizes #8 through #14, royal coachman, brown and gray hackles, cow dung, queen of water, ginger quills, professor, grizzly king, bee, and black gnat are used with success in many waters of the Parks. A fighting trout on a light fly rod amidst nature's unadulterated splendor is an experience open to everyone.

Fishing tackle consisting of rod, reel, line, and lure may be rented at the Lake McDonald and Glacier Park Lodges, the Many Glacier

Hotel, and the Apgar and Two Medicine Lake docks, and at the Rising Sun and Swiftcurrent Camp Stores. Fishing equipment may be purchased in Waterton townsite and in the towns and cities near the two Parks, as well as at all camp stores, hotels, and lodges.

As previously stated, the beautiful lakes, surrounded by towering mountains, are home for hardy trout. Here the fisherman, while trolling, may feast his eyes on some of the most outstanding scenery in the world. The thrill of a big one taken in this ideal setting cannot be duplicated. Red and white daredevils, plugs, and spinners are used with success. Bait casting from either shore or boat often yields desired results. Josephine, Swiftcurrent, Waterton, Red Eagle, St. Mary, Two Medicine, Kintla, and Bowman Lakes are outstanding for either trolling or bait casting. Up-to-date fishing information as well as the lakes and streams to fish, can be obtained from Park Rangers and Wardens.

FISHING REGULATIONS

In *Glacier National Park,* no fishing license is required. The general angling season extends from late May to October 15, although special seasons apply to some waters. For instance, Hidden Lake, Logging Creek from the head of Logging Lake and including Grace Lake, and Quartz Creek between Lower Quartz Lake and Quartz Lake is open generally only from July 1 to October 15, while Kintla Creek between Kintla Lake and Upper Kintla Lake can be fished from July 1 to August 31. Some streams such as Midvale and Hidden Creeks are closed to fishing at all times. Because the open season on various waters is subject to change occasionally, visitors are advised to consult Park rangers or inquire at the Park visitor centers or headquarters regarding those that can be fished.

The limit for each fisherman per day is 10 pounds of fish (dressed weight with heads and tails intact), or one fish, not to exceed a total of ten fish of same weight. The possession of more than one day's limit of fish is prohibited. There is no minimum size for fish that can be retained except in the case of Dolly Varden, which must be at least 18 inches in length with head and tail intact. Fishing hours are between 5 A.M. and 10 P.M. daily.

You can obtain *complete* fishing regulations from the Superintendent, West Glacier, Montana 59936, or at entrance stations or visitor centers.

153

In *Waterton Lakes National Park,* a fishing license is required for all persons who are 16 years of age or over, and it costs $2 for the entire season. It can be purchased at the information center, the Park license office in the administration building, the Park entrance station, and from all Park wardens. The fishing regulations themselves are constantly being revised, chiefly in regard to size, the limit of the catches, and open seasons on certain waters. When you get your license, ask for a summary of the regulations and study it. The complete regulations may be consulted at the administration building in Waterton Townsite.

In both Parks, fishing is allowed by hook and line only—the rod or line being hand-held. In Glacier, salmon eggs may be used as long as fished on the hook only (not used as chum). In Waterton Lakes National Park, the use or possession of salmon eggs or other fish eggs or any preparation therefrom or imitation thereof, or any kind of live or dead fish for bait, is prohibited. You should *not* dig worms in either Park; however, they may be purchased locally. In Glacier, be sure to contribute to the success of the Park's fishery management program by supplying creel census information. Creel census forms are available in boxes placed at various locations along the lake shores, from any ranger, and at ranger stations and visitor centers.

BOATING IN THE PARKS

Boating is a popular sport in both Waterton and Glacier National Parks. *Motorboats* are permitted only on Kintla, Bowman, McDonald, Sherburne, Swiftcurrent, St. Mary, Two Medicine, and Waterton Lakes. The latter includes the main Waterton Lakes chain plus the Waterton River and Maskinonge Lake. A permit must be obtained to operate a motorboat on the Canadian portion of Waterton, but they are issued free by district Park wardens. (A permit is required on all water in this Canadian Park.) *Nonmotorized boats* are permitted on all other waters in both Parks.

Launching ramps are located on Lake McDonald (near Apgar village), St. Mary Lake (at Rising Sun Boat Landing), Two Medicine Lake, Swiftcurrent Lake, and Waterton Lake (at Waterton Townsite). Mooring buoys are available at Apgar dock on Lake McDonald and in Emerald Bay in Waterton Lake. Fuel and boating supplies can be had at Waterton Townsite and the Apgar dock. Boat rentals are available (rowboats, with or without outboard motors) at McDonald (at Lake McDonald Lodge and Apgar

154

docks), Two Medicine, St. Mary (at Rising Sun Boat Landing), Swiftcurrent, and Waterton Lakes.

Water skiing is permitted only on Lake McDonald and St. Mary Lake from sunrise to sunset. Two competent persons must be in the towing boat and each person being towed must wear a lifesaving device. (If the device being worn is not approved by the U. S. Coast Guard, an approved device must be readily available in the towing boat.) Towing is prohibited within 500 feet of swimming areas and harbors and within 100 feet of any person in the water. Turning direction must always be counterclockwise.

In *Glacier National Park,* state and federal boating regulations apply. The boating regulations will be found in full in Title 36, *Code of Federal Regulations,* and are available at Park headquarters and permanent ranger stations. Below are a few of the important items to remember.

Prohibited Operations

1. *Reckless* or *negligent* boat handling so as to endanger or be likely to endanger the lives and property of others.

2. Boat handling by any person *under the influence of intoxicants or narcotics.*

3. Riding on *gunwales, transom,* or *foredeck* while boat is in operation.

4. *Swimming* from a boat while underway.

5. *Interference* with other boats or with free and proper navigation of waterways.

6. Operating motorboats *closer than* 500 feet to a swimming area.

7. *Leaving* a boat *unattended* for more than 24 hours without specific authority from the superintendent.

8. *Launching* and *recovery* of a boat at a site other than an established boat launching ramp.

9. *Unsafe loading* of boats.

10. Placing any *obstruction whatsoever* in the water.

11. Removal of wheels from boat trailers except for making repairs.

12. *Discharging* untreated *toilet wastes* into the water closer than ½ mile from shore.

13. *Depositing trash, refuse,* or *debris* of any kind in the water.

Required Boat Equipment

1. *Registration number* for boats with motor of more than 10 h.p.
2. For each person on board, one good, serviceable, and readily accessible *lifesaving device* approved by the U. S. Coast Guard.
3. *Oars* or *paddles, bailer,* and *waste receptacle.*
4. *Flame arrester* (U. S. Coast Guard approved) on each carburetor of inboard engines.
5. *Fire extinguisher(s)* (B-1 type) or a fixed fire-extinguishing system for all inboard engines and outboards with enclosed fuel compartments.
6. *Sound-producing device* for each motorboat 16 feet and longer.
7. *Navigation lights* on motorboats for use between sunset and sunrise.
8. *Flashlight* or *lantern* for hand-propelled boats used between sunset and sunrise.
9. *Anchor light* for boats anchored at night.
10. Internal combustion engines must be effectively *muffled.*

Law Enforcement

1. The U. S. Coast Guard's Rules of the Road apply to all waters in the park as well as Title 36, *Code of Federal Regulations.*
2. Boating regulations applicable in Glacier National Park may be *enforced by any uniformed employee.*
3. If *judged guilty* of violating any boating regulation, the person so judged may be *fined $500* or *imprisoned for 6 months or both* and assessed the *cost of the proceeding.*
4. The superintendent or his authorized representative may *inspect* or *board* any boat for the purpose of examining documents, licenses, and/or other permits relating to the operation of the boat and to inspect the boat to determine compliance with regulations.

In *Waterton Lakes National Park,* all boats operating on the lakes must carry proper safety equipment and conform with *Canadian Federal Navigation Regulations.* (They are very similar to U. S. Coast Guard regulations.) A copy of these regulations may be obtained from the Canadian Government Travel Bureau, Ottawa 4, Ontario, Canada, or at the administration building in the Park. Emerald Bay in the townsite area of Upper Waterton

Lake is a restricted boating area. As a safety measure boats are restricted to a maximum speed of 5 m.p.h.

LAUNCH CRUISES

Scenic launch cruises are available on Lake McDonald, St. Mary, Swiftcurrent, Josephine, Two Medicine, and Upper Waterton Lakes.

Lake McDonald. The excursion launch *De Smet* leaves from and returns to the dock at Lake McDonald Lodge on five scheduled trips daily. On this 45 to 60-minute scenic cruise, areas of the Park not visible from the roadways are seen, and informative narrations are given on three tours by a Park naturalist and on two tours by the boat captain. Schedules are posted at Lake McDonald Lodge and all visitor centers.

St. Mary Lake. Two cruisers, *Red Eagle* and *Curley Bear,* operate on this lake. On the 1-hour sightseeing tour, they travel for 10 exciting miles around the lakeshore, viewing Sexton Glacier, numerous waterfalls, primitive forest, steep cliffs rising a mile above the lake level, and many other natural features. A special photographic cruise is scheduled every morning, as well as a special trail-boat trip. On the latter, a Park naturalist accompanies the group around the end of St. Mary Lake for 7 miles along the Red Eagle Trail. Baring, St. Mary, Virginia, and other small waterfalls are seen along the route of this 6-hour excursion. There are other cruise-trail trips here, too. On one, the passengers take a guided nature walk with a Park naturalist to Baring Falls from Sun Point Dock. (Total time required is 2½ hours with walking distance 1½ miles.) All boat tours are from the Rising Sun Boat Landing, and the schedule of these sailings may be obtained here or at the visitor centers in the Park and the Rising Sun Motor Inn.

Two Medicine Lake. The launch *Rising Wolf* makes three trips daily (9:30 A.M.; 1:30 P.M.; 3 P.M.) from the Two Medicine boat dock to the upper end of the lake and back. The last afternoon trip includes a Park naturalist talk and an opportunity to take a 2-mile walk to Twin Falls.

Swiftcurrent and Josephine Lakes. The cruiser *Altyn* plies the waters of Swiftcurrent, while the launch *Chief Two Gun* sails on Josephine Lake. They operate concurrent schedules. That is, the *Altyn* leaves the Many Glacier Hotel dock and cruises to the head of Swiftcurrent Lake in time to meet the *Chief Two Gun* for its

tours to the head of Josephine Lake. A short walk is necessary between the lakes. Hikers going to Grinnell Glacier save almost half the hike by taking the two launches. Several of the *Altyn* cruises have a Park naturalist on board. Complete information on the sailing times of the two boats may be obtained at the information desk at the Many Glacier Hotel or at the visitor centers in the Park.

Waterton Lake. The large powerboat *International* and the smaller launches *Miss Waterton* and *Deeidra* operate on full schedules of trips to the head of this 7-mile lake. As your powerboat pulls away from the dock and turns directly southward into the main reach of the lake, you may notice the low ground on which the Townsite of Waterton National Park is built. This is the delta that formed from the sand, gravel, and boulders which were carried down Cameron Creek by the glacial meltwaters and were spread around by waves in the lake. As you travel away from the delta, its flat fanlike shape becomes clearer. Passing still farther down the lake, you notice that brooks have built deltas which stick out into the lake at the mouth of each major valley as low flats with rounded outlines. Here and there, such as at the mouth of Hell Roaring Creek, the white of waterfalls may be seen. These falls, at the edge of the main lake, were all formed when the small tributary streams reoccupied preglacial drainage valleys only to find that the main valley system had been deepened very considerably by the ice. A little more than halfway down the lake you cross the international boundary, marked by posts on the shores of the lake, and a 20-foot swath clear of trees. This is the 49th parallel of latitude which, from near Vancouver all the way to Lake of the Woods east of Winnipeg, forms the boundary between Canada and the United States. After a short stop in the United States at Goat Haunt Landing, the vessel makes the hour return trip down Upper Waterton Lake. As the powerboat nears the Townsite again, the massive, gabled Prince of Wales Hotel can be plainly seen on a bluff high above the lake. To the hotel's right is the Bosporus, connecting Upper and Lower Waterton Lakes. Information as to sailing times for this 2-hour cruise may be obtained at the Waterton boat dock area, the Park Information Center, or at the Prince of Wales Hotel.

Passengers boarding the launch International *for a trip down Upper Waterton Lake. The Prince of Wales Hotel can be seen standing proudly over the lake.* Glacier Park, Inc., photo.

Chapter 8.

Accommodations and Services
in the Parks

As you have read, there is lots to do and see in the Land of Shining Mountains. Sight-seeing is unlimited. There are also launch cruises, fishing, hiking, horseback riding, and daily naturalist activities. In addition, there are accommodations to fit anyone's desires—beautiful large hotels, motel units, mountain chalets, rustic cabins, and campgrounds at many places in Glacier-Waterton Parks.

ACCOMMODATIONS IN GLACIER
NATIONAL PARK

The concessioners within the Park operate under the supervision of the National Park Service, which keeps careful check on the rates, features, and quality of services, equipment, liability, and other items.

HOTELS

Glacier Park, Inc., operates Many Glacier Hotel and Lake Mc-Donald and Glacier Park Lodges in or near Glacier National Park, and Prince of Wales Hotel in Waterton Lakes National Park. These hotels are open from about June 15 to about September 10, and the facilities are as follows:

Glacier Park Lodge. Located at East Glacier Park, Montana, near the southeast entrance to Glacier National Park. The lodge is surrounded by beautifully landscaped grounds silhouetted against

160

Assembly of saddle horses awaits riders at Many Glacier Hotel. Chalet-style architecture is typical of many of Glacier Park's accommodations. Glacier Park, Inc., photo.

snowcapped peaks. Attractively decorated and newly furnished rooms with private bath. Rooms have telephones and are steam heated. Dining room, coffee shop, gift shop, and cocktail lounge in the lodge. Entertainment for all: dancing, golf, pitch-and-putt course, shuffleboard, riding and hiking, outdoor heated swimming pool.

161

Many Glacier Hotel. Located in the heart of Glacier National Park on the shore of Swiftcurrent Lake, 12 miles west of Babb, Montana. All rooms have private bath, steam heat, and have been recently remodeled or refurbished and equipped with new furnishings. There is a telephone in each room. A dining room, coffee shop, gift shop, and cocktail lounge are conveniently located in the hotel. Activities include scenic launch cruises, boating, riding, hiking, and fishing.

Lake McDonald Lodge. Located 11 miles northeast of West Glacier, Montana, on the east shore of Glacier's largest lake. Rooms with bath are available in the lodge as well as in the adjoining cottages. All rooms have been refurbished and newly furnished. There is a dining room, gift shop, and cocktail lounge in the lodge and a coffee shop, post office, and camp store on the grounds. Entertainment includes naturalist talks, movies, launch trips, boating, swimming, riding, and hiking.

MOTELS AND CABINS

Motel units and cabins operated by Glacier Park, Inc., are available at Swiftcurrent, Rising Sun, and Apgar. The facilities include the following:

Swiftcurrent Motor Inn. Located 1¼ miles from Many Glacier Hotel in Swiftcurrent Valley. Accommodations for auto tourists include completely furnished, attractively decorated motel units, each with shower bath and thermostatically controlled heat. There are also two- and three-room housekeeping cabins. Two-room cabins have a kitchen and one bedroom with double bed. Three-room cabins include kitchen and two bedrooms each with a double bed. Cabins are equipped with pillows, linen, and blankets. Kitchens have a combination cooking and heating stove, table, benches, sink, and cold running water. Wood is furnished. Kitchen facilities are suited for preparing light meals. However, no cooking utensils or dishes are furnished. A limited assortment of cooking utensils and dishes is sold at the camp store. Public rest rooms with shower are provided for cabin occupants.

Rising Sun Motor Inn. Located just off the Going-to-the-Sun Road, 6½ miles west of St. Mary Junction on the north shore of St. Mary Lake. The facilities include modern motel units, each with private shower bath, attractively decorated and comfortably

Lake McDonald Lodge has an atmosphere of the Old West. Glacier Park, Inc., photo.

furnished, and cabins that have two non-connecting rooms with or without shower bath. Rooms without shower have cold running water and half bath. Pillows, linens, and blankets are furnished. No cooking is permitted in the motel or cabin rooms. There is a coffee shop, general store, gift shop, and service station in the area.

Village Inn. Located in Apgar village at the foot of Lake McDonald. This modern motel has one-bedroom, two-bedroom, kitchen-bedroom, and two-bedroom–living-room units available. All units have private shower baths, and are attractively decorated and comfortably furnished. The facilities of Apgar village—general store, cafes, and boat dock—are nearby.

Reservations are usually necessary for hotels, motels, and cabins. For rates and reservations, write Glacier Park, Inc., from June 1 through October 1, at East Glacier Park, Montana 59434; from October 2 through May 31, at P. O. Box 4250, Tucson, Arizona 85719. A deposit of the first night's room rent is required on all reservations.

Chalets. Chalets at Sperry and Granite Park are open for use of hikers and horseback parties from about July 1 through Labor Day, and are reached by trail only. Sperry Chalets are 6.5 miles from the Lake McDonald Lodge. Granite Park Chalets are 7.4 miles from Logan Pass. Mountain goats are a familiar sight at Sperry Chalets. Rare indeed is the day or night that goats are not on hand to amuse visitors. Meals are served at both places.

While reservations are not required, they are desirable due to the wilderness-area location of these chalets. For reservations, write to B. Ross Luding, P. O. Box 37, Martin City, Montana 59926. Deposit on reservations is *not* required.

There are several cabins and motels available on private lands within the Park at Apgar village and near Lake McDonald Lodge. These are not authorized concessioners and do not operate under the supervision of the National Park Service. In addition, most of the neighboring towns and cities have hotels, motels, and tourist courts with modern facilities. For information, address inquiries to the chambers of commerce of nearby towns in Montana: Kalispell, Havre, Cut Bank, Whitefish, Columbia Falls, or East Glacier Park.

The Swiftcurrent Motel and Cabin Camp near Swiftcurrent Lake. Allen Mountain (right), Wynn Mountain (center), and East Flattop Mountain (far distance) are also shown. Great Northern Railway photo.

ACCOMMODATIONS IN WATERTON
LAKES NATIONAL PARK

The Park's accommodations—hotels, chalets, lodges, and bungalow cabins—are located within the Waterton Townsite. There are some eighteen different accommodation facilities available, including the world-famous Prince of Wales Hotel. This Swiss-style structure has a very picturesque lobby, dining room, and cocktail lounge. Each of the rooms has private bath and telephone. It is operated by Glacier Park, Inc.

Publications containing details of the name, rates, capacity, and plan for the other tourist accommodations in Waterton Lakes National Park may be obtained at the Park's information bureau, or from the Canadian Government Travel Bureau, Ottawa 4, Ontario, Canada. It is advisable to arrange advance accommodations if you plan to stay overnight in the Park.

CAMPGROUNDS IN GLACIER
NATIONAL PARK

Glacier's major campgrounds, located at Apgar, Fish Creek, Sprague Creek, Avalanche Creek, St. Mary, Rising Sun, Many Glacier (Swiftcurrent), and Two Medicine, have fireplaces, tables, sanitary facilities, and running water. Coffee shops, soda fountains, and camp stores are located near Many Glacier (Swiftcurrent), Rising Sun, Two Medicine, Sprague Creek, and Apgar Campgrounds.

Smaller campgrounds for those desiring quiet and solitude are located at Kintla Lake, Bowman Lake, Bowman Creek, Mud Creek, River (North Fork), Quartz Creek, Logging Creek, and Cut Bank. These primitive camps have fireplaces, tables, and toilets. Trailer space is available in all campgrounds *except Sprague Creek,* but there are no utility connections. The dirt road from Fish Creek Campground to Kintla and Bowman Lake Campgrounds (North Fork area) is too narrow for large housetrailers. Before you attempt this route with a housetrailer, consult a Park ranger. Campsites cannot be reserved; they are operated on a first-come, first-served basis. There is *no* charge for use of any of the campgrounds in Glacier, but be sure to register at the campground entrance.

Campground*	No. of Campsites	Flush Toilets	Trailers Permitted	Piped Water
Apgar	198	Yes	Yes	Yes
Avalanche Creek	143	Yes	Yes	Yes
Bowman Creek	6	No	Yes**	No
Bowman Lake	48	No	Yes**	Yes
Cut Bank	19	No	Yes**	No
Fish Creek	182	Yes	Yes	Yes
Kintla Lake	9	No	Yes**	Pump
Logging Creek	7	No	Yes**	No
Many Glacier (Swiftcurrent)	117	Yes	Yes	Yes
Mud Creek	6	No	Yes**	Pump
Quartz Creek	6	No	Yes**	Pump
Rising Sun	82	Yes	Yes	Yes
River (North Fork)	7	No	Yes**	Pump
Sprague Creek	45	Yes	No	Yes
St. Mary Lake	100	Yes	Yes	Yes
Two Medicine	98	Yes	Yes	Yes

* Locations given in the logs which appear in Chapter 3.
** Unimproved access road, too narrow for large housetrailers (except at Cut Bank). These sites are in the North Fork area. Group camping sites are available at St. Mary and Apgar. Backcountry campfire sites are listed on pages 100-102.

Campground Regulations Enforced in Glacier National Park

1. *Designated Campsites.* Camping is permitted only at designated sites equipped with a fireplace and table, and at designated backcountry sites, where a campfire permit is required.

2. *Tables.* Each campsite is equipped with one table which may not be moved from the site.

3. *Fires.* Fires are permitted only in the fireplace provided.

4. *Vehicles.* It is prohibited to drive or propel or park any wheeled vehicle off the paved roads or parking areas, except "pop-up" trailers which have to be staked.

5. *Water and Electric Hookups.* Individual water sewage and/or electrical hookups to camps or trailers are not permitted.

6. *Digging.* The natural terrain shall not be altered in any way. Leveling of the ground or digging for any purpose is prohibited.

7. *Disturbance of Plant or Animal Life.* Plants or animals shall not be disturbed in any way. The driving of nails into trees or the stripping of bark, leaves, or branches from trees or shrubs is prohibited.

167

8. *Drainage and Refuse from Trailers*. Trailer owners must provide receptacles for catchment of waste water. Such waste shall be disposed of only at public rest rooms, and at the sewage disposal units at all major campgrounds.

9. *Hours of Quiet*. Quiet must be maintained between the hours of 10:00 P.M. and 6:00 A.M.

10. *Dogs, Cats, and Pets*. All dogs, cats, and other pets must be kept on leash or under physical restrictive control at all times while in the Park. Pets are not allowed on trails.

11. *Unattended Camps*. Camps may not be left unattended for more than 48 hours without specific authority of the campground ranger.

12. *Camping Limit*. No person or party may camp longer than 14 days in the Park during July and August, in a single period or combination of periods.

13. *Clean Camps*. Campers are responsible for maintaining a clean camp at all times and for cleaning their campsite, including removal of all camping equipment, debris, and refuse before leaving.

14. *Use of Hydrants*. Cleaning fish and washing dishes or clothes at water hydrants is prohibited. The use of hot-air dryers in the comfort stations for drying clothes or dishes is prohibited.

15. Only dead and downed wood may be gathered for firewood.

CAMPGROUNDS IN WATERTON LAKES NATIONAL PARK

Four campgrounds readily accessible to the motoring public are available in the Park. The main campground is located in the southern part of the Waterton Townsite and covers an area of more than 35 acres. It is traversed by Cameron Creek and is part of an alluvial fan upon which the townsite is laid out. A gravel subsoil ensures good drainage, and there are sufficient trees to provide shelter for tents. This campground is fully serviced with electricity, modern plumbing in most of the service buildings, laundry facilities, and showers. Kitchen and community shelters are equipped with tables, stoves, and fuel. Trailer sites, equipped with water, sewer, and electrical connections, are located on either side of Cameron Creek. A caretaker and matron service is maintained throughout the summer season. A fee is charged for the use of facilities in this serviced campground.

Semi-serviced campgrounds, equipped with kitchen shelters,

stoves, and fuel and sanitary facilities are located at Cameron Lake, Mount Crandell, and Belly River. All are within a reasonable distance of the townsite (see the mileage logs in Chapter 3), and there is no charge for their use.

Campground	No. of Campsites	Flush Toilets	Trailers Permitted	Piped Water
Townsite Campground*	250	Yes	No	Yes
Townsite Trailer Area*	95	—	Yes	Yes
Cameron Lake	10	No	No	No
Crandell Mountain	132	Yes	No	No
Belly River	24	No	No	Yes

* Serviced campground—fee is charged.

Visitors who wish to camp away from the road will find primitive campsites with kitchen shelters and sanitary facilities at many of the high lakes such as Alderson, Bertha, Crandell, Crypt, and Twin Lakes. While there is no charge for the use of these primitive campsites, you *must* register your overnight trip with the Warden Service prior to leaving and check in with the warden when you return.

The campground rules are very much the same as those in Glacier National Park. Where a self-registration system is employed at the campgrounds, be sure that you insert a registration card in the appropriate slot indicating that the site of your choice is in use. Please remove it when you leave the campground at the end of your stay and drop it in the box provided for this purpose at the entrance gate. If you are leaving or re-registering, please do so by 2:00 P.M. Stays at the campgrounds are limited to two weeks.

Four public campground and picnic sites have been established on the Blackfeet Reservation. They are located: *Two Medicine,* on lake 5 miles from U.S. Route 2, 24 camping and 40 picnic units; *Duck Lake,* 4 miles from U.S. Route 89, 26 camping and 20 picnic units; *St. Mary,* on lake and U.S. Route 89, 100 camping and 500 picnic units; *Twin Lakes,* 10 miles from U.S. Route 89, 16 picnic units. There is a $3 tribal permit cost for the use of the sites. For information, write Blackfeet Tribe or Indian Agency, Browning, Montana.

169

SERVICES IN GLACIER
NATIONAL PARK

Meals and Supplies. Groceries, film, camping supplies, and other items are available in stores at Swiftcurrent, Rising Sun, Lake Mc-Donald, and Two Medicine. Meals may be obtained at the coffee shops at Swiftcurrent, Lake McDonald, Rising Sun, and in all the hotels. Box lunches are available at all hotels and motor inns. Coffee, soup, and sandwiches may be obtained at the camp store at Two Medicine. Additional eating facilities, and general stores carrying complete lines of campers' supplies and photographic film, are available on private lands within the park at Apgar village and near Lake McDonald Lodge.

Transportation. Bus service is maintained between all hotels, including the Prince of Wales Hotel and Two Medicine Lake. At Two Medicine Lake, the bus stops long enough to give you the opportunity to do some fishing or to enjoy a launch trip and short hike with a park naturalist (see page 157 for additional information).

If you do not have your own transportation and would like to do some independent exploring of the Park, you can obtain rental cars from Glacier Park, Inc.

Medical Service. During the Park season, there are qualified nurses at the hotels on both sides of the Park, and a resident physician is at the Glacier Park Lodge. Nearest hospitals are at Cut Bank and Cardston on the east side of the Park, and at Whitefish and Kalispell on the west side of the Park.

Religious Services. Protestant and Roman Catholic church services are conducted at several places in the Park on Sundays. Protestant services are sponsored by the National Council of Churches. Times and locations of the services are posted in the principal gathering places within the Park, and Park rangers will have this information.

Post Office, Telephone, and Telegraph. Post offices are located at East Glacier Park 59434, West Glacier 59936, Babb 59411, Polebridge 59928, and (from June 15 to September 10) Lake McDonald 59921. Mail for guests at Glacier Park Lodge, Many Glacier Hotel, and Rising Sun and Swiftcurrent Motor Inns should be addressed to East Glacier Park, Montana 59434, in care of the hotel at which the guest is staying or in care of Glacier Park, Inc., if the hotel is not known. Mail for guests at Lake McDonald Lodge should be addressed to the Lake McDonald P. O., Montana 59921, in care of the lodge. Village Inn's mailing address is West Glacier, Montana 59936. Outgoing mail leaves all the hotels once a day. The mail drop is at the front desk.

Telephone and telegraph services are available at all hotels and motels. Telegrams for guests at the Glacier Park Lodge, Many Glacier Hotel, and Rising Sun and Swiftcurrent Motor Inns should be addressed to them at the hotel, lodge, or inn, in care of Glacier Park, Inc., East Glacier Park, Montana. The telegraph address for the Lake McDonald Lodge and Village Inn is West Glacier, Montana.

Check Cashing. Travelers' checks are accepted. Personal checks will be honored only to the extent of hotel bills, contingent on presentation of acceptable identification. Hotels reserve the right to refuse acceptance of personal checks.

United States and Canadian Exchange. Canadian funds will be accepted in Glacier National Park and United States funds will be accepted in Waterton Lakes National Park in payment for accommodations and purchases at current rates of exchange.

Baby-Sitters. Given reasonable notice, the front desk in the various hotels can *usually* provide baby-sitters from among their college-student employees, at reasonable rates.

Barber-Beauty Shop. There is a beauty shop on the ground level at Glacier Park Lodge, and there are both barber and beautician at the Many Glacier Hotel.

Gift Shops. They are operated at Glacier Park Lodge, Many Glacier, Lake McDonald, Swiftcurrent, Rising Sun, and Two Medicine. They also handle outing clothes, tobacco, candy, newspapers, books, magazines, souvenirs, fishing tackle, cameras, film, etc. Film developing and printing accepted.

Drugs. Closest pharmacists are at Browning on the east and Hungry Horse on the west. The gift shops cannot fill any prescriptions but offer *almost* everything else from aspirin and deodorant to toothpaste and baby oil.

Laundry and Valet Service. This service is available at Glacier Park Lodge and Many Glacier Hotel.

Hayrides. From Glacier Park Lodge, there is a hayride every night —great fun for the kids and guaranteed to bring back memories for adults. It starts right at the door. At Many Glacier Hotel, an ancient surrey (with a fringe on the top) makes fun trips around Swiftcurrent Lake during the day. This coach was first used in the early 1900's between Browning and points west.

Launch Cruises and Boat Rentals. See Chapter 7.

Golf. There is a fine nine-hole course at Glacier Park Lodge. There is also a pitch and putt course located on this lodge's front lawn.

Swimming. There is a heated swimming pool at Glacier Park Lodge. Glacier's lakes are fed by melting snow and ice; therefore, for any but the hardy, they are too cold for swimming. There is one exception: Lake McDonald, on the west side, is not so cold.

Saddle-Horse Trips. See Chapter 4.

Service Stations. Within the Park, there are service stations at Two Medicine, Rising Sun, Lake McDonald, Apgar, and Swiftcurrent.

Photography. You will want to get out your camera the minute you set foot in Glacier, for the amazing extravagance of wildlife, wildflowers, and superb mountain scenery will present more subjects than you can possibly photograph during your visit. Glacier's intense blue skies provide ideal atmospheric conditions for the camera artist. Here, too, you will find sharp contrasts for both black-and-white and color shots. Photo supply shops in each of the hotels and camp stores operated by Glacier Park, Inc., will take care of your film needs and provide developing service.

Train Reservations. A ticket office is maintained at Glacier Park Lodge, where arrangements may be made for tickets and reservations.

All one-way and round-trip tickets are good for stopover at East Glacier Park and West Glacier (Belton) Stations.

All-Expense Tours. The Park concessioners have jointly arranged attractive all-expense tours, which include bus fare, meals, hotel lodging, launch excursion, and horseback riding. Trips that include the Prince of Wales Hotel in Waterton Lakes National Park are also available. You may obtain information concerning rates or reservations from Glacier Park, Inc. (see page 165).

SERVICES IN WATERTON LAKES NATIONAL PARK

In the Waterton Lakes Townsite, the visitor will find the following business establishments: four china and novelty shops, three dry-goods stores, four fishing tackle dealers, three garage and service stations, two grocery and meat stores (combined), one pharmacy, one hardware dealer, two Laundromats (one in the main campground), one liquor vendor, and one barber and beauty shop. There are three restaurants, plus the dining room facilities in the Prince of Wales Hotel. In addition, cocktail lounges can be found at the Prince of Wales Hotel and Kootenai Lodge. A seasonal branch of the Canadian Imperial Bank of Commerce is located in the hotel of the Lakeshore Village and is open from 10:00 A.M. to 3:00 P.M., Monday through Friday, plus additional hours on Friday from 4:30 P.M. to 6:00 P.M. While the nearest doctors and hospitals are at Pincher Creek and Cardston, about five doctors have cottages in the Park, and one of them can usually be located when emergencies arise. Anglican, United, Roman Catholic, and Latter Day Saints services are held each Sunday during the tourist season. Twenty-four-hour telephone and telegraph service is available in Waterton, and there is a post office in the townsite.

Golf. A golf course operated by the Natural and Historic Resources Branch of Canada is situated on the rolling slopes at the base of Mount Crandell, and has a fine scenic setting. It is an eighteen-hole course and has an exceptionally attractive clubhouse, which is open to visitors. Light refreshments are served. A moderate fee is charged for a round of eighteen holes (continuous) with comparable rates for daily, weekly, and seasonal periods.

Tennis. Tennis courts owned and operated by the Park are available free of charge. They are situated near the Royal Canadian Mounted Police Barracks in Waterton Townsite.

Swimming. A modern outdoor swimming pool which has been erected in Waterton Townsite is available to Park visitors, at slight cost, during the summer season. The water in the pool is heated, chlorinated, and in continuous circulation. Dressing rooms containing showers and other facilities are provided for the use of patrons. A wading pool for children, separate from the main pool, has been incorporated in the development. Lifeguard services are also provided. The beach at Lake Linnet, a short distance north of the townsite, is suitable for bathing and swimming but is not supervised.

Entertainment. Movies are shown nightly in the townsite theater. Outdoor and naturalist programs are held several times a week in the amphitheater located in the southwest corner of the main campground. A dance is held on Saturday night, as well as one other night during the week, at the Waterton Pavilion. A playground for children is available in the center of the townsite. It is equipped with slides, swings, and other facilities for children's enjoyment; there is also a spray pool for tots.

Boating, fishing, trail hiking and riding, and scenic launch trips, which are all popular in Waterton Park, are fully discussed in earlier chapters. For those who like a hayride, the Timberline Stables conducts them several times a week.

SUMMARY OF NATURALIST PROGRAM IN GLACIER

As described in previous chapters, the National Park Service provides naturalist-conducted activities in several areas of the Park, from about June 15 until September 10. These services are free except for the boat rides, and for lodging in connection with overnight trips to Sperry Glacier and Granite Park. Schedule leaflets are available at entrance stations, information offices, hotels, cabincamp offices, Visitor Centers. For your convenience, the following is a summary of the naturalist program in Glacier:

Area	*Activities and Places of Interest*
Headquarters	Naturalist's office
Apgar-Fish Creek	Evening program at amphitheaters, Apgar and Fish Creek Campgrounds

(*continued*)

Area	Activities and Places of Interest
Lake McDonald; Avalanche Campground	Nature walk to Avalanche Lake Naturalist-accompanied boat trips from Lake McDonald Lodge Evening programs, Lake McDonald Lodge and Avalanche Campgrounds Self-guiding nature trail, Avalanche Campground
Sperry Glacier	Naturalist-conducted overnight trip from Lake McDonald Lodge to Sperry Chalets and Sperry Glacier
Logan Pass	Visitor center; Orientation path Free telescope during open hours Nature walks along the Garden Wall Naturalist-led all-day or overnight hike along Garden Wall to Granite Park Chalets
St. Mary; Rising Sun; Sun Point	St. Mary Visitor Center; Sun Point—photographic point, viewfinder, and old chalet site Naturalist-accompanied boat and combination boat and trail trip, St. Mary Lake Evening programs, St. Mary Visitor Center and St. Mary and Rising Sun Campgrounds Self-guiding trail to Baring Falls
Many Glacier	Nature walks to Grinnell Glacier, Iceberg Lake Appekunny and Redrock Falls Naturalist-accompanied boat and trail trips to Grinnell Lake Evening programs, Many Glacier Hotel, and Swiftcurrent Campground Self-guiding nature trail along Swiftcurrent Lake Other walks as announced

(*continued*)

Area	Activities and Places of Interest
Two Medicine Lake	Nature walks to interesting places
	Naturalist-accompanied combination boat and trail trip to Twin Falls
	Evening program, Two Medicine Campground
	Trick Falls Self-Guiding Nature Trail
East Glacier Park	Evening talk once a week, Glacier Park Lodge
Waterton Lake	Interpretive shelter, viewfinder

SUMMARY OF NATURALIST PROGRAM IN WATERTON

Self-guided nature trails have been developed at Cameron Lake and Red Rock Canyon to help visitors gain a better understanding of the wonders of nature. Labels on trees and shrubs identify various species, and a Park naturalist conducts guided tours in summer. Nature talks illustrated by colored slides and motion pictures are presented in the evenings at the Park amphitheater near the Townsite Campgrounds.

An exhibition herd of plains buffalo occupies a fenced area on the northern boundary of the Park, just west of the highway to Pincher Creek. Visitors may enter the paddocks from 9 A.M. to 6 P.M.

If you are a fisherman, you will want to visit the fish-rearing station, located southeast of Cameron Falls in the townsite.

WHAT TO WEAR

As a rule, Glacier-Waterton visitors are inclined to carry too much. We suggest a very inexpensive and simple outfit: comfortable clothes and stout shoes. You will need light clothing for sunny days and indoors, and a warm jacket, sweater, or topcoat for cool nights. On trails, afoot or on horseback, you will appreciate a wool shirt, slacks or levis, a brimmed cap, a raincoat, and sunglasses. Late spring or early fall visitors should pack warmer clothing.

PUBLICATIONS OF THE GLACIER
NATURAL HISTORY ASSOCIATION, INC.

The Glacier Natural History Association, Inc., was organized for the purpose of cooperating with the National Park Service by assisting the Division of Interpretation of Glacier National Park in the development of a broad public understanding of the geology, plant and animal life, history, Indians, and related subjects bearing on the Park region. It aids in the development of the Glacier National Park Library and wayside exhibits; offers books on natural history for sale to the public; assists in the acquisition of non-federally owned lands within the Park in behalf of the United States Government; and cooperates with the Government in the interest of Glacier National Park. Revenues obtained by the Glacier National History Association are devoted entirely to the purposes outlined. Any person interested in the furtherance of these purposes may become a member upon payment of the annual fee of one dollar. Gifts and donations are accepted for land acquisition or general use. Books and pamphlets available at present are listed as follows:

ANIMALS

Bears, Pete and Repete, the National Park Bears—Powell—Portfolio of 12 wash drawings of cub bears, including poems. $1.00

Birds of Glacier National Park—Parratt—86 pp, 25 color, 2 black-and-white illustrations. 1.25

Fishing Guide to Glacier National Park—Kinnie—32 pp, 11 illustrations, 3 maps. .25

Mammals of Glacier National Park—Lechleitner—87 pp, 42 drawings. 1.00

TREES AND FLOWERS

Trees and Forests of Glacier National Park—Robinson—48 pp, 27 black-and-white illustrations. .50

Wildflowers of Glacier National Park—Sharpe—40 pp, 101 black-and-white drawings. .50

GEOLOGY

Geologic Story of Glacier National Park—Dyson—24 pp, black-and-white illustrations. .25

Glaciers and Glaciation in Glacier National Park—Dyson—24 pp, 16 black-and-white illustrations. .35

177

GUIDES AND MAPS

Guide to Going-to-the-Sun Road—Beatty—illustrated.   .35
Climber's Guide to Glacier National Park—Edwards—135
   pp, black-and-white illustrations.   4.95
Hiking Trail Map.   .50
Topographic Map of Glacier National Park—U. S. Geologi-
   cal Survey.   1.00

GENERAL

Climate of Glacier National Park—Dightman—12 pp, 30-yr.
   summary.   .30
Framing Prints. 11″ x 14″, full color—St. Mary Lake, Lake
   McDonald, Rocky Mountain Goat.   ea.   .25
Nature Trail Leaflets—Trick Falls, Swiftcurrent, Trail of the
   Cedars, Water Ouzel Trail, and Hidden Lake Overlook.
   (Please indicate choice.)   ea.   .10
Place Names in Glacier National Park—22 pp.   .50
Through the Years in Glacier National Park (*Park History*)
   —Numerous black-and-white illustrations.   1.50

All mail orders should be addressed to, and remittances made payable to, Glacier Natural History Association, West Glacier, Montana
59936. Other publications available. Write for price list.

INDEX

The index below covers both Glacier and Waterton Lakes National Parks. To distinguish those entries relating to Waterton Lakes National Park alone, they are set in italics.

179

181

182